A Brief History of
THE WESTERN WORLD

NINTH EDITION

Thomas H. Greer

MICHIGAN STATE UNIVERSITY

Gavin Lewis

JOHN JAY COLLEGE,
CITY UNIVERSITY OF NEW YORK

WADSWORTH
CENGAGE Learning

AUSTRALIA • BRAZIL • JAPAN • KOREA • MEXICO • SINGAPORE • SPAIN
UNITED KINGDOM • UNITED STATES

WADSWORTH
CENGAGE Learning™

A Brief History of the Western World,
9th Ed.
Thomas H. Greer and Gavin Lewis

Publisher: Clark Baxter
Senior Development Editor:
    Sue Gleason
Assistant Editor: Paul Massicotte
Editorial Assistant: Richard Yoder
Technology Project Manager:
    Melinda Newfarmer
Marketing Manager: Lori Grebe Cook
    and Caroline Croley
Marketing Assistant: Mary Ho
Advertising Project Manager: Stacey
    Purviance and Brian Chaffee
Project Manager, Editorial Production:
    Kimberly Adams
Print/Media Buyer: Judy Inouye
Permissions Editor: Sarah Harkrader
Production Service: Orr Book Services
Text Designer: Kaelin Chappell
Photo Researcher: Image Quest
Copy Editor: Bruce Emmer
Illustrator: Graphic World and Maps.com
Cover Designer: Irene Morris
Compositor: Thompson Type

Cover Image: Detail from Ambrogio
Lorenzetti's fresco *The Blessing of Good
Government* (1338) in the Palazzo Pubblico,
Siena. Erich Lessing/Art Resource, NY.

For product information and technology assistance,
contact us at
**Cengage Learning Customer & Sales Support,
1-800-354-9706**

For permission to use material from this text or product,
submit all requests online at **cengage.com/permissions**
Further permissions questions can be emailed to
permissionrequest@cengage.com

Library of Congress Control Number: 2004108726

ISBN-13: 978-0-534-64236-5
ISBN-10: 0-534-64236-5

Wadsworth
25 Thomson Place
Boston, MA 02210
USA

Cengage Learning is a leading provider of customized
learning solutions with office locations around the globe,
including Singapore, the United Kingdom, Australia,
Mexico, Brazil, and Japan. Locate your local office at:
International.cengage.com/region

Cengage Learning products are represented in Canada by
Nelson Education, Ltd.

For your course and learning solutions, visit
academic.cengage.com

Purchase any of our products at your local college store
or at our preferred onlone store **www.ichapters.com**

Printed in the United States of America
3 4 5 6 7 11 10 09

In memory of
Thomas H. Greer
1914–2004

BRIEF CONTENTS

CONTENTS

Part Two

MEDIEVAL CIVILIZATION

Part Three

THE REMAKING OF EUROPE

CHAPTER 7

The Transformation and Expansion of Europe   291

CHAPTER 8

The Renaissance: Upsurge of Humanism   335

Part Four

THE RISE OF THE MODERN WEST

Part Five

THE WEST AND THE WORLD IN THE ERA OF GLOBAL CIVILIZATION

MAPS

TIME CHARTS

PREFACE

Those who cannot remember the past are condemned to repeat it.

GEORGE SANTAYANA
1863–1952

What is the nature of the Western world? How has it shaped the men and women who are its heirs? What is its role in the larger worldwide civilization of the present day? The search for answers to questions such as these is not new; it traces back to the ancient Greeks. Inscribed on the temple of Apollo at Delphi were the words of the god: *Know yourself.* And one way to self-knowledge and knowledge of the world in which we live is to learn of the past experiences of humans like ourselves. As William Shakespeare observed, *What's past is prologue.*

A Brief History of the Western World aims to present a clear, concise account of truly meaningful human experiences relevant to the society in which we live that will also serve as a guide and companion for deeper explorations of the human past. Accordingly, the book focuses on the outstanding institutions, ideas, and creative works that have formed (and expressed) Western civilization, as well as on Western interactions with other civilizations in the past and the present.

Extensive changes have been made in this edition to meet the developing needs of instructors and students, while maintaining full continuity with the content, organization, and features of earlier editions.

A new Prologue, "What Is Western Civilization?" provides students with guidance on fundamental questions involved in the study of Western history: the significance of encounters and borrowing between different cultures in Western civilization's growth; the role of Western civilization in world history; the main stages of Western history; the usage of the terms "Western" and "civilization"; controversies over the historical record of Western civilization; and the role of continuity and change in Western history.

New part overviews, together with revised chapter overviews, explain how the material in each part and chapter relates to the themes discussed in the Prologue. The Prologue, part overviews, and chapter overviews together enhance understanding of the overall pattern of Western history.

To provide more succinct coverage and clearer analysis of historical issues, many paragraphs have been broken into smaller portions that allow for easier comprehension. In addition, new subheads appear throughout the text, making it easier for students to find and reference key topics. Defined terms appear in italics within the text and are highlighted with asterisks in the Index. Each chapter concludes with descriptive Recommended Reading, references for use with InfoTrac® College Edition, and a reminder about the electronic resources available with the text.

Many other revisions have been made throughout in response to suggestions by helpful colleagues. In the treatment of ancient times, the rise of monotheism among the Israelites is now treated in Chapter 1 as part of the discussion of changes within Middle Eastern civilization after 1200 B.C. The experience of the Jews under Greek and Roman rule is still discussed in Chapter 4, both as background to the rise of Christianity and as an introduction to the development of rabbinic Judaism. Fuller discussion has been provided of the final century of the Roman republic in Chapter 3, by way of background to the rise of the imperial monarchy.

In the treatment of the medieval and modern periods, the discussion of Byzantine eastern Europe has been reorganized so as to keep it more closely in step chronologically with that of western Europe. The section dealing with the sixteenth- and seventeenth-century wars now appears as part of the treatment of the Reformation in Chapter 9, to enable the student to better appreciate both the religious aspect of the wars and the way in which the religious aspect came to be overshadowed by secular ambitions. The discussions of the revolutions and ideologies of the seventeenth and eighteenth centuries, and of those of the early nineteenth century, now appear separately in Chapters 11 and 12, to make this complex material easier to assimilate. In addition, there is fuller discussion of social and political tensions within the Old Regime leading up to the French Revolution.

In recent and contemporary history, the Second World War now appears at the end of Chapter 14 so as to form part of the discussion of divisions within Western civilization during the era of imperialism and the rise of communism and fascism. Chapter 15, covering the era of the Cold War and decolonization, has been extensively revised to stress the themes of the continuing divisions within Western civilization and their overcoming at the end of the Cold War, as well as the various relationships of cooperation and conflict between the West and the rest of the world.

A new final chapter, "Western Civilization in the World of Today," covers two main themes of contemporary history. One is that of changing political and economic relationships within the West, and between the West and the rest of the world, since the fall of communism. This is treated as the latest stage in a lengthy merging process between Western and worldwide civilization. The other theme is the rise of Postmodernism in thought, literature, and art since the 1960s. As with the *Brief History of the Western World*'s treatment of cultural matters in earlier periods, the student is introduced to specific Postmodern thinkers, writers, artists, and works in such a way as to put these in their context of Western cultural traditions.

The narrative is supplemented throughout by visual features that have been strengthened in several ways in this edition. The number of maps has been more than doubled, so that students are made more fully aware of Western history's geographical aspect, and new "spot maps" have been added to focus on details not evident in larger maps. In addition, the maps are fully captioned to explain their significance, and globe icons indicate maps that appear in interactive form on the Book Companion Web Site. Chronologies at the beginning of each part of the book show the chronological relationships of notable individuals, events, and works in various fields of politics, society, religion, and culture in the periods concerned. Timelines at the top of pages within chapters show the sequence of events related to individual historical developments.

Every work of art discussed in the narrative is illustrated, and additional illustrations add a visual dimension to many other subjects. New captions explain how the illustrations exemplify the themes discussed in the text. And all illustrations, maps, timelines, and chronologies appear for the first time in full color.

A Brief History of the Western World is available in single-volume and two-volume editions to suit the differing needs of colleges and instructors. In addition, Volume II begins with a special Introduction, "The Background of the Modern West," which reviews Western history prior to 1300.

Teaching and learning ancillaries include the following:

Instructor's Resource CD-ROM with Exam-View®. Includes the *Instructor's Manual*, Resource Integration Guide, *ExamView®* testing, and Microsoft® *PowerPoint®* slides with lecture outlines and images. *ExamView* allows instructors to create, deliver, and customize tests and study guides (both print and online) in minutes with an easy-to-use assessment and tutorial system. It offers both a *Quick Test Wizard* and an *Online Test Wizard* that guide instructors step-by-step through the process of creating tests, while its "what you see is what you get" capability allows users to see the test they are creating on the screen exactly as it will print or display online. Instructors can build tests of up to two hundred and fifty questions using up to twelve question types. Using *ExamView*'s complete word-processing capabilities, the user can enter an unlimited number of new questions or edit existing questions. Additional images are available at the Western Civilization Resource Center at **http://history .wadsworth.com.**

Instructor's Manual with Test Bank. Prepared by Thomas H. Greer and Gavin Lewis with the assistance of John Soares, the manual includes chapter outlines reflecting the main chapter headings; learning objectives; lecture and discussion topics; and examination questions (essay, short answer, thirty true/false, and thirty multiple-choice, the latter with correct answers and text page references). Also available on the *Instructor's Resource CD-ROM.*

Full-Color Map Acetate Package. Map commentary provided by James Harrison, Siena College. Each package contains more than one hundred four-color map images from the text and other sources.

CNN® Today Videos for Western Civilization. Professors can launch lectures with riveting footage from CNN, the world's leading twenty-four-hour global news television network.

History Video Library. A completely new selection of videos for this edition, from Films for the Humanities & Sciences and other sources. Includes "The Huns Are Coming," "Gypsies and the Freedom to Hate," "Cursed Ground, Hallowed Ground: Nazi Death Camps Revisited," and "Putin: A Bitter Decision."

Sights and Sounds of History. Short, focused video clips, photos, artwork, animations, music, and dramatic readings are used to bring life to the historical topics and events that are most difficult for students to appreciate from a textbook alone.

Music CD-ROMs. Available to instructors upon request, each of these CD sets includes musical selections to enrich lectures, from Purcell through Ravi Shankar. A correlation guide is available in the instructor's area of the Book Companion Web Site.

The Greer/Lewis Book Companion Web Site. Both instructors and students will enjoy the Book Companion Web Site for the ninth edition, at **http://history.wadsworth.com/ greerbrief09/**, with its chapter-by-chapter resources that take learning beyond the pages of the text. Text-specific content for students includes interactive maps and timelines, simulations, "At the Movies" movie activities, tutorial quizzes, glossary, hyperlinks, *InfoTrac College Edition* exercises, and Internet activities. Instructors also have access to the *Instructor's Manual,* lesson plans, and Microsoft *PowerPoint* slides. Additionally, users have unlimited access to the Western Civilization Resource Center home page (accessible at **http:// history.wadsworth.com/western**), where instructors and students can access many selections, such as an Internet Guide for History, a career center, lessons on surfing the Web, the Western Civilization Image Bank, and links to great history-related Web sites.

History Interactive: A Study Tool. Prepared by Sandra Pryor, Old Dominion University, this valuable student CD-ROM is packaged free with every copy of the text. It includes numerous primary source documents; interactive maps and timelines; chapter summaries; How to Read a Document; How to Read a Map; analysis of primary source documents; study tips; the Western Civilization Image Bank; simulations for Western civilization; map questions and analysis; a self-test quiz, including matching, fill-in-the-blank, and chronology exercises; and two samples from *HistoryNow: Online Explorations in Western Civilization,* a new offering that allows students to experience history interactively.

HistoryNow: Online Explorations in Western Civilization Correlation. A user's guide and access code provide students with access to interactive multimedia modules to complement any college-level Western civilization course. The user's guide provides a complete index to the interactive modules, as well as a correlation guide to *A Brief History of the Western World.* Contact your Wadsworth representative for more information.

Magellan Atlas of Western Civilization. Available to package with the text, this booklet contains forty-four full-color historical maps, including "The Conflict in Afghanistan, 2001" and "States of the World, 2001."

Map Exercise Workbook. Prepared by Cynthia Kosso, Northern Arizona University, this workbook has been thoroughly revised and improved. Over twenty maps and exercises ask students to identify important cities and countries. Available in two volumes.

Document Exercise Workbook. Prepared by Donna Van Raaphorst, Cuyahoga Community College, this collection of exercises based on primary sources is available in two volumes.

Documents of Western Civilization. This reader, containing a broad selection of carefully chosen documents, can accompany any Western civilization text.

Exploring the European Past: Text & Images (ETEP). This fully customizable, second-generation reader brings to life the events, people, and concepts that defined Western civilization. ETEP integrates written and visual materials into one product. The ETEP program consists of printed primary and secondary sources, plus online visual sources provided via our secure Web site. Visit **http://custom.cengage.com/etep/** for a preview.

The Journey of Civilization CD-ROM. Prepared by David Redles, Cuyahoga Community College, this exciting CD-ROM takes students on eighteen interactive journeys through history. Enhanced with QuickTime movies, animations, sound clips, maps, and more, the journeys allow students to engage in history as active participants rather than as passive observers.

MapTutor: Western Civilization. This interactive map tutorial helps students learn geography by having them locate geographical features, regions, cities, and sociopolitical movements. Each map exercise is accompanied by questions that test knowledge and promote critical thinking.

InfoTrac College Edition. This fully searchable database offers twenty years' worth of full-text articles from almost 5,000 diverse sources, such as academic journals, newsletters, and up-to-the-minute periodicals, including *Time, Newsweek, Science, Forbes,* and *USA Today.* This incredible depth and breadth of material—available twenty-four hours a day from any computer with Internet access—makes conducting research easier than ever. And incorporating *InfoTrac College Edition* is easy as well—references to this virtual library are built into every chapter of the text. Both instructors and their students receive unlimited access for four months. In addition, students now have instant access to critical-thinking and paper-writing tools through *InfoWrite.*

Acknowledgments

This edition of *A Brief History of the Western World,* like all its predecessors, owes a great deal to the discerning suggestions of colleagues who are both experienced instructors and knowledgeable scholars. It is a pleasure to thank the following for their work in reviewing this edition:

David D. Bartley, Indiana Wesleyan University

Richard Cándida Smith, University of California, Berkeley

Eric Carlsson, University of Wisconsin—Madison

Sean L. Field, Marquette University

Richard M. Filipink, Jr., St. Bonaventure University

Beverly Garrison, Oral Roberts University

Gregory Guzman, Bradley University

George Kaloudis, Rivier College

Brian A. Pavlac, King's College

Elizabeth L. B. Peifer, Troy State University

Sandra Strohhofer Pryor, Old Dominion University

Kimberly D. S. Reiter, Stetson University

Leslie Schuster, Rhode Island College

B. Ann Tusty, Bucknell University

Warren Treadgold, Saint Louis University

William Benton Whisenhunt, College of DuPage

Michael Zaccaria, Cumberland County College

The editorial and production people at Wadsworth, a part of Cengage Learning, have welcomed this newcomer to their list. Clark Baxter has devoted unstinting attention to this one among countless projects, and has been a constant guiding presence. Sue Gleason has seen this edition through a complex process of revision with unfailing helpfulness, inexhaustible good humor, and much more tactful prodding than she had a right to expect she would have to do. Kim Adams has made the task of coordinating author, editors, design, and production seem easy. John Orr, of Orr Book Services, has been outstandingly helpful and professional in the task of production. Irene Morris and Kaelin Chappell have created exceptionally attractive and elegant cover and text designs, respectively. And Paul Massicotte coordinated a suite of ancillary items of unprecedented size and complexity.

The preparation of this edition has also been a family project. Nadezhda Katyk Lewis and Dorothea Lewis did a large share of the time-consuming task of repaginating the lengthy index. The former, in addition, gave decisive inspiration for the subjects of the cover art, as well as permitting the borrowing, in the sections on contemporary literature, of ideas that she developed in the course of her scholarly work.

This is the first edition of *A Brief History of the Western World* to have gone through the process of revision and publication without the participation of its original author, Thomas H. Greer. It was the first brief Western civilization book to be published, and it is still the only one to have been written from the start in the brief format. The basic idea, and most of the present text, are his. This will always be Tom Greer's book, and this edition is dedicated to his memory.

Gavin Lewis

PROLOGUE

What Is Western Civilization?

This book deals with the history of Western civilization from its 5,000-year-old Middle Eastern origins right up to the present day, when "the West," centered in North America and western Europe, wields power and influence across the world.

It is a story not just of one civilization, but of a whole series: the Middle Eastern civilizations of Mesopotamia and Egypt, the Mediterranean civilization of Greece and Rome, then Christian Europe, and finally the modern West. Each of these civilizations was located in a different region of the world, each had its own rich individuality that made it profoundly different from the others, and each interacted intensively with still other civilizations. Yet together these civilizations form a continuous line of development from the ancient Middle Eastern past to the modern North American and western European present.

This Western development has had a momentous impact on the human race as a whole, for most of the changes for good or ill that have swept across the world in modern times, from democracy and the abolition of slavery to dictatorship and genocide, were the outcome of this development. It also has a direct impact on everyone living in North America, whatever their personal background and heritage, for it is the West that has formed the countries in which they live. In addition, the story of Western development is a controversial one, for the Western and worldwide changes of modern times have led to fierce conflicts within the West itself, and have made the West both admired and hated throughout the rest of the world.

Clearly this is a story that needs some explanation in advance. What kind of human group is a "civilization," and what does it mean to speak of a series of "civilizations"? What is the meaning of "the West" and "Western," and why are these names applied to several different civilizations? Is Western civilization the hero or the villain of world history? What is the relevance of the lengthy Western past to the swiftly changing Western present? The answers to these questions will make the details of the story easier to follow, and the pattern of the whole easier to grasp.

"CIVILIZATION" AND "CIVILIZATIONS"

Civilization in General

All human groups, no matter how small they are and how simple their ways of life, possess such features as beliefs and values, social organization, knowledge of the world around them, technology, and art. But some human groups are larger and more complex than others. Their beliefs and values are more elaborate, their knowledge is more extensive, their society is more highly structured, their technology is used on a larger scale, and their art is more refined. The farther a human group has evolved in all these ways, the more likely we are to speak of it as civilized.

There is no exact dividing line between civilized human groups and those that are not civilized, but there are some rule-of-thumb ways of telling the difference. If a human group has a large population, some of whom live in cities; if it is ruled by a highly organized government; if it builds large and impressive religious and public buildings; and if it keeps written records, it is generally considered to have reached the state of civilization.

Judged by these standards, civilization first arose in the Middle East about 5,000 years ago—that is, human groups already living in that region were the first in the world to grow large and complex enough that we speak of them today as civilized. Later on, civilization also arose in the Far East and in Central and South America. From these original centers civilization spread to other parts of the world—that is to say, peoples who were not yet civilized adopted civilized ways as a result of peaceful or warlike contact with civilized neighbors. As a result, by about 2,000 years ago most people in the Eastern Hemisphere were living in civilized societies, and 1,000 years later, most people in the Western Hemisphere were doing so as well.

Individual Civilizations

As civilization arose in new centers, the specifics of its features were different from those in older centers. Furthermore, when peoples who were not yet civilized adopted civilized ways of life from their neighbors, they often changed and improved upon what they learned. In these ways, civilized peoples came to possess different beliefs and values, have different kinds of knowledge, use different writing systems, live under different types of government, and create different styles of art. In cases where there were many such differences between civilized peoples—though, again, there is no exact dividing line—we speak of these peoples as having had different individual "civilizations."

An individual civilization, in this second meaning, usually originated among one people in one territory, but then became the property of many peoples across a whole region of the world. The territory where a civilization originated often became that civilization's heartland—a model for outlying territories, and even their actual ruler. Sometimes, too, it lost the status of heartland to some upstart outlying territory. Civilizations in neighboring regions influenced and interacted with one another, as well as with peoples on their borders who were not yet civilized.

Over time, civilizations not only arose and flourished, but also passed out of existence. They were undermined and then destroyed by one or more of such misfortunes as internal strife, economic problems, loss of confidence in their own beliefs and values, and invasions by outsiders. When a civilization ceased to exist, however, that did not usually mean that the peoples who formed part of it stopped being civilized. Instead, they rejected many of their existing civilized traditions and adopted different ones, so that a new civilization emerged out of the old one. But these changes were never total. Always, peoples who made them kept a good deal of their old civilized ways of life. In this way, some of the traditions of earlier civilizations continued on into later ones.

The Western Series of Civilizations

Western civilization has been formed by all of these processes. It consists of a series of individual civilizations, each of which arose, flourished, and fell, as civilization in general spread westward from its earliest point of origin to peoples who were not yet civilized. When any one of these civilizations was replaced by the next, some of its traditions were lost, but others continued into later civilizations. The Western series of civilizations is therefore a genuine line of succession—that is, each civilization emerged out of the one before it.

The succession began with the Middle Eastern "parent" civilizations of Mesopotamia and Egypt, continued with the Mediterranean civilization of Greece and Rome, and then moved on to the civilization of Christian Europe (that is, Europe in the era in which Christianity wielded unchallenged power over that region's values, culture, and society). All of these civilizations also had peaceful and warlike contacts with civilizations outside the Western line of succession. The Greeks and Romans, for example, were very much influenced by civilized peoples of the Middle East, and Christian Europe by Islam. Eventually, Christian Europe spread westward to the Americas, conquered the civilizations of the Western Hemisphere, and at the same time remade itself to form the present-day West.

TRADITIONAL CIVILIZATION, MODERN CIVILIZATION, AND THE WEST

Traditional Civilization

In spite of their many differences, for several thousand years all individual civilizations that arose throughout the world, including those in the Western succession, had some important features in common above and beyond the fact that all of them were large and complex human groups. These additional common features were so widespread and persistent that they amounted to a worldwide traditional pattern of civilization in general.

All civilizations were agrarian societies—that is, the vast majority of their people were farmers, providing food and other supplies for the cities and the elite. All civilizations possessed technologies without which they could not have survived, but their stock of technical know-how increased only very slowly.

All civilizations also had elites that enjoyed most of the benefits of civilization, such as leisure, comfort, and education. It was these elites, too, that ruled the rest from the top down, and that were responsible for most of the achievements and misdeeds of civilization that fill the history books. All civilizations practiced slavery, and in all of them, women were in one way or another subordinated to men.

In all civilizations, religion was the single most important source of inspiration for most areas of thought and values. Rulers wielded authority as servants of whatever divine power they believed in, and as a result, rulers themselves were considered to be holy or even divine.

Furthermore, both mutual influences and also conflicts among civilizations were mostly between those that were neighbors. Among those that were farther away from one another, the influences and conflicts were weak or nonexistent.

Modern Civilization

As late as five hundred years ago, this traditional pattern of civilization was still shared by the six major civilizations that existed at the time—in the Eastern Hemisphere, those of China and the Far East, India and southern Asia, Islam, and Christian Europe; and in the Western Hemisphere, those of Mexico and Central America, and of the Andes Mountains in South America.

About that time, however, Christian Europe gradually began to break with the traditional pattern within itself, so as to form the modern West. The changes were slow at first, but gathered speed until in the last two hundred years they have run at a breakneck pace.

A new kind of society arose—industrial society, in which the vast majority of people were white-collar and blue-collar workers, and farmers were a tiny minority. Science and technology began to leap forward, and their advance became the main engine of changes in values and ways of life.

Leisure, comfort, and education ceased to be monopolies of the elite. Though there was still an elite, it shared the power to rule and take decisions with the rest of society—consumers, shareholders, voters. Slavery was abolished, and the subordination of women began to be replaced by equality.

Though religion continued to inspire much of the thought and values of civilized societies, its influence was challenged by secular (nonreligious) ideologies that claimed to guide behavior and culture alongside religion or in opposition to it. Governments gave up the claim to rule as servants of divine power, and ruled instead in the name of whatever secular ideology they believed in.

The Modern West and the World

Over the five hundred years in which Europe remade itself into the modern West, European exploration and empire building caused these changes to spread—not just to neighboring civilizations as in the past, but to every civilization throughout the world. In this way, a new and worldwide pattern of civilization began to come into being, a process that continues at the present day.

As with earlier regional interactions between civilizations, this worldwide one has involved exchanges that went both ways, but the balance of exchanges has so far favored the West. "Imports" from the rest of the world such as religious and philosophical ideas from the Far East, music and art from Africa, and basic foodstuffs from the Western Hemisphere have certainly changed the life of Western societies in important ways. But the changes brought to the rest of the world by such Western "exports" as science and technology, democracy and gender equality, and Christianity have been more far-reaching.

This does not mean that the modern pattern of global civilization is being simply imposed by the West on the rest of the world. In its early stages, the rise of modern global civilization did mainly involve conquest, settlement, and domination by Westerners in distant parts of the world. More recently, however, it has been a matter of the rest of the world to a greater or lesser extent actively adopting Western ways and avoiding or escaping from Western domination as a result. In Africa south of the Sahara, for example, more people now practice Christianity than any other religion—and worldwide Christian churches are increasingly influenced by the views of their African believers. Likewise, Far Eastern countries like Japan have adopted and adapted Western models of democracy and capitalism—and have become both partners and rivals of the Western countries in the global economy.

Of course, many people outside the West, such as Islamic fundamentalists in Muslim countries and Hindu nationalists in India, seek to turn back such Western influences as gender equality, secular ideologies, and Christianity. On the other hand, most of them have nothing against technology, industrialism, nationalism, and material well-being for the masses—all of which are also Western values. Even their preferred forms of government are borrowed from the West—democracy in the case of Hindu nationalists, and more or less dictatorial regimes in the case of Islamic fundamentalists. Thus even anti-Western movements in the modern world cannot help being deeply influenced by the civilization that they despise.

Since the modern pattern of global civilization is still in the making, no one can know for sure what its ultimate shape will be. But the outline of the past is clear enough. Stretching across the 5,000 years of traditional civilization, one particular succession of civilizations, interacting with other civilizations and with many not yet civilized human groups, finally produced the modern West. Many traditions of these earlier civilizations went to make the modern West, which has grown out of them rather than simply rejecting them and starting afresh. All the same, with the rise of the modern West, the 5,000 years of traditional civilization are coming to an end, and a new pattern is forming across the world. How and why all this happened is what this book is about.

WHAT MAKES WESTERN CIVILIZATION "WESTERN"?

"Western" and "Non-Western" Civilizations

Most civilizations are identified by the region of the world that they occupy, or by their dominant religion—Chinese or Islamic civilization, for example. The civilization of the West, however, has come to be known by a name that does not make a straightforward statement about where it is located, let alone about its religion. Instead, the name raises a question: To the west of what? Western civilization, it seems, is defined in relation to a "somewhere else" that it lies in a particular compass direction away from—a place or civilization other than itself.

About two hundred years ago, when the "West"/"Western" label first began to be used, that was certainly true. At that time, the western European countries were becoming increasingly secular-minded, and their traditional collective name for themselves—"Christendom" or the "Christian commonwealth"—

had fallen out of use. At the same time, these countries had already spread their civilization westward to North and South America, and now they were turning eastward to dominate the civilizations of Islam, India and southern Asia, and China and the Far East. Accordingly, they started using "the West" and "Western" to define themselves against these civilizations, which they lumped together as "the East."

Later on came the twentieth-century era of world wars followed by the Cold War. The rising North American countries as well as many in western Europe found themselves allied in a series of struggles, first against Germany and later against Soviet Russia. Both struggles involved conflicts between important values and interests, such as democracy against fascism, and capitalism against communism. As a result, it became standard usage on both sides of the Atlantic to speak of the common values and interests of North America and western Europe as those of "Western civilization" or "the West." The individuality of other civilizations of the world was recognized more than before, but as a group they came to be thought of as "non-Western."

Of course, the North American and western European countries had countless victims, enemies, and critics—in the non-Western world, in outlying territories of Western civilization, and even at home. These opponents had many different reasons for despising the West, but all of them thought that the "West"/"Western" label was a good one for defining what they despised. With both admirers and despisers agreeing to use these labels, the labels themselves were bound to stick.

The Geography of Western Civilization

In origin, then, "the West" and "Western" were rallying cries, both for and against the countries that these labels defined. But the common identity that the labels stood for obviously had not come about overnight, and the peoples of North America and western Europe shared many features of their identity with peoples in other parts of the world. Accordingly, "the West" and "Western civiliza-

tion" came to be stretched backward in time and outward in space. In the process, the meaning of these labels became both broader and vaguer.

The Geography of the Western Past. As soon as the North American and western European peoples began to think of themselves as "Western," they began to think of earlier civilizations from which they derived major features of their way of life as being "Western" too. In particular they identified the civilization of Greece and Rome and that of Christian Europe as earlier "Wests"—as forerunners of the West of their own time. This was partly because these civilizations had arisen out of the westward spread of civilization from its Middle Eastern point of origin, and also because many of their traditions had continued without interruption into the civilization of the modern West.

As a result, the "West"/"Western" label has come to be used to describe the entire succession of civilizations from the Greeks to the present-day West, and the term "Western civilization" is applied to them all. The earlier Middle Eastern civilizations of Mesopotamia and Egypt, whose traditions have been less directly transmitted and whose offspring also includes the non-Western civilization of Islam, are not considered to be part of Western civilization even though they are ancestral to it.

Because of this westward spread of civilization, the "West"/"Western" label is used today to refer to different geographical areas at different times in the past. For many centuries of Greek civilization, the heartland of Western civilization was the Greek homeland in the eastern Mediterranean, with outlying territories stretching wherever Greeks settled and made their influence felt from the Atlantic Ocean to the Middle East. When the Roman Empire was at its height, the Western heartland included Italy as well as Greece, and its outlying territories included the rest of the empire—western Europe, North Africa, and the Middle East. In the era of Christian Europe, the Western heartland moved northwestward to the countries of western Europe, and Eastern Europe formed the main outlying territory of Western civilization.

The Geography of the Present-Day West. Even at the time that it was invented, the "West"/ "Western" label was almost meaningless when applied to the present. There were too many regions of the world that lay in some direction other than "westward," but shared many features of their civilization with the countries of North America and western Europe that now formed the Western heartland.

There were the vast southern lands of Latin America, whose civilization was mainly derived from the western European countries of Spain and Portugal. For that matter, there were also the twentieth-century adversaries of the North American and western European countries, Germany and Russia. Germany shared so much of its identity and history with the rest of western Europe that it clearly counted as part of the Western heartland. And even Russia, stretching eastward from Europe all the way to the Pacific Ocean, was inspired by many traditions of Greece, Rome, and Christian Europe. Was it not also to be regarded as part of Western civilization?

There are many arguments among historians about whether and how much of Russia, Eastern Europe, and Latin America belong to the West. In this book, all these countries and regions are counted as part of Western civilization. Latin America, Eastern Europe, and Russia are treated as outlying territories with their own regional versions of Western civilization. And the twentieth-century struggles that brought the term "Western civilization" into common use are treated as conflicts within Western civilization itself.

By now the "West"/"Western" label has stuck so fast that it is unlikely ever to be removed. But Western civilization is in fact an intercontinental one that stretches to all points of the compass, and all other civilizations of the world have become, to at least some extent, "Westernized." This is the single most easily identifiable of the great changes in worldwide civilization that the West is bringing about. Instead of many civilizations, each interacting only with its closest neighbors, a single civilization now interacts with the entire world, and is seemingly merging with the others to form a new, global civilization.

ACHIEVEMENTS AND MISDEEDS OF WESTERN CIVILIZATION

The intercontinental extent and worldwide influence of the present-day West are among the few things about Western civilization that are not vigorously disputed. Almost everything else one can say about what Western civilization is like and how it evolved is likely to start an argument between believers in two opposing images of the West. Even Westerners themselves, let alone non-Westerners, are divided between admirers of the Good West and despisers of the Bad West.

Each of these images is based on a different moral judgment about the course of Western history. As often happens with images of history that are based on moral judgments, both are highly oversimplified. Since they inspire a great deal of present-day discussion and debate about Western civilization, however, it is necessary for readers of this book to come to grips with them.

The Good West

The image of the Good West is as old as the use of "the West" and "Western" as North American and western European rallying cries, and it has continued to be proclaimed by "patriotic" Westerners ever since.

The features of the Good West include, for example, freedom, democracy, respect for law, reasoned debate, forgiving one's enemies, scientific discovery, technical progress, pluralism, gender equality, and material comfort and leisure for all. Among its heroes are such figures as Socrates, Jesus, Leonardo da Vinci, Abraham Lincoln, Susan B. Anthony, Albert Einstein, Winston Churchill, and Martin Luther King.

To accomplish these achievements and produce these heroes, its admirers say, Western civilization has built up a rich inheritance over thousands of years, to which today's West is the heir. The Greeks, for instance, contributed democracy and reasoned debate, the Romans contributed respect for law, and the Judeo-Christian tradition contributed forgiving one's enemies. Non-Western civilizations also contributed some of their achievements, so that the best achievements of the human race as a whole have become part of the Western heritage.

Today, according to its admirers, Western civilization is flourishing as never before. It has defeated and destroyed its enemies within—would-be corrupters and destroyers of its unique heritage such as fascism and communism. Now it is struggling to pass on its heritage to the other civilizations of the world. All that is best in the non-Western world is on the side of the West, say its admirers, and those who oppose the West are the next fearsome adversary that the West must destroy.

The Bad West

This is the image of the West as seen by its victims, enemies, and critics. The features of the Bad West include imperialism, class conflict, the manipulation of the masses by the elite, genocide, racism, ethnocentrism, sexism, environmental pollution, consumerism, and dumbed-down mass entertainment. Among its misdeeds over the centuries are gladiatorial combats, the burning of heretics, the African slave trade, the Nazi death camps, million-gallon oil spills, porno Web sites, Third World sweatshops, and the atom bomb.

These evils were gradually built into Western civilization, according to those who despise it, by all the Wests of the past—sexism and slavery by the Greeks, for example, and ethnocentrism and intolerance by Christian Europe. So far as the West ever did anything right, it was as a result of stealing ideas from non-Western civilizations without giving them any of the credit.

At the present day, its despisers claim, the West is showing unmistakable signs of decline—frenzied pleasure seeking, the loss of traditional standards and values, and even the bloated wealth and power that make it such a threat to the rest of the world. For even in its decline, they say, the West is arrogantly trying to remake the non-Western world in its own ugly image, causing worldwide misery and committing worldwide cultural genocide in the process.

A More Complex West

Anyone who studies the past has a right, perhaps even a duty, to make moral judgments about its deeds. When making moral judgments of any kind, however, it is best to recognize the complexity of the facts and issues that one is dealing with. Accordingly, the image of the West in this book—one that readers will of course accept, reject, or amend depending on how convincing they find it—is more complex than either the Good or the Bad images.

It is the image of a West that is both good and bad—like all civilizations and for that matter all human beings. Western history includes both Jesus and the burning of heretics, Leonardo da Vinci and dumbed-down mass entertainment, Lincoln and slavery, Susan B. Anthony and sexism, Einstein and the atom bomb. Each civilization in the Western succession has produced its share of achievements and misdeeds, some of which were imitated and built on by subsequent Wests.

Civilizations in the Western succession before the modern West also often imitated and built on the achievements and misdeeds of non-Western civilizations. For this reason, Western civilization cannot take all the credit for all of its past achievements. The Greeks learned to carve statues from the Egyptians, for example, and Christian Europe learned about printing from China. But learning is not the same as copying: a Greek statue is a very different work of art from an Egyptian one, and the European printing process was an improvement on that of the Chinese. As usually happens when one people learns from another, Western peoples changed what they learned from non-Western peoples, and made it distinctively their own.

Nor does Western civilization have to take all the blame for its past misdeeds. Besides printing, Christian Europeans also learned from China how to use gunpowder to kill people—though they made big improvements in that process too. And many of the misdeeds of which Western civilization stands accused, such as slavery and sexism, were common to all Western and non-Western civilizations of the past, because they were built into the way traditional civilization worked.

What the West can take the main credit and must take most of the blame for, however, are the achievements and misdeeds of modern global civilization so far, because modern global civilization originated in the West. Democracy and racism, gender equality and terrorism, modern scientific discovery and genocide—all began in the West with little or no help from non-Western peoples. But non-Western peoples are more or less swiftly "modernizing" themselves—that is, they are learning from the achievements and misdeeds of the West. If the past history of peoples learning from one another is anything to go by, the future achievements of non-Western peoples within global civilization will be just as impressive as those of the West. Many non-Western misdeeds, notably of genocide and terrorism, have already been just as horrifying.

THE CONTINUITY OF WESTERN CIVILIZATION

One thing that admirers of the Good West and despisers of the Bad West agree about is that present-day Western civilization is the result of 5,000 years of continuous development in every field of human thought and action. There is plenty of argument over whether this development has been to the advantage or disadvantage of the human race. But both sides agree that, one after another, civilizations from Mesopotamia and Egypt onward have contributed to the development of Western civilization by handing on some of their traditions to later civilizations, thereby building up a massive inheritance that finally came down to the present-day West.

There are also those who argue, however, that there is no such thing as a continuous history of Western civilization. Some of these critics are historians who argue that the supposed Western forerunner civilizations were profoundly different from one another and even more so from the West of today. Thus we distort the reality of these civilizations by rummaging in their history for the roots of the modern West. Other critics declare that the present-day West is changing so swiftly and has broken with so much of traditional civilization that it makes no sense to look for its roots in a 5,000-year past. Essentially, they agree with Henry Ford that "history is bunk"— that the past is distant, alien, and dead, and has no relevance to the present.

The story that this book will tell is one of Western development proceeding from one civilization to the next. All the same, the disbelievers in Western continuity are right to point out that the forerunner civilizations were very far from being simply earlier versions of the present-day West. They were deeply alien to the modern West in many ways, and it would falsify their story simply to pick out those of their features that happen to have come down to the present.

On the contrary, the fascination of Western history comes partly from forgetting about the present and simply studying the rich and strange life of the civilizations of the Western past as they were in themselves. But it is also fascinating to see how the civilizations of the Western past, so different from one another and the present-day West, nevertheless built up an inheritance of achievements and misdeeds that still inspires and burdens the swift-changing Western present.

How the West Was Formed

Western development did not take place, however, by the forerunner civilizations "contributing" or "handing on" their traditions to the modern West. That is not how traditions pass from generation to generation, since earlier generations have no control over what later generations will do. Instead, it is later generations that decide, in accordance with their own beliefs and needs, what will happen to traditions of earlier ones—sometimes rejecting traditions of the past, sometimes keeping them going, and sometimes reviving them.

Rejecting Traditions: Polytheism. The process of rejecting traditions has been just as important as the persistence of traditions in forming Western civilization.

Polytheism (the worship of many gods and goddesses), for instance, was once a basic Western tradition. Seventeen hundred years ago, however, the peoples of Europe began turning against this tradition. Gradually they all became Christian, and it is now Christianity that is the basic religious tradition of the West. Today, Westerners are liable to see many religious customs of the pre-Christian Wests as foolish or even wicked—the Roman practice of honoring some of their emperors as gods, for instance. But of course, to wise and civilized Romans at the time, honoring emperors as gods seemed a righteous and sensible thing to do, and it was those who would not do so, in particular the early Christians, who seemed foolish or wicked.

One does not have to agree with the Romans, but one has to take their ideas into account if one wants to understand how their emperors wielded power, why they persecuted the Christians, and why they finally changed their minds and accepted Christianity. In this way, knowing about rejected traditions is part of understanding both the richness and strangeness of the Western past, and the processes of change whereby present-day Western civilization was formed.

Keeping Up Traditions: The Alphabet. If a tradition suits the beliefs and needs of later generations, however, they will keep it up for thousands of years. In spite of all differences among civilizations, the present-day West possesses many such traditions dating from the distant past. Often they involve things so basic that people today usually take them for granted, such as the alphabet.

The scribes (writing experts) belonging to a now-anonymous people living on the northeastern borders of Egypt who originally invented the alphabet 3,500 or more years ago had no notion that we would still be using it today. Most likely, they saw it simply as a vast improvement on complicated existing writing systems, since it enabled anything that was thought and said to be expressed with a mere couple of dozen signs. Middle Eastern trading peoples such as the Phoenicians, and then the Greeks and Romans, Christian Europe, and the modern West—not to mention many non-Western civilizations—also found the system to be simple and flexible, so they kept on using

it. That is how this 3,500-year-old innovation has become a basic Western tradition.

Reviving Traditions: Democracy. When later generations decide that a long-rejected tradition does suit them after all, this, too, can have a momentous impact on the development of civilization. The modern West, for example, has reached far back into the past to revive the tradition of democracy. The democratic tradition began 2,500 years ago in ancient Greece, but after a couple of centuries the Greeks abandoned it. For the next 2,000 years democracy was despised by the Greeks themselves, the Romans, and Christian Europe, as a system of government that had been tried and failed. The modern West, however, has completely reversed the verdicts of all these forerunner civilizations and has made democracy its one and only legitimate form of government.

Tradition, Change, and Western Continuity

Western development, therefore, has taken place through an endless process of later generations rejecting, upholding, and reviving the traditions of earlier ones. No two generations have exactly the same beliefs and needs, however, so that when later generations uphold or revive a tradition, they also change it in ways that earlier generations never imagined.

The alphabet, for example, as originally invented in the Middle East, had no vowels, word spaces, punctuation, or capital and lowercase letters. All these improvements were made by later civilizations to meet their changing reading and writing needs. Likewise, the Greek pioneers of democracy would certainly have been shocked by many features of democracy in the present-day West—for instance, the participation of women as well as men. Greek civilization, however, was a traditional one, whereas the West has revived democracy in the course of pioneering a new pattern of civilization that includes the equality of women and men. The basic Greek tradition of mass citizen participation in government suits the modern West, but the West has other beliefs and needs that can be met only by drastically changing the tradition.

Without such changes to meet changing needs, however, it would have made no sense to revive democracy or to go on using the alphabet. The same applies to every persistent or recurring Western tradition. All of them are here today because they have been able to absorb the changes imposed on them by different civilizations in the Western succession. Tradition and change, in fact, are not enemies but allies. Traditions cannot survive without changing, and even the greatest changes are often brought about by altering existing traditions.

It is these persisting but changing traditions that have provided the continuity of Western history from Mesopotamia and Egypt down to the present day. The same combination of persistence and change is what makes it possible for the modern West to be inspired by traditions of its 5,000-year past, even as it pioneers the transition from traditional to modern civilization. And that is also why it makes sense to treat the history of Western civilization as a single story—though it is a story without an ending, for it is still continuing today.

Fig. I.1. A Roman Emperor Sacrifices to the Gods. Marcus Aurelius, who ruled Rome late in the second century A.D., is shown burning incense before ritually slaughtering the bull in the background. Some of the meat will be offered to the gods, and the rest will be shared among the worshipers so that they may feast together with the divine beings. The image expresses beliefs that were common to all ancient civilizations—a sense of dependence on divine power and of the need for communities and their rulers to serve and honor that power.

Part One

THE ANCIENT WORLD

MIDDLE EASTERN AND

MEDITERRANEAN CIVILIZATION

PART ONE

The Ancient World

An essential first step toward understanding the past is to divide it up into *periods*—longer or shorter stretches of time that mark off important stages in the development of human activities and ideas. Of course, activities and ideas are complex things that change continually, so that the stages of their development are often difficult to recognize. In addition, what makes such stages "important" is to some extent a subjective matter—it depends on what seems important about the past to ourselves, looking backward from the present day. All the same, we have to define historical periods as accurately and objectively as possible, for unless we do so, we cannot arrange facts about the past into any meaningful pattern.

The generally agreed-upon large-scale pattern of Western history is made up of three main periods, each more or less aligned with the lifetime of one or more civilizations in the Western succession. The 3,500 years of the early Middle Eastern civilizations and of Mediterranean civilization make up the *ancient* period (3000 B.C.–A.D. 500). The thousand years of Christian Europe (500–1500) are the *Middle Ages*—the "in-between times" separating the ancient from the *modern* period (1500 to the present). This last period consists of the five hundred years (so far) of the rise of the modern West and its remaking of civilization across the world.

The dates that mark off these periods are simply convenient benchmarks, and nothing in particular happened at any of them. At each of them, however, large-scale and fast-moving changes were taking place in many fields of activity and ideas, so that the transition from one civilization to the next was well under way. However, the fact that a particular historical period began and ended with spectacular changes does not mean that in between, everything stayed the same. On the contrary, massive changes took place within these large-scale periods, so that historians often divide them into smaller-scale ones—"early," "middle," "late," and so on. But except in the case of the modern period, such changes within large-scale periods were never quite so far-reaching as those under way at the beginning and ending dates.

In the case of the ancient period, the initial sudden and world-changing development was the rise of the first Middle Eastern civilizations in Mesopotamia and Egypt, which took place over several centuries around 3000 B.C. Over many centuries civilized ways of life spread to many peoples of the Middle East, and underwent many changes. Political structures formed in Middle Eastern civilization that ranged from city-states (small self-governing communities) to extensive empires. Technical skills developed that were as varied as ironworking and alphabetic writing. Religious beliefs arose that were as different from each other as the worship of god-kings by the Egyptians and the monotheism of the Israelites (Jews). All these features were taken up by later Western and non-Western civilizations.

Eventually civilized life spread westward from the Middle East, taking new forms as it did so, until the brilliant Mediterranean civilization of Greece and Rome (often called "Greco-Roman") emerged and went through its own lengthy development.

Greco-Roman civilization was the first that today counts as geographically and culturally "Western." Citizen participation in government; the disciplines of science, philosophy, and history; magnificent new styles of architecture; works of art and literature that conveyed human experiences and perceptions with unprecedented vividness and power—all originated with the Greeks. The Romans then imitated and developed these and other achievements of Greek civilization to the point where they often equaled and sometimes surpassed the Greeks. Rome, in turn, became an inspiration and model for civilization's further development—above all in Western Europe, the future heartland of Western Civilization.

In two basic respects, however, Greco-Roman civilization had more in common with contemporary Middle Eastern civilizations than with later Western ones. First, the Greeks and Romans worshiped not one God but many gods and goddesses, as did most peoples of the ancient Middle East. Secondly, besides adapting the Middle Eastern government model of city-states, the Greeks and Romans also continued the rival Middle Eastern tendency to form vast empires ruled by limitlessly powerful monarchs. The final result was the mighty Roman Empire, which united the Mediterranean lands, Western Europe, and a good deal of the Middle East under one rule. In these ways, Greco-Roman civilization was both "Western" and "ancient."

Eventually, over about three hundred years around A.D. 500, there came another series of world-changing events. The peoples of the Roman Empire converted to Christianity, with its belief in one almighty God. The empire itself was then broken apart by less advanced European peoples invading from the north, and by Arab conquerors from the south who brought with them another religion that worshiped one God—Islam. Countless traditions of Middle Eastern and Mediterranean civilization persisted, but the changes were drastic enough to bring an end to the existing civilizations of both regions. Out of the old ones, two new civilizations arose, whose future destinies would be closely linked. One was the non-Western civilization of Islam. The other, and the next in the Western succession, was that of Christian Europe.

	POLITICAL, SOCIAL, AND ECONOMIC DEVELOPMENTS	RELIGION, SCIENCE, AND PHILOSOPHY	HISTORY AND LITERATURE	ARCHITECTURE, ART, AND MUSIC
3000 B.C.	Earliest civilization in Mesopotamia and Egypt	Creation and flood myths (Sumer)	Invention of writing	First temples and palaces
		Belief in immortality (Egypt)	Epic of Gilgamesh	Early megalithic monuments (Europe)
	Beginning of spread of Indo-European peoples			Pyramids of Giza (Egypt)
2500	Minoan (Cretan) civilization begins	Beginning of mathematical sciences		
		Foundations of medical sciences		
	First appearance of Indo-European-influenced tribal groups in Europe			
				Ziggurat of Ur (Sumer)
2000				Palace of Knossos (Crete)
	Babylonian kingdom	Abraham	Development of alphabet (Middle East)	
	Law code of Hammurabi			
	Achaean migrations into Greece			Stonehenge (England)
1500	Mycenaean civilization			Temple of Karnak (Egypt)
		Akhenaten		
		Moses and the Hebrew Covenant		
1200	Crisis of Middle Eastern civilization (1200–900)			
	"Dark Ages" of Greece (1200–800)			
	Trojan War (legendary)			
1000	Hebrew kingdoms (1000–600)	Beginning of Iron Age	Widespread use of alphabet	
		David		
		Solomon		
800	"Homeric Age" of Greece	Amos	Homer and Greek epics	
	Greek city-states founded	First Olympic Games honoring Zeus		
	Greek colonization of the Mediterranean and Black Seas			
	Rome founded		Lyric poetry begins	
	Assyrian Empire			
		Zoroaster (Persia)		
600	Solon of Athens	Thales of Miletus		Early Greek style of sculpture
			Sappho of Lesbos	
	"Babylonian Captivity" of the Jews		Greek drama emerges	
	Persian Empire	Growth of mystery cults (Greece)		
				Palace of Persepolis (Persia)

POLITICAL, SOCIAL, AND ECONOMIC DEVELOPMENTS	RELIGION, SCIENCE, AND PHILOSOPHY	HISTORY AND LITERATURE	ARCHITECTURE, ART, AND MUSIC	
		Aeschylus		500 B.C.
Roman Republic established	Parmenides of Elea	Herodotus	Greek lyre and pipes	
Twelve Tablets of law (Rome)	Heraclitus of Ephesus	Sophocles	Classical style:	
Persian Wars in Greece; Darius, Xerxes	Hippocrates of Cos	Aristophanes	Phidias	
Athenian supremacy and empire		Euripides	Parthenon	
Pericles		Thucydides	Erechtheum (Porch	
Peloponnesian War	Protagoras and Sophists		of Maidens)	
Plague of Athens	Aristippus of Cyrene		Myron	
	Socrates			
	Plato			400
	Aristotle		Praxiteles	
Philip of Macedon				
Alexander the Great				
Hellenistic kingdoms	Epicurus, Zeno (Stoicism)		Hellenistic style	300
Urbanization	Cyrenaic school (hedonists)			
Punic Wars begin (Rome vs. Carthage)				250
		Plautus		200
		Terence		
Punic Wars end		Polybius		
Reforms of the Gracchi in Rome				
Civil Wars in Italy				100
Rome completes conquest of the Mediterranean world	Cicero	Virgil		
Julius Caesar's conquest of Gaul	Lucretius	Horace		
Overthrow of the Roman Republic		Ovid		
Augustus and the foundations of the Roman Empire		Livy		
Pax Romana (27 B.C.–A.D. 180)				
	Birth of Christ	Plutarch, Suetonius		A.D.
	Peter and Paul	Tacitus		
Tiberius		Juvenal		
		Seneca		
Nero				
Trajan				100
Hadrian	Ptolemy		Colosseum	
	Galen		Trajan's Forum	
Epidemics in Italy begin	Marcus Aurelius		Pantheon	
			Pont du Gard	200
Period of rival emperors	Rivalry of Mithraism and Christianity			
Attacks by Germanic tribal confederacies	Last great persecution of the Christians		Baths of Diocletian	
Diocletian: Reconstruction of the empire	Anthony (hermit monk)			

	POLITICAL, SOCIAL, AND ECONOMIC DEVELOPMENTS	RELIGION, SCIENCE, AND PHILOSOPHY	HISTORY AND LITERATURE	ARCHITECTURE, ART, AND MUSIC

300	Constantine
	Constantinople founded
	
	Theodosius
		Toleration decreed for
		  Christians
		Council of Nicaea
		
		Christianity becomes official
		  Roman faith
		Pagan religions outlawed		

400	Beginning of Germanic takeover
	  of the Western Roman Empire
	
	Sack of Rome by Visigoths
	
	Sack of Rome by Vandals
	
	End of Western Roman Empire
		Jerome and Vulgate
		Augustine
		Recognition of papacy in
		  the West		

500	Roman law codified by Eastern
	  emperor Justinian
	Bubonic plague
		Benedict and his monastic
		  rule
				Sant'Apollinare
				  basilica

CHAPTER 1

The Birth of Civilization
in the Middle East

OVERVIEW

Even the earliest civilizations were a very recent turn in the long road of human evolution and development. Accordingly, this chapter begins long before ancient times, with *prehistory*—the millions of years in which human beings appeared on the earth, spread across the planet, and advanced in organization and skills. Language, religion, art, technology, farming, village communities, and other basic features of human existence right down to the present—all originated in prehistoric times.

This earliest development led around 3000 B.C. to the rise of societies that were so advanced that they count as the first *civilizations*—those of Mesopotamia and Egypt. In these Middle Eastern lands, there appeared complex social and economic structures, effective and lasting governments, compelling religious beliefs, impressive scientific and technical achievements, and sophisticated literary and artistic styles, all of which influenced many later civilizations, both Western and non-Western.

In addition, from these first civilized peoples, civilization soon began to spread to less advanced ones. This was not a one-way process in which civilized peoples did all the work. To come under the influence of civilized peoples at all, less advanced ones had to be at least wealthy enough to be worth the trouble of trading with or conquering. In fact, less advanced peoples were often skilled and powerful enough actually to conquer their civilized neighbors—but that, too, brought them under the influence of civilization. Furthermore, since less advanced peoples were so active in adopting civilized ways of life, they often brought something of their own ways of life to the types of civilization that they adopted. Thus, as civilization spread, it was liable also to change.

In these ways, by 1200 B.C. civilization had spread far beyond Mesopotamia and Egypt. There came into existence an international civilized "world," with many local versions of Mesopotamian and Egyptian civilization. This world stretched right across the Middle East and neighboring territories, including the eastern shores of the Mediterranean Sea—and there was no reason for the spread of civilization to stop there.

The Middle Eastern civilized world then underwent a crisis, involving both internal troubles and outside invasions. It emerged from the crisis larger, more advanced, and more expansive than before. From the recovering civilized world, the commercial and seafaring Phoenicians explored and traded ever farther among the less advanced lands and peoples of the Mediterranean Sea. Meanwhile, two empire-building peoples, first the Assyrians and then the Persians, united the Middle East under their rule. Individual empire builders might fall as well as rise, but by 300 B.C. most peoples of the Middle East were getting used to the idea of living as the subjects of one or other "universal" empire.

In the changing world of the Middle East after 1200 B.C., there also appeared a new religious belief—that of _monotheism_—in a single almighty God as the creator and ruler of the world. The rise of monotheism took place mainly among one people that first became prominent in the recovering civilized world after 1200 B.C., the Jews. Both their triumphs and their disasters in the power struggles of the era strengthened their belief in one God and in themselves as his Chosen People. By 300 B.C., the Jews were wholeheartedly committed to monotheism, and many of the features of later monotheistic religions were already part of the beliefs and practices of Judaism.

The Prehistoric Era

Viewed in relation to more ancient life forms (fish, reptiles, insects) and in relation to the age of the planet, humans are latecomers. Though the age of the earth (about four billion years) is beyond comprehension, the human-to-earth time relationship can be grasped through a drastic reduction in the time scale. If we reduce the age of the earth to the period of our familiar twenty-four-hour day, the time that elapsed prior to the appearance of humans is twenty-three hours and fifty-eight minutes. And of the two remaining minutes, representing the time of humans on earth, the period of civilization is less than the last half-second!

Why was civilization so long in coming on this planet—some billions of years? An answer takes form as we peer back through those thousands of centuries. We see that civilization was neither a chance happening nor a happening of nature; it was, rather, an extraordinary creation by one species. After developing physically and completing a series of successful responses to the environment, human beings were at last able to take the first important steps toward civilization.

A key step was the invention of writing. Because written language led quickly to historical records, it established a clear dividing line between "historic" and "prehistoric" epochs. Drawing on nonwritten evidence from geology, paleontology, anthropology, and archaeology, we will first look briefly at the long prehistoric period—from the first appearance of human beings to the dawn of civilization.

THE ORIGINS AND "AGES" OF HUMAN BEINGS

To discover the origins of humans, we must first identify them as a biological type. In the current scientific scheme of classification, their type is designated (in Latin) as

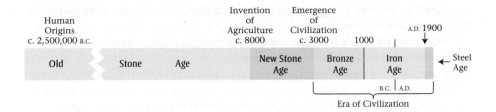

Homo sapiens sapiens, "thinking thinking human being." *H. s. sapiens* (the abbreviated form) is so called because it is the most advanced and the only surviving subspecies of the species *Homo sapiens,* "thinking human being," and the genus *Homo.* Excavations of fossils (remains of organisms) at a number of locations indicate that *H. s. sapiens* goes back only about 30,000 years. But archaeologists tell us that related subspecies of *Homo sapiens* first appeared about 160,000 years ago and that the first hominids (humanlike creatures) appeared about 2.5 million years ago. They differed from *Homo sapiens* chiefly in the size of their skull, which limits the size of the brain. The brain of today's species is nearly twice as large as that of the earliest species (and four times that of our closest biological relations, the great apes). This larger brain, which accounts for superior intelligence, is the reason why classifiers agreed on the term *sapiens* ("thinking") to distinguish modern *Homo* from earlier species.

Classification and comparison among advanced biological types may be based on criteria other than brain size. One of those criteria is the use of tools, a product of intelligence. Though certain other animals (notably apes) can and do make limited use of simple implements, humans clearly surpass them in conceiving, fashioning, and employing tools. Since humans are comparatively weak physically, this toolmaking ability proved crucial in the struggle for survival amid natural environments that were often unfriendly, as well as against competing, tougher creatures. Small in size (except for their brains), humans have used tools, as well as countless other devices such as weapons, vehicles, machinery, and buildings, as extensions of their mental and physical being—as ever more powerful levers for subduing competitors, constructing worlds of the imagination, and increasing the comfort and convenience of life. Owing to this persistent inventiveness, the stock of devices at the disposal of the human race has increased over time—at first very gradually and in recent times with dizzying speed. Most of the developments in human history described in this book—in the social and economic realms, in government, politics, and warfare, and even in culture and the arts—have taken place to a greater or lesser extent under the impact of this progress in technology.

Given the significance of tools as technology, it is fitting that the past ages of human beings have been identified and classified according to the development of materials used for making tools, as determined by excavation of early human remains and the tools found alongside them. Standard methods of dating such remains include investigating the geological stratum (earth layer) in which they are found or subjecting them to laboratory tests that reveal their approximate age.

The earliest (and longest) prehistoric period is called the Old Stone (Paleolithic) Age. This era reaches back to the beginnings of the earliest human types, who used tools made of chipped stone. Humans made many improvements over the passing thousands of years, and the pace of progress speeded up with the appearance of *Homo sapiens.* Stone tools became ever stronger, sharper, and more specialized for different tasks, until by 8000 B.C. they had advanced so far that archaeologists refer to the subsequent period as the New Stone (Neolithic) Age.

When metals finally replaced stone as the principal tool material, the Neolithic Age was followed by the Bronze Age (about 3000–1000 B.C.) and then the Iron Age (after 1000 B.C.). (All these dates refer to developments in the Middle East; other regions of the world, either by imitating advances made there or through independent invention, passed through similar stages at somewhat later periods.)

Archaeological evidence indicates that the earliest humanlike species originated in East Africa. A later species, currently designated *Homo erectus,* appeared there about 1.5 million years ago and by half a million years ago had spread to much of Europe and southern Asia. At some later time—when, where, and how are as yet unknown—*Homo erectus* evolved into *Homo sapiens,* a new and more advanced species. Several subspecies of *Homo sapiens* are known to have existed, but by about thirty thousand years ago—again, for reasons that are much discussed but quite uncertain—these subspecies were replaced by or developed into a single subspecies, *Homo sapiens sapiens,* first in the Middle East and Europe and not long after that throughout Africa and Asia. This subspecies then made its way across a "land bridge" that at that time linked the eastern tip of Asia with Alaska to pioneer the human colonization of the Americas. In this way, *H. s. sapiens* became the first and only type of human to spread throughout the whole world.

During the course of its worldwide expansion, *H. s. sapiens* developed different physical characteristics in different regions of the world. Among these were the color of the skin and the shape of various external physical features that form the basis of the present-day distinctions among whites, blacks, orientals, and other races. These racial differences represent only a small part of the total genetic variations among human populations. In fact, "white" western Europeans actually have more genes in common with "black" West Africans than with their fellow "whites" from eastern Europe. In any case, by comparison with the variation that exists within many other species, the genetic variations among human beings are small, amounting to only minor differences within a single subspecies.

Humans of the *H. s. sapiens* subspecies, like earlier human types, lived for thousands of years as migratory (wandering) hunters, fishers, and gatherers of edible plants, wholly dependent for food and shelter on whatever the land and water happened to offer. For purposes of hunting, protection, and child rearing, they usually combined into small groups of perhaps twenty to thirty. (The "pack," rather than the single family, was probably the basic social unit of most early hunter-gatherer societies.) These groups fashioned shelters where they could—in caves or crude huts, with room for storing their tools and provisions.

Observation of hunting and gathering societies that have survived into recent times suggests that among prehistoric hunter-gatherers there was a rough equality between females and males, resulting partly from food-acquiring methods and partly from child-rearing practices. Women would have been responsible for gathering plants and the technologies required to store them and prepare them for eating, and men would have been responsible for hunting as well as the manufacture of tools and weapons that were needed for killing and butchering animals. In addition, pregnancies would have been few and far between. In the absence of easily digestible cereal or milk foods, children had to be breast-fed until they were old enough to eat normal adult food, and

AP/Wide World Photos

Fig. 1.1 Prehistoric Cave Painting. These images of rhinoceroses and a panther were painted about 25,000 years ago deep in a cave in southern France. Nearer the entrance, people had their dwellings, but they would only have seen these pictures on special occasions. To judge from animal bones thrown away in caverns used as dwellings, the painters did not hunt the beasts depicted, but perhaps they saw them as powerful beings and the images were used in worship. Layers of paint suggest that the paintings were continually restored, so they must have been very important objects.

since women are less likely to conceive while breast-feeding, during that period they would produce fewer children. Playing an equal part with men in ensuring the survival of the group, and with few children to take care of, women probably enjoyed much the same status and power within the hunting and gathering bands as men did.

Among the various abilities of *H. s. sapiens,* perhaps the most important was the capacity for language. There is no way of knowing precisely when and how this means of communication came into use—whether it was inherited from earlier human types or unique to the new type. Either way, it proved extremely useful to humans in hunting, fighting, and other cooperative enterprises. Language was also essential to the creation of abstract ideas—such as the concepts of guardian spirits, magic, and life after death. Along with these creations came the development of forms of aesthetic expression, themselves probably connected with religion and magic, such as cave paintings (*Fig. 1.1.*).

THE NEW STONE AGE: THE AGRICULTURAL REVOLUTION

As we have seen, accelerated toolmaking skills brought such a change in techniques that archaeologists have named the period after 8000 B.C. the Neolithic or New Stone Age. Along with these advances in toolmaking went fundamental alterations in human social organization and way of life. During the next two or three thousand years, substantial portions of the human species shifted from migratory hunter-gatherer patterns of existence to forms of settled agrarian life. This giant step, which involved the cultivation of plants, the taming of animals, and the breeding of both so as to adapt them to human needs, led to the founding of agricultural villages (such as Jericho, in Palestine) and the growth of more highly organized community relations. As a result of this Agricultural Revolution, humans no longer lived in the wild; they became food makers instead of food finders.

This change in the manner of providing nourishment brought greater security and stability to individuals and groups. It increased the supply of food (and other commodities) from what nature offered to what humans, with nature's help, could produce. One major consequence was a steep rise in actual and potential population. Total numbers of humans on earth, probably no more than four million at the close of the Old Stone Age, have grown to six billion today.

The Agricultural Revolution took place not once but on several different occasions throughout the world; the first such revolution, however, began in the Middle East. It was preceded and conditioned by important geological and climatic changes. The earth's most recent ice sheet, which had covered much of Europe after 70,000 B.C., began to melt and withdraw northward around 10,000 B.C. By 8000 B.C., the glaciers (which are still melting) had pulled back more or less to their modern limits. Europe was left cold and rainy; North Africa, formerly cooled and watered by glacial influence, began to dry up. The most favored areas lay in the Mediterranean latitudes, which include the Middle East (*Map 1.1*). In locations with fertile soil and a good water supply, the inhabitants had an opportunity to cultivate crops. Similar opportunities had existed countless times before. But only now did humans possess the combination of mental capacity, tools, and will that permitted them to make a successful response.

We can only imagine how farming began. Wild grasses bearing nourishing seeds flourished naturally in the grasslands above the river valleys of the Middle East. The grains would probably have been collected and stored by the women of hunting and gathering bands, who then observed that seeds that fell to the ground in the soft and well-trampled soil around the storage containers often sprouted into plants. The women would then have begun cultivating garden patches of these grasses, always preferring to put back into the soil the seeds of the plants that grew best and were easiest to harvest. Thus, over many generations, there emerged the first deliberately bred grain crops, wheat and barley. Gradually, tools were fashioned that made it possible to accomplish more work more efficiently and therefore to grow the new grain crops on a larger scale—stone-bladed hoes to break the soil for seeding, and flint-edged sickles to cut the edible seeds from the stalks.

Closely linked with crop production was the domestication of animals. Wild dogs were the first animals to be tamed by humans, probably by the men of hunting bands, who used them to help in finding and killing prey. With the Agricultural Revolution, however, sheep, goats, pigs, and cattle became more important—first as "prey" that did not need to be hunted as a source of food and then as providers of wool, skins, and milk. Finally, toward the end of Neolithic times, humans began to make use of the muscular strength of large animals in agriculture and transportation. Most likely the first animals to be used in this way were cattle, particularly oxen (bulls that were castrated to make them unaggressive and responsive to training).

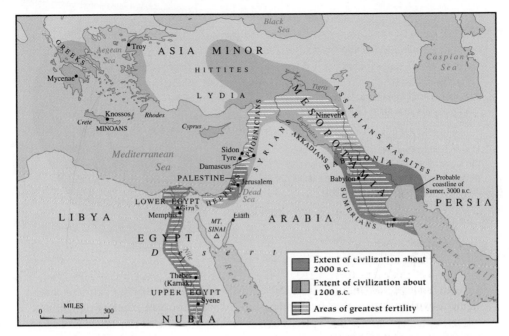

Map 1.1 The Civilized World of the Middle East, 3000–1200 B.C. In the course of 1,800 years, civilization spread from its original centers in the river valleys of southern Mesopotamia and Egypt to the mountainous interior of Asia Minor and to the coasts and islands of the eastern Mediterranean. Many different civilized ways of life arose in these regions, but they were all linked by common cultural features, peaceful and warlike contacts, and trade by land and sea.

But selecting and training animals was not enough. In addition, devices had to be invented that would make their strength available for transporting people and goods, and for tilling the ground. Around 3500 B.C., two such devices appeared: the wheel, first used in the grasslands on the borders of Europe and Asia, and the plow, which is first known to have existed among the villagers of Neolithic Europe (pp. 56–57). With the development of the plow, which turned over the soil for seeding faster and more thoroughly than hoes, cereal crops like wheat and barley changed from being garden crops that formed only a small part of the diet to field crops, providing the main foodstuffs for far larger populations than before.

Along with farming and the domestication of animals there arose a whole range of new technologies to make the products of the fields and pastures fit for human use. Bread, beer, wine, cheese, edible oils, woven cloth, leather, fired-clay pottery for cooking and storage, clay bricks for house building—all of these items of food, clothing, and equipment that we take for granted today were first used by the early farmers of the Middle East. When one bears in mind how many complex operations are involved in turning wheat into bread or the wool of a sheep into a garment, it is clear that the Agricultural Revolution was one of the most decisive eras of technological advance in human history. In addition, such practical enterprises stimulated artistic expression, whose character and quality are preserved in the pottery of the New Stone Age (*Fig. 1.2*).

Fig. 1.2 Neolithic Storage Jar. Pottery making, developed at the time of the Agricultural Revolution, made possible the storage of plant and animal products that were now available in much larger quantities than before. In addition, as with this jar, which was made in Egypt about 4000 B.C., pottery surfaces gave painters a new medium for artistic creation (compare *Fig. 2.4*, p. 75).

Kestner Museum/Hanover Germany

Last but not least, looking after crops and animals required more or less permanent settlements within easy reach of field and pasture. Around 6000 B.C. the first agricultural villages appeared, consisting typically of huts made of sun-dried clay bricks and a few special-purpose buildings such as granaries and shrines of local gods and goddesses.

The social and intellectual consequences of the Agricultural Revolution were far-reaching. The typical village, with two or three hundred inhabitants, required greater control and organization than the earlier hunting packs of twenty to thirty persons. Authority probably rested in the hands of male elders and village chiefs. The farmlands were most likely considered common property and would have been worked cooperatively. Since individual and community survival depended on closely coordinated efforts, the lives of the villagers would have been regulated by complex systems of tradition and custom, out of which the law and ethics of civilized societies ultimately grew.

In addition, the Agricultural Revolution was probably accompanied by profound changes in the division of labor between men and women and hence in their shares of power in the family and society. The reason for these changes seems to have been that agriculture could feed many more people than hunting and gathering and needed many more people as laborers; it also shortened the period of breast-feeding by providing foods that young children could eat, thereby causing women to become pregnant at shorter intervals than before (pp. 10–11). Consequently, pregnancy, childbirth, and child rearing took up far more of women's time and effort than in earlier times, and this would have had the effect of confining them, at least partially, to a new sphere of activity that had itself come into existence along with settled village life: the home.

Women tended to concentrate on tasks that could be accomplished in and around the home and which could be combined with looking after children. Among these were garden cultivation and the care of barnyard animals, all phases of food preparation from grain grinding to cooking, and the crafts of yarn spinning and cloth weaving. Tasks that required distance from the home came to be done mainly by men: tending to field crops and herd animals, most kinds of skilled crafts, and trade, as well as politics, government, and war. Once this pattern was established, it became a basic feature of most societies until the changes in the division of labor between women and men that began with the rise of industrial society in recent times (p. 640).

This division of labor was never absolutely hard and fast. It could be broken down by emergencies, such as the death of male or female members of households. It could shift over time; thus, in many societies, cloth weaving eventually became a male occupation. Individuals could always break through the barrier, notably the many upper-class women of later civilized societies who became rulers of kingdoms and empires. Nevertheless, the distinction between "men's work" and "women's work" persisted, and perhaps because it placed the main responsibility for the survival of the household and for community affairs on men, it gave them power over women of a kind that they may not have had before. From the Neolithic Age up to recent times, values, customs, and laws concerning the relationships of women and men would vary greatly at different times and places. But the variations would usually be within a basic framework of female dependence on males.

Religious beliefs and rituals were closely associated with food production. As hunters, humans had displayed a respect for animal spirits in their daily pursuit of game. As farmers, they worshiped the spirit of the earth—the fruitful Great Mother who brought forth the harvest. Worship of the Great Mother expanded quickly, and priests came into being to seek her favor. Countless other spirits and deities were revered by farmers and herders. Of particular importance were sky objects, especially the sun and moon, whose movements provided a visible and regular calendar—and a calendar is indispensable for the accurate timing of plantings and harvests. The sun, through its rising and setting and its yearly movement across the various constellations (patterns of stars in the sky), made it possible to reckon the days, seasons, and years; the moon, through its phases, enabled people to keep track of passing weeks and months. Eventually, the early sky watchers noticed that the roughly twenty-nine days that it takes the moon to go through its phases do not divide evenly into the roughly 365 days that it takes the sun to return to the same position in a particular constellation. The problem of adjusting the months so that they would stay in step with the seasons and years became humanity's first "scientific" endeavor.

Over many centuries, the Agricultural Revolution and the changes that went with it spread outward from the region of their origin—notably to the Neolithic peoples of Europe, who adapted wheat and barley to the cooler and wetter conditions of that continent. In Africa, tropical Asia, and eventually also the Americas, separate agricultural revolutions based on local crops such as yams, rice, corn, and potatoes brought settled village life to the humans of those regions as well.

In this way, the small agricultural community, with its farms, established routines, watchful priests, and dependence of women on men, became the typical way of life of the human race throughout much of the world. In spite of countless changes in farming methods, customs and traditions, and religious beliefs, this way of life persisted for thousands of years down to the time of the Industrial Revolution (pp. 505–506), and it is still to be found in many parts of the world today.

The Neolithic villages also prepared humans for their next cultural leap: the rise of the first true civilizations. This was not a simultaneous worldwide development. On the contrary, throughout human history, it has only rarely happened that a prehistoric society of farmers and villagers has evolved on its own into an advanced civilization. For

this to happen seems to require a stimulating combination of advantages and difficulties, which are encountered only at certain times and places. There must be favorable
conditions of soil and climate that make primitive farming unusually productive,
thereby enabling farmers to produce the wealth necessary for advanced civilization;
but there must also be difficulties and problems in exploiting these conditions, which
force people to develop new technical and cultural abilities.

The best-known "cradles of civilization" of this kind are the river valleys of the
Middle East about 3500 B.C., where the earliest known civilizations arose; those of
northern India and northern China about a thousand years later; and the plains,
forests, and mountain valleys of Central America and the Andes toward 500 B.C. All of
these played major roles in world history, but the Western civilization of modern times
is directly descended from the early civilizations of the Middle East: those of Mesopotamia and Egypt.

The Earliest Cities: Mesopotamia

The civilizations of Mesopotamia and Egypt emerged at about the same time (from
roughly 3500 B.C. onward), seemingly independent of each other. They lasted down to
the beginning of the Christian era, leaving a massive inheritance of cultural achievement, technical and scientific knowledge, and religious belief that has influenced
many subsequent civilizations down to the present day. For many centuries, all direct
knowledge of ancient Mesopotamia and Egypt was lost until in recent times archaeologists dug up their cities and scholars deciphered their writing systems and languages.
As a result, recorded history now goes back almost to the beginnings of these earliest
known civilizations. In the case of Mesopotamia, it is even possible to reconstruct how
civilization arose out of the earlier village life of the region.

The scene of this momentous development was a vast plain stretching between
two great rivers of the Middle East, the Tigris and the Euphrates. These "twin" waterways follow generally parallel courses for about 600 miles from their headwaters in
present-day Turkey, until they finally enter the Persian Gulf (*Map 1.1, p. 13*). The area
bounded by them forms the heartland of the modern states of Syria and Iraq, but in
ancient times the Greeks aptly named it Mesopotamia, "the land between the rivers."

About 3500 B.C., several thousand years after the Agricultural Revolution began,
Mesopotamia and the region surrounding it already had many prosperous villages. But
the leap to civilization began in a much smaller area: the southernmost portion of
Mesopotamia, where the twin rivers ran close to each other before entering the gulf.
This was an unattractive district: the land was flat, marshy, and open to disastrous floods.
Rainfall was slight, and the summers were hot and humid. To live here at all, the local
farmers relied on irrigation. Seasonal river flooding deposited water and the rich silt
(earth materials containing plant nutrients) that had washed down from distant hill-
sides; the villagers diverted the water onto their fields and palm groves, which were
the most productive of the entire Middle East. But because of the sheer size of the rivers,
there were not many places where the water was controllable enough for irrigation to

be practicable, so that villages and patches of cultivation were actually fewer and farther between than elsewhere in Mesopotamia.

What began the rise to civilization was a change in the local climate, which became slightly colder and drier about 3500 B.C. With less water flowing through them, the twin rivers, especially the Euphrates, became easier to harness for irrigation. The effects were dramatic. In two or three centuries around 3000 B.C., the population of this area expanded tenfold. Many new villages were founded, some older villages grew into small towns, and a few of the towns grew still further. They became the first true *cities* in the history of the world, with populations estimated as high as forty thousand people. With growing population and wealth came technical innovation, cultural development, and more complex social organization.

Eventually, as the landscape continued to dry out and water actually became scarce, the wealth and population ceased to grow. But the waters never retreated so far as to make city life impossible. Instead, the cities responded to the new problems with new solutions. They built large-scale, centrally controlled water conservation and irrigation systems. Intensive warfare also began among them for control of scarcer resources. Governments developed that were powerful enough to plan and organize these undertakings. Nurtured by a favorable environment and then toughened by harsher conditions, there grew up in southern Mesopotamia a new kind of society, so much more advanced than the older one that today it counts as one of the world's first true civilizations.

SUMER (3500–2400 B.C.)

The ancient name of the southern portion of Mesopotamia where the new civilization arose was Sumer, and the people who created it are therefore known as the Sumerians. They seem to have arrived in southern Mesopotamia sometime after 3500 B.C., conquering or absorbing the earlier inhabitants. We have no evidence regarding their origins, but it is possible that they came from somewhere in central Asia; very likely, they were attracted to their new homeland by its growing wealth and fertility as the environment there began to change. They settled in and ruled over the communities of the region, including its growing cities, each of which became the seat of government for a surrounding area of villages and countryside. The ruins of many of these cities have been excavated in recent times, with especially spectacular discoveries of buildings and works of art at the city of Ur on the Euphrates River. For over one thousand years the Sumerians controlled the southern parts of Mesopotamia, and for long periods, much of the north as well. They shaped the basic ideas and institutions—political, economic, social, religious, and artistic—that would become the models for civilization throughout Mesopotamia and, later, Europe.

Rise of a Complex Society. As the population of Sumer grew, there was a heightened need for social direction, regulation, and discipline. At first, this was exercised mainly by a specialized priesthood. The power of the priests originally came from their status as servants of the gods and goddesses—the personified forces of nature (p. 21) upon whom the Sumerians believed that the survival of their communities depended. As these communities became more prosperous and powerful, they devoted much of their new resources to the service of the gods and goddesses, thereby greatly increasing the power and wealth of the priests and priestesses. They, for their part, were far from confining themselves to matters of ritual and belief. It was they who directed the building of unprecedentedly large temples to house the gods and goddesses, employed craftsmen to furnish the temples with costly and beautiful works of art, managed vast properties, introduced technological innovations, and were responsible for the invention of writing. In Sumer, the priesthood led the process of social, technical, and cultural innovation out of which civilization emerged.

In time, however, as the waters retreated and resources grew scarcer, there arose another group of leaders whose power was originally based on military might rather than on religious belief. As the landscape became drier, the cities of Sumer became increasingly tempting to roving gangs of bandits and wandering peoples, and the Sumerians fought among themselves over rival land claims and water rights. And as the competition for resources grew more intense, so did warfare among the cities and with foreign peoples. In each city, soldiers and armies appeared. Military chieftains, arising as defenders of their communities, won power and rewards. By 2500 B.C., these military leaders had come to be called "kings," with power not only in war but also in the peacetime governance of the cities. Their relationship with the priests seems to have been one of both partnership and competition. Like the priests, the kings claimed that they ruled under the direction of the gods; to make sure of divine support, they built temples and took a leading part in temple rituals. At "divine command," they also taxed the people and built impressive palaces for themselves. In varying forms, palace and temple have continued to be the dual houses of social power in virtually every civilization since Sumer.

In this way, each major city of Sumer, together with its surrounding countryside, acquired its own government and armed forces, independent of—and, indeed, fiercely competitive with—others of its kind. It was the first appearance in history of the *city-state,* a form of government that would continually recur wherever conditions favored it, whether in the Middle East, ancient Greece, or Italy of the Middle Ages and Renaissance (pp. 41–42, 64, 67, 309, 311).

Priests, kings, and the artisans and soldiers whom they employed all depended for their food on the cultivators of the soil—who made up about 90 percent of the population. The farmland surrounding most cities was divided into one section worked for the temple priests, another for the king, and the remainder for large private landowners. Most people were tenant farmers who worked on one of these sections and received a share of the crop for their labors—the rest went for the upkeep of the other groups or into vast temple storehouses from which the community as a whole could draw in time of famine or siege. The farmers were prosperous enough to purchase pottery, textiles, and tools manufactured by skilled artisans; some became craftsmen themselves, employed in temples and palaces to produce tools, weapons, works of art, and other articles for use by the priests and rulers. Others turned to commerce, shipping surplus produce beyond the city in exchange for commodities (such as metals, timber, and stone) that the city lacked. Finally, some people—mostly farmers—who had fallen into heavy debt sold themselves (or their children) as payment for debt and labored as artisans or domestic servants for fixed periods of time. They shared this early, limited form of slavery with captives of war.

In this way, with its priests and kings, soldiers and craftsmen, merchants and farmers, Sumer developed one of the main features that distinguished civilized from primitive societies: the division of labor and specialization of social functions. Out of this, in turn, there developed a system of ranks of prestige, authority, and power. At the top, acting in the name of the city's chief god or goddess, were the king, the high priests, and their principal officers and agents. Next in order were the private men of wealth—great landowners and merchants. Then came the largest group by far—the commoners, consisting mainly of farmers (peasants) and a smaller number of free craftsmen. At the very bottom were the slaves, who were regarded as the property of their masters.

As Sumerian society grew more complex and sophisticated, women began to occupy some of the roles of authority and prestige that they would fill in many subsequent civilized societies. They had an important part to play in religion: the temple rituals of male gods were entrusted to priestesses who were held in great veneration. There were wealthy female landowners, as well as kings' wives, who administered large estates. But the priestesses and wealthy women occupied specialized niches within a general structure of female subordination. In Sumer, there were only kings and no queens, and unlike the priests of goddesses, the priestesses wielded no power outside the temples. Furthermore, with the Sumerian development of writing, there arose a whole new area of civilized life from which women seem to have been mostly excluded—that of education and literary culture.

Technology. Along with the advances in social and political organization came progress in technology. In ancient times, civilized societies had no monopoly on technical inventiveness, and the Sumerians benefited greatly from a series of epoch-making innovations, originating among socially and politically less advanced peoples, that changed the ways of life of many societies across Asia, Africa, and Europe from about 3500 B.C. onward. Among these were the wheel and the plow (pp. 57–58), which early written documents indicate were widely used in Sumer by 3000 B.C. Another such innovation, which revolutionized the making of tools and weapons, was the development of metalworking.

As early as 6000 B.C., people living in the ore-bearing mountains that fringed Mesopotamia had learned to use loose pieces of copper that they found lying on the ground. By hammering the metal, either cold or heated, they managed to create a variety of useful articles. The supply of pure copper was limited, however, and tools made of copper are rather soft. A first breakthrough came about 4000 B.C. with the discovery that copper as well as other metals, notably tin, could be smelted—that is, extracted from ore (rock in which metal is combined with other materials). Later on came a further discovery: that copper and tin could be alloyed (blended) to make a much harder and stronger metal—bronze. Heat-resistant ovens, or kilns, had to be developed, which could withstand the extremely high temperatures required to smelt and alloy metals; new processes of working the metals also had to be devised, such as casting (pouring the molten metal into molds to produce articles of the desired shape). Gradually the problems were solved, and by 3000 B.C. the use of the new metal had spread to Sumer. Mesopotamia, as well as many other lands of western Asia, northern Africa, and eastern Europe, had entered the Bronze Age (p. 10). By 3000 B.C. several other metals besides copper and tin—notably gold, silver, and lead—were also being worked for use or decoration. But bronze remained the king of metals until the general adoption of iron tools and weapons after 1000 B.C. (p. 41).

The Birth of Writing. In addition, the Sumerians were themselves responsible for yet another great invention: one of the world's first systems of writing.[1] For such a momentous innovation, the origins of Sumerian writing were surprisingly humdrum. Nearly all of the earliest known written documents of Sumer (dating from about 3100 B.C. onward) are accounting records, providing information on supplies delivered to temple storehouses or consumed by temple officials. Thus it seems that writing was developed in response to the increased prosperity of Sumer and the increased need for direction and control—both of which the wealthy and powerful Sumerian priesthood would have been particularly well aware of.

Even before the rise of civilization, Neolithic villagers had used a simple record-keeping system based on clay counters with pictograms (drawings of objects, such as sheep or bales of cloth) scratched into them. In the Sumerian temples, which had much more property to keep track of and consequently a greater need for detailed records, this system of counters developed into something much more sophisticated. The pictograms were simplified so that they could be more easily and quickly "drawn." Eventually, each symbol became no longer a picture but simply a series of wedge-shaped marks; hence Sumerian writing is known as "cuneiform" (from *cuneus,* Latin for "wedge"). Some of the symbols came to be used as ideograms (symbols for ideas, such as "life"); in time, others were adapted to become phonograms, which stood for the sounds of words or syllables. Just as important, the new symbols were no longer written singly, each on its own small counter. Instead, any desired combination of symbols was scratched with a sharpened piece of reed, or stylus, into a larger piece of moistened clay, known as a tablet. The tablet was then dried to form a permanent record of complicated transactions involving any number of items.

But as a result of all these improvements, the system had outgrown its original purpose. By 2600 B.C., a writer could produce a visual statement not just of business dealings but of anything that was spoken. In addition to keeping accounts, writing could now express any human thought or feeling.

By present-day standards, cuneiform writing was clumsy and hard to learn. Writing was practiced only by professional scribes who had to master hundreds of symbols (characters) and the delicate skill of imprinting them on moist clay. But so valuable was the practice of writing, for keeping records and preserving ideas in religion, law, and literature, that other peoples of the Middle East later borrowed the cuneiform symbols and adapted them to their own languages. For thousands of years, cuneiform writing remained the main vehicle of communication throughout much of the Middle East, and it was not until after the beginning of the Christian era that it finally fell out of use.

Written laws, which are essential to the very concept of civilization, were among the fruits of the invention of writing. They first appeared as statements of the customary rules and practices of early Sumerian society. Judicial officers, usually members of the privileged priestly class, may have felt little need for written guides as they inter-

---

[1] The Egyptian writing system, which dates from about the same time period as that of Sumer, is discussed on pp. 34–35.

preted traditional rules and decided on penalties in the cases brought before them. But the commoners no doubt insisted on the protection afforded by written statements of those rules; to use a modern phrase, they sought "a government of laws, not men." By 2500 B.C., most city-states had begun to assemble summaries, or codes, of accumulated law.

Religion. Law and life in Sumer were geared to an intensely religious view of the universe and humanity. Civic order, maintained by human authority, was viewed as part of universal order, upheld by divine power. The Sumerians believed not in a single all-powerful god, like the God of the later Jewish, Christian, and Muslim faiths, but in hundreds of deities. This type of religion, which is called *polytheism* (belief in many gods), as distinguished from monotheism (belief in one God), was inherited by the Sumerians from their more primitive ancestors. It probably originated in the belief, which seems to date back to the earliest times of the human species, that powerful living beings, both friendly and hostile, caused the workings of nature. In addition, Sumerian religion had two other characteristics, which probably originated with the rise of civilization and were passed on to subsequent peoples. It was anthropomorphic, regarding the deities as humanlike in character and appearance; and among its deities, a dozen or so great gods and goddesses were considered to excel all the others in power and holiness.

Many of the Sumerian deities are described in surviving religious writings. The highest among them was the god of heaven (or sky), named An. Important also were Enki, the god of the waters, and Inanna, goddess of fertility. These and other leading gods and goddesses were believed to be concerned chiefly with their own affairs; the role of humans was to serve and amuse them. They had homes (temples) in particular cities. There they were served by priests and priestesses who sought their favor through prayer, sacrifice, and ritual. The will of the gods could be revealed and interpreted (by means of divination) through signs (omens) that appeared in dreams, the entrails of animals, and the stars. It was in Sumer that such mystical arts, including astrology, made their appearance.

Humans could expect neither immortality nor rewards and punishments after death. Rather, the Sumerians believed that the spirits of the dead descended to a dark underworld, where they eventually passed into nothingness. (This view of the afterlife was a forerunner of the ancient Greek Hades; p. 76.) And so the Sumerians generally made no effort to prepare the bodies of the dead for a voyage beyond the grave. The only true life for humans was life on earth, and that life was brief, hard, and uncertain; this view was in some measure a product of the unpleasant physical environment of Mesopotamia. The gloom of daily existence was reinforced by religious myths of the Creation and the Flood, each showing humanity at the mercy of divine powers.

Though passive "acceptance" was no doubt the main popular mood, the surviving literature of the Sumerians reveals a many-sided humanity. Fables, legends, psalms, and proverbs were passed down mainly by word of mouth. The most impressive literary creations of these people, recited by bards and minstrels and recorded on clay tablets, are their epic poems. This form of expression, dealing with heroes and their ambitions and struggles, is common to many societies. Most of the Sumerian epic poems concern the career of an early king, Gilgamesh. Though Gilgamesh was probably a real person, in epic poetry he becomes a semidivine character who embodies the values and aspirations of the people of Sumer. He fights for his city-state, slays hostile humans and animals, and displays bravery, cunning, and a sense of fairness and mercy. The king's quest for immortality—a principal theme of the epic—ends in failure, as it does for all people. The epics of Gilgamesh, along with the religious myths of the Sumerians, provided a rich cultural inheritance for later civilizations in the Middle East. Through direct contact with Mesopotamia and indirectly through the Syrians and Jews, the Greeks and Romans shared that inheritance.

Science. In addition to their pioneering contributions to writing, law, religion, and literature, the Sumerians established the foundations of mathematics, science, and engineering. These developments were direct responses to their practical needs in cultivation, irrigation, and commerce. The Sumerians devised the basic processes of arithmetic: multiplication, division, and the square and cube root. It was they who first divided the hour into sixty minutes, the minute into sixty seconds, and the circle into 360 degrees. They also derived the formula for computing the hypotenuse of a right triangle and worked out the method for calculating the area of a rectangle.

A lunar ("moon-based") calendar provided for a month of about twenty-nine days, the time taken by the moon to go through all its phases. Since twelve months of this length did not quite add up to one solar (sun) year, the approximately 365 days taken by the sun to return to the same position against the background of the stars (p. 15), an extra month had to be added every few years to keep the lunar months in step with the solar year. The seven days of the week were named for heavenly bodies (Sun Day, Moon Day, and so forth), and the most prominent sky objects were charted by official astronomers. These trained observers also charted the twelve divisions (signs) of the zodiac— the constellations through which the sun passes in the course of the year—which are still familiar to the followers of astrology.

The Sumerians accomplished little in the field of medicine, for they were ignorant of the physical basis of disease. They believed that sickness was caused by spirits entering the body. The physician, accordingly, prescribed magical charms (or bitter-tasting drinks) to exorcise the culprits. Surgery was sometimes employed, but progress was retarded by severe penalties imposed on the surgeon in the event of failure.

Architecture and the Arts. Architecture and the arts served both everyday purposes and religious and political needs. The construction of simple mudbrick (adobe) houses and walls was not a very difficult problem, but the raising of mighty temples to gain the favor of the gods or palaces to display the power of kings was a challenge that brought forth some spectacular monuments. We know of these only through fragmentary remains because the Tigris-Euphrates region contains no durable stone. Even the most ambitious structures, such as hundred-room palaces for kings, were built of mudbrick, which is neither a beautiful nor a durable material. The builders used as basic forms the self-supporting arch, the tunnel-shaped vault, and the dome, but they did not exploit those forms as the Romans would many centuries later (p. 137).

We know from remains and records that temples were the most distinguished structures. The principal temple of a Sumerian city was invariably built at the center of the city, with structures for priests and temple craftsmen surrounding it. Typically, it consisted of an enclosure placed atop a man-made "mountain," a kind of step-pyramid called a *ziggurat* (*Fig. 1.3*). The first level of the ziggurat at Ur was a solid mudbrick mass some 50 feet high and 200 by 300 feet at its base. It supported two ascending setback levels, the higher one serving as a pedestal for the shrine (house) of the deity. (A structure of this type was probably the model for the biblical Tower of Babel, with its "top in the heavens," described in Genesis 11:1–9.) This general type of mountain-temple has reappeared throughout the world over long stretches of time, notably in Mexico and India, and perhaps in all cases it reflects similar beliefs about the relationship of the human and the divine. The hundred-step ramps of the ziggurat suggest a sacrificial climb as the worshiper approaches the deity or perhaps the descent of the deity from heaven to be present among the people; the sheer mass of the monument symbolizes the power and rank of the god in comparison with ordinary mortals.

The Sumerian temples were dominated by statues, which the faithful believed embodied divine personalities. The sculptors displayed extraordinary skill in creating highly stylized humanlike forms; deities, high priests, and kings were their main subjects. In all of the statues, the most prominent feature is the eyes; the pupils are magnified enormously, perhaps reflecting the dominance of eye function in human perception and communication (*Fig. 1.4*). Because durable stone was hard to come by in Mesopotamia, sculptors often used sandstone or clay, adding shells, alabaster, and semiprecious stones for dramatic effect. Other artisans crafted exquisite jewelry and metalwork, chiefly for use in the temples and palaces.

FEET
0   50   100

Fig. 1.3 Reconstruction of the Ziggurat at Ur. The temple at the top rests on three platforms, each of them a solid mass of sun-dried clay (adobe) bricks. The careful design and large scale of the structure show the skills, organization, and wealth of early Sumerian civilization.

Fig. 1.4 Sumerian Temple Statuettes. These miniature statues, the largest of them 30 inches high, date from about 2700–2600 B.C. Each statue represents a worshiper who has donated it to the god of the temple. By placing these images of themselves in the temple, worshipers proclaimed their loyalty to the god and hoped to gain his protection and support.

BABYLONIA (2400–1200 B.C.)

One of the most remarkable features of Sumerian civilization is that it served as a base for all later cultural growth in the Middle East, as well as that of neighboring territories to the east and west. It absorbed numerous infiltrations and conquests by peoples from outside Mesopotamia, but the patterns of work, class structure, law and government, religious and literary traditions, and art forms persisted pretty much unbroken. For more than three thousand years, from the earliest city-states until the last days of the Persian Empire (330 B.C.), the institutions established at Sumer provided a groundwork of civilization from the Persian Gulf westward to the Mediterranean and Black seas.

The early Sumerian city-states were frequently at war, but no one of them managed to keep down the others. After 2400 B.C., that balance was destroyed by conquerors from an area just north of Sumer, called Akkad. These conquerors spoke a Semitic language (one of the major linguistic branches) that was common to the inhabitants of the Arabian peninsula (*Map 1.1*, p. 13). They had migrated over a period of centuries from Arabia into the Akkad region. About 2350 B.C., one of their military chieftains, Sargon, began to attack the Sumerian cities. His ruthless campaigns won for him not only Sumer but also the rest of the Mesopotamian region. Sargon was history's first great military conqueror. His empire fell within a century, however, to be followed by a long period of struggles for control over the Tigris-Euphrates valley. It was not until about 1900 B.C. that order and security were once again restored. This was the accomplishment of the Amorites, another tribe of Semitic nomads, who had settled near the city-state of Babylon, on the midcourse of the Euphrates River.

The Amorite kings of Babylon forced into submission the cities of Sumer to the south. The greatest king of their line was Hammurabi, who built up an empire that included much of Mesopotamia by 1700 B.C. Akkadian, a Semitic tongue, now became the language of the new empire of Babylonia, and the Sumerian language was afterward used only by priests and scholars. Now the Creation myth was revised, and Marduk, patron god of the city of Babylon, was portrayed as the Maker of All Things. He soon became the foremost deity of Mesopotamia and was commonly called Ba'al (Lord).

Hammurabi was the most impressive ruler in the history of Babylonia. He developed an efficient civil service, permitting effective administrative control over his far-flung empire. The fundamentals of Sumerian culture remained intact; only minor cultural shifts are reflected in the Code of Hammurabi, the best-known collection of laws of the ancient world. We know that Sumerian law codes existed several centuries earlier, but only Hammurabi's code has been recovered in its original form (*Fig. 1.5*). The code is engraved (in cuneiform writing) on a 7-foot-tall black stone pillar; a single relief sculpture at the top shows the Babylonian god of justice, Shamash, holding the symbols of divine authority while dictating the laws to King Hammurabi.

Hammurabi's Empire

The intention of the sculpture is clear: the rules engraved on the black stone represent the will of the god coming through the person of a divinely sent king. Actually, the laws of Hammurabi are a summation of legal concepts and practices that had grown out of centuries of human experience in the Tigris-Euphrates valley. The chief importance of the code is that it provided a uniform standard of law, in place of differing local interpretations, for the whole empire of Babylonia.

Hammurabi's code is divided into nearly three hundred clauses, or "case laws," dealing with the administration of justice, social classes, property, trade and commerce,

© Réunion des Musées Nationaux/Art Resource, NY

Fig. 1.5 A King and His God. This carving is from the top of a stele (stone slab) on which the laws of King Hammurabi (c. 1780 B.C.) are inscribed. The picture shows the Babylonian god Shamash (seated at right) giving the laws to Hammurabi. It expresses the Mesopotamian concept of kingship, which was inherited by Western civilization and persisted down to modern times—that kings, though mortal, rule as servants of divine power and must therefore be honored and obeyed.

assaults, wages, and marriage and the family. Marriages, we find, were arranged by parents, the marriage contract specifying the price of the bride and the amount of her dowry. Husbands could divorce their wives freely and were complete masters of their unmarried children. A wife, however, could seek separation only on charges of cruelty or neglect, and if the court found her to be at fault, she was subject to death by drowning. A sterile wife could find a concubine (female companion) for her husband to bear him a child; the concubine and her offspring were accepted as legitimate members of the family. Though women were legally barred from engaging in business, records show that some did so and that some held property in their own name.

Punishments for criminal acts were quite different from modern practices. Neither imprisonment nor forced labor was imposed; rather, penalties took the form of physical acts against the person judged guilty. The supporting principle was "retaliation in kind" (Latin, *lex talionis*); as passed on to the Hebrews, it was expressed as "eye for eye, tooth for tooth" (Exodus 21:23–25). Mutilation was common for a variety of offenses, depending on the nature of the crime. A son who struck his father might have his hand cut off; a snooper or a spy might have an eye put out. Capital offenses (such as murder, treason, vandalism, disorder, or theft) were punished in a number of ways— to fit the crime. These ways included drowning, burning, hanging, crucifying, and impaling. Some of King Hammurabi's forms of punishment persisted through ancient times and survived in Europe until the eighteenth century. They have also influenced Islamic law and continue to do so today.

The high state of government, law, and economy achieved by the Babylonian empire did not prevent its falling apart soon after the death of Hammurabi. Less civilized peoples were attracted, as they had been previously, by the wealth of the Tigris-Euphrates valley. By 1600 B.C., the non-Semitic Kassites, from the mountains to the east of the Tigris, had conquered most of Babylonia. They adopted the Babylonian culture, language, and religion and dominated Mesopotamia for four hundred years down to 1200 B.C.

In this way, the civilization that had begun at Sumer flourished in spite of the many changes of rulers and nations that followed the downfall of the Sumerian city-states in 2400 B.C. In fact, from about that date, Mesopotamian civilization—as it is usually called, in reference to this later period—also spread far and wide among less advanced peoples in the lands that fringed the region to the north and west. Momentous changes were taking place among those peoples, above all as a result of the arrival of invaders from still farther north. Though these newcomers belonged to many different tribes and nations, they spoke related languages belonging to the widespread Indo-European linguistic group (p. 58). They brought with them a domestic animal that was so far unknown to civilized peoples, the horse, as well as a formidable new weapon of war, the chariot, which carried warriors wielding bows, spears, or axes. For a while the invaders were unbeatable, until every civilized nation as far away as Egypt adopted horse-drawn chariots as the main striking force of their armies. Eventually the newcomers settled down on the northern and western fringes of Mesopotamia, established organized kingdoms, adopted the institutions and culture of Mesopotamian civilization, and adapted cuneiform writing to their various languages.

Of the many Indo-European-ruled kingdoms, the most powerful and longest lasting was that of the Hittites in Asia Minor (present-day Turkey, *Map 1.1*, p. 13). In Asia Minor, civilization had to adapt to a very different natural environment from that of Mesopotamia. This was a land of mountains, forests, and high plateaus, where the most valuable resources were metals: copper, gold, and silver were plentiful, though tin was scarce. For centuries, local peoples and then Indo-European invaders had struggled for control of the mining districts, the routes by which tin was imported to make bronze

(p. 19), and the profitable export routes to Mesopotamia, as well as to Syria and Pales-tine on the eastern shore of the Mediterranean.

By about 1600 B.C., the Hittite kings had won this competition, and at the height of their power, they dominated almost all of Asia Minor. They ruled with the help of powerful nobles living in mountaintop strongholds, but in time they acquired almost absolute authority, as effective as that of any Mesopotamian king.

With the wealth they acquired from the trade in metals, they built an army of charioteers and well-trained infantry numbering as many as thirty thousand men and fought wars with Egypt to control Syria and Palestine. In the heavily fortified cities of the Hittite homeland, priests tended to gods and goddesses and practiced rituals that were partly Hittite and partly Mesopotamian. Scribes translated Babylonian versions of the tales of Gilgamesh and other Mesopotamian heroes into the Hittite tongue and composed letters in Akkadian (pp. 24–25) for the kings to send to foreign rulers—for the Semitic tongue of Mesopotamia had become the international language of trade and diplomacy in a civilized world that by 1200 B.C. stretched from the Persian Gulf to the Aegean Sea (*Map 1.1*, p. 13). And among the rulers with whom the Hittite kings cor-responded most often were their partners and rivals who ruled the other great civiliza-tion that had arisen at the same time as that of Mesopotamia—the pharaohs of Egypt.

Land of the Pharaohs: Egypt

The valley of the Nile River, like the twin valleys of Mesopotamia, was a center of early civilization. Its people were of mixed stock, having entered the area from Arabia (to the east), Nubia (to the south), Libya (to the west), and Palestine and Syria (to the north). Accordingly, the Egyptians were of both white and black racial origin, with the white probably predominating in the north of the country, and the black in the south, as is still the case today. They spoke an Afro-Asiatic tongue, one of a large group of languages spoken across northern Africa and the Middle East, which also includes the Semitic languages.

During the Neolithic era, the people of the Nile had moved toward civilization in response to the same influences that gave rise to the cities of Sumer, some 900 miles to the east (pp. 16–18). But the subsequent development of the two civilizations was quite different. For three thousand years, Egypt remained a unified, conservative, and rather insulated society. Political and sectional conflicts did not usually break the country's unity; for many centuries, foreign invasions were few and far between, and cultural in-fluences from abroad were welcomed or kept at arm's length, as seemed best to the lit-erate elite. Thus for the first two thousand years of its existence, Egypt enjoyed a conti-nuity and stability that gave its inhabitants a sense of permanence, even perfection, in their institutions and way of life; occasional times of trouble and change, far from de-stroying Egyptian civilization, provided an invigorating challenge. This sense of per-fection enabled Egyptian civilization to flourish even in its last thousand years of exis-tence, when the country was repeatedly invaded and for long periods under foreign rule. Thus the culture of the Nile contrasts in some critical respects with that of the Tigris-Euphrates; Western peoples are heir to both.

THE NILE AND THE "TWO LANDS"

The Nile River itself played a role in Egypt similar to that of the rivers of Mesopotamia. The cycle of labor and of life itself depended on the river's annual flooding and receding. The mighty Nile, the longest river in the world, rises in central Africa and winds northward for thousands of miles before descending into the torrid Egyptian desert. From that point it continues as a single navigable stream for some 500 miles until it flows, about 100 miles from the Mediterranean Sea, into a fan-shaped pattern of waterways, or delta (*Map 1.1*, p. 13). The country is thus divided into two distinct geographical sections, called by the ancient Egyptians the "Two Lands": Upper Egypt (the Valley) and Lower Egypt (the Delta). Lower Egypt is a triangular area of rich soil (deposited by the Nile); Upper Egypt is long and narrow, averaging no more than twelve miles in width. Beyond those areas of fertile land, Egypt was (and is) a barren wasteland.

The Egyptian rulers drew their strength both from "the gift of the Nile," which gave them the resources necessary for power, and from the desert barriers that for many centuries no foreign nation was able to cross in force. Behind these barriers, Egypt witnessed an early consolidation of increasingly wealthy communities, scattered along the river, into the kingdoms of Upper and Lower Egypt. Around 3100 B.C., the Two Lands were unified under a single king. The country's rulers from then on are usually known by the name later used by the Egyptians themselves: the pharaohs. One of the early pharaohs built a new capital at Memphis, south of the Delta and close to the boundary between the Two Lands, as the center of government for the entire country. Thus unlike Mesopotamia, where civilization began with independent city-states, Egyptian civilization, almost from the start, was linked with a single state under a single ruler.

GOVERNMENT BY A GOD-KING (3100–30 B.C.)

To hold the Egyptian state together for many centuries on end was no easy matter. That the Egyptians were able to do so was not only the result of the wealth of the Nile and their desert defenses. It was possible also because of their beliefs about the pharaoh, whom they both obeyed as a man given power by the gods and venerated as a god who dwelt among men.

Throughout most of the three thousand years of Egyptian civilization, every pharaoh was identified in different ways with three of the country's ruling deities. By birth, he was the son of the sun god, Re, who was also the king of all the other gods and goddesses. At his succession, he became the incarnation (living embodiment) of Horus, the falcon-headed ruler of the sky. When he died, he became one with Osiris, who reigned as pharaoh of the underworld. Thus before, during, and even after his reign, one or other mighty god was always linked with or actually present in the person of the pharaoh.

Yet the pharaoh was also a human being, empowered by and responsible to the gods; and this, too, gave him a unique position among the Egyptians. Alone among humans, they believed, it was he whom the gods and goddesses had appointed to conduct the rituals and sacrifices that won their favor and inclined them to do their work of upholding the universe. Of course, in hundreds of temples up and down the Two

Lands, thousands of priests and priestesses daily tended to the gods and goddesses in their shrines. But they did so only as delegates of the pharaoh: not even the most trivial ritual act they might perform was of any effect unless done in his name.

In his double capacity as god and man, the pharaoh had awesome responsibility and power. The stability and harmony of their state, the Egyptians believed, was part of the stability and harmony of the universe as a whole. The judges dealing out fair and impartial justice in the courts, the tax collectors levying no more from the peasants than was due, the Nile flooding in exactly the right amount to deliver its riches on schedule, even the sun rising on time in the morning and setting on time in the evening—all were simply different aspects of this same universal stability and harmony, which the Egyptians called *maat*. It was up to the pharaoh, by properly performing the rituals as a man and properly exercising his authority as a god, to uphold all these aspects of *maat* against the forces of chaos and confusion.

These convictions about the pharaoh were reflected in the way the country was governed. All of Egypt belonged to the pharaoh as his personal property, in which he tended "the cattle of god"—his subjects. The economy, the military, and the priesthood were closely supervised by his household staff. The pharaoh, of course, could and did delegate many of his functions to others. His chief deputy (vizier) directed most royal affairs; his high priests regulated religious matters.

The royal administrators and priests made up a kind of aristocracy (nobility) between the monarch and the commoner (peasant) class. Minor officials, soldiers, artisans, and laborers were drawn from the commoner class, but most commoners toiled as sharecroppers on the pharaoh's land. (Slaves, captured in wars, formed a small underclass.) No distinct business class emerged, as it did in Mesopotamia; foreign trading expeditions, mining, and similar large enterprises were conducted by select companies of the royal household. All exchanges and payments were in kind (goods). As a consequence, no cities of commerce arose in Egypt; the urban centers remained essentially administrative capitals or extensive temple compounds.

Egyptian women had a relatively high degree of freedom and independence. Monogamous marriage (one spouse) was the rule, and women could own property, bring lawsuits, and divorce their husbands. More often, seemingly, than in Sumer (p. 19)—though still not nearly so often as men—upper-class women learned to read and write. Harems (with multiple wives as well as concubines) were a feature of upper-class households, but there was always a principal wife who held high status and authority—especially in the royal household, since in order to avoid "diluting" the divine blood of the pharaoh, the principal wife was often the ruler's own sister. Thanks to this touch of divinity, Egyptian princesses and queens often wielded real power, especially when there was no male of the royal blood to inherit the throne or when the heir was still a child. But as usual, this was within a general framework of female subordination. The only woman to wield the full authority of a pharaoh, Hatshepsut, who enjoyed a long and successful reign shortly after 1500 B.C., was described in inscriptions and depicted in monuments not as a queen but as a "king"—evidently because masculinity was an essential feature of the god-king of Egypt.

The Egyptian political and social system did not always work smoothly. Like any hereditary monarchy, that of Egypt was from time to time shaken by incompetent pharaohs, disputes over the succession, disloyal courtiers, and self-seeking officials.

Whole dynasties of pharaohs (family lines involving many individuals) were often cut down by failure to produce heirs or even sometimes by violent turnovers—in all, over three thousand years, no less than thirty dynasties succeeded one another in power. There were even periods of total collapse, when the Egyptian state would dissolve into fragments. But to the Egyptians, such a state of affairs seemed profoundly abnormal and wrong. It was a disturbance of the order of the universe, which must sooner or later give way to the stability and harmony of *maat,* under a single all-powerful god-king.

As a result, the rhythm of Egyptian history was one of lengthy periods of stability and unity, interrupted by much briefer intervals of slippage and change. After several hundred years of early state building, the power of the pharaohs first reached its height in the period known to modern scholars as the Old Kingdom, beginning about 2700 B.C. In total command of the country's resources and having few foreign enemies to contend with, the pharaohs used their power to build the most gigantic of Egyptian monuments, the pyramids (pp. 36–37). About 2200 B.C., however, a series of weak pharaohs allowed power to pass to local administrators, who came to regard their positions as hereditary. For more than a century, Egypt remained in turmoil, until about 2050 B.C. It was then that a dynasty from the upriver city of Thebes brought the whole country under its rule, to form the "Middle Kingdom."

By this time, the world outside Egypt was changing, with the spread of Semitic tribes and the growth of many powerful states throughout the rest of the Middle East (pp. 24–28). Accordingly, the god-kings of Egypt faced a new challenge as part of their general task of upholding universal order against the forces of chaos: that of what they called "treading on" foreign nations. The pharaohs of the Middle Kingdom rose to this challenge and poured the spoils of their conquests into building and magnificently equipping the temples of the Nile. Finally, however, internal conflict was renewed about 1800 B.C. Semitic immigrant tribes known as the Hyksos (from the Egyptian words for "chiefs of foreign lands") were able to move into Lower Egypt, and the Middle Kingdom came to an end. Following the usual pattern of tribal conquerors of advanced civilizations, the Hyksos adopted Egyptian culture, and for a time their chieftains ruled Lower Egypt as pharaohs. Native Egyptian pharaohs continued to rule Upper Egypt from Thebes, and in 1600 B.C. they were able to defeat the Hyksos rulers and bring the nation into its imperial era, the New Kingdom.

More than ever before, the rulers of Egypt acted as conquerors. Their armies moved south into Nubia and vied with the Hittites of Asia Minor (pp. 27–28) for control of Palestine and Syria. Along with this aggressive warfare and bid for military glory came more open contact with the world beyond the Nile: for example, the pharaohs took to breeding horses and riding chariots, just like their Hittite rivals. Yet again, the wealth of the world went to the benefit of the gods and goddesses of the Nile. Though no longer builders of pyramids, the pharaohs of the New Kingdom instead had their mas-

sive tombs hewn out of solid rock in the Valley of the Kings near Thebes, and they constructed vast new temples like that of the Theban god Amon at Karnak (p. 37). Partly
because of this dedication of wealth to religion, the power of the priests eventually
came to overshadow that of the pharaohs. This, together with the inability of the then-
ruling dynasty to produce heirs, led to the end of the New Kingdom about 1100 B.C.

After the New Kingdom, Egypt became a frequent victim of power struggles in the
Middle East and northern Africa. It was dominated at different times—though with
intervals of independence—by its western and southern neighbors, the Libyans and
the Nubians, and by the Assyrians of Mesopotamia (pp. 43–45). In 525 B.C., Egypt
became a province of the universal empire of Persia (pp. 45–48); from 333 B.C., it
was ruled by the Greeks; and finally, in 30 B.C., it was conquered by the Romans
(pp. 101–103, 124–125).

Even so, Egyptian civilization continued to flourish. Libyan and Nubian rulers,
who were much influenced by Egyptian ways even in their homelands, governed as
genuine pharaohs, upholding the country's power and independence against enemies
in the Middle East. Later conquerors, though belonging to different civilizations, found
it wise to rule Egypt in accordance with the country's traditional beliefs and customs.
The last great temples of the Nile were built after 250 B.C. by Greek kings acting as Egyptian pharaohs, to uphold the stability and harmony of the universe by tending to the
needs of the gods.

Thus despite the ebb and flow of the nation's fortunes, the core institutions of
Egypt remained essentially unchanged until the onset of irreversible decline under the
Roman Empire. Over the very long period of time between 3100 and 30 B.C., the whole
of Egypt shared in a single civilization.

RELIGION AND LAW

Like the Mesopotamians, the Egyptians believed in the existence of numerous divine
forces and beings (polytheism). Many of their deities, tracing back to the Stone Age,
were originally conceived in the form of animals; during historic times, the divine images often bore animal heads or bodies. The sky god Horus, for example, is usually represented with the head of a falcon, and the pharaoh himself was sometimes portrayed,
as in the Great Sphinx (*Fig. 1.6*), with a human head on a lion's body. Other important
gods included the sun god Re and the wind god Amon, who came to be worshiped as a
combined god, "Amon-Re, King of the Gods." Sometimes the two were even joined together with a third, the craftsman god Ptah, to make a single, overwhelmingly mighty
deity.

This custom of worshiping different deities in a single combined form arose partly
out of the way in which Egypt itself had come into being. The many Egyptian deities
had originally been local ones, and as the different communities of the Nile combined
to form a single state, it made sense to believe that the god or goddess of one community was in fact the same as that of another with which it was now united. Furthermore, in spite of their varying appearances and powers, the Egyptian deities did not
have strong individual "personalities" such as the Greek gods and goddesses later displayed, so it did not seem odd to combine them.

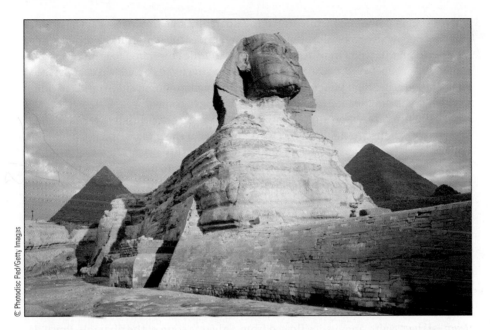

Fig. 1.6 The Great Sphinx. This famous monument, carved out of solid rock in the royal burial area at Giza, expresses the Egyptian belief in the pharaoh as god-king. The sphinx's body is that of a lion, symbolic of the god Re, and its face is that of King Khafre (c. 2500 B.C.), who as pharaoh was thought of as the "living image" of the god. The pyramid to the left of the sphinx is Khafre's royal tomb. To the sphinx's right is the pyramid of Khafre's father Khufu.

In fact, Egyptian priests and rulers often speculated that behind all the different deities they worshiped, there lay a single divine power: one god who had created all the others, perhaps, or who ruled, protected, and nourished all the nations of the world. A pharaoh of the New Kingdom, Akhenaten, who identified the supreme god with Aten, the shining disk of the sun, took this idea so far that he actually tried to abolish the worship of other leading deities. He failed in this "religious revolution," but even so, Egyptian polytheism always had an underlying urge toward the opposite form of belief, monotheism (pp. 48–49).

Furthermore, over time, Egyptian religion became increasingly ethical (demanding virtuous behavior). Originally, the Egyptians did not believe that the gods had such expectations of them. The divine beings had created the universal order and continued to regulate it benevolently so long as the human race, in the person of the pharaoh, performed specified services. Ethical ideas, however, gradually crept into the religious teachings. The major gods, especially Re, came to be associated with the ideals of truth and justice.

Additional motivation for living a virtuous life was provided by the growing hope of immortality. At first it was believed that only the pharaoh, being a god, was immortal, though he could confer everlasting life on his close associates. But the time of troubles at the end of the Old Kingdom inspired a creative new idea: local administrators who now held power independently of the pharaoh came to expect that they would also live independently of him after death. Even under the powerful rulers of the Middle Kingdom, this belief in wider access to the afterlife continued to grow. Every person, it was now believed, possessed a supernatural life force or soul (*ka*) that persisted after the body died; and preserving the body (through mummification) and providing it with comforts in the tomb would help it in the life to come.

Furthermore, by 1800 B.C., Egyptians had come to believe that the soul of every deceased person had to stand before Osiris, the ruler of the underworld, for judgment. The soul recited its good deeds and denied doing anything evil (cheating, adultery, lying). The heart (character) of the person was then weighed in a balance to measure the soul's truthfulness. If the soul passed this test, it was admitted to everlasting life in a garden paradise; otherwise, it was cast into the crocodile jaws of a monster.

The Egyptians' idea of a single divine power, their belief in rewards and punishments after death, and their expectation of immortality were major contributions to the religious beliefs of the world. They were passed on to later civilizations and clearly influenced ideas about life after death and the nature and role of divine power in the universe.

Though the Egyptians had a stong desire for social order and harmony, they developed no system of law comparable to that of Mesopotamia. The reason was that for them, all law, right, and justice flowed from only one source: the pharaoh. Royal decrees and court decisions were recorded and collected for judges to consult, but their principal guides were custom and the will of the ruler.

However, since even the all-powerful god-king could not be everywhere at once, judges and administrators were free much of the time to decide matters as they thought best. Court procedures as we know them did not exist. One account of the trial of a man accused of treason suggests how the judges behaved: "They examined his crimes; they found him guilty; they caused his sentence to come upon him." On the other hand, arbitrary and corrupt behavior by officials was regarded as highly destructive of *maat* (the right order of the universe; p. 30) and hence displeasing to the gods. Even mighty pharaohs feared the judgment of Osiris if they failed to deal fairly with their subjects.

LITERATURE

Writing, the indispensable tool of civilization, probably started in Egypt around 3100 B.C. Though the idea may have been borrowed from Sumer (pp. 20–21), Egyptian writing developed independently, producing several different scripts.

The oldest of these scripts was the *hieroglyphs* (from the Greek for "sacred carvings"). As their name suggests, the hieroglyphs were first devised as part of carvings and paintings intended for religious purposes—above all, to benefit the pharaohs as god-kings of Egypt. In the mind of the pharaohs, as for all Egyptians, religion was closely connected with magic. By having themselves depicted in a particular scene—for example, together with a god who was promising them immortality—they believed that they could make that scene actually happen, in a magical world beyond the accidents of time and place. Obviously, the magic would be all the more effective if the actual words of the god could also be "depicted."

Probably for this reason, the hieroglyphic characters consisted of pictures of real-life or mythical creatures and objects, which were often very detailed and realistic (*Fig. 1.9*, p. 40). Most of the characters, however, were used to represent either whole words or separate sounds of speech. In this way, they could communicate anything that could be thought or said. Most often they were used in temples and other monuments (*Fig. 1.7*, p. 38), and the thought and speech they conveyed were always religious—their Egyptian name, in fact, was "the writing of the words of god."

Soon after the invention of the hieroglyphs, "shorthand" versions of the characters were developed that could be much more easily and quickly written. These are known as the "hieratic" (priestly) script. In spite of its name, the hieratic script was used not only by priests but also for general literary and administrative purposes. Much later, after the era of the New Kingdom, an even faster shorthand, the "demotic" (popular) script, came into use. Thus, writing was as much part of the everyday life of civilization in Egypt as it was in Mesopotamia.

Apart from the differences in the speed of writing, all the Egyptian scripts worked in the same way, employing hundreds of characters according to complex rules. But about 1700 B.C., individuals in an unidentified nation in the Middle Eastern lands bordering on Egypt used some of the hieroglyphs as the basis for developing the first alphabet. Through the Phoenicians (p. 42), this invention was handed on to Western peoples, so that the letters used to print this book are actually distant descendants of Egyptian hieroglyphs.

Most Egyptian writing, especially the hieratic and demotic scripts, was done not on buildings or stones but on papyrus. (It is from this Greek word that our word *paper* derives.) The Egyptian technique of preparing writing scrolls from the stems of the water-grown papyrus plant was a major cultural breakthrough. The Mesopotamians had never advanced beyond using clay or stone as materials to write on. The convenience of papyrus was soon recognized everywhere, and papyrus scrolls (rolls) became the books of the ancient world (*Fig. 2.3*, p. 75).

The easy availability of writing materials no doubt encouraged the Egyptians to create a national literature. Much of it served religious purposes, for example, tales about the gods and books of rituals and spells to aid the passage of the soul to the afterworld. But virtually all forms of literature arose: philosophical essays, books of "wise sayings," manuals for personal conduct, tales of adventure, romances, texts on medicine and magic, poems, and songs. The Egyptians, strangely, produced no heroic masterpiece to equal the Sumerian epics of Gilgamesh (pp. 21–22), but they excelled in the scope and quantity of their literary creations.

SCIENCE AND TECHNOLOGY

The Egyptians were skilled in practical geometry. Surviving texts explain how they computed the areas of fields, the volumes of various shapes, and the properties of pyramids. A major Egyptian contribution was the invention of a solar calendar of 365 days. They divided the year into twelve equal months of thirty days, adding five "free" days at the end. This was the most successful solution yet devised to the problem of keeping the months in step with the seasons of the year (pp. 15, 22), and its basic principles are still used in our present-day calendar. In addition, they divided each month into three "weeks" of ten days each and each day into twenty-four hours. They also invented sundials, of the kind still seen today, for telling the hours of the day. Although they charted the heavens and recorded the daily rising of certain stars, they seem to have had no interest in a general science of the skies (astronomy).

Medical science was a different matter; some writers declare that the Egyptians were the founders of scientific medicine. They understood nothing of germs or infections, and the "demonic" theory of sickness that prevailed in Mesopotamia (p. 22) prevailed also in Egypt. But alongside the magic formulas and priestly exorcists were some healing drugs and trained physicians and surgeons. The Egyptians also developed systematic procedures for handling cases of illness, wrote books about diseases, and established medical libraries and schools. One reason for the superiority of their medical techniques, no doubt, was the anatomical knowledge (unique in the ancient world) derived from the Egyptian practice of mummification. Prior to embalming with special preservatives, the body of the deceased was opened and the internal organs (except the heart) were removed.

The Egyptians were also pioneers in important fields of technology. For instance, the growing wealth of their civilization led them to devise ways of improving water transportation along their main artery, the Nile. They began by building boats that were larger than the traditional dugout canoes by fastening wooden planks together to make the hulls. To propel these heavy craft upstream, by 3100 B.C. they had equipped them with masts and sails to catch the wind, which in the Nile valley usually blows against the current of the river. Thus they became the first known people to harness the power of the wind to human purposes (though the Sumerians may also have built sailboats). By 2500 B.C., the Egyptians had adapted these sailboats to travel the open sea to the Mediterranean's eastern shoreline, which was a source of timber and other valuable products. It was the first of many times that the Mediterranean would serve as a highway linking the civilizations of the Middle East with less advanced peoples to the north and west.

ARCHITECTURE AND THE ARTS

The most spectacular Egyptian technical feats, however, were in the field of building. Their inspiration here was mainly religious—above all, the fact that their god-king (and as time went on, many other important personages) must have a stone tomb as a final resting place. The best-known tombs are the giant royal pyramids—the structures that come most readily to mind when we think of Egypt. These masterpieces of practical engineering (and social discipline) sum up, in many ways, the character of that ancient civilization. They were built to last forever by a people who believed that they and their ways would go on forever. The four-sided, pointed design of a pyramid was the most stable and resistant structural form they could conceive; limestone was the most durable material within reach. The architecture of the Egyptians was, indeed, "art for eternity."

The largest of the pyramids was built by order of King Khufu, who ruled about 2650 B.C. Located at Giza (near modern Cairo), the Great Pyramid measures 476 feet in height and 760 feet on each side of its base (*Fig. 1.6*, p. 33). This mountain of stone consists of some 2.3 million cut blocks, each weighing about 5,000 pounds! The sides of the pyramid were originally coated with polished marble, but that was stripped away by Muslim rulers in the Middle Ages to build the mosques and palaces of Cairo. (The royal tomb within was robbed by thieves in ancient Egyptian times.) Close by is the Great Sphinx, another type of monument, carved soon afterward for another king, Khafre. The enormous head of this man-beast, cut from the cliff of the valley wall, rises 66 feet from its base.

Religious shrines (with their special rituals) were the primary architectural concern of Egyptian priests and worshipers. Temple buildings were usually supported by the "post-and-lintel" method, with horizontal beams (lintels) held up by columns (posts). This method had been known to Mesopotamian architects, but it was not practical for their structures, which were made of brick. (They had to use solid walls or self-supporting brick arches to hold up the roofs of their buildings.) The method was very suitable, however, for stone structures, and Egyptian builders, unlike the Mesopotamians, had easy access to immense supplies of stone.

The temple of Amon at Karnak (near Thebes) was begun about 1530 B.C. and completed about 1300 B.C. (*Fig. 1.7*). The largest religious building ever constructed, it covered a ground area of 1,220 feet by 340 feet (about 10 acres) and enclosed a space large enough to contain four of the huge Gothic cathedrals that were built more than 2,500 years later in Europe. The roof of the main hall rested on 134 columns, each made of elaborately carved stone drums; the central (nave) columns are 70 feet high and 12 feet in diameter. As the builders intended, the gigantic proportions of Karnak overwhelm its viewers and make them feel insignificant.

Sculptors and painters worked under the direction of architects to fulfill the aims of each kind of building. They did much of their work for the interiors of royal and noble tombs. Representations of the deceased were believed to contribute to the welfare of the soul of the dead; therefore, stone statues of the individual (and members of the household) were usually placed within the tomb. The walls of the tomb were painted with scenes of Egyptian life related to the career of the deceased. Though lifelike, these representations were seldom naturalistic (the way persons and objects normally look to the eye). Sculptured portraits, for example, had to be made according to set rules. Rather rigid postures were required, and the figures were placed so as to be viewed from the front (this is known as "frontalism"). Usually the left foot was placed forward; wigs and beards were treated in a standard stylized manner. Yet the human quality of these statues comes through despite the somewhat stilted forms (*Fig. 1.8*).

This humanistic quality is evident also in the tomb paintings, from which we have learned many details about Egyptian civilization. There was no attempt to provide perspective, or depth, in these pictures; artists were free to arrange their compositions as they thought best within the assigned space. Thus some scenes might be laid out on a line parallel to the base line of the picture frame, some (in the same picture) on a line perpendicular to the base line. Also, individual figures might be drawn to different scales, although the king was always shown as the largest person in a given frame.

A governing principle of Egyptian painting was that a representation must reflect established knowledge of the object and must be shown from the angle that best reveals that knowledge. For example, the face is always shown in profile, except for the eye, which is shown as it appears frontally. Shoulders and torso are viewed from the front, legs and feet in profile (*Fig. 1.9*).

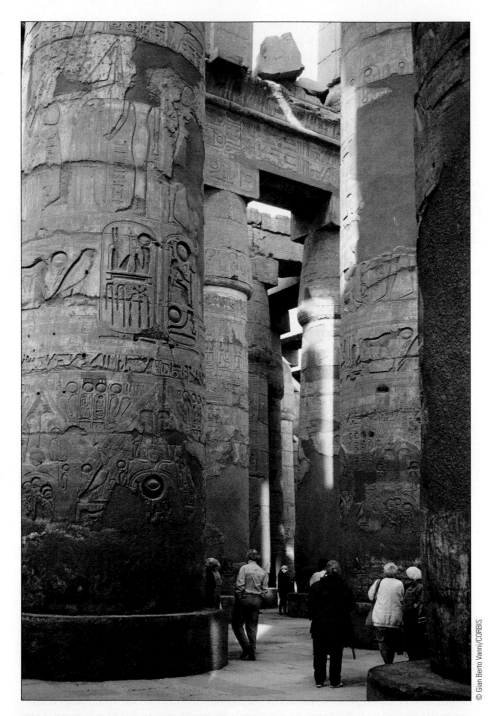

Fig. 1.7 The Temple of Amon at Karnak. This vast building was constructed about 1600 B.C., at the height of the wealth and power of the New Kingdom. The photograph shows the Hypostyle Hall (Hall of Columns), a gigantic porchlike structure leading from the temple's outer courtyard to a series of inner shrines where the actual worship took place. In the dimly lit hall, priests prepared themselves to perform the holy rituals of the god.

Pair Statue of King Menkaure and His Queen; From Giza, Dynasty IV, 2599–1571 B.C. Slate Schist, 54½ in. Harvard MFA Expedition. Courtesy, Museum of Fine Arts, Boston.

Fig. 1.8 King Menkaure and His Queen, 2500 B.C. The queen has her arm protectively around her husband, a typical pose in Egyptian statues of married couples that testifies to the status and power of upper-class women. The king's pose, with arms at his sides, fists clenched, and left foot forward, remained typical of Egyptian male statues for thousands of years and influenced early Greek sculpture (compare *Fig. 2.7*, p. 92).

These strict rules were probably intended to make sure that painting fulfilled the religious and magical purposes that lay behind much of Egyptian art. By depicting the various parts of a human body from the different angles at which each of them was most fully seen, the artist could make a person most fully present on a two-dimensional surface, even if the whole body was not seen, as it would be in real life, from a single viewpoint. In any case, the Egyptian painters, within their rules, developed techniques of line, design, and color that were extraordinarily effective. The artistic creations of the Egyptians, including jewelry, metal, and glass, became admired models for the ancient world—both East and West.

Fig. 1.9 The Tomb of Sebekhotep. This was the resting place of an official during the New Kingdom who was important enough to lie in a cemetery near the tombs of the pharaohs themselves, across the Nile from Thebes. Servants carry papyrus reeds and poultry; the smaller pictures at right are hieroglyphs. The picture and the words were intended to remain forever in darkness, unviewed and unread, but according to Egyptian belief they would bring about what they depicted and described—the continuation of Sebekhotep's life and activities into eternity.

The First Universal Empires: Assyria and Persia

Around 1200 B.C., a new and dramatic phase opened in the ancient Middle East. The brilliant civilizations of Egypt and Mesopotamia had already spread to many neighboring peoples, from the eastern Mediterranean to the shores of the Indian Ocean. This international civilized world now underwent a massive crisis. It was weakened by internal conflicts, less advanced peoples attacked it from north and south, old established kingdoms were swept away, and in some areas civilization itself vanished for a time.

Gradually, the civilized world recovered from the crisis, but it was a different world than before. It possessed new technical skills that would be basic features of many future civilizations, such as the use of iron and alphabetic writing. It was more closely knit together by trade and travel, controlled by networks of flourishing commercial city-states. And the new skills and international contacts helped make it possible for conquering peoples to build universal empires, which sought to control all of the civilized world that they could reach.

From time to time, there were spectacular reversals of fortune when one empire fell and another arose to take its place. But the idea took hold that the civilized world was a single world and that it was normal for the world to have a single mighty ruler. This was an idea with a long future ahead of it.

CRISIS AND RECOVERY OF THE CIVILIZED WORLD (1200–900 B.C.)

Around 1200 B.C., the Hittite kingdom in Asia Minor (pp. 27–28) fell to mysterious invaders who arrived by land and sea from the Aegean region and elsewhere in the coasts and islands of the Mediterranean. These invaders belonged to no single nation and had perhaps been displaced by overpopulation and war among the barbarian peoples of Europe (p. 59). In any case, the newcomers were well armed and desperate, and from Asia Minor they went on to spread havoc in Syria and Palestine. Finally they attacked Egypt, where they were known as the "Sea Peoples" and where they were eventually repelled or assimilated. At about the same time, the Kassite kings of Mesopotamia were overthrown by civilized eastern neighbors, who, however, were not strong enough to replace them as rulers of that entire region. Of the three great powers of the civilized world, two had been destroyed, and the third, Egypt, was weakened by rivalry between the pharaohs and the priests (p. 32).

In Mesopotamia, new groups of Semitic nomads appeared out of the desert—the Aramaeans from Syria and the Chaldeans from present-day Arabia—and took advantage of the collapse of Kassite rule to overrun much of the region: the northern part fell to the Aramaeans and the south to the Chaldeans. In Asia Minor, the disruption of the trade in metals that had supplied much of the wealth for civilization led to several centuries of decline and decay, made worse by new invasions of nomadic peoples from farther north.

But invasions and the disruption of trade also brought world-changing advances in technical skills. The nomadic warriors who attacked Asia Minor brought with them a new way of exploiting the speed and strength of the horse in battle: instead of using it to pull chariots, their archers and spearmen rode on its back (p. 58). Once again, this was an advance that at first dismayed civilized peoples until they adopted it themselves.

About the same time, metalworkers in the devastated lands of Asia Minor, who were short of the imported tin that they needed to make bronze, began to take an interest in another metal: iron. This metal had been known for many centuries and was far more plentiful than copper or tin, but it had never been popular because it was difficult to smelt and work. Forced by necessity, the bronzesmiths started to experiment with improved processes for smelting iron, as well as hardening and toughening it, until they ended with a metal that was superior to bronze and available in far larger quantities. In this way, out of the chaos wreaked by the Sea Peoples, tools and weapons advanced from the Bronze Age to the Iron Age (p. 10).

Meanwhile, in the Middle East, the Aramaean nomads adapted, like so many invaders before them, to the civilized ways of Mesopotamia. In the vacuum created by the collapse or decline of the great powers, they established a network of prosperous city-states that dominated land trade throughout the Middle East.

Likewise, on the Mediterranean coast, another Semitic-speaking people, the Phoenicians, also benefited from the absence of great powers (*Map 1.1*, p. 13). For many centuries, the Phoenicians had lived by seaborne trade, above all with Egypt, and they seem to have been in some way subject to the pharaohs. Now their wealthy seaports became independent city-states, using the forests in the coastal mountains—the famous "cedars of Lebanon"—to build fleets that were the last word in two thousand years of progress in shipbuilding.

The Phoenician ships were no longer the converted riverboats of the Egyptians (p. 36) but had stout internal timber frameworks to strengthen their hulls against wind and wave. The merchant vessels were escorted by purpose-built seagoing warships propelled not only by sail but also by crews of oarsmen, sitting in two rows one above the other, to provide speed and maneuverability. In battle, they sank enemy vessels with bronze-tipped rams projecting from their bows or hooked up alongside and put soldiers aboard.

In their seaworthy vessels, Phoenician merchants ranged throughout the Mediterranean and out into the Atlantic in search of timber, metal, and slaves. They set up trading stations on the coastlines of Africa and Spain that eventually turned into colonies—most notably, the North African city of Carthage (*Map 2.2*, p. 63; p. 113). Both as traders and as settlers, the Phoenicians played a leading role in the spread of civilization to the less advanced nations of Mediterranean Europe (p. 64).

In addition, both the Aramaeans and the Phoenicians played a vital role in the transmission of the new and simplified system of writing, the alphabet. The new system, which used a maximum of thirty signs, in contrast to the several hundred employed by other contemporary writing systems, had been developed in the Middle East, as an improvement on Egyptian hieroglyphs, several centuries earlier (p. 35). After 1200 B.C., the Aramaeans brought the alphabet to Mesopotamia, and the Aramaic tongue, with its easily learned alphabet, which could be written on convenient leather or papyrus scrolls (p. 35), replaced Akkadian as the international language of the civilized world. Eventually, Aramaic even became the everyday speech of many Middle Eastern peoples, including the Jews at the time of Jesus. Meanwhile, the Phoenicians handed on alphabetic writing to less advanced Western peoples with whom they came into contact, above all the Greeks (p. 64). All the alphabets in use in the Western world at the present day, whether Greek, Latin, or Cyrillic, are ultimately derived from that used by the Phoenicians (*Fig. 1.10*).

Phoenician	Greek	Roman
𐤀	A	A
𐤁	B	B
𐤂	Γ	G
𐤃	Δ	D
𐤄	E	E
𐤅	[Y]	F
𐤆	Z	Z
𐤇		H
𐤈	I	I
𐤉	K	[K]
𐤊	Λ	L
𐤋	M	M
𐤌	N	N
𐤍	O	O
𐤏	Π	P
𐤐		Q
𐤑	P	R
𐤒	Σ	S
𐤓	T	T
	Y	U,V
	X	X
	Ω	

Fig. 1.10 Development of the Alphabet. The alphabet was developed by Semitic peoples from Egyptian hieroglyphs. For example, the second letter from the top in the Phoenician alphabet had originally been a diagram-like hieroglyph meaning "house." The Phoenicians still called the letter by their word for house, *bet*, but they used it to represent only the first sound of that word, *b*. The Greeks took over the letter as well as its name (*bēta*), though they changed its shape. The Romans then adopted the Greek version, which has remained standard in the West ever since.

By 900 B.C., the civilized world once again stretched from the Persian Gulf to the Aegean, and in many ways it was actually more advanced than it had been before the crisis. The time was ripe for new great powers to arise, who would not merely compete with each other as the Egyptians, Hittites, and Kassites had done, but each of which would seek to unite the civilized world under its rule.

ASSYRIA (900–600 B.C.)

The Assyrians lived for centuries along the middle and upper reaches of the Tigris River (*Map 1.1*, p. 13). Their location astride trade and invasion routes between Mesopotamia and neighboring lands exposed them to frequent attacks by nomadic tribes to the north and east, as well as by civilized states to the south and west. Though they were essentially farmers, herders, and traders, they grew into tough soldiers as they defended their lands. But the weakening of the great power centers in the Middle East after 1200 B.C. gave Assyria an opportunity to turn to the offensive. Assyrian leaders saw that rich profits were to be reaped from controlling the trade routes between western Asia and the Mediterranean. And as they gradually accomplished this aim, they began to conceive of the larger object of a universal empire. As one of their rulers would declare, "I am the legitimate king of the world . . . of all four rims of the earth . . . king of kings."

The rise of Assyria to universal empire began shortly after 900 B.C. with the overthrow of the Aramaeans in northern Mesopotamia. Then the Assyrians struck north and west and took over the southern portion of Asia Minor, as well as Syria, Phoenicia, and part of the Israelite territories in Palestine (pp. 51–52). By 700 B.C., they had also added the Chaldean-ruled territories of southern Mesopotamia, including Babylon, to their possessions. The empire reached its greatest extent in the seventh century B.C., when the rest of Palestine and most of Egypt fell under its control (*Map 1.2*).

During the turbulent period of conquests, insurrections, and frontier wars, the Assyrians faced the endless task of holding a widespread empire together. Drained of their strength at last, they were overcome by a rebellion of their old enemies, the Chaldeans, aided by the Medes (pp. 45–46) attacking from the east. In 612 B.C., their high-walled capital at Nineveh, on the Tigris, was broken into and burned. Most of their army and royal family were wiped out, and the Assyrian nation sank into obscurity, never to rise again.

The terrible vengeance brought down on the Assyrians by their conquerors was in large measure a response to the way they ruled their empire. The basis of Assyrian power, from its beginning, was armed force and terror. Assyria was the first truly military state. All adult males were subject to military service, commanders were rewarded with the best lands and the highest honors, and war was glorified and pursued as the principal business of the kingdom. The Assyrians, with their passion for war, became the most advanced people of their time in the arts of weaponry and military tactics. Their army was a mixed force that did not rely on chariots alone but on the combined striking power of chariots, light infantry (archers and slingers), and massed heavy infantry clad in bronze helmets and armor and wielding iron swords and spears. As time went on, the Assyrians also made use of the new horse-riding cavalry, and their engineers devised the first battering rams and movable siege towers to break down the defenses of cities.

As the nation's manpower was reduced by its wars, the imperial masters relied increasingly on drafted or hired troops drawn from subject peoples. A fatal weakness in the Assyrians' system was that they were too small a nation to enforce their rule over

Map 1.2 The Assyrian and Neo-Babylonian Empires. The rulers and armies of Assyria and then of Babylonia were able to conquer empires that included most of the Middle East. Both empires collapsed, but they prepared the way for the rise and fall of other world conquerors, the Persians and later the Greeks.

the vast reaches of their conquests. To compensate, they pursued a policy of deliberate terror. They used and boasted of inhuman practices—skinning and mutilating bodies, torturing, impaling, burning alive, and displaying stacks of human skulls. Their behavior was excessive even by the normal standards of warfare through the ages, and Assyrian palace art still proclaims their acts of violence in superb and explicit wall reliefs (*Fig. 1.11*). The "propaganda of the deed" was no doubt an effective source of power; it made the Assyrians the most feared people of the ancient world. But they themselves were at last destroyed by the storm of hatred they had aroused.

And yet, whatever their methods and motives, the Assyrian kings succeeded in bringing together the largest collection of peoples ever united up to that time. This was the first truly imperial government. Conquered lands were usually organized as provinces, with Assyrian nobles appointed as governors by the king. Some of the "tribute states" were permitted, in return for regular payments, to keep their own rulers, under the watchful eyes of Assyrian officials. Systematic intelligence and administra-

Fig. 1.11 Assyrian Siege Warfare. This wall sculpture from the palace of King Tiglath-Pileser III (c. 745–728 B.C.) shows the king's army attacking a city wall with scaling ladders (left), and a wheeled siege tower (right). Behind the siege tower, captured defenders are impaled on tall stakes. The siege equipment continued to be used by armies for two thousand years down to the invention of the cannon (compare Fig. 7.4, p. 308).

tive reports flowed to the capital city of Nineveh from all corners of the empire—helped by a well-developed road system, for the Assyrians were forerunners of the Persians and Romans in grasping the importance of good roads for great empires (pp. 47, 138).

The Assyrians made few original contributions in literature, culture, and the arts. However, as heirs to the ancient Mesopotamian civilization, they played a vital role in preserving it and transmitting it to future generations. The world's first known great library was established by the Assyrian ruler Assurbanirpal at Nineveh about 650 B.C. It contained some twenty thousand tablets with texts in the Sumerian as well as the Akkadian languages, and provided the key to present-day knowledge of Mesopotamian writing, history, and culture when it was excavated in the nineteenth century A.D.

PERSIA (550–330 B.C.)

After the fall of Assyria, the peoples of the Middle East returned again to their separate ways. The Chaldeans, having liberated Babylonia, stimulated a rebirth of industry and the arts. The vigorous King Nebuchadrezzar II (the Old Testament's Nebuchadnezzar) renovated his capital city of Babylon and reached out to destroy the kingdom of Judah, in Palestine (p. 52). But the power of the Chaldeans' "Neo-Babylonian empire" was short-lived; like the rule of the Medes in the upper region of Mesopotamia, it shortly fell to the Persians.

The Medes and Persians were closely related peoples of Indo-European origin (p. 58) who had moved into the territories to the east of Mesopotamia from about 1000 B.C. onward. As with Asia Minor, the natural environment was very different from that of civilization's Mesopotamian heartland. Media and Persia formed the western part of a

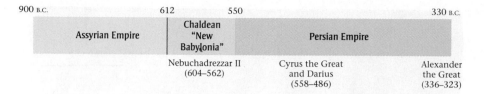

900 B.C.	612	550	330 B.C.
Assyrian Empire	Chaldean "New Babylonia"	Persian Empire	
	Nebuchadrezzar II (604–562)	Cyrus the Great and Darius (558–486)	Alexander the Great (336–323)

vast plateau, much of it desert and fringed to the north and west by mountain ranges, that stretched all the way to India. But the region was rich in metals, and farmers there had adopted ingenious methods of exploiting underground water sources. As the wealth and population of the Medes and Persians grew, the rulers became sophisticated enough to take an interest in Mesopotamian civilization and strong enough to intervene in the power politics of their western neighbors.

After the Medes had helped the Chaldeans crush the Assyrians, the Persian king, Cyrus (the Great), moved to take over all the surrounding lands. He defeated the king of the Medes in 550 B.C. and made their capital at Ecbatana his own. In so doing, Cyrus also sought the support of the Medes for his further ambitions. By treating them generously, he won their sympathy and aid and even their partnership—the Greeks used either name, "Persians" or "Medes," to describe their powerful eastern neighbors. Thus in his very first step, Cyrus showed that he meant to reject the Assyrian way of taking power. Rather than terrorizing his opponents, he sought to win them over by reasonable and decent treatment. As a result, Persian rule was quickly accepted. Within twenty years after his victory over the Medes, Cyrus was in control of the Middle East from the Indus valley to the Mediterranean. Four years later (525 B.C.), his son Cambyses added Egypt and Libya to the new universal state, making it larger by far than any previous empire (*Map 1.3*).

This second attempt at political unification resembled the Assyrian effort in many ways. Governmental form was essentially the same; the style of monarchy practiced for centuries in Mesopotamia found its final embodiment in the Persian absolute ruler. He was the "Great King," the "king of kings," identified with divine will and justice, though not himself considered a god like the Egyptian pharaohs. He sat on a gold and blue throne in a huge palace, dressed in purple cloth and laden with jewels. In his presence, ordinary mortals were required to lie, face down, before him; his royal word was an unquestioned command.

Standing ready to carry out the commands of the throne were the Persian army and civil servants. The military forces were similar in organization and weapons to those of the Assyrians; tough Persian troops constituted the backbone of the heavily armed infantry, which operated together with bow-wielding cavalry and charioteers. But large supporting forces, including fleets of warships, were drawn from the conquered populations, including Syrians, Phoenicians, Egyptians, and Greeks. Because of the moderate nature of Persian rule, these forces were generally loyal. Once established, the empire seldom engaged in offensive wars, and insurrections by the conquered peoples were few. In consequence, the state did not develop a militaristic character. The monarchs preferred to spend their energies and resources on public buildings, roads, and services rather than on military campaigns. Unlike the Assyrian rulers, they advertised their peaceful accomplishments, not their bloody battles.

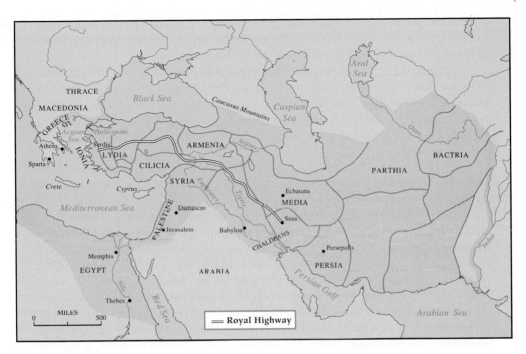

Map 1.3 The Persian Empire. The Persian Empire was far larger than any earlier Middle Eastern empire. From their homeland on the border between the Middle East and the rest of Asia, the Persians moved west to conquer most of the civilized world that had grown up in the Middle East and the eastern Mediterranean. They also moved north and east into vast lands of nomadic peoples in central and southern Asia.

For administrative purposes, the realm was divided into some twenty provinces known as *satrapies*. The king placed a nobleman (usually a Persian) as governor (satrap) in charge of each province; the satrap ruled with a light hand, however, under the guiding principles of restraint and tolerance. Taxes and military supplies were rigorously collected, but local customs, language, and religion were left alone. As a further measure of administrative control, the monarchs also appointed royal inspectors, the "king's eyes," who supervised the work of the satraps and reported directly to the royal palace. The work of the "king's eyes" was eased by an excellent road network. The most famous of these roads, the Royal Highway, ran 1,700 miles from Susa, near the Persian Gulf, to Sardis, not far from the Aegean Sea (*Map 1.3*), and a system of messengers and relay stations enabled royal orders and the reports of satraps to cover the entire distance in only a week.

In religion, the Persians, like the Jews (p. 49), began to break away from the traditional polytheism of the peoples of the Middle East. The Persian religious thinker Zoroaster, who is believed to have lived in the seventh century B.C., transformed the ancient beliefs and superstitions of his people into a noble and inspiring faith in one God, the author of good and evil. His followers turned this faith into a dualism that taught that the world was the scene of two rival forces: Ahura Mazda, god of goodness and light, and Angra Mainyu, demon of evil and darkness. At the end of time, Ahura Mazda would triumph, Angra Mainyu would be made harmless, and all of humanity would be raised to enjoy eternal bliss. At the approach of the last days, a savior would appear, miraculously born, to prepare the way for the Final Judgment. All this had been revealed and written down in the Avesta, the Persian holy book.

Zoroastrianism was an ethical religion that praised truthfulness, love, and the "Golden Rule" (treat others as you would want them to treat you) and condemned pride, lust, and avarice. Whether a person's soul went to heaven or hell upon death was determined by conduct during life. All people, however, would ultimately be saved by Ahura Mazda's goodness; unlike the later Christian damnation (p. 163), the Persian hell was not forever.

With the sweep of Persian conquest in the sixth century B.C., the religion of Zoroaster was carried to all the peoples of the Middle East. For several centuries it worked its influence on those peoples, including the Jews.

Babylonian astronomers continued, with Persian encouragement, to advance their knowledge of the heavens; one result was their learning how to calculate and predict eclipses of the moon. Persian art and architecture were chiefly adaptations of existing styles and techniques. The most magnificent example, the royal palace at Persepolis, was a successful combination of building and sculptural elements from Assyria, Babylonia, Egypt, and Greece. The Persians used cuneiform writing (adapted to their language) for inscriptions on royal monuments, but for purposes of administration and government, they used the Aramaic language and alphabet (p. 42), which remained standard for commerce throughout the Middle East. This was good for trade, as was the Persian development of coinage. Prior to this time, payment for goods was generally made in kind (goods) or with bars of precious metal. Coins, to make payment easier, had been invented by the Lydians of Asia Minor in the seventh century B.C.; their Persian conquerors adopted the use of coins and carried it to all parts of their domain.

The Persian Empire lasted for two centuries until it fell in its turn—for some of the same reasons that later empires, like that of Rome, also fell. It had to contend with human aggressiveness and corruption, as well as the immense difficulty of managing large numbers of diverse peoples. It was weakened by internal conflicts among the Persians themselves and declining loyalty to their own king. At last, in 330 B.C., a Greek, Alexander the Great, brought down the failing empire in a brilliant military campaign (p. 100).

All the same, the Persian Empire set the standard for a successful world state. The civilized Middle East of Persia's time had grown into an economic and cultural unit, and the empire's subjects showed a longing for unity, peace, and the freedom of movement and ideas that unity permits. The Persian Empire satisfied that longing while permitting its subject peoples to maintain their own identities. United yet diverse, enriched by many different cultural traditions that had grown up over the centuries, the Persian Empire was the culmination of three thousand years of civilization in the Middle East.

The Jews and Monotheism (1200–330 B.C.)

Of all the changes that took place within the new world of the Middle East after 1200 B.C., the one with the most lasting impact was the rise of a new kind of religious

c. 2000 B.C.   c. 1200   c. 1000 c. 900   587   531   333 B.C.

Hebrew Nomadic Tribes   Settlement of Palestine   Israel and Judah   Persian Rule

United Kingdom   Exile

belief. Alongside traditional polytheism, the belief in many gods and goddesses, which remained unchanged among most peoples in the Middle East and elsewhere, there appeared the belief in one God, or *monotheism*.

The new belief involved far more than just the question of how many divine beings were to be worshiped. The one God was thought of as eternal, almighty, all-knowing, the creator of the whole universe, infinitely good, pure spirit yet somehow masculine. For unsearchable reasons, he had allowed an opposing evil power to gain dominion over the human race. He would save from evil those humans who believed in and obeyed him, however, and at the end of time, he would send a mighty savior to crush the evil power and all who served it.

Meanwhile, humans must renounce their allegiance to the gods and goddesses—who did exist but were evil beings—and accept the one truth about the one God. Humans would be helped in this by the fact that although God was utterly beyond human knowledge and understanding, he spoke to them through angels, prophets, and authoritative books—and on a more everyday level, through religious leaders who acted as guides to understanding and obeying his will.

Several Middle Eastern peoples were involved in developing these ideas, and it took time for the ideas to come together to form a single belief. About 1800 B.C., the Egyptian pharaoh Akhenaten had worshiped a single divine power that ruled the whole universe, though his innovations had been rejected after his death (p. 33). A thousand years later, the Persians saw the world as a place of struggle between mighty good and evil forces (p. 47). But above all, the features of monotheism developed out of the beliefs and practices of the Jews, and out of their experiences of victory and defeat in the endless power struggles of the Middle East.

THE RISE AND FALL OF ISRAEL, 1200–587 B.C.

Amid the turmoil of the civilized world about 1200 B.C., as archaeological surveys indicate, the previously empty hill country of Palestine (*Map 1.4*), lying inland from the Mediterranean coast, filled up with settlers fleeing war and invasion in other regions. Among the settlers, it seems, were Semitic emigrants from Egypt, whose traditions said that they had already existed as a group for many generations. They had originated, according to these traditions, in Mesopotamia. From there they had wandered to Palestine as a small nomadic clan headed by their forefather, Abraham. Later on, famine had forced them to move to Egypt, where they had stayed for a long time and grown to be a numerous people. One of the pharaohs had begun to mistrust and oppress them, but a great prophet, Moses, had arisen to lead them out of Egypt, thus enabling them eventually to make their way back to Palestine.

Map 1.4 The Israelites and Their Neighbors. About 1000 B.C. the Israelites controlled a sizable territory in the interior of the Mediterranean coastal region of the Middle East. They were mostly an inland farming people, unlike their seafaring neighbors, the Phoenicians, and their rivals the Philistines, who controlled most of the actual coastline of Palestine.

Most of the other settlers in Palestine came to identify with the emigrant group from Egypt. They adopted the group's name for itself—the "children of Israel," the "Israelites," or just "Israel."[2] They also began to worship the group's powerful god, Yahweh.

The Israelites' beliefs about Yahweh may well have been influenced by Egyptian and Mesopotamian ideas, but it seems clear that even in these early times, he was unique among the gods and goddesses of the Middle East. Many Egyptian deities were "hidden," veiling their true being in mystery; only Yahweh was so deeply "hidden" that he could not even be depicted. Many Egyptian deities required from humans both

---

[2] "Israel" ("He Who Strives with God") was the name taken, according to tradition, by Abraham's grandson Jacob. Down to about 500 B.C., it was the most usual name for the people that claimed descent from him. The name "Jews" (from the part of Palestine known as Judah) came into use after that date. The name "Hebrew" (from a Semitic word meaning "wanderer") is often used today to refer to the Israelites down to about 500 B.C. but was not usual at the time. The language of the Jews at all periods is known as "Hebrew."

ritual purity and righteousness (pp. 33–34); only Yahweh's requirements were so detailed and specific that they came to have the status of laws.

Likewise, it was not unusual for Mesopotamian peoples to owe special allegiance to a particular god or goddess who was the rival and enemy of other deities. Only Yahweh, however, was so "jealous" that he actually forbade his people to worship other deities at all. And while the deities of all peoples promised benefits in return for obedience, only Yahweh had bound himself by specific covenants (agreements) with Abraham, Moses, and others, promising the Israelites favor and protection as his Chosen People so long as they gave him their exclusive allegiance.

Yet as impressive as Yahweh was, many or most of the early Israelites did not, in fact, give him the exclusive allegiance that he demanded. Even kings like David and Solomon combined the worship of Yahweh with that of the traditional gods and goddesses of Palestine. In the centuries after the settlement of Israel in Palestine about 1200 B.C., the prophets of Yahweh—his chosen messengers, who received word directly from him—struggled for the people's soul against the gods and goddesses. In the course of this struggle, Yahweh revealed himself to be a vastly grander being even than before. Instead of simply forbidding his people to worship other gods and goddesses, he declared that they were "abominable" beings and that no real deity existed beside himself. Far from being merely the powerful protector of Israel, he was the almighty creator and ruler of the universe. It was in this way that Jewish monotheism began to take shape.

What gave the victory to the prophets, however, was not just this new monotheistic belief in Yahweh but also the triumphs and disasters of Israel from 1200 B.C. onward as the Middle East recovered from its earlier crisis and then came under the rule of universal empires (pp. 40–48).

Like other Middle Eastern peoples, the Israelites became more advanced and prosperous than before. They used the newly popular alphabetic writing (p. 42) to record their traditions about Yahweh's dealings with them in the past and his continued guidance in the present. They used iron weapons to do battle with neighboring peoples, in particular the Philistines, who had also moved into Palestine about 1200 B.C., in their case from somewhere westward in the Mediterranean. And as Israelite society grew increasingly complex and conflicted, the prophets began to call in Yahweh's name for justice between rich and poor.

For a brief splendid period under the reigns of David and Solomon, about 1000 B.C., the Israelites also tasted military triumph and worldly power. David extended his kingdom until it included most of the eastern coastlands of the Mediterranean, and ruled his territories from the newly conquered city of Jerusalem. On Mount Zion, in the heart of the city, Solomon raised the Temple, a magnificent shrine to Yahweh, where priests served him with plentiful offerings and sacrifices like any other leading Middle Eastern deity. But in the midst of the Temple, instead of a sacred image, stood the Ark of the Covenant, a wooden chest containing documents that recorded Yahweh's agreements with his people.

In an age of emerging universal empires, however, other peoples were more consistently successful in Middle Eastern power struggles than the Israelites. Internal discontents and rivalries led Solomon's kingdom to split in two after his death—one part, which kept the name Israel, in the north, and another, Judah (including Jerusalem and the Temple), in the south. In 722 B.C., the Assyrians destroyed the northern kingdom of Israel. More than a century later, the Chaldeans of Babylonia invaded Judah, and in 587, they captured Jerusalem and destroyed the Temple.

Both disasters were followed by massive deportations of Israelites, many of whom merged with other peoples of the Middle East, while others formed a large community centered on the city of Babylon. Many more Israelites took refuge in Egypt, whose recent pharaohs had generally been friendly to the kings of Israel and Judah. In this way, the Israelites became a scattered people, striving to worship Yahweh and preserve their identity as a minority living among foreign nations.

THE JEWS AS A SCATTERED PEOPLE, 587–330 B.C.

It was the experience of defeat and exile that for the first time made the monotheistic worship of Yahweh the exclusive Israelite religion. Far from proving that Yahweh was weaker than the gods and goddesses of other nations, the disaster, so the Israelites came to believe, was in fact proof of his power. They had not been overcome by foreign deities; rather, they were being punished by the one almighty God for breaking their covenants with him. The Assyrians and Babylonians—in fact, all peoples and all nations—were simply his instruments. Once the Israelites turned their hearts back to God and fulfilled their covenanted duties to him, he would restore them to the land that he had given them.

Sure enough, when the Persians overthrew the Chaldeans and established the largest and most tolerant universal empire so far (pp. 45–48), they permitted the Israelites to return to Palestine. By 515 B.C., the Temple had been rebuilt, and once again the one God was served with offerings and sacrifices in the city of David—though the Ark of the Covenant had not survived the troubles, so that the "Holy of Holies" now consisted simply of an empty chamber.

All the same, the disaster had brought about permanent changes in the way of life of the Jews. Their territory now consisted of no more than Judah (or Judaea, as the Greeks and Romans called it), from which they took their new name. They were ruled not by kings but by the high priests of the Temple, who were appointed by the Persian rulers. In any case, many Jews did not return from Babylonia, and few or none, seemingly, from Egypt. The majority of Jews now lived permanently in what came to be known as the _Diaspora_ (dispersion). In Babylonia, and later to a considerable extent in Judaea as well, they gave up their Hebrew tongue in favor of the internationally spoken Aramaic language (p. 42), and in Egypt, they eventually came to speak Greek. Thus the Jews remained a scattered people, held together not by a common language or possession of territory but by religion.

More ardently than before, the Jews turned to the worship of the one God. They zealously studied the writings about God's dealings with his people, which by this time had grown into a large mass of documents recording his laws, his utterances through his prophets, and his raising up and casting down of rulers and nations. Many of these documents were combined, reedited, and rewritten while the Jews lived under Persian rule to form "books" of the present-day Hebrew Bible—the Old Testament of the Christian Bible.

Above all, the Jews strove to follow more devoutly than before the laws of righteousness and ritual purity contained in the "instruction" (Torah), the first five books of the present-day Bible. (Among these laws were the Ten Commandments, the requirement of male circumcision, and the prohibition of eating the flesh of "unclean" animals.) And because the Law was so important, for the first time the Jews took to holding themselves apart from Gentiles (non-Jews) who did not follow the Law—refusing, for instance, to intermarry or eat with Gentiles. Yet now that the Jews were more of a religious than a national group, it also became possible for a Gentile to "join the house of Israel" through circumcision and obedience to the Law.

Since the actual worship of God with offerings and sacrifices now took place only in the Temple, everyday Jewish religious practice came to consist mainly of study of the holy writings and prayer to God. It became customary to meet for these purposes on the Sabbath, the seventh day of the week, which God had commanded to be kept holy. In time, the buildings where the Jews met for prayer and study, and the communities that met in these buildings, came to be known as synagogues (from the Greek word for "meeting-houses"). An elite of leaders of prayer and study grew up—men who could read and write and who were respected in their communities for obeying and understanding the Law. These religious guides replaced the prophets and gradually came to rival the Temple priests as leaders of the Jews.

Besides causing the Jews to rally round their religious beliefs, the experience of exile and return also led them to develop those beliefs in new ways—in writings that today also form part of the Hebrew Bible. How was it, for example, that when God punished his people, the righteous suffered along with the wicked? Some Jews argued that the answer to this question was an unsearchable mystery. Others, influenced by the beliefs of the world-conquering Persians, proclaimed that the sufferings of the righteous were the fault not of God but of an evil opposing power, "the Adversary" (Satan). Eventually, God would send his "Anointed One" (Messiah) to triumph over the forces of evil, and the righteous would rise from the dead in their own bodies to enjoy blessedness forever.

In these ways, many present-day features of Judaism as a way of life came into existence in Persian times. Some of these were to remain common to all future monotheistic religions. Among them were an authoritative holy book, prayer and study as the main religious practices, ministers of religion who acted as leaders of the community and interpreters of the holy book, religious buildings that were meeting places for prayer and study rather than the "residences" of gods and goddesses, the conversion of nonbelievers, and the idea of the world as a place of struggle between good and evil, which would be won by a savior sent by God.

For the moment, these were the beliefs of a scattered minority in a world where most people still worshiped the traditional gods and goddesses. All the same, monotheism was one of the two longest-lasting legacies to later civilizations from the changing world of the Middle East after 1200 B.C. The other was the spread of civilization to a European barbarian people living on the northwestern edge of the civilized world: the Greeks.

RECOMMENDED READING

The Prehistoric Era An up-to-date treatment of human evolution is R. J. Wenke, *Patterns of Prehistory: Humankind's First Three Million Years* (1999). R. Leakey, *The Origin of Humankind* (1994), is a brief and readable account by a leading archaeologist. B. Fagan, *Snapshots of the Past* (1995), is an enjoyable description of the kinds of problems with which archaeologists deal and their methods of solving them. M. Ehrenberg, *Women in Prehistory* (1987), explains the theories of modern researchers on changes in the position of women in Neolithic times and summarizes the evidence.

The Earliest Cities: Mesopotamia   S. N. Kramer, *The Sumerians: Their History, Culture, and Character* (1971), is the work of a leading scholar, stressing the evidence of written documents; H. Crawford, *Sumer and the Sumerians* (1991), uses archaeology to explain geography, the environment, and settlement patterns.

A. L. Oppenheim, *Ancient Mesopotamia: Portrait of a Dead Civilization* (1977), covers all aspects of Babylonian civilization; J. Bottéro, *Mesopotamia: Writing, Reasoning, and the Gods* (1987), surveys the mental world of Babylonian civilization while telling the story of the science of Assyriology and archaeological discovery in Mesopotamia. On religion, see the classic work of T. Jacobsen, *The Treasures of Darkness: A History of Mesopotamian Religion* (1978).

A readable and well-illustrated account of the Hittites is J. G. McQueen, *The Hittites and Their Contemporaries in Asia Minor* (1996).

Land of the Pharaohs: Egypt   Of the many histories of ancient Egypt, A. Gardiner, *Egypt of the Pharaohs* (1961), is a classic account by a renowned scholar. A more recent, splendidly illustrated survey is S. Quirke and J. Spencer, *The British Museum Book of Ancient Egypt* (1992). Books on particular features of Egyptian civilization include P. Clayton, *Chronicle of the Pharaohs* (1994), a reign-by-reign account that covers much of Egyptian government, history, and beliefs about the pharaohs; C. Aldred, *Egyptian Art* (1980); I. E. S. Richards, *The Pyramids of Egypt* (1961); S. Quirke, *Ancient Egyptian Religion* (1992); and B. Watterson, *Women in Ancient Egypt* (1991).

The First Universal Empires: Assyria and Persia   W. E. Dunstan, *The Ancient Near East* (1999), gives a succinct account of all aspects of the crisis of the civilized world between 1200 and 900 B.C., as well as of the Assyrian and Persian empires. The development of the alphabet is briefly and clearly described in J. F. Healey, *The Early Alphabet* (1990). G. Markoe, *The Phoenicians* (2000), and J. Curtis, *Ancient Persia* (1989), are up-to-date accounts.

The Jews and Monotheism (1200–300 B.C.)   An excellent brief introduction to the history of the Jews as a people and Judaism as a religion is D. Cohn-Sherbok, *The Jewish Heritage* (1988). H. Shanks, ed., *Ancient Israel* (1988), has essays by leading scholars on the Israelites as a nation, incorporating the results of archaeology.

☝ INFOTRAC COLLEGE EDITION

Visit the source collections at **http://academic.cengage.com/infotrac,** and use the Search function with the following key terms:

antiquities	Babylonian	Assyrian
Mesopotamia	Egypt history	Persian
archaeology	Phoenicians	Hebrews

🌐 WESTERN CIVILIZATION RESOURCES

Visit the Brief History of the Western World Companion Web Site for resources specific to this textbook:

http://history.wadsworth.com/greerbrief09/

Also, the CD in the back of this book and the World History Resources Center at **http://history.wadsworth.com/west_civ/** offer a variety of tools to help you succeed in this course, including access to quizzes; images; documents; interactive simulations, maps, and timelines; movie explorations; and a wealth of other sources.

CHAPTER 2

The Greek Beginnings
of Western Civilization

OVERVIEW

The Greeks began as yet another less advanced people that came into contact with the world of Middle Eastern civilization and adopted a civilized way of life. Originally, they were a European barbarian people—that is, they had a distinctive way of life based on farming and warfare which they shared with most other peoples of Europe. About 2000 B.C., they began to migrate into Europe's southeastern corner, only a short sea trip from the Middle East. As a result of contact with civilization, the Greeks began to adopt a civilized way of life—something that would happen to European barbarian peoples over and over again in the next three thousand years, until civilization spread right across Europe.

The earliest Greek civilization was very much an offshoot of the civilization of the Middle East. It shared in the international crisis and recovery of civilization across the Middle Eastern civilized world (pp. 41–43) and finally emerged as "classical" Greek civilization about 800 B.C. Every feature of this renewed Greek civilization was still deeply influenced by Middle Eastern peoples, but this time the Greeks had created something new and distinctive. Within classical Greek civilization there appeared ideas, art forms, and forms of government whose influence on Western civilization has lasted down to the present day.

Thus, Greek city-states (small self-governing communities) were the first to practice citizen participation in government—on a restricted basis in oligarchies like Sparta and on a much freer and wider basis in democracies like Athens. Greek thinkers and writers, reflecting on their nation's religious traditions and observing the natural and human world around them, originated the disciplines of science, philosophy, and history. From ancient religious rituals and epic tales, as well as from the close-knit community life of the city-states, there emerged the new art form of drama. The need to honor the gods and goddesses, as well as the urge of newly wealthy city-states and individuals for prestige and display, produced magnificent new styles of architecture and sculpture. And since the city-states also traded and colonized along the northern coastlands of the Mediterranean Sea, they brought their distinctive civilization to many barbarian peoples of Mediterranean Europe—above all, Italy.

The city-states were also innovators in warfare, developing methods of fighting by land and sea that shortly after 500 B.C. enabled them to preserve their independence against the mighty kings of Persia, at that time the rulers of the Middle Eastern civilized world (pp. 41–43). But the city-states also fought endlessly among themselves, and the longest and most brutal of these conflicts, the Peloponnesian War, between opposing alliances under Athens and Sparta, led to the end of the heyday of the city-states around 400 B.C. As a result, the city-states eventually fell under the rule of the Greek-influenced northern kingdom of Macedonia.

This did not mean the end of Greek civilization or of Greek power in the world, however. On the contrary, King Alexander of Macedonia led the Greeks to the conquest of Persia, and though his empire split up after his death, its separate territories came to be ruled by spectacularly wealthy and powerful Greek kings. By 300 B.C., Greek civilization had entered a new phase, the Hellenistic era, in which their culture dominated those of the nations they ruled but was also influenced by them. And the Greeks themselves had evolved from a barbarian people on civilization's northwestern edge to become the dominant nation of a civilized world that now included the Mediterranean coastlines as well as the Middle East.

The European Barbarians

During the three thousand years from early Sumer and Egypt to the Persian Empire, people living within civilized societies grew to be a substantial proportion, perhaps even a majority, of the human species as a whole. Apart from the expanding civilized world of the Middle East, civilizations arose also in India, China, and the Western hemisphere (pp. 325, 328). Elsewhere, however, humans still lived the prehistoric village life that had emerged from the Agricultural Revolution (pp. 11–16)—including those who inhabited the territory of Europe.

The sophisticated rulers, priests, and scribes of the Middle East probably thought of these early Europeans merely as distant suppliers of raw materials and slaves and as occasionally troublesome raiders and invaders—if they bothered to think about them at all. Yet it was out of the encounter between the peoples of prehistoric Europe and the great civilizations of the Middle East that Western civilization would eventually be born.

For many centuries before this historic encounter, Europe was only distantly affected by the rise of civilization in the Middle East. Even so, the way of life of the peoples of Europe underwent many changes and advances. By 4000 B.C., farming and village life had spread throughout the continent. With them came an increase in population and wealth, as well as technical inventiveness that was sometimes actually ahead of that in the Middle East. By 3500 B.C., there were peoples in western Europe who were numerous and well organized enough to construct ceremonial monuments consisting of circles and rows of huge upright boulders, as well as massive earthen tombs and for-

© Royalty–Free/CORBIS

Fig. 2.1 Stonehenge. The most famous of megalithic structures was built by an illiterate farming and trading people in the west of England about 2000 B.C., contemporary with the beginning of the Babylonian empire in Mesopotamia and the founding of the Middle Kingdom in Egypt. The urge to build great monuments and the wealth, skills, and organization to do so were no monopoly of civilized peoples in ancient times.

tifications. Many of these "megalithic" structures (from the Greek words for "large boulder") have survived to the present day. Underneath some of the earthworks, archaeologists have discovered traces of furrows in the soil on which they were originally built—evidence that the peoples of this region were the first to use plows to break up the ground more quickly and more thoroughly than with the traditional hoes, and thereby to make agriculture more productive.

Perhaps the most famous single achievement of the early Europeans was the building of the great open-air monument of Stonehenge, in the west of England. Stonehenge was built, probably as a religious center, and then repeatedly rebuilt over a period of several hundred years, by a prosperous people of farmers and traders who inhabited the region, until it reached its final form about 2000 B.C. The monument consists of about 160 massive boulders, weighing up to 50 tons each, all of which had to be dragged many miles to the site. Forty of the largest boulders were trimmed with stone tools to form neatly rectangular structural components. These were set upright with others placed horizontally on top of them as crosspieces (similar to the post-and-lintel construction of Egyptian temples; p. 37). Together with the other boulders, they were arranged in four circular or horseshoe-shaped groups one inside the other, all carefully aligned to the movements of the sun and the moon. The whole vast structure, much of which is still standing today (*Fig. 2.1*), is testimony to the level of wealth, organization, and skills attainable by the peoples of prehistoric Europe.

Both the villagers of Europe and the city-dwellers of the Middle East were frequently the victims of a third group of peoples. These were the migratory herders, or nomads, who inhabited the steppes (prairie grasslands) that stretched for thousands of miles from eastern Europe almost to the Pacific Ocean. The nomadic way of life arose from 4000 B.C. onward as farming peoples moved onto the steppes and found that the grassy plains were best exploited by herding large numbers of animals.

Among the animals these settlers herded was one that was native to the steppes, the horse. By 3800 B.C., the steppe peoples were keeping the horse for its meat and hide. By 3500 B.C., they were harnessing it to the earliest known wheeled vehicles. By 1200 B.C.—having bred it to be larger and stronger than before—they had learned to ride it. As the partnership of human and horse grew closer, the steppe peoples concentrated more and more on herding. On light chariots and later on horseback, they could follow larger herds farther across the grasslands in search of grazing and water, and over the generations, they gave up settled village life altogether.

Megalithic Europe

The nomads who had the most far-reaching influence on Europe were a prehistoric people or group of peoples known today as the Indo-Europeans. Probably originating in the steppes of present-day southern Russia, they spread outward from their homeland over many centuries between 4000 and 1000 B.C., as raiders, conquerors, and rulers. Some of them moved south into the civilized Middle East and eastward as far as India (pp. 27). Those who moved into these lands, such as the Hittites, Medes, and Persians (pp. 27, 45), usually adapted to the ways of the civilizations they encountered. Other Indo-European peoples moved westward into Europe, and by 1000 B.C. they had occupied most of the region.

Everywhere they moved, the Indo-Europeans brought great changes, above all in the languages of the peoples they encountered. Throughout vast areas of Europe and Asia, the inhabitants abandoned their original tongues and came to speak that of the Indo-Europeans, as their descendants still do at the present day. Languages as different as English and Bengali, or Russian and Spanish, are all derived from dialects spoken by the prehistoric Indo-Europeans.

The impact of the Indo-European nomads was especially strong on the villagers of Europe. From 2500 B.C. onward, under the influence of the newcomers, the settled peoples of the region began to form themselves into new ethnic groups whose way of life was a mixture of their traditional patterns and the new Indo-European influences. On the one hand, they did not become nomads—which would have been impossible in the forests, mountains, and swamps of Europe—but continued to live the settled village life of their ancestors. On the other hand, in place of their earlier tongues, they now spoke languages of Indo-European origin. In other ways, too, their way of life and social organization underwent important changes.

Throughout much of Europe, there appeared elites of warriors—often charioteers and horsemen—whose lives centered around strength and courage, comradeship and loyalty, contests and battle. In addition to the deities of earth and fertility, and the

dominant mother goddesses (p. 15) that many European peoples had traditionally worshiped, the warriors turned also to gods of fatherhood and thunder, metalworking and
war. When a leading warrior died, his horses and chariot, his bronze (or later, iron)
swords and daggers, his gold and silver drinking cups, would all go to the grave with
him—presumably so that he could go on riding, fighting, and drinking as a comrade
of the gods in the afterlife. And to judge from the reports of Greek and Roman writers
about the less advanced European peoples of their time, women shared these warrior
values. They went to war along with the men—not only to bring them food and bind
their wounds but also to force them back into the fight if they panicked, and sometimes to join in the fighting themselves.

Of course, war as such was nothing new to Europe or any other part of the world.
But it seems that the peoples of the continent now came to regard it not only as necessary and profitable but also as honorable, noble, and pleasing to the gods—that is, as
enhancing the value of the warrior as a human being.

Even for the most warlike Europeans, however, the main business of life was farming, adapted in various ways to the different regions of the continent. They lived in villages or in big farmsteads housing several related families; generally, the settlements
were widely scattered, for the population was thinner than in the civilized Middle East.
Groups of villages or farmsteads formed tribes, held together by common interests, traditions, and ties of kinship. A tribe would meet from time to time to conduct its common business and celebrate the festivals of a local god or goddess, and would often
build itself a hilltop stronghold.

Tribes, in turn, formed larger groupings, mainly for purposes of warfare, under
warrior kings—or occasionally warrior queens—and their battle comrades. In good
times, the tribal groupings fought each other for metals, slaves, and other items that
brought prestige to their possessors or could be exported to the Middle East in return
for some of the luxuries of civilization; in bad times, overpopulation and famine sometimes drove them to massive armed migrations such as those of the Sea Peoples (p. 41).

Thus Europe came to be inhabited by peoples who spoke mostly Indo-European
languages; who were skilled in farming, metalworking, trade, and warfare; and who
lacked cities, written records, and fixed structures of government, though they were
fairly well organized on the local level. The relatively advanced prehistoric peoples
who followed this way of life are customarily referred to as the European *barbarians*.
The word comes from the Greek *barbaros,* which originally meant "non-Greek." Today,
the word refers to people believed to be less intelligent, refined, or humane than oneself. Scholars, however, use the word with no contemptuous overtones to mean the
tribal groups and way of life that emerged in Europe from about 2500 B.C.

One by one, over a period of three thousand years from 2000 B.C. right down to
A.D. 1000, the European barbarian peoples came into contact with civilization. As with
the earlier spread of civilization to less advanced peoples of the Middle East (p. 7), the
contacts were sometimes peaceful and sometimes warlike, and if the contacts were
warlike, the barbarians were sometimes the conquerors and sometimes the victims.
But the results were always the same: one by one, the barbarian peoples of Europe became civilized. The chieftains and warriors of one era became the leaders and defenders of civilization in the next, often making their own contribution to the civilization
they had acquired. And in this way, civilization eventually spread throughout Europe.

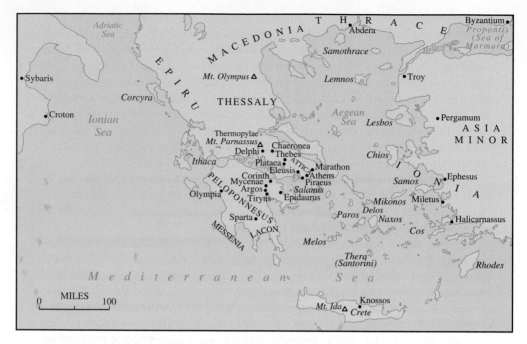

Map 2.1 The Greek Homeland. The Greeks settled in the regions of Thessaly, Attica, and the Peloponnesus from about 2000 B.C. onward, coming as migrants from somewhere farther north. Between 1200 and 800 B.C., they spread to the islands of the Aegean Sea and the western coast of Asia Minor. In later times, the Greeks continued to migrate across Europe and Asia from the western Mediterranean to the borders of India, but the Aegean region remained the center of the Greek world.

The first such barbarian warrior people to make contact with civilization were the Greeks. As a result of their encounter with the civilized peoples of the Middle East from 2000 B.C. onward, the Greeks developed a distinctive civilization of their own—the first that counts as definitely "Western."

The Aegean Background

The scene of the encounter between the Greeks and Middle Eastern civilization was the territory surrounding the Aegean Sea, an arm of the eastern Mediterranean leading to the Black Sea (*Map 2.1*). The Aegean region was very different in landscape and climate from civilization's river-nourished homelands in Mesopotamia and Egypt. To the west, the mountainous peninsula of mainland Greece jutted southward from the European landmass; the Aegean Sea itself was strewn with hundreds of islands; and on the east lay the coastal plains of Asia Minor. With its rocky soil, its hot, dry summers, and its cold, wet winters, most of the region had only a limited amount of agricultural wealth to provide a foundation for civilized life. Over many centuries from about 3000 B.C. onward, however, the farmers of the Aegean and elsewhere in the Mediterranean had

Fig. 2.2 The "Master of the Animals." In this heavy gold pendant, about 2½ inches across and made in Crete about 1700 B.C., a powerful being holds a goose in each hand, while two pairs of bull's horns loom behind him. The depiction of his body and the lotus flowers at his feet show Egyptian influence. The elegance of this piece of jewelry, and no doubt its luck-bringing power, were valued far from its homeland. It was found in the Greek island of Aegina, 200 miles across the sea from Crete.

found a way to get the most from their land by cultivating grain together with olives and grapes. In addition, southeastern Europe was rich in metals and in timber for shipbuilding. As a result, the Aegean peoples had traditionally supplemented their agricultural livelihood with metalworking, lumberjacking, trade, and piracy. This had early on brought them into contact with the Middle East, so that before 2000 B.C., the Aegean had come to be a fringe region of the international civilized world, inhabited by relatively advanced and prosperous peoples—none of whom, as yet, were Greeks.

About 2200 B.C., the Aegean region began to advance still further when a distinct civilization, known today as Minoan (from Minos, a legendary king), arose under Middle Eastern influence on the island of Crete. Minoan civilization drew its wealth from control of the surrounding seas and from thriving trade with many eastern Mediterranean lands, above all Egypt. As in Egypt, trade was controlled by the rulers, whose business records were written in a script developed locally under Egyptian influence. The ruins of luxurious palaces, as well as elegant jewelry and other surviving objects (*Fig. 2.2*), indicate a rich, refined civilization—one that was free, seemingly, of internal wars, since neither the palaces nor the nearby settlements were fortified. Artistic remains suggest a pleasure-loving society in which women played a prominent role—a society devoted to spectacular games and the worship of a fertility goddess.

At the same time that Minoan civilization arose, great changes were taking place on the Greek mainland. While some Indo-European peoples moved into the Middle East, other Indo-European-speaking immigrants or invaders arrived in the Aegean— the Greeks. There is no way of knowing exactly when, where, or how the Greeks developed into a separate ethnic group, but at the time that they made their way into their new homeland, they seem to have been a European barbarian people much like any other (pp. 56–59). By 1600 B.C., however, their chieftains had established fortified settlements along the mainland's southern shore and on some of the islands, and these settlements had become the centers of a new civilization—the Mycenaean civilization, so called from Mycenae, the earliest site to be excavated in modern times.

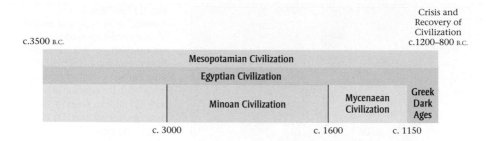

The Mycenaean Greeks were a warlike people whose leading warriors rode into battle in horse-drawn chariots and who protected their settlements with extraordinarily massive walls. They buried their rulers in huge, stone-lined underground chambers together with rich treasures of bronze weapons, as well as magnificent gold and silver personal adornments and eating and drinking vessels—proof of a skilled and wealthy society. The Mycenaeans also adopted many features of Minoan civilization, including its writing, which they adapted to their own early version of the Greek language.

But the Mycenaeans also struggled with the Minoans for control of the commerce of the eastern Mediterranean until the rivalry ended about 1400 B.C. with the destruction of the Minoan towns, perhaps as a result of Mycenaean conquest. Crete became Mycenaean in civilization and eventually Greek in language, and the riches of every land between Egypt and the Black Sea (*Map 2.2*) now came by ship to the Mycenaean chieftains of the Greek mainland.

Mycenaean civilization lasted until shortly after 1200 B.C., when it fell victim to the same crisis of the civilized world that brought about the downfall of the Hittites and the attacks of the Sea Peoples on Egypt (p. 41). Exactly what happened in the Aegean is unknown. Perhaps, as later Greek tradition declared, fresh waves of warlike Greeks overran the region as part of the many armed migrations of barbarian peoples that troubled the Mediterranean at this time. Or perhaps the Mycenaean chiefdoms were weakened internally by overpopulation and warfare and themselves supplied uprooted warriors to the raiding and invading forces. What is certain is that in about 1150, Mycenae was sacked and all the other fortified settlements were deserted. The population dropped, the ships no longer sailed, and writing fell out of use. Just as in Asia Minor (p. 41), the crisis led to the eclipse of civilization for nearly four centuries—a period known as the "Dark Ages" of Greek history.

But the Greeks themselves survived and even expanded their territory: fleeing the chaos on the mainland, many of them settled across the Aegean on the western coast of Asia Minor, which became part of the Greek homeland. In addition, many Mycenaean religious and cultural traditions lived on. The people continued to worship deities whom their ancestors had brought with them to Greece—like the thunder god, Zeus—or whom they had taken over from earlier Aegean peoples—like the war goddess, Athena. Minstrels sang songs of heroic deeds done in the days of "golden Mycenae"— above all of a grand expedition of allied chieftains from Greece to besiege and capture the flourishing city of Troy on the northwestern coast of Asia Minor. And the minstrels' listeners absorbed the traditional values that the heroic songs celebrated—the values of a warrior aristocracy that was at home on both land and sea.

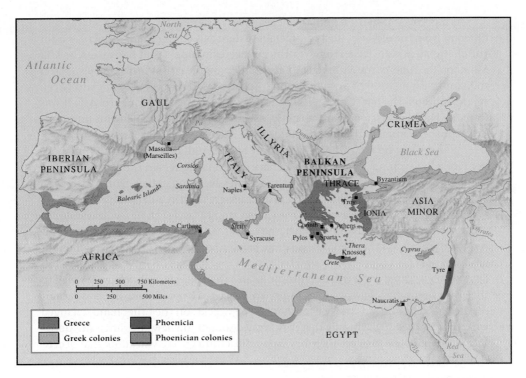

Map 2.2 Greek and Phoenician Overseas Migration. In the eighth and seventh centuries B.C., as their civilization became more advanced and their population grew, the Greeks joined the Phoenicians as traders, travelers, and
settlers across the sea. By 600 B.C., Greek city-states were flourishing along the coasts of southern Italy and Sicily,
southern Gaul (present-day France), North Africa to the west of Egypt, and the Black Sea. As the philosopher Plato
said shortly after 400 B.C., "We Greeks live around the [Mediterranean] sea like frogs round a pond."

By about 800 B.C., as in the rest of the civilized world (though somewhat later),
the Aegean was on the way to recovering from the crisis. Again the population expanded—so rapidly this time that it outran the skimpy food supply. Greek settlements
often grew beyond supportable limits, and when that happened, the city fathers usually
sent out expeditions to find a suitable spot for the founding of a daughter settlement
(colony). For two centuries emigration continued, until by 600 B.C. the Mediterranean's shores had come to be dotted with Greek colonies from the Black Sea westward to the coast of Spain, and the Greeks had joined the Phoenicians as the leading
commercial and seafaring nation of the civilized world (*Map 2.2*).

In spite of their wide dispersion, however, the Greeks maintained a sense of oneness, which was expressed above all by their common religion. From all over the Mediterranean, Greek athletes came to compete in the Olympic Games, held every fourth
year in honor of Zeus at Olympia in southern Greece. Warriors and statesmen visited
the oracle of the sun god, Apollo, at Delphi in central Greece to learn whether their
undertakings would succeed. Ordinary people went on pilgrimage to Eleusis, not far
from Athens, to gain the hope of eternal life by sharing in the rites of the fertility goddess, Demeter. These practices, all dating from not long after 800 B.C., formed the main
binding force in the renewed civilization of the Greeks.

As much as it inherited from the Aegean past, this renewed civilization was very different from the old one—to a considerable extent as a result of new influences from the changing Middle East. From wealthy civilized kingdoms that had arisen in Asia Minor on the ruins of the Hittite state, Greek settlers on the coast learned the use of iron tools and weapons as well as coined money (pp. 41, 48). From the Phoenicians Greek sailors imitated the latest shipbuilding and naval warfare techniques (p. 42). It was from the Phoenicians, too, that the Greeks relearned the art of writing—this time in its new alphabetic form, with adaptations to fit the needs of the Greek language (*Fig. 1.10*, p. 42). And after 700 B.C., when Egypt threw off Assyrian rule and became independent for a time (pp. 32, 43), Greek mercenary soldiers who served the pharaohs came home with stories of huge stone temples and impressive stone statues, which stirred the architectural and artistic ambitions of the increasingly wealthy rulers of the homeland.

This is not to say, however, that the Greeks simply "stole" their civilization from other nations in Asia and Africa. Rather, the Greeks did what the Babylonians, the Hittites, and countless other peoples had done before them. Migrating into a region that brought them into contact with the civilizations that had begun in Mesopotamia and Egypt, they learned from these civilizations and then adapted what they learned to their own needs. But earlier peoples had generally ended by producing mere variations on the older civilizations they encountered. The Greeks, on the other hand, changed what they learned so drastically that they created something new and different. Alongside Mesopotamia and Egypt there now appeared a third great civilization: that of classical Greece.

The City-State

With the recovery of Greek civilization about 800 B.C., the family-, clan-, and tribe-based communities of the Dark Ages began to develop into well-organized, independent city-states. The mature Greek city-state, or *polis,* was more than just a government, a trading center, or a place to live. It ranged in extent from a few square miles to 1,200 square miles or so, an area about the size of Rhode Island (in the cases of Athens and Sparta). Where possible, the city proper was built around a protecting hill, with a fortress crowning the summit, or *acropolis* (*Fig. 2.3*). The surrounding countryside, the mountains, and the sea nourished the city with agriculture and commerce. The population of both town and country ordinarily numbered only a few thousand, though the largest, Athens, may have reached 250,000.

Social and political units of this kind were not unique to Greece. They had tended to arise wherever there was no powerful kingdom or empire to limit their independence—notably among the Sumerians and Phoenicians. But the major Greek city-states differed from those of other peoples in one important respect: for the Greeks, the city-state was a community in which *all* citizens had a share and in which all were entitled to participate to a greater or lesser extent. Each city-state regarded itself as a *sovereign* (independent) community, entitled to the undivided loyalty and obedience of all its inhabitants. But the citizens did not regard this subjection to the community as a restriction on their liberty or an interference in their private lives, because they also had the right and duty to participate in community affairs. True, the rich usually

Fig. 2.3 The Acropolis of Athens. The citadel and main religious center of the Athenian city-state was already ancient when these buildings were constructed at the height of Athens's wealth and power during the fifth century B.C. At right, a staircase slopes up to the Propylaea, a ceremonial gateway leading through the citadel's walls to the Parthenon, the temple of Athena. The small building at left housed several religious cults, including that of Erechtheus, an early king whom the Athenians venerated as a "hero," or semidivine human being.

participated more than the poor, the well educated more than the illiterate, and men far more than women. Even so, the Greeks generally viewed the city-state as a community enterprise of all the citizens. In fact, the very idea of citizenship, in this sense, is of Greek origin.

This notion of citizen participation seems to have originated partly in the geography of the city-states. They first developed at exactly the time when the Assyrians were reaching for power across the civilized world (p. 43), but the Greek city-states were protected from the Middle Eastern conquerors by many miles of land and sea. With no universal empire to keep them in order, they were free to quarrel endlessly among themselves. Furthermore, they occupied a land that was far less wealthy than Mesopotamia or Phoenicia. In their conflicts with each other, the Greek city-states could not afford professional soldiers or large cavalry forces. Instead, they came to rely mainly on infantry armies made up of their own citizens.

Citizens who could afford to serve as *hoplites* ("men-at-arms") equipped themselves with bronze helmets and armor, round shields, long spears with iron blades, and short iron swords; they fought in formidable shock units of several hundred men each, known as *phalanxes,* or "rollers." Poorer citizens fought as light-armed infantry, harassing the enemy ahead of the phalanx's charge or covering its vulnerable flanks. This way of fighting was not new. In fact, much of the hoplite's equipment seems to have been modeled on that of the Assyrian heavy infantry (p. 43). But among the Greeks it was the ordinary male citizens who fought this way—and if arms-bearing citizens wanted to participate in other community activities besides warfare, they could not very well be told to mind their own business.

The sense of the city-state as a community of all its citizens, which existed even in such large city-states as Athens, was reinforced by tradition and myth. Each city-state was believed to have been founded and developed by a family or a clan—a kinship group—and most of its citizens claimed to trace their ancestry back to common fore-fathers. In the fully developed city-state, citizenship was in fact a matter of birth: the status of a father usually determined that of his children. Thus the citizens could think of themselves as distantly related members of one big family. They saw no more reason for conflict between the individual and the state than between the individual and the family. The "good life" for the individual was a life of active participation in civic affairs.

The city-state was also the citizens' "church." Although Greeks everywhere be-lieved in the same pantheon (group of gods), they paid special reverence to the partic-ular god or goddess who was associated with their own city. Local legend almost in-variably held that the founder of the community was divine or semidivine, and that a certain deity gave favor and protection to the city. The goddess Athena, for example, was the patron (guardian) of Athens, and all Athenians were therefore united in a spe-cial faith and ritual. The temple priests, moreover, did not form a class apart from the state; rather, they were state officials.

Just as the citizens were involved in the city-state's military, religious, and social affairs, they also took part in its government. In the earliest times of classical Greek civilization, the communities that would become city-states were ruled by kings (tribal chieftains) and their leading companion warriors, as described in the epics of Homer (pp. 84–85). But with the development of citizen armies, *monarchy* (government by kings) gave way to new forms of government that distributed power more widely among male citizens. One of these forms was *oligarchy* (rule by a few, from the Greek word for "few," *oligos*). In this form, a minority of citizens dominated the government, and the power of the majority was limited in various ways. Many city-states in main-land Greece were oligarchies, above all Sparta (pp. 67–69).

But other city-states, particularly those that developed into large commercial cen-ters, gave far more power to the majority. In such cities, the common people (in Greek, the *dēmos*) were too numerous and active to ignore, and the ruling groups were often divided among factions that competed for the commoners' support. Besides, big com-mercial cities needed navies as well as armies and depended in wartime on even the poorest citizens as oarsmen in the triremes. These were massive fighting vessels that fought in the Phoenician style, by ramming or boarding enemy ships (p. 42), but were larger and stronger than the Phoenician warships: instead of two banks of oars, the triremes had three. Since each trireme needed 170 men to row it, there was no way that a city-state could maintain a powerful fleet without the willing cooperation of the commoners.

In these large city-states, social conflicts sometimes led to the emergence of *tyranny*—the rule of a "tyrant." A ruler of this kind was not necessarily a tyrant in our present-day sense of a wicked and oppressive ruler. He was more what we would call a self-proclaimed dictator, who held power partly by force, partly by exploiting internal divisions, and partly by providing efficient government. But tyranny was often only a passing phase on the way to *democracy* (literally, government by the common people), in which all government decisions were made by the majority of male citizens. The most powerful and successful of democratic city-states was Athens (pp. 69–74), but there were many others, particularly among the Greeks of Asia Minor and elsewhere on the Mediterranean coastline.

It is not surprising that Greeks cherished their city-state, with its harmonious design for living. True, it was in a sense a narrow and exclusive type of political community. Women generally participated on a much more limited basis than men (pp. 68, 73–74); immigrants—including immigrants from other Greek city-states—had the duties but not the rights of citizens; and slaves were not considered members of the community at all. When a colony was settled abroad by citizens from a mother city, the new settlement became a separate, independent state. And when one city conquered another, it extended its control but not its citizenship. In the end, these tiny states exhausted one another through endless rivalry, jealousy, and war—for each had its own armed force as well as its own law. But in the course of their warfare, they developed exceptional organizational and fighting skills that enabled some of them, notably Athens and Sparta, to act for a time as great powers, alongside even the universal empire of Persia.

Although the Greek city-states had many features in common, each was individual in character and had its own personality. Athens brought forth in the course of a century more enduring creations of the human mind and spirit than any city before or since. Yet Athens was by no means the only center of creativity; there were, for example, Miletus and Ephesus in Asia Minor and Thebes, Argos, and Corinth on the mainland. But the power that contended with Athens for supremacy in Greece was Sparta. Though both were city-states, their particular institutions and ways of life were strikingly different. Before examining the remarkable achievements of Athens, we will look at its polar opposite in the Greek world.

SPARTA: THE MILITARY IDEAL

The Spartans were the chief descendants of warlike Greeks who had conquered the southern mainland. The land surrounding Sparta, known as Laconia, forms part of the Peloponnesus, a hand-shaped peninsula attached to the mainland by the Isthmus of Corinth (*Map 2.1*, p. 60).

The Spartans, in the eighth century B.C., were a minority of landholders (less than ten thousand adult males) ruling over a subject majority of *helots*. These were descendants of earlier Greek immigrants who were now bound to the land by the Spartan state and compelled to work for the landholding citizens. Since much of the land in their territory of Laconia was infertile, the Spartans pushed westward into the broad and fertile plains of Messenia. They subjugated its inhabitants, who were also Greeks, and turned them into helots too, so that in all, the Spartan citizens were outnumbered by the noncitizens about ten to one.

The conquerors became prisoners of their own success. Though the Laconian helots were relatively well treated and even fought in the army, the Messenians were harshly exploited, never accepted their defeat, and often rebelled. This situation required the Spartans to place themselves under a rigid system of life that would enable them, through the use of terror, to hold down a population much larger than their own. This demanded cultivation of their physical strength and endurance (for soldiering), strictest discipline, and a continuous watch (indeed, spying) on every individual. The Spartans rarely wavered, over several centuries, from their self-imposed way of life. The very name "Spartan" became a byword for courage, stamina, sternness, and determination.

Because their control over conquered people was often threatened, the Spartans hesitated to tamper with any of the institutions on which that power rested. They kept their dual kings, for example, long after kings had disappeared elsewhere in Greece—though they did limit the royal powers. While the kings continued to command in battle, policy decisions were taken over by a council of elders. This consisted of the kings, along with some thirty other men chosen for life (by the citizens) from among the leading families. The elders had to be at least sixty years of age. And the five officials called *ephors* (overseers), who held executive authority in the city, were usually old men too (elected annually). Although there was an assembly, which was open to all adult males of the citizen minority, those who attended were not even permitted to debate. Instead, the council of elders drew up all proposals and then presented them to the Assembly for approval or disapproval only—and this was given not by vote but by a shout. Thus the Spartan government was a leading example of oligarchy (p. 66).

The Spartans tried to seal off their city from outside influences. Compared with other Greek cities, Sparta had little contact with foreigners; it discouraged trade and showed visitors little hospitality. Its citizens feared that "subversive" ideas might upset the delicate internal balance, and they resorted to secret police and physical isolation to keep ideas out. But they were not motivated by fear alone; most Spartans *wanted* to preserve intact their system of government, their way of life, and their ideal of virtue (personal excellence).

Spartan men were required by law to serve as professional soldiers; all other occupations were closed to them. Property was fairly evenly divided among them, and any tendency to luxury was frowned on as a sign of softness. Their farms, as noted, were worked by the helots, while a middle class of aliens (noncitizens) was permitted to conduct such little business as there was.

One of the most curious features of the Spartan social system was the family life (or lack of it) among the ruling class. The men, when they were not out fighting, lived in barracks until they reached the age of thirty. They might then have some home life with their wives and children (they were permitted to marry after age twenty), but they still had to take their chief meal each day at a soldiers' mess. Infants who showed any sign of weakness were abandoned to die of exposure—a common Greek practice. Boys were taken by the state at the age of seven; they were taught manly behavior and reading and writing and were started on a lifelong routine of physical toughening and military instruction. Bachelors were punished, and the state encouraged the mating of the best human specimens. All this regimentation, this denial of personal choice and decision, was directed toward one main goal: the production of hoplites (p. 65) who would be fitter, better trained, and more highly disciplined than those of any other city-state. In fact, for as long as the city-state system was at its height, the Spartan army remained the most respected in all of Greece.

Girls were also required to participate in drills and exercises, which were designed to develop them into healthy, childbearing women. Partly for this reason and partly because for most of their lives they lived apart from their husbands, Spartan women led active, energetic lives and were considered scandalously "liberated" by other Greeks. But they fully shared the militaristic ideal of their menfolk. The story was told of the Spartan mother whose parting words to her son, as she sent him off to battle, were that she expected him to return to her either *with* his shield (that is, as a victor) or *on* it (as a corpse).

Although the Spartans paid a high price for security, their system did what they wanted it to do. For centuries, Sparta dominated the Peloponnesus, and in the desperate struggle with democratic Athens during the Peloponnesian War, the Spartans came through weakened but victorious.

Many other city-states in the Peloponnesus and elsewhere in Greece, including important centers like Corinth and Thebes, were also oligarchies, though on a somewhat different pattern than Sparta's. In Sparta, all citizens were relatively wealthy landowners who accepted almost total domination by a few among themselves so as to preserve discipline and hold down the helots. In other oligarchies, the way of life was far less harsh and rigid, and there were middling and poor citizens as well as wealthy ones. In these oligarchies, the power-holding "few" were generally the wealthiest citizens, who monopolized public office, and the assemblies in which the "many" gathered had more power of debate and initiative than in Sparta. But even the most liberal oligarchy gave far less power to the majority of citizens than the main alternative form of government, democracy, as practiced most famously in Athens.

ATHENS: THE GLORY OF GREECE

To the Athenians, the Spartan life was not worth living. One of their favorite quips was that the life led by the Spartans explained their willingness to face death. The Athenians themselves fought many wars, but they also sought a more balanced life. The contrasts between the two cities are endless. Sparta was agricultural and landlocked; Athens carried on a prosperous commerce and had direct access to the sea. Sparta had the more powerful army; Athens's chief strength was its navy. Sparta sought cultural isolation; Athens welcomed foreign ideas and visitors. And while the Spartans cultivated physical fitness and military courage, from Athens flowed the daring inventiveness, the glorious literature, the stunning creations of mind and hand that have so enriched our heritage.

The Athenian homeland was the peninsula of Attica, which is located about 100 miles northeast of Sparta, and which juts out into the Aegean Sea from the central portion of mainland Greece (*Map 2.1,* p. 60). Since Mycenaean times, Attica had been divided among many separate communities, but in the period of renewal of Greek civilization about 800 B.C., they merged to form a single city-state that was known by the name of the most important community, Athens.

Over the next three centuries, Athens passed through several stages of political growth, including both oligarchy and tyranny. But through all these stages there was one clear trend: the extension of political power to all adult male citizens. One of the main reasons for this was that in spite of many social conflicts, the Athenian aristocrats (leading citizens) allowed and even encouraged the trend to democracy. The aristocrats were descendants, usually rich, of prominent and long-established Athenian families. Though they prided themselves on being "fine and noble," many of them felt a sense of community with *all* Athenian citizens, and in addition they were divided among rival factions that often sought the commoners' support against each other.

One important stage on the road to democracy was a series of reforms, passed about 600 B.C. by the wise and respected aristocrat Solon. At a time of severe economic and political crisis, with poorer citizens losing their farms through debt and demanding a share of political power, Solon was appointed to arbitrate the crisis and reform the laws. He acted first to cancel existing debts and prohibit enslavement for nonpayment of debt in future. Then he altered the constitution by granting increased influence over government decisions to the Assembly—in which all adult males were entitled to take part—though confirming for the aristocrats the sole right to public office. Though Solon's reforms did not permanently solve the persisting political problems of the city arising from the disputes between rich and poor, they were crucial steps along the path to majority rule.

Around 500 B.C., another aristocratic statesman, Cleisthenes, led the way to complete democracy with a series of reforms that opened public office to all adult male citizens while giving ultimate power over all government decision making to the Assembly. Not long afterward, rich silver mines were discovered in Attica, and the democratic Assembly decided to spend the windfall on building a war fleet of unprecedented size, which the newly empowered commoners willingly manned. The commanders, as well as most of the influential politicians of democratic Athens, came from the aristocracy, for even though the *dēmos* now controlled the state, they voluntarily relied on the leadership of wealthy and educated men. Unlike in Sparta, freedom and democracy unleashed the enthusiasm and commitment of all social groups, and it was this above all that for the next hundred years would make Athens a "great power."

In those hundred years there were two turning points in the life of Athens and the rest of Greece, both military. The first was the Persian Wars, in which Athens led the Greek city-states to victory over the mighty oriental empire. This exhilarating success was followed by the Age of Pericles (460–430 B.C.), a period of the highest confidence, power, and achievement in Athens. That period was cut short by the second turning point, the Peloponnesian War between Athens and Sparta. But let us now view Athens at its best. The signal that set Athens on the path to glory was the Persian attack.

The Persian Wars. In the sixth century B.C., the rulers of Persia had succeeded in conquering most of the civilized world of the Middle East (p. 46). For the first time, a Middle Eastern universal empire had come within striking distance of the Greeks, and the Persians were able to bring the Greek-settled territories on the eastern shore of the Aegean Sea under their rule. The "Great King," Darius I, determined (about 494 B.C.) to extend his control into mainland Greece, for the Athenian upstarts had recently aided a rebellion against him by the Greek cities of Asia Minor. Darius, and later his son Xerxes I, sent two expeditions by land and sea against the mainland Greeks; the Persians lost the first decisive battle to the Athenians at Marathon in 490 B.C. (The original "marathon" was run by a messenger sent to seek Spartan help, who sped the 140 miles from Athens in thirty-six hours—but the reinforcements came too late.) Ten years later, in a sea battle near Athens (off the island of Salamis), the Athenian navy smashed the Persian fleet (supplied mainly by the Phoenician city-states, the former rulers of the sea).

Sparta, which shared with Athens the leadership of the Greek defense, also contributed to the defeat of Persia. The Spartans' suicidal stand at Thermopylae (480 B.C.) remains a symbol of heroism, and soon after Thermopylae, the Spartan hoplites routed a more numerous but less heavily armed and armored Persian army in the pivotal land battle of Plataea. But in the course of the long war, Athens made the greater sacrifices, and by 445 B.C., when final peace was made with Persia, Athens was the controlling power of the Aegean Sea.

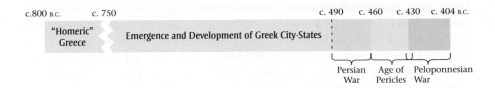

The courageous and resourceful little state had demonstrated surprising capacity in fighting the Persian forces. At the height of the wars, the Athenians had fled their homes and watched the enemy burn their city to the ground, but they had come through victorious. With their victory came a new-felt power. How had they, so few in number and so limited in wealth, turned back the power of the Great King, with his millions of slavish subjects? To the Athenians, flushed with confidence and pride, there could be only one answer: they and their free institutions were superior. A new sense of mission and assurance inspired the architecture, sculpture, drama, and philosophy of these remarkable years. True, the Golden Age of Athens had been for centuries in gestation, but it was the crisis successfully met, the thrill of triumph, that brought it to splendid life.

The Golden Age. Pericles, whose name is synonymous with the Golden Age, was the leader of Athens after the victory over Persia. It was largely through his initiative and guidance that the ambitious public works program on the Acropolis was carried through. An aristocrat of wealth and learning, Pericles nevertheless identified with the popular faction in politics. By virtue of his personal influence and his long tenure in important elective offices, he acted as the city's guiding force during the thirty-year period of Athenian supremacy in Greece. His death in 429 B.C., soon after the start of the Peloponnesian War (p. 98), signaled the end of the Golden Age.

It was in Pericles' time that democracy came into fullest effect in Athens. Though the government system worked very differently from those of twenty-first-century democratic states, it nevertheless provided a precedent and example of democracy in action that have lasted—like the word itself—down to the present day.

In Athenian democracy, ultimate government power rested in the Assembly of adult male citizens. All major decisions were made there: for peace or war, for sending forth expeditions, for spending public money, and for every other aspect of public affairs. Even the building of the Parthenon, the great temple of Athena on the Acropolis of Athens (pp. 89–91), was decided not by any religious authority but by the Assembly. Meetings were held about once a week, and the number of citizens present was usually less than five thousand. Although many more were eligible to attend, men who lived in the country districts of Attica were often unable to come to town. At first, the Assembly met in the marketplace (*agora*) of Athens, later on the slopes of a nearby hill (Pnyx). Although it could draw up laws on its own, ordinarily it discussed proposals put before it by a committee of the Council of Five Hundred. The latter body was chosen annually by lot to draft the laws and to supervise their administration.

Debates in the Assembly were often spirited. Naturally, those with a talent for public speaking enjoyed a great advantage over their fellows. The members of the Assembly, highly critical and not always polite, might express their disagreement with an argument by jeering or whistling. But a shrewd and skillful orator like Pericles could win and hold the favor of the Assembly. And once he had done so, he became the most powerful man in Athens, for the decisions of the Assembly were final. Voting was usually by a show of hands, and a simple majority determined the outcome.

The Athenian citizens insisted on *direct* democracy (personal participation) not only in making laws but in administering them. There were up to a thousand public officials in Athens—tax collectors, building inspectors, and the like—and all but a few of them were chosen annually by lot. (Those chosen must have volunteered to serve and were subject to examination for fitness by the courts.) Since these officials were paid for their services, poor men as well as rich could afford to hold office. Here was a system of "rule and be ruled," the full application of a deep faith in the political capacity of every male citizen.

The Athenians did not, however, trust to lot in selecting their chief executive officers. These were the Ten Generals (*Stratēgoi*), who were chosen each year by vote of the male citizens. They commanded the army and the navy, managed the war department, and exercised extensive control over the treasury. The Ten Generals chose their own chairman; the popular Pericles was elected general by the citizens and chairman by his fellow generals for sixteen years in succession.

The laws of Athens, then, were made by the male citizens, and it was the male citizens who also administered the laws. Athenian courts differed from American courts in several respects. They were much larger in size, usually about five hundred members. This served to make bribery or coercion difficult and to guarantee a broad cross section of citizen judgment. The court for each trial was chosen by lot from a long list of names. There was no officer, like a judge, to decide questions of law; the Athenian court was judge and jury combined. By majority vote, it ruled on all issues of procedure, legal interpretation, guilt or innocence, and type of punishment. There were no lawyers, either. Every citizen argued his own case—another reason why the ability to speak effectively was so valued in Athens.

The Athenians practiced what they preached about political democracy. In fact, they *invented* democracy (both the concept and the word itself). Civic and political participation was part of the Athenian way of life for all adult male citizens. We have no statistical records, but estimates suggest that during the Age of Pericles, the number of adult male citizens was only about 40,000 out of a total citizen population (including children) of perhaps 100,000. Beneath the citizens in status were resident aliens, chiefly artisans and tradespeople, who may have numbered 50,000. At the bottom of the social structure were the slaves, who were perhaps equal in number to the citizen class. Thus the estimated 40,000 male citizens controlled the government of a state of possibly 250,000 inhabitants. And yet, even though female citizens, aliens, and slaves were excluded, there were doubtless more individuals actively participating in government in Athens than in any other city of comparable population before or since.

Slavery in a Democracy. Slaves were found in all the city-states, as they were throughout the ancient world. They were chiefly non-Greeks, usually descended from captives of war. The Athenians (including the philosopher Aristotle) justified slavery by arguing that Greeks were superior to non-Greeks and that it is good and right for superiors to rule inferiors. Slaves, Aristotle declared, were necessary "instruments" for the use of their superiors. By taking over the dull and heavy tasks, they freed their masters for greater leisure and cultural attainments. Most of the slaves in Athens were household servants; some worked in the fields; some were craftsmen; about ten thousand of them worked in the silver and lead mines of Attica. The mine workers were driven cruelly, but the others seem to have been treated humanely. Slaves were legally the property of their owners, and they worked and lived pretty much as their masters chose. A few were permitted to rise to positions of considerable importance in Athens, and many were set free as a reward for faithful service. At any rate, there were no slave revolts like those that occurred in Sparta and in most other places where slavery has existed. The orator Demosthenes claimed that Athenian slaves enjoyed greater freedom than the citizens of many other lands, and he was probably right. A favorite taunt by the Spartans (in a way, a compliment) was that on the streets of Athens, one could not tell a citizen from a slave. As a matter of fact, the Athenians did not stress social or economic differences. The majority of citizens were people of limited means: small farmers, artisans, or merchants.

Daily Life in Athens. The Athenian economy was diversified and balanced; its chief products were wine and olive oil. By the fifth century B.C., Athens had become well known also as a manufacturing center. Free men and slaves, working in small shops, produced excellent metal weapons, pottery, and hand-wrought articles of silver, lead, and marble. Most of these were sold abroad in return for grain, meat, fruit, textiles, and lumber. Many citizens made their living by building or sailing ships, for Athens was a leading maritime power. Wages and profits were generally low, but so was the cost of living.

And the Athenians had simple needs. Wraparound garments and a single pair of sandals made up the typical wardrobe. They took but one main meal each day, consisting normally of grains, fruits, vegetables, and fish. Wine was consumed daily; meats were reserved for holidays. Recreation was free at the civic festivals, which included athletic contests, dances, and dramatic performances. What most Athenian males sought was not great wealth but leisure: time for talk, for exercise and games in the public gymnasium, and for engaging in the affairs of their city. Living standards did vary, of course, and there was always some feeling of hostility between rich and poor—hostility softened, however, by common devotion to the community and by the fact that the wealthy paid for festivals, dramatic shows, and ships for the navy. (The state received additional revenue through court fines, customs duties, an annual tax on aliens, and certain sales taxes—including one on prostitution.)

Women did not share in the freedom and democracy enjoyed by Athenian men. Free women with Athenian fathers counted as citizens and played an important part in the city-state's religious affairs, notably as priestesses of various deities. But they could not take part in the proceedings of the Assembly or the law courts, let alone hold public office. Poor women sometimes worked in trades outside the home, as weavers, innkeepers, and vendors in the marketplace; in the countryside, they did the women's work (p. 14–15) of the farms. Well-off Athenian women lived a more restricted life than those of Sparta and had less favorable property rights than those of Egypt. They were not supposed to socialize with men other than their fathers, brothers, and husbands; male visitors to a house had to keep to a special "men's room." If a woman left the house, she had to be escorted by a close male relative or be in a group with other women; and she had to have a specific reason, such as buying supplies, taking part in public religious celebrations, or attending drama performances. Women held property under the control of a male "guardian"—usually a father, brother, or husband—and they could plead in the law courts only through these guardians.

Though mutual respect and affection were normal between spouses, marriage was viewed primarily as a practical partnership for producing heirs and keeping house, and marriages and divorces were arranged by men. The sexual liberty of the husband was taken for granted. In addition to his wife, he had access to his household slaves as well as to public prostitutes (noncitizens). And if he found his wife boring and could afford to do so, the husband might take up with more engaging female companions (*hetaerae*). These women, usually noncitizens from Asia Minor, were schooled in the arts of conversation and entertainment. The most famous of them was the intelligent and charming Aspasia, the consort and mistress of Pericles.

The effect of all this, however, was not just to make aristocratic women dependent on men. It also meant that these women lived in a separate female world, with its own social life, activities of household management, and religious observances. Those who lived successfully within this world were considered to possess "virtue"—that is, excellence as human beings—on the same level as men.

Besides their relationships with women, well-off Athenian men, like all other upper-class Greeks including the Spartans, could without dishonor form homosexual ties, as long as these were of a particular sort. Perhaps because of their relatively restricted family life, the Greeks found it normal and even praiseworthy for adult men to fall in love and have sexual relationships with teenage boys. Sooner or later, when the boy grew up, a relationship of this kind was supposed to turn into ordinary friendship, and homosexuality between "consenting adults" was generally frowned on. Within these limits, male homosexuality played an important part in the sexual and emotional life of the Greeks.

Aristocratic Athenians lavished great care on their children, especially their sons. Though the girls received little formal training, most upper-class boys were instructed in private schools or individually by tutors (*Fig. 2.4*). They were taught to exercise, to play games, and to compete in sports. They were also instructed in reading, writing, and speaking, as well as in the popular legends, music, and the poems of Homer. After reaching eighteen years of age, the young men were assigned to special companies for two years of military and civic training. As far as is known, the less well-off majority, both male and female, was for the most part illiterate. But the city itself was the principal school for young and old, aristocrats and commoners.

THE CITY-STATE WAY OF LIFE

In Athens we find the full flowering of Greek genius, but there were scores of other city-states in which the way of life was similar. And although Greek civilization expressed itself through these independent city-states, we should not lose sight of the "oneness" of the culture. Each city paid special respect to its favorite gods, but all sacrificed to the same chief deities, just as they shared common shrines and oracles and celebrated such all-Greek festivals as the Olympic Games. All claimed a common forefather, Hellen, and all had a common inheritance in the heroes and history of Homer.

The same language bound these freedom-loving people together and set them apart, in their own view, from outsiders. Those who did not speak Greek they called

Fig. 2.4 Athenian Education. Greek pottery was often decorated with scenes of everyday life—in this case, a school. At left, a boy is learning to play a harp-like instrument, the lyre. At center, another boy recites by heart while his teacher follows the text, written on a papyrus scroll. At right, a slave who has escorted one of the boys to school waits patiently for the lesson to finish. Hanging on the wall are lyres, a basket, a flute in a case, and two-handled drinking cups like the one on which this scene appears.

barbarians (*barbaroi*) (p. 59). This was not necessarily a term of discredit or blame, for the Greeks applied it to refined and sophisticated Persians as well as to primitive and untamed tribes. It meant simply that those outsiders could not speak Greek, from which it followed that they could not think Greek and hence could not know or live the Greek way.

What was this Greek way? How did it differ from the Eastern way? The cardinal distinction lay in the Greek view of the individual. In the ancient cultures of the Middle East, ordinary people were of small account. The ruler of Egypt, the pharaoh, owned and regulated the land and its inhabitants through divine right. The idea of personal liberty had little meaning to the mass of his subjects, and no one in authority regarded them as capable of governing themselves (p. 30).

But Greek citizens would be slaves to no person and to no state. They believed in law and in an orderly society protected by the gods, but they generally insisted on a substantial measure of freedom and political participation (for adult males). The city-state was more than a means of government; it was in itself a way of life—the only "good life." And the Greeks believed that all free and intelligent members of their nation were capable of enjoying this good life. They did not take the view, characteristic of the East, that individuals must resign themselves to a fate altogether beyond their control. In a limited way, the Greeks were optimistic about the world and about what a man could do on his own—if he did not presume too far.

Greek Religion

While the Greeks' view of life was reflected in their politics, it was expressed most fully in their religion, philosophy, and art. Greek religion by the Age of Pericles (fifth century B.C.) had become a well-developed institution of the state. It ordered the daily lives of citizens, inasmuch as the community undertook no important act without giving thought to the gods, but there was no authoritative body of dogma, no "Word of God," and no special class of priests. Prayers, rites, and festivals were rooted in customs that could be traced back to the misty beginnings of Greek history and were preserved in the works of early poets. The greatest of these poets, Homer (pp. 84–85), drew portraits of the gods and told colorful tales about them. Another poet, Hesiod, wrote more directly about the ancestry of the gods and the creation of the universe. These works and those of several lesser writers were generally accepted by the Greeks as highly respected accounts of the divine scheme of things.

GODS AND GODDESSES

From earlier civilizations, the Greeks inherited the basic ideas of polytheistic and anthropomorphic religion (p. 21). They believed that the natural world and human affairs were controlled by hundreds of living beings, similar to humans in appearance and character except for their immortality; among these, a few were thought to be superior in power and majesty. Though far from being the first to personify the forces of nature and fortune in this way, the Greek poets and artists surpassed all others in their appealing imagery.

The gods lived close by—the great ones on top of Mount Olympus, the highest peak of Hellas (*Map 2.1,* p. 60). There, behind a veil of clouds, Zeus, father of the gods, presided over his divine family. The Olympian deities were usually perfect and beautiful in shape, but they also displayed human frailties and emotions. They knew ambition, pride, and jealousy, and they took an active interest in affairs on earth. Though they were not all-powerful, they merited the respect of mortals. Human and divine beings alike, moreover, were thought to be subject to the mysterious and irresistible force of *Moira* (Fate).

Zeus (Jupiter, as the Romans later called him), whose special zone was the sky, shared overlordship of the world with two of his brothers: Poseidon (Neptune) ruled the sea, and Hades, or Pluto (Dis), ruled the underworld. The underworld was a dark, forbidding place where spirits of the departed lingered for an uncertain period. There was, generally, no expectation of immortality for humans and no system of rewards and punishments after death. But the gods could inflict their power for good or ill on a person during life, and therefore it was important to win their favor through sacrifices, honors, and prayers.

As Zeus embodied the patriarchal (fatherly) principle, his wife Hera (Juno) embodied the matriarchal (motherly) principle. She was regarded as the protector of womanhood and marriage. But she was also something of a shrew, and Zeus found comfort in extramarital romance—which resulted in numerous divine offspring. His favorite daughter was Athena (Minerva), a spirited virgin noted for her wisdom, armed and martial in bearing, the consoler of maidens and the protector of Athens. The Athenians raised many monuments in her honor; the most perfect was the temple of the Parthenon (from the Greek word for "virgin"), which still crowns the Acropolis of Athens.

The legends of the love affairs of Zeus and of other gods and goddesses had doubtless grown up as a way of explaining the special character of individual deities and their relationships to one another. But the Greek poets gave extraordinary color and vigor to these legends. They told, for example, how Leto, one of the companions of Zeus, had presented him with a splendid pair of twins—the handsome Apollo and his sister Artemis (Diana). Apollo, later associated with the sun, was widely worshiped as the god of poetry, music, art, and manly grace. Artemis, associated with the moon, was the goddess of wild nature, a hunter, and the model of athletic girlhood.

A female of quite another type was Aphrodite (Venus), goddess of beauty and love. Aphrodite tried her charms on many men and gods, among them the bluff and powerful Ares (Mars). But the god of war, "the curse of men," preferred the thrill of killing to the pleasures of lovemaking. More companionable was the fleet Hermes (Mercury), messenger of the gods and patron of athletes. He had the lithe form of a perfect runner, and he glided on winged sandals over land and sea. Dionysus (Bacchus) was a son of Zeus by a mortal woman, Semele. It was in part this mixed parentage that made him so popular and beloved among the Greeks. Many legends were mingled in Dionysus: he was the god of wine and indulgence; he was also associated with the fertility principle in nature, with the suffering of death, and with the joy of rebirth. It is not surprising that "mystery" cults (worship groups) promising personal immortality grew up in connection with Dionysus.

PRIESTS, ORACLES, AND MYSTERY CULTS

The Greeks had no churches—neither organizations nor buildings—as we think of them. And because they had no rigid teachings, people could believe what they pleased so long as they did not openly deny or insult the official deities. (Such acts were forbidden because they might bring down divine punishment, not only on the offending individual but on the whole community.) The temple, the chief place of worship, was designed as a "home" for the personal use of the god it honored. A statue of the god was normally placed in the interior, which was seldom entered by the public. An appointed priest was responsible for the care and protection of the statue and the sacred temple area.

Ceremonies in honor of the god were usually performed in front of the temple, where the worshipers presented the priest with gifts—pottery, garments, whatever might be pleasing to the god or goddess. They also offered up prayers and animal sacrifices to win divine favor and assistance. After a sheep or pig had been roasted and the aroma had reached the nostrils of the god, the priest and the worshipers ate the meat in a common sacred meal. (The only food and drink taken by the gods themselves were the divinely perfect "ambrosia" and "nectar," believed to nourish their immortality.)

Some priests and priestesses claimed that they had the power to see into the future by interpreting certain signs (omens) or by verbal communication with the gods.

The Greeks took special interest in these seers (oracles) and paid them high honor and respect. The most famous oracles in all Greece were the priestesses of Apollo who lived at Delphi (*Map 2.1*, p. 60). Politicians, generals, heads of families—the mighty and the lowly alike—went or sent to Delphi for advice on such matters as whether or not to undertake a military campaign or what they must do to end a plague. A priestess would fall into a trance, relay the question to Apollo, and then utter the answer received from him. The utterance was usually unclear and had to be interpreted for the questioner by a priest. The Delphic oracles won a high reputation for accuracy, partly because the advice and predictions were in such vague, ambiguous terms that they could be made to fit almost any later event.

The official religion thus offered mortals a glimpse of the divine will. It also explained the mysteries of nature and provided a means of gaining the favor and help of superhuman forces. What it did not provide was consolation to those who lost the game or suffered misfortune. Nor did it hold any promise of life other than the one on earth; only the gods enjoyed eternal life. As if to balance these shortcomings, various cults grew up alongside the official religious beliefs and practices. Because their rituals were usually known only to the initiated, these came to be called mystery (secret) cults.

Dionysus, the central figure of worship in most of these cults, was associated with seasonal death and rebirth (winter and spring). His followers believed that they could identify themselves with the god, and thus share his rebirth, by means of ritualistic experiences; these included undergoing severe physical tests, becoming intoxicated with wine or drugs, eating a sacred meal, and witnessing a dramatic representation of the god's death and resurrection. At the end of such ordeals, the worshiper sensed a mystic union with the god and the assurance of everlasting life. The mystery religions supplemented, rather than replaced, the official religion, and probably only a minority of the citizens underwent the initiation rites.

Other Greeks were more interested in the relation of religion to morality. The gods of Homer had shown slight concern for customary moral standards, but by the time of the Golden Age, they had become more closely identified with ideas of right and wrong. Zeus was regarded as the upholder of justice, especially of the sanctity of oaths. Human crimes were frowned on by most of the Olympians, and divine punishment would surely fall on the murderer, perjurer, or arrogant individual. Even so, the official religion, with its accounts of strange and questionable acts performed by the gods themselves, did not fully satisfy the moralists. Greek dramatists and philosophers ("serious" thinkers) began to challenge the traditional beliefs, insisting that religion should include a definite *moral* order. Failing to find it in the Greek legends, they either rejected the gods or made them subordinate to a "higher power" of justice.

The Founders of Western Philosophy

The earliest Greek philosophers (in the sixth century B.C.) began by criticizing the popular nature myths. They found it hard to believe that earthquakes were caused by the stamping of Poseidon or that lightning was a bolt from Zeus. They made the intellectual leap from a primitive view of nature to a reasoned, analytical view.

PIONEERS OF RATIONAL THOUGHT

One of the questions the Greek philosophers sought to answer concerned the composition of the physical universe. They were convinced that nature, in its unseen being, is far simpler than it appears to be—all material things are made up of a small number of basic elements. Around 600 B.C., Thales of Miletus (in Asia Minor) theorized that water is the basic element. This was a logical notion, since water seems to be present, in various forms, throughout the world of space and matter. It fills the sea, rivers, and springs; it falls from the sky; it is found in the flesh and organs of animal bodies. Though later philosophers rejected Thales' belief that everything can be reduced to water, they agreed that he was on the right track. Some believed the prime substance to be air or fire; others concluded that there are four basic elements: earth, air, fire, and water.

But during the fifth century B.C., Democritus of Abdera (in Thrace) developed the theory that all physical things are formed by combinations of tiny particles, so small that they are both invisible and indivisible. He called them *atoms*. Democritus' atoms are identical in substance but differ in shape, thus making possible the great variety of objects in the world. They are infinite in number, everlasting, and in constant motion. They account, said Democritus, for everything that has been or ever will be. Democritus offered no concrete evidence to prove the existence of atoms, but the fact that he could arrive at this remarkable idea demonstrates the far-reaching achievement of Greek reasoning.

Rational thought was also applied to diseases. In the fifth century B.C., Hippocrates of Cos (an island in the Aegean) openly challenged traditional supernatural explanations of illness. He insisted that *natural* causes be looked for and that natural means be used to treat disease. He was one of the first physicians to stress the influence of the environment (climate, air, and water) on health. His most notorious theory, however, was that of "humors." The human body, Hippocrates believed, contains four humors (fluids): blood, phlegm, yellow bile, and black bile. When these are in proper balance, the individual enjoys normal health. But when the balance becomes disturbed, the physician must use his skill to restore it. This unproved theory was widely accepted in the West until the eighteenth century—and sometimes brought suffering or death (from bloodletting).

Turning to more abstract and universal matters, the philosopher Parmenides of Elea (in southern Italy) tackled the controversial issue of permanence versus change in the world. He convinced himself that everything in the universe must be eternal and unchangeable. Change requires motion, he reasoned, and motion requires empty space. But empty space equals nonexistence, which by definition does not exist. Therefore, he concluded, motion and change are impossible. Parmenides readily admitted that some things *appear* to move and change; but this must be an illusion of the senses, he said, because it is contradicted by logic. And logic, the Greek philosophers thought, is the most reliable test of truth.

Logic did not always lead to the same answers, however. While Parmenides satisfied himself that matter was unchanging and permanent, another Greek reached the opposite conclusion. Heraclitus of Ephesus (in Asia Minor) insisted that the universe, instead of standing still, is in continuous motion. He declared that a person cannot step into the same river twice—in fact, the river is changing even as one steps into it.

This doctrine proved most disturbing, for if everything is constantly changing (including ourselves), how can we gain true knowledge of anything? By the time our mind has been informed, the object of our attention is no longer what it was!

THE SOPHISTS

Uncomfortable suggestions like these led many Greeks to abandon the effort to find absolute or final truth. A group of professional teachers, called Sophists because they claimed to make their pupils wise (*sophos*), played a leading part in this shift. Most of them, as teachers, had visited various cities of the Mediterranean area in order to earn their living. Hence when they settled in Athens, as many did, they held more cosmopolitan views about the world than did ordinary Athenian citizens. Prominent among the Sophists was Protagoras. He is famous for having declared, "Man is the measure of all things, of what is and of what is not." Completely skeptical (doubting) of general truths, even about the gods, he insisted that truth is different for each individual. What was true (or right) for a Spartan might well be false (or wrong) for an Athenian. Furthermore, as Heraclitus had suggested, our bodies and minds are changing every moment, and our perceptions and ideas change with them.

The Sophists thus rejected the established view that there existed a common, "objective" reality that all persons can grasp in the same way. They concluded, therefore, that it is pointless to look for absolute truth about either nature or morals. Because truth is relative to each individual, it is important only to know what one finds agreeable and useful, such as the arts of persuasion or how to achieve "success." And one leading Sophist, Aristippus of Cyrene (in North Africa), equated success with pleasure. He and his followers (the Cyrenaic school) were convinced that the only sensible goal for each individual is personal enjoyment. They were not the first humans to come up with such an idea, but they may have been the first to justify it with reasoned arguments. Because they claimed *hēdonē* (pleasure) to be the "highest good," they and people of like mind are often called *hedonists*.

The Sophist teachings that equated morality with success or pleasure and contradicted traditional beliefs about truth, standards, and duty were radical for the times. As news of these teachings circulated in Athens and elsewhere in Greece, the more conservative citizens were shocked and alarmed. Such ideas smacked of impiety (disrespect for the gods) and threatened to subvert the laws and moral code of the state. Protagoras protested that his theories did not call for the denial of authority (anarchy) and cautioned his pupils, "When in Athens, do as the Athenians." Social order, he agreed, requires reasonable conformity to the laws of the community, whether or not they are absolutely true or right. But the conservative elders were not reassured. It upset them to think that one person's ideas are as "true" as another's. And the laws of gods and mortals, they argued, cannot be properly respected and upheld unless the citizens believe them to be true and just—in an absolute sense.

SOCRATES AND PLATO

The greatest teacher of the fifth century was Socrates, who met the Sophist view of how to get on in life with the full force of his intellect and will. He was not a defender of the Olympian religion or of traditional morality; he was convinced, rather, of the existence of a higher truth. Socrates did not claim to know this truth but spoke of himself only as a seeker after knowledge. Because of his skeptical approach and his primary interest in human affairs, Socrates was often mistaken for one of the Sophists. He believed that knowledge must proceed from doubting, and he was forever posing questions and testing the answers people gave him. The Athenians resented having to justify their ways and ideas to Socrates, and he became increasingly unpopular. But he persisted in his arguments and discussions, for, he felt, "the unexamined life is not worth living."

Socrates believed that a technique of careful questioning can lead to the discovery and elimination of false opinions, which often pass for "truth." He cross-examined his associates on their definitions of justice, right, and beauty, moving them constantly toward answers that seemed more and more certain.

This "Socratic method," sometimes called the "dialectical method," is simply a procedure for reaching toward truth by means of a dialogue or directed discussion. Socrates did not believe it necessary to observe and collect data in order to find absolute knowledge; he had a deep conviction that truth is implanted in the mind but becomes hidden by erroneous sense impressions. The function of the philosopher is to recover the truth that lies buried in the mind.

Socrates' theory of knowledge is closely related to his idea of the soul (the seat of the mind). Almost all we know about his idea of the soul, as well as his other views, comes to us through the writings of his brilliant pupil, Plato. In the dialogue of the *Phaedo,* Plato describes the final hours of his great teacher. Condemned to death by an Athenian jury on charges of corrupting the youth and doubting the gods, Socrates faces his fate cheerfully. He does so because he believes the soul is immortal, though during life it is hindered by the troubles and "foolishness" of the body. Death brings release for the soul and the opportunity to see the truth more clearly than before. And for Socrates, the real aim of life is to know the truth, rather than to seek the satisfactions of the body. His devotion to the search for truth persisted unto death.

Almost all we know about Socrates' views comes to us through the writings of Plato. It is difficult to say where the ideas of Socrates end and those of Plato begin. Plato wrote masterly literary works in the form of dialogues in which Socrates usually appears as the chief speaker. It seems clear that Plato took up the main thoughts of his teacher and carried them through a full and positive development. After traveling widely through the Mediterranean lands, Plato founded a school at Athens in 385 B.C. The Academy, as it was called, became the most influential intellectual center of the ancient world. It endured after its founder's death for over nine hundred years, and it served as a model for similar schools in other cities.

Plato continued the Socratic attack on the Sophist theory of relative truth. He refused to admit that the world consists of nothing more than imperfect nature in a constant state of flux. Turning back to the controversies of earlier Greek thinkers, who had been concerned with the "stuff" of the universe and with the question of permanence and change, Plato felt that the imperfect *surface* of things conceals a perfect, absolute, and eternal order. With daring imagination, he constructed a picture of the universe that satisfied the demands of his intelligence and his conservative temperament.

In his famous "Doctrine of Ideas," Plato conceded that the *physical* world is just what Heraclitus and the Sophists suggested: imperfect, changeable, and different in appearance to every individual. But the physical world is superficial, possibly only an illusion of our senses; above and beyond it, Plato asserted, is the "real" world of *spirit*. This world consists of perfect Ideas (Forms) authored by "God," which exist unchanged through all the ages. There are, for example, the Ideas of Man, Horse, Tree, Beauty, the State, Justice, and the highest of all Ideas—Goodness. These exist independent of individuals and can be known to them only through the mind (soul). The physical objects that the senses report are at best imperfect reflections or copies of the master Ideas; hence, though they may offer clues to the Ideas, they have no value in themselves. Philosophers should turn away from these sensory impressions and focus on the discovery and contemplation of the perfect, the eternal, the real. It is in the Ideas (Forms) that they will discover *absolute* truths and standards. Plato and thinkers of similar outlook have found this conception sublimely illuminating and satisfying. Centuries later, Plato's view was to prove adaptable to the teachings of Christianity (pp. 161–162), for the Christians, too, subordinated physical things and urged believers to reflect on the world of spirit—the "other" world of divine order and perfection.

Affairs on earth, according to Plato, are best guided by absolute principles as interpreted by true philosophers. Partly to provide a model society and government (state), he wrote the best known of his dialogues, the *Republic.* Plato believed that human institutions should aim not at complete individual freedom and equality but at social justice and order. Justice, to Plato, meant *harmony of function* within each individual and among the individual members of a state. (An aristocrat by birth and inclination, Plato admired Spartan institutions and had contempt for democratic ways.) Reflecting his view of the state as an *organic* unity, he argued that the foot should not try to become the head—nor the head the stomach. Every part of the human body and every member of the body politic should do the job it was designed to perform. Only then can friction, envy, and inefficiency—the chief sources of human and social sickness—be eliminated.

To reach this objective, Plato felt, the state must be structured according to natural capacities. The bulk of its citizens would make up the class of Workers (producers), who would be sorted into various occupations according to their aptitudes. Above them would be the Guardian class, which would be trained in the arts of war. From this disciplined class would be chosen, with the greatest care, the rulers of the state (Plato's "philosopher-kings"). While the Workers would be permitted to live "naturally," procreating and raising families, the Guardians would follow a most austere and regulated life. Matings among them would be arranged by the state, to ensure the production of superior offspring. Any infant showing a physical defect would be left to die of exposure, and normal infants would be taken from their mothers and placed in a community nursery. Parents would not be permitted to know their own children, nor would they be allowed to possess personal property. Such extreme measures are necessary, thought Plato, if rulers are to become truly selfless and dedicated to the welfare of the whole community.

The education of the Guardians, the same for males and females, was to be closely controlled. Only the "right" kind of music, art, and poetry would be taught, so that pupils would receive the desired moral indoctrination. Men and women chosen from this class to be the rulers would have additional training in philosophy and would serve a period of political apprenticeship before taking their places as directors of the state. Plato's Republic remains to this day an example for believers in aristocracy, planned society, equality for women, and state control over education and the arts. It was the first of a series of utopias, or model states, that have offered radical solutions for the problems of human society.

ARISTOTLE

Born in Stagira (in Thrace), Aristotle made his way early to Plato's Academy in Athens; years later, he founded a school of his own there—the Lyceum (335 B.C.). Far more than his teacher, Aristotle was interested in the evidence of the senses. He was, in fact, the greatest collector and classifier in antiquity. His interests ranged from biology to poetry, from politics to ethics.

Aristotle accepted Plato's general notion of the existence of Ideas (Forms), but he held that physical matter is also a part of reality and not to be despised. Matter, he thought, constitutes the "stuff" of reality, though its shapes and purposes come from the Forms that Plato had set forth. By logical thinking, people can gain knowledge of the purposes of things and of their interrelations, knowledge that will give meaning and guidance to their lives and bring them at the same time closer to God—whom Aristotle conceived as pure spirit and the source of the Forms. To Aristotle, logic is the indispensable key to truth and happiness. For this reason, he worked out precise and systematic rules for logical thinking, rules that have been respected by philosophers for centuries.

In his study of society and government, Aristotle began by examining existing constitutions and states. In his classic work, the *Politics*, he analyzed and evaluated the major types of political organization. He did not draw from these a model organization suitable for all cities; rather, he recognized that there are differences in local conditions and classes of inhabitants. Aristotle identified three basic types of government: rule by *one person* (monarchy), by the *few* (oligarchy), and by the *many* (democracy). Each of these types, if devoted to the general welfare, he considered legitimate, but any one of them becomes a "perversion" when the rulers pursue their own interest alone. (The worst government of all, he thought, is a perversion of rule by the many.) Under whatever constitution, Aristotle favored a strong role for the "middle class" of citizens. The more numerous poor, he stated, lack experience in directing others; the very rich are not used to obeying. The middle class knows what it is both to command and to obey and may be counted on to avoid political extremes.

The same spirit of moderation—"nothing in excess"—marks Aristotle's comments on what constitutes the "good life." In accordance with his theory that all things have a purpose, he taught that every organ and creature should function according to its design. The function of the eye is to see; the function of the ear is to hear; the function of a human is to live like a human. This last calls for a harmonious balance of faculties (abilities) of both body and mind. But since the mind is the crowning and unique part, it is clear that individuals should be governed by reason rather than by their appetites and emotions. Further, Aristotle insisted, it is not enough just to be a human; the "good life" must be *nobly* lived, with every action aimed at excellence.

But what makes an action excellent (virtuous)? Aristotle admitted that this is a difficult question that cannot be answered by any exact rule. He advised that in general, excellence in a particular activity lies somewhere between extremes. In battle, a warrior should exhibit neither a lack of nerve (cowardice) nor an excess (foolhardiness). Rather, he should strike a happy medium (courage). A work of sculpture or architecture should be judged by asking whether it might be improved, either by taking something away or by adding something to it. If it cannot, the work is "just right"—excellent.

Aristotle warned that his advice did not apply to things that are good or bad in themselves. Truth and beauty, for example, should be sought in the highest degree, while murder, theft, and lying are evil in any degree. But in most activities, each person should find, through trial and self-criticism, the desired mean (midpoint) between extremes. This has come to be called the Golden Mean. It does not signify a pale average or a mediocre standard; rather, it calls for the *best* performance of mind and body working together in harmony.

Greek Literature

Aristotle did not invent the Greek ideals of excellence, but he did reflect and express them. Everywhere around him, especially in literature and art, he observed the products of Greek genius. Western drama, prose, history, and poetry are Greek in origin; painting, sculpture, and architecture, too, have drawn heavily from Hellenic models. The Greeks believed that each art form enjoyed the patronage (support) of a minor goddess, or Muse, sprung from Zeus himself.

EPIC AND LYRIC POETRY

The Greeks recognized and made use of various types of poetry suited to different moods and purposes, but their earliest and greatest was the *epic*. Almost every people has at least one major epic—a long poem telling a story of great deeds and heroes in the national past. Sometimes it is based on ancient traditional tales, originally sung with instrumental accompaniment by illiterate minstrels, like the French *Song of Roland* (pp. 273–274). Sometimes an epic is the creation of a single author, like the *Aeneid* of the Roman poet Virgil (p. 131). Either way, the greatest epics become treasured possessions of the peoples among whom they originate—sources of national pride, of subjects for later poets, and even of moral guidance.

The father of the Greek epic, and of all Western literature, is Homer. His *Iliad* and *Odyssey* came to be known and recited by nearly every Greek of the Golden Age. Respected as fountains of wisdom, they provided later Greek writers with countless plots, themes, and characters. No one knows exactly who Homer was, although his authorship of the two epics is firmly established by tradition. It is generally believed that he was blind and lived in one of the Greek cities on the coast of Asia Minor, perhaps about 800 B.C. Most likely, the *Iliad* and the *Odyssey* were epics that evolved out of earlier tales sung by minstrels, who would have partly memorized and partly improvised the tales, so that every minstrel and every generation had a different version of them. What Homer probably did was to combine these tales into two great narrative poems, setting his stamp on the ancient stories more than any minstrel before him. In addition, Homer or others soon after him had access to the new skill of alphabetic writing, so that his version became the standard, one which has lasted unchanged for thousands of years.

The general setting of his poems is the Trojan War, a struggle between early Greeks and the defenders of Troy (Ilium), in Asia Minor, which purportedly took place in the twelfth century B.C. (p. 62). In the *Iliad,* Homer concentrates on the decisive point of the struggle, during the tenth (and last) year of the war: the wrath of Achilles and its consequences for the Greeks and Trojans. Homer's sequel, the *Odyssey,* skips the overthrow and destruction of Troy and tells a story of high adventure, the return of the Greek war heroes to their homes. The central figure is the wily and brave Odysseus (in Latin, Ulysses), king of Ithaca.

The *Iliad* is the tale of the wrath of Achilles, the mightiest warrior of the Greeks besieging Troy. Achilles sulks and refuses to fight because King Agamemnon, the commander of the Greeks, has deprived him of a beautiful slave, his prize in battle. Neither man will give in. The Trojans, led by the powerful Hector, take heart upon learning that Achilles has quit the field. Only after his dearest friend, Patroclus, is slain and dishonored does Achilles return to the battle, to seek vengeance and to avert disaster. With the help of the goddess Athena, the Greek hero succeeds in killing Hector but takes pity on Hector's father, Priam, the Trojan king, and gives him Hector's body for honorable burial.

Exploiting the richness and precision of the Greek language, Homer presents the human traits of courage, pride, envy, sacrifice, and love with striking realism. But the gods, too, are very much a part—if not the leading part—of the epic. Homer thus sketched, in the story of Achilles, a typical Greek view of mortals and gods, morals and fate. That view was to be restated, many times over, in classical literature, drama, and art.

The Greeks created lyric poetry as well as epic poetry. It is called *lyric* because it was normally sung to the playing of a lyre (a plucked, harp-type instrument). The distinguishing mark of this poetry is its personal nature. Instead of recounting the deeds of others, as in epic poetry, lyric poets express their own thoughts and feelings about life, love, patriotism—even the consolations and pleasures of wine.

Solon, the Athenian lawgiver (pp. 69–70), was as famous for his poetry as for his statesmanship. One of his verses is a proud defense of his record in politics. Referring to Athenians he had released from slavery, he wrote, "These I set free; and I did this by strength of hand, welding right law with force to make a single whole. So have I done, and carried through all that I pledged." But Solon's favorite subject was individual happiness and how it is won and lost. Foreshadowing later Greek dramatists, he advised his listeners "to call no man happy until the day of his death." Every life is uncertain, takes unexpected turns, and must be judged in its entirety.

Sappho of Lesbos, the first female poet of record, lived in the time of Solon (sixth century B.C.), but she expressed herself in a more private and passionate manner than Solon. She sang mainly of romantic love—frequently of beautiful youths preparing for their weddings. Her language is remarkable for its moving imagery; for example, Sappho describes her jealous passion while watching an adored young woman sharing intimacies with a young man: "To watch has made my heart a pounding hammer in my breast. . . . My silent tongue is broken, and a quick and subtle flame runs up beneath my skin. . . . I drip cold sweat, and a trembling chases all through me. I am greener than the pale grass and it seems to me that I am close to death."

Though Sappho loved both women and men, her most erotic feelings appear to have been aroused by the beautiful girls who formed her circle of companions. This did not seem abnormal to the ancient Greeks, any more than did the accepted form of male homosexuality (p. 74). Later generations, however, would sometimes use the word *lesbian* in referring to women of Sappho's sexual temperament. (The poetess and her companions lived on the Aegean island of Lesbos.)

DRAMA: TRAGEDY AND COMEDY

Though Aristotle admired poetry, he regarded tragic drama as a higher form of art. In addition to being read or sung, Greek drama was acted out, and its tighter structure gave it superior unity and impact. It enabled the audience, he thought, to see with a sense of detachment the common destiny of themselves and others.

Greek tragedy grew out of ancient religious ceremonials. It began in the sixth century B.C. as part of the annual spring festival in honor of the god Dionysus. On those occasions, it was customary for a choral group to sing hymns about the gods and heroes of Greek legend. As the chorus sang, it danced in dignified fashion around a circular plot of ground called the *orchestra* (derived from the Greek word for "dance"). Drama was born when the leader of the chorus was permitted to step out from the group and carry on a kind of conversation (in song) with the chorus.

By the beginning of the fifth century B.C., the choral dramas might have several individual characters, although no more than three actors plus the chorus took part at any one time. Thus the ancient, repetitive ceremonial became a medium for expressing new ideas. Gradually, the connection with Dionysus faded away, and writers of tragedy were allowed to choose whatever serious themes suited their purpose. The religious origins were not forgotten, however, and tragedy remained moral in purpose and character.

Comedy, the other form of Greek drama, grew from a different side of the Dionysiac tradition. The rites in his honor (both spring and winter) included not only somber dances and chants but also raucous processions and frenzied revels. It was out of these joyful celebrations that Athenian comedy was born. The earliest comedies were crude slapstick performances, but gradually they became clever and biting satires. Aristophanes, the chief writer of comedy whose works have come down to us, used his plays to make fun of local politicians, poets, and philosophers with whom he disagreed. Ridicule was his weapon of criticism. A good example is *The Clouds* (423 B.C.), a hilarious satire on the supposed teachings of the Sophists (p. 80). Another example is the frank *Lysistrata* (412 B.C.), an antiwar comedy. Its plot revolves around a sex strike by the wives on both sides of a war between Athens and Sparta. Their warrior-husbands at last give in: they agree to stop fighting in return for an end to the strike.

The comedies and tragedies were presented during the Dionysiac festival season in open-air amphitheaters. The theater of Athens was located on a slope of the Acropolis. Rows of seats, arranged in a semicircle, descended from the top of the hill to the orchestra. (The best-preserved Greek theater, at Epidaurus, is shown in *Fig. 2.5.*) Beyond the orchestra, across the open end of the theater, stood a *skēnē*, or actors' building; in front of it was a porch, or platform, from which the speakers usually recited their lines.

The Greek actors (all men) wore masks that identified their roles and were shaped to help them project their voices. The performances were colorful, with grand speeches, music, graceful dancing and singing, and rich costumes and headdresses. The effect was more that of opera than of modern stage acting. The author himself wrote the music as well as the text and also trained the cast.

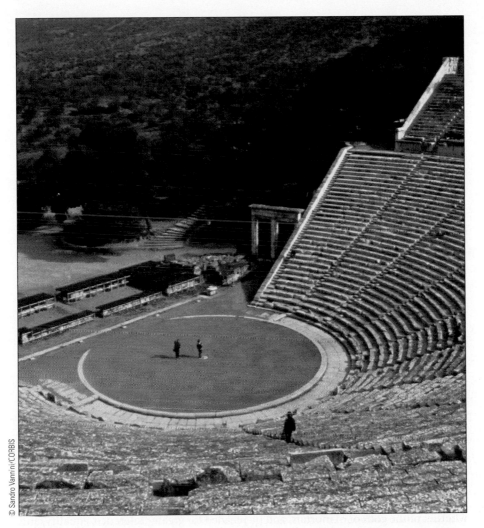

Fig. 2.5 The Theater of Epidaurus. The theater was built in the fourth century B.C. for dramatic contests at the festival of the healer-god Asclepius and is still in use today. The circular area is the orchestra, and behind the orchestra are the foundations of the *skēnē*. The semicircle of benches seats about eight thousand. The architect, Polyclitus the Younger, laid out the theater so ingeniously that a person speaking in a normal voice from the *skēnē* can be clearly heard 70 yards away in the rear benches.

During the standard three-day festival of Dionysus, dramatic performances began each morning and lasted until nightfall. There was no curtain or lighting and very little scenery. Usually, three playwrights competed on successive days, and a prize of great honor was awarded to the one who was judged best.

Three of the greatest playwrights of Western history were Greek. They all lived in one century, the fifth century B.C., and in one city, Athens. Aeschylus, Sophocles, and Euripides wrote nearly three hundred plays, although only about thirty have survived. The earliest tragic dramatist was Aeschylus, whose plays transform suffering and death into inspiration and the will to live. That, in fact, is the measure of true tragedy. A play that merely presents pain and grief with a sense of despair or baseness may be "dramatic" and "pathetic," but it is not "tragic." The Greek play, and its successors in the tragic spirit, generally show a hero of high rank, a great struggle, and intense suffering. But justice triumphs in the end, and there is reason beneath the suffering. One leaves Aeschylus with the feeling that individuals pay for their crimes—that the gods and the moral law are hard but that one can face fate bravely and nobly.

In the Orestes trilogy—*Agamemnon,* the *Libation Bearers,* and the *Eumenides*—Aeschylus' central theme is the family crimes of the royal house of Atreus. The plot, well known in Greek legend, revolves around the murder of King Agamemnon by his wife when he returns from the Trojan War. Wife, son, and daughter are involved in the crimes that follow; all of them can justify their acts, but all are nonetheless guilty. To Aeschylus, these crimes and the suffering they bring are divine punishment for violations of the moral order. In the final play of the trilogy, Athena herself intervenes to protect the murderer Orestes, son of Agamemnon, and to stop the terrible cycle of crime and punishment. Primitive revenge is transformed into the justice of the city-state, and Orestes is restored to respectability.

Because Sophocles reflected the Greek ideal of "nothing in excess," he has been called the "most Greek" of the three playwrights. He focused on the consequences of exaggerated pride. In the tragedy *Oedipus the King,* Oedipus thinks he can avoid his fate, which has been foretold by the Delphic oracle of Apollo. A man of good intention, he tries to escape from the shocking prophecy that he will kill his father and marry his mother. But in the end, the truth of his moral crimes, which he has committed unknowingly, is brought to light by his own insistent searching. He realizes at last the folly of his conceit and savagely blinds himself as punishment for the foulness of his deeds.

Euripides, the youngest of the great Greek tragedians, probably had the deepest insight into human character. He has been called "poet of the world's grief." Euripides was also considered something of a radical, for he challenged the traditional religious and moral values of his time. He opposed slavery and showed the "other side" of war. In *The Trojan Women,* the battle ends with a brokenhearted old woman sitting on the ground holding a dead child in her arms. Euripides was keenly sensitive to injustice, whether of the gods or of mortals, and he pleaded for greater tolerance, equality, and decency.

HISTORY

The Greeks rank high in historical writing as well as in dramatic literature. The "father of history," Herodotus, was born in 485 B.C. in Halicarnassus, a Greek city on the shore of Asia Minor. A great traveler, he visited various parts of the Persian Empire—Mesopotamia, Syria, and Egypt. He also toured Greek colonies from the Black Sea to southern Italy. Having lived through the time of the Persian Wars, which ended in the triumph of Athens and its allies (pp. 70–71), he decided to set down a record of that struggle and of the events that led up to it.

Herodotus called his work the *Historia,* which means, in Greek, "investigation." Until his time, the legends of poetry had been accepted as true accounts of the past. He set out to separate fact from legend, to write an account based on direct observation and evidence. The sources he used were not all reliable, to be sure, but he usually warned his readers when he was passing along doubtful information. The major portion of the *Historia* is a survey of Herodotus' world: political and military affairs, social customs, religious beliefs, and leading personalities. In the final portion of his work, he tells the story of the Persian Wars in a manner sympathetic to both Persians and Greeks, though presenting it as a dramatic contest between slavery and freedom.

A generation later, the Athenian Thucydides lifted the writing of history to a much higher critical level (though at some sacrifice of literary charm). In the first "scientific" history, he wrote about the long and cruel war between Athens and Sparta that had broken out soon after their joint victory over Persia (pp. 96–98). An exiled general of Athens, he had traveled widely to gather information during the war.

His subject matter is far more limited than that of Herodotus, but his account has greater unity and depth. And he excluded all suggestion of supernatural interference; history, he insisted, is made by human beings. Thucydides was convinced that human nature could be understood through careful study of the past and that the knowledge so gained could be useful as a guide to understanding the future. He presented his facts from both sides, showing the reader the causes, motives, and consequences of the war. But his work is more than military history; it deals with the still-relevant questions of imperialism, democracy, and the whole range of social relations.

Architecture and Sculpture

As we have seen, the Greeks regarded community activities as more important than private affairs; hence they put their best efforts into public structures. The temple, which represented a strong bond between religious and patriotic feelings, was their supreme architectural achievement. But they constructed other types of public buildings as well: there were the open marketplaces, enclosed on four sides by a covered colonnade; the outdoor amphitheaters (*Fig. 2.5,* p. 87) for dramatic festivals; and open-air gymnasiums, race courses, and stadiums. The Greeks seemed least interested in private dwellings, which were small, simple, and built of light materials. Plumbing and sanitary facilities were primitive or nonexistent.

Up to the sixth century B.C., even the most important buildings were usually made of wood. Gradually, however, limestone and marble took the place of timber in public structures. This was a natural development because the country's forests were thinning out, whereas there were ample supplies of stone. The Greeks used the post-and-lintel method for supporting the roofs of their buildings, meaning simply that the horizontal members (beams or lintels) rested on vertical posts or columns. A series of columns placed at close intervals could thus support a roof of considerable weight. The effectiveness of this building method had been demonstrated centuries earlier by Egyptian architects (p. 37).

TEMPLE BUILDING: THE PARTHENON

The Greek temple represents the perfection of post-and-lintel construction and of the refinements of the stone column. The early buildings had a rather heavy appearance,

Fig. 2.6 An Early Doric-Style Temple. This temple of the goddess Hera is one of a magnificent group of shrines, overlooking the sea not far south of Naples, that formed the religious center of a Greek colony, Posidonia (Roman Paestum). The temple was built in the sixth century B.C., when Greeks were settling in large numbers in the fertile and thinly populated coastal lands of southern Italy and Sicily. It has the massive appearance typical of early Greek stone temples.

as in the sixth-century temple at Paestum, Italy (*Fig. 2.6*). Gradually, however, the pro-portions of the temple, and of the columns especially, were modified. The finest result of this development was the Parthenon of Athens (*Fig. 2.7*). In this shrine for Athena, a perfect balance of architectural elements was achieved.

The exterior columns of the Parthenon, which form a continuous colonnade on all four sides of the temple, are of the Doric "order." This was the earlier of the two basic styles, Doric and Ionic, that the Greeks developed. The differences lie in the *base, shaft,* and *capital* of the columns and in the *entablature* (horizontal structures) that they support. The Greeks later developed a third order, called Corinthian; it was simi-lar to the Ionic except for the column capitals, which were decorated with stylized leaves of the acanthus plant.

The floor plan of the Parthenon is simple. It divides the interior into two rectan-gular enclosures. The principal enclosure (*cella*) originally contained a statue of the goddess and has but one entrance, facing east. The smaller cella, whose entrance faces west, contained the treasury of Athens. The roof of the building was gabled (slanted) and supported by a wooden framework. It was closed at each end by a triangular slab of marble, called the *pediment.*

The Parthenon was designed about 450 B.C. by the architect Ictinus as part of Per-icles' plan for rebuilding the Acropolis after the Persians had destroyed the earlier sa-cred structures there. Though ravaged by time and war, it still embodies the Greek ideal of the Golden Mean. It is not a huge structure, measuring only 100 by 230 feet, but it was perfectly suited to its purpose and position. The pediments and portions of the

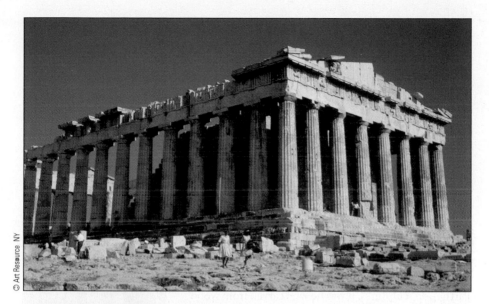

Fig. 2.7 The Parthenon. Built in honor of the virgin goddess Athena, from whom the city-state of Athens took its name, the Parthenon ("Place of the Maiden") was a cherished project of Pericles. It was he who about 448 B.C. persuaded the Athenian Assembly to authorize its construction and to employ two well-known architects, Ictinus and Callicrates. They achieved a combination of solidity and gracefulness that has made the Parthenon a model of classic dignity and beauty from ancient times to the present day.

entablature were decorated with sculpture, and pastel paints were applied to add warmth and interest. The paints have long since faded, but the weathered marble now provides attractive color of its own.

The wonder of the Parthenon comes, in part, from the painstaking details of its design. Subtle curves, rather than straight lines, avoid any impression of stiffness. The diameter of each column, for instance, diminishes gradually as it rises to its capital in a slightly curving line (*entasis*). The Greek builders had discovered that a perfectly straight profile makes a column look too rigid. They had also found that by adjusting the spacing between columns, they could improve the visual effect of the entire structure. Hence in the Parthenon, the space between each corner column and the column next to it is *less* than the space between other columns, and this gives a feeling of extra support at the points of extra stress. The fact that the builders went to such pains to satisfy the demands not only of engineering but of aesthetics as well is testimony to their desire for excellence.

IMAGES OF GODS AND HUMANS

Little has survived of Greek painting other than the charming miniatures on pottery vases (*Fig. 2.4*, p. 75). But the Greeks' passion for beauty, interest in human forms, and striving for the ideal are clearly reflected in their sculpture. Only a few originals—and these in mutilated condition—have come down to us, but hundreds of copies of Greek statues, produced in Roman times by Greek artisans, still survive. The Greek originals, or what we know of them, have served through the centuries as models for Western sculptors.

Early Greek statues reveal an Egyptian influence. The Egyptians sought solidity and permanence in their figures; they did not aim to reproduce natural appearances (pp. 37). This same purpose is apparent in the many statues of young men, probably victorious athletes, that have been unearthed in Greece (*Fig. 2.8*). But the Greeks grew dissatisfied with this kind of representation and turned steadily toward greater naturalism, movement, and grace in their figures. The statues carved during the fifth century B.C. were chiefly of gods and goddesses; like the deities themselves, they resembled mortals—not actual individuals, but *idealized* men and women.

Phidias, the most highly respected sculptor of Athens in the Age of Pericles, was put in charge of the Parthenon sculptures. It was he who carved from wood the gigantic statue of Athena (some 35 feet tall) that was placed in the main cella. Although the original was lost long ago, ancient descriptions tell us that it was richly decorated with ivory, gold, and jewels. Phidias also planned and supervised the carvings of the marble pediments and the marble frieze (band) that ran around the outside of the cella walls. Fragments of this sculpture are still in existence (*Fig. 2.9*). They form parts of a carved procession of young women and men, some on horseback, moving toward a platform on which various deities are seated. The sense of ease and motion and the splendid proportion and form are evident even in these fragments.

Better known is *The Discus Thrower* by Myron, another sculptor of the time of Phidias (*Fig. 2.10*). The original bronze casting has been lost, but the figure was so much admired that many marble copies were made. In this statue, Myron chose to portray the athlete at the moment before he made his supreme effort, so that he would appear dynamically poised and in full self-control. The statue is not an accurate picture of a real discus thrower; rather, it is an ideal representation of the male figure—a masterpiece of line and form.

© Borromeo/Art Resource, NY

Fig. 2.8 Early Greek Sculpture. This 5-foot-high marble statue from about 600 B.C. depicts a successful athlete. Such statues were often placed in temples, thereby making the athlete into a personal "servant" of the god or goddess, in thanksgiving for victories in contests such as the Olympic Games (compare *Fig. 1.4,* p. 24). The pose of the statue, with arms hanging at the sides, fists clenched, and left foot forward, imitates Egyptian sculpture (compare *Fig. 1.8,* p. 39). The nudity—reproducing the nakedness of Greek athletes—is a Greek innovation.

After about 400 B.C., Greek sculptors tended toward a more natural and graceful style, as well as a wider choice of subjects. The leading developer of this new style was Praxiteles. His most famous work, *Hermes with the Infant Dionysus* (*Fig. 2.11,* p. 94), does not have the masculine strength of *The Discus Thrower,* but it is so natural and relaxed, yet perfectly balanced, that it seems godlike all the same. As part of this tendency away from idealized masculinity, it was probably Praxiteles who broke with the tradition of

Fig. 2.9 **The Parthenon Frieze.** The horsemen are riding in solemn procession to the Parthenon in honor of Athena—the high point of Athens's religious year. It was customary among ancient peoples to decorate temples with scenes of religious ceremonies, probably as a magical way of making sure that the deity would always be receiving worship. Under the supervision of the renowned sculptor Phidias, the carvers of the frieze brought to this tradition the freedom and gracefulness of the newly developed Greek style of sculpture.

Fig. 2.10 *The Discus Thrower.* This statue was much admired in the ancient world, and the photograph shows one of several marble copies made in Roman times. The bronze original, which does not survive, was made by Myron, a contemporary of Phidias, about 450 B.C. Unlike the early statue shown in *Fig. 2.8*, with its conventional pose, this is an idealized study of the naked male body in action.

Fig. 2.11 *Hermes with the Infant Dionysus.* This is the only surviving Greek statue that can be identified as an original work by a famous master—the fourth-century B.C. sculptor Praxiteles. The statue was found in the nineteenth century A.D. in the ruins of the temple of Zeus at Olympia, at the same spot where the travel writer Pausanias had seen it 1,700 years earlier. Unlike the idealized figures of Phidias and Myron, Praxiteles' Hermes is portrayed in a relaxed yet graceful pose, and Dionysus reaches toward him as a baby naturally would.

Fig. 2.12 *Venus de Milo.* This famous statue, probably dating from about 100 B.C., may originally have depicted the goddess holding up a polished shield as a mirror. Perhaps so as to hold the shield while she looks into it, she has twisted her body slightly and shifted her weight to her right leg. Her left knee is thrust forward, keeping her low-slung garment from slipping off her hips. Yet this complex pose is so perfectly balanced that it produces an effect of goddess-like serenity and power.

portraying women and goddesses fully clothed, and introduced an entirely new subject of sculptural art—the naked or half-naked female body. At their most successful, as in the famous *Aphrodite of Melos (Venus de Milo)* of about 100 B.C. (*Fig. 2.12*), Greek sculptors achieved an idealization of feminine strength and serenity that paralleled the earlier idealization of the male body.

Along with the trend toward a more natural style there developed an interest in portraiture, emotional expression, and representation of ordinary people—street ven-

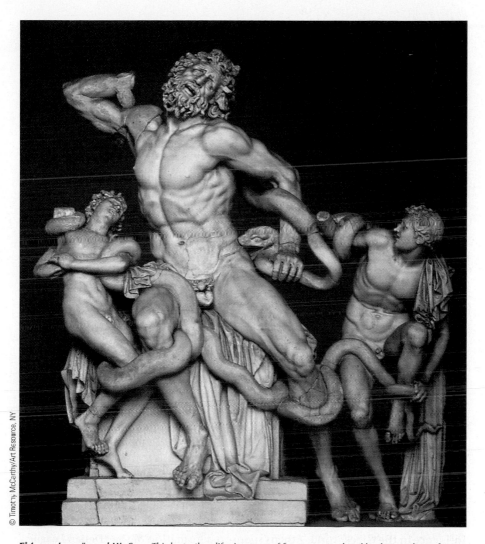

Fig. 2.13 *Laocoön and His Sons.* This larger-than-life-size group of figures was produced by three sculptors from the island of Rhodes—Athenodorus, Hagesander, and Polydorus—about 50 B.C. It is one of the finest examples of the later Greek taste for sculpture that depicted powerful emotions and dramatic events of history or mythology. In a distant future, this style of sculpture would deeply influence the art of seventeenth-century Europe (compare *Fig. 9.7*, p. 392).

dors, dancers, and common soldiers. The sculptors of the fifth century B.C. had carved only deities and heroes. They had also avoided showing facial expression and, generally, any indication of pain or suffering. But with the passing of centuries, exact likenesses became popular, and more and more statues showed intense emotion.

Probably the most famous example of work of the latter kind is the marble group known as *Laocoön and His Sons* (about 50 B.C.). This group shows a Trojan priest and his young sons being crushed by two deadly serpents (*Fig. 2.13*). (According to legend, the serpents were sent by the goddess Athena. The Greeks, whom she favored, had schemed to take Troy by hiding soldiers inside a giant wooden horse offered as a gift, and Laocoön had warned his fellow Trojans not to bring the horse into the city.)

The Decline of the Greek City-States

Art during and after the fourth century B.C. reflected an attitude toward life that was considerably different from the attitude of Greeks during the Age of Pericles (fifth century B.C.). The change was an outgrowth of the Peloponnesian War and its aftermath. The Persian Wars had brought confidence and glory; the Peloponnesian War left disillusionment and decay. Most of the Greek city-states were caught up in the conflict, but the principal antagonists were Athens and Sparta.

The Athenians called it the "Peloponnesian" war because their chief enemies were Sparta and its allied cities of the Peloponnesus and neighboring areas (*Map 2.3*)—the "Peloponnesian League." There had been earlier conflicts between Sparta and Athens, but the long struggle that opened in 431 B.C. and lasted until 404 B.C. ended with the final defeat of Athens.

THE PELOPONNESIAN WAR

The underlying cause of the Peloponnesian War, and of the endless wars that preceded and followed it, was built into the Greek city-state system. Each city had its own military forces and asserted its complete independence of any higher authority. When differences developed that could not be settled by agreement, either party might resort to war. Some cities managed to subdue their neighbors temporarily by force of arms, but the defeated communities refused to be absorbed and waited patiently for a chance to regain their independence. Hence, the Greek world was in a constant state of war. The cities refrained from fighting one another only when it was necessary to join together against a foreign foe. It was through such a general alliance that they had, with difficulty, met the Persian threat in the first half of the fifth century B.C. (pp. 70–71).

Soon after Athens became the accepted leader in 478 B.C., it moved to solidify its influence in the Greek world. Athens sponsored formation of the "Delian League," which consisted of most of the Greek cities on the Aegean coasts and islands (*Map 2.3*). (The League was named, by modern historians, after the island of Delos, sacred to Apollo, where the alliance was founded.) Members agreed to contribute money annually for the construction of triremes (p. 66), which were placed under Athenian command. The city thus gained control of several hundred vessels with their crews—by far the largest fleet to sail the Mediterranean at the time.

In 445 B.C., after the Persian threat had passed, the League members announced that they would make no more payments. But Athens threatened to use force should they cease sending money. What had been contributions for the common defense against Persia were thereby transformed into tribute to Athens.

Many of the city-states of mainland Greece were aroused by the Athenians' behavior—especially as these city-states were generally ruled by oligarchies, and the Athenians usually insisted that their subject cities practice democracy. The smaller mainland

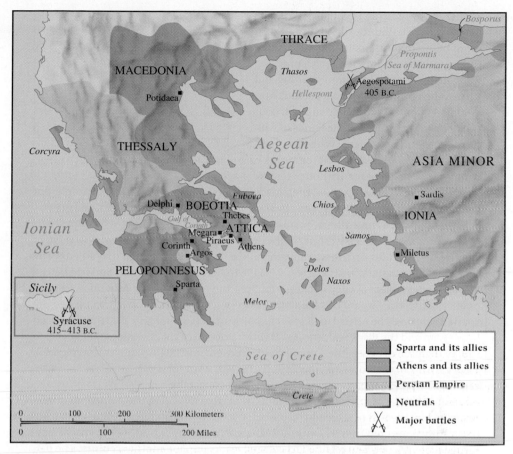

Map 2.3 The Peloponnesian War. The war was a conflict between the land power of Sparta and its allies, mainly in southern Greece, and the sea power of the Athenian alliance of city-states in the coasts and islands of the Aegean. Because of their different fighting strengths, it was hard for either side to strike a decisive blow until Athenian naval losses in Sicily, as well as money and supplies from the still mighty Persian Empire, enabled Sparta to build a navy that could defeat Athens.

cities appealed to the Spartans (who headed the Peloponnesian League) to put a check on Athens. At last the Spartans decided to support their ally, Corinth, which had become involved in a naval war with Athens. The Athenians, with their league of allies (forced and voluntary), took up the challenge.

In the course of the war (431–404 B.C.), the Athenians, under the guidance of Pericles, at first showed caution and sound strategy. The city of Athens and its nearby harbor, Piraeus, formed a single stronghold. The Spartans, unbeatable on the battlefield but not equipped for siege warfare, often raided Attica but could not capture the city itself or cut its links with the sea. Meanwhile, the Athenians used their navy to guard the sea routes that supplied them with grain, and to raid Sparta and its allies. Their most serious reversal was not by arms but by disease. A terrible plague struck the city in 430 B.C. Though the exact nature of this infection remains uncertain, it is known to have come by sea from Egypt to Piraeus. The plague was brief but deadly, killing thousands of inhabitants, including a quarter of the army. Pericles himself was a victim.

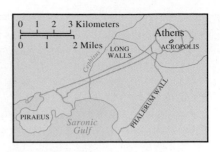

Athens and Piraeus

The plague came without warning and turned the optimism of the Athenians into gloom. As public confidence slipped, control of the city passed into the hands of willful and reckless politicians. When the Spartans on several occasions offered terms of compromise and "peace without victory," these Athenian leaders spurned their offers and held out for a clear-cut triumph. But such hopes were shattered in 413 B.C. by the annihilation of an expedition against Syracuse (in far-off Sicily), an ally of Sparta, which cost Athens two-thirds of its ships. With financial aid from the Persians, who considered Athens the most dangerous to them of the Greek city-states, Sparta was able to build a fleet strong enough to challenge the shrunken Athenian navy. Athens was still able to hold off the Spartans and win battles at sea. But dependent as they were on supplies from overseas, if the Athenians lost just one sea battle, they would be doomed. The decisive defeat came in 405 B.C. when the Spartans crushed the Athenian fleet at the battle of Aegospotami in the straits between the Aegean and the Black Sea. Stripped of the protection of their warships and unable to supply themselves by sea, the Athenian citizens were starved into surrender (404 B.C.). They gave up all their outlying possessions, pulled down their defensive walls, and became forced allies of Sparta under a harshly ruling oligarchy.

But Athens was not alone in defeat. The victors as well as the vanquished were weakened by the loss of men and resources. Greek civilization in its traditional form never fully recovered from the ruinous struggle, even though Athens eventually returned to democracy and retained its cultural leadership for another century. The pattern of Greek life could not be restored. Sparta for a while, and then Thebes, tried unsuccessfully to exert leadership and maintain order. But it was only a matter of time until the quarreling Greek cities were to fall before foreign powers (first Macedonia, then Rome) and to surrender for good their cherished independence.

The citizens tended to turn inward, to regard politics and civic affairs as things apart from themselves and their families. And they found little solace—no promise of a better world to come—in their traditional religion. The Olympian gods may have defended the Greeks against the Persians, but they had not preserved them from self-destruction. Many people turned to more personal and hopeful faiths—mystery cults, the worship of foreign gods and goddesses, and in the subsequent age of the Hellenistic states, even the veneration of kings and queens as divine (pp. 102, 121).

Disillusionment spread in other directions as well. The search for truth, the appeal to reason, and the counsel of moderation had not brought the anticipated satisfactions and happiness. Democracy itself came in for a share of blame because the leaders of democratic Athens were held chiefly responsible for bringing on and prolonging the disastrous war. Sparta and its allies, on the other hand, had favored oligarchy (p. 66). The military triumph of the Peloponnesians strengthened aristocratic attitudes and weakened the democratic cause in most parts of Greece. And in every city where democratic and oligarchic factions still vied for power, the struggle was intensified by bitter memories of social division and civic betrayal during the war.

Even as the city-states and their traditional values declined, Greek civilization continued to flourish, and the Greeks as a nation became more important in the world than ever before. To the north of the weakened city-states, a new power was rising, the kingdom of Macedonia, which would soon put an end to the independence of the city-states. But under Macedonian leadership, the Greeks would enjoy a brief moment of unity that would enable them to replace the Persians as the dominant nation of the international civilized world.

THE RISE OF MACEDONIA

Macedonia was a border territory between civilized Greece and the still-barbarian peoples farther north in Europe, and though the Macedonians probably spoke Greek, they and the Greeks regarded each other as different nations. The country was several centuries behind Greece in its political development: it was ruled in the traditional manner, by kings and warrior nobles. But it was also larger and richer in resources than any city-state, and its kings had always admired the Greeks and longed to associate themselves with them. In 359 B.C., Macedonia came under the rule of King Philip II, a shrewd man of broad vision who determined to gain control of the weak and divided city-states and to lead the Greeks and Macedonians in a united force against the weakening empire of Persia. In the course of fighting against barbarian peoples to the north, he strengthened his army by adopting the phalanx tactics of the Greeks, improving the weapons of his hoplites, and building up a stronger cavalry force than any city-state possessed. This also enabled him to bring the nobles of his kingdom into line while he made careful plans for infiltrating and conquering Greece.

Philip's agents worked to prevent the city-states from joining forces against him. One eloquent Athenian, Demosthenes, recognized the peril and repeatedly warned his fellow citizens. But the traditional reluctance of the city-states to work together, combined with their failure to take the new menace seriously, played into Philip's hands. At last he was ready to move. Through diplomacy and military pressure, Philip thrust into northern and central Greece. The Athenians, aroused at last, formed an alliance with the Thebans in an attempt to stop him. It was too late. At the battle of Chaeronea (338 B.C.), the Macedonians won a decisive victory. What remained of Greek independence was left for Philip to decide.

The Macedonian king used his newly won power wisely. After advancing into the Peloponnesus, he established himself as the president of a league of Greek states. He treated the Greek cities considerately and let them manage their own affairs except in the conduct of foreign policy. Philip, now at the head of a powerful alliance, vowed to avenge the insults and injuries inflicted on Greek temples and sanctuaries by the invading Persians more than a century before (pp. 70–71). But as he stood at the very brink of fulfillment, Philip was assassinated in 336 B.C. His son, Alexander III, only twenty years old, succeeded him and proceeded to carry out his father's grand design.

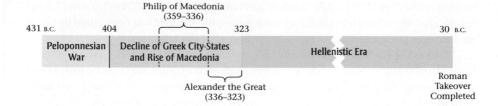

Philip of Macedonia
(359–336)

431 B.C.   404   323   30 B.C.

| Peloponnesian War | Decline of Greek City-States and Rise of Macedonia | Hellenistic Era |

Alexander the Great
(336–323)

Roman
Takeover
Completed

Alexander the Great and the Wider Spread of Greek Culture

After dealing with disturbances in Macedonia and Greece that had broken out after his father's death, Alexander crossed into Asia Minor (334 B.C.) to launch the campaign that would make him one of the greatest conquerors in history. True, the Persian Empire had declined in military power, but the combination of heavily armed phalanxes, fast-moving cavalry, and Alexander's daring and genius succeeded beyond anyone's expectations. His army of about 35,000 Macedonians and Greeks—small in comparison with what it accomplished, though far larger than that of any individual city-state—broke the power of the Persian king within four years. Asia Minor, Syria, Egypt, and Mesopotamia fell before him (*Map 2.4*). Pushing on through Persia to the frontiers of India, he was checked only by the grumbling and protests of his own men. At the age of thirty-three, Alexander died of a fever (probably cholera) in the city of Babylon, which he had chosen for his imperial capital.

ALEXANDER'S DREAM OF "ONE WORLD"

Alexander had established certain principles of government for his new world-state—a successor to the universal empires of Assyria and Persia (pp. 43–47). Though he believed in the superiority of Greek culture, Alexander had no intention of destroying the cultures of the East. Rather, he hoped to fuse the best features of each civilization into a new culture. To achieve this end, he founded cities in the regions he conquered and sent Greeks or Macedonians to colonize them. Their military garrisons would serve to maintain order in the surrounding countryside, and the cities themselves would serve as cultural "melting pots." He made Greek the official language and distributed Greek books and works of art throughout his empire; he hoped by these means to spread Hellenic ideas and standards, at least as a veneer, over the oriental pattern of life. He encouraged intermarriage and led the way himself by marrying an eastern princess, Roxana.

But after Alexander's death, his "One World" was soon divided. Though he left a son, the boy fell victim to power struggles among his father's leading generals. In decades of bitter warfare, three major states emerged, each ruled by a dynasty of kings descended from one or other of the Greek generals.

These states were based, respectively, on Macedonia, Egypt, and the lands stretching eastward from Syria; alongside them, other rulers, both Greek and non-Greek, carved themselves smaller shares of territory (*Map 2.4*). The three major dynasties continued to be rivals and from time to time fought each other on a scale that dwarfed even the Peloponnesian War. As a result of these rivalries, the city-states of Greece it-

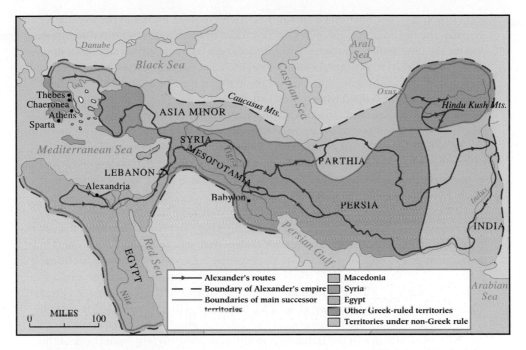

Map 2.4 The Greeks in the Middle East. With the conquests of Alexander (334–323 B.C.), the Greek world expanded 2,000 miles eastward. Even though Alexander's empire fell apart after his death, most of it remained under the rule of Greek kings, and Greek cities sprang up across the Middle East from Egypt to the borders of India. The Greeks and their culture remained a dominant influence in much of the Middle East for a thousand years until the rise of Islam in the seventh century A.D.

self managed to regain some freedom of action. But their citizen armies and navies were no match for the massive forces of Greek mercenary soldiers and slave-rowed warships that the kings maintained. Even once-mighty Athens and Sparta generally bowed to whichever king was most powerful at any given time. This balance of power survived through the last two centuries B.C., when the Romans gradually took over the eastern Mediterranean (p. 115).

THE HELLENISTIC STATES

Although Alexander's dream of "One World" was never fulfilled, his conquests had a profound effect on the development of the West. In the centuries of the emergence of the city-states, Greeks had already emigrated westward across the Mediterranean (p. 63); now, summoned by Alexander's successors, who needed them as soldiers, officials, and traders, they left their overpopulated homeland for the East as well. By 200 B.C., Greeks were scattered across the world from the coasts of Spain to the borders of India. In the Middle East in particular, they now lived side by side with ancient civilizations—those of Mesopotamia and Egypt—from which their own had partly arisen. A new era in the history of Greek civilization had begun—one for which historians have invented the term *Hellenistic* (from a Greek word meaning "to behave like a Greek"), so as to suggest a fusion of Greek and non-Greek cultures in which Greek influence predominated. Actually, the fusion of cultures never became more than an imperfect mixture. Greek became the international language of business and government, which ambitious non-Greeks would learn so as to get ahead in those fields. But otherwise the ways of the East persisted as in the past. In Egypt, for example, temples were built and decorated, and gods and goddesses tended within them, all according to age-old tradition, as if the several hundred thousand Greeks who now lived in the country had never arrived; even the Greek kings were venerated and obeyed by the Egyptians as native pharaohs (p. 32). As for the Greeks, they were mostly content to study Homer by the banks of the Nile or to applaud the plays of Aeschylus and Sophocles, performed by traveling actors in amphitheaters in Syria and Lebanon that looked exactly like those of Greece itself (*Fig. 2.5*, p. 87)—or of Sicily and Spain.

Still, in the long run, the fact that the Greeks were now an internationally dominant nation could not help but bring about changes in their civilization. With the immense resources at their disposal, the Greek rulers were able to support researchers in many fields and to build libraries that preserved the legacy of their nation for future generations. With their new and wider horizons, Greek scholars studied the past and present of many Middle Eastern lands. Thus Hellenistic civilization achieved great things in science and technology, geography, history, and literary scholarship, as well as carrying on the earlier achievements of the Greeks in philosophy and the arts.

The political forms of the Hellenistic world were also different from those of the Greek past. Democracy and oligarchy, the traditional Greek forms of government, were both put down by the new order of things. Absolute rule was accepted as the only effective means of governing large areas. The fate of the world was now in the hands not of city-states but of great kings. It was only fitting that the Greeks should venerate these mighty monarchs and their queens as living gods and goddesses—more clearly visible, and more obviously powerful to help or harm, than the fading deities of the city-states. Probably this Greek version of divine kingship developed independently from similar practices among the nations they ruled. But it certainly fit in well with existing Eastern traditions of rulers entrusted with power by the gods or of actual god-kings (pp. 25, 29–30, 46).

In the long run, too, the Greeks could not help absorbing influences from the nations they now dominated—above all, in the field of religion. The Hellenistic world abounded with international cults of non-Greek gods and goddesses—for example, the Egyptian deities of the underworld and fertility, Isis and Osiris. The Greeks believed such deities to be the same as their own, only in foreign guise: thus Isis and Osiris were identified with Demeter and Hades, who had much the same powers among the Greek gods and goddesses. But the foreign versions of the gods and goddesses had come to seem to the Greeks themselves more powerful, holy, and helpful to humans than the native, Olympian ones. These international cults were a precedent for the spread of Eastern religions, including Christianity, in the Roman Empire (pp. 161, 166–170).

The economy of the Hellenistic age was also markedly different from that of earlier times. The new and more extensive political units encouraged large-scale production and trade. The Greeks had carried on a far-flung commerce, ranging from the Black Sea to Gibraltar, but now the gates were opened eastward—as far as India. The vast new market stimulated enterprise: huge fortunes were made, banking and finance were expanded, and a kind of capitalism took shape. The heads of the great states had a keen interest in business affairs. They promoted commerce by aiding navigation and transport and made up their expenses by taxing the enterprises.

Although wages and general living standards remained low, the growth of industry and trade created many new jobs in the cities. As a result, thousands of peasants moved from the countryside into the urban centers of the Middle East.

The typical Greek city-state had been a community of perhaps five or ten thousand citizens, but the *metropolis* (great city) now became the central unit of social organization. Many such cities grew up around the centers Alexander had tried to establish. The largest and most renowned was Alexandria, which he had founded near the delta of the Nile River, in Egypt. Its population may have approached one million by the beginning of the Christian era, and it rivaled imperial Rome in size and magnificence. Alexandria was the economic and cultural hub of the eastern Mediterranean; for centuries, its marvelous library and "museum"—a kind of research institute endowed by the rulers—were centers of scholarship and scientific study.

The Hellenistic era is considered to have come to an end with the Roman takeover of Egypt, the last of the Greek-ruled states to become subject to them, in 30 B.C. (p. 119). But even though the Hellenistic world submitted to the Romans and paid them tribute, it was otherwise little affected by the conquest. It was here that the Romans found the culture—the philosophy, science, literature, and art—that they were to absorb and pass on to western Europe, as well as the political forms of universal monarchy and divine kingship that were to inspire their own empire (pp. 119, 121–122, 149). Within the Roman Empire, the Hellenistic world remained a distinct cultural region, dominated by Greek civilization. When that empire finally divided, its Greek-dominated eastern half continued for several centuries until the Muslim conquest, and even then, the Hellenistic legacy was preserved by the empire of Byzantium (pp. 198–203).

RECOMMENDED READING

The European Barbarians B. Cunliffe, ed., *Prehistoric Europe: An Illustrated History* (1998), covers, authoritatively and readably, the entire prehistory of Europe from the Old Stone Age to the barbarians of Roman times. On the origins and spread of the Indo-Europeans and their influence on the language and way of life of the peoples of Europe and Asia, see J. P. Mallory, *In Search of the Indo-Europeans* (1989).

The Aegean Background Z. Archibald, *Discovering the World of the Ancient Greeks* (1991), is a short and well-illustrated account of archaeological discovery. T. R. Martin, *Ancient Greece: From Prehistoric to Hellenistic Times* (1996), is an introduction to Greek civilization that includes thorough and up-to-date treatment of early Aegean developments. R. F. Willetts, *Everyday Life in Ancient Crete* (1969); J. Chadwick, *The Mycenaean World* (1976); and A. Snodgrass, *Archaic Greece: The Age of Experiment* (1980), are short and readable accounts by leading scholars. Also brief and readable is W. Burkert, *The Orientalizing Revolution* (1992), a classic work on early Greek civilization by a distinguished scholar.

The City-State P. Cartledge, ed., *The Cambridge Illustrated History of Ancient Greece* (1998), covers all aspects of the life of Greek city-states in the period of their heyday and decline. S. Blundell, *Women* *in Ancient Greece* (1998), is a comprehensive survey, against the background of the city-state. V. D. Hanson, *The Western Way of War: Infantry Battle in Classical Greece* (1989), vividly evokes the experience of city-state warfare and the way in which it molded the community life of citizen soldiers.

A. H. M. Jones, *Athenian Democracy* (1957), is a classic brief account of the workings of Athenian government in the age of Pericles and after; M. I. Finley, *Democracy Ancient and Modern* (1985), looks to Athens for lessons for present-day democracy. J. W. Roberts, *City of Sokrates* (1998), is an introduction to the history, culture, way of life, and urban setting of classical Athens; A. Powell, *Athens and Sparta* (1988), contrasts the government systems and ways of life of the two rival city-states.

Greek Religion P. Easterling and J. Muir, *Greek Religion and Society* (1985), and S. Price, *Religions of the Ancient Greeks* (1999), are excellent introductions to the various forms of Greek religion and their relations with other areas of life and culture. L. Zaidman and P. Pantel, *Religion in the Ancient Greek City* (1992), deals with religion in the life of the city-states, above all Athens; W. Burkert, *Ancient Mystery Cults* (1987), introduces this aspect of Greek religion. Fritz Graf, *Greek Mythology: An Introduction* (1993), deals with the role of mythology in religion and other areas of Greek life; for the myths themselves, see R. Graves, *Greek Myths* (1960).

The Founders of Western Philosophy R. Sowerby, *The Greeks: An Introduction to Their Culture* (1995), briefly surveys the philosophy, literature, and art of ancient Greece. Specifically on philosophy, B. Russell, *A History of Western Philosophy* (1967), may be recommended for its simple explanations and its lively style. W. K. C. Guthrie's classic, *The Greek Philosophers: From Thales to Aristotle* (1950), is a readable survey; T. Irwin, *Classical Thought* (1988), is a more recent treatment covering a longer period. E. Hussey, *The Presocratics* (1972), is a brief and authoritative account of the early philosophers; C. C. W. Taylor, R. M. Hare, and J. Barnes, *Greek Philosophy: Socrates, Plato, Aristotle* (1999), includes accounts of those thinkers by leading scholars.

Greek Literature K. J. Dover, ed., *Ancient Greek Literature* (1997), is a brief and authoritative survey covering all fields of literature from Homer to the Byzantine period. C. R. Beye, *Ancient Greek Literature and Society* (1987), is an attractively written account, stressing the nature of Greek literature as a public and social activity. Tragic drama is surveyed as both literature and performance in B. Zimmermann, *Greek Tragedy: An Introduction* (1991).

Architecture and Sculpture J. Boardman, *Greek Art* (1996), surveys all forms of Greek artistic creation up to Hellenistic times, from architecture and sculpture to vase painting and jewelry. A. W. Lawrence, *Greek Architecture* (1996), is a short, clear, and well-illustrated standard work; for a concise, readable, and well-illustrated general history of architecture, see I. Sutton, *Western Architecture: From Ancient Greece to the Present* (1999). Brief, clear, and authoritative guidance on sculptural techniques and styles is found in J. Boardman, *Greek Sculpture: The Archaic Period* (1975), *The Classical Period* (1985), and *The Late Classical Period* (1995), and in R. R. R. Smith, *Hellenistic Sculpture* (1991). J. J. Pollitt, *Art and Experience in Classical Greece* (1972), and N. Spivey, *Understanding Greek Sculpture: Ancient Meanings, Modern Readings* (1996), relate the Greek artistic achievement to its cultural and social background.

The Decline of the Greek City-States A. Powell, *Athens and Sparta* (1988), includes an up-to-date analysis of the rise of the Athenian empire, the rivalry with Sparta, and the course of the Peloponnesian War. L. A. Tritle, ed., *The Greek World in the Fourth Century* (1997), deals with the decline of the city-states and the rise of Macedonia.

Alexander the Great and the Wider Spread of Greek Culture L. Tritle, ed., *The Greek World in the Fourth Century* (1997), includes a brief and clear account of Alexander's conquests and the breakup of his empire. P. Green, *Alexander of Macedon* (1974), is an exciting piece of storytelling by a leading scholar; N. Hammond, *The Genius of Alexander the Great* (1997), analyzes the conqueror's military and political methods. V. D. Hanson, *The Wars of the Ancient Greeks* (1999), describes the development of Greek battle tactics up to Alexander. G. Shipley, *The Greek World After Alexander, 323–30 B.C.* (2000), gives a clear and comprehensive picture of Hellenistic civilization.

☞ INFOTRAC COLLEGE EDITION

Visit the source collections at **http://academic.cengage.com/infotrac,** and use the Search function with the following key terms:

Greek history   Peloponnesian War

Greek mythology   Alexander the Great

WESTERN CIVILIZATION RESOURCES

Visit the Brief History of the Western World Companion Web Site for resources specific to this textbook:

http://history.wadsworth.com/greerbrief09/

Also, the CD in the back of this book and the World History Resources Center at **http://history.wadsworth.com/west_civ/** offer a variety of tools to help you succeed in this course, including access to quizzes; images; documents; interactive simulations, maps, and timelines; movie explorations; and a wealth of other sources.

CHAPTER 3

The Roman Triumph and Fall

OVERVIEW

Roman civilization and that of Greece were twin versions of a single "Greco-Roman" civilization, in which the Greeks were the originators and the Romans, to begin with, were the followers. The rise of Rome, in fact, began as a continuation of classical Greece's early westward expansion through the Mediterranean Sea. This brought the Greek model of civilization to the peoples of Italy during the eighth century B.C.— among them the barbarian tribal community of Rome.

The Romans not only imitated Greek civilization but also improved on it—at least so far as government and warfare were concerned. About 500 B.C., Rome became a Greek-style city-state that was no longer ruled by kings, but the Roman government system—the *Republic,* as they called it—was for several centuries more stable and more effective than any in Greece. The war-fighting methods of Roman armies were more consistently successful than those of the Greeks, and Rome's treatment of conquered enemies was usually more generous. As a result, by the beginning of the Christian era, Rome had become the wealthy and luxurious center of an empire that stretched from the Middle East to the Atlantic Ocean.

But by that time, endless expansion had also led to social conflict, political crisis, civil war, and unstable rule by powerful army commanders. Finally, one of these commanders, Augustus Caesar, managed to turn military rule into a workable system of government by a single man. The new system kept many features of the Roman Republic, allowed subject peoples a good deal of self-government, and brought Rome's destabilizing expansion to a halt. The empire lasted in its new form for four hundred years— long enough to bring about historic changes in civilization among the peoples it ruled.

Within the empire, the Roman version of Greco-Roman civilization prevailed in the western territories, and the Greek version was dominant in the East. The empire-wide civilization destroyed and replaced the traditional barbarian cultures of western Europe, it undermined ancient civilizations in the Middle East, and it also interacted with them to produce new forms of culture and religion—among them Christianity.

In Greco-Roman civilization itself, Roman literature and art, philosophy and law, architecture and engineering were often inspired by Greek models. But Roman achievements in these fields eventually equaled or surpassed those of the Greeks and became in their turn an inspiration and model for civilization's further development, above all in western Europe, the future heartland of Western civilization.

Like every expanding civilization before it, that of the Roman Empire brought changes to peoples living outside as well as inside its borders. In particular, the Germanic barbarians of northern Europe became increasingly advanced and powerful exactly as a result of hundreds of years of living as Rome's neighbors. From about A.D. 200, they became such a formidable threat that the emperors could hold them off only by building up the army, replacing self-rule by centralized government, and openly ruling as absolute monarchs. But the threatened empire was still strong enough to bring about the last and greatest of the changes in civilization that took place under Rome's rule: the conversion of its peoples to Christianity.

Eventually, the burden of government and the army became too heavy to bear, the barbarian attacks grew too fierce to be resisted, and the empire began to collapse. Over about a century down to A.D. 500, the entire western half was gradually taken over by Germanic invaders. In the seventh century A.D., the surviving eastern half lost its Middle Eastern and African territories to the new religion and empire of Islam. But the Germanic rulers of the West accepted the Latin-speaking culture of Rome, as well as the empire's recently acquired Christianity. What was left of Rome's territories in the East survived as the long-enduring Greek-ruled empire of Byzantium. Instead of dying, the Mediterranean civilization of Greece and Rome began to change, and to spread among many still-barbarian northern peoples, until it became the Christian Europe of the Middle Ages.

The Rise of Rome

The question of why Rome "fell" has challenged scholars for centuries. An even more fascinating question is how Rome *rose* from the status of a small Italian city-state to become the master of its world. Rome built an enduring order of astonishing size, given the technology of the time. How did the Romans surpass all that had gone before them?

ITALY AND ITS PEOPLES

While the Greeks were moving down into the Aegean area, tribes speaking another Indo-European dialect (p. 27) made their way from the north into central Italy. There they mingled with earlier inhabitants to form the Latin people. Some of them settled near the mouth of the Tiber River (*Map 3.1*, p. 108), building a cluster of huts on low-lying hills along the river—the famed "Seven Hills ." These settlements joined together to form a city-state around 750 B.C. By 500 B.C., Rome had grown to be the chief power of Latium, an area reaching some 100 miles southward.

The natural resources of the Italian peninsula, though not abundant, are superior to those of Greece. Most of the land is mountainous, with the Apennines forming a

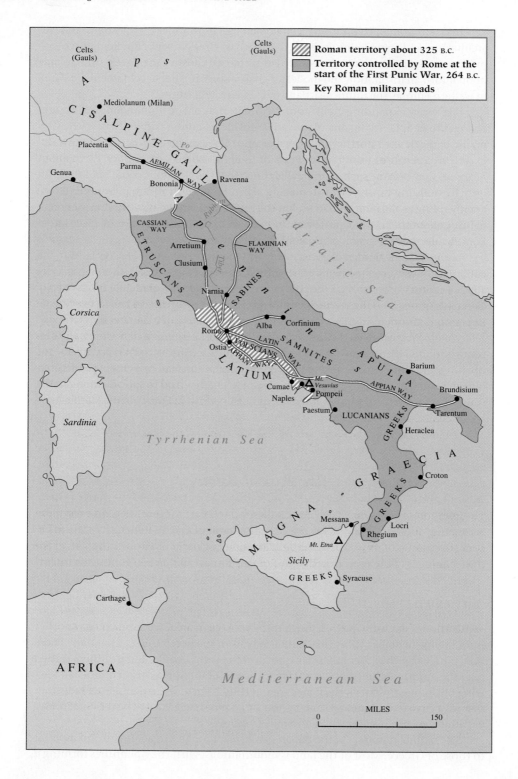

Celts
(Gauls)

Celts
(Gauls)

▨ **Roman territory about 325** B.C.

**Territory controlled by Rome at the
start of the First Punic War, 264** B.C.

══ **Key Roman military roads**

A l p s

C I S A L P I N E   G A U L

• Mediolanum (Milan)

Placentia •

Genua •

Parma •

AEMILIAN WAY

Bononia •

Po

• Ravenna

Adriatic Sea

CASSIAN
WAY

Arretium •

Clusium •

Narnia •

Rubicon

Tiber

A p e n n i n e s

FLAMINIAN
WAY

SABINES

ETRUSCANS

Corsica

Roma •

Ostia •

Alba •

• Corfinium

VOLSCIANS

LATIN
WAY

LATIUM

APPIAN
WAY

Cumae •

Naples •

S A M N I T E S

A P U L I A

• Barium

Mt.
Vesuvius △

Pompeii •

Paestum •

LUCANIANS

APPIAN WAY

Brundisium •

Tarentum •

Sardinia

Tyrrhenian Sea

GREEKS

Heraclea •

GREEKS

M A G N A

G R A E C I A

• Croton

GREEKS

Messana •

Locri •

Rhegium •

Mt. Etna △

Sicily

G R E E K S

• Syracuse

Carthage •

AFRICA

M e d i t e r r a n e a n   S e a

MILES

0   150

spiny barrier from the Po valley in the north to the very toe of the Italian boot. But there were extensive pasturelands and fields, and the peoples who settled this country were self-sufficient from their very beginnings.

Rome itself was strategically situated on the peninsula. Lying 14 miles from the sea, the city was fairly easy to defend; it was even better adapted to offense, for it controlled the principal routes of travel. The Italian peninsula itself was to serve as a superb base for Rome's far-ranging conquests. Astride the Mediterranean, it commanded every direction: southward and eastward to the territories of Greek and Middle Eastern civilization, northward and westward to the lands of barbarian Europe.

The Romans did not have the peninsula to themselves, however. Besides the Latins, many other peoples lived in Italy, of which two in particular were to have a decisive influence on the growth of Roman civilization. the Etruscans and the Greeks.

The Etruscans, whose background is mysterious, apparently arrived in Italy from somewhere to the east in about the ninth century B.C. They gained control of the north-central portion of the country, established city-states under the rule of kings, and built up a civilization that combined native features and Greek influences. In the seventh century B.C., they struck out in all directions, including southward: they conquered Latium, and for a time Etruscan kings ruled Rome itself.

Around 500 B.C., the Etruscans were ejected from Rome by an uprising. But they possessed a superior, urban culture that was readily absorbed by the Romans. From the Etruscans the Romans learned a great deal about war, politics, religion, and agriculture, and they adopted such specific features as a street plan for cities, the insignia of authority (*fasces*), the triumphal procession, gladiatorial combats, and the masonry arch.

The Romans also borrowed directly from the Greeks. As part of their expansion across the Mediterranean (p. 63), the Greek city-states had begun to plant colonies in southern Italy as early as the eighth century B.C., and these spread northward up the coast almost to the borders of Latium (*Map 3.1.*). It was from the Greeks that the Latins first learned the alphabet and something of the Olympian gods. And in dealing with the Greek colonies, the people of Latium came into direct contact with the civilized life of the Greek city-state. The Romans, realizing that this civilization was more advanced than their own, gradually absorbed Greek ideas and arts into their culture.

Map 3.1 Rome in Italy. When Rome became a republic about 500 B.C., Italy was a region of many different city-states and small ethnic groups. Rome itself was a city-state in Latium, the ethnic territory of the Latins. In 250 years, Rome united Italy under its leadership by a system of alliances, by emigration and settlement, and by roads that speeded the movement of goods, news, and above all armies. These were methods of unification that Rome would later apply in many lands of the Mediterranean, western Europe, and the Middle East.

THE GOVERNMENT OF THE EARLY REPUBLIC

Under the influence of the Etruscans and the Greeks, the Romans acquired the skills that enabled them to build their unique political institutions. For several centuries, they were governed by kings whose authority resembled that of the rulers of Homeric Greece. The king served as high priest of the state religion, military commander, supreme judge, and chief executive. He was advised by a council of elders called the Senate (from the Latin *senex,* meaning "old man") whose members were drawn from the leading families (the patricians). When a king died, his successor was chosen by the Senate from among its own members, subject to approval by an assembly of all male citizens— for, like the Greek city-states, Rome relied on its own citizens as fighting men and therefore had to give them at least some share in government (pp. 65–66).

Around 500 B.C., when the Etruscans were expelled, the monarchy was also abolished. From then on, the Roman city-state, though influenced by the government systems of the Greeks, developed according to its own unique pattern. Military and executive power was transferred to two chief magistrates (consuls), elected annually by another body of male citizens, the Assembly of Centuries (groups of one hundred men into which the citizens were formed for government, taxation, and military purposes). The Romans created this plural executive to guard against tyranny, and they empowered each consul to veto any lawmaking proposed by the other. But the Romans extended this practice by electing two or more men (*collegae,* or colleagues) to every important office of the Republic (*res publica,* or commonwealth). Those who shared a given office were usually given separate duties, but on important matters of common concern, they were required to act in concert. This principle of joint responsibility in administration sometimes led to costly delays or even paralysis. To correct this weakness, the Republic permitted the appointment of a "dictator" in time of emergency. The dictator was chosen by the consuls with the advice of the Senate, and his term was limited to six months.

The evolution of government under the Republic reflected the serious social struggle that was taking place among the Romans. On the one side were the upper-class citizens, the *patricians* (aristocrats), who belonged to the oldest and noblest Roman families and who alone could perform the religious rituals on which the safety of all depended. On the other side were the common citizens, the *plebeians* (from the Latin *plebs,* meaning "commoners")—everyone who did not have the hereditary status of patricians, including workers, small farmers, and even quite wealthy citizens.

The patricians, though they made up only a tiny fraction of the total citizenry, dominated Roman politics. The several citizen assemblies, which included the plebeians, held the powers of approving laws and electing public officials, but their voting procedures were usually arranged to favor the patricians. Further, magistrates could be named only from the upper class, and they were expected to act under senatorial advice. The Senate consisted of a fixed number (about three hundred) of the heads of patrician families; senators were appointed for life by the consuls.

The plebeians, who felt that they were being treated as second-class citizens, were determined to win equal rights. They resorted to various means of putting pressure on the patricians, including acts of passive resistance and threats to secede and start a rival settlement. Since they managed, however, to stay within the bounds of law and order, the Republic was not subverted.

Among the chief complaints of the plebeians was that they lacked legal protection. Before the fifth century B.C., there had been no written code of law to which an accused person could turn for guidance or defense. The sacred traditional laws were interpreted by judges, who were, of course, patricians. Understandably, the plebeians protested that they were not receiving equal treatment in the courts. About 450 B.C., in response to their demand, the laws of Rome were set down in writing. According to tradition, the new code was engraved on twelve tablets (made of wood or bronze) and mounted in the chief public square, the Forum, for all to see. These Twelve Tablets served as the foundation for the elaborate system of Roman law that grew up in the centuries to come (pp. 135–136).

The plebeians also demanded admission to the major public offices (magistracies), especially the consulship. Although the patricians firmly resisted this demand, they did agree to let the plebeians elect officials of their own, called *tribunes*. Immune from interference when in the pursuit of their duties, the tribunes had power to protect any citizen whom they thought was being wronged by a patrician magistrate. Later the tribunes acquired the further right to initiate laws in the Assembly of Tribes (yet another citizen assembly, where plebeians had a majority of the votes)

This compromise, like others that gradually admitted the plebeians to greater power, was characteristic of the Roman approach to politics. Instead of abolishing or radically altering an old institution, the Romans preferred to install a counterweight. This habit exasperates modern political scientists who try to analyze precisely how the Republic worked, but the Romans themselves were little disturbed by the complex checks and balances, the contradictions between political form and reality, and the unplanned growth of offices. They had a lingering affection for traditional ways, and their system showed a flexibility and resilience often lacking in more logical political structures. Their "mixed" government, as it was called on account of its combination of oligarchic and democratic features (p. 66), was widely admired in ancient times and continues to influence government systems today. The separation of powers in the U.S. Constitution (p. 455) derives ultimately from the checks and balances between different branches of government in the Roman city-state.

By 250 B.C., the plebeians had won the main objectives in their contest with the patricians: eligibility for *all* public offices, the right to marry into the patrician class, and admission to the Senate itself. The citizen assemblies played an important role in legislation, as well as electing the consuls, tribunes, praetors (judges), pontiffs (priests), and other magistrates for one-year terms; and to be appointed a senator, a man had to have served as a magistrate. Since the Republic depended on its ordinary citizens to serve in the army, this democratic element in the government was vital to Rome's stability and power.

But this did not mean that Rome was a democracy. Control of the Republic still rested in the hands of the Senate, and since only well-off plebeians could afford to join the Senate, it was now an oligarchy of wealth. Running for the public offices that qualified a man for the Senate was expensive. To seek the votes of the citizens, a candidate had to spend large sums for displays and popular entertainments. In addition, he needed to follow the long-standing Roman practice of supporting *clients* (dependents); these were normally less wealthy citizens, protected and paid by a rich patron for personal services and campaigning. And once a candidate got himself elected, he had to pay the costs of his magistracy out of his own pocket, since it carried no salary. Due to such heavy costs, only the rich could afford to belong to the Senate.

Those who did make it sat in the seats of the mighty, for the Senate was a body of enormous prestige and influence. No matter how restricted a group it might be, until the final centuries of the Republic it governed firmly and effectively, exercising wide powers that it had acquired not so much by law as by general consent. The members of the Senate set long-range policies and made immediate decisions on pressing matters. They appointed and instructed the military leaders of the Republic, received foreign ambassadors, and concluded treaties. They supervised finances and investigated high crimes. In all these ways, the Senate functioned as the balance wheel in the complicated machinery of the Roman state.

ROMAN EXPANSION

The Romans were, above all, a military people—patriotic farmer-soldiers. The first campaigns that we know much about were essentially defensive—against the Etruscans, Gauls, Greeks, and competing Italic tribes. Then, as the Romans secured their position at home, they began to reach out for territories and allies. Along the way, they encountered ever more enemies, for across each new frontier stood a new danger. The Romans, of course, lost as well as won battles, but they invariably won the war.

In addition to the toughness of its soldier-citizens and the shrewdness of its Senate, Rome had a superior military organization. At the beginning of the Republic, the citizens usually served for short periods and without pay, and the best-off soldiers seem to have armed and trained themselves to fight in Greek-style phalanxes, each numbering several hundred men. But in the course of numerous wars that were fought ever farther from home, the Romans began to pay their citizen draftees so as to permit longer campaigns and better training; and by combining the fighting methods of the various enemies they encountered, they developed formidable new tactics.

By 250 B.C., Roman soldiers fought in small units of about one hundred men (centuries), each under the command of a centurion. They wore light armor and carried large, oblong shields, and rather than using long thrusting spears like the hoplites (p. 65), they attacked their enemies from a distance with javelins before closing in for hand-to-hand fighting with swords. The centuries were combined into bigger units, of which the largest was the *legion,* of about four thousand; thus Roman armies were highly maneuverable yet also well coordinated, unlike the unwieldy Greek phalanxes. But what most distinguished the Roman army was its combination of iron discipline with treatment of the soldiers as citizens who deserved respect. The soldiers elected their own centurions, yet once chosen, a centurion had almost absolute power. Penalties for cowardice or neglect of duty were severe and cruel; on the other hand, there were generous rewards and promotions for the brave and victorious.

The Romans applied this same incentive-deterrent system to the peoples they conquered in war. The rule of conquest, booty, and massacre that had usually prevailed in the ancient world was supplanted by an improved formula: in exchange for "coopera-tion," the Romans offered protection and self-rule. Those who remained loyal and con-tributed the most aid were given the highest privileges; those who wavered or deserted were punished or annihilated. In fact, Roman rule had many advantages. In place of bloody anarchy, it brought order, roads, prosperity, and a share in the benefits of further conquests. It was this principle of two-way benefit that the Romans would extend, step by step, to the whole Mediterranean world. The army was the foundation of Roman power, but the conquered domains were cemented to Rome by mutual interest and service.

The new conquerors refrained from interfering with local laws, religions, or cus-toms, insisting only that the defeated communities submit to Rome's direction of ex-ternal relations and provide troops for the Roman forces—both heavy infantry of the Roman type, as well as light infantry and cavalry, which the Romans lacked. They tight-ened their control over the Italian peninsula by creating a network of colonies of set-tlers from Rome that served both as garrisons and as models of Roman civic organiza-tion. Both the colonists and the allies raised soldiers on the same scale as Rome itself, so that the Roman forces increased in step with their conquests. This was another rea-son why Rome always won its wars in the end: however disastrously its armies might be defeated, there were always other armies to take their place.

The Roman colonists enjoyed rights of citizenship that were almost equal to those of citizens who lived in Rome itself. Gradually, forms of participating citizenship were also offered to the non-Roman inhabitants of Italy until by the middle of the first century B.C., most of them counted as Roman citizens, and the status of "ally," sepa-rate from the Romans, disappeared. Thus Rome, unlike the exclusive Greek city-states (p. 67), became an expanding, *absorptive* political entity.

Roman methods of conquest and administration paid handsome dividends, for by 250 B.C., all of Italy south of the Po valley was in Roman hands. But no sooner had the Romans secured their position on the peninsula than they were challenged by a power beyond the sea: Carthage, a rich empire with its capital on the north coast of Africa (*Map 3.1*, p. 108). The city had been founded about 700 B.C. by colonists from Phoenicia (modern Lebanon), a trading folk of Semitic origin who had built up a thriv-ing commercial civilization (pp. 41–42). Organized as an oligarchic republic similar in form to Rome, Carthage spread its influence across North Africa, southern Spain, Sar-dinia, Corsica, and Sicily. It was the Carthaginians' interest in Sicily, lying between Africa and Italy (*Map 3.1*, p. 108), that brought them into conflict with the Romans. The Greek city-states of Sicily had for centuries been struggling with Carthage for con-trol of the island, and the Romans had inherited the struggle when they took over re-sponsibility for protecting their Greek allies. Thus began the fateful Punic Wars (264–146 B.C.), which lifted Rome into the position of a "world" power. (The term *Punic* derives from *Poeni,* the Latin name for the Phoenicians, the settlers of Carthage.)

But more was at stake than the harbors and hills of Sicily. These two proud and ag-gressive antagonists were fighting for command of the whole western Mediterranean. The struggle was waged on land and sea, in three vicious rounds, and in one phase of the war, the Carthaginian general Hannibal invaded Italy, defeated several Roman armies, and brought Rome to the brink of defeat. But Rome's system of alliances proved strong enough to meet the test. The loyalty of the Romans' allies, the perseverance of

Map 3.2 Roman Expansion. Notice the rhythm of Rome's expansion—250 years to unify Italy (500–264 B.C.); 140 years of much faster growth from the outbreak of the Punic Wars to the death of Gaius Gracchus (264–121 B.C.); 140 years of triumphant conquest even as the Republic collapsed (121–44 B.C.) and Augustus took over (44 B.C.– A.D. 14); and in the following century of imperial monarchy, the gradual end of expansion (A.D. 14–117). All the civilized Mediterranean lands and the Celtic barbarians of western Europe came under Roman rule. The Germanic barbarians, the steppe nomads, and powerful Middle Eastern civilized states remained unconquered and would eventually bring the empire down.

their own forces, and their greater manpower—for they were able to draw citizen and allied soldiers from all of Italy, while Carthage relied on smaller mercenary armies— enabled them to triumph. In a final act of vengeance, the victorious Roman general leveled the city of Carthage to the ground and sold the survivors into slavery.

The former possessions of Carthage in Sicily, Spain, and Africa became the first Roman provinces. These administrative units did not enjoy the status of Rome's allies in Italy; instead, they were ruled as conquered lands by proconsuls (governors) appointed by the Senate. They paid tribute to the Roman state, contributed cavalry and light infantry units (auxiliaries) to the Roman forces, and provided opportunities for influential Roman citizens to build up private fortunes. It was not until the time of Augustus, after 27 B.C., that the provinces began to share in the benefits of Roman order (p. 121). But for Rome, the conquest of the western Mediterranean meant an enormous increase in both resources and military power.

In Spain and neighboring territories in the south of Gaul (*Map 3.2*), Rome for the first time gained a substantial foothold among the peoples of barbarian Europe. But even before the final defeat of Carthage, venturesome Romans were looking also to the civilized eastern Mediterranean for new areas to exploit. The prospect in that direction was promising, for the Hellenistic world (pp. 100–101) was in turmoil.

Rome's first involvement was in Greece, and it grew out of a special invitation. Around 200 B.C., ambassadors from various Greek city-states appealed to Rome for aid in resisting the king of Macedonia, who had been allied with Carthage. Moved by admiration for Hellenic culture as well as by greed, the Romans replied by sending an army. Their professed aim was to secure the liberties of the proud and quarrelsome Greek cities and then to withdraw. But they soon became entangled in the politics and conflicts of the East. In the course of endless maneuvering and fighting, the Romans carved one province after another out of the Hellenistic kingdoms, until by the early first century A.D., they were supreme in the eastern Mediterranean. From Gibraltar to Jerusalem fell the shadow of mighty Rome.

The Overthrow of the Republic

Rome's triumphs abroad had a profound effect on society at home. In former days, the farmer-soldier had been the backbone of the state. But the social and economic revolution that followed the Punic Wars and Rome's adventures in the East changed all that.

THE IMPACT OF WAR AND CONQUEST

The Punic Wars and then the endless conquests in Greece and Asia enormously increased the burden of military service on the Roman farmer-soldiers. Once drafted, they now served for years at a time until the particular conflict for which they had been called up came to an end. Many never came back; those who did often found their farms spoiled by neglect. Some farmers remained stubbornly on their land, but most gave up and drifted into the cities, especially Rome. Many of these became clients of the well-to-do (p. 112) and began to look to the politicians for security and entertainment ("bread and circuses").

While small independent farmers were disappearing, a new social group was rising to prominence in Italy. It consisted of war profiteers of various sorts—contractors to the armed forces and dealers in booty. They used their wealth to buy up ruined farms, restock them, and turn them to new purposes. Small plots on which independent farmers had raised grain were often merged into large tracts known as *latifundia* for use as vineyards, olive groves, or pasturelands for livestock. The new owners, who operated their holdings as capitalistic enterprises, had little interest in the displaced farmers either as tenants or as hired hands. Most of the labor was now performed by gangs of slaves, who had become plentiful and cheap as a result of Rome's conquests overseas.

By 150 B.C., the social composition of Rome and the peninsula as a whole had undergone a drastic alteration. Rome was now the largest slaveholding society in the ancient world; slaves made up nearly one-third of the population of Italy. They labored mainly on the *latifundia,* where they were generally treated little better than beasts of burden. In the cities, slaves were better off, working as household servants or in various commercial occupations (including prostitution). The master had a right to a slave's earnings, but he sometimes permitted the slave to withhold a portion. By this means, some slaves saved enough money to purchase their freedom and with it Roman citizenship. Thereafter they were called "freedmen" or "freedwomen" and normally kept their place in the labor force.

Within the body of citizens, the number of small farmers continued to fall. At the same time, the capitalists and landowners mounted in importance, and the property-less urban mob (proletarians) steadily swelled in size. The senatorial families, which had guided Rome through its long wars, still held the highest rank and power—though their war-connected prosperity would soon corrupt their character.

From the earliest days of the Republic, the noble families of Rome had valued honesty, simple living, and strict moral conduct. But few could resist the lure of the riches that now poured into Rome from across the seas. Many of them found ways of sharing in the new opportunities for profit—especially those who secured appointments as provincial administrators. Gradually, the old republican virtues of plain living and discipline gave way to indulgence and moral decay, while the gulf between the rich and the poor widened dangerously. Some Roman moralists held that the growing influence of Greek attitudes and ideas was responsible for Rome's plight. But this influence was probably of minor significance. The fact is that the Romans had become subject to powerful new forces within themselves; their change in moral outlook was a direct consequence of their rise to imperial fortune. The Republic paid for its good fortune with its life, for the new wealth and corruption upset the balance of Roman society. Had the Senate been able to meet the problems that came crowding in on Rome, its position would have remained secure. But the senators, absorbed in seeking personal gain and privilege, proved unequal to the broader challenges of their times.

The first sign of political breakdown appeared toward the end of the second century B.C. Tiberius and Gaius Gracchus (the Gracchi), sons of a patrician family, thought that a partial solution to Rome's troubles would be to resettle many of the city's poor, as well as discharged army veterans, on small farms and to provide a subsidy of grain for those who remained in Rome. Such a program, they hoped, would raise the number of independent farmers and reduce the gap between rich and poor. Though unable to win Senate support for these measures, the Gracchi proposed them directly to the Assembly of Tribes. Tiberius, who was elected tribune of the people in 133 B.C., initiated the reform effort. But his term as tribune, limited by custom to one year, did not allow sufficient time to carry through his long-range program. Moreover, the Senate attacked him as a dangerous troublemaker. Tiberius decided to break custom and stand for reelection as a tribune; in so doing, he gave his opponents an excuse to instigate and condone his murder, along with those of hundreds of his supporters. His younger brother, Gaius, carried forward the reform crusade; he, too, fell under attack by the Senate and met a violent death in 121 B.C.

Having defeated the well-meaning reform efforts of the Gracchi, the Senate then found its power drifting away to more ruthless challengers, as the decline of the small farms led to a change in the character of Rome's armed forces. Instead of the farmer-soldiers of old, it was now landless and propertyless citizens who were drafted to fill the ranks of the legions. This new type of soldier proved just as courageous and tough as the old one, and throughout the first century B.C., Rome's empire expanded faster than ever into barbarian Europe and the civilized Middle East (*Map 3.2*, p. 114). But Rome's citizen-soldiers were now "semiprofessionals," so to speak, who fought to a large

Roman Republic   Roman Empire

Punic Wars
(246–146)

extent in the hope of bettering themselves through pay, loot, promotion, and above all grants of land or money to provide them with a living when they were discharged. And small farms for veterans were precisely what the Senate had shown itself too greedy and shortsighted to provide.

Instead, the soldiers began looking for these benefits to their own commanders, who were themselves mostly senators but who stood to gain politically by meeting the needs of their troops. Many army commanders turned into what amounted to independent warlords, sure of the personal loyalty of their soldiers and hence more powerful than the Senate itself. Since there was usually more than one such warlord at any given time, their rivalries led to bouts of destructive civil war, in each of which the winner became the one and only supreme warlord and hence the one and only ruler of Rome. But government by supreme warlords was bound to be brief and unstable—unless one of them could turn military dictatorship into legitimate power.

The first of the civil wars took place between 88 and 82 B.C. The main contenders were Gaius Marius, a plebeian by birth, who had led his legions to brilliant victories in Africa and western Europe, and Lucius Sulla, a patrician who had served under Marius but became his rival for an army command in Asia Minor. Marius claimed to represent the interests of the people and the common soldiers, while Sulla had the support of the Senate. In fact, both warlords set aside the republican government while they settled their dispute by military force. After vicious fighting in Greece, Italy, and Spain, and following Marius's (natural) death, there was no one left to challenge Sulla, and he was appointed dictator (p. 110). He abolished the traditional limits on the power of the Senate but also made sure to pay off his soldiers with generous land grants. In reality, the only unlimited power in Rome was his own. He ruled by terror, making systematic use of proscription—an outlawry procedure involving the public posting of the names of those selected for death and the confiscation of their property. The victims included many senators as well as men of lower standing—opponents, possible opponents, and anyone who was rich enough to make it worthwhile to eliminate him.

After two years, Sulla felt safe enough to retire from office, and he died in 78 B.C. Rome's first experiment with one-man rule had not been encouraging, and the Senate and the other institutions of the Republic returned to their traditional functioning. Soon, however, a new generation of army commanders and would-be army commanders was struggling for power. With no external enemy able to challenge Rome, it nevertheless seemed likely to tear itself apart from within. But among the new contenders was Marius's nephew by marriage, a resourceful young man whom Sulla had proscribed but who had managed to escape and lie low until the dictator was dead—Julius Caesar. In time, Caesar would become the most spectacular of the warlords and Rome's second and more statesmanlike, though still ultimately unsuccessful, supreme ruler.

JULIUS CAESAR

Julius Caesar came from an old patrician family that had come down in the world, and he entered the city's politics as a young man determined to regain the fame and power of his ancestors. As he grew in maturity and experience, however, he also came to identify Rome's key problems at home and abroad. In the social struggles, he sided with the poorer citizens and used his influence with them to advance his own cause. But he was also a flexible politician, and in 60 B.C., he formed an alliance with two of Sulla's former henchmen. One was Marcus Crassus, who had grown rich from the confiscated property of victims of proscription. The other was Gnaeus Pompeius (Pompey), an officer promoted by Sulla who had become Rome's most brilliant general, the conqueror of much of the Middle East, including the kingdom of the Jews (p. 159). Together these political allies formed a *triumvirate* ("Three-Man Board") that was for a time the dominant political force in Rome.

With the help of his new friends, Caesar won an appointment as proconsul with a military command, which opened the way for him to become a warlord in his turn. His province included the southern regions of Gaul, a territory stretching all the way from northern Italy and the Mediterranean coast to the Rhine River and the Atlantic Ocean (*Map 3.2*, p. 114). The Gauls, as the inhabitants were called, were a branch of the Celtic peoples, the predominant barbarian ethnic group across most of western Europe and the British Isles. The Gaulish tribes outside the Roman-ruled areas were powerful and advanced enough that they might one day become dangerous to Rome, and were wealthy enough to be a tempting target. In eight years of brilliant and brutal campaigns, Caesar conquered Gaul and even made forays into Britain and Germany. By 50 B.C., most of western Europe was under Roman rule, and Caesar had built a powerful army personally devoted to him .

Meanwhile, Crassus had also become an army commander but had died after a crushing defeat in the Middle East, while Pompey had stayed in Rome, growing increasingly jealous of Caesar and forging alliances against him in the Senate. Finally, with Pompey's support, the Senate ordered Caesar to disband his army and return to Rome. Instead, he decided to come back with part of his army. This was contrary to Roman law. As he crossed the Rubicon River, the southern boundary of Gaul, he declared fatefully, "The die is cast." It was the beginning of another round of far-flung civil wars.

Pompey was hastily commissioned to defend the Senate, but his forces were no match for Caesar's veterans. Forced to flee from Italy, Pompey was later defeated by Caesar in Greece and murdered in Egypt where he had taken refuge. After subduing supporters of Pompey and other opponents in Egypt, Asia Minor, Africa, and Spain, Caesar returned to Rome in triumph in 46 B.C. The Senate, which had once branded him an outlaw, now hailed him, however reluctantly, as the "father of his country."

Caesar moved swiftly to consolidate his position and launch a program of reform. Publicly he rejected the offer of a royal crown, but by indirect means he gathered to himself the authority of a king. He secured the republican office of consul, then that of dictator (for ten years). He had himself appointed to the office of tribune, censor, and *pontifex maximus* (chief priest of the state religion). He altered the functions of most of the republican institutions, though he was careful to preserve their form. A citizen assembly, for example, continued to exist, but under Caesar it did little more than endorse his proposals. The Senate, now enlarged by his own appointees, paid him noble compliments, and its members vowed to risk death in defense of his person. For his part, Caesar showed respect to the Senate but treated it as a mere advisory body.

Caesar used his new powers to attack the grave problems facing Rome. He took care to keep the loyalty of the soldiers and prevent the rise of rival warlords by resettling war veterans on farmlands in Italy and the provinces. He extended Roman citizenship to portions of Gaul and Spain, appointed provincials to the Senate, and tried to make Romans more conscious of the world beyond Italy. He gave the Romans splendid public buildings and roads, and he introduced reforms into every department of administration.

Romans at home and abroad applauded Caesar's deeds, but there remained a stubborn core of older senators who were disturbed by the dictator's successes. Their personal prestige and privilege had been reduced, and they saw Caesar as a destroyer of the Republic. Their concern deepened further when in 44 B.C. he secured a vote from the Senate making him dictator for life. Caesar himself, though he never ruled by terror like Sulla, grew ever more arrogant in manner. He permitted a religious cult to be established in his honor, like the rulers of the Hellenistic monarchies (p. 102), and he wore the purple robe of the ancient Roman kings. These acts were in defiance of republican tradition, and the diehard senators found them intolerable. At last, some sixty of his enemies entered into a conspiracy to assassinate him when he visited the Senate House on the Ides of March (March 15), 44 B.C. In spite of urgent warnings, Caesar appeared, unarmed and unguarded, according to his custom. The conspirators, crying, "Tyrant!" struck him down with their daggers.

Caesar's murder did not restore the Republic; instead, it produced yet another crop of contenders for power and yet more bouts of civil war. Cassius and Brutus, the leaders of the plot, spoke of themselves as liberators, but the populace and the army, urged on by Caesar's fellow consul Mark Antony, turned against them. Antony soon faced a rival for the loyalty of Caesar's supporters, however—the youthful Octavian Caesar, the murdered dictator's grandnephew and adopted son. The two leaders at first fought each other in Italy, but then they joined forces. They formed another triumvirate together with a lesser warlord, Marcus Lepidus, which eliminated opponents in a new reign of terror in Rome, and defeated Cassius and Brutus in battle in Greece.

The partners then divided the Roman world, with Octavian based in Rome, Lepidus in North Africa, and Mark Antony in Alexandria. Their cooperation soon turned to rivalry, however, and the balance of power began swinging toward Octavian. Antony's passionate love affair with Queen Cleopatra, one of the last descendants of the Greek rulers of Egypt, made him unpopular in Rome, and his efforts to win prestige by making Middle Eastern conquests ended in failure. Meanwhile, Octavian pushed Lepidus out of power and successfully began expanding Rome's frontiers northward toward the Danube (*Map 3.2*, p. 114). Finally, in 31 B.C., the rulers of the East and the West went to war. Octavian's forces defeated those of Antony and Cleopatra in a decisive naval engagement near Actium in Greece (*Map 3.3*, p. 125). Antony and Cleopatra returned to Egypt, and within a year both had committed suicide. Octavian was now the sole master (*Fig. 3.1*, p. 120)—the third to rule Rome, and the one who finally managed to turn military dictatorship into legitimate and permanent monarchy.

Fig. 3.1 Coin of Octavian Caesar. In a world without mass media, rulers used coins to spread news and propaganda. This one, dating from between 30 and 27 B.C., celebrates Octavian's victory over Antony and Cleopatra. The obverse ("heads" side) shows "Caesar" (Octavian) and an emblem of religious authority—the crooked staff carried by the augurs, the official soothsayers of the Roman city-state. The reverse ("tails" side) shows a crocodile, the symbol of the Nile, and the words *Aegupto capta* ("Egypt conquered").

The Imperial Foundations

Octavian completed the reforms and reconstruction begun by Caesar. Familiar with civil strife from an early age, he matured rapidly into a shrewd and subtle statesman. Once in sole command, Octavian set about advancing the new order at home and abroad. Soon after his triumph at Actium, the Senate conferred on the young man the title of *augustus* ("revered"), which had formerly been reserved for the gods. Over the many years of his rule, the title came to be regarded as his own personal name, and he has gone down in history as Augustus Caesar. The main lines of the "Augustan settlement" had emerged by 27 B.C., the year generally accepted as the end of the Republic and the beginning of the rule of the Roman emperors.

THE AUGUSTAN POLITICAL SETTLEMENT

Though Augustus founded the new system of one-man rule in *fact,* he took pains to deny it. He recognized that affection for the Republic persisted, especially in high places, and he chose to utilize that sentiment rather than resist it. But he also knew that Rome and its subjects were eager for peace—for an end to the violent conflicts of rival factions. He could have ruled, as others had before, by military force alone. Instead, having used ruthless means to secure power, he chose to direct that power toward making a peaceful world of "law and justice." The Roman citizens, for their part, recalling the fate of Caesar and the shameful disorder that followed his death, felt that the time had come for tolerance and compromise, rather than defiance and conspiracy.

Following his victory at Actium, therefore, Augustus announced that his aim was to restore peace and the Republic. He refused the offer of kingly honors and referred to himself simply as *princeps* ("first citizen"). From time to time he accepted election or appointment to the principal republican offices, including consul, censor, and pontifex maximus, though the only one that he continuously held, and used as the legal basis of his power, was that of tribune of the people. By arrangement with the Senate in 27 B.C., he was confirmed as commander in chief *(imperator,* from which the English word *emperor* is derived) of the armed forces, which included civil and military control of all provinces with garrisons. In return, he permitted the Senate to supervise Italy and the city of Rome, as well as provinces where no soldiers were stationed.

Augustus kept all his arrangements flexible, but no one doubted where the real authority lay. By cloaking his authority in traditional trappings, he gained the backing of conservatives, thereby strengthening his power and reducing the danger of assassination. His prudence brought genuine harmony to Rome. On his way to supreme power, he had proscribed and put to death many opponents in the Senate and replaced them with his friends and allies. Now he could afford to consult the Senate frequently and give it genuine government power. The citizen assembly, meanwhile, faded into oblivion. In contrast to the royal manner affected by Caesar, Augustus wore the toga (robe) and insignia of a consul and lived like any other wealthy patrician. Although he was essentially an innovator bent on creating a new world order, in his own time Augustus was known as a divine *restorer* and *preserver* of the republican tradition.

REFORM, RECONSTRUCTION, AND THE END OF EXPANSION

Augustus strove for peace throughout the empire as well as harmony at home, and one of his principal aims was to bring just administration to the empire's far-flung territories. During the days of the Republic, as we have seen, the provinces had suffered under grasping governors and dishonest officials, who amassed private fortunes at the expense of the people they governed. Caesar had made a start at correcting this abuse; Augustus began a whole series of carefully planned reforms.

First, in appointing governors for the imperial provinces, Augustus chose men of demonstrated ability and loyalty and paid them ample salaries. Though his appointees came mostly from leading and wealthy families and were not professional civil servants, they had to make their way, under his eye, up a ladder of government ranks, including both civil positions and military commands, until they reached the highest offices.

Second, in the course of numerous personal tours of the provinces, Augustus showed his respect for local institutions and encouraged provincial leaders to fulfill their responsibilities. He kept control over the affairs of the empire as a whole in Rome, but control over local affairs he left to the individual provinces; in fact, it is estimated that the entire vast empire needed no more than a couple of thousand Roman officials to run it.

It is hardly surprising that Augustus was respected in Rome and worshiped in the provinces. In the East especially, people were soon looking upon him as a divine being. Tradition had long accustomed them to venerate god-kings, such as the Egyptian pharaohs and the Greek rulers of the Hellenistic monarchies (pp. 29, 102), and Augustus was quickly given a place among the deities of the Hellenistic world. Temples were built in his honor, and groups dedicated to his cult sprang up throughout the eastern provinces. Augustus approved of these and promoted their spread to the western provinces. The cult of the emperor (more strictly, of the emperor's *genius,* or "spirit") was thus established as part of the state religion. Whatever Augustus himself may have thought about his divinity, he realized that this strong religious feeling would foster loyalty and unity throughout the empire.

Augustus also tried to restore the ancient Roman virtues, which had been corrupted by the spoils of conquest. Through personal example, he strove to guide the Romans back to the virtuous paths of the old Republic. He had stricter laws passed on personal behavior, adultery, and divorce, and he encouraged poets to praise high-mindedness, noble conduct, and love of country. In these efforts, however, Augustus was less successful than in his other undertakings.

Ultimately, what enabled Augustus to rule Rome and the provinces so flexibly and liberally was the fact that he alone held military power, and accordingly, one of his most important areas of reconstruction and reform was the army. After the battle of Actium, Mark Antony's troops came over to Augustus, who found himself at the head of a combined army of 600,000 men. Half were Roman citizens serving in about sixty legions, and the rest were provincials serving in auxiliary units (p. 114). Such a large army was impossible to pay for or keep under control, and its men would soon become a danger to peace and order. Augustus quickly cut the troop strength in half, and since tens of thousands of unemployed veterans would also be a danger to the state, he paid off the men he discharged with grants of land and money.

Then Augustus gradually phased in a radical reform of the conditions of service: instead of filling the army with draftees whose term of service was uncertain since it lasted as long as a particular conflict, in future he would rely on volunteers who would serve for long but fixed terms. The army would be more stable and reliable, since every man would serve willingly and would know when to expect his release and his discharge grant. The turnover of soldiers would be smaller, so there would be fewer discharge grants to pay and the army would be less expensive to maintain. And of course, every soldier would swear permanent obedience to Augustus and look to him for pay, maintenance, and veterans' benefits. In this way, Augustus created a force that was personally loyal to him and his successors and broke with the Roman tradition of soldier-citizens to create the world's first professional standing army.

Even after Augustus' troop cuts, his army was still far larger than the forces that Rome had usually maintained in the past. Part of it, the legion-sized Praetorian Guard, he kept in Rome to back up his power at the empire's center. But after Actium, Augustus moved most of his forces to the frontiers of the empire, for he fully intended to continue Rome's tradition of seemingly endless conquest. Egypt, the lands stretching from Italy and Greece to the River Danube, a wide swath of Germany to the east of the Rhine (*Map 3.2*, p. 114)—all these territories were added to the empire by Augustus' legions. But toward the end of his reign, many of the newly won territories in Europe rebelled, and in a memorable disaster, an entire Roman army was destroyed by German barbarian insurgents. Augustus seems to have realized that his forces had been overstretched by his conquests and that a still larger army would be so expensive and so uncontrollable as to endanger his power. He did not try to reconquer Germany beyond the Rhine, and after his death, his will was found to contain a recently added clause advising the Senate and his successors that the empire should be confined within its existing boundaries.

For the most part, Augustus' successors followed his advice. In the next century, most additions to the empire were takeovers of client kingdoms, states whose rulers already held power in allegiance to Rome. The only large independent territories that Rome permanently added to its empire were the southern half of the island of Britain (present-day England), beginning in A.D. 43; and most of Dacia (present-day Romania) by 108. The conqueror of Dacia, the unusually aggressive Trajan, also briefly held Mesopotamia and Armenia, but when he died in A.D. 117, his successor, Hadrian, immediately evacuated these territories (*Map 3.2, p. 114*). After that, there were no more conquests, and the Roman Empire settled down within the borders of the African desert in the south, the Atlantic Ocean in the west, the Rhine and Danube in the north, and the Euphrates in the east. The army's 300,000 men were stationed in hundreds of larger and smaller encampments strung out along what came to be thought of as the permanent frontiers of the empire. Though Roman forces often campaigned beyond the frontiers, it was nearly always to deter or punish attackers from the other side, for in principle the army's mission had changed from conquest to defense. In this way, the advent of monarchy, with its stress on internal political stability, brought five centuries of Roman expansion to an end.

Approach to One World: The Pax Romana

The very success of the reforms introduced by Augustus raised in people's minds a worrisome question: Who would take his place when he died? Legally and constitutionally, he held his immense powers simply as a gift of the Senate. Theoretically, when the princeps died, power would go back to the Senate until that body named his successor or even decreed a return to the traditional functioning of the Republic. But either way, the door might well be opened to renewed civil war, and in any case, the reality was that the power of the princeps in fact belonged to a particular family line. Augustus himself would never have come to power if he had not been Julius Caesar's grandnephew and adopted son; and whatever the laws and the constitution might say, the soldiers of the army, who were represented in Rome by the Praetorian Guard, felt a hereditary loyalty to the descendants of Caesar.

Lacking sons of his own, Augustus followed a common custom of wealthy, powerful, and sonless Roman men, and decided to adopt a son and heir as Julius Caesar had done with him—only in this case, his heir would also be his successor as princeps. He settled on his stepson Tiberius, a leading general who was well known to the army, and arranged his appointment to a series of important public offices. In this way he hoped to give Tiberius both hereditary standing, constitutional legitimacy, and control of the army so that the Senate would have no choice but to proclaim Tiberius his successor. Sure enough, when Augustus died in A.D. 14, the Senate declared Tiberius the new princeps, and he assumed full authority without challenge.

Most of the emperors who succeeded Tiberius during the first century A.D. emerged—usually after brutal family intrigues—from among the descendants of Julius Caesar and were then confirmed by the Senate as Tiberius had been. Eventually, Caesar's last descendant, the notorious Nero, was overthrown after a tyrannical reign, but by that time the Romans had become so used to one-man rule that no one seems to have thought of restoring the Republic. Instead, after a brief interval of civil war among rival army commanders in A.D. 69, the winner founded another dynasty, the Flavians.

By the beginning of the second century, the Flavian family, too, was extinct. Subsequent rulers for much of that century happened to have no sons by blood who survived them, so they followed the example of Augustus and adopted sons whom they also designated (proclaimed) as their successors. Such an adopted son immediately became a junior emperor with what had now become the imperial title *caesar,* and when his senior colleague died, he took full charge as *augustus.* This custom of "adoption and designation" produced a long series of outstanding emperors. The great Spaniard Trajan, who became emperor in A.D. 98, was the first; he had been picked by a wise predecessor, Nerva. His selection reflected the widening base of political participation, for he was the first non-Italian to sit on the imperial throne. Trajan, in turn, exercised sound judgment in selecting Hadrian (another Spaniard) as his junior colleague and ruler-elect. Hadrian was followed by the wise Antoninus and the philosopher-statesman Marcus Aurelius. But adoption and designation made no difference to the basically hereditary character of the emperorship. From the late second century, when emperors often had better luck with their sons by blood, they tried to arrange for these sons to succeed them, though this did not guarantee that their wishes would be respected.

Regardless of whether the empire was ruled by a Trajan or a Nero, the governing structure that Augustus had built remained remarkably stable for nearly two centuries after his time. The army generally confined itself to defending the frontiers and for the most part loyally upheld the power of the reigning princeps, while the imperial administration, in partnership with local agencies of self-government, tended to the daily business of the empire. This era of stability has gone down in history as the *Pax Romana,* the era of the Roman Peace.

THE EMPIRE: EXTENT AND COMPOSITION

At its greatest extent during the second century A.D., the Roman Empire measured nearly 3,000 miles from east to west and nearly 2,000 miles from north to south, and its total land area was about half that of the continental United States (*Map 3.3*). Its population at this time, when it was at its most prosperous, had increased from perhaps 50 million under Augustus to as high as 70 million. This was small by present-day standards—the total population of the lands once ruled by Rome is now about 530 million. At the time, however, only the empire of China had a population as large as Rome's (though probably not larger), and no other human group under a single government was as large as these two.

Beyond the frontiers, there were as yet no enemies capable of making any permanent breaches in Rome's defenses. To the south, the desert tribes of northwestern Africa made no more than occasional raids; in the Nile valley, the Nubian rulers were mostly friendly. The Germanic barbarian tribes beyond the European frontier (pp. 145–146) were still not advanced and powerful enough to challenge the empire. The chief antagonist in the East was the empire of Parthia, carved by nomadic invaders out of territories that had once been conquered by Alexander (p. 100). Though a stubborn foe, Parthia was a mere "regional power" compared with the intercontinental empire of Rome.

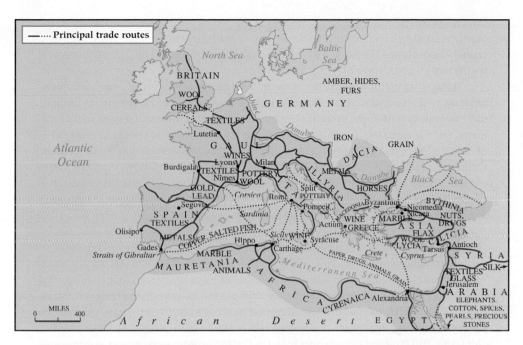

Map 3.3 The Roman Empire at Its Height. The map shows the empire at the beginning of Hadrian's reign (A.D. 117). The road network now stretches from Britain to the Middle East. But transport by water is even more efficient, and the Mediterranean, the Rhine, and the Danube are highways, not barriers. The network of trade and travel does not stop at the empire's frontiers but stretches deep into barbarian Europe, down the Red Sea to Arabia and India, and across the Middle East and central Asia all the way to China.

Beyond Parthia, the Romans had sea links to India and Ceylon, and by land, they were in touch with the horse-riding nomads of the steppes (pp. 57–58). These peoples had become increasingly wealthy and well organized and had formed swift-moving warrior nations that dominated hundreds or even thousands of miles of territory, and their westernmost tribes were neighbors of Rome on the lower Danube (*Map 3.2,* p. 114). But for the time being, the steppe peoples fought mainly with each other or with Rome's Far Eastern counterpart, the empire of China. As for China itself, then enjoying power and prosperity under the Han dynasty as great as those of Rome itself, it was a distant land, known to the Romans only through the reports of middlemen in the overland silk trade. Thus the intercontinental balance of power among the peoples and states of Asia, Africa, and Europe for the moment favored the peace and stability of the Roman Empire.

The peoples of the empire fell into three broad cultural groups, each having many dialects, religions, and ways of life. The Eastern group consisted mainly of Egyptians, Jews, and Syrians. All of these peoples were deeply affected in one way or another by Roman rule: Egypt's ancient civilization, for example, which was based on a system of belief centering around the pharaoh (pp. 29–30), finally began to wither away under the government of the distant Roman emperors. But none of the Eastern peoples assimilated to the culture of Rome. Instead, it was Greek civilization that was the dominant international one throughout the East—a tradition dating from the Hellenistic era, which outlasted the Roman Empire itself and was continued by its Eastern successor, Byzantium (pp. 198–201).

The second cultural group, the Hellenic, included the Aegean Sea area and southern Italy, where Greeks were the majority population. Both here and elsewhere throughout the eastern half of the empire, Greek civilization was influenced only slightly by Rome. On the contrary, it was the Romans who learned from the Greeks in most fields of culture (pp. 131–134), as well as absorbing Eastern influences that came to them through the Greeks—Persian and Egyptian ideas of sacred monarchy, many religious cults and beliefs, and finally Christianity itself (pp. 29, 46, 102). Culturally at least, the Greeks were partners rather than subjects of the Romans, and accordingly, the empire's dominant civilization is usually referred to as "Greco-Roman."

The third cultural group occupied the largest geographical area: the Western, or "Romanized," section of the empire, stretching from Italy northward all the way to distant Britain, westward to Spain, and southward to North Africa (*Map 3.3*, p. 125). Throughout this area, Roman armies, officials, and colonists moved in, bringing with them cities, organized government, and writing—the distinguishing features of civilization. The Celtic barbarians who occupied most of western Europe (p. 118) had already been advancing toward civilization before the Roman conquests. Their wealthy chieftains and landowning warriors took readily to the Roman language, culture, and way of life. In time, even ordinary people came to see themselves as Romans and to speak Latin, and out of the Latin they spoke there developed in later centuries the Romance languages of medieval and modern Europe (p. 273). The Berber tribes of North Africa were much more resistant to the ways of the conquerors, but there, too, the upper classes and the cities were Roman. Everywhere throughout the western half of the empire, the stamp of Rome was unmistakable.

CITIES OF THE EMPIRE

Although the empire was administered through some forty provinces, the basic unit of government and of social and economic life was the city (*civitas*). Where cities existed in conquered territories, the Romans strengthened them as centers from which to control the surrounding districts; where there were no cities, the Romans created new ones in the image of Rome. In contrast to the self-destroying independence of ancient Athens or Sparta, there was an even balance between municipal self-government and centralized power under the early empire.

The cities of the empire were bound together by a network of sea lanes and highways, with Rome, the magnificent capital, at the center. During the prosperous second century, nearly a million people lived there. Augustus is said to have found Rome a city of brick and to have left it a city of marble. And the emperors who followed him lavished gifts on the capital, building temples, forums, arenas, monuments, public baths, and palaces to honor themselves and to please the populace. There were, in addition, the elegant private estates of the wealthy, both in the city and in its suburbs. True, not everyone lived in villas; the poor lived in wretched tenements. But Rome gave a stunning impression of affluence and grandeur.

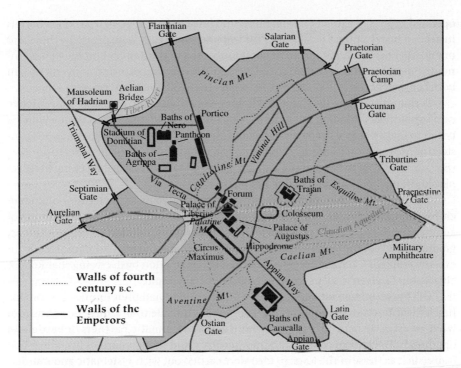

Imperial Rome

Only a few cities approached Rome in size. Whether large or small, the cities of the empire were alike in their social and political organization. In each city, a senate managed local affairs, and in each, there was a rigid structure of social classes. In the oriental and Greek cities, the old patterns of society persisted. But the cities of the West—in Italy, Gaul, Spain, and Africa—strove to copy Rome. Each had its forum and senate house, its baths, arena, and temples. The excellent water supply and underground sewage systems explain the comparatively good health of the imperial population until late in the second century. The remains of these admirably planned cities are still to be seen, notably at Pompeii and Herculaneum (Italy), Segovia (Spain), and Nîmes (France).

THE MEANING OF THE ROMAN PEACE: PROSPERITY, TECHNOLOGY, CITIZENSHIP

What was the Roman world like in the period of the Roman peace? For one thing, it was a relatively prosperous world. The empire cleared the broadest area of trade known until that time, opening up distant markets that enabled agriculture and industry to flourish as never before. Olive groves in Spain supplied oil to the citizens of Rome; legions stationed on the Danube received part of their grain rations from North Africa; workshops in Gaul turned out cheap earthenware bowls, jugs, and lamps for use in households throughout the empire.

Large markets also encouraged technical invention to make production and transportation easier and more convenient. Water-powered mills to grind grain, screwoperated presses to extract oil from olives and juice from grapes, light wooden barrels instead of heavy pottery jars to carry oil and juice once they were pressed—these and many other devices first came to be commonly used in the Roman Empire. Roman innovations in building technology—likewise often stressing ease and convenience, in both construction and use—are discussed later in this chapter (pp. 137–139).

Perhaps the single most notable Roman contribution to ease and convenience came in the field of reading and writing. Sometime in the first century A.D., the Romans began to make books with pages that could be turned as one read (*Fig. 4.1*, p. 168), instead of the traditional lengthy scrolls that had to be wound from one roller to another (*Fig. 2.4*, p. 75). By the end of the empire, the new reading device had completely replaced the old one and has remained standard ever since.

The flow of people, goods, and ideas was stimulated by the extension of Roman citizenship. Intermarriage, as well as the award of citizenship to discharged veterans of auxiliary units (p. 114) or to those who made themselves useful in local government, gradually blurred the legal distinction between Romans and non-Romans. Finally, in 212, the emperor Caracalla completely erased the distinction by decreeing that Roman citizenship be given to *all* freeborn inhabitants of the empire.

Of course, Roman universality and enlightenment had their limits. The Romans had little interest in or knowledge of the peoples outside their frontiers, apart from what was strictly necessary to deal with them as diplomatic partners or battlefield opponents. Occasional conquests of new territory and suppressions of internal rebellions (such as those of the Jews; p. 160) were carried out with systematic and murderous ferocity. And it was the elite and the townspeople who benefited most from the universality of the empire, while the peasants paid heavily for the splendor of the emperor, the upkeep of the army, and the beautification of the cities. Soon after Caracalla made citizenship universal, a new distinction grew up between what were called the "more honorable" citizens—the aristocrats, the government officials, and the military, including even common soldiers—and the "humbler" citizens, which meant everyone else. True, a person did not have to come from Rome or Italy to count as "more honorable." All the same, these were official legal categories that guaranteed a privileged status to the wealthy, educated, and arms-bearing few against the majority of Roman citizens.

Even so, the consciousness of being Roman seems to have spread widely through the population in general, as the widespread adoption of the Latin language suggests. And among the elite, ancient tribal and local loyalties were transcended by a new sense of belonging to the human family. The Greek biographer Plutarch, writing in the second century, remarked, "I am a citizen, not of Athens or of Greece, but of the world."

Roman Character and Thought

Unless we dismiss the Romans' achievement as a mere accident of history, we must conclude that it was in some measure the product of their character. What was the "inner" nature of those remarkable conquerors and governors?

RELIGION, MORALITY, AND FAMILY LIFE

The Romans, from earliest times, accepted the existence of powers outside themselves that had to be treated with respect. They regarded themselves neither as completely free agents nor as pawns of supernatural forces. In their primitive period, they had viewed the world as teeming with spirits (*numina*), each with a special function. There were protective spirits of the hearth, the cupboard, the house; other spirits were active in the fields, in the woods, and on the battlegrounds. The Romans sought the help of these forces through certain rites, prayers, and sacrifices; the head of the family (*paterfamilias*) usually acted as priest.

These practices lasted down to the victory of Christianity (p. 150), but as Rome developed into a city-state, some of the spirits came to be seen as having power to help (or harm) the entire community and hence as entitled to worship from all the citizens. Such were the sky god Jupiter (whose name meant "Divine Father"), the fertility goddess Juno, and the wise and skillful goddess Minerva. More changes came after 300 B.C., when the Romans came into closer contact than before with the Greeks of southern Italy. They began to identify their gods and goddesses with those of the Greeks. Jupiter, they believed, was the same being as Zeus, the Greek lord of the sky; Juno was Hera; and Minerva was Athena. These and other Roman gods and goddesses took on distinctive personalities like their Greek counterparts. The Romans also took to worshiping personifications of valued qualities and "powers," usually represented as goddesses—also originally a Greek practice. Among these were Fortuna (Luck), Salus (Health), Felicitas (Success), Victoria (Victory), and Pax (Peace). And the citadel of the city of Rome, the Capitol, like the Acropolis of Athens, became the center of worship of the city-state, with a splendid stone temple of the three main deities—Jupiter, Juno, and Minerva.

The Romans' ideas about their gods remained within the bounds of their old-fashioned values. They could not accept as proper, for instance, the rather scandalous image of the gods and goddesses portrayed by Homer. For the Roman character was traditionally marked by moral strictness. And what the Romans held to be moral was generally what had been done—what was recorded about Rome's heroic farmer-soldiers. Even during the late Republic and the empire, when Roman morality declined, this conviction did not wholly disappear. Certainly the noblest and truest Romans embodied the virtues of the early Republic.

The moral quality most valued by the Romans was *virtus*. This meant, literally, "manliness," but it carried the special sense of bravery in battle. This quality was considered of such importance that the term came to suggest, in time, the character of moral goodness as a whole; hence the broader meaning of our modern word *virtue*. Manliness was tempered by *pietas*, a disciplined acceptance of the authority of higher powers, both human and divine. Also valued was *gravitas*, a sense of responsibility and seriousness; every matter at hand, however small, had to be weighed with care. The best Romans might be good-humored and easy in manner, but they were rarely light-minded or impulsive.

Home and family (which meant all members of a household, including slaves) were a more intimate part of life in Rome than in Greece. The father was responsible for the education and devotions of his children and, in theory at least, was absolute

Fig. 3.2 A Roman Husband and Wife. This portrait of Publius Paquilius Proculus, a wealthy bakery owner, and his wife was preserved by lava that buried their house (and presumably killed them both) when the nearby Mount Vesuvius erupted in A.D. 79. Notices painted on house walls announced that Paquilius was running in municipal elections, and the scroll he is holding suggests that he already held city office. His wife holds wax tablets and a stylus (a sharp instrument for writing on wax), indicating that she can read and write and is proud of it.

master of his household. He alone (as in Greece) decided the fate of newborn infants. Those showing physical defects were ordered abandoned; sons were more likely than daughters to be chosen for rearing. Significantly, upper-class daughters were not given personal names. They were called simply by the names of the aristocratic clans (groups of related families) to which they belonged, and identified by such terms as "the elder" or "the third," or by the names of indvidual families to which their fathers or husbands belonged. Thus, Augustus' third wife, who came from the Livius clan, was known either as Livia or as Livia Drusilla, after her father's family name, Drusus. If spared at birth, girls were expected to marry in their early teens and to bear children soon afterward. But Roman women of the upper class did enjoy social respect, freedom, legal rights, and access to education (*Fig. 3.2*); they could, for example, own property outright and were often consulted by their husbands about important family matters.

The role of women and the character of family living evolved with Rome's growing wealth. The simple "country life" of the early Republic gave way to more costly and varied styles of living—and to greater personal independence. By the time of Augustus, upper-class wives had become frequent targets of moralists and satirists (all male) because of their "libertarian" behavior. They also shared increasingly in the lavish feasts and entertainments of the large cities.

Though Roman women possessed, legally, no political rights, some in the imperial family wielded awesome power behind the scenes. Augustus' wife Livia plotted to ensure that Tiberius, her son by a previous marriage, would become Augustus' successor (p. 123); it was even thought that she may have poisoned Augustus to clear the way. Later in the first century A.D., three of the most influential persons in the court of the emperor Nero were his mother, Agrippina; his wife, Octavia; and his mistress, Poppaea. In contrast to the political impotence of most Roman women, these women demonstrated that neither gender nor law necessarily weakens the will to power.

LITERATURE AS MORALISTIC EXPRESSION

Roman literature reflects their moralistic qualities of mind and action. It is less imaginative than Greek literature, and though it includes examples of sensual and emotional writing, a substantial portion is sober and moralistic in tone.

Among the first Roman writers was Livius Andronicus, a poet of Greek origin who wrote in the third century B.C. It was Livius who translated Homer's *Odyssey* into Latin. Roman poets were soon writing epics and dramas of their own; during the second century B.C., for instance, Plautus and Terence authored comedies that are still performed today. The republican age produced two more memorable poets during the first century B.C.: one was the philosopher Lucretius, of whom we will speak again (p. 132); the other was Catullus, a writer of sensitive and passionate lyrics.

The greatest prose writer of the first century B.C. was Cicero. A distinguished figure in public life during the last troubled days of the Republic, he was best known for his speeches in the law court and the Senate. In addition, he wrote long philosophical essays on the art of government, justice, and theology, in which he provided digests of the best Hellenistic thought. These essays gave the Romans a literature of philosophy that they had lacked before and made Greek thought available to future generations.

Historical writing in Rome, though lively, was less reliable than that of the best Greek historians (pp. 88–89). Livy's *History of Rome,* for example, is hardly an objective inquiry; it is moralistic in character, drawing chiefly from previous histories and well-worn legends about ancient heroes.

Three outstanding poets adorned the reign of Augustus (27 B.C.–A.D. 14): Virgil, Horace, and Ovid. Virgil was the eloquent spokesman of the Romans' spiritual tradition and of their love of the soil. He was also the prophet of Rome's mission and destiny. At a time when the old republican order was lying in ruins, his desire, like Livy's, was to promote a regeneration of patriotic values. Although the spirit of Virgil's masterpiece, the *Aeneid,* is Roman, he took Homer's epic form as his model, and the adventures of his hero, Aeneas, parallel those of Odysseus after the fall of Troy (p. 85). Guided by the gods, Aeneas wanders to Italy, where he and his companions become the "fathers" of the "Roman race."

The lyric poems of Horace (the *Odes*) range over a variety of moods: trivial, moralizing, and romantic. His patriotic verses consistently reflect the spirit of the Augustan revival and sing of the destiny of Rome. Ovid's erotic poems, published under such titles as *Loves* and *The Art of Love,* deal in a playful, witty, adult manner with the life of the senses. In an age when official policy was committed to the restoration of morality, these poems seemed highly immoral. It was partly for this reason that Augustus banished Ovid to a remote town on the west coast of the Black Sea.

Though the literature of the century after Augustus' death is usually judged inferior to that of the preceding century, it was not lacking in distinction. The philosopher Seneca was known for his epigrams (cleverly turned phrases), and his polished letters are considered the forerunners of the essay form in Western literature (p. 359). He also wrote melodramas based on the Greek myths. Catering to the Roman taste for plotting and violence, Seneca emphasized passion and horror in his plays.

Biographical writing was of higher quality and proved popular with the upper classes. The Greek Plutarch, a man of cosmopolitan tastes, wrote *Parallel Lives,* some fifty short biographies of Greek and Roman statesmen and generals. Appearing about A.D. 110, these served to remind his readers of the glory of ancient Greece and to compare the talents of the best Greek and Roman leaders. Suetonius, who lived about the same time as Plutarch, wrote short biographies (*Lives of the Caesars*) of the Roman rulers, from Julius Caesar to Domitian (who died in A.D. 96). Unlike Plutarch, Suetonius refrained from making interpretations, confining himself to personal details and anecdotes, many of them of a scandalous nature.

The scandals of the empire brought blistering attacks from the satiric poet Juvenal (who wrote after A.D. 100). In his verse, we find once more that continuing trait in Roman literature, a longing for the past and its ideals. Juvenal, in his satires on the moral lows of "high" society, the "wickedness" of women, and the indignities of life in the great metropolis, pointed again and again to the "good old days" of early Rome.

ROMAN EPICUREANISM AND STOICISM

The Romans borrowed freely from Greek philosophy as well as from Greek literature. But it was not the thought of Plato or Aristotle that attracted them. Rather, they were drawn to the more individualistic philosophies of the Hellenistic period. One of these was Epicureanism, which enjoyed a vogue among educated Romans. Epicurus, who had taught in Athens around 300 B.C., concentrated not on cosmic problems but on ways of achieving individual happiness. (In this aim, he followed the lead of the earlier Greek Sophists; p. 80.) The chief promoter of his teachings in the West was the Roman poet Lucretius (first century B.C.), who articulated them in his eloquent *De Rerum Natura* (*On the Nature of Things*). This poem is also a hymn to Epicurus himself, whom Lucretius praises for having liberated the human mind from superstitious fears.

Epicurus had presented a "scientific" and materialist view of the universe. Setting aside mythological explanations, he accepted the principle of Democritus of Abdera (p. 79), which reduces all matter to atoms. To Epicurus, all forms of existence are temporary combinations of minute, imperishable particles. Only the laws of motion and chance determine the shape and character of things, and there is no governing "purpose" on earth or in the heavens.

In such a universe, Epicurus believed, the only logical aim for the individual is to strive for personal happiness. As a guide in the search for happiness, Epicurus formulated this basic equation: happiness equals pleasure minus pain. He suggested that the major way to secure happiness is by decreasing the pain factor of the equation, rather than by increasing the pleasure factor. Though he conceded the existence of bodily aches, Epicurus taught that fear, the "ache of mind and heart," is the deepest source of human pain, and fear feeds on ignorance and superstition.

Religious teachings, Epicurus had charged, were aimed at frightening simpleminded believers with tales of darkness, terror, and punishment. Priests and magicians played on the fear of death in order to serve their own purposes. Epicurus was no atheist; he did not deny the existence of the gods (whom he thought of as made of atoms). But, he insisted, the gods live far from humans and have no concern for them. Prayer is useless, for one cannot expect help from the gods. To dispel the dread of death, Epicurus insisted that death is nothing—simply a separation of atoms: "Death, usually regarded as the greatest of calamities, is actually nothing to us; while we are, death is not, and when death is here, we are not."

The pursuit of pleasure—the other factor in Epicurus' "happiness equation"—is an art more difficult than the avoidance of fear. Epicurus warned that what he called "dynamic" (restless) pleasures such as eating and drinking are usually self-defeating, for they stimulate appetites that act as fresh sources of pain (until they have been satisfied). Rather than feed these appetites, he thought it wiser to discipline them to reduce their influence on behavior.

Epicurus urged the cultivation of the "passive" (quiet) pleasures, such as literature, recollection and meditation, personal friendship, and the enjoyment of nature. He shunned the pursuit of wealth or public office, for it often brings disappointment, trouble, and pain. Epicurus valued, above all, calmness, poise, and serenity of mind.

The most influential of the philosophies Roman intellectuals imported from the East was Stoicism. One reason, no doubt, is that its ethical code paralleled the traditional Roman virtues. We might almost say that the Romans had practiced Stoicism before hearing of it. The term itself derives from the porch (*stoa*) in Athens where Zeno, the founder of Stoicism, had taught (about 300 B.C.). Zeno, like Epicurus, had a materialist view of the universe. But passive matter, he held, contains an active principle known variously as "divine fire," "providence," "reason," and "God." The universe is not chaos; rather, it functions according to a plan of goodness. Although people cannot control what is beyond themselves, they are masters of their own beings: they can hold themselves ignorant, rebel against nature, or live in harmony with it.

Harmony and happiness, declared the Stoics, are achieved by striving for virtue rather than pleasure. Virtue, according to their definition, consists of understanding nature through reason, accepting by self-discipline God's purpose, and living in accordance with duty, truth, and natural law (justice). They regarded all persons as inherently equal, because all share, in common with God, the spark of reason. Consequently, they challenged the ancient practice of slavery and taught that all individuals should tolerate, forgive, and love one another as brothers and sisters. The ideal Stoic is self-sufficient, dutiful, compassionate, and calm.

The followers of Stoicism included Cicero, the noble lawyer and senator; Seneca, the writer and adviser to the emperor Nero; and Epictetus, once a learned slave in

Nero's court. But the Roman who most closely lived a Stoic life was an emperor—Marcus Aurelius. The last of the "good emperors" of the second century (p. 124), he embodied Plato's dream that kings should be philosophers, or philosopher-kings (p. 82). Day by day, he set down his innermost thoughts in a little book, called *Meditations* (thoughts to himself). The work of God (providence), wrote Marcus Aurelius, is in its totality good. But specific events may seem harmful to the individual who is immediately affected by them. In order to live in wisdom and harmony, individuals must learn to accept such events as necessary to the total good. Then personal suffering will actually give them a sense of participation in the greater works of providence. No matter what their lot, they will bless God and conduct themselves calmly.

Stoicism, as formulated by Marcus Aurelius, was quite in accord with the ancient Roman virtues. "Let it be your hourly care," he advised, "to do stoutly what the hand finds to do, as becomes a man and a Roman, with carefulness, unaffected dignity, humanity, freedom, and justice. . . . Perform every action as though it were the last of your life, without light-mindedness, without swerving through force of passion from the dictates of reason." The individual should live one day at a time, leaving the past to itself and entrusting the future to providence. Every man, whether emperor or slave, must do his duty as it falls to him. Thus nature's plan is served, and the individual's life is blended with that of the universe.

Stoicism made a significant mark on Roman times and influenced the future; it offered a noble standard of conduct and in its ethics anticipated Christianity. Perhaps the most direct influence, however, was on Roman legal thought, in which the Stoic idea of "natural law"—law identical with reason and God—was of high importance.

SCIENCE AND MEDICINE

In literature and philosophy, we have seen that the Romans were essentially preservers and carriers of Hellenistic culture. The same is true in the sciences. While Athens remained the leading center for philosophical studies, Alexandria (in Egypt) continued as the hub of scientific and medical works. It was there, in the second century A.D., that the Greek astronomer and geographer Claudius Ptolemy compiled his marvelous *Almagest.* (The title is Arabic, meaning "the greatest [work]," for the book was neglected in Europe after the fall of Rome but continued to be studied and admired by Muslim scholars; p. 208.) Bringing together the accumulated learning of the Greeks about the earth and the heavenly bodies, Ptolemy set forth a model of the universe that was generally accepted in the West until the scientific revolution of the seventeenth century (pp. 418–424).

Of equal influence was a series of books written about the same time by a Greek physician, Galen of Pergamum (in Asia Minor). Galen stressed the importance of personal hygiene to health, and his views on anatomy and physiology were accepted until the emergence of scientific biology in the seventeenth century (p. 424).

Roman Law

The Romans were vigorous originators in the field of law, and their most enduring contribution to Western institutions lay in legal theory and practice.

THE EVOLUTION OF ROMAN LAW

In the later Republic, the Romans gradually developed the idea that the law of the state should reflect what is right according to universal reason. Hence they used the word *justitia,* which is related to *justus,* or "right." According to Cicero's definition, "Law is the just distinction between right and wrong, made conformable to most ancient nature."

As we have seen (p. 111), the "customary" laws that the patrician judges had been observing were recorded in the Twelve Tablets during the fifth century B.C. This code included the rules of evidence in judicial hearings; provision for the calling and questioning of witnesses; specification of crimes and their punishments (involving the death penalty for numerous kinds of acts); and the special rights of husbands and fathers (including the right of "life and death" over their children and the right to divorce their wives for any given reason). The Twelve Tablets remained the basis of Roman law for centuries. Although it provided for harsh penalties, the judges gradually modified them through interpretation. The rulings of the courts thus conformed ever more closely to *justitia.*

After 366 B.C. a special magistrate, called a *praetor,* was elected annually to administer justice to the citizens of Rome. He was expected to follow the code of the Twelve Tablets but was given some freedom in interpreting it. Each praetor, at the start of his term, was required to announce his own interpretation of the law. Through this interpretive decree and through his daily decisions, he adapted the original tablets to the cases before him. By 246 B.C., another praetor had been established, to deal with disputes between Roman citizens and foreigners under Roman jurisdiction. This official had a still wider basis for interpretations, for he could draw on the various foreign laws, as well as on Roman law, in arriving at fair decisions and settlements. Thus there grew up, in the days of the Republic, two distinct bodies of law: the law of citizens, or *jus civile,* and the law of "peoples," or *jus gentium*

Because the law of peoples drew from broader sources than the law of citizens, the Roman praetor for citizens tended to be guided more and more in his own decisions by the *jus gentium.* By the first century A.D., the basic provisions of the two bodies of law had been brought close together; after 212, when all free inhabitants of the empire were declared Roman citizens, the dual system disappeared. From that time on—in theory, at least, and usually in practice—one system of law prevailed throughout the empire.

Under the empire, the ancient statutes of the Republic were further expanded by the decrees and interpretations of rulers and by the opinions and commentaries of legal experts. The praetors themselves were not always professional lawyers, and even during the first century B.C., they had established the custom of consulting men who were "skilled in the law" (*jurisprudentes*). The emperors regularly appointed outstanding legal scholars to advise magistrates on specific cases. Since the Romans had profound respect for the law and for experts in law, the commentaries carried considerable authority. The judicial traditions of the West owe much to the clarifying and humanizing influence of these fair-minded and dedicated scholars.

THE IDEA OF "NATURAL LAW"

Most of the jurists were well-educated men who felt at home with Stoic philosophy. They observed that the laws of nations had many elements in common and that the laws themselves were gradually fusing into the single law of the empire. This similarity in legal ideas among the peoples of the empire coincided nicely with the Stoic belief that there was one law in nature, the law of reason. From this the jurists inferred the reality of "natural law" and concluded that human rules could and should conform to this "higher law." Thus the Roman experience, supported by Hellenistic philosophy, gave rise to the doctrine of natural law, or *jus naturale.*

This doctrine, which has deeply influenced legal theory in the West, is the basis of the idea of law and human rights contained in the United States Declaration of Independence. Cicero, in the *Laws,* observed, "Law and equity have been established not by opinion but by nature." The regulations of states that do not conform to reason, he declared, are not truly laws and do not deserve obedience. Clearly, this doctrine is a two-edged sword: it gives added authority to laws that citizens regard as right but in the case of laws they believe to be *wrong,* it opens the door to disobedience (and rebellion).

CODIFICATION OF THE LAWS

Over the centuries, several emperors tried to bring a degree of order into the mounting accumulation of laws, interpretations, principles, and procedures. But it was not until the sixth century (after the division of the Roman Empire) that a complete codification was carried through, under the emperor Justinian (p. 198). Justinian's *Corpus Juris Civilis* (*Body of Civil Law*) consists of several parts: the *Digest,* a summary of judicial opinions and commentaries; the *Code,* a collection of statutes from Hadrian to Justinian; the *Novels,* a collection of statutes enacted after the publication of the *Code;* and the *Institutes,* a brief discussion of legal principles, designed for law students. Justinian's great codification became the foundation for the legal systems that were later developed throughout Europe. Hundreds of millions of people today live under systems that are modeled, in whole or in part, on Roman law as found in the *Corpus.*

Architecture and Engineering

The Romans built their state, their law, and their public structures for eternity, and there is no more impressive proof of their sense of power and permanence than their architecture. After centuries of erosion and vandalism, the ruins of hundreds of Roman buildings still stand on three continents—from the shores of the eastern Mediterranean to the Scottish border. Although the architects of Rome borrowed and adapted techniques from a wide variety of styles, the primary influences were Etruscan and Hellenistic. The Romans built on a larger scale than the Greeks, however; while the typical Greek city-state had to provide public structures for only a few thousand citizens, the population of Rome numbered hundreds of thousands. The Romans, moreover, developed a taste for grandeur, elegance, and display, and they expressed this taste freely in their architecture.

Construction materials were readily available: the Italian peninsula had plenty of timber and stone, as well as good clays (for brick) and lava and sandy earth (for concrete). Other materials, such as decorative marble, were often imported. Brick and concrete faced with stucco or marble veneer were the materials most commonly used in Rome itself.

© Adam Woolfitt/CORBIS

Fig. 3.3 The Pont du Gard. Completed in 19 B.C. as part of a 30-mile aqueduct supplying the city of Nemausus in southern Gaul (present-day Nîmes, France), this bridge carried a water channel for 300 yards across the 160-foot valley of the River Gard. The top tier of arches slopes slightly to allow the water to flow rapidly and stay clean. The bridge is built of accurately cut stones that hold together by their own weight without cement, yet the structure is so strong that the bottom row of arches carries a roadway used by modern motor vehicles.

ARCHITECTURAL FORMS AND AIMS

Although the Romans made some use of the post-and-lintel method of construction (p. 37), their preference in large buildings was for the *arch, vault,* and *dome*—all first used in ancient Sumer (p. 22). They realized that an arch formed of bricks, stones, or poured concrete could carry a far heavier load than a stone beam supported at either end by a post or column. And they discovered that a series of arches placed side by side could carry a bridge or an aqueduct across a deep valley (*Fig. 3.3*).

The vault is actually an extension of the arch. The typical tunnel, or barrel, vault is an arch extended in depth to produce a tunnel-shaped enclosure of the desired width and length (*Fig. 3.4a,* p. 138). Because this type of vault admits light only at the two ends, however, it is of limited usefulness in public structures. To overcome this difficulty, Roman architects devised the *cross-vault* plan, which permits light to enter from the sides as well. It consists of one or more short vaults intersecting the main vault at right angles (*Fig. 3.4b,* p. 138). This kind of structure can be carried to a substantial height and can be made to enclose a huge space with no need for supporting members between floor and ceiling.

Another architectural form used by the Romans to provide an uncluttered enclosure was the dome, which is simply a hemisphere resting on a cylindrical wall or on a circle of supporting arches (*Fig. 3.5,* p. 139). A large dome was built up of a series of progressively smaller horizontal rings of brick, stone, or concrete. When completed, the parts formed a single unit firmly set in place.

Fig. 3.4 Roman Vaulting Systems. (a) Barrel vault; (b) cross-vault. These structures, developed in countless different ways, continued to be basic features of large public buildings for many centuries down to the nineteenth-century invention of steel-frame construction. For cross-vaulting, see, for instance, *Fig. 6.3,* p. 259; and for barrel vaulting, *Fig 9.9,* p. 394).

⏐ The Romans were especially clever in designing structures to serve the practical needs of the population. To provide their cities with water for public baths and orna-mental fountains and also to ensure a good supply of drinking water, they built great aqueducts leading down from distant mountain springs. Much of the way, the water descended through pipes or channels in the mountains or hills, but across a valley or a plain it flowed through a channel carried by an aqueduct. Since the Romans had no me-chanical pumps, the aqueduct had to be engineered so that the water flowed steadily by force of gravity alone. The famous Pont du Gard (*Fig. 3.3,* p. 137) is part of a Roman aqueduct that once carried water across the Gard River and valley to the provincial city of Nîmes, in southern Gaul (France). The upper level of arches supported a covered water channel 900 feet in length. The entire structure, 180 feet high, was built of stone blocks fitted together without mortar.

Roman engineers also reduced the spread of disease from marshy areas, especially south of the capital. Mosquitoes, the carriers of malaria, breed easily in wetlands. By means of extensive drainage works, the Romans—without understanding the mecha-nism of the disease—hit at the source of malaria.

⏐ Perhaps the most impressive practical achievement of the Romans was their wide-ranging network of roads. Like the Assyrians and Persians before them (pp. 45, 47), they needed a swift and reliable means of overland movement to control, defend, and expand their empire. Over the centuries, they built or improved some 50,000 miles of roads, reaching out from Rome to the farthest corners of the empire. Constructed by a variety of methods, the typical roadbed was about 15 feet wide and 5 feet deep. Broken stone and gravel were packed down to form a foundation and then carefully graded to ensure solidity and good drainage. The surface was usually of dirt, except in the neigh-borhood of towns, where traffic was heaviest and thick blocks of hard stone were used.

The army, government officials, and the emperor's messengers had priority in the use of the strategically planned system of roads, but roads were also open to the public in general. The roads were regularly patrolled, and on the major arteries, there was a stable every 10 miles and a hostel every 30 miles for the use of official travelers. No road system comparable to the Roman highways was to be undertaken again until the twen-tieth century.

Fig. 3.5 The Pantheon. Emperor Hadrian built this temple in Rome about A.D. 120 after fire had destroyed an earlier one dating from Augustus' time. Out of Roman reverence for the past, Hadrian had an inscription carved above the entrance columns that names only the original builder: "Constructed by Marcus Agrippa in His Third Term as Consul." The Pantheon's dome is a shallow one, as if the builders were cautiously experimenting with an unfamiliar structural form. Nevertheless, the dome is the ancestor of its much younger neighbor, the dome of Saint Peter's Basilica (*Fig. 8.14*, p. 357).

In domestic architecture, the wealthy Romans found their model in the dwellings of the ancient Etruscans. The basic plan of the Roman villa, with its central court (*atrium*) partly open to the sky, was Etruscan in origin. Such homes were extremely comfortable and luxurious, as we can tell from the remains of the splendid houses at Pompeii, located near Naples. (An eruption of Mount Vesuvius in A.D. 79 buried the city in layers of lava and ashes, preserving it virtually intact.) Excavations have revealed the well-designed homes, with their fountains, sculptures, wall paintings, mosaics, and metalware. The great mass of the urban populations, however, lived in crowded apartment buildings. Examples of these have been uncovered at Ostia, a port and suburb of Rome.

CIVIC ARCHITECTURE AND MONUMENTS

It is in public buildings, however, that we find the grandest and most enduring monuments of Roman architecture. Every major city of the empire had a public square—a *forum*—that served as a civic center. The Roman Forum, for example, was a marketplace in the early days of the Republic, but it was gradually transformed into an impressive meeting place with handsome statues, temples, and halls of government. Overlooking the Forum was the sacred Capitoline Hill, topped by the temple of Jupiter, while across the Forum, on the Palatine Hill, stood the palaces of the emperors.

Several emperors constructed their own forums in Rome as memorials to themselves. One of these, the Forum of Trajan, was built early in the second century A.D. on a spacious site near the Capitoline Hill. Symmetrically laid out, it included a large area for shops, an imposing public hall (*basilica*), a library, and a temple dedicated to the deified emperor. Dominating all the rest was the towering marble Column of Trajan, with a spiral band of sculptured relief (3 feet high and 650 feet long) retelling the emperor's conquests.

Most of the public meeting halls in Rome and the other cities of the empire were built in the style of the basilica or "imperial hall" (from *basileus,* the Greek word for "emperor"). This was a rectangular building constructed either on the cross-vault principle or with a roof supported by columns in the Greek manner. In either case, there was a wide central aisle (*nave*) running the length of the building, with narrower side aisles. By lifting the roof of the center aisle higher than the roof of the side aisles, the architects were able to admit light through a series of "clerestory" windows. A semi-circular area, called an *apse,* was joined to one end; sometimes there was an apse at each end. Covered by a half-dome, the apse was frequently walled off from the central hall and used as a chamber for courts of law. In the fourth century, when the Christians were finally permitted to build public houses of worship, they adapted the basilica to their own needs. The congregation stood in the open rectangular area, and the apse was used to house the altar and sacred objects. This plan of church architecture persisted for centuries (*Fig. 3.6*).

The usual Roman temple resembled the Greek, but it followed more precisely an Etruscan plan. Though columns were used to support the roof, the Roman temple stood on a higher base (*podium*) than the Greek and faced in only one direction. The most impressive of all Roman temples, however, has a design unlike that of earlier structures. It is the Pantheon in Rome (*Fig. 3.5,* p. 139), a temple dedicated to all the gods (from the Greek *pantes theoi,* "all the gods"). The present building is actually a reconstruction ordered by the emperor Hadrian about A.D. 120 to replace the original temple, which had been destroyed by fire.

The Pantheon consists of a round central hall, or *rotunda,* capped by a vast concrete dome. To carry the great weight of the dome, the rotunda wall was built 20 feet thick. The height of the dome and its diameter are identical (140 feet), assuring geometric balance, and the dome is pierced by an eye (*oculus*) 30 feet across, which serves as the source of light. Originally, it is believed, statues of the seven "planetary" deities stood in the seven niches cut into the wall. There is a single doorway, which is approached through a Greek-style porch. From the outside, the Pantheon has a squat, heavy appearance, but the interior gives a dramatic impression of space and buoyancy.

The civilization of the empire, as we have seen, was mainly urban, and elaborate structures were erected to satisfy the recreational needs of city people. Particularly popular were the public bathhouses (*thermae*), which were equipped with steam rooms and small pools filled with hot, lukewarm, or cold water. The emperors courted popular favor also by donating magnificent pleasure palaces that housed not only baths but large indoor and outdoor swimming pools, gymnasiums, gardens, libraries, galleries, theaters, lounges, and bars. Because these recreational centers were especially attrac-

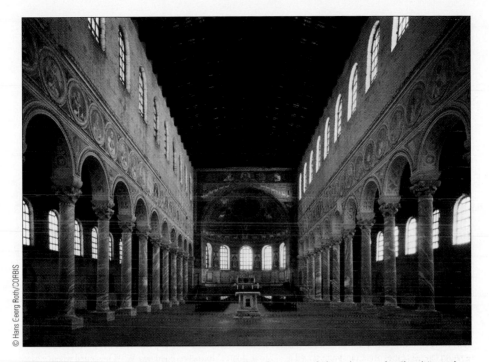

Fig. 3.6 Sant'Apollinare in Classe. This church was built in the seaport of Classis (present-day Classe) in north-eastern Italy, to honor the town's first bishop, Saint Apollinaris. The church dates from A.D. 535–538, nearly five centuries after Apollinaris and seventy years after the last emperor reigned in Rome, but it is modeled on a traditional Roman type of public building, a basilica. Classis had once been an important imperial naval base, and the church's construction was a sign of the town's continuing wealth and civilization in spite of the empire's troubles.

tive to the lower classes and to idlers, their reputation in polite society was not altogether respectable.

The best-preserved pleasure palace in Rome is the complex of buildings known as the Baths of Diocletian, built in the late third century A.D. Its main hall, which once enclosed a huge swimming pool, is constructed on the cross-vault principle. It is 300 feet long, 90 feet wide, and 90 feet high. It is estimated that the baths could accommodate three thousand bathers in lavish surroundings of gilt and marble.

One of the most popular pastimes of the Romans was watching the chariot races of the circus and the gory combats of the arena. As the theater symbolized the cultural tastes of the ancient Greeks, the arena best symbolized the cultural tastes of the Romans. Although every city of the empire had places for mass entertainment, the most famous arena was the Colosseum of Rome (*Fig. 3.7*). This huge structure, which covers about 6 acres and seated more than fifty thousand spectators, was the largest of its kind. The crowds made their way to their seats through some eighty entry vaults, and the stairways were arranged so that the stadium could be emptied in minutes.

A variety of materials was used in the construction of the Colosseum. Key areas of stress, such as archways and vaults, were generally of brick; other sections were of concrete and broken stone. The outer facing was divided into three stories topped by a high wall of stone blocks. Between the arches of each story, and above them in the high

© Historical Picture Archive/CORBIS

Fig. 3.7 The Colosseum. A new imperial dynasty, the Flavians, built this famous arena in A.D. 72–82 to win popularity in the city of Rome by providing mass entertainment on a spectacular scale. The entertainment—mainly gladiatorial combats, wild beast hunts, and mock sea battles—continued until 523, when the city's decay ended them. In later centuries, the Colosseum served as a "stone quarry" for newer buildings. What remained when preservation eventually replaced quarrying, as seen in this engraving of 1761 by Giovanni Piranesi, was still a huge and impressive structure.

wall, were placed Greek-style half-columns. Sockets set inside the high wall once held great poles, on which protective awnings could be mounted. A coating of marble originally covered the exterior of the Colosseum, but the marble (and other building material) was carried off over the centuries for use in other structures.

Underneath the arena floor, which was made of wood covered with sand, lay a maze of corridors, chambers, and cells, where animals and humans (mainly slaves or criminals) awaited their turn at combat. These contests were usually fought to the death, but the crowd's appetite for violence was hard to satisfy. "Roman holidays," about one hundred a year, were lengthy affairs, lasting from early morning till dark. Wealthy donors seeking popularity usually paid the bills, including the cost of food and refreshments.

To impress the citizens and the thousands of visitors who flocked to Rome, the emperors ordered monuments built in their own honor—triumphal arches, columns, and statues (*Fig. I.1*, p. xxx). These edifices are still to be found in abundance in the Eternal City, as well as in the provinces. Like the mighty Column of Trajan, they carry a sense of pride, power, and permanence. To the Roman rulers, works of sculpture were also viewed as a medium of propaganda. They might relate the events of a military campaign or simply present the unaffected portrait of a man. Figures of gods and goddesses were based on Greek models, and the same idealized style might be used to represent the rulers themselves (*Fig. 3.8*). Most Roman portraits, however, are extremely

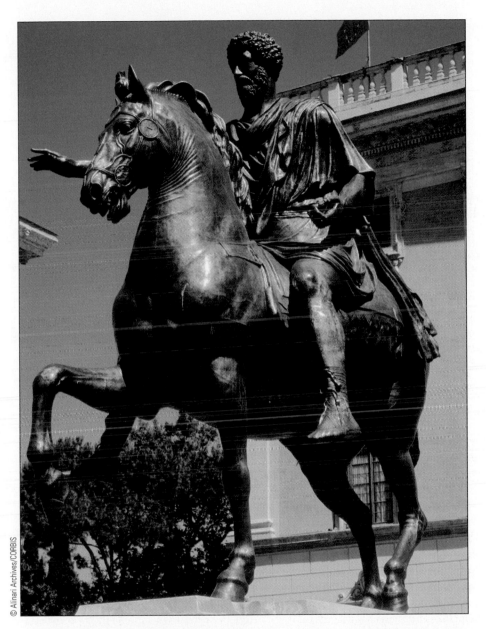

Fig. 3.8 Emperor Marcus Aurelius. The strength and eagerness of the horse express the power and authority of the rider who controls it, and the rider's high-browed, bearded face (modeled on depictions of Greek philosophers) and his outstretched arm speak of wisdom and mercy. This bronze equestrian (horse-riding) statue has inspired many other masterpieces since it was set up in Rome about A.D. 165 (*Fig. 8.7*, p. 350). Michelangelo, who designed the statue's present pedestal, was supposedly so taken with the horse's lifelike quality that when the pedestal was ready, he commanded the animal to walk forward onto it.

Fig. 3.9 Portrait of a Roman. This carving, from about 80 B.C., depicts an unknown patrician. By long-standing religious custom, when a patrician died, his family had a wax death mask made, exactly rendering his face, which was carried in his own and later funeral processions. But wax was perishable, and the custom grew up of reproducing the masks as marble busts. A fine artist would carve not just a replica but a study of character—in this case, an aged but strong-minded, shrewd, and perhaps grimly humorous noble Roman.

© Alinari/Art Resource, NY

lifelike (*Fig. 3.9*). The National Museum of Naples possesses a superb collection of original busts of emperors, each bearing the mark of an individual personality.

The End of Rome and the Beginning of Europe

With the death of Marcus Aurelius in A.D. 180, the great age of the Pax Romana ended and the era of "decline and fall" began. But the weakening of the Roman Empire was a lengthy and gradual process marked by periods of recovery. For much of the time, the average citizen had no sense of sudden catastrophe; despite the many ills of the empire, life went on much the same. Scholars have written hundreds of volumes on the problems the empire faced; their evidence suggests that several weakening forces were at work.

THE PROBLEMS OF THE EMPIRE

One of these factors was the economic weakness of the western portion of the empire. Under the Republic, Italy had been able to live off the profits of conquest, but after Augustus' time, these mostly came to an end. In provinces such as Spain and Gaul, there was a period of prosperity following on the Roman conquest as cities were founded, agriculture flourished, and commerce developed. Even so, the West had fewer people, cities, and economic resources than the East. To meet the needs of the army and the civil government, tax rates had to be raised. This led to gradual impoverishment of tax-payers, which the government tried to make up for by boosting taxes still further.

Besides these economic problems, the empire began to suffer from an inability to ensure stable and effective leadership. Toward the end of the second century, the line of emperors by adoption and designation came to an end when Marcus Aurelius' son by blood, the worthless Commodus, outlived him and became emperor. Commodus was murdered after twelve years of irresponsible rule, and rival generals then fought one another to take over the imperial office. Even successful and capable emperors were beholden to the soldiers of the armies that won them the supreme power; the result-ing gifts and pay raises increased the burden on the empire's resources. These difficul-ties, in turn, made it harder for the empire to deal with a third major problem: the still-unconquered barbarian peoples who lived to the north of its European frontiers. These were the Germanic peoples, who spoke closely related Indo-European languages and had much the same way of life as other Indo-European barbarians like the Celts—or, for that matter, the Greeks and Romans before they became civilized (pp. 57–59).

The Germanic peoples were farmers, livestock breeders, and warriors, living a set-tled life in villages but liable to move around in search of new land or as a result of de-feat in war or natural disasters. Neighboring villages formed more or less permanent tribes (p. 59), and each tribe also had a nobility based on birth. In addition, there were some individuals who were "bound" to do labor for others in payment for debt; and there were slaves who had been captured in battle.

The Germans also had their characteristic political and military institutions. Within the tribe, each village held a monthly assembly, open to all free males, which served as both a council and a court of justice. (There were no written laws until after the Germans moved into the empire.) The principal tribal military unit was the *comi-tatus* or war band, a group of elite warriors who pledged themselves to follow a tribal chieftain and defend him with their lives. The chieftain, in turn, supported the war-riors and gave them a share in the spoils.

Before historic times, the Germanic tribes had lived in Scandinavia and northern Germany, but by the time of Caesar, they had spread into the broad area between the Baltic and North seas and the Rhine-Danube frontier. In the third century A.D., they moved into eastern Europe as well. The Romans applied the name of one of the tribes, the *Germani,* to the tribes in general and spoke of their homelands south of the Baltic Sea as *Germania* (Germany)—a considerably larger area than the present-day country of that name (*Map 3.2,* p. 114).

As soon as the Romans, for their part, reached north of the Alps, they came into close contact with the Germanic tribes. These contacts were just as often friendly as hostile, for the tribes had no feelings of solidarity among themselves and no deliberate intention of destroying the empire. Many Germans joined the supporting forces of the Roman army, and some enlisted in the legions themselves. It became a common prac-tice for the Romans to permit—or sometimes even compel—fairly large groups to settle within the frontier as a buffer against further encroachment.

Over the centuries, contact with Rome brought changes among the Germanic tribes. Whether as enemies or as soldiers of Rome, the Germanic warriors learned the empire's methods of fighting and adopted its weapons. Trade, loot, and Roman subsi-dies to friendly tribes brought greater wealth to Germany than before. Warfare among the tribes became more profitable, fiercer, and broader in scale. From late in the second century A.D., the tribes began to form larger confederacies led by powerful chieftains and their war bands. Thriving on warfare, wealthy from loot or Roman subsidies, and eager to spend their wealth on the luxurious trappings of the upper-class Roman way of life, the members of the war bands became an elite that stood somewhat apart from the average Germanic warrior-tribesmen. With the ability to field armies as large as twenty thousand warriors, the tribal confederacies had formidable war-making capacity, both against each other and against Rome. Ironically, the more advanced the Germanic barbarians became under Roman influence, the more dangerous they were to the empire.

About the middle of the third century, the combination of diminishing resources, political divisions, and growing barbarian strength brought about a crisis that almost destroyed the empire. The economic situation was made even worse by a decline in population. This came about mainly from repeated outbreaks of disease, spread through much of the empire by Roman troops who had campaigned in Syria. Political collapse set in as provincial armies battled to advance their favorite candidates, and the imperial succession was determined by the clash of legions. Surprisingly, many of the emperors so chosen proved to be effective leaders. This did not save them from violent death, however, and their terms of office were generally short.

Profiting from the civil wars, barbarian tribal confederacies devastated the empire from Gaul to the Black Sea. Even territories far from the frontiers, such as Spain, Greece, and Italy itself, were looted by barbarian war bands. In the East, meanwhile, the Parthian kingdom (p. 124) had been overthrown by a revived Persian kingdom, whose rulers looked to revive the great empire of earlier centuries (pp. 45–48) at Rome's expense and now ravaged the provinces of the Middle East. The entire empire seemed on the brink of falling apart.

RECONSTITUTION OF THE EMPIRE BY DIOCLETIAN AND CONSTANTINE

At last, in A.D. 284, a ruler came to power who in origin was simply another victor in the struggle for power but who had the shrewdness and good fortune to avoid sudden death, and the vision and determination to rescue the failing empire. Diocletian was in many ways a typical third-century emperor. Born in Illyria (modern Croatia; *Map 3.3*, p. 125), the son of a freed slave, he enlisted in the ranks, worked his way up, and was at last proclaimed emperor by his troops. Rivals contested his claim to the throne, but he subdued them all. After a reign of some twenty years, he retired voluntarily to a palatial estate at Split, in his native Illyria. Diocletian is often credited with undertakings that were begun before his time, but all the same, he was the principal agent in shoring up the crumbling foundations of the empire.

Diocletian found that most of the empire's sources of support during the era of the Roman peace—above all the Senate and the cities—had been undermined by the calamities of the third century. Instead, he was obliged to use and strengthen the only means left to him: the imperial bureaucracy, the army, and his imperial authority. Consequently, the "late empire" took on the character of a centralized and militarized sacred monarchy.

The End of the Augustan Settlement. Diocletian's first major step was to overhaul the civil administration. The empire was now too big, he decided, for one man to administer, so he divided it in two. In theory, Diocletian was still monarch of the entire empire. But he moved his capital to Nicomedia, close to the Bosporus (*Map 3.3,* p. 125), taking direct charge of the eastern portion, and in 286, he appointed a fellow general, Maximian, as joint ruler to govern the western portion from Milan. (Milan was closer than Rome to the threatened frontiers.) After 293, these two senior emperors or *augusti* were each assisted by a junior colleague (a *caesar*), who was assigned to rule a specified subportion (*prefecture*). Thus began the separation of East and West, which became complete and permanent in 395.

Diocletian reduced the size of the individual provinces, increased their number, placed them under closer supervision, and stripped the provincial governors of their former command of troops. The 120 provinces were grouped into twelve units called *dioceses;* the dioceses were in turn grouped into four prefectures, each ruled by one of the augusti or caesars. This arrangement of ascending ranks of authority (*hierarchy*) ensured stricter control from the top and reduced the possibility of provincial revolts, which had plagued the third century.

In his reform of the military establishment, Diocletian broke with centuries of Roman military tradition. The third century had brought new threats—more numerous and better-armed Germanic barbarian raiders and Persian attacks spearheaded by forces of heavily armed and armored cavalry. Diocletian began a series of reforms to meet these threats that by early in the fourth century produced what amounted to a new Roman army.

The old legions were broken up into smaller units. Some of these were stationed in heavily fortified outposts along the frontiers, others were assigned to mobile armies in each diocese, and still others to central reserve forces in the imperial capitals. Infantry arms and armor were lighter and fortifications much stronger than before; cavalry—in particular, Persian-style heavy cavalry, the forerunners of the knights of the Middle Ages—was far more important than in the days of the legions. All this required an increase in troop strength, to perhaps as much as double what it had been since Augustus' time (p. 122). To reach these numbers, more and more of the soldiers had to be recruited from the barbarians, and in time many of them became loyal Romans and rose to positions of high command (*Fig. 3.10,* p. 148).

In this way, Diocletian and his successors managed to restore order in the empire and on the frontiers. But it was at the price of breaking the limits on the size of the bureaucracy and the army that every emperor since Augustus had more or less kept to, and thereby imposing on the citizens a heavy burden of tax payments and supply deliveries. To increase the yield of taxes, Diocletian ordered a new survey of the empire's population and wealth and revised the methods of tax collection. A thousand years

© Alinari/Art Resource, NY

Fig. 3.10 Stilicho, Honorius, and Flaccilla. The Roman general Stilicho was by birth a Vandal (one of the Germanic tribal confederations). This ivory diptych (two-part picture customarily commissioned by officials of the late empire to commemorate important promotions) probably dates from A.D. 395, when the former tribal warrior (*left*) became the effective ruler of the empire's western half as guardian of the youthful emperor Honorius (*right*, with his mother, Flaccilla). Eventually, Stilicho was killed by a rival at court, but the diptych shows the "merger" of Romans and barbarians already well under way.

later, his innovations would be studied and imitated by many European rulers when they, too, wanted to collect more taxes so as to provide for larger armies (p9. 409–410). But neither Diocletian nor his advisers knew enough about economics to deal with the deeper problems.

A tough old soldier, Diocletian tried to deal with economic problems as if they had been barbarian invaders—by giving orders. In a heroic attempt to check inflation, he issued an "edict of maximum prices," which froze the price level of all basic commodities. To reduce tax evasion and banditry, he ordered that critical occupations be made hereditary and that all persons remain at their jobs. These sweeping decrees discouraged business owners, destroyed the mobility of the labor force, weakened what was left of individual incentive, and made workers virtual slaves to their jobs. Strict enforcement proved impossible, though substantial efforts were made to put the decrees into effect.

Sacred Monarchy and the Worship of the Gods. From the beginning of his reign, Diocletian realized that he had to strengthen respect for imperial authority if he was to hold the empire together and win acceptance of his reform decrees. Following the trend of centuries, he transformed the imperial office into a sacred monarchy. He was not content, as Augustus had been, simply to accept the veneration of the citizens for his genius (pp. 121–122). Instead, he claimed to be Jupiter in human form, while Maximian (his joint ruler) was Hercules. Diocletian expected all citizens of the empire, whatever other deities they might worship, to be devoted to Jupiter as the father and ruler of the traditional gods and goddesses of Rome and to himself as Jupiter's earthly embodiment. And he built or restored many temples of other gods and goddesses, a form of piety that the emperors had neglected amid the succession struggles and barbarian invasions of the third century.

The emperor's court ceremonial matched his new divine status. The title of princeps, preferred by Augustus, gave way to *dominus* (lord). At Nicomedia, Diocletian built a two-thousand–room palace of oriental splendor, set in a vast park. From the ancient Persian monarchs he copied regalia (kingly garments and emblems) dating back to the Great King, Darius (p. 46). On state occasions, the emperor sat on an immense throne beneath a canopy of Persian blue and the glittering emblem of the sun. He wore a magnificent costume, gold fingernails, and a crown of pearls. Visitors, after being screened by the secret police, were brought to the throne room through a maze of chambers, doorways, and corridors. When at last they came into the emperor's presence, they were required to lie flat on the floor before his sacred person. These arrangements served to overwhelm the emperor's visitors with a sense of mystery and majesty.

In these ways, Diocletian probably hoped to give stability and legitimacy to imperial rule. He himself, his colleagues, and their successors would no longer be successful contenders for power who had been chosen by the armies; rather, they would be gods chosen by the gods. Furthermore, as a pious traditional pagan, Diocletian undoubtedly felt that Rome's troubles were above all due to the fact that by neglecting the gods, it had lost their favor. By rallying the citizens around the city's traditional deities, he would win back the support of the divine power that ruled the universe.

Constantine and Christianity. Diocletian succeeded in reestablishing imperial authority. But like his predecessors, he failed to solve the troublesome succession issue. He had planned an orderly procedure, with the caesars becoming augusti as the senior rulers retired or died and then appointing new caesars who would eventually become augusti in their turn. But the system was not proof against power struggles among the rulers themselves, which broke out as soon as Diocletian's guiding hand was removed. After years of dreary fighting, one among the various claimants to power, Constantine I, emerged as sole victor. By 324, he had disposed of all rivals, and for a brief period there was again one empire and one emperor.

Constantine carried forward most of Diocletian's reforms. His major departure, inaugurating a basic change in the nature of Roman civilization itself, was in the empire's policy toward Christians. (The rise of the Christian Church is discussed in Chapter 4.) Diocletian had persecuted the Christians in the belief that they were undermining his efforts to win back for the empire the favor of the gods. But in 313, Constantine ordered complete freedom of worship throughout the territories under his control (Edict of Milan). During his reign, however, Constantine increasingly showed his preference for Christianity, and pagan religion fell into disfavor. When he founded his new capital on the Bosporus (New Rome, later called Constantinople), he made it a Christian city from the start.

In his religious policy, Constantine was following exactly the same aims as Diocletian, namely, to strengthen his own and his successors' authority as emperors and to win for the empire the support of the divine power that ruled the universe. The momentous change, however, was in the means. Probably because the Christians had withstood the power of the emperors, Constantine came to the conclusion that it was their one God, not the crowd of pagan deities, who was truly almighty. It was the Christian God, then, around whom the citizens of the empire must be rallied; and it was the pagan cults that Constantine and his successors came to view as subversive of the empire's relationship with divine power. Though pagan religion survived for another century or more, it did so under growing imperial disapproval and finally outright prohibition and persecution: in 381, Constantine's successor Theodosius made Christianity the sole legal religion.

Likewise, Constantine continued Diocletian's tradition of sacred monarchy. In the decisive battle of the civil war that brought Constantine to power, his soldiers had fought with the cross of Jesus painted on their shields—because, it was said, the emperor had seen the cross in a dream and heard a voice that told him, "In this sign you shall conquer!" In this way, Constantine, like Diocletian, could claim to be not just another victor in the power struggles of the generals but an emperor divinely chosen to rule—only it was the one true Christian God who had chosen him, instead of the false pagan deities. Of course, as a Christian, he could not expect to be venerated as a god himself. Still, he retained the majesty and mystery of Diocletian's court, and the bishops themselves proclaimed that Constantine deserved to be revered as God's chosen instrument and the Church's protector. As such, they willingly accepted his right to intervene in the Church's government and arbitrate its disputes (pp. 175–176).

The Burden of Empire. The Christian version of sacred monarchy had a long history ahead of it. Right down to the beginning of the twentieth century, European kings and emperors would claim to wield power over their peoples and over the Christian Church as the chosen ones of God (pp. 201, 212, 417). But the adoption of Christianity could not solve the immediate problems of the Roman Empire: rivalries and warfare among emperors and would-be emperors, the economic decline of the West, and the rising threat of barbarian invasions.

Worst of all, Christianity did not alter the overriding fact that like most highly centralized, regulated, and militarized states, the empire of Diocletian and Constantine was squandering its most precious asset: the willingness of the citizens to bear the burden of keeping it going. Particularly in the West, high taxation and rising prices were as destructive and demoralizing in the long run as the most savage barbarian attacks. Already in the third century, the prosperous cities of the early empire had been reduced to heavily fortified outposts whose citizens had lost all real self-government. With the triumph of Christianity, the cities began to find a new source of civic leadership in the persons of the bishops (p. 171). But rather than bolstering the authority of the government, the bishops often had to act as substitutes for it. They occupied themselves with matters of social welfare, to which the government paid no attention, and with protecting the citizens, in the name of Christian mercy, from excessive government demands.

Meanwhile, the country-dwellers, bankrupted by the endless demands of the tax collectors, came under the domination of a tiny elite of landowners—those who were wealthy enough to carry the burden of taxes or influential enough to gain tax exemptions. The debt-ridden peasants sold out to these wealthy men and became sharecroppers or laborers—giving up part of their harvest or doing farmwork in return for continuing to occupy their holdings. Though they were not human property like the slaves who worked alongside them (p. 115), the peasants became bound to their landlords by ties of personal obedience and subjection. The landowners usually dealt with the government on behalf of their peasants. They often shielded them from the tax collectors as best they could, if only in order to exploit the peasants more effectively themselves.

In spite of their power and wealth, there were limits to the sacrifices that the landowners were willing to make for the emperor. Many emperors—and often the shrewdest and most successful ones—kept the landowners out of the most important government positions. The high army commands went to barbarian generals, and the leading administrative positions to the ruler's trusted personal advisers. The landowners had to be content with local positions in the regions where they were influential, especially those of *count*—an official in charge of a city and its surrounding territory—and bishop. Members of wealthy families now served the Church with the same self-sacrificing sense of duty that leading citizens had formerly brought to the service of the empire.

In this way, landowners and bishops came to form a kind of interlocking elite over much of the western half of the empire. They were strongly attached to the ideal of Rome and far from disloyal to the emperors, but in practical politics, what counted most for them was not the empire as a whole but their local power and local responsibilities. Increasingly, it was to this elite, not to the army, the bureaucracy, or the emperor, that ordinary citizens in the West looked for help and protection and to whom they acknowledged a duty of loyalty and obedience.

Thus in reaction against the overmighty state of Diocletian and Constantine, some of the features of the European society of the Middle Ages were already beginning to appear—notably the power of landowners over peasants and the institution of serfdom (pp. 137–138) and the deep involvement of the Church in matters of worldly government (pp. 255–257).

GERMANIC INVASIONS OF THE WEST

Thanks to the reforms of Diocletian and Constantine, the empire held off barbarian attacks for most of the fourth century. During this time, there was plenty of brutal and exhausting warfare between the Romans and their barbarian neighbors, but in many ways they were becoming increasingly alike. Leading Romans began to take up barbarian ways: even the emperors, when not dressed for court ceremonies, now wore the cloak, tunic, and pants of Germanic chieftains instead of the traditional Roman toga. For their part, the Germanic chieftains, when chosen as such by their warriors, would be raised on the back of a shield to receive the warriors' acclamation—a custom that they had picked up from the Roman legions, who saluted a newly chosen emperor in this way. Many of the tribal confederacies living nearest to the empire even became Christian, though they usually adopted the unorthodox, Arian version of the new religion that Rome itself had rejected (pp. 175–176). The historical stage was being set for a "merger" between Rome and the barbarians. When it came, the merger was a vast and long drawn-out process involving the entire western half of the empire and taking more than a century to accomplish. At some times and in some regions, it took the form of bloody conquest; at other times and in other regions, it resembled a peaceful takeover.

The Germanic barbarians began to move in on the empire not because of any deliberate plan of conquest but as a result of a momentous shift in the intercontinental balance of forces that had helped Rome endure for so long (pp. 124–125). Shortly before the beginning of the Christian era, a nomadic nation living to the north of China, the Huns, had been defeated in conflicts with other nomads who were backed by the Chinese emperors. As a result, they began to move away from China, westward across the steppes (pp. 57–58), and as often happened with nomad peoples, once they had left their homeland, they gradually migrated and fought their way farther westward. Finally, in 370, they burst into Europe. Though earlier nomad conquerors had ruled parts of eastern Europe, none had been so well organized, ruthless, and ambitious as the Huns. For three-quarters of a century, they dominated a region stretching from Europe's eastern borders all the way to the Rhine (*Map 3.4*), and the impact on the barbarian peoples of the region was devastating. The Huns subjected and destroyed some Germanic tribal confederacies in this region and caused others to flee.

Among those who fled were the Visigoths, a tribal confederacy that lived on the lower Danube River, which in 376 begged to be admitted to Roman territory. Their plea was granted, but the starving tribespeople were ruthlessly oppressed by corrupt Roman officials and provision merchants. Finally, the Visigoths took up arms; at the battle of Adrianople, their horsemen won a crushing victory over the imperial foot soldiers, killing the emperor Valens. His successor, Theodosius I, decided to make the best of the situation. First, he gave the Visigoths a substantial grant of land in the Eastern empire, and then he used them as allies against a rebellious army commander in the West.

Theodosius was also the last emperor to rule a united empire. Before he died in 395, he made a permanent division, splitting the empire along the lines established earlier by Diocletian and naming one of his sons emperor of the West (at Milan) and the other emperor of the East (at Constantinople) (*Map 3.4*). After his death and the division of the empire, the Visigothic leader Alaric began to exploit the weakness of Theodosius' successors to gain yet more land and power in the empire. He did so sometimes by playing off the Eastern against the Western emperor, sometimes by helping both against their foes, and sometimes by warfare or blackmail against them. Sensing the greater weakness of the West, Alaric finally concentrated his efforts there, and in 408, he led the Visigoths into Italy.

Meanwhile, the West was being penetrated from another direction. In 406 and 407, taking advantage of the Western emperor's problems with the Visigoths, several other Germanic tribal confederacies crossed the frontier on the Rhine River. By 410,

Map 3.4 Invasions of the Western Empire. The map shows the locations of the main invading groups when the invasions started in A.D. 376 (*italic names*) and the regions that they eventually came to occupy (underlined names). The shading shows the territory dominated by the Huns just before Attila's death in 453 and their retreat into Asia. The territories inside the empire occupied by Germanic peoples are shown as of 533—after 150 years of struggles with the Romans, with each other, and with less successful invading groups, and just before Eastern Roman efforts at reconquest began.

they had spread far and wide into Gaul and Spain. In that year, too, the Visigoths, angered by what Alaric saw as the Western emperor's unreasonable refusal to grant them land and Roman civil and military titles, captured and sacked the city of Rome itself. This was a disaster that, perhaps for the first time, made the empire's citizens seriously doubt its permanence.

During the fifth century, the story of these opening moves in the barbarian take-over was repeated, with variations, over and over again. The leaders of the tribal confederacies were not deliberately trying to destroy the empire but rather to extract concessions from its rulers. Depending on circumstances, they would fight the Romans or each other, make deals with emperors or local Roman commanders, or even set up puppet emperors of their own to get whatever particular advantages they wanted. The last emperor in the West, Romulus Augustulus, was such a puppet emperor. His name, ironically, combined that of the legendary founder of the city of Rome with a diminutive version of the name of the founder of the empire. He was deposed in 476 when his Germanic master had no further use for him.

As for the Romans, they simply no longer felt their old sense of urgency to expel the barbarians. Instead, rival emperors or would-be emperors would often seek the help of the invading tribal confederacies in wars against each other. The Eastern emperors did not hesitate to rid their territories of barbarian armies by persuading them to move to the West. Even when the Romans defeated some barbarian group, the victors would not force the invaders to leave the empire but rather settled them within its frontiers. And in 451, at the battle of Châlons, Romans and Germans even fought side by side to hold off an invasion of Gaul by the Huns under their famous and terrible ruler Attila. This victory marked the beginning of the end of the Hunnish menace that had given the original impetus to the Germanic takeover. Within two years, Attila was dead and his people began to retreat back into Asia and disperse.

If anything, the defeat of the Huns made the Germanic takeover of the West more acceptable to the Romans. But in any case, the Romans in the West no longer felt a strong need to defend the empire. The ordinary citizens were crushed by the tax burdens imposed by Diocletian and Constantine. The wealthy landowners, while clinging to Roman culture, thought more of their local power and position than of the empire as a whole. For the bishops, the Church, not the empire, was their main concern. To all these, the empire seemed hardly worth saving—particularly since the barbarian chieftains were found to be "men one could do business with."

By the early sixth century, the Western empire had been carved up into a number of territories, each dominated by one or another Germanic tribal confederacy. Africa belonged to the Vandals; the Ostrogoths now held Italy; the Visigoths had moved on to occupy Spain; the Franks were supreme in most of Gaul as well as across the Rhine, in the western lands of barbarian Germany; and the Angles and Saxons had sailed across the North Sea to conquer Britain (*Map 3.4*, p. 153). Most of the Germanic rulers had won some kind of recognition and official titles from the emperors in Constantinople, and hence they were in theory the emperor's subordinates. In practice, however, they all acted independently, and they all bore the Germanic title of *king,* signifying leadership in war and, among tribes that were still pagan, the favor of the gods.

The Germanic kings assigned portions of the lands they occupied to their followers: leading warriors gained vast properties, while the mass of tribal fighters were given small freehold homesteads. In most of the regions they took over, the Germanic settlers were a small minority of the population, with their own status, customs, and laws, which—at least to start with—were different from those of the Romans among whom they lived. (Britain, where the Angles and Saxons assimilated or drove out the local population, was an exception.)

Yet the Romans were not treated as a mere conquered people. Roman government and institutions continued to function in the service of the Germanic kings. Roman culture survived: the conquering chieftains revered it, and even if they were illiterate themselves (which was not always the case), their sons and daughters became educated people of Latin culture. Roman landowners kept their inherited power and status, and although they had to give up a great deal of land for the benefit of the Germanic settlers, they remained exceedingly wealthy. Thus, over the centuries, the Germanic invaders were absorbed into the mass of the Roman population; but their laws, customs, and traditions significantly influenced the emerging European society of the early Middle Ages (pp. 194–195).

Of all the institutions of the Roman Empire that survived the Germanic takeover, the single most important was the Christian Church. In fact, the Church not only survived but prospered. Still-pagan conquerors, notably the Franks, were baptized into the orthodox form of Christianity that prevailed in the Roman West. Those, such as the Visigoths, who were already unorthodox (Arian) Christians (p. 176), clung to their version of the faith for several generations, and this was the main source of conflict between them and their Roman subjects. But in this conflict, it was the rulers who yielded, in time conforming to the Roman version of the faith. Thus by A.D. 600, though the Roman Empire had fallen, the Christian Church was more or less united in its beliefs, and had emerged as the principal binding force among the diverse peoples and kingdoms of the West.

RECOMMENDED READING

The Rise of Rome A. Kamm, *The Romans: An Introduction* (1995), is an excellent brief introduction to all aspects of Roman life; M. Le Glay, *History of Rome* (1996), is a readable and up-to-date account; and social and economic conditions are clearly described in H. C. Boren, *Roman Society: A Social, Economic, and Cultural History* (1977). All these books cover the entire period of the rise and fall of Rome.

Specifically on the rise of the Republic, its political and social life, and its overthrow, the best short treatment is M. Crawford, *The Roman Republic* (1992). L. J. F. Keppie, *The Making of the Roman Army* (1984), describes the army's fighting methods, organization, and role in politics from its origins to the time of Augustus.

The Overthrow of the Republic A clear survey of the transition from the Republic to imperial monarchy is D. Shotter, *The Fall of the Roman Republic* (1994). The growth of Rome's imperial possessions and its government under the Republic is described in A. W. Lintott, *Imperium Romanum: Politics and Administration* (1993). C. Meier, *Caesar: A Biography* (1995), is scholarly and readable. For a survey of the inhabitants of Gaul, see D. Dumville, *The Celts* (1992).

The Imperial Foundations Augustus' reforms are clearly outlined in D. Shotter, *Augustus* (1991); an up-to-date account of his life and times is P. Southern, *Augustus* (1998). His changes in the provinces are dealt with in A. W. Lintott, *Imperium Romanum: Politics and Administration* (1993).

Approach to One World: The Pax Romana F. Millar, *The Roman Empire and Its Neighbors* (1981), surveys the empire's government, the integration of its subject peoples, and its most powerful neighbors in Europe and the Middle East. P. Garnsey and R. Saller, *The Roman Empire: Economy, Society, and Culture* (1987), is a brief and authoritative account of these aspects of imperial Rome; J. E. Stambaugh, *The Ancient Roman City* (1988), covers urban life under the Republic and the empire; Y. le Bohec, *The Imperial Roman Army* (1994), is a standard survey of the organization, fighting methods, and political and cultural role of the army from Augustus to Diocletian. L. Casson, *Everyday Life in Ancient Rome* (1998), is an attractive portrayal of different types of people throughout the empire.

Roman Character and Thought A good survey of Roman culture, setting it against the background of social and political developments, is P. Jones and K. Sidwell, *The World of Rome: An Introduction to Roman Culture* (1997). R. M. Ogilvie, *The Romans and Their Gods in the Age of Augustus* (1969), surveys religious belief and practice at that period; K. Dowden, *Religion and the Romans* (1992), covers a longer time span. Roman women are dealt with in S. B. Pomeroy, *Goddesses, Whores, Wives, and Slaves: Women in Classical Antiquity* (1975). An excellent account of Roman writers, and of the readers for whom they wrote, is R. M. Ogilvie, *Roman Literature and Society* (1980). Philosophy is briefly and clearly covered in T. Irwin, *Classical Thought* (1989).

Roman Law Three short and nontechnical books may be recommended. O. Tellegen-Comperies, *A Short History of Roman Law* (1993), outlines the development of the law. D. Johnston, *Roman Law in Context* (1999), sets it against its background of social life. Its enduring influence is surveyed in a work by a leading scholar, P. Stein, *Roman Law in European History* (1999).

Architecture and Engineering N. H. Ramage and A. Ramage, *Roman Art: Romulus to Constantine* (1991), and H. Stierlin, *The Roman Empire* (vol. 1 of the *Taschen History of Architecture*) (1996), are attractively written and lavishly illustrated surveys. M. Grant, *Art in the Roman Empire* (1995), deals briefly with all forms of art and architecture. E. D'Ambra, *Roman Art* (1998), explains the role of art as expression of political power and social status. L. Sprague de Camp, *The Ancient Engineers* (1963), includes a nontechnical account of Roman engineering.

The End of Rome and the Beginning of Europe E. Gibbon, *The Decline and Fall of the Roman Empire* (6 vols., 1776–1787), is a monumental classic of historical literature (available in paperback in a one-volume abridgment, ed. D. Womersley, 1995). A. Cameron, *The Later Roman Empire, A.D. 284–430* (1993), and *The Medieval World in Late Antiquity, A.D. 395–600* (1993), are up-to-date surveys. P. Brown, *The World of Late Antiquity, A.D. 150–750* (1971), is a highly readable and well-illustrated work that stresses religion and culture. The development of the Germanic peoples and their relations with Rome, from the first encounters through the period of the invasions to the establishment of the barbarian kingdoms, is covered in H. Wolfram, *The Roman Empire and Its Germanic Peoples* (1997).

INFOTRAC COLLEGE EDITION

Visit the source collections at **http://academic.cengage.com/infotrac,** and use the Search function with the following key terms:

Rome history	Roman Empire	Roman mythology
Roman Republic	Constantine	Roman law

WESTERN CIVILIZATION RESOURCES

Visit the Brief History of the Western World Companion Web Site for resources specific to this textbook:

http://history.wadsworth.com/greerbrief09/

Also, the CD in the back of this book and the World History Resources Center at **http://history.wadsworth.com/west_civ/** offer a variety of tools to help you succeed in this course, including access to quizzes; images; documents; interactive simulations, maps, and timelines; movie explorations; and a wealth of other sources.

CHAPTER 4

A Conquering New Faith: Christianity

OVERVIEW

The rise of Christianity was part of a historic change in religion that began many centuries before Jesus, produced not one but three new faiths, and spread far beyond the civilizations of the Western succession. The core of this revolution was the replacement of traditional *polytheism,* or belief in many gods and goddesses, by belief in one God, or *monotheism.* The change involved countless aspects of religious belief, practice, and organization. Given the central importance of religion in civilization, the rise of monotheism also had a vast impact on culture, social life, and government in the regions where it took hold. It was perhaps the greatest single change in civilization since the dawn of civilization itself.

Monotheism developed as the religion of a single people, the Jews, in the changing world of Middle Eastern civilization after 1200 B.C. (pp. 44–53). This was now followed by monotheism's spread, in the new form of Christianity, to become the predominant religion of the peoples of the Roman Empire, as well as of all later civilizations in the Western succession.

Christianity began as a group within Judaism at a time of division and uncertainty among the Jews arising out of their encounter with the dominant civilization of Greece and Rome. Jesus himself lived and taught as a Jew, although he set his own unique stamp on the Jewish teachings of his time. After Jesus' death, under the influence of the apostle Paul the believers in him as the promised Savior turned away from Judaism and toward the Greco-Roman world, seeking converts among all peoples of the empire.

As Christianity grew, it suffered occasional persecution by the Roman authorities and was often divided by disagreements over belief—above all concerning the nature of the one God and his relationship to Jesus. Even so, by A.D. 300, Christians were to be found in every city of the empire—still a minority of the population, but well organized in the Catholic (universal) Church, with a powerful guiding structure of priests and bishops.

Not long afterward, the emperor Constantine accepted the Christian God and Savior as the true divine power on which the troubled empire should rely. By A.D. 400, Christianity had become the official religion of the state and the majority of its subjects. In accordance with the claim of monotheism to be the one truth about the one God, the worship of the traditional gods and goddesses had been outlawed, and what was now the rival monotheism of Judaism was only grudgingly tolerated.

True, the change did not save the Roman Empire; in fact, the empire's collapse followed almost immediately. But this only strengthened the Church and made its message more convincing. The Christian thinker Augustine developed the idea of the Church as a community of believers who were predestined (chosen in advance) by God for salvation, regardless of the fate of any empire. Christian men and women began to live a life of closeness to God and freedom from the distractions of the world as monks and nuns, providing the Church with a new elite that would give it inspiration and leadership in difficult times. The barbarian invaders themselves eventually adopted the Catholic beliefs of the peoples they had conquered. By A.D. 600, Christianity had the inner strength that would enable it to survive its next great trial, the loss of countless Middle Eastern and North African believers to the new rival monotheism of Islam—and also to seize its next great opportunity, the conversion of the increasingly advanced and powerful barbarian peoples of northern Europe.

Sources of Christianity

Christianity first appeared as a *sect* (a dissident religious group) among the Jews. As it grew, it also incorporated various practices of contemporary mystery religions and ways of thinking that were inspired by Greek philosophy. But above all, Christianity as a monotheistic religion was the product of many centuries of Jewish experience in the Middle East, as well as their more recent experiences under the power of Greece and then Rome. So, too, was the development of the specifically Jewish type of monotheism, which has continued to flourish, and to influence Western civilization, down to the present day.

THE JEWS IN THE WORLD OF GREECE AND ROME

Christianity began as one of many Jewish religious groups, each of which had its own answer to a disturbing question that faced their people as a whole: What were the plans and purposes of God for his Chosen People in a world that was dominated by the religion and culture of Greece and the military power of Rome?

The Jews already had answers to these questions, which had stood the test of time (on the earlier development of Jewish beliefs, see pp. 48–53). God, it seemed, wanted the Jews to live scattered through the world under the rule of more powerful peoples, from Egypt, through their homeland of Judaea in Palestine, all the way to Syria and Babylonia. Around them, he would raise up and cast down world-ruling nations, but he would preserve and protect his Chosen People as long as they obeyed his Law and worshiped him in his Temple in Jerusalem.

The Jews had, in fact, outlasted the Assyrian and Persian universal empires, and they had prospered under the Greek-ruled kingdoms that divided the conquests of Alexander. At the time of Jesus, there were probably about five or six million of them—as many Jews as Egyptians or Italians, though less than a million actually lived in Palestine. The Jews did not go out of their way to make converts, but it was not at all unusual for Gentiles to join them or to follow their way of life without actually being circumcised.

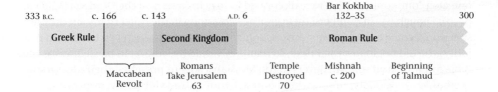

| 333 B.C. | c. 166 | c. 143 | A.D. 6 | Bar Kokhba 132–35 | 300 |

Greek Rule | Second Kingdom | Roman Rule

Maccabean Revolt | Romans Take Jerusalem 63 | Temple Destroyed 70 | Mishnah c. 200 | Beginning of Talmud

Within their scattered communities, leaders of prayer and study held unchallenged authority. The Temple in Jerusalem, with its long-lived dynasties of priests and its endless round of sacrifices to the God of Israel, was one of the world's most magnificent shrines.

In all these ways, the place of the Jews in the world seemed assured. But during the second century B.C., the world had begun to change yet again, and the old answers had come to seem less certain.

Jewish Disputes in a Changing World. The change began when the Greeks started to lose their place as rulers of the civilized world. For a hundred years, until the Romans replaced them, there was a power vacuum in the Middle East. For the first time since the days of David and Solomon almost a thousand years before, a strong Jewish kingdom arose. The rise of the new state began when a king of Syria unaccountably broke with the usual Greek broad-mindedness in matters of religion by banning the practice of Judaism in his territories, which included Judaea, and setting up an image of Zeus in the Temple. In 166 B.C., a revolt broke out, led by the priestly family of the Maccabees. In the course of a heroic and brutal twenty-five-year struggle, the Temple was recaptured and purified, the Greek forces were driven out, and Judaea became independent under Maccabean rule. The descendants of the Maccabees went on to conquer more territory than David had done, and proclaimed themselves kings.

Eventually the dynasty fell victim to family disputes, and the Romans stepped in, capturing Jerusalem in 63 B.C. But even this was not the end of this second Jewish kingdom. Its most famous ruler, Herod the Great, reigned in allegiance to the new masters of the world for more than thirty years, until shortly before the beginning of the Christian era.

Yet for all its greatness, the new kingdom produced discontent and division among the Jews. The Jewish kings could not help being influenced by the dominant Hellenistic culture of the international world in which they were so powerful and respected. Herod, for instance, rebuilt the Temple to be more splendid than ever before—but for his additions to the shrine, he used a Greek style of architecture. Most of the kings also held the office of high priest and manipulated the priestly aristocracy in the interests of bolstering their power. In addition, they made the Jewish peasants pay heavily for their building projects and their wars.

Many of the leaders of prayer and study who were now so influential with ordinary Jews distrusted the rulers and the Temple priests. More than ever before, they stressed study of and obedience to the Law as the heart of Jewish religion. Though they usually called on the people to obey the rulers and make offerings in the Temple, to some extent they stood apart from both. Perhaps for this reason, they came to be known as *Pharisees,* from a Hebrew word meaning "separators."

Other groups separated themselves far more drastically from the rulers and the Temple, and set up communities in which they lived lives of obsessive ritual purity. Their way of life is known from the famous Dead Sea Scrolls, the relatively well-preserved records of one such community, which were discovered in 1947 in caves near the Dead Sea (*Map 1.4*, p. 50). Though few in numbers, these groups were strong in the belief that soon the Messiah would come to sweep away Greeks, Romans, Jewish kings, and even the Jewish majority who did not follow their rules, so that they would live forever in blessedness as the Bible foretold. And some believers in the Messiah's advent preached their ideas to the overburdened peasants, among whom unrest, banditry, and violence were growing.

Eventually the Romans broke up the Jewish kingdom and made Judaea a province of the empire (p. 118). Rome respected Jewish religion as the Greeks and Persians had done, and most of the Jewish leaders of prayer and study preached obedience to the emperors as the latest instruments of God's almighty power. But Rome's taxation was heavy and its governors were corrupt, inspiring hatred among the peasants and hope among those who expected that these troubles heralded the advent of the Messiah. The result was two massive uprisings that were at one and the same time revolts against Rome, social revolutions, ethnic and religious wars between Jews and Gentiles in Palestine, and civil wars among the Jews themselves.

Both uprisings were crushed by the legions and also resulted in religious disaster. The first ended in A.D. 70 with the destruction of the Temple, and the second in A.D. 135 with Jerusalem turned into a Roman city—complete with a shrine of Jupiter on the Temple site—which Jews were not allowed to enter. The traditional Temple worship, with its daily offerings and sacrifices to God, had come to an end, never to be resumed.

The Rise of Rabbinic Judaism. It was during the period of conflict and dispute leading up to the revolt of A.D. 70 that Jesus lived and taught and that his followers ultimately broke with traditional Jewish religion. Most Jews, however, did not join these dissidents. Instead, they continued the rich life of prayer, praise, and obedience to the Law that had grown up alongside the Temple worship and which now completely replaced it as the heart of Jewish religion.

The leaders of prayer and study in Palestine had opposed both revolts and insisted that there was no way of knowing whether the Messiah would come soon or in the distant future, and events had proved them right. Favored and respected by the Romans, who continued to tolerate Jewish religion even while they crushed the strivings for independence, the leaders of prayer and study became more than ever an elite among the Jews. It became customary to address them as "My teacher!" (*rabbi*), and this respectful form of address became their title of honor.

The rabbis' interpretations of and additions to the Law themselves acquired binding legal authority and were collected about A.D. 200 in a book known as the "Repetition" (*Mishnah*). This, in turn, gave rise to two enormous works explaining and expanding the Mishnah. One of these was produced in Palestine in the third and fourth centuries, and the other in Babylonia between the third and sixth centuries; each was known as a "Commentary" (*Talmud*). Between them, the Mishnah and the Talmuds extended the original Law into every detail of Jewish life, while also preserving many nonlegal customs, beliefs, and stories and giving opportunity for endless further debates and explanations. Judaism as a monotheistic religion was now based entirely on the Torah and the works that explained it, rather than on the Temple worship, and the Jews as a people were now led by rabbis, rather than by priests, prophets, or kings. This new, "rabbinic" form of belief and practice has remained the basic pattern of Judaism down to the present day.

True, the Jews survived as a people scattered among the nations and in time became a minority in Palestine itself. Probably because the rabbis did not want to provoke the

Roman authorities (and later those of Christianity and Islam), the practice of convert-ing Gentiles gradually died out, though it was never formally prohibited. Still, in the course of its own development, Judaism had originated or transmitted beliefs and prac-tices concerning God, his dealings with humans, and how he was to be worshiped that were to become the common inheritance of both Christian and Muslim monotheism.

MYSTERY RELIGIONS

Apart from its roots in Judaism, Christianity was also influenced by the practices and beliefs of traditional "mystery" religions. All these religions grew out of ancient vege-tation myths; all told of a god who had died and was resurrected, as the cold death of winter is followed by the warm life of spring. All taught that the individual worshiper, through initiation and secret rituals, might win eternal life. They provided a message of hope and consolation and a promise of better things—if not in this life, then in the next. People throughout the Roman Empire were particularly responsive to the tales of *miracles* that clustered around such deities as the Persian Mithra, the Phrygian Cybele, and the Egyptian Isis and Osiris (p. 34). These religions interacted with Christianity for several centuries and influenced its development.

An especially popular mystery religion was Mithraism, which mingled the Zoroas-trian beliefs of Persia (pp. 47–48) with Greek and oriental polytheism. Carried west-ward from Asia Minor after the first century B.C. by soldiers and merchants, it flour-ished in the empire, particularly among the Roman legions, until Constantine threw his support to Christianity (p. 150).

The divine Mithra was believed to be a lieutenant of the Persian supreme god Ahura Mazda, but he attracted worshipers in his own right. According to legend, he was born of a rock and was first attended by shepherds. Mithra was also associated with the sun, and his followers marked Sunday as his day of worship. They called it the "Lord's Day," for Mithra was known to them as "Lord." Only men were admitted to this faith, and initiates had to undergo secret and terrifying rituals designed to instruct them and to test their will. Among the milder ceremonies were baptism in holy water and the partaking of a sacred meal of bread and wine. After passing through successive ordeals, converts were "born again" in Mithra. This experience charged them with new hope, for, though Mithra had ascended to heaven, he had promised to return and guide his loyal followers to their reward in *paradise* (a Persian word).

GREEK PHILOSOPHICAL THOUGHT

Greek philosophy, too, had an effect on Christianity, especially as the new faith began to expand beyond Palestine into more thoroughly Hellenized lands. Plato's Academy, founded in the fourth century B.C., continued to train scholars far into the Christian era, and the impact of Plato's thought on Christianity was immense. Plato had been the first to elaborate the concept of an eternal "soul" distinct from the body (p. 82). In his "Doctrine of Ideas," he spoke of an eternal spiritual order of perfection, presided over by the Idea of Goodness (God). He considered the human body a source of dis-traction and evil, a view that reinforced the *ascetic* strain in Christianity (p. 180).

Stoicism also exerted a strong influence on Christianity. Belief in a cosmos ruled by providence, emphasis on universal love and on the virtues of justice, compassion, and restraint—all were central to its teachings (pp. 133–134). Stoicism was widespread among the educated classes of the Roman Empire, and its numerous parallels with Christianity helped to prepare the way for the new faith.

The Life and Teachings of Jesus

After we have sifted through all the historical influences, however, we must recognize Christianity as a religion with its own integrity and power. Jesus (the Latin version of his Hebrew name, Joshua) is not a vague mythological figure like Mithra but a person who lived and taught in Roman times. And it is his life, character, and message that stamp the Christian faith with its unique meaning.

Jesus left no writings of his own. What is known of his career is contained in the four New Testament Gospels attributed to Matthew, Mark, Luke, and John. Biblical scholars are not certain as to the actual authorship and dates of composition of these books, but they were obviously written by true believers. In explaining the relationships of the Gospels to one another, scholars generally agree that Mark's Gospel was the first to be written, probably shortly before the destruction of the Temple in A.D. 70, and that (possibly together with another, undiscovered book) it was used as a source by Matthew and Luke. John's account, which was written later (at the close of the first century), reflects a more developed theology, with emphasis on the divine nature of Jesus and his affirmations of immortality.

THE "NATURE" OF JESUS

But there are gaps even in this composite biography. The Gospels focus on the birth of Jesus , the brief years of his ministry, and his death and resurrection; the disciples felt no need to set down all the details of his life, for to them the Gospel required no "historical" proof. Faithful converts would later accept him as the Christ (the Anointed One—the Greek version of the Hebrew "Messiah"; p. 53), the true God in human form (incarnate). Some biblical scholars have found it hard to go behind the Jesus of the Gospels to determine the nature of the historical Jesus. For example, since the Gospels were written between forty and seventy years after Jesus' death, it is possible that their accounts were influenced by beliefs about Jesus that had already arisen among Christians. Moreover, though the Gospels agree in general outline, they differ somewhat in their accounts of Jesus' personality and identity. Did he, for example, represent himself as God (or the "Son of God")? Some Gospel passages (notably, Matthew 16:15–17 and John 17:1) appear to say this, yet Jesus also speaks of God as the Father of all who love him (Matthew 6:6). The nature of the historical Jesus, then, remains open to various interpretations. Was he "Son of God," "son of man," inspired teacher, religious reformer, humanitarian idealist—or, as his Jewish critics insisted, a "false prophet"? A final answer, acceptable to all, cannot be drawn from the available sources.

THE SERMON ON THE MOUNT

The *ethical* teachings of Jesus are best summarized in the Sermon on the Mount (Matthew 5–7). The Gospel of Matthew brings together the best-remembered sayings, stories, and moral advice of Jesus. What manner of life is most pleasing to God? What virtues does he value most highly? Jesus answered these questions directly and precisely, in the context of his own place and time. In Palestine during the years of Jesus' ministry, when discontent and discord among the Jews were building toward the first great revolt against the Romans (pp. 159–160), he was not the only one to answer these questions, but the answers he gave were very much his own. Like the Pharisees, he obeyed the Law, visited the Temple, and called for acceptance of Roman rule while standing apart from the priestly aristocracy and condemning the exploitation that had grown up around the Temple worship. But he also denounced the Pharisees for their efforts to extend the Law to cover every detail of life, which he saw as pedantic and hypocritical. Like the radical sects, he seems to have expected the long-predicted end of time to come very soon, but he was far from preaching a war of liberation that would eliminate the sufferings of the poor and overthrow the Romans. And he expressed his views not as an aloof divinity but as a Jewish teacher, speaking directly to the people with whom he came into contact.

Blessed are the meek, he declared, the merciful, the peacemakers, and the pure in heart. In other words, he was telling his listeners to turn away from the warrior ideal exemplified by Achilles, Alexander, and Caesar, since righteousness and love are more precious in God's sight than worldly success and honor. Moreover, Jesus assured his listeners that there was no conflict between his teaching and that of the Hebrew prophets of old, that he came not to destroy "but to fulfill." His moral demands, indeed, were based on the traditional ethics of Judaism, but he carried them beyond ordinary human reach. Obeying the Law and the Commandments was not enough. In the "new testament" that Jesus taught, one must love not only the Lord but one's enemies; one must refrain not only from adultery but from lustful thoughts; one must not only give up the search for material goods but give away all possessions; one must not merely resist evil but "turn the other cheek."

This code of conduct makes extreme demands on the human spirit. Did Jesus actually expect men and women to live up to it? To this question, too, there is no clear-cut answer. The view generally taken by Christians is that Jesus' teachings form an ideal toward which all should strive but which none can attain. Therefore, all will fall short—yet all may be saved by repentance (sorrowful regret) and God's mercy.

Like other Jewish teachers, Jesus challenged the Temple priests who wielded considerable power under Roman rule. The Gospels state that the priestly authorities finally seized him and handed him over to the Romans, who crucified him—their standard method of execution—on charges of posing as king of the Jews. His twelve closest disciples all failed him. Judas betrayed him to the temple priests, Peter denied all connection with him, and the ten others abandoned him in terror and despair. But according to the Gospels, the crucified Jesus rose from the tomb and showed himself several times to his disciples before ascending to heaven. His reappearance renewed the faith of his followers that he was truly "the Christ, the son of the living God" (Matthew 16:16), come to save the world from evil and death. Soon they came to believe that Jesus would come again to fulfill the role that Jewish tradition gave to the Messiah, but even more spectacularly. At his Second Coming the world would come to an end and the dead would rise from their graves in their own bodies, to be judged worthy to live with him in his kingdom forever, or be condemned to fire eternal. In this way, the disciples regained the will to obey Jesus' last instruction as recorded in the Scriptures: "Go ye into all the world, and preach the gospel to the whole creation" (Mark 16:15), so as to gather in the harvest of converts to await his coming.

The Early Church and Its Expansion

The Acts of the Apostles, which tells the story of the early Church, states that the disciples were at first dismayed by Jesus' command to set forth as missionaries. How could they, a handful of despised and humiliated men, succeed in such a task? They were simple and uneducated Jews, with little knowledge of foreign lands or languages. So they waited patiently, mindful of Jesus' promise: "But you shall receive power when the Holy Spirit has come upon you" (Acts 1:8).

MISSIONARY BEGINNINGS: PENTECOST

According to Scripture, the missionary work started at Pentecost (fifty days after Jesus' resurrection). The Book of Acts relates that the Holy Spirit descended upon the disciples like "the rush of a mighty wind" (2:2). The Spirit gave them the gifts of wisdom, languages, and healing, thus distinguishing them from other men and preparing them for their task. But the mission was not easy. Three thousand, the Scriptures say, were baptized in the faith of Pentecost. These first converts, however, were all Jews, and soon the apostles were faced with a thorny question: Could they share food with Gentiles, contrary to the Jewish law, and baptize them directly in Christ? Or must Gentiles first become Jews as in the past, by circumcision and observance of the Law (p. 53)? Peter, the first disciple of Jesus, leaned toward the latter view. But a vision taught him his error, and he began to baptize Gentiles as well as Jews. The issue was finally settled by a council of apostles and elders at Jerusalem in A.D. 44, which decided that Gentile converts were not to be bound by the Jewish Law.

Peter continued to hold that those who had been born to the Law should hold to it, but the trend moved steadily away from the observance of the Law by Christians. For example, Easter, celebrating the resurrection of Christ, displaced the Jewish Passover, which commemorates the deliverance of the ancient Israelites from Egyptian bondage. Similarly, the Jewish Sabbath (seventh day) gave way to Sunday as a day of rest and worship, for according to the Gospels it was on the "first day of the week" that Christ arose from the dead.

The destruction of the Temple in A.D. 70 was an important moment in the separation of the two religions. For the Christians, it was God's punishment of the Jews for refusing to recognize Jesus as the Messiah. For most Jews, on the other hand, it made strict observance of the Law more important than ever and confirmed the belief that the coming of the Messiah was still in the future (p. 160). A minority of Jews, especially in the Diaspora, still became Christians, and to judge from the complaints of early Church leaders, it also happened that some Christians went over to Judaism. But from late in the first century onward, when a Jew became a Christian or vice versa, it was by way of "conversion." For Christianity and Judaism had become rival religions, both believing in the one God but each accusing the other of falsifying the one truth about him and disobeying his will.

THE APOSTLE PAUL

Paul, the "apostle to the Gentiles," led the way in making clear the differences between Christianity and Judaism. It was not a role that he had expected for himself in his early life. He was not one of the original twelve, nor even a native of Palestine, but a Jew born in the city of Tarsus, in Asia Minor. He claimed Roman citizenship and apparently came from a well-to-do, educated family. Trained in both Hebrew and Greek, he was familiar with the religions and philosophies of the Hellenistic world, and as a Pharisee, he shared the prophetic hope that the God of the Jews would one day be accepted by all humankind.

Paul first came to know of Christianity while studying in Jerusalem shortly after the death of Jesus. At first he bitterly opposed the new sect and helped to repress it, until he had a sudden change of heart. According to Scripture, the risen Jesus himself struck Paul blind, reproached him for his deeds of persecution, and then cured him and announced that he had become a "chosen vessel" to bear the name of Christ to the Gentiles. Paul became a Christian of passionate conviction, and undertook the religious conquest of the non-Jewish world.

The Epistles (letters) of Paul, in the New Testament, reflect the enthusiasm and skill he brought to his missionary task. He had become convinced that Christ represented the fulfillment of historical Judaism—but a Judaism made pure and universal. He declared that the Gospel had superseded the Law—even for Jews. No one can be saved by the Law, Paul taught; the Law can only bring people to an understanding of their dependence on Christ. With the barrier of the Law taken away, and with the "good news" of Jesus as the Messiah, the true religion could now be carried to the Gentile world.

An enthusiastic and able organizer, Paul made hard journeys by land and sea and founded numerous Christian congregations in Asia Minor and Greece. His task was made easier by the existence of the Pax Romana and the imperial roads, and by the fact that the Greek language was universally spoken in the eastern parts of the empire. Still, these means would have been worthless had it not been for his fearless devotion to the cause of Christ.

In the course of his missionary work, Paul became of necessity an interpreter of the new faith, for Jesus had left few stated doctrines. When Paul carried the Gospel to the curious Greeks, he was met by all kinds of questions—many of which are recorded in his Epistles, or letters. He answered the questions humbly, explaining that he spoke only as the Lord gave him power.

The First Epistle to the Corinthians illustrates the manner in which Paul developed his interpretations. The congregation at Corinth had asked him numerous questions: Is virginity more seemly to God than marriage? Are women by nature subordinate to men? In what *kind* of body will believers be raised from the dead at Jesus' Second Coming? In his patient answers to these and countless other questions, Paul set forth doctrines that would carry down through the centuries. Among them were his support for the tradition of male supremacy in both worldly and spiritual matters and his acceptance of the practice of slavery: "Wives, be subject to your husbands, as to the Lord. . . . Slaves, be obedient to those who are your earthly masters. . . ." (Ephesians 5:22; 6:5). According to his teachings, however, the Gospel *transcends* all worldly relationships; all individuals are equal in the eyes of Christ.

As the bringer of the "good news" to the Gentiles, Paul demanded no particular style of life, no legalistic rules of conduct. It was enough that individuals simply have faith in Christ as their Savior. Paul thus laid the foundation for the belief that salvation depends exclusively on *faith,* rather than on following the Law or doing "good works." This belief was to raise a problem for Christian ethics and discipline, because one may well ask, "Why, then, bother to obey the rules and teachings of the Church?" Paul's answer would be that good works will flow naturally from faith, but it is *faith,* not works, that leads to salvation.

Paul's position led him unavoidably to another problem: How do individuals *receive* faith? Do they earn it through their own efforts, or is it a gift freely granted by God for his own secret reasons? Paul believed that faith was a gift of God, a conviction that was confirmed by his own experience. Why had Paul, a stony-hearted enemy of Christ, been chosen by the Lord to see the light of conversion? The only answer, Paul felt, lay in God's secret will. As Paul expressed it in his Epistle to the Romans, "So then he has mercy upon whomever he wills, and he hardens the heart of whomever he wills" (9:18). This view, variously referred to as the doctrine of "predestination" or of "election," was to become a source of controversy within the Church. Augustine (in the fifth century), Martin Luther, and John Calvin (both in the sixteenth century; pp. 179, 371, 376–377) are among those who have pursued Paul's line of thought most vigorously, but the idea that some human souls are excluded from all hope of salvation has proven unacceptable to many Christians.

THE SPREAD OF CHRISTIANITY

Paul did not labor alone in his efforts to bring Christianity to the Gentiles. Tradition holds that Peter reached Rome and founded the congregation there; other churches claiming to have been founded by apostles were those of Jerusalem, Alexandria, Damascus, and Antioch (*Map 4.1*). Other missionaries were also at work, and by the end of the first century, there were about fifty Christian congregations. Most of them were in the towns and cities of Palestine and western Asia Minor, though there was also a congregation in Rome.

Appeal and Rejection in the Age of the Pax Romana. Most of the places where Christianity had spread were home to communities of Jews living alongside other ethnic and religious groups, all of which used Greek as their common language. Following the destruction of the Temple in A.D. 70 (p. 160), some of these Jews seem to have heeded the Christian claim that God was punishing them precisely for holding to the Law rather than to the teachings of Jesus. Likewise, some Gentiles in the eastern cities longed to worship the same mighty and perfect God as the Jews, but did not see why he required such detailed and complex observances.

For such people, Jew or Gentile, Christianity was a compelling faith. It put trust in one God of justice and mercy, taught compassion and love, and promised life everlasting in a better world. Instead of the Jewish Law or the equally complex rituals of the traditional gods and goddesses, it demanded only faith in Jesus as the Savior from evil and death. Yet the new religion also contained elements that had been made familiar by Judaism, and as it developed, it also acquired features of the popular mystery religions and absorbed many ideas from the revered philosophy of the Greeks.

The *universalism* of Christianity also brought converts to the new religion. In a world of stark contrasts between Roman and non-Roman, "more honorable" and "humbler" citizens, men and women, Christianity accepted these differences as God-given yet preached equality in the eyes of Christ. This was not simply hypocrisy, for at least in the time of the early Church, the Christian minority did succeed in bridging these differences better than the polytheist majority.

Map 4.1 The Spread of Christianity. The map shows areas in which Christian communities were thickly scattered in A.D. 200 and in 325 (the Council of Nicaea), the region where Christianity was the predominant religion in 600, and areas outside the empire to which Christianity had spread by that date. Christianity spread slowly during the Pax Romana down to 200, much faster in the troubled times of the third century, and fastest of all during the era of imperial favor and barbarian invasions down to 600.

From early times, both middle-class and poor people, and even the occasional aristocrat, joined the Christian communities. The very first Christian converts, looking forward to the Second Coming, had sold their possessions and given the money to their congregations. This urge toward *community property* soon faded when it appeared that the Savior's return would not be as speedy as was first thought. All the same, the teaching and practice of charity—especially caring for the sick—held rich and poor together within the Christian communities.

Likewise, although Christianity accepted the subordination of women to men, the doctrine of equality in Christ made a real difference to the position of women in early Christian congregations. Christianity denounced the common practice of infanticide, of which girl babies were usually the victims, and preached that adultery by husbands was as sinful as by wives. Both Christian and non-Christian observers agreed that women formed the majority of converts, and they played an important role as *deaconesses,* assisting in religious services and administering charity in the early congregations. Even Paul took it for granted that women should be deaconesses, and praised and respected them in this role.

In spite of its spirit of charity and relative equality, however, the new religion did not at first have widespread appeal. On the contrary, it was actually repellent to the vast majority of Jews and Gentiles alike. The main reason was that converts to Christianity had to make a radical, and for most people pointless and unjustified break with their own past lives and the rest of society.

Fig. 4.1 Jesus and His Apostles. Painting from a catacomb, an underground Christian cemetery built near Rome about A.D. 300. Catacombs were perhaps originally intended to be hidden, but most were built after the persecutions had ended—possibly to continue the tradition of earlier, "underground" times. Jesus is shown as an intense, authoritative, relatively short-haired young man, unlike the later serene and long-haired figure (*Fig. 8.11*, p. 353). He holds a Bible—not the traditional scroll (*Fig. 2.4*, p. 75) but the recently invented book with pages.

Like all groups who stand apart from society, the Christians were exposed to ignorant and prejudiced accusations. They were accused of cannibalism and incest, and the respected first-century historian Tacitus declared that they felt "hatred for the human race." Occasionally, they were victims of mob violence. But most of what the majority had against the Christians was true. Christians often refused to associate with non-Christians, and they condemned such popular amusements as the public baths and the combat arenas. Even in death, they avoided the public cemeteries, preferring to await resurrection separately from pagans, who would awake to judgment and eternal fire (*Fig. 4.1*). They spoke out against the practice of venerating the emperor as a god and refused to take part in religious rites before the imperial images. They proclaimed that the empire itself was doomed to inevitable destruction when Jesus should return to replace it with his everlasting kingdom—something that they expected to happen very soon. They declared that the gods and goddesses were false—not in the sense of denying their existence, which would have been bad enough, but in the sense of claiming that they were truly existing wicked demons in disguise. True, the Jews, too, despised pagan belief and would not treat the emperor as a god. The Jews had more or less given up making converts, however, whereas the Christians were above all missionaries seeking to gather in the harvest of the Gentiles.

But during the second century—a time when the empire was strong and stable, the gods and goddesses seemed powerful and kindly, and the emperors ruled with godlike justice—most Gentiles had no desire to be gathered in. They preferred their ancient polytheistic traditions or newer mystery religions that accepted the existing order. As for the Jews, they had to make painful adjustments in their beliefs and practices following the destruction of the Temple, but the overwhelming majority followed the call of the rabbis for stricter observance of the Law, not the call of the Christians to do away with it.

As a result, Christianity spread only very slowly. By A.D. 200, most Christian congregations were still to be found in Palestine and western Asia Minor, and even there they were a minority among Jewish or pagan majorities (*Map 4.1*, p. 167). In the entire western half of the empire, there were still only half a dozen or so congregations, in cities with large communities of Greek-speaking immigrants. Even in Rome, the Christian congregation was still using Greek as its main language.

Growth and Persecution in the Empire's Time of Troubles. From the late second century onward, Christianity's message came to seem more convincing as the empire began to suffer from endless struggles over the succession to imperial power, devastating epidemics, and seemingly unstoppable barbarian attacks (p. 146). In this new and cruel world, many people began to look for certainty, hope, and peace elsewhere: to the Christian Church, which took such loving care of the sick; inside themselves, to the experience of love and mercy offered by the one God and his saving Son; or to the Second Coming of Jesus, which Christian prophecy said would be heralded by great wars and disasters. The numbers of converts mounted, and Christianity grew more widespread. By the early fourth century, Christian congregations were thickly scattered through Egypt, Syria, Greece, and Asia Minor. In the West, they had spread along the Danube and Rhine frontiers, along the Rhone and Seine rivers right across Gaul, across prosperous regions of Africa and Spain, and to many Italian satellite cities of Rome itself (*Map. 4.1*, p. 167).

The faster Christianity spread, however, the more the pagan majority disliked and distrusted it. Pagan philosophers who had earlier regarded Christianity as beneath their notice now took it seriously enough to write books attacking it. To patriotic Roman citizens and earnest pagan believers who felt that the way to solve Rome's problems was to repair its relationship with the traditional deities, the Christians no longer seemed simply an objectionable fringe group, but a real danger to the empire. They were subversive and fanatical deniers of the gods and goddesses, who provoked divine anger against not only themselves but also the community that tolerated them.

The imperial government, which had long outlawed Christianity but had only rarely bothered to enforce the ban, now made more vigorous efforts to reverse the spread of the new religion. The practice began of ordering people suspected of being Christians to prove their loyalty or renounce their faith by sacrificing to the emperor, and executing those who refused. Campaigns of denunciation and coercion against Christians spread across whole regions from time to time. Several of the most energetic and conscientious emperors carried out such campaigns throughout the empire, and these efforts culminated in seven years of vicious persecution under Diocletian from 304 to 311. It was the first time that a government had ever set to work to destroy a religious movement by large-scale repression.

But the emperors had too many other problems to carry out the kind of persistent, long-term persecution that might have crushed the new religion. Bouts of persecution were followed by lengthy periods of toleration or at least neglect. Christians who had fled from persecution or had lain low could safely return or come into the open and rebuild their congregations. Those who had saved their lives by sacrificing to the emperor could safely repent and once again be Christians. And all who survived were inspired by the memory of those who had perished—the martyrs who had borne witness to the faith. Each persecution ended with the Christian congregations becoming larger and more numerous than before.

All the same, early in the fourth century, Christianity was still the religion of a minority. There were still many regions, especially in the West, where Christian congregations were thinly scattered. Away from the complex life of the towns, most of the peasants were content with their ancient cults. (That was why the Christians came to use the Latin word *paganus,* "country dweller," as a contemptuous name for worshipers of the gods and goddesses—hence the English word *pagan.*) Even in regions where there were many congregations, the Christians remained a minority, though by now a prominent and powerful one. There is no way of knowing exactly how many of them there were altogether, but it is very unlikely that they made up more than 10 percent of the population—probably about the same proportion as the Jews. The Christians could survive and even prosper in spite of the emperors' fitful persecutions, but to become predominant they would need the emperors to move in a new direction—that of consistently supporting them.

The Growth of Christian Organization and Doctrine

As befitted a widely distrusted new religion, the first Christian congregations usually met in private homes or halls. There, accepting one another as brothers and sisters, they prayed, sang psalms, and took part in simple rituals. Though the ceremonies were not at first uniform, two were performed by every congregation. One was baptism, the purifying rite of Christian initiation; the other was the partaking of bread and wine, in keeping with the Gospel story of Jesus' last supper with his disciples (Mark 14:17–25). This second ritual came to be known in the Greek service as the Eucharist, and in the Latin service as the Mass.

From such beginnings, the Church had developed an elaborate system and structure by the time of the emperor Constantine (fourth century). The Mass remained the central ceremony, but a host of companion rites and practices grew up. The developing liturgy—that is, the forms of worship—reflected the influence of Judaic tradition and of the Greek and oriental mystery religions. Incense, bells, and ritual garments came into use, along with holy water, oil, candles, and prayer beads. And gradually the religious calendar, with its cycle of fasts and feast days, was worked out. From birth to death, the Church provided the faithful with guidance through a ceaseless round of services and observances. In short, the *idea* of Christianity took solid form as an *institution*.

THE RISE OF THE PRIESTHOOD AND THE EMERGENCE OF BISHOPS

It would have been impossible to accomplish all this without strong leadership and organization. In the beginning, little formal structure was necessary; but as the gospel spread throughout the Roman world, a need arose for supervision and direction. As long as the congregations were small and the Second Coming was still believed to be near at hand, all the members probably shared in the management of local affairs. But as the congregations grew larger and as ritual became more complex, it was natural to develop a specialization of talents and responsibilities. Those who were assigned special functions came to be known as the *clergy* (from the Greek word for "property," probably because they were thought of as the special property of God); the rest of the congregation was called the *laity* (from the Greek word for "the people").

Differences in degrees of authority were also recognized. The early groups viewed all their members as equal in authority, but they gave special status to the apostles, who were reported to have been filled with the Holy Spirit at Pentecost, thereby gaining special powers of wisdom and healing. These powers, it was believed, could be passed on to others by the solemn act of the "laying on of hands."

The theory of *ordination* (admission to the Christian ministry) that grew out of these traditions justified the special role and authority of the priesthood. The priests were believed to have received, through the laying on of hands, the power to perform the miraculous rites of the Church. This theory strengthened the clergy's authority over the laity and ensured at the same time that unauthorized persons would not be able to assume roles of leadership.

At first, the priests and lesser officials were elected (or approved) by their congregations, but as time passed, the clergy grew more and more independent of the laity. They sensed a need for closer association among themselves and for superior levels of authority. They believed that by these means they could better hold the scattered congregations together against external attacks and internal divisions. And so there grew up over the years a system of rising ranks and jurisdictions—the *hierarchy* (sacred rule) of the Church.

Before the end of the second century, each city in which there was a Christian congregation had a chief priest who was recognized as its bishop (in Greek, *episkopos,* or "overseer"). He was selected by the priests of his community and aided by the laity, and he held his position for life. Responsibility and authority in local affairs went increasingly to the bishop. He was ordained to the office by other bishops, and the theory gradually developed that the bishops together constituted the *successors* of the original apostles. (The church of each bishop, by tradition, was believed to have been founded by an apostle or by the companion of an apostle.) The bishops alone possessed the power to ordain others. They taught that priests, deacons, and lesser clerics received, through the bishops, a *portion* of apostolic authority but that only the bishops possessed it in full. This explanation of the authority of bishops came to be known as the doctrine of *apostolic succession.*

A third-century bishop was a busy man. He oversaw the preaching of the gospel, the performance of religious rites, the care of the sick and the poor, the management of church property, and the improvement of Christian morals. He spoke for the faithful in dealings with civil authorities and represented them at larger religious gatherings. His area of jurisdiction, known as a *diocese,* normally included the city in which his church was located and the surrounding district. The diocese was divided into *parishes,* each with its local congregation and priest (pastor). Because both clergy and laity were required to obey the bishop, he held full control over the Christian community.

In coordinating their religious activities, the bishops turned to the model of Roman imperial administration. As Diocletian grouped several provinces into a civil diocese, the bishops (reversing the terms) grouped several dioceses into a *province.* Over this larger jurisdiction reigned the bishop of the chief city in the province. Since a great city was known as a "metropolis," this bishop took on the higher title of *metropolitan* (later, *archbishop*).

By the time of Constantine, there were five leading metropolitans: the bishops of Jerusalem, Alexandria, Antioch, Constantinople, and Rome. Their importance led to their being designated as *patriarchs,* a title and rank above that of the other metropolitans. Thus from the parish priest upward there were four distinct levels in the Christian hierarchy, just as there were in the hierarchy of the late empire (p. 147). Both church and state achieved, at about the same time, closely supervised and authoritarian systems of control.

ROMAN SUPREMACY: THE POPE

The theory of apostolic succession ensured a framework of legitimate authority that could settle differences and enforce discipline at the local level; the bishops exercised control within their dioceses by assuming the right to *excommunicate*—that is, to exclude individuals from church fellowship and services. But when issues arose that divided the bishops themselves, serious troubles ensued.

A question had come up, for instance, around the year 150, regarding the correct day for celebrating Easter. The Gospels were contradictory on this point; the churches of the East observed one day, the churches of the West another. It seemed odd, if not unholy, for one group of Christians to be feasting while another was fasting. Later in the second century, Victor, bishop of Rome, decided to settle the question by excommunicating the Eastern churches on the grounds that the authority of the Roman bishop was superior to that of all others. In any event, the Eastern churches accepted Victor's date for Easter, and the excommunication was lifted.

Thus unity of practice was achieved through the acceptance of a higher authority. Of the five patriarchs, Rome seemed to have the strongest claim to exercise this power. The Eternal City still enjoyed great prestige among the communities of the empire; Rome was the scene of the missionary work and martyrdom of the two leading apostles, Peter and Paul; and according to tradition, the Roman diocese had been founded by Christ's *first* disciple, Peter. Furthermore, the Roman bishops interpreted a passage in the Gospel of Matthew (16:18–19) to mean that Christ had founded his Church on Peter and had entrusted to him alone the "keys of the kingdom of heaven." This, they insisted, made Peter supreme among the apostles. And since each bishop of Rome was the direct successor of Peter, the bishop of Rome was clearly supreme among the bishops of the world.

The rival patriarchs rejected Rome's assertion of supremacy, pointing out that such a sweeping claim could hardly be justified by a brief passage appearing in only one of the Gospels. They argued further that during the early days of the Church, all important decisions were made by a council in Jerusalem, in which Peter had participated but had not ruled. The patriarchs of the East conceded that the successors to Peter had a right to sit at the "head of the table," so to speak, as *first* among *equals,* but ultimate power, they contended, resided only in *general councils* of bishops, such as the Council of Nicaea (p. 175). The Roman bishop, however, was not satisfied with this; he continued to insist on his supremacy, on being recognized as the "Vicar (deputy) of Christ" on earth.

In the West, where there was no rival, Rome achieved that supremacy. By the fifth century, the Roman bishop had begun to reserve to himself the title of *papa* (pope). This word, meaning "father," had formerly been used to refer to any bishop or priest, but henceforth it was used only for the bishop of Rome, in the broader sense of father of the Church. And from this usage arose the term *papacy* to refer to the office of the pope.

Following the Muslim conquest of Alexandria, Antioch, and Jerusalem in the seventh century (p. 204), the pope and the patriarch of Constantinople were left as the two most powerful bishops, heading the Latin and Greek churches, respectively. In spite of many rivalries and disagreements, Rome and Constantinople for several centuries thereafter accepted each other as fellow members of a single all-embracing Christian Church. Eventually, new and bitter disputes arose over the claim of the popes to rule the whole church. These disputes led to a split which has lasted down to the present day (pp. 278–282).

THE CANON OF SCRIPTURES

The administrative authority given to the Church hierarchy was paralleled by the development of biblical authority. At last, in the fourth century, the *canon* (that is, the authorized list) of Scriptures was established. Previously, a great many "holy" books and epistles had been in circulation, but the bishops agreed that if the unity of the Church was to be preserved, these writings would have to be screened for certification. How were they to decide which had been inspired by God and which had not? Some of the bishops objected to accepting the Hebrew Scriptures, but these writings were so well established by tradition that it was finally decided to accept them. From the Christian point of view, they dealt with the "Old Covenant" (p. 51) of God with the Jews as opposed to his "New Covenant" with the Christians. The Latin word for "covenant" is *testamentum;* hence the English names Old and New Testament.

For the New Testament there was no such guide in tradition, so the bishops resorted to authority. They decided that only writings by apostles or their companions, clearly inspired by the Holy Spirit, would be admitted. Although this rule at once eliminated many disputed books of uncertain origin, it did not work automatically. For example, when a certain gospel attributed to Peter was found to favor a doctrine offensive to the bishops, they simply declared that Peter could not have been its author. On the other hand, books and epistles that struck the bishops as "right" in doctrine were readily attributed to an apostle—and thereby included in the canon. In the same way, the Jews had earlier made Moses the author of all the sacred books on law, David the author of the psalms, and Solomon the author of the books of wisdom. But in the final analysis, it was the judgment of the bishops that determined whether a particular writing was admitted into the canon.

The bishops did not reach final agreement on the canon until near the end of the fourth century, when the pope proclaimed that Jerome's Latin translation (p. 182) was the standard text for the Church. In the West, where Latin was the common language, Jerome's version became known as the Vulgate (from *vulgatus,* meaning "common").

DOCTRINAL DIFFERENCES: ORTHODOXY AND HERESY

Even with its priestly hierarchy and canon of Scriptures, the Church was frequently split by serious disputes over doctrine. These ranged over a broad area: religious ritual, rules of Christian conduct, and the complex field of Christian theology—that is, explanations of God, the Creation, sin, and salvation. For centuries, the existence of conflicting positions disturbed the leaders of the Church. If there is to be one Church believing one truth about the one God, there must be one doctrine, defined as "orthodox" (from Greek words meaning the "correct opinion"). Views differing from orthodoxy are "heresies" (from a Greek word meaning "to choose for oneself" rather than following the consensus), and heresies must be false. One of the earliest, most persistent, and most radical of the heresies was *Gnosticism* (from the Greek *gnōsis,* "knowledge").

The Gnostics were a religious-philosophical group with origins distinct from those of Christianity. Influenced by Platonic thought (pp. 81–83), they believed that the universe is divided between spirit and matter. Spirit is the only true good; matter came into existence as a kind of casting off from spirit when the physical world, including human bodies, was created. The body (as Socrates had taught) imprisons the soul and is the source of evil; the true aim of life is to gain knowledge by which the soul may liberate itself and join with the *universal spirit.* But, said the Gnostics, this knowledge cannot be attained through reason; it comes only as *mystical* insight, which the initiate achieves after passing through secret rites. Similar notions had appeared in Persian thought, particularly in the dualism that followed Zoroaster's teaching (p. 47).

Gnostics, like Christians, were to be found mainly in the cities of the eastern half of the empire, and many of them made their way into the Church, where they formed factions and held to secret teachings that made use of certain Christian ideas. They interpreted Christ as the Savior who would emancipate humankind from the prison of the flesh (sin). Moreover, because Christ is all good, he could not have had a body; hence, the Incarnation, Jesus' life as a man, and his human suffering were only *appearances.* They could not have occurred, logically, for goodness consists of pure spirit.

This view clearly ran counter to basic Christian doctrines, and it alarmed the Church leaders. During the second and third centuries, the bishops struck hard at such unauthorized teachings. When the Gnostics declared that their wisdom had come to them through "chosen" persons, the bishops replied that no one but the apostles and their successors could speak for the Church. The ordained bishops stood firm, and at last the Gnostics were driven out of the Church. In varying forms, however, the central idea of this heresy continued. It cropped up in the fourth century as Manichaeism and again in the thirteenth as the Albigensian heresy (pp. 254–255).

The persistence of such deviations arises from the fact that the orthodox Christian position itself rests on a delicate balance between spirit and matter, soul and body. This position holds that both exist and that both are essentially good, for both are the handiwork of a perfect God. Yet there is a clear tendency in the Scriptures, in the preachings of Jesus and Paul, to place spirit *above* matter, although *how far* above is not made clear. Given this lead, some Christians have tended to praise the soul as the true home of God and to put down the body as the "devil's workshop." Those who follow this line to the extreme show contempt for *all* worldly things, including food and drink, sexual activity, and care of the body. A practical outlet for this impulse, within the limits of Church control, is *monasticism* (pp. 179–184).

No sooner had the Gnostic threat been suppressed than a heresy of a different sort erupted: the Donatist heresy, named after Donatus, bishop of Carthage (in Africa). During the persecutions under Diocletian, some African bishops had given up their holy books at the demand of the Roman authorities, thereby saving their own lives. Their surrender was regarded as an act of treason to the Church, and although the bishop of Rome reinstated the offenders after they had shown due repentance, many members of the African Church refused to accept them. Worse, Donatus and his followers insisted that all the rites performed by the bishops after their sinful acts were *invalid.* Thrown into question were ordinations of priests (p. 170), marriages, baptisms—all the sacred rites of the Church. Here was a challenge that could not be ignored.

In 313, a council of bishops at Arles (in southern France) considered the question and decided against the Donatists. They declared that priests who had surrendered to persecution might be restored and that their ritual acts were in no way affected by personal guilt or innocence: "Once a priest, always a priest." This appears to be the only position the Church could have taken. If the council had ruled that a priest must be in a state of goodness (grace) in order to discharge his duties, the validity of any ceremony he performed would be open to question. The decision at Arles sealed the powers given by ordination and set at rest the doubts of the faithful. The Donatists, however, stubbornly refused to accept the ruling, and the Church authorities, supported by the newly Christian emperors, determined to suppress them. The result was the first systematic persecution of Christians by Christians, which continued long enough to reduce the Donatists from a rival church to an underground movement. The heresy smoldered, however, until the seventh century, when the Islamic tide rolled over North Africa (p. 204).

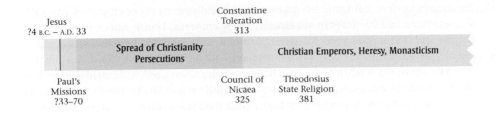

Jesus ?4 B.C. – A.D. 33	Constantine Toleration 313	
Spread of Christianity Persecutions	Christian Emperors, Heresy, Monasticism	
Paul's Missions ?33–70	Council of Nicaea 325	Theodosius State Religion 381

THE COUNCIL OF NICAEA AND THE TRINITARIAN CREED

The doctrinal dispute that came nearest to splitting the Church was over the nature of Jesus and his relationship to God. We have already seen that the Gnostics believed Jesus to be pure spirit and denied his human nature. In direct opposition to that view was the idea that Jesus was *only* a man, although a man of superior moral stature, who had been adopted by God for his divine purposes. Between these extremes were countless other points of view, most of which subordinated the Son in some manner to the Father. All the variety and subtlety of Hebrew and Greek tradition were brought into play in this crucial theological debate. For how could Christians worship as one body unless they agreed on the nature of the godhead?

The argument was still raging three centuries after the birth of Christ. By the early fourth century, however, opinions had been reduced to two main views. One was set forth notably by Athanasius, bishop of Alexandria, and the other by Arius, a learned priest of the same city. Athanasius held that Father and Son were two equal persons but *one substance.* Arius insisted that because Christ had been "begotten," there must have been a time when he did not exist. Because he was not coeternal with the Father, he could not be coequal.

When the emperor Constantine learned of this religious division, he was deeply distressed. After accepting Christianity in 313, he had given the Church legal status (p. 150), fully expecting that it would serve as a unifying force in the empire. But now he found it, instead, a source of discord. Most of the East leaned to Arius; the West supported Athanasius. How could Constantine heal the spirit and restore Christian unity?

He knew that the dissension could not be bridged by means of reason, for logical arguments were being spun out endlessly by both sides. Realizing that as in matters of discipline, the final resort would have to be to authority, he summoned the leaders of the Church to a meeting at Nicaea (in Asia Minor) in 325. This was the first general (worldwide) council of the Church, and more than three hundred bishops attended. On the question put before them, the majority sided with Athanasius. A formal *creed* (statement of belief) was drawn up, declaring that the Son is of one being, or essence, with the Father but also stressing the nature of Christ as *both* man and God, thus striking at Gnostic teachings. The creed also included the Holy Spirit, thus completing the concept of the godhead as a Trinity: one *substance* in three equal but distinct *persons.* The Nicene Creed, as amended at the Council of Constantinople (381), remains the orthodox view and is recited in most Christian churches to this day.

The Council of Nicaea did not immediately succeed, however, in restoring unity on the issue of the Trinity. When Arius and several other priests at Nicaea refused to sign the creed, Constantine banished them. Ten years later, an Eastern council at Tyre (in modern Lebanon) reversed the decisions of Nicaea and exiled Athanasius instead of Arius. Constantine's successors held differing opinions on the issue, and for some forty years, the banishing or recalling of bishops turned on the decisions of the emperors. Athanasius was banished six times in all. Finally, a new emperor, Theodosius I, reunited the empire and summoned a second general council. This meeting, held at Constantinople in 381, reaffirmed the Nicaean decision and put an end to the exhausting debate.

The divisions within the Church nevertheless persisted stubbornly. Rejected within the Roman Empire, Arian missionaries took their faith outside its frontiers, to the Germanic barbarians who eventually took over the empire's western provinces (pp. 151–155). Meanwhile in the East, new differences arose over the exact relationship of the divine and the human in Christ. The popes and the Western Church maintained that he was both fully divine and fully human, and eventually the Eastern emperors and the patriarchs of Constantinople came to share this view—which has remained Christian orthodoxy ever since. In Alexandria, Antioch, and Jerusalem, however, it was generally believed that Jesus' divinity predominated over or even excluded his humanity. In the sixth century, the Eastern emperors tried by force and persecution to convert the heretics of Egypt and the Middle East to what was now the orthodox view. In doing so, the emperors aroused such fury and hatred among their subjects that in the seventh century, when the Muslims conquered the region (p. 204), they were welcomed by most of the people as liberators. But the views on the Trinity and the nature of Christ that were hammered out in the fourth and fifth centuries have remained Christian orthodoxy ever since.

The Worldly Victory of the Church

By the end of the third century, Christianity had grown to be a well-organized movement in the cities of the Roman Empire, and the emperors had to decide what they were going to do about it. Either they must crush it, because tolerating it would bring the empire into disfavor with the traditional gods or goddesses; or they must join it, because it alone could guarantee the empire the favor of the one true God. In the end, the emperors made the second choice, and it was this that enabled Christianity to change from a minority faith to the dominant religion of the empire.

THE ALLIANCE WITH THE STATE

The emperors tried hard to make the first choice work before settling for the second. But none of them was able to crush the new religion, and after Diocletian's persecution died down, it was clear that the Church could not be broken. The Christian God, it seemed, was more powerful than the Roman emperors. Perhaps it was his favor, not that of the pagan deities, that the empire needed.

At last, after Constantine came to power and issued his edict of toleration in 313, the emperors came to accept the Christian God as the one whom they should worship and who would protect the empire (p. 150). It took no more than a hundred years for the elite and the people in the cities to fall into line. From the start, of course, the emperors had the backing of the Christian minority, but for a long time they did not risk open pagan resistance by actually forbidding the traditional rites. Still, they favored Christian rather than pagan officials and army commanders for rewards and promotion; they donated property to churches rather than temples, or even confiscated temple property and handed it over to churches; they took advice from bishops rather than pagan interpreters of the will of the gods; and they replaced pagan with Christian ceremonies and symbols on state occasions. Public entertainments, which were an important part of the life of cities and closely connected with religion, became subject to Christian restrictions. The Colosseum (pp. 141–142), with its bloody combats, had traditionally been one of the main gathering places of Rome, but the people of the new Christian city of Constantinople had to make do with chariot races in the Hippodrome. Meanwhile, the bishops did their part to edge out popular pagan festivities as painlessly as possible. It was now that they began celebrating Christmas on December 25—a date never mentioned in the Gospel accounts of Jesus' birth, which was, however, the same as that of a joyous winter festival of pagan Rome.

It took until 381 before Theodosius I legalized the Christian victory by making Christianity the religion of the state and forbidding pagan rites. Now the tables were turned. Mobs began vandalizing pagan temples, smashing idols, and attacking worshipers. The Church, which had once protested to emperors about their intolerance of Christians, now joined with the state to stamp out rival faiths. Pagan worship continued in the countryside, though Christianity was finally spreading there too as wealthy landowners converted and made their dependent peasants (p. 151) follow the new religion. But the traditional cults that mighty emperors had practiced only a century before now survived only as rural superstitions. By A.D. 600, Christianity was probably the religion of the majority in most of the territories that belonged or had once belonged to the Roman Empire, and it was spreading beyond those territories to Mesopotamia in the east and Ireland in the west (*Map 4.1*, p. 167).

However, harassment and persecution by the Christian state and Church were not the main reason why traditional polytheism collapsed so fast. Rather, its collapse was the result of the polytheist way of thinking about the gods and goddesses. From Constantine onward, the emperors, who had previously claimed to be both gods themselves and responsible to the gods, denied their own divinity and the deities of Rome. From the pagan point of view, these were deeds that deserved divine vengeance. If the Roman Empire had begun to fall in the time of Constantine, that would have confirmed the pagan belief in their deities and might well have delayed or even prevented the Christian victory. When the empire did finally start to collapse, those pagans who were left did indeed explain this as the vengeance of the gods, but by then it was too late. For a lifetime after Constantine, the Christian emperors had challenged the gods and goddesses and most of the people of the Roman Empire had followed them, yet life had gone on just the same. Traditional polytheists could not conceive of truly powerful deities as being content with the worship of a minority of the human race or as being long-suffering if their worshipers turned against them—those were monotheist concepts. So long as the Christian emperors prospered, for many pagans that was proof that the gods and goddesses were weak, or indifferent, or nonexistent—in which case, what was the point of resisting Christianity?

There was, however, one religious group that did have the inner conviction to survive the Christian victory: the Jews. Even when Rome became officially Christian, the problem for the Jews remained basically the same as it had always been—that of surviving alongside a majority religion which they considered to be false. The Christian point of view was more complicated. On the one hand, Christians believed that the religion of the Jews was false inasmuch as they had rejected Christ and continued to observe the Law. In addition, the Jews were still liable to convert Christians who found the one God of Judaism easier to believe in than the Trinity, and the burden of the Law no harder to bear than the rule of bishops and priests. All this was reason enough to punish the Jews. However, many Christian thinkers believed that God himself already had the punishment of the Jews in hand. It was his will that they should wander the earth to the end of time, deprived of the land he had given them and of his presence in the Temple, all the while pointlessly submitting to the restrictions of the Law from which Christ had freed the human race. Thus by actually suppressing Judaism, the Christians would in fact be frustrating God's purpose.

With this in mind, Theodosius ordered that the religious practices of the Jews be tolerated and that they be protected against attacks by Christian mobs. Soon afterward, steps were taken to limit the contacts and influence of Jews. They were forbidden to seek converts or to build new synagogues, intermarriage between Jews and Christians was severely punished, and Jews were excluded from government service. In this way there began an ambivalent Christian policy toward the Jews, which was to continue for centuries to come—one of harassing, restricting, and humiliating them while not usually seeking to convert or destroy them.

AUGUSTINE: THE PHILOSOPHER OF CHRISTIAN VICTORY

Augustine, one of the Fathers of the Church, symbolizes the Christian triumph. His own life, with its pagan beginnings and ultimate acceptance of Christ, parallels the larger struggle within the empire. Born of a Christian mother and a pagan father, Augustine was attracted at one time or another by the leading philosophies of his day until about 387, when he was converted and rose swiftly to a position of importance in the Church. A man of extraordinary intellectual power, he influenced succeeding generations even more than his own, for his ideas have helped shape the theology, morals, politics, and philosophy of the Western world. A prolific writer, he set down his major thoughts in his *Confessions* and *The City of God*.

Augustine grew up in a small town in North Africa. There he plunged into the study of classical literature and the arts of logic and argumentation, which were to serve him later as an advocate of Christian doctrine. During those same years, he indulged his taste for pleasure and delved deeply into pagan thought. When at last he felt the pull of Christianity, he discovered that he could not make his way to God by himself; the *Confessions* tells the story of his inner struggle.

Augustine's youthful association with Manichaeism (a dualistic philosophy related to Gnosticism) gave him a lifelong bias toward dualism (pp. 173–174), which influenced his interpretations of his personal history and of world history. He saw the struggle within himself between two sides of his character: his love of worldly things versus his love of the Lord. Ultimately, by God's grace, the higher love won out, and the tortured young man was baptized a Christian. Thanking the Lord for this gift, Augustine confessed, "For so completely did thou convert me to Thyself that I desired neither wife nor any hope of this world, but set my feet on the rule of faith." He became a priest and later bishop of Hippo, in North Africa (*Map 4.1*, p. 167).

From his personal experiences Augustine concluded that bodily appetites (as well as false philosophies) distract people from the contemplation of God. Their only hope for release from the enormous burden of sin is to pray for God's help in bringing them to repentance and self-denial. Augustine himself gave up family and possessions and lived like a monk.

His own experience also led him to embrace Paul's doctrine of predestination—that the Lord chooses those who are to be saved (p. 166). The original sin of Adam, wrote Augustine, condemned all men to eternal punishment—but "the undeserved grace of God saved *some* therefrom." Thus Paul was chosen from among the Pharisees and Augustine from the Manichaeans to become servants of God. Neither felt he had earned grace through his own behavior, so both gave full credit to the Lord's mercy.

Augustine expanded this idea of the "elect" and the "nonelect" into a comprehensive yet profoundly simple philosophy of world history. Following his inclination to view matters in a dualistic way, he declared that all of humanity—the dead, the living, and the unborn—is divided into two communities. The first is moved by love of self; the second, by love of God. These conflicting loves, he argued, are more important than the superficial attachments to race, nation, and class. He called one community the "Earthly City" and the other the "Heavenly City" (the City of God). Though the members of these two communities are intermixed in the present world, they have separate fates. The first will suffer everlasting punishment with the devil, and the second will live eternally with God.

It was in this light that he explained the sacking of Rome by the barbarian Visigoths in 410 (p. 153). That calamity, occurring only a generation after Theodosius had made Christianity the state religion, shocked and disheartened many Christians, and surviving pagans whispered that it was a punishment sent by their gods. Augustine indignantly denied their claim and began to write his monumental book, *The City of God,* which put the fall of Rome into a larger perspective. With immense labor, he listed the earlier reverses and disasters of Rome, thus "proving" that the city's troubles were not the result of its having embraced Christianity. In fact, Augustine assured the faithful, the sack of Rome was a spectacular confirmation of basic Christian teachings: it demonstrated that even the most powerful of earthly cities must sooner or later crumble and fall. The only true Eternal City is the City of God, and the whole earthly show of history is a passing thing. To some, Augustine's interpretation implied that they should simply stand by and let events take their course ("God's will be done"). But he reminded them that the empire, whatever its past sins, was now a Christian state and a protector of order; he therefore urged all its citizens to resist the barbarians who were bringing plunder and anarchy.

But, some critics objected, are not fighting and killing contrary to the commandments of God? Augustine, interpreting Scripture, answered that God's law against killing applies only to *personal* behavior. A war declared by officials of the state can be morally "right," and in a "just war," killing is permissible. Augustine's idea of the "just war" carried an inescapable implication: if one side is just, then its enemy must be unjust. He thus laid the foundation for Christian approval of wars and the "good-versus-evil" view of disputes between nations.

Augustine's concepts of predestination and the Two Cities guided Christian thinking for centuries to follow. More immediately, his example and teachings lent support to an emerging institution of the Church—monasticism.

Early Christian Monasticism

Monasticism has been a recognized way of life in both Western and non-Western cultures for centuries, answering the needs of a sizable minority of people. Monks and nuns have also served the needs of society as a whole—as religious leaders, as transmitters of the culture and knowledge of the past, as pioneer settlers in empty lands, and in many other roles. But the basic motivation of the monastic is to escape from society, to pray and contemplate in solitude, and so to come nearer the desired spiritual goal. In the rise of Christian monasticism, this goal was a purer life, as understood through faith. And the desire for this goal, in turn, sprang from two forces: love for God and fear of damnation.

THE ASCETIC IDEAL

The holy life, in the Christian view, is not easily attained. It requires, above all, self-discipline—strict control over the natural self and its appetites. The very term *ascetic* is derived from the Greek word for the exercise practiced by a trained athlete. Just as the discus thrower must discipline his muscles, so the "perfect" Christian must gain control over his or her entire body and mind. Only then will that individual be free from sinful thoughts and acts—free to follow Christ's commands and perhaps to know the ecstasy of heavenly visions.

Why have some Christians thought of perfection in such "unnatural" terms? In most cases, they have taken their lead from the example of Christ. Jesus was no monk, but his teachings had a decidedly ascetic quality. As we have seen, his ethical teachings called for a degree of selflessness that few humans have been able to achieve: "If you would be perfect, go, sell what you possess and give to the poor, and you will have treasure in heaven; and come, follow me" (Matthew 19:21). Added to this original emphasis was the influence of Paul. He distinguished two standards of Christian conduct, the permissible and the heroic, and set the second above the first. While conceding, for instance, that it is "better to marry than to be aflame with passion" (1 Corinthians 7:9), he ranked virginity above the married state. "It is well," Paul advised, "for a man not to touch a woman" (7:1). Finally, the impact of Gnostic views, which identified the body with evil (p. 173), reinforced the ascetic tendency in Christianity.

THE HERMIT MONKS: ANTHONY

In the early days of Christianity, a man who aspired to the ascetic ideal simply abandoned civilization. In Egypt, where Christian monasticism was exceedingly popular during the third century, this was an easy matter, for the empty desert was close at hand. There, exposed to the burning heat and sand, the hermit could punish his body and strengthen his will. One of the most celebrated hermit monks was Anthony, whose biography by Bishop Athanasius was widely read throughout the empire. The son of an aristocratic family of Alexandria, Anthony became a devout Christian in about 270. After selling all his possessions, he headed for the desert and spent the rest of his life subjecting his body to increasingly severe discipline. So famous did he become that thousands sought him out, hoping for cures and advice from this "holy man." To preserve his privacy, he was forced to move deeper and deeper into the desert.

Anthony's hardest struggle was with sexual desire. His biographer reported that the devil would appear to him at night in the "form and deportment of a woman." But Anthony stubbornly resisted, and at last he cried out so fiercely that the devil "fled in terror." Other monks, too, were bedeviled by the sexual urge, which more than any other symbolized to them the disturbing appetites of the body. Monastic chronicles are full of anecdotes about the monks' torments of desire and their efforts to dispel them.

One way was to keep from looking at a woman. But as Anthony discovered, this did not shield the mind from provocative fantasies. A surer way was to keep the body weak, bruised, and exhausted—a solution that also enabled the monk to display his contempt for the flesh.

Anthony was a model Christian hermit, fasting constantly and wearing a prickly hair shirt beneath his leather outer garment. He never washed his body and was at pains to keep even his feet out of water. His solitary life of prayer and contemplation was frequently rewarded, we are told, by divine visions. This way of life must have agreed with Anthony, or else he was of very hardy stock: at the age of one hundred, writes Athanasius, the hermit at last fell ill and died in his desert cell.

Stirred by the example of Anthony and other world-renouncing hermits, a multitude of Christians throughout Egypt and the East began to abandon the cities and take up a solitary life. Many inflicted such hardships on themselves that it is hard to imagine how they survived. For their fellow Christians, however, their hardships and survival proved them to be holy men, whose closeness to God gave them power on earth. One of the most famous of all the hermits was Simeon Stylites (the "Pillar-Dweller") of Syria, who tried to limit his contacts with the crowds of pilgrims who came to visit him by living on a small, unenclosed platform at the top of a pillar. He stayed there for thirty-six years until he died, and was revered across the Christian world and respectfully visited even by emperors.

REGULATED COMMUNITIES: BASIL, JEROME

Not all who felt called to asceticism, however, had the strength to live a life of hardship on their own, but needed the support of a community. And so in time, the first monasteries, for men only, were founded. Here each monk had a private cell for devotions, but during certain hours of the day he joined his fellow monks for common meals and labor. Eventually, similar homes (*convents*) for women (known as *nuns*) were established.

The earliest religious "houses" were organized in the fourth century. One of these was founded by Pachomius, a desert hermit, who built a crude compound on an island in the Nile River. A former soldier, Pachomius laid the place out like an army camp and imposed a strict schedule and discipline on his Christian "recruits." The regulations came to be known as the Rule of Pachomius and were later adopted and modified by Basil, a bishop of Asia Minor. The Basilian Rule became the basis of monasticism in the East and has remained so to the present day.

The ascetic impulse spread westward across the Mediterranean world, spurred by the changing relationship between Christianity and the empire. Constantine's recognition of Christianity was followed by Theodosius' decision to make Christianity the empire's official religion. By making it safe to practice the faith, these measures brought into it large numbers of converts who lacked the sincerity and conviction of the earlier Christians. In other words, as the Church advanced into the world, it became more worldly. Even the clergy began to fall to corruption and ambition as the doors to wealth and power opened before them.

Christians who wished to imitate Christ and the holy martyrs were upset and repelled by the growing worldliness of the Church; after the fourth century, many of them chose monasticism as a substitute for martyrdom and as a refuge from the distractions of worldly affairs. The life of the monk or nun, in fact, was often described as "white" (bloodless) martyrdom, as against the "red" martyrdom of the person who gave his or her life for the faith. Church leaders in the West gave warm support to this ascetic trend. Augustine established a monastic community in North Africa and practiced rigid self-discipline himself. The scholarly Jerome, who lived in the same period, gave up a comfortable life in Rome to become a hermit.

The earlier hermits had shown contempt for all books other than the Scriptures. Anthony, for instance, was an uneducated man who believed that all a devout Christian needed was a sound mind and the inspiration of the Spirit. His attitude was in keeping with the teachings of Jesus, which might be characterized as anti-intellectual. And Paul, like Jesus, had put faith and love above reason and learning. Jerome, however, could not bear to leave his library at home, so he carried it with him to the Holy Land. But his passion for the classics at last filled him with anxiety, and he decided that he must be either a "Ciceronian" or a Christian. He determined therefore to give up his attachment to pagan literature. Yet as soon as he stopped studying, he was tormented by visions of Roman dancing girls. Like Anthony, he tried to beat down his lustful thoughts by starving and mortifying his body. Nothing helped until he hit upon the idea of learning Hebrew. Because Hebrew was the language of the Scriptures, he believed that this study would be pleasing to the Lord. Furthermore, it required such mental concentration that his tantalizing visions began to fade.

Eventually Jerome was able to look at women without desire. When he was called to Rome on Church business in 382, he took the opportunity to spread the gospel of asceticism among the noble ladies of the city and persuaded many of them to turn their lives to Christian purity. "Marriage fills the earth," he counseled; "virginity fills heaven." On his return to Palestine, he founded, in partnership with a rich widow named Paula, several monastic communities in Bethlehem—some for men and some for women.

Jerome's most famous literary work, completed about 400, was a translation of the Bible into Latin from the Hebrew and Greek sources. Jerome decided to set the monks and nuns to work on scholarly projects also. His success in turning the energy of monasticism to productive literary enterprise established an important precedent. During the Middle Ages, monasteries helped safeguard the cultural heritage of the West by preserving and copying manuscripts and by providing basic schooling for the clergy.

BENEDICT AND HIS RULE

The most influential founder of European monasticism was Benedict of Nursia. The son of a noble Italian family, he began early in life to follow Anthony's example. Sickened by the vice he saw in Rome, he fled to the nearby hills and imposed on himself a rule of physical self-punishment and spiritual dedication. So famous did the austere hermit become that he attracted other young men who wished to share his way of life. Convinced at last that asceticism was better practiced in groups, he left his solitary cave and established several small communities for his disciples.

The monastery at Monte Cassino (*Fig. 4.2; Map 4.1*, p. 167), which Benedict founded about 529, served as the center of his work. It has been rebuilt many times (most recently, after the Second World War), and it still stands on a towering hill overlooking the town of Cassino, between Rome and Naples. There Benedict drew up a set of regulations to govern the lives of his monks. This Benedictine Rule reflected the ideals of love, humanity, and piety that inspired the life of its author. It struck a balance between solitary meditation and group activities. The Rule proved so successful that it

Fig. 4.2 The Monastery of Monte Cassino. Founded by Benedict of Nursia in A.D. 529, Monte Cassino was where he developed his Rule, which became the most widespread pattern of monastic life in the Christian world. The monastery was repeatedly destroyed over the centuries—by barbarian invaders not long after Benedict's death, by Muslim raiders in the ninth century, by a fourteenth-century earthquake, and by Allied bombing during the Second World War. Nevertheless, the monks of Monte Cassino still follow Benedict's Rule today.

became the model constitution for all other religious orders in the West, and within a few centuries, nearly 40,000 monasteries and nunneries were governed by it.

Any free man or woman was eligible to commit his or her life to the Rule. After spending a probationary (testing) year to ensure that they were equal to its rigors, aspiring monks or nuns took three perpetual vows: chastity, poverty, and obedience. In addition they pledged "stability," which meant that they had to remain on the monastery grounds unless given permission to leave. The monk or nun thus surrendered sexual gratification, private property, and personal freedom for the chance of living a life more pleasing to God and of gaining salvation through discipline.

Benedict felt that control by one person made for the greatest serenity and harmony within the monastic community. Consequently, he granted authority over the monks to a "superior," known as an *abbot*. The abbot was chosen by the monks to serve for life, and Benedict advised the utmost care in his selection. He also gave the abbot advice on how to govern. The abbot, said Benedict, ought "rather to be of help than to command"; he should "exalt mercy over judgment . . . and strive rather to be loved than feared." He should always be aware of his own imperfection and should keep himself from becoming troubled and anxious; if he grows jealous or suspicious, he will have no rest. He should use moderation in assigning labor to his monks: "He shall so temper all things that there may be both what the strong desire, and the weak do not shrink from" (*Rule,* LXIV).

On all matters of importance, Benedict urged, the abbot should consult the assembled brothers, as the monks were known, and weigh their advice seriously: "Do all things with counsel, and you shall not thereafter repent" (*Rule,* III). At the same time, he warned the abbot against shutting his eyes to the vices of the monks. In dealing with a rebellious monk, the abbot should first correct him and, next, exclude him from association with his brothers. If these steps, supported by prayer, did not cause the offender to obey, the abbot was authorized to use the lash and, as a last resort, to expel him from the monastery.

Though Benedict left the abbot some measure of discretion, he set down in detail the standard monastic routine. The most important activity of all was the saying of Divine Office (obligatory daily prayers); seven times a day the toll of bells called the monks to their knees. During meals they were to observe the rule of silence while one of them read aloud from the Scriptures. Certain hours of the day they were to spend alone in their private cells reading and meditating. To Benedict, the monastery was a "school for the service of the Lord."

Since each monastery depended on its own resources, the monks had to spend much of their time growing and preparing food and providing for their other material needs. From four to eight hours a day were set aside for manual labor, which, Benedict thought, would provide a wholesome balance to their intellectual and spiritual activities. The monks cleared new land for cultivation; aided the sick, orphans, and widows; learned the arts of agriculture; and preserved ancient handicrafts in their workshops. Their services to Western civilization during the Middle Ages were immense, for they also served as missionaries, preserved and copied ancient writings, and carried on scholarly tasks after the example of Jerome.

Yet direct service to God remained the primary aim of the Benedictine houses and of the religious orders that arose later. The monastics devoted their lives to prayer and charity, providing a model for Christians outside the cloister. They also exercised a corrective influence on the more worldly priests and bishops of the Church. Because they lived under a special rule (*regula*), they came to be called the "regular" clergy. Clerics who were not monks and were therefore thought of as belonging to this world (*saeculum*) came to be known as the "secular" clergy.

By the sixth century, the very existence of the Church depended heavily on the regular clergy. Some of the most vigorous and devoted leaders of the Church came up through the Rule—men like Gregory the Great, who became bishop of Rome in 590 and was a molder of the medieval papacy. After the collapse of imperial power, the survival of Western civilization itself rested largely on the three organized forces within Christianity: the papacy, the secular clergy, and the monastic orders. Ironically, it fell to the Church, whose primary mission was to open the way to the *next* world, to safeguard the civilization of *this* world.

RECOMMENDED READING

Sources of Christianity S. J. D. Cohen, *From the Maccabees to the Mishnah* (1987), is an authoritative account of the development of Judaism as a religion in Hellenistic and Roman times.

P. Clark, *Zoroastrianism* (1998), outlines the main features of Persian religion, and T. Irwin, *Classical Thought* (1989), deals with the influence of Greek philosophy on Christian doctrine.

The Life and Teachings of Jesus H. C. Kee, *What Can We Know About Jesus?* (1990), is a brief account by a leading scholar of what is known of the writing of the Gospels and their reliability as evidence; E. P. Sanders deals with Jesus' life and teachings in *The Historical Figure of Jesus* (1993). P. Perkins, *Jesus as Teacher* (1990), discusses his ethical message and his own understanding of his mission. J. Riches, *The World of Jesus: First-Century Judaism in Crisis* (1990), puts Jesus and his teaching against the background of Jewish history and religion.

The Early Church and Its Expansion H. Chadwick, *The Early Church* (1967), is a classic and readable account, covering the entire period of the rise of Christianity. E. G. Hinson, *The Early Church* (1996), and G. Vallée, *The Shaping of Christianity* (1999), are excellent recent treatments. E. P. Sanders, *Paul* (1991), is a brief assessment by a leading scholar. B. Withington, *Women and the Genesis of Christianity* (1990), discusses the role of women in the life and teachings of Jesus and Paul and in the Gospel narratives. J. F. Kelly, *The World of the Early Christians* (1997), deals with the social background of Christianity.

The Growth of Christian Organization and Doctrine The books by Chadwick, Hinson, and Vallée listed in the last section all cover organization and doctrine. B. Schimmelpfennig, *The Papacy* (1992), is a short history that includes the period of the early Church. R. MacMullen, *Christianizing the Roman Empire (A.D. 100–400)* (1984), discusses the spread of Christianity and pagan reactions to it. A good general account of the emergence of Christianity out of the Jewish and Gentile worlds is R. Doran, *Birth of a Worldview: Early Christianity in Its Jewish and Pagan Contexts* (1995).

The Worldly Victory of the Church P. Brown, *The Rise of Western Christendom, A.D. 200–1000* (1996), begins with the victory of the Church. R. MacMullen, *Christianizing the Roman Empire (A.D. 100–400)* (1984) and *Christianity and Paganism in the Fourth to Sixth Centuries* (1997), discuss the end of paganism and the imposition of Christian belief.

M. Downes, *The Doctrine of the Trinity* (1999), outlines the disputes over the nature of God and the person of Jesus. C. Harrison, *Augustine: Christian Truth and Fractured Humanity* (2000), sets the development of theology in its cultural and social context. M. T. Clark, *Augustine* (1994), outlines his life and thought.

Early Christian Monasticism C. H. Lawrence, *Medieval Monasticism* (1989), is a readable introduction that includes treatment of monastic origins. M. de Dreuille, *From East to West* (1999), discusses the relationship between Christian monasticism and similar ways of life in other religions.

INFOTRAC COLLEGE EDITION

Visit the source collections at **http://academic.cengage.com/infotrac**, and use the Search function with the following key terms:

early Christianity

Constantine

WESTERN CIVILIZATION RESOURCES

Visit the Brief History of the Western World Companion Web Site for resources specific to this textbook:

http://history.wadsworth.com/greerbrief09/

Also, the CD in the back of this book and the World History Resources Center at **http://history.wadsworth.com/west_civ/** offer a variety of tools to help you succeed in this course, including access to quizzes; images; documents; interactive simulations, maps, and timelines; movie explorations; and a wealth of other sources.

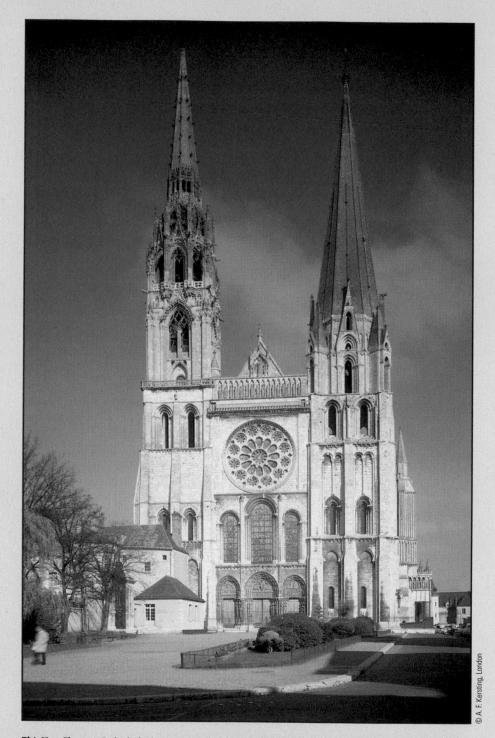

Fig. II.1. Chartres Cathedral. The western end of the nave (central hall) stands 120 feet high, but much of it is glass rather than stone so as to flood the building's interior with light—symbolic of the light that flows from God himself. Tall stone arches piled on top of each other and capped by slender timber-framed spires form the 360-foot bell towers, which dominate the town of Chartres and the nearby countryside. This thirteenth-century French cathedral bears witness to two leading features of medieval civilization: powerful religious beliefs and daring technical inventiveness.

Part Two

MEDIEVAL CIVILIZATION

PART TWO

Medieval Civilization

The conversion to Christianity of the peoples of the Roman Empire and the Germanic invasions of the empire's western territories were completed by about the year 500. Together with the conquest of the Middle East and North Africa by Islam about a century later, they bring us to a new phase of Western history. These shifts in civilization opened the thousand years of the Middle Ages—the "in-between times" separating the ancient from the modern period (p. 2).

Geographically, the Middle Ages were the European phase of Western development, when a new and distinctive civilization emerged on the soil of Europe, spread throughout that region, and reached the highest levels of cultural achievement. In religion, this was the era when the Christian faith and Church spread through all of Europe and when their ascetic and other-worldly view of life set the tone of Western civilization in every activity. In government and social life, it was the heyday of an elite whose power came mainly from the fact that its members were owners of land and leaders of warriors—the social group that came to be known, on account of its overwhelming prestige, as the *nobility*. It was also a time when Western civilization came into closer touch with the other civilizations of the Eastern Hemisphere than before, but was inferior to them in wealth, practical knowledge, and social organization.

In these ways, the Christian Europe of the Middle Ages was very different from the secular-minded, democratic, and world-dominating West of the present day. The modern West is separated from the Middle Ages by a new series of spectacular shifts in civilization that began about two hundred years before 1500 (the "official" end date of the Middle Ages), went on for more than a century afterward (see Part Three), and were followed by yet more shifts that have continued down to the present. Because of these shifts, Christian Europe is often regarded today as the most alien of the Wests of the past. We often use the word *medieval* (from the Latin for "Middle Ages," *medium aevum*) to mean the same as "brutal," "superstitious," "closed-minded," "unhygienic," and other unpleasant adjectives that supposedly no longer apply to Western civilization.

In fact, many of the things that are thought of today as typically "medieval" in the bad sense were widespread features of traditional civilization in general. Disease, poverty, and torture were just as common in ancient Greece and Rome, for instance, as in the Middle Ages, and in reality they are not exactly unknown at the present day. Christian Europe also shared many of its more praiseworthy features with other civilizations. It inherited many of its cultural and intellectual traditions from ancient Greece and Rome and developed these traditions in many creative ways. In spite of religious hatreds, Christian Europe learned a great deal from the neighbor and rival civilization of Islam. But the civilization with which Christian Europe has the most in common, in spite of all shifts and changes, is the present-day West.

The list of basic features of the West of today that originated in medieval times is a long one. It was in the Middle Ages that Western civilization first came to be made up of many ethnic groups, each with its own version of a common culture, and of many independent states, all competing fiercely with each other. English, Spanish, and most of the other languages of the West were first spoken and written in Christian Europe. England, France, Russia, and many other present-day European countries first came into existence and practiced the earliest forms of representative government. Christianity itself remains the overwhelmingly predominant religion of the West. Everyday practices of today, such as arranging lists in alphabetical order so as to make the items easy to find, or putting hops into beer to make it taste interestingly bitter, also began in medieval times. In all these and many other ways, the modern West is still the child of the Christian Europe of the Middle Ages.

	POLITICAL, SOCIAL, AND ECONOMIC DEVELOPMENTS	RELIGION, SCIENCE, AND PHILOSOPHY	HISTORY AND LITERATURE	ARCHITECTURE, ART, AND MUSIC
A.D. 500	Kingdom of the Franks established by Clovis			
	Justinian's temporary reconquest of the western Mediterranean	Benedict and his monastic rule		Hagia Sophia
	Bubonic plague			
	Slavs spread through eastern Europe (550–900)			
600		Muhammad and the Koran		Gregorian chant (monophony)
	Islamic conquest of Middle East and Mediterranean world	The Hegira		
	Rise of Carolingian dynasty			
700	Charles Martel and the repulse of the Muslims in France			
		Donation of Pepin ("States of the Church")		
800	Charlemagne crowned "Roman Emperor" by Pope Leo III			Palace of Aachen
	Division of Islamic conquests			
	Breakup of Charlemagne's empire			
	Invasions of western Europe by Vikings (Norsemen), Muslims, and Hungarians			
900	Emergence of feudal and manorial systems	Monastic reform movements: Cluny		
	Partial recovery of central authority in France and Germany			

POLITICAL, SOCIAL, AND ECONOMIC DEVELOPMENTS	RELIGION, SCIENCE, AND PHILOSOPHY	HISTORY AND LITERATURE	ARCHITECTURE, ART, AND MUSIC	
Revival of trade		Growth of vernacular literature		1000
Norman conquest of England	Ecclesiastical reform; Hildebrand (Gregory VII)			
Rise of towns and guilds	College of Cardinals created		Romanesque style of architecture	
Rise of feudal states	Cistercian order			
The crusades (1096–1291)	Widespread persecution of Jews and Christian heretics	Chivalric romances: Chrétien de Troyes	St. Trophîme Cathedral (Arles)	1100
		Goliardic poetry	Gothic style	
	Rise of universities		Medieval Latin hymns	
	Impact of Muslim scholars: Averroës		Goliardic verses	
	Final separation of Greek and Latin churches	*Song of Roland*	Chartres Cathedral	1200
Magna Carta	Papacy at height of power: Innocent III	Omar Khayyám (Persia)	Chivalric troubadours	
Mongol invasions of eastern Europe	Franciscans and Dominicans (friars)			
Emergence of capitalism	Grosseteste			
Growth of banking	Thomas Aquinas			
	Scholastic philosophy dominant			
Origins of Parliament	Papal Inquisition			
	Roger Bacon			
	Decline of papal power: Boniface VIII	Dante		1300
	Development of cannon and clocks	Chaucer		
		Christine de Pisan		

CHAPTER 5

The Creation of Europe:
Political and Social Foundations

OVERVIEW

The fall of Rome was the beginning of a lengthy upheaval that affected all of Europe—both the civilized Christian lands that Rome had ruled and the pagan barbarian lands beyond the empire's frontiers. As with the Middle Eastern upheaval two thousand years before (pp. 41–43), this one ended not in a collapse but in a renewal of civilization.

For more than five hundred years after the fall of Rome, Germanic and Slavic barbarian peoples, as well as nomads from Asia, continually raided, conquered, and settled in the civilized lands that had once belonged to the empire. As with earlier invasions, however, what enabled these less advanced peoples to make such inroads was the fact that they were already growing in organization and skills as a result of contacts with civilization, and they ended by adopting the way of life of the civilized peoples they attacked. By 1000, civilization had spread throughout Europe, and the three-thousand-year-old European barbarian way of life had come to an end (pp. 56–60). Because they were conquerors rather than victims of conquest, however, most of the once barbarian peoples formed separate kingdoms that were independent of the older civilized lands. As a result, the renewed European civilization was one of many vigorous ethnic cultures and many powerful competing states.

Christian Europe was not the only new civilization that arose out of the fall of Rome. It was what was left over after the Christian Middle East and Christian North Africa were overrun by Islam in the seventh century. From then on, Christian Europe faced a fearsome adversary to its south and east—a civilization of intercontinental size, in some ways more advanced than itself, and inspired by an aggressive rival monotheism. But exactly because Islam was larger and more advanced, it was also a source of trading wealth and cultural inspiration to Christian Europe, and a gateway to more distant civilizations of the Eastern Hemisphere.

The upheaval affected eastern and western Europe in different ways. What was left of the eastern half of Rome's empire evolved without a break into the Greek-ruled empire of Byzantium. Throughout the era of invasions, Byzantium was able to keep up many traditions of the Eastern Roman Empire—its Greek culture, its bureaucratic government, and its subordination of the Church to the emperor. These traditions, in turn, influenced many successful barbarian peoples of eastern Europe.

In the West, the effects of the upheaval were more drastic. The cities declined; education, literature, and art found refuge in the monasteries; and there were no more emperors in Rome. The most successful of the Germanic invaders of the empire, the Franks, formed an unstable and fragile kingdom, ruled by an uneasy balance of power between kings, nobles, and Church leaders. Around A.D. 800, the Frankish warrior-king Charlemagne was able to dominate the nobles and the Church, conquer barbarian peoples in central Europe, act as champion of Roman and Christian civilization, and take the title of Roman emperor. But many other Frankish rulers were mere helpless figureheads, and in the end the Frankish state fell apart.

Exactly because the crisis was worse in the West, however, the renewal of civilization went furthest there. Under the stress of turmoil and invasion, new skills, new ideas, and new social structures arose. In place of the emperors, the popes took over as rulers in Rome and eventually became independent heads of the Church. In the kingdoms that arose in and around the former territories of the Frankish state, the interplay of rulers, nobles, and Church leaders came to be regulated by rules and customs so formal and binding that they were regarded as laws. As a result, a new pattern of social life and government arose—that of *feudalism*. Between 1000 and 1300, feudalism enabled many of the new kingdoms to become well-organized states.

Meanwhile, in the countryside, changes in the organization and technology of farming led to an increase in food production and hence in population and wealth. Through the institutions of *serfdom* (an unfree but farm-holding peasantry) and the *manor* (a type of agricultural estate), the kings, nobles, and Church leaders were able to gain control of this growing wealth and to use it for purposes of government, warfare, religion, and culture. And the increase of farming wealth, together with closer contacts with the world outside Europe, led to an increase in trade and a revival of urban life. By 1300, western Europe, with its centralized Catholic Church, its powerful feudal kingdoms, and its prosperous towns and cities, had become the heartland of a new civilization, as brilliant as any in the past.

The Germanic Kingdoms of the West

We have already discussed the Roman and Christian ingredients of medieval civilization (Chapters 3 and 4). Now let us look at the new element—the Germanic. The Germanic barbarians—together with their eastern counterparts, the Slavs (pp. 199–201)—were the last major wave of northern barbarians to move into the lands of the south. Even though the invaders were in time mostly assimilated by the Roman peoples they conquered, some of their traditions lasted—and these same traditions persisted more strongly among Germanic peoples farther north in Europe, who did not enter the empire. Either way, the way of life of the Germanic barbarians influenced various features of the emerging civilization of Europe.

THE GERMANIC BARBARIANS

Over several centuries of close contact with the Roman Empire, the Germanic tribes had formed large groups or *confederacies,* led by an elite of powerful chieftains and their "war bands" of leading warriors (p. 145). When the tribal confederacies took over the empire's western territories in the fifth century, the chieftains shared newly acquired land with the members of their war bands, who became owners of vast properties. They took up Roman ways and often intermarried with Roman aristocrats. Even though the Germanic warriors eventually lost their separate identity, they changed the way of life of the relatively unmilitary Roman landowners. The members of the new western European elite were both landowners and warriors whose power came partly from their control of economic resources and partly from their skill in warfare and military leadership. Consisting as it did of warriors, the elite was generally unruly and given to feuding and private warfare, but it was also held together by the warrior virtues of honor, comradeship, and loyalty.

The more "democratic" tribal institutions, notably the regular assemblies of rank-and-file warriors and farmers (p. 145), did not long survive the move into the Roman Empire. Even among the tribes that did not move into the empire, the spread of Christian and Roman civilization enhanced the power of chieftains and their favored warriors at the expense of tribal assemblies. All the same, a tradition of popular participation in government lingered on, especially in the field of law and justice. In many western European countries in the early Middle Ages, groups of ordinary freemen would be summoned and sworn to reveal their collective knowledge of the truth, in such matters as identifying the originator of a blood feud, establishing ownership of property, or accusing wrongdoers.

Like most other ancient peoples, the Germanic tribes were polytheists, worshiping a pantheon of human-like deities (p. 21). Even after the adoption of Christianity, many traditions persisted in Germanic folklore and symbolism. Thus in the English language, the names of Tiu, the Germanic war god; Woden, who was thought to take a special interest in the affairs of the human race; Thor, the thunder god; and Frigg, the fertility goddess, are still honored in the names of four days of our week: Tuesday, Wednesday, Thursday, and Friday. Even the climactic day of the Christian calendar received its name, in many northern lands, from Eastre, the ancient German goddess of spring.

Perhaps the most important consequence of the Germanic takeover was that in the long run, it led to the disappearance of the already crumbling frontier between civilized and barbarian Europe. In Germany, the Low Countries, and the Scandinavian lands farther north, there remained many Germanic peoples who had not moved into the Roman Empire. These barbarians now began to look southward in their turn for trade, conquest, Roman culture, and Christianity. The more or less civilized Germanic rulers of former Roman lands, for their part, were less cautious than the Romans had been about expanding their power north and east of the Rhine and Danube rivers. Thus by a strange and momentous twist of fate, the fall of the Roman Empire actually led to the spread of Roman and Christian civilization beyond its frontiers.

THE KINGDOM OF THE FRANKS

Most of the half-dozen or so barbarian-ruled kingdoms that emerged from the fifth-century invasions had a relatively short life. In the following two hundred years, they fell victim to Byzantine efforts at reconquest (p. 198), to the power of Islam (p. 204), or

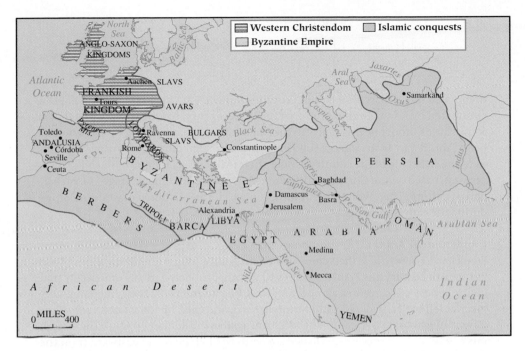

Map 5.1 Western Christendom, Byzantium, and Islam About 750. The map shows the new division of the civilized region earlier occupied by the Roman Empire and its Middle Eastern neighbors. The largest share now belongs to Islam, which has swallowed more than half the lands once ruled by Rome. The remaining countries of predominantly Greco-Roman culture and Christian religion now stretch in a narrow and discontinuous band from Ireland to Byzantium, sandwiched between Islam to the south and powerful European barbarian and Asian nomad peoples to the north.

to each other. In the end, only two Germanic nations succeeded in building permanent states on former Roman territory: the Anglo-Saxons and the Franks (*Map 5.1*). It was these two nations, together with the non-Germanic Irish, that played the leading role in preserving Roman and Christian civilization and spreading it beyond the former frontiers of the Western empire.

England and Ireland. From the area that is now Denmark and northwestern Germany, two tribal groups, the Angles and the Saxons, sailed over the North Sea and invaded Britain during the fifth century (*Map 3.4*, p. 154). They overran the native Britons, who were quarreling among themselves, and established several kingdoms of their own. Unlike in other conquered regions of the Roman Empire, it was the natives who were assimilated by the invaders, except in outlying territories that came to be known as Wales and Scotland. Elsewhere, Germanic dialects and customs took firm root, and the country came to be known as "the land of the Angles," or England. Though pagan when they first settled, most of the Angles and Saxons became Christian during the seventh century, partly as a result of missionary efforts sponsored by the papacy from 595 onward and partly under the influence of two neighboring, already Christian nations: the Irish and the Franks.

Ireland was the first territory outside the frontiers of Rome to which Christian civilization spread when the empire collapsed. A remnant of the Celtic peoples who had

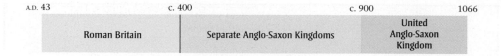

A.D. 43   c. 400   c. 900   1066

| Roman Britain | Separate Anglo-Saxon Kingdoms | United Anglo-Saxon Kingdom |

dominated much of western Europe centuries earlier (p. 118), the Irish had never been conquered by Rome. In the turmoil of the fifth century, the missionary and (later) Saint Patrick brought Christianity to the island. (Patrick was a native Briton who had been captured by Irish raiders.) Following this, Christian monasteries came to dominate the tribal life of the country. Under their influence, a unique Irish civilization grew up, based on the Christian faith, Roman literature, and the heritage of Irish barbarian culture. This civilization, in turn, came to influence much of western Europe during the early Middle Ages.

Clovis and the Franks. The most powerful state to arise in the West was that of the Franks, who were to give their name to modern France. When the big invasions began in the fifth century, the Franks were joined together in a loose tribal confederacy that controlled an extensive area along the lower Rhine River. One of their chieftains, Clovis, welded the confederacy into a unified force and then in 486 started campaigns against neighboring Germanic kingdoms and against the Romans in Gaul. The victorious Clovis and his successors pushed south to the Pyrenees and eastward from the Rhine until they ruled all of present-day France and much of western and southern Germany. As the Franks became Christian and adopted Roman ways, so also did some of their subject tribes to the east of the Rhine. In this way, the spread of Christian and Roman civilization beyond the empire's former frontiers began on the mainland of western Europe.

Clovis now began to build a stable system for governing his territories. He shared the conquered land with his principal warriors, as Germanic custom required, but made sure that the lion's share went to himself and his descendants. Instead of overthrowing the existing Roman elite of landowners, counts, and bishops (p. 151), he let them keep much of their property and their positions in church and state; he then made use of their services in governing his kingdom. Clovis's power over his conquered territories was further strengthened by his early conversion to orthodox Christianity, which helped gain him the support of powerful Romans (*Fig. 5.1*). The bishops encouraged Clovis to regard himself as the preserver of both Christian and Roman traditions. The alliance between the Church and the Franks provided the West with a new base of power to replace the shattered authority of Rome.

The Kings, the Nobles, and the Church. When Clovis died, however, much of what he had done to restore stability was destroyed. Following Germanic custom, he divided his kingdom among his four sons, treating political authority as though it were private property. This practice was to plague the Frankish kingdom throughout its life, since the sons usually quarreled over their shares and gave the leading nobles of the kingdom a chance to play off one brother against another.

The Frankish nobility developed out of the gradual merging of Clovis's followers and the old elite of Roman Gaul. As landowners, they had since late Roman times possessed power not only as landlords but also as rulers and protectors of the peasants. As

Bibliothèque Nationale, Paris, France

Fig. 5.1 The Baptism of Clovis. This is a medieval French depiction of what was considered the founding event of the Christian kingdom of France. The king is naked and up to his waist in water, expressing the purity and thoroughness of his conversion. He is surrounded by the kingdom's main power wielders. On the left are bishops led by Saint Remigius of Reims, who performed the baptism. On the right are nobles, one of whom carries the royal crown. Above, the Holy Spirit in the form of a dove bears holy oil.

warriors, they had their own followers who would fight for them and owed them loyalty and obedience. The kings needed the cooperation of these powerful leaders to govern effectively. In order to win their support, the kings had to give them government positions, royal lands, and the right to control these lands without royal interference. In addition, the kings, who as Catholic rulers had authority over Church appointments, also had to give wealthy and powerful positions as bishops to men from this same leading group.

As a result, a vicious circle set in. The rulers' lands, revenues, and control over the government and the Church gradually dwindled. This forced them to depend still more on the leading nobles and to concede to them still more land and power. By the end of the seventh century, the Frankish kings were mere puppets of their chief officials, the "mayors of the palace." The mayors were themselves usually the heads of powerful factions among the nobles. But these factions feuded ferociously with each other, and there was usually more than one rival mayor, each associated with one or another rival king, so that even the power of the mayors was insecure. In consequence, the authority of the central government became increasingly weakened, with each family of nobles acting as a power unto itself.

Compared with the Roman Empire in its most glorious days, the Frankish kingdom and the many small kingdoms of England and Ireland were feeble political structures, yet their role in the building of European civilization was important. The kings and nobles of the Franks, the Anglo-Saxons, and the Irish were Christian believers and respecters of Roman tradition. They invested an extremely large proportion of their resources in monasteries that harbored learning, culture, and religion. The Franks passed these practices on to the neighboring Germanic nations to the east and north, often with the help of Anglo-Saxon and Irish missionaries.

Even in politics and government, the Frankish kingdom in particular was of more importance than its history of conflict and disintegration might suggest. Within the kingdom, the main elements of the feudal state, with its decentralized authority and its constant interplay of monarch, powerful nobles, and leading churchmen, were already coming into existence. In one form or another, monarch, nobles, and churchmen would dominate political and social life in most European countries down to the nineteenth century (see Chapters 11 and 12).

Byzantium and Its Neighbors

While the new Germanic rulers tried to restore order in the West, Roman emperors in Constantinople still ruled a mighty empire in the East, stretching from the Danube to the Euphrates and the Nile (*Map 3.4,* p. 153). The strength of the empire rested on foundations that had been laid by Diocletian and Constantine and before that by the rulers of the Hellenistic states (pp. 102, 146–150). Centralized control was assured through an absolute monarchy sustained in oriental splendor at the grand court of Constantinople. The emperor commanded a professional bureaucracy and well-trained armies and navies. Moreover, his productive realm provided him with sufficient revenues to support administration and defense. He was supported, too, by the powerful Greek Church (p. 172), of which he was the formal head.

In the sixth and seventh centuries, the empire first tried and failed to regain the lost Roman territories of the West, and then lost all of its Middle Eastern and North African territories to the new religion and empire of Islam. From that time on, all it was left with was part of southeastern Europe and most of Asia Minor (*Map 5.2*). But it still remained the wealthiest and (together with the Frankish kingdom) the most powerful state in the emerging Christian Europe of the early Middle Ages. At the time it was thought of as simply "the Empire," or even "Rome," but today it is usually called by the old Greek name of its capital city, Byzantium.

THE SURVIVAL OF BYZANTIUM

Reconquest and New Invasions. The emperors at Constantinople continued to claim authority over East and West alike, and several of them tried to recapture portions of the West—above all, the energetic Justinian. This man of extraordinary talent and determination, who came to the throne in 527, took seriously his role of God-appointed despot and determined to strengthen and expand his empire. At severe cost in men and resources, he succeeded in wresting Italy and northwestern Africa from their Germanic masters. His armies and navies also won the western Mediterranean islands, including Sicily, and gained a foothold in Spain. The Mediterranean world became once more the province of the "Romans."

But Justinian's fleets and garrisons had been spread too thin, and the lengthened frontiers of empire invited attack at many points. In addition, beginning in 542, the resources of Byzantium had been sapped by waves of bubonic plague. Since this rat-

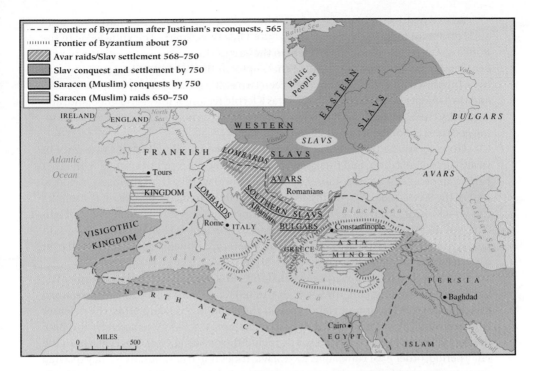

Map 5.2 Byzantium and Its Invaders, 565–c. 750. Locations of invaders when they began their attacks are shown by *italic* names, and their final locations by <u>underlined</u> names. In the mid-sixth century, Byzantium still ruled most of Rome's universal empire, but in 750 it was struggling to hold the Balkans and Asia Minor. Most of Byzantium's losses were to the new universal empire of Islam. To the north, Byzantium confronted a combination of Asian nomadic invaders and European barbarian peoples—above all the Slavs, who became predominant across most of central and eastern Europe.

borne disease had not previously penetrated the Mediterranean world, the population was especially vulnerable to it. The plague first reached Egypt from Ethiopia or India. From there it spread throughout the Mediterranean area and to much of western Europe. The toll was staggering, equaling that of the later Black Death (p. 294).

Late in the sixth century, new attacks on Byzantium's overexpanded frontiers began. The first invasions came from Europe, where barbarian nations were once again set moving by nomadic invaders from Asia, as in the time of the Huns and the Visigoths (p. 152). This time it was the Avars, a people akin to the later Turks, who followed the trail blazed by the Huns and set up an empire in central and eastern Europe. In 568, the Germanic tribal group known as the Lombards, in flight from the Avars, conquered most of Byzantine-held northern Italy (*Map 5.2*). Like earlier Germanic invaders, the Lombards eventually became the rulers of a civilized Christian kingdom, and Byzantium managed to hold a few coastal areas of northern Italy, together with southern Italy, Sicily, and northwestern Africa. But it was the end of Byzantine efforts to reconquer the empire that had once been ruled by Rome.

The Slavs. Caught up in the Avar invasion was another, much larger barbarian tribal group than the Lombards, which would eventually come to dominate eastern Europe just as the Germanic barbarians dominated the West: the Slavs.

Like so many other European barbarian peoples, the Slav tribes had a language and customs of Indo-European origin (p. 58). They first came to the knowledge of the Romans, as a people living somewhere to the east of the Germans, during the second century A.D. By the time of the fall of the empire in the West, the Slavs are known to have inhabited an area stretching between two eastern European rivers, the Vistula and the Dnieper (*Map 5.2*, p. 199). This was a fertile region of forest and grassland, and originally the Slavs seem to have been farmers, living a simple tribal life and worshiping gods and goddesses of weather and fertility.

From about the third century onward, however, the Slavs began to advance in wealth, in organization, and finally in power—mainly as a result of contact with other barbarian peoples who were more sophisticated and warlike than themselves. To the west of the Slavs lived the Germans; to the east lived the nomadic peoples of the steppes (pp. 57–58). More than once the Slavs were conquered and subjected by these neighbors, but they did not lose their identity. Instead, they served their various overlords in peace, fought under them in war, followed them on campaigns of conquest all over eastern Europe, and finally inherited their dominion.

The Slavs began their warlike expansion as foot soldiers of the Avars. Under the leadership of the nomadic invaders, in the sixth and early seventh centuries they moved south from their homeland, crossed the Danube River, and broke the defenses of Byzantium. They took over most of the empire's provinces in southeastern Europe— the region known today as the Balkans—including for a time even Greece itself. In the same period, other Avar campaigns took Slavic tribes north and west until they reached the Baltic Sea and threatened the eastern frontier of the Frankish kingdom. More slowly and peacefully, yet other Slavs settled the vast forest region that stretched for hundreds of miles northeast of their homeland. By 800, the Slavs had occupied almost all of eastern and central Europe (*Map 5.2*, p. 199).

Whereas the Germanic tribes had been absorbed and lost their identity nearly everywhere they migrated, in eastern Europe it was the Slavs who assimilated the earlier peoples of the region. As a result, most of the peoples of eastern Europe are still ethnically Slavic at the present day.

Here and there, old established ethnic groups managed to avoid assimilation by the Slavs. In swamps and forests along the southern and eastern shores of the Baltic Sea, earlier Indo-European settlers survived to become the Baltic nations of today. In remote mountain valleys on the east coast of the Adriatic Sea, tribes that had never been fully assimilated by Rome eventually developed into the present-day Albanians. Along the lower Danube, where the Latin language had been spread by Roman soldiers and settlers, it continued to be spoken by mountain shepherds and by farmers in the plains, the ancestors of the Romanians. In Greece, where persistent Byzantine efforts of reconquest eventually succeeded, it was the Slavs who were absorbed and turned into Greeks.

Meanwhile, the widely scattered Slavic tribal confederacies were themselves beginning to divide into different groups, each with its own version of the single original Slav language. There was a western group, the forerunner of such modern nations as the Czechs and Poles; a southern group, including tribes that already called themselves Croats and Serbs; and an eastern group, out of which the Russians, Ukrainians, and other nations would in time evolve (*Map 5.2*, p. 199). In this way, with the Slavic invasions there began to come into existence the present-day ethnic mosaic of eastern Europe and the Balkans.

During the seventh century, the Slavs who moved south of the Danube began to rebel against their Avar overlords, and in time, Byzantium was able to gain influence over the Slav invaders (pp. 224–225). But Italy and southeastern Europe were not the only regions where Byzantium was under attack. Its hold was also weakening on its territories in northern Africa and the Middle East.

Persian and Muslim Invasions. Late in the sixth century, the Middle Eastern empire of Persia, continuing its feud with Rome (p. 146), launched an assault on Justinian's successors. In a series of vicious wars, the Persians conquered both Syria and Egypt but were eventually driven out in 630. But both sides were so exhausted that Byzantium's Middle Eastern and North African territories, as well as the entire Persian Empire, fell easy prey to the Arabs a short while later (p. 204). By 750, all that was left to Byzantium was Asia Minor, Constantinople and its outskirts, a few other coastal footholds in the Balkans, and its possessions in Italy and Sicily (*Map 5.2,* p. 199).

But the Byzantine rulers were upheld, in spite of all disasters, by a mystical faith in themselves and their empire. They still thought of themselves as Roman emperors, but their Rome, they believed, was not a passing "Earthly City" as it had been considered earlier by Augustine (p. 179). Rather, it was a true reflection on earth of the Heavenly City of God, which would *never* perish. And as rulers of that city, the emperors—like Constantine and Theodosius before them—saw themselves as rulers of the Church as well as the state. While the Roman popes, in response to the decline of civil authority in Italy, became more and more independent of the state, the Byzantine emperors appointed the patriarch of Constantinople (p. 172), decided theological disputes, and enforced clerical discipline. Both the emperors and the patriarchs rejected the claim of the popes to supremacy in religious matters (p. 172). For the time being, the Greek and Latin branches of Christianity still saw each other as part of one and the same Christian Church, but they were drifting apart in their relations to the state as well as to each other.

Though harassed on every side, Justinian's successors managed to reform the machinery of government so as to support the armies and navies that would enable them to hold on to what was left of their empire, and they even regained some lost territories in Greece and eastern Asia Minor. Warfare and diplomacy held off Asiatic nomads, Slav barbarians, and Muslim conquerors. Though defeats did occur, Persians and Arabs, Slavs and Avars were still brought to a halt before the gates of Constantinople, surrounded by water on three sides and defended on the fourth by massive fortifications. This Byzantine determination and persistence were fortunate for Europe, since it was Byzantium that guarded the continent against assaults from the East. It was not until the eleventh century that the empire again began to shrink, and it took until 1453 for Constantinople to fall to another nation of Muslim invaders, the Turks (pp. 278–282, 298).

BYZANTINE CULTURE AND ARCHITECTURE

Byzantium played a major cultural role in the development of Western civilization. It was Justinian, in his role as Roman emperor, who was responsible for the codification of Roman law, the *Corpus Juris Civilis* (p. 136), which still forms the foundation of the legal systems of most Western countries at the present day. In addition, Byzantium inherited from the Hellenistic past the internationally dominant Greek culture of the eastern Mediterranean and the Middle East (pp. 101–104, 126). Even when the Greeks lost this international dominance to the new, Arab-dominated civilization of Islam (pp. 207–208), Byzantium continued to serve as the main custodian of classical Greek

Fig. 5.2 Cathedral of Hagia Sophia. Justinian's cathedral, later a mosque and now a museum, was the work of two architect-mathematicians, Anthemius of Tralles and Isidorus of Miletus. Using their knowledge of the geometry of curves, they designed a structure that a contemporary, Procopius of Caesarea, found overwhelming. The huge dome on its four arches, he wrote, was "marvelous in its grace, but by reason of the seeming insecurity of its composition altogether terrifying. For it somehow seems to float in the air on no firm basis, but to be poised aloft to the peril of those inside it."

© Zefa/Robertstock.com

culture. The rich literature of ancient Greece was conserved in archives and libraries, and Byzantine scholars enriched their heritage by adding their own commentaries and summations. Greek learning continued to serve as the foundation of education in the empire. Though Justinian, in his role as Christian ruler, closed the philosophical schools of Athens, a great Christian university grew up in Constantinople.

Byzantium not only conserved and developed the culture that it had inherited from the past but also contributed to the education of western Europe. All through the Middle Ages, there was constant interchange between East and West—by way of clergy, warriors, pilgrims, traders, and scholars. Though there was more antagonism than affection between the two, both were heirs of ancient Greek culture. And it was Byzantium that guarded their common cultural endowment.

The Byzantines also had impressive accomplishments in the decorative arts and architecture. Byzantine craftsmen produced superb objects in gold, silver, and enamel of exquisite color and design. Visitors from the West were dazzled by the magnificence of Constantinople, the "city of cities." Justinian himself had launched an ambitious building program for the capital. The principal monument, to the glory of God (and the pride of the emperor), was the mighty church of Hagia Sophia (Holy Wisdom) (*Fig. 5.2*). An elaborately planned structure, it employs domes and half-domes to create a vast interior space. The most striking feature is the main dome, over 100 feet in diameter and 180 feet in height. It does not rest, like the dome of the Pantheon (p. 139), upon a cylindrical wall. Instead, it rests on four giant arches, which mark off a central square beneath the dome. The arches carry the downward thrust to four stone corner piers,

395   1453

| Byzantine Empire |
| United Saracen Empire |

          622   c. 1000

which are reinforced by massive stone supports on the outside. Arched windows, piercing the base perimeter of the dome, crown the interior with a halo of light.

Built in only six years' time, under the urging of the impatient emperor, Hagia Sophia is one of the world's architectural wonders. It combines the building principles of the Romans with the decorative splendor of the Persians. The columns of the interior are of richly colored marble taken from various parts of the Mediterranean world. The vaultings are covered by multicolored mosaics, which have survived the whitewash of later Muslim conquerors. This temple inspires, in its own fashion, the sense of marvel and holy mystery that the cathedrals of Europe were to achieve centuries later, and has served as a model for thousands of churches and mosques in Middle Eastern lands.

The Book and Sword of Islam

At the same time that Rome and Byzantium were growing apart to produce different versions of European civilization, the largest single section of the old Roman Empire, its North African and Middle Eastern territories, developed in an entirely different direction. This region became the seat of a new and different form of civilization as a result of another great invasion—this time, from Arabia. The Arabs (or Saracens, as the Romans called them) brought a militant faith and succeeded in building a brilliant and distinctive culture—both known by the name of *Islam*. Both as a warlike adversary and as a peaceful neighbor, it had a profound effect on the development of the West.

THE ARABS AND MUHAMMAD

At the opening of the seventh century, most of the Arabs were nomadic tribesmen. Because they conquered and adapted to an advanced civilization, there is a parallel between their role in the Mediterranean world and that of the Germans in western Europe. There are significant differences, however. The Arabs, instead of being converted by the Christians they conquered, were fired with a religious zeal of their own and sought to impose what they considered to be a superior spiritual truth on the peoples they overcame. (Islam, like Christianity, is one of the few *missionary* religions in world history.)

The founder of the faith was Muhammad (known simply as the Prophet), a man who was destined to transform the lives of millions. Born about 570 in Mecca, a trading center near the western coast of Arabia, he apparently grew up with no formal education. He did, however, learn something of the teachings of Judaism and Christianity, which had sifted down from Palestine and Syria. When he was about forty years old, he turned from his life as a merchant to become a religious hermit. Spending days in lonely meditation, he began to experience visions that he believed to be direct revelations from God (Allah). In one of these visions, the archangel Gabriel directed him to carry these messages to his people, and from that time on, he abandoned all other activities.

Most Arabs, however, were polytheists who worshiped idols and nature spirits, and Muhammad soon found himself a prophet "without honor in his own country." His insistence that "there is no God but Allah, and Muhammad is his Prophet" proved offensive to them. He became especially unpopular in the city of Mecca, where a building known as the Kaaba housed idols and a black stone considered holy by the Arabs. When he denounced this shrine, he was branded a blasphemer and a disturber of the peace. Faced with this opposition, Muhammad left Mecca in 622, "shaking its dust from his feet," and fled northward to Yathrib (later renamed Medina, "City of the Prophet"). There he was able to preach freely, and his band of disciples began to grow—and to follow his example of seeking to convert others.

Muhammad's purpose was to wipe out primitive superstitions, put an end to tribal feuds, and unite the Arabs under a single pure faith. This could be done only if the Arabs would surrender to the will of Allah as revealed by the Prophet. The Arabic word for submission is *islam,* and the word for one who has submitted is *muslim.* These are the terms used to identify, respectively, the faith and the believer.

Though Muhammad viewed himself as a spiritual leader, he became a political and military chieftain as well. His disciples responded to his words without question; and he was persuaded through revelation that the use of force, if necessary, against unbelievers was one of many forms of religious "striving" (in Arabic, *jihad*) that were approved by Allah. (Other forms of *jihad* included everything from unwarlike efforts to convert unbelievers, through the struggle for justice in society, to the individual's striving for personal righteousness.) Soon Muhammad was leading his followers on raids against desert caravans. The proud Meccans were at length compelled to yield, and the Prophet returned to Mecca in triumph. He ordered that all the idols in the city be destroyed, but he preserved the Black Stone as a symbol of the new faith. Attracted by his militant methods and by his vision of bringing the whole world under Islam, the desert tribes began to flock to his leadership. By the time of his death, in 632, he had extended his personal control over a large portion of Arabia.

THE SARACEN EMPIRE

Once the pattern of expansion had been established, the movement spread with lightning speed. Muhammad, though many times married, had left no son to inherit his mantle, so his disciples chose a successor (*caliph*) from among his close relatives. Family connection with Muhammad was accepted from the beginning as a mark of political legitimacy. Under the first two caliphs, Abu Bakr and Omar, the Arabs carried their holy war to the neighboring peoples of the Middle East. Within a decade their hard-riding horsemen had conquered Persia and had taken Egypt and Syria from the Byzantine Empire. Though outnumbered in almost every battle, the crusaders for Islam succeeded in routing their opponents. At the end of two generations, their empire (*caliphate*) stretched from India in the east across North Africa to Gibraltar in the west (*Map 5.1,* p. 195). By 720, they had taken Spain from the Christianized Visigoths and were sending raiding parties across the Pyrenees into France. Near Tours, in 732, they were stopped by Frankish warriors under Charles Martel (p. 211).

All this was only the beginning of Muslim expansion. Where the warriors stopped, the traders took over. By 1000, Arab merchants, looking in distant lands for exotic commodities to bring to the Middle Eastern centers of the Islamic world, had spread the religion of the Prophet to the gold- and ivory-producing kingdoms of western Africa, to the spice islands of the Far East, and to the empire-building Turkish nomads of central Asia.

How can we explain the amazing Arab conquests? They were due, in part, to the faith that sparked the invaders. Every Muslim warrior knew that he would share in a rich booty if his side was victorious, and he believed that if he fell in battle his soul would fly straight to paradise. But there are other reasons as well. The effects of the bubonic plagues of the preceding century have already been mentioned (pp. 198–199). Byzantium and Persia, the only substantial powers in the area, had weakened each other militarily by years of bitter warfare and could offer no effective resistance. Further, many of the peoples of the Middle East and Africa were discontented under their old rulers. Syrians and Egyptians, for example, resented the heavy Byzantine taxation and the continuing persecution of Christian heretics, and welcomed the Saracens as liberators.

Though determined to drive out paganism and eager to convert all peoples to their faith, the Saracens offered toleration to Jews and Christians (upon payment of a special tax). Within a few generations, however, most Christians in the conquered territories embraced Islam. There were legal and social advantages in becoming Muslims, and the religion appealed to many Christians. The conversion was to prove lasting; except for Spain, the lands that fell to the Arabs are still lands of the mosque.

ISLAM AND CHRISTIANITY

What were the teachings of this new faith? A radical monotheist, Muhammad never claimed divinity for himself but insisted only that he was the last and greatest of Allah's prophets. He set his revelations in the context of Judaism and Christianity, identifying Allah with Yahweh (Jehovah) and accepting the line of Jewish prophets from Abraham through Jesus. Instead of claiming that he was introducing a *new* religion, he insisted that his work was the fulfillment of the old. His position with respect to Judeo-Christianity was similar to that of Jesus with respect to Judaism. His message, as recorded in the Koran, might be viewed in this light as a *sequel* to the Old and New Testaments.

The central spiritual appeal of Islam is its stress on the *oneness* of God. Most of the Koran is given over to describing and praising Allah, who alone is the supreme reality, all-knowing and all-powerful. The true believer must submit unreservedly to Allah's will as expressed through the Prophet. This could be done simply and without doubting; unlike Christianity, Islam raised no questions concerning the nature and persons of the godhead (pp. 175–176).

Similarly, there were no arguments over what made up the sacred canon (authorized holy books). Muhammad's revelations were memorized by his disciples and written down in final form shortly after his death; this original Koran, in Arabic, remains the only authorized version. Shorter than the New Testament, it is a poetic book, which millions have memorized (hence its name, which in Arabic means "Recitation"). Though today Muslims are outnumbered by Christians two to one, the Koran is undoubtedly the most-read book in the world. It serves not only as a record of divine inspiration but as a guide to morality, legislation, and science. In some Muslim countries, the Koran is the supreme law of the land; the legal code (*Sharia*) is based on it and is applied, notably, in Iran today.

ISLAMIC SOCIAL AND ETHICAL IDEAS

Muhammad's ethical teachings are in the Judeo-Christian tradition, and the Koran repeats many of the proverbs and stories of the Bible. Because the Prophet had a practical mind, the model life that he described is within the reach of the faithful. While stressing love, kindness, and compassion, he did not insist on self-denial beyond the powers of most people. He saw no particular virtue, for instance, in sexual abstinence. He did, however, try to moderate the traditional Arab practice of polygamy. This custom had arisen chiefly from the imbalance in the number of men and women among the Arabs, whose tribal feuds resulted in a chronic shortage of men. One means of providing security for the surplus females was to permit each male to take several wives. The practice had eventually led to sexual promiscuity, however, and the Prophet declared that a man should have no more than four wives at a time. (The quota did not apply to Muhammad himself, who was exempted by a special revelation.) No limit was set on the number of concubines a man might have. Though women possessed some property rights, Muslim society was (and is) a "man's world."

A characteristic of Islam that appealed to many is the absence of a formal priesthood. Every Muslim stands as an equal before Allah—though in practice, religious scholars and "holy men" (*mullahs* and *ayatollahs*) enjoy special respect and authority. There are no saints mediating between humans and God (as in Catholic Christianity; pp. 249–250); and because there are no priests, there are no mysterious rites that only priests can perform. To increase the worshiper's concentration on Allah, statues and images are banned from Muslim art. The place of worship—the mosque—is devoid of anything that resembles an idol.

All this led Muslims to feel that their faith was spiritually purer and more democratic than Christianity. They scorned the Christians as people addicted to wrangling over doctrine, content to worship three or more divine figures, and cloaked in pagan superstition.

OBLIGATIONS OF THE FAITHFUL

The religious duties of Muslims, known as the Five Pillars of Faith, are clearly stated in the Koran. The first is the familiar profession of belief, "There is no god but Allah, and Muhammad is his Prophet." By accepting and repeating these words, the convert is initiated into the faith.

Daily prayer—at dawn, midday, midafternoon, sunset, and nightfall—is the second duty. At the appointed hours, from atop slender minarets (towers) the muezzins (criers) call upon the faithful to bow down, turn toward Mecca, and say the prayer in Arabic. The prayer itself, which is not unlike the Christian Lord's Prayer, usually includes the short opening verse of the Koran, praising Allah and asking for guidance along the "straight path." This formula is repeated many times each day. The only public religious service is the midday prayer on Fridays, which must be attended by all adult males (and is closed to females). Inside the mosque, standing in self-ordered rows, the congregation prays aloud in unison; then the leader, a layman, delivers a brief sermon. After the service, normal everyday activities may be resumed.

The third duty is giving to the poor. At first, almsgiving was practiced as an individual act of charity, but it gradually developed into a standard payment. In the Islamic states, the money was collected through regular taxation and was used to help the needy and to build and maintain the mosques. The usual amount was one-fortieth of the individual's income.

Fasting, the fourth pillar of faith, ordinarily is confined to *Ramadan*, the ninth month of the Muslim lunar (moon) calendar (p. 22). It was during Ramadan that Allah gave the Koran to the archangel Gabriel for revelation to Muhammad. For thirty days, no food or drink may be taken between sunrise and sunset. Fasting, which was not practiced by the Arabs before Muhammad, was adopted from Jewish and Christian custom.

Finally, every Muslim who can afford it must make a pilgrimage to the Holy City of Mecca at some time during his or her life. Over the centuries, this practice has had a unifying effect on the different peoples that embrace Islam. Rich and poor, black and white, Easterner and Westerner—all come together in the Holy City.

In the early stages of Muslim history, a *sixth* duty was required of all able-bodied men: participation in *jihad,* in the sense of war against unbelievers. It was this requirement that sparked the first explosive conquests of the Arabs. Each caliph believed it his obligation to expand the frontiers of Islam and thus reduce the infidel "territory of war."

The Five Pillars of Faith are only the *minimum* requirements of Islam. In all things, true believers must seek to do the will of Allah as revealed in the Koran. They must also believe that God has *predestined* the ultimate fate of all humankind, to be revealed in the Last Judgment. Muhammad left vivid descriptions of hell and heaven. Unbelievers will burn eternally in a great pool of fire; believers who die in sin will also suffer there for a time but will finally be released. In the end, *all* Muslims (male and female)—who have accepted Allah—will enjoy the pleasures of paradise. Muhammad, drawing from Persian sources, pictured paradise in sensual terms as an oasis of delight, with sparkling beverages, luscious fruits, and dark-eyed beauties.

RELIGIOUS AND POLITICAL DIVISIONS

In spite of the comparative simplicity of Muhammad's teachings, they were open to conflicting interpretations as the years passed. The major disagreements arose over the principle of succession to the caliphate, religious doctrines, and the proper way of life for Muslims.

The main division was between the Sunnites and the Shiites, a division that still disturbs the Muslim world. The Sunnites were associated with the Umayyad dynasty, which seized the caliphate in 661 and moved the capital of Islam from Medina to Damascus, in Syria. They accepted as valid certain traditions (Sunna) that had grown up outside the Koran. The Shiites, on the other hand, held strictly to the Koran and insisted that only descendants of the Prophet could become caliphs. The Abbasid family, of the Shiite sect, gained power in 750 and moved the capital again, this time to the new city of Baghdad (*Map 5.1,* p. 195), in the modern state of Iraq.

After the eighth century, the Saracen empire began to break up. The ousted Umayyad family established itself in Spain and broke off political connections with Baghdad. Similarly, a descendant of Muhammad's daughter Fatima later declared himself an independent caliph in control of Egypt, Syria, and Morocco. Provinces in Arabia and India also fell away until by 1000, the Abbasid ruler controlled only the area surrounding Baghdad.

THE MUSLIM LEGACY TO THE WEST

Despite all these political divisions, Muslim civilization reached its height in the ninth and tenth centuries. The unifying faith, the common Arabic language, and the relative stability that the Saracen conquerors provided served to bring about a revival in the Middle Eastern world. The Islamic achievements of this period are a blend of various traditions, especially Hellenic, Syrian, and Persian. But out of this blend there emerged a distinctive new civilization, which replaced that of Greece as the internationally dominant culture of northeastern Africa and the Middle East, as well as of the vastly larger area to which Islam eventually spread.

Islam and Europe. The rise of Islam was almost as important an event for European peoples who remained Christian as for those of Africa and Asia who actually became Muslims. The Islamization of North Africa and the Middle East had the effect, for many centuries, of confining Christianity, and most of the traditions of Greco-Roman civilization, to the territory of Europe. The Christian European nations now lived on the fringes of a mighty intercontinental civilization that was alien to and more advanced than their own. Islam was a world far larger than that of the Roman Empire before it—one that eventually stretched from western Africa all the way across the Eastern Hemisphere to the Pacific; it included lands far wealthier, with far older and deeper cultural traditions, than western Europe.

It was no wonder, then, that for Christian Europe, Islam was a formidable enemy. For a thousand years, Islam and Christendom fought bitter wars against each other. The warlike prowess of medieval European society was steeled by the endless conflict, and European states like the Frankish kingdom and Byzantium devoted much of their energies to it.

Yet Islam was also a neighbor from which Europe benefited in many peaceful ways. Trade, inventions, fashions, pastimes, scholarly and scientific discoveries, all spread rapidly across the world of Islam—whether they originated within it or in some neighboring, non-Islamic civilization. Part of the reason that Europe was able to advance during the Middle Ages was that it had come to belong to a group of civilizations, linked together by the intercontinental civilization of Islam, that stretched across the Eastern Hemisphere all the way to China.

The list of advances that came to Europe from or through Islam begins with long-distance commerce. Trade routes in the Islamic world were made secure; Arab traders traveled between Spain and western Africa and between the Middle East, China, and the East Indies; as a result, exotic goods came within reach of merchants from Europe (p. 239). A valuable scientific advance that came to Europe by way of Islam was the introduction from India of what we now call Arabic numerals—an innovation that freed mathematicians from the awkward Roman system. In fact, there was hardly a branch of learning that was not advanced by the Muslims, with results that soon came to be known in Europe. The Muslims took notable steps in medicine. Scholars translated into Arabic the writings of such ancient Greek physicians as Hippocrates and Galen (pp. 79, 134). Muslim doctors wrote useful books of their own; best known is the *Canon* of Avicenna (ibn-Sina), a summary of the medical knowledge of his time (eleventh century).

Islam preserved and developed many other scientific and philosophical writings of the ancient Greeks. Enlightened rulers commissioned Arabic translations of writers such as Aristotle and Ptolemy (pp. 83–84, 134). Great centers of learning sprang up, notably at Cairo (Egypt), Toledo (Spain), and Palermo (Sicily), where scholars studied these works, developed them further, and related them to Muhammad's religious teachings. Gradually, European scholars made their way to Spain and Sicily to gain access to this Arab learning. As the Muslim tide receded from those areas after 1000, the

Institut Amatller d'Art Hispanic, Barcelona

Fig. 5.3 The Great Mosque, Córdoba. The building dates from the eighth to tenth centuries, when Córdoba was a leading city of the Muslim world and the largest city in western Europe. Its magnificence expresses the piety and power of the Umayyad rulers of Spain. The illustration shows the holiest part of the mosque, the prayer niche or *mihrab*, where the ruler as leader of prayer faced toward Mecca.

Christians of the West seized on the rich intellectual deposit and made it their own. Europe recovered through Arabic translations—retranslated into Latin, the scholarly language of western Europe, by Spanish and Sicilian experts—many of the treasures of Greek learning that had been lost for centuries.

Islamic Culture. Western artisans and builders were also impressed by what they discovered in Muslim countries. In the tenth century, when most of Christian Europe was busy trying to fend off attacks from every quarter, Muslim Spain was enjoying unequaled prosperity. Its capital, Córdoba, the largest city of Europe after Constantinople, boasted magnificent mosques and palaces, public baths, colleges, libraries, and private homes. Córdoban leather, textiles, and armor were famous everywhere. Scholars, poets, and musicians were generously patronized by the rulers.

Muslim architecture, a blend of Persian and Mediterranean styles, was distinguished by its graceful variations of the Roman dome and arch—typically pointed, a form that was taken up by European architects to produce the Gothic style (pp. 262–263), or in the shape of a horseshoe (*Fig. 5.3*). Walls were richly decorated with marble, precious stones, and glazed tiles. Since Muhammad had forbidden the representation of human or animal figures, painting and carving consisted mainly of geometric and floral designs (arabesques).

Muslim literature mirrored a broad sweep of attractive subjects: desert life, bustling cities and bazaars, mosques, fierce warrior horsemen, and mysterious veiled women. The literary forms included prose for history, philosophy, and religion; fantastic and romantic stories; and colorful poetry. Among the stories, the *Arabian Nights* has become the one most widely read in the West: an enchanting collection drawn from many times and places of the Islamic world. (Its best-remembered characters, no doubt, are Sinbad the Sailor, Aladdin, and Ali Baba.)

Popular also are the charming verses of the Persian Omar Khayyám, a mathematician and astronomer of the twelfth century—as well as a poet. His *Rubáiyát,* composed of a thousand quatrains (four-line verses), expresses a scientific-determinist point of view. Omar has few illusions about the universe or humanity. In memorable figures of speech, he accepts, yet protests, both fate and death. To Omar, one's life was part of a caravan traveling from nothingness to nothingness. Therefore, he concluded, we should

Make the most of what we yet may spend,
Before we, too, into the dust descend . . .

In other words, one should plunge into the pleasures of the present. The poet urges his beloved:

Come, fill the cup, and in the fire of Spring
The winter garment of repentance fling:
    The Bird of Time has but a little way
To fly—and lo! The Bird is on the wing.

Omar's philosophy connects, across centuries and cultures, with the ideas of two philosophers of ancient Greece: the materialist Epicurus and the hedonist Aristippus (pp. 80, 132–133).

The Carolingians

While Islam was spreading across Africa and Asia and Byzantium was struggling to remain the most powerful Christian state in the East, its western counterpart, the kingdom of the Franks, was seemingly falling apart as its kings lost power to competing factions among the nobles.

What finally put an end to this situation was the triumph of one particular noble family in the continual struggles for power. From the name of the family's most famous member, Charles the Great (Charlemagne; p. 213), the family is usually known as the Carolingians (*Carolus* being the Latin for Charles). It was the Carolingians who rebuilt the Frankish kingdom, and used their power to spread Christian and Roman civilization throughout much of western and central Europe. Though the power of the Carolingian rulers melted away in its turn, their achievements outlasted them. It was they who began the rise of western Europe to become the heartland of Western civilization.

THE RISE OF THE CAROLINGIAN DYNASTY

Late in the seventh century, the Carolingians were able to become the wealthiest and most powerful of all noble families and to unite the various positions of mayor of the

c. 50 B.C.   c. A.D. 486   751   987

Roman Gaul	Frankish Kingdom and Empire

Clovis's Dynasty   Carolingian Dynasty

palace (p. 197) in the person of the head of their family. They thereby restored unity to the Frankish kingdom and established a hereditary claim on the office. In 714, the "mayoralty" descended to Charles Martel ("the Hammer"), grandfather of Charlemagne. In bitter fighting, Charles had been able to crush the opposition of rival claimants and secure firm control of the kingdom. With the legal ruler (the king) pushed ever more into the background, the actual ruler turned to the grim task of reconstruction.

In 732, Charles Martel faced a historic challenge when the Saracens swept north from Spain and made raids into the Frankish kingdom (p. 204). They found the richest booty in the treasuries of churches and monasteries and were riding toward the abbey of Saint Martin of Tours, the richest in the country. Charles Martel commanded a defense force that consisted of foot soldiers supported by a small number of horsemen. The Saracen cavalry had superior mobility and striking power, but Charles maneuvered it into launching an attack on a fort surrounded by implanted wooden stakes. The raiders, badly hurt by a shower of arrows and javelins, decided to pull back to Spain.

Charles suspected that more attacks were coming and determined to build up a large force of heavy cavalry in order to oppose them. Horsemen of this type wore body armor and wielded close-quarters weapons such as swords and spears, in contrast to light cavalry forces, which were armed mainly with bows and arrows. Heavy cavalry had originally appeared among the horse-riding peoples of the steppes (pp. 57–58) about the beginning of the Christian era, and the Persians and Romans had used them against each other in many Middle Eastern wars (p. 147). The Avars (p. 199) had brought to Europe another nomadic invention, *stirrups*—iron foot rests hanging from the saddle—which made heavy cavalry fighting easier as they gave horsemen a more stable platform from which to wield their weapons. The Saracens, with their Middle Eastern background, were also users of heavy cavalry, and now the ruler of the most powerful kingdom in western Europe decided to equip his forces to fight in this way. But heavy cavalrymen needed elaborate coats of armor and specially bred horses. Wealth existed mainly in the form of land, it took a large amount of land to provide for just one horseman, and Charles needed thousands of them. Somewhere he needed to find enough land to maintain a heavy cavalry army.

The Church caught his eye at once. Bishoprics and monasteries, as a result of generous gifts and legacies, now held from a third to a half of all the land in the realm. When the Church leaders refused to give him the land he wanted, he seized many Church properties and distributed them as military grants (benefices) to noble warriors. In return, each warrior bound himself to supply a body of armed cavalry when called upon. Thus was laid the basis of the "feudal compact" (pp. 227–228), in which the use of land was exchanged for military equipment and service.

Within a century, the Frankish army had been converted into a force of mounted warriors, or *knights,* as they came to be known in English. For the next five centuries, the cavalry was to be the "queen of battles." So long as physical defense depended on armored cavalry, and so long as land remained the principal source of wealth, landholding would be closely associated with the knights.

THE ALLIANCE OF THE FRANKS AND THE PAPACY

Charles Martel's son, Pepin, decided that the time had come for the *actual* power in the kingdom to be recognized as the *legal* power. But it was not a simple matter to take the crown from the descendants of Clovis. Though they were only figureheads, they were respected as the rightful possessors of the kingship, and all the powerful men of the kingdom—bishops, nobles, and mayors of the palace—had sworn loyalty to them.

Pepin, anxious to avoid another civil upheaval, tried to win the Frankish bishops over to his side before deposing the reigning monarch. But the bishops were still angry over Charles Martel's seizure of Church lands and had no intention of supporting his son. Pepin then went over their heads and appealed directly to Rome. The pope, for his own reasons, approved the deposition in 751.

Pepin was shortly thereafter crowned and anointed (holy oil placed on him) by a clergyman who was close to both himself and the pope: the monk, missionary, and (later) saint, Archbishop Boniface of Fulda. This was the first time in the history of the Frankish kingdom that a king inaugurated his reign with a solemn religious ceremony conducted by a leading clergyman (representing the pope). The ceremony was deliberately patterned after the consecration of the Israelite kings at God's command as described in the Old Testament. Against the hereditary legitimacy of the descendants of Clovis, Pepin now claimed a special holiness and authority from God. It was not long before clerical coronation and anointing became the normal ceremony for inaugurating kings throughout Europe. The idea behind the ceremony, that the power of kings came from God, strengthened royal power for many centuries to come, though in the Middle Ages, the popes always stressed that this divine authority was conferred by the Church (pp. 255–257).

Later it was Pepin's turn to do the pope a favor. The Lombard kings of northern Italy (p. 199) were pushing southward, depriving the popes of their power in Rome and in nearby territories. Because the Byzantine emperors still claimed Italy, the pope, Stephen II, might have appealed to Constantinople for aid. But the rivalry between the Latin and Greek churches (p. 172) had strained relations between East and West; moreover, the Eastern emperor had military problems of his own. So Stephen turned to Pepin for protection. Stephen journeyed to the Frankish court in 754, reanointed the king, and won promises of military help.

Two years later, Pepin fulfilled his obligation to the papacy by crossing the Alps, defeating the Lombards, and transferring a strip of territory across central Italy to the governing authority of the pope (*Map 5.3*). Thus by the so-called Donation of Pepin, the States of the Church came into being as a sovereign political entity. They remained so for over a thousand years—until the unification of Italy in 1870 (*Map 12.4*, p. 500). At about the same time as Pepin's gift, the papacy justified its right to govern this territory with a far bolder claim. It asserted that the emperor Constantine, when he moved to Byzantium, had bequeathed *all* of the West to Pope Sylvester and his successors. As proof of this claim, the papal court produced a signed document. The Donation of Constantine, as this paper came to be known, also declared the pope to be the superior of all other bishops and of the emperor himself. In the fifteenth century, the document was shown to be a forgery (p. 341), but in the meantime it served to advance the ambitions of the papacy.

The Donation of Pepin, however, was genuine and had immediate results: it sealed the alliance between the Frankish state and the papacy, the two strongest forces in the West. The outcome of this alliance was the empire of Charles the Great.

Map 5.3 Charlemagne's Empire. Charlemagne ruled far less territory than the original Roman emperors, but he widened the strip of civilized Christian lands that stretched between the Islamic world and the pagan barbarians and nomads of northern and eastern Europe (compare *Map 5.1*, p. 195). Furthermore, his empire was twice the size of contemporary Byzantium. Even after his death and his empire's gradual collapse, the new boundaries of Christendom did not shrink, and the balance of power within Christendom did not swing back to the East.

CHARLEMAGNE

Charles, Pepin's son and Charles Martel's grandson, stands as one of the towering figures of history. Through the force of his personality and the challenges of a long reign (forty-six years), he contributed mightily to the evolution of western Europe. Descendant of Frankish barbarian invaders, warrior against heathens and Muslims, and holder of the revived office of emperor, Charles personified the merging of Germanic, Christian, and Roman elements in the western European civilization (*Fig. 5.4*, p. 214).

Tall, fair-haired, and blue-eyed, Charles was proud of his German heritage. His given name was Karl, and though he knew Latin, he preferred to speak in his native Frankish tongue. All the same, he is usually referred to in English by the French name that first appeared more than a century later: Charlemagne (Charles the Great).

Conquests: Italy, Germany, Spain. Charlemagne was almost constantly at war. Ruthless and cruel in battle, he fought not only for territory and spoils but also for what he considered the higher goals of Christianity and universal order. As a result, he expanded the boundaries both of Christianity and Frankish power outward in all directions by military force.

Fig. 5.4 A Frankish Ruler. This bronze statuette depicts either Charlemagne or his grandson Charles, king of the western Frankish territories. The rider wears a crown and carries an orb, Christian symbols of royal power. The horse is also a symbol of power, modeled on the second-century horse of Marcus Aurelius (*Fig. 3.8*, p. 143). It was made separately from the rider—perhaps in late Roman times, since its harness does not include stirrups. The combination of older Roman and newer Christian symbolism expresses the Frankish empire's double claim to power.

© Erich Lessing/Art Resource, NY

Not all of Charlemagne's victims were pagans or Muslims. When advised by the pope that the Lombards were again threatening papal territory, he led his armies into Italy in 774 and broke the Lombard power. Now he called himself king of the Lombards as well as king of the Franks, and extended his authority over most of Italy (*Map 5.3*, p. 213).

His hardest campaigns, which lasted some thirty years, were against the Saxons. These tough warriors, some of whom had crossed the North Sea to Britain in the fifth century, lived on the northeastern boundary of the Frankish kingdom (*Map 5.3*, p. 213). Unlike the Saxons in England, they clung stubbornly to their heathen religion. Charlemagne, encouraged by the Church, was determined to transform the Saxons into Christian subjects. He succeeded, but only after laying waste to Saxony, massacring countless captives, and relocating thousands of families in other parts of his empire. At last the Saxons accepted Christianity, and the Frankish clergy moved in to establish bishoprics and monasteries.

Farther south, Charlemagne attacked the nomadic nation of the Avars, who had invaded central and eastern Europe in the sixth century (p. 199). As with the Huns before them (p. 154), the defeat of the Avars caused most of them to retreat and disperse, but they left behind Slavic tribes who had accompanied them on their campaigns of conquest (p. 200). All along its eastern frontier, from the North March to the East March, Charlemagne's empire now confronted Slavic peoples, whether as enemies to be conquered or as neighbors to be influenced and converted (pp. 223–224).

To defend his conquered territories, Charlemagne set up military zones called *marches* or *marks* along the lengthened frontiers, many of which developed into new European countries. The mark that separated the conquered Saxons from their northern neighbors, the Danes, eventually gave its name to the Christian kingdom of Denmark. The North March (*Nordmark*), set up on the eastern frontier of Saxony as a defense against the Slavs, was to become the duchy of Brandenburg (later, Prussia). The East March (*Ostmark*), carved out of territories conquered from the Avars, became the duchy of Austria. And south of the Pyrenees, Charlemagne erected the Spanish March as a wall against the Muslims. From this foothold, Christianity gradually expanded into the kingdoms of Aragon and Castile.

Government: The Church and the State. Charlemagne concerned himself with domestic matters as well as with military campaigns. Recognizing the Church as the only institution that was accepted by all his subjects, he worked to strengthen its leadership and extend its activities. Though a devout and submissive Christian in private life, he believed that as king he must act as head of the Church. Viewing the religious structure as part of his royal administration, he appointed bishops, issued reform orders to the clergy, and assumed, in general, the same attitude the Byzantine emperors took toward the Greek Church (p. 201). He treated bishops and abbots as agents of his government and saw to it that they received copies of all his imperial decrees.

Aside from Church law and imperial decrees, Charlemagne issued no uniform legal code for his sprawling territories, leaving the various peoples—Franks, Lombards, Saxons, Romans—to govern themselves according to their own laws. One regular feature of his government, inherited from earlier kings and late Roman rulers, was the role played by his counts (pp. 151, 196). Each *count* represented the crown in a given region, called a *county*. He presided over a court that met once a month, collected fines, and in time of war, assembled the knights of his county for military action. Sometimes, for purposes of defense, several counties were grouped into a larger unit headed by a *duke* (leader). Both counts and dukes were selected from the local landed nobility.

As a check on the honesty and efficiency of these officials, the king appointed royal inspectors, who visited all his territories once a year. Traveling in pairs (a nobleman and a clergyman), they investigated the performance of the counts and dukes and reported their findings to Charlemagne. By acting vigorously in response to this intelligence, he succeeded in holding together his far-flung empire.

Because there was no general system of taxation, the king had to draw most of his revenue from the crown lands, which he kept as his own. He held thousands of estates, most of them concentrated between the Seine and Rhine rivers (*Map 5.3*, p. 213). Understandably, he was keenly interested in the efficiency with which his properties were managed, and he prepared detailed instructions for the guidance of his royal stewards (estate managers).

Art and Literature: The Carolingian Renaissance. Charlemagne made his capital at Aachen, which was surrounded by productive crown lands in the heart of the ancient Frankish territories. His palace chapel at Aachen, which still stands, was the first important stone building to be erected north of the Alps after the fall of Rome (*Fig. 5.5*, p. 216). This fact in itself indicates the slow recovery of the West. The chapel was modeled on the church of San Vitale in Ravenna, a Byzantine outpost on Italy's east coast. San Vitale, in turn, was built in the same general style as the grand Hagia Sophia (*Fig. 5.2*, p. 202). The king was so impressed when he first saw San Vitale—a rich church, glistening with mosaics—that he directed his builders to duplicate the plan in his own capital. Thus the art of Constantinople found its way to Aachen and the Frankish heartland.

Fig. 5.5 Charlemagne's Palace Chapel. Built about A.D. 800 in Charlemagne's capital of Aachen in the west of present-day Germany, the chapel imitates an earlier Byzantine building in Italy. However, the designer was a Frankish architect, Odo of Metz, who evidently possessed sophisticated knowledge and skills. In later times, Charlemagne was believed to lie buried beneath the center of the building, which remained for many centuries a monument to the dream of a revived Roman Empire.

By importing artisans and artists from Italy, Charlemagne stimulated the development of the arts in northern Europe. He was concerned, as well, over the low level of education and scholarship in his realm and issued a decree instructing bishops and abbots to improve the training of the clergy. In Aachen itself, around 780, he set up a palace school that would become a center of intellectual activity. (The students, like most of those who received any kind of schooling at the time, all belonged to the clergy. It was unusual even for high nobles and rulers to be literate: Charlemagne himself only learned to read as an adult and never mastered the art of writing.) The school came under the guidance of a monk named Alcuin, who was the leading scholar of his day. Charlemagne had called him from the cathedral school of York, the finest in England.

Alcuin trained a staff of expert scribes (copyists), who brought back the monastic tradition of reproducing ancient manuscripts. This was perhaps his principal contribution to Western culture. Most of the ancient Latin literary works that we possess have come down to us from Carolingian copies, carefully preserved in monastic libraries, and the easily readable handwritten letters designed by the Carolingian scribes still form the basis of the lowercase letters that we use at the present day. Alcuin also established a course of studies, based on that of the monastic and cathedral schools, for selected young men of the Frankish nobility. The faculty of the school at Aachen was made up of distinguished scholars drawn from all over Europe. Many of their pupils became outstanding teachers themselves in other intellectual centers of Germany and France. Though

Charlemagne's empire barely survived him, the "Carolingian Renaissance" of the arts and scholarship provided a lasting impetus to the cultural development of Europe.

THE RESTORATION OF THE "ROMAN EMPIRE"

The most dramatic event of Charlemagne's rule—one that captured the imagination of Europe—was his coronation as "Charles Augustus, Emperor of the Romans." The event took place on Christmas Day, 800, while the Frankish king was attending Mass in Saint Peter's Basilica in Rome. Apparently he had not planned the coronation beforehand; his biographer, Einhard, reports that Pope Leo III, without warning, placed the crown on his head and pronounced him emperor.

The pope had his own reasons for taking this historic step. He still needed a strong protector in Italy, but there was also the possibility that the Franks themselves might prove dangerous. By taking the initiative in 800, the pope succeeded in defining the relationship between the restored (Western) empire and the Church. By setting himself up as a *donor,* he secured the *superior* position: Charlemagne received the crown from the hand of the pope, thereby putting the emperor under obligation to the papacy. The action also gave force to the later claim that the papacy had a right to *withdraw* what it had given. Later popes, making this claim, would unseat emperors.

Though Charlemagne may have been surprised by the circumstances of his crowning, there is no evidence that he was displeased. From the time of Clovis's conversion to Christianity in the fifth century (p. 196), there had been close ties between the Franks and the papacy. Together they had worked to spread the faith and to reestablish order. By Charlemagne's time the Frankish state had become large and strong enough to lay claim to being a restored version of the Roman Empire, and the fact that it made this claim demonstrates the historical force of an idea. Through four centuries of struggle and near anarchy, the *idea* of universal law and order had lived on. At the first sign of its becoming a reality, the restoration was proclaimed, even though the restored empire in fact had a very different structure from the old one. In extent, it was substantially less than the Western half of ancient Rome; missing were North Africa, Sicily, Spain, and Britain, though territories east of the Rhine that had never been controlled by Rome were part of Charlemagne's rule. In Charlemagne's territories, there was no single citizenship, no unified law, no professional civil service, and no standing army. There were few cities, and the roads had fallen into disrepair. Christianity was the main unifying force in the new empire, and yet the agencies of the Church could not make up for the absence of firm political institutions. Charlemagne's empire was held together chiefly by the strength of his personality. Soon after his death in 814, the empire fell apart, leaving but a fiction of unity and an ideal.

Even so, Charlemagne's coronation was a truly historic event. There was, after all, another "Roman emperor" in Constantinople. At the time, a woman, Irene, was reigning over Byzantium, contrary to strict Roman tradition under which females were considered ineligible to rule. The pope may therefore have seized the moment to elevate Charlemagne to a "vacant" throne. But in any case, by accepting the title of emperor, Charlemagne was not just restoring the old empire. For the first time, a barbarian-descended western European king was claiming equality with, or even supremacy over, the Eastern emperors. Between the Byzantine East and the barbarian West, the balance of power was beginning to change.

Europe Takes Shape

After Charlemagne died, the promise of order and stability that his rule had held out faded in the dusk of renewed civil wars and invasions. Yet out of the conditions that accompanied the collapse of his empire emerged the main features of medieval European civilization that would govern Western life and thought until the fifteenth century.

THE DISSOLUTION OF CHARLEMAGNE'S EMPIRE

Internal Collapse and Renewed Invasions. The troubles of the ninth century sprang in part from the inner weaknesses of the restored empire and in part from external forces. Charlemagne was succeeded in 814 by his only surviving son, Louis the Pious. Louis was a good emperor, but he lacked the determination of his father. Though he tried to hand on the bulk of his territories and titles to his eldest son, Lothar, this led to warfare with his younger sons, who were determined to get equal shares in accordance with Frankish custom (p. 196). Finally, after Louis's death, his sons arrived at a settlement that marked an important early stage in the development of the countries of western Europe. By the Treaty of Verdun (843), Lothar was confirmed as emperor and given the middle portion of the empire; this included Italy and territory north of the Alps that came to be called after him, Lotharingia (Lorraine). The second son, Louis, received the portion of the empire east of the Rhine, which would become Germany. Charles, the youngest son, inherited the western third, which would become France.

But the Treaty of Verdun did not prevent continued fighting among the sons of Louis the Pious and among their descendants. Within a short time, the middle kingdom (Lotharingia) disappeared altogether, and most of its territory was ultimately taken over by the rulers of the eastern portion. The disintegration of Charlemagne's empire was speeded up by ferocious attacks from outside. One arm of invasion came from the Mediterranean, where Muslim raiders from North Africa had established themselves in Sicily and Sardinia. They preyed on shipping, struck at the coastal towns of Italy and southern France, and made off with everything they could carry. In 846, they captured Rome itself and pillaged the surrounding countryside. In desperation, Pope Leo IV built a wall around the heart of Rome. The rest of the city, however, lay open to the Muslims when they returned some years later.

On the eastern frontier, there appeared yet another nation of Asiatic nomads , the Magyars or Hungarians. They took over the same territory that the Huns and Avars had occupied before them—a large plain about halfway along the course of the River Danube which still makes up present-day Hungary. From here they sent plundering expeditions throughout Germany, some-

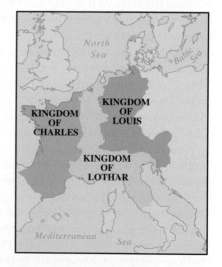

The Treaty of Verdun, 843

Map 5.4 Invasions of the Ninth and Tenth Centuries. Locations of invaders when they began their attacks are shown by italic names and their final locations by underlined names. Muslim sailors attacked the Christian coastlines of the western Mediterranean. Magyar horsemen raided westward from the middle Danube, the traditional staging area for nomad invaders of Europe (compare *Map 3.4*, p. 153, and *Map 5.2*, p. 199). Norsemen traveled the coasts and rivers of western Europe, made lengthy river voyages through eastern Europe to the Black Sea, and "island-hopped" across the Atlantic to North America.

times striking as far as the Netherlands and southern France. For much of the tenth century, they kept central Europe in turmoil.

The Norsemen. By far the strongest blows against Europe came from the Norsemen or Vikings ("men of the North" or "pirates" in their own language), the fierce barbarian warriors of Scandinavia. The Norsemen were the northernmost branch of the Germanic peoples, and now, with the northward spread of Christianity and Roman culture, they found themselves—like the Greeks, the Romans, and other European peoples before them—on the fringe of the civilized world (p. 59). As a result, they in turn became more advanced. By the ninth century, though still pagan and mostly illiterate, they had become a formidable nation of seafarers, traders, and warriors. Moreover, their numbers had grown, so that there were too many of them for the scanty harvests of their northern homeland to support. Consequently, they struck out on what proved to be the last great barbarian invasion of civilized Europe.

From 800 on, the long, high-prowed vessels of the Norsemen began to appear all along the coastline of western Europe (*Map 5.4; Fig. 5.6*, p. 220). The warriors who leaped ashore demanded tribute from the inhabitants and carried off what they could. From the coasts, they moved up the rivers and carried their raids deep into the interior.

Fig. 5.6 A Viking Longboat. This Norwegian warship was buried with its owner about A.D. 900 and dug up and restored in 1870. It has a mast to hoist a sail and 32 oar holes along the upper edge of the hull. Allowing for 64 oarsmen to row in shifts, the 75-foot-long boat probably carried at least that many warriors, with wooden chests for their clothes and bedding which doubled as rowing benches, on lengthy open-air trips on stormy seas and treacherous rivers. In 1893, a replica of a similar vessel crossed the Atlantic.

Finally, the Viking raids turned into regular campaigns of conquest in which they seized and settled whole territories.

No part of northern Europe was safe from the Viking attacks. Their western tribes, the Norwegians, mainly sailed westward and took over much of Scotland and Ireland; by 1000, their westward urge had taken them across the Atlantic to Iceland, Greenland, and "Vinland" (North America). The southernmost Norse tribes, the Danes, generally moved southward to the coastlands of the North Sea and the Channel: England, France, and the Netherlands. The Anglo-Saxons were forced to surrender the eastern half of England (the Danelaw) to the invaders, and the Frankish rulers were compelled to yield a large territory along the Channel: it was called, after the Norsemen, the duchy of Normandy (*Map 5.4*, p. 219). The Vikings of the east, the Swedes, traveled across the Baltic Sea and thence upriver to a watershed territory far inland, where other rivers led them hundreds of miles south to the Black Sea. They won power over the Slavic tribes who had settled this vast region of eastern Europe (pp. 200, 225), and in 860, their longboats attacked Constantinople.

Shift of Power to Leading Nobles. Throughout the territory of Charlemagne's empire, the struggles among his descendants, as well as barbarian and Muslim attacks, made violence and danger more than ever a normal condition of life. Everywhere, people turned from the distant and helpless central government to whoever was near enough and strong enough to offer them some protection. Free peasants bound themselves and their descendants to labor on the lands of local warriors as *serfs* (p. 237). Lesser warriors agreed to serve greater ones in war and peace as their *vassals* (pp. 227–228) and in turn received from the greater warriors secure possession of land. Everywhere, effective power came to be exercised by the strongest warrior nobles, who could gain the allegiance of the largest number of lesser warriors to swell their armies. They could then use their armies to assert control of the most important resources: land, the labor of peasants, and the goods and treasure obtainable by trade or pillage.

The leading warrior-nobles also increased their power at the expense of the rulers of the various Carolingian kingdoms. Partly by grants from Carolingian rivals who sought their support, and partly by simple seizure from feeble rulers, the leading nobles took over royal lands, collected royal revenues, and exercised royal powers of justice. And they treated all these new resources and powers, as well as the rights they acquired over lesser warriors and peasants, as family property. The *hereditary possessor* of such a property was known as a *lord*. The leading lords also took over such former royal offices as duke and count (p. 215) and converted these into hereditary titles.

Finally, in both the eastern and the western Frankish kingdoms, the succession to the kingly office itself came to be determined through election by the great lords. When the direct descendants of Charlemagne died out—in the eastern kingdom in 911 and in the western kingdom in 987—the great lords chose new (and powerless) kings from among themselves.

THE RISE OF WESTERN EUROPE

The dissolution of Charlemagne's empire did not mean the end of civilization in Europe. On the contrary, as in the case of the fall of Rome in the fifth century, the collapse of the empire and barbarian invasions actually led to the wider spread of civilization.

Government itself did not simply disintegrate but rather developed into new and in the long run more effective forms. The great lords, eager to pass on their newly acquired powers and possessions to their descendants, began to give up the Germanic custom—previously followed by nobles as well as kings—of dividing their properties among their children. Instead, during the eleventh century, the custom grew up of handing the bulk of the property to the eldest son. This was known as the right of *primogeniture* (from the Latin for "firstborn"). As a result, dynasties of great lords emerged that were able to control fairly stable blocks of territory over several generations. Sooner or later, any individual dynasty would usually fall victim to defeat in war or failure to produce male heirs. As a group, however, the great lords came to constitute a class of regional potentates, presiding effectively over a chaotic but dynamic warrior society. They defended their possessions against Norsemen, Hungarians, and Saracens; they undertook counteroffensives, such as the reconquest of Spain or the Crusades; and they fought continually against each other.

But these lords did more than wage wars. They generously endowed monasteries and supported movements of reform and reorganization in the Church. They pushed the peasants on their lands to carve new farms and villages out of the wilderness that at that time covered much of Europe, and they even took a hand in founding towns as centers of trade and industry. The role of these leading nobles in the building of medieval European civilization was an important one.

Revival of Royal Power: France, England, the Holy Roman Empire. As for the central authority of kings, though much diminished for a time, it never entirely disappeared and eventually revived. In the *western* Frankish kingdom—now coming to be known by the modern name of France (*Map 5.5*, p. 222)—the new king, who replaced the last

Map 5.5 Europe About 1000. The division between civilized Christian Europe and pagan barbarian Europe has almost vanished (compare *Map 5.1*, p. 195, and *Map 5.3*, p. 213). The increasingly advanced Slavs, Norsemen, and Magyars have formed Christian kingdoms on the model of their civilized neighbors. More have followed the model of the Latin than of the Greek Church so that the boundary between the two runs a long way east. To the south, the rival monotheism of Islam has yielded little ground. Europe is taking shape between the Atlantic, the Mediterranean, and Russia.

Carolingian in 987, was Hugh Capet, count of Paris. Though Hugh wielded little power outside the area of northern France that he controlled as count, he did at least succeed in persuading the great lords to elect his son king during his own lifetime. Later Capetian rulers managed to dispense with the need for election altogether so as to hand on the kingship—whole and undivided, like the rest of their possessions—by hereditary right. Having thereby won "independence" from the other great lords, the Capetians would lead the way, by the thirteenth century, to the establishment of a strong hereditary monarchy and state in France (pp. 230–231).

Elsewhere in western and central Europe, the revival of central authority was much swifter. In fact, the very same Norse and Hungarian attacks that helped demolish the power of the Carolingians also led to the appearance of new forms of central government so as to defend whole countries against these barbarians.

Already in ninth-century England, King Alfred of the southern kingdom of Wessex led all the Anglo-Saxons in resistance to the Danes. Even though he had to concede the Danelaw to the invaders (p. 220), it remained under his overlordship, and his tenth-century successors were able to recover the lost territory and build for the first time a united English state.

In the eastern Frankish kingdom, feeling the need for strong leadership against the Hungarians, the great lords finally permitted the most powerful family among them, the dukes of Saxony, to fill the office of king. The ablest of that family, Otto I, defeated the Hungarians decisively in 955, ending their raids into Germany. Otto next reclaimed the "Roman" imperial title, which had fallen into disuse, and was crowned emperor by Pope John XII at Rome in 962. Actually, Otto's holdings included only Germany and the northern and central portions of Italy, and the empire he founded came to be known as the Holy Roman Empire of the German Nation, or the Holy Roman Empire (*Map 5.5*). Though its rulers were never consistently able to enforce the principle of hereditary succession against that of election by the great lords, they remained powerful down to the later Middle Ages and kept alive the universal political ideal of Augustus and Charlemagne. From the thirteenth century on, the Holy Roman Empire grew progressively feebler, but it was not finally abolished until 1806. Soon after, the heartland of its territory was reunited to form a very different entity the modern national state of Germany (pp. 475–476, 499–500).

Barbarian Conquerors and the Spread of Civilization. Even where the barbarian invaders were able to take over parts of western Europe, this did not put an end to effective government or to civilization as such. As so often before, barbarian conquerors ended by adopting the civilization of the areas they conquered.

In the principal western European territories seized by the Vikings—the Danelaw and Normandy—the Norse settlers agreed to become Christian in return for recognition of their conquests by the English and French kings. In England, Danes and Anglo-Saxons became so mixed in language and customs that within a few generations they were hard to tell apart; in Normandy, the sons and daughters of the invaders already spoke French. From England and France, and under the influence of the adjoining Holy Roman Empire, Christianity and Roman civilization spread back to the Norse homelands, so that by 1000, Norway, Denmark, and Sweden were on the way to becoming Christian kingdoms.

Among the Norse conquerors, the Normans in particular went on to make an important contribution to the development of civilization in the West. In 1066, Duke William of Normandy conquered the Anglo-Saxon kingdom of England, coming not as a barbarian invader but with his banners blessed by the pope, as a claimant to the country's Christian kingship. Building on the institutions of the Anglo-Saxon kingdom, the Norman conqueror and his successors made innovations in the fields of administration and justice that have influenced the laws and government of England, and of countries inheriting English traditions, down to the present day (pp. 232–233).

Meanwhile, other Normans acting independently of their dukes wrested Sicily from Muslim control, and together with warriors from other parts of France, they gave fresh vigor to Christian efforts at the reconquest of Spain (p. 276). In this way, the descendants of barbarian conquerors became Christian warriors, helping their adopted civilization take the offensive against the forces of Islam.

In central Europe, barbarian conquerors were absorbed in much the same way as in the West. After their defeat by Otto I in 955, the Hungarians still held a region extending from the frontiers of the Holy Roman Empire to those of Byzantium (*Map 5.5*). Instead of retreating and dispersing as earlier defeated nomads had done, the Hungarians held on to the territory they had conquered and won acceptance from the Holy Roman Empire by adopting its Latin Christianity and culture. So also, during the ninth and tenth centuries did the rulers of various groups of Slav tribes that in earlier centuries had settled in the lands on the empire's eastern borders (pp. 200, 214): to the southeast, the

Slovenes and Croats; to the east, the Czechs (in Bohemia) and their eastern neighbors the Slovaks; and to the northeast, the Poles.

With many of these barbarian peoples, the process of adopting civilization was far from peaceful. Among the Norsemen and Hungarians, at least some of the leading warriors opposed the change. They clung to traditional pagan beliefs, and they rightly suspected that their rulers would swell from mere chieftains into kings who would demand obedience in peace as well as war. Throughout Scandinavia, and in Poland and Hungary as well, the coming of Christianity led to rebellion and civil war, and the triumph of the new religion was military as well as spiritual. But the upshot was that the ninth- and tenth-century invasions ended with the boundary of Latin Christianity expanding northward into Scandinavia and a long way into eastern Europe and the Balkans (*Map 5.5*, p. 222).

THE RISE OF BYZANTINE EASTERN EUROPE

Beyond the eastern borders of Latin Christendom, the general pattern of successful barbarian peoples attacking civilized states, yet also reaching toward Christianity and civilization, was much the same. The difference was that the Christianity and civilization they were reaching for were those of Byzantium.

In Byzantium as in the civilized states of western Europe, central power grew stronger under the stress of external attack. The emperors reorganized their administrative and military system from the seventh century onward. By about 800, they had regained control of Greece from the Slav invaders, and their rulers were experts in playing the Slav tribes and nomadic invaders of eastern Europe against each other. During the ninth and tenth centuries, with many setbacks, they gradually pushed their borders northward against the Slavs and eastward against the Arabs.

The Conversion of the Slavs. In dealing with the Slavs, the Byzantines did not rely on warfare and diplomacy alone. As with so many other pagan barbarian conquerors, the very success of the Slavs had uprooted them from their traditional way of life. Migration and war had fostered among them the growth of a wealthy and powerful elite of chieftains and warriors, and this elite was now in direct contact with Byzantine civilization. Like the Germans before them (pp. 143–146), the chieftains of the Slavs had no desire to destroy the civilized state they threatened. They might fight against it, but they also wanted to participate in its way of life. The armies and navies of Byzantium could never banish the Slav threat, but the Christian religion and the Greek heritage might at least bring them under the empire's spiritual and cultural sway.

In the ninth and tenth centuries, the Byzantine emperors and leading clergymen of the Greek Church deliberately set about the task of bringing Christianity and Greek culture to the Slavs. So eager were the Byzantines to make their message acceptable that they even allowed the Slavs to worship in their own language, rather than in Greek—unlike the Latin Church, which usually insisted that no other language than Latin be used in public worship. Byzantine monks also adapted the Greek alphabet to the sounds of the Slav language. The result was the Cyrillic alphabet (named for the missionary Cyril, one of the leaders in the project of converting the Slavs); it has remained the standard script in Russia and several other Slav countries ever since.

These Byzantine gifts of religion, culture, and literacy were usually combined with others that were just as appealing: military alliances, commercial treaties, and prestigious imperial titles for the Slav chieftains. In the long run, the combination proved irresistible. One by one, the chieftains invited Byzantine missionaries to their lands or came in person to Constantinople to be baptized. As in western Europe, pagan warriors often clung to their traditional customs, but their opposition faded away or was crushed. More serious competition came from the Latin Church, which was able to attract the westernmost Slav tribes into its orbit (p. 223). Elsewhere it was Byzantium that triumphed.

The Balkans. In the Balkans, for a time, Byzantium had a formidable rival. North of Byzantium's recovered territory of Greece many Slav tribes had been united into a powerful state by yet another nation of nomadic invaders, the Bulgars. The Slav majority eventually assimilated their overlords and accepted Christianity from Byzantium. Even so, the Bulgarian *tsars* (the Slav version of the Latin title *caesar,* inherited by Byzantium from ancient Rome; p. 124) struggled with the Byzantine emperors for control of the Balkan region. Around 1000, in the last of many brutal wars, Byzantium finally conquered Bulgaria, though in language and culture the Bulgarians remained Slavic.

To the west of the Bulgarians there lived another Slavic tribal group that had become Christian under Byzantine influence, the Serbs. Long overshadowed by the powerful Bulgarians, the Serbs were now able for the first time to build a unified state. It fell victim to internal tribal rivalries within less than a century—but not before its rulers had come into conflict with the rulers of the neighboring Slav people to the west, the Croats. Both kingdoms laid claim to the Slav-settled land of Bosnia, which lay between them. In addition, between Serbia and Croatia there ran the dividing line between Latin and Greek Christianity; and while the Serbs counted as vassals of Byzantium, from about 1100 Croatia was ruled by the kings of Hungary. Thus although the Serbs and Croats were closely related tribal groups whose descendants still speak almost identical languages today, they eventually developed into separate and sometimes rival nations.

Russia. Byzantium's greatest success was with the Slavs of northeastern Europe, between the Baltic and Black seas. These Slavs came to be known by the name of a group of Swedish Vikings who conquered them in the ninth century (p. 220): the Rus or Russians. The Swedish conquerors formed their territories into a powerful state, which they ruled from the important commercial center of Kiev (*Map 5.5,* p. 222). Like the Norse conquerors of Normandy, those of Russia quickly adopted the language and customs of their subjects (in this case, Slavic), but they did not lose their Viking appetite for trade and warfare.

The main trading partner of the Russians, and the frequent victim of their raids, was Byzantium. However, the Russian rulers also admired the empire's way of life and respected its ancient glory. Finally, in 988, Prince Vladimir of Kiev made a bargain with Byzantium: in return for the exceptional honor of marriage to the emperor's own sister, he threw down the pagan idols of Kiev and was baptized into the Greek Church. Thus Russia became the easternmost of the states that shared in the religious and cultural heritage of Byzantium.

By 1000, most of the eastern European peoples formed a religious and cultural community on much the same level of civilization as that of western Europe—but one that looked to Constantinople instead of to Rome. What held this community of Byzantine-influenced states together was not, as in the West, the inheritance of Roman civilization, the Latin Church, and obedience to the pope. Instead, the peoples of Byzantine eastern Europe were held together by the inheritance of Greek civilization, the Greek Church, and reverence for the Byzantine emperor (or in some cases his actual overlordship). Thus there appeared in the East a variant of European civilization that was noticeably different from the Western variant. The cultural divergence between the two areas that grew up in the early Middle Ages still persists today.

THE END OF THE BARBARIAN WAY OF LIFE

In this way, the turmoil of the ninth and tenth centuries produced a surprising result: by 1000, three thousand years of interaction—in which Europe had been both the meeting place and the arena of conflict between civilized and barbarian peoples—had all but come to an end (p. 59). In the regions immediately south and east of the Baltic Sea there still lived pagan tribes of Slavic and other ethnic origins. But they were neither powerful nor numerous enough to present a serious threat to civilization, and in the following centuries they would mostly fall victim to their Christian neighbors.

Apart from these remnants of the traditional barbarian way of life, all of Europe had come within the orbit of civilization, and this civilization had already developed distinctive features that have characterized it ever since. The Christian religion and the inheritance of Greece and Rome, in spite of all divergences between Rome and Byzantium, gave European civilization its basic unity. Numerous different ethnic groups and independent states supplied the vigor of diversity and competition, as well as the destructive urge to conflict and domination.

It is time now to turn to the political, social, and economic institutions on which this new civilization was built, especially those that had emerged in western Europe; for it was these institutions that would govern Western life and thought until the fifteenth century and exert a continuing influence well into modern times.

Feudalism

The word *feudalism* was coined by historians, long after the end of the Middle Ages, to describe the type of government institutions, as well as the general social and political relationships, that existed at that period among the dominant warrior-landholders in much of Europe. Feudalism came into being in northern France during the tenth century, following the breakup of the Carolingian empire. It spread outward from its "homeland," partly through campaigns of conquest by French, and especially Norman, warriors (p. 223) or by imitation on the part of warrior-landholders in other countries who found that it met their needs. By the twelfth century, not only France but also England, the Holy Roman Empire, Spain, Sicily, and even Byzantium were governed according to feudal principles.

Feudalism was not a tidy unified system spelled out in any decree or constitution. In all cases, however, feudal institutions and relationships worked according to two basic principles, each affecting one of the two things that were of most concern to warrior-landholders, namely, warfare and land.

As warriors, feudalism bound them by personal ties of mutual trust and loyalty. Lesser warrior-landholders were supposed to show loyalty to a greater one, enabling him to rely on them as his personal army; but the greater warrior-landholder was expected to show them loyalty in turn, protecting and helping them individually so that they would not have to stand against enemies on their own. In addition, feudalism bound members of the upper class together as landholders by giving them mutual rights over and interests in the most important of all resources, the land and the peasants who worked it. Lesser warrior-landholders did not actually "own" their land but "held" it on condition of doing military and other service to a greater one. So long as these conditions were met, however, the greater warrior-landholder was obligated to guarantee and protect the lesser ones in the secure hereditary possession of their estates. Through feudal ties of this kind, kings and great lords could assure themselves of the services of the mounted knights who formed the backbone of armies at this period (p. 211), by guaranteeing to the knights the wealth and social status that made them, too, part of the ruling warrior-landholder class.

Relationships of exactly the same kind also existed between rulers of countries and the great lords within the countries they ruled. Since the great lords had taken over so much of the powers of government (pp. 220–221), it was only through these ties that monarchs were able to hold their countries together. In any country, in fact, there existed a host of miniature governments, each ruled by one or another great lord and loosely associated under the monarch by the ties of feudalism. In spite of its decentralized operation, feudal government afforded some measure of security and justice for millions of Europeans, and held many countries of Europe together as political units, for five hundred years. It even succeeded in producing powerful states, in which effective central authority was grafted onto the decentralized feudal structure with its stress on mutual rights and responsibilities between holders of power and those subjected to them.

THE FEUDAL COMPACT

At first, the practice of exchanging property for personal service was extremely vague, consisting of unwritten agreements among greater and lesser landholders that were subject to a wide range of interpretations. By the eleventh century, however, the *feudal compact,* or contract, as this aspect of feudalism is called, had evolved into a fairly standard arrangement. Whoever granted land to someone stood in the position of *lord;* the recipient of the land was his *vassal*. A piece of land granted by a lord to a vassal was called a *fief* (Latin, *feudum*).

In addition to its economic benefits, the fief carried with it certain political responsibilities. The vassal was expected to protect the inhabitants of his fief, collect revenues, and dispense justice. Thus, under feudalism, political authority was linked to landholding. In addition, each vassal, in return for the benefits of his fief, owed important obligations to his lord.

Chief among these was military service. Every vassal was expected to serve his lord in person, and the holder of a large fief was required, in addition, to furnish a body of armed men. In this way, the kings and the great lords, who found it impracticable to pay for standing armies, were able to raise fighting forces when needed. At first the vassal's obligation to fight when called on by his lord was unlimited, but gradually it was set by custom at about forty days' service each year.

The holder of a fief was obliged also to serve on the lord's *court,* which was usually held once a month. This court heard disputes among the lord's vassals, often over land and interpretations of feudal rights. It also heard criminal charges. The lord presided in all cases, and his vassals acted as judges. It then became the lord's duty to enforce their decision, but should the losing party refuse to accept it, armed conflict could result.

Medieval court procedures rested on custom, growing out of ancient Germanic practices. One practice, for example, was the testing of accused persons by "ordeal." When evidence was lacking, the court might require individuals to walk barefoot over hot coals, thrust their arm into boiling water, or risk personal injury in some other way. It was believed that God would save them from harm if they were innocent and telling the truth. But bodily damage from such a test was seen as proof of *guilt,* and the court then imposed the customary penalty for the alleged crime. Not until the thirteenth century did the Church withdraw its support of trial by ordeal. In many countries, this led to a revival of the procedures of Roman law, which dealt with the problem of getting evidence by the routine use of torture; and in England, to the development of jury trial (p. 232).

Under the feudal compact, the lord had no general right to collect taxes from the vassal or the peasants who lived on the vassal's fief, but in some strictly defined circumstances, a vassal was required to make payments to his lord. After receiving his fief, he normally paid its first year's income to the lord by way of "*relief.*" When the lord's eldest son was knighted or his eldest daughter was married, or if the lord was captured in battle and had to be ransomed, the vassal had to make payment. In addition, for a given number of days each year, the lord and his family and attendants could demand food, lodging, and entertainment from the vassal.

HOMAGE AND KNIGHTHOOD

The granting of a fief, with all its requirements, was accompanied by the vassal's doing *homage* to his lord. Usually the vassal knelt down, put his hands between those of his lord, and offered himself as the lord's man (in Latin, *homo*). The lord accepted the vassal's homage, told him to rise, and embraced him. Next, it was customary for the vassal to make a Christian vow of fealty (faithfulness). The lord, in exchange for the declaration of vassalage, customarily presented his vassal with a clod of earth or some other symbolic object to serve as the "investiture," by which he invested ("clothed") the vassal with the right to govern and use the fief. With its use of symbol and ritual, its embracing and hand-clasping and taking of vows, the act of homage was not unlike a wedding. In fact, the intention was much the same: to reinforce a legally binding contract between two individuals by a strong personal bond—one that would survive disputes, conflicts, and even the occasional breach of the terms of the contract.

The feudal contract remained in effect so long as lord and vassal honored their mutual obligations or until one of them died. By the custom of primogeniture (p. 221), the eldest son of each came to enjoy the right of succession to his father's position with respect to a fief. But whenever a lord or a vassal died, new pledges of homage and new acts of investiture were necessary.

Only professional warriors (by now called *knights*) could become vassals and fiefholders. Before a young man could qualify for knighthood, he had to serve an apprenticeship as squire to his father or some other fighting man and then undergo severe tests of courage and military skill. From the eleventh century onward, the young man would then be knighted—initiated into the professional caste of warriors, usually by being presented with a sword by an already qualified knight.

This ceremony soon developed spiritual and religious overtones. By the middle of the twelfth century, the knight's sword was usually placed on an altar before the presentation, implying that the knight was obliged to protect the Church. By the thirteenth century, the ritual was normally performed in a church or a cathedral, rather than in a manor house or a castle. The initiate spent a night of vigil and prayer before the day of the ceremony, emerging from the ritual as a "soldier of Christ." The behavior of the warriors seldom measured up to the ideals of the Church, but the transformation of the knighting ceremony into a religious ritual tended to improve the conduct of Europe's military aristocracy.

When a vassal died and left an heir who was not a qualified knight, special arrangements had to be made. If the heir was a son who had not yet attained his majority, the lord would normally serve as guardian until the youth could qualify as a knight and become his vassal. If the sole heir was a daughter, the lord would serve as guardian until he found her a knightly husband. Then her husband, through the act of homage, would receive the fief as the lord's new vassal. Such marriages were one of the chief means of expanding individual and family power during the feudal age. When a vassal died leaving no heir, the fief reverted to the lord, who could keep it for himself or grant it to a new vassal on the same terms.

THE FEUDALIZATION OF THE CHURCH

Land held by the Church was also bound up in the feudal pattern. Church lands were held as fiefs by archbishops, bishops, and abbots who had sworn fealty to counts, dukes, princes, or kings. But how, one might ask, could clergymen perform military duties and *kill* on the field of battle? They were not trained knights, and Church law forbade the shedding of blood by the clergy.

The higher clergy were usually the sons of noblemen and familiar with the ways of war. During the ninth and tenth centuries, in fact, they often ignored the Church prohibition and engaged in personal combat. Archbishop Turpin, in the epic *Song of Roland* (p. 273), wields his sword against the infidel and dies a hero's death along with Charlemagne's lay vassals. However, with the reform movement of the eleventh century (see Chapter 6), clerical vassals were directed to satisfy their military obligations by assigning portions of their properties as fiefs to *warrior-nobles*. These warriors pledged, as vassals, to perform the required military services. Lay and spiritual lords became closely associated at all levels of authority.

FEUDAL STATES

Any feudal monarch who wanted to be truly the ruler of his country, rather than a mere figurehead, faced daunting problems. He might claim to be the supreme ruler, but in fact his actual power was limited by the extent of his hereditary family territories within the kingdom. It was only in these territories that he was entitled to do justice, levy taxes, recruit knights, and in general exercise government authority. Outside these territories (the "royal domain"), it was the great lords, or *barons,* as they were called, who held these powers. Of course, all the barons were vassals of the monarch as overlord, holding their properties as fiefs on condition of doing him military service and bound to him by the personal tie of homage. But it was hard for the monarch to compel them to meet their obligations, given that their combined knightly armies— and quite often those of individual barons—were greater than his own.

All the same, a feudal monarch did have certain assets that he could use to maintain and gradually increase his power. He could exploit the fact that the barons actually needed an effective overlord, to settle their quarrels and lead them in war. He could use the authority he gained in this way to favor more obedient vassals and undermine less cooperative ones. He would use every chance to increase the size of the royal domain so that his personal wealth and power would outweigh those of his vassals. And if things went wrong, the barons rebelled, and he was defeated, he was almost certain not to be killed or overthrown. For of all the warrior-landholders in his country, he alone was holy: chosen by God, crowned, anointed like King David of old (p. 212), and even credited with the miraculous power to heal disease by his mere touch.

A feudal monarch who built up his assets in this way could not only be a powerful ruler but also create government institutions to ensure that his power would outlive him. In this way, there developed within feudalism effectively governed *states,* of which the most important were the Holy Roman Empire, France, and England. All of these states were vulnerable to disruptions of various kinds, above all resistance and rebellion on the part of vassals, and disputes with the Church, which was both a partner and a rival institution. But only the Holy Roman Empire was permanently enfeebled by these problems. In France and England, on the other hand, the problems were solved by political and governmental innovations that enabled them to survive as strong states into modern times and to provide models of statehood for other European countries.

France: The Strengthening of Monarchy. In France, the homeland of feudalism, the "system" worked for a long time against effective royal power. The descendants of Hugh Capet (p. 222) had enough to do ensuring that the kingship would remain in their family and strengthening their control of the royal domain, a 50-mile stretch of countryside around the city of Paris. Outside that area, the barons governed their territories—often ably and effectively—and struggled for power among themselves, paying little heed to the wearer of the crown.

It was only in the twelfth century that the power of the rulers began to grow—mainly because outside threats caused the barons to cluster more closely as vassals around their overlord, the king. The Holy Roman emperors coveted territory in eastern France and even dreamed of restoring the united empire of Charlemagne. In the south, militant heretics, the Albigensians (pp. 254–255), challenged Catholicism and feudalism alike. Above all, France was threatened with gradual takeover by rival foreign rulers who were also overmighty French vassals: the kings of England.

It was in the duel with the English kings that a powerful French monarchy was forged. Ever since Duke William of Normandy (a territory that was part of France) had conquered England in 1066 (p. 223), his descendants had been both fully independent rulers of England yet also, so far as their French possessions were concerned, vassals of the king of France. In the twelfth century, by marriage and inheritance, the English kings added to Normandy a whole series of other fiefs that gave them control of the entire western half of France. Although vassals, they were easily powerful enough to destroy their overlords. Therefore, as a matter of survival, their overlords set out to destroy them.

It was King Philip Augustus who finally succeeded in doing this. Patiently, in the later decades of the twelfth century, he exploited his powers as overlord against his dangerous vassals, rallying other French barons against them, and hearing appeals from the English king's own French vassals against high-handed acts by their overlord. He even encouraged the disobedient and warlike sons of his English rival, Henry II, in rebellions against their own father. The climax of Philip's campaign came in 1204. Using feudal procedures, he declared one of Henry's successors, King John, a rebellious vassal in his capacity as duke of Normandy. Philip then confiscated that territory and summoned his other vassals to come with their knights to enforce the judgment. Normandy and other French possessions of the English kings were conquered—and much of them was then added to the French king's royal domain. Though the English kings still held extensive fiefs in southwestern France, it would be more than a century before they again challenged the French monarchy (p. 314).

The French kings had become the most powerful warrior-landholders in their country, to whom even the greatest barons looked for leadership, and this, in turn, gave them the chance to build a strong, centrally controlled state. The famous thirteenth-century King Louis IX, courageous crusader, generous giver to the poor, fighter against injustice and corruption in his own government, who was eventually recognized by the Church as a saint, was also the mightiest ruler in Europe. His royal courts were open to all free subjects, regardless of the courts maintained by barons in their fiefs. Paid officials throughout the country enforced the king's decisions, carried out his orders, and saw to it that the central power of the king overrode the local power of the barons. Even so, Louis maintained the barons' support—because he personally was a model of the Christian warrior virtues that they admired and because on the whole he kept within the limits of feudal custom and tradition. In this way, Louis and other thirteenth-century French kings, while still operating in many ways as feudal overlords, laid the foundations of the absolute monarchy of later times (pp. 314–315, 409–418).

The Holy Roman Empire: The Weakening of Monarchy. In the same centuries during which the kings of France changed from figurehead rulers to truly powerful monarchs, the Holy Roman emperors moved in exactly the opposite direction. The empire's founder, Otto I (p. 223), and his tenth-century successors had been truly powerful rulers, exploiting from the start the kind of assets that it took the French kings generations to acquire. The emperors already owned massive domain territories, and the great lords needed their leadership against outside enemies, above all the Slavs and Hungarians (pp. 223–224). In addition, the emperors controlled the Church, thus ensuring that the Church leaders, with their extensive properties and large knightly armies, would in effect be agents of the ruler's power throughout the empire.

True, for a long time, the lords were outright owners of their territories, rather than holding these on condition of service to the ruler. But the twelfth-century emperor Frederick I Barbarossa ("Red-Beard"), a contemporary of Philip Augustus and Henry II, remedied this. He obliged the great lords to accept the status of vassals to him as overlord, holding their territories as fiefs—and on one occasion, like Philip Augustus, he was able to deprive an overmighty vassal, Duke Henry the Lion of Saxony, of his fief and drive him into exile. The empire, too, it seemed, was on its way to becoming a powerful feudal state.

In their efforts to build their power as feudal rulers, however, the emperors faced a persistent and formidable adversary: the popes. In Charlemagne's time and for long afterward, the popes had been willing to accept the protection of the emperors and often their supervision. But with the eleventh-century Church reform movement, the popes began to seek independence from and even supremacy over the emperors (pp. 255–256).

In the long run, the assets of the emperors as feudal monarchs were gradually eroded by the lengthy struggle. Their control of Church positions was disrupted; the great lords lost the habit of looking to them for leadership; they diverted energy and resources into vain attempts to establish power bases in Italy, from which they hoped to overawe both their German vassals and the popes. Worst of all, the emperors were not able to enforce the principle of hereditary succession but instead had to live with election by the great lords; and from the middle of the thirteenth century onward, the great lords took care to elect emperors who would leave them alone. Each fief, each bishopric, each city in the empire's territories, whether in Germany or northern Italy, became in practice a small independent state—often well governed and fairly powerful, but individually not nearly so formidable as the large feudal states of France and England.

England: The King's Government and the Common Law. In England, as in the Holy Roman Empire, feudalism arrived as a foreign import, and from the start it actually favored the growth of royal power. It was Duke William of Normandy who introduced feudalism when he conquered England. As the leader of a victorious army, he could tailor the "system" to his own advantage as king. He kept no less than one-sixth of the country in his own hands as royal domain. He also set up his leading Norman vassals as barons in England, with generous fiefs; however, these mostly consisted not of solid blocks of territory but of smaller parcels scattered across the country so that they were practically impossible to govern independently of the king. Thus in England more than any other feudal country, the barons needed the central government services that the king provided. Conveniently enough, William inherited from his native English predecessors a highly efficient government system. The whole country was divided into counties, or *shires,* with a royal official, the *shire reeve* (sheriff), transacting business in accordance with written royal orders or *writs.*

William's successors, particularly the contemporary and rival of Philip Augustus, King Henry II, built on this basis the most complex and efficient of medieval states. On the whole, they got the cooperation of the barons in this because the state provided both the barons and lesser folk with services that they could not provide for themselves. Most notably, by the beginning of the thirteenth century, the king was providing his subjects with standardized justice operating according to standardized rules and precedents (the "common law"). The king's legal experts, or *justices,* regularly traveled the country to hear cases.

When a justice would arrive in a county to hold a court session, the sheriff would summon sworn groups of freemen (p. 194), known as *juries* (from the Latin *jurare,* "swear an oath"), to give truthful evidence before the justice that would establish the rights and wrongs of disputes over property or to present before them those suspected of serious crimes (*felonies*). Criminal suspects were normally sent for trial by ordeal (p. 228) until, early in the thirteenth century, the Church threw the English criminal justice system into temporary paralysis by declaring the practice of ordeals to be superstitious and ungodly. Hastily, the king's legal experts thought up a new procedure. From then on, the guilt or innocence of suspects would be determined by summoning juries not to *reveal* what they knew or believed but to *render a verdict,* under the guidance of the justice, on the truth of testimony given by others. In this way, the feudal English state inaugurated the modern jury system.

With these and other changes in law and administration, the English kings extended their power over everyone throughout their country. But they were still feudal rulers whose power came from their overlordship of vassals, and their innovations also led to problems and tensions with their vassals, which exploded early in the thirteenth century into a major political crisis.

The Crisis of English Feudal Monarchy: Magna Carta. The English rulers used their new government machinery not just to benefit their subjects but also to exploit the resources of the country to the fullest—above all so as to be able to maintain armies that would protect their possessions across the sea in France. Henry II and his famous elder son, Richard I (the "Lion-Hearted"), had made their English subjects pay heavily for these wars, stretching their powers as overlords, for instance, to demand money as well as military service from their vassals. But at least they had been mostly victorious—an important quality in a feudal overlord. In 1204, however, Richard's younger brother, King John, lost the greater part of his French territories and subsequently failed to win them back. As a defeated overlord, he lost the respect of his vassals—"Lackland," they scornfully called him—and he had to rule by increasing oppression and terror.

Between overlords and vassals, outright oppression and terror were always counterproductive: the end result, in 1215, was a rebellion on the part of many leading barons in which the king found himself deserted and alone. But the barons, true to feudal tradition, could not bring themselves to kill or depose their crowned and anointed king. Instead, following complex negotiations, the armed barons came to an agreement with their king that was enshrined in a famous document: Magna Carta, the "Great Charter."

What the barons wanted from the king was not for him to dismantle his complex and efficient government machine. Rather, they wanted him to ensure that it worked to their benefit, by operating within the traditional feudal framework of mutual rights and responsibilities between overlord and vassals. Some of the king's concessions were of historic importance. He promised that in future, should he need to collect money from his vassals other than for the traditional feudal purposes of knighting his eldest son, marrying his eldest daughter, or ransoming himself, he would do so only with the consent of a council composed of the vassals themselves. And he also promised that he would not deprive any freeman of life, liberty, property, or protection of the law, "unless by legal judgment of his peers or by the law of the land."

Of course, King John granted these things because he could only get the armed barons to demobilize by promising whatever was demanded of him. He and the barons were soon at war again, and conflicts of this kind continued to break out regularly during the thirteenth century. But just as regularly, at the end of every crisis between the English kings and their barons, as a trust-building gesture, the Great Charter would be solemnly renewed, and in time it became part of the political instincts of kings and barons alike.

Only a powerful king heading an effective government, they came to believe, could ensure peace, justice, and prosperity in the kingdom. But as part of his duties as overlord, the king must respect the rights of his vassals—including their right to share with him the responsibility for governing the country—and he must strictly observe his own legal procedures. The king, then, was under the law, and he needed the consent of at least his leading vassals before taking measures that were not expressly part of his rights as overlord. In this way, out of the collision between the newly powerful state and the traditions of feudalism, England took its first steps toward constitutional and parliamentary government (pp. 316, 446–451).

Manorialism

In the Middle Ages, society was thought of as being divided into three *estates* (social groups), each making its particular contribution to the welfare of the whole. Highest were "those who pray"—the clergy, whose lives were the most honorable because they were the guardians of people's souls. Next came "those who fight"—the feudal nobility, from mighty kings to simple knights, who protected life and property. Lowest in status were "those who work"—the common people in town and countryside, including everyone from wealthy merchants and lawyers to landless farm workers, whose labors supported the clergy and nobles as well as themselves. The people of this low estate had little political voice and even less social prestige, but it was they who made possible the achievements of medieval civilization. Like every great civilization before it—those of Sumer and classical Greece, for example (pp. 12, 63)—the civilization of medieval Europe owed its rise to an increase of population and agriculture and a growth of cities and trade. These developments provided the wealth for a complex society, a well-organized government, and an advanced culture. Accordingly, it is to the life, labor, and forms of community of "those who worked" that we now turn—beginning with the most numerous group, probably forming 90 percent of the population in most countries: the ones who worked in the countryside.

THE MANORIAL ESTATE

In medieval Europe, most of the agricultural population worked as members of families that occupied small farms—that is, they belonged to the type of rural social group that is known as *peasants*. But the peasant families did not work their farms individually, nor did they own them as private property. Instead, the principal farming property and social unit was the manorial estate or *manor*, belonging to a member of the feudal nobility or to a Church institution. A relatively humble member of the nobility—a simple knight, for instance—might possess no more than a single manor or even a fraction of one. A great fief, on the other hand, consisted of hundreds of these estates. And so far as the peasants were concerned, anyone who owned a manor, no matter how high or low his status in the feudal hierarchy, was their *lord*.

Manorial estates ranged in size from about 300 acres to perhaps 3,000. The average estate was probably about 1,000 acres, supporting some two or three hundred people. The estate had to be large enough to support its manorial community and to enable its lord to fulfill his feudal obligations, but it could not be so large as to be unmanageable as a farming unit.

Farming Methods: Wheeled Plows and the Three-Field System. The productive heart of the manor consisted of the arable (plowable) fields, and more than half the estate was normally used for crops. Crop yields were boosted by technical innovations that had spread widely through much of western Europe since the fall of Rome, regardless of the turmoil of the times. Ironworking had become so common that blacksmiths were to be found on most estates, turning out sturdy tools that made it easier to clear forests and work the soil. In particular, iron was used to make plowshares (soil-cutting blades) for big wheeled plows that turned over the wet, heavy soils of northern Europe far more thoroughly than earlier types of plow, which merely scratched a shallow furrow. Iron horseshoes and new types of harness made it possible to use horses as work animals, though it was long before horses replaced the less powerful but hardier oxen. Water-powered grain-grinding mills, first used on a large scale in the Roman Empire and widespread throughout much of Europe by 1000, relieved peasant women from endless hours of grinding grain by hand—time that they could devote to more productive women's work (pp. 14–15) such as dairying or weaving.

The most important innovation of the Dark Ages that increased the agricultural wealth of western Europe was the *three-field system* of cultivation. The arable lands of the manor were usually divided into three large, unfenced open fields. In a given farming year, one of these fields would be planted in the fall, another would be planted in the spring, and the third would be left fallow (unseeded) to regain its fertility. The following year, the fallow field would be planted in the fall, the previous fall field would be planted in the spring, and the previous spring field would be left unseeded; and in the third year, the three fields would be rotated yet again. Thus each year, two-thirds of the arable lands were in use while one-third was lying fallow. This simple conservation measure helped to maintain the fertility of the soil, as did the use of animal manures.

Individual peasants did not have compact areas assigned to them. Instead, they held long, narrow strips in each of the three fields (*Fig. 5.7,* p. 236). This was partly because work animals were scarce and small (by modern standards), so that plowing and harvesting had to be done on a cooperative basis. Peasants had to have land in each of the three fields to ensure that they had a regular supply of fall crops and spring crops each year. In addition, the strip system made it possible to distribute the good and poor areas of land fairly among the peasants.

The shape of the strips was apparently governed by the techniques of cultivation. One long furrow could be plowed more efficiently than several short ones. The typical strip was a rod wide (about 17 feet), allowing ample turning space for a team of oxen or horses, and 40 rods long (a *furlong,* or one-eighth of a mile). A unit of these dimensions could be plowed comfortably in a morning or an afternoon, which meant that the workday could be conveniently planned. The lord of the manor, according to his privilege, usually retained a special plot of land for his exclusive use (the *close*). This, together with his strips in the open fields, was known as the lord's *demesne.* Other strips were set aside for the benefit of the resident priest ("God's acre").

Land and Buildings. In addition to the arable lands, supporting areas were essential for the estate. There was a common forest or *woodland* where the peasants were permitted to gather fuel, a *meadow* to provide hay for the work animals, and a *pasture* where the sheep and cattle grazed. A water source (usually a stream or a pond) was indispensable, as well as an area for dumping waste. Only a small section of the estate was occupied by the thatch-roofed, mud-walled homes of the village. Around these windowless cottages the villagers kept small vegetable gardens and raised a few hens, pigs, or goats to supplement their diet. The food grown in the open fields consisted chiefly of staples: wheat, rye, oats, barley, peas, or beans. The common beverage was homemade beer or wine.

Many villages had a manor house for the lord, as well as a church or priest's house. If there was no church or the lord did not actually live in the manor—or if the "lord" was not an individual person but an institution such as a monastery or bishopric—there would at any rate be barns to collect the produce that was due to the lord and the priest. Then there were the mill and the smithy, as well as a bake oven and a wine press—all provided by the lord for a fee. In addition, the priest, the miller, the blacksmith, and the baker had their own agricultural holdings.

Fig. 5.7 Plan of a Manor. The plan shows the main resources that peasants used: cultivated strips in the open fields belonging to each household (the holdings of one household are shown in black), and the meadow, pasture, and woodland which all households used in common. Also shown are features that enabled the lord to live off the peasants' labors: his demesne land, which they cultivated, and a bridge and grain mill, which they used in return for produce or money. This layout originated in medieval times but lasted until the mid-twentieth century.

THE PEOPLE OF THE MANOR

The records of village life prior to the thirteenth century are meager. But we do know that in those mute centuries, the basic habits of work, law, worship, and play evolved into established custom. And we have abundant evidence that village life as it existed in the thirteenth century persisted with little change for the following five hundred years. The rise of trade and the growth of cities, the emergence of national states, the struggles between religious factions—all seem to have had slight effect on the basic patterns and rhythms of rural life. One of the striking facts about medieval life, in contrast to modern times, was the general lack of privacy. Homes were tiny, consisting usually of one room. Adults, children, and animals often spent the night under the same roof.

The Lord and His Family. The lord of the manor was presumably guided by the rules of God and by custom; in any case, his word was law. Whether a simple knight or a noble of high degree, he was often away from home for long periods of time. He was a warrior as well as a landlord and had his feudal obligations to fulfill. When he was not performing those duties, his favorite pastime was hunting. He typically took little direct interest in farming and left the management of his lands and local justice to his overseers (*stewards* or *bailiffs*). The lord's wife spent most of her days in the manor house supervising the servants, household operations, and entertainment of guests. If she was a lady of high rank, she might also act as a partner in the conduct of her husband's political and administrative affairs.

From his own farms and payments by the peasants in kind (crops), the lord normally took about half the total produce of the estate. He also maintained a *reserve* of grain in his barns so that in years of crop failure, he would be able to provide the peasants with food. He could not allow them to starve, for aside from humane considerations, they represented his labor force.

Peasants and Serfdom. Most of the peasants were serfs (Latin, *servi*), whose special status and ties to the soil were inherited. The origins of serfdom can be traced back to the western provinces of the Roman Empire in the third and fourth centuries (p. 151); by 1000, it had spread beyond the empire's former frontiers and was normal throughout most of Europe. During the turbulent times of the early Middle Ages, whole communities of farmers had placed themselves under powerful warriors for protection (p. 220). In addition, in territories that had once belonged to the Roman Empire, many serfs were descended from earlier generations of slaves who had worked on the estates of great landowners (p. 151); in their case, serfdom represented an improvement in status. Nevertheless, a serf was legally unfree. The lord could free a serf when he chose, but otherwise serfs were held to their obligations.

The main obligation of the serfs was to cultivate the strips in the open fields that belonged to the lord. In addition, they could be called on to build roads, clear forests, and do other work, and they had to give the lord fixed amounts of any valuable items that they produced, such as spun yarn or poultry. The serfs' children were likewise bound to the manor; no members of their families could leave the estate or marry without the consent of the lord. A serf's eldest son normally inherited the rights and duties of his father.

Peasants whose ancestors had managed to avoid serfdom had the status of *freemen.* This did not necessarily mean that they were better off; some, in fact, lived on the edge of starvation. If the freeman farmed land, he did so as a farm *tenant,* paying rent to the lord in the form of a share of his crop. The lord could evict a freeman whenever he saw fit, whereas a serf could not legally be separated from his land.

Free or not, the peasants of a manorial village shared a hard and isolated life. Husbands and fathers exercised primary rights in their households, but men, women, and children alike toiled together in the fields. Illiterate and uneducated, they knew little of the outside world, save for news and gossip brought by the lord, the priest, or traveling peddlers and clerics. The course of their lives was shaped by the pattern of labor, the seasons, the cycle of religious holidays, and the round of births, marriages, and deaths.

Manorialism and Increasing Wealth. In spite of the harsh life to which it condemned the peasants, manorialism was a highly successful form of economic and social organization. The three-field system was more productive than earlier farming methods. More secure than freemen and with far greater property rights than slaves, the serfs had an incentive to found families and increase the amount of land they farmed. Partly for these reasons, the emergence of manorialism by 1000 was followed by three centuries of agricultural boom. Throughout Europe, the serfs cut down forests, drained swamps, and brought grasslands under the plow. Thousands of new villages sprang up, and by 1300, the population of Europe had risen from roughly forty million to about one hundred million.

This *internal colonization,* as it is called, was very much in the interests of the lords, as it increased the amount of productive land that they controlled. Usually it was they who founded new manors on uncultivated land and moved serfs into them. But to get the cooperation of the serfs, the lords had to offer them concessions, such as larger holdings, smaller crop deliveries, and fewer hours of work. So profitable was it for the lords to bring new land under cultivation that they did not hesitate to offer these concessions. In time, the lords even found it preferable to abolish servile obligations altogether and turn their serfs into free tenants, paying rent in produce or cash. (The lords, however, usually retained manorial powers of government and justice, as well as ultimate ownership of the land.) In western Europe, this eventually led, by the end of the Middle Ages, to the almost complete disappearance of serfdom (p. 303).

In addition, European society as a whole had become much wealthier and also more complex and diverse. As the population swelled and peasants and lords both prospered, commerce and industry also began to grow, and the number of people who made a living by these activities increased. Alongside the manor, the typical community of peasants and lords, there appeared another type of community, formed by merchants and craftsmen: the town.

The Rise of Trade and Towns

With the reopening of trade routes and the appearance of new marketing centers in the eleventh century came the emergence of the towns that were destined to convert Europe from a rural to an urban society. The lords and peasants who remained on the manors played a mainly indirect role in the growth of these towns, as producers and consumers of goods that were bought and sold in them. An expanded cast of characters gradually appeared there, consisting of merchants, bankers, lawyers, artisans, and unskilled laborers. In the thirteenth century, these groups made up but a fraction of Europe's population (less than 10 percent), but their numbers were destined to grow until by the twentieth century they would be a majority (p. 514).

In some areas, notably northern Italy, where trading opportunities were particularly rich and the authority of the feudal ruler, the Holy Roman emperor, was usually feeble, the towns grew into cities. They extended their power over the neighboring countryside, acquired their own armies and navies, and thus became true *city-states* (pp. 18, 64–67). More commonly, the towns had to find themselves a place within the existing structure of feudal monarchy. But their place was often an important one: it was in the towns that kings set up their government offices, bishops built their cathedrals, and scholars gathered to form universities (pp. 266–268). Thus the rural-based civilization of the early Middle Ages became a city-based civilization, like those of earlier Greece and Rome—or neighboring Byzantium and Islam.

THE GROWTH OF TRADE

The revival of trade and towns was closely connected with the rise in population and production in the European countryside. With more land being cultivated by improved methods, the owners of manors and even better-off peasants had more to spend on the luxuries that the towns had to offer. Likewise, with some assurance that crops could be marketed in the towns, peasants and lords had an additional incentive for increasing farm output. Church lords and nobles, instead of consuming all the food and supplies that the peasants produced for them, sold some of the produce in the towns, in return for cash; or instead of receiving their income in goods and services, they freed their serfs and charged them rents to be paid in money. Gold and silver were being mined and coined again and were passing into circulation with the speed-up in trade. Money, little used in the early Middle Ages, was now seen as the key to new comforts and delights.

Long-Distance Trade. Many luxuries came from the Mediterranean world and the wider intercontinental world to which the Mediterranean gave access. Byzantium and Islam, which dominated the sea's eastern and southern shores, were vigorous commercial societies and manufactured elegant articles for export; in addition, they controlled trade routes that led overland across central Asia to China and by sea across the Indian Ocean to India and the spice islands of the Far East (pp. 320–321). Their merchandise was brought to western Europe overland through Spain or, more commonly, through Venice and other port cities of northern Italy (Map 5.6, p. 240). Constantinople was the main source of luxury goods, which found a growing market among European aristocrats. Those who could afford them sought spices (pepper, ginger, and cinnamon); silks and satins; precious jewels; statues; and rugs and tapestries.

In return for these imports, the Europeans began to export woolens and linens, horses, weapons and armor, timber, furs, and slaves. (The word *slave* is derived from *Slav* because Slavs, captured in wars among themselves or with their German and Hungarian neighbors, often ended up being sold by Italian merchants in the slave markets of Byzantium and the Muslim world.) From all parts of Europe, caravans carried goods across the Alps, chiefly to Milan, Pisa, and Venice, for transshipment to the East. Northern Italy thus became the commercial gateway between western Europe and the rest of the Eastern Hemisphere.

Industry and Technology. The wool and textile industries provided the bulk of European exports. These industries centered in the Low Countries, where conditions were favorable for sheep-raising. In time, this region gained fame also for its manufacture of woolen cloth, and Flemish producers finally had to turn to outside sources of raw wool to satisfy their needs. English farmers and landlords met this demand by converting more of their holdings into pastureland. After the thirteenth century, both in England and on the Continent, there was a growing cash market for wool. A single peasant, with only a few sheep, might thus become a participant in the new trading economy.

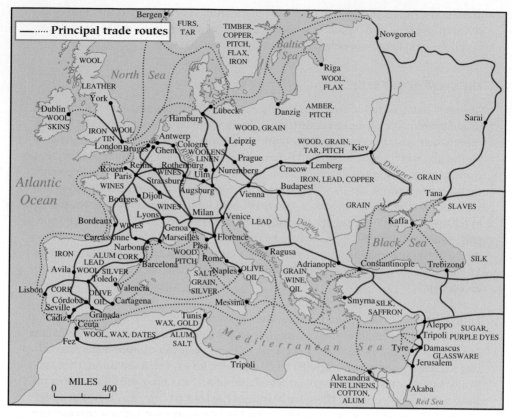

Map 5.6 Trading Routes and Towns, 1300. At the height of Europe's medieval economic boom, the network of land and sea routes and important towns is still densest in areas that once belonged to the Roman Empire— through southern and western Europe and across the Mediterranean to the Islamic world. But the network has also extended to places that were far from civilization in Roman times—Scandinavia and the Baltic, as well as eastern Europe as far as Russia.

The increase in wealth brought about by the growth of agriculture and trade also fostered a spirit of technical progress, which was shared in not only by "those who worked" but also by "those who fought" and "those who prayed." Enterprising craftsmen, wanting to save labor and increase production in their workshops, devised ingenious mechanisms to adapt the waterwheel, long used for grinding grain (pp. 127, 235), to all sorts of other tasks. Hammering raw iron to remove impurities, beating rags into pulp to make paper, stamping on woolen cloth to thicken it—all these and many other manufacturing processes came to be done by water-powered machinery. Feudal lords wishing to besiege the castles of their rivals equipped their forces with *trebuchets*— huge wooden contraptions that used the counterweight principle to hurl boulders weighing as much as a ton. Though stone-throwing devices had been used as "artillery" since Hellenistic times, their main targets had been enemy soldiers; trebuchets, on the other hand, were the first war machines that could do significant damage to stone fortifications. And bishops and abbots, desiring their cathedral and monastery towers to be heard as well as seen across miles of countryside (p. 263), urged on metalworkers to develop methods of large-scale bronze casting that would produce monster bells. The spurt of technical progress that began in the Middle Ages continued and accelerated without a break until it ended in the Industrial Revolution of the eighteenth and nineteenth centuries (pp. 304–307, 504–508).

THE LOCATION AND APPEARANCE OF TOWNS

The medieval towns were essentially trading posts where local produce could be sold and foreign merchandise purchased. Traveling merchants, moving along familiar land and water routes, carried imported goods from northern Italy to such trading sites as the junction of highways, the confluence of rivers, or the capital of a duchy or a kingdom (*Map 5.6*). The merchants, in turn, attracted laborers and craftsmen—generally landless commoners, most of whom came from manorial villages. Ancient Roman cities that happened to be well located reawakened as bustling towns. The community surrounding a cathedral (that is, the headquarters of a bishop or an archbishop) might also become an important trading center. In some parts of Europe, particularly "frontier" areas such as eastern Germany (p. 223) where towns had strategic value, kings and nobles cooperated in founding them but rarely took part in their actual government. In other regions, the townspeople had to struggle for many generations to win from the landed aristocracy a degree of self-government for their communities.

Physical protection for the merchants was of course a necessity. They usually set up their shops in the shadow of a castle or a fortified settlement and then raised walls around their "new" town, linking it to the old. The English word *town* derives from the Anglo-Saxon *tun* ("fortified enclosure"). The remains of these town walls may still be seen in many of the old cities of Europe, notably Carcassonne in France (*Fig. 5.8*, p. 242), Avila in Spain, and Rothenburg in Germany.

Understandably, space was at a premium in these towns. Streets and passageways were kept as narrow as possible so that a maximum number of buildings could be erected. And the buildings themselves had as many stories as safety would permit. Even so, housing was painfully cramped—tighter, sometimes, than the space in peasants' cottages. There was very little town planning, and sanitation was notoriously poor. From the very earliest times, European cities faced problems of congestion, traffic jams, infectious diseases, and slums.

Nevertheless, there was a certain order in most medieval towns. By the thirteenth century, a typical pattern had appeared. The town was usually dominated by the towers or spires of its main church. Next in importance were the town hall and the buildings of the various trading and industrial organizations (the *guilds;* pp. 242–243). The heart of the town was the central marketplace and shops. At first most of these were the places of traders, but artisans of all kinds (weavers, smiths, bakers) soon found they could sell their services in town, and they set up workshops there. Thus towns became centers of industry as well as trade.

A NEW SOCIAL ELEMENT: THE BOURGEOIS

Unlike the peasants, all townspeople were legally free. Yet the towns had a social structure of their own—though one not quite so rigid as that of the manor (pp. 236–237). At the top were the leading merchants and moneylenders and the heads of the guilds. Beneath them were skilled artisans and clerks, and at the bottom were apprentices and unskilled laborers.

© Adam Woolfitt/CORBIS

Fig. 5.8 Carcassonne. This town in the south of France near the Spanish border dates from Roman times. The inner walls were originally built to defend the town from barbarian invaders and were reconstructed in the twelfth century when the town lay on a main route of reviving trade (*Map 5.6*, p. 240). These walls run for about 1,400 yards around an area of about 1/20 of a square mile—a reasonable size for a medieval town. The outer walls were added in the thirteenth century and made the town almost impossible to capture using medieval siege methods.

The members of the highest group dominated civic affairs and are usually called by the French word for townspeople in general: the *bourgeois.* They constituted a new social element in European society, which gained in wealth and power as the centuries passed. Even so, the bourgeois were regarded as *commoners,* legally and socially inferior to the clergy and the nobility.

Because the whole pattern of life in the towns was different from that of the feudal estate, a new plan for government had to be devised for the new communities. The townspeople sought special *charters* that would free them from the customary obligations of the feudal relationship and would permit them to establish appropriate rules of their own. These charters, granted by the king, nobleman, or bishop holding authority over the area, recognized the citizens of the town as constituting a political body, or *corporation,* with legal privileges and powers. In return for these privileges, and in place of feudal services, the corporation made regular payments of money to the grantor. The form of government differed from one town to another, but in most places, control rested in the hands of a governing *council* and an official called a *mayor.* Though voting rights (for adult males only) were often quite liberal, it was uncommon for any but the leading bourgeois families to hold important offices.

ECONOMIC THEORY AND CONTROL: THE GUILDS

The governing council imposed strict political control on the community. Legally, the citizens of a town were free individuals, but the idea of *collective* responsibility and regulation was accepted in town and countryside alike. Merchants and craftspeople formed special corporations called *guilds.* The guilds limited production and sale of goods to their members, upheld standards of business practice and quality of merchandise, and set prices for every commodity.

The principal organization in most towns was the *merchant guild,* which established rules governing the marketplaces. These rules controlled the times and places at which goods could be sold, the standard weights and measures, and the grades and prices of the commodities sold. At first the merchant guild included most of the tradespeople in a given town. With growing specialization, however, one group after another split off from the parent unit to form independent *craft guilds:* weavers, dyers, tailors, carpenters, masons, silversmiths, bakers, barbers, and the like. By the thirteenth century, there might be as many as thirty or forty guilds in a single town.

The primary function of a craft guild was to supervise the production of goods and the training of artisans. Craftsmen were classified as masters, journeymen, or apprentices. Only masters had the right to operate workshops and train others; they alone were voting members of the guild and directed its policies, and their coveted status was won by other craftsmen only after long experience and proof of excellence. Before the masters certified a journeyman to their rank, they customarily required him to submit an example of his workmanship. This effort, the finest he was capable of, was called his *masterpiece.* Journeymen were licensed artisans who had served an apprenticeship. They were employed by the masters and were usually paid at a fixed rate per day (French, *journée*). Before becoming a journeyman, an individual was obliged to work for a specified period of time, ranging from two to seven years, as an apprentice (learner) in the shop of a master. In return for their labor, apprentices received only food and lodging. Though women of the towns were permitted to perform some skilled and unskilled services, they were generally excluded from guild membership.

The guilds were primarily economic units, but they also performed personal and social functions. If a member fell sick, was put in jail, or got into some other kind of trouble, he could count on help from the guild brotherhood. The guilds provided proper ceremonies on the occasions of births, marriages, and funerals; they conducted social affairs; and they celebrated Church festivals as a body. Each one, moreover, honored a particular Christian saint who was associated by tradition with a given craft. (Saint Joseph, for example, was honored by carpenters.) The guilds often dedicated altars or chapels in the town church to their special saints. In all their varied activities, they embodied the corporate and community spirit so characteristic of medieval society.

RECOMMENDED READING

The Germanic Kingdoms of the West M. Todd, *The Early Germans* (1992); J. M. Wallace-Hadrill, *The Barbarian West* (1985); and P. J. Geary, *Before France and Germany* (1988), are readable accounts of the Germanic peoples, the barbarian-ruled successor states of Rome, and the Frankish kingdom. R. Fletcher, *The Barbarian Conversion* (1997), surveys the spread of Christianity beyond Rome's former frontiers.

Byzantium and Its Neighbors An excellent general survey of Byzantine history and culture is R. Browning, *The Byzantine Empire* (1992). T. F. Mathews, *The Art of Byzantium: Between Antiquity and the Renaissance* (1998), is a splendidly illustrated brief guide to art and architecture. D. Obolensky, *The Byzantine Commonwealth: Eastern Europe, 500–1453* (1971), analyzes the Byzantine influence on the Slavs and other eastern European peoples. All these books cover the entire period of the Byzantine Empire down to the fall of Constantinople. J. Moorehead, *Justinian* (1994), is a good brief biography.

The Book and Sword of Islam D. Norcliffe, *Islam: Faith and Practice* (1999), is a good survey of beliefs, practices, and culture down to the present; B. Lewis, *The Arabs in History* (1993), covers the nation most closely associated with Islam; T. Andrae, *Mohammed: The Man and His Faith* (1936), is brief and balanced. D. Sourdel, *Medieval Islam* (1983), discusses ethnic, geographical, political, and social factors in the spread of Islam.

The Carolingians J. Le Goff, *Medieval Civilization, 400–1500* (1988), is an up-to-date introduction to all aspects and periods of the Middle Ages; P. Brown, *The Rise of Western Christendom, A.D. 200–1000* (1996), describes the early medieval transformation of the Roman world into the civilization of western Europe.

The best account of the rise, achievements, and decline of the Carolingians, covering government, religion, culture, and society, is P. Riché, *The Carolingians: A Family Who Made Europe* (1993); the ways of life of all social groups in the Frankish empire are readably described in P. Riché, *Daily Life in the World of Charlemagne* (1978).

Europe Takes Shape F. D. Logan, *The Vikings in History* (1993), is a brief and vivid account, ranging from Constantinople to the New World; P. Sawyer, ed., *The Oxford Illustrated History of the Vikings* (1997), gives more detail and is splendidly illustrated.

R. Bartlett, *The Making of Europe: Conquest, Colonization, and Cultural Change, 950–1350* (1993), is an up-to-date interpretation of the recovery and expansion of Christian western Europe; D. Obolensky, *The Byzantine Commonwealth: Eastern Europe, 500–1453* (1971), deals with the recovery and expansion of Christian eastern Europe.

Feudalism Two classic short books on the workings of feudalism may be recommended: F. L. Ganshof, *Feudalism* (1952), which analyzes feudal institutions in France and the Holy Roman Empire, and C. Stephenson, *Mediaeval Feudalism* (1942), a readable general introduction to feudalism as a legal, government, and social system and a way of life.

Another classic, S. Painter, *French Chivalry* (1940), readably describes the values and rituals of knighthood; M. Keen, *Chivalry* (1984), is an excellent introduction to the values and practices of the feudal elite throughout western and central Europe; and J. Le Goff, *Medieval Callings* (1990), describes the way of life of knights, among many other medieval social types. On women of the feudal elite and other social groups, see S. Shahar, *The Fourth Estate: A History of Women in the Middle Ages* (1983), and the attractive portrayals of individuals in E. Power, *Medieval Women* (1975).

On individual feudal states, see G. Duby, *France in the Middle Ages* (1991), and P. Frame, *The Political Development of the British Isles* (1990).

Manorialism W. Rösener, *The Peasantry of Europe* (1994), traces changes in farming technology, peasant life, and relations of peasants and lords from early medieval times to the present; G. Duby, *The Early Growth of the European Economy* (1974), deals with the same themes in more detail, concentrating on the period of the growth of manorialism. The books by Le Goff, Shahar, and Power listed in the last section cover the ways of life of men and women in the countryside.

The Rise of Trade and Towns J. H. Mundy and P. Riesenberg, *The Medieval Town* (1958), is a brief introduction to the rise of towns, covering economic and social life, government, and the urban setting; D. Nicholas, *The Growth of the Medieval City* (1994), is an authoritative recent survey. The ways of life of urban men and women are dealt with in the books by Le Goff, Shahar, and Power listed in the section on feudalism. R. S. Lopez, *The Commercial Revolution of the Middle Ages* (1971), is an excellent brief account of the expansion of trade and its relationship to developments in agriculture.

ℹ INFOTRAC COLLEGE EDITION

Visit the source collections at **http://academic.cengage.com/infotrac**, and use the Search function with the following key terms:

Middle Ages	Carolingian	feudal, feudalism
Byzantium	Charlemagne	
early Christianity	Vikings not Minnesota	

🌐 WESTERN CIVILIZATION RESOURCES

Visit the Brief History of the Western World Companion Web Site for resources specific to this textbook:

http://history.wadsworth.com/greerbrief09/

Also, the CD in the back of this book and the World History Resources Center at **http://history.wadsworth.com/west_civ/** offer a variety of tools to help you succeed in this course, including access to quizzes; images; documents; interactive simulations, maps, and timelines; movie explorations; and a wealth of other sources.

CHAPTER 6

The Flowering of Medieval Culture

OVERVIEW

As with all earlier civilizations, the single most important influence on the culture of western Europe in the Middle Ages was religion—in this case, the Christianity of the Latin or Catholic Church (p. 172). With the renewal of civilization came an upsurge of new developments in the Church's beliefs, practices, and organization. The conversion of barbarian peoples, the rise in population, the agricultural boom, and the revival of trade brought more territory, believers, and wealth to the Church. More humanly appealing forms of devotion appeared, which made heaven seem more accessible to believers and strengthened the authority of the clergy who controlled this access. New orders of monks and nuns were founded—some to make up for the failings of existing orders that had been spoiled by increasing wealth and others to adapt monasticism to the needs of the growing towns.

All these changes gained approval and backing from the popes, who were striving to bring the whole Church under their central control. Their efforts ran into determined resistance from their partners and rivals, the rulers of the western European feudal states. All the same, the popes acquired such power over the Catholic Church that they became for a time the most powerful rulers in western Europe.

The inspiration of religion, combined with increasing wealth, technical progress, and the revival of urban life, created the conditions for cultural achievements that equaled those of any earlier civilization. The renewed civilization of western Europe invested much of its newfound wealth and skills in magnificent religious buildings—the churches and cathedrals of the Romanesque and Gothic styles. New urban institutions of learning, the universities, supplied skilled professionals to meet the needs of a complex society and also nurtured advances in knowledge and thought. Literacy became normal for nobles and better-off townspeople, who provided authors and a public for masterpieces of literature in both Latin and the developing vernacular (native) languages of Europe.

Religion and the advance of civilization also combined to produce two other features of medieval western European civilization: its bitter internal disputes and its urge toward outward expansion. New *heresies* (dissident Christian religious movements) arose which denied the authority and holiness of the clergy and the centralized Church. Rivalries between Christians and Jews in the growing towns led to frequent explosions of anti-Jewish violence. And on the frontiers of Christian Europe stood yet more religious enemies—above all, Islam.

Accordingly, western Europe also invested its wealth and skills in formidable attacks on its religious foes. The Church tribunals of the Inquisition devised complex procedures of investigation and punishment to enforce religious conformity. Rulers of powerful feudal states used their government machinery to expel the Jews from entire countries. Above all, the main forces in medieval society—the Church, the feudal warriors, and the towns—combined to undertake a series of unprecedented long-distance expeditions against religious enemies—the Crusades.

These holy wars failed in the most famous of the purposes for which they were fought: to regain the Holy Land permanently from Islam. They led to a *schism* (break) with the Greek (Orthodox) Church, which the Catholic West came to see as a religious enemy because it would not accept the universal rule of the pope. But the Crusades also brought colonists and missionaries to conquered territories in Muslim Spain and remaining pagan regions in eastern Europe, as well as traders to seaports in the eastern Mediterranean. In this way, the Crusades set a precedent of colonizing and converting non-Christian lands, and of long-distance overseas trade, which was to be followed by empire building among western European nations at the end of the Middle Ages.

The Medieval Church

In Chapter 5, we concentrated on the material side of life in the Middle Ages. But medieval men and women were more concerned with what lies *beyond* this world; they looked toward life eternal. And because the central role of the Church was to guide souls to everlasting salvation, the Church was regarded as the primary institution in society.

Never before had the Church been so dominant in the affairs of Westerners, nor has it been so since. Though priests and bishops looked toward eternity, they paid close attention to what happened on earth. For what people did in the here and now could bear on their fate in the hereafter. Consequently, the clergy felt they had a duty to examine the heart and deeds of every Christian and to ensure that human institutions reflected the will of God.

THE SACRAMENTS

The extraordinary power of the medieval Church rested solidly on the trust of the people. The rich left it generous gifts, and bishops and abbots thereby acquired vast properties in land, serfs, animals, and buildings. The Church had deeper and broader sources of strength, however—among them, the direct and intimate relationship with every inhabitant of the "Christian commonwealth."

It was the bishops and priests who held in their keeping the *sacraments*—the holy rituals through which God's *grace* (divine aid) was made available to the human race. The sacraments had developed over a thousand years from the rituals practiced by the early Christians (p. 17). By the eleventh century, a general theory of the sacraments had appeared. According to this theory, God had created the sacraments as a means of providing divine aid (grace) to sinful men and women to enable them to be saved. In addition, God had instituted his priests as the principal administrators of these rites.

Seven sacraments were recognized. Through *baptism* the individual was initiated into church membership (usually as an infant) and cleansed of the stain and penalty of past sin. The second sacrament was *confirmation,* administered to baptized people later on, so as to confirm them in their acceptance of Christ and strengthen them in faith by the Holy Spirit. *Ordination* was the sacrament whereby bishops conferred on priests their miraculous power to administer sacraments. Because ordination, baptism, and confirmation each left a special mark upon the soul that was believed to be indelible, these sacraments were administered only once during a person's lifetime.

The other four sacraments could be repeated. Foremost among them was the *Eucharist (Mass),* which was believed to provide food for the soul. The Church taught that at a certain moment in the rite, the bread and wine were transformed (*transubstantiated*) into the body and blood of the Savior. The recipient, sharing in the strength of Christ himself, would thus be aided in doing good and resisting evil. Christians were required to take the Eucharist at least once each year. But the Eucharist was beneficial only if received worthily—that is, only if the individual was in a "state of grace," forgiven for past sins. To prepare for the Eucharist, the individual took the sacrament of *penance,* which consisted of inward repentance (sorrowful regret) for misdeeds, oral confession, and acceptance of a penalty. The person was then pardoned by the priest. When Christians appeared to be on the point of death, they were given the sacrament of *extreme unction* (last rites), which granted them final forgiveness for the sins of their lifetime.

The seventh sacrament was *matrimony,* the joining together of husband and wife. (In this ceremony, the individuals being married actually administer the sacrament to each other, but a priest must be present for it to be held legitimate by the Church.) The clergy compared the matrimonial bond to the union between Christ and the Church and held it to be unbreakable so long as the two partners lived. Should one of them die, the survivor could take another spouse by repeating the matrimonial rite. This sacrament and that of ordination were not essential to the individual's salvation. But the other five were compulsory, and the clergy taught that only through them could a Christian reach heaven.

CHRISTIAN DEVOTIONAL LIFE

The sacraments were central to the spiritual life of medieval men and women. They were part of many religious observances that followed the calendar and the clock. These included all the formal worship services (*liturgy*) of the clergy and the laity; the most important of these services was the Mass. Though Masses were performed every day, the main service was on Sunday, when attendance was required of all Christians.

The experience of the Mass strengthened human associations in the Age of Faith. Clergy and laity were joined in a common drama as men and women of all social classes participated together under one roof. They were taught that the sacrament was a mystic union—a holy communion—between Christ and themselves. No other ritual has symbolized more completely the intimate association between human and divine beings. Around the official devotions surrounding the Mass were countless informal practices, which made up the popular religion of the times. These devotions grew out of

Fig. 6.1 The Gero Crucifix. This life-size wood carving, made toward the year 1000, is one of the earliest appearances in art of the figure of Christ suffering on the Cross. Traditionally, artists had treated the Crucifixion as a scene of the divine Savior triumphing over death. Here, by contrast, Jesus is shown with his arms stretched back, his knees giving way, and his head hanging down—a human being in the last agony of a cruel death.

the beliefs, fears, and hopes of the common people, but they were generally regulated by the priesthood.

The cult of the Crucifixion, for example, grew out of a deep and spontaneous sympathy for Jesus as a *man*. In earlier centuries, theologians had tended to stress the role of Jesus as *God*. His life, death, and resurrection were seen as part of a grand design by which he overcame the devil and opened the way to salvation. The Crucifixion, in this view, was an act of divine majesty—above the fears and pains of ordinary human beings. Early Christian art usually portrayed the Savior as the risen Christ sitting in royal dignity upon the heavenly throne (*Fig. 6.4,* p. 261). Sometime after the year 1000, a new view began to gain attention. It emphasized Jesus' *human* experiences—his struggles, humiliations, and physical sufferings. Both theologians and the common people drew fresh meaning from the Passion (suffering) of their Lord, recognizing in his agony their own anguish and miseries. Artists increasingly showed the dying Christ hanging heavily from the Cross. Gradually the crucifix, which aroused in pious hearts the deepest feelings of compassion and love, became the most popular devotional object (*Fig. 6.1*).

In the same way, the infant Jesus in early portraits appears as a kingly figure, but during the Middle Ages he was made to look like any infant held in the arms of a loving mother. And his mother, Mary, was presented in an ever more tender and human light.

The cult of the Virgin was exceedingly popular in the Middle Ages. The monasteries played a leading role in developing it, but ordinary people responded warmly to the appeal of Mary. Aside from her role as the mother of God, she personified the Christian ideals of womanhood, love, and sympathy. During an upsurge of religious fervor in the thirteenth century, many of the great new cathedrals were dedicated to Mary. A rich literature and a host of legends came into being that told of the countless miracles of the Virgin. She was pictured as loyal and forgiving toward all who honored her and ready to give earthly benefits and heavenly rewards to those who prayed to her. From time to time, the higher clergy grew concerned over the intensity of this Marian cult. There was always the risk that honoring the Virgin might compete with worship of God. The bishops nonetheless encouraged the cult as part of general reverence for the saints.

Mary ranked highest among the saints, but there were hundreds of lesser figures who also attracted prayer and devotions. These practices reflected the strong *will to believe* among medieval people. Faith in marvels, omens (signs), and supernatural appearances was nearly universal; devils and demons were thought to lurk everywhere; and miraculous cures and resurrections of the dead were reported almost daily. These wonders, many of which were credited to the saints, fired the imagination of all true believers.

The saints included the twelve apostles and the early martyrs, as well as a host of later men and women. Their individual fame as preachers, hermits, and workers of miracles became established by tradition; it was not until the thirteenth century that the popes assumed the exclusive right to identify them formally as saints (canonization). The bishops, from early times, required Christians to show the saints the special honor of *veneration* (deep reverence). Though it was taught that veneration should not become *worship* (which was reserved for God), medieval Christians directed a large share of their devotions to the saints.

The Church taught that saints had the power to perform miracles after their deaths as well as during their lives on earth. In heaven, because of their privileged position, they could win divine aid for mortals by interceding (pleading) with God. Hardly any act was undertaken in the Middle Ages without first calling upon the saints. Moreover, some of their power was thought to stay on earth in their physical remains (*relics*). Oaths and treaties were sworn on saintly remains; townspeople carried them in religious processions; knights often inserted holy fragments in the hilts of their swords; people traveled hundreds of miles on pilgrimage to the shrines of famous saints where their relics were preserved (p. 275).

The skulls, bones, and hair of saints were the most common relics, but other items were preserved as well: the sweat, tears, and umbilical cord of Jesus; Saint Joseph's breath; and the Virgin's milk. Pieces of the "true" Cross seemed to be everywhere—enough, it was said later, to build a ship. Several heads of John the Baptist were claimed, as were the entire skeletons of many lesser saints. No church or monastery was without its collection of relics—its "spiritual endowment." To this day, the treasuries of many European churches are rich with golden reliquaries (containers) and their precious contents. It was only toward the close of the Middle Ages that some devout Christians began to express doubts of the authenticity of the more unlikely relics.

MONASTIC REFORM MOVEMENTS

In addition to providing spiritual guidance, the medieval Church served society in numerous other ways. The secular clergy (p. 184) acted as counselors and administrators for rulers; bishops and archbishops functioned as vassals of kings and emperors. Different sorts of services were carried on by the regular clergy (p. 184), who lived in the great monasteries that by now existed all over western Europe, most of which followed the Benedictine Rule (pp. 182–184). Although the monasteries' primary function was to serve as a refuge for ascetics seeking to devote themselves to God, the monks dwelling there answered the needs of the times by taking on other important functions as well.

The regular clergy preserved and copied manuscripts (p. 260) and provided elementary schooling for youths planning to enter the clergy, thus keeping literacy and learning alive. At the same time, they preserved in their workshops the useful arts of weaving, pottery-making, and metalworking, and in the fields they developed more efficient tools and techniques of farming. Over the centuries, the religious houses became large landholders, and though the monks themselves were bound by vows of poverty, the corporate (collective) wealth of the monasteries rose steadily.

Wealth, Power, and Corruption. As a result of this growing wealth, the monastic establishments became more and more involved in the affairs of the world. The head of a monastery—the abbot—held the monastery's property as a fief from some overlord, and he had the usual military, financial, and political responsibilities of a vassal. He met his obligations, in part, by granting some of the monastery's lands to knights, who, as vassals of the abbot, performed the required military duties. From the ninth to the twelfth century, military units from monastic fiefs were important components of feudal armies, and kings and the feudal barons frequently chose their administrators from among members of the regular clergy (as well as the secular).

These developments improved the stability of the government and the economy, but they tended to interfere with the ascetic way of life once so characteristic of the regular clergy. Wealth brought the ways of the world into the religious orders themselves. Some abbots lived as elegantly as great nobles, and ordinary monks enjoyed the produce of the prospering estates. Plenty of food and wine led to a broader pursuit of pleasure. Obedience to monastic rules weakened, the vow of chastity was taken less seriously, and physical labor grew less attractive. The monks tended, at the same time, to neglect the arts of reading and writing.

During the tenth century, standards of learning and conduct fell to an even lower level among the secular clergy. The appointment of bishops and archbishops was generally controlled by powerful nobles, who often sold these offices (positions) to the highest bidder. Some of these "successors of the apostles" were more active in politics than in spiritual matters. Many parish priests also fell short of their responsibilities; some were unable to read; some, contrary to Church law, had wives and families. The popes, as the monarchs of the Church, might have tried to correct these abuses, but they were as open as other bishops to the influences of the times (p. 253).

Cycles of Reform: Cluny, Cîteaux, and the Friars. Distressed by widespread corruption within the Church, a few conscientious rulers, bishops, and abbots started a program of reform. The most far-reaching of these efforts was undertaken in the Burgundian monastery of Cluny, founded in 910 by the duke of Aquitaine. The first abbot, Berno, set out to revive the strictness of the Benedictine Rule. His efforts were carried on by a series of extraordinary abbots, whose reputation for holiness brought generous support and gifts from wealthy nobles throughout western and central Europe.

In order to protect individual monasteries from falling under local political influences, the Cluniac monks placed themselves under the direct authority of the pope. For the same reason, the abbots of Cluny did not allow newly founded monasteries to become independent, as Benedictine monasteries had traditionally been. Instead, they were "daughter" houses subject to the "mother" house. Within a century, there were some three hundred Cluniac houses spread across western Europe, but only the mother house was called a *monastery.* The daughter houses were called *priories,* and the priors (subabbots) who governed them were appointed by the Great Abbot of Cluny.

From Cluny, the move for reform spread to all parts of the clergy. Heads of the older Benedictine houses also came under the influence of the reform spirit; bishops, too, and the papacy itself were caught up in this revival of Christian purpose and discipline. The Cluniac movement was a striking success. Monastic life was restored to something like its original rigor, simony (the selling of Church services or offices) was exposed and reduced, and the rule of priestly celibacy (prohibition against marriage) was more strictly enforced. But in the end, Cluny's very success brought about its decline as a model of reform. By the twelfth century, surrounded by mounting wealth and influence, the monks of Cluny slipped into the ways of material ease.

Repeating the Cluniac pattern, a new order now appeared. This order arose in a barren area of Burgundy (southeastern France) with the founding of an abbey at Cîteaux (Latin, *Cistercium*) in 1098. Its daughter houses expanded spectacularly under the leadership of the saintly and charismatic Bernard of Clairvaux, who was to promote the Second Crusade of 1147–1149 (p. 281). The Cistercians, as they were called, wore white robes to distinguish themselves from the black of the Benedictines. There was acute rivalry between the two orders, with the Cistercians at first deploring the riches of Cluny. But the white robes, too, became soiled by economic success, gifts, and worldly power. Within a century of the abbey's founding, the Cistercians had fallen to the comforts of wealth.

A third reform effort followed a similar course. Early in the thirteenth century, a young Italian, Francis of Assisi, felt himself called to live his life in imitation of Christ. The son of a wealthy merchant, Francis gave up his home, his fine clothing, and the security of his family to travel about in voluntary poverty, supported by begging alone. Soon he was joined by companions of like mind, forming a company of twelve. Rejecting the routine of monks in some remote cloister, they chose instead to work among the needy of the towns. In the expanding centers of trade, the Franciscans preached and served the poor, stressing the ideal of Christian love and brotherhood.

Francis was reluctant to found an order, for he believed that formal organization tends to hold down individual freedom of action. He also feared the effect of wealth— even collective wealth—on the ideal of holy poverty. The papacy, however, was worried about what Francis and his followers would do if they were permitted to carry on' their activities without supervision by the Church. Consequently, the papacy authorized Francis to establish an order under his direct control. Soon the brothers (friars) of the new order, who had previously lived by begging, began to accept gifts of property and buildings. Within a century, the Franciscans became another wealthy religious order, and their devotion of poverty and simplicity gave way to increasing concern for material things.

Francis himself was a *mystic*—one who seeks God's truth through inner inspiration and revelation. He and his fellow mystics, who had substantial influence in the Middle Ages, were doubtful of book learning and human reason. Of a contrary view was the Spaniard Dominic, a contemporary of Francis. Dominic was an intellectual who saw God's truth as a *reasoned* ideology, and the order of friars he founded was devoted chiefly to scholarship, teaching, and preaching. Alarmed by the spread of heretical doctrines in his time, Dominic believed he could best serve the Lord by guiding the thoughts and education of Christians. Francis appealed mainly to people's *hearts;*

529		910	Accession of Pope Gregory VII 1073	Death of Pope Boniface VIII 1303	1417
	Spread of Benedictine Monastic Houses		Cluniac Reform Movement	Pope and Emperor Struggle for Supremacy	Avignon Papacy and Great Schism

Dominic appealed more to their minds. Both the gray friars (the Franciscans) and the black (the Dominicans) became familiar figures on the streets and highways of Europe.

THE PAPAL MONARCHY

The most significant reforms of the medieval Church were associated with the papacy itself. For centuries, the local nobles of Rome had competed with one another for control of that office, and their rivalries and intrigues had produced many disreputable popes. The nobles were restrained only by the powerful Holy Roman emperors of the time (pp. 223, 231), who would occasionally intervene to appoint their own candidates—most of them worthy and conscientious churchmen. It was one such imperial appointee, Pope Leo IX, a German bishop much influenced by ideas of the Cluniac type, who toward the middle of the eleventh century first put the papacy at the head of the movement for Church reform.

The Independent Papacy: Gregory VII. But to the more radical reformers, it seemed a wicked defiance of the will of God that the successors of Peter and vicars of Christ (p. 172) should be under the control of any worldly ruler, even reform-minded emperors. The chief promoter of these ideas was the Italian Hildebrand. As archdeacon of Rome, a key office in the Church's administration, he proved himself a shrewd planner and tactician. In 1059, thanks largely to his efforts, a new system was brought into being for the election of popes—the College of Cardinals.

Prior to that time, the popes had been elected, theoretically, by the entire clergy of the Roman diocese, subject to the approval of the city's populace—an arrangement that lent itself readily to interference by local nobles and the emperors. But from then on, the papal electors were to be restricted to the *cardinal* clergy—a small number of the ranking priests of Rome. The cardinals were appointed by the pope, and when a pope died, they met in seclusion to name his successor. Because they usually chose from their own membership, the body automatically furnished select candidates for the papal office.

In 1073, the cardinals chose Hildebrand as Pope Gregory VII. Conditioned by his earlier training at Cluny, he applied himself to a sweeping reform of the Church. One of his main objectives was to strengthen the papacy, to make it a monarchy in fact as well as in theory. Under his guidance, the central administration of the papacy came to be handled through a number of bureaus, departments, and assemblies—called, collectively, the papal *curia* (court or council). The officers in charge of these agencies were usually chosen from among the cardinals and formed, in effect, a kind of "cabinet" for the pope.

The Popes and the Church. Beyond Rome, papal authority reached into every diocese of Western Christendom. According to the doctrine of apostolic succession (p. 171), the bishops constituted the core of the Church. But all were subordinate to the supreme bishop, the successor to Peter: the pope. He kept in touch with them through continual correspondence—the papal letters run to thousands of volumes. Bishops (and arch-bishops) were also required to make regular visits to Rome, which often involved arduous travel. In order to boost his influence outside Italy, Gregory initiated the practice of sending forth papal *legates* (ambassadors) to conduct inquiries and see that the pope was being obeyed in the territories they visited.

In addition to the income from their extensive properties in Italy, the popes received large revenues from all over Europe, including such special levies as "Peter's pence," an annual tax on Christian families in England. The popes also collected a substantial sum from every newly appointed *prelate* (high-ranking cleric). Countless other payments flowed to Rome: fees for appeals from bishops' courts, for dispensations (exemptions) from canon law, and for papal *indulgences*. These last were certificates, issued to Christians through agents of the pope, that were believed to reduce the punishments suffered after death for sins committed in one's life (pp. 371–372). All these revenues were used for various purposes—administrative and political as well as religious, charitable, and artistic.

Papal influence over medieval society was reinforced by sweeping disciplinary power. The pope (and the bishops) could *excommunicate* Christians and thus deprive them of the benefit of the sacraments. Since the sacraments were considered essential to salvation, excommunication was regarded as a fearful penalty. The threat or use of excommunication usually brought obedience from clergy, noblemen, and commoners alike—even from kings and emperors.

If excommunication did not bring a ruler to his knees, the pope could resort to the *interdict*. This was an order closing the churches and suspending the sacraments for an entire area. A ruler, no matter what his own religious convictions, could scarcely ignore the interdict, for his subjects, fearing that their souls were in danger, would press the ruler to yield so that the churches might be reopened. Moreover, should the ruler continue his defiance, the pope could declare the ruler *deposed* and release his subjects from obedience to him.

The disciplinary power of the pope had certain limits of effectiveness, however. A person who had been excommunicated could beg forgiveness; if he or she showed evidence of genuine repentance, the pope was virtually obliged to lift his order. And extreme measures like the interdict often boomeranged. If a ruler who was in dispute with the pope had the sympathy and support of his people, the interdict might cause them to rally to the ruler's side.

Nevertheless, through the channels and agencies of the Church, the papacy could exert a powerful influence on popular thought and behavior. By means of proclamations, letters, and speeches, for example, the pope could spread his ideas and exert active leadership. At his command were the bishops, the religious orders, the church schools, and the parish priests—all of them in contact with the people.

Heresy and the Inquisition. As the Church grew stronger and better organized, however, there also appeared movements of rebellion against it—new or revived heresies (pp. 172–174) that denied the Church's beliefs and despised the priests, bishops, and pope. One of the most widespread of these, perhaps descended from the Gnostics and Manichaeans of early Christian times (p. 174), proclaimed a *dualistic* picture of the universe: only spirit, its supporters believed, was good, whereas matter was by nature evil. Beliefs of this kind spread widely in medieval Europe and were viciously persecuted wherever they occurred. They were found in the Balkans throughout the Middle Ages

(p. 298); in western Europe in the twelfth century, they were widespread in southern France, where they were called the "Albigensian heresy," named for the cathedral town of Albi.

Pope Innocent III proclaimed a crusade (p. 278) against the Albigensians, and French nobles from the north cruelly suppressed the rebellion by 1226. But heresy smoldered even after the crusade was over. To snuff out the remaining embers, Innocent's successor, Pope Gregory IX, established a permanent court for finding and trying heretics: the Inquisition.

The pope's grand inquisitor was placed at Carcassonne, in the south of France. He sent deputies, drawn chiefly from the new Dominican order (p. 252), to the towns and cities of the area. In the public square of each place, the deputies would announce their mission and then call for people to testify regarding suspected heretics. In pursuing their inquiries, the deputies followed common judicial practice of the period in using torture to wring confessions from uncooperative suspects and in denying accused persons legal counsel and the right to call or confront witnesses (p. 228). Proceedings were usually conducted in secret. Lucky prisoners would confess early, repent, and forfeit only their property.

Those who proved stubborn or who lapsed again into heresy after repenting were excommunicated and turned over to the civil authorities for more severe punishment, since canon law (Church law) forbade the clergy to take life. Because heresy was often associated with popular discontent or rebellion, the civil authorities regarded it as equivalent to _treason_ and therefore set the penalty of death for convicted heretics. The most common means of execution was burning at the stake—a means that gave heretics a chance to make a final repentance as the flames reached higher and higher. They might then have time to beg for God's forgiveness and the salvation of their souls. But in no case would the fire be quenched; the body of a "confirmed" heretic was already forfeit.

The procedures and penalties of the Inquisition appear cruel and inhumane to most persons today, including religious leaders. In the view of medieval churchmen, however, the end—rooting out heresy—justified the means. Even the "angelic doctor" of the Church, Thomas Aquinas (p. 270–271), held that extreme punishments were necessary to protect souls from the contamination of false beliefs. His was no doubt an honest argument. But the Inquisition was also open to the foulest abuses. To level the accusation of heresy became a convenient way of injuring or getting rid of personal enemies, and the accusers were never identified by the court. Despite the justifications advanced by its defenders, the Inquisition was generally abandoned after the seventeenth century.

THE STRUGGLE FOR SUPREMACY OVER THE STATE

Gregory VII, as we have seen, worked to strengthen the control of Rome over the Church and to free it from secular interference and corruption, in accordance with the aims of the pervasive Cluniac reform movement. But Gregory aspired to go much further. Cluny had concentrated on the reform of the clergy and had tended to accept the secular world as it was; Gregory sought to give to the Church—and to its monarch, the pope—the responsibility and the power to purify the _whole_ of Christian society. This inevitably brought him into collision with the other main authority in Christian society, the state.

Ever since the time of Constantine (p. 150), Christian teaching had given civil monarchs a sacred character as well as secular authority. The emperor Charlemagne, who was held up as a model, had appointed bishops and abbots to their offices and had employed clergymen as administrators and as teachers in his palace school. Mutual support between the nobility and the clergy existed at all levels of feudal government. It was this relationship that Gregory and his successors sought to change.

By various historical arguments and documents, including the falsified Donation of Constantine (p. 212), Gregory claimed to be the overlord of the rulers of western Europe. He declared, for example, that the Holy Roman emperor, Henry IV, was his vassal, on the grounds that Charlemagne, Henry's predecessor, owed his crown to Pope Leo III (p. 217). He objected particularly to Henry's control over the selection of German bishops, who were important fief-holders and vassals of the emperor. Henry was exercising a traditional right when he influenced their selection and invested (clothed) them with their symbols of office. Gregory insisted, however, that bishops were *spiritual* officers and could be invested with ring and staff, the symbols of their religious authority, only by the pope. What he sought, of course, was papal control over the elections themselves. This *investiture* issue set off a prolonged conflict between Rome and the European monarchs, but it was only one aspect of the papal bid for supremacy.

Gregory employed every means at his command to bring Henry down. He plotted with the emperor's enemies in Germany, subjected him to excommunication and deposition (1076), and turned to the Normans in southern Italy for military assistance against Henry's forces. After his excommunication, Henry outmaneuvered his adversary by crossing the Alps in winter and appearing as a penitent before Gregory at the palace of Canossa (in northern Italy). Standing barefoot in the snow, he begged the pope to forgive him for his offenses and restore him to communion with the Church. Gregory granted the request, but the contest shortly resumed, and the pope once again excommunicated Henry. In the long run, Gregory lacked sufficient armed power to transform occasional triumphs into lasting victory. The investiture argument was settled later by compromise: Henry's successor agreed in 1122 to give to the pope the investiture of religious symbols, but he retained the emperor's traditional influence over the selection of German bishops.

Even so, the papacy's growing control over the Church gave it greater power against emperors and kings than ever before. During the reign of Innocent III the papacy reached its height of prestige and power. Its strength was shown by the humbling of King John of England, who, after a bitter dispute with Innocent over the election of the archbishop of Canterbury, was forced to submit. John was deposed; afterward, in 1213, he was granted the realm of England as a fief from Rome, but only after pledging homage to the pope. Such was the international authority of Innocent III that John's subjection to the pope actually strengthened the king's hand in his ongoing disputes with his discontented barons (p. 233).

Papal claims were carried even further by the aggressive Boniface VIII. He met his match, however, in King Philip (the Fair) of France. Philip, who was waging war against England, levied a tax on church properties in 1296. Boniface answered this bold move, which was contrary to existing law, with angry denunciations. The violent dispute reached its climax a few years later when Boniface issued a papal *bull* (pronouncement) titled *Unam sanctam,* which included the most extreme claims of Gregory and Innocent. Boniface declared that *all* secular rulers were subject to the pope and that the pope could be judged by God alone. He concluded, daringly, "We declare, state, define, and pronounce that it is altogether necessary to salvation for every human creature to be subject to the Roman pontiff." Yet Boniface's words did not prevail over Philip's deeds. Philip, realizing that no peaceful solution could be reached with Boniface, sent a military force across the Alps to seize the aged pontiff. Roughly treated and humiliated by the French soldiers, Boniface died of shock soon afterward in 1303.

These events set the stage for a rapid decline of the papacy. The popes had overreached themselves in their pursuit of worldly power, and the fourteenth and fifteenth centuries would see the unhappy consequences of papal extremism. They had failed to win supremacy over secular rulers or even to put an end to the power of those rulers within the Church. Even so, the position of the papacy *within* the Catholic Church had permanently changed. The popes had won for themselves a position as true monarchs of the Church, governing and supervising its operations throughout the Catholic world, which they have retained to the present day.

Christian Art

Despite the later decline of the papacy, the Church was a powerful creative force throughout the Middle Ages. Nowhere is this force displayed more clearly than in the arts—above all, in architecture.

For several centuries after the Germanic invasions of the West, most new buildings north of the Alps were built of timber; the first stone structure of importance was Charlemagne's chapel at Aachen, completed around 800 (*Fig. 5.5,* p. 216). With the return of stability and security in the eleventh century, architecture began to revive—most notably in the form of great churches, which sprang up rapidly throughout Europe.

Though the church builders reused some of the architectural forms and techniques of Rome, they did not look for inspiration to the specifically religious buildings of antiquity. The reason was that Christian churches differed widely from pagan temples, not only in regard to the god they glorified but also in terms of the purpose they served. A pagan temple was the "home" of a god or goddess, which the ordinary worshiper might never enter (p. 77). But the Christian God, like that of other monotheistic religions (p. 53), dwelt "in a house not made with hands." It was not God but his worshipers who needed a building—one that would bring them close to him. Hence the church was intended to communicate to believers something of the nature of God and the universe he ruled. Paintings and sculptures taught these lessons to the mass of illiterate believers. The educated, too, were meant to perceive in the church, with its ordered structure centered upon the altar, an image of the universe ruled by God. It was this theory that was responsible for the overwhelming impression that the great churches of the Middle Ages still create today: an impression of orderly and logical perfection and yet also of mystical and inexpressible holiness.

THE ROMANESQUE STYLE

The monastic reform movement that originated at Cluny provided the main impulse for the revival of building activity from 1000 onward. Though secular structures of various kinds were erected, the most important buildings of this period were monastery churches.

Fig. 6.2 Plan of a Romanesque Church.
The Church of Saint-Sernin (Saint Sat-
urninus) in the southern French city of
Toulouse was begun by local monks about
1070 to attract pilgrims to the shrine of
Toulouse's first bishop, martyred about
A.D. 250. The pilgrims' contributions, at
a time when trade and travel were reviving,
financed the construction of Europe's
largest Romanesque church. It has a nave
(the long central space) and four rows of
side aisles, as well as transepts on each side
and a semicircular apse at the end, furnished with projecting chapels of Saturni-
nus and other saints.

© Marburg/Art Resource, NY

The predominant style of building, which lasted down to about 1200, is known as
the *Romanesque,* and it found expression in painting and sculpture as well as architecture. The term *Romanesque* is somewhat misleading, for this first European style was
based only partly on Roman examples.

The relationship is most apparent in architecture, where the round arch and the
vault served as basic structural elements. But the builders of the Middle Ages used these
elements in a manner quite different from that used by the ancient Romans.

Though Romanesque churches were ultimately based on the pattern of the Roman
basilica (*Fig. 3.6,* p. 141), developments in worship services led to a shift to the cruciform (cross-shaped) plan (*Fig. 6.2*). The nave (central hall) and the side aisles were kept,
but the apse (the semicircular space at the end of the nave) was enlarged, and chapels
were built into its perimeter. A transept, or cross arm, was introduced at right angles to
the nave, with entrances at either end. This new plan provided more space for the
clergy participating in the Mass, members of the choir, and worshipers making private
devotions. It became, with numerous variations, the favored plan for large churches all
over the West.

Aside from its functional merit, the cruciform plan had obvious symbolic meaning. When the faithful entered the church, they were "returning to the Cross." The
façade (front) of the building usually had *three* main portals, symbolizing the Trinity.

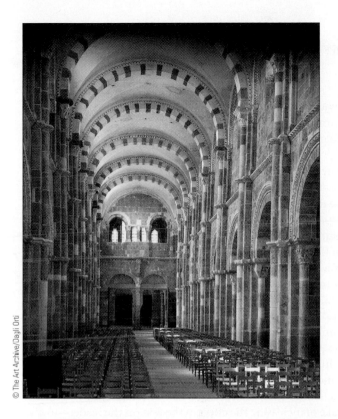

Fig. 6.3 Romanesque Structural Design. The nave of the Church of Sainte-Marie Madeleine (Saint Mary Magdalene) at Vézelay in eastern France was completed about 1145. The light- and dark-colored round arches divide the ceiling into bays. Additional round arches running diagonally across the bays strengthen and lighten the structure, but each bay is nevertheless built of 45 tons of stone. To support this load, the side walls have to be thick, with narrow slits for windows that widen on the inside so that shafts of light swing across the interior as the sun moves across the sky.

Whenever possible, the cross plan was located so that the nave ran from west to east, with the altar at the eastern end. Thus the worshipers faced more or less in the direction of Jerusalem.

Elements of Roman architectural forms may also be seen in the rounded doorways and windows of Romanesque churches and in the arches and tunnel vaults used to support the roof. The roofs of earlier churches had generally rested on a framework of timber; the Romanesque architect, seeking greater permanency, chose stone. But how could the massive weight of a stone ceiling be held up? One way was to bridge the nave by means of a tunnel (barrel) vault . Such a vault placed severe stress on the stonework below, which usually had to be supported by half-vaults built over the side aisles. It also followed that the size of windows was strictly limited, for large openings would have made the walls dangerously weak. Hence scant daylight found its way into the nave.

To admit more light, medieval architects often divided the nave into a series of rectangular spaces, or bays. The stone ceiling over each bay was formed by a Roman-type cross-vault (*Fig. 3.3b,* p. 138). This type of construction permitted larger openings in the clerestory portion of the nave—that is, the part rising above the side-aisle roofs.

The round dome, which also goes back to Roman times, was frequently used by Romanesque builders. More characteristic of the Romanesque style, however, was a new architectural feature, the *tower,* from which bells called the worshipers to prayer. In Italy, the graceful campanile (bell tower) stood by itself a few feet away from the church; elsewhere in Europe, the tower was an integral part of the main building. It was sometimes built over the "crossing," where the nave and the transept cross, but more commonly a tower or a pair of towers formed part of the front of the building. In some areas, bell towers were capped by a soaring *spire*. Church towers remain to this day a symbol of Western Christianity.

Along with architecture, painting and sculpture were also revived. The renewed interest in these art forms was prompted by the accelerated pace of church building; in fact, painting and sculpture remained subordinate to architecture until the close of the Middle Ages.

Sculpture was used almost exclusively for religious purposes: the glorification of God and the instruction of the faithful. Overcoming the barrier of illiteracy, each medieval church was virtually a "Bible in stone." Nowhere is the atmospheric contrast between the medieval world and the ancient world more sharply displayed than in Romanesque sculpture. The "idealistic" style of the Greeks and the "naturalistic" style of the Romans (pp. 92, 143–144) are both absent. Few ancient statues were available to the sculptors of the eleventh and twelfth centuries; they took as their models the illustrated figures of medieval manuscripts.

The tradition of furnishing written documents with illustrations dates back to ancient Egypt, where scribes most likely used it for magical purposes—to give additional force to the rituals and spells that their manuscripts contained (p. 34). The idea of illustrating books for the sake of increasing the effect of the text on the reader—to give visual form to the ideas it contained or simply to break the monotony of the endless procession of words on a page—seems to have originated not long after the invention of books with pages (p. 128). In the early Middle Ages, this kind of illustration flourished, producing powerful religious images that were then reproduced in stone (*Fig. 6.4*).

The strange animal figures that often appear in Romanesque sculpture came directly from the northern barbarian tradition. Numerous books were available describing hundreds of imaginary beasts, and sculptors copied them in stone. The upper walls of Romanesque churches were studded with *gargoyles* (from a French word for "throat")—frightening monsters and demons whose open mouths spouted water draining from the roof and which looked all too real, no doubt, to the congregation.

Romanesque sculptors mingled the natural and the supernatural, the earthly and the unearthly. Hence the real may look unreal and the unreal real. To ensure that the idea or story they were illustrating would be correctly interpreted, sculptors relied heavily on symbols. Although they might show Saint Peter in a number of poses, they always identified him by giving him a set of keys. Matthew was consistently shown as an angel, Mark as a lion (*Fig. 6.4*). Having identified a figure with its traditional symbol, the artist could then treat it in an individual manner.

This freedom presented an opportunity for creativity quite unknown in classical art. Romanesque sculptors, though often showing inferior technique, were not bound to exacting artistic rules or naturalistic representations. This also permitted them greater liberties in overall *composition*—a freedom shared by painters and other artisans of the period.

Fig. 6.4 Romanesque Sculpture. Late-twelfth-century statue from a tympanum (space above a doorway) in the west façade of the cathedral of Saint-Trophîme in the southern French town of Arles. Christ is shown crowned as a king and seated upon a throne as he blesses the world and holds a Bible on his knee. He is surrounded by winged creatures symbolic of the Evangelists (authors of the Gospels)—an angel (Matthew), a lion (Mark), an ox (Luke), and an eagle (John). Compare the more informal early Christian portrayal (*Fig. 4.1,* p. 168), and the suffering Savior in *Fig. 6.1,* p. 249.

THE GOTHIC STYLE

The Romanesque style marked a break with the past, but in less than two centuries, out of the Romanesque came the later style of the Middle Ages—the *Gothic.* This style showed itself first in architecture, around 1150, reached its prime by 1300, and declined in vitality with the closing of the Middle Ages.

The term *Gothic* was invented in the eighteenth century, when Greek and Roman models of culture were the most admired. It was originally applied to the culture of the Middle Ages in general and meant much the same as "barbaric." The name continues to be used, without the contemptuous overtones, to describe the style of architecture and art that is now recognized as the grandest expression of medieval civilization.

While the Romanesque style had flourished in the monasteries, the Gothic style flourished in the towns. There the bishops and their cathedrals became the centers of attention, and the ascetic spirit was now overshadowed by a more worldly one. Insecurity was giving way to a new confidence: Gothic cathedrals were built to the glory of God, but they reflected the pride of humans.

But Gothic cathedrals also represented a new way of giving expression to religious belief. The educated clergy of the twelfth century wanted to build churches that would be a true image of the universe as they thought of it: a vast structure, designed by its creator to be perfectly harmonious in every detail and glowing with light that flowed from

Fig. 6.5 Web of Stone. In Gothic cathedrals, structural stresses are transmitted mostly downward from intersecting stone ribs, shaped as pointed arches, to vertical pillars resting on bedrock. The spaces between the ribs and pillars are filled with brick or glass surfaces that carry no structural loads. At the thirteenth-century cathedral of Amiens in northern France, the system makes possible a nave that is 50 feet wide and 140 feet high.

© Angelo Hornak/CORBIS

God himself. Only a building of this kind, they thought, would truly lead the worshipers to the knowledge and love of God.

Judged by this standard, existing Romanesque churches were inadequate. Their thick walls often gave a feeling of confinement, their massive arches seemed ill-proportioned, and their relatively small windows did not provide a rich illumination. But any attempt to alter this pattern raised difficult technical questions. How could architects increase the spaciousness and height of a building, reduce the thickness of the supporting walls and arches, and enlarge the area of the windows? They found their answer in *rib vaulting*.

In the twelfth century, Romanesque builders had developed a better system than cross-vaulting (p. 259) for supporting a heavy roof. They marked off each rectangular bay by four vertical stone pillars. From the top of each pillar, they connected ribs of arching stone to the tops of the other three; then they filled in the ceiling areas between these ribs with light brick. The weight of the roof was carried to the ground through the ribs and pillars, and no force was exerted on the areas between the pillars (*Fig. 6.5*).

Gothic architects developed the full potential of the new method. This revolutionary plan of construction enabled them to lift roofs to soaring heights and to make the walls of the clerestory into softly glowing sheets of stained glass. They could discard the idea of a building as a stone mass enclosing static space and think of it instead as a web of stone with space and light flowing freely through it. Among the refinements they developed to carry out their idea were the *pointed arch* and the *flying buttress*.

Ironically, the graceful pointed arch, the hallmark of the Gothic style, had first been used by Muslim builders to construct ever larger and more splendid mosques. But it was also perfectly suited to the spiritual and aesthetic purposes of Christian cathe-

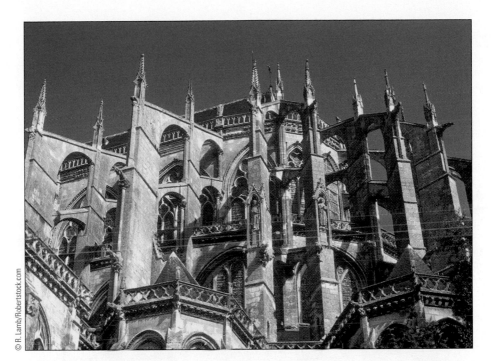

Fig. 6.6 Flying Buttresses. These structures were an engineering necessity, to help prop up the nave of a Gothic cathedral while straddling the lower side aisles—essentially, they were outward extensions of the internal web of stone. At the west end of the thirteenth-century cathedral of Le Mans in northern France, the resulting tangle of tall stone pillars and slanting arches also has a visual effect. It draws the eye upward, making the building look higher but also less massive than it actually is.

dral builders, since it accentuated the vertical lines of their structures and lifted the vaults to greater heights than could be achieved with the round arch. With the pointed arch, the direction of thrust is more downward than outward, decreasing the danger that the supporting pillars will collapse. Moreover, the pointed arch is far more adaptable to rib vaulting, for the steepness of its curving ribs can be fitted to varying distances between the pillars, whereas the round arch follows a fixed curve.

To make the soaring vaults safer, French architects added external buttresses (props) of masonry. They could not place these buttresses directly against the pillars of the nave, because the side aisles, with their separate, lower roofs, stood in the way. So they erected massive pillars at intervals *outside* the side aisles. They rose almost to the level of the nave ceiling and were connected to the pillars of the nave by stone ribs. (An example of this may be seen at Le Mans; *Fig. 6.6.*) Since the ribs appear to be suspended over the side aisles, they are commonly called "flying" buttresses. Though they support the stone framework at critical points, they interfere only slightly with the flow of light through the great clerestory windows.

The Gothic cathedral, pointing to heaven, stood high above the houses huddled in the town, symbolizing the commanding position of the Church in the lives of medieval men and women. As travelers approached a cathedral town, the first sight they saw on the horizon was the spire (or spires) reaching hundreds of feet into the sky (*Fig. II.1,* p. 186). Then the whole of the cathedral would gradually come into view. If the travelers were pilgrims, they would approach the west façade and reverently prepare to enter.

Fig. 6.7 Gothic Sculpture. Thirteenth-century statues from the west façade of Reims Cathedral in northern France. Left, the Annunciation: a smiling Archangel Gabriel tells a solemn Virgin Mary of the coming birth of Christ. Right, the Visitation: the Virgin (inner statue) is greeted by Saint Elizabeth, John the Baptist's mother—an elderly woman, as described in the Gospel. In keeping with the trend to more human forms of religious devotion than earlier in the Middle Ages, the sculptors revived the goal of Hellenistic and Roman sculpture—to depict human emotion and interaction in stone.

Set into the façade were stone sculptures representing figures from the Bible. Gothic artists preferred a more naturalistic style than Romanesque artists. Although the figures could still be identified by certain symbols, they looked more lifelike than their Romanesque counterparts (*Fig. 6.7*). The artisans of this period relied less on copybook drawings and looked more to live models—as did manuscript illustrators, whose work, often miniaturized to fit into crowded text or even inside individual letters, became both vividly naturalistic and exquisitely detailed (*Fig. 6.8*). Artistic technique and general craftsmanship rose steadily in excellence.

Inside the cathedral, the emphasis was on space, light, and color (*Fig. 6.5*, p. 262). Here one forgets the calculation and engineering wisdom that made possible the complicated thrust and counterthrust of arches, vaults, and buttresses. One is absorbed by the vastness, rhythm, and splendor of the interior. Stained glass is the special glory of the Gothic. By daylight, the upper levels of the interior glow with luminous blues, reds, greens, and golds. The windows, of varying shape and size, consist of mosaics of colored glass. The glass pieces are held together by lead strips and bars creating geometrical designs (*Fig. 6.9*). The function of the windows, like that of the sculpture, is to illustrate biblical events, but the figures are often absorbed into the broader patterns of line and color. Thus in its immensity, its harmonious beauty, and its glowing illumination, the building conveys something of the image of the universe and its creator that inspired the builders.

Fig. 6.8 Words and Pictures. In medieval books, illustrations and text were closely intertwined. In this fourteenth-century service book, the red text at top gives instructions for the opening procession of a church consecration service, and a picture shows the procession approaching the newly built church. A prayer follows (black text below), beginning "Omnipotens sempiterne Deus" ("Almighty and everlasting God"). In the initial "O," a bishop is shown reading from a book held up by an assistant. Evidently the book is this one, and the bishop is reading this very prayer.

Fig. 6.9 "Our Lady of the Lovely Window." This stained glass window in Chartres Cathedral depicts the Virgin Mary crowned and enthroned with the infant Jesus. It is a 7-foot-high "jigsaw puzzle" of pieces of glass that were colored while still molten, cut to fit the design, and fastened together with strips of lead. Important features such as faces were then painted onto the surface of the glass. The intention was to proclaim the twelfth-century French cult of the Virgin as Queen of Heaven in a way that would glow with the light of divine revelation.

Thought and Education

Medieval education, like the arts, was dominated by the Church. At no other time in Western history have the channels of communication and education been so completely in the hands of one institution. From the eighth to the twelfth century, members of the clergy made up the only literate and educated class of society, and even after that they staffed virtually all the schools, libraries, and centers of higher learning. But the feudalistic and local character of the times counterbalanced what was in theory the monolithic force of the Church. The methods of long-distance communication were primitive, and the Church itself was split into many authorities, orders, and factions. Although basically only a Catholic point of view could be professed in western Europe, a wide range of intellectual inquiry and debate was still possible.

During the troubled centuries immediately after the fall of Rome, the monasteries had conserved precious manuscripts and provided at least the rudiments of education to the clergy, the only class of society that was thought to have need for it. Around 800, Charlemagne gave strong support to the revival of interest in intellectual matters (p. 216). Though advance was slow, it may be said that by 1200, Western civilization had reached the general level of learning of ancient times and had begun to match that of the Muslims. The monasteries still provided elementary education, and cathedral schools were beginning to respond to a growing desire for education in the towns. But the most significant development was the rise of the university.

THE RISE OF UNIVERSITIES

The earliest steps toward higher education were taken in southern Europe, where access to Muslim and Byzantine learning was easiest. Medical instruction started at Salerno, in the south of Italy close to Muslim-ruled Sicily, in the ninth century, and late in the eleventh century, training in the law began in the northern Italian town of Bologna, not far from Ravenna, which had a long Byzantine tradition. The universities founded at these centers were professional in nature, and satisfied the demand for physicians and lawyers to serve Italian princes and merchants, as well as the rising papal monarchy.

The university movement then spread northward from Italy to Montpellier and Paris. It was in Paris during the thirteenth century that Europe's foremost institution of learning was established. Its faculty was made up of professors drawn from the cathedral school and from local monastic schools, along with lay lecturers in law and medicine. Whereas Salerno and Bologna limited themselves initially to professional training in medicine and law, Paris was the first university to offer the four major curricula that have become identified in the West with the idea of a university: medicine, law, theology, and liberal arts. The last two earned for Paris its high reputation. From Paris, which served as the model in the north, the movement spread to England, Germany, and the rest of western Europe (*Map 6.1*). By 1300, eighteen universities had been founded, and by 1500 the total number of universities, many of which are still in existence, exceeded

Map 6.1 Religious and Intellectual Centers in Western Europe, 1300. The map shows all eighteen universities that now existed, most of them founded in large towns in the previous hundred years. Forty-eight leading shrines that attracted pilgrims from a distance are also shown—an indication of the scale of travel in the Middle Ages. In addition there are eleven monasteries and thirty-nine cathedrals—a small selection of the most important among many hundreds of monastic institutions and main churches of bishoprics.

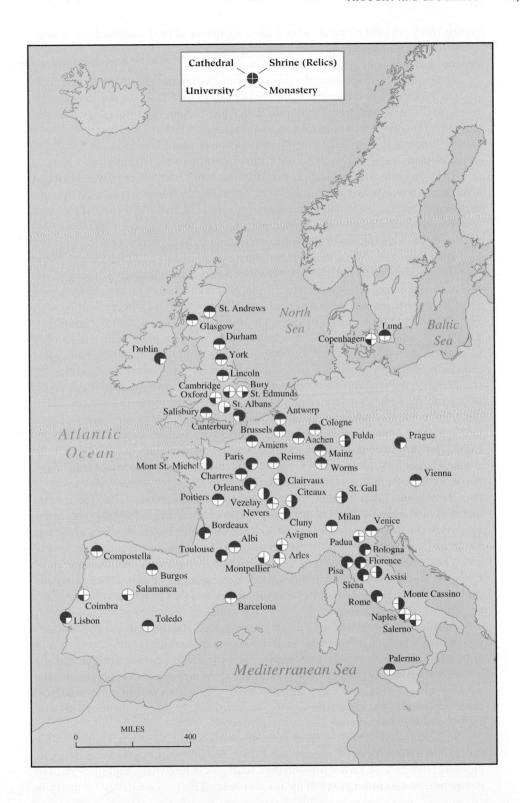

Cathedral — Shrine (Relics)
University — Monastery

St. Andrews
Glasgow
Durham
Dublin
York
Lincoln
Cambridge
Oxford
Bury St. Edmunds
St. Albans
Salisbury
Canterbury
Brussels
Antwerp
Cologne
Amiens
Aachen
Fulda
Prague
Paris
Reims
Mainz
Mont St.-Michel
Worms
Vienna
Chartres
Clairvaux
Orleans
Citeaux
St. Gall
Poitiers
Vezelay
Nevers
Cluny
Milan
Venice
Bordeaux
Avignon
Padua
Albi
Arles
Bologna
Toulouse
Montpellier
Florence
Compostella
Pisa
Assisi
Burgos
Siena
Salamanca
Rome
Monte Cassino
Coimbra
Barcelona
Naples
Lisbon
Toledo
Salerno
Palermo
Lund
Copenhagen

North Sea
Baltic Sea
Atlantic Ocean
Mediterranean Sea

MILES
0   400

eighty. Unlike the old monastic schools (p. 216), nearly all of the universities were located in important towns and cities, reflecting the connection between the rise of universities and that of trade and towns (pp. 238–239).

Each university operated under the protection of a charter granted by a ranking official of the Church or the state (usually the pope or a king). Thus the universities were freed, for the most part, from the jurisdiction of local courts and local clergy. One justification for this exempted status was that teachers and students came from all over Europe, making the universities truly international. Moreover, most students held minor clerical rank and therefore could claim immunity from civil authority.

The word *universitas* was simply the Latin word for a body or corporation, such as a guild, and the organization of a university controlled by teachers paralleled that of a craft guild (pp. 242–243). The guild *masters* (professors) had the sole right to award qualifying certificates, or "degrees." The *apprentices* (students), upon earning the appropriate degree, were eligible to become masters in a teaching corporation (university).

The liberal arts curriculum of the university was normally a prerequisite to the professional courses. Its outlines had been developed in the monastic schools, which had in turn followed late Roman educational practices. The liberal arts subjects were seven in number: grammar, rhetoric, and logic (the *trivium*); and arithmetic, geometry, astronomy, and music (the *quadrivium*). Grammar, of course, meant Latin grammar. This was the language used by members of the clergy, lawyers, physicians, and scholars all through the Middle Ages. But the trivium went beyond the mechanics of language; it included the study of works of philosophy, literature, and history. The quadrivium was based on the reading of ancient texts and was almost entirely theoretical. Today we refer to the subjects of the trivium as *humanistic* studies and to the subjects of the quadrivium (excepting music) as *mathematical* studies.

Whatever subject they were studying, the students had few books and no laboratories. They inscribed their lecture notes on wax tablets and then transferred them to sheets of parchment. More stress was placed on memorizing and analyzing a small number of highly respected books than on extensive reading.

The students in medieval universities earned their degrees on the basis of comprehensive oral examinations. After attending lectures and reading for several years in the subjects of the trivium, a student would ask to be examined by the members of the faculty. If he performed satisfactorily, he was granted the preliminary degree of *bachelor of arts,* a prerequisite for going on to the quadrivium. After several additional years of study, the student would present himself for examination once again. If he passed, he was awarded the degree of *master of arts,* which certified that he was qualified to teach the liberal arts curriculum.

The higher degrees were, similarly, *teaching* degrees. The Latin word *doctor* (teacher) was customarily used for the degrees in theology, law, and medicine. (The doctor of philosophy degree came later, "philosophy" meaning advanced study in the liberal arts area.) Each of these degrees normally required four or more years of study beyond the master's and was also awarded on the basis of the candidate's performance in a rigorous examination. The candidate usually presented a *thesis,* or proposition, which he explained and defended orally before a faculty board.

Student life was quite different from what it is today. Since most females were thought to have no need for a formal education, the universities were for males only. Professors lectured—at least at first—in their homes or in hired halls, and students lived independently, according to their means and tastes. This unregulated life sometimes led to ill health, "immoral" conduct, or both. As a corrective, private donors established residential "colleges" for scholars at many universities.

The first notable "college" was founded about 1250 by Louis IX's chaplain, Robert de Sorbon; he provided it with a dormitory in which theology students at the University of Paris could live. Later, faculty members were assigned to the college, and lecture and library facilities were added. Thus the "Sorbonne" became a separate living-and-learning unit under the university's general control. This pattern was adopted for students in other curricula at Paris, and it gradually spread to universities beyond France. It took firm root in England (at Oxford and Cambridge), where it has persisted to the present day.

SCHOLASTIC PHILOSOPHY

Of special interest to scholars were some of the ancient classics that had reappeared in the West during the eleventh and twelfth centuries. Growing contact with Constantinople and the Muslim world prompted Latin translations, from Greek, Arabic, or Hebrew, of many of the works of Aristotle as well as books of Hellenistic science, mathematics, and medicine (pp. 201–202, 208–209). These were accompanied by original writings and commentaries by leading Muslim and Jewish scholars who had formerly been unknown in western Europe.

Chief among the Muslim commentators on Aristotle was the twelfth-century philosopher Averroës (ibn-Rushd), a Spanish-born Arab. But many Christians were disturbed by his doctrine, drawn from Aristotle, that the universe had always existed and was therefore *not created*. He also denied the immortality of the human soul. More acceptable to Christians were the writings of Averroës' contemporary, the Jewish philosopher-physician Maimonides (Moses ben Maimon). His *Guide for the Perplexed* addresses the "big" philosophical and religious questions that confront Jew and Christian alike: What is the purpose of God's universe? Will it last forever? How is God's will related to natural causes? Maimonides' answers to such questions consist of a closely reasoned mixture of Aristotle, the Old Testament, and traditional Jewish authorities (Sages).

The stimulus from the East lifted the intellectual life of Europe beyond the level of earlier monastic and cathedral education. The creative response by scholars (schoolmen) gave rise to the major philosophical method of the Middle Ages, called *scholasticism*. The scholastics were primarily interested in religious matters. Thus, Anselm, a learned Italian monk and one of the first scholastic philosophers, put together arguments to prove logically the existence of God. In another treatise written about 1100, he explained why God had chosen to take on human form as Jesus. In defense of his studious efforts, Anselm asserted that understanding was a proper supplement to Christian believing.

Reason and Faith, Words and Things. In the twelfth century, the French scholar Abelard argued that the authorities of the Church should not be read without questioning, for they often contradicted one another. He demonstrated this in an influential writing that put many such conflicting answers to theological questions alongside one another; he called this work *Sic et Non* (Latin for "Yes and No"). Abelard insisted, therefore, that all writings be subjected to the light of logic. "By doubting," he observed, "we come to examine, and by examining we reach the truth." Thus Abelard had returned to the position of Socrates, who had sought knowledge through persistent questioning. Abelard sought to replace the general medieval habit of ready belief with an insistence on critical examination; no subject henceforth would be shielded from doubt and reason.

Though theological matters remained the focus of scholastic concern, medieval philosophers debated every subject under the sun—some grand and divine, some trivial and worldly. One of the most absorbing issues was that of "universals." Do "Man," "Horse," "Beauty," and "Justice" exist *independently* of particular things? Or are these terms merely convenient *symbols* for referring to various classes of objects and characteristics? The argument paralleled the ancient one between Plato and the Sophists (pp. 80–82). Plato believed that Ideas (Forms) have a perfect and independent existence, while the Sophists thought that only particular things exist. In the Middle Ages, those who held that universals are real were called *realists;* those who declared that they are just names (*nomina*) were called *nominalists.*

The argument was (and is) important to one's philosophical outlook. The extreme realists attached little importance to individual things and sought through sheer logic or divine revelation to know the universals. The extreme nominalists, by contrast, saw only specific objects and refused to admit the existence of unifying relationships among particular things. The realists tended to ignore the observed world; the nominalists could scarcely make sense of it.

Most scholars took a middle position on this question. Among the moderates, Abelard expressed a view approximating that of most scientists today. It is called *conceptualism.* Abelard held that only particular things have an existence in and of themselves. The universals, however, are more than mere names. They exist as *concepts in individual minds*—keys to an understanding of the interrelatedness of things. Thus the concept "Horse" exists in our minds and adds something to our understanding of all quadrupeds of a certain general description. Once we have identified such a creature, we can assign to it the specific features drawn from our concept. By means of many such concepts, inferred from individual observations, we can make the world (to a degree) comprehensible, manageable, and predictable.

Harmony of Faith and Reason: Aquinas. Thomas Aquinas, the greatest of the scholastic philosophers, was a moderate realist. Born near Monte Cassino (Italy) of an aristocratic family, he joined the order of Dominican friars in 1244 (p. 252). A brilliant pupil, he studied at Cologne and Paris and spent his adult life teaching at Paris and Naples. He wrote an enormous number of scholarly works. Reflecting the medieval desire for unity (oneness), Aquinas sought in these works to harmonize various approaches to truth and to bring all knowledge together. In his most comprehensive work, *Summa Theologiae* ("Theological Summary"), he clarified Church teachings about the nature of God and humanity.

Following the lead of Anselm, Abelard, and other scholastics, Aquinas set a high value on human reason. By this time, the full impact of Aristotle (pp. 83–84) and the new learning from the East had struck the schools and universities of Europe, and Christian teachings were being challenged by pagan, Jewish, and Muslim logicians—especially Averroës (p. 269). Instead of answering their arguments by denying the power of reason, Aquinas adopted Aristotelian logic and turned it to the defense of his faith. He sought to demonstrate that divine law (*jus divinum*)—as revealed in the Bible—is never in conflict with logic, *properly exercised.* Both faith and reason, he argued, were created by God, and it is illogical to hold that God could contradict himself.

Aquinas's methodology is most plainly set forth in the *Summa Theologiae,* in which he divided each major subject into a series of questions. For each, he explained the arguments *pro* and *contra,* in accordance with the usual scholastic method of presentation. The arguments are generally *deductive* in form—that is, they rely on reasoning from basic propositions assumed in advance to be true, because they are found either in the Bible or in the works of thinkers (both pagan and Christian) who are considered authoritative (pp. 341, 422). Thus in an effort to support a particular point, Aquinas may join a generalization from Aristotle's *Politics* with Jesus' Golden Rule. He presented his own conclusion for each of the questions he posed—a conclusion that generally agreed with accepted Christian teachings. The *Summa* is a masterful combination of quotations from Scripture, formal logic, and common sense. Aquinas's grand synthesis ("harmonization" of knowledge) stands as an impressive monument to the discipline and resourcefulness of the human mind.

By the end of the thirteenth century, the intellectual life of the West had achieved a new vigor. The communities of university scholars had succeeded in their efforts to preserve and advance learning. The scholastic philosophers had refined the methods of logical thought and had laboriously collected, compiled, and classified sources of information. Above all, they had established the essentials of scholarship: comprehensive research and precise expression.

Modern thought owes much to these medieval seekers after truth. They built upon classical learning, reconciled it with Christian teachings, and absorbed new ideas from the Muslim world. Bernard of Chartres once compared himself and his fellow scholars with the philosophers and scientists of ancient times. "We are like a dwarf," he said, "standing on the shoulders of a giant." There is modesty in this statement but also pride—pride in the fact that he and his colleagues could see a bit farther than their intellectual ancestors.

MEDIEVAL SCIENCE

The scholars of the Middle Ages cannot be called scientists in the modern sense. In the first place, they were not *specialists;* they regarded the *whole* of knowledge as their field of inquiry. Secondly, they did not observe what has come to be known as the "scientific method," which depends on the processes of observation, experimentation, and verification (pp. 422–423). Yet certain scientific knowledge passed on by the ancient Greeks and the Muslims attracted their attention, and a few medieval scholars, in the course of their studies, did contribute to that body of knowledge.

The German scholar Albert the Great (a teacher of Thomas Aquinas) wrote on the broad range of philosophical and theological questions that challenged thirteenth-century thinkers. But he also found time to observe systematically many of the animal species of western Europe, including bees, spiders, hawks, beavers, whales, and eels. Albert rejected medieval accounts of mythical animals like "griffins" and "harpies" simply because he had never observed any.

Robert Grosseteste, an outstanding English scholar of the same period, wrote commentaries on the Bible, Aristotle, and a wide variety of philosophical topics. But he wrote, too, about the sun, weather, tides, colors, comets, and other aspects of nature. Grosseteste was a pioneer teacher (and chancellor) at the new Oxford University, where he helped establish the study of science and mathematics. A generation afterward, his pupil, Roger Bacon, continued to emphasize experimental methods. Bacon, who died in 1294, is remembered also for his predictions of such technological innovations as flying machines and powered ships. Other, lesser-known scholars of the Middle Ages made modest advances in optics, astronomy, and medicine.

Language and Literature

The language common to western Europe during the Middle Ages was Latin. Passed down from pagan Rome, it had been carried beyond the old Roman frontiers by the Church. Although it remained the formal language of education, law, medicine, and commerce, Latin began to disappear from spoken conversation. It was gradually supplanted by a variety of regional tongues (*vernaculars*), from which the modern languages would develop. By the thirteenth century, the vernaculars had gained predominance in popular literature as well as in everyday speech.

LATIN WRITINGS

Medieval Latin did not hold to the classical standards of ancient Rome. The study of pagan authors was sometimes viewed with suspicion; some, such as Cicero and Virgil (p. 131), continued to be widely read because it was felt that in spite of being pagan, they had valuable moral lessons to impart. Christian writers who had lived at the time of the Roman Empire, such as Augustine and Jerome (pp. 178–179, 181–182), were deeply studied for the religious guidance they offered. But pagan or Christian, the ancient authors were not read for the sake of their language and style. As a result, the writing of classical Latin was neglected, and a modified Latin evolved that itself became the medium for notable literary achievements.

The finest creations in medieval Latin were the prayers and hymns of the Christian worship services. Some of these were incorporated into the Mass and are notable for their poetic beauty (*Stabat Mater* and *Dies Irae*). Latin was also used in new forms of religious drama: "Passion" plays (which grew out of the Easter ritual), dramatizations of the lives of the saints, and Christian "morality" plays. Classical dramas were not performed in the Middle Ages and did not begin to influence European literature until the fifteenth century. By then a secular (worldly) branch of dramatic literature had grown out of the religious performances and had detached itself from the Church.

Though Latin was the language of worship, it also was used to express dissent from Christian ideals. A substantial body of verse written by wandering scholars began to appear in the twelfth century, the best of which is known as Goliardic poetry because it was dedicated to a mythical patron, Saint Golias. Although few of the poets have been identified, it is clear that they were men of learning, schooled in Latin and familiar with the classics. One Goliard refers to his band as a "vagrant order" of runaway students and clerics. Their verses were mainly satirical, aimed at the clergy and the ascetic ideal. They were pagan in spirit, lauding the pleasures of drinking, eating, and love-making. One of the Goliardic poets, called "the Archpoet," declared:

> My intention is to die
> In the tavern drinking;
> Wine must be at hand, for I

Want it when I'm sinking.
Angels when they come shall cry,
At my frailties winking:
"Spare this drunkard, God, he's high,
Absolutely stinking!"[1]

VERNACULAR WRITINGS

Goliardic verse could be understood only by the educated few who knew Latin, but literature in the vernacular tongues could reach a much wider audience. These tongues fell into two broad groups: the Romance and the Germanic. The boundary between the two was roughly the frontier of the ancient Roman Empire. In areas that had long been occupied by Rome, spoken Latin served as the foundation of the vernacular tongues. It was modified only slightly as a result of the Germanic invasions, and it evolved, as living languages do, into local dialects. In areas to the north of the Roman imperial frontiers, the Germanic-speaking peoples continued to use their age-old tongues. Western Europe to this day remains divided into these linguistic groups: the national languages of Italy, Spain, Portugal, and France are "Romance" languages that have evolved from Latin; those of the Netherlands, Germany, and Scandinavia emerged from the Germanic tongue of the barbarian peoples of northwestern Europe. Eastern Europe was occupied mostly by the Slavs, whose dialects developed into Slavic languages such as Russian, Ukrainian, Polish, Czech, and Bulgarian. Latin as well as the original Germanic and Slav languages were in turn descended from Indo-European dialects spoken by different groups of barbarian tribes in prehistoric times (p. 58).

England, in the west, is a special case. It was less thoroughly Romanized than the other portions of the empire, and the Anglo-Saxon invaders were able to impose their Germanic dialect upon the native Britons. The later Danish and Norman conquests (pp. 220, 223) brought additional influences—including French, which was spoken by the Normans. By the middle of the fourteenth century, Anglo-Saxon (Old English) had become modified into what we now term "Middle English." Out of this evolved *modern* English, a mixture of Germanic and Romance elements.

Epic and Romance. As early as the eleventh century, the spoken vernaculars began to be set down in writings that at first appealed chiefly to the nobility. A leading work was the epic *Song of Roland (Chanson de Roland),* written around 1100 by an unknown author in the dialect of northern France. Like the *Iliad* and the *Odyssey* eighteen hundred years before (p. 84), the *Song of Roland* grew out of traditional songs memorized and continually altered by generations of illiterate minstrels—*chansons de geste* ("songs of great deeds") about the earlier hero-king Charlemagne and his courtly companions. Like the epics of Homer, too, this poem about heroes of the past in fact expresses the values of the time at which it was written—in this case, the ideals of medieval Christian knights.

Its chief hero is Count Roland, nephew of Charlemagne. Roland personifies the warrior ideals of bravery, loyalty, and military prowess—and the Christian faith in God and salvation. The field of battle runs red with the blood of the courageous, and

---

[1] From George F. Whicher, *The Goliard Poets.* Copyright 1949 by George F. Whicher. Reprinted by permission of New Directions Publishing Corporation.

Roland's fellow vassals observe strictly the code of honor and revenge. Other national epics were written at about the same time in neighboring countries: the *Nibelungenlied* ("Song of the Nibelungs") in Germany and the *Poema del Cid* ("Poem of the Cid") in Spain.

But the troubadours (professional singers) of the Middle Ages did not confine themselves to epic tales. They also sang of "courtly" manners and *romantic love* (from *romance,* which originally meant a tale, as opposed to a learned work in Latin). For the first time since the days of the pagan authors, a poetry of passion appeared in Europe. But it was for the most part passion on an "elevated" plane. The romantic knight placed his ideal woman on a pedestal and adored her from afar—with thoughts of physical fulfillment repressed or postponed. This "cult of love" also brought forth elaborate manuals of behavior for lovers. Courtly love, it should be noted, was a pastime for the nobility only; commoners were considered unsuited to the delicate art of romance. Even so, the code of conduct that held love as a noble ideal made a distinguishing mark upon the whole of Western culture.

Clearly, the hearty masculine culture of the early Middle Ages was giving way to a more tranquil, confident, and leisurely society. The noble's castle was becoming less of a barracks for fighting men and more of a theater for refined pleasures. Aristocratic ladies were accorded more and more attention and were able to exercise greater control over the men.

The feudal society of the later Middle Ages is splendidly portrayed in the so-called Arthurian romances, a cycle of prose stories composed in the twelfth and thirteenth centuries by French and Norman writers. The central figure of the romances is King Arthur, a Celtic chieftain of sixth-century Britain who fought against the Anglo-Saxon invaders (p. 196). But the legends of Arthur's Round Table are told in the manner of the late Middle Ages; they are tales of forbidden love, knightly combats, and colorful pageantry. One of the first and best of the romance writers was Chrétien de Troyes, who lived for a time at the court of the countess of Champagne, in eastern France, and who also enjoyed the patronage of the strong-willed Eleanor of Aquitaine. (Eleanor, who had been queen of France before becoming queen of England, regarded herself as the queen of courtly love and its laws of conduct.) Chrétien's most popular story, *Lancelot,* helped shape the heroic mold of that mythical knight.

Realism and Satire. Toward the close of the Middle Ages, the narratives of chivalric love became less fanciful and more realistic than the Arthurian tales. Most successful was the work of Christine de Pisan, the first woman to support herself entirely from her earnings as an author. Born in Italy, she spent most of her years at or near the French court in Paris. Her best-known story, *The Book of the Duke of True Lovers* (c. 1400), reads much like the earlier aristocratic romances. But it is based on actual events rather than legend, and its lovers act in response to common sense rather than to the dictates of passion and the cult of love.

These aristocratic tales were of little interest to the bourgeois. Finding little of their own lives in such stories, they turned to a different sort of secular literature. This, too, originated in France and consisted of *fabliaux* (fables). Unlike the heroic and idyllic tales of chivalry, the fabliaux were about everyday life. Frank, sensual, and witty, they ridiculed both courtly and priestly life. One of the most popular fables was *Aucassin and Nicolette,* by an unknown author. Its hero, Aucassin, spurns knighthood in order to pursue his passion for a beautiful young Muslim captive. Indifferent to his soul's sal-

Fig. 6.10 "Upon an Ambler Easily She Sat . . ." Geoffrey Chaucer's *Canterbury Tales* was a best seller as a handwritten book—eighty-four copies, an unusually large number, still exist today—and was one of the first works in English to get into print. This illustration from a luxury manuscript of about 1400 shows one of the pilgrim storytellers, the Wife of Bath. Forceful, independent, and five times married and widowed, she is depicted as Chaucer describes her, with wide-brimmed hat, hair in a net, and riding astride, not side-saddle as was expected of medieval ladies.

vation, he subordinates everything to his desire for union with Nicolette. He even prefers hell to heaven, on the ground that the company there will be more attractive and entertaining.

Chaucer and Dante. Two works of the late Middle Ages rise above ordinary classification. One is *The Canterbury Tales* of Geoffrey Chaucer, written in the fourteenth century. This collection of stories is in the general spirit of the fabliaux but includes all classes of society and a wide range of topics. Born of a merchant family, Chaucer spent most of his life in the service of the English aristocracy. He read broadly and traveled extensively on the Continent. His outlook was cosmopolitan and urbane, and he displayed a rare combination of scholarship, insight, and humor. In the *Tales,* a group of people exchange stories as they ride on a pilgrimage to the shrine of a revered saint, Thomas Becket, at Canterbury (p. 250). The stories, of "good morality and general pleasure," appealed to all literate persons in fourteenth-century England. In them—and in the tellers of the tales, all of them typical people of the time (*Fig. 6.10*)—they could see themselves and their society as in a mirror.

The other monumental work of the period is the *Divine Comedy* of Dante, which is regarded as the supreme masterpiece of Italian literature. More profound than Chaucer's work, the *Comedy* is a grand synthesis of medieval theology, science, philosophy, and romance. Dante, a Florentine scholar and poet, was immersed in the political and intellectual currents of his time. His heroic poem is an *allegorical* tale describing the experiences of human souls after death. Escorted by the Roman poet Virgil (p. 131), Dante travels in his poem through the regions beyond the grave. He descends into the terrible Inferno (hell), where the damned suffer eternal punishments that fit their crimes. Then he moves on to Purgatory, where the souls of pardoned sinners suffer for a limited time until their souls are cleansed of guilt. At last, he is permitted to enter Paradise (heaven), where the blessed enjoy, in fitting ways, the gifts of God. For this final portion of the journey, Dante must leave the pagan Virgil behind. Now he is guided by the pure Beatrice, his ideal of Christian womanhood, who represents the blending of romantic and spiritual love that leads Dante at last to a climactic vision of God.

Dante called his work a "comedy" because he believed the story suggests a happy ending for all who choose to follow Christ. (Later admirers added the compliment "divine.") It is a moving and intensely personal story. At every turn of the narrative, Dante makes sharp comments on the characters of history and myth, who serve as dramatic symbols for his moralizing. Readers may agree or disagree with Dante's judgments, but they will long remember the vivid images created by his words.

West and East: The Crusades

The flowering of European literature and art reflected the mounting self-confidence of the West. Latin Christendom had come a long way from the troubled, precarious days of the ninth century, when western Europe had been a besieged fortress, struggling to hold out against determined invaders (pp. 218–221). As between the two variants of European civilization that had come into existence by the year 1000, that of the Latin West and the Byzantine East (pp. 225–226), the balance of power was swinging toward the West, and the West was even strong enough to take the offensive against the rival religion and civilization of Islam.

THE WESTERN COUNTEROFFENSIVE

To a large extent, this counteroffensive was the work of the feudal society that had grown up in the turmoil of the early Middle Ages. Kings and great lords were eager to enlarge their holdings and acquire land with which to reward their vassals. Among lesser warriors, there were crowds of younger sons and landless knights who dreamed of finding fiefs that would enable them to acquire the wealth and status of landholders. Thus there was a tendency among feudal warriors, once the pressure of outside attack slackened, to go immediately over to the offensive—not just to eliminate enemies but to conquer and colonize land. Any non-Christian nation, whether pagan or Islamic, was regarded as fair game for this purpose. That was why, during the tenth century, Norman warriors hastened to Sicily to reconquer it from the Saracens, and great lords and knights from all over Europe participated in the gradual reconquest of Spain (*Map 6.2*).

But feudal warriors were not the only ones involved in the Western offensive. Conquest and colonization usually also opened the way for trade and were therefore in the interests of the townspeople as well. Especially in the south, the pushing back of the frontiers of Islam cleared the western Mediterranean for the rising commerce of Christian Europe. In the eleventh century, while feudal knights were fighting to reconquer Spain and Sicily, the islands of Sardinia and Corsica were seized from the Saracens by an Italian city-state, Pisa.

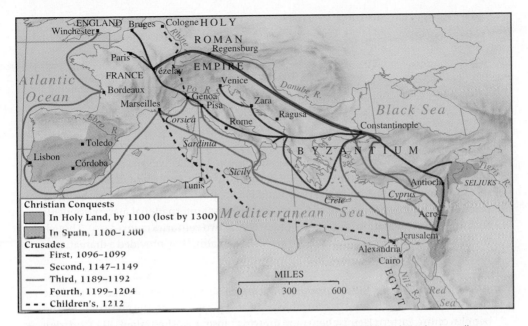

Map 6.2 The Crusades, 1096–1213. Western European efforts to conquer and hold the Holy Land, 2,000 miles away in the Middle East, were on a vast scale. Large forces had not marched, sailed, and fought across such distances since the time of the Roman Empire—a sign of western Europe's reviving wealth and skills. Crusades on this scale continued during the thirteenth century, but by 1300, the Muslims prevailed. Meanwhile at the other end of the Mediterranean, however, Christian campaigns of reconquest drove the Muslims from most of present-day Spain and Portugal.

Besides feudal land hunger and commercial enterprise, the West was also possessed by religious faith. The power of religion in guiding the Western offensive is shown by the fact that religion was sometimes actually strong enough to rein the offensive in. Pagan tribes several times saved themselves from attack by timely conversion; this was one of the reasons why the Poles and Hungarians adopted Latin Christianity (pp. 223–224).

But of course, religion also drove the warriors forward, particularly once theologians redefined the Church's teaching about war against non-Christians. Traditionally, the Church had thought of this as simply a variety of "just war" as defined by Augustine (p. 179)—that is, as an evil activity that became permissible or necessary in a good cause but could never be good in itself. In the expanding Christendom of the eleventh century, however, theologians proclaimed that war against pagans and Muslims was not merely a necessary evil but a deed that was pleasing to God, and that to die in the course of such a war was a form of martyrdom. For the first time, Christianity had a concept of "holy war" that was similar to the Muslim doctrine of *jihad* (p. 204).

But in the Christian understanding, "holy war" was still a form of "just war"—and no war could be "just" unless it was declared by an authority with legitimate power over the entire community. Western Europe in the late eleventh century had such an authority—the papacy. Once the popes took on the role of declarers of war against the enemies of Christendom, the stage was set for the most dynamic forces in western European civilization—the feudal warriors, the townspeople, and the Latin Church—to cooperate in a vast but ill-fated enterprise: the Crusades.

TRIUMPH AND TRAGEDY IN THE HOLY LAND

Although crusades were proclaimed and fought in the Middle Ages against various non-Christian enemies in different regions of Europe, the most important of them were directed against the Muslims in the Holy Land for the purpose of recapturing the birthplace of Christianity. These "great" Crusades were in fact international mass movements that fired the imagination of all classes of society for two centuries (1095–1270). Though the Crusades in the Holy Land failed to achieve their aim, they provided a dramatic expression of the confidence and zeal of the reviving West.

Western Christendom, Byzantium, and the Turks. The series of events that sparked the Crusades had its beginning in central Asia. In this period when the civilizations and peoples of the Eastern Hemisphere were drawing closer together, Islam, like Christian Europe, was subject to invasion by increasingly powerful nomads of the steppes (pp. 199, 218–219). During the ninth century, a nomadic people that had recently come to prominence in the steppes, the Turks, had entered Persia from the north. They were quickly converted to Islam and for more than a century held control over a portion of the Islamic empire. In the eleventh century, the Turkish Seljuk dynasty conquered Baghdad and won the title of *sultan,* or ruler, from its caliph (p. 204). Members of this warlike family pushed westward from Baghdad into Syria, Palestine, and Asia Minor. They established themselves as sultans of several small states in those areas and were less tolerant of Christian minorities than earlier Arab rulers had been. In particular, they began harassing the growing numbers of Christian pilgrims to the Holy Land.

While resentment mounted in western Europe against the infidels who ruled the holiest shrines of Christianity, to Byzantium the expansion of the Turks was a formidable new threat. It arose, moreover, at a time when its relations with the Latin half of the Christian world were going from bad to worse. The sources of conflict were many: disputes over the religious allegiance of eastern European peoples; the rising self-confidence of the Westerners, to whom the Byzantines seemed decadent, pompous, and effeminate; the threatened sense of superiority of the Byzantines, to whom "the Franks," as they called the Westerners, still seemed to be rude and grasping barbarians.

But the main reason for conflict between Byzantium and the West was the increasingly bitter religious rivalry between the Latin and Greek churches (p. 172). In the eleventh century, the popes not only tried to make good their claim to be the rulers of Christian society in the West but also insisted more than before on their supremacy over the whole Christian Church. This brought them into collision with both the emperors and the patriarchs in Constantinople. In 1054, papal representatives in Constantinople formally excommunicated the patriarch, whereupon the document of excommunication was solemnly burned by the Greeks, and the patriarch in turn excommunicated the pope's representatives. Though neither side intended this as a complete

Frontier between the Byzantine and Abbasid
empires, c. 930

Areas of Anatolia occupied by the Abbasids in 1070

Areas of Anatolia occupied by the Seljuk Turks in the
early thirteenth century

Byzantium and the Turks

break between the two halves of the Church, they began to see each other, much more
than before, as religious adversaries. The Norman rulers of Sicily, having conquered the
island from the Muslim Saracens, now went on to wrest southern Italy from Christian
but "schismatic" Byzantium.

Now, on top of all these problems from its fellow Christians in the West, Byzantium suddenly found itself in deadly danger from its new Muslim neighbors to the
East. In 1071, the Turks crushed a Byzantine army at Manzikert in eastern Asia Minor
and then began to move toward the imperial capital itself. In this emergency, the eastern emperor, Alexius, decided to mend his relations with the Christian West and sent
an urgent appeal for help to Pope Urban II.

The First Crusade. The pope heard the plea of Alexius' ambassador early in 1095
and found the idea of sending a rescue force to the East well suited to his own far-
reaching aims. Heir to the Cluniac reform movement and to the policies of Gregory VII (pp. 251–256), Urban realized that a successful holy war against the Turks would
do more than free Palestine and reopen the roads of pilgrimage. It would in all likeli-
hood compel the Byzantine emperor, in repayment, to recognize the supremacy of the
pope over the whole Christian Church. Moreover, the triumph would lift the prestige
of the papacy to such a height that the ideal of Church supremacy over the state would
surely be realized.

Later in the year 1095, Urban used the Council of Clermont, in central France, as
his forum for launching the First Crusade. His speech, a masterpiece of persuasion and
emotion, appealed to both the highest and the lowest of human motives. As he ad-

dressed the assembled clergy, he was really speaking to all the classes and interests of Europe. He knew that some of the churchmen listening to him at Clermont had a deep dislike of violence. Yet his call for action was so effective that as he ended the oration his listeners shouted, "God wills it!" This became the battle cry of the crusaders.

In his speech, the pope kindled ugly prejudices and fanned them into a flame of hatred for the Turks. He reported, in horrific detail, atrocities that the "vile" and "accursed" race had allegedly committed against Christians. In the name of Christ, Urban appealed to men of all ranks, rich and poor, to exterminate the infidels. He reminded his listeners that such a response would be in keeping with the grandest traditions of Western Christendom: Charlemagne, for example, had proved his manhood and achieved glory by destroying paganism and extending the territory of the Church (pp. 213–215). The same objectives could be accomplished once more—and with a guarantee of safety for the soul of each participant. The pope, citing his authority as Vicar of Christ, declared that all who died while journeying or fighting on this "holy pilgrimage" would be automatically pardoned for all their sins.

Urban was aware, however, that it would take more than religious excitement to defeat the Turks. He aimed his call directly at the military class—the knights and landholders. Quoting Scripture, Urban told them that they must not hold back because of their concern for family or possessions: "Everyone that has forsaken houses, or brothers, or sisters, or father, or mother, or wife, or children, or lands for my name's sake shall receive a hundredfold and shall inherit everlasting life." Then Urban observed that Europe was a narrow and confined space—too small to support its growing population. For this reason, he explained, you "murder and devour one another" in endless private warfare. Let your quarrels and hatreds cease, the pope concluded: "Enter upon the road to the Holy Land; take it from the wicked race, and keep it for yourselves. That land which, as the Scripture says, 'flows with milk and honey,' was given by God into the possession of the children of Israel."

Thus presented, the crusade appealed to many Europeans' desire for wealth, for Christian unity, for personal honor and sacrifice, for excitement and adventure, and for spiritual salvation. The Italian merchants, though Urban had not been addressing them directly, saw a special advantage to themselves in the crusade. They would gain profit by providing ships and supplies. And if the crusaders succeeded, fabulous commercial opportunities would be opened to them.

The crusading spirit possessed other classes of society as well. Early in 1096, a motley crowd of commoners set out from southern Germany for Constantinople. Their enthusiasm, sparked by the pope's call to arms, was whipped to a fury by a maverick preacher known as Peter the Hermit. The Peasants' Crusade, as it came to be called, distinguished itself chiefly by the massacre of Jewish communities along the way. Lacking provisions of their own, these commoners lived off the country as they marched. When they at last reached Constantinople, the Byzantine emperor grew alarmed and hastily ferried them across the Bosporus waterway to Asia Minor. There the Turks made quick work of the misguided peasants.

Meanwhile, however, a more formidable force was assembling. French noblemen, responding to the call of Urban (who was himself a French aristocrat), made up the main body of crusaders. Godfrey, duke of Lorraine, joined by other dukes, counts, and barons, set out in 1096 with an army of some fifteen thousand knights. It was this army of feudal warriors that fought and won the First Crusade, the only crusade that temporarily, at least, attained its goal.

The crusaders traveled down the Danube and then across the Balkans to Constantinople, where they met other groups of knights that had taken different overland routes, and then crossed into Asia Minor to confront the Turks (*Map 6.2,* p. 277). On the way across Asia Minor, they suffered severe hardships, disease, and some defeats, but they were at last victorious. Their leaders, having turned back the Turkish threat to Constantinople, moved on to establish dukedoms in eastern Asia Minor and abandoned their original plan to march on to Jerusalem. The survivors of lesser rank, however, insisted that the crusade be resumed. Responding at last to their demands, Raymond, count of Toulouse, advanced on Jerusalem and took the city, after a six-week siege, in 1099.

The crusaders' entry into the Holy City was an orgy of looting and killing of Muslims and Jews. One crusader reported in his journal:

> The amount of blood that they shed on that day is incredible. . . . Some of our men (and this was more merciful) cut off the heads of their enemies; others shot them with arrows, so that they fell from the towers; others tortured them longer by casting them into the flames. Piles of heads, hands, and feet were to be seen in the streets of the city. . . . It was a just and splendid judgment of God that this place should be filled with the blood of unbelievers, since it had suffered so long from their blasphemies.

With the help of fleets from Venice, Genoa, and other Italian cities, the crusaders moved on to take the coastal towns of Palestine and Syria. (For this aid the Italians received, as they had hoped, rich privileges in the trade of the Orient.) The various conquered territories were then drawn together into a loose feudal state called the Latin Kingdom of Jerusalem. Baldwin of Flanders was chosen as its first king and accepted the usual homage and services of the landholding nobility. The feudal system of western Europe was thus transplanted to this Christian beachhead in the Middle East.

Later Crusades. The First Crusade was followed by countless other expeditions to the East, only some of which have been assigned a number by historians. Most of these later crusades to the Holy Land were intended not to expand the Christian territories but to defend them against fierce Muslim campaigns of reconquest. The Second Crusade (1147–1149)—called in response to Turkish success in recapturing part of the gains of the First Crusade—was inspired by a reforming monk, Bernard of Clairvaux (p. 252). An extraordinarily persuasive man, he induced two leading feudal rulers, the king of France and the Holy Roman emperor, and thousands of fighting men to "put on the Cross." The main force of this expedition was cut to pieces as it moved across Asia Minor. Bernard, convinced that his cause was just, concluded that the failure must have been due to the sinfulness of the crusaders.

Bernard's view was accepted by his more ardent followers. Some of them went still further: they reasoned that if purity of soul was a requirement for victory, young children would be the most favored of all crusaders. In accordance with this notion, thousands of innocent German and French boys marched off on the Children's Crusade in 1212. They never reached the Holy Land, however, for they fell victim to accident and disease or were captured by slave dealers along the way.

The climax of the struggles in the Holy Land came somewhat earlier, however, with the Third Crusade (1189–1192). Until not long before this crusade, most of the Muslim resistance to the invaders had come from Asia Minor and Syria. Now, however, Muslim Egypt joined the struggle under its ruler Salah-ed-Din—Saladin, as the crusaders called him. Saladin was a pious Muslim, an ambitious statesman, and a formidable warrior who was a hero to Muslims and admired even by Christians. If he could expel the unbelievers from Jerusalem, to Muslims the "Glorious Place" from which the Prophet had ascended to heaven, he would both fulfill his duty of *jihad* and strengthen his position as the dominant Muslim ruler in the Middle East. Accordingly, in 1187, he crushed the army of the Latin Kingdom and went on to capture Jerusalem.

Once again, armies set out from the feudal kingdoms of western Europe—overland from the Holy Roman Empire and from France and England by sea routes that the Italian cities had opened across the Mediterranean (*Map 6.2*, p. 277). Saladin fought them all to a standstill, and finally the most famous Christian warrior of the time, King Richard I of England ("the Lion-Hearted"; p. 233), had to make an agreement with the Egyptian ruler that left most of the Holy Land, including Jerusalem, in Muslim hands.

The Fourth Crusade, organized a few years later by leading French barons, involved a change of strategy: instead of going to the Holy Land, it would travel by sea from Venice to attack the center of Muslim power in Egypt (*Map 6.2*, p. 277). But a combination of factors—the ambition of Venice to dominate the eastern Mediterranean, an appeal for help from a deposed emperor in Constantinople, religious hatred of the Greek Church, as well as the feeling that Constantinople would be an easier prize than Cairo—caused the leaders, while on their way, to change their plans. In 1204, the imperial capital was stormed by the very men whose forefathers had promised its rescue a century before.

Untold treasures of gold, silver, and holy relics were seized during the subsequent pillage and rape. Vandalism and fire consumed irreplaceable works of Greek art and literature. The city and the European portion of the empire were then divided among the chieftains of the crusade, and these remnants were brought together as the Latin Empire of Constantinople. The count of Flanders was proclaimed its first emperor, and a new patriarch (head) of the Greek Church was installed—one who was loyal to the pope in Rome. Venice secured special trading privileges, and the farmlands were parceled out in feudal fashion to the plundering knights. Thus long-desired and ill-concealed goals were momentarily realized by the papacy, the Venetians, and the French aristocracy—all at the expense of Byzantium.

The Latin Empire of Constantinople was a freak of history, and its life was even briefer than that of the Kingdom of Jerusalem. What the Western forces really accomplished by this infamous crusade was a fatal weakening of Europe's key point of defense against the Turks. A Byzantine emperor carried on in exile, clinging to a small piece of territory in Asia Minor, and in 1261, he managed to regain Constantinople and the area around it. But Byzantine power had been so shattered that it proved unable to check a later advance by the Turks (p. 298), and the rivalry between the Greek and Latin churches hardened into outright schism (p. 295).

Additional crusades intended to maintain or expand the Christian presence in the Holy Land continued throughout the thirteenth century. They all came to nothing, however, and the last Christian foothold, the fortress of Acre, fell in 1291. After that, the popes continued to proclaim crusades—against eastern European pagan peoples, against Christian heretics, and even against local rivals in Italian power struggles. From the fifteenth century, however, as European rulers built up centralized governments and became the main focus of loyalty within their countries, they no longer needed or wanted to act under the authority of the pope (p. 370). Christians and Muslims, and later on Catholics and Protestants, still fought wars of religion against each other, but formal crusades became a thing of the past.

THE ANTI-JEWISH CRUSADE

The Christian expeditions against the East were accompanied by rising hostility toward the Jews in Europe. During the early Middle Ages, following a grudging decree of toleration by the Roman emperor Theodosius I (p. 178), the Jews and their culture had survived. Remaining outside the Christian community and restricted by special laws and customs, they were spared the abuses and outrages that came later. The Jews remained small in numbers, constituting perhaps 1 to 2 percent of western Europe's population by the year 1000.

Medieval Jews were usually forbidden to hold land, serfs, or slaves, and were in fact a class entirely separate from the Christian social order. Cut off from the land, they had sought to establish themselves in the towns. The professions, guilds, and most other occupations were closed to them, however, so they supported themselves in enterprises that were for the most part shunned by Christians—above all, moneylending (p. 301).

The Jews congregated in their own quarters of medieval towns, partly to enhance their physical security and partly to maintain their distinctive pattern of life. There they were allowed a kind of autonomy by the governing officials. Despite the limitations on their freedom of action, some Jews rose to positions of power and distinction in commerce and royal administration. These individuals, however, could not match the achievements of the Spanish Jews, who enjoyed the generous tolerance of Muslim rulers (prior to the Christian reconquest of Spain). Notable Jewish scholars, poets, philosophers, and statesmen made, in Muslim Spain, a golden age of Jewish history. They contributed, at the same time, to the intellectual development of Christian Europe by helping bring the wisdom of the ancient Greeks into circulation in the West (p. 269).

The Christian attack on the Muslims in Spain (p. 223) and the expeditions to recapture the Holy Land brought a disastrous end to the relative security of Jews everywhere. The First Crusade, launched in 1096, set off a spasm of religious fanaticism and violence (p. 280). During the next two centuries, as prejudices against Jews were stirred up by Christian leaders, mob attacks on Jewish communities became commonplace.

Sporadic outbursts of anti-Semitic feeling had occurred in earlier times, but now the burnings and massacres became epidemic. In 1215, the Fourth Lateran Council of the Church encouraged public humiliation of the Jews by ordering that they must wear a yellow patch or cap for identification. In most countries of Europe, strict laws were enacted confining Jews to a marked-off zone (*ghetto*) in each town—usually the foulest and most congested part. Punishment and intimidation often took the form of seizing and burning copies of the Talmud (ancient rabbinical commentaries on the Jewish Scriptures; p. 160), on the ground that the contents were offensive to Christ. At last, because they were thought to be an intolerable "contamination" to Christians, all Jews who refused conversion to Christianity were expelled from country after country: England in 1290, parts of Germany in 1298, France in 1306, Spain in 1492, and Portugal in 1498. Compelled to leave their their property behind, thousands of Jews migrated to eastern Europe and the Middle East (pp. 296, 298).

Some Christians were, of course, shocked by the violence and injustice directed toward the Jews and gave them aid and protection when they could. But from the twelfth century onward, the Jews could expect repeated humiliations and persecutions from the Christian societies in which they lived. This record is one of the longest and gloomiest chapters of Western history—a compound of Church teachings, popular grievance, mob hysteria, and individual aggression.

RECOMMENDED READING

The Medieval Church The best short introduction to the religious and cultural world of the Middle Ages is R. W. Southern, *The Making of the Middle Ages* (1953). More detailed treatment will be found in J. Le Goff, *Medieval Civilization, 400–1500* (1988).

Specifically on the Church, J. H. Lynch, *The Medieval Church: A Brief History* (1992), is an excellent introduction. The veneration of saints and other popular religious practices are analyzed in P. Brown, *The Cult of the Saints* (1981), and A. Vauchez, *The Laity in the Middle Ages* (1993).

C. H. Lawrence, *Medieval Monasticism* (1989), includes all forms of monastic life; on the religious, social, and cultural influence of the friars, see his *The Friars* (1994). J. Le Goff, *Medieval Callings* (1990), includes treatment of monks and saints.

G. Barraclough, *The Medieval Papacy* (1968), is brief and readable; B. Schimmelpfennig, *The Papacy* (1992), is a more recent account that includes the medieval period. The issues in and general significance of the dispute over investiture are discussed in G. Tellenbach, *Church, State, and Christian Society at the Time of the Investiture Contest* (1940).

Christian Art A. Petzold, *Romanesque Art* (1995), and M. Camille, *Gothic Art: Glorious Visions* (1996), are excellent introductions to both art and architecture. X. Barral i Altet, *The Romanesque: Towns, Cathedrals, Monasteries* (1998), and G. Binding, *High Gothic: The Age of the Great Cathedrals* (1992), concentrate on architecture. A. Erlande-Brandebourg, *Cathedrals and Castles: Building in the Middle Ages* (1995), describes the processes of planning and construction. All these books are concise and splendidly illustrated. On the beliefs and values that the Gothic cathedrals expressed, see the classic works of E. Panofsky, *Gothic Architecture and Scholasticism* (1951), and O. von Simson, *The Gothic Cathedral* (1998).

Thought and Education The best introduction to medieval universities is C. H. Haskins, *The Rise of Universities* (1973). J. Le Goff, *Intellectuals in the Middle Ages* (1993), vividly portrays the intellectual concerns, social background, and daily life of the academic world of the Middle Ages.

D. Knowles, *The Evolution of Medieval Thought* (1988), is a readable and reliable introduction; D. E. Luscombe, *Medieval Thought* (1997), is a brief and clear recent account. C. F. J. Martin, *An Introduction to Medieval Philosophy* (1996), briefly explains the difference between the aims and methods of philosophy in the Middle Ages and later times; G. R. Evans, *Philosophy and Theology in the Middle Ages* (1993), concisely discusses the medieval relations between these two fields of inquiry; and E. Grant, *The Foundations of Modern Science in the Middle Ages* (1996), discusses the medieval contribution to the development of science.

Language and Literature A readable and interesting general introduction to medieval literature is C. S. Lewis, *The Discarded Image* (1964). The following books are excellent introductions to specific types of literature: N. Daniel, *Heroes and Saracens: An Interpretation of the Chansons de Geste* (1984); P. Krueger, ed., *The Cambridge Companion to Romance* (2000); S. Gaunt and S. Kay, eds., *The Troubadours: An Introduction* (1999); and H. Waddell, *The Wandering Scholars* (1955), on the Goliards. C. C. Willard, *Christine de Pizan: Her Life and Works* (1984); D. Brewer, *Chaucer and His World* (1978); and S. Bemrose, *A New Life of Dante* (2000), are concise biographies, putting the works of these authors against the background of their lives and times.

West and East: The Crusades T. F. Madden, *A Concise History of the Crusades* (1999), is an up-to-date introduction; J. Riley-Smith, ed., *The Oxford Illustrated History of the Crusades* (1995), covers social and cultural as well as religious, military, and political aspects of the crusading movement. M. Foss, *People of the First Crusade* (1997), is a vivid narrative. R. W. Southern, *Western Views of Islam in the Middle Ages* (1962), deals with Christian attitudes to the rival monotheism.

R. I. Moore, in *The Formation of a Persecuting Society* (1987) and *Origins of European Dissent* (1985), analyzes persecution and the rise of heresy. E. Peters, *Inquisition* (1988), is a brief introduction dealing with both medieval and later times; A. C. Shannon, *The Medieval Inquisition* (1991), concentrates on the Middle Ages. L. B. Glick, *Abraham's Heirs: Jews and Christians in Medieval Europe* (1999), and M. R. Cohen, *Under Crescent and Cross: The Jews in the Middle Ages* (1994), are excellent surveys of medieval Jewry and its relations with the dominant monotheisms of Christianity and Islam.

INFOTRAC COLLEGE EDITION

Visit the source collections at **http://academic.cengage.com/infotrac,** and use the Search function with the following key terms:

early Christianity   Middle Ages   Crusades

WESTERN CIVILIZATION RESOURCES

Visit the Brief History of the Western World Companion Web Site for resources specific to this textbook:

http://history.wadsworth.com/greerbrief09/

Also, the CD in the back of this book and the World History Resources Center at **http://history.wadsworth.com/west_civ/** offer a variety of tools to help you succeed in this course, including access to quizzes; images; documents; interactive simulations, maps, and timelines; movie explorations; and a wealth of other sources.

Fig. III.1. A Renaissance Gentleman. Jean de Dinteville, an aristocrat portrayed in Hans Holbein's painting *The French Ambassadors* (1533), is shown as a man of wide interests. He carries a dagger, symbolic of prowess in combat, but other objects display his knowledge of geography, science, and music. An oriental rug proclaims his access to exotic luxuries of the world that is opening up beyond Europe. But as a Christian, he knows that human knowledge and achievement do not last forever: the distorted object at his feet, when viewed at an angle, reveals itself as a skull.

Part Three

THE REMAKING OF EUROPE

PART THREE

The Remaking of Europe

Unlike the Roman world, the Christian Europe of the Middle Ages did not "fall." There were no waves of invading barbarians, no collapse of empires, no decline of trade and cities. Instead, many old established and gradually developing traditions of medieval civilization reached "critical mass"—and gradual development turned into spectacular change.

Two of the most famous events connected with this change, Christopher Columbus's voyage of 1492 and the beginning of the Protestant Reformation in 1517, took place around the turn of the fifteenth and sixteenth centuries. For this reason, the year 1500 has become the benchmark date of the "end" of the Middle Ages and the "beginning" of the modern period (p. 2). In fact, however, medieval civilization began to change as early as 1300, and it took 350 years for a recognizably more modern pattern of civilization to appear. A whole series of further changes then followed, which have gone on right down to the present. Unlike the ancient and medieval periods, the modern period has so far been one of continual shifts in civilization, each just as massive as the ones before it.

In the three and a half centuries of the first series of modern shifts in civilization, Europe's social and political structure, as well as its place in the world, were all transformed. Out of the booming agriculture and bustling cities of the Middle Ages came the freeing of the serfs in western Europe and the rise of international banking and capitalism. The competition of powerful feudal states led successful rulers to rely on royal bureaucrats, mercenary armies, and national taxation rather than the services of warrior-landowners—and in many countries, to seek backing from their subjects through representative institutions.

Meanwhile, stronger links with the other civilizations of the Eastern Hemisphere brought technical ideas from distant lands that Europe turned into revolutionary advances—firearms, printing, clocks. And out of the urge to make these links even stronger, as well as the need to counter the growing power of Islam, came exploration and overseas empires, so that Christian Europe replaced Islam as the world's farthest-flung intercontinental civilization.

The changes in culture and religion were just as drastic, and their roots in the past were just as deep. Medieval scholars and thinkers had always felt themselves to be the heirs of Greece and Rome, and this finally led them into a determined effort to revive all that was left of the ancient traditions—the Renaissance. Out of this encounter with the Greco-Roman past came new ideals of human personality and behavior, new philosophical ideas, new questions about Christian belief and practice, and new forms of art and literature that challenged the cultural traditions of the Middle Ages.

Likewise, the Catholic Church of western Europe, for all its stress on unity of faith, had a long-standing history of inner conflict that finally exploded in the religious revolution of the Protestant Reformation. Protestantism failed to take over the entire Church or even to remain a united movement, but out of its disunity came countless new forms of Christian belief and practice. The Reformation also strengthened the state in its partnership with both the Catholic and the Protestant churches, and in the long run, it helped make religious diversity and freedom of conscience accepted Western values.

All these changes also strengthened the position that western Europe had won in the Middle Ages as the heartland of Western civilization. The Renaissance and Reformation began in western Europe and hardly affected the Orthodox countries of the East. The centers of finance, trade, and technical innovation, as well as the rulers with the best-organized governments and armies, were all to be found in the West. It was the western European countries that reached overseas for trade and empire, while eastern Europe served as their buffer zone against one expanding Islamic land empire after another—above all that of the Turks. And among the western European countries, a few exceptionally successful ones, above all France and England, were beginning to emerge as the "heartland of the heartland" of the West.

These shifts in civilization were far from being a triumphant progress toward modernity. The international capitalist economy brought bitter class struggles and vicious repression in town and countryside, and in eastern Europe, it helped serfdom grow ever more oppressive. Better-organized and better-armed states were able to fight more destructive wars than ever before. The short-term result of the Reformation was two hundred years of religious hatred, persecution, and war. Europe's closer links with the rest of the world led to devastating intercontinental epidemics, the destruction of the civilizations of the Western Hemisphere, and the beginning of the Atlantic slave trade. In all these ways, the era was as tormented as any in history.

All the same, by 1650, a new kind of civilization, possessing unprecedented technical skills, worldwide power, and a willingness to deliberately alter its own ways of life, was coming into being. Christian Europe was on the way to remaking itself into the modern West.

	POLITICAL, SOCIAL, AND ECONOMIC DEVELOPMENTS	RELIGION, SCIENCE, AND PHILOSOPHY	HISTORY AND LITERATURE	ARCHITECTURE, ART, AND MUSIC
1300	Travels of Marco Polo			Florence Cathedral
		"Babylonian Captivity" of papacy (1309–1376)		Giotto
	Black Death (bubonic plague) Hundred Years' War (1338–1453) Decline of feudal and manorial systems	Renaissance humanism (1350–1600)	Petrarch Boccaccio	
	New weapons of war: longbow and crossbow	Great Schism (1379–1417) Wiclif		Madrigals (polyphony) Renaissance style of architecture: Brunelleschi
1400	Domestic system of production (1400–1750)	Hus		Donatello Masaccio van Eyck Ghiberti
	Age of despots in Italy: Cosimo de' Medici Francesco Sforza	Platonism (Florentine Academy)	Valla Gutenberg	
	New-style armies: cannon and muskets Fall of Constantinople to Ottoman Turks Christian reconquest of Spain Jacob Fugger	Ficino Pico della Mirandola Machiavelli		
				Botticelli
1500	Overseas exploration: Columbus, da Gama, Magellan		Erasmus Castiglione	Leonardo
	Establishment of European colonial empires: Cortés, Pizarro Rise of national monarchies: Henry VIII, Francis I	Luther (beginning of Protestant Reformation) Calvin Pope Paul III (beginning of Catholic Reformation) Copernicus Loyola and Society of Jesus	More Rabelais Cellini	Michelangelo Titian Holbein St. Peter's Basilica
	Charles V, Holy Roman emperor	Council of Trent	Montaigne	
	Philip II Elizabeth I Spanish Armada			Brueghel Escorial Palace
				Baroque style
1600		Bacon Kepler, Galileo	Cervantes Shakespeare Jonson	Globe Theater
	Religious wars (Thirty Years' War in Germany)	Descartes		Rubens
				Rembrandt Bernini
1650	Peace of Westphalia Louis XIV			Taj Mahal
				Versailles Palace

CHAPTER 7

The Transformation and Expansion of Europe

OVERVIEW

In the late Middle Ages—that is, the fourteenth and fifteenth centuries—Europe was shaken by a series of disasters. The increase in population that had begun in the early Middle Ages broke through the limits of what existing farming methods could support, and the result was famine, social conflict, and peasant revolts. The Black Death, the famous mid-fourteenth-century pandemic outbreak of the plague, ravaged the entire Eastern Hemisphere and killed as much as a quarter of the people of Europe. Islam, now led by powerful nomad peoples of the Asiatic steppes, was more dangerous than at any other time since the original Arab conquests, and most of eastern Europe came under the rule of the Muslim Tartars and Turks.

But these crises did not stop the continuing evolution of civilization in western Europe, and in some ways they even spurred it on. Merchants reinvested their profits in industry and banking as well as trade, so that a capitalist sector of the economy began to appear alongside the agrarian and guild-based economy of the Middle Ages. Partly in order to serve the needs of this new economy, and helped by its ability to mobilize resources and create markets, late medieval inventors came up with a series of world-changing devices: three-masted sailing ships, firearms, printing presses, and mechanical clocks. All these inventions built on inspirations from Islam and the Far East, but for the first time they gave Europe technological leadership among the civilizations of the world.

Capitalism and new technology also helped change the way in which rulers governed their countries. Rulers began to rely on taxes and loans from bankers as well as on the services of vassals. New infantry weapons overthrew the battlefield supremacy of mounted knights. The invention of cannon made the castles of nobles vulnerable to attack, as well as being too expensive for anyone but leading rulers to afford. The Italian city-states came under the rule of efficient despotic governments that practiced the naked pursuit and use of power. The rulers of western European countries followed Italian models as they began to build up centralized governments, hire mercenary soldiers, and collect taxes directly from their subjects.

However, the feudal notion persisted that subjects had rights against rulers, and that rulers could not do things that affected these rights without their subjects' consent. Accordingly, to get the backing of their subjects for their new measures, rulers in many countries began to summon representative assemblies—most famously, the English Parliament.

Finally, increased contact with the Far East, the renewed Muslim threat, the capitalist pursuit of profit, and the competitive ambitions of powerful western European rulers all led to the single most momentous undertaking of late medieval Europe: the exploration of new routes across the Atlantic Ocean to distant continents. The explorers not only succeeded in their original goal of finding routes to the Far East that would bypass Islam, but also came into contact with the civilizations of the Western Hemisphere, which were less advanced than those of the Eastern Hemisphere and therefore easy to conquer.

The result was a historic change in the position of Christian Europe among the civilizations of the world. The capitalists of western Europe gained worldwide profits. The region's governments fought worldwide wars against each other for control of worldwide trade and empire. The Christianity of western Europe, both Protestant and Catholic, became a worldwide religion, for the first time outreaching Islam. The eastern European countries became well organized and strong enough to conquer the Tartars and hold off the Turks, stabilizing the land frontier with Islam while Western civilization broke out from Europe across the oceans to spread its influence around the globe.

Crises and Problems of the Late Middle Ages

Deep-running historical currents were already transforming European institutions by 1300, but the events of the years that followed hastened the process. The fourteenth century was a time of turmoil and disaster, comparable to the late fifth century B.C. in Greece (pp. 96–99) and the turbulent third century A.D. in Italy (pp. 144–146). Social unrest and epidemic disease threatened the very foundations of the political and economic order, while Asiatic invaders menaced the very existence of Christian Europe.

THE CALAMITOUS FOURTEENTH CENTURY

Social unrest, growing out of the deprivations and indignities that the common people had suffered for centuries, grew acute in western Europe after 1300. Revolts by peasants against their feudal masters had occurred at various times and places throughout the Middle Ages. Now, however, they took place on a larger scale than ever before.

The trouble started with the weather. Early in the century, arctic cold and heavy rains swept across Europe, flooding farmlands and shortening the growing season. For the three preceding centuries, the population had grown, and more and more land had been taken under the plow to feed it (p. 238). But now there was no more wild territory that could be turned into productive fields, and the available farmland had reached the limit of what it could produce with the methods in use at the time. The combination of bad weather and population increase that strained the limits of resources led to

Fig. 7.1 Crushing an Uprising. This manuscript illustration shows the capture of a town in fourteenth-century France. Foot soldiers hack at rebels and throw them into a river; mounted knights patrol the streets, and noble ladies, dressed in the height of fashion, look on unconcerned.

widespread hunger and starvation. The resulting famine had further effects: lower human resistance to disease, severe dislocations in agriculture and commerce, and fiercer competition among individuals, classes, and nations.

In 1320, a peasant uprising started in northern France. Its leaders expressed the grievances of the poor and a religious hope that the lowly would overthrow the highborn and establish a "Christian commonwealth" of equality for all. Farmers and poor people from the cities joined excited mobs as they made their way across the countryside. The rebels seized arms, attacked castles and monasteries, and destroyed tax records. As tales of atrocities circulated, the nobility and the clergy grew alarmed. Finally, after Pope John XXII had condemned the outlaws, mounted bands of knights took to the field and ruthlessly slaughtered the weary peasants (*Fig. 7.1*). But the resentment and anger of the poor persisted.

Another uprising occurred about a generation later, in 1358. It was called the *Jacquerie, from Jacques, the* popular catch-name for a peasant. Kindled in a village near Paris, the revolt spread like wildfire across the country. At its peak, perhaps 100,000 men, women, and children were on the rampage. Though better equipped and better organized, the Jacquerie suffered the same fate as the earlier rebellions. For two months, both the peasants and the avenging nobles engaged in burning, looting, and killing.

France was not alone in its ordeal. Similar uprisings occurred all over Europe throughout the century. In England, the Peasants' Revolt of 1381 followed the pattern of the Jacquerie. Marked by murders and burnings, it was finally crushed by the ferocity and treachery of the nobles and the king.

Adding to these miseries were the drawn-out struggles between the English and French monarchs. (This prolonged conflict, which began in 1338, was later referred to as the Hundred Years' War.) Though combats were limited mainly to the noble class, they brought ruin to the farms and towns of France, the principal battlefield. The long-term political consequences of the Hundred Years' War will be discussed later in this chapter (pp. 314–316); the widespread physical damage was the immediate and most distressing result.

But the cruelest blow of all to fourteenth-century Europeans was the bubonic plague, or *Black Death*. The plague was part of a pandemic (universal) outbreak of the disease that had begun in southwestern China about 1340 and spread in a few years throughout the Eastern Hemisphere. It took about seven years to reach the Black Sea region, from where merchants from the city of Genoa brought it to Europe.

The infection, which is carried by black rats but is spread by fleas from rats to humans, had already devastated much of Europe in the sixth century (pp. 198–199). For several centuries thereafter, there were no massive outbreaks; but now the plague spread in about four years to all parts of the Continent and to the British Isles. Having had slight prior contact with the infection, people were highly susceptible, and their capacity for resistance had been weakened by widespread malnutrition. The first symptom of the disease is the appearance of *buboes,* painful swellings in the lymph glands, often in the groin. Fever and chills follow, along with dark spots on the skin. (Since the dark spots usually precede death, the pestilence came to be known as the "Black Death.") After the primary form of the plague has become established in humans, it can be transmitted directly by breath to other humans. This second form, which invades the lungs, is even more lethal than the first and causes death within a few days.

The plague continued to flare up from time to time until the late seventeenth century—one of the last outbreaks was the Great Plague of London in 1665. It killed perhaps a quarter of all the inhabitants of Europe during the fourteenth century (25 million out of a population of 100 million), and it was not until the sixteenth century that the population reached its earlier level. In addition to its toll in death and suffering, the plague had drastic economic, social, and psychological effects. Death became a universal obsession. Many people interpreted the plague as a punishment from God that called for severe personal penitence; some thought the end of the world was at hand.

By the close of the fourteenth century, the effects of the plague had diminished, and life returned more or less to normal. But the medieval patterns of society had been severely strained by the plague and by the other catastrophes that had struck the people of Europe. The bonds holding people and institutions together were close to the breaking point: between serf and lord, journeyman and master, noble and king, layman and priest, priest and pope. The bonds held for yet a while. But new forces, new ideas, and new relationships were on the rise; with the gradual recovery of European strength and confidence, the new ways would shortly overcome the old.

EASTERN EUROPE IN THE LATE MIDDLE AGES

The crisis of the late Middle Ages affected eastern Europe even more severely than western Europe. Whereas the western countries mastered the crisis and rebuilt European civilization, those of the east never completely recovered. Instead, they took on the role in European civilization that they have retained down to the present day: that of "junior partners" to the western European countries and of bulwarks against threats to Europe from farther east.

Byzantium and Orthodoxy. The differences between western and eastern Europe were partly religious and cultural, originating in the divergences between Roman and Byzantine civilization and the schism between the Latin (Catholic) and Greek (Orthodox) churches (pp. 172–201, 282). The capture of Constantinople by western crusaders in 1204 led to more than two hundred years of chaos in the Balkans, a region that Byzantium had earlier dominated but which the Latin Empire of Constantinople and the restored Byzantine Empire after 1261 were both too feeble to control (p. 282). Serbia and Bulgaria, both already important earlier in the Middle Ages (p. 225), reappeared for a time as powerful independent kingdoms, but eventually they disintegrated as a result of disputes over the succession to their thrones and rivalries among their nobles. Other rulers held power over less prominent Balkan ethnic groups—the Slavic Bosnians and the non-Slavic Albanians and Romanians (p. 200)—which thereby took their first steps toward independent nationhood. Meanwhile, on the outskirts of the Balkans, powerful neighbors—Venice, Hungary, and most menacingly, the Turks (pp. 298–299)—took advantage of the situation to gain power and influence in the region.

Yet the spiritual and cultural hold of Byzantium over the Orthodox peoples of eastern Europe was as strong as ever. The most successful Bulgarian and Serbian rulers took the title of *tsar* or "emperor" (p. 225), surrounded themselves with Byzantine pomp and ceremony, and dreamed of ruling in Constantinople. They established national "Bulgarian" or "Serbian" Orthodox (as opposed to "Greek Orthodox") churches, and appointed "autocephalous" (independent) patriarchs to run these churches. They built splendid cathedrals and monasteries, where glowingly colored frescoes and icons (holy pictures) seemed to give believers a glimpse of the other world, and where monks wrote chronicles and lives of saints in the ancient Slavic religious language and the Cyrillic alphabet used by all the national Orthodox churches (p. 224). In many ways, the late Middle Ages were the golden age of Slavic Orthodox culture.

As a result of the disaster of 1204, this flourishing Orthodox world now viewed the Catholic Church as an enemy and a traitor to Christianity. The Bulgarian, Serbian, and restored Byzantine rulers sometimes struck bargains with the popes, submitting to papal religious authority in return for western military and political support. But these bargains never lasted, for suspicion and hatred of Rome were firmly anchored in the hearts of the Orthodox faithful. Thus the estrangement between the Catholic and the Orthodox churches hardened into bitter religious hostility.

Eastern European States and Societies. The divergence between western and eastern Europe was also social, economic, and political. With the rise of a dynamic urban trading and industrial economy from 1000 on, western Europe forged ahead of the east. While the ruling families of western Europe came to accept the principle of primogeniture (p. 221) in the eleventh and twelfth centuries, those of eastern Europe continued to divide their dominions among numerous heirs until the end of the Middle Ages, thereby weakening their dynastic power. Europe came to be divided into a group of stronger and more highly developed western countries and a group of weaker and less highly developed eastern countries. The second group included not only the Orthodox countries but also Catholic Poland and Hungary and the eastern territories of the Holy Roman Empire (*Map 5.5*, p. 222). This division has persisted down to the present day.

In the Middle Ages, the western countries gained many advantages from the presence of a group of less advanced countries on their eastern borders. For western Europe, the east provided territories for colonization and emigration and sources of foodstuffs and raw materials. In the twelfth and thirteenth centuries, crusaders from the Holy Roman Empire conquered many still pagan tribes on the southern and eastern shores of the Baltic Sea (*Map 5.5*, p. 222). Throughout these eastern borderlands of the Holy Roman Empire and on into Poland and Hungary, masses of German colonists moved in, clearing the land for agriculture and founding new towns and cities—a migration that nationalist-minded German historians centuries later christened the "Drive to the East." Along with the migration of Germans, there was also a mass movement of Jews, fleeing eastward from western European anti-Semitism (p. 283).

In the newly colonized territories, and throughout much of the rest of northeastern Europe, farmers grew grain and flax, and lumberjacks logged timber, for export westward. The towns of eastern Europe functioned as trading outposts of the important German coastal cities that headed the dominant commercial organization of northern Europe, the *Hansa* (p. 300). Farther south, the commerce of Hungary, Serbia, Bulgaria, the Byzantine Empire, and the Black Sea regions (*Map 5.5*, p. 222) was controlled in the same way by the Italian city-states (pp. 309–310).

Sometimes this western expansion into eastern Europe led to conflict. For more than two hundred years, the rulers of Poland vied for control of the Baltic coastlands with the Teutonic Knights, a group of crusading warriors that had led the German conquest of the pagan tribes of that region. The kings of Hungary likewise contested the hold of Venice on the eastern shores of the Adriatic Sea, Hungary's main outlet for seaborne commerce. In Bohemia, which was inhabited mainly by the Slavic Czechs, resentment at German immigration, along with religious disputes, led eventually to a bitter internal and international struggle, the Hussite Wars (p. 369).

But these conflicts were exceptional. So long as the rulers of eastern Europe did not feel directly threatened with the loss of their local power and independence, they usually accepted western immigration and commercial domination. The kings of Bohemia, Poland, and Hungary welcomed and even invited Germans and Jews to settle in their countries, for the sake of the increased prosperity—and increased tax revenues—that the newcomers brought. Noble landowners were glad to supply foodstuffs and raw materials to the west; and with the kings weakened by the division of their territories and family disputes, it was often the nobles who wielded the greatest share of power. Following the Black Death, there were far fewer peasants available to grow the profitable crops. For this reason, from the fifteenth century onward, the nobles of eastern Europe began to reimpose the burdens of serfdom, which had earlier been loosened there as in the western countries (pp. 238, 303). As a result, from the eastern territories of the Holy Roman Empire through Poland, Hungary, and on into Russia, serfdom persisted down to the nineteenth century (pp. 373, 416, 431, 495, 514).

Moreover, in eastern Europe, social differences were also ethnic. In any particular region, the peasants belonged to one ethnic group and the townspeople to other groups—usually German, Jewish, and in the Balkans also Greek—and it was not unusual for the nobles and rulers to belong to yet another ethnic group. In the Middle Ages, eastern Europe was on the whole more tolerant of ethnic and religious diversity than western

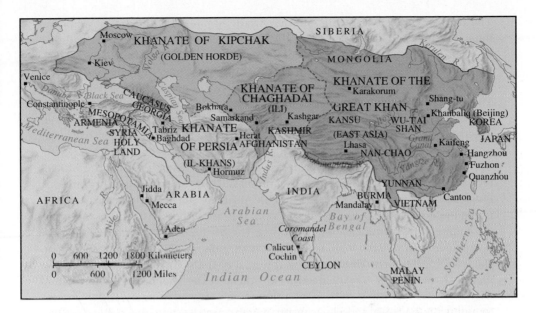

Map 7.1 The Mongol Empire. The Mongols built a larger empire than any conquering people before them. From his capital of Khanbaliq ("City of the Ruler"—the modern Beijing), the Great Khan ruled China, Korea, and the Mongol homeland. Lesser khans, loosely subject to the Great Khan, ruled territories stretching across the steppes as far as Russia. The empire was stable and secure for most of the thirteenth century. For the first time in history, so far as is known, Europeans (including Marco Polo) could visit the Far East.

Europe. But in modern times, under the impact of religious, nationalist, and class ide- ologies of western European origin—combined, in the Balkans, with the lasting effects of Turkish conquest (pp. 298–299)—eastern Europe would be torn by savage strife.

Mongols, Tartars, and Russia. There was another important difference between east- ern and western Europe: the eastern countries, unlike the western ones, were constantly exposed to attack from the increasingly advanced nomadic peoples of the steppes (pp. 57–58). This threat reached its height in the thirteenth century when a pagan nomadic people from the Far East, the Mongols under Genghis Khan, built an em- pire that stretched from China to Europe (*Map 7.1*). Between 1237 and 1240, Genghis's grandson Batu Khan devastated much of eastern Europe and conquered Russia.

It was not long before the Mongol empire broke up, but Russia's ancient capital city of Kiev and most of the country's southern territories (present-day Ukraine) remained under the rule of the Tartars or Kipchak Turks (known to the Russians, supposedly be- cause of their luxurious encampments, as the "Golden Horde"), a Muslim people eth- nically related to the Turks who were allied with the Mongols. The northern regions, however, were held by native Russian vassals of the Tartars, most prominent among whom were the rulers of the city and surrounding territory (principality) of Moscow. Over the generations, even while acknowledging Tartar overlordship, Moscow ex- tended its power over most of northern Russia. The new state was in close contact with the Byzantine-influenced Slavs of the Balkans and shared in their flourishing religious and cultural life, but its rulers already controlled far more people and territory than the Bulgarian and Serbian monarchs who so proudly called themselves tsars. Eventu- ally, the Russian rulers would take—and keep—that title (p. 414).

The Turks in Europe. Meanwhile, another Asiatic empire was forming that would be not much smaller than that of the Mongols but would last far longer—that of the Turks. By origin yet another nomadic people of the steppes, the Turks had entered the Middle East and become Muslims in the ninth century (p. 278). Under the Seljuk dynasty in the eleventh and twelfth centuries, they had already conquered most of Asia Minor. Then, in 1299, they came under the rule of a new dynasty, the Ottomans. Combining the warlike prowess of their nomadic ancestors with highly civilized diplomatic and governing skills, the Ottoman Turks expanded their empire by stages rather than all at once—and their first target was the chaotic and divided Balkans.

The Turks first landed in Europe in 1352 and quickly took over most of the limited territories that the restored empire of Byzantium still possessed. Within fifty years, the Bulgarians and Serbs were conquered, and the Albanians not long after that. There followed Byzantium's final destruction. In 1453, the last outpost of the thousand-year-old empire, Constantinople itself, was taken. The city founded by Rome's first Christian emperor became the capital of the Ottoman sultan, and Justinian's cathedral of Hagia Sophia was turned into a mosque (pp. 202, 203). Outlying areas of the Balkans, such as Greece and the Romanian territories, still had to be "mopped up," but by 1500, the Turks were ready to turn their attention to new targets: Hungary, the lands surrounding the Black Sea, and a huge swath of Arab countries stretching right across the Middle East and North Africa. Once again, Christian Europe confronted a vast and expanding Islamic empire.

For the Christian peoples of the Balkans, life as subjects of this empire had its advantages. The Turks brought unity and peace such as the region had hardly ever known since Roman times, and with unity and peace came prosperity, trade, and low taxes. Trade flourished and towns burgeoned. Constantinople, where a shrunken population had lived amid abandoned buildings at the time it was conquered, grew to a size of three-quarters of a million, thereby regaining its long-lost position as Europe's largest city.

Turkish rule even brought religious benefits, for the sultans, in accordance with Muslim principles (p. 205), tolerated other monotheistic religions. The Orthodox majority not only could practice their religion freely but were also sheltered by Turkish power from Catholic efforts to make them accept the supremacy of the pope. Furthermore, under Muslim law, the Orthodox faithful constituted a separate community, governed in secular as well as spiritual matters by their own religious leaders. As a result, the Orthodox bishops, headed by the patriarch of Constantinople, actually wielded greater worldly power under the Turks than they had ever enjoyed under the Christian emperors. Jews, too, fleeing Christian persecution around 1500 in Spain and Portugal, found the Turkish-ruled Balkans a haven of tolerance, and were far more prosperous and respected there than those who fled western Europe for Poland and Hungary.

All the same, most non-Muslim ethnic groups in the Balkans now had a status of second-class citizens from which there was only one way of escape: conversion to Islam. Most noble landowners in the Bulgarian, Serb, Bosnian, and Albanian territories seem to have accepted the new religion so as to maintain their privileged status, and eventually became Turkish in language and customs as well. Christian heretics, who were numerous in Bosnia (p. 254), probably also converted in large numbers without losing their ethnic identity; so did Albanians moving eastward, out of their mountainous homeland along the Adriatic Sea, into the nearby Serb-inhabited plain of Kosovo.

There was one non-Muslim group that was highly favored: the wealthy Greek upper class, which became almost a second ruling group of the Balkans under the Turks. Now that Venice was kept at bay by Turkish power, Greek merchants and bankers controlled the region's trade and finance, and provided men and ships for the Turkish merchant and war fleets. Likewise, Greek patriarchs and bishops held religious and worldly power throughout the Balkans, regardless of whether the local faithful were Greek or not. The other Orthodox nations of the Balkans now consisted almost entirely of peasants, with no leadership apart from their parish priests, and little literate culture except what survived in monasteries. What mainly kept their national identities alive was a flourishing oral culture of epics and folktales, telling and retelling of the tragic events and defeated heroes of the struggle against Turkish conquest.

In all these ways, new religious and national divisions, coupled with inward-looking ethnic identities and long memories of defeats to be avenged, grew up throughout the Balkans. When Turkish rule grew weak and oppressive in the eighteenth and nineteenth centuries, and finally disappeared early in the twentieth century, this mixture would flare into frequent murderous conflicts.

Throughout the centuries of Mongol and Turkish expansion, the western European countries on the whole left eastern Europe to its fate. The popes generally strove for friendship with the pagan Mongols, in hopes of converting them to Latin Christianity and turning them against the Muslims. Such western help as came to the Balkans against the Turks was generally too little and too late—and was usually coupled with highly unwelcome demands that Orthodox rulers and their subjects submit to the pope. Up to the end of the Middle Ages, what prevented the invaders from advancing still farther into Europe was above all the huge size of their empires: both the Mongols and the Turks found their territories difficult to control, and they had to fight wars on many other fronts besides Europe. Later, in the sixteenth century, powerful central and eastern European rulers emerged who mounted effective resistance to the Asiatic conquerors (pp. 318, 412–413, 416). Thus, with little effort of their own, the western countries were insulated from attacks from the east as they pursued the innovations that would create modern Western civilization.

The New Economy

We have already pointed out that the rise of trade and towns was a crucial development of the eleventh and twelfth centuries (pp. 238–241). But from 1200 onward, European commerce began to take on a new look. Medieval guilds and merchants had generally operated within limited areas and had been subject to local regulation (pp. 242–243). The system fostered the growth of trade and industry while Europe was still relatively backward, but by 1200, its very success was beginning to reveal its limitations. The masters of the workshops paid money wages and hoped to make a profit from their enterprises, but most prices were fixed, and the scale of business was small. As a result, the master's profit was seldom large, and whatever he made usually went to the upkeep of his shop and the care of his family. Though capital was used in trade and industry, very little capital *surplus* could be built up. The *entrepreneur* (organizer of a business) still thought primarily in terms of production for use in a limited market; he had not yet grasped the idea of the unlimited accumulation and expansion of capital. The true capitalist had not yet emerged.

THE BIRTH OF MODERN CAPITALISM

Italian merchants had taken the lead in the revival of trade in the eleventh century (p. 239), and in the thirteenth, they pioneered the development of capitalism. They dominated the profitable trade of the Mediterranean, and many of them made quick fortunes in their dealings. Finding that they could not spend all their profits immediately, they hit upon the idea of *reinvesting* the surplus.

This novel idea made it possible for the successful trader to launch new, more ambitious enterprises. Soon he was no longer traveling about as an ordinary merchant but was minding his account books at home as a "capitalist." He directed his energies to extracting profits from his varied enterprises and reinvesting them to gain *more* profits. Thus emerged the features that have characterized the "capitalist system" for the past five centuries: its boundless profit seeking and its dynamic spirit.

What the Italians achieved as the middlemen between Europe and the Far East, the merchants of the port cities of Germany achieved in the Baltic Sea area. They found that by pooling their resources, they could build fleets and win joint trading privileges abroad, and by the fourteenth century, the leading towns of northern Germany had formed an effective commercial league, the *Hansa,* which dominated the trade of northern Europe from England to Russia. The cities of the Hanseatic League monopolized the foreign trade of northern Germany and set up outlets in the trading centers of Russia, Poland, Norway, England, and the Low Countries. From these far-flung outposts, rich profits flowed in to the capitalists of northern Germany (p. 296).

The merchants of the Low Countries prospered too. The wharves of Antwerp and Bruges saw a steady stream of Italian ships carrying oriental spices and silks, and vessels from the Baltic loaded with furs, timber, and herring. The industries of England and the German Rhineland also sent their products into the Low Countries. By the fifteenth century, a truly international commerce had developed—extensive enough to provide for the accumulation of profit surpluses and for the growth of a capitalist class.

INNOVATIONS IN BUSINESS ORGANIZATION

The new leaders of enterprise scrapped many of the traditional methods of doing business. In the eleventh and twelfth centuries, the masters of each guild, collectively, had served as its directing force, and within a framework of rules, individual masters had run their own shops. After 1200, several industries cast off the shackles of the guilds. Still, entrepreneurs found that they could seldom go it alone. Commerce was becoming more extensive and complex, requiring a pooling of capital and of managerial talent. Gradually the *partnership* came into favor as a unit of business organization. A special form of partnership, the family firm, was the most common. A group of relatives could best handle matters demanding secrecy and mutual trust, and could ensure the continuance of the enterprise.

The displacement of guild control is best illustrated by the woolens industry, in which the traditional association of master weavers, journeymen, and apprentices had disappeared in most areas by 1400. The industry was taken over by enterprising merchants who bought the raw wool and put it out to semiskilled laborers for processing—first to spinners and then to weavers, dyers, and cutters in succession. The workers were paid by the piece or by measure, but ownership of the materials stayed with the merchants. They sold the finished cloth or garments in the international market at whatever price they could get.

The wool merchants thus reaped the profits of both industry and commerce. They paid the laborers at a low rate and permitted them no say in the conduct of the business. Moreover, the laborers were forbidden by law to organize or strike. This "putting-out" or "domestic" system was the principal mode of production in early modern Europe. It destroyed the close relationship between master and journeyman that had existed in the medieval guilds. It made profit the sole concern of the entrepreneur and diminished the worker's sense of creativity. The antagonisms that grew up between these entrepreneurs and the workers foreshadowed the fierce conflicts that were to mark the later industrial world.

THE RISE OF BANKING AND BANKERS

As Europe moved from a largely self-sufficient economy to an economy geared to trade, the old techniques of exchange and finance proved inadequate. By 1200, money had come back into general use, but the further expansion of enterprise depended not so much on money itself as on new instruments of exchange and credit.

Perhaps the most important substitute for money payments was the *bill of exchange,* which was similar to a modern bank draft or check. A merchant with branch offices in various countries usually made a side business of selling drafts that were payable by his firm in some other city. A Venetian who bought linen from Antwerp, for example, would find it inconvenient to ship money to the Low Countries every time he placed an order. Instead, he could go to a Venetian firm that did business in Antwerp and purchase a draft payable by its office there. The seller of the linen in Antwerp was perfectly willing to accept this bill of exchange, for he knew he could collect on it in his own city. Rather than demand cash for it, however, he would probably endorse the bill (sign it on the back) and hand it over to someone else to whom he, in turned, owed money. Thus the bill would become a kind of paper money.

The first bankers were successful merchants who had accumulated a profit surplus and who wished to reinvest it. They found that the business of moneylending, though risky, could bring high returns. Commencing in the thirteenth century, large-scale moneylending became normal. It had been practiced in earlier times, but on a smaller scale—partly because the economy was not so prosperous and partly because the Church condemned *all* interest-taking as usury (lending at an excessive rate). In consequence, lending at interest had been done chiefly by Jews, whose faith did not forbid it. This particular role of the Jews no doubt contributed to the periodic anti-Semitic outbursts in Europe (pp. 283–284).

With the expansion of commerce, however, many people came to realize that lending was a useful and acceptable activity. The traditional argument against interest payments was based on a revulsion against taking high rates from individuals "in distress." But loans to businessmen engaged in profitable enterprises, or to kings and popes, were obviously of a different sort. These loans could be *productive,* and they exposed the lender to risks that justified some reward. Many theologians agreed that this kind of lending was not sinful, and the popes themselves were among the biggest borrowers. Consequently, small-scale Jewish moneylending came to be overtaken by large-scale Christian banking.

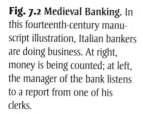

Fig. 7.2 Medieval Banking. In this fourteenth-century manuscript illustration, Italian bankers are doing business. At right, money is being counted; at left, the manager of the bank listens to a report from one of his clerks.

Italian merchants first moved into the banking business during the thirteenth century (*Fig. 7.2*). In the next century, Florence became the leading center of international finance. The Bardi and Peruzzi families, for example, advanced huge loans to King Edward III of England. Later, Edward refused to repay the loans and thereby forced those families into bankruptcy. But in the fifteenth century, a new house of bankers, the Medici, emerged in Florence. This family restored the financial power of the city and came to dominate its political and cultural life.

Banking spread north from Italy to the rest of Europe. Jacques Coeur, a French merchant who had made a fortune in trading with the Far East, was appointed royal treasurer by King Charles VII of France in 1439. Taking advantage of his position at the court, Coeur acquired extensive holdings in mines, lands, and workshops and thus became one of Europe's most powerful international bankers. He used his enormous wealth for the benefit of his family and built a palace worthy of a king in his native town of Bourges.

The wealthiest and most famous banker of the period was Jacob Fugger of Augsburg. Southern Germany, in the fifteenth and sixteenth centuries, was sharing in the prosperity of growing commerce—and had the added resource of copper and silver mines. Some years earlier, capital had been put into the mining industry for the first time, permitting miners to dig more deeply and more efficiently with improved tools. The leading entrepreneurs of the industry soon took control of smelting and metalworking as well as mining, concentrating the direction of all operations in a few hands. The workers, who had formerly been independent producers, now became voiceless employees of the capitalists.

The Fugger family drew immense wealth from these and other enterprises and channeled their surplus into banking. Jacob pushed the family business beyond Germany by opening branch offices in the major commercial centers of Europe. He ventured into buying, selling, and speculating in all kinds of goods, and he provided financial services to merchants, high clergy, and rulers. One of his most spectacular operations was to lend half a million gold coins to King Charles I of Spain. Charles wanted to "buy" the office of Holy Roman emperor through payments to the imperial electors

(p. 317). A good capitalist, Jacob was also a good philanthropist. He and his brothers built, as evidence of their piety and generosity, an attractive group of dwellings for the "righteous" poor of Augsburg. They still stand, near the center of the city, as a memorial to the Fuggers' wealth and charity.

THE IMPACT ON SOCIAL STRUCTURE AND VALUES

The forces released by the rise of capitalism not only undermined the guilds, they also weakened the manorial system (pp. 234–238, 242, 243) and undermined the values that the Church had traditionally tried to promote in economic life.

The End of Serfdom in Western Europe. The most far-reaching change, which affected all relationships between nobles and peasants, was the substitution of money for payments in goods or services. Traditionally, the serfs were required to cultivate the lord's demesne, the land reserved exclusively for his benefit. Toward the close of the medieval period, the nobles often found it advantageous to rent out their demesnes to free tenants, who were now able to sell their produce at nearby markets and pay their rents in cash (pp. 238). The serfs preferred this arrangement because it released them from extra work; the lords preferred it because they could usually find cheap day labor and still have cash left over from the serfs' payments.

The next step was the emancipation (freeing) of the serfs. Now that the nobles no longer depended on forced labor, they were willing to grant the serfs freedom. In most instances, the freedman remained on the land as a tenant and in exchange for his freedom paid his lord a lump sum or extra rent. But in so doing he normally lost his former hereditary right to stay on the land, which meant that he could be ousted when his lease expired.

By 1500, serfdom had disappeared from England and had become a rarity in western Europe. The medieval lord, with his rights to the produce and services of the peasantry, had become a capitalist landowner living off his rents. Though many of the great estates remained intact, the pattern of relationships had been changed. In short, the spirit of commercial enterprise had spread to the countryside. Merchants began to buy estates and play the role of landed aristocrats, while intermarriage between bourgeois and landed families further blurred the old distinctions. Serfs were becoming freemen, merchants were becoming landholders, and noblemen were becoming capitalists. (The different development in eastern Europe, where trade and capitalism actually strengthened the bonds of serfdom, is discussed on p. 296.)

The Challenge to Medieval Values. Dislocations in society led to dislocations in ethics. The merchants and bankers of the early modern period made profit their immediate and constant concern; they separated commercial dealings from Christian ethics. In their desire for gain, they differed only in degree from the landlords and rulers of medieval times. The latter, however, could cover their activities under the cloak of feudal and royal rights and customs; the upstart bourgeois had no such camouflage at hand. The religious ideals of meditation, prayer, and giving were overtaken by the goals of hard work, punctuality, and saving. One might suppose that the Church would have mobilized its forces against this challenge to its ancient ideals, but it no longer wanted to. The popes and the higher clergy, like almost everyone else in Europe, were dazzled by the new riches and became obsessed with wealth, elegance, and power.

The active carriers of the new morality were the bourgeois. Some members of this class, like Jacques Coeur and Jacob Fugger, attained high levels of influence, equal to that of counts or princes. The position of the class as a whole, however, advanced much more slowly. So long as land and its products remained the main forms of wealth, and so long as successful bourgeois invested their profits in buying land and sought to acquire noble titles, the nobles would keep their traditional position as the leading group in society. But from the sixteenth century onward, bourgeois ideals had a growing influence on society as a whole.

The New Technology

The rise of capitalism, like the rise of trade and towns earlier in the Middle Ages (pp. 239–241), went hand in hand with technical progress. Now, however, increased contact, both peaceful and warlike, with the intercontinental civilization of Islam exposed Europe to the often superior technology not only of the Arabs but of the Far East as well (p. 208). Like many earlier peoples, the Europeans adapted and improved on advances that they learned from other civilizations, and in this case the result was a whole series of world-changing technical innovations. Sea transport, warfare, book production, the measurement of time—all were revolutionized by the Europe of the late Middle Ages.

Navigation and Ship Design. One of the basic needs of growing medieval trade, in an age when transport was far more efficient by water than by land, was for reliable methods of navigation—for sailors at sea to be able to know where they were and what direction they must sail in to get to the ports for which they were bound. Building on geographical techniques developed by the Greeks and transmitted and improved on by Arab scientists, European mapmakers began to produce accurate charts of the Atlantic and Mediterranean coastlines. New instruments of navigation came into use. One was the north-pointing *magnetic compass,* a Chinese invention, which helped the navigator set and hold the course of his ship. Another was the *astrolabe,* a sighting instrument devised by Arab astronomers, which enabled the navigator to calculate his latitude (his position north or south of the equator) by determining the height of the sun and stars above the horizon. Both these aids to navigation were in common use on the seaways of Europe by the early fifteenth century. Soon they would help guide sailors across oceans to distant continents.

Growing trade also needed ships that were large, strong, and easy to handle. Shipwrights in Venice and Genoa, whose craft had to be able to carry goods to and from western Europe, combined features of ship design from both the Mediterranean and the stormier Atlantic waters. They borrowed the triangular sails of their Mediterranean neighbors the Arabs, which made for easy maneuvering, as well as the stout hulls and square, wind-catching sails of Atlantic ships . The result was a new kind of vessel, the *carrack*—the first three-masted sailing ship, which appeared about 1400 and would soon become the workhorse of overseas exploration (*Fig. 7.3*). Carracks had a combination of speed, maneuverability, and seaworthiness that was unmatched by the vessels of the most advanced non-European civilizations. And eventually, three-masted ships would also become unbeatable fighting vessels, once they were equipped with another late medieval invention—cannon.

Fig. 7.3 An Oceangoing Ship. Sixteenth-century engraving showing a carrack, the workhorse of European overseas exploration. The two forward masts carry square sails for speed, and the mast nearest the stern carries a triangular sail for maneuverability. The vessel is armed with cannon along the sides and at the stern.

Firearms. The Chinese invention of gunpowder first became known to Europeans in the twelfth century, when Christian warriors in North Africa and Spain found their Muslim foes using the quick-burning substance against them as an incendiary (fire-starting) weapon. The idea of confining the powder so that it would actually explode, and using the force of the explosion to hurl a projectile, seems to have been a European one. At any rate, "firepots" or "tubes" (Latin, *canones*) are first mentioned in Italian documents of the 1320s.

Up to around 1400, cannon were too small, inaccurate, slow to operate, and dangerous to their users to make much real difference to warfare, but in the fifteenth century, improvements came quickly. Makers of church bells began using their knowledge of large-scale bronze-casting methods (pp. 240–241) to manufacture guns that were solid and safe to use. Ironworks started turning out cannonballs that were heavier in proportion to their size, more accurately spherical, and far quicker to make than stone ones. Carpenters devised wheeled gun carriages that made the weapons mobile and absorbed the recoil when they were fired. Water-powered hammermills (p. 240) were adapted to crush charcoal, sulfur, and dried animal droppings so as to produce gunpowder by the ton. Mathematicians tackled the problems of weight and motion involved in accurate aiming. By 1500, cannon could be relied on to smash any stone castle or town wall—let alone the wooden hulls of sailing ships—and scaled-down versions of the big weapons were beginning to appear, which were small and handy enough for a single soldier to load, aim, and fire.

Printing. European traders and warriors earlier in the Middle Ages had learned from the Muslims of peaceful as well as warlike Chinese inventions—most notably, of paper and of woodcut printing. Paper, made mainly from rags that were beaten to a pulp with water and various chemicals (p. 240) and then dried into sheets in special frames, was much faster and cheaper to make than parchment (the skin of lambs or calves), the traditional European writing material.

Likewise, printing with woodcut blocks was faster than writing out books by hand. The process involved carving a whole page of text and illustrations in mirror image out of the surface of a single block of wood, then smearing the block with ink, and pressing a sheet of paper onto the block with a roller. By 1400, small books and items such as playing cards (an Arab pastime that had spread to Europe) were commonly produced in this way. But woodcut printing was an expensive way to produce large books with many pages, since hundreds of blocks had to be painstakingly chiseled and then thrown away when the job was finished.

Supposing, however, that each individual letter were made in mirror image on its own tiny block, many such blocks could then be put together to form the text of a page, and taken apart and reassembled any number of times to make new pages. The printing process would become fast and cheap, even for the longest books.

This had already occurred to printers in China and Korea, but the idea had never caught on there—partly because of the large number of characters in Far Eastern writing systems, which made it hard to manage all the different blocks. When the same idea struck Johann Gutenberg, a businessman in the German city of Mainz, he had the basic advantage of belonging to a civilization that used an alphabetic writing system with relatively few characters (p. 42). Even so, it took twenty years of tinkering and much technical wizardry to put the idea into practice. Gutenberg's greatest inspirations were to make the tiny single-letter blocks ("types") out of metal so that they could be quickly cast in molds rather than laboriously carved, and to adapt the centuries-old olive or grape press (pp. 127–128) to apply quick and accurate pressure to the paper lying on the ink-smeared type. By about 1450, he had developed a reliable system of printing with "movable" (reusable) type.

The new method of printing, with its drastically reduced costs, for the first time made it possible to mass-produce books, and the international trading and credit networks of early capitalism enabled books to find a mass market. By 1500, there were more than a thousand printers at work in Europe, and nearly ten million books had been printed. The influence of the printed word was infinitely greater than that of the written word had been before. The spread of religious and cultural movements like Renaissance humanism and the Protestant Reformation, as well as the growth of powerful centralized governments with their need for law books and many kinds of standardized paperwork—all were helped along by the Gutenberg printing process.

Clocks. Along with printed books and firearms, the late Middle Ages also saw the introduction of history's first widely used automatically operating machine, the mechanical clock. The basic idea of the clock seems to have come from astrolabes, which used dials with revolving pointers as sighting devices to measure the motion of the sun, moon, and stars across the sky. Sometime late in the thirteenth century, inventors in various countries began tinkering with ways to make the pointer actually "imitate" these heavenly bodies—in particular the sun—by moving around the dial. Since the hours and days were reckoned by the motion of the sun, the effect would be that the motion of the pointer would measure the passage of time.

Of course, for this to happen, the pointer would have to be made to turn by itself. A falling weight, attached to a cord wound around a spindle, could provide the necessary turning power. But there would also have to be mechanisms to slow the weight's fall and "wind it up" again when there was no more cord left to unwind, and gearwheels to slow the turning motion still more, so that the pointer would move round the dial no more than once in a day.

It seems to have been mechanically minded English monks, looking for improved ways of regulating their communities' complex daily routines of work and prayer (p. 184), who first came up with practicable solutions to these problems around 1300. But it was not long before the lives of townspeople, with their hours of work fixed by guilds or settled privately between capitalists and their employees, also came to be regulated by the new time-measuring machine. High in a tower of town hall or cathedral, it was visible to all as its hand (usually only one of them) moved, with no human intervention, in step with the movement of the sun itself; and all could hear its tones as, thanks to an improvement that was not long in coming, it struck the changing hours of the day.

In these ways, late medieval Europe took the first steps toward the modern age of automation, mass production, mass communications, and firearms. And already by the end of the Middle Ages, firearms and the new sailing ships were helping rulers to build powerful centralized governments and sailors to explore and conquer across the world.

The New Politics

Intimately bound up with economic evolution and expansion were new developments in the patterns of government. The fact that all classes of society now made payments in money, coupled with the rise of trade and banking, made it easier than before for rulers to mobilize the resources of their countries. They could collect rents from peasants on their personal landholdings (p. 303), like other landowners. They could levy tariffs on trade, or even get involved in commerce themselves. They could find ways to collect money from their subjects who lived on the lands of other lords, by way of national taxation. And if the money from all these sources fell short or was slow in coming in, wealthy bankers like the Bardi, the Peruzzi, or the Fuggers could come up with loans that were big enough to tide them over.

With all this money available, rulers no longer had to rely on personal service from independent-minded vassals. Instead, they could do government business through officials who were bound to obey orders; and they could apply capitalist methods to warfare, making contracts with mercenary captains to supply trained soldiers complete with weapons.

In practice, these new methods were often no more efficient than those of feudalism. Most officials were not paid from the central government treasury but were expected to charge the public fees which they put directly into their own pockets—a license for every kind of fraud and corruption. Military contractors might take the money but not provide the soldiers—or they might provide the soldiers but not get their money, in which case the soldiers would mutiny for lack of pay. But the new system did have one

© The Granger Collection, New York

Fig. 7.4 Infantry, Cavalry, and Artillery. Early sixteenth-century woodcut showing "state-of-the-art" warfare. In front, opposing masses of foot soldiers wielding pikes and halberds (axes on poles) have come to grips; where they meet, there is a grim "killing zone." Behind them, cannon are emplaced to bombard a walled town; to left of the town, more pikemen are shown, leveling their weapons for the charge. At rear, armored knights charge against each other in the traditional way.

great advantage over feudalism: it put control of the government and the armed forces directly in the hands of the major rulers.

This growth of centralized government was also furthered by dramatic new developments in warfare (*Fig. 7.4*). So long as rulers needed knights on horseback to win battles and nobles could rely on their castles as safe refuges, neither the independence nor the lands of the feudal elite could be touched. But during the fourteenth and fifteenth centuries, new weapons came into use that acted as "equalizers" between foot soldiers and horsemen. First was the *longbow,* which could penetrate the armor of knights and disable their horses at a distance. Then came the *pike* (a long spear against which horses would refuse to charge), and various types of axes, knives, and hooks on long poles, which could be wielded against men on horseback. Finally, by 1500, cannon had revolutionized siege warfare by their ability to smash stone fortifications. In these ways, the feudal nobles lost their ability to win battles or to hold out in their castles. Furthermore, the new weapons, particularly siege cannon or cannon-armed ships, were so expensive that only governments, supported by taxation and loans, could afford them.

None of these developments deprived the nobles as a group of their leading place in society and government. Bourgeois officials and bankers usually invested their profits in land, and expected to be rewarded for their services to rulers with titles of nobility; nobles did not find it beneath their dignity to be royal officials or captains of mercenary soldiers. Sometimes, nobles were able to prevent the growth of centralized government, as happened in the Holy Roman Empire, or to roll it back for a time, as in sixteenth-century France (pp. 396–397, 410). But countries that remained without strong central government for any length of time were bound to become dominated by more powerful neighbors, or even to be swallowed up by them. From the late Middle Ages on, the successful European countries would be ones where feudalism, with its divisions into small, loosely centralized units, gave way to larger units of centralized power.

ABSOLUTISM IN PRACTICE: ITALY

Ironically, it was in one of Europe's most politically fragmented regions that the new politics began, for the theory and practice of strong government were pioneered by city-states, popes, and kings in Italy. It was here, too, that the modern practice of *diplomacy* and the development of the body of law that would one day govern *international relations* first began. A tribute to the early ambassadors is the portrait by Hans Holbein the Younger (*Fig. III.1*, p. 286).

Ever since the end of the Roman Empire, Italy had been the scene of continual struggles for power among barbarian, Muslim, and Norman invaders, Byzantine emperors, Holy Roman emperors, and last but not least, the popes, who remained constant foes of Italian unity down to the nineteenth century. As a result, Italy had become a permanently divided country (*Map 7.2*, p. 310).

City-States and the Rise of Despotism. In the north of the peninsula, with its commercial and industrial wealth (p. 239), many cities had the resources to defend and govern themselves. Thus in the Middle Ages, northern Italy developed into a collection of rival city-states struggling against each other for survival and mastery. Like the ancient Greeks, citizens of Italian city-states identified strongly with the city of their region rather than with any broader territorial unit. The city was near and familiar; it was worthy of reverence and sacrifice. Dante, for example, was more a Florentine than an Italian.

During these turbulent years, significant changes occurred in the internal politics of the Italian cities. By the end of the thirteenth century, most of the cities had won self-rule from the feudal nobility and had emerged as *sovereign* (independent) republics. Their citizens, however, proved incapable of stable self-government. The usual source of trouble was the rivalry among factions: the bankers and capitalists, rising rapidly in wealth, tried to take political control from the more numerous small merchants, shopkeepers, and artisans. At the same time, wealthy families competed with one another for special advantage.

Out of the struggle, political "strong men" had emerged during the fourteenth century. Sometimes they were invited to assume power by one or another of the factions looking for an alternative to chaos; sometimes they invited themselves. In the main, they supported, and were supported by, the bankers and capitalists. The rest of

Map 7.2 Fifteenth-Century Italy. A thousand years after the fall of Rome, Italy was still in some ways the center of Europe. Two city-states, Milan and Florence, were Europe's main banking centers. Two others, Genoa and Venice, controlled Mediterranean empires and sea routes. The popes, rulers of the States of the Church, also governed the international Catholic Church. But the world of these "great powers" was threatened by still greater ones—the Ottoman Turks, France, and Aragon (in Spain), which already ruled the south of Italy.

the citizens submitted (except for occasional plots and uprisings), for they, too, preferred stability to the disorders of freedom.

The new rulers, generally known as *despots,* used an iron hand to restore peace and economic well-being and relied on hired soldiers to preserve their power. Since there was no citizen militia to speak of during this period, professional mercenary warriors decided the conflicts within and between cities.

The soldiers were organized in armed bands led by enterprising captains (*condottieri*). With no sentimental attachments, they generally sold their services to the highest bidder. On occasion, they turned down all bids and seized power for themselves. These hardened and crafty adventurers, thirstier for money than for blood, remained an unpredictable force in the politics of Italy.

One of the most famous was Francesco Sforza, who made himself ruler of Milan in 1450. Assuming the title of duke, which a preceding despot had purchased from the Holy Roman emperor, he governed from his moated *castello* ("fortress-palace"). Under the shrewd policies of Sforza and his heirs, Milan enjoyed a half-century of peace and prosperity. In the fashion of the times, the despot supported the arts and attracted scholars to his city.

The city of Florence, though it had experienced numerous upheavals and short-lived tyrannies, remained a republic. In 1434, authority settled in the hands of Cosimo de' Medici, heir to a wealthy banking family. He and his successors generally held no major political office, but controlled the machinery of government through persuasion, manipulation, bribery, and force. The Medici advanced their own financial interests and the interests of their supporters, and treated rival groups harshly. Despite their methods, they enjoyed the support of most citizens, for they put an end to the rioting and confusion that had previously prevailed in the city. The most illustrious member of the family, Lorenzo the Magnificent, was a man of extraordinary ability and artistic taste. Under his rule, in the latter part of the fifteenth century, Florence reached its peak as the cultural center of Italy.

The only major city to escape the trend toward absolutism was Venice, whose government had been stable since the beginning of the fourteenth century. A small group of rich merchants managed to keep political control over the city and saw to it that the rest of the citizens were excluded from participation. The constitution of Venice, the envy of its less fortunate rivals, provided that the city be governed by councils and committees elected from and by the merchants. The "official" head of state was a *doge* (duke), who was chosen for life by the leading families. Though the doge was treated with respect, he had no independent authority.

Despotism in Central and Southern Italy. In the middle of Italy, the States of the Church, originating in the eighth-century Donation of Pepin (p. 212), were under the rule of the pope. In the south of the peninsula was the feudal Kingdom of the Two Sicilies, ultimately descended from territories conquered by the Normans in the eleventh century (p. 223).

In the States of the Church, the pattern of despotism was barely distinguishable from that in the rest of the country. The popes hired condottieri to reduce subject cities to obedience, engaged in wars and alliances, and used their office to further the wealth and rank of their families. The Borgia pope, Alexander VI, was notorious for his faithlessness and immoral behavior; Julius II had a fondness for waging war; and the Medici Leo X was noted as an elegant connoisseur of the arts. Such qualities were hardly those of Peter the fisherman, but they were typical of the despots of the new era.

South of Rome, the Kingdom of the Two Sicilies was equal in area to all the rest of Italy (*Map 7.2*). It was created in 1435 when Alfonso of Aragon, the ruler of Sicily, won a major victory in the Italian power struggle by acquiring the kingdom of Naples on the mainland. Though the southern Italian countryside was agrarian and backward, under Alfonso's "benevolent" despotism, cultural life flourished in the capital at Naples.

By the middle of the fifteenth century, the stronger Italian states had expanded their boundaries, absorbing weaker neighbors. A kind of balance of power developed among the three leading city-states, Milan, Florence, and Venice, together with the States of the Church and the feudal Kingdom of the Two Sicilies. It was the interplay of these states with each other and neighboring states, as well as the despotic methods of their rulers, that formed the background to the thought of Niccolò Machiavelli.

THE THEORY OF ABSOLUTISM: MACHIAVELLI

Fifteenth-century Italy valued individual achievement above all—in commerce, in learning, in the arts. And yet in politics there was a pronounced tendency, as we have seen, to curb individual freedom. The citizens of the northern Italian city-states were proud and competitive men who by no means relished submitting themselves to absolute authority. But their long experience with factional rivalries and political instability had been disheartening, so that one city after another had accepted the rule of a despot.

In the judgment of many Italians, their whole nation would benefit from a unified, absolute government. Despotic rule had put down internal dissension in Milan and Florence, for example, but in relations between cities, anarchy still reigned. If a despot could bring all of Italy under his rule, these wasteful conflicts would cease. After 1500, the argument for unity grew stronger. The French and Spanish monarchs found that they could sweep into the Italian peninsula and easily subdue the divided cities, which were protected only by corrupt mercenaries. The invaders, with their loyal, well-equipped armies, kept Italy in turmoil for a century.

The most able spokesman for Italian unification and political absolutism was a Florentine, Niccolò Machiavelli, a onetime diplomat and a close observer of Italian affairs. He set down his basic views in a kind of manual, which he intended as a guide for the despot who would one day liberate Italy. *The Prince,* written in 1513, was dedicated to the Medici rulers of Florence.

The Secularization of the State. Machiavelli's book marks a sharp turn in Western political thought. Medieval philosophers had seen government as one aspect of God's administration of human affairs: the Church and its officers direct Christians toward *spiritual* salvation, which is eternal; the state looks after their physical well-being, which is *temporal* (limited in time). Yet both branches of authority are subject to divine law.

Thomas Aquinas had discussed this matter in his *Summa Theologiae* (pp. 270–271). He reasoned that temporal power is invested by God in the people as a whole, who delegate it to suitable persons. The state, then, whether monarchical, aristocratic, or democratic, is not a power in itself. It receives its authority from God (through the people), and it must exercise its power for Christian purposes and in a Christian manner. To be sure, medieval practices often seemed to contradict this doctrine, but these were explained away as the result of human frailty or error.

Machiavelli met the doctrine head on, rejected it, and stated the "modern" view of politics and the state. He felt no uneasiness in breaking away from traditional Christian teachings. He blamed the papacy for keeping Italy divided and felt that Christian teachings, in general, did not contribute to good citizenship. In his commentary on the ancient Roman Republic (*Discourses*), Machiavelli observed that the pagans had encouraged civic pride and service, whereas the early Christians had urged people to turn away from public affairs. The state, he thought, does not rest on any *supernatural* authority. It provides its own justification, and it operates according to rules that have grown out of the "facts" of human nature. He thereby removed politics from Christian ideology and placed it on a purely secular (worldly) level.

Machiavelli's view of government was influential in his own time and prophetic of the evolution of the state in future times. Largely through his influence, the word *state* came into use to mean "a sovereign political unit." And the evolution of European states from the sixteenth century onward moved in the direction outlined by Machiavelli. The state was to become the central force of modern times, a law unto itself, subjecting both institutions and individuals to its will.

The Pursuit of State Power. Means, as well as ends, were a matter of concern to Machiavelli. As he saw it in *The Prince,* the central problem of politics is how to achieve and maintain a *strong* state. Much depends on the character of the citizens. He admired the Romans of the ancient Republic and the self-governing Swiss of his own day, but he concluded that a republican form of government could prosper only where the citizens possessed genuine civic virtue. But Machiavelli regarded the Italians of his day as corrupt beyond correction (except, possibly, by a strong prince). He wrote that they were, in general, "ungrateful and fickle, fakers, anxious to avoid danger, and greedy for gain; they offer you their blood, their goods, their life, and their children, when the necessity is remote; but when it approaches, they revolt." With citizens of such character, how was a state to be founded and preserved?

Machiavelli advised that a ruler first turn his attention to military strength. The prince, he believed, must devote himself to the training and discipline of his troops and must keep himself fit to lead them. He must practice maneuvers and study the decisive battles of the past; it was thus that Caesar had learned from Alexander. Machiavelli had only contempt for the condottieri and their hirelings, for they had proved ruinous to Italy and incapable of defending the country from invasion. He advised the prince to build an army of citizens drawn from a reserve of qualified men under a system of compulsory military training, for their interests would be bound up with his own. Machiavelli thus introduced to modern Europe the ideas of universal male conscription (draft) and the "nation in arms."

Military strength is not enough in itself, however. For the prince must be both "a lion and a fox." The lion, Machiavelli explained, cannot protect himself from traps, and the fox cannot defend himself from wolves. A ruler, in other words, must have both strength and cunning. Machiavelli noted that the most successful princes of his time were masters of deception. They made agreements to their advantage, only to break them when the advantage passed. He declared that the ruler should hold himself *above* normal rules of conduct, Christian or otherwise —that the only proper measure for judging the behavior of a prince is his *power*. Whatever strengthens the state is right, and whatever weakens it is wrong; for power is the end, and the end justifies the means.

Machiavelli cautioned the prince never to reveal his true motives and methods, for it is useful to appear to be what one is not. Though the prince must stand ready, when necessary, to act "against faith, against charity, against humanity, and against religion," he must always *seem* to possess those qualities. Machiavelli summarized his advice to the ruler as follows:

> Let a prince therefore aim at conquering and maintaining the state, and the means will always be judged honorable and praised by everyone. For the vulgar [common people] is always taken in by appearances and the result of the event; and the world consists only of the vulgar, and the few who are not vulgar are isolated when the many have a rallying point in the prince.

BUILDING THE NATIONAL MONARCHIES

The rising monarchs of Spain, France, and England were cut to the Machiavellian pattern. Building on the inheritance left by strong rulers of feudal times (pp. 229–233), they were aided in their efforts to extend state power still further, in each country, by growing national sentiment.

The Unification of Spain. In Spain, the spirit of patriotism had been ignited during the fierce struggle to expel the Muslims. When the kingdoms of Castile and Aragon, which had led the fight, were linked through the marriage of Queen Isabella of Castile and King Ferdinand of Aragon in 1469, the way was open for a unified Spain. With popular backing, Ferdinand and Isabella broke the independence of the feudal lords, who had taken over most of the lands from the defeated enemy. They also reformed the Spanish Church, gaining the right to name its bishops. So vigorous were the centralizing efforts of the two rulers that the foundations of royal absolutism were completed by the close of Ferdinand's reign (1516).

France: The Monarchy and the Nation. In France, the richest and most populous kingdom of Europe, with some twelve million inhabitants, the most powerful stimulant to national feeling was the Hundred Years' War (1338–1453). This lengthy off-and-on struggle with the English arose out of conflicting feudal claims. The English rulers had long resented the loss in 1204 of their northern French fiefs (p. 233); in the fourteenth century, stronger than they had been before, they decided to regain these territories. Their king, Edward III, laid claim to the throne of France as well. (The succession was in doubt, and Edward was the grandson of an earlier French king.) And so the long campaigns began. By 1420, the English had triumphed, and most of France north of the Loire River (*Map 7.3*, p. 318) was given to Henry V, now the English king. The French forces also agreed to accept Henry as heir to their throne.

This humiliation at the hands of foreigners brought forth a surprising reaction among the French people, who had traditionally been indifferent toward feudal struggles. After the throne fell vacant, they found an inspiring leader in a peasant girl called Joan of Arc, who in 1429 persuaded Charles, the disinherited son of the former French king, to march to Reims (the ancient crowning place of French monarchs). Claiming divine guidance, Joan herself took command of a small military force and vowed to drive the English from the soil of France. The young prince, responding to Joan's appeal, was crowned in Reims Cathedral as Charles VII and went on to lead his armies to final victory over the English. Joan did not live to see that day, however. Soon after Charles's coronation, she fell into the hands of the English, who tried her as a witch and burned her at the stake. The martyred Joan has been revered for centuries as the glorious symbol of French patriotism.

The Hundred Years' War was frightfully destructive to France (p. 294) and interrupted the growth of royal authority. But when it was over, Charles VII and his son, Louis XI, were able to proceed more rapidly than before with the work of political centralization.

In their efforts, the kings of France were able to take advantage of the new developments in warfare to build armies that were more than a match for any aristocratic opponent. Such armies required more revenue than the monarch had ever received through ordinary feudal dues, but Charles succeeded in raising this revenue. In preparing for his final thrust against the English, he summoned the Estates-General of France in 1439. This body, which represented the three estates, or classes, of France (p. 234), had the sole power to authorize new taxes. In a burst of patriotic fervor, the Estates-General approved Charles's national army and voted a permanent tax for its support. This tax was called the *taille* ("cut"); it was a kind of land tax levied mainly on commoners. With this substantial new revenue, supplemented by income from his own lands, Charles could now afford to act independently of the nobles. He acted by deception, threats of force, and marriage alliances to bring the great fiefs back into the royal domain (his personal holdings).

Louis XI pursued his father's methods and more than doubled the size of the royal domain. His final victory was to win back the duchy of Burgundy, which had long been

751	987	1328	1589
Carolingian Dynasty (Frankish Kingdom)	House of Capet (Kingdom of France)	House of Valois	

Hundred Years' War
(1338–1453)

independent even though it was legally subject to the French crown. Its last duke, Charles the Bold, had tried to expand his holdings into a major state between France and Germany. But his plans had miscarried; and when he died without a male heir in 1477, Louis took over the duchy.

The success of the monarchy in consolidating its power changed the role of the nobility. Wealthy bourgeois gave financial aid to the monarchs. (Jacques Coeur, it will be recalled, was Charles VII's treasurer and financed his later military campaigns, p. 302.) And the expanding towns became firm allies of the king. But nobles who cooperated kept their ancestral estates and inherited titles, were awarded favored positions as military or civil officers of the king, and together with the Church, were exempt from the *taille*. The monarch, for his part, now had at his command the services of an *elite* class.

The Estates-General lingered on, meeting from time to time at the request of the crown. It might have developed into a constitutional body of importance, as did Parliament in England, but class and sectional rivalries, coupled with skillful manipulation by the monarch, prevented this from happening. The Estates-General never became a serious challenge to royal authority, and it was to be swept into the dustbin of history in 1789 (pp. 460–462).

Nothing now checked the king's control over secular matters. But absolute power, to be absolute, must embrace ecclesiastical matters as well. While taming the nobility, Charles did not overlook the clergy. The archbishops, bishops, and abbots held vast properties in France and had a strong influence over the people. They generally supported the king in his efforts to centralize authority and end feudal warfare. They were jealous, however, of their own privileges, and they wavered in their loyalty between king and pope.

After the extreme ambitions of the papacy collapsed at the end of the thirteenth century (p. 257), the French clergy had tended to act independently of Rome. Although the French bishops and abbots had no thought of overturning traditional Church doctrines and institutions, they resented papal interference in local administrative affairs. The popes, however, continued to insist on the right to fill important ecclesiastical offices, a privilege that brought them handsome fees. They also siphoned off a substantial proportion of Church revenues to Rome.

As national feeling grew in the country, there was mounting sentiment for establishing a self-governing "Gallican" (French) Church. In 1438, the clergy, with Charles's approval, formally declared its administrative independence of the pope at the Council of Bourges. The decree limited papal interference and forbade payments and appeals of local decisions to Rome. This move gave clear control of the Gallican Church to the French bishops under royal protection. Louis XI revoked the decree, however, and his successor, Francis I, struck a bargain with the pope that extended the influence of the crown over the Church. In a treaty with the pope (the Concordat of 1516), Francis secured the right to appoint French bishops and abbots. In return for this right, the papacy was granted the first year's income of Church officeholders in France. The pope thereby gained additional revenue and the alliance of a powerful monarch; the king, outflanking his own clergy, brought the Church within his grip.

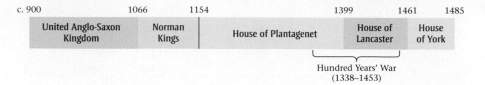

c. 900		1066	1154		1399	1461	1485
United Anglo-Saxon Kingdom		Norman Kings	House of Plantagenet		House of Lancaster	House of York	

Hundred Years' War
(1338–1453)

England: The King and Parliament. In England as in France, the Hundred Years' War had strengthened national feeling, but in the end, because the war was lost, it had weakened the position of the monarch. In addition, in order to raise the substantial sums of money needed for the expeditions to France, the kings of England had been compelled to make concessions to Parliament.

The origins of Parliament go back to the thirteenth century. Already in 1215, the Magna Carta had expressed the idea that the king needed the advice and consent of his barons before taking measures such as the levying of unaccustomed taxes (p. 233). Later in the century, as both king and barons sought to enlarge their bases of support in the country, the custom grew up of inviting representatives of the shires (counties) and boroughs (towns) to such meetings. In 1295, Edward I held the precedent-setting "Model Parliament," and during the next century, Edward's successors called Parliament frequently in their need for additional funds to carry on the war in France. Parliament evolved into two chambers: the House of Lords and the House of Commons. In the former sat the great barons and clerics of the country—lords who held fiefs and offices directly from the crown. In the latter sat representatives of the shires and of certain towns. The Lords were the more important house for several centuries, but the Commons would ultimately have the upper hand in lawmaking.

The king had to turn to Parliament for approval of new revenues, and its members took advantage of that to gain privileges and redress of their grievances. It will be recalled that the Estates-General, a similar body in France, voted a royal income tax without demanding concessions from the monarch. England's Parliament did not agree so readily to the desires of the king and kept a firm hold on the purse strings. Its control over lawmaking and general administration came only slowly, however. At the close of the Hundred Years' War, England suffered a series of calamities. Confidence in the crown was shattered by the defeat in France, and the nobles proceeded to slaughter one another in civil warfare led by the house of York against the house of Lancaster (known as the Wars of the Roses). Henry Tudor, who would become Henry VII, was a relative of the Lancasters. When he at last emerged victorious from these wars in 1485, the strength of the nobles had been broken, and the nation was yearning for peace and unity.

Henry restored law and order and put an end to private warfare, and the sixteenth century, the century of Henry VIII and Elizabeth I, was an era of despotic power in England. But unlike the rulers of France, those of England continued to rely on Parliament, using it both as a safety valve for grievances and to give legitimacy to their actions. Parliament actually became more important and more deeply involved in government than before, and in the century to follow, it would replace royal absolutism with parliamentary government.

THE ECLIPSE OF THE UNIVERSAL EMPIRE: GERMANY AND THE HABSBURGS

Strong central government did not come for centuries to other parts of Europe. Neither Germany nor Italy became a unified state until 1870. The reasons for this contrast

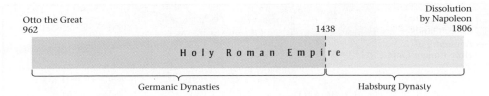

Otto the Great
962

1438

Dissolution
by Napoleon
1806

Holy Roman Empire

Germanic Dynasties   Habsburg Dynasty

with the rest of western Europe were many and complex, but the main one was the failure of the Holy Roman emperors to turn their territories into an effectively governed feudal state during the Middle Ages (pp. 231–232).

As a consequence, while Spain, France, and England were growing into strong centralized powers, Germany lingered on as a patchwork of hundreds of fiefs. There were landed nobles with a bewildering array of ranks and titles, wealthy officials governing "free" cities under imperial charters, and powerful Church lords. The ranking princes of the empire had won the status of permanent *electors* as the result of an imperial decree of 1356 (known as the Golden Bull). Three of these electors were ecclesiastical: the archbishops of Cologne, Mainz, and Trier. Four were lay: the Count Palatine of the Rhine, the duke of Saxony, the margrave of Brandenburg, and the king of Bohemia. When an emperor died, these seven men met to choose his successor. This was often an occasion for lengthy bargaining—even bribing (p. 302), for the imperial office, though its power was declining, remained the political position of highest prestige in the West.

Dynastic (family) considerations, more than concern for national feeling, guided the politics of central Europe. The family that played the dynastic game most skillfully was the Habsburgs, whose influence on the Continent endured for centuries. Rudolf of Habsburg, a south German prince, had been elected Holy Roman emperor in 1273. The main reason for his being chosen was that he was a minor figure who could be counted on not to create trouble for the independent-minded barons and bishops. And in fact he took his imperial responsibilities lightly, choosing to concentrate on expanding his family holdings. In a struggle with a defiant vassal (Ottokar of Bohemia), Rudolf won the duchy of Austria and surrounding territories. He assigned these lands to his sons as imperial fiefs, and Austria thus became the base of the family properties.

The Habsburgs' mounting power worried the electors, who, when Rudolf died, chose an imperial successor from another, less affluent family. For nearly two centuries the Habsburgs were then passed over, but in 1438 another member of the family (Albert) was elected emperor. Thereafter, until the end of the Holy Roman Empire in 1806, the Habsburgs managed to keep the office in their possession while extending their wealth and power by means of carefully arranged marriages.

The family holdings reached their greatest extent when they passed to the young man who was to become Emperor Charles V. His inheritance included the ancestral lands on the Danube River, Luxembourg, and the Netherlands, as well as Spain (with Hispanic America), Sardinia, Naples, and Sicily. When he secured the imperial title in 1519 (by buying the votes of the electors), he added to his family's domains the overlordship of Germany and northern Italy (*Map 7.3,* p. 318). In 1526, the death (in battle against the Turks) of the king of Hungary and Bohemia, to whom Charles was related by marriage, brought him the title to those two kingdoms as well. This was by far the greatest aggregation of territory, both in and outside Europe, that any European monarch had ever ruled.

Map 7.3 Europe in 1526. Two "great power" dynasties now dominated Europe—the Habsburgs, reinforced by the worldwide resources of Spain, and the Ottomans, Muslim rulers of the Balkans as well as the Middle East and northern Africa. Their rivalry gave room for four competing middle-sized powers: England, France, Poland, and Russia. But this balance of power was liable to be upset by western European struggles for worldwide power, by competition for control of the small states of Italy and the Holy Roman Empire, and by the beginning religious conflicts that led to the Reformation.

But the aggregation proved exceedingly hard to control. The emperor encountered an endless series of political, military, and personal frustrations, and he at last retired to a monastery in 1556. Before abdicating, Charles divided the Habsburg properties into an eastern and a western portion. The western portion consisted of Spain, the family's other territories in western Europe and the Mediterranean, and the vast Spanish overseas empire. The eastern portion included Austria, Bohemia, Hungary, and the rule of the Holy Roman Empire.

Far from weakening the Habsburgs, the division of their territory into more manageable portions actually strengthened them. Working closely together, the Spanish and Austrian branches of the dynasty dominated Europe for a hundred years. It was they who sustained the Roman Catholic Church against the Protestant revolt, fought the Turks to a standstill, and organized the Spanish empire in the New World (pp. 326–327, 328–329, 413). In these ways, the Europe and the world of today still feel the effect of their power.

The New Geography

The expansion of Europe was the climax of the outward political, cultural, and religious thrust of European civilization that dated back to the tenth century. In addition, it was the final outcome of the gradual strengthening of Europe's links with other civilizations, which had been going on since the fall of the Roman Empire (pp. 208–209, 224–225). And it also came about as a combined result of all the other changes that took place toward the end of the Middle Ages. The need to respond to the renewed challenge of Islam, the vision of ever-growing markets and fathomless riches supplied by capitalism, and the rivalries of powerful centralized governments in western Europe all provided incentives for exploration and empire building in distant continents. Technical progress provided ships, navigational instruments, and weaponry for exploration, as well as printed books and maps to publicize the explorers' discoveries and stir up public opinion for yet more voyages.

Neither earlier Western civilizations nor non-Western ones of the fifteenth century were ripe for sustained exploration leading to domination of distant parts of the world. The reported landing by the Norwegian Leif Ericson around 1000 (p. 220) made only a slight impression in Europe. Likewise, a fifteenth-century non-European venture, in which the Ming emperors of China sent several powerful fleets ranging across the Indian Ocean from the East Indies to the African coast, came in the end to nothing. But in the fifteenth and sixteenth centuries, Europe—or at least a group of leading western European countries—was hungrier than ever before for contact with the outside world. Nothing in the history of world relations proved more fateful than the resulting far-flung encounter between Europe and other continents.

THE IMPULSE TO OVERSEAS EXPANSION

The expansion of Europe was partly the result of internal developments and partly also of changes in the wider community of civilizations of which Europe had come to be a part. Ever since the rise of Islam and of the nomadic peoples of the steppes had linked the civilizations of the Eastern Hemisphere, Europeans had benefited in many ways from membership in this wider community. They had tasted sweets, spices, and other luxuries from afar; they had enjoyed exotic pastimes such as card games and chess; and they had made use of non-European knowledge and inventions such as Arabic numerals, paper, and printing.

But Europeans had for long known little or nothing of the distant lands from which these things came to them. The Crusades (pp. 276–283) had carried them to the Middle East and excited their curiosity about the lands beyond. They knew the Black Sea and, of course, the Mediterranean. But the areas beyond were great blanks on their maps—reaching eastward and westward, perhaps to the "edges of the earth." Popular conceptions about the uncharted world were full of fanciful suggestions. Tales of sea monsters abounded, and sailors, fearful of the unknown, hugged the coasts in their tiny vessels.

Wider Horizons. In the thirteenth and fourteenth centuries, this European ignorance of the outside world began to change. The main reason was the rise of the intercontinental empire of the Mongols. As devastating as the Mongol conquests were to their victims in eastern Europe and the Middle East (p. 297), once established, their empire maintained peace and secure communications across the steppes for a hundred years (*Map 7.1,* p. 297). The civilizations of the Eastern Hemisphere were drawn together as never before. For the first time, Europeans were able to visit the lands beyond Islam and return to tell what they had seen.

Marco Polo, a thirteenth-century merchant of Venice, contributed more than anyone else to Europe's awareness of these lands. Members of the Polo family, after establishing trading contacts with the Mongol empire in western Asia, decided to journey to the far side of the empire. A long trek by caravan took them from the Black Sea to the Chinese capital of Beijing, where the Mongol ruler Kublai Khan held court as emperor. The Polos were welcomed with courtesy, and Marco remained there for many years before returning by way of Southeast Asia and the lands of the Indian Ocean. Once back in Italy, he wrote of his travels and revealed to astonished Europeans the fabulous wealth of the Orient.

Not long afterward, Europe received the same revelation about another hitherto unknown part of the world with which it did indirect business—West Africa (the lands in the bulge of Africa south of the Sahara). Early in the fourteenth century, the ruler of the powerful Islamic empire of Mali, fulfilling his obligation to visit Mecca (p. 207), passed through Cairo, where there was a large Italian trading community. Soon the news reached Europe that the wealthy pilgrim had handed out so much gold by way of gifts that the gold-based Egyptian coinage had temporarily lost a quarter of its value. Much else was reported about the ruler, his empire, and its resources. From this, as well as the reports of Marco Polo and other travelers, Europeans began to get a distinct idea of the distant lands and peoples of the Eastern Hemisphere—together with the uncomfortable but enticing feeling that among the intercontinental family of civilizations to which they belonged, they were, so to speak, poor relations.

Venice's Monopoly and the Muslim Threat. In the middle of the fourteenth century, the Black Death swept through Asia, Africa, and Europe (p. 294), leading to an intercontinental decline in prosperity and trade. Disputes among the successors of Genghis Khan led to the gradual collapse of the Mongol empire, and the rising power of the Turks (pp. 298–299) blocked off the western end of the overland routes to the Far East. Trade and other contacts between Europe and the Orient came to be channeled mainly through Egypt. Thus as Europe gradually recovered from the Black Death, it found the door to the outside world partly closed. But in the countries of western Europe, the effect was actually to increase their hunger for contact with distant lands.

Among the Italian city-states that had traditionally dominated the routes to the Middle East (p. 239), competition to control the chief remaining link with the Orient grew intense. The two largest cities, Venice and Genoa, fought a series of wars that ended in the victory of Venice. That city now became Europe's main gateway to the rest of the world. Venetian strongpoints and harbors were scattered along the coasts and islands of the eastern Mediterranean, guarding the sea routes, attracting the commerce of neighboring areas, and creating a Venetian trading monopoly in the region.

But the Venetians not only traded, they also developed new resources. In the Venetian-owned island of Cyprus, a fabulously profitable crop of Middle Eastern origin, sugarcane, was grown on plantations worked by gangs of slaves imported from countries to the north of the Black Sea. In these ways, Venice set an example of empire building and colonial exploitation that was carefully studied by the increasingly powerful and prosperous countries of western Europe—even while they envied the city's newfound monopoly of links with the East. As for Genoa, it was confined to the western Mediterranean and the sea routes leading from there to the lands of Europe's Atlantic coast. It was no coincidence that Christopher Columbus came from Venice's Atlantic-oriented rival city.

Furthermore, the fifteenth century saw a hardening in western European attitudes toward the neighbor and rival civilization of Islam. The Muslim world, for so long the connecting link between Europe and other civilizations of the Eastern Hemisphere, came to seem an irksome obstacle now that western Europeans had some idea of what lay beyond it. At the same time, the Turkish drive into eastern Europe left no doubt that Islam was a stronger and more dangerous enemy of Christendom than ever before— one against which it would be most desirable to find non-European allies.

New Routes to the East. In Portugal and Spain, France and England, dreams began to grow of acquiring the luxuries of the Orient direct from the producers— and paying for them with the gold of West Africa, obtained in return for European goods also sold on the spot. In this way, the middlemen's profits of Venice and Islam would be eliminated, going instead into the pockets of the western European nations. Besides, somewhere in the world beyond Islam, there might be powerful Christian rulers, or non-Muslim ones ripe for conversion to Christianity, who would join Europe's struggle against the followers of the Prophet.

To bypass Venice and Islam, it would be necessary to find new routes to distant destinations, leading through waters to which the western European countries had direct access—the Atlantic Ocean. No doubt this would be a difficult task, but at the same time as the western European countries were becoming hungry for access to distant lands, the development of three-masted sailing ships and cannon, as well as the improvement of aids to navigation, were giving them the knowledge and technical abilities necessary for exploration at sea.

By the fifteenth century, a race was under way to find sea routes between western Europe and the Far East. Europeans knew that no water passage existed between the Mediterranean and the Indian Ocean; hence, only two possibilities lay open. One was to try the way *south,* around Africa, then eastward to India. This was a relatively conservative plan, since ships could hold close to land during most of the voyage. The other was a much bolder, more theoretical plan: sailing due *west* across the open Atlantic. Though Africa and the Indian Ocean appeared on existing maps of the world, the Atlantic was uncharted. Geographers agreed that China must lie on the far side, but none knew for sure what distances or barriers might have to be crossed before reaching it.

The prizes to be won by whoever solved these geographical riddles were glittering indeed. The merchants of each western European nation hoped to win control of any newly discovered sea route, each excluding the merchants of the other nations, just as Venice monopolized the existing Mediterranean route. But the alternative possible routes were costly and risky to test, and merchants were often reluctant to finance voyages of exploration on their own. In any case, this could be better done by governments, because to set up commercial routes and bases, as the Venetian example also showed, would require political and military power.

The ambitious monarchs of western Europe grasped the opportunity. They hoped that by bringing wealth to their lands, they could strengthen the economic base of their countries and hence their own personal power and glory—not least, of course, against each other. In backing exploring ventures, the kings had the blessing and encouragement of the Church. Not only did the clergy support the idea of finding non-European allies against Islam; in addition, responding to the scriptural obligation to spread Christianity (p. 164), they were eager for new converts. Indeed, in the European religious turmoil of the sixteenth century (see Chapter 9), both Catholic and Protes-

tant missionaries, and even different Protestant churches and Catholic religious orders, would each strive against the other to baptize the maximum number of converts.

Thus three central motives combined to launch the brave sailors and their ships:
the desire of the clergy to combat Islam and spread the Gospel, the ambition of the
monarchs for power and glory, and the hunger of the merchants for gold—all sharpened by the spur of competition. That was why the expansion of Europe, once started,
spread so far and so fast.

THE VOYAGES OF EUROPEAN DISCOVERY

Once the voyages of exploration started, they produced many surprises. Africa turned
out to be a huge continent, stretching much farther into the Southern Hemisphere
than geographers and sailors had suspected. The westward distance from Europe to the
Indies was far greater than even the most pessimistic estimates had allowed, and that
vast stretch of ocean contained an unsuspected "New World." The world as a whole revealed itself as far larger, yet also far more accessible, than anyone, European or non-
European, had imagined.

Portugal and the African Route. The little kingdom of Portugal took the lead in sponsoring exploration. It had only a short history of independence, having emerged when
the Muslims were being expelled from the Iberian peninsula. Portugal had been a fief
for a period, subject to the Christian rulers of Castile, but in the twelfth century its
count proclaimed himself a king. The Portuguese monarchy, with its capital at Lisbon,
reached the height of its power during the sixteenth century. With astounding will,
enterprise, and ruthlessness, the Portuguese exploited vast territories and peoples overseas. Portugal became the early model of that form of worldwide cultural aggression
known as Western imperialism.

The Portuguese favored the relatively conservative plan of looking for a route
southward around Africa and then eastward to India. This would enable ships to hold
close to land so as to fill their holds with food and fresh water whenever they ran short.
It also held the promise of making direct and profitable contact with the wealthy peoples of West Africa. Exploration started early in the fifteenth century, but proceeded
slowly, partly because the African coastline proved far longer than expected, and partly
because the Portuguese rulers had many other concerns besides sponsoring exploration. In the course of developing the route, Portuguese forces occupied the nearby
Madeira Islands and the Azores and opened trade for gold, ivory, and slaves along the
coast of West Africa.

At last, in 1488 Bartolomeu Dias sailed farther southward than any earlier Portuguese sailor, and turned back only after the coastline turned northward, giving good
reason to hope that he had found the way round the continent. Ten years later, Vasco
da Gama followed the same route, continued onward until he reached Arab trading
cities in East Africa, and sailed across the Indian Ocean to the west coast of India (*Map
7.4*), thereby linking Europe with the Orient.

Spain and the Atlantic Route. Even before Vasco da Gama's voyage, Christopher Columbus had put into effect a much bolder plan, to sail *westward* to China and Japan. The
son of a weaver in Genoa, he had turned to the sea and to dreams of fame and fortune.
Finding his way to Lisbon, the center of activity in geography and navigation, Colum-

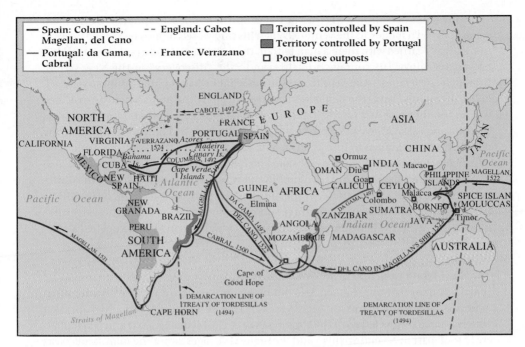

Map 7.4 European Explorers and Empires, 1492–1534. The early sixteenth century was the first era of Western-led globalization. Portuguese eastward explorers sailed round Africa, spread out across the Far East, and began building an intercontinental network of trading footholds among powerful peoples and states. Westward explorers inspired by Columbus's dream of a shortcut to the Indies ranged the coastlines of the Americas, across the Pacific, and eventually around the world. Vast New World territories fell to conquerors from the least wealthy and powerful of the civilizations of the Old World.

bus went into the business of making maps and sea charts. On occasion he accompanied ship captains on voyages down the African coast. He also gained sufficient social status to marry a daughter of the governor of Madeira, thereby gaining access to the royal court of Portugal.

When Columbus described his bold project to the king and asked for ships and provisions, the royal advisers pronounced his plans unsound. This was not because they thought that Columbus would fall off the edge of the flat earth. Like all educated people in Europe since contact with the Muslims had brought renewed knowledge of Greek philosophy and science (p. 269), the advisers new perfectly well that the earth was round. The question was: On the surface of the round earth, how far away was Asia from Europe, going westward? Columbus believed China to be about 3,000 nautical miles west of Lisbon—just near enough for a ship to arrive without resupplying with food and water. His critics put the figure at about 6,000 miles, much too far for a ship to sail without resupplying. (The actual distance is more than 12,000 miles.)

Though disappointed, Columbus was not a man to give up. He turned next to the Spanish rulers, Ferdinand and Isabella, who were now driving the last of the Muslims from the Iberian peninsula (pp. 313–314). His proposal was at first rejected by a commission of experts, for the same reason that had been advanced by the Portuguese. However, when the queen learned that Columbus was journeying north to offer his plan to the French king, she called him back and agreed to fund his expedition.

Columbus personified the early modern spirit. A modest capitalist, he invested some of his own money in the venture. When his tiny vessels dipped below the horizon in 1492, they carried with them a high faith in the individual—and a passion for wealth, power, and glory. His courage brought him to the "discovery" of the New World, though he never understood the true nature of what he had found. By a bizarre coincidence, he sighted land (the Bahama Islands) at precisely the point where he expected to find the shores of Asia (*Map 7.4,* p. 323). This convinced him that his geographical theories and calculations were correct and that he had reached his true destination. Yet if a continent unknown to him had not lain across his path, the admiral would have returned to Spain empty-handed—or sailed on to his death.

Still seeking Japan or China, Columbus spent several months exploring the Caribbean, whose islands he mistook for the "Indies." He sighted and claimed Hispaniola (Haiti) as well as Juana (Cuba). On three subsequent voyages, he strengthened Spain's claim to the Western Hemisphere. He died in 1506 still believing he had opened a westerly route to Asia.

The "New World" and the Pacific Ocean. After 1500, most geographers were convinced that Columbus had not reached Asia but had stumbled across a hitherto uncharted landmass. Among them was Amerigo Vespucci, a Florentine adventurer and mapmaker who was once connected with the banking firm of the Medici (p. 302) and who apparently took part in several Spanish and Portuguese voyages along the mainland coasts of the hemisphere, from Brazil to Florida. Vespucci wrote colorful letters about what he saw and coined the term "New World." Copies of his letters were widely circulated in Europe, and literate persons were soon discussing the "land of Amerigo," or America.

Conflicts quickly arose over the rival overseas claims of Spain and Portugal. To avoid trouble, the monarchs of the two countries agreed, in 1494, to draw a line between their spheres of interest. In the form of a circle of longitude, the Demarcation Line of the Treaty of Tordesillas passed through a point approximately 1,500 miles west of Cape Verde, the westernmost tip of Africa (*Map 7.4,* p. 323). The Portuguese were to confine their claims to territories *east* of the line, while the Spaniards would limit themselves to areas *west* of the line. The Spaniards believed that this division would give them all the lands in the area of Columbus's discoveries; they had miscalculated the eastward extension of the southern continent. As it turned out, a large portion of it (Brazil) reached into the Portuguese zone. Lisbon thus gained, unexpectedly, a claim in the Western Hemisphere.

After Vasco Nuñez de Balboa sighted the Pacific Ocean from the Isthmus of Panama in 1513, Europeans came to realize that beyond the New World lay another great stretch of water. The Spanish were disappointed that Columbus had failed to reach the Orient and still hoped that portions of it might fall within their treaty sphere. It was mainly with this in mind that Ferdinand Magellan set out in 1519 to find a passage to the Pacific through which he might sail on to Asia.

Magellan, a Portuguese in the service of Spain, guided his fleet of five ships down the coast of South America. He managed the hazardous passage around the southern tip of the continent into the Pacific (through straits ultimately named in his honor) and then sailed northwestward into the greatest of oceans. Following a frightful crossing of about one hundred days, during part of which his men lived on leather and rats, Magellan reached the island of Guam. With fresh provisions, he sailed on to the Philippine Islands, claiming them for Spain. There he was killed in a skirmish with the natives, but the expedition pushed on to the Spice Islands (the Moluccas), and the one remaining vessel, with a remnant of the original crew, finally returned to Spain by continuing westward around Africa (*Map 7.4*, p. 323). Magellan's expedition demonstrated conclusively that the earth was round, it dramatized the vastness of the Pacific, and it gave a truer idea of the globe's size.

Though Spain and Portugal felt that the overseas world was to be shared by them alone, the northwestern countries of Europe did not intend to stand idly by. The English, the French, and the Dutch were also seeking routes for direct trade with the Orient. A Genoese mariner, whom the English called John Cabot, was sent out in 1497 to seek a "northwest passage" to the Indies. Cabot touched the shores of the New World somewhere around Labrador and Newfoundland and thereby provided England with a claim to North America (*Map 7.4*, p. 323).

Shortly afterward, a Florentine, Giovanni da Verrazano, explored the North Atlantic coast for the king of France. Neither he nor anyone else ever discovered another water passage, but the search led to a close examination of the hemisphere's eastern shores from Labrador to the Straits of Magellan. It was only after hope of finding a shorter passage had been abandoned that the French and English took steps to settle the northern lands.

THE COLONIAL EMPIRES

The Portuguese and Spanish discoveries were followed by empire building. A network of Portuguese harbors and citadels arose along the coastlines of the powerful peoples and states of the Old World, while Spain overthrew entire vulnerable civilizations in the New World.

The Portuguese in the Far East. The Portuguese had won the race to the Orient when Vasco da Gama brought his ship into the harbor of Calicut, India. They had seen their goal clearly, attained it, and exploited their victory to the full. What they wanted was a monopoly over the richest trade in the world, and this they held for more than a century.

When the Portuguese arrived in India, they found a fabulously wealthy territory, which was not unlike Europe in that it comprised many different peoples and states, most of whom were held together by a common civilization and religion—that of Hinduism, which also dominated all of Southeast Asia. The peoples of India had only been united under one government for brief periods—usually imposed by foreign conquerors. The conquerors, after the tenth century A.D., consisted of successive armies of either Turks or Mongols, all converts to Islam. A Muslim sultan (ruler) at Delhi controlled most of India from about 1250 until 1398, when Delhi's power was smashed by yet another Mongol raider, Tamerlane (Timur).

At the moment of the Portuguese landing in 1498, India was once again divided into a number of separate kingdoms and was torn by hostility between Hindus and Muslims, friction among the various castes (classes), and warfare among local warlords. Even so, the local rulers were too strong for the Portuguese to conquer. With their superior warships, however, the newcomers were able to exploit the local turmoil so as to establish permanent trading settlements along the western (Malabar) coast.

The next strategic step for the Portuguese was to get control of the trade in luxury goods from the Indian ports to the Middle East and Africa. Having seized much of this trade from the Arabs, they extended their operations eastward to the Spice Islands and entered the ports of China and Japan. Here, too, they sought to gain control of the commerce in goods such as silks, lacquer, and spices. By about 1530, the coastlines of the Eastern Hemisphere from western Africa to the Far East were dotted with Portuguese-controlled harbors, naval bases, and trading stations. It was a repetition of what Venice had done in the eastern Mediterranean, only on an enormously larger scale—and, of course, to the great disadvantage of the Italian city. For it was the Portuguese who now monopolized the trade between Europe and the East, and it was Lisbon, not Venice, that had become Europe's gateway to the Orient (*Map 7.4*, p. 323).

The New World Empires. The Spanish looked on enviously as the Portuguese piled success on success. The demarcation treaty of 1494 had tied their hands east of the dividing line, and Columbus's failure in the west had for the time being destroyed their dream of breaking through from that direction. True, Magellan had finally arrived in the Orient, and Spain was eventually able to reach across the Pacific and acquire the Philippines as a foothold in Asia. But at first, the New World appeared to the Spaniards as a monstrous obstacle to their ambitions.

The Caribbean natives were peaceful enough, but they offered little of value to European traders. The only hope left to the Spanish adventurers was to fall upon some precious store of wealth—gold, silver, or gems. This they did in a manner and on a scale that surprised even those hardy soldiers of fortune. It was Hernán Cortés who first struck it rich. Attracted by rumors of wealth on the mainland, he organized and equipped a small expeditionary force in Cuba. He sailed off in 1519, without authorization from his superiors, and made for Mexico; there he had his soldiers proclaim him the legitimate ruler of the land, subject only to the king of Spain. Then he scuttled his ships so that his men had no means of escape.

Cortés's conquest of the Aztec empire was both daring and cruel. The Aztecs were a civilized people who boasted rich cities, splendid temples and palaces, and superb artistic creations. In the Caribbean islands, the Spanish had looted and destroyed as they pleased, but in Mexico, they faced an organized power, capable of resistance. The Aztecs suffered serious disadvantages, however. They had not invented the wheel, could not make iron utensils or weapons, and lacked horses and cattle. The government was oppressive and constantly threatened by tribal unrest. Finally, like the other natives of the Western Hemisphere, the Aztecs had not been exposed to European diseases; they therefore lacked resistance to the deadly germs that the invaders brought with them.

Cortés played upon the natives' superstitious fears, drew up his cannon, and set one tribe against another. In the face of constant personal danger, he succeeded in overthrowing the emperor, Moctezuma. While the defenders were falling ill with smallpox, Cortés then destroyed the Aztec capital and laid out a new one on the old site, which later became Mexico City. Rich prizes were sent back to the Spanish court, and the king recognized Cortés as captain-general and governor of "New Spain." Within a decade, his lieutenants had taken over most of Central America, from the Rio Grande to Panama (*Map 7.4*, p. 323).

This caesar of the New World had many freebooting companions and rivals, though none surpassed him as a conquistador (conqueror). South of the Panamanian isthmus, the most notorious adventurer was Francisco Pizarro. Learning of gold and silver in the Inca territories, he organized an expedition with royal approval. The Inca empire, like that of the Aztecs, rested upon an advanced society; it stretched southward along the

Andes Mountains from Ecuador through the modern states of Peru and Bolivia. Pizarro discovered, however, that the empire was torn by internal unrest and infected with smallpox—to which his own soldiers were resistant. Like Cortés, he made the most of the situation. Armed with superior weapons, Pizarro's men captured the ruler, Atahualpa, and held him for an extravagant ransom. After Pizarro had received tons of gold and silver, carried in from all parts of Peru, he had his prisoner baptized a Christian and then had him strangled. He next marched to the magnificent Inca capital of Cuzco, looted it, and took over the empire in 1534.

The Newcomers: England, France, and Holland. For much of the sixteenth century, the efforts of the English, French, and Dutch to explore, trade, and colonize overseas were overshadowed by the fabulous successes of Portugal and Spain. Yet these northwestern European countries were just as ambitious in this respect as the southwestern countries. France and England were powerful national monarchies whose rulers, nobles, and merchants were all eager for land and profits overseas. The Dutch rebelled against Spanish rule in the second half of the sixteenth century (pp. 295–396), formed their own independent republic (officially the Netherlands, but commonly known, from the name of its largest province, as Holland), and became the most dynamic commercial nation of Europe. Three such competitors could not forever be kept on the sidelines.

As the sixteenth century drew to a close, the English, French, and Dutch redoubled their efforts to gain a share of world trade and world empire. They explored the coastlines of North America and northern Europe, vainly searching for northwest or northeast sailing passages—routes not dominated by Spain and Portugal—that could take them to the Indies. (Though such routes do exist, they are too icebound to have been used by sixteenth- and seventeenth-century ships.) More successfully, the northwestern countries began to *settle* in areas not yet occupied by Spain and Portugal, chiefly in North America. In addition, the new competitors began to encroach on the trade and territories held by the Spanish and Portuguese themselves. An era of "world wars" began, in which European armies and navies fought for control of distant overseas lands.

By the end of the seventeenth century, England, France, and the Netherlands had successfully stepped into the inheritance of Portugal and Spain. They now dominated the trade of the Far East, and most of Portugal's possessions there were now in the hands of the Dutch or the English. The northwestern countries had driven the Spanish from much of the Caribbean, and Dutch ships carried much of the overseas trade of the Portuguese and Spanish empires in South and Central America. English, French, and Dutch colonies in North America were thriving, with those of the English already harboring tens of thousands of settlers.

The northwestern countries struggled as fiercely with each other for trade and empire as they did with Spain and Portugal. During the eighteenth century, with the Dutch exhausted by wars within Europe, the overseas struggle narrowed to one between France and Britain (from 1708 on, Britain was the name for the union formed by England and Scotland; p. 447). Every major eighteenth-century war, including those of the American and French revolutions (pp. 452, 464, 470–471), was part of a worldwide conflict between these two most powerful western European nations. By the end of the eighteenth century, in spite of the loss of its American colonies, Britain had come off best. It had won the position it was to keep down to the twentieth century, as the world's leading commercial and imperial nation.

OVERSEA CONSEQUENCES OF EUROPE'S EXPANSION

In the long run, the European discoveries and conquests were to have a profound impact throughout the world. As Europe became the heart of an expanding system that reached into all parts of the globe, changes occurring at the center of the system reverberated in far-off places.

The Americas: The Triumph of Europe. In the sixteenth century, however, the impact of the Europeans was felt above all in the Western Hemisphere. The European conquest of the Americas was in fact more devastating than any other invasions of recorded history. The killing, burning, looting, raping, and enslaving were not unusual. But there was, in addition, a rare psychological shock, arising in part from the clash of very different cultures.

The trauma was intensified by the suddenness and strangeness of the encounter. The dark-skinned natives had no knowledge of the existence of the white men and no warning of their coming. When the conquerors stepped ashore from the great ocean—with their pale skin and unfamiliar dress—it was as if they had descended from another planet. They rode animals never before seen, wore armor stouter than anything known to the natives, and spoke in the name of the "one true God," who was stronger than all the rest. The astonished natives readily became believers when they observed that the white Christians stayed relatively healthy while they themselves died in terrifying numbers from smallpox and other diseases.

In fact, the confrontation between the Europeans and the Americans was really a clash between the Old World and the New World, in which the advantage was overwhelmingly on the side of the former. Europe was but *one* among many Old World civilizations, which over the centuries had influenced each other in many ways and which had a longer and broader history than those of the New World. At the time of the European discovery of America, about 4,500 years had passed since the civilizations of Sumer and Egypt had first arisen, whereas it was only about 2,500 years since the earliest civilizations had appeared in the Western Hemisphere (p. 16). The European horses that amazed the Indians had first been domesticated in central Asia; the invaders' armor was made of iron, a metal first worked in the Middle East; and the gunpowder for their terrifying firearms had been invented in China. Thus the Europeans had behind them the collective achievement of all the Old World civilizations. Furthermore, the diseases that the Europeans brought with them were common throughout the Old World but unknown in the New. It is believed that, having no resistance to these diseases, the native population of the Americas was reduced by as much as 90 percent in the first hundred years of European rule—a staggering blow to their ability to resist.

After the era of conquest and plunder was over, the Spanish monarchy, in intimate partnership with the Church, endeavored to bring Western culture and Christian salvation to their subject millions. On the whole, considering the immense geographical distances involved, they succeeded remarkably well. The *Pax Hispanica* (Spanish Peace) covered an area far broader than the Roman Empire. And whereas Rome imposed its civilization upon only a portion of its domain, Spain determined to Christianize and Westernize the whole of the Americas.

The Spaniards, in a sense, carried the historic Roman mission to the New World in the sixteenth century. Heirs to Rome, they would build as well as or better than their forebears. During three centuries of rule, they organized new cities and towns, churches and missions, plantations and industries. They constructed fine bridges, aqueducts, and highways. While destroying the native civilizations, the Spanish (and the Portuguese) brought to America, long before anyone else did, the Western legacy of art, literature, and learning. These contributions were enjoyed mainly by a privileged few—the European-born whites. For the colonial administrations differed from those of the Roman Empire in one vital respect: Rome permitted the native peoples to participate in the imperial prosperity (p. 128); Spain viewed them primarily as "wards" of the monarchy—to be Christianized and "civilized" but to serve the interests of the crown and its supporters.

After 1600, the Portuguese, too, turned their attention from commerce to the longer, harder task of developing the wealth of America. They established in Brazil a system of autocratic control similar to that of the Spanish. In both colonial empires, the natives were forced into virtual serfdom, working huge estates (*encomiendas*) for the white landlords. In Brazil and the Caribbean, which were thinly populated by less advanced peoples than those of Mexico and Peru, the Native Americans quickly succumbed to the maltreatment and disease of the whites. They were replaced, over time, by millions of Africans, brought to the Western Hemisphere as slaves (pp. 330–331). As a result, blacks and mulattoes today make up about one-sixth of the total population of Latin America, while whites constitute about one-quarter; most of the remainder are mestizos (mixed white and Native American). From early times, the Spanish and Portuguese permitted intermarriage between Europeans and Christianized nonwhites.

Asia: The Limits of European Power. While the impact of the Europeans in the Western Hemisphere was catastrophic, in Asia it was at first hardly noticeable. The reason, once again, was that Asia and Europe both belonged to the same community of civilizations. The Europeans had most of their knowledge and skills, and even their diseases, in common with the peoples they encountered; indeed, the wealth of India, the statecraft of China, and the military organization of Japan, for example, were all superior to their own. Thus the Europeans held no massive advantage that would have enabled them, as a handful of newcomers, to undermine and destroy the Asian civilizations. The most they could do was to use their superiority in the single area of sea warfare to corner the trade in luxuries between Asia and Europe itself, and to make inroads into the regional commerce of the Orient. But apart from the Spanish in the relatively backward Philippines, Europeans were unable to conquer and Christianize any Asian territories other than their tiny commercial footholds.

Heroic missionaries, like the Jesuit father (pp. 384–385) Francis Xavier, traveled incredible distances and learned many (to Europeans) extraordinarily difficult languages so as to preach the Gospel throughout the East. But without the help of conquering armies, cultural shock, and deadly diseases, as in the New World, the missionaries had little effect on the great religions and flourishing cultures of Asia. True, in the seventeenth century, the rulers of China and Japan began strictly controlling contact with the newcomers, as well as (in Japan) viciously persecuting Christian converts. This was a sure sign that in those countries, the elites took the Europeans seriously as a potential threat. But it was not until the eighteenth century and, especially, the nineteenth century, that the Europeans gained a margin of superiority sufficient to turn the potential threat into a real one (pp. 551–555).

Africa and the Slave Trade. In the last major area of the world where the Europeans were newcomers, black Africa south of the Sahara, they also encountered civilizations and cultures that they could not destroy. In West Africa, civilized Islamic states with a literate elite had existed for centuries, and at the time of the arrival of the Europeans, pagan central and southern Africa were also advancing in prosperity and sophistication. Stable governments and powerful tribal chiefdoms, centered on permanent capital cities like Timbuktu in western Africa or Zimbabwe in the southeast, were an increasingly common feature of the region. Iron, horses, and of course Old World diseases were more or less familiar throughout most of Africa. Even with their firearms, when Europeans tried to conquer black African nations, they were generally defeated. Thus they had to treat the states and kingdoms of the region as partners to be dealt with on the basis of mutual interest rather than as victims to be destroyed.

Above all, this mutual interest lay in trade. Black African rulers had traditionally built their power partly on the control of those resources of their region that were most highly valued in the outside world, namely, gold, ivory, and slaves. European traders had originally been attracted to Africa above all by the lure of gold, but following Venice's example, they had soon begun buying slaves to work on sugar plantations—in this case, located in various newfound islands of the Atlantic. Then, in the sixteenth century, the rulers of the new European empires in the Americas turned from plunder and commerce to developing new sources of wealth. In Brazil, the Caribbean, and North America, there was endless land suitable for growing not only sugar but also other profitable crops like tobacco, coffee, and later cotton; but there were few, if any, natives who could be compelled to grow them. However, all along the Atlantic coast of Africa were densely populated regions where states and chiefdoms were rising in power, conquering land and people as they did so. The result was the appearance of the most massive and systematic traffic in human beings that the world had ever seen: the African slave trade.

The African slave trade was one of the most extensive population movements in human history, second only to the later European emigration to the New World. Between 1523, when the first Africans were shipped across the Atlantic, and the 1880s, when the trade finally came to an end, at least twelve million people were transported from Africa to the Americas. This was also the most systematically brutal of all forms of slavery. Although many civilized societies have made widespread use of slavery, it has often been moderated in practice—for example, by the close association of slaves and owners in ancient Athens (pp. 72–73). African slavery had none of these moderating features. Captured by enemy warriors in the course of plundering their villages, the victims—mostly young men, though young women were also taken—were marched down to the nearest coastal trading station and sold to European (mainly Portuguese, English, and Dutch) dealers. They were packed lying on their backs into the holds of the slave ships for a voyage of many weeks: at least one in six could expect to die on the way. Once arrived and sold to a plantation owner, another one in three could expect to be dead of overwork and underfeeding within three years. But that did not matter to the owners. Until competition among traders drove up the price in the late eighteenth century, new slaves could always be bought cheaply from the African suppliers.

For Africa, the result of the slave trade was a debilitating loss of human resources. Many other warlike and rapidly advancing societies, including that of medieval Europe (p. 239), had profited by selling captives to foreigners as slaves. But to do so on such a vast scale helped bring to an end several centuries of social and political advancement in black Africa. For the Americas, the result was a corresponding gain, especially from the late eighteenth century, when the African survival rate began to rise. In the end, a distinctively African element emerged in the culture of many nations from Brazil to the United States. For the western European countries that ran the slave trade, the result was enormous profits that helped make them the economic center of the world. In addition, the unchecked exploitation of Africans led to the growth of the belief in white racial superiority and the related feeling that the rest of the world was at Europe's disposal to do with as it wished. It was these notions that fueled the intensive imperialism of the nineteenth and twentieth centuries (pp. 549–550).

CONSEQUENCES FOR EUROPE

What effects did the overseas expansion have on Europe itself? The most immediate motive for the explorations had been economic, and their first effect was economic: expansion nourished the roots of capitalism. As trade with the Orient and the Americas increased, profits accumulated; and the huge investments required for the long voyages and the colonial ventures brought handsome gains to bankers and capitalists. The flow of gold and silver from the New World stimulated general business activity. By 1600, the volume of money in existence in Europe had risen to nearly $1 billion (in today's terms). This more adequate supply of coins promoted trade and strengthened the incentive of all classes to produce for the market, and it also made for price inflation. This, in turn, gave an added push to business, for merchants and investors are eager to buy goods and properties when they see that prices are moving upward.

The overseas trade brought an abrupt shift in the geographical distribution of prosperity and power. Venice, Florence, Genoa, and the smaller Italian cities had long enjoyed a strategic position between the Middle East and northern Europe. Italy had sparked the revival of trade in the eleventh century and had helped the growth of early capitalism (pp. 239, 300). But after the Portuguese reached the sources of Oriental commerce in the sixteenth century, the Mediterranean routes dwindled in importance; for the countries of western Europe facing upon the Atlantic now had the advantage of geographical position. Venice, the queen of the Adriatic, fell into decline.

As Britain, France, and Holland became the main trading gateways between Europe and the rest of the world, the center of prosperity and power shifted to northwestern Europe. Antwerp, Amsterdam, and London were to become the leading financial centers of expanding world commerce. These cities had the first organized "money markets" in which large private and government loans were arranged. Exchange houses arose there for trade and speculation in commodities, currencies, bonds, and stocks. Stocks began to appear in the seventeenth century with the creation of *joint-stock companies,* the forerunners of the modern corporation; these companies made it possible to raise large sums of capital for long-term investment. Though limited at first to commercial ventures, joint-stock companies were later formed in the mining and manufacturing industries.

The triumph of capitalism was assured by the acceleration of trade and production. The wealth of Europe mounted steadily, and the variety and quantity of goods increased with every day. Commodities and habits (like tobacco), formerly unknown in Europe, were introduced from both America and Asia. New foods added nourishment and novelty to European diets, notably potatoes, Indian corn, tomatoes, citrus fruits, chocolate, coffee, and peanuts. (Syphilis was also introduced from America—in exchange, perhaps, for the European gift of smallpox to the Indians.) Chinaware, orien-

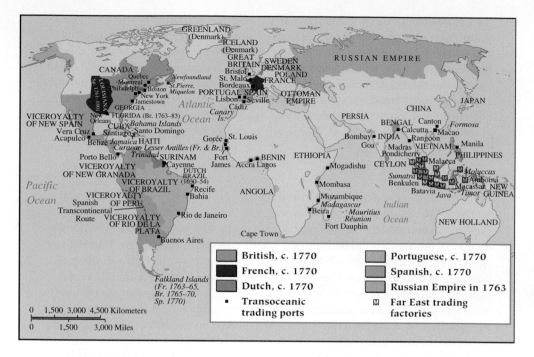

Map 7.5 Worldwide Trade and Empire About 1770. Three centuries after Columbus, European rule had spread through the Americas, Russia stretched all the way to Alaska, there were European trading footholds all along the coasts of Africa and Asia, and Britain had replaced Spain as the leading worldwide power (compare *Map 7.4*, p. 323). Soon there would be drastic changes in this global pattern centered on Europe: independence in the Americas, imperialistic conquest in the interior of Africa and Asia, and new centers of trade and empire in North America and the Far East.

tal furnishings, and art objects began to appear in the homes of the privileged classes. The taste for luxuries had been whetted by medieval commerce, and the well-to-do could now indulge it to the full.

In these ways, overseas penetration triggered the expansion of capitalism into a worldwide system (*Map 7.5*). The fact is that after 1500, the world became a treasure house for the West. Europe, whose people made up a tiny fraction of humanity, was in a position to seize and exploit vast areas of the globe. In no other period of history has a major cultural group enjoyed so favorable a ratio between its population and its available resources. Although the Europeans were to squander this advantage on endless wars, it served to lift their standard of living and their sense of power.

Just as important as the economic results of the expansion of Europe were its religious and cultural ones. All of a sudden, though not quite in the way that the earliest explorers had expected, the position of Christianity among the world's great religions was transformed. After many centuries in which Christianity had been almost entirely confined within the narrow limits of Europe (p. 208), between 1500 and 1600 it replaced Islam as the world's farthest-flung intercontinental religion.

In addition, the growth of Europe's worldwide power had the effect of strengthening the nonreligious elements in Western culture. Europe's newfound success had a profound effect on the outlook and psychology of Western men and women. By confirming the usefulness of curiosity, daring, and ruthlessness, it raised the value they placed on these traits. The success also strengthened *materialism* by making more widespread the enjoyment of wealth and the chances of acquiring it. It broadened the intellectual horizons of Europeans to some degree but contributed little to their respect for non-Western ideas and institutions. On the contrary, the startling victories of the Europeans fortified their optimism and strengthened their faith in their own superiority.

In both its religious and its nonreligious aspects, Western civilization now became a worldwide civilization. For the first time in history, a civilization was to leap every barrier of race and geography and spread its influence around the globe. Some areas, of course, would be touched only superficially, but European values and ideas would become familiar almost everywhere. And within the emerging world of associated cultures, the West would continue to serve as the chief carrier and transformer of ideas and institutions.

RECOMMENDED READING

Crises and Problems of the Later Middle Ages The best short introduction to all aspects of the transformation and expansion of Europe is E. F. Rice and A. Grafton, *The Foundations of Early Modern Europe* (1994); D. Nicholas, *The Transformation of Europe* (1999), is an excellent detailed survey.

Specifically on late medieval times, J. Huizinga, *The Waning of the Middle Ages* (1927), is a work of subtle insight, dealing with cultural aspects. W. C. Jordan, *The Great Famine* (1996), and D. Herlihy, *The Black Death and the Transformation of the West* (1997), discuss the effects of plague and famine on economy, society, and culture; P. Ziegler, *The Black Death* (1969), and B. W. Tuchman, *A Distant Mirror* (1978) (a more general account), vividly describe the horrors of the fourteenth century. For the effects of disease on human cultures from the earliest times to the present, see W. H. McNeill, *Plagues and Peoples* (1976). R. Hilton, *Bond Men Made Free* (1973), analyzes medieval peasant movements throughout Europe, in particular the English uprising of 1381.

On eastern Europe, R. Milner-Gulland, *The Russians* (1997), is an excellent general account of Russian civilization, stressing the medieval period; R. H. Davison, *Turkey* (1968), includes brief and readable treatment of the Ottoman expansion.

The New Economy N. J. G. Pounds, *An Economic History of Medieval Europe* (1994), is a good introduction. E. S. Hunt and J. M. Murray discuss changes in business organization and methods in *A History of Business in Medieval Europe, 1200–1550* (1999); E. S. Hunt, *The Medieval Super-Companies* (1994), vividly describes the rise and fall of the Peruzzi banking firm. J. Le Goff, *Your Money or Your Life* (1998), explores changing religious attitudes to usury in the era of the medieval origins of capitalism.

The New Technology F. Gies and J. Gies, *Cathedral, Forge, and Waterwheel* (1994), is an excellent nontechnical account of the development of technology throughout the Middle Ages; A. Pacey, *Technology in World Civilization* (1990), discusses the intercontinental flow of technical innovation in the Middle Ages and the rise of the West to technical supremacy. C. M. Cipolla, *Guns, Sails, and Empires* (1965), and D. Cline, *Navigation in the Age of Discovery* (1990), deal with the evolution and impact of seafaring and sea warfare technology. P. Contamine, *War in the Middle Ages* (1984), is a readable standard work that includes treatment of the development of firearms. W. Chappell and R. Bringhurst, *A Short History of the Printed Word* (2000), covers the origins of printing in Europe; L. Febvre, *The Coming of the Book* (1976), is a classic account of printing's cultural and economic impact. D. S. Landes, *Revolution in Time* (1983), includes both technical aspects and discussion of the impact of clocks on civilization.

The New Politics D. Hay and J. Law, *Italy in the Age of the Renaissance, 1380–1530* (1989), and G. Mattingly, *Renaissance Diplomacy* (1955), are good introductions; D. Waley, *The Italian City-Republics* (1988), covers the medieval city-states. On individual city-states, see G. Brucker, *Renaissance Florence*

(1969), and F. C. Lane, *Venice: A Maritime Republic* (1973). Q. Skinner, *Machiavelli* (1981), is an authoritative short account.

For the growth of government power outside Italy, see H. Kamen, *Spain, 1469–1714: A Society of Conflict* (1991); D. Potter, *A History of France, 1460–1560: The Emergence of a Nation-State* (1995); G. Elton, *England Under the Tudors* (1991); and J. Bérenger, *A History of the Habsburg Empire* (1994).

The impact of changing methods of warfare on government, society, and the economy is dealt with in J. R. Hale, *War and Society in Renaissance Europe* (1985). C. Allmand, *The Hundred Years' War* (1988), is a brief account of the war's course and impact. G. Parker, *The Military Revolution: Military Innovation and the Rise of the West, 1500–1800* (1996), gives insight into the long-term impact of changes in warfare on both Western and non-Western civilizations. M. Howard, *War in European History* (1976), is a brief interpretation by a leading scholar that includes treatment of late medieval changes in warfare.

The New Geography D. J. Boorstin, *The Discoverers* (1983), is a brilliant account of *all* discoveries about the world and humankind. J. L. Abu-Lughod, *Before European Hegemony* (1989), discusses the intercontinental developments in the Old World that led to European exploration and empire building. J. H. Parry, *The Age of Reconnaissance* (1981), describes the beginnings of exploration; a brief biography of the most famous of the explorers is S. E. Morison, *Christopher Columbus, Mariner* (1983).

G. V. Scammell, *The First Imperial Age* (1989), surveys European exploration and worldwide empires up to the early eighteenth century. H. S. Klein, *The Atlantic Slave Trade* (1999), gives an overview of the economic, social, and cultural impact of the trade on Africa, the Americas, and Europe. P. Bakewell, *A History of Latin America: Empires and Sequels* (1997), is an excellent account of the Spanish and Portuguese conquest of the New World and its impact on Latin America down to the twentieth century.

INFOTRAC COLLEGE EDITION

Visit the source collections at **http://academic.cengage.com/infotrac,** and use the Search function with the following key terms:

Hundred Years' War	Machiavelli	medieval Germany
Black Death	medieval England	

WESTERN CIVILIZATION RESOURCES

Visit the Brief History of the Western World Companion Web Site for resources specific to this textbook:

http://history.wadsworth.com/greerbrief09/

Also, the CD in the back of this book and the World History Resources Center at **http://history.wadsworth.com/west_civ/** offer a variety of tools to help you succeed in this course, including access to quizzes; images; documents; interactive simulations, maps, and timelines; movie explorations; and a wealth of other sources.

CHAPTER 8

The Renaissance:
Upsurge of Humanism

OVERVIEW

From about 1300 onward, scholars, thinkers, writers, and artists began to turn away from the literary and artistic styles, and to some extent from the accepted values, of medieval civilization. Instead, they sought inspiration in a deeper knowledge of Christian Europe's forerunner civilization, that of pagan Greece and Rome. This endeavor began in Italy, but by 1600, most of the educated elite of Catholic and Protestant Europe had come to share in it. To those who took part in the endeavor, it seemed so exciting that they spoke of literature, thought, and the arts as having been "reborn" after many centuries of medieval "barbarism."

In fact, the culture of the Middle Ages was a brilliant one, and its critics were simply taking to a new level the existing medieval habit of borrowing ideas and knowledge from the Greek and Roman "ancients." All the same, the revival movement rediscovered so much of the neglected or forgotten past of Greece and Rome that today we still call the movement by the French word for "rebirth"—the _Renaissance._

The Renaissance involved far more than simply resurrecting the past, however, for there was no way that the admirers of pagan Greece and Rome could separate themselves from the living Christian European civilization of their own day and age. The result was an extraordinarily diverse cultural achievement. Scholars rediscovered the classical ideal of the fully developed human being whose character was formed by literary study and education, and grappled with the implications of this ideal for the otherworldly values of the Christian faith. Idealistic philosophers inspired by Plato sought an ultimate truth that would reconcile pagan wisdom and Christian faith. Earnest believers sought to renew Christianity by bringing it back to its roots in the ancient world. Painters depicted the naked female body sometimes as an emblem of worldly sensuality, and sometimes as a symbol of divine beauty and truth. Writers longed to "equal or surpass the ancients" in the beauty of their Greek and Latin style, but they wrote just as eloquently in English, Spanish, French, and many other native languages of Europe. And most often what they wrote about was the life and characters of their own times— the hypocrisy and corruption of monks, for example, the foolishness of a would-be knight errant, or the tragic flaws of an all too thoughtful prince of Denmark.

By reviving and adapting the traditions of the Greco-Roman past, the scholars, thinkers, writers, and artists of the Renaissance also changed the traditions of the European present—and thereby contributed in many ways to the remaking of Christian Europe into the modern West. Their efforts to renew Christianity helped bring about both the Protestant Reformation and the reform and reaffirmation of Catholicism. Their rediscovery of ancient mathematical knowledge and military tactics helped make possible the Western revolutions in science and warfare. Their ideals set precedents for basic cultural values of today—belief in the ennobling effect of education, literature, and art on the human personality; respect for civilizations different from one's own; and distrust of received wisdom and preconceived ideas. And though the writers and artists of the modern West have traveled far from the aims and methods of their Renaissance forerunners, the best of Renaissance literature and art provides an understanding of the human condition and an ideal of beauty that will never cease to console and inspire.

The Renaissance View of Human Nature

At the core of the Renaissance as a movement of cultural change was an upsurge of *humanism*. The humanist way of thinking can be most broadly defined as any view that puts the human person (*humanus*) at the center of things and stresses the individual's creative, reasoning, and aesthetic powers. Such a view is at least as old as the Greeks and Romans. Although the word *humanism* was not used in the classical age, Cicero (p. 131) referred to *humanitas* as the quality of mind and spirit that distinguishes human beings from mere animals. That quality, he thought, is best nurtured and expressed through literature (including history, philosophy, and oratory). Renaissance scholars, following Cicero's lead, identified the study of classical literature (both Greek and Latin) with humanism, and they applied the term *humanist* exclusively to classical scholars.

THE REVIVAL OF INTEREST IN THE CLASSICAL WORLD

Interest in the classics had not altogether disappeared during the Middle Ages. By the twelfth century, many scholars had made themselves familiar with works of antiquity, and Dante and Chaucer drew heavily from the Latin poets. Before the fourteenth century, however, there had been little to equal the enthusiasm of Renaissance scholars for classical writings. It was in those works that they caught their "new" vision of humanity. Moved by this vision, they searched eagerly for ancient documents and developed a deep respect for the literary culture of antiquity. Their enthusiasm was not stirred primarily by dramatic finds of "new" documents; it resulted, rather, from a quickening change in the European *state of mind.*

The medieval intellect, steeped in a God-centered, otherworldly view of the universe, had been largely closed to the naturalistic, pagan spirit. The schoolmen fingered classical manuscripts through thick gloves, so to speak; their religious training normally kept them from a truly sympathetic contact (p. 272). But with the passing of the Middle Ages, the ideals of asceticism and Christian poverty receded before advancing worldliness.

Caught up in this trend were many groups among the educated elite of Europe. In the developing towns, the bourgeois found medieval ideals increasingly unattractive and were looking for standards closer to their hearts. Kings and nobles glimpsed through the classics the worldly elite of Greece and Rome, whose elegance, refinement, and heroic achievements they hoped to imitate. Even popes and bishops, coming as they mostly did from bourgeois and noble families, often dropped their suspicion of the pagan ancients and became patrons of humanist learning. Bourgeois, aristocrats, and high churchmen all hoped, by imitating the best in ancient thought and behavior, to re-create classical standards in their own times. They failed to bring back the past or even to imitate it faithfully, but their efforts to do so helped shape modern values.

The good life, according to most Renaissance thinkers, is the life that is pleasing to the senses, intellect, and aesthetic capacities. Human desires are generally good, though they need to be cultivated and kept in balance. Well-born and educated individuals, Renaissance humanists believed, should be free and proud. They should strive for mastery of all the worthy arts, because their ultimate value as human beings would be measured not in humility, but in talent and accomplishments. Successful individuals, as the Italian humanists put it, possess the quality of *virtù* ("strength, virtuosity"). Their minds are so filled with thoughts of this world that they have little time (or desire) to think about the next.

The ideas of the humanists plainly ran counter to many Christian teachings. They seemed to reject the doctrine of original sin and natural human sinfulness. They suggested that individuals could perform mighty deeds without divine assistance. And yet, especially in northern Europe, a Christian humanism developed alongside this secular humanism. Some pious scholars shared the growing enthusiasm for the classics and ancient languages. They shared, too, the heightened appreciation of human capabilities, especially the powers of reason and creativity. But they insisted that all human powers were a gift of God—and that this life, though rewarding, fell short of the glory of heaven.

THE NEW SCHOLARSHIP: PETRARCH, BOCCACCIO

It is no accident that the Renaissance arose in Italy. The forces of social change were most advanced there; the development and spread of urban life, for example, had progressed further in Italy than in northern Europe. There was another reason, however, independent of those forces: the growing consciousness of *nationality*. Although this consciousness did not produce a unified state in Italy (as it did in Spain and France), it caused Italians to embrace their past more warmly than ever before. As Italian humanists studied the Latin classics, they began to dream of restoring the grandeur of ancient Rome. Few Italians had forgotten those glories, for their land offered eloquent architectural reminders. The humanist "road back to Rome" was shortest in Italy, and it was traveled by patriotic pilgrims.

Francesco Petrarca (Petrarch), who is regarded as the founder of Renaissance humanism, was born in 1304 of an exiled Florentine family. Urged by his bourgeois father to study law, he came upon the works of Cicero in the course of his reading. His admiration for Cicero's thought and style led to a passion for all the classics, and when his father died, Petrarch gave up his study of law and turned to a life of scholarship.

It was Petrarch who first undertook the collection of ancient manuscripts. He persuaded others to join him in a search through monastic and cathedral libraries that took him all over Italy and into France and Germany as well. Among his finds were some lost orations and letters of his beloved Cicero. He employed copyists in his home and built up an admirable collection of pagan documents and books. His private library, the first of its kind, became a model for scholars and other intellectuals. Following his example, many of the well-to-do took up the search and began to build their own libraries.

Petrarch set the style as a scholar as well as a collector. Though he led a busy life and spent much of his time in cities and at the courts of aristocrats, he expressed a love of solitude and the peace of nature. But this was a different solitude from that prescribed by the ascetic ideal; it was closer to the ancient Roman model. He spent his private hours not meditating and praying but studying literature; for isolation without books, he declared, was "exile, prison, and torture." He alternated writing with reading, in the fashion of the modern scholar. What a glory it was, thought Petrarch, "to read what our forerunners have written and to write what later generations may wish to read."

He preferred to write in classical Latin because he had only contempt for the vernacular tongues (p. 272) and the corrupted Latin of the Middle Ages. Many of his writings were in the form of epics, dialogues, and letters patterned after the style of Cicero and Virgil (pp. 131–132). He is hardly remembered for those efforts. More successful were his love poems (sonnets), which he wrote in Italian. He addressed most of them to Laura, a beautiful young married woman whom he loved and idealized (though she was unaware of his passion). A record of his most intimate thoughts upon seeing her and thinking of her, these sonnets to Laura became a model for many generations of romantic poets.

One of Petrarch's followers, Giovanni Boccaccio, was among the first Westerners of modern times to study the Greek language. The son of a Florentine banker, Boccaccio grew bored with the humdrum of credits and debits and set out to learn Greek. Once he had done so, he instructed his tutor to translate Homer into Latin and thus helped to introduce his generation to their first reading of the *Iliad* and the *Odyssey* (pp. 84–85). Like Petrarch, Boccaccio searched far and wide for ancient manuscripts. One of his prized discoveries was a work of the historian Tacitus, which he uncovered in the monastery library at Monte Cassino. When he first saw the neglected condition of the archives there, he burst into tears.

Though Boccaccio was nominally a Christian, his own writings are markedly pagan in spirit. *Fiammetta,* which is sometimes called the first psychological novel of the West, makes no reference to the world of Christian faith and morals. When the heroine is torn by the question of whether to give herself to her lover, she is answered not by the Virgin but by Venus. The characters in *The Decameron,* Boccaccio's best-known work, are similarly un-Christian in outlook and behavior. The tales in this collection, which Boccaccio borrowed from various countries of Europe and the Middle East, feature sensual escapades, deceits, and clever revenges.

Now other Italian scholars began to study Greek. By 1500, nearly all the Greek authors had been recovered by the West and translated into Latin and Italian. This was an accomplishment of lasting importance. Although medieval scholars had become familiar, through Arabic, with many of the writings of Aristotle and the Hellenistic scientists, they had no direct knowledge of Greek *literature*. It was the humanists who restored to our Western heritage the works of Homer, Herodotus, Thucydides, Aeschylus, Sophocles, Euripides, and Plato.

HUMANISTIC EDUCATION AND THE "GENTLEMAN"

This new body of knowledge challenged traditional patterns of education and thought. For medieval Europe as a whole, religion was the focus of higher learning. The trivium and quadrivium centered on scriptural texts, the writings of the Church Fathers, and the logic of Aristotle (p. 83). But the Italian humanists made up the first substantial body of *secular* (nonreligious) scholars in Europe. Most of them were sons of the middle class or the nobility and had no connection with the clergy. In Greek and Roman literature they saw the means of providing students with a truly *liberal* education.

It was fairly easy to eliminate scholasticism from the Italian universities, for it had never taken deep root there. The new learning was introduced in its place by humanist professors of rhetoric (speaking and writing), whose lectures drew enthusiastic students from all over Europe. The humanists were not welcomed at most northern universities, however. In the scholastic strongholds of Paris, Cologne, and Heidelberg, the faculties looked with disdain upon the unfamiliar Greek studies. Some Oxford masters condemned them as "dangerous and damnable." Not until the end of the sixteenth century did Greek and Latin literature—the "classics"—supersede philosophy as the foundation of liberal education in the north.

Humanism reached into elementary as well as higher education. The private schools that arose in the towns to serve the sons of the well-to-do were secular in tone and concentrated on Latin and Greek studies. But they aimed at more than the cultivation of the intellect. The schoolmasters saw the ancient statesmen (like Pericles and Cicero) as models to inspire young men to lives of fruitful citizenship. The Greeks and Romans had lived in cities and had enjoyed a sophisticated social life; so it was their example, rather than that of the monks and saints, that seemed best to follow. Literature and moral instruction were balanced by training in music and athletics. The Greek ideal of the well-rounded man, mentally and physically fit, was at the heart of humanistic education.

During the sixteenth century, this pattern of education spread from Italy throughout western Europe. Like the classical model on which it was based and the privileged society it served, the private school was aristocratic in purpose and style, and although the curriculum of Greek and Latin studies often became rigid and sterile, it helped shape a new type of personality: the "gentleman." As an ideal, the gentleman now took the place of the medieval knight or the ascetic holy man. Leading noblemen, like the sixteenth-century French aristocrat in Hans Holbein's *The French Ambassadors* (*Fig. III.1*, p. 286), had artists portray them not just as well dressed and well armed but also as well educated. Whether of noble or bourgeois background, the ideal gentleman was a man of refinement and self-control. Just as chivalry had tamed the warriors of the Middle Ages (pp. 228–229), humanistic education taught the new landowners and capitalists the ways of urbane living.

The true gentleman possessed a disciplined mind, graceful manners, and excellent taste. For those impatient to acquire such virtues, manuals of proper behavior began to appear; the most influential of them, *The Courtier,* was published in 1528 by an Italian nobleman, Baldassare Castiglione. As Machiavelli was advising rulers on the art of state-craft, Castiglione advised young aristocrats, both male and female, on education and manners. The gentleman and the lady would flourish as admired types in the West for some four hundred years.

PHILOSOPHY: THE APPEAL OF PLATONISM

In philosophy, the main effect of the recovery of Greek learning was to put Plato (pp. 81–83) in Aristotle's place as the foremost philosopher. Aristotle had ruled over the medieval universities because his methods of logic proved so useful to the scholastic thinkers (p. 269). His works were better known than Plato's, and his moderation appealed to men like Aquinas. But the humanists found his writings difficult and without literary appeal. As the complete dialogues of his teacher, Plato, became available during the fifteenth century, the humanists were struck by their charming style as well as their ideas. Here was philosophy that was at the same time literature and literature that was philosophy. Plato became the new master.

Florence was the leading center for Platonic studies. Cosimo de' Medici, a scholarly ruler who was keenly interested in Plato, founded the Platonic Academy there about 1450. The Academy served as a center for the translation of Platonic writings and for discussions of Plato's philosophy. Named after Plato's own circle of disciples (p. 81), it consisted of only a few select scholars, subsidized by the Medici, and their circle of friends. And yet the influence of the Academy was substantial—especially in art and literature. Almost every artist of the later Renaissance was influenced by Platonism, and some, like Botticelli and Michelangelo, became deeply absorbed in it. Through them the Platonic influence passed on to later generations—ultimately to such nineteenth-century writers as Wordsworth and Goethe (pp. 482–484).

Marsilio Ficino was the shining light of the Academy. Chosen by Cosimo at an early age, he was carefully educated and then installed in a villa in the hills near Florence. From that time until his death, he devoted himself to translating Plato's writings and explaining his doctrines. He presided over polite seminars at the villa and corresponded with notables all over Europe, seeking to demonstrate that Platonic teachings were in agreement with Christianity. For those who could not accept religion on the basis of "revelation," he suggested that Plato could open another way.

Pico della Mirandola, a disciple of Ficino, went beyond his master and attempted a synthesis, a bringing together, of *all* learning, Eastern and Western. This genius of the age knew Arabic and Hebrew as well as Greek and Latin, and he studied Jewish, Babylonian, and Persian records. He refused to ignore any source of truth merely because it was not labeled "Christian." He emphasized human freedom and capacity for learning, and, by breaking through the bounds of medieval theology, he opened a door to the study of *comparative* religion and philosophy.

Like the other members of Cosimo's circle, Pico embraced the Platonic view of creation and existence, which held that humans had become separated from their divine home of pure spirit by some accident of prehistory. Though each soul (spirit) had fallen prisoner to matter (the body), it struggled for liberation and a return to God. This view corresponded to the Christian doctrine of the Fall and the human longing for salvation.

An interesting offshoot of this idea had a profound effect on the arts. The feeling for *natural beauty,* said the Platonists, came from the soul's remembrance of the *divine beauty* of heaven. Hence aesthetic expression and enjoyment took on a religious connection. Finally, the Platonists linked the emotion of physical love to the higher urge that moves individuals toward their divine source (Platonic love). According to the Florentine intellectuals, art stimulates appreciation of beauty, and *love* brings the individual closer to the ultimate goal of spiritual reunion with God.

The widespread acceptance of this idea helps to explain the Renaissance "cult of beauty" and the toleration by devout Christians of a frankly sensual art. It reinforced the naturalistic thrust of humanism and the rising secular taste of the times. Thus by the fifteenth century, most painters and sculptors had turned their backs on the otherworldly style of art and had plunged eagerly, sometimes ecstatically, into *realistic* representation.

THE CRITICAL SPIRIT AND THE BEGINNINGS OF EMPIRICISM

Also of great importance for philosophy were the methods of scholarship that were introduced by the humanists, although the philosophical implications of those methods were not fully recognized at the time. Petrarch, Boccaccio, and the others who collected classical manuscripts sought to re-create, from the various documents, *correct* texts of the ancient authors. Their intention was simply to reassemble old learning, but their method led to a more critical attitude toward the written word and greater attention to observed facts. The downfall of scholasticism, with its system of knowledge based on authority and reason, encouraged later scholars to find truth by *empirical* methods (observation and experiment; pp. 422–423).

The Roman humanist Lorenzo Valla was a pioneer of modern textual criticism. An expert on Latin style, he abhorred the carelessness of medieval writers and was bold enough to attack even the Latin of the Vulgate (the Bible as translated by Jerome; p. 182). He also challenged the popular belief that the Apostles' Creed, the traditional confession of Christian beliefs, had actually been composed by the apostles. His most shocking discovery, in 1440, was that the Donation of Constantine (p. 212) was a forgery. This document, which served as a basis for papal claims to secular supremacy over the West, had stood unchallenged for centuries.

Using his new tools of scholarship, Valla demonstrated that the *language* of the Donation could not have been that of the fourth century but was more likely that of the eighth or ninth. Going beyond grammatical analysis, he also pointed out (as a careful scholar should) that the manuscript contained terms of a period later than the date when it was supposedly written. In the words of the Donation, the emperor Constantine assigns vast powers to Pope Sylvester before leaving Rome to build a new capital at Byzantium. Yet he declares that the pope shall have supremacy over all patriarchs, including the one at "Constantinople." How could this be, asked Valla, when at that time Constantinople was not yet a city and there was no such patriarch? So conclusive was Valla's criticism that the Donation was recognized by all as a fraud.

It speaks for the spirit of the age that the popes made no move to punish Valla. On the contrary, they asked for the scholar's services. He was secretary to King Alfonso V of Naples when he published his exposé of the forgery. Afterward, Pope Nicholas V hired him away and brought him back to Rome to translate the ancient Greek historian Thucydides (p. 89). Nicholas, a patron of humanism, also founded the Vatican (papal) Library as a depository for ancient manuscripts.

Valla was bold, critical, and independent, but as a practicing humanist, he limited his attention to what could be learned from the literature of the past. The methods of

Niccolò Machiavelli as a political thinker, basing his view of government and the state on recorded history and personal experience (pp. 311–313), went further. Though he lacked the system, precision, and control of modern social scientists, Machiavelli, by generalizing from collected data, was clearly moving toward a new conception of knowledge and its verification.

He was not alone in this. Leonardo da Vinci, a fellow citizen of Florence, grew discontented with bookish learning and determined to see things for himself. Though Leonardo is best known for his great paintings (pp. 351–354), his love of art was matched by his desire to unlock the secrets of nature. In order to improve his skill in drawing human and animal bodies, he dissected cadavers and set down his on-the-spot sketches and comments in notebooks. He found dissection difficult and distasteful, but he insisted that observation was the only means to true knowledge. He also experimented with mechanics and drew up plans for ingenious practical inventions. A man of his times, Leonardo both typified Italian humanism and foreshadowed the age of empiricism.

CHRISTIAN HUMANISM: ERASMUS

So far we have spoken about humanism only in Italy, without tracing its spread beyond the Alps. During the fifteenth century, a number of northern scholars journeyed to the Italian centers of learning and carried home with them the seeds of the new scholarship. But the soil of the northern countries produced a different variety of humanism—the pagan flavor, so strong in Italy, was missing.

When humanism came to the north, the intellectual leaders there were filled with Christian piety (deep reverence) and were eager to reform the Church. Dissatisfied with scholasticism, they seized on the rediscovered classics of antiquity. Unlike the scholars of Italy, however, they were not looking for models of sophisticated secular life. Rather, they sought guides to a purer religion, and found in the ancient writings those ideals that would encourage *spiritual* reform.

There were many devout and vigorous humanists in the north, especially in Germany and England. But the greatest of them all was Desiderius Erasmus. Born in Rotterdam in 1466, he became a cosmopolitan scholar, at home in many lands. His learning and scholarship won him acclaim throughout Europe as the "prince of humanists."

Erasmus, an illegitimate child, had little knowledge of his family background. His father, of middle-class origin, was a priest at the time of Erasmus's birth. Little is known of his mother. Sent off to school as a boy, he lacked the comfortable bourgeois background characteristic of the Italian humanists. His school was supervised by an order of devout laymen, the Brethren of the Common Life. The Brethren, who were dedicated to a pious, mystical Christianity, taught that individual lives should be modeled on the example of Jesus. While subjecting themselves to rigid spiritual discipline, they emphasized the ideals of service and love. Erasmus was deeply touched by this early influence, and he adopted the "philosophy of Christ" as his lifetime ideal.

After Erasmus left school, he was persuaded to enter an Augustinian monastery, where he received little formal instruction but was free to read as he pleased in the classics, both Christian and pagan. At the age of thirty, looking to wider and deeper scholarship, he secured a release from his monastic vows. He went to the University of Paris, where he completed a course in theology. From then on, he devoted his life to research and writing, visiting the major centers of learning. Though he was an ordained priest,

Erasmus never served a parish. He lived, sometimes meagerly, on the support of patrons and on income from his books.

In the classics, Erasmus found models of behavior that could well be followed by genuine Christians. Socrates, Plato, and Cicero were worthy, he thought, of a place among the saints. But he read the ancient writings as a firm believer, and he was persuaded that such studies should serve to strengthen faith, not undermine it. Above all, he sought to use the new linguistic and textual skills developed by the Italian humanists as a means of establishing a "truer" Bible. He hoped with these tools to cut away the "false growths" of medieval religious practice and to restore thereby a "pure" Christianity.

Erasmus used his scholarly skills to prepare a more accurate version of the New Testament. Like Valla, he felt certain that the Vulgate Bible, respected though it was, contained errors. After collecting a number of the earliest available New Testament manuscripts in the original Greek, he produced a fresh Greek version based on a comparison of texts. He finished this work in 1516, along with his own Latin translation and commentary, hoping that these efforts would lead to a clearer understanding of the message of Christ—and to translations in the vernacular tongues. He was one of the first to believe that the Bible should be read by the people themselves.

Erasmus carried on an extensive correspondence with fellow scholars, and the influence of his ideas, expressed in clear, polished Latin, was extraordinary. He was feared by suspicious conservatives among the clergy but was welcomed everywhere by admiring humanists. Unlike many of them, however, Erasmus was not content to bask in the adulation of an elite; he wanted to make his thoughts available to all literate people.

He published a great many works, often satirical, through which he tried to call attention to the need for reform. He wished to cleanse the Church and society of selfishness, cruelty, hypocrisy, pride, and ignorance—and to replace them with tolerance, honesty, wisdom, service, and love. Repelled by violence and disorder, he hoped that appeals to *reason* would bring about peaceful change. But he sometimes questioned if reform could be achieved peacefully. His most widely read and most entertaining work, *In Praise of Folly* (published in 1509), is filled with doubts and double meanings. Paraded before the reader are the lovers of Folly, a character who personified for her creator the strongest forces in human nature. Erasmus has Folly sing her own praises: "Without me the world cannot exist for a moment. For is not all that is done among mortals, full of folly; is it not performed by fools and for fools?" Society rejects the person who pulls off the masks in the comedy of life; the "well-adjusted" person adapts to the game, mixes with others, and encourages their delusions.

Erasmus spoke of the foolishness of war and warmakers and of the peculiar conceits of individuals and nations, but he reserved most of his barbs for the clergy. The Church, he thought, had grown unduly fond of Folly and had drifted far from the teachings of Christ. He criticized the hair-splitting theologians, the vain and ignorant monks, and the power-loving bishops and popes (p. 250). He also ridiculed the excesses of the popular cult of the saints and their relics and the purchase of indulgences (pp. 371–372).

The literate men and women who read Erasmus's books were impressed and amused, but neither they nor the Church nor society at large were much changed by his sharp words. His criticism of clerics, it is true, helped to bring on the Reformation, but that religious revolt took a shape that he despised. What he hoped for was a *peaceful* reform of Christianity *as a whole*. He wanted a purified Church, not a divided one.

Erasmus was just as critical of the passions and violence aroused by Martin Luther as he was of the errors of the popes. This made him appear to be, in the eyes of Protestant reformers, a moral and physical coward who would not stand up for his convictions. Actually, Erasmus stood fast upon his own convictions—that Christian unity should be upheld, reason promoted, and rebellion shunned.

The Revolution in Art

The spirit of humanism could not be confined to literature and philosophy, and as early as the fourteenth century, it burst forth splendidly in the visual arts. It appeared first, as one might expect, in Italy—in Florence, the capital of humanism, which remained for some two hundred years the leading center of European art. Few places on earth, over a comparable period, can match that city's output of painting, sculpture, and architecture.

THE PIONEER OF NATURALISM: GIOTTO

In point of time, Giotto di Bondone was a medieval man, living in the early fourteenth century, at the same time as Dante. But his influence touched every artist of the Renaissance and extended beyond mere technique. He established himself as a model to follow: the artist as hero, a famous individual. Medieval painters and sculptors had rarely put their names on their works, but Giotto, in the new spirit of the times, signed his paintings and amiably accepted popular acclaim.

In 1305, he was commissioned to paint biblical scenes, mainly from the lives of Christ and the Virgin Mary, on the inside walls of the Arena Chapel in Padua. This was an enormous task, calling for some thirty-five separate scenes. Giotto worked in a common technique known as "fresco." Each morning, a small area of the wall which the artist planned to finish that day, was freshly plastered (*fresco* means "fresh"). Paint consisting of powdered pigment mixed with water was then applied to the wet plaster and became part of the wall surface when it dried. Because of its size and excellence, Giotto's work in the Arena Chapel was a milestone in European painting. Later artists would be commissioned to follow Giotto's grand example; their efforts reached a peak in Michelangelo's stupendous fresco on the ceiling of the Sistine Chapel (pp. 354–355).

Giotto was not satisfied with the flat look of medieval altar panels and the painted figures of manuscripts. He wanted to re-create an actual scene, to give the viewer the feeling of being an eyewitness. In order to accomplish this, he sought to produce the illusion of depth (perspective) on a flat surface and to make the figures look solid and real. This he did by skillful use of light and shadow and by *foreshortening* the hands and feet (painting the parts supposed to be nearer to the viewer larger than those farther away). He also gave careful attention to the *composition* of each scene, arranging individual figures and groups as in a stage setting. Finally, he suggested the emotional state of his subjects through careful attention to facial expression and gesture (*Fig. 8.1*).

In his own day, Giotto was hailed by the citizens of Florence for having achieved a revolution in artistic technique. His tomb in the cathedral of Florence bears this inscription: "Lo, I am he by whom dead painting was restored to life, to whose right hand all was possible, by whom art became one with nature." He demonstrated, further, the humanist ideal of the many-sided genius, the person of *virtù*. A man of many skills, he became the official architect of Florence and designed the graceful campanile (bell tower) of the cathedral. Rising some 400 feet, it overlooks his beloved city and the valley of the Arno River (*Fig. 8.2, p. 346*).

Fig. 8.1 "Dead Painting Restored to Life." In Giotto's *Lamentation*, the followers of the dead Christ surround him in dramatic attitudes of grief, while the sky above is turbulent with mourning angels. The painter has used revolutionary techniques of arranging figures in groups and producing a three-dimensional appearance so as to create an image of overwhelming sorrow. His work also has roots in the medieval past, however—he has found a way to reproduce in two dimensions the naturalism and human interaction of Gothic sculpture (*Fig. 6.7*, p. 264).

NEW ARTISTIC TECHNIQUES: BRUNELLESCHI, MASACCIO, VAN EYCK

Giotto left a technical challenge to his successors: How could painting be made more naturalistic? It was not until a century later that a significant advance in this direction was made. Again it was a Florentine, Filippo Brunelleschi, who pointed the way. A master of sculpture and architecture as well as painting, he designed a stunning dome to match Giotto's tower (*Fig. 8.2*). But he shared with his fellow humanists a distaste for medieval forms. After a close study of existing Roman buildings, he set out to create a new style of church architecture that adopted many Roman elements while keeping something of the light and graceful quality of the Gothic style (*Fig. 8.3*).

Brunelleschi made a unique contribution to drawing and painting through his study of *perspective*. He was the first to lay down the mathematical rules governing the reduction in size of pictured objects, according to their placement toward the rear of a scene. The ancient Romans, and Giotto, had been skillful in suggesting depth and distance, but they did not have at their command precise mathematical laws. Brunelleschi formulated them by means of observation and measurement, the "new tools" of Renaissance learning.

Fig. 8.2 Florence Cathedral. Medieval and Renaissance styles here combine to produce a harmonious and majestic group of buildings. A late-thirteenth-century architect, Arnolfo di Cambio, designed the nave exterior to echo the Romanesque baptistry (beyond the picture at left). The interior, and Giotto's fourteenth-century bell tower, are Gothic. The dome, planned by Arnolfo but designed and built by Filippo Brunelleschi in the fifteenth century, revives a Roman tradition (*Fig. 3.5*, p. 139) but is higher than any Roman dome—partly because this Renaissance structure has the Gothic features of stone ribs and a pointed shape.

Fig. 8.3 A Renaissance Church. Brunelleschi's Santo Spirito (Holy Spirit) Church in Florence breaks with medieval building traditions and revives those of imperial Rome. Instead of reaching upward to a vault, the columns and arches march forward under a flat ceiling, as in Roman government halls and early Christian churches (*Fig. 3.6*, p. 141). The building's harmonious proportions, like those of ancient temples, are intended to reflect the harmony of the universe, but for a Christian purpose—to give a glimpse of the mind of the Creator whose Spirit pervades all things.

Fig. 8.4 Surpassing the "Ancients." Countless late medieval pictures showed scenes like this one, but Masaccio's version (about 1425) is framed by correctly designed Greco-Roman columns and an arch like those of Brunelleschi (*Fig. 8.3*). Masaccio has also followed Brunelleschi's rules of perspective. He gives a "real-life" view of the donors (wealthy citizens who paid for the picture) kneeling outside the columns, the figures grouped round the crucified Christ just inside them, and the high vault fading into the background. No Greek or Roman painter could create such a convincing illusion of height and distance.

One of the first painters to make use of the laws of perspective was Masaccio, some years younger than Brunelleschi. In 1427, he finished a fresco in the church of Santa Maria Novella in Florence. It was a startling innovation. The subject matter was common enough: the Holy Trinity, with the Virgin Mary, Saint John, and the donors of the painting (*Fig. 8.4*). What was striking about it was that it presented the illusion of a Roman tunnel vault reaching back through the church wall. Perspective drawing is familiar to us today, but its unveiling in the fifteenth century provoked amazement. As viewers stood back from the wall, they must have gasped at what seemed to be a group of sculptured figures placed within a classical, three-dimensional chapel.

In northern Europe, artists were taking a different approach to naturalism. Among the most influential was Jan van Eyck, a painter of Flanders (in the Low Countries). Well-to-do patrons began to appear in prosperous commercial Flanders (p. 300) as in Italy, and Flemish art set the style for northern Europe during most of the Renaissance period.

Van Eyck's realism was distinct from that of the Italians. Giotto and Masaccio sought to give their figures roundness and solidity, set against a receding and darkened background. Van Eyck, less radical than Masaccio, observed most of the traditions of late Gothic painting, but he carried the recording of precise detail to an unprecedented degree. He treated objects in the background of his paintings with the same close attention that he gave to those in the foreground. His work has been described as both micro-

Fig. 8.5 Appearance and Reality. In *Giovanni Arnolfini and His Bride* (1434), Jan van Eyck uses the new technique of oil painting to reproduce the subtlest variations of color and the finest details. Many of the details raise questions, however. Why is the bridegroom shoeless—and the bride, too, as her cast-off clogs prove? And why is a candle burning in the chandelier by daylight? The marriage chamber is holy ground where one must go barefoot, and it is surveyed by the all-seeing eye of Christ, represented by the candle. Behind van Eyck's correctly rendered appearances there lies another world of mysteries and symbols.

© Erich Lessing/Art Resource, NY

scopic and telescopic. In the detail from one of his portraits, *Giovanni Arnolfini and His Bride* (*Fig. 8.5*), he seems to have counted every hair on the little dog, and he shows each one in a precise gradation of light and shadow.

In his efforts to achieve such effects, van Eyck experimented with various paint materials. He was among the first to develop and use *oil* paints. Before this time, painters had mixed powdered pigments with plain water or water "tempered" with egg yolk (*tempera*). The latter gave fairly good results but dried out rather quickly. Van Eyck discovered that by mixing his pigments with linseed oil, he could work more slowly and produce the special effects he desired. The quality and brilliance of his painting, as well as its accuracy, soon led most European artists to follow his lead.

THE LIBERATION OF SCULPTURE: DONATELLO

Sculpture, even more than painting, can be used for the faithful reproduction of nature. Sculptors have no need to create an illusion of depth, for they work in three dimensions. Yet medieval sculptors usually had to fit their figures into the narrow spaces assigned to them by architects and were therefore unable to realize the full potential of their art. Donatello, a contemporary of Masaccio and Brunelleschi, restored sculpture to an independent status and gave to his art the character of naturalism and humanism.

Donatello made a careful study of the remains of Roman sculpture. Discarding the copybook methods of medieval workmen, he also began to work (as the Romans and

© Scala/Art Resource, NY

Fig. 8.6 *The Feast of Herod.* Donatello's bronze relief was made about the same time as Masaccio's wall painting shown in *Fig. 8.4* (p. 347). Like the painting, it uses perspective to make the scene more lifelike and has a background of Roman arches and columns. In Giotto's tradition (*Fig. 8.1*, p. 345), it is a dramatic scene with individual figures expressing similar emotions—in this case, disgust and horror—in different ways.

Greeks had done) from live models. His fame spread swiftly from his native Florence, and he was commissioned to work in one city after another. One of his most striking early works, *The Feast of Herod* (1425), is part of the baptismal font (holy-water basin) of the cathedral of Siena (*Fig. 8.6*). It is a bronze *relief* sculpture—a flat panel in which some of the objects depicted, especially human figures, are raised above the surface. In the biblical scene shown, King Herod is being presented with the head of John the Baptist. Herod had reluctantly ordered John's beheading at the urging of his stepdaughter, Salome, because John had condemned the king's unlawful marriage to Salome's mother. Now Herod and his guests, seated at the banquet table, recoil in horror. Though Donatello's panel measures only about two feet on each side, it is rich in dramatic detail. The partly three-dimensional human figures stand out vividly, but in addition, having learned the trick of perspective from his friend Brunelleschi, Donatello created a marvelous illusion of depth. One can look through the rounded arches to Herod's musicians and beyond, through other archways, into the far background.

Near the close of his life, Donatello spent some ten years in Padua, which was then part of the Venetian Republic. There he produced a monumental equestrian statue in bronze (*Fig. 8.7*, p. 350). The rider, Gattamelata, is a Venetian general (*condottiere*) with the assured bearing of a Caesar. One of the first equestrian statues to be made since ancient Roman times, it was modeled after a monument to the emperor Marcus Aurelius

Fig. 8.7 *Gattamelata.* Donatello's bronze monument to a Venetian general is meant to recall a famous statue of the Roman emperor Marcus Aurelius (*Fig. 3.8*, p. 143), and the horse's hoof rests upon an orb, the symbol of imperial power. But since Marcus's time, the world has changed. Instead of a weaponless philosopher-ruler restraining an eager mount, Donatello shows a heavily armed and armored soldier astride a ponderous charger. The image is no longer one of peaceful rule over a vast empire, but of warlike power in a land of competing city-states.

© Cameraphoto/Art Resource, NY

(*Fig. 3.8*, p. 143). That splendid work, the only one of its kind to survive from the ancient world, had remained for more than a thousand years in its original location in Rome—most likely because until fifteenth-century humanists correctly identified it, the statue was thought to be of the first Christian emperor, Constantine.

ART TRIUMPHS OVER NATURE: BOTTICELLI, LEONARDO

The painters and sculptors of the late fifteenth and early sixteenth centuries were challenged by a task even greater than that of their predecessors. Masaccio, van Eyck, and Donatello had shown the way to naturalistic representation—an impressive achievement, made possible by intensive study and technical innovation. But once naturalism had been established, it revealed its own limitations. A "literal" presentation of subject matter did not necessarily result in harmonious composition, and it did not always carry a message, mood, or emotion in the most effective way.

Sandro Botticelli, a fifteenth-century Florentine, did much of his work for the Medici rulers and was very much influenced by the Platonism of their Academy (pp. 81, 340). He wanted to preserve the liveliness and realism typical of the work of the Renaissance pioneers, yet as a Platonist, he also wanted to create an art that would transcend (rise above) nature. This meant taking liberties with the actual appearance of things, subordinating realism to form and color, and even injecting elements of mystery. It also led him to become one of the first painters to use figures from classical mythology in major works, among them his *Birth of Venus* (*Fig. 8.8*).

The work is full of color, movement, and grace. In the center, being wafted to shore on a seashell, stands the goddess of love. The picture is harmonious and unified, and it conveys the mystery of beauty that so fascinated the Florentine intellectuals, who associated love of beauty with man's desire for reunion with the divine. Venus, symbolically, was the fountain of beauty and love. Though Botticelli used a flesh-and-blood model, his Venus appears detached, unearthly—an *idealized* beauty. In this way, Botti-

© Scala/Art Resource, NY

Fig. 8.8 *The Birth of Venus.* Botticelli's painting echoes descriptions of the love goddess's birth from the sea foam by classical and Renaissance poets. Zephyrus, god of the West Wind, wafts her toward the land, and a nymph starts to fling a garment about her. The figure of Venus is inspired by Hellenistic statues depicting her as modest rather than erotic— compare her thoughtful eyes with the bold glance of Titian's *Venus* (*Fig. 8.9*, p. 352). Her beauty is no image of bodily desire but one of spiritual love that springs from the mind of God.

celli revived the classical tradition of depicting the naked female body as beautiful, noble, and divine (*Fig. 2.12*, p. 94).

Medieval artists had occasionally depicted female nudes, but not with the intention of showing their beauty—their commonest subject was Eve, the mother of fallen humanity. For an artist to rejoice in the beauty of the female (or male) body, they believed, was mere pagan lustfulness. In fact, ancient Greek and Roman nudes had not usually been particularly erotic. In the Renaissance, however, the idea persisted that a depiction of a beautiful female body must excite desire—and now that Botticelli had made female nudes respectable, artists soon began painting them in ways that were frankly sensual. The Venetian painter Titian is a notable example. His *Venus of Urbino* (*Fig. 8.9*), which he painted in 1538, concentrates the viewer's attention on a reclining, seductive nude. This is not the spiritlike Venus of Botticelli; in fact she is probably not meant to be Venus at all—the picture acquired its title long after it was painted, and must originally have celebrated the beauty of a mistress of the duke of Urbino, a minor Italian state. In any case, she is an enticing woman who seems aware of her naked loveliness and the eyes of the viewer. Titian's remarkable technique is revealed in his flesh tones and textures. His works were to serve as models for every painter of nudes who followed him.

The leading experimenter in both art and nature, however, was Leonardo da Vinci, who fulfilled the humanist ideal of the "universal genius" (p. 337). His notebooks demonstrate the astonishing breadth of his curiosity. He began his artistic training toward the end of the fifteenth century as an apprentice in a Florentine workshop, where

© Scala/Art Resource, NY

Fig. 8.9 *Venus of Urbino.* Titian used his supreme mastery of Renaissance artistic techniques to give this painting its sensual power. Perspective makes the viewer feel the closeness of the naked woman by showing the depth of the room behind her. The subtle tones of oil painting reveal her body's softness and strength. The arrangement of the figures makes a contrast between the woman looking toward the viewer and her servants who turn away, thereby adding to the intimacy of her glance. The result is a memorable depiction of the female nude as an image of desire.

he learned, under the guild system of supervision (pp. 242–243), the standard methods of observing and sketching models and objects. He studied the optics of perspective, the mixing of colors, and the techniques of metalwork. But when he left the shop of his master, Leonardo had only started his education. For he was less interested in the surface appearance of things than in what lay underneath, and so he undertook his ceaseless exploration of anatomy, physiology, and nature (p. 342).

He left many of his projects unfinished. We have only a few of his major paintings, and some of these are in poor condition. In those we have, his genius is clear. He resolved the difficulties of combining lifelike representation with artistic form and an element of mystery. In his use of light and shadow, Leonardo found that shading lends grace and softness to facial features and reduces stiffness of line. By blurring his contours, especially at the corners of the mouth and eyes, he left something to the imagination of the viewer. Each time we look at his *Mona Lisa* (*Fig. 8.10*), her expression (and thought) seems to change.

Leonardo's most famous painting is *The Last Supper,* completed in 1497 (*Fig. 8.11*). This sacred subject had been treated countless times before. How could an artist do anything special or original with it? Most earlier paintings had shown Christ and his disciples quietly seated around the supper table in varying settings and kinds of dress. Leonardo introduced drama and excitement. He chose the precise moment after the Lord had said, "One of you will betray me" (Matthew 26:21). While Christ sits calmly at the center of the picture, waves of disbelief, amazement, and distress sweep to the

Fig. 8.10 *Mona Lisa.* According to Leonardo da Vinci, "The good painter has essentially two things to represent: the individual and the state of that individual's mind." Here Leonardo puts his advice into practice. His refined oil painting technique gives the illusion of life to the sitter's physical appearance yet also creates a veiled, misty effect. His artistic perception probes her inner nature—including the element of mystery at the core of every human personality. This revealing yet mysterious quality is what has given the portrait its enduring fascination and fame.

Fig. 8.11 "Is It I?" Leonardo's *Last Supper* depicts the disciples reacting to Jesus' announcement that one of them will betray him. To convey the drama of this moment, Leonardo used the "stagecraft" skills of Giotto and Donatello (*Fig. 8.1,* p. 345; *Fig. 8.6,* p. 349). He made countless preliminary drawings, "rehearsing" individual disciples in expressions and gestures of protest, astonishment, disbelief—and in Judas' case (third from left), obstinate defiance. For the Milan monks who commissioned this work for their dining hall, it was an unforgettable reminder of the most sacred of all meals.

Photo Vatican Museums

Fig. 8.12 *The Creation of Adam.* Michelangelo's depiction gives visual form to a humanist version of Christian beliefs about the human race and its creator. God, borne by angels on a rushing mighty wind, reaches toward the first man; the mortal body stirs and reaches toward God; and the immortal soul passes from its divine originator to its human recipient. In the crook of God's arm, the still uncreated Eve looks intently toward Adam, the mother of humankind gazing upon its father. Beyond her, God's finger rests on the infant Christ, humankind's future redeemer.

right and left of him. Only Judas, among the disciples, is motionless. And even with the agitation and tension of the recorded instant, the painting forms a harmonious whole.

THE ARTISTIC CLIMAX: MICHELANGELO

Though Leonardo was the most versatile of Renaissance figures, he was overshadowed as an artist by Michelangelo Buonarroti. Leonardo observed and investigated nature as a whole; Michelangelo concentrated on anatomy, convinced that the inmost urges and sensitivities of human beings could best be expressed through the human figure.

Michelangelo preferred to represent the body in three dimensions of sculpture, but he was required to do numerous works as a painter. In 1508, he was called to Rome from his native Florence by Pope Julius II—himself a Renaissance man of *virtù* who was no saint, but a statesman, general, and patron of the arts and architecture. The pontiff wanted Michelangelo to make him a monumental tomb, but complications arose, and Julius asked Michelangelo to paint the ceiling of his private chapel instead. The chapel had been built by Pope Sixtus IV (hence the name "Sistine"), and its walls had been painted by an earlier generation of masters (including Botticelli). The ceiling vault, however, remained blank.

Michelangelo, disappointed when his sculpting commission was put off, accepted the new task with reluctance. But having once decided to undertake it, he plunged into the work with his customary vigor. Some four years later, the fresco was finished. It covers about 10,000 square feet and includes more than three hundred figures. In plan, execution, and magnitude, no other painting in history by a single individual has surpassed it.

In the Sistine Chapel painting, as in all his creations, Michelangelo expressed his deep religious concern about humankind. Tormented by a sense of sin—his own and that of the human species—he suffered from a feeling of personal frustration, of unfulfilled ambitions. His conviction that individuals struggle helplessly against destiny led

Fig. 8.13 *David.* The Israelite hero was a traditional symbol of the Florentine city-state, which prided itself on fighting off such neighboring "Goliaths" as the popes. Statues usually showed David with the head of the defeated Goliath at his feet, but the twenty-six-year-old Michelangelo carved him dauntlessly facing the approaching giant. Michelangelo was inspired by serenely balanced poses that he had seen in Roman copies of Hellenistic statues (*Fig. 2.11*, p, 94), but this David is not at rest. His balanced pose is that of a fighter poised to swing into ferocious combat.

him to a tragic view of life. He felt that the human spirit, of divine origin, desires to return to God but is held fast by the sins of the flesh. In *The Last Judgment,* which he painted late in life on the end wall of the Sistine Chapel, he portrayed a severe and muscular Christ condemning crowds of sinners to the eternal fires of hell.

Michelangelo was clearly influenced by the Platonism of the Academy (p. 340). In an effort to reconcile his Christian convictions with the teachings of the Platonists, he merged the two in his pictorial layout for the chapel vault. The main feature, on the ceiling proper, is a series of nine panels showing the stories of the Creation and the Flood. Perhaps the most appealing of these panels is *The Creation of Adam* (*Fig. 8.12*). God the Father, borne by the heavenly host, is about to bring the inert Adam to life by the touch of his finger. Evident here is Michelangelo's ability to suggest latent (reserved) power and to inject light and movement.

After finishing his backbreaking labor on the Sistine scaffolds, Michelangelo returned to his first love, sculpture. From solid blocks of marble, he began to carve several figures for the projected tomb of Julius II. The special quality of his sculpture can be understood in part by his attitude toward the stone: before taking up his chisel, he always visualized the human form within each block. He then proceeded, with furious energy, to "liberate" the form from the stone.

One of his finest works, carved some years earlier, expresses the spirit of athletic youth. His 18-foot-tall *David* (*Fig. 8.13*) was at first placed in the main piazza of Florence. A copy stands there today, but the original is housed in a Florentine museum. The *David* shows the influence of Greek sculpture on Michelangelo's work—in particular its celebration of the naked male body, a theme that had first been revived by Donatello. Later creations, such as the figures for Julius's tomb, show the influence of Platonism. In one of these, known as the *Dying Slave,* Michelangelo shows a mature, powerful body falling into repose as death approaches, releasing the slave from life's futile struggle. Among Michelangelo's other sculptural works are a *Pietà* (the sorrowing Virgin Mary mourning for the dead Christ) and a wrathful, monumental *Moses.*

Later in life, having won fame as a painter and a sculptor, Michelangelo turned his attention to architecture. Here, too, he was without peer. He continued the development of the Renaissance style that had been initiated by Brunelleschi. Much of his work was done in Rome, and the touch of his hand is revealed there in countless places, but his greatest masterpiece was the dome of Saint Peter's Basilica.

The new Saint Peter's (replacing the original church of the fourth century) was planned early in the sixteenth century by the tireless Julius II. He wished to erect, over the tomb of the first apostle, a structure that would surpass all others in Christendom. Several architects had a hand in the design, but in 1547, Michelangelo was put in charge. During the remaining years of his life, he devoted most of his energies to planning the mighty church.

The floor plan was for a colossal structure laid out in the form of a Greek (square) cross. A central dome was to be the crowning feature. Earlier schemes had called for a shallow dome modeled on that of the Pantheon (*Fig. 3.5,* p. 139), but Michelangelo wanted something greater for the "capitol" of Christendom. Inspired by Brunelleschi's dome in Florence (*Fig. 8.2,* p. 346), he planned one even steeper and higher—one that would tower over every other building in the Eternal City.

Although he died before Saint Peter's was completed, the dome was finished according to his designs. The square plan of the basilica, however, was altered into a Latin (oblong) cruciform plan (*Fig. 6.2,* p. 258), which meant that a long nave (central aisle) had to be constructed. As a result, the view of the dome from the front of the church is partially blocked. The view of Saint Peter's from the rear (*Fig. 8.14*) shows the dome as it would have appeared from all sides had the original plan been carried out.

The magnificent dome, the largest in the world, has been copied by architects everywhere. Equal in diameter to that of the Pantheon, it rises 300 feet higher. It stands as a splendid symbol of Christianity and a fitting monument to Michelangelo.

Literature and Drama

While the visual arts of the Renaissance were reaching their climax in Italy, striking accomplishments in literature were appearing beyond the Alps. The north could not match the best painting and sculpture of the south. It proved equal or superior, however, in the *written word*—the impact of which was enormously increased by the invention of printing with movable type (pp. 305–306). Erasmus probably had more contemporary readers than any previous writer, and now that there existed a mass market for books, he was soon joined by other humanist authors whose works became "best-sellers."

THE LIBERTARIAN HUMORIST: RABELAIS

In France, the most popular author was François Rabelais, an enthusiastic humanist with a talent for satire and parody. Though his books were condemned by religious

Fig. 8.14 Saint Peter's Basilica. In 1503, Pope Julius II decided to tear down the thousand-year-old basilica of the Roman emperor Constantine and replace it with a more splendid building. His chosen architect, Donato Bramante, planned a dome that would dwarf that of another ancient Roman structure, the Pantheon (*Fig. 3.5*, p. 139). It was Michelangelo who actually carried out most of this daring Renaissance undertaking—not just to bring the "ancients" back to life, but to destroy one of their most revered works in order to outdo them.

and civil authorities, they had a warm appeal to readers. Rabelais was (and still is) a most popular author.

Like Erasmus, who was born a generation earlier, Rabelais knew the Church and the universities from the inside. From a middle-class family, he had entered a Franciscan monastery in order to become a scholar. But he was a rebel from the beginning; his absorption in the classics disturbed his superiors and led to trouble. He switched from one religious order to another, for a time wore the garb of a priest, studied at various universities, and later took up law and medicine. His career, like his writing, followed no visible plan. With a vast appetite for life and learning, he was the personification of a vigorous and spontaneous humanism.

Though Rabelais loved the classics and knew them intimately (especially those of Rome), his own temperament was by no means classical. He wrote in vernacular French, rather than classical Latin, and he detested all rules and regulations. One should follow, he insisted, one's own inclinations. Rabelais thus represented a humanism that did not copy classical models (or any other) but stood as a purely *individualistic* philosophy. Rejecting the doctrine of original sin (and most other doctrines), he stressed *natural goodness;* he held that most people, given freedom and proper education (in the classics), will live happy and productive lives.

This idea is central to Rabelais's great work, *Gargantua and Pantagruel.* The story, about two imaginary giant-kings, was published in several volumes over a period of

© Scala/Art Resource, NY

c. 1350	1520	1650
Era of Renaissance Humanism	Reformation and Religious Wars	

c. 1600

years, beginning in 1538. He wrote the work primarily for amusement, because he believed that laughter (like thought) is a distinctively human function. However, in telling of the heroes' education and adventures, he voiced his opinions on the human traits and institutions of his time. In a tumble of words, learned and playful, he mingled serious ideas with earthy jokes and jibes.

Monasticism was a prime target for Rabelais, as it was for most humanists. Its stress on self-denial, repression, and regimentation was to him inhumane and hateful. He had Gargantua give funds to a "model" institution that violates monastic practices in every possible way. At this "abbey of Thélème," with its fine libraries and recreational facilities, elegantly dressed men and women are free to "do as they please." Monks, hypocrites, lawyers, and peddlers of gloom are barred from the abbey; only handsome, high-spirited people are admitted.

Rabelais disliked pretense and deception and praised the natural instincts and abilities of free persons. Rejecting the ascetic ideal, he expressed humanism in its most robust and optimistic form. In doing so, he also anticipated the modern appetite for unlimited experience and pleasure (pp. 654–655).

THE SKEPTICAL ESSAYIST: MONTAIGNE

Michel de Montaigne, born a generation after Rabelais, lived through the same troubled times of religious struggle between the Protestants and Catholics and shared Rabelais's keen interest in the classics. But his temperament was nearer that of Erasmus (pp. 342–344). Both men remained loyal to the Roman Catholic Church, and both were dedicated scholars, though Montaigne was more secular-minded and detached than Erasmus. The son of a landowning family near Bordeaux, Montaigne received a superb education. His father held public office, traveled abroad, and believed in a humanistic upbringing for his children. When his father died, Michel inherited the family estate and was able to retire at the age of thirty-eight to his library of a thousand books.

Privacy and leisure, which Montaigne treasured above all else, gave him an opportunity to read and think. He chose only books that gave him pleasure—pleasure in the Epicurean sense (pp. 132–133). These were the Latin authors (and some Greeks in translation), whom Montaigne considered superior in style and content to other writers. From his reading, he developed a desire to live his personal life according to classical ways, and like Petrarch, he began to record his own thoughts and observations.

Out of this activity came the first two volumes of *Essays* (1580). Unlike Rabelais's books, these were models of clear French prose. They were immediately popular, and Montaigne was encouraged to publish a third volume soon afterward. Altogether, he wrote more than a hundred essays on such topics as the emotions, superstition, customs, education, marriage, scholarship, and death. His usual manner was to begin with the opinions of traditional authorities on the topic, inserting quotations from their works, and then to explain his own views. Sometimes he would present opposing answers to a given question and then suggest a compromise solution—or perhaps no solution at all.

Montaigne's essays were a new form of literature, though they owed much to the example of Seneca, a Roman writer of the first century A.D. (p. 132). Montaigne did not attempt to change the minds of his readers but wrote in large measure for his own satisfaction. And because the essays were based on his own experiences and thoughts, they were also a form of *autobiography.* The notion that every person of worth should pass on some record of his or her life and ideas became widespread during the Renaissance. The boastful Florentine artist Benvenuto Cellini was among those who accepted this idea; he dictated his *Autobiography* in 1560. Gradually, the *essay* and the *memoir* became standard literary forms, further expressions of the individualism and self-confidence of the age.

In one of Montaigne's most notable essays on the subject of knowledge and reason (Volume 2, Essay 12), he showed himself to be a philosophical *relativist* (p. 80). He spoke of the limits of reason in efforts to comprehend the universe: neither theology, classical wisdom, nor science can provide final answers to the "big questions"; all knowledge is subject to uncertainty and doubt. The human mind, observed Montaigne, is erratic; and the senses, which are unreliable, often control the mind. Beliefs, no matter how firmly held, cannot be regarded as constant, for they, too, have their seasons, their birth and death. He thus challenged the self-assurance of both Christians and earlier humanists.

Montaigne did not suggest that people should not use their minds. On the contrary, he thought that every individual capable of reason should seek answers satisfactory to that individual. The thinking person should never embrace the ready-made views of others, no matter how impressive their authority; rather, one ought to consider various ideas and then make a choice. And if one feels unable to make a choice, one should remain in doubt. The uncertain character of knowledge ought to teach us, above all, that *dogmatism* (absolute self-assurance) is unjustified—and that persecuting people for differing beliefs is wrong.

Montaigne made his eloquent plea for tolerance in the midst of the frightful struggle among religious fanatics that raged through sixteenth-century France. He could see that war and homicide are often the outcomes of absolutistic thought and belief. Like Erasmus, Montaigne was a political conservative and opposed to violence; he felt that firm authority was indispensable to peace and order. Though he cherished independence of thought, he did not rebel against established institutions, hoping that those who held power would see the light, ultimately, of moderation and decency. In any event, he stuck to his personal philosophy—a blend of skepticism, Epicureanism, and Stoicism (pp. 132–134)—and remained aloof from other people. In the quiet and security of his library, Montaigne could meditate on one of his favorite sayings: "Rejoice in your present life; all else is beyond you."

Rabelais and Montaigne were among the few writers on the Continent whose devotion to humanism was not disturbed by the religious upheavals that broke out around 1520. Another was Miguel de Cervantes, the greatest author of Spain. He began his masterpiece, *Don Quixote,* well past midlife (about 1600). It was a satire on the tales of chivalry (p. 274) that were still being written (and read) in his native land. Cervantes's hero is a caricature of the romantic *knight;* he imagines windmills to be evil giants and vainly charges against them. While Don Quixote is a hopeless idealist, his squire, Sancho Panza, sees the world in simple, down-to-earth terms. (As the story unfolds, the dialogue between them produces a reversal of values in each.) Cervantes succeeded in ridiculing chivalric literature and revealed, through the Don's adventures, a panorama of the Spain of his day. On the philosophical level, the contrasting and shifting values of Panza and Quixote remind one of the relativity of truth that Montaigne had noted in his essays.

THE MASTER DRAMATIST: SHAKESPEARE

Humanism came late to England. It had hardly been established there by 1500, and it might even have vanished in the religious turmoil that erupted shortly thereafter. One of the casualties, indeed, was Sir Thomas More. A dedicated scholar and a friend of Erasmus, he wrote the visionary *Utopia,* under the influence of Plato's dialogues and his *Republic* (p. 82), in which he set down the humane features of a decent, planned society (p. 517). But he later paid with his life for refusing to swear loyalty to the king as head of the Church of England (p. 381). Humanism proved hardy, however, and attained its full expression in literature around 1600. The leading genius of this expression was William Shakespeare.

Shakespeare was not a classical scholar. As his friend (and rival playwright) Ben Jonson said, he knew "small Latin and less Greek." But he was familiar (in the original or in translation) with many of the ancient authors. Moreover, he was filled with the spirit of humanism, which characterized the Elizabethan Age (1550–1600). Shakespeare's plays contain elements of the classical and the timeless, but they speak in the voice of the Renaissance.

The roots of Elizabethan drama go back to the Romans and the Greeks, for during the Middle Ages, there had been only religious pageants and Passion and morality plays. But the classical revival of the fifteenth century stimulated the reenactment of Roman dramas at the courts of Italian rulers, and in time, a new form of secular drama, based on the Roman model, came into being and spread across Europe.

Although the Italian playwrights followed the classical tradition of lengthy recitations, a chorus, and little action, the English introduced modifications to suit their national taste. They also began to build permanent theaters for dramatic performances; none had existed in medieval times. When Shakespeare arrived in London about 1590, both the new drama and the new way of designing theaters were approaching maturity.

The Globe Theater of his day is a good example of the Elizabethan playhouse. Like the plays that were performed there, it drew inspiration from the Greeks and Romans but met the needs and tastes of its own times. In contrast to the theater of Epidaurus and the Colosseum, with their spacious accommodation for audiences of tens of thousands (*Fig. 2.4*, p. 87; *Fig. 3.7*, p. 142), the Globe held a maximum of three thousand, with considerable overcrowding. Instead of being a religious or public monument to which spectators were admitted free, it was an admission-charging private business (in which Shakespeare himself owned a one-eighth share), located in a theater and red-light district safely across the River Thames from London itself. Circular in outward plan, it faced inward on a large courtyard (*Fig. 8.15*). The stage, or platform, was built on one side of the inner circle and projected some 20 feet into the yard; ringing the yard were three tiers of covered galleries or boxes. Spectators who could not afford boxes (the "groundlings") stood or sat in the yard itself.

Hamlet, Shakespeare's Globe 2000, photo © John Tramper

Fig. 8.15 The Globe Theater. In this modern replica of Shakespeare's theater, the groundlings stand in the open and the quality folk sit in covered galleries. Behind the stage are curtains for Polonius to spy on Hamlet and a balcony where Juliet can be overheard by Romeo. Besides this minimal scenery, there were occasional special effects that could go badly wrong. In 1613, a cannon that was fired to liven up a battle scene set the roof alight, and the theater burned to the ground.

The stage lacked the scenery and equipment available in our contemporary theaters. A curtained area in the rear could serve as a chamber or an inner room; when closed off, it became the backdrop for a setting on the main stage. The front of the platform often served as a street or passageway. Because there was no main curtain, the script had to provide action to clear the stage at the end of each scene.

A balcony directly above the stage could represent the window of a house, the deck of a ship, or the top of a castle wall, while trapdoors in the floor and roof of the stage enabled witches and spirits to ascend and descend. Lighting was no problem, since this was an open-air theater and performances were given in the afternoon. Though much of the setting was left to the viewer's imagination, the Elizabethan theater proved remarkably flexible and enabled the actors to establish close contact with their audience. As in classical drama, all the roles were played by men or boys. (The stage was not considered a fit place for females, and "respectable" women were seldom seen in the audience.)

Shakespeare's dramas differed from ancient drama in significant ways. They were not associated with religious festivals, as Greek drama had been (pp. 86–88), and though they often dealt with moral issues, their spirit was markedly secular. They lack any doctrinaire Christian tone; in some of them, there are even hints of religious doubts and fatalism.

The range of Shakespeare's themes and locales is greater than that of the classical dramatists. "All the world's a stage," declares one of his characters (Jaques, in *As You Like It*)—speaking to an audience that had daily reports of adventures in newly discovered lands. Many other features of his work reflect the values and concerns of humanism. The urge to power is the central theme in many of his plays, and the rising sense of nationality, or patriotism, fills his historical dramas. Shakespeare's deep interest in character and inner psychological conflict reflects the Renaissance concern with individualism. Finally, he demonstrates the same concern for realism displayed by the humanist painters and sculptors.

Hamlet, one of Shakespeare's greatest tragedies, illustrates his dramatic methods. The story comes out of a medieval Danish history book, though Shakespeare probably based his work on an English dramatic adaptation of the early sixteenth century. *Hamlet* is a tragedy of revenge, a type of drama popular at the time. Shakespeare gave it the elements of conflict, suspense, violence, and poetic imagery that his audience enjoyed. Since the audience consisted chiefly of well-read individuals, he was able to bring moral and philosophical ideas into the course of the dramatic action.

As a character, Hamlet typifies the ideal gentleman of the new Europe (pp. 339–340). He also embodies the conflict between meditation and action that fascinated the intellectuals of the age. Hamlet knows that it is his duty (by custom) to avenge his murdered father, but he insists on using the humanistic tool of reason to guide his actions. While he delays acting, a series of miserable deaths occurs. Shakespeare leaves it to his audience to decide whether reason should bow to custom and whether humans are the masters of their destiny.

We know little about Shakespeare's life except that he prospered in London and retired to his native Stratford some years before his death in 1616, but we do have the legacy of his works. No one has had a surer feeling for the sense and sound of the English language, and his collected writings have been referred to as the "English secular Bible." The Renaissance, which admired the individual genius, produced one in Shakespeare. Moreover, as Ben Jonson observed, he was "not of an age but for all time."

RECOMMENDED READING

The Renaissance View of Human Nature J. Burckhardt, *The Civilization of the Renaissance in Italy* (1860), is a readable masterpiece whose influence on understanding of the Renaissance has lasted to the present; the best reprint is that of 1990, with an introduction by P. Burke that assesses the validity of Burckhardt's approach. Burke's own *The European Renaissance: Centers and Peripheries* (1998), provides an authoritative present-day interpretation. J. Kraye, ed., *The Cambridge Companion to Renaissance Humanism* (1990), contains brief essays by leading scholars describing the impact of humanism on many fields of thought and art. P. Burke, *The Italian Renaissance: Culture and Society in Italy* (1999), relates culture and art to social and political institutions.

The best short treatment of philosophy in the Renaissance is P. O. Kristeller, *Renaissance Thought* (1961); a longer and more recent account is B. P. Copenhaver and C. P. Schmitt, *Renaissance Philosophy* (1992).

On individual humanists, J. McConica, *Erasmus* (1991), and A. Kenny, *Thomas More* (1983), are good brief accounts, both available in J. McConica et al., *Renaissance Thinkers* (1993).

The Revolution in Art The best introductions to all forms of Renaissance art and architecture throughout Europe are P. Murray and L. Murray, *The Art of the Renaissance* (1963), covering the fourteenth and fifteenth centuries; and L. Murray, *The High Renaissance and Mannerism* (1977), covering the sixteenth century. Specifically on architecture, see P. Murray, *The Architecture of the Italian Renaissance* (1980).

On individual artists, the following books are recommended. G. Gaeta Bertel, *Donatello* (1998); L. Bellosi, *Giotto* (1982); K. Clark, *Leonardo da Vinci* (1968); L. Murray, *Michelangelo* (1985); F. Pedrocco, *Titian* (1993); and F. Zollner, *Botticelli* (1998).

Literature and Drama   W. A. Coupe, *The Continental Renaissance, 1500–1600* (1991), surveys literature in Italy, France, Spain, and Germany. M. J. Heath, *Rabelais* (1996); P. Burke, *Montaigne* (1981); M. Duran, *Cervantes* (1974); and G. Greer, *Shakespeare* (1986), are good short introductions giving cultural and social background.

P. Hyland, *An Introduction to Shakespeare: The Dramatist in His Context* (1996), is an excellent short account of Shakespearean drama, including Elizabethan staging and the theatrical profession. A. Burgess, *Shakespeare* (1970), is a well-illustrated biography by a distinguished present-day man of letters.

INFOTRAC COLLEGE EDITION

Visit the source collections at **http://academic.cengage.com/infotrac,** and use the Search function with the following key terms:

Renaissance   humanism   Leonardo da Vinci

William Shakespeare

WESTERN CIVILIZATION RESOURCES

Visit the Brief History of the Western World Companion Web Site for resources specific to this textbook:

http://history.wadsworth.com/greerbrief09/

Also, the CD in the back of this book and the World History Resources Center at **http://history.wadsworth.com/west_civ/** offer a variety of tools to help you succeed in this course, including access to quizzes; images; documents; interactive simulations, maps, and timelines; movie explorations; and a wealth of other sources.

CHAPTER 9

The Reformation:
Division and Reform in the Church

OVERVIEW

The Protestant Reformation began as an explosion of long-standing grievances against the Catholic Church—grievances that had grown worse with the changes in medieval civilization after 1300. Rival popes backed by opposing groups of powerful rulers had brought the papacy into discredit. Social revolts had merged with and strengthened heretic movements. Renaissance scholars had contrasted the Church's wealth and corruption with the simple ways of early Christianity. From 1517 on, Martin Luther turned the grievances into a rebellion by proclaiming the revolutionary idea that the Church was leading souls to hell rather than heaven, and must therefore be "reformed in head and limbs."

Luther preached the equality of all Christians—their equal helplessness to please God by their own deeds, and their equal freedom and holiness once they put their faith in God's mercy to save them all the same. The Church's belief that Christians could help themselves and others into heaven—by living as monks or nuns or unmarried priests, for instance, or by giving gifts to the Church—was a devilish deception. Instead of obeying the popes who upheld this deception, Christians must be guided into heaven by God himself, speaking through their own consciences and their own understanding of the word of God in the Bible.

As Luther's protest spread, however, his followers interpreted his message of "reformation" in different ways. Were unworthy humans helpless even to have faith unless God gave it to them himself, so that it was he who predestined them to go to heaven or hell? Did God want the Church to be restructured on the self-governing model of early Christianity, did he want it to be governed from above by bishops, or did he want no clergy and Church government at all? Did Christian equality and freedom apply also to worldly matters—to relations between peasants and nobles, for instance, or between subjects and rulers? These questions seemed to affect the salvation of souls just as much as those in dispute between Protestants and Catholics, and the Protestant arguments over them were just as bitter. Instead of reforming the whole Church as they had originally wanted, the Protestants came to be divided into many different churches, each with its own beliefs and organization.

Meanwhile, by far the largest of the churches was still the Roman Catholic Church. In response to the Protestant challenge, it rallied around its traditional beliefs and practices as the only way to heaven, and around the traditional authority of the papacy as the only guide of Christians. It abolished some of the worst abuses that had brought the clergy into contempt, and developed new religious orders, above all the Jesuits, that were powerful instruments of education and propaganda. And although it lost most of northern Europe to Protestantism, it gained millions of new believers in Latin America.

About 1650, after more than a century of controversy, propaganda, persecution, and war, the struggle among the churches ended in stalemate. The survival of Protestantism was assured, as a third branch of Christianity alongside Catholicism and Orthodoxy. This was the greatest single change in Western religion since the rise of Christianity itself. It was also one that affected many other areas of civilization apart from religion, as the Reformation interacted with the other changes involved in the remaking of Europe—sometimes pushing them forward, sometimes holding them back, and sometimes changing their direction.

For the time being, the Reformation strengthened the growing power of both Protestant and Catholic rulers, since it was they above all who had the power to choose and uphold one or other church. The partnership between Church and state grew even stronger than before—except that now the state was the senior partner. But social rebels, political dissidents, and religious refugees kept alive the idea that Christian freedom and equality applied to this world as well as the next. As the struggles of the churches died down, the idea got a wider hearing, and in time it came to influence the structure of states and societies.

Likewise, the Reformation at first blighted many ideals of the Renaissance, such as tolerance and understanding among religions and optimism about the possibilities of human nature. But as the religious disputes died down, the idea of toleration revived and was even strengthened by the Protestant belief in freedom of conscience. Religious persecution and war came to seem evils of the past, which had been overcome as human nature changed for the better. To some, religious arguments themselves came to seem pointless—as if the Christian beliefs that were argued about could never be proven and perhaps were not even true.

Background of the Reformation

From the view of the established Catholic organization, the Protestant reformers were *heretics* who defied the pope. Differences on matters of doctrine had arisen early in the history of Christianity, and in the Middle Ages, the Christian Church had come to be divided between the Catholic West and the Orthodox East (p. 282), but for many centuries, unity had been maintained in the West. To preserve Western unity, the popes and bishops had exercised continuous watchfulness and strong discipline. During the Middle Ages, thousands of heretics had been burned at the stake in the name of Christian purity and unity. How was it that the Protestant heretics survived where their predecessors had perished? One reason is that the late medieval Church had suffered a fateful decline.

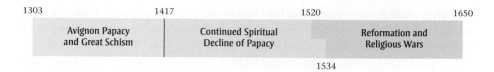

DECAY OF THE CHURCH

During the thirteenth century, the medieval Church had reached the height of its power. This was when the great cathedrals were built, when powerful reform orders were founded, and when scholastic philosophy achieved its greatest influence. Under Pope Innocent III, the papal monarchy had dominated the rulers of Europe as well as the Church organization (p. 256). But the fourteenth and fifteenth centuries saw a steady fall in the condition of the Church, and by 1500, the organization had reached its low point.

The fortunes of the Church as a whole were closely tied to those of the papacy. Medieval popes like Gregory VII and Innocent III had done much to strengthen the Church's structure. But the popes of later centuries had been less successful in their undertakings, and their failures affected the entire institution. Boniface VIII, for example, was defeated in his struggle with the French king Philip the Fair (pp. 256–257). After Boniface's death in 1303, Philip moved to avoid future trouble with Rome by forcing the election of a French bishop as Pope Clement V. The new relationship was demonstrated shortly thereafter when Pope Clement V transferred his court from Rome to Avignon, a papal holding on the lower Rhône River, just east of the border of the French kingdom. Clement secured a French majority in the College of Cardinals (p. 253), and for some seventy years, a succession of French popes reigned at Avignon.

Outside France, these popes were looked upon with suspicion and hostility. Because the pope holds office by virtue of his being the bishop of Rome, it seemed improper that he should reside anywhere but in the Eternal City. Clement had left Rome voluntarily, chiefly because conditions there were unsafe, and the Avignon popes acted quite independently. But his move confirmed a widespread feeling that the papacy had become a captive of the French monarchy. The Italian humanist Petrarch labeled the popes' stay at Avignon "the Babylonian Captivity," a reference to the forced removal of ancient Jewish leaders to Babylonia (pp. 51–52).

More serious embarrassments to the Church were yet to come. In 1377, Gregory XI decided to return the papal court to Rome; upon his death there, the Roman populace pressured the cardinals into choosing an Italian as pope. But the French cardinals then fled the city, pronounced the election invalid, and chose a pope of their own. This one, with his supporting cardinals, moved to Avignon, while the Italian pope, with his cardinals, stayed in Rome. Each declared the other to be a false pope and excommunicated him and his followers.

The Great Schism (split), as this division was called, lasted some forty years (1378–1417). Europe now endured the spectacle of a Church divided into opposing camps, with two popes and two colleges of cardinals. Conscientious Christians were distressed, for they had no way of being certain who was the pope and who was the "antipope." Civil rulers supported whichever side seemed more useful politically. Thus France and its allies recognized Avignon, while England and the German princes recognized Rome. The schism was at last settled by a general council of the Church at Constance, which deposed both rival popes and elected a new one. But by this time, the papacy had suffered serious damage. The foundation of papal power had previously been its immense moral authority. That position was now gravely weakened, opening the way to contempt and defiance.

The humiliation of the papacy contributed to the decline of the clergy as a whole—a decline that had begun after 1300. Worldliness and abuses had swept the Church once more, and the brave reform efforts of earlier centuries were forgotten (pp. 251–253). The monastic orders, traditionally the conscience of the clergy, fell into scandal, corrupted by comfortable living. Many of the seculars (priests and bishops) also slipped into self-indulgence, lust, and greed. While there doubtless remained thousands of honest, chaste, and pious clerics, the general situation was nevertheless distressing.

Vigorous reform of these abuses became urgent. But the popes of the fifteenth century, themselves deep in worldliness, were not interested in reform. The "princes" of the Church were more interested in politics, wealth, and art than in spiritual affairs. The Medici pope, Leo X, is reported to have said, after his election in 1513, "As God has seen fit to give us the papacy, let us enjoy it!"

THE AWAKENING REFORM SPIRIT

Many devout Christians realized that moral reform of the Church would have to start at the top, but they feared that the papacy lacked the will to reform. As a consequence, they began to turn inward in their devotions. In northern Europe, the fifteenth century saw a revival of *mysticism* (p. 252) and *pietism* (deep reverence). One response there was the founding of the Brethren of the Common Life (p. 342), whose members turned away from the formalism of established rituals. They joined together in semireligious communities stressing Christlike simplicity, purity of heart, and direct communion with God. Other Christians were moving, at the same time, toward a new idea of what the Church should be. Their model was "primitive" Christianity as practiced during the first century after Christ. The Brethren stayed within the Church, but others went into open rebellion. In England, the followers of John Wiclif became for a time a widespread movement, and the Bohemian supporters of the Czech reformer Jan Hus were able to take and hold an entire country.

John Wiclif. A leading Oxford scholar and teacher, Wiclif was among the first to question openly the need for a priesthood. After a lifetime of study, Wiclif concluded that the Church was suffering from more than just the misbehavior of some of its clergy. He challenged the established role and powers of the clergy itself—arguing that God and Scripture (the Bible) are the sole sources of spiritual authority. And to enable ordinary English people to read Scripture for themselves, he made an English translation of the Vulgate Bible (p. 343).

More important, Wiclif urged laymen to read the Bible for themselves. Every individual, he said, can communicate directly with the Lord and can be saved without the aid of priests or saints. For challenging the accepted doctrines of authority and salvation, he was condemned and forced to retire from teaching. Civil disturbances in England and the Great Schism in the Church saved him from more drastic punishment, but many of his followers in England (who were known as Lollards) were burned as heretics—a penalty that was specially introduced by an alarmed Parliament. Systematic repression caused the movement to die out before the Reformation began.

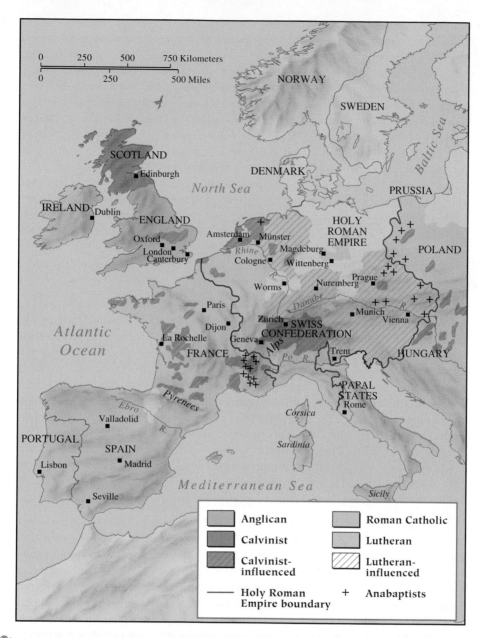

Map 9.1 Catholicism and Protestantism in 1560. The map shows the religious division of Europe when the Reformation was approaching its height. The Lutheran, Calvinist, and Anglican reformations are dominant in much of northern and western Europe, and only Italy and Spain are still entirely Catholic. But the struggle is still undecided in the regions shown as Lutheran- and Calvinist-influenced, and a Catholic religious revival and the support of local rulers will eventually bring most of them back into the Catholic camp.

Jan Hus. The fate of the reform movement that began with Jan Hus, the hero of Bohemia, was different. Hus was a priest and a professor at Charles University in Prague (*Map 9.1*), in the kingdom of Bohemia. Already active in efforts to reform the clergy, he was inspired by the writings of Wiclif to launch stronger, more radical attacks. Hus

Fig. 9.1 Heretic and Martyr. Burning, the standard penalty for unrepentant heretics from the thirteenth century onward, symbolized the hellfire that supposedly awaited preachers of false doctrine, but this seventeenth-century depiction of the burning of the Czech heretic Jan Hus in 1415 shows him calm and dignified amid the flames. For the Protestants who looked back to Hus as their forerunner, the fire of his burning had become a beacon of persecuted Christian truth. The picture is a woodcut—one of thousands of copies printed from an engraved wooden block as religious propaganda.

had the support of most of his compatriots, partly because many of the clerics he criticized were Germans, whereas the majority of the population in Bohemia were Czechs (p. 296).

Bohemia was part of the Holy Roman Empire, and Emperor Sigismund had grown disturbed by the mounting agitation among the Bohemians. When Hus was summoned by the Council of Constance in 1414 to stand trial on charges of heresy, the emperor promised him safe-conduct to and from the trial. After a long and cruel imprisonment in Constance, Hus was tried and found guilty. The emperor did not keep his promise of protection, and Hus, refusing to recant (withdraw) his beliefs, went to his death at the stake (*Fig. 9.1*). The reaction in Bohemia was instantaneous. Anti-German and antipapal sentiments were inflamed. A bloody uprising erupted, which eventually took over the country, fought off Catholic campaigns against it, and eventually merged into the Reformation. This was but the beginning of a long series of political-religious wars in Europe.

During the fifteenth century, the criticisms by heretics like Wiclif and Hus were reinforced by the writings of the Christian humanists (pp. 342–344). Erasmus poured ridicule on the high clergy, monasticism, and popular devotional cults. But his intellectual approach did not stir the common people, and he never challenged the authority of the Church. For these reasons, and because of the humanistic leanings of the Renaissance popes, Erasmus escaped personal harm.

Nevertheless, the leaders of the Protestant revolt found justification for their actions in Erasmus's call for a purer religion, one freed from ritualism and superstition. They were prepared, of course, to go much further than Erasmus: they would defy authority and split the Christian community if necessary in order to achieve their goals.

THE INFLUENCE OF POLITICAL AND SOCIAL FORCES

By 1500, ideas for religious reform were in broad circulation, and a century after Hus, the political and social conditions in Europe were also shifting. The new situation would permit the rise of religious founders instead of religious martyrs.

National sentiment and political absolutism were working against the principle and practice of the universal Church. As distinctively national cultures took shape, people grew increasingly conscious of belonging to a particular *nation*—a nation independent of all others. The citizens of the northern countries, especially, came to regard the popes as "foreigners" who had no proper business outside Italy.

This popular feeling supported the desire of kings and princes to gain control over the Church in their own territories and to build state churches. By 1520, the monarchs of Spain and France had virtually achieved this end by securing the right to appoint the bishops within their kingdoms. One reason for the failure of heresies in those two nations is simply that their kings had nothing to gain from religious changes. In Germany and England, however, where the kings and princes expected to enlarge their powers in the event of a religious break with Rome, heresies were to prove successful.

The higher social classes also began to sense that they might benefit from a break with Rome. In Germany, the Church was immensely wealthy, holding from one-fifth to one-third of the total real estate. The landed aristocrats looked on those holdings with covetous eyes, and members of the middle class disliked the fact that Church properties were exempt from taxes. And all classes of German society deplored the flow of Church revenues to Rome; the feeling that the "foreign" papacy was draining the homeland of wealth thus created another source of support for a religious revolt.

These economic, social, and political factors must be kept in mind if we are to understand the nature and success of the Protestant reform movements. The reformers, to be sure, did not act upon a calculation of these factors; they acted, rather, in response to their religious thoughts and feelings. But this had been true also of the less fortunate heretics who preceded them. The success of the Protestant leaders was due primarily to the new political and social forces. The time was ripe for religious revolt in northern Europe; the division of the Roman Church was at hand.

The Revolt of Luther: "Justification by Faith"

Martin Luther, like the other Protestant reformers, did not intend, at the outset, to divide the Church or to start a new church. He believed that he had the correct vision of the *one true* church, and he set out to convert all Christians to his point of view. But because Luther could not, in fact, convert all Christians, and because other reformers then arose whom he could not dominate either, the end result was the division (and subdivision) of the Church.

LUTHER'S SPIRITUAL SEARCH: HIS DOCTRINE OF SALVATION

The fact that Martin Luther originated Western Christianity's first successful rebellion against the Catholic Church was due in part to his temperament. He relished a fight and was capable of quick, violent, and sustained anger. He was also a man of instinctive frankness and courage. But his beliefs were mainly the product of a long spiritual pilgrimage marked by doubt, agony, and finally conviction.

Luther was of peasant stock. His father, who had once been a miner, made wise investments and became a respected bourgeois. He wanted his son to study law in preparation for a career as a middle-class civil official. But Martin, who had attended a school run by the Brethren of the Common Life (p. 342), had fallen into deep spiritual fears in his early years. By the time he completed his liberal arts course at the University of Erfurt in Saxony, he had decided to abandon secular life and enter a monastery. His decision was sealed, he later explained, when he was caught in a violent thunderstorm and, terrified, interpreted the thunder as a call from God.

Luther took vows at an Augustinian monastery in Erfurt. Fearing that his soul was in danger of damnation, he hoped that an ascetic life would afford him a better chance of salvation. But he found no peace of mind either as a monk or as a priest. No matter how strictly he fasted, prayed, and punished himself, his sense of unworthiness persisted. The Church taught that salvation could be achieved only by God's grace (p. 248), known through faith, and by "good works," including the partaking of the sacraments. Luther despaired of doing enough good works to gain God's favor. While he was in this torment, he was sent by his superior to a new university in Wittenberg that had been founded by Frederick, the elector (ruler with the right to take part in the election of the Holy Roman emperor—p. 317) of Saxony. After receiving his doctor's degree there in 1512, he stayed on as professor of theology.

At Wittenberg, Luther began to discover his path to spiritual peace. While preparing some lectures on the Bible, he was struck by certain passages that seemed to suggest an answer. In Paul's Epistle to the Romans, for example, Luther read, "The just shall live by faith" (1:17). After days and nights of pondering, he concluded that "by grace and sheer mercy God justifies [saves] us through faith." The whole of Scripture, he later explained, then took on new meaning for him. Whereas the "justice of God" had formerly filled him with hate, it now became "inexpressibly sweet in greater love. This passage of Paul became to me a gate to heaven."

Now Luther understood why his own self-punishment and works as a monk had gained him nothing. Man, by his nature, cannot please God without faith; but faith, a free gift of God's mercy, "justifies" a person and ensures salvation. We are saved not by works, concluded Luther, but by *faith alone,* freely given us by God. From our love of God, we will perform good works—not because we need to but because we want to.

Ideas of this kind had a long history in Christianity, dating back to the apostle Paul and to Augustine, the leading Christian thinker of the late Roman Empire (pp. 165–166, 179). But although these ideas brought Luther immense personal relief, when he began to apply them to the institution of the Church, he grew troubled. If people received faith according to God's secret judgment, of what use was the ordained priesthood? If every Christian was, in effect, a priest, were not the claims of the clergy absurd and hateful? And what good were the special vows and way of life undertaken by monks and nuns? If works were no help to salvation, what was the benefit of sacraments, pilgrimages, and papal indulgences?

THE PROVOCATION: THE SALE OF INDULGENCES

It was in fact the issue of indulgences that set religious passions aflame. A Dominican friar (p. 252) named Tetzel, who was selling indulgences in Germany, came to Wittenberg

(*Map 9.1*, p. 368). In Catholic teaching, indulgences may reduce or eliminate penalties due for sins, both on earth and in purgatory. (Purgatory, in Catholic doctrine, is a temporary state or condition, after death, for the cleansing of pardoned souls on their way to heaven.) Tetzel, however, made extravagant claims for indulgences, implying that they would *automatically* remove a sinner's guilt as well as the penalty.

For Luther, the idea that a believer could purge himself of guilt in the eyes of God in return for the "good work" of paying money to an indulgence seller was a flagrant distortion of religious teachings. Up to this point, he had shared his views only with his students; now he felt compelled to speak out. And so it was that he prepared, in a traditional form for academic debates, his "Ninety-five Theses" (reasoned propositions or arguments) criticizing the sale of indulgences and reportedly nailed them to the door of the Wittenberg Castle church.

Luther charged that the money from Tetzel's sale of indulgences was going to Rome for the building of a new Saint Peter's Church (p. 356). But he also challenged indulgences in general, implying that they were of doubtful value. His charges brought an immediate attack from the clergy, but they struck a sympathetic chord with the laity. Copies of the "Ninety-five Theses" were distributed throughout Germany; the revolt from Rome, aided by the new technique of printing, was under way.

THE WIDENING SPLIT WITH ROME

Pope Leo X, whose main interests appeared to be in art, hunting, and politics, was in no hurry to deal with Luther. He referred scornfully to the dispute over indulgences as a "squabble among monks." In addition, as a professor at Wittenberg, Luther enjoyed the protection of the elector, Frederick of Saxony; and the pope, for political reasons, was trying to stay on friendly terms with Frederick. But while the pope delayed, the seemingly unimportant incident set off a chain reaction of dissent and rebellion throughout Germany.

To begin with, Leo simply directed that a reply be made to Luther's theses. In answering this reply, and in the series of exchanges of theological pamphlets that followed, Luther broadened his attack on the Church, especially the papacy. At the same time, he appealed to the German nobles (in his *Address to the Christian Nobility of the German Nation*), and to the laity in general, by speaking of the "priesthood" of all baptized Christians. Ordained priests and bishops, he argued, had no more special powers than other Christians; they were simply fulfilling the duties of their office (as princes fulfilled theirs). He also attacked monasticism and declared that priests should be permitted to marry.

In addition to challenging the doctrines of apostolic succession (p. 171) and "good works," Luther struck directly at the number and meaning of the holy sacraments (pp. 247–248). Of the seven traditional sacraments, he asserted that only *two* were called for by Scripture: baptism and the Eucharist. And contrary to Catholic doctrine, he insisted that in the Eucharist there is no miraculous change of substance (*transubstantiation*) from bread and wine into the body and blood of Christ. Luther taught, instead, that the "Real [Corporeal] Presence" of Christ was physically present *along with* the bread and wine. He insisted, furthermore, that the Real Presence is not brought into being by the priest, for God is present everywhere and always.

In 1520, Leo finally ordered Luther excommunicated. Luther responded by burning the bull (the papal document of excommunication) before the city gates of Wittenberg, thus demonstrating his defiance of Rome. The clergy now called on the Holy

Roman Emperor, Charles V, to seize Luther (it was considered the duty of the civil ruler to punish confirmed heretics), but Luther had such strong support among all classes of the laity that the emperor hesitated. The elector Frederick then insisted that Luther receive a hearing before the Imperial Diet (assembly of princes of the empire). At the Diet of Worms in 1521, Luther was afforded a last chance to recant his heresies. He refused, declaring eloquently that Scripture was the sole source of authority and that he must obey his conscience. The Diet then condemned Luther and issued a decree prohibiting all new religious doctrines within the Holy Roman Empire.

Luther had been guaranteed safe-conduct on his journey to Worms. After he left the assembly, however, the emperor ordered him put under the ban—which meant that he was branded an outlaw. Subjects of the empire were forbidden to shelter him, and, if seized, he could be killed. Frederick, however, had planned for Luther's safety in advance. His soldiers kidnapped Luther as he left Worms and took him secretly to Frederick's castle at Wartburg, where Luther remained for about a year working on a German translation of the Bible. His "people's" version of Scripture was printed in many thousands of copies, and helped shape the modern German language as well as Protestant doctrines.

BUILDING THE LUTHERAN CHURCH

When Luther thought it safe, he returned to Wittenberg to lay plans for a reformed church. He spent the rest of his life not as a rebel but as an organizer and administrator. It was in this part of his career that he met some of his severest tests. Many of his followers had responded in unexpected ways to his teachings of the "priesthood of all believers" and the sole authority of Scripture. Some developed disturbing notions about Christian practices and about the relation of religion to society. Numerous sects began to appear, not only in Germany but in Switzerland and the Low Countries as well.

The principal group went under the general name of *Anabaptists*—a name derived from their views on baptism. They insisted that baptism was meaningful only after someone old enough to comprehend Christian doctrines had made a voluntary confession of faith. They therefore opposed infant baptism and held that adult Christians who had been baptized as infants must accept the rite again (the Greek prefix *ana-* means "again"). The sects within the Anabaptist group varied considerably in their social ideas, which often proved troublesome to established laws and customs. Some applied New Testament teachings literally to their own times, refused military service, and sought to establish a more egalitarian community. Other sects advocated acts of violence against "ungodly" persons and against officials who declined to punish them.

Luther, who was extremely conservative in his views on the social order, was alarmed by such proposals. He believed in unquestioned obedience to the state and opposed any sort of rebellion against established political authorities. In 1524, Luther responded angrily to a peasant revolt that swept through Germany; the serfs were seeking relief from new burdens laid upon them by their feudal lords, especially in eastern Germany, where, as in the rest of eastern Europe, serfdom was growing more oppressive at this time (p. 296). He urged the aristocracy to put down the violent uprising without mercy, to slay the rebels as they would "mad dogs." He later admitted that it was he who had commanded the slaughter of the peasants: "All their blood is on my head. But I throw the responsibility on our Lord God, who instructed me to give this order." (Luther also urged harsh measures against Jews, reinforcing the popular anti-Semitism of his times.)

He was equally severe with preachers who disagreed with his doctrines. He considered them "blasphemers" and believed that they, like persons guilty of rebellion against the state, should be executed. Though claiming for himself the freedom to interpret Scripture, he denied it to those whom he judged to be not properly "qualified." The Lutheran Church developed an orthodoxy of its own, resting on the Augsburg Confession of 1530. This document, largely the work of Luther's friend and disciple Philipp Melanchthon, was a moderate statement of Luther's doctrinal views, including those on justification (salvation), sacraments, and the relation of faith and works.

The emperor Charles, though busy with war and politics outside Germany, still hoped to suppress the Lutheran Church by force. In 1529, Charles and the Catholic members of the Imperial Diet reaffirmed the earlier Worms decree prohibiting all new religious doctrines in Germany. The Lutheran princes of northern Germany protested this action and thus acquired the name "Protestant." In time, this name came to be used for all the rebellious creeds.

Soon Germany was split into armed alliances; Catholic states lined up against Lutheran states. By the time the emperor could send his forces against the Lutheran princes, he found them too powerful to overcome. The result was a truce, known as the Religious Peace of Augsburg (1555), in which the members of the Imperial Diet agreed to leave each prince free to choose either Catholicism or Lutheranism for his realm. (Other doctrines were still prohibited.) Under the Peace of Augsburg, religious warfare among the German states was suspended for some sixty years.

The people living in the Lutheran states found no great difficulty in accepting the decisions of their respective princes. Though the peasants had been embittered by Luther's harsh attitude toward them, their bitterness softened with time. For their part, the princes, nobles, and bourgeois enthusiastically supported the reformed church. It appealed to German patriotism by rejecting the Roman papacy, and its support of the established order pleased all who held office or wealth. The laity as a whole tended to feel comfortable in Luther's church. According to his doctrine, all baptized Christians were on the same spiritual level as their ministers; the devout man of property could feel superior to the ascetic, propertyless cleric whose way of life, according to Luther, was actually displeasing to God. Religion was still the dominating influence in society, but the Church was no longer an independent power.

The kings of Scandinavia recognized the advantages of a state church, and they, too, established the new faith as their official religion. In each Lutheran country, the ruler appointed superintendents to oversee his religious establishment—thus subordinating church to state. The formerly Catholic religious buildings and grounds were assigned to the new churches, but the extensive landholdings of the bishops and abbots were seized by the crown.

In accordance with Luther's views, monastic orders were abolished in all these states, and ministers were permitted to marry. Luther himself married a former nun, who bore him six children. By his acts and teachings, he raised the value placed on marriage and upheld the rights of wives to sexual satisfaction; he did not, however, urge any basic changes in the social role of women. The veneration of saints and relics (pp. 249–250) and all manner of formal "good works" were rejected. Luther did, however, retain the principle of Church authority and many semblances of medieval religious practice. The worship service, in German, was not much different from the Catholic service. Unlike some other reformers, Luther also kept art and music in his church;

he composed a notable book of hymns as well as several catechisms (handbooks for oral expression of Church teachings).

Calvin and the Elect: "Predestination"

Luther was by no means the only religious rebel at work during the 1520s. And although he tried to impose his doctrines on the others, he failed to do so outside northern Germany and Scandinavia. The logic of his own thought, in fact, worked against a unified reform movement. He had taught that each individual, guided by the Holy Spirit, must see the truth of Scripture according to his or her own conscience. While the papal theory of Petrine supremacy (p. 172) had offered a logical basis for *one* interpretation of truth and for *one* Church, Luther's view led naturally to *many* churches. Once papal authority had been overthrown, there was no logical limit to the number of creeds and denominations.

Of the countless separations that followed Luther's revolt, two require special attention because of their far-reaching historical impact. One of these is the Church of England, the most conservative of the major splits from Rome. The other, initiated by John Calvin, departed most radically from the Catholic tradition—in doctrine, spirit, organization, and ritual.

CALVIN: THE INTERNATIONAL REFORMER

Younger than Luther by some twenty-five years, Calvin (*Fig. 9.2*) was born and raised a Frenchman. As a young man, he prepared for the priesthood in Paris and then, at his father's urging, turned to the study of law. But he found a career in law distasteful and instead became active in humanistic scholarship (p. 338). After receiving his law degree, he took up the study of Greek and Hebrew. A year later, in 1533, Calvin had a sudden conversion to the idea of religious reform. France, like the rest of Europe, was the scene of heated disputes about the Church; the writings of Erasmus and Luther had stirred the youthful Calvin.

Calvin remained a keen scholar all his life, but after his "conversion," Calvin the humanist gave way to Calvin the reformer. He turned to a systematic explanation of his religious views and finished the first edition of the *Institutes of the Christian Religion* when he was only twenty-six years old. This work was to stand as the principal statement of Protestant theology for some three hundred years and as such is comparable to the Catholic statement by Thomas Aquinas, the *Summa Theologiae* (p. 270).

By that time, fear of persecution by the Catholic king had forced him to flee France, and he eventually settled down in the Swiss city of Geneva in 1536, the same year that he published the *Institutes*. The city, which had just revolted from its feudal overlord (a bishop), was in the midst of political and religious turmoil. Within a short time, Calvin and his version of reformed Christianity achieved dominance in the community. For some twenty years, until his death in 1564, he guided the Church, the state, and the Academy (university) of Geneva (*Map 9.1*, p. 368).

Calvin's influence extended far beyond the boundaries of his city. He corresponded with rulers and theologians alike, and reformers from all over Europe came to Geneva to study his doctrines. When they returned to their homelands, they carried

Fig. 9.2 John Calvin. Woodcut portrait published in Germany in 1574, two years after a famous massacre of Protestants in Paris. The caption underneath says: "Jan Hus converted the Czechs, Luther taught the Germans, Calvin spread the faith in France and defended it against Antichrist—that's why Antichrist does unheard-of diabolical murders." It is a powerful propaganda message—of the true Protestant faith leaping from nation to nation, with "Antichrist" (the popes) vainly trying to stop it by spilling innocent blood.

Snark/Art Resource, NY

Calvinism with them. Calvinism thus became the leading Protestant force in France, the Netherlands, Scotland, and England.

THE DOCTRINE OF GOD'S OMNIPOTENCE

Calvin was very close to Luther in his basic theology. He saw the Bible as the sole source of authority and rejected a priesthood based on apostolic succession. Calvin agreed, too, with Luther that salvation was determined by God's grace alone, unaffected by human works. Like Luther, he scorned monasticism and such "Romish" practices as pilgrimages, indulgences, and the veneration of saints and relics (pp. 249–250).

The difference between the two men, and it was a real one, lay in what each chose to emphasize. Luther was obsessed with his soul's salvation, and it was this that led him to his doctrine. Calvin, on the other hand, was obsessed with a sense of God's omnipotence (unlimited power) and human depravity (wickedness). Calvin's position may well have been a reaction to his contact with humanism, which praises human abilities. But he drew his vision of God's glory and perfection directly from the Old Testament, and no other theologian has followed through the implications of that vision with such relentless logic.

The best known and most controversial of Calvin's doctrines is predestination and election. Like justification by faith, this doctrine was not new but had been proclaimed by Paul and Augustine (pp. 165–166, 179). More than any other Christian thinker, however, Calvin made it the center of his system of religious belief. God, declared Calvin, foreknows and determines everything that happens in the universe—even events ordinarily credited to chance. It follows that he determines who shall be saved and who shall be forever lost. All individuals, because of Adam's sin and their own wickedness, would disobey God if left to their own puny powers. But God gives to those he "elects" the ability to persevere in his service. The rest, for his own reasons, he allows to fall. Calvin unflinchingly defined this doctrine in his *Institutes:*

> Predestination we call the eternal decree of God, by which he has determined in himself, what he would have become of every individual of mankind. For they are not all created with a similar destiny; but eternal life is foreordained for some, and eternal damnation for others. Every man, therefore, being created for one or the other of these ends, we say, he is predestinated either to life or to death.

In his discussion of predestination, Calvin warned that the subject is dangerous and delicate, since it touches on a guarded secret of the Almighty. To the charge that God could not be so unfair as to condemn most of humankind to damnation, Calvin answered that no one *deserves* salvation and that it is only through God's gracious mercy that some are saved. Further, it is wrong to question the plans and judgment of God. Man has only a worm's-eye view of Creation. Whatever God has willed is right, because he has willed it. Calvin admitted that the Lord's predestination was an "awesome decree," but he held that all must nevertheless accept it.

But many would not accept so harsh a doctrine. Luther accepted it, though he did not stress it in his teachings. Most Protestant groups, in time, would turn away from the doctrine for two reasons: it is very gloomy, and it denies free will. The Roman Catholics (including Erasmus) condemned Calvin's teachings, declaring that they reduce human beings to mere puppets. Catholics did not deny that God's grace is indispensable to salvation, but they believed that it is offered more generously than Calvin suggested. They also insisted that each individual can either cooperate (through good works) in achieving salvation or can refuse to cooperate. By refusing, a person chooses the path to hell, but this is the person's own doing. Calvin answered that the Catholic argument is an insult to God's majesty. It suggests that God's will is not all-powerful and that his grace, alone, is insufficient.

In reply to the charge that his doctrine would destroy all incentive for following a worthy Christian life and cause some people to throw themselves into reckless indulgence, he declared that nothing in the doctrine of predestination excuses any person from striving to obey God's commandments. On the contrary, Calvin argued, no one knows for certain who is of the "elect" and who is "reprobate" (condemned). All individuals, therefore, should act as if they enjoy God's favor. If they do enjoy that favor, they should want their lives to be shining examples to others; if they do not enjoy it, they should obey God anyway. It is surely the duty of those who feel moved by the Spirit to do God's will themselves and to see that others, whether or not they are to be saved, also honor God. The divine will can be clearly read in Scripture; all should shape their lives accordingly, regardless of the decree of predestination.

CALVINIST ETHICS: THE PURITAN DISCIPLINE

Calvin applied this line of reasoning with strict logic to the entire field of Christian morals. Though a person's behavior is not the means of his salvation, it must nonetheless be subjected to close scrutiny. Puritanism as a social discipline was thus developed by Calvin, for he wanted the behavior of all Christians to be held under tight control.

To Calvin, God is a righteous, demanding judge, under whose searching eye Christians should conduct themselves humbly and soberly.

Calvin criticized any form of decoration lest it lead to vanity and pride—and any form of card playing lest it lead to gambling. The theater, because of its historical associations with paganism, was closed down in Geneva; art was seen as a distraction from God's word. Drinking was condemned as a prelude to intoxication, and dancing was prohibited as a stimulant to desire. The clothing of women had to be plain and ample; he regarded the display of personal ornament or the exposure of flesh as a signal to sexual instincts. In living a "puritanical" life, concluded Calvin, one follows the teachings of the Lord, who "condemned all those pleasures which seduce the heart from chastity and purity."

Yet a "puritanical" life was not the same as the traditional idea of an ascetic life (p. 180). Like Luther, Calvin despised the way of life of the monk or nun and expected Christians to live their disciplined lives within the world. In addition, Calvin accepted business as a normal Christian vocation. He took for granted (as Luther and the Catholic theologians did not) the functions of capital, banking, and large-scale commerce. Though urging entrepreneurs to be honest and reasonable in their dealings, he did not question the morality of their occupation. He was the first theologian to praise the capitalist virtues: hard work, thrift, and the accumulation of money. He praised the creation of wealth through industry so long as that wealth was not used for self-indulgence. Like every other Christian, the businessman should be sober and disciplined, dedicated to the "service of the Lord."

Calvin's faith suited the economic realities of the day and was attractive not only to solid businessmen but also to colonial pioneers. Carried to New England in the seventeenth century, Calvinism (Puritanism) contributed significantly to the shaping of American life. To Calvin, a person's conscience was the prime defense against ungodly distractions and against sin itself. But if the individual could not avoid wrongdoing, Calvin believed, it was up to other Christians to be their "brother's keeper." As chief pastor in Geneva, he used his pulpit to warn and frighten potential sinners. When his sermons failed, he resorted to force in prohibiting unseemly acts and words. The Consistory of Geneva was a special body of pastors and lay elders responsible for public morals and discipline. Alleged offenders were called before this court, which might reprimand the accused or impose bread-and-water sentences upon them. Common offenses were profanity, drunkenness, dozing in church, criticizing ministers, dancing, and other "immoral" acts.

More serious offenses were handled by the town council. One man, accused of placing an insulting placard on Calvin's pulpit, was tortured until he confessed; later, he was beheaded on a further charge of conspiring against Calvin. Accused heretics were also brought before the council. The most notorious trial was that of the Spaniard Michael Servetus, who challenged the Christian doctrine of the Trinity. Calvin, after warning Servetus to stay away, had him arrested when he visited Geneva. Calvin then charged him with heresy and supported his conviction and execution (1553). With firm logic, Calvin justified the destruction of "false prophets" by referring to the harsh thirteenth chapter of Deuteronomy:

> God makes plain that the false prophet is to be stoned without mercy. We are to crush beneath our heel all affections of nature when his honor is involved. The father should not spare his child, nor the brother his brother, nor the husband his own wife, or the friend who is dearer to him than life.

The Protestant reformer had come full circle to the papal position of intolerance toward dissenting doctrine. By excommunicating "wrongdoers" from his church, Calvin drove most of his critics from Geneva; refugees from Catholic persecution, meanwhile, kept slipping in from other lands. By the end of Calvin's rule (1564), most of the citizens of Geneva supported his principles and policies. They admired and respected him for defending Christian doctrine and imposing strict rules of conduct on all the residents of the city.

RELATIONS OF CHURCH AND STATE

Though Calvin dominated both religion and government in Geneva, he held no public office. He opposed the union of spiritual and civil authority, but like Pope Gregory VII (pp. 255–256), he believed that ministers of the Church must stand as teachers and judges of civil rulers. To Calvin, the purpose of government was to regulate society according to the will of God, and the Church was the appointed interpreter of God's will: "Great kings ought not to think it any dishonor to humble themselves before Christ, the King of Kings, nor ought they to be displeased at being judged by the church. . . . They ought even to wish not to be spared by the pastors, that they may be spared by the Lord."

Geneva was legally a republic whose principal governing organ was the elected town council. As we have seen, the council served to protect Calvin's church against critics, rebels, and heretics. And in the manner in which Pope Gregory VII had held the threat of excommunication (and disgrace) over kings and princes (p. 256), so Calvin held it over the politicians of Geneva.

For some twenty years, Geneva served as a model of theocracy (a church-controlled state). The organized Church, Calvin asserted, is essential for the supervision of the state as well as for the salvation of souls. This view, too, paralleled the papal pronouncement that individual salvation is possible only within the Church. The idea of dependence on Church membership may seem to contradict Calvin's doctrine of predestination and election. If God has already determined that a person is to be saved, why must that person remain in Calvin's church (or any other church)? Calvin's explanation was simple: it is God's will that the elect be saved through the True Church. And through its inspired teaching and discipline, the ways of Heaven might be reflected on earth.

CALVINIST MINISTRY AND RITUAL

Calvin saw nothing inconsistent in holding to certain Roman Catholic principles. But he differed sharply from them with respect to the ministry and ritual of the Church. Calvin accepted, with Luther, the principle of the "priesthood of all believers"; his church gave to its ministers no special powers that set them apart from baptized laymen. Their authority came only from their assigned office, just like the authority of civil officials.

Calvin guarded against preaching by self-proclaimed ministers. A "legitimate ministry," he declared, is formed when suitable persons are appointed by the lay elders, subject to the approval of the congregation and the pastors of the community. In the administration of each church, the minister was assisted by elders elected by the congregation. Thus developed the *presbyterian* form of Church government. (*Presbyteros* is the Greek word for "elder.")

Calvin insisted that Church ritual be based exclusively on Scripture. He found, with Luther, that only baptism and the Eucharist are clearly established there as sacraments. (But unlike Luther, he held that the presence of Christ in the Eucharist is spiritual, not physical.) Beyond the administration of these two rites, Calvin permitted little except the singing of psalms and the preaching of sermons. He believed that music, art, and ornamentation had no place in the Church; the awesome Catholic cathedrals, with their stained glass, gilt, and statuary, he branded as pagan temples. Jesus and Paul, according to Scripture, had conducted their ministries in simple fashion by preaching. And preaching was the core of the Calvinist service. There were no processions, genuflections (bending of the knee), embroidered garments, incense, or Latin chants. The minister wore simple black and spoke only in the ordinary language of his congregation (as Jesus had). The typical Calvinist service was once described by a critic as consisting of "four bare walls and a sermon."

Henry VIII and the Church of England

Calvinist austerity found little acceptance among Lutherans or among English reformers. While Protestant ideas from the Continent influenced the doctrine of the Anglican Church (Church of England), its organization and ritual remained close to the Catholic tradition. Thus the Anglican Church came to represent a sort of compromise between extreme Protestantism and Roman Catholicism. Radical reformers would criticize it as a muddled and illogical institution, subservient to the state; Roman Catholics would condemn it as divisive and heretical. The Anglicans, however, insisted that theirs was the True Church, that it was both Catholic *and* reformed.

HENRY'S DESIRE FOR INDEPENDENCE

Although John Wiclif had preached reform during the fourteenth century (p. 367), there was no English counterpart to Luther or Calvin in the sixteenth century. Religious reform in England, though supported by numerous critics of the Catholic Church, was carried through by its monarchs. From the time of Henry VIII, who initiated the reform, to the time of Elizabeth I, who completed it, changes were prompted primarily by the wishes of the crown.

The first Tudor monarch, Henry VII, had laid the foundations for royal absolutism (p. 316). His policies were vigorously pursued by his son and successor, the youthful Henry VIII. Henry proved to be a popular king, a robust Renaissance despot. He had had some training in theology, for as a younger son in the royal family, he had been started by his father on a career in the Church. The plan was dropped on the death of his elder brother, Arthur, which left Henry heir to the throne. His interest in religious matters continued, however, and after his coronation, he formally defended the Catholic view of the sacraments against Luther's public attack (1521). As a reward, Leo X gave Henry the title "Defender of the Faith."

But Henry soon came to resent Roman interference in the affairs of his kingdom. In Spain and France, the monarchs controlled the Church within their borders, but in England, the pope still confirmed the appointment of high-ranking clergy. Appeals from Church courts (in keeping with canon law) and a portion of Church revenues continued to go to Rome.

But it was a personal matter, related to the welfare of the state, that led Henry VIII to break with Rome. In order to preserve the alliance between the ruling families of England and Spain, he had married Catherine of Aragon, his elder brother's widow. Because it was contrary to canon law to marry so close a relative, he had sought and received a papal dispensation (p. 254) permitting the union. In the course of their marriage, Catherine bore six children, but all except one were stillborn or died in infancy. The single survivor was a girl, Mary. The English had only recently emerged from a bloody civil war over the succession to the throne, and they feared that a female ruler might prove unable to maintain national strength and unity. When it appeared that Catherine would have no more children, Henry and his advisers began to think about his taking a new wife.

Henry's sense of duty was accompanied by his fondness for Anne Boleyn, an attractive young lady-in-waiting to the queen. In 1527, he decided to marry her and directed his chancellor (chief minister) to have his marriage to Catherine annulled (declared invalid). The Church did not permit divorce, but if it found a marriage to be invalid, both partners were free to marry again. Because the marriage to Catherine had been contrary to canon law, it would have been easy enough for papal lawyers to find some defect in the earlier dispensation.

But the infatuated Henry was to be disappointed. The Habsburg emperor, Charles V, was Catherine's nephew. He informed the pope that there were no proper grounds for annulment and that such action would be cruel and insulting to his aunt and his family. Charles did not wish Henry to remarry, for Henry's daughter, Princess Mary (Charles's cousin), was heir to the English throne. If Henry had no son, Mary would ultimately become queen, bringing another state into the Habsburg circle of power.

Charles was busy at the time in a campaign to win control of Italy, and his army happened to be in Rome when Pope Clement VII received Henry's appeal. But Clement decided to do nothing, hoping that something would happen to spare him from making the choice. After nearly six years of waiting, Henry's patience ran out. He married Anne Boleyn in 1533, after his newly appointed archbishop, Thomas Cranmer, had declared his marriage to Catherine annulled. Clement promptly excommunicated the king and released Henry's subjects from their obligation of obedience to the crown.

BREAK WITH ROME: THE ACT OF SUPREMACY

Infuriated by the pope's delaying tactics and by what he considered Clement's interference in state affairs, Henry determined to free himself of the pope once and for all. He was backed by both Parliament and the people, for the papacy had become exceedingly unpopular in England. Having first submitted the issue to the assembled English clergy, Henry had the Act of Supremacy passed by Parliament in 1534. This act declared that the king was the "only supreme head on earth" of the Church of England and approved his power to "repress, redress, and reform" all errors, heresies, and abuses in religion.

A series of supplementary acts made the break with Rome complete. Communication with the pope (who was now referred to as the Bishop of Rome) was forbidden; payments to Rome were stopped; the crown was given sole right to appoint bishops and abbots; and any denial of the king's supremacy was labeled as treason. Sir Thomas More, a Christian humanist (p. 360) and former chancellor, refused to take the required oath of supremacy and was beheaded. Other men of strict principle followed More to the cutting block, and some minor rebellions had to be put down. But Henry imposed his will on the clergy, Parliament, and his subjects.

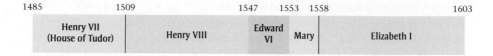

1485	1509	1547	1553	1558	1603
Henry VII (House of Tudor)	Henry VIII	Edward VI	Mary	Elizabeth I	

Henry's taking control of the Church of England did not mean that he wished to reform its doctrine. On the contrary, he disliked the Protestant tendencies in the country and had Parliament pass the notorious Six Articles, which required all the king's subjects to accept such Catholic beliefs as transubstantiation, celibacy of the clergy, and the necessity of oral confession in the sacrament of penance (p. 248). Henry thus showed his determination both to rule the Church and to keep it "true." Those who challenged his authority were sent to the block as traitors; those who questioned Catholic doctrine were sent to the stake as heretics.

Henry's only important departure from Catholic tradition was his suppression of monasticism. The monks had acquired an unfavorable reputation, the religious houses possessed great wealth and extensive lands, and Henry was hard pressed for money. His obedient Parliament voted to close the monasteries and to turn over their property to the crown. Most of it was taken for the king's own purposes or distributed to his favorites and supporters.

Henry—a shrewd manipulator of people and institutions, a true Machiavellian prince (pp. 311–313)—was thus able to create new ranks of landed noblemen who now had a vested interest in his break with Rome. In those troubled times, moreover, many of the English (like many Italians) preferred despotic power to liberty and disorder. The success of Henry's undertakings, as well as his hearty manner, endeared him to most of his subjects despite his greed, cruelty, and marital misadventures.

Three years after marrying Anne, he accused her of adultery and treason, had her beheaded, and then went on to take, in succession, four more wives. Anne Boleyn had borne him a daughter (Elizabeth), and Jane Seymour gave him a son at last. But the boy proved frail. He came to the throne as Edward VI when only ten years old (1547), and his powers had to be exercised by a guardian regent (an appointed officer acting for the crown). He died before coming of age, and the crown passed, after all, to his elder sister Mary, the daughter of Catherine of Aragon.

THE STRUGGLE OVER DOCTRINE: PROTESTANT ADVANCE AND CATHOLIC REACTION

During the regency period of Edward, Protestant factions in England brought about significant changes in the Anglican Church. Cranmer, the archbishop of Canterbury, had Lutheran leanings; after Henry's death, he led the way to reform by persuading Parliament to repeal the Six Articles and to pass the Act of Uniformity (1549). This law required that all Church services follow a uniform text, composed in English by Cranmer himself; this was then put into the *Book of Common Prayer,* which is still (as revised) the basis of Anglican ritual. All subjects of the kingdom were required by the act to attend services regularly; other forms of public worship were outlawed.

When Mary succeeded Edward in 1553, the religious pendulum swung back. Mary, who had been raised a devout Catholic, was determined to restore the nation to allegiance to Rome. She arranged for her subjects to be ceremoniously pardoned for their heresy and restored to communion with Rome. She replaced Protestant-minded bishops with Catholics and compelled the clergy to give up their wives. (Under Cranmer, priests had been allowed to marry, in keeping with the Lutheran practice.) Latin replaced English in the services of the Church. Mary's most unpopular act was to wed her relative, Philip, the Habsburg heir to the Spanish throne and a bitter enemy of Protestantism.

In the face of Mary's ruthless policy against dissenters, most people adjusted their beliefs to avoid execution; but several hundred, including Cranmer, went to the stake for their convictions. The monarch thus earned the name (among Protestants) of "Bloody Mary." She was no more ruthless than her father, Henry, but she offended national feeling by subjecting the country once again to the pope and by marrying a despised foreigner. As Mary bore no child, her reign proved to be only a reactionary interlude whose net effect was to make Catholicism more unpopular than before.

THE ELIZABETHAN COMPROMISE

Elizabeth, the daughter of Anne Boleyn, inherited the crown upon Mary's death in 1558. She had been raised a Protestant but, unlike her half-sister, was neither devout nor fanatical. During her early years, she could observe for herself the frequent shifting of loyalties in religion and politics. As queen, she stood firmly for a Protestant Church and independence from Rome. But her first concern was for the security of the crown and the unity of her subjects.

A true child of Henry, she managed Parliament and her ministers shrewdly. She had Mary's Catholic legislation repealed and the Act of Supremacy reenacted (1559). But she avoided giving unnecessary offense to those of her subjects who were pro-Catholic. Her new laws established the Elizabethan Compromise (or Settlement), which remains to this day the foundation of the Anglican Church.

Parliament, with Elizabeth's approval, enacted a revised summary of official doctrine known as the Thirty-Nine Articles, which was designed to satisfy all but extremists. The Thirty-Nine Articles were Lutheran or Calvinist on certain matters, including the exclusive authority of Scripture, salvation by faith alone, the number of sacraments, and the freedom of the clergy to marry. There was also a firm insistence on respecting the traditions of the Church, except those that were clearly "repugnant to the Word of God."

Internally, the Anglican Church was organized much like the Roman Catholic Church. The monarch was its "supreme governor," but only in the sense that she was responsible, under God, for ruling all classes (religious and secular) in the country. This idea was similar to the position of Constantine, Theodosius, and Charlemagne in relation to their empires (pp. 150, 215).

The actual ministering of the Word and the sacraments was restricted to the ordained priesthood, in accordance with the doctrine of apostolic succession. Most other Protestant groups developed a presbyterian form of Church government (p. 379), but the Anglican bishops traced their authority back to the twelve apostles, as did the Roman Catholic bishops (and those of the Orthodox Church). The Anglicans rejected, however, the theory of Petrine supremacy, which was the cornerstone of papal claims to universal authority (p. 172).

The Elizabethan Settlement brought stability because most of the English (who by this time were weary of religious quarreling) were prepared to conform. Only a handful of the clergy—who had called themselves Catholic under Mary—now refused to accept the new Act of Uniformity. Elizabeth, who cared little about the private views and doubts of her subjects, was content with outward obedience. She would not tolerate open dissent, but penalties were softened and offenders were few. Not until the seventeenth and eighteenth centuries would new religious stirrings disrupt the established Church.

The age of Elizabeth also brought England to the threshold of world power. Philip, who had become King Philip II of Spain in 1556, sought the hand of Elizabeth after the death of his wife, her half-sister Mary. Elizabeth had held him off, so Philip finally decided to take her kingdom by force. (The pope excommunicated Elizabeth in 1570, declared her deposed, and thus opened the way to Philip's adventure.) In 1588, Philip sent a mighty fleet, the Spanish Armada, against England, expecting that once his soldiers had landed on the island, the thousands of unhappy Catholics in the country would rally to his banner. But the Armada was routed in the Channel by the English navy and was smashed by storms on its return home. With Spain, the leading power of the Continent, thus humbled, the English became conscious of their strength on the seas. Elizabeth's reign marked a turning point in the nation's history. Thereafter, English sea power, commerce, and diplomacy were to exercise a mounting influence over European and world affairs.

The Roman Catholic Response: Reform and Reaffirmation

Within half a century after Luther's challenge at Wittenberg, most of northern Europe had broken away from the papacy. Protestants dominated the cities of Switzerland; they formed a militant minority in France; and a few had even penetrated the Catholic strongholds of Spain and Italy.

Finally, the Roman Catholic Church, after hesitation and uncertainty, moved to check the spreading revolt. Too late to reverse the major losses, these efforts did recover some ground and kept the remainder of Europe loyal to Rome. The response took two main courses: reform within the Catholic Church and countermeasures against Protestantism.

Catholic reforms were inspired, in part, by the same ideas and ideals that had motivated Luther and the other religious rebels. As we have seen, the condition of the late medieval Church had caused widespread discontent and sharp criticism. But though some aims were common to both the Catholic and the Protestant reform movements, there were important differences between them. The Protestant leaders wanted a reconstruction of the Church, in accordance with unorthodox theories of authority, priesthood, and salvation. The Catholic reformers, on the other hand, accepted the central doctrines, traditions, and organization of the Church. What they desired was a purer Christian life within the existing Church, in keeping with its historic tradition of self-reformation.

LOYOLA AND THE SOCIETY OF JESUS

While the Protestant movements arose in the north, Catholic reform efforts were centered in Spain and Italy. The Spanish reformation had begun in the late fifteenth century, led by Cardinal Ximenes (archbishop of Toledo), with the full support of the monarchy. The Spanish reform served as a model for Catholic action elsewhere in Europe. This was reform distinctly in the medieval tradition: it included a rigorous campaign to improve the morals and education of the clergy, military action against infidels (the Muslims; p. 313), and a strong effort to wipe out heresies.

In Italy, too, some churchmen had urged similar actions. But the Renaissance popes had dampened the hopes of reformers, and the princes of Italy were either indifferent or unwilling to make the necessary effort. As in the Middle Ages, however, new and reformed religious orders now arose to improve the quality of Christian life. One was the priestly order of Theatines, which was dedicated to education. Another was the order of Capuchins, a reformed branch of the Franciscan friars (p. 252). The Capuchins modeled themselves on Francis of Assisi and carried his message of love, piety, and simplicity to the common people.

One man and one order above all others, however, were to play a decisive role in the Catholic Reformation and in stemming the Protestant tide. Ignatius Loyola, a Spanish nobleman and soldier of the king, was the founder of this new order. At about the time Luther was standing before the Diet of Worms (1521), Loyola was seriously wounded in a battle. His leg was shattered by a cannonball, and he lay for months in painful convalescence, during which time he experienced a profound spiritual conversion.

Loyola was burdened, as Luther had been, by a sense of sin and unworthiness. After a lengthy period of confession, fasting, and nightly vigils (watches), visions of Christ and Mary appeared to him and relieved him of his fears. Now he resolved to give up all thought of resuming his former life and enlisted himself as a "soldier of the Lord." He turned the strong military and chivalric traditions of his country to a spiritual purpose, dedicating his services to the Virgin as a knight would to his lady. And he held also to the Spanish tradition of religious orthodoxy, finding satisfaction not in revolt but in absolute obedience to God and the pope.

Loyola realized that if he was to save souls from heresy or indifference, he would need a thorough religious education. After preparing himself in Latin, he went on to the University of Paris, where he studied for some seven years, gathering about him a small band of devoted followers. Working at first as an informal association bound by common vows, they formed a regular religious order in 1540.

The order was named the Society of Jesus, and its members were commonly called Jesuits. Loyola was elected its general, or commander, for life, and he placed himself and his society at the service of the pope. The general shaped the internal organization along strict military lines, with a "chain of command" reaching down to the ordinary Jesuit "soldier."

The Jesuits took the usual monastic vows of chastity, poverty, and obedience and required, in addition, absolute acceptance of orthodox doctrines and the authority of the pope. In his manual for members, Loyola laid out both "spiritual exercises" and rules of conduct. One of the rules stated, "To be right in all things we ought to adhere always to the principle that the white which I see I will believe to be black if the Church so rules."

When Loyola died in 1556, the Society of Jesus had grown to nearly fifteen hundred members. All were carefully selected men, well trained and well disciplined, who could be counted on to serve the broad purpose of the Society of Jesus: "to employ itself entirely in the defense of the holy Catholic faith." The Jesuits sought to accomplish this goal chiefly through widespread education and preaching. They founded schools and colleges to inculcate young minds with the "true" doctrine, and they sent out missions to convert heathens and heretics (p. 329). The Jesuits also tried (mainly through oral confessions) to keep wavering Catholics on the path to correct belief. And by serving as confessors and advisers to civil rulers, they tried to guide states in policies favorable to the Church. Though the Jesuits were highly effective in their education and preaching, these political activities ultimately brought heavy criticism and attacks.

THE REFORMING POPES

The papacy, whose leadership was essential to effective self-reformation of the Church, had long remained indifferent. But when Paul III became pope in 1534, he was forced to respond to the events in both Germany and England. Unlike his predecessor, Clement VII, he committed himself seriously to reform. He found a report by a committee of cardinals on abuses among the clergy so shocking that he decided to keep it secret. He did, however, launch an overhaul of papal administration, and he summoned a council to deal with reform and heresy.

Many Catholics, as well as Protestants, felt that a church council might help settle the deep troubles of Christendom. The conciliar (council) tradition was long established; the first general council, held at Nicaea in 325 (p. 175), had successfully faced a serious division over doctrine. The Council of Constance (p. 366) had faced an equally trying problem in 1414 with respect to the Great Schism of the Church. Some believed that another meeting of all the high clergy might once again restore unity and purity to the Church.

Others, however, though they favored a reform of practices, feared that a council might be drawn into a compromise on doctrine. The pope was hesitant for an additional reason: past councils had tried to limit the papal monarchy and to establish the council itself as the supreme authority in the Church. Although Paul III at last summoned a council to meet in the northern Italian city of Trent, he made sure that the papacy would control it.

The Council of Trent. The Council of Trent met, with interruptions, over a period of some twenty years (1545–1563). The Jesuits at the council sought to keep a balance favorable to Roman policies; they were aided in this by the facts that papal ambassadors presided over the sessions and that Italian bishops outnumbered those of any other nationality. (The French clergy, who were committed to a "national" church, did not participate fully.) Because the Italians (and Spaniards) were loyal to Rome, they could be relied on to support the papacy.

By the time the council opened, the pope had decided on a definite course of action. Earlier, a few of his advisers had recommended that some effort be made to bring about reconciliation with the Protestants, but this had proved futile. The pope settled instead on a program of reform and reinvigoration, while refusing to compromise on doctrine. He was willing, apparently, to accept the Catholic setbacks for the time being and to concentrate on holding the line against further losses. This, he thought, could best be done by correcting abuses and by restating beliefs.

The Council of Trent sent its final decrees to the pope for approval, thereby reaffirming the supremacy of his authority. In general, the decrees gave the papacy what it wanted. They fell into two main parts: reform decrees and statements of doctrine. Bishops were ordered to regain strict discipline over their clergy in such matters as keeping vows, morals, behavior, and dress. (Special attention was given to the problem of restoring chastity and putting aside concubines.) And they were required to provide better education for the priesthood by establishing a seminary (theological school) in each diocese. Among the higher clergy, the practice of simony—the sale of Church positions—was forbidden. Also forbidden was the holding of more than one office at a time. The Council of Trent, in addition, outlawed the selling of papal indulgences while affirming that the spiritual grace granted by indulgences was genuine and worthy of continued belief and practice. Had these reforms been launched fifty years earlier, they might have blunted the criticisms of Erasmus and other conscientious Christians. In any case, Trent was a turning point in Catholic history, and the clergy and laity both experienced a reawakening of piety and devotions.

Although the Protestant revolt no doubt stimulated the reform and revival of the Church, it also prompted a hardening of Catholic doctrine. The Council of Trent made no compromise with Luther or Calvin on theological issues; in responding to the Protestant challenge, it not only reaffirmed traditional doctrines but stated them more distinctly. The special powers of the priesthood, the necessity of the Roman Church and the seven sacraments, the doctrine of transubstantiation (p. 372), the veneration of saints and relics, the belief in purgatory and indulgences (p. 372)—all were specifically confirmed by the council. At the same time, the council condemned the opposing Protestant doctrines. The result was to make orthodoxy clearer and narrower and to leave Catholic theologians with less freedom of interpretation than they had had before Trent.

Repression and Censorship. In addition to the Jesuits, two other agencies worked to crush heresy and to keep the faithful safe in traditional Catholic beliefs. The first was the Inquisition, of medieval origin (p. 255), which was now revived in Spain, Italy, and the Low Countries. Directing its efforts against those accused of heretical ideas, its secret trials, torture, and burnings aimed at conformity through terror. In other Catholic countries, there were no special tribunals, and the traditional burning of heretics gave way to less spectacular but just as effective methods of persecution. The local clergy and religious orders were constantly on the watch for religious dissidents, while actual intimidation and punishment were the work of the state. Troops would be sent to Protestant districts to harass the people into conforming; Protestant ministers would be given life sentences as galley slaves; and if all else failed, the Protestants of whole regions would be given the choice between conversion and expulsion. Catholics in Protestant countries suffered the same kind of treatment. In England, for example, Catholic families could be ruined by huge fines for not attending Anglican services, and priests were cruelly put to death as traitors.

In addition, the Catholic authorities introduced systematic censorship of books, which had been ordered by the Council of Trent. The council authorized an index (list) of prohibited books, including all those that attacked the Roman Church or contained ideas contrary to its doctrines, and it established the Congregation of the Index to publish the list and keep it current. Church members were forbidden to read any work named in the Index, which soon came to include much of the serious literature of Europe. Censorship, of course, had long been used by both Catholics and Protestants, but the new effort was more comprehensive and was executed with greater energy than ever before. Although the prohibited books continued to circulate even in Catholic countries, the Index no doubt contributed to a narrowing of the exchange of ideas. It remained in force until 1965, when it was dropped by order of the Second Vatican Council (p. 653).

Headed by the papacy, the Church was now prepared to carry out the reform decrees of Trent and to restore Catholic doctrines throughout Christendom. Under the zealous popes of the second half of the sixteenth century, the Church moved from stagnation and defensiveness to a bold offensive. The vigorous response of the Roman Church to the Protestant challenge prevented further Catholic losses, and the religious divisions of about 1560 (*Map 9.1*, p. 368) generally remain today—though it took another century before all sides accepted them as more or less final (pp. 398–400).

Art During the Reformation

For many Protestants, sacred paintings and sculpture were associated with Rome, and the revolt against "popery" was often accompanied by attacks (both physical and verbal) on art images. Calvin, as we have seen, saw works of art as a distraction from the word of God. He objected to any attempt to "paint or carve" subjects that went beyond ordinary observation: "God's majesty, which is too exalted for human sight, may not be corrupted by fantasies which have no true agreement therewith."

The Protestant reformers (and some pious Catholics as well) were also offended by the sensuality in some Renaissance art. The "cult of beauty" (pp. 340–341, 350–351) had produced works that were shocking to puritanical viewers, and a reaction now set in against the portrayal of nudity. Reforming popes of the sixteenth century ordered artists to paint clothes on the figures in numerous Renaissance masterpieces, and many of these works simply disappeared from public view.

THE IMPACT OF PROTESTANTISM: HOLBEIN, BRUEGHEL

In spite of the loss of church patronage and Calvinist disapproval of paintings and decorations, Protestant artists could still find themes for painting, and even develop new ones, that the churches did not frown on. The career of the German painter Hans Holbein is illustrative. Born in 1497, he mastered the techniques of his day and produced works that combined the best of the Italian and the northern styles. Most of his early paintings were designed for church altars, but with the coming of the Reformation, Holbein had to turn to portrait painting. By good fortune and with the help of Erasmus (pp. 342–344), he was able to move to England, where he secured commissions from the aristocracy; eventually, he became court painter to Henry VIII. He produced hundreds of lifelike portraits of the monarch, his family, and the royal courtiers (close officials of the king). Working with oils and in the realistic tradition established by Jan van Eyck (pp. 347–348), Holbein usually showed his subjects in their customary setting and surrounded by the symbols and tools of their office or profession. A notable example is *The French Ambassadors* (*Fig. III.1,* p. 286).

Other Protestant painters explored the possibilities of landscapes and scenes of ordinary life (*genre* painting). The Flemish master of genre painting was Pieter Brueghel; though he produced many splendid landscapes, he is best known for his pictures of common folk. Brueghel was himself a townsman, but he showed a keen understanding of plain, unsophisticated peasants. His interest in rustic subjects is evident in his paintings of peasants at work and at rest and in his scenes of hunting, feasting, and playing. Brueghel's *Wedding Dance* (*Fig. 9.3*), painted in 1566, near the end of his life, is a striking example of perspective and organization. With its lively movement and rhythm, it suggests the healthy animal spirits of the dancers. Brueghel was one of the first artists to break with the aristocratic tradition of Renaissance painting to show us, bluntly and honestly, the ordinary men and women who made up the bulk of European society.

DEVELOPMENT OF THE BAROQUE: RUBENS, REMBRANDT

Although many Catholic painters were also skillful at treating secular subjects, they were encouraged to direct their talents to religious art. The Catholic Church, after the Council of Trent (pp. 386–387), was eager to check the spread of Protestant ideas, and one way was to bring the teachings of the Church directly to the faithful. Art had pro-

Fig. 9.3 *The Wedding Dance.* Medieval artists usually showed peasants at work, to celebrate such themes as orderly government or the seasons of the year. Pieter Brueghel shows peasants at play—dancers uproariously flinging themselves about, quietly sociable groups of neighbors, everyone in their Sunday best. He is celebrating peasants themselves, with their spontaneous high spirits, their sense of community, their modest prosperity—and also their social pretensions. Some of the men wear tight-fitting outfits complete with suggestively upstanding codpieces, as was the fashion among nobles of the day.

vided religious instruction during the Middle Ages; it was now called upon to renew its role in defense of Catholic teachings.

The response was an outpouring of magnificent art, ranging from the mystical to the sensual. Though the new artists built on Renaissance models, they threw off the restraints of classical rules. Their work came to be called *Baroque*—meaning "excessive" or "ornate." But the movement generated its own standards and must not be measured by classical norms. At its best, Baroque has an impressive originality and impact.

The leader of Baroque art was the Flemish painter Peter Paul Rubens. In 1600, as a young man of twenty-three, he journeyed to Italy, where he learned to create heroic, large-scale canvases. After returning to his native Antwerp, Rubens combined the traditional Flemish attention to detail with his newly learned Italian style. He worked chiefly for the court of the ruling Habsburgs, the Flemish aristocrats, and the Church. A man of enormous energy and versatility, he created fine portraits, altar paintings, and huge murals for palaces and religious houses. His subject matter ranged from romantic and mythological themes to the central mysteries of the Catholic faith. So great was the demand for Rubens's work that he set up a well-organized workshop in which he trained specialists to paint certain elements—heads, hands, animals, or backgrounds. He supervised the production of each work and finished the key features with his own hand. He was blessed by good fortune and a happy disposition, and his paintings are charged with movement and vigor. His well-nourished nudes reflect the spirit with

Fig. 9.4 *The Rape of the Daughters of Leucippus.* Rubens depicts Castor and Pollux, horse-riding sons of Zeus, kidnapping Phoebe and Hilaera as brides. Almost every detail contributes to an image of helplessly protesting womanhood overwhelmed by irresistible male passion. Even the horses, white in the original ancient Greek myth, are a more masculine-looking chestnut and gray. But one detail tells a different story. The men, too, are helpless—mere puppets of the mischievous boy-god Cupid (left), whose name means "Desire."

Alte Pinakothek, Munich/Joachim Lavel Krotothek

which he viewed the world. In his treatment of a traditional subject from Greek legend, *The Rape of the Daughters of Leucippus* (*Fig. 9.4*), he arranged powerful men, horses, and women into a tight group of solid figures. There is little "philosophical" intent in this kind of painting, but it combines exciting elements of form and movement.

As Rubens was the artistic master of Catholic Flanders, Rembrandt van Rijn was the master of Protestant Holland. But a greater contrast in personalities can hardly be imagined. A generation younger than Rubens, Rembrandt won substantial recognition early in his career. After his beautiful and well-to-do wife died in 1642, however, his fortunes began to decline. He fell into debt, his popularity vanished, and he turned more and more inward in his thoughts.

Yet it was in the dark days of tragedy and self-examination that Rembrandt did his most profound work. He often painted religious subjects, but even his nonreligious works possess a mysterious spiritual quality. Unlike Rubens, he usually took his subjects from the middle or lower classes. He portrayed them with remarkable economy of line and without affectation, shunning bright colors and extravagant movements and relying on contrasting light and shadow. His colors appear dark or drab to those who see his paintings for the first time; Rembrandt favored browns, dark reds, and golds. He did not wish the surface of his canvases to blind the viewer to the "inner" person. When we look closely at a Rembrandt portrait, we sense the essential character of the subject (*Fig. 9.5*).

Rembrandt spent most of his life in Amsterdam, but he put into his work many of the qualities of Italian painting. These included careful organization and balance and, above all, psychological interest (as stressed by Leonardo; p. 352). An illustration of Rembrandt's religious painting is the *Supper at Emmaus* (*Fig. 9.6*). A good Protestant, he was a devout reader of the Bible, and in this picture he dramatized a moment from

Fig. 9.5 *Portrait of the Artist.*
In this self-portrait, Rembrandt
goes outside himself and looks
inward. He shows himself, like
any other sitter, in the dress
and with the instruments of his
calling. He flatters himself a little
with a freehand-painted circle
to proclaim his technical skill.
But he mainly uses his skill, as
well as his artistic perception, for
a deep and sympathetic exploration of his own character. He
has applied Leonardo da Vinci's
advice (*Fig. 8.10*, p. 353), to paint
"the individual's appearance and
the state of his mind," to himself.

Fig. 9.6 *Supper at Emmaus.*
The risen Christ reveals himself
to two followers after walking
with them unrecognized to a
village near Jerusalem. Baroque
artists usually depicted this
scene as a moment of drama,
but Rembrandt, the sober
Protestant, deliberately under-
states it. Instead of the traditional close-up with different
poses of utter astonishment, he
shows an intimate group in a
corner of a shadowy room, with
Christ's followers too absorbed
by the sight of him to be amazed.
Perhaps they have quietly and
joyfully realized that they knew
who he was all along.

Fig. 9.7 *The Ecstasy of Saint Theresa.* "The pain was so great that I screamed aloud; but at the same time I wished the pain to last forever. . . . It was the sweetest caressing of the soul by God." Giovanni Bernini, the passionate Catholic, boldly uses theatrical devices to reenact the words of the sixteenth-century Spanish mystic. The figures are poised on a cloud with no apparent support, divine rays (and actual light) flood down from above, and the saint's face and the angel's smile echo the commonest human experience of unbearable pleasure.

© Alinari/Art Resource, NY

the life of Christ as recounted in Luke (24:13–31). The Gospel states that on the day of the Resurrection, Jesus appeared, unrecognized, along a road. There he joined two of his disciples, who invited him to eat with them at an inn. Rembrandt shows Jesus at the moment when he blessed and broke the bread and was revealed to his disciples as the risen Christ.

BAROQUE SCULPTURE AND ARCHITECTURE: BERNINI

The main source of the Baroque style was Rome, where the Catholic Reformation was centered. The climax of that style came during the seventeenth century in the work of the sculptor and architect Giovanni Lorenzo Bernini (1598–1680).

A leading characteristic of Baroque artists was their effort to fuse architecture, sculpture, and painting into a single structure of grandeur and "truth." Bernini was trained as a sculptor, but he thought of himself as an artist who combined several talents. "I render marble as supple as wax," he declared, "and I have united in my works the resources of painting and sculpture." Bernini's most distinctive contribution was the revival of the Italian sculptural tradition, which had fallen into decline with the passing of Michelangelo (pp. 354–356). In the cold, hard medium of stone, Bernini succeeded in catching the fleeting instant, the throbbing passion, the rhythm of movement.

He learned much from the muscular, twisting figures of Michelangelo, but his work displayed even wider range and inventiveness. By means of extraordinary technical skill, he brought sculpture to new heights of drama and emotion. *The Ecstasy of Saint Theresa* (*Fig. 9.7*), which Bernini prepared for a chapel in a small Rome church, shows the

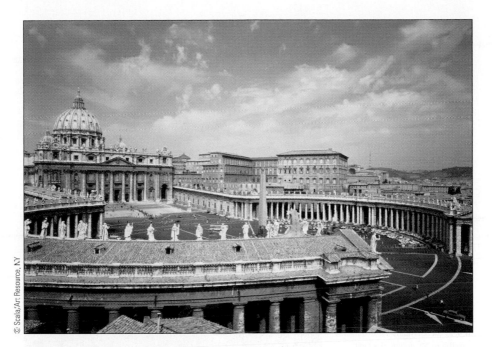

Fig. 9.8 The Church's Embrace. The approach to Saint Peter's Basilica begins with Bernini's vast oval plaza surrounded by massive columns. At the center is an ancient Egyptian obelisk, brought to Rome in imperial times and set upright and tipped with a cross during the Renaissance. The colonnades are linked with the basilica by a straight-sided space, which widens toward the still loftier columns of the western entrance. At the universal Church's center, the architecture proclaims that the Church has outlasted Egypt, triumphed over Rome, and spread around the world to embrace the human race.

mystical Spanish nun after her heart has been pierced by the arrow of divine love. As a smiling angel looks on, the face and body of the saint express indescribable rapture.

As an architect, Bernini was also a master of dramatic effect. Late in his life, he fashioned the vast oval piazza that stands before Saint Peter's Basilica, the largest church in Christendom. (More than 100,000 people crowd into this space on special days to await the blessing by the pope.) To enclose its two sides, Bernini constructed a huge, curving colonnade (*Fig. 9.8*), consisting of 284 Greek-style columns. They carry a roof more than 60 feet high, surmounted by seventy giant-sized statues. Visitors entering the piazza from its open end are embraced, symbolically, by the "arms" of the Church.

Baroque architecture (like Baroque painting and sculpture) was an adaptation of Renaissance models. Such classical elements as columns, pediments, and arches were used freely, but without following strictly the ancient "rules" for their use. From the late sixteenth century to our own day, many of the public buildings of the West have been designed in this flexible style—mainly because the spectacular effects that it makes possible are well adapted to proclaiming the glory and power of the buildings' users.

For this reason, the monarchs of Europe were quick to adopt the style. Philip II of Spain, the most powerful ruler of his time (p. 383), started in 1563 to build a new royal palace, choosing for its site the village of Escorial, in the mountainous country near Madrid. Philip's architects laid out a vast complex of buildings and courtyards, with an elegant church at its center. Beneath its main altar was placed a burial vault in which the Spanish kings and queens have since been entombed. The Escorial complex also

Fig. 9.9 The Hall of Mirrors, Versailles. This 80-yard-long marbled and mirrored chamber for court ceremonies and festivities, with its ceiling paintings of Louis XIV's government achievements and victories over rival rulers, proclaims "the king supreme in France and France supreme in Europe." Its symbolic meaning for friend and foe has been long-enduring. In this hall in 1871, the invading king of Prussia was proclaimed emperor of Europe's new dominant power, united Germany, and in 1919, France and its allies summoned the Germans back to sign the treaty ending the First World War.

© Erich Lessing/Art Resource, NY

included a monastery, a seminary, and a library. Its architectural style is generally restrained, but its plan is Baroque.

A better-known monument to royal glory is the Versailles Palace, built a century later by Louis XIV. The French monarchy had by then replaced the Spanish as the leading royal house of Europe, and Louis wanted to erect a residence and a center of government and the arts that would surpass all existing palaces. Like the Escorial, Louis's residence was built in the countryside (about 20 miles southwest of Paris). It was a high point of the secular Baroque style, combining architecture, landscaping, sculpture, painting, and the minor arts into a grand synthesis.

Built at staggering cost, Versailles matched Louis's love of display. The enclosed areas cover 17 acres and housed some ten thousand people. The formal gardens, courts, parade grounds, and surrounding woods stretch over many square miles. The overall plan is a masterful realization of the Baroque idea of "integrated" design. While the exterior of the Versailles Palace is relatively modest, the interior is lavish in the extreme. One of the most dazzling chambers is the Hall of Mirrors (*Fig. 9.9*), a shimmering room designed to overawe visitors to the French court.

Religion, Politics, and War

In spite of all the Reformation changes, most of the contending religious groups continued to believe in two traditional ideas about the place of religion in the community.

The first was that there was only one religious truth, that all members of a community should confess it, and that deviation from it was a danger to souls. The second was that the rulers of a community had a duty to uphold religious truth in partnership with the Church, if necessary by coercing those who deviated from the truth.

Now that there was no longer a single religion but several "religions," as they were called, each with its own version of religious truth, these beliefs in unanimity and partnership actually made for conflict. Rulers of countries with different dominant religions might make war on each other as part of their duty of upholding religious truth. Within countries, rejected old religions or rising new ones, facing a hostile partnership of Church and state, might rebel and even seek help from sympathetic foreign rulers, both to protect themselves from persecution and to impose their own version of truth on the community. All these motivations made the Reformation an era of civil and international *wars of religion*.

Meanwhile, however, rulers continued their endless nonreligious struggles for power, land, and trading opportunities, as well as for personal, dynastic, and national glory. Within their countries, furthermore, their partnership with powerful subjects—especially nobles—continued to be full of frictions just as it had been in the past. Religious disputes did not replace all these conflicts but became entangled with them. Religious and nonreligious rivalries reinforced each other, and the wars of religion were all the longer and more embittered as a result.

In every country, there were also idealistic humanists who were in principle against settling religious disputes by force, as well as prudent statesmen who feared that religious war would weaken their countries in nonreligious struggles. But their voices got a hearing only at times when the rival religious groups had fought each other to a standstill and compromise of some kind seemed inevitable. And even when compromises came about, new nonreligious disputes and new religious conflicts supplied new reasons for war, and new wars of religion would begin.

As a result, the wars of religion were fought in three main stages, each inspired by one or other of the main religious movements of the time. First came the wars in the Holy Roman Empire arising from the spread of Lutheranism, which ended in the first effort at religious compromise, the Peace of Augsburg of 1555 (p. 374). Then, in the second half of the sixteenth century, the spread of Calvinism resulted in civil and international wars involving the Netherlands and France. Finally, as the Counter-Reformation gathered strength, Catholic efforts to recover lost territory led in the first half of the seventeenth century to new struggles in the Holy Roman Empire that reached their height in the Thirty Years' War.

When the Thirty Years' War ended in stalemate, efforts to change the religious balance internationally at last came to seem so costly and destructive that they were clearly harmful to the nonreligious interests of whoever pursued them. As a result, in the second half of the seventeenth century, religion gradually ceased to play a role in international conflicts. In this way, out of the religious wars of the Reformation there grew a new, secular European state system.

THE CALVINIST WARS: THE NETHERLANDS AND FRANCE

The Netherlands were a center of trade and industry which formed a wealthy part of the Habsburg domains (p. 317), and the region's powerful cities had a long-standing tradition of self-government. Protestantism first spread there from Germany and then grew rapidly under Calvinist leadership *(Map 9.1,* p. 368). At about the same time, the Netherlands came under the rule of the Spanish Habsburgs following the division of the territories of Charles V (p. 318), and in 1567, King Philip II of Spain responded to the spread of Calvinism with cruel repression. In addition to admitting the Inquisition (p. 387) to the area, he introduced harsh political and economic restrictions. In reaction to this challenge to their self-government, both Catholics and Calvinists rebelled in 1566 under the leadership of a local aristocrat and Habsburg official, William "the Silent," prince of Orange-Nassau.

There followed nearly half a century of wars, in which the Netherlands gradually divided. Spanish armies and growing Catholic mistrust of the Calvinists recovered the southern Netherlands for the old rulers and the old religion. In the north, however, the defiant Calvinists, with English help, fought the Habsburg forces on land and sea. In 1581, they declared independence, but it took nearly thirty years before a truce gave them de facto Spanish recognition in 1609. A new country had appeared, the United Provinces of the Netherlands—often known as Holland, the name of its largest province.

Holland's commercial wealth made it a leading contender in European power struggles throughout the seventeenth century, and it became one of the main challengers of Spain and Portugal for control of worldwide trade and empire (p. 327). There were still many Catholics in Holland, many disagreements among the dominant Calvinists, and many dissident Protestant groups. Persecution would risk renewed civil war in a small country that was still vulnerable to Spanish attack, and would also be very bad for business. Instead, therefore, Holland became Europe's first country to hold consistently to a policy of religious toleration, though the government stayed under Calvinist control.

Meanwhile, the Catholic southern Netherlands remained under Habsburg rule until the time of the French Revolution. Afterward, following a brief period of reunion with Holland, they won independence as the country of Belgium (p. 429).

Religion and politics were similarly mixed in France. Early in the Reformation, persecution by the Catholic rulers had kept Protestantism from spreading, but after the death in 1547 of Francis I, the country had a series of weak rulers, and noble factions began to spring up that sought either to limit the monarch's power or to bring the government under their control. At about the same time, the Frenchman John Calvin was making the French-speaking Swiss town of Geneva into a model Protestant community, and Calvinist missionaries began to spread their beliefs in France *(Map 9.1,* p. 368). Soon there was a growing Huguenot (a French slang word for "Swiss") movement in France, in which Calvinist ministers supplied religious fervor and powerful nobles provided military power.

The Huguenots never made enough converts or gained enough victories to take over the government, but the rulers were too weak, and had too many independent-minded Catholic nobles to deal with as well, to be able to crush them. The result was a series of civil wars and foreign interventions that continued on and off for most of the second half of the sixteenth century. The very existence of France as a powerful independent country seemed to be threatened by religious struggles, and a school of thinking grew up, known by the French name *politiques* (because it put politics before religion) which sought religious compromise for the sake of national unity. Finally, King Henry IV, legitimate ruler by inheritance but also a Huguenot, brought the wars to an end by following a *politique* strategy. He defeated Catholic forces in battle but himself became a Catholic so as to win the loyalty of the strongest religion. To keep the support of the Huguenots, by the Edict of Nantes (1598) he guaranteed them civil rights, religious tolerance, and even the possession of military forces and strongholds.

In this way, Henry was able to restore both national unity and royal power, but after his death, this second effort to keep religious disputes separate from political struggles broke down. The French rulers became fervent Catholics as the Counter-Reformation took hold, and Cardinal Richelieu, the powerful minister of Henry's successor, King Louis XIII, viewed the Huguenots as an obstacle to royal power—a "state within the state." In renewed civil war, he broke the military power of the aristocratic Huguenot faction. For the time being, Huguenots were still tolerated, but they now faced a strong Catholic government that favored those of its own religion. From a powerful faction under noble leadership, the Huguenots became a dwindling minority of middle-class townspeople.

THE COUNTER-REFORMATION WARS:
THE HOLY ROMAN EMPIRE AND THE THIRTY YEARS' WAR

As Calvinism spread and the Counter-Reformation got under way, the Peace of Augsburg began to break down. As we have seen, this settlement (p. 374) had left each German prince free to decide whether the religion of his subjects would be Lutheran or Catholic. Over the next sixty years, the Catholic princes, guided by the Jesuits (p. 385), stamped out the remnants of Protestant dissent in their territories. The zeal of the Lutheran princes, on the other hand, was weakened by bitter squabbles with Calvinist minorities. Sensing danger, some of the Protestant princes joined together in an armed league in 1608, an action promptly countered by the formation of a Catholic league.

As each camp eyed the other, watching for any move that might upset the religious and territorial balance, revolt exploded in Bohemia, a self-governing kingdom within the Holy Roman Empire. Most of the population of Bohemia were Czechs who were both anti-German and antipapal, and the trouble there had its roots in the Hussite rebellion of the fifteenth century (pp. 296, 368–369). During the sixteenth century, the Protestants of Bohemia had enjoyed toleration under moderate Catholic rulers. But when Ferdinand of Styria, a Habsburg and a zealous Counter-Reformation Catholic, was forced upon them as king, they feared that their religious and political rights were in jeopardy. Accordingly, in 1618, the Bohemian nobles announced their open defiance of Ferdinand and chose a Calvinist prince of the Rhineland to be their king.

The Catholic league of princes moved swiftly to help Ferdinand crush the poorly organized rebellion, and the support of the Spanish Habsburgs, as well as Ferdinand's election as Holy Roman Emperor in 1619, gave him added strength. The imperial armies moved into the Rhineland to attack the possessions of the defeated rival Bohemian king. Ferdinand hoped to overthrow Protestantism throughout the empire and in the process to reverse the empire's gradual breakup and turn it into a powerful Catholic state under his own rule. And Catholic victory in the empire, so he and his Spanish relatives as well as the papacy hoped, would be the key to Catholic victory throughout Europe.

But what the Habsburgs hoped for, many other rulers—both Protestant and Catholic—feared. The king of Denmark decided to intervene in Germany in order to protect Lutheranism and to acquire territory for himself. He was promised help by the English and the Dutch, who also wanted to check the advance of Habsburg (and Spanish) power. Later, Sweden joined the struggle against Ferdinand. Meanwhile, the Catholic princes of the empire regularly lost enthusiasm for the struggle whenever it seemed that Ferdinand was too successful and might threaten their independence. Catholic France, where Cardinal Richelieu put political interest above religion in his international dealings, actually joined the war on the Protestant side. Richelieu wanted to build a powerful Catholic monarchy at home, but he was determined not to let Ferdinand do the same in the Holy Roman Empire. All of the empire's neighbors became involved at one time or another, but the balance of forces was too even, and none was able to win a lasting victory. Germany was turned into a ghastly battlefield, endlessly fought over by mercenary armies.

THE PEACE OF WESTPHALIA AND THE END OF WARS OF RELIGION

It took thirty years, from 1618 to 1648, for the contenders finally to give up hope of decisive victory. The Peace of Westphalia, which concluded the war, is a landmark in European history. In Germany, the terms of the Peace of Augsburg were restored and extended to include Calvinism as well as Lutheranism and Catholicism. Each prince retained the right to prescribe one of these faiths for his subjects, but conditions throughout the country were so wretched that none of them used force to compel conformity. Thus a kind of religious coexistence emerged from the exhausting struggle.

The end of the wars left Germany in a desperate condition. Having long suffered from political disunity, the country had then endured the ravages of warfare, plunder, famine, and pestilence (typhus). The population had been reduced by a third, and the loss of property had been severe. At the Peace of Westphalia, the German princes won recognition as independent sovereigns, and the Holy Roman Empire was thus reduced to a shell. Switzerland and the Netherlands, which had once been subject to the Habsburgs, were also recognized as independent states. With the decline of Germany and of Habsburg power, the Bourbon dynasty (founded by Henry IV) took the lead in Europe, and a century of French dominance was at hand.

The settlement, whose principal provisions lasted until the Napoleonic Wars (pp. 470–471), marked a shift in the balance of dynastic power and the emergence of the modern European state system. Religious wars were still occasionally fought. Thus, late-seventeenth-century struggles between English-backed Protestants and French-backed Catholics in Ireland, for example, ended in more than a century of second-class citizenship for the Catholic majority and in resentments that are still alive today. Vicious coercion of out-of-power religions also continued for the time being, for instance in France, where King Louis XIV turned from toleration to persecution of the Huguenots. In 1685, he formally revoked the Edict of Nantes, and tens of thousands of refugees "defected" to Protestant countries. But for the most part, religious disputes among Christians ceased to play the leading role in international and civil conflicts that they had played since the sixteenth century.

Map 9.2 Europe After Westphalia (1648). After more than a century of wars of religion since 1526 (*Map 7.3*, p. 318), changes are under way in the pattern of European power struggles. The Habsburgs have divided their territories, and their dominant Spanish branch has been overstretched by war. The Ottoman Empire and Poland still look large but are weakened by internal disputes. The future belongs to Russia and the Austrian Habsburgs, to the newly arisen United Netherlands (Holland) and Brandenburg-Prussia, and above all to the rising western European "superpowers," France and England.

Already in the Middle Ages, wars of religion among western European rulers had been unusual, but that had been because the rulers had shared a common faith. Now that there was no longer a common faith and no hope of reimposing one, European countries and rulers more or less deliberately excluded religion from their conflicts. Rulers no longer thought of themselves as belonging to a single Christendom, whose harmony was liable to be disturbed by quarrels arising from sinful human nature. Instead, they thought of themselves as sharing a single territory, Europe, whose "balance of power" depended on successful adjustment of mutually competitive interests (*Map 9.2*). Gone were the remains of imperial and papal claims to authority over the political life of Europe; each state was now free to wage war or make peace and generally to act in a sovereign manner.

A miniature model for the new European state system had appeared in Italy during the Renaissance, when city-states such as Florence, Milan, and Venice had worked out a system of relationships among themselves as sovereign powers (p. 309). The powerful states beyond the Alps that now dominated Europe drew on the Italian experience in shaping their own international relations.

With the end of any kind of common authority, the seventeenth century also saw the emergence of the idea and practice of international law, aimed at regulating relations among these independent states by mutual agreement. Some rulers, of course, were more careful than others in following the law, but the law at least provided standards that were widely respected. The classic statement of those standards is the *Law of War and Peace* (1625), written by the Dutch lawyer Hugo Grotius partly in response to the atrocities committed during the Thirty Years' War. Though Grotius recognized war as a "legitimate" state of affairs, he distinguished between just and unjust conflicts and laid down some guidelines for "humane" methods of waging war. Grotius condemned such acts as poisoning wells, mutilating prisoners, and massacring hostages. Drawing on the ancient Roman principles of natural law (p. 135), he also spelled out the rights of neutral states and of civilians in war zones.

In the eighteenth century, wars of religion ceased altogether. With the predominant religion fully secure in each country, minority religions gradually came to be tolerated, though their believers were usually excluded from public office, and the partnership between the state and the predominant religion remained in effect. Only the newly formed United States went so far as to dissolve the partnership, with the First Amendment to its Constitution proclaiming that "Congress shall make no law respecting an establishment of religion." Few European countries followed this example, but in the nineteenth century, they mostly granted religious minorities, Christian and non-Christian, full toleration and civil equality. Religious freedom and equality became generally accepted Western values, which were violated more often by supporters of new secular ideologies than by religious believers. Such, ironically, was the final result of the wars of religion of the Reformation era.

RECOMMENDED READING

Background of the Reformation J. Bossy, *Christianity in the West, 1400–1700* (1985), is an excellent brief overview and interpretation of religious change throughout late medieval and early modern times. R. H. Bainton, *The Reformation of the Sixteenth Century* (1952), and O. Chadwick, *The Reformation* (1964), are readable brief accounts by leading scholars; a more recent and detailed treatment is E. Cameron, *The European Reformation* (1991). A. E. McGrath, *Reformation Thought: An Introduction* (1993), is an excellent guide to theological issues, as well as to Protestant and Catholic ideas on society and government. For the general history of the period, see E. F. Rice and A. Grafton, *The Foundations of Early Modern Europe* (1994), and the more detailed account by G. Elton, *Reformation Europe* (1999).

Specifically on the background of the Reformation, F. Oakley, *The Western Church in the Later Middle Ages* (1979), is an excellent survey dealing with all aspects of both Catholic and dissident religion.

The Revolt of Luther: "Justification by Faith" R. H. Bainton, *Here I Stand* (1950), is a readable and reliable classic; R. Marius, *Luther* (1974), is a more critical interpretation. W. R. Estep, *The Anabaptist Story: An Introduction to Sixteenth-Century Anabaptism* (1996), is a scholarly and sympathetic survey of the radical Reformation movements.

Calvin and the Elect: "Predestination" W. Bouwsma, *John Calvin: A Sixteenth-Century Portrait* (1988), insightfully depicts Calvin as a man of his time; A. E. McGrath, *A Life of John Calvin: A Study of the Shaping of Western Culture* (1990), stresses Calvin's thought and its impact. J. T. McNeill, *The History and Character of Calvinism* (1954), is a good short account of Calvinism's theology, church organization, and impact throughout Europe and the New World.

M. Weber, *The Protestant Ethic and the Spirit of Capitalism* (1930), is the classic statement of the relationship between Calvinism and capitalism; the 1998 reprint has an introduction by R. Collins assessing the validity of the Weber thesis. See also the books by Bainton, Chadwick, and Cameron listed in the first section and McGrath's book listed here.

Henry VIII and the Church of England A. G. Dickens, *The English Reformation* (1991), and C. Haigh, *English Reformations: Religion, Politics, and Society Under the Tudors* (1993), survey not only the policies of rulers and the activities of religious leaders but also the response to the Reformation at the grass roots: Dickens stresses popular acceptance of religious change, and Haigh emphasizes popular resistance to it. An excellent brief guide to the much-disputed question of when and how the English people became wholeheartedly Protestant is D. Rosman, *From Catholic to Protestant: Religion and the People in Tudor England* (1996).

The Roman Catholic Response: Reform and Reaffirmation A. G. Dickens, *The Counter-Reformation* (1969), is a good brief introduction to the activities of rulers, religious leaders, and artists, which covers both religious and cultural aspects; M. D. W. Jones, *The Counter-Reformation: Religion and Society in Early Modern Europe* (1995), also includes material on the popular response to and acceptance of the Counter-Reformation, with source selections. R. Po-chi Hsia, *The World of Catholic Renewal, 1540–1770* (1998), discusses the practice and culture of Counter-Reformation Catholicism and its differences from the Catholicism of the Middle Ages.

Art During the Reformation The best introduction to Baroque art and architecture is G. Bazin, *Baroque and Rococo* (1964). J. R. Martin, *Baroque* (1977), deals with the distinguishing features of Baroque style. On individual artists, see H. Hibbard, *Bernini* (1965); W. Stechow, *Pieter Brueghel the Elder* (1990); C. White, *Rembrandt* (1984); and C. Scribner, *Rubens* (1989). On the commercial and patronage side of Baroque art, see S. Alpers, *Rembrandt's Enterprise: The Studio and the Market* (1988).

Religion, Politics, and War H. G. Koenigsberger, *Early Modern Europe, 1500–1789* (1987), is an excellent brief overview of the period covered by this chapter; R. Bonney, *The European Dynastic States, 1494–1660* (1991), and J. Black, *Eighteenth-Century Europe, 1700–1789* (1990), are more detailed surveys. G. Parker, *The Thirty Years' War* (1984), includes social as well as military and political aspects; and his *The Military Revolution: Military Innovation and the Rise of the West, 1500–1800* (1996), deals with the impact of military changes on politics and government.

INFOTRAC COLLEGE EDITION

Visit the source collections at **http://academic.cengage.com/infotrac**, and use the Search function with the following key terms:

Reformation	Martin and Luther not King	Elizabeth I
Counter-Reformation	John Calvin	Thirty Years' War

WESTERN CIVILIZATION RESOURCES

Visit the Brief History of the Western World Companion Web Site for resources specific to this textbook:

http://history.wadsworth.com/greerbrief09/

Also, the CD in the back of this book and the World History Resources Center at **http://history.wadsworth.com/west_civ/** offer a variety of tools to help you succeed in this course, including access to quizzes; images; documents; interactive simulations, maps, and timelines; movie explorations; and a wealth of other sources.

Fig. III.1. Remaking the Universe. In this diagram by Thomas Digges, a sixteenth-century follower of Copernicus, the earth orbits the sun, and the stars, "far excelling our sun both in quantity and quality," extend "infinitely" upward. To make this picture believable, Digges claims it not as a scientific breakthrough but as "most ancient doctrine" of Greek philosophers. The stars are also "the habitacle [dwelling] of the elect"—those predestined to salvation, according to the Protestant reformer John Calvin. Digges mixes scientific discovery with religious belief and an appeal to traditional authority. The rise of science is still beginning.

Part Four

THE RISE OF THE MODERN WEST

The Rise of the Modern West

The seventeenth, eighteenth, and nineteenth centuries were an era of further spectacular shifts in civilization, following upon those that had already altered the medieval pattern. These new shifts eventually brought into being all the basic features of the modern West.

In those three centuries, violent revolutions and peaceful reforms undermined Europe's traditional government structure of kings and nobles claiming authority from God. European settlers in North and South America revolted against their distant rulers and founded independent countries. The ancient institutions of slavery and serfdom were abolished. Secular ideologies—nonreligious systems of thought and belief—arose to challenge Christianity as the central belief of Western civilization. The slow-moving pace of technical advance and scientific discovery turned into a headlong rush, and the traditional agrarian way of life gave way to an industrial society.

All these shifts in civilization sprang from the earlier ones that had already altered the medieval pattern. The rise of industrial society was made possible by the technical advances of the late Middle Ages, the worldwide markets opened up by overseas exploration and empire building, and the financial resources of burgeoning capitalism. The astronomers who overturned the traditional earth-centered model of the universe, and in the process developed new ways of gaining scientific knowledge in every field, were inspired by the Renaissance revival of ancient Greek science and philosophy. The revolts and revolutions that shook the traditional order were reactions against the burdens and inequalities of absolute monarchy, the high point of the long-standing growth in the power of hereditary rulers. The first of the secular ideologies, the Enlightenment belief in reason, progress, and human fulfillment in this world, was developed by eighteenth-century thinkers impressed by Europe's growth in knowledge, wealth, and power up to their own time.

In addition, the new shifts in civilization interacted with one another—usually in such a way as to drive all of them onward. The increase of scientific knowledge contributed to the rise of secular ideologies, and the resulting breakdown of consensus over Christian belief made it pointless for governments to claim to rule in the name of God. Industrialization speeded travel and brought mass media into existence, making it easier for political leaders to rally citizens of large countries to influence governments. Enlightenment principles helped inspire the abolition of slavery and serfdom, and millions of workers became free to move from plantations and villages into factories.

As a result of all these changes, a new kind of civilization grew up within the West that was different from all others of its own time and of the past, including the earlier "Wests" themselves. In this new civilization, the majority of the population lived in cities and worked in factories and offices rather than on farms, and the traditional division of status and power between men and women was beginning to break down. It was wealthy enough to have realistic expectations of health, education, leisure, and abundance for the masses as well as the elite. Its governments ruled in the name of the people and the nation, and had more control of their citizens' lives than ever before—compelling them to go to school, supporting them in sickness and poverty, drafting them into the army. Citizens, in turn, were equipped with rights and freedoms that enabled them to wield greater power over governments than ever before, above all through more or less democratically elected representative assemblies.

More than any earlier civilization, this one had a double and often conflicting view of the order of the universe and the destinies of the human race. It still regarded these things as the fulfillment of divine purposes to be interpreted through religion, but it also saw them more clearly than ever before as the outcome of natural processes to be understood through science. And it was the first civilization to pin its hopes and fears for its own future on the production of a limitless flood of technical advances and scientific discoveries.

In this civilization, the traditional understanding of the meaning and purpose of literature and art was also beginning to change. In its most admired works of art, the affirmation of generally accepted beliefs and values was beginning to give way to questioning. Recognizable depiction of the appearance of things was being replaced by the expression of the perceptions and inner world of the artist. Alongside the continuing influence of traditional styles and themes, a self-conscious break with the past was under way. The progress of science and technology was giving rise to new artistic media, as well as to a whole new area of artistic creation: mass entertainment.

The geography of the Western heartland had also changed. It was now to be found in those regions where the shifts in civilization had gone farthest, and whose wealth, power, and cultural influence had consequently grown the most—no longer western Europe alone, but also the formerly outlying territory of North America.

	POLITICAL, SOCIAL, AND ECONOMIC DEVELOPMENTS	RELIGION, SCIENCE, AND PHILOSOPHY	HISTORY AND LITERATURE	ARCHITECTURE, ART, AND MUSIC

1600	Religious Wars:
	  Thirty Years' War in Germany
	Grotius and emergence of
	  international law
	
	Peace of Westphalia
		Copernicus (died 1543)
		Bacon
		Kepler
		Galileo
		
		Descartes
				Baroque style of
				  architecture
				
				Monteverdi (opera)

1650	English Revolution Cromwell Mercantilism Louis XIV Age of absolutism	Royal Society founded Hobbes Bossuet Locke Newton		Versailles Palace Wren

1700	Rise of Prussia and Russia:
	  Peter the Great
	  Frederick the Great
	
	Enlightened despotism
		The Enlightenment:
		
		Deism
		
		Montesquieu
			Age of classicism:
			  Racine
			  Pope
				St. Paul's Cathedral
				Handel
				Rococo style:
				  Watteau
				  Boucher
				  Fragonard
				
				Reynolds

POLITICAL, SOCIAL, AND ECONOMIC DEVELOPMENTS	RELIGION, SCIENCE, AND PHILOSOPHY	HISTORY AND LITERATURE	ARCHITECTURE, ART, AND MUSIC	
Industrial Revolution and beginnings of factory system	Rousseau Smith	Voltaire Diderot		1750
American Revolution			Classical revival style of architecture	
		Jefferson		
	Kant		David	
U.S. Constitution			Jefferson	
French Revolution	Condorcet Burke			
			Haydn Mozart	
Napoleon I and empire of the French Conservative reaction	Ricardo	Goethe	Beethoven Schubert Chopin	1800
		Age of romanticism:	Romanticism in art:	
Congress of Vienna	Hegel Dalton	Wordsworth Scott	Goya Gothic revival style:	
Metternich System "Concert of Europe"	Schwann	Byron Shelley	Houses of Parliament	
	Utopian socialists: Saint-Simon Fourier Owen	Keats		
			Turner, Constable	
Spread of political and economic liberalism Growth of nationalism Early Industrial Revolution in Britain	Comte Mazzini	Balzac	Delacroix	
	Marx, Engels, Bakunin Darwin	Dickens	Berlioz Wagner Tchaikovsky	1850

CHAPTER 10

Absolute Monarchy, Science, and Enlightenment

OVERVIEW

Among the most spectacular new shifts in civilization in the seventeenth and eighteenth centuries were the rise of absolute monarchy, the beginning of modern science, and the emergence of the secular worldview of the Enlightenment.

Absolute (unlimited) monarchy was a continuation of the late medieval increase in the power of rulers, in response to fierce struggles over religion, territory, and trade in Europe and overseas. To meet these challenges, rulers cast off traditional restrictions on their power, such as representative assemblies. They treated nobles and churches at best as junior partners, though until late in the eighteenth century, they upheld the long-standing privileges of the nobility, clergy, and wealthy bourgeoisie. They taxed the rest of the population more heavily than ever, built up massive standing armies and navies, and declared their actions to be authorized by God himself. They helped other Western changes onward by generously supporting science, scholarship, and art and by fostering trade and industry as best they could. Furthermore, the increase in government power that absolute monarchy brought about became a permanent feature of Western states.

Meanwhile, the intellectual changes that had begun with the Renaissance were leading to a momentous and unexpected result: the Scientific Revolution. Under the influence of the revived ideas and knowledge of the Renaissance, investigators from Nicolaus Copernicus to Isaac Newton brought about a revolution in one particular field of natural knowledge: astronomy. They did not just prove that the earth moved around the sun, but developed a whole new understanding of the universe as a vast self-regulating entity, whose rules of operation could be discovered by observation and experiment and described in the language of mathematics. Thus in addition to revolutionizing astronomy, the investigators launched the whole modern enterprise of scientific discovery.

This new understanding of the natural universe in turn helped lead to a new understanding of humanity and God—that of the eighteenth-century Enlightenment. In place of an almighty God who directed the workings of nature and the destinies of the human race, the writers and intellectuals of the Enlightenment put a remote deity who had created the universe, established its laws, and left it to itself. In place of faith in the unseen, they put human reason which could limitlessly discover the unknown. In place of original sin and redemption they put the ideas of progress and human perfectibility. The Enlightenment was the first serious challenge to Christian belief since ancient times, but it was also an attractive way of thinking that influenced all classes of society. Few people shed their religious beliefs, but even nobles, bishops, and absolute monarchs began to work for such reforms as widespread education, religious toleration, and the abolition of serfdom.

In the cultural field, Europe continued its Renaissance revival of Greco-Roman art and thought, and continued to reinterpret the traditions of the ancients in accordance with its own changing needs. The passion and drama of the Baroque style were inspired by the revived Catholicism of the late sixteenth and early seventeenth centuries (pp. 388–389). The order, clarity, and precision of classicism were suitable to an age of reason and exact science. The elegance and refinement of the eighteenth-century Rococo style reflected the luxurious court and noble life of the eighteenth century. In addition, improvements in musical instruments and notation for the first time gave composers the same scope for creativity as writers or painters.

In some of its basic features, the seventeenth- and eighteenth-century West was still a traditional civilization. Farming remained the main source of wealth, the vast majority of the population still consisted of peasants, and absolute monarchy rested on the long-standing partnership of rulers, nobles, and churches. Even so, the changes in knowledge, thought, art, and government power were impressive, and more than ever before, they radiated outward from the countries of western Europe. Shortly before 1700, the ruler of an outlying territory of Western civilization, Tsar Peter I of Russia, visited the countries of the heartland and determined to reshape his own country in their image. For the first time, the European West was providing a model to be envied and imitated in another region of the world.

The Rise of Absolutism

The era of religious struggles leading up to the Thirty Years' War and the continued nonreligious conflicts that followed it (pp. 384–401) saw a renewed strengthening of royal government throughout most of Europe. The main reason was that only by increasing their power to control their countries could rulers hope to prevail in their endless competition—and this, in turn, was to a large extent because only powerful governments could mobilize the resources necessary to fight wars.

The changes in methods of warfare that had begun in the late Middle Ages (pp. 305–306, 308–309) had gone on into the sixteenth and seventeenth centuries, making warfare ever more costly. Shipbuilders had learned to build vessels large enough to carry whole batteries of artillery; engineers had devised cannon-resistant methods of fortification; gunsmiths had developed small firearms (muskets) that were handy and reliable enough for foot soldiers to use effectively. Already in the sixteenth century, the long time it took to build ships and train their crews had led governments to maintain standing navies. Late in the seventeenth century, the unreliability of the mercenary armies that had fought the Thirty Years' War meant that governments began to keep standing armies as well. From now on, the increased cost of war had to be borne also in peacetime.

The result was that rulers began to tax their countries ever more heavily and to do so at their own discretion. In countries where representative assemblies like the French Estates-General existed, which were supposed to give their consent to taxation (pp. 314–315), the rulers stopped calling them together, or reduced them to rubber-stamp bodies. The rulers bought off the most powerful likely opponents, the nobles and Church leaders, by leaving untouched their traditional privileges: tax exemption; favored access to government, military, and Church positions; the power to repress religious minorities; and authority over the peasants. And unquestionably, many subjects of all social groups felt that this takeover of power by rulers was much better than the likely alternatives—civil war, foreign conquest, and unwelcome changes of religion. It was in this way that *absolute monarchy*—"absolute" in the sense of "unrestricted"—rose to be the predominant European form of government. (The very different development in England is discussed in Chapter 11, pp. 446–451.)

THE ABSOLUTE MONARCH: LOUIS XIV

Of all the seventeenth-century absolute monarchies, the most powerful, and for a long time the most successful, was that of France. The wealthiest and most prosperous of the western European nation-states, France had moved toward political centralization during the fifteenth century and collapsed into civil war following the Reformation (pp. 314–315, 396–397). Once the wars were settled, the trend toward absolute monarchy resumed during the seventeenth century. Cardinal Richelieu, the astute minister of Louis XIII, led the way in crushing provincial and aristocratic revolts and in fashioning effective instruments of royal power. His aim, he declared simply, was "to make the king supreme in France and France supreme in Europe." Richelieu died in 1642, but his work was continued during the reign of Louis XIV.

The idea of absolutism was not new, but in Louis it found its most spectacular fulfillment. Having come to the throne as a boy in 1643, he took personal charge of state affairs in 1661. Louis held firm control for more than half a century down to 1715, laboring ceaselessly at perfecting his royal image and performing his royal tasks. His style of governing became the model for all Europe, as did the French army, language, manners, and culture.

Louis ignored the traditional checks on royal power as he concentrated all authority in the crown, which became the symbol of national power. (He is credited with having declared, *"L'état, c'est moi"*: "I am the state.") Louis overawed the nobles (whose fathers had notions of regaining their independence), though he maintained their privileges and surrounded himself with men and women of the oldest and wealthiest noble families at his magnificent court. In spite of lavish additions, his existing palace in Paris, the Louvre, still did not seem to him a splendid enough setting for the court, so he built the greatest of Baroque palaces outside the city, near the village of Versailles (*Fig. 9.9*, p. 394). In many respects, Versailles proved to be highly functional. Though wasteful of the nation's resources, it helped the king to centralize his authority within France, and it strengthened the role and image of France as the cultural leader of the West. A milestone in politics as well as in civic planning and the arts, Versailles called forth a hundred imitations by the monarchs and princelings of Europe.

Louis's minister of finance, Jean Baptiste Colbert, strengthened the tax system and promoted economic development. Internal trade was aided by improved roads and waterways, colonies and trading companies were founded overseas, and French industries were sheltered by protective tariffs and export subsidies.

The purpose of Colbert's program was to increase employment, profits, and state revenues—and to secure for France a "favorable balance of trade" with other countries. (This means selling goods abroad whose total value is more than that of goods purchased abroad; the balance due must then be paid in gold or silver, which were thought to be especially useful by the monarchs and experts on trade of the day.) Regulation of business was not novel in Europe; the towns and guilds had practiced it for centuries (pp. 242–243). But the chief economic controls now shifted to the *national* governments; this system came to be called *statism* or *mercantilism*. It was well established in seventeenth-century France and was also practiced in similar ways in Spain, Holland, and England.

Louis had a passion for territorial expansion and a love of war and glory. His driving desire was to gain and hold France's "natural" frontiers—the Rhine River, the Alps, and the Pyrenees. During his long reign, Louis was able to push France's frontiers farther east and north than ever before, and when the Habsburg rulers of Spain died out, he was able, after many years of war, to win the succession for a branch of his own Bourbon dynasty. Throughout the eighteenth century, the size and strength of France, and its alignment with Spain, its former rival and now its subordinate ally, were basic facts of the balance of power (*Map 10.1*). Louis's opponents—above all Britain, Holland, and the Austrian Habsburgs—were able to limit his gains, however. Strong barriers to French expansion remained in the Netherlands and northern Italy. France had greater weight in the European power balance than ever before, but Louis had failed to make France "supreme in Europe." In fact, by siphoning off the nation's wealth and manpower into costly military adventures, he spoiled many of the accomplishments of his long reign. And on his death in 1715, France lay exhausted, its military power spent. Though it recovered and fought many more wars, the power and prestige of its absolute monarchy began a long decline that ended in revolution (pp. 457–459).

EASTERN EUROPE

From the sixteenth to the eighteenth centuries, as in the Middle Ages, eastern Europe remained a distinctive region, though closely linked to the dominant western countries. Barred by geography from ready access to worldwide trade and empire, the eastern countries looked to western Europe for overseas products; to pay for these, they sent grain, timber, and cattle westward in ever-larger quantities. The rulers and nobles of the region, for whom these exports were their main source of income, redoubled their efforts to control and exploit the producers of these valuable resources: the peas-

Map 10.1 Europe in 1763. In the century since 1648 (*Map 9.2*, p. 399), the Bourbons have replaced the Habsburgs as Europe's farthest-flung dynasty, though different branches rule in France, Spain, and Italy. The Austrian Habsburgs, however, have reconquered Hungary from the Turks and kept former Spanish Habsburg territories in the Netherlands and Italy. The Prussian lands are now scattered from the Rhine to the eastern Baltic, and Russia is beginning to push westward into Poland. England has become Scotland's senior partner in the union of Great Britain, which is now the leading worldwide power.

ants. By the beginning of the eighteenth century, serfdom in eastern Europe, far from dying out, had become more oppressive than it had ever been in the Middle Ages.

In eastern Europe, as in the western countries, the leading rulers worked to build up absolute monarchies and struggled with each other for control of territory. Their task was complicated by the fact that the nobles were stronger and even more independent-minded than those of western Europe (p. 296). In addition, religious passions were even more disruptive than in western Europe, as the Protestant Reformation and the Catholic countermeasures brought militancy to a region where Christians were already divided between the Catholic and Orthodox churches (p. 295) and which was also home to most of Europe's Jews (p. 296). Tens of thousands suffered exile or death as a result of campaigns of expulsion and massacre directed by Catholics, Protestants, and Orthodox against each other and by Catholics and Orthodox against Jews. Some rulers, unable to overcome these problems, became vulnerable to external attack. From the late seventeenth century, the formidable Turkish empire went into decline, lost part of its European possessions, and became more intolerant than before toward its Christian subjects in the territories that were left to it. And Poland, a leading contender for power in eastern Europe until the eighteenth century, was actually swallowed up by its rivals (p. 416).

But the ruling dynasties of three other states—the Hohenzollerns of Brandenburg-Prussia, the Habsburgs of Austria, and the Romanovs of Russia—proved more successful. By the end of the eighteenth century, they had built up states that, at least in terms of military power, could stand comparison with the wealthy imperial countries of western Europe.

Prussia. The Hohenzollern dynasty rose to power from comparatively small beginnings in the Middle Ages, as vassals of the Holy Roman Emperors. The center of their properties was the North German princedom of Brandenburg, but the family also held the territory of Prussia to the east and claimed several smaller territories in western Germany. Through the Peace of Westphalia, Prince Frederick William gained additional lands and then spent the rest of his life tightening his control over the family's holdings. He regulated economic activities, raised a large and well-equipped army, and demanded strict discipline from his soldiers and subjects. Prussia's landed aristocrats accepted the monarch's authority in return for complete control over their serfs. They also supplied the king with a hereditary officer class. By 1688, when Frederick William died near his capital of Berlin, Brandenburg-Prussia had become the most efficient state in Germany. His successor joined the coalition against Louis XIV, and the Holy Roman Emperor awarded him the title of "King in Prussia" (in addition to "Prince of Brandenburg"). The higher title soon displaced the lesser one, and the name Prussia soon was applied to the whole of the Hohenzollern lands.

Frederick II (the Great), who was crowned king of Prussia in 1740, personified the new ideal of power. With Machiavellian keenness, Frederick expanded his possessions to the east at the expense of the less efficient Habsburgs of Austria and the dissolving state of Poland. He proved shrewder than Louis XIV, to whom he first looked as a model. In his palace at Potsdam (in a vast park whose design had been inspired by Versailles), he could boast at the end of his reign that he had made Prussia a power of the first rank in Europe (*Map 10.1*).

Austria. The Thirty Years' War had left the Austrian Habsburg rulers mere figurehead emperors of the Holy Roman Empire (p. 398), and in spite of many years of war after the Spanish branch of their dynasty died out, they finally had to yield Spain to the Bourbon dynasty (pp. 317, 411). But they were able to take over some of the Spanish Habsburg possessions in the Netherlands and Italy, they held their own hereditary lands in central and eastern Europe in spite of rebellions by Protestant nobles and peasants, and they gained territory from the Turks in Hungary and the Balkans (*Map. 10.1*) Together, these Habsburg lands formed a large block of territory (usually known for convenience as Austria, the name of some of the dynasty's ancestral possessions within the Holy Roman Empire), but their government was unwieldy and inefficient. In the eighteenth century, defeats at the hands of Frederick II of Prussia galvanized the Habsburgs into making administrative and social reforms. Empress Maria Theresa and her son Joseph II made considerable progress in centralizing control of their territories, improving the administrative and tax systems, and limiting noble exploitation of the serfs so that the latter would be able to pay higher taxes to the government (p. 431). In this way, the Austrian rulers hoped to build up an army that would be a match for Prussia's. Though Habsburg Austria never achieved the degree of unity and discipline to be found in Prussia, it nevertheless counted as one of the leading European powers.

Map 10.2 "From Sea to Shining Sea." From the late sixteenth century onward, Russia became a continent-sized country. First it defeated Muslim states on the borders of Europe and Asia. Then it expanded swiftly across Siberia, empty of people but rich in gold and furs, and on into Alaska, though the central Asian Muslim states and China were barriers too strong to overcome. Finally, in bitter European struggles with Sweden, Poland, and Turkey, Russia gained less territory but many more taxpaying subjects, as well as access to the Baltic and Black seas.

Russia. Perhaps the most spectacular change in eastern Europe was the rise of Russia. At the end of the Middle Ages, the principality of Moscow, from which modern Russia originated, had been a tributary state of the Asiatic Tartars (p. 297). But the Muscovite princes were ambitious men, with a strong sense of mission and strong religious and cultural ties to Constantinople (p. 297). Following the Turkish capture of that city and the end of the Byzantine Empire in 1453, the Muscovite ruler Ivan the Great (who died in 1505) married Sophia, the last emperor's niece. Powerful, Byzantine-influenced Slav rulers of the Middle Ages had often called themselves *tsar* ("caesar"), so it was natural that Ivan should now take that title, as the heir of the Byzantine emperors. The Byzantine rulers had themselves been regarded as the legitimate successors of the emperors of ancient Rome, and accordingly, a Russian writer of Ivan's time referred to Moscow as the "third Rome." Thus, from early times, Moscow was driven by a sense of imperial mission.

Over the generations, in spite of many setbacks, Ivan's successors were true to this mission. In the sixteenth century, they first threw off the overlordship of the Tartars, and then made the Tartars their subjects. Russian colonists penetrated ever farther east into the wilderness of Siberia, until by the beginning of the eighteenth century the tsar's dominions stretched all the way to the Pacific Ocean. (Together with contemporary conquests by the powerful Qing emperors of China, this brought to an end thousands of years of nomad domination of the steppes and nomad invasions of the settled peoples of Europe and Asia; pp. 57–58.) At the time, this vast land empire was not nearly as profitable to its owners as the overseas empires of the Western countries. All the same, it made Russia what it has remained ever since: a country that dwarfs (geographically) all the other countries of Europe and whose sheer size has made it impossible to conquer (*Map 10.2*).

Scan courtesy of Dr. Alexander Boguslawski

Fig. 10.1 Russia and the West. In this propaganda woodcut, a traditionalist Russian has seen the error of his ways. He wears Western-style jacket, breeches, and cloak as Peter the Great has ordered, and now he wants a Western-style shave: "Cut off my beard, barber—if you don't, I'll call the police!" But the barber willingly obeys the tsar: "I'll be glad to give you a shave!" Peter was the first of many rulers across the world to compel his subjects to look like Westerners, hoping that they would eventually act and think like Westerners.

From the accession of the first tsar of the Romanov dynasty in 1613, however, the efforts and ambitions of Russia's rulers were focused mainly on Europe. They struggled with two principal competitors, Poland and Sweden, for control of the territories lying between the Black and Baltic seas. Though not always the aggressors in this struggle, the tsars were ultimately the victors. By the end of the seventeenth century, they had reached the coasts of the Black Sea and were pressing forward to the Baltic. In the eighteenth century, Peter the Great, the most energetic and ruthless of the Romanov tsars, at last broke through.

Russia's rival in the Baltic area was Sweden. In the sixteenth century, under the Vasa dynasty, the Swedish monarchy had succeeded in making itself the dominant power of the Baltic region. But a grand alliance of eastern states, including Russia, put a hold on Swedish imperialism. After a lengthy war, in 1721, Peter took from Sweden the eastern Baltic provinces of Karelia, Estonia, and Livonia (*Map 10.2*). In this region, close to the border of Finland, he built a new capital, Saint Petersburg. This "window on the West" was a symbol of his determination to make his empire into a well-organized state on the western European model, and if possible to make his subjects themselves into Westerners (*Fig. 10.1*).

When Peter died, a bitter struggle broke out between those Russians who supported a Western orientation and those who opposed it. Catherine II, who became tsarina in 1762, looked toward Europe. She had gained the throne after marrying a grandson of Peter, and though she was the daughter of a German nobleman, she devoted herself to the interests of her adopted country. Within the limits of her subjects' tolerance, Catherine followed Peter's lead in encouraging Westernization. Forced to compromise with stiff-necked nobles, she never managed to secure the same degree of internal control that prevailed in France and Prussia.

In external affairs, Catherine continued the Romanov policy of expanding their power further into Europe. In wars against the Turks, many of whose subjects shared the Orthodox Christianity and Slavic ethnic origins of the Russians (pp. 297, 298–299), she extended her territories to the south. On Russia's western frontier, Catherine intervened in the neighboring country of Poland. Once one of the strongest powers in eastern Europe, Poland had gradually been reduced to anarchy and helplessness as a result of the overweening power and endless factional disputes of its nobles, whom the rulers could never bring under control. Between 1772 and 1792, Poland was "partitioned" (divided up) among its neighbors. Russia gained the largest share, and the rest was taken over by Prussia and Austria (partly to prevent Russia from advancing still farther westward). By the end of the eighteenth century, Russia had become a major force in the power balances of Europe and the Middle East.

For all their successes, Prussia, Austria, and Russia remained in some ways weak and vulnerable. This was partly because the rulers of these eastern European states had built on societies that were backward and poor compared with the Western countries. In spite of the efforts they put into reorganizing their governments, increasing the yield of taxes, and recruiting and training soldiers, the eighteenth-century Hohenzollern, Habsburg, and Romanov rulers could not fight a war for any length of time without massive financial help from one or other of the western European rival countries, Britain and France. In spite of their autocratic government, the eastern rulers could not overcome the resistance of their nobles to abolishing serfdom. And this was a reform, as the wiser of these "enlightened despots" (pp. 431–432) well understood, that offered the main hope of modernizing their economies and making their countries truly wealthy and powerful.

A further handicap, for the Habsburgs and Romanovs in particular, was linked to the fact that they had expanded into regions of eastern Europe that were ethnically very mixed. Once-powerful independent nations—Poles, Czechs, Hungarians, Ukrainians, and many others—were now under the rule of foreigners. Russia and Austria were not national but *multinational* states in which no single ethnic group formed a majority of the population.

In the seventeenth and eighteenth centuries, serfdom and the subjection of nations to foreign rulers were generally accepted as legitimate, but in time this would change. In the serf societies and multinational states of nineteenth- and twentieth-century eastern Europe, social and national conflicts would arise that would dwarf the earlier religious struggles; instead of tens of thousands, millions of people would be expelled or killed.

JUSTIFICATIONS FOR ABSOLUTISM: BOSSUET, HOBBES

In the seventeenth and eighteenth centuries, absolutism appeared superior to other forms of government for very practical reasons: despots were able to check civil strife within their realms, and in the struggles with competing rulers, they could command the full resources of their states. Nevertheless, no form of government enjoys the unquestioned respect of every subject. Consequently, the absolute monarchs sought ideological justification for their rule. They wanted to show why it was *right* for subjects to submit to them. They might have turned to the absolutist theory of Machiavelli, who had viewed politics as a purely secular art and science (pp. 311–313). But they preferred a higher justification for their authority, and they found it in the doctrine of *divine right.*

This was not, however, a return to medievalism. In the Middle Ages, all authority was thought to be sent from heaven, but authority was believed to be *distributed* and *limited.* The theorists of the seventeenth century went further: they sought to reconcile *absolutist* concepts and practices with traditional Christian doctrine. James I of England, the Stuart king who succeeded Elizabeth I in 1603, did not hesitate to speak out for himself. "The state of monarchy," he lectured Parliament, "is the supremest thing on earth, for kings are not only God's lieutenants upon earth, but even by God himself are called gods."

It was in the France of Louis XIV, the "Grand Monarch," that divine right truly held sway. The theory was stated most precisely by a favored bishop of the court, Jacques Bossuet. In *Politics Drawn from Holy Scripture*, a booklet prepared about 1670 for the instruction of Louis's heir, Bossuet set down the royalist arguments. Referring to the Bible as the ultimate truth, he supported his points with appropriate quotations. Royal authority, he concluded, is sacred, fatherly, and absolute. The king's judgment is subject to no appeal on earth, and the king must be obeyed for reasons of religion and conscience. Whoever resists the king's command in reality *resists God.* For, declared Bossuet, "the royal throne is not the throne of a man, but the throne of God Himself."

The monarchs of France and other European states found these ideas appealing and, having heard them from childhood, probably believed them. They were less enthusiastic about the secular argument for absolutism developed by Thomas Hobbes. An English scholar and philosopher, Hobbes was a royalist who supported the Stuart kings. His writings (around 1650) did them little good; nevertheless, his analysis proved significant for later generations.

Hobbes broke completely with religious traditions and drew instead on the mathematical and scientific advances of his time (pp. 418–425). In a sense, Hobbes took up where Machiavelli had left off; accepting politics as a purely secular matter, he tried to make of it a deductive science, resting on materialism and mechanism.

Hobbes held that every human being is a kind of machine, whose feelings, thoughts, and actions are the result of complex motions and countermotions. What drives these machines is above all an instinctive need for self-preservation. From this it follows that the physiology and psychology of human beings are the true bases of political organization and consequently the true bases of the state. As Hobbes wrote in his classic study, *Leviathan,* "I put for a general inclination of all mankind, a perpetual and restless desire of power after power, that ceases only in death." In a "state of nature," with no coercive governing authority, the general human condition is a "war of every man against every man." To Hobbes, such a life was "solitary, poor, nasty, brutish, and short." He did not look at history or primitive cultures to prove his generalizations; his method was logical rather than empirical, deductive rather than inductive (p. 422). His dismal picture of the original (precivilized) condition of human beings arose from his assumptions regarding their physical makeup.

Fortunately, said Hobbes, humans have a power of reason that enables them to provide an alternative to the anarchy of nature. Because they are selfish egoists, unable to trust one another, they cannot create a cooperative society of equals. What they can do is agree to surrender their personal strength to a higher authority, which alone will have the power to curb individual aggression. Hobbes believed that human society, the state, and civilization itself arose from this imaginary "contract" of each individual with all others:

> I authorize and give up my right of governing myself, to this man, or to this assembly of men, on this condition, that you give up your right to him, and authorize all his actions in like manner. . . . This is the generation of that great Leviathan, or rather (to speak more reverently) of that Mortal God [king] to which we owe under the Immortal God, our peace and defense.

Once civil government is established in this manner, all subjects are bound by their contracts to obey it. They do so not for moral or religious reasons but, again, because of the underlying motive of self-interest. Law is preferable to anarchy because it better serves the individual. Hobbes supported absolute monarchy, or any other authority, on these grounds. But it is clear why his logic was not appreciated by the monarchists of his day: he demolished their claim to divine right and brushed aside all moral arguments, appeals to tradition, and personal sentiments. Though a royalist, Hobbes was in fact a most radical Englishman. While defending the old (monarchy), he turned people's minds to the new (in politics).

The Scientific Revolution of the Seventeenth Century

The Scientific Revolution of the seventeenth century produced a radically different view of the universe and a new mode of thinking. These intellectual changes influenced Hobbes's ideas and would have a profound effect on Western life and thought.

The methodology of modern science seems natural enough to educated persons of the twenty-first century. Because we are accustomed to it, we do not appreciate how *unnatural* it is and how difficult it was to achieve. Our unaided "common sense" could never have produced science (any more than it could have produced theology or philosophy). In fact, one of the greatest barriers to scientific thinking was the tendency of human beings to accept as truth the judgments of their senses. The fantastic world that science reveals to us is often concealed under natural appearances. Through countless centuries, in every corner of the globe, people accepted the "obvious": that the earth, for example, stands still while the sun and stars wheel past overhead. It was only through a rare combination of circumstances and high creative impulse that science was "invented." The methodology has not been perfected even yet, but the decisive period of its development was the seventeenth century. The fertile minds of that time produced a stunning intellectual triumph and made the West the teacher of the world.

This achievement rested, of course, on a rich intellectual heritage, starting with the science of the Greeks, which had been recovered in the Middle Ages (pp. 78–83, 269). The medieval philosophers added refinement in *logic,* strengthened the idea of an *ordered* universe, and made modest contributions in some scientific fields (pp. 272–273). Renaissance artists then stressed the precise observation of nature, and Renaissance scholars rediscovered Greek mathematics and sharply advanced this indispensable tool of the mind. Equally important, the founders of science displayed the ability to see old things in new ways. The result was the overthrow of a universe—that of Aristotle and Aquinas. As the new universe took form (*Fig. IV.1*, p. 402), the methods that produced it became a new way of thinking.

DISCOVERERS OF A NEW COSMOS: COPERNICUS, KEPLER, GALILEO

Aristotle's system must be looked at before the revolution of the seventeenth century can be understood. That system was far more in harmony with the world of appearances than the system that would take its place. As adapted by Ptolemy, a second-century Greek astronomer (p. 134), Aristotle's scheme placed the solid, immovable earth at the center of things. Rotating about the earth, in perfect circular motion, were the luminous heavenly bodies, each embedded in a transparent sphere. Closest to earth was the sphere that carried the moon; then, at successive intervals, came the spheres of Mercury, Venus, the sun, Mars, Jupiter, Saturn, and the fixed stars. Beyond the sphere of the fixed stars was the *Primum Mobile* (Prime Mover)—a sphere whose daily rotation from west to east drove all the other spheres in the opposite motion, from east to west. Beyond the Primum Mobile was the *Empyrean* (the highest heaven).

This ancient view fitted everyone's ordinary observations, and by means of clever adjustments, it could be made to correspond to observed data. Moreover, it suited people's awe of the heavens by placing the heavenly bodies in a "higher" zone, distinct from the earth. Scholars taught that change, imperfection, and decay ruled over the human zone, whereas in the revolving spheres, all was permanence, regularity, and harmony. This in turn made it easy to accept the view into Christian thought, according to which the real mover of the whole system was God himself, located in the highest Heaven beyond the visible universe.

Ptolemy also knew of a heliocentric (sun-centered) theory of the universe that had been taught by Aristarchus, an earlier Greek astronomer, in the third century B.C. According to his theory, the apparent motion of the heavenly bodies was due to the earth's rotation on its axis. But Ptolemy rejected this theory, as did other astronomers, because it did not fit his recorded observations so well as the geocentric (earth-centered) theory. Further, it was impossible to reconcile Aristarchus's notion of earthly rotation with existing beliefs about motion. Again, the authority of Aristotle was decisive. He had held that earthly objects remain in a state of rest unless they are moved by a force and that continued motion requires continued force. Because it was held that these rules did not apply in the heavenly zones, the rotation of the crystalline spheres presented no difficulty. But in the earthly zone, motion depended on force; and the astronomers could find no existing force strong enough to keep the earth's mass turning. Because of this, and because of the appearance that the earth stood still, the heliocentric theory had failed to convince the ancient thinkers.

Copernicus. Nevertheless, Nicolaus Copernicus revived it in the sixteenth century. A learned Polish cleric with a passionate interest in astronomy, Copernicus grew dissatisfied with the geometric complexities and discrepancies of Ptolemy's system. He allowed himself to imagine various patterns and found that the heliocentric one offered the simplest geometric explanation of observed movements. His major work, *Concerning the Revolutions of the Celestial Bodies,* was published in the year of his death, 1543. Although other astronomers of the time shared his dissatisfaction with the Ptolemaic system, they did not accept the Copernican theory.

Copernicus's book was condemned by religious leaders, including Luther and Calvin, on the grounds that it contradicted Scripture and thus offended God. In one respect, his theory was but a limited departure from the accepted view: It did not challenge the motion mechanics of Aristotle. Copernicus accepted the idea of the revolving spheres and only exchanged the positions of sun and earth. This alteration, however, upset the traditional view, for it shifted the earth into the heavenly zone of laws and forces—and that made his theory unacceptable.

A further objection was that Copernicus could furnish no observational proofs of his belief. If, as he thought, the earth revolved around the sun, then the position of the fixed stars should show a shift when sighted from opposite sides of the earth's orbit. As astronomers know now, they do shift; but the shift is so small (because of the enormous distances) that Copernicus could not detect it. Copernicus also faced a problem that had baffled the ancients: How could he account for a force sufficient to keep the earth in rotation? He offered an answer, but it was hardly persuasive. He argued that it was the "nature" of spheres to rotate and that the earth could not keep from doing so.

Kepler. Though Copernicus did not overcome the limitations of traditional science, he inspired later generations to resume the search for a simpler and more satisfying truth. Toward the end of the sixteenth century, a Danish astronomer, Tycho Brahe, made new and more comprehensive observations of the skies. These were assembled and analyzed by his coworker, the brilliant German mathematician Johannes Kepler. As a test of the Copernican theory, Kepler tried to fit Brahe's data on the planets to *circular* courses (orbits) around the sun. When that effort yielded a negative result, he tried fitting the data to *elliptical* orbits. This gave him a positive result, and his finding came to be known as Kepler's First Law (1609).

Kepler next studied the data in order to find if there was consistency in all planetary motions. His resulting Second and Third Laws define in precise mathematical terms how the speeds of planets vary according to their distance from the sun. Kepler thus appears as the first man to work in the manner of modern scientists: he first formulated hypotheses and then tried to check the deduced consequences empirically (by observation). He also bridged the supposed gap between heavenly bodies and the earth by demonstrating the consistency of mathematical relationships throughout the solar system. Of still broader significance, he was the first to glimpse the universe as a vast, intricate machine subject to exact and knowable laws.

Though Kepler described the movements of the planets in precise mathematical terms, he was less successful in explaining what made them move. He assumed that some force might be holding the planets in orbit and moving them continuously along their courses. This force he concluded to be the sun, a view that he based largely on the experiments of William Gilbert, an English physicist. Around 1600, Gilbert had built a spherical magnet and had noted that its magnetic properties were similar to those of the earth. He reasoned that the heavenly bodies must also resemble the earth in this respect, each one exerting a pull toward its own center. The moon, he said, keeps the same face toward us because of its magnetic attraction to the earth. But the sun, the largest body in the solar system, is the focus of magnetic power. It was a giant rotating magnet; as it turned, it pulled the planets along in their orbits. In adopting Gilbert's view, Kepler was reaching toward the modern concepts of universal gravitation and inertia.

Galileo. But it was left to the Italian genius Galileo Galilei to complete the overthrow of Aristotle, confirm the heliocentric theory, and bring the laws of motion to the point of a grand synthesis. A contemporary of Kepler, Galileo was less a mathematician and more an observer and experimenter. An astronomer as well as a physicist, he was the first, in 1609, to construct a telescope that could be used to examine the heavens. (The instrument itself had been invented a few years earlier by Dutch lensmakers.) Galileo's telescope was a lead tube about 3 feet long, with a 2-inch glass. Crude and low-powered by modern standards, it nonetheless revealed a world previously unknown to earthlings.

To his excitement, Galileo saw that the surface of the moon was scarred with "imperfections" in the form of mountains and craters and that the planets were spherical bodies just like the earth—as if the earthly and heavenly zones of the universe, instead of being completely different, were in fact much the same. By discovering moons revolving around Jupiter, Galileo provided support for the idea that there could be more than one center for heavenly orbits. And as he peered into the depths of space, looking past the fixed stars, he was overwhelmed by the incredible distances revealed by his telescope. Tens of thousands of stars, previously unseen, came into view, and he was convinced that uncounted millions lay beyond. The familiar, closed universe of the Greek and Christian worlds vanished forever; earth and humans were now seen as wanderers through dark and boundless space.

The Catholic Church was quick to challenge Galileo's proofs and to condemn his conclusions. Because its authority and doctrines were linked to the Ptolemaic system, it regarded the new ideas as a menace to Christian truth and salvation. Galileo fell into trouble after publishing his *Dialogue on the Two Chief Systems.* In 1633, he was charged with heresy and brought before the Roman Inquisition; threatened with torture, he formally recanted. Through the *Dialogue,* however, his devastating attack on the conventional astronomy continued to spread. The book was placed on the Index (p. 387), along with the works of Copernicus and Kepler, where it remained until 1835. But the banning of a book could not alter the order of the heavens.

After his ordeal before the Inquisition, Galileo was allowed to work quietly in a villa near Florence. During these years, he turned to a subject that in itself would not disturb the authorities but that opened the way to the ultimate victory of the new view of the universe. The subject was motion. It was clear that the overthrow of Aristotle's universe must include the rejection of his ideas about motion, but no one had yet shown how that was to be done.

Earlier in his life, Galileo had experimented with falling bodies. He later built special structures in order to study the acceleration of polished balls rolling down frictionless wooden surfaces. These permitted him to make more precise measurements of time and distance than he could make when objects were dropped through the air. In 1638, he published the results of his experiments and set forth his general conclusions on the subject of mechanics. He rejected the traditional beliefs that objects are "normally" in a state of rest, that there are "natural" directions of motion for certain substances, and that heavy objects fall faster than light ones.

His observations convinced him that a body in motion (with friction disregarded) continues at a constant speed without any continuing force; a change in either velocity or direction requires a force. He also found that falling bodies accelerate as they descend, and described in precise mathematical terms the rate at which they accelerate.

Galileo did not quite see that his "law of falling bodies" was the same law that kept the planets in their orbits. But he contributed the important new idea of *inertia* (the tendency of objects to remain in their existing state of either rest or motion).

MAKERS OF SCIENTIFIC METHOD: BACON, DESCARTES

Although the most striking accomplishments of the Scientific Revolution were in astronomy and mechanics, swift advances were taking place along the whole frontier of knowledge. One of the most significant was the development of science itself as a *methodology.* Here two men stand out: Francis Bacon and René Descartes.

Bacon, born in England in 1561, was a man of wide interests, a public official as well as a scholar. But his chief concern was the advancement of learning. He complained of the stagnation of knowledge, blaming the condition on undue reverence for the ancients—above all, as we have seen, for the authority of Aristotle. While Aristotle's ideas were being upset by Kepler and Galileo, Bacon struck at the root of his system— its methodology—thereby adding force to the intellectual revolution.

Bacon favored the practices of observation and experiment that had sprung up during the Renaissance (pp. 341–342). Experiments in themselves were not new, but he saw in them the foundation for a planned structure of useful knowledge. He criticized Aristotle's reliance on deduction, which he viewed as a mere manipulation of words. Bacon's proposed system called for *induction*—that is, repeated experiments that would lead to a general statement or conclusion. Following each induction, new observations and experiments would be undertaken that would permit further inductions to be made. In this fashion, a total system of descriptive truth could be built up, he thought, in a relatively short time.

Bacon was mistaken in many of his own beliefs about nature, but he was confident that future experiments would correct his errors. He also urged scientists to record their experiments and to exchange data, in the interest of mutual assistance. True, he subordinated the role of mathematics in scientific activities, but that fault was remedied by the Frenchman René Descartes.

The advance of science requires, indeed, two modes of thought. One of these is induction, stressed by Bacon; the other, emphasized by Descartes, is deduction. Descartes was a brilliant mathematician, and his accomplishments in mathematics affected his approach to knowledge as a whole. A private scholar of independent means, he was disgusted by the absence of certainty and precision that he found in most areas of study. In his *Discourse on Method,* published in 1637, he tried to apply to other subjects the methods of geometry and arithmetic, which start with "clear and simple" propositions of unquestioned truth. From these propositions, all consequences are deduced; plane geometry, for example, is built upon a single axiom (self-evident assumption): "A straight line is the shortest distance between two points."

In adopting the method of mathematics, therefore, one must commence by doubting all present ideas (a method of thinking known as "Cartesian doubt," from its originator's name); the slate must be wiped clean, so to speak. If an idea can be questioned for any reason at all, it must be discarded. Descartes did just that, reducing knowledge to a single idea that he could accept absolutely: "I *think*"—from which he deduced, "therefore, I *exist.*" Upon this foundation he set out to construct, by a series of logical steps, a complete picture of the universe (including God).

In this ambitious effort, Descartes committed errors and fell short of success. But his rejection of existing knowledge, intellectual authority, and traditional ways of reasoning undermined those old ways of looking at the world. Especially challenging was his vision of a *mechanical* universe governed by *mathematical* rules, a vision that would profoundly influence philosophy and religion as well as science.

THE GRAND SYNTHESIZER: NEWTON

The final statement of seventeenth-century science was left to Isaac Newton, who perfected and refined the new cosmic system first outlined by Kepler and Galileo. It was Newton also who established the rules of scientific method as a union of Baconian and Cartesian theory.

Newton was a simple country youth whose rare talents won him a place at Cambridge University. After earning his degree, he became deeply absorbed in mathematics and shortly developed the system of calculus, which is essential for the continuous measurement of complex variable quantities. While still in his twenties, he was appointed professor of mathematics at the university, where he continued his far-ranging research. He soon turned his inquiring mind to the puzzles posed by the new astronomy.

Galileo had virtually established the principles of earthly motion but had failed to demonstrate how those principles applied to bodies beyond the earth. Why did the planets move in curved orbits rather than in straight lines? Galileo mistakenly answered that curved motion was as "natural" as straight-line motion and therefore had its own kind of inertia. The solution to the mystery lay in the combination of straight-line inertia with the pull of gravity. Although Galileo recognized and gauged the earth's gravity in his observations of falling bodies, he had not made the stupendous leap to the concept of universal gravitation.

Suspecting that the relationship between inertia and gravitation was the key to understanding planetary motion, Newton studied the problem over a period of years. In order to prove his theories, he had to translate masses and motions into mathematical terms. He succeeded in calculating the masses of the sun, the planets, and their satellites. As a result, he was able to define mathematically how the sun's gravitational pull must decrease with distance so as to cause the planets to move in their orbits according to Kepler's laws. He next applied this gravitational formula to the motion of the moon around the earth. Treating the moon as a body with inertial movement in space, he theorized that its curved orbit was due to a continuous "falling" toward the earth. And after making due allowance for its distance from the earth, he concluded that the moon behaves in the same way as falling bodies on earth. Newton thus linked Galileo to Kepler, eliminated the barrier between forces acting in space and those on earth, and established by empirical and mathematical proof the existence of universal laws.

Such was the message of Newton's *Principia* (*Mathematical Principles of Natural Philosophy*), published in 1687. In this work, he unraveled the mysteries of planetary motion and demonstrated the fact that human beings have the means to achieve far greater understanding. For he demonstrated that on the basis of experiments conducted in a tiny corner of the universe and aided by the lever of mathematics, he had discovered the nature of gravitation *everywhere*. Newton also set down rules of scientific reasoning to guide others in finding the fundamental principles embodied in nature, stating those principles mathematically and verifying them through observation and experiment.

Not surprisingly, Newton was hailed by his generation as a lawgiver, a scientific Moses. As his contemporary, the English poet Alexander Pope, put it:

> Nature and nature's laws lay hid in night;
> God said, "Let Newton be," and all was light.

The *Principia* soon became the undisputed source and symbol of science—the new testament of a new faith. Most of Newton's ideas about matter and motion have been modified by twentieth-century physicists (pp. 642–644), but his methodological principles remain a model.

THE ORGANIZATION OF SCIENCE

The story of science since Newton has been one of continuous acceleration in the growth of knowledge. Even in Newton's time, discovery was proceeding in numerous fields, and findings in one subject suggested and aided investigations in others. Robert Boyle identified physical "elements" and thereby fathered chemistry. William Harvey explained the function of the heart and the circulation of the blood, thus beginning the science of physiology. The Greek physician Galen (p. 134), whose authority had ruled for centuries, fell from favor; medicine and pharmacy now achieved a scientific foundation.

Rapid strides were also made in optics, and the development of the microscope (as well as the telescope) opened promising new areas of exploration. The microscope paved the way for the sciences of botany and zoology, and made it clear that human beings stand near a midpoint on the scale of size in the universe—halfway between the giant stars and the tiniest particles of matter. And the idea of the laboratory, where experiments could be conducted under controlled conditions, took shape by the end of the seventeenth century.

The universities were painfully slow in promoting the new learning, however. Still in the grip of religious and humanist traditions, they were generally hostile or indifferent to science. In the education of young men, two centuries were to pass before the "classical" curriculum (pp. 339–340) would make room for scientific subjects, and new institutions had to be created for the support and coordination of experimental studies.

The earliest societies for the advancement of research were founded in Italy. Rome set up an academy in 1603, of which Galileo was a member; a half century later, the Medici established a scientific institution in Florence. More influential and longer-lasting, however, was the Royal Society of London, which was chartered in 1662. It consisted of scientists and mathematicians, as well as interested merchants, nobles, and clerics. In an effort to support Francis Bacon's idea for building up a total system of knowledge (p. 422), the society aided experiments, listened to learned discussions, corresponded with foreign societies, and published a scientific journal. These developments reflected the growing *interdependence* of scientific investigators and their equipment. The isolated, casual experimenter of the Renaissance (like Leonardo; p. 352) had given way to a new type. No matter how proud or self-centered scientists might become, they fully recognized that science was a *social* enterprise. The Royal Society was interested in the practical applications of science as well as in "pure" research. Bacon himself had declared that the true goal of science was to give human beings greater power for human benefit. And Robert Boyle, an early member of the Royal Society, confessed that he did not desire merely to talk and write about nature—he wanted to learn to

	Copernicus		Newton	
c. 1350	c. 1543		c. 1687	c. 1789

		Scientific Revolution	The Enlightenment
Era of Renaissance Humanism			

c. 1600

master it. Traditional philosophy, he pointed out, had been barren of practical advantage to humanity. Science, properly understood, would strengthen the useful arts and raise people's standard of living.

This emphasis on practical applications attracted support from commerce, industry, and government on the Continent as well as in England. Louis XIV, at the suggestion of his finance minister, Colbert, endowed the French Academy of Science in 1666, and similar institutions were founded in other European states. Thus science (the search for understanding of nature) and technology (the search for ways to control nature) began to experience a mutual attraction, though the actual marriage of the two had to wait until the nineteenth century (p. 507).

The Impact of Science on Philosophy: The Enlightenment

The revolution within science also led to revolutionary changes outside it, in the general ideas, values, and attitudes of society. For science gave to educated Westerners a radically new view of their universe and the forces that move it. Since their way of looking at life came from their underlying beliefs about the nature of the universe, from this new base they proceeded to construct a new philosophy and a new society.

Of course, the new scientific vision of the universe, as well as the philosophical ideas derived from it, penetrated much more slowly among the general population. Even among the educated, many did not totally accept the new views, and some actively opposed them—mainly because these views conflicted with established religious teachings. But even opponents could not help being affected by the consequences of the change. A new intellectual climate enveloped Europe in the eighteenth century, which in the long run affected all classes, and spread outward to the ends of the earth.

The scientists themselves had little to do directly with the new way of looking at life that took shape during this era. Nor did professionally trained philosophers play a very significant role. The shift in thinking was mainly the work of gifted amateurs—"literary" persons. Most of them were French, and although they did not establish any formal system of philosophy, they came to be known in their country and eventually in the English-speaking world as the *philosophes* (philosophers).

The philosophes were so dazzled by Newton's brilliance that they considered themselves to be living in an unprecedented "age of light." It was this notion that gave rise to the term "Enlightenment" as a name for the century from 1687, the date of Newton's *Principia,* to 1789, the start of the French Revolution. Those who glimpsed the new vision of the universe thought of themselves as the "enlightened" ones, and they were eager to spread the light to others.

A REVISED COSMOLOGY: THE "WORLD-MACHINE"

The universe that the philosophes held up to view contrasted sharply with the traditional Christian one. The most evident and disturbing differences were that the new universe extended through boundless space. The devoutly religious mathematician Blaise Pascal had confessed, "I am terrified by the eternal silence of those infinite spaces." But the humanist as well as the Christian felt humbled: humanity was no longer at the center of nature's plan. The architecture of Newton's universe made humans appear insignificant, both in time and in space. It was still possible to believe that a personal God existed, that he had a special plan for humanity, and that human life had supreme value. But such a faith was no longer supported by the evidence of astronomy. It seemed, rather, to be *contradicted* by the extravagant dimensions of the cosmos.

Other supports for traditional beliefs collapsed. With Aristotle's laws of motion overthrown, no role remained for a Prime Mover (p. 419). The hand of God, which once kept the heavenly bodies in their orbits, had been replaced by universal gravitation. Miracles had no place in a system whose workings were automatic and unvarying. Governed by precise mathematical and mechanical laws, Newton's universe seemed capable of running itself forever.

People had long been familiar with such complex machines as watches and clocks. Was it not logical, after Newton, to believe that the universe itself was a grand machine? Not all its rules of operation had yet been discovered, but scientists knew enough to be able to sketch the nature of the whole. The French astronomer Pierre Laplace expressed the mechanistic idea of the eighteenth century when he said, "Give me the present location and motion of all bodies in the universe, and I will predict their location and motion through all eternity."

THE VIEW OF GOD: DEISM

The "enlightened" concept of the universe raised disturbing questions about religious convictions. What was to become of the beliefs of Christianity? Many scientists and intellectuals found it extremely difficult to bring together the Newtonian system and Christian theology, to fit Christian teachings and practices into the new cosmology. The "world-machine," it seemed, had no *need* for supernatural guidance, prayer, priests, sacraments, or penance; these now seemed superfluous, if not contradictory. The philosophes, therefore, persuaded that they could not logically reconcile Christianity with scientific truth, rejected the former.

This did not mean that they necessarily gave up the idea of God. Because common sense still made it difficult for people to think of something as existing that had not been *made,* the question of creation remained unanswered. Newton himself stated that the First Cause is not mechanical and suggested that God, "in the beginning," had formed matter in the particular way he desired. It was equally logical for those in scientific circles to believe that he had established the governing rules of the universe as well as its substance. But—to use a comparison often made at the time—having designed the watch, built it, and wound it up, God had then left it to run on its own. Since God had removed himself from the affairs of the physical universe, only *nature* remained—so it was nature that must be understood and respected.

This was a religion of sorts, but it was clearly not Christianity, Judaism, or any other revealed system of belief and worship. Vaguely labeled *Deism,* this new religion got its start in the seventeenth century. An Englishman, Lord Herbert of Cherbury, who died in 1648, tried to make of it a universal faith that would include and surmount all the others. He posed five basic truths as common to the foremost religions of the world—and not incompatible with science: the existence of a Supreme Power, the necessity of worship, the requirement of good conduct, the benefit of repentance of vices, and the existence of rewards and punishments after death.

Lord Herbert's efforts failed to bring all believers together. He had dreamed of an end to sectarian strife and of accord among all people of goodwill. Though Deism became popular with such eighteenth-century intellectuals as Voltaire, Franklin, and Jefferson, for most churchgoers it was an inadequate substitute for traditional religion. It lacked mystery, ritual, emotional appeal, and discipline. And it was offensive to the clergy of all denominations, for it challenged the authority of their sacred books, doctrines, and offices.

Deism gradually lost its appeal even to the converts of science. By the close of the eighteenth century, many of them had decided that there really is no need even for a Creator. Newton had shown that motion is as natural as nonmotion. Is not matter, then, as natural as nonmatter? Was it not old-fashioned to think that things must be *created*? The universe and its motion had always been and always would be. This line of reasoning led some to deny God absolutely (*atheism*); others said they could not or did not know whether God existed (*skepticism* or *agnosticism*). For the first time since Rome's conversion to Christianity, religious doubt became a force in Western civilization.

True, many among the educated did not agree that science and Christianity contradicted each other, as the philosophes claimed. Newton himself, for example, was all his life a believer who hoped through his discoveries to confirm the wonders of the Almighty. In fact, he divided his energies between scientific pursuits and deep study of the Bible, through which he hoped, among other things, to achieve the traditional Protestant goal of proving that the Catholic Church was a perversion of true Christianity.

As for the churches and synagogues, they continued to be the main influence on the way of life of most people in Europe. Indeed, the age of the Enlightenment was also a time of religious revival. In different faiths, religious mass movements arose, inspired by beloved leaders whose preaching stirred up the fervor of many thousands of men and women. In Protestant England, for example, there was the Methodist minister John Wesley; in Catholic Italy, the Redemptorist father Alfonso Liguori; among the Jews of Poland, the Hasidic rabbi Israel ben Eliezer. All three had in common the ability to interpret the traditional beliefs of their respective religions in deeply personal and moving ways that made sense to ordinary believers. All of them, moreover, had a permanent effect on their respective faiths, through organizations of their followers who have continued their work down to the present.

Nevertheless, as proofs of the Newtonian system continued to accumulate, religious leaders had no choice but to make their peace with the results of scientific discovery. At the level of basic belief, they rejected the notion of the philosophes that the new view of the universe made Christianity harder to believe in. But at the level of social and political thought, many religious leaders, and educated believers in general, could more or less accept such Enlightenment ideas as religious toleration, more widespread education, or the use of scientific knowledge to improve the condition of the human race. It was through adaptations of this kind that the ideas of the Enlightenment spread beyond the relatively small circles of the philosophes, to become part of the general climate of opinion among educated people in eighteenth-century Europe.

THE VIEW OF HUMAN SOCIETY

If God played an inactive role (or none at all) in the view of the philosophes, the place and powers of humans were dramatically enlarged. Followers of the tradition of the Renaissance humanists (pp. 336–339), after recovering from the initial shock of Newton's astronomy, saw that humans became more important as God's role declined. Writers began to emphasize the grandeur of reason, which had enabled human beings to unveil the mysteries of the universe. Though humans could not control its movements, they had touched the cosmos with their minds. And through science and technology, they could improve their well-being and press nature itself into their service.

Human beings might be viewed as not only stronger but better. The philosophes did not deny the existence of evil in human affairs, but they generally blamed it on bad social institutions. Nature, as revealed by Newton, is orderly and harmonious. Because of ignorance, however, humans had failed to follow nature's ways and had made customs, laws, sanctions, and beliefs that twisted and shackled the individual. Humans would regain their birthright and exhibit their true character when the chains of unreason were broken.

This growing optimism about human prospects had its roots in the Renaissance, but it was strengthened by the new science. The doctrine of original sin appeared out of place in the new cosmos, and the observed laws of motion showed no built-in movement in the direction of evil. Within the boundaries of human freedom, it seemed likely that individuals would choose good rather than bad—so long as they followed nature and reason. Some of the philosophes took an extreme position: as knowledge advanced, they held, individuals would become increasingly capable of good, and when at last they reached complete harmony with nature, they would be judged perfect. Thus, they concluded, humans are not only good but also perfectible.

No doctrine of the eighteenth century proved more controversial than this doctrine of human perfectibility. It runs counter to traditional Christian teaching and is hard to reconcile with much of history. The ablest thinkers among the philosophes did not accept such an extreme view, but they joined with others in working for social improvement. They became tireless reformers, aiming to remake social institutions according to the lights of reason. The humanitarian movement, as an organized force, was in large measure a product of eighteenth-century thought. Voltaire in France (p. 434) and the marquis de Beccaria in Italy, for example, worked for more effective ways of dealing with crime and punishment. The reformers focused attention, too, on helping the poor, the orphaned, the enslaved, and the sick; in these efforts they were often supported by traditional Christians acting in the spirit of holy charity. The philosophes worked, above all, for broad freedom of expression, tolerance, and a cosmopolitan outlook.

FAITH IN NATURE AND REASON

The humanitarian and ethical goals of the Enlightenment were similar to those of Christianity. But whereas the latter evolved out of centuries of human experience, the philosophy of the Enlightenment sprang from the newly found method and vision of science. The essential differences may be summed up this way: Christianity rests its faith in the power of God as known through *revelation;* the Enlightenment puts its trust in nature as understood through *reason.* The supreme goal of Christianity is *heaven* (spiritual bliss after death); the goal of the Enlightenment is *progress* (physical happiness in life on earth).

To the ancient Greeks, as well as to the Christians, nature had been an uncertain force, more likely to be hostile than friendly. To some thinkers of the Enlightenment, nature had virtually replaced God and had been shown to be regular and knowable. They believed that the secrets of nature could be discovered and applied usefully to ordinary affairs—the farmer, for example, could make the soil more productive by observing and following physical laws. They believed, too, that legislators and judges could provide justice by applying moral and social "laws" to human relations. This confusion of moral principles with physical laws was to lead to bitter disappointments.

The eighteenth-century "cult of nature" was an outgrowth of excessive enthusiasm. Respect for the harmonious motions of the heavenly bodies led some philosophers to an unscientific, sentimental attitude toward all objects in nature. Alexander Pope (p. 433) attributed to nature a grand—and ultimately benevolent—intelligence and purpose:

> All Nature is but art, unknown to thee;
> All chance, direction which thou canst not see;
> All discord, harmony not understood;
> All partial evil, universal good.

Most eighteenth-century intellectuals, however, kept their eye on the central idea: the extension of useful knowledge through the exercise of reason. Perhaps the most exciting discovery of the age was that nature behaves in a reasoned, even mathematical, manner; therefore, its workings correspond to human logic. From this the philosophes concluded that reason is the key to nature's secrets and powers and is the proper means of judging and regulating human affairs.

An acceptable model for explaining the working of the mind was supplied by the Englishman John Locke (pp. 450–451). Though interested in science, Locke followed the guide of common sense rather than a strict methodology. He studied medicine, economics, political theory, and philosophy, and he associated with many of the leading political figures of his country. Perhaps because of his familiarity with practical affairs, his writings were readily received by the educated public, and several generations of hardheaded revolutionaries found reassuring arguments in his political writings. His ideas about the nature of human knowledge were especially persuasive, for he rested his case on the ordinary sense experience of his readers. Locke may not have been profound, and he was certainly not scientific. Nevertheless, his writings swept away many ancient beliefs and showed what the "new" reason could do when it was applied to questions about human beings and society.

In his *Essay Concerning Human Understanding* (1690), Locke stated that all knowledge comes from experience. This was in line with Bacon's empiricism (p. 422) and challenged long-established convictions that knowledge is inborn, as Socrates and Plato had taught, or revealed by God, as Christianity claimed. Locke supported a rival concept that is often called the *tabula rasa* ("blank writing tablet") theory, though he himself used a slightly different comparison. The mind at birth, he said, is like "white paper, void of all characters, without any ideas." The ideas that come to be written on this paper come from but one source: experience—that is, knowledge that comes to us through our senses and is then sorted and arranged by our minds. In this way, we learn to understand and control the world about us.

Locke's notion of the "thinking machine" was oversimplified, but it suited the eighteenth-century view that people are shaped by their environment. According to Locke, ideas are totally dependent on outside stimuli. Hence, if the correct environment is provided, the individual will receive only the "right" ideas. This suggests, in turn, that through the reform of institutions, especially education, rapid improvements can be made in human nature and society.

These beliefs help explain the devotion of eighteenth-century intellectuals to both science and education. To them, ignorance had replaced sin and the devil as the principal enemy. Sinners were to be redeemed not by the grace of God, but by human reason. Research had to be encouraged so that investigators could learn more; education had to be overhauled and extended so that the new knowledge could be carried everywhere. The philosophes threw themselves into these endeavors with the enthusiasm of missionaries. They felt that education should be for adults as well as for children. As propagandists of "truth," they took to writing pamphlets, books, and encyclopedias. (The most notable encyclopedist was the brilliant French editor and critic Denis Diderot.) The world would never be quite the same again; the belief in science and education became a feature of the modern world.

THE VISION OF PROGRESS

The extreme apostles of reason had no doubt that they were on the path to paradise on earth. No Christian heaven existed in their philosophy, but they found its counterpart in their vision of progress—a vision they expected to fulfill within a few generations.

Progress, as these philosophes understood the term, was a new idea in history. The ancients, if they wished to think of something better than their own lives, had looked backward rather than forward, to an age of heroes or a Garden of Eden. Christianity had taught that sinful mortals must live in this world as "pilgrims" awaiting perfection in the world to come. Even the humanists of the Renaissance, for all their high estimate of human capacity, had looked backward to Greece and Rome as the time when that capacity had been most fully realized.

But seventeenth-century science at last broke the spell of antiquity. Scientists began to point out how much more they knew than the ancients. They felt that it was the Greeks and Romans who were "children" in time; the most recent generations, those who had the advantage of the accumulated experience of earlier generations, were actually "older" than the ancients. Science thus dissolved the myth of classical superiority in knowledge and, with its new tools, pointed the way toward a grander future.

The marquis de Condorcet made the most eloquent statement of this unbounded faith in progress. A well-educated nobleman trained in mathematics and science, Condorcet served as secretary of the French Academy of Science. He is especially remembered for his *Progress of the Human Mind,* written, ironically, during a chaotic year of the French Revolution (1794). Though an active reformer, Condorcet had broken with the more radical leaders of the revolution and was then in hiding as a fugitive. But he wrote that his sorrow over temporary injustices and barbarities was overbalanced by his vision of the future.

Condorcet's expectation of universal happiness on earth would prove mistaken, but his writing was nonetheless prophetic. He declared that nothing could stop the advance of knowledge and power "as long as the earth occupies its present place in the system of the universe, and as long as the general laws of this system produce neither a

general cataclysm nor such changes as will deprive the human race of its present faculties and its present resources." He forecast that rapid technological advances would lead
to a world in which "everyone will have less work to do, will produce more, and satisfy
his wants more fully." He saw the eventual achievement of equal rights for women, the
abolition of poverty, and the ordering of economic affairs so that every individual,
guided by reason, could enjoy true independence. And he predicted an end to warfare,
declaring that wars would "rank with assassinations as freakish atrocities, humiliating
and vile in the eyes of nature."

POLITICAL RESPONSES TO THE NEW PHILOSOPHY: ENLIGHTENED DESPOTISM

The Enlightenment is an outstanding example of how philosophical ideas conceived by
writers and intellectuals can have an overwhelming impact on practical affairs. In the
long run, the philosophes helped to bring about massive changes in Western politics,
government, and society. The philosophes' emphasis on reason and education, as well
as on perfectibility and progress, naturally led them to judge the social and political institutions of their own time. Did these institutions, they asked, contribute to the moral,
intellectual, and material progress of the human race? Needless to say, they mostly condemned what they found.

Only one major European country met with some degree of approval from the
philosophes. This was Britain, whose seventeenth-century revolution (pp. 446–451)
had produced a government and social system that met their standards, at least in some
respects. On the basis of the British experience, Enlightenment thinkers developed
ideas about government and the social order that in turn had a major impact on the
eighteenth-century revolutions in America and France, as well as on subsequent revolutionary changes in Europe and elsewhere. (These theories are discussed further in
Chapter 11, pp. 450–451, 462.) But Enlightenment ideals influenced not only revolutionary opponents of the existing order. The same ideals also inspired the bureaucrats,
nobles, and absolute monarchs who dominated most countries of eighteenth-century
Europe. Many members of this elite became dissatisfied with the very social and political order they ruled, producing a reform within the system that later historians called
"enlightened despotism."

The most famous enlightened despots were among the rulers of central and eastern Europe: Frederick II of Prussia, Maria Theresa and Joseph II of Austria, and Catherine II of Russia (pp. 413, 415–416). All of them sought, to a greater or lesser extent, to
put into practice such enlightened reforms as religious toleration, improvements in
the condition of agriculture and the peasantry, and wider access to education. The
high point of enlightened despotism was the reign of Joseph II in Austria. In ten years
of whirlwind reform between 1780 and 1790, Joseph introduced changes so drastic as
to amount almost to a peaceful revolution. Among other things, the emperor, himself
a Catholic, granted religious freedom to his Protestant, Orthodox, and Jewish subjects;
dissolved hundreds of Catholic monasteries, with much of their funds going to education; and gave the serfs freedom to marry and leave their manors without the consent
of the lords (though other features of serfdom, notably labor service, survived until
1848; p. 495).

Partly, the reason for reforms such as these was that, like so many others among
the educated elite, the rulers themselves could not escape the influence of the
philosophes. Some, like Frederick II and Catherine II, became Deists who made no

secret of their contempt for Christian belief; others, like Joseph II, were Christian in their basic beliefs but eagerly accepted enlightened social and political ideas (pp. 428–431). Either way, to this new generation of absolute monarchs, it seemed absurd to say, as Louis XIV had done, "I am the state." Instead, Frederick II spoke for all of them when he described himself, more modestly, as "the state's first servant."

Naturally, in adopting enlightened ideas, the rulers were thinking also of their own power. No less than earlier monarchs, they were enthusiastic makers of war. It did not escape them that a reformed state—with well-fed, well-educated, and productive citizens, with believers in different faiths living peaceably and tolerantly side by side, and with the nobles acting as real social leaders rather than as pampered courtiers—would probably win any war it fought with an unreformed state. And as the "first servants" of such a reformed state, the enlightened despots did not intend to give up even the smallest fragment of their absolute power. On the contrary, they expected to be more truly in control of their dominions than the divine-right rulers of traditional absolute monarchies.

Like all efforts at reforming a system from within, enlightened despotism worked only so long as it did not go too far and too fast. Joseph II, the most radical of the despots, ended with his government paralyzed by the opposition of the nobles; those who did not meet such opposition, like Frederick II and Catherine II, left many of their countries' traditional institutions unchanged. Still, it was the enlightened despots who first put some of the ideas of the philosophes into practice, and thereby began to undermine the surviving elements of the social and political order that had emerged in early medieval Europe (Chapter 5).

The Rational Spirit in Literature and Art

The new ideas in science and philosophy had a marked effect on the literature of the seventeenth and eighteenth centuries. The leading cultural fashion was *classicism,* an extension of Renaissance ideals given fresh force by the new stress on logic and universal laws. The philosophes sought, through the use of reason, to construct a view of humanity that would be universally valid. Likewise, Bernard Fontenelle, who preceded Condorcet as secretary of the Academy of Science, called attention to the significance of mathematical principles for literature:

> The geometric spirit is not so tied to geometry that it cannot be detached from it and transported to other branches of knowledge. A work of morals or politics or criticism, perhaps even of eloquence, would be better (other things being equal) if it were done in the style of a geometer. The order, clarity, precision, and exactitude which have been apparent in good books for some time might well have their source in this geometric spirit.

The leaders of classicism also sought to perfect exact forms of expression, based on ancient models, and to give to modern languages the precision and charm of classical tongues. Rejecting the force of current usage in determining what is "correct," they looked instead to recognized judges of style and taste. In the late seventeenth and early eighteenth centuries, Nicolas Boileau in France and Alexander Pope in England were respected critics whose opinions were taken as literary law. Each wanted to be the Newton of his art. And at the end of the eighteenth century, Condorcet insisted that all expression must accept "the yoke of those universal rules of reason and nature which ought to be their guide."

The advocates of classical standards favored the founding of national academies to promote and enforce those standards. This idea appealed to the monarchs of the period—Louis XIII, for example, created the Académie Française in 1635. Because patronage flowed chiefly from the court and its dependent aristocracy, most writers now felt compelled to observe the official rules of style and taste. The Académie succeeded in imposing classical standards on French writers for more than a century.

CLASSICISM: RACINE, POPE

As we saw earlier in this chapter, France was the center of European power and culture during the seventeenth century (pp. 410–411). And classicism had its strongest roots in France, inspiring one of the richest periods in French literature. In addition to philosophical writers like Descartes and Pascal, there were outstanding individuals in every branch of letters. Chief among them was Jean Racine, France's greatest dramatic poet and a leading promoter of classicism.

Educated by a Catholic religious order, Racine received thorough training in Greek and Latin, as well as in theology. His middle-class family wanted him to become a priest, but an urge to write poetry took him to Paris in 1663. When a poem written to Louis XIV brought him to the attention of the king, Racine's literary career was launched. He received a post at the court the following year and was elected to the Académie Française in 1673.

The plots of Racine's tragedies were drawn mostly from classical themes and invariably centered on a single moral issue. Like other plays of the period, his were intellectual in nature, with long speeches and little action on stage. He relied on the spoken word to reveal character and passion under stress. The simplicity, precision, and dignity of his poetry led Voltaire to comment: "Beautiful, sublime, wonderful."

Classicism was expressed in another literary form by Alexander Pope. In *An Essay on Criticism* (1711), he set down his guidelines for critics and, later, in *An Essay on Man,* he put forward in verse a rationalistic view of the universe. Pope, an English Catholic by birth but strongly influenced by Deism (pp. 426–427), tried to reconcile the discoveries of science with the idea of a benevolent God. He stressed the elements of order in nature, which had been confirmed by the mathematics of Newton. But while admitting the power of reason, he urged his readers to restrain their curiosity and pride: God's works are ultimately beyond understanding; it is best to accept one's limited place in the scheme of things and to believe that "Whatever is, is Right."

Pope's *Essay on Man* is classical in form as well as substance. It consists of hundreds of rhyming couplets, many of which are cleverly turned and well remembered:

Know then thyself, presume not God to scan;
The proper study of mankind is man.

Hope springs eternal in the human breast;
Man never is, but always to be blest.

The work as a whole illustrates the strengths and weaknesses of *didactic* verse (poetry with a "message")—and the classic form. Strict form has a power and beauty in itself; at the same time, it may limit the development of ideas and feelings.

SATIRE: VOLTAIRE

Literature in the eighteenth century, responding to the Enlightenment and increasing rates of literacy as education became more widespread, reached out to an ever-widening public. A group of writers appeared whose chief aim was to digest important ideas and put them in readable form for the public. Along with encyclopedias, dictionaries, and surveys of knowledge, there was a rapid spread of newspapers and magazines.

The most successful and famous of the new writers was Voltaire. The son of a Parisian lawyer, he was schooled by Jesuits, who evidently sharpened his talent for argumentation. But his real education began in England. In trouble in France because he had insulted a nobleman, Voltaire accepted exile across the Channel in 1726. Through private study and conversation, he quickly absorbed the ideas of English philosophy and politics.

When Voltaire returned to France, he began to write all sorts of works—plays, histories, poems, scientific surveys, and philosophical essays. The best known and most widely read of his more than a hundred books is the satirical novel *Candide* (1759), which reflects his reasoned outlook, his irony, and his strong convictions. The story is a swift-moving, rollicking caricature of an idea popularized by Pope—that "this is the best of all possible worlds." The "hero," Candide, is an innocent young man who has been brought up to believe that "everything is for the best." In the course of incredible misadventures, he learns differently. At the story's end, Candide and his companions are living on a small farm trying to shut out the stupidities and indecencies of the world. One of them concludes that the only way to do this is to "lose oneself" in some form of satisfying work. "It's the only way to make life endurable."

In the novel, Voltaire struck out with rapier and bludgeon at many targets: the bigotry and hypocrisy of organized religion, the atrocities of war, the "inhumanity of man to man." He expressed contempt for arbitrary authority and disgust with ignorance and prejudice. Though a man of the Enlightenment, he criticized many of the new ideas as well: he ridiculed "pseudo" reason, which spins out unsupportable theories and seeks to find "cause" and "effect" in every event; scoffed at the nature cult; and turned the dream of "progress" into a nightmare.

Yet Voltaire had faith in the method of science and the power of reason. He stood courageously for freedom of expression; he admired simple honesty, moderation, humaneness, and tolerance. "Tolerance," he wrote in his *Philosophical Dictionary* (1764), "is the natural attribute of humanity. We are all formed of weakness and error; let us pardon reciprocally each other's folly. That is the first law of nature. It is clear that the individual who persecutes a man, his brother, because he is not of the same opinion, is a monster." If Voltaire sometimes grew bitter, it was because the world seemed so full of what he hated and so empty of what he loved. Like Erasmus, he was no revolutionist, but he and his fellow philosophes nevertheless helped prepare the ground for revolution.

THE ARCHITECTURE OF REASON: WREN, JEFFERSON

The Enlightenment was only partly reflected in the visual arts. On the Continent, the style of Baroque architecture (pp. 392–394) carried over into the eighteenth century and was gradually modified into the lighter, more delicate style of *Rococo* (from *rocaille*, a French word for the pebble- or shell-lined walls of grottoes that were a fanciful feature

Fig. 10.2 Saint Paul's Cathedral, London. This, the first cathedral built in England since the Reformation, was completed in 1710, when the "United Kingdom" of Britain was consolidating Protestant domination, strengthening parliamentary government, and rising to worldwide power. The cathedral, with its stately mixture of classical and Baroque design, became a British national shrine where victories were celebrated and heroes had their funerals. The architect, Sir Christopher Wren, became a national hero himself. He is commemorated by a simple Latin inscription carved into the cathedral's floor: "If you seek a monument, look around you."

©A. F. Kersting, London

of aristocratic garden design). Both styles were elaborate and elegant, suited to the pomp of monarchs and aristocrats. By 1750, however, the classical spirit in the other arts led architects back to the simplicity of Roman and Greek models.

In England, the Baroque had been more restrained, and the return to classicism came earlier there than on the Continent. The most influential architect of the time was Christopher Wren. The Great Fire of London (1666) gave him a unique opportunity; as the king's principal architect, he was charged with replanning the city and rebuilding Saint Paul's Cathedral. As might be expected, Wren had to accept many compromises, and his master plan for London was never realized. He did, however, succeed in having many of the city's churches constructed according to his designs.

Wren's triumph was Saint Paul's (*Fig. 10.2*), completed in 1710. The clergy had wanted a tall Gothic building (like Chartres Cathedral; *Fig. II.1,* p. 186), but he won approval for a plan that was essentially classical. Wren was influenced by Michelangelo's plan for Saint Peter's in Rome and by later Italian architects, but he shunned the curving lines and extravagance of the Baroque. He desired a simple though impressive structure crowned by a great dome. In order to satisfy the clergy, he placed tall bell towers above his classical façade and a tall "lantern" on top of the dome. The result was something of a hybrid, though Wren strove to preserve the basic harmony of the plan.

Subsequently, the trend was toward a strict classicism. The preferred manual of taste was now a book by the Renaissance architect Andrea Palladio, who had methodically measured ancient ruins. The "Palladian manner," with its Roman-style porches, rotundas (circular halls), and domes, became the standard for eighteenth-century En-

© Royalty–Free/CORBIS

Fig. 10.3 American Classicism. Thomas Jefferson's design for the Virginia State Capitol in Richmond was inspired by the Maison Carrée ("Square Building"), constructed in the southern French town of Nîmes seventeen centuries earlier to commemorate two grandsons of Augustus who had been deified (declared divine) after their deaths. Jefferson's simple and dignified building, which originally had no side wings, closely resembled the original. In this way, the design of a building that had served the cult of an all-powerful ruler's divine offspring was reused to proclaim the "Roman" wisdom and virtue of the new American republic.

gland. Noblemen who built villas in this style believed that their homes were a reflection of an age of reason—the reason of Newton and Pope.

Thomas Jefferson was one of the many intellectuals who became enamored of the classical style. On a visit to France in the 1780s, he saw the ancient Roman temple, the Maison Carrée, in the provincial town of Nîmes. He reported that he gazed at it for hours at a time, "like a lover at his mistress." When Jefferson returned to his home, he designed numerous public and private buildings, thus popularizing the classical style in America. His plan for the Virginia State Capitol at Richmond (*Fig. 10.3*) was inspired by the Maison Carrée, and his design for his home at Monticello was patterned after the Roman Pantheon (*Fig. 3.5*, p. 139). The public architecture of Washington, D.C., has borne the impress of Jefferson and the classical revival. Officials of the newly independent United States were proud to demonstrate visually their enthusiasm for the Enlightenment and its ideals of reason and order.

ACADEMY PAINTING: PORTRAITS OF ARISTOCRATIC ELEGANCE

In the eighteenth century, painting was less affected than the other arts by the radical changes in science and philosophy. The grandeur and drama of the Baroque (p. 393) were no longer in fashion, and eventually, the French Revolution would make classicism for a time the preferred style of painters in France (p. 484). But for the moment, in France and elsewhere, royal and aristocratic patrons preferred the elegance, charm, and grace of the Rococo style.

Fig. 10.4 *The Music Party.* Watteau here depicts a type of scene that he originated, and which the French Academy of Painting officially named "elegant entertainment"—a theme dear to the hearts of aristocrats in eighteenth-century France. Fine clothes, beautiful young women, handsome young men, pretty children, friendly animals, a pleasant countryside, wine served by a "negro page" (an aristocratic status symbol in his own right), and music—all combine to form a stage-like tableau whose original title was *The Delights of Life.*

The Belgian master Antoine Watteau was the finest representative of this style. He came to Paris in 1715 and went to work on various projects for the nobility. As a designer of interior decorations for courtly festivals and pageants, Watteau caught the spirit of refined ease and gallantry associated with the aristocratic ideal. He began to create oil paintings of picnics in the woods, music parties, and mythical scenes peopled by graceful ladies and gentlemen in lustrous silks and satins (*Fig. 10.4*). But these are not lifelike portrayals. They arise out of a dream world, where ugliness is absent and beauty touches all.

Watteau worked, like his fellow artists in France, under the watchful eye of the Academy of Painting. Yet his paintings have an unmistakable individuality with an air of melancholy. Destined to die in his thirties of tuberculosis, Watteau seems to have sensed the fleeting character of life and beauty.

More sensual and lighthearted—but no more realistic—were the paintings of François Boucher and his contemporary, Jean-Honoré Fragonard (*Fig. 10.5*). These artists painted mythical subjects and the frivolities of the nobility in a delicate and delightful manner. Their works, corresponding to the aims and taste of their patrons, had no important function other than playful entertainment.

Painting in England was more sober, solid, and "classical." The leading figure there was Joshua Reynolds, who became the first president of the Royal Academy of Art (1768). Reynolds is best known for his portraits of the wealthy and for his support of tradi-

© The Frick Collection, New York

Fig. 10.5 *The Meeting.* An eager young gentleman arrives for a rendezvous with an enticingly bashful young lady. Love, in this fantasy landscape of feathery trees, riotous flowers, and an antique statue, seems both playful and dreamlike. This painting was one of a series, *The Progress of Love,* that Jean-Honoré Fragonard completed in 1773 for the mansion of Madame du Barry, Louis XV's intimate female friend. The paintings did not please, and were returned—perhaps because, as a contemporary writer suggested, they hinted too broadly at "the adventures of the mistress of the house."

tional "laws" of painting. "I would chiefly recommend," he told the Academy, "that an implicit obedience to the Rules of Art, as established by the practice of the great Masters, should be exacted from the young students." He regarded the Italian Renaissance, rather than ancient Greece or Rome, as the "classic" source for the rules of painting. But he agreed with the classicists that there existed universal standards of taste and excellence.

The English upper classes were willing to pay a good price to have their portraits painted in what Reynolds himself called the "grand manner." Reynolds felt that historical or mythological subjects offered a greater challenge to his intellect, but he made

Fig. 10.6 *The Duchess of Hamilton.* A pose like a classical statue, and a relief with a mythological scene, lend a great lady the ideal nobility of Greece and Rome, while her ermine cloak proclaims her an actual noblewoman. This duchess's high standing was recently acquired, however. She was one of two propertyless daughters of an Irish commoner family who went off to London, created a sensation by their beauty, and quickly made splendid marriages. To be painted by Joshua Reynolds in his "grand manner" was confirmation of her social triumph.

his fortune by painting the rich. With high skill in texture and composition, he created hundreds of flattering portraits. His *Duchess of Hamilton (Fig. 10.6)* is typical of Reynolds's "classical" style.

The Classical Age of Music

The seventeenth and eighteenth centuries, taken together, constitute the classical age of European music; during that formative period, most of our modern instruments and forms of composition were established. If, however, we use the term *classical* in a narrower sense to mean the musical style corresponding to the style of classical literature and architecture, we find that it applies to the eighteenth century only. The music of that century, as we shall see, echoed the general accent on order, balance, and restraint. Seventeenth-century music, on the other hand, is usually called Baroque because its variety and power corresponded to similar elements in Baroque art and architecture (pp. 388–394).

MUSIC IN WESTERN CIVILIZATION

Music has always been a vital part of the life and expression of Western culture, but we have very little information about the musical instruments and compositions of ancient and medieval times. Almost all the music and instruments we hear today go back no further than the Renaissance. Yet ancient and medieval peoples believed that music had important powers. They used it for both sacred and secular purposes, and composers from the Renaissance onward built on their achievements.

Though we possess only a few fragments of ancient Greek music, we know that music held a high place in the Greek scale of values. Belief in its power is symbolized by the ancient myth of Orpheus; his playing on the lyre (harp) tamed wild animals and even secured the rescue of his wife, Eurydice, from the underworld. Music was customarily used to heal sick bodies and minds, and was thought to influence the development of character and temperament. Greek epic and other poetry was intended to be sung to the accompaniment of a lyre rather than recited. Playing and singing were indispensable to Greek religious and civic processions, and they were vital parts of the drama. Aristotle stressed the psychological impact of various combinations of harmony and rhythm: some depressed the emotions, some inspired enthusiasm, others produced a moderate mood. For all these reasons, the study of music was fundamental to Greek education.

Greek music, like that of the Orient, was primarily vocal, as might be expected of the Greeks, who were a highly verbal people. (Plato considered melody and rhythm useless, except as accompaniment for words.) Most Greeks were amateur musicians, but there were professional singers and players as well. Wandering poets recited or sang their tales to the accompaniment of the lyre (pp. 84–85). The only other standard instrument was the pipes, which usually consisted of two slender tubes joined at the player's mouth. Its sound, scholars believe, was something like that of the modern oboe.

The oldest music that can still be heard today is Christian sacred music from the sixth century A.D., just after the fall of the Roman Empire in the West. This music originated in a variety of oriental sources, chiefly Hebrew. Exclusively vocal, it was used only in liturgical services (the Mass) and canonical prayers (the Offices), and it was sung without accompaniment by the priest, the choir, or the congregation. It was first collected and organized by Pope Gregory the Great, the leading figure in shaping the medieval Church.Known as the Gregorian chant, it has been for centuries the principal sacred music of the Roman Catholic Church.

Nonreligious music presumably continued to be performed among civilized European peoples, though no record of it survives; and the barbarian peoples certainly sang epic and other poetry, like the early Greeks. With the revival of European civilization from the eleventh century onward, nonreligious music began to be written down. Many works survive that were performed by the troubadours, originally minstrel singers of epic poems and later on of love poems and romances of chivalry. Poems and songs were also presented by wandering scholars, who called themselves Goliards (p. 272–273).

But about the same time, a new and more complex form of music made its appearance in Europe. From the ancient Greeks to the troubadours, music had been *monophonic,* consisting of a single tune, without harmonizing chords—as is still the case with music outside Western civilization. *Polyphony* ("part" music, in which singers or players perform different but harmonizing notes or tunes) had its beginnings in the tenth century. This more complex form demanded a superior means of musical notation, and during the twelfth and thirteenth centuries, the basis was laid for the modern system, with its staff, time signature, and sol-fa syllables. Meanwhile, improved instruments were appearing, notably the pipe organ—a complex machine that furthered the development of polyphonic music. Its mechanism enabled a single person to play many "instruments" at once by replacing human lungs with bellows, and the direct touch of the fingers with a keyboard and foot pedals.

During the Renaissance, polyphony reached its full development in both sacred and secular music. It was applied to scriptural texts, Masses, and dramas of the Lord's Passion. The most popular songs were "madrigals," which consisted of secular poems put into "part" singing. Instrumental music (written mainly for dances) also gained favor. The recorder, a wooden relative of the flute, was introduced at this time, and the most common stringed instrument was the lute, similar to a mandolin. Renaissance polyphony also furthered the development of instruments that combined the keyboard principle of the organ with the strings of lutelike instruments. This would in time lead to the development of clavichords, harpsichords, and eventually pianos.

BIRTH OF THE "MODERN" STYLE: MONTEVERDI, HANDEL, BACH

The transformation of music to its "modern" form began rather late in the Renaissance and reached full force during the Baroque era of the seventeenth century. So sweeping were their innovations that the Baroque composers believed they were bringing about a musical revolution. In fact, they referred to the Renaissance manner as the "old style" (in Italian, *stile antico*) and to their own as the "modern style" (*stile moderno*).

In contrast to the even-tempered, complex themes of traditional polyphony, Baroque compositions were marked by a heavier stress on a dominant melody. Elaborate harmonic chords and dramatic effects were also characteristic, and in order to create a wider range of tonal effects, larger numbers and types of instruments were used: flutes, oboes, trumpets, and bassoons, as well as violas, violins, and the harpsichord. Composers now began to write instrumental music for *listening,* not just for dancing. Reflecting the growing social role of the bourgeois, concerts were held in public halls as well as in the private courts of royalty and nobility.

Perhaps the most important cultural development of the time was the appearance of a new art form: the opera. This "music drama," consisting of expressive speech heightened by melody and rhythm, originated in Italy. Its chief creator was Claudio Monteverdi, who had spent the earlier years of his life writing madrigals and Masses but who in middle age turned enthusiastically to the modern style. The most appealing of his operas, *Orfeo* (*Orpheus*), was first performed in 1607. Exhibiting most of the elements of modern opera, it contained the first operatic overture (musical introduction) and a number of instrumental passages to heighten dramatic action. Monteverdi, who was also a singer, string player, and conductor, supported the operatic action with an effective combination of instruments. His ensemble (musical group) was close to that of the modern orchestra.

Opera, however, did not find ready acceptance outside Italy. Nearly a century passed before the new art form spread north of the Alps, thanks partly to the work of George Frideric Handel. Of German origin, Handel spent much of his youth in Italy before settling in England early in the eighteenth century. Admired by the king and aristocrats who acted as his patrons—and beloved also by the growing English middle classes who attended his performances—Handel was enormously successful in his adopted country, and died a wealthy man. Endlessly prolific and versatile, Handel could express in music almost any situation and emotion. These ranged from the sensual passion that marks many of his operas, through the magnificence of his works for royal occasions such as the *Water Music,* to the religious grandeur of his sacred music, notably the oratorio *Messiah.*

Meanwhile, another prolific German composer was writing in every form except opera. Handel's contemporary Johann Sebastian Bach was a giant of the Baroque period and one of the great musicians of all time. A devout Lutheran, he composed profound and inspiring scores for religious texts (cantatas and oratorios), Masses, and Passions. Bach was equally talented in secular music, creating superb pieces (chamber music) for performance by small groups at aristocratic courts. He is notable for the power and grandeur of his expression and for his mastery of polyphonic themes.

THE CLASSICAL SPIRIT: HAYDN, MOZART

The death of Bach in 1750 marked the end of the Baroque and the beginning of yet another style of musical expression. As in the visual arts, a reaction had set in against the elaborateness and complexity of seventeenth-century music. The Enlightenment valued rationality, clarity, and restraint; in France, the Academy of Music attempted to impose these qualities in a manner similar to that of the Academy of Painting. Melodies and rhythms were simplified, and form rather than content was stressed. Music, the classicists believed, should not be disturbing but should express balance and repose through perfect craftsmanship. The compositions of this era, which were mainly secular, were designed for enjoyable listening. They appealed as much to the intellect as to the heart.

Not surprisingly, instrumental music was more highly regarded than singing. The sections of the modern orchestra were well established during the eighteenth century, when the first important symphonies were written. Most popular, however, was music intended for chamber performances, normally given in small halls. The string quartet was the leading new musical form; the violin was the chief ensemble instrument, and the piano was the foremost keyboard instrument.

Among the most gifted of all the classical composers were Franz Joseph Haydn and Wolfgang Amadeus Mozart, both Austrians. Haydn, the lighthearted Viennese composer, brought the chamber and symphonic forms to a high point of perfection and in doing so created works of enduring appeal. Mozart, a child prodigy, was composing serious works before the age of five. Though he died in 1791 at the age of thirty-five, he created an astonishing number of magnificent compositions.

Mozart was himself a superb harpsichordist and pianist and wrote many pieces for keyboard instruments. He was a master of all types of composition, however, and displayed the clarity and grace of classicism at its best. But his ultimate triumph was in opera, where his understanding of human character combined with his gift for melody to produce immortal works. Among his most popular operas today are *Don Giovanni, The Marriage of Figaro,* and *The Magic Flute.* Though he was truly a man of the eighteenth century, trained in classicism, Mozart transcended both the style and the age.

RECOMMENDED READING

The Rise of Absolutism P. Goubert, *Louis XIV and Twenty Million Frenchmen* (1970); G. Ritter, *Frederick the Great* (1968); and M. S. Anderson, *Peter the Great* (1995), are brief and authoritative biographies.

On individual states, see R. Briggs, *Early Modern France* (1998); S. B. Fay, *The Rise of Brandenburg-Prussia to 1786* (1937); C. Ingrao, *The Habsburg Monarchy, 1618–1815* (1994); and C. E. Ziegler, *The History of Russia* (1999).

W. M. Spellman, *European Political Thought, 1600–1970* (1998), deals with theories of absolutism. A. Martinich, *Thomas Hobbes* (1997), is a brief account by a leading scholar.

See also the books listed in Chapter 9 under "Religion, Politics, and War."

The Scientific Revolution of the Seventeenth Century H. Butterfield, *The Origins of Modern Science, 1300–1800* (1957), and S. Shapin, *The Scientific Revolution* (1996), are brief interpretations; Butterfield voices the "classic" view of the seventeenth-century changes in science, and Shapin explains how far that view is still regarded as valid. A. R. Hall, *The Scientific Revolution, 1500–1800: The Formation of the Modern Scientific Attitude* (1962), surveys the specific changes that took place in each field of science; J. R. Jacob, *The Scientific Revolution: Aspirations and Achievements, 1500–1700* (1998), is briefer and more recent. T. S. Kuhn, *The Copernican Revolution: Planetary Astronomy in the Development of Western Thought* (1957), describes and interprets the field of science where the most spectacular and decisive changes took place. All these books are nontechnical, though they assume basic scientific knowledge.

The Impact of Science on Philosophy: The Enlightenment Two excellent general surveys are N. Hampson, *The Enlightenment* (1968), which considers philosophy against its social and political background, and D. Outram, *The Enlightenment* (1995), which includes discussion of the role of women and non-Western civilizations in Enlightenment thought. On individual thinkers, J. J. Jenkins, *Understanding Locke* (1983), and E. Goodell, *The Noble Philosopher: Condorcet and the Enlightenment* (1994), are good brief biographies; P. S. Woodhouse, *The Empiricists* (1988), has brief essays on Locke and Hume, among others. J. B. Bury, *The Idea of Progress* (1932), covering one of the main themes of Enlightenment thought, is still well worth reading.

The Rational Spirit in Literature and Art F. Kermode, *The Classic: Literary Images of Permanence and Change* (1983), explores the concept of classicism in literature, including the eighteenth century. On individual writers, see L. Goldmann, *Racine* (1972); F. Rosslyn, *Pope: A Literary Life* (1990); and H. Mason, *Candide: Optimism Demolished* (1992).

Two excellent introductions to art and architecture are M. Levey, *Rococo to Revolution: Major Trends in Eighteenth-Century Painting* (1966), and J. Summerson, *The Architecture of the Eighteenth Century* (1986). On individual artists and architects, see J. Massengale, *Fragonard* (1993); R. Wendorf, *Sir Joshua Reynolds: The Painter in Society* (1995); and M. Whinney, *Wren* (1971).

The Classical Age of Music A. Einstein, *A Short History of Music* (1937) (from ancient times to the late nineteenth century); N. Anderson, *Baroque Music: From Monteverdi to Handel* (1994); and J. Rushton, *Classical Music: A Concise History from Gluck to Beethoven* (1986), are excellent introductions by leading scholars. Brief and authoritative biographies of leading composers are D. Arnold, *Monteverdi* (1975); M. Boyd, *Bach* (1983); W. Dean, *The New Grove Handel* (1982); J. P. Larsen, *The New Grove Haydn* (1982); J. Rosselli, *The Life of Mozart* (1998) (stressing his musical creation and career); and P. Gay, *Mozart* (1999) (analyzing his inner personal development). All books listed are nontechnical, apart from occasional musical examples.

INFOTRAC COLLEGE EDITION

Visit the source collections at **http://academic.cengage.com/infotrac,** and use the Search function with the following key terms:

Louis XIV	Galileo not Jupiter	René Descartes
Copernicus	Isaac Newton	

WESTERN CIVILIZATION RESOURCES

Visit the Brief History of the Western World Companion Web Site for resources specific to this textbook:

http://history.wadsworth.com/greerbrief09/

Also, the CD in the back of this book and the World History Resources Center at **http://history.wadsworth.com/west_civ/** offer a variety of tools to help you succeed in this course, including access to quizzes; images; documents; interactive simulations, maps, and timelines; movie explorations; and a wealth of other sources.

CHAPTER 11

The First Modern Revolutions

OVERVIEW

The seventeenth and eighteenth centuries, when absolute monarchs became supreme within the traditional partnership of rulers, nobles, and churches, were also the era when this long-standing Western power structure first began to be seriously undermined. The main agent of destruction was a series of violent *revolutions*—spectacular collapses of the existing power structure followed by lengthy struggles over the shape of a new one—in England, North America, and France.

Revolutions sometimes happened in earlier periods—notably the Jewish revolts against ancient Rome and the Hussite wars in medieval Bohemia (pp. 160, 296)—but they have become much more common in modern times as massive shifts in civilization have produced deep conflicts within the West and across the world. The seventeenth- and eighteenth-century revolutions were followed by many more in the nineteenth century, and in the twentieth century non-Western as well as Western countries have undergone revolutions.

The English, North American, and French revolutions were the outcome of conflicts arising from shifts in civilization that had begun in the late Middle Ages. Actual or threatened increases in central government power often provoked resistance on the part of wealthy and educated people whose interests and authority were harmed, such as English country gentlemen, American merchants, and French aristocrats. The growing scale and cost of warfare led to conflicts over who had the right to levy taxes and who had to bear the burden of paying them—the king of England or the Parliament, American colonists or the British government, French nobles or the peasants who worked their lands. These discontents among both the elite and the masses made even powerful governments liable to collapse.

Meanwhile, the Reformation and the Enlightenment made governments illegitimate in the eyes of those who did not share the religious beliefs or ideological views of their rulers, and inspired opposing parties with idealistic fury—Catholics against Protestants, philosophes against Christian believers, different kinds of Protestants or philosophes against each other.

These political, social, and ideological tensions reinforced each other, leading to the collapse of governments followed by years of strife, and in England and France, to many changes of government. Radical dictatorships claimed to build a new heaven and a new earth; military strongmen used their armies to uphold their own visions of a new order and tried to win general acceptance by foreign conquest; and counter-revolutionary regimes staged would-be restorations of the old order.

In England, the turmoil of its seventeenth-century revolution ended in a compromise that pointed the way toward a new power structure that would eventually replace the old one. The rulers of England (and later of the United Kingdom of Britain) were still effective hereditary monarchs backed by a powerful class of landowning nobles and country gentlemen, allied with the established Protestant Church and able to tax their subjects heavily so as to fight worldwide wars. But they were "limited" or "constitutional" monarchs who were bound to respect their subjects' rights including freedom of religion, and Parliament authorized them to collect taxes in return for constant legislative oversight.

Impressed by this new pattern of British government, Enlightenment thinkers developed theories according to which society was an arrangement among individuals to secure the earthly goals of life, liberty, and property; rulers were agents of society who could be resisted if they overstepped their limits; and checks and balances between different branches of government were necessary to protect the liberty of the people. In the late eighteenth century, the American Revolution put these ideas into effect in a more far-reaching way than ever before. It produced the first democratic republic to govern a large territory and the first community that did not practice a specific form of religious worship. But the American republic, like the British constitutional monarchy, was a compromise, designed to uphold the country's existing society and values—its many ex-colonial governments, its religious diversity, its commercial interests, and the institution of slavery.

At the end of the eighteenth century, Europe's most powerful absolute monarchy collapsed in France, and in the next quarter century, the turmoil of revolution eventually spread through much of the mainland of Europe. Unlike the revolutions of England and North America, the French Revolution ended not in compromise but in defeat—its foreign enemies victorious, France itself occupied, and its old rulers restored. But the shifts in civilization that had undermined the partnership of king, nobles, and Church in France could not be turned back, and defeat only continued the conflicts of the revolution—not just in France, but to a greater or lesser extent in the rest of Europe as well. The traditional order that had developed fifteen hundred years before out of the merging of Greco-Roman civilization and the warrior societies of barbarian Europe was coming to an end, but the struggles over a new order were just beginning.

The English Revolution: Parliamentary Supremacy and the Bill of Rights

The English Revolution of the seventeenth century began as a religious and political struggle, like many others that arose in the wake of the Reformation (pp. 395–400). In this case, the religious conflict was between different versions of Protestantism, and

1485			1603	1642	1660		1714
House of Tudor			House of Stuart	Civil War and Cromwell	House of Stuart Restored		

the political disputes involved the rival claims to government power of the ruler and the Parliament. Like other seventeenth-century religious and political struggles, this one ended in compromise. The power of the ruler and the official Church diminished and the power of Parliament and the rights of subjects increased, yet the government was more stable and stronger in both war and peace than before. It was this combination that made the outcome of the English Revolution a precedent for change in the traditional power structure in many lands of Western civilization.

CHALLENGE TO THE DIVINE RIGHT OF KINGS: THE CIVIL WAR AND CROMWELL

In the era of the Reformation, the Tudor rulers of England had built a form of government that relied on the cooperation of the traditional English representative institution, the Parliament (pp. 316, 381–384). After the death of Elizabeth I in 1603, however, cooperation gradually gave way to political and religious disputes in the relations between the ruler and Parliament. Elizabeth was succeeded by her nearest relative, James I of the Stuart family, who was already king of Scotland. (England and Scotland remained separate kingdoms, though ruled by one and the same monarch, down to 1708, when they merged to form the "United Kingdom" of Britain.) James upheld the royal tradition of *divine right* (p. 417), but he was not an Elizabeth or a Henry VIII (p. 381): he failed to win the personal following they had enjoyed, and Parliament refused to agree to his demands. The House of Commons consisted of elected representatives of the gentry (small to medium rural landholders) and of middle-class townsmen. Most of them were Puritans, English supporters of the international Calvinist Reformation, and they had no affection for the religious compromises of the Church of England as reorganized by Queen Elizabeth I (pp. 384–385). Moreover, they disapproved of James's foreign policies and his extravagance. When he asked them to approve new taxes to support his projects, they stubbornly refused. And so James governed without Parliament during most of his reign.

James's son, Charles I, fared worse. Unable to make Parliament do his bidding on new taxes, he resorted to forced "loans" and to increases of established taxes. Resentment toward Charles was aggravated by what the House of Commons considered his violation of English constitutional traditions that went back to the Magna Carta of 1215 (p. 233). The Magna Carta had indeed proclaimed the feudal principle that kings should rule according to law and respect the rights of their vassals, including the right to be consulted. But Parliament had not existed in 1215, and what was now breaking down was a tradition of cooperation between ruler and Parliament that dated from the late Middle Ages. When Charles summoned a Parliament in 1640, after a decade of ruling without it, the stage was set for an open clash between the king and his opponents.

The Long Parliament (as it was later called) proceeded to enact measures against the king's ministers and against the king's exercise of illegal power. When, in 1642, Charles tried to arrest the parliamentary leaders, the House of Commons answered by raising a citizens' army for its own protection. Charles, with a minority of the Commons and most of the House of Lords, then withdrew to Oxford; the rest of the Commons held

London and prepared for war. In the main, Charles was supported by the great nobles, the high clergy of the Anglican Church, and the Roman Catholics. Parliament was backed by the bourgeois, by most of the gentry, and by Puritan dissenters from the Anglican Church. In strictly political terms, the Civil War was a showdown between two rival power groups and two theories of government. The king and his hereditary lords were defending their privileges and the idea of absolute monarchy; Parliament, representing the smaller landholders and businessmen, was fighting for rule by a broadened aristocracy.

Civil War in England

In the test of arms, the parliamentary forces kept control of the chief cities and seaports and the prosperous country districts of southern and eastern England, and they enjoyed the support of the navy. On land, their campaigns were fought by a "new model" army, which had been organized by Oliver Cromwell—a landowner, militant Puritan, and member of Parliament. The first citizen army to be recruited in the era of revolutions, this force consisted chiefly of volunteer yeomen (independent farmers) who disliked royal absolutism and the established Church. Showing Puritan zeal and discipline, Cromwell's army decisively defeated Charles's forces in 1646.

But the victorious coalition could not agree on what to do next. Cromwell and his army fell out with the majority of Parliament over questions of religion and the future of the king. Calvinism replaced Anglicanism as the state religion for a few years, but in 1649, a limited sort of religious toleration was adopted. Leadership of the revolution fell more and more upon Cromwell himself. At last, he decided that Charles must be executed, on the grounds that he was untrustworthy and attracted "ungodly" persons to his cause. When Parliament balked, Cromwell drove out the members who opposed him. The surviving "Rump" Parliament of some sixty members put the king on trial (*Fig. 11.1*) and had him executed in 1649. It then declared the title and office of king abolished and proclaimed England a republic (the "Commonwealth").

The execution was the work of a determined minority, and the majority of the nation's subjects recoiled from the deed. With the revolutionaries divided among themselves, Cromwell found that he could maintain orderly government only through strong personal rule backed by the army. He sought to institutionalize his control through several written constitutions, including one that called his government a "Protectorate"—in fact, a kind of renewed monarchy. He conducted foreign affairs to the general satisfaction of his subjects, and he advanced the interests of the business class by encouraging trade and shipping. But this was not the kind of state that the Puritan opponents of the Stuart kings had wanted.

THE RESTORATION OF THE MONARCHY AND THE GLORIOUS REVOLUTION

Sentiment in England swung steadily toward a restoration of the Stuart monarchy (and a "free" Parliament). Shortly after Cromwell's death in 1658, a new Parliament assembled—the first in twenty years to have been freely elected. One of its early acts was to invite the dead king's son, an exile in France, to return as Charles II. He was cheered on

Fig. 11.1 A King on Trial. King Charles I of England, wearing his hat to show his disrespect for a court he does not recognize, faces his judges. No king had been put on trial before, let alone for treason—by making war "to uphold an unlimited and tyrannical power to rule according to his will, and to overthrow the rights and liberties of the people of England." The sentence was also unprecedented—that Charles "be put to death, by the severing his head from his body." Ten days later, the sentence was carried out.

his arrival in 1660 by an emotional show of loyalty on the part of his subjects, and the nightmare of regicide (king-killing) and Puritan tyranny faded into the English past.

Parliament did not intend, of course, to restore divine right. It made clear to Charles that his was to be a *constitutional* government, based on the traditional rights of the crown, Parliament, and the people. Though the Anglican Church became once again the established church, it no longer upheld political absolutism. Bloody revolution and Cromwellism may have been viewed as mistakes, but few desired to turn back the clock to 1600.

Charles II accepted all this on the surface, though he was suspected of having private reservations. Whatever his inner convictions, he could not forget the shadow of exile or the block; hence he avoided extreme policies. The same cannot be said for his younger brother, who succeeded him as James II. A convert to Roman Catholicism, James raised the fear that "popery" might return to England. Moreover, he antagonized both the Anglican clergy and major factions of Parliament, justifying his unpopular acts by claiming that the king was "above the law."

Though his critics were exasperated by James's behavior, they expected that matters would improve after his death. His probable successor was his Protestant daughter, Mary, the wife of William III of Holland. But in 1688, a son was born to the middle-aged English king, who had him baptized a Catholic. Now faced with the prospect of continued political reaction and "Romanization," the leaders of Parliament secretly invited William to land military forces in England. After William's landing, James found himself without support and quickly sailed for France. Parliament, alleging that James had "abdicated," then declared the throne vacant and offered it to William and Mary. Thus was the Glorious Revolution of 1688 carried out—glorious because it was decisive and bloodless.

Determined to keep the new rulers in check, Parliament in 1689 passed the Bill of Rights, which declared parliamentary supremacy over the crown and spelled out English civil liberties. This historic measure completed the revolution that had started in 1642. It stated that the king could suspend laws, raise armies, and levy taxes *only* with the consent of Parliament; it also provided for frequent meetings of the lawmakers and unlimited debate within their houses. The Bill of Rights also guaranteed every citizen the right to petition the monarch, to keep arms, and to enjoy "due process of law" (trial by jury and freedom from arbitrary arrest and cruel or unusual punishment). This was a restatement of the guarantees in the Magna Carta (p. 233), but they were now expressed in more specific language.

The triumph of Parliament in 1689 was important for two main reasons. It put an end to absolutism and established a governing aristocracy (of property owners); at the same time, it strengthened the exercise of individual freedoms for all. The wider enjoyment of civil rights led, eventually, to a demand for wider sharing of political power as well (p. 493). Thus the Glorious Revolution prepared the way for truly representative government in England.

LOCKE'S JUSTIFICATION OF REVOLUTION

A by-product of the English upheaval was John Locke's political theory, which would have a profound influence on future revolutions. Locke, as we have seen (pp. 429–430), was in touch with the scientific, philosophical, and political ideas of his day. He approved of Parliament's fight against absolutism and felt that both the Puritan Revolution and the Glorious Revolution were justifiable. In 1690, in order to defend the parliamentary settlement, he published *Two Treatises on Government*. The first treatise (study) rejected the theory of divine right, and the second defended the right of rebellion and became an ideological handbook for revolutionists everywhere.

Like his older contemporary Thomas Hobbes (pp. 417–418), Locke saw the state in a purely secular light and denied that it had been founded by God. Both insisted that the miserable condition of people in the "state of nature" had given rise to an agreement to establish civil government. Both also shared an *atomistic* view of society, regarding it as a collection of self-serving individuals bound together by a "social contract."

But although Locke accepted the theory of social contract, he disagreed with Hobbes about its terms. Hobbes had reasoned that human aggressive tendencies had made life unbearable under "natural" conditions; hence, he argued, individuals must have turned over *all* their rights to the state as a means of securing order. Locke, on the other hand, held that all people possess certain "natural rights," just as physical objects possess certain natural properties (mass, density, shape, and so forth). Individuals had retained most of their natural rights and powers and had agreed (in the contract) to transfer only *one* power to society: the power to preserve their life, liberty, and property. A society, said Locke, holds this power as long as the society lasts, but it delegates the use of this power to political agents. Should any agent (such as a king) push beyond set limits, the society is free, legally and morally, to resist. Who should decide whether a ruler's action is in fact a step beyond the set limits? "The people shall judge," Locke replied, and if, in face of this judgment, a ruler refuses to yield, the people have the ultimate right to resort to force—to "appeal to Heaven."

Thus by building on the ancient Roman ideas of natural rights and natural law (pp. 135–136), on the seventeenth-century style of reasoning, and on appeals to common sense, Locke constructed a "universal" political theory. Though it rested neither on scientific facts nor on actual historical events, it served as a fiction to justify the acts of the parliamentary side in England's civil war. In the next two centuries of revolution, the Lockean "myth" was heartily embraced by Thomas Jefferson and many other revolutionary leaders as a "self-evident," absolute truth.

A French Enlightenment thinker who lived somewhat later than Locke would also exert an important influence on the political thought of the following period. He was the Baron de Montesquieu. A distinguished aristocrat, actively involved in political affairs of the nobility, he was deeply concerned about the dangers of any form of despotism. In his famous work *The Spirit of the Laws* (1748), he argued that there is no single form of government suitable to all times and places. But he insisted that some arrangement of *separation of powers* is essential, in every situation, as a guard against tyranny. Montesquieu thought of England as a model of this principle—with its division of authority among king, lords, and commons, and the separation of legislative, executive, and judicial functions of government. These ideas had a direct impact on the writing of the United States Constitution (p. 455).

The American Revolution and Constitution

Though he wrote the Declaration of Independence nearly a century after Locke's treatise appeared, Thomas Jefferson formed a direct intellectual link between the English and American revolutions, for he expressed many of the ideas of Locke and the Enlightenment and gave them wider circulation. This, however, was but one element of the American Revolution of 1776. That rebellion also brought about the first expulsion of a European colonial power, replaced monarchical government with a republic, and established the principle and practice of popular sovereignty (democracy). As a result of these achievements, the American Revolution served as a beacon and a model for later revolutions around the world.

THE AMERICAN COLONIES AND THEIR ASPIRATIONS

The overseas expansion of Europe had brought English settlers to the North American continent in the seventeenth century. Many were "nonconforming" Christians seeking freedom from the strictures of the established Anglican Church (pp. 383–384). Most of them, after driving back the Native Americans and carving homesteads from the wilderness, inhabited the thirteen colonies of the Atlantic seaboard between Nova Scotia and Florida. By 1750, the white population of these colonies (including emigrants from the Continent as well as Britain) amounted to about two million. Viewed from London, they made up but one part of a far-flung empire; some thirty chartered colonies and companies, in America and Asia, were then controlled by the king and Parliament. (The total number of Britain's subjects was approximately fifteen million at the time.)

In accordance with the economic doctrine of mercantilism (p. 411), colonies were considered valuable chiefly as a source of raw materials and as a market for exports, both of which would be monopolized by Britain. But the costs to the mother country for defense and administration were heavy, the colonists broke through trading restrictions by means of wholesale smuggling, and they showed little desire to provide for their own military defense. After 1750, therefore, Parliament tightened the regulation of trade and the collection of taxes.

Not surprisingly, the colonists resented British efforts to collect existing taxes or to impose new ones. This was especially true after 1763, when the close of the French and Indian War—the American theater of one of many eighteenth-century worldwide struggles for trade and empire between Britain and France (p. 327)—brought victory to Britain. With French power on the North American continent broken, there was no longer a serious foreign threat to the thirteen colonies. Feeling more secure than before, the Americans grew defiant toward their absentee rulers.

Parliament passed various new taxes and then repealed them in the face of American protests, with the exception of a tax on imports of tea, which it retained for symbolic reasons—to emphasize its right to tax British subjects everywhere (*Fig. 11.2*). But the Americans, who sent no members to the distant British Parliament, refused to admit that right. "No taxation without representation!" became the rallying cry of colonial protest.

English leaders argued in vain that the colonies enjoyed "virtual" representation, since members of Parliament, in theory, represented not individual electoral districts but national and imperial interests as a whole. Actions and counteractions were building to more entrenched positions and heightened emotions. Though a minority remained loyal to the British flag and British law, most colonists were moving toward the point of no return. They saw themselves as heirs of the Glorious Revolution of 1688 and the British king and Parliament as tyrants who went beyond their legal limits.

The Americans at first sought redress of their grievances, but gradually they began to think of seizing control of their own destiny through self-rule. Members of the urban middle class took the lead. They realized that British mercantilism would check their own economic development, and that under colonialism, their general well-being would always be subordinated to imperial aims. Thomas Paine, a shrewd revolutionary propagandist, described the situation in a geographical perspective. Using the language of the Enlightenment, he declared that America's subjection to England was "contrary to reason." He went on:

> There is something absurd in supposing a continent to be perpetually governed by an island. In no instance has nature made the satellite larger than its primary planet; and as England and America, with respect to each other, re-

Fig. 11.2 Story of a Revolution. In this rueful British cartoon published when America won independence, Father Time gives a "magic lantern" (slide) show. This slide, he explains, features "the little hot spitfire teapot that has done all the mischief." Other slides show "the stamped paper that helped to make the pot boil," "the British Lion basking before the American bonfire while the French cock is blowing up a storm about his ears," "Miss America grasping at the Cap of Liberty," "the British forces flying before the Congress men," and "the Thirteen Stripes and Rattlesnake exalted."

verse the common order of nature, it is evident that they belong to different systems. England to Europe; America to itself.

Paine did much to advance the cause of rebellion in America. Later he aided the radicals in France and England, thus becoming the first international revolutionist of modern times.

WAR AND THE DECLARATION OF INDEPENDENCE

By 1774, the colonists had begun to commit acts of violence and sabotage (notably the Boston "Tea Party"), and the British responded with tough measures. Parliament passed what Americans called the Intolerable Acts, which closed the port of Boston and virtually canceled the charter of Massachusetts. The British may have thought that this hardline policy would bring the colonists to their senses, but it had just the opposite effect. Protests and opposition grew in Massachusetts, and shortly thereafter, representatives from all the colonies assembled at a Continental Congress in Philadelphia. There they drew up a statement of grievances and formed an association to cut off all trade with Britain. The conflict of words had given way to direct action.

When the British governor of Massachusetts ordered its legislature dissolved, the legislators defiantly met again and proceeded to raise a defense force of "Minutemen." This step was, of course, illegal; it brought into existence a condition of armed rebellion.

The first clash of arms occurred in April 1775, when British troops set out from Boston to destroy a reported supply of rebel weapons stored near Concord. They accomplished their mission but suffered heavy losses to sharpshooters on their return march. The war for independence was on.

The Continental Congress reassembled shortly after the skirmish in Massachusetts. The Minutemen around Boston were enlisted as the core of a Continental Army, and George Washington, a distinguished officer of the Virginia colonial militia, was appointed its commanding general. The war dragged on for six years. Britain, though a leading European power, was hampered by long lines of communication and uneven generalship. The colonials suffered from the internal differences that normally divide revolutionists, and the Continental Congress was unable to provide enough troops, supplies, or money. Although the rebels fought bravely and endured severe hardships, they could hardly have won without the aid of foreign powers.

The French monarchy, eager to even the score with Britain after the humiliation of 1763 (p. 327), decided to aid the rebels. The first significant American victory, at Saratoga, was won chiefly with French weapons. Impressed by the American success in that battle, the French became formal allies and declared war on Britain. Spain and Holland followed, swinging the European balance in the Americans' favor. The surrender of the encircled troops of Lord Cornwallis at Yorktown (Virginia) in 1781, which ended the British military effort, was forced by a French fleet controlling the waters offshore. Two years later, by the Treaty of Paris, the United States of America won recognition as a sovereign nation stretching from the Atlantic Ocean to the Mississippi River.

The independence of the new government, as well as its bid for allies, had been formally proclaimed in 1776. In fact, the most memorable achievement of the Continental Congress was its adoption of the Declaration of Independence. Drafted by Jefferson, it aimed to justify the resort to force against Britain and to win support abroad as well as at home. It is significant that the preamble gives this reason for publishing the document: "a decent respect to the opinions of mankind. . . ." In 1776 (as today), the influence of foreign opinion on the outcome of a struggle for independence could not be ignored.

The Declaration of Independence is a masterpiece of revolutionary literature fitted to the American cause. Jefferson omitted any mention of the colonists' reluctance to pay their share of defense costs; overlooked the long story of smuggling, civil disobedience, and provocative acts; and gave no hint at all of the deeper motives of the rebel leaders. He knew that Parliament had been supreme in England since 1689 (p. 450), yet he shrewdly focused his charges of wrongdoing upon the *king.* He did so because the king, in an era of absolute monarchs, could more readily be painted as a tyrant.

The ringing paragraph that links the American Revolution with "universal truths" is a paraphrase of Locke, but Jefferson's version is marked by greater simplicity, clarity, and power. Jefferson declares:

> We hold these truths to be self-evident: That all men are created equal; that they are endowed by their Creator with certain unalienable Rights; that among these are Life, Liberty, and the pursuit of Happiness.—That to secure these rights, Governments are instituted among Men, deriving their just powers from the consent of the governed,—That whenever any Form of Government becomes destructive of these ends, it is the Right of the People to alter or abolish it. . . .

In these few lines, Jefferson sets forth a view of humanity, government, and revolution that remains an inspiration to believers in human dignity, liberal principles, and progressive social change.

THE CONSTITUTION OF THE UNITED STATES

The Americans emerged from their war of independence with relatively few scars. Serious divisions had appeared within the colonies, but they were moderate compared with those of revolutions elsewhere. The fact that the enemy was an *absentee* ruler served as a unifying force among Americans of all classes. Even so, there was a minority of die-hard "loyalists" (loyal to Britain) who opposed the "patriots" (revolutionists). Subjected to confiscation of their property and rough treatment by the majority, some sixty thousand fled to Canada. Their departure eased the internal conflict in the colonies, and most of the émigrés (refugees) did not return to stir up trouble. (Canadian colonists remained loyal to Britain.)

After independence, the most pressing need of the former colonies was to agree on a plan for self-government. Each new state drew up a written constitution for itself, but there was disagreement over what form the union of the states should take. Having previously lived in separate colonies, many citizens preferred complete independence for their states but grudgingly accepted the idea of a loose union, as provided by the Articles of Confederation. When the Confederation proved unable to meet the common needs of commerce and defense, the states sent delegates to Philadelphia (1787) to revise the Articles. Instead, they drafted a new constitution aimed at forming a closer union.

The federal constitution, approved after bitter debate in the thirteen states, was the earliest *written* constitution of a major country—and is the oldest still in use. The very act of Americans' framing their own basic law fired the imagination of European intellectuals. Here was Locke's social contract made real! Here also was a reasoned statement of the new doctrine of popular sovereignty (rule by the people). Starting with a clean political slate, the Americans rejected the notion of any privileged persons or bodies. The foreword identifies the sole source of civil authority in its opening words: "We, the people . . . do ordain and establish this Constitution for the United States of America." The new document also launched a successful experiment in federalism, in which individuals hold citizenship both in their state and in the nation. The authors of the Constitution tried to strike a balance between powers delegated to the central government and those reserved to the states. With changing conditions, the balance has had to be readjusted through constitutional interpretation or amendment. Nevertheless, federalism stands as a noble endeavor to harmonize the requirements of centralized planning and power with the desire for local control.

Above all, the Constitution followed Jefferson's maxim, which became the foundation of nineteenth-century liberalism (pp. 496–497), "That government is best which governs least." Fearing possible tyranny by one person or one body and influenced by the ideas of Montesquieu (p. 451), the framers put their trust in a system of "checks and balances." The best protection against the human urge to power, they thought, is to establish separate political authorities and to leave them in jealous competition. Thus the states were to keep a watchful eye on the national power; and within all government units, a division of executive, legislative, and judicial powers was established.

Although the Constitution provides defenses against the invasion of individual rights, fears of an overly strong central government continued to be voiced. And so, at the insistence of many citizens, the Bill of Rights was added to the Constitution in 1791. Comprising the first ten amendments, it clarifies and extends the principles of the English Bill of Rights (p. 450). Strongly supported by church leaders, freedom of worship and freedom from an established church head the list. Every person is also guaranteed freedom of expression, petition, and assembly; the right to keep and bear arms; security of person and home; and due process of law.

By and large, the liberal principles embodied in the Constitution proved well suited to the self-reliant temper of the American people and to the conditions of life during the republic's first hundred years. With no strong enemies on their borders and with vast resources to be exploited, Americans were free to exercise their inventiveness and talents. The federal power survived secession and civil war during the 1860s. But great forces were not needed for external defense, for eliminating counterrevolutionary elements, or for restraint of private powers. Not until the end of the nineteenth century—with the closing of the frontier, the swelling of the population, and the rise of giant industry—did conditions develop that were less suitable to limited government.

The French Revolution: "Liberty, Equality, Fraternity"

The American Revolution helped to spark the French Revolution of 1789, which proved to be the most violent and far-reaching upheaval so far. The French Revolution brought drastic changes in the legal, social, and economic order of France, the largest and most populous country in western Europe. The struggle was intensified by passionate opposition at home and by the intervention of foreign powers. Even more than the English or American revolutions, it was a watershed in the flow of Western history. As the nineteenth-century French political thinker Alexis de Tocqueville later wrote, "The French Revolution had no territory of its own; indeed, its effect was to efface, in a way, all older frontiers. It brought men together, divided them, in spite of law, traditions, character, and language—turning enemies sometimes into compatriots and kinsmen into strangers. . . ." Not until the Russian Revolution of 1917 was an uprising to have such an impact on the Western world. What, then, were the main causes, phases, and consequences of the movement that began in 1789?

THE OLD REGIME AND ITS PROBLEMS

Before the Revolution, France lived under a version of the same political, social, and economic order that had prevailed in most of western Europe since the early Middle Ages. In this traditional order, the rulers, the nobles, and the Church shared power over a predominantly agrarian society, where the land was the main source of wealth, most people were peasants, and townspeople were a minority.

The Three Estates. The superiority of the nobles and the Catholic clergy to the rest of the king's subjects was a legally recognized fact. The status of all French people in the eyes of the law depended on which of three "orders" or "estates" they belonged to: the First Estate, made up of about 100,000 Catholic clergy; the Second Estate, consisting of 400,000 nobles; and the Third Estate, which included the rest of the 26 million people of France. The members of the First and Second Estates enjoyed various privileges over those of the Third Estate, the most important of which was exemption from the *taille,* a tax on land and other property that was one of the government's main sources of revenue. Yet as lords of manors holding rights of government and justice (p. 238), the nobles and clergy were able to extract much of the wealth they needed for their upkeep from the very same peasants who paid the largest share of taxes. In addition, the legal division of society expressed the feeling of nobles, in particular, that they stood far above the rest of the king's subjects: without noble status, even a wealthy banker, a learned judge, or a writer renowned throughout Europe was still a mere commoner, part of the 98 percent of the population who stood in third place below the nobles and the clergy.

The reason that this system had survived so long was that two things had kept it from being so starkly unfair in practice as it was in principle. First of all, most members of the privileged orders had not really lived in splendid isolation above the rest of society. Besides bishops and abbots from noble families who were too busy at court to visit their dioceses or live in their monasteries, there were tens of thousands of parish priests and nuns who worked devotedly among the peasants and townspeople to whom they themselves belonged by birth. In addition to courtier-nobles who scrambled for access to the king so as to win positions as ambassadors, bishops, and generals, there were farm- and factory-managing nobles, shipowning nobles, and even poverty-stricken nobles who plowed their own fields. And alongside "nobles of the sword" who prided themselves on their own or their forebears' prowess, there were "nobles of the gown" who earned law degrees and worked as judges and administrators.

Secondly, inequality was an accepted feature of society at all levels. In families high and low, husbands controlled the property of wives, and younger children were not supposed to marry before older ones. In the villages, peasants with larger holdings intermarried to form hereditary "dynasties" that looked down on families with smaller holdings or none at all. Rather than expecting equality for everyone, most people hoped for privileges for themselves, and over the centuries the traditional order had to some extent satisfied this hope. Wealthy townspeople, for example, could buy official positions from the king that turned them into tax-exempt "nobles of the hat," looking down upon humble taxpaying commoners though still despised by nobles of the sword and the gown.

Over many centuries, these safety valves had often failed to work, and force had been used to uphold the existing order against peasant revolts, religious dissidents, and discontented nobles (pp. 293–294, 396–397, 410). Such rebels, however, had mostly turned to violence to make the existing order better serve their interests or ideals, but not to destroy it. In the eighteenth century, by contrast, France was feeling the effect of gradual changes, some of them under way since the Middle Ages and others more recent, that were causing pressures to build up and safety valves to become clogged. The result would be an explosion of unprecedented suddenness and violence. The existing order, still generally assumed to be permanent as late as the 1780s, would in the 1790s come to be seen as a thing of the past—the "Old Regime."

The Undermining of the Old Regime. One of these changes was the increase in the power of rulers and the problems that it brought. Like all systems of rule by one person, absolute monarchy depended very much on the character of the monarch, and France's eighteenth-century kings were not such dominating personalities as Louis XIV. The

Sun King was succeeded by a child, his grandson Louis XV, who grew up to be a capable but pleasure-loving ruler; his own successor was the well-meaning but indecisive Louis XVI. The monarchy retained its claim to divine-right absolutism, but in practice, both kings were guided by powerful courtier-nobles and courtier-clergy. The splendid court of Versailles, designed by Louis XIV to keep the nobles out of government, became the vehicle for them to make their way back into power. Meanwhile, away from Versailles, nobles of the gown in the *parlements* (superior law courts in Paris and each province of France) reasserted their traditional right, which Louis XIV had suppressed, to limit the king's power by registering his decrees before they went into effect.

None of this prevented the absolute monarchy from continuing to fight wars, in which there were many victories but also many defeats—above all at the hands of two countries, the enlightened despotism of Prussia and the constitutional monarchy of Britain (pp. 413, 431–432, 449–450). These defeats made rulers, clergy, nobles, and commoners alike feel the need to restructure the French version of absolute monarchy at the same time as the government faced an increasingly urgent short-term problem, that of paying for its wars.

Like every absolute monarchy, that of France had met the growing cost of war both by increasing taxes and by heavy borrowing, but by the middle of the eighteenth century, both sources had reached their limit. For more than a century, the burden on the main taxpayers, the peasants, had been growing. Many landowners, worried that the peasants might react by skimping on payments to them, had recently been using their power as lords of manors to extract every penny that the peasants owed them. Meanwhile, as the monarchy's debts mounted, so did the cost of repaying them— which also had to be met by the taxpayers.

Crippling government debts, oppressive taxation, and shifts in power within the partnership of ruler, nobles, and Church were nothing new, but this time the traditional order was under pressure in other ways as well. A group outside the traditional ruling partnership, the wealthy and well-educated business and professional people who belonged to the Third Estate, was outgrowing its traditional humble position in the government and social order. At the same time, the new ideology of the Enlightenment was throwing many traditional beliefs and values into doubt.

The growth of the business and professional classes was related to many other developments that had been under way since the late Middle Ages. Absolute monarchy needed officials and lawyers; cannon-equipped armies and navies needed engineers and navigators; the growth of trade within Europe and across the world increased the opportunities for manufacturers and merchants. By the late eighteenth century, nearly a quarter of France's population lived in towns, and the *bourgeoisie* (the French for "townspeople," in particular the urban elite) was larger and wealthier than ever before— and was finding the existing order more constricting than ever before. Manufacturers were hampered by guild rules and price controls, which the absolute monarchy maintained so as to keep the urban poor from rioting. Traders' profits were cut by tariffs on goods passing from one province to another inside France, which were an important source of government revenue. Meanwhile, nobles tried to prevent the sons of the bourgeoisie from entering military academies and began to resent the long-standing royal practice of creating nobles of the hat even while impoverished nobles sold their manors to wealthy townspeople or "manured their land" by marrying their sons to bourgeois heiresses.

In addition, the literate public, high and low, was reading the books of the philo-sophes and being inspired both to idealistic hopes for future change and to cynicism and resentment at existing realities. Many royal advisers began to envy the efficient and reforming enlightened despotism of Prussia. Louis XVI's queen, Marie Antoinette, under the influence of the "cult of nature" (p. 429), had a rustic village built at Ver-sailles, where she and her ladies frolicked as milkmaids—to the scorn of haughty no-bles and serious-minded bourgeois alike. More than a few nobles began to believe that their privileges had become a bar to progress, and sought to lead France toward the British model of constitutional monarchy with a dominant but taxpaying aristocracy and an honored place for other social groups. Some of the clergy—mostly the offspring of noble families, holding high Church positions—were no longer Christian believers, a development that inspired fury among humble parish priests while only increasing contempt for religion among less privileged unbelievers. And bourgeois facing the in-creasingly irksome restrictions of absolute monarchy, as well as growing fear and resent-ment from nobles, were liable to console themselves with the unaccustomed thought that all people were endowed with natural rights to freedom and equality.

All these hopes, fears, and resentments came to a head in the second half of the eigh-teenth century, when the ruling partnership of king, nobles, and Church was strained to the breaking point over the question of what to do about the government's debts.

In 1763, King Louis XV and his advisers were faced with the problem of paying for a worldwide war (including the French and Indian War in North America) that had ended badly for France. They did not believe that the problem could be solved at the expense of the peasants, who would revolt at yet another tax increase, or of the bankers, who might never again lend their money if the government defaulted. That meant that the solution would have to come at the expense of the privileged orders, and as a first step, the government announced a tax on land belonging to nobles. The nobles' response came from the *parlements*, in particular the Parlement of Paris, which told the king that "to levy a tax without consent" was "to do violence to the constitution of the French government" and to "injure . . . the rights of the Nation." This was language that had been heard a hundred years before from English gentry and Puritans, and would soon be heard again from North American colonists. But the ones who were using it now were members of the privileged orders of France.

This particular conflict ended in a compromise that enabled the government to raise enough new revenue to avoid bankruptcy. The basic problems remained, how-ever, and for the next quarter of a century, the nobility and the monarchy struggled in-decisively over reform of the public finances, which inevitably raised questions about reform of the government system in general. The nobles proclaimed the ideal of gov-ernment by consent, but for many of them, the idea of giving up their privileges to be-come the dominant force in a constitutional monarchy seemed a risky gamble. The rulers and their advisers announced several reform plans that would have made the government into a more efficient and equitable version of absolute monarchy, but they did not have the stomach for a break with their traditional partners in the privi-leged orders. As a result, the problems remained unsolved, while both sides fell into the dangerous habit of publicly criticizing each other. Both absolute monarchy and the privileges of nobles and clergy became subject to discussion in the court of public opinion—which meant the opinion of the wealthier and better-educated members of the Third Estate.

THE OVERTHROW OF THE KING AND THE NOBLES

The final crisis came after the absolute monarchy fought another expensive war against Britain, this time in support of American independence. The war was successful, but the debts were overwhelming, and in 1786, the government announced yet another reform plan, the centerpiece of which was a permanent tax on land, to be levied on all subjects alike. As usual, the privileged orders protested and resisted, and this time they had a trump card to play in the battle for public support. In 1787, the Parlement of Paris declared that the new tax could not become law unless it was discussed and accepted by the ancient national representative assembly of France, the Estates-General. This body had been an important part of the government in the Middle Ages (pp. 314–315), but as the rulers' power grew, they had found it a nuisance and had not convened it since 1614. To revive it now, therefore, would in effect mean the dismantling of absolute monarchy.

With this proposal, the privileged orders briefly became the leaders of the nation against the king. Bourgeois who wanted a larger place in the power structure and freedom for industry and trade, the urban poor who were suffering from high food prices caused by bad harvests, peasants hoping for relief from taxes and payments to landowners—all could hope for redress of grievances from the Estates-General, and the demand that the king summon it became widespread and clamorous. Facing open disobedience from nobles, with tax revenues shrinking and bankruptcy threatening, and afraid to use force, in 1788 King Louis XVI agreed to summon a meeting of the Estates-General, to be held at Versailles the following year.

The Triumph of the Third Estate. As planning for the meeting went ahead, a split opened between the nobles and the bourgeoisie. Traditionally, the Estates-General had been an assembly of representatives of the First, Second, and Third Estates, with each estate meeting and voting separately, and the consent of all three (as well as the king) required for decisions to become law. This system, which enabled the First and Second Estates to dominate the proceedings, had seemed fair enough in 1614. Now, however, in the age of the Enlightenment and bourgeois self-confidence, the lawyers and other professional men who emerged as spokesmen for the Third Estate wanted it revised. They argued that there should be twice as many representatives of the Third Estate as of the other two, and that all three estates should meet in a single assembly. The privileged orders would still have far more representatives than their numbers warranted, but reform-minded noblemen and clergy would vote with the Third Estate, so that the Third Estate would dominate the decision making.

The king granted the demand for double representation of the Third Estate, but the Parlement of Paris, to which the issue was referred, ruled in favor of the traditional voting method. The arguments continued, however, as elections got under way throughout France to choose the members who would represent the Third Estate at Versailles. The members were chosen by provincial assemblies that were themselves elected on a fairly wide suffrage, including small businessmen and heads of peasant households. Now, if not before, the common people in general became aware that their votes might not carry as much weight as those of the nobles and the clergy. The stage was set for a conflict that would involve not just the king, the privileged orders, and the bourgeoisie but the entire nation.

After the session opened—to the accompaniment of riots caused by bad harvests and high bread prices in many parts of France—matters soon came to a head. Unable to persuade the two higher estates to sit and vote with them as one body, the representatives of the Third Estate (most of whom were lawyers) decided to walk out of the Estates-General. Stating that they were the only true representatives of the people, they then declared themselves to be the "National Assembly" of France. This proclamation (on June 17, 1789) was the first act of actual revolution, for by law the power to determine the procedure of the Estates-General rested with the king. Louis XVI was thereby faced with a crisis of decision.

Forced to choose sides between the nobility and the bourgeois, Louis sided with the nobility. His initial response was to lock the meeting hall of the building where the Third Estate had been sitting. But the action failed; the Third Estate found another meeting place at an indoor tennis court nearby. There the members swore the "Tennis Court Oath," pledging not to return home until they had drafted a new constitution for France. Within a few days, the National Assembly was joined by many priests from the First Estate and by some of the nobles. Having failed to persuade the rebels to back down, Louis next tried to intimidate them by a show of force. Toward the end of June, he called some twenty thousand soldiers to Versailles.

The National Assembly was rescued by the people of nearby Paris—not just the wealthy bourgeois, but also the small business owners and their workers who made up the bulk of the city's population. They had often rioted in the course of earlier disturbances, such as the civil wars of the Reformation (pp. 396–397), and now they were aroused by the threat to the Third Estate. Excited by rumors of troop movements, crowds began to roam the streets of the capital in search of weapons, and on July 14, they demanded arms from the Bastille. Though the old fortress was no longer of military importance, it was a hated symbol of despotism. When its commander refused to turn over arms, the mob attempted to push its way in. After an exchange of gunfire, in which about a hundred of the crowd were killed, the commander agreed to surrender. Then the mob rushed in, killed members of the small garrison (including its commander), cut off their heads, and carried them on spear points through the city streets.

Thoroughly alarmed, and doubting that his troops would fire on the people, Louis yielded. He sent his forces away from Versailles. He played for time by pretending to yield to the demands of the Paris mob and the Third Estate. The king recognized a self-appointed citizens' committee as the new city government of Paris, and directed the representatives of the privileged estates to sit in the new National Assembly. Thus the revolutionary movement was saved for the time being and was strengthened by a new and powerful influence—the Parisian populace.

The final blow to the Old Regime came from the largest social group in France, the peasants. At least since the elections, they had known of the issues at stake, and though it took time for news to spread to remote country districts, many of them knew that the Third Estate was in some way threatened. Earlier they had rioted to stop merchants exporting scarce grain from country districts, but now they turned directly on the nobles. By late July, it was rumored that the landlords were gathering hired ruffians to attack the peasants. While many of the nobles were away at the capital, the peasants seized the initiative. During the "Great Fear" of late summer, they vandalized the manor houses of the nobles and destroyed the hated records of their required payments and services.

As the king had appeased the Paris populace, the National Assembly now tried to quiet the peasants. Many of the bourgeois, as well as the nobles, held landed estates. Frightened by the disorders in the country, they realized that they would have to take drastic action to save their families and properties. At a single night session (August 4), the National Assembly removed all special privileges in landed property. Reform-minded noblemen led the way by surrendering their historic rights to peasant fees and labor, hunting on farmland, tax exemptions and advantages, and special courts of law for the nobility. A final decree, approved overwhelmingly, declared that "feudalism is abolished." Thus a drastic overturn in property rights was the first major reform of the National Assembly. The chief losers were, of course, the nobles; the beneficiaries were the peasants, who now had a substantial interest in defending the revolution.

The Rights of Man. Now the National Assembly could turn to its original task: the framing of a new constitution. Although this effort was to prove trying and divisive, there was wide agreement on the major principles. Those principles were summarized in the Declaration of the Rights of Man and the Citizen. Drafted as a preface to the constitution, it served as a guide to the new order.

The Declaration was the French counterpart of the English and American bills of rights. It went beyond them, however, in setting forth specific principles of government. After stating the "natural, inalienable, and sacred rights of man," it defined the duties of individuals in a society. "Every citizen summoned or seized according to law ought to obey instantly," but law must be an expression of the "general will." *All* citizens have the right to participate in the making of law, and its administration must be the same for all. (This statement, however, was not generally understood to include women—in spite of some feminist demands at the time.) "The source of sovereignty is essentially in the nation," the Declaration continues; "no body, no individual can exercise authority that does not proceed from it in plain terms."

This emphasis on the "general will" reflected in large measure the influence of the French-Swiss philosopher Jean-Jacques Rousseau, who was the first to use this term. Rousseau had died in 1778, eleven years before the revolution, but his political ideas had stimulated the rebels of his own day and lived on in his writings. Rousseau's *Social Contract* dealt with the same question of rights and authority that had been treated in differing ways by Hobbes and Locke (pp. 417–418, 450–451).

For Rousseau, the "general will" meant the collective will of a community, in which every individual has a share. Since all individuals contribute to the general will, they must obey it because it is their own will; and for the same reason, even if they do obey it, they are still free. Upon examination, the "will" of Rousseau turns out to be a vague, mystical notion, bound to "moral principles" and the "welfare of the whole society." The chief difficulty lies in discovering how, in practice, the general will is to be found. Rousseau's interpreters have set forth three broad possibilities, each connected with a different form of government: the general will can be identified with the *decision of a majority* (democracy), it can be "revealed" by a charismatic *individual* (dictatorship), or it can be determined by a chosen *elite* (one-party rule). Thus the National Assembly, Napoleon the self-made emperor who eventually took over the Revolution, and the Communist parties of recent times (pp. 574–575) could each speak in the name of the "general will" of the people.

Rousseau's ideas were raised against all political institutions that rested on a divine or historical right rather than on the general will. His arguments gave philosophical support to the French Revolution and served to justify the National Assembly's claim to sovereign authority. The planners of the new constitution accepted it as their duty to create a framework of government that would respond to and express the general will of France. But from the beginning, there was sharp disagreement on how the

Fig. 11.3 **"Let's Go Get the Baker!"** In October 1789, seven thousand Parisian market women joined an armed march to Versailles to force King Louis XVI to act against high bread prices, approve the National Assembly's revolutionary measures, and come with his queen, Marie Antoinette, and the heir to the throne to live in Paris. After tense negotiations, the king agreed to all the demands. For a century, Versailles had been the seat of France's absolute monarchy, but the marchers ended this under the contemptuous slogan "Let's go get the baker, the baker's wife, and the little baker boy!"

framework should be built. Some wanted the new government modeled after that of England, with an upper and a lower house, and a king with executive and veto powers. Others, fearing that this arrangement would give undue power to the nobility, wanted a single legislative chamber and a figurehead king.

The rising distrust of Louis XVI shifted the balance toward the single-chamber (unicameral) plan. The leaders of the National Assembly were properly suspicious of the monarch's loyalty to the revolution; his brother, the Count of Artois, had already fled the country, along with many other nobles. These émigrés proceeded to urge foreign powers to intervene in France, and Louis himself hesitated to accept either the Declaration of Rights or the Assembly's decrees abolishing feudalism. Demonstrating their doubts about Louis, crowds marched from Paris to the Versailles palace in October 1789 and compelled him and his queen to move to the city palace of the Tuileries (*Fig. 11.3*).

From Monarchy to Republic. The growing fear for the fate of the revolution put increasing power in the hands of radical factions, of whom the most influential were members of the Jacobin Society. (The name came from that of a former convent in Paris where the society met, which had belonged to the Jacobite religious order.) Founded in 1789, this society soon had local chapters throughout France. By 1793, it had nearly half a million members and had become virtually a government within the revolutionary government. Serving as propagandists and administrators, the Jacobins were a prototype (model) for the revolutionary parties of the twentieth century.

As the revolution grew more radical, resistance to it also began to grow. Over 100,000 aristocrats left France, including more than half of the officers of the army, but they hoped to return one day to recover their lost positions and lands. Within the country, many people who would otherwise have supported the revolution were turned against it by its religious measures. In 1790, monastic orders were suppressed, and the properties of the Church were confiscated as a means of financing the revolutionary government. In addition, the clergy were placed under a "Civil Constitution," with *elected* priests and bishops and with salaries paid by the state. These measures provoked not only the anger of most clerics but widespread popular opposition, particularly in the devoutly Catholic western and southeastern parts of the country. Far from acting as the agent of the "general will," the revolutionary government was becoming the leader of one side in an increasingly divided nation. The constitution completed in 1791 provided for a unicameral legislature and a suspensive veto for the king. (He could only delay, not prevent, legislation.) At the same time, the well-to-do members of the National Assembly managed to limit the right to vote. Moreover, candidates for the "electoral college," which was to name the legislators and administrative officials, had to be male citizens of substantial property. (Only fifty thousand men qualified as candidates in the first elections.) The reason given for these restrictive provisions was that the great majority of the people were uneducated; the effect was to hand control to the wealthy families of the country.

Louis XVI, who was named the titular ("official") head of the new government, had sealed his fate earlier in 1791 by attempting to escape from France. Captured near the northeast frontier and brought back to Paris in humiliation, he thus destroyed any serious hopes for a successful constitutional monarchy. Soon this government foundered, the king was deposed, and a new assembly was called (1792) to draft another constitution. (In the election of these delegates, *all* adult males were permitted to vote.) The new body, named the National Convention, met and proclaimed the (first) French Republic. The Convention governed France during troubled years of reform and war and completed its work in 1795 by approving a constitution for the Republic.

FOREIGN WAR AND INTERNAL DISORDER

Reaction abroad deeply affected the course of the revolution. Whereas outside intervention had assured the success of the American Revolution (p. 454), it had destructive consequences for the French. It stimulated extremism and internal splits within the revolution, and it helped to bring about panic, dictatorship, and ultimately, military defeat.

Some individuals outside France sympathized with the aims and deeds of the revolution, but the most influential groups—the royal and privileged ones—had become increasingly alarmed. Their feeling was strengthened by blood ties with the captive Bourbon king and by warnings from the émigrés. Foreign sentiment had led to a military threat in the Declaration of Pillnitz (August 1791). In this document, Leopold II of Austria, the Holy Roman Emperor, stated that if the other European powers would join him, he would use force to restore the Bourbon rulers to their full rights. Busy with matters in Austria, the emperor did not really wish to send troops to France, but his declaration encouraged the émigrés and alarmed the French leaders.

It also strengthened the hand of the more aggressive revolutionists in France, who hoped that foreign war would restore national unity behind the revolution and believed that the reforms could not be made secure in France unless they were also carried abroad. They pictured French armies carrying the banner of "liberation" into neighboring lands and uniting with native radicals to overthrow established governments. The government accordingly declared war on Austria in April 1792, thereby launching a period of continental revolution and war that lasted for twenty-three years.

At first, the war went against the French, producing panic and disorder in Paris and the provinces. In the autumn, a mob rushed the royal palace of the Tuileries and massacred the king's Swiss Guard. Later a band of enthusiastic army recruits invaded the Paris jails and seized a thousand or more prisoners who had been rounded up as suspected sympathizers with the aristocracy. After mock trials, these unfortunates were put to death. The winds of violence, released by the revolution and whipped by nationalist hysteria, now swept across France. When the National Convention first met in September 1792, it faced the immediate problems of dealing with the king, restoring law and order, and conducting the war.

Louis's trial for treason opened a major split between the moderates and the radicals. The leaders of the Convention were all radical Jacobins, but they were divided into factions reflecting a broad range of philosophies, interests, and temperaments. Louis was voted guilty by unanimous decision, but the order of execution was passed by only a narrow margin. The majority of the Convention members thereby marked themselves as regicides (king killers); the others were thereafter regarded as halfhearted or even counterrevolutionary. The seeds of mutual distrust and hostility were thus sown within the revolution, and the rival leaders proceeded to devour one another.

The guiding spirit of the Convention, the radical Maximilien Robespierre, ruled over the near anarchy of 1793 and 1794. By this time the forces of Prussia, Spain, Britain, the Netherlands, and Sardinia had joined Austria, forming the First Coalition of powers against revolutionary France. Violent uprisings erupted in the strongly Catholic parts of the country, out of opposition to the Convention's measures—including efforts to replace traditional religion with a state-sponsored Deism (pp. 426–427)—and the growing concentration of power in Paris. Revolutionary trial courts were set up around the country to limit lynchings and to stifle the rebellions. Probably as many as forty thousand heads fell under the guillotines, usually on charges of treason (aiding the country's enemies) or sedition (rebellion against authority). Thousands more perished during the uprisings in the provinces.

To oppose the First Coalition, the National Convention approved the drafting of all able-bodied men. The French draftees, fired by revolutionary spirit, soon showed themselves more than a match for their enemies. By June 1794, they had turned the tide of battle and were overrunning the Low Countries. As foreign peril declined, internal hysteria declined with it, and within weeks, the foes of Robespierre (both left and right) put an end to his political domination. He was outlawed by vote of the Convention and was executed along with many of his associates.

The fall of Robespierre marked the end of "the Terror" and the return to power of the moderates. It was the moderates, chiefly representatives of the well-to-do, who secured the Convention's final approval of the republican constitution of 1795. The government so established (known as the Directory) restricted political participation to men of substantial wealth, even fewer in number than those who had held power under the constitution of 1791.

NAPOLEON AND THE REVOLUTIONARY EMPIRE

France under the Directory was a very different country from what it had been only six years earlier. The monarchy had been abolished, and feudal property rights, titles of nobility, and special privileges had been swept away. The traditional administration, with its chaotic mixture of royal authority and noble privilege, had been replaced by self-governing cities and "departments"—units about the size of American counties. Craft guilds, labor organizations, and the mercantilist regulations of the late monarchy had all been scrapped.

But what kind of country France would become, and whether it would provide an example of reform that other countries would want to follow, were still very uncertain. The leaders of the Directory were mostly ex-Jacobins who were themselves involved in the killing of the king, the persecution of the Church, and atrocities against Catholic and royalist peasants; but they had also killed Robespierre and repressed his followers among impoverished urban workers. They were therefore widely hated and despised both by opponents of the revolution and by its most radical supporters. Yet by restricting the suffrage, the bourgeois men of property who now ran the government had deliberately closed the door to building up widespread popular support. Furthermore, the government of the Directory lacked effective leadership, since many sincere reformers had either dropped out of public affairs or been destroyed in the rivalry of factions. The politicians who remained were largely men of narrow vision and self-interest who showed themselves lazy, corrupt, and incapable of solving the nation's problems.

Among the people, high hopes had been turned into disappointment, animosity, and bloodshed. Economic conditions had worsened for the poor, families had been torn apart, and mothers, especially, bore a heavier burden of securing food and shelter for their children. Emotionally exhausted by years of fevered excitement, many citizens fell into a mood of indifference or cynicism. The only institution of the republic that inspired trust or admiration was its army, which won victory after victory and brought Switzerland and much of Italy, as well as the Netherlands, under its control (*Map 11.1*). Ruling a mostly hostile or indifferent country, the Directory clung to power only with the aid of the military.

The Rise of Napoleon. The most successful of France's conquering generals, Napoleon Bonaparte, was quick to grasp the facts of the political situation. He had first defended the government in 1795 against attacks by royalist mobs. (Afterward he boasted that he had dispersed them with a "whiff of grapeshot.") Two years later, his troops were called on to enforce illegal measures that had been taken by the Directory, and in 1799, he plotted with some of its leaders to take over the state by a coup d'état (sudden seizure). The conspirators believed that only a strong government headed by a general could hold off royalism, establish internal order, and defeat France's foreign enemies. Napoleon proclaimed himself "First Consul," a title borrowed from the ancient Roman Republic (p. 110); later, after receiving a national vote of approval, he proclaimed himself emperor in 1804 (*Fig. 11.4*, p. 469). With warm public support, he ruled for fifteen years as a virtual dictator.

Born on the Mediterranean island of Corsica in 1769, only a year after its annexation to France, Napoleon had become a fervent French nationalist. He distinguished himself as an officer of artillery; the defection of many aristocratic officers opened the

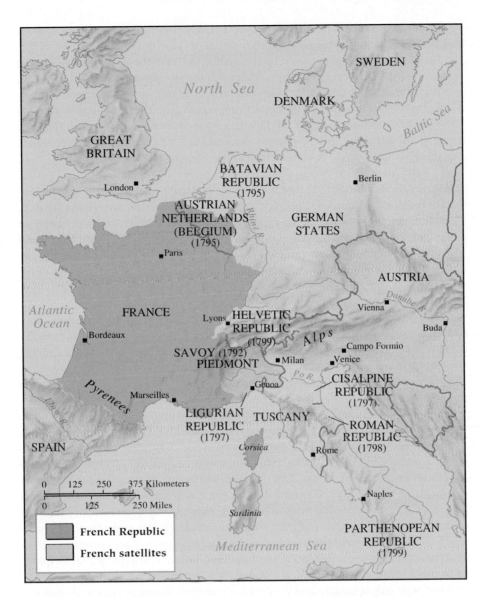

Map 11.1 Conquests of the French Republic. By 1799, revolutionary France and the leading European monarchies had been at war for seven years. The result was an expanded France and a belt of satellite republics, stretching from the Netherlands (the "Batavian Republic") to Italy, called by the names of their territories in Roman times. France had, in fact, changed into a conquering republic like ancient Rome—and as with Rome, the power of its conquering armies had grown to overshadow the authority of its republican institutions.

grades above him, and the far-ranging wars of the Republic offered him uncommon opportunities. Owing his rapid advancement to the overthrow of the Bourbon monarchy, he heartily declared himself a "son of the revolution." Napoleon was a master of politics and cunning, but there is no reason to doubt the sincerity of his professed devotion to revolutionary goals. He despised inherited and artificial privilege and was impatient with the inefficiency of the former government. He favored equality of opportunity, with careers (like his own) open to talent. Interpreting its meaning in his way, he readily embraced the revolutionary slogan of "Liberty, Equality, Fraternity."

Napoleon was a child of the Enlightenment as well as of the revolution—a skeptic, a rationalist, and a believer in progress. There was a strain of mysticism in him, too, an ever-present faith in himself as a "man of destiny." Viewing himself as above ordinary people, he felt free from ordinary morality. He was the intellectual and moral heir of Caesar, Machiavelli, and Voltaire. With a firm sense of drama and history, he built an image of himself as the creator of a new Pax Romana—a *Pax Francica* (French Peace). This image, in turn, was to be transformed into a living myth.

Stabilizing the Revolution. The new master of France had no use for either the old aristocracy or the new democracy. Though his various constitutions gave voting rights to all adult males, the voters elected only lists of candidates, from which his government named the legislators and officials. Napoleon saw to it that only men loyal to him and to his purposes were appointed and advanced in office. This democratic charade gave satisfaction to the populace and brought honor to his favorites, but Napoleon himself was the real power. Scornful of the democratic interpreters of Rousseau (p. 431–432), Napoleon presented *himself* as the spokesman of the general will of France.

It is inaccurate to conclude that Napoleon snuffed out democracy in France, for it had never existed there before. The great majority of the people—illiterate and uneducated—had enjoyed no political power under either the monarchy or the Republic. Napoleon's overthrow of the Directory meant that a nonnoble but propertied aristocracy had been displaced by an enlightened despot (pp. 431–432). Declaring a general political amnesty, he invited back to France all the émigrés who were willing to work faithfully for their homeland. He called to his service men of widely varying backgrounds (from royalist to regicide) who would cooperate in consolidating the new order.

His first task was to secure domestic peace and order. He arranged to have his opponents silenced by means of selective deportations, "exposure" of alleged plots, and the efficient work of his secret police. Catholic disaffection, springing from the earlier measures that had been taken against the Church, was dissolved by a dramatic concordat (agreement) with Pius VII in 1801. In this agreement, Napoleon formally accepted the fact that the Roman Catholic faith was the principal religion of the French. Church seminaries were reopened, and public religious processions were again permitted. Priests who had submitted to the revolutionary Civil Constitution were left to papal discipline, while those who had remained loyal to Rome were recognized as legitimate.

The pope, in return, accepted the new status of Catholicism in France. He dropped Rome's claims to confiscated church property and gave the French government the right to nominate bishops. He tried but failed to eliminate the toleration of all faiths that had been secured by the revolutionary regimes. Although the settlement was criticized by some on both sides of the dispute, it established a peace between state and Church in France that lasted for over a century.

Napoleon, privately a nonbeliever, recognized the importance of religion to the people and appreciated the advantage of having the Church on the side of the state. But he would not allow it to be the primary force in the shaping of citizens. The state, through its own schools, had to provide for the education and patriotic instruction of the young. He approved the earlier closing of Church schools by the National Convention and put into effect its comprehensive plans for a national educational system. By 1808, his subordinates had completed the structure of state-supported primary and

Fig. 11.4 Revolutionary Coronation. Jacques-Louis David's painting shows Napoleon's version of the thousand-year-old ceremony of coronation. The pope is present (behind Napoleon) to show the Church's approval, but to avoid any implication of receiving power from the Church, Napoleon has set the crown on his own head and is about to crown his empress, Josephine. A throng of cardinals, generals, ambassadors, courtiers, and relatives is depicted, including the emperor's mother (seated at top left). In fact, "Madame Mother," the only person to whom Napoleon did not dare to give orders, loathed her daughter-in-law and refused to attend the ceremony.

secondary schools as well as public institutions of higher learning. The entire system, supervised from Paris, remains the basis of French education to this day.

Napoleon also carried through the plans of revolutionary leaders for reorganizing French law and administration. His appointed commissions cut through the centuries-old accumulation of rules and regulations and brought to completion the Napoleonic Code. This collection of laws and principles relating to persons and property was the product of a gigantic labor of sorting, eliminating, and condensing. The code would become the new basis of law in major parts of Europe (and America) and is comparable to the ancient Roman codes that inspired it (p. 136). In later years, Napoleon regarded the code as his most durable accomplishment. While in exile he wrote, "My true glory is not in having won forty battles; Waterloo has effaced the memory of so many victories. What nothing can efface, what will live eternally, is my civil code."

Under Napoleon, the modern techniques of administering a centralized state took shape. The historic provinces of France, the local courts and offices, the administration of justice—all had been swept away by the revolution. Salaried officials ("prefects") responsible to the central government now presided over the cities and departments. The reform of public administration extended to taxation, expenditure, and money and banking; the day of the bureaucrat was at hand, and with it the equality of citizens before the law. All these changes, along with a grand design for public works, were in keeping with the rationalism (logical thinking) of the Enlightenment and with bourgeois ideas of efficiency.

The Struggle for Europe. If Napoleon brought peace and order at home, he caused turmoil abroad. At the very outset of the revolution, a sharp tension had developed between France and the rest of Europe. Any revolution, if it is a true revolution, creates such tension, for it is a threat to established social systems. The privileged classes of Europe, as we have seen, reacted in fear to the events of 1789; the French leaders, in turn, had declared war in the expectation of being attacked. In the warfare that followed, the armies of the revolution extended the frontiers of France to the Rhine River and to central Italy, but the outcome of the struggle was still undecided when Bonaparte took over in 1799.

His first move in foreign affairs was to break the Second Coalition of powers (Britain, Russia, Austria, Portugal, and Naples), which had come together against France. By swift military moves and skillful diplomacy, he had achieved this goal by 1802. For the first time in a decade, there was peace between France and its neighbors. But it proved to be an uneasy truce.

The French state now held more territory than the Bourbon kings had dreamed of, and Napoleon could have chosen a defensive military posture, against which his enemies might have struck in vain. But defense of the revolution merged, in Napoleon's mind, with personal and imperial glory, and he began to dream of dominating all of Europe (*Map 11.2*). His political and military moves led to another break with Britain, renewal of the war, and the rise of the Third Coalition against France.

Napoleon's genius and the confusion of his enemies brought him near to his goal. But the stubborn defiance of the British and their control of the seas, exhausting warfare against popular uprisings in Spain and Portugal, and the vast manpower and distances of Russia brought about his downfall.

A critical defeat for Napoleon was the bloody naval battle off Cape Trafalgar (1805), near the Atlantic entrance to the Mediterranean Sea. Ships of the British admiral, Lord Horatio Nelson, destroyed the French and allied fleets after Nelson himself was killed in battle. Compelled by this loss to abandon plans for invading Britain, Napoleon then tried to bring down the island nation through an economic blockade—ordering all ports on the Continent closed against British exports. The British took countermeasures, however, and his "Continental System" proved a failure by 1810.

Napoleon's second failure was in Spain, which he invaded in 1807. His troops easily crushed the regular Spanish army, but the people of that country and neighboring Portugal continued to resist the French, using the methods of what they called the *guerrilla,* or "little war." Their tactics were those of ambush, surprise, and retreat before superior forces, and they were backed by the British with money, supplies, and an expeditionary force of regulars. As a result, the guerrillas held down tens of thousands of troops that Napoleon badly needed elsewhere.

Frustrated in the west, Napoleon turned eastward in a land attack on Russia in 1812. This proved to be his fatal blunder. After initial victories, his "Grand Army" of French and allied troops was annihilated by the terrible winter, disease (typhus), and the stamina of the Russian guerrillas, using tactics similar to those of Spain and Portugal. Napoleon fought more battles after his disastrous retreat from Moscow, but his chance for final success was buried in the Russian snows (*Map 11.2*).

After abdicating as emperor in 1814, Napoleon was banished to the Mediterranean island of Elba. Escaping a short while later, he raised a new army in a foolish gamble against the odds of power. On the battlefield of Waterloo (in modern Belgium), his last minutes as a maker of history ran out, and he was again shipped away—this time to

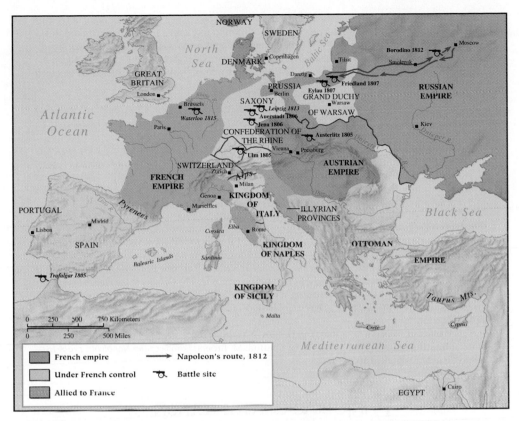

Map 11.2 Napoleon's Europe. By 1807, France had absorbed much of Germany and Italy; its satellite states stretched from Spain to Poland; Austria, Prussia, and Russia were its obedient allies; and only Britain stood against it. When the ancient Roman Republic had given way to a single ruler, Rome's conquests soon slowed and then stopped, and its emperors had ruled for centuries. Napoleon's conquests reached right across Europe, but his empire lasted only a dozen years. The battle names in Roman type mark Napoleonic victories, and those in italics are milestones of retreat.

the far-off isle of Saint Helena, in the South Atlantic Ocean, where he died in 1821, a man of not much more than fifty. But Napoleon had planted the seeds of a new order in Europe, and the Continent would never again be the same.

RECOMMENDED READING

The English Revolution: Parliamentary Supremacy and the Bill of Rights On revolutions in general, the following books are recommended. C. Brinton, *The Anatomy of Revolution* (1952), identifies common features of the English, American, French, and Russian revolutions; A. Todd, *Revolutions, 1789–1917* ((1998), does the same for all European revolutions during that period; and C. Tilly, *European Revolutions, 1492–1992* (1993), traces the course and impact of revolutions throughout modern times.

Specifically on the English Revolution, C. Hill, *The Century of Revolution, 1603–1641* (1980), concisely analyzes the seventeenth-century changes in government, economic, religious, and cultural life; M. Kishlansky, *A Monarchy Transformed: Britain, 1603–1714* (1997), is a readable and up-to-date survey, tracing both changes in the government and social order and the emergence of the

British state. N. Carlin, *The Causes of the English Civil War* (1999), is an excellent summary of the current thinking of historians on the process of revolution in England. On the strengths and weaknesses of two dominant rulers, see C. Haigh, *Elizabeth I* (1998), and P. Gaunt, *Oliver Cromwell* (1996).

Locke's political ideas are discussed in W. M. Spellman, *John Locke* (1997). W. Prest, *Albion Ascendant: English History, 1660–1815* (1997), describes all aspects of the state and society that emerged from the English Revolution.

The American Revolution and Constitution R. Middleton, *Colonial America* (1996), is a standard survey; J. A. Henretta and G. H. Nobles, *Evolution and Revolution: American Society, 1600–1820* (1987), deals with the social aspect of the emergence of the American nation.

On the period of the revolution, E. S. Morgan, *The Birth of the Republic, 1763–1789* (1977), is a classic brief account; a more recent introduction is C. Bonwick, *The American Revolution* (1991). R. Horsman, *The New Republic* (2000), describes the government and social order that emerged from the revolution. N. Risjord, *Thomas Jefferson* (1994), and the classic C. Becker, *The Declaration of Independence* (1922), deal briefly with the ideas of the Declaration and its drafter.

The French Revolution: "Liberty, Equality, Fraternity" N. Hampson, *A Social History of the French Revolution* (1963) (to 1799), and J. D. Popkin, *A Short History of the French Revolution* (1995) (to 1815 and after), are excellent introductions to events in France; N. Hampson, *The First European Revolution, 1776–1815* (1979), and P. M. Pilbeam, *Themes in Modern European History, 1780–1830* (1995), cover the revolution's impact throughout Europe. G. Lefebvre, *The Coming of the French Revolution* (1947), is a noted work by an outstanding scholar; W. Doyle, *The Origins of the French Revolution* (1999), is more recent. W. Doyle, *The Oxford History of the French Revolution* (1999), is a more detailed account.

J. Hardman, *Robespierre* (1999), and G. Ellis, *Napoleon* (1997), are brief biographies of two of the dominating figures of the revolutionary period. M. Broers, *Europe Under Napoleon, 1799–1815* (1990), is a more detailed account.

INFOTRAC COLLEGE EDITION

Visit the source collections at **http://academic.cengage.com/infotrac**, and use the Search function with the following key terms:

American Revolution	Rousseau	Napoleonic Wars
French Revolution	Napoleon	

WESTERN CIVILIZATION RESOURCES

Visit the Brief History of the Western World Companion Web Site for resources specific to this textbook:

http://history.wadsworth.com/greerbrief09/

Also, the CD in the back of this book and the World History Resources Center at **http://history.wadsworth.com/west_civ/** offer a variety of tools to help you succeed in this course, including access to quizzes; images; documents; interactive simulations, maps, and timelines; movie explorations; and a wealth of other sources.

CHAPTER 12

Conservatism, Liberalism
and Nationalism

OVERVIEW

In the first half of the nineteenth century, the struggles that accompanied and followed the French Revolution led to the rise of three new ideologies (secular systems of belief) that were also international political movements: conservatism, liberalism, and nationalism. Out of the interaction of all three, a new Western government and social order gradually began to develop.

Conservatism was the instinctive belief of rulers, nobles, clergy, and many of lower rank whom the turmoil of the French Revolution had turned against Enlightenment ideals. Conservatives proclaimed the virtues of tradition and community, and the limits on people's ability to change the world or govern themselves. At first, conservatives tried to uphold the traditional order by repression and force, but in time, they turned from resisting change to trying to guide it. They formed political parties that competed with liberals and nationalists for seats in representative assemblies. Rulers, for their part, hoping to avoid revolution and outdo one another in their continuing rivalries, reinvented themselves as leaders of social reform and national power.

Liberalism was the ideology of those who still supported Enlightenment ideals of reason and progress in spite of revolutionary turmoil. Middle-class business and professional people, as well as others of both higher and lower standing, were often liberals. They trusted that if individuals were given equal chances, control over the actions of governments, and the maximum freedom to pursue their own interests, the result would be a prosperous, harmonious, and efficient society. As a means of bringing this about, liberals put their faith in the British and American model of representative institutions, legally guaranteed rights and freedoms, and legally binding constitutions.

The rise of *nationalism* was a result of changes that revolution and liberalism brought to the long-standing Western tradition of different nations sharing a common civilization. Revolutionaries and liberals acted in the name of the united and self-governing "people," but always "the people" meant the English, the American, or the French people—in other words, the people making up a specific nation. Self-government and unity, it seemed, were rights of nations just as much as of peoples. This ideal of the united and independent nation-state soon spread to the Germans and Italians, large but divided nations to whom it offered equality with other large nations like the French. It also appealed to smaller nations living under imperial rule like the Poles, the Greeks, and European settler communities in Latin America, to whom it held out the hope of developing their national cultures and interests as they saw fit.

All three political movements were influenced by a wider cultural trend, that of *Romanticism*. The Romantic movement began as a rebellion against some aspects of the thought and art of the Enlightenment. It valued emotion and imagination above reason, community above individualism, and spontaneity above established rules. Romantic thinkers stressed the limits of reason and observation as ways of knowing the world, or they looked for some higher reason to be found in history or nature rather than individual humans. Writers, painters, and musicians celebrated such themes as the drama of nature, the passions and torments of sensitive souls, the horrors of war, or the fleeting joys of youth. Romantics might be liberals or conservatives, depending on whether they saw untamed human fancy and feeling as a hope for the future or an endangered tradition of the past. They might be deeply religious or enthusiastically nationalist, according to whether they believed in Christianity or the nation as the guardian of community traditions.

In the middle of the nineteenth century, the dismantling of the old power structure gathered speed. Eastern European serfdom, New World slavery, and the legal privileges of nobles and clergy were all abolished. Latin American empires disintegrated into independent nations, Germany and Italy were unified into powerful nation-states, and many subject nations of eastern European multinational empires laid claim to independence. In nearly every European country, rulers yielded a larger or smaller share of power to more or less widely elected representative assemblies. The original revolutionary countries, Britain, the United States, and France, evolved toward full democracy.

These changes came about through continued turmoil of revolution and war, as well as through peaceful reforms. Liberalism and nationalism benefited some social groups and nations but harmed others, and often the result was bitter social resentments and international power struggles. In only two major countries, Britain and the United States, did a generally accepted new power structure arise. Elsewhere, the shape of the future Western social, political, and international order was still uncertain and contested. As it had developed so far, it mainly reflected the ideals of liberalism and nationalism. Would it live up to these ideals, or would it bring social, ethnic, and international conflict on a scale never seen before?

The Conservative Reaction

While Napoleon was making his dash from Elba to final defeat in the spring of 1815, the victorious powers were assembled at the glittering Congress of Vienna. Here the crowned heads of Europe and their chief ministers were trying to restore the Continent to what it had been before the revolutionary disturbances. But Napoleon had planted the seeds of a new order in Europe, and the Continent would never again be the same.

METTERNICH AND THE "CONCERT OF EUROPE"

Though there were many signers of the settlement of 1815, the management of the treaty was in the hands of the four major powers that had brought about Napoleon's defeat: Britain, Russia, Prussia, and Austria. Prince Clemens von Metternich, the chief minister of Austria, was the leading spirit of the conference. An aristocrat of distinguished family, he had been a career diplomat in the service of the Habsburg dynasty (p. 317). He had demonstrated his shrewdness when Napoleon was at the height of power (1810) by arranging a marriage between the conqueror and Maria Louisa, daughter of the Austrian emperor. Then, after Napoleon's disastrous defeat in Russia, Metternich threw Austria's weight against him. Though beaten many times by the French, Austria thus came out of the wars in a victor's role; and Metternich, to clinch the advantage, persuaded the allies to hold the peace congress in Vienna, the Austrian capital.

Metternich's cunning was matched by that of the clever Prince Talleyrand. Talleyrand was loyal only to himself and to France. He had served as a bishop under Louis XVI, as a statesman of the revolution, and as Napoleon's foreign minister. When it appeared that the French emperor was overreaching himself, Talleyrand offered secret aid to Napoleon's enemies abroad, thereby preparing a place for himself in the postwar government. When the emperor fell, Talleyrand urged the victors to restore the Bourbon rulers in France; this, he explained, would follow the principle of legitimacy (legality). He hoped, by applying that principle, to hold for France the territories it had possessed before the revolution.

The allies accepted the principle of legitimacy and restoration of the Bourbons. The heir to the throne of France was King Louis XVIII, the eldest surviving brother of the executed king, who had been living as an émigré in England. (The late monarch's young son, who had died in 1795, was considered by the royalists as Louis XVII.) The Bourbon ruler was brought back to Paris in 1814 by courtesy of the victors and at once rewarded Talleyrand by appointing him foreign minister.

At Vienna, Talleyrand played skillfully on the differences among the four principal victors, thus giving France, the defeated nation, a role in the settlement. The chief concerns of the conference were to restore, so far as practicable, the legitimate holdings of all titled rulers and the European balance of power. That balance, which had been established by the Peace of Westphalia (Map 9.2, p. 399), had aimed to secure the independence of European states by preventing one or more of them from gaining too much power. In the course of the Vienna conference, for example, Talleyrand joined Metternich and Lord Castlereagh of Britain in a secret pledge to go to war should Prussia and Russia carry through their joint plans for expansion in central Europe. When word of the agreement leaked out, a compromise plan was proposed and accepted.

The Congress of Vienna by no means restored the borders of Europe exactly as they had been before 1789; it provided territorial compensations for the states that had contributed the most to toppling Napoleon. Russia, for example, was allowed to take Finland from Sweden, and Sweden was awarded Norway in exchange. (Norway regained its independence in 1905.) The redrawn map of Europe (Map 12.1) was to remain in effect, save for minor alterations, for half a century. The most unstable boundaries proved to be those in central Europe. There Napoleon had given the final blow to the Holy Roman Empire in 1806 and had merged many of the smaller German states into a league of minor kingdoms known as the Confederation of the Rhine. The Congress kept this

Map 12.1 Europe After the Congress of Vienna. The peacemakers of 1815 tried to restore the old balance of power among European monarchies in hopes of preventing further wars and revolutions. Many small states in Germany and Italy were restored, and France itself lost none of its eighteenth-century territory (*Map 10.1*, p. 412). But in central Europe, instead of an empire that called itself Roman, there was now a confederation that called itself German, and within it, Prussia was far larger than before. A new Germany, a new Europe, and new wars and revolutions lay ahead.

general arrangement, which was joined by Austria and Prussia and renamed the German Confederation. Subject mainly to Austrian control, this grouping forestalled for the moment Prussian desires for dominance in Germany.

Metternich was realistic enough to know that he could not completely undo the effects of the French Revolution. In France, the restored King Louis felt it necessary to grant a constitution that made the country a *limited* monarchy. The legal, administrative, clerical, and educational reforms of the revolution were retained. And beyond the borders of France, the ideas of liberalism could not be altogether erased. Still less could Metternich prevent the rising sentiment of nationalism, which had been strengthened by the revolution's stress on "fraternity" and by Napoleon. The peoples of Germany and Italy, especially, were impressed by the power and accomplishments of the French nation-in-arms and exhilarated by the sense of national solidarity that came from resistance to the French conquerors. All across Europe, patriotic societies arose to champion the cause of national unity and independence.

But for the time being, liberal and nationalistic movements were kept down. The privileged classes and the rulers of multinational states (p. 416) saw these movements as threats to their interests and agreed at Vienna to keep a close eye on them. Metternich arranged a "Concert of Europe" (in actuality, a Quadruple Alliance of Austria, Prussia, Russia, and Britain) that would use diplomacy and force against moves to change boundaries or social systems. Accordingly, several conferences ("congresses") of those states under Metternich's guidance were called to meet threats to the established order. Until the middle of the nineteenth century, the so-called Metternich System thus provided a type of collective security for the nations of Europe.

THE REJECTION OF REVOLUTION AND RATIONALISM: BURKE

Opposition to liberal ideas found wide support among ordinary people as well as intellectuals. This was natural enough, for Napoleon, who personified the triumph of the revolution, had fallen. Victory had passed to the defenders of privilege and the old order, and the ideals of the Enlightenment had been dimmed by the realities of revolution, politics, and war. Many who had sympathized with the ideals now recoiled from the bloody cost of attempting to put them into practice. The liberals, who stressed science and reason, equality and democracy, now stood in opposition to those who stressed tradition and sentiment, aristocracy and authority—the conservatives.

One of the ablest spokesmen of the conservative point of view was the British thinker and statesman Edmund Burke. Opposing from the beginning the underlying principles of the revolution, he had feared that those ideas might win favor in his homeland. His *Reflections on the Revolution in France* appeared in 1790 and has remained to this day an important statement of conservative principles.

Burke's first point of attack was the doctrine of natural rights, which John Locke (pp. 450–451) and the revolutionary leaders had used to justify their actions. The liberties of the English people, wrote Burke, were those that had been slowly forged in the fire of history; he saw them as part of a specified "inheritance," handed down from generation to generation. And that inheritance was by no means equal for all. The king, the lords, and every other group within the English social body had the right to enjoy the particular privileges and liberties passed on to it from "a long line of ancestors." Burke thus expressed his belief in aristocracy and attacked efforts made in the name of equality to interfere with "legitimate" privilege.

Burke warned against undue reliance on human reason. He felt that each person's private stock of reason is pitifully small and therefore a poor guide to action. He much preferred the wisdom deposited in the "general bank and capital of nations and ages"—by which he meant tradition. It is arrogant for reform-minded thinkers, said Burke, to try to reconstruct institutions out of their own minds; such "progress" as might result from their efforts would prove a cruel disappointment. It is far better, he concluded, for people to follow the "prejudices" (established convictions) that bind them to tried and tested institutions.

Burke reserved his bitterest scorn for the Lockean-Jeffersonian belief in the right and benefit of revolution. Denouncing the social atomism of both Hobbes and Locke (p. 418), he thought of individuals as parts of a larger organism—society. He saw the state as a divine creation, binding past, present, and future generations. He referred to it as a partnership embracing all human purposes and not to be broken by individual human wills.

The state, being sacred, must be regarded with awe and reverence. It should not be "hacked to pieces" by would-be innovators; such recklessness can lead only to anarchy. And, Burke felt, the absence of firm social control is "ten thousand times worse" than the blindest and most stubborn government. A devout Anglican, he held to the doctrine of original sin and rejected the Enlightenment faith in human goodness and progress. Only by strict social discipline, he believed, is the individual made decent and civilized. And once restraints are broken, people fall back to beastlike behavior. Thus, Burke argued, revolution leads to an intolerable chaos, which can be ended only by some form of despotism.

Burke did not think, however, that institutions should remain frozen. His view of society as an organism led him to think in biological terms. Useless growths should be cut off, and new shoots and branches should be allowed to develop. He was, therefore, a flexible conservative. He even stated that conditions in a given society might become such that a resort to revolution would be permissible. But it should never be a calculated action. Mystically (and dangerously), he declared that the justification for revolution must be "the first and supreme necessity only, a necessity that is not chosen, but chooses, a necessity paramount to deliberation, that admits no discussion, and demands no evidence." In other words, he placed his ultimate reliance on intuition (inner conviction), thus giving his approval to irrational social action.

Other writers soon joined in the assault on Enlightenment beliefs. The English clergyman Thomas Malthus attacked the idea of human perfectibility, which had been put forward by some eighteenth-century writers (pp. 430–431). Noting the general misery of the poor, Malthus found the explanation in the pressure of population growth. Because of the sexual urge, said Malthus in *An Essay on the Principle of Population* (1798), people tend to increase faster than food supplies. Population growth is held down mainly by the "positive checks" of starvation, disease, and war. Seeing no way out of this condition (save the unlikely prospect of sexual restraint), Malthus predicted continued suffering for the human race. And without a favorable balance between food and people, the material foundation for happiness (and perfectibility) is missing. Malthus thus called attention to one of the root problems facing the modern world.

A NEW PHILOSOPHICAL SYNTHESIS: KANT, HEGEL

The conservative reaction was also strong on the European continent, where the intellectuals of the Enlightenment were held responsible for the unhappy events of revolution and war. After 1815, liberal writers and critics were regarded with official hostility and general suspicion. The frequent persecution of authors and the suppression of their works were products of the haunting fear of new social upheavals. Defenders of the restored order concluded also that the weakening of religious faith had eased the way to social subversion. They therefore encouraged the revival of religious fervor that had arisen as a reaction to the secularism of the Enlightenment and the revolution. The Roman Catholic Church, traditionally conservative, played a leading role in this renewal of piety, morality, and respect for authority.

European philosophy was affected even more deeply than religion by the reaction against eighteenth-century thought. A German professor, Immanuel Kant, was a key figure in the shift from the outlook of the Enlightenment to that of the nineteenth century. Born in East Prussia, he spanned in his long lifetime (1724–1804) the confident period of science and rationalism as well as the aftermath of disenchantment. His keen, analytical mind, coupled with a profound moral and religious sense, gave his philosophy its special shape.

Deeply impressed by the achievements of Newtonian science (pp. 423–424), Kant retained much of the rationalist spirit and methodology. However, he set limits on its use and marked off areas of knowledge where religion and moral conviction applied. It was the skepticism of the eighteenth-century Scottish philosopher David Hume that first awakened Kant to the limitations of reason and observation as means of knowing. Hume had argued that science has no way of *proving* causal relationships; it can only note that a certain event is *preceded* by another. This relationship in time and space may be witnessed over and over again; yet the idea of causation remains a suggestion of the mind, not a proven fact.

Kant carried the point further, asserting that even "perceived objects" are in large measure a reflection of the mind. Kant criticized Locke's belief that knowledge comes from experience, received through the senses (p. 429). He insisted that our minds, independent of experience, establish certain internal structures, which impose their patterns on our perceptions. For example, we have the concept of "time"—which cannot be perceived and is therefore mental rather than experiential. Yet this concept, along with many others, controls and puts in order all our observations.

From this Kant concluded that scientific knowledge, though highly useful, is not knowledge of the "real" world but a creation of the human mind, drawn from bits of observation. While science thus provides a restricted means of knowing about material things, it cannot even ask the questions that go beyond material things. On such issues as the existence of God, immortality of the soul, and moral responsibility, science is mute. In these vital matters, Kant declared in his *Critique of Pure Reason* (1781), the individual must rely chiefly on conscience and intuition.

Following Kant's lead, German philosophy in the nineteenth century reached its fullest development in the work of another professor, Georg Wilhelm Friedrich Hegel, an energetic and imaginative man who helped make the University of Berlin a center of philosophical activity. In response to the doubts and contradictions current among serious thinkers, he attempted to reconcile opposing philosophical tendencies and bring them into a unified system. He found that approach in the historical method.

Hegel steeped himself in the study of history, convinced that true understanding of any subject—whether politics, art, or religion—can be found only through examining its historical development. (This idea came to be known as *historicism*.) He saw the general history of an age as more than a collection of events; politics, art, and religion are related parts of a cultural whole—guided by a unifying Reason, or Spirit (*Zeitgeist*), which is itself the fulfillment in time of a divine and logical Idea.

The Idea may be invisible to most individuals before it takes shape as historical happening. Hegel illustrates this point by declaring, "Great revolutions which strike the eye at a glance [like the French Revolution] must have been preceded by a quiet and secret revolution in the Spirit of the Age [*Zeitgeist*], a revolution not visible to every eye. . . . It is a lack of acquaintance with this spiritual revolution which makes the resulting changes astonishing." The human individual, so precious to the philosophes (pp. 425, 430), was reduced by Hegel to a relatively minor role in history. Great leaders, acting on their own purposes and passions, can nevertheless accomplish notable deeds; political genius consists in identifying oneself with a developing idea. In this way, Hegel would explain the greatness of a Caesar, a Jefferson, or a Napoleon.

Hegel's thought is related to that of Plato, with its Doctrine of Ideas, and that of the Christian philosopher Augustine, who had also seen history as the unfolding of divine will (pp. 81–82, 179). Hegel's special contribution was his development of the notion of *dialectic*—the conflict of opposing forces—in history. He defined those forces as opposing ideas, which become ever more inclusive at successive stages of the struggle. The dominant idea at any given stage he defined as the *thesis,* which (because it is imperfect and incomplete) calls forth a negative or opposing idea—its *antithesis.* In the conflict between the two, neither is entirely destroyed; the opposing elements are reconciled and absorbed into a higher idea, the *synthesis.*

As an example of his theory, Hegel suggested that the idea of oriental despotism had been opposed by the Greco-Roman idea of limited freedom (*aristocracy*); both were being superseded by the German-Christian idea of universal freedom under monarchy. His concept of freedom was an *ordered* freedom governed by law. Hegel in this sense glorified the state and taught that it was approaching perfection in the Prussian monarchy of his day (p. 413). Though discarding the eighteenth-century concept of progress and reform as naive, he regarded the dialectic of history as leading surely to a freer and happier condition for humanity. (This condition would not include equality for women, whom he regarded as, by nature, inferior to men.)

Since Hegel saw the development of ideas as the guiding force and the underlying reality of history, he is usually classified (like Plato) as a philosophical idealist—as distinguished from a materialist. "Whatever is rational is real, and whatever is real is rational." But he did not deny material existence; he merely subordinated it to the superior reality of ideas and logic. Human reason, in the eighteenth-century sense, he discounted, putting in its place the Reason of history. Hegel insisted that history provides its own solutions to problems that even the wisest of thinkers can understand only dimly.

Hegel's thought was a blend of many elements that had previously been regarded as contradictory. It assigned value, on the one hand, to science, reason, and individual freedom—and on the other hand, to faith, intuition, and authority. As might be expected, this comprehensive philosophy had a broad appeal: Hegel's books provided stimulus and support for a wide range of ideas. After his death in 1831, his disciples branched off in many directions.

The Romantic Spirit in Literature, Art, and Music

The reaction against the Enlightenment showed itself not only in philosophy but also in the arts, where it was to take on the name of Romanticism. The Romantic movement included an extraordinary variety of creative expressions in the life and work of individual artists, some of whom were political and social conservatives, while others were supporters of liberalism.

ROMANTICISM IN LITERATURE

Appeal to the Heart: Rousseau. The pioneer of Romanticism was Jean-Jacques Rousseau, whose impact on the French Revolution we have already mentioned (p. 462). Though he lived during the Enlightenment, Rousseau's career was in part a revolt against the dominant thought of his age.

A man of little formal education or personal discipline, Rousseau had reacted spontaneously against the eighteenth-century emphasis on reason and science. Through a stormy career, which we know largely through his own *Confessions,* he found time to write hundreds of letters, as well as essays and books. His attacks on rationalism struck home not because he wrote from deep knowledge, but because of the power of his language and his appeal to inner experience. Science, he declared, gives people knowledge that they are better off without. The only knowledge worth having is knowledge of virtue (moral goodness)—and for this, science is not needed. The principles of virtue are "engraved on every heart."

Readers who were unmoved by the theories of science and philosophy responded warmly to Rousseau's emotional outpourings. In his novel *The New Héloïse* (1761), the hero is madly in love with one of his pupils, but she must marry another. The two frustrated souls experience many temptations and torments that end only after the death of the heroine. The theme of passion and suffering, of morbid self-examination, became a mark of Romantic prose and poetry in the nineteenth century.

Another theme of *The New Héloïse* is Rousseau's criticism of sophisticated society and his glorification of nature. The hero of the novel seeks relief from his anguish by wandering through a wilderness. This provides the author with an opportunity to fashion eloquent word pictures of lakes, mountains, and flowers, which inspired such Romantic nature poets as William Wordsworth. Rousseau's Romantic worship of wildlife also inspired the "back to nature" movement of the nineteenth and twentieth centuries, with its love of hiking and camping as ways of bringing one nearer to earth, rocks, and scenery unspoiled by human beings.

Rousseau's individualism and his rejection of imposed patterns of behavior are best expressed in his famous novel *Émile* (1762). From infancy to manhood, the fictional Émile is cared for and taught in a manner contrary to the educational practices of the eighteenth century. Rather than forcing the boy into a succession of studies corresponding to the "knowledge" of the day, his teacher encourages Émile to learn for himself. When the need or desire strikes him, the youngster asks for instruction in reading, writing, and nature studies. Meanwhile, he lives a spare, simple, athletic life in the country. The teacher refrains from punishing his pupil for destructive acts, confident that such errors will be corrected through the boy's own experience of consequent loss. There are no naturally bad boys; real vices are learned from "civilized" elders.

Rousseau held that girls as well as boys deserved a sound education. But it must be suited to the female role in life, which he sharply distinguished from the male role. In *Émile,* he states that girls should be taught only what they will need as women, namely:

> To please men, be useful to them, and make themselves loved and respected by them; to educate them when they are young, care for them when grown, counsel and console them, and make life agreeable and sweet to them. . . . The search for abstract and speculative truths, principles, and scientific laws is beyond the capacity of women; all their studies therefore ought to be of a practical sort.

There is much of Rabelais (pp. 357–358) in Rousseau's ideas about educational methods, but Rousseau wrote seriously rather than playfully, as Rabelais did. His permissiveness appealed to Romantic individualists and impressed a number of educational reformers. Rousseau's religious sentiments, too, influenced succeeding generations. His was a Romantic brand of Deism, rejecting theology and sacred books. As taught to Émile (at the appropriate time), this religion consisted of a simple faith in God and immortality. All that needs to be known about the deity and his commandments, wrote Rousseau, can be found in one's heart and in the study of nature.

Rousseau's insistence on the divinity and beauty of nature and on unrestricted human emotion was echoed by the writers of the early nineteenth century, and their typical means of expression was lyric poetry. As a literary form, lyric poetry traces back to ancient Greece—to Solon and Sappho (pp. 85–86). It was perfectly suited to the needs of Romantic writers, who desired to tell others of their innermost feelings and visions. Prose forms, especially the novel, also flourished, but many leading novelists were also poets.

English and Scottish Romantic Writers. William Wordsworth was one of the first Romantic poets; his most moving verses deal with the excitement and meaning of wild nature. But Wordsworth sensed something beyond the colors and movements of a landscape. His perceptions of nature opened the way to moral and spiritual insights, and partly for this reason, he shared Rousseau's contempt for formal learning as well as his passion for nature. In "The Tables Turned," he wrote:

> Books! 'tis a dull and endless strife:
> Come, hear the woodland linnet,
> How sweet his music! on my life,
> There's more of wisdom in it. . . .
> One impulse from a vernal wood
> May teach you more of man,
> Of moral evil and of good,
> Than all the sages can.
> Sweet is the lore which Nature brings;
> Our meddling intellect
> Misshapes the beauteous forms of things—
> We murder to dissect.
> Enough of Science and of Art;
> Close up those barren leaves;
> Come forth, and bring with you a heart
>   That watches and receives.

Beauty, youth, and rebellion were common themes of three other poets—Keats, Byron, and Shelley—each of whom died young. John Keats saluted the ancient Greek ideal of beauty in a poem honoring a painted vase ("Ode on a Grecian Urn," 1820). Addressing this classical work of art, Keats concludes with these words:

> When old age shall this generation waste,
> Thou shalt remain, in midst of other woe
> Than ours, a friend to man, to whom thou say'st,
> "Beauty is truth, truth beauty,"—that is all
> Ye know on earth, and all ye need to know.

Lord Byron (George Noel Gordon) lived a turbulent life of passion and adventure, corresponding to the Romantic quality of his writings. He died in 1824 at the age of thirty-six while taking part in the Greek war for independence from the Turks (p. 491). His famous poem *Don Juan* includes a stanza (canto 4:12) that proclaims his admiration for youth and his contempt for life "after thirty":

> "Whom the gods love die young" was said of yore,
> And many deaths do they escape by this:
> The death of friends, and that which slays even more—
> The death of friendship, love, youth, all that is,

> Except mere breath; and since the silent shore
> Awaits at last even those who longest miss
> The old archer's shafts, perhaps the early grave
> Which men weep over may be meant to save.

Byron's young friend, Percy Bysshe Shelley, also lived an unconventional life—devoted to the cause of unrestricted personal freedom. Expelled from Oxford University because of his open profession of atheism (p. 427), Shelley continued to rebel against all forms of authority. He spent his last years in Italy, where he composed his most eloquent poems. In one of these ("Hellas," 1822), he ends by expressing anguish over the human sufferings of the past and hope that a better world may be dawning (signaled by the Greek war for independence):

> Oh, cease! must hate and death return?
> Cease! must men kill and die?
> Cease! drain not to its dregs the urn
> Of bitter prophecy.
> The world is weary of the past,
> Oh, might it die or rest at last!

Shortly after writing this poem, at age thirty, Shelley drowned while sailing in the Mediterranean Sea.

Shelley's young wife, Mary Wollstonecraft Shelley, survived him. She, too, was a Romantic writer and an active feminist. (Her mother, Mary Wollstonecraft, had written *A Vindication of the Rights of Woman* in 1792 as an answer to the sexist views of Jean-Jacques Rousseau.) Mary Shelley's best-known book is *Frankenstein*, the story of a medical student who creates and brings to life a manlike monster.

Though Romantic writers sometimes focused on themes of horror, mystery, and death, they more often wrote about broader human experiences. One of the most popular prose writers in Britain was Sir Walter Scott, whose works made him a Scottish national hero. He created the historical novel, choosing the Middle Ages and the turbulent border country between Scotland and England as the setting for many of his books. Novels such as *Waverley* (1814) and *Ivanhoe* (1820) show the drama, color, and imagination that marked his best romances.

Goethe. In Germany, the leading literary figure was Johann Wolfgang von Goethe. Born in the middle of the eighteenth century, he grew up during the Enlightenment and lived on into the age of Romanticism. Goethe came from a well-to-do family of lawyers and administrators; his "conversion" to Romanticism took place while he was studying law at Strasbourg. He later became a member of the court of Saxe-Weimar, a small German duchy. He remained for most of his life in Weimar, the capital of the duchy, where the duke's generosity allowed him freedom to study, travel, and write.

A man of high intelligence and feeling, Goethe wrote beyond the limitations of most Romantic authors. But his personal life was notably romantic—a series of passionate love affairs, many of which he described in his writings. Goethe's lyric poetry reflects his fascination with love, nature, and death. In prose, the most striking expression of his youthful Romanticism is *The Sorrows of Young Werther* (1774), which describes the extravagant sufferings of a forlorn hero tortured by frustrated passion.

Faust, a dramatic poem on which Goethe worked during most of his long life, parallels the conflicts and growth that took place in his personal development. Part One, published in 1808, retells the Renaissance legend of a learned professor, Doctor Faust, who bargained his soul with the devil in return for youth and power. (This portion was set to music by several Romantic composers.) Part Two, which was not published until after the author's death in 1832, carries Faust on a kind of philosophical excursion in search of man's ultimate purpose and way to happiness. The soul of the hero, in Goethe's poem, is saved at last because he loves God and humanity and tries, in spite of errors, to serve both. Goethe's Faust is a literary model of "modern" man—the individual who seeks to understand and experience the lowest and the highest and to harmonize sensual and spiritual urges.

Pushkin. The Romantic spirit in literature also brought forth an impressive response from Russian writers. As a result of Russia's turning toward the West (p. 415), eighteenth-century Russian literature had been largely imitative of the French. In the nineteenth century, however, it developed its own character. Alexander Pushkin (who died in a duel in 1837, at the age of thirty-eight) was the first Russian writer to command serious attention in western Europe with his Romantic poems, plays, and short stories. In his homeland, he is still revered both as a writer of genius whose own short life was filled with Romantic passion and adventure, and as the forefather of modern Russian literature in general.

REBELLION AND ROMANCE IN PAINTING

Artistic styles in painting developed more slowly than in literature. The eighteenth century was the era of the elegant, frivolous Rococo style (pp. 436–438), and classicism first appeared in the era of the Revolution, when French painters turned away from the aristocratic Rococo and sought inspiration in ancient Roman and Greek sculpture.

The classical revival in French painting may be said to have begun with the exhibition in 1785 of a heroic painting of Roman warriors in the *Oath of the Horatii* (*Fig. 12.1*), by Jacques-Louis David. David, a middle-class man who sympathized with the radical political reforms of the period, was elected to the National Convention (p. 464) and helped abolish the royal Academy of Painting. The leaders of the revolution regarded art primarily as an instrument of propaganda; they destroyed the academy because it upheld aristocratic traditions. In its place they established the École des Beaux-Arts (School of Fine Arts), which adopted the classical style and sought to impose it on all French painters.

David reached the height of his influence later, under Napoleon. The emperor thought classicism suitable to his role as a "modern Caesar" and wanted the art and architecture of his reign to be different from the Baroque and Rococo styles of earlier French rulers. As "First Painter of the Empire," David made portraits of the emperor, supervised the national galleries, arranged imperial ceremonies, and saw to the licensing of artists who wished to exhibit their works. After Napoleon's fall, David was ordered into exile, and the Academy of Painting was restored.

Classicism remained influential in both art and architecture, but already during the revolutionary era a reaction began against the values of the eighteenth century in the visual arts, as earlier in philosophy and literature.

Romantic painters everywhere revolted against classicism, against official styles of any sort, and against academic rules of painting. One of the earliest rebels was Fran-

© Réunion des Musées Nationaux/Art Resource, NY

Fig. 12.1 *Oath of the Horatii.* The Horatius brothers swear on their swords, held aloft by their father, to fight to the death as Roman champions against three brothers from a rival city who are their relatives by marriage. Jacques-Louis David emphasizes the hard determination of the men by contrasting them with the soft and languishing women of the household, who mourn the coming bloodshed. The figures are "frozen" as if carved in marble, giving the picture's message of manly patriotism above womanly family feeling the timelessness of a classical statue.

cisco Goya, a Spanish contemporary of David. Heir to the rich legacy of Spanish painting of the Baroque period (pp. 388–392), Goya preferred it to the restraints of classicism. However, he did not paint in the traditional aristocratic manner, which aimed to ornament or glorify. His portraits of Spanish royalty and nobility are proofs of his extraordinary honesty and powers of observation.

Goya's active social conscience also made him sensitive to the tyranny, civil strife, and poverty that he saw on every hand in his native land. In his painting *The Third of May, 1808* (*Fig. 12.2*), he presented an execution scene in the streets of Madrid; Napoleon's soldiers had been attacked by civilians the day before and are shown making their reprisal. Goya chose to dramatize the horror of war and the human capacity for brutality—a side of war that David had preferred to ignore.

The Romantic style achieved its fullest expression in France during the generation after Napoleon's downfall. Its most brilliant exponent was Eugène Delacroix. After a classical education, he decided to become a painter and began his training in Paris, which now eclipsed Rome as the art center of Europe. He became almost at once an enthusiastic convert to the new style. "If by Romanticism is meant the free expression of my personal feelings, my aloofness from the standardized types of paintings prescribed by the Schools, and my dislike of academic formulas," he wrote later, "I must confess that not only am I a Romantic but that I already was one at the age of fifteen!"

Fig. 12.2 *The Third of May, 1808, at Madrid.* Massacres were traditionally depicted as panoramas (*Fig. 7.1*, p. 293), but Goya focuses on a single moment of horror. A group of prisoners faces a French firing squad. A minute before, they were among the background figures; in the foreground, we see what will become of them in another second. The night sky, the buildings and hillside, and the line of soldiers bar the viewer's eye from escaping the central scene. In an era of revolutionary violence, Goya has found a new way to depict man's inhumanity to man.

Delacroix first gained public attention in 1822 through the showing of his *Dante and Virgil in Hell.* This scene, illustrating a passage from Dante (p. 275), shows a group of tormented individuals writhing in the dark waters of hell's River Styx. Friendly critics saw in this work suggestions of the figures of Michelangelo and the colors of Rubens, the opposites of classical serenity. In his historical painting *Entry of the Crusaders into Constantinople* (*Fig. 12.3*), Delacroix raises the emotions of the viewer by contrasting the triumphant invaders with their crouching victims (in the Fourth Crusade, p. 282). Responding to the Romantic taste for the exotic (foreign), Delacroix once traveled to Algiers, in Africa. Some of his most popular works, paintings of lion hunts and of the Muslim court and concubines, grew out of that experience.

The love of nature, which was a central feature of Romanticism, was best expressed in painting by the English artists J. M. W. Turner and John Constable. Turner's paintings are visionary rather than realistic. A superb colorist, he gave his landscapes and seascapes a sense of grandeur and mystery. He often used a sentimental subject for his canvases, as in *The Fighting Téméraire* (*Fig. 12.4*), painted in 1839. English patriots were stirred by this picture of the ghostly *Téméraire,* a sailing ship of Lord Nelson's battle fleet (p. 470), being towed away for destruction. It is led to its inglorious fate by a squat black tug, symbol of the triumph of steam over sail, iron over timber, efficiency over beauty. Turner showed the ship against a sweep of sky and sea. The time, symbolically, is sunset, and a reddish light is cast on the water. Turner's imaginative treatment of na-

Fig. 12.3 *Entry of the Crusaders into Constantinople.* Delacroix excelled in the Romantic art of creating "atmosphere." Here, like Goya, he depicts a grim event, but actual brutality is only the background to a menacing group of horsemen advancing on cowering captives. The sky is smoke-filled, the horsemen drag other captives along, and the foremost horse—no noble beast in the tradition of equestrian images (*Fig. 8.7*, p. 350)—viciously threatens two captives. Delacroix leaves the viewer to imagine what exactly may happen next, but everything suggests that it will not be good.

ture proved extremely popular; he sold hundreds of paintings and etchings and built up a fortune during his lifetime.

Constable, Turner's contemporary, approached nature in a different manner. His love of the English countryside was akin to that of his good friend, the poet Wordsworth, but he studied nature with the eye of a scientist, and though he finished his canvases indoors, he worked from oil sketches prepared in the open. His paintings were so strikingly different from the commonplace studio landscapes of the period that they created a sensation at first showing. When *The Hay Wain* (*Fig. 12.5*) was exhibited in Paris in 1821, French painters were astonished by its truth to nature, and many set out to imitate Constable's technique.

Constable referred to Turner's works as "airy visions, painted with tinted steam," while he based his own painting on "observable facts." He wanted nature to speak for itself, without artificial effects. Limiting his subject matter almost entirely to rural scenes, he painted rich canvases—with people and animals (as in *The Hay Wain*) fitting into a scheme clearly designed for human satisfaction. The atmosphere of Constable's paintings is often set by his treatment of the sky, which he believed was "the key note, the standard scale, and the chief organ of sentiment."

Fig. 12.4 *The Fighting Téméraire.* For Romantic artists, natural scenery expressed the "sublime"—the awesome vastness of nature, of which humans and their doings are only a tiny part. In Turner's painting, the sailing ship fades into the sky above it, and the steam tug merges with its reflection in the sea. The scene is dominated by the setting sun and the glow that it casts over sky and sea. Turner was fascinated by the "sublime" effect of misty, all-pervading light, and his colleague John Constable described his paintings as "airy visions, painted with tinted steam."

Fig. 12.5 *The Hay Wain.* In the Romantic manner, Constable makes the wain (wagon) and its riders part of a larger landscape. It is a more human scene, with its cottage and its field with ripening crops, all depicted in meticulous detail, than Turner's misty seascape. But above it there stretches a wide sky with billowing clouds whose light is reflected and transformed in countless ways by the details of the scene below. For Constable, humans are very much a part of nature's larger harmony.

Fig. 12.6 Houses of Parliament, London. This nineteenth-century building proclaimed the antiquity of British parliamentary government by reviving the Gothic style of medieval England, but no medieval government building had had such impressively regular and symmetrical façades as this one. Three hundred years of Baroque and classical architecture had inspired the instinctive belief that to express the pride of nations, buildings had to be orderly in appearance. Like the Renaissance revivers of Roman architecture before them, the Romantic revivers of Gothic architecture adapted an earlier style to ideas and needs of their own time.

THE GOTHIC REVIVAL IN ARCHITECTURE

In the nineteenth century, architectural style became more and more a matter of individual taste or fancy. This was a time of vast activity in construction, especially in the industrial cities; most of the older buildings still standing in Europe today were erected during the nineteenth century. They represent a confusing variety of styles springing from several architectural revivals. The architect sometimes aimed at a "pure" style, sometimes at a mixed one, and sometimes at an original design. But by mid-century, certain "associations" had developed: banks and government buildings, for instance, were usually built in the Greek or Roman manner; churches and colleges, in the Gothic.

Of the various styles, the Gothic is most often associated with Romanticism. The Gothic revival first appeared in England before the French Revolution, as a reaction to the classical Palladian style (pp. 435–436). After the turn of the nineteenth century, the Romantic movement gave new force to the Gothic revival. The outstanding example of this period is the Houses of Parliament in London *(Fig. 12.6)*. When the old building burned down in 1834, the lawmakers, remembering that English liberties and

Parliament itself traced back to the thirteenth century, decided to rebuild it in the medieval style. And feeling a Romantic attachment to the medieval past, Horace Walpole, a writer and the son of a noted statesman, remodeled his house in the manner of a Gothic castle. The result, like many such efforts, was anything but "pure" Gothic, despite the addition of spires and towers. At about the same time, across the North Sea in Germany, numerous "medieval" castles began to appear. All over Europe and America the Gothic revival proved popular.

ROMANTICISM IN MUSIC: BEETHOVEN, WAGNER

The eighteenth-century classical style in music, as we have seen (p. 442), stressed order, grace, and clarity; the nineteenth century cast off restraint and released the emotional power of music. The classical style did not disappear altogether, but it was submerged in the tide of Romanticism. Ludwig van Beethoven, born in Bonn, Germany, in 1770, bridged both styles. His early works are similar to those of Haydn and Mozart, and he followed established compositional forms throughout most of his life. But he responded to the Romantic spirit, and his later works are marked by heightened drama, suspense, and brilliant climaxes. But Beethoven never lost control of his musical themes; his works throb with energy but are contained within an orderly pattern. For this reason, he is sometimes called a "classical Romantic."

Orchestral compositions in the Romantic style called for more volume and range of sound than earlier works; Beethoven's orchestra was nearly twice the size of Haydn's. Although few new instruments were introduced—with the notable exception of the modern piano—the number of strings, winds, and percussion instruments was enlarged. The symphony became the most popular form, but pieces for solo performance also found favor. Melodies were highly expressive and original, harmonies were rich and often dissonant, and rhythms were subject to sudden or subtle changes.

Leading composers in the Romantic style were an Austrian, Franz Schubert; a Pole, Frederic Chopin; a Frenchman, Hector Berlioz; and a Russian, Peter Ilich Tchaikovsky. Much of the serious music performed today—in the concert hall, on the air, and on records, CDs, and tapes—is by Romantic composers. The high point of Romanticism, however, appeared not in the symphony hall but in the opera house. Richard Wagner, born in Leipzig, Germany, in 1813, created a new concept of opera—or music-drama, as he preferred to call it. Wagner personified the deepest yearnings of the Romantic spirit. Above all, he stressed the idea of the unity of thought and feeling and believed that this unity should be reflected in all art forms. He had contempt for art as mere entertainment or spectacle—"effects without cause." His new kind of opera, which was modeled on the performances of Greek tragedy (pp. 86–88), joined poetry, music, scenery, and action into one unified whole.

Wagner's "Ring cycle," a sequence of operas drawn from Germanic legend, best illustrates his idea of form. Here the drama—which is concerned with the curse of gold and the lust for power—is central. Voices and orchestra combine to carry forward the powerful themes; instead of writing separate speeches, arias, choruses, and accompaniments, Wagner created an "endless melody" out of all the musical elements. His music is rich and complex, full of passion and suspense, wholly Romantic.

Italian opera, too, reflected the new stress on emotion and the enlarged capabilities of the orchestra. Giuseppe Verdi, Wagner's artistic rival, is probably the most successful of operatic composers; his spectacular *Aïda* has been performed more often than any other opera. Verdi chose plots that focused on the most elemental human feelings and set them to thrilling vocal music. A political activist, he also used stories in his operas that inspired the rising desire for liberty and nationhood in Italy (p. 500).

The Spread of Liberal Democracy and Nationalism

The defeat of revolutionary France and the conservative reaction that followed slowed the momentum of liberal and national revolution but in the long run could not reverse it. The forces of change were too strong to contain. These included the resentment of the middle classes against absolutism and privilege, continued deprivation among the urban poor, the growing discontent of eastern European serfs, and the appeal of liberal Romantic ideas to educated young people of all classes. On the other side, the conservative rulers and nobles, divided by traditional power rivalries and inclined to waver between repression and reform as the best way of preventing renewed violent revolution, were not so united and determined as they seemed. Down to 1871, the nineteenth century saw the gradual crumbling of conservative resistance and the emergence of a new Europe, dominated by the hopes and ideals—and the ambitions and rivalries—of liberalism and nationalism.

REVOLUTION AND REFORM

In the first decade after the Congress of Vienna, most uprisings in favor of liberal democracy and national unity were quickly suppressed (as in Naples, Spain, and Russia). Revolutionary successes were achieved only in Greece (against the Ottoman Turks; pp. 298–299) and overseas, where the Spanish and Portuguese colonies in Latin America gained their independence by 1825. But the struggle began to turn with the victory of liberal forces in France in 1830.

Even with the restoration of the Bourbon king, Louis XVIII, in 1814, France had preserved the principal reforms introduced by the revolution and Napoleon. Louis reigned as a constitutional monarch, with a legislature that represented the restored nobility and well-to-do members of the business class—an arrangement close to what the moderate bourgeois had sought in 1789. It was threatened in 1824, however, when Louis was succeeded by his brother, Charles X.

As Count of Artois, Charles had been a leader of the émigrés who had urged other European nobles and princes to attack revolutionary France after 1789 (p. 464). After becoming king, he and his reactionary friends moved to turn back the clock. They sought to require the government to make annual payments to former nobles whose lands had been confiscated during the revolution, and they favored a return of clerical influence in education and politics. Charles himself, proud and stubborn, was contemptuous of the popular criticism his measures caused. When the elective Chamber of Deputies refused, in 1830, to bend to his will, Charles dissolved the Chamber, censored the press, and changed voting rights to strengthen the power of the former nobles.

The Revolutions of 1830. Paris responded to this revival of absolutism by throwing up barricades in the streets. The "July Revolution" of 1830 lasted only a few days, for the

1804	1814	1830	1848	1852	1870
First Empire (Napoleon I)	Bourbon Restoration	July Monarchy (Louis-Philippe)	Second Republic	Second Empire (Napoleon III)	

troops and police refused to fire on the populace. Charles, who had no desire to share the fate of Louis XVI, promptly abdicated and left for England. The rebels now found themselves divided on what to do next. The workmen, students, and intellectuals who had hoisted the revolutionary tricolor (red, white, and blue flag) at the city hall demanded that the monarchy give way to a republic. The bourgeois politicians, however, opposed such a change, feeling that their interests would be safer under a constitutional monarchy. All they wanted was a different kind of king, one who would serve their purposes. The politicians found such a man in Prince Louis-Philippe, who, though a member of the Bourbon family, had fought on the side of the revolution in 1789. They persuaded an aged and respected national hero, the Marquis de Lafayette, to support Louis-Philippe. This helped to make the "left-wing" Bourbon prince acceptable to those who wanted a republic.

The reign of Louis-Philippe brought a modest extension of liberal and democratic practices. Though the number of voters was still only a small fraction of the total citizenry, it was double what it had been before. The chief significance of the July Revolution was that it decisively ended the threat of counterrevolution in France and shattered the principle of legitimacy, hallowed at Vienna in 1815—Louis-Philippe became king upon the *invitation* of an elected Chamber of Deputies. The French thus struck a blow against the Metternich System (p. 477), and their success encouraged liberals and patriots elsewhere.

The first uprising outside France occurred in the Belgian Netherlands. This territory, for centuries under either Austrian or Spanish control, had been joined to the independent Dutch Netherlands by decision of the Congress of Vienna. Metternich and his colleagues had hoped that a united Netherlands would serve as a barrier to the French, whose rulers had frequently sent armies northward toward the Rhine River. But the Dutch were mainly Protestant, while the Belgians were mainly Catholic; and the French-speaking population of southern Belgium (the Walloons) resented the required use of the Dutch language in most areas. Discontent with the Dutch king, William I, led to street riots in Brussels shortly after the July uprising in France.

At first, the Belgian leaders demanded only local self-rule. But when William took up arms against them, they declared for complete independence. With French and British backing, the Belgians managed to hold off the Dutch king. Finally, in 1831, an international conference in London provided for an independent Belgium, with a German prince (Leopold of Saxe-Coburg) as constitutional monarch. In 1839, King William also recognized the new state, and its independence and neutrality were guaranteed by the major European powers.

Polish patriots, meanwhile, had tried and failed to reestablish the independence of their homeland (p. 412). At the Congress of Vienna (pp. 475–476), most of Poland had been given over to Russian control as a separate kingdom—under the personal rule of Tsar Alexander I. Early in 1831, the Polish assembly of nobles (the Diet) rejected Alexander's successor Nicholas I as their king; Nicholas sent a large army and crushed the brave but divided Polish forces. Revolutionary stirrings were also put down by force in 1830 in various parts of Germany and Italy. But the widespread agitations demonstrated that liberal nationalist forces were rising throughout Europe, kept in check only by political repression and military measures.

Liberal Reform in Britain. Liberal ideas and practices made a striking advance in Britain, where substantial change could be brought about through legislation. Already during the 1820s, Parliament moved away from a mercantilist economy toward free international trade. It also gave to Catholics and dissenting Protestants political rights equal to those of Anglicans. But the most significant single act was the Reform Bill of 1832, which altered the voting franchise and the system of representation in the House of Commons.

The act assigned seats to the growing urban and industrial centers of the North and the Midlands at the expense of districts in the South. The individual right to vote remained tied to property ownership, but more lenient requirements almost doubled the number of eligible voters (men only), to nearly one million. The new voters were chiefly of the middle class; the Reform Bill raised its share of power in the Commons to roughly that of the landed gentry (p. 447). It also opened the door to further liberal and democratic reforms during the ensuing decades, including extension of the vote to women. Although the British achieved this transformation without revolution or civil war, at critical moments the threat of violence was no doubt decisive. In 1832, for example, the Reform Bill was driven through Parliament under the pressure of street demonstrations and signs of possible insurrection.

Some of these pressures came from the English "Radicals" of the time, who wanted to go far beyond the liberals in overhauling British society and politics. The Radicals—chiefly from the working class, along with some of the new industrialists like Robert Owen (p. 518)—were both philosophical and action-minded. Inspired by such older writers as the American Tom Paine (pp. 452–453) and their own countryman Jeremy Bentham (p. 496), they demanded radical changes in voting laws, Parliament, courts, prisons, the Anglican Church, and the privileges of the lords. Many of these changes were brought about later in England. But for the time being, in 1832, the controlling powers in Parliament showed enough skill to permit mild reforms rather than face the risk of rebellion.

The Revolutions of 1848. On the Continent, the strongholds of privilege proved more unbending. Rather than submit to change or attempt to guide its course, the conservatives generally sought to repress it. Liberal and nationalist discontent continued to build up, however, and another and more widespread series of explosions came in 1848 (Map 12.2).

In France, Louis-Philippe, the "citizen-king," had become exceedingly unpopular. The critics of the government fell into two groups: the radicals, who wanted to discard the monarchy and establish a republic with universal voting rights, and the liberals, who wanted only a limited extension of voting rights. Had Louis-Philippe yielded to the liberals, he could have gained broader support and kept his crown. But he stubbornly rejected any constitutional change, and in February 1848, the streets of Paris bristled once again with barricades.

In a virtual repetition of the events of 1830, the royal troops refused to march against the people, and the king sensibly sailed for England. The victors were again

Map 12.2 Revolutions of 1848–1849. Before the nineteenth century, revolutions had usually broken out in one country at a time, but in the highly charged atmosphere of Europe after 1815, revolution was liable to spread. In 1848, the collapse of the monarchy in France led to outbreaks in fifteen other cities across Germany, Italy, and the Austrian Empire, where educated middle-class people and urban workers joined forces to call for government and social reform and for national liberation and unification. The revolutionaries mostly failed to achieve their aims, but they set the pattern for future change in Europe.

split between monarchists and republicans, but this time the disagreement developed into deeper civil conflict. The republican leaders of Paris were concerned about social as well as political reforms. They spoke for the growing number of workers who had been drawn into the capital. The victims of low income, insecurity, and poor working conditions, these "proletarians" were generally anticapitalist and antibourgeois.

In 1848, the republicans in Paris overcame monarchist opposition and forced the proclamation of a republic. They then arranged for the election, by a universal male vote, of a Constituent Assembly to frame a new basic law for France. The Assembly, which met in May, no doubt represented the sentiment of the nation as a whole, which was much less radical than Paris. It favored democratic political changes but no substantial social or economic reforms. This view was assailed by the aroused workers of the city, most of whom wanted the government to establish industrial workshops as a means of providing employment.

Fearing that the majority of the Assembly would reject their demands, groups of workers attacked it, and yet again the barricades went up. This time, however, the result was very different. An ugly class war started in Paris, and some ten thousand people were killed or wounded in several days of bloody street fighting. The regular army, called upon to defend the Assembly, crushed the revolt and thereby earned the bitterness of most of the urban workers. The bourgeois, for their part, were shaken by the threat of social revolution.

After those bloody "June Days," the Constituent Assembly drafted a new constitution that provided for a legislature and a president with strong powers. Presidential elections were soon held, and the victory went to the candidate who promised the most to both sides in the civil struggle. Prince Louis Napoleon Bonaparte, a nephew of the famous Corsican, represented himself as standing for both social order and social change. Capitalizing on his family name, he swamped his rivals and became president of the Second Republic in December 1848. Three years later, he brought about the dissolution of the legislature and had himself elected for a new term of ten years. In 1852, this shrewd politician proclaimed the Second Empire, taking the title of Napoleon III. (His cousin, Napoleon II, the son and direct heir of Napoleon I, had died in 1832.)

The cycle of revolution and counterrevolution was repeated beyond the borders of France. In central Europe, liberal demands were mixed with nationalist hopes. Revolutionists rushed into the streets in a dozen capitals, proclaiming political rights and calling for the unity and independence of their own national groups. Monarchs and ruling classes were at first frightened by these demonstrations and generally responded by offering concessions or new constitutions. But the protesting movements lacked the internal cohesion and the organized force needed to hold their gains. When it became clear that they could be stopped by military action, the authorities recovered their poise, withdrew their concessions, and put down the rebels with troops and police. In the course of these uprisings, peasants who were still serfs won their freedom, but liberal reforms and progress toward national self-determination were checked.

Nevertheless, the movements of 1848 had significant consequences. The Austrian Empire felt the greatest shock, a warning of things to come. Until 1848, Prince Metternich (p. 475) had remained the outstanding leader of "legitimacy" and conservatism. Yet a liberal uprising in Vienna so unnerved him that he hurriedly resigned as imperial chancellor and departed for London. The flight of Metternich brought joy and hope to the advocates of change everywhere. These feelings were premature, however, for within two years, imperial troops had suppressed the disturbances in the Habsburg domains, and Metternich could return to his beloved Vienna to write his memoirs. But he was no longer in power, and the Metternich System was broken.

Nationalist aspirations, though frustrated, were intensified throughout central Europe. Hungarians, Czechs, Italians, Serbs, Croats, and Romanians became more dissatisfied within the Austrian Empire. Many Germans, meanwhile, were looking toward the creation of a large united German state. The various German territories (including Austria proper) sent delegates to Frankfurt in 1848 with the aim of setting up a German federal union. Political disagreements, power rivalries, and the suspicion of the existing authorities frustrated its work, and it broke up in 1849 having achieved nothing. Nationalist sentiment had nonetheless been stirred, and within a generation, a united Germany would be created by the more "realistic" methods of diplomacy and war (pp. 499–500).

THE LIBERAL IDEAL: MILL

The immediate aims and actions of the liberal and nationalist movements were in keeping with their maturing ideologies. The liberal demands were for extension of voting rights, free expression, guarantees of legal protections, and constitutional checks on government power; the nationalist demands were for the political union and independence of distinct cultural groups. Neither set of aims can be fully understood without a knowledge of its underlying system of thought.

Nineteenth-century liberal thought was the outcome of a trend that had started in the Renaissance or even as far back as the late Middle Ages. It was represented in succeeding stages by men like Erasmus, Rabelais, Locke, and Jefferson (pp. 342–344, 356–358, 450–451, 454–455). Central to the thinking of these men was their stress on human personality and its free development. This idea could be realized, they believed, only through each individual's exercise of personal freedom. The nature of freedom and the proper conditions for its use had been outlined before the French Revolution; after Napoleon, those views had to be modified considerably.

Nineteenth-century liberals were bitterly aware that "Liberty, Equality, Fraternity" had led to bloodshed and dictatorship—but they clung to the same basic beliefs while studying the mistakes that had been made. They became more respectful of history than earlier liberals had been, observing that human rationality is not sufficient to overcome, in a short time, the lasting power of old institutions and habits of thought. They were also more wary of popular tyranny, concluding that the will of the majority can be as wrong and oppressive as that of a despot. Many liberals emphasized, finally, that freedom must be guided by morality if it is not to go astray.

In England, the leading country of peaceful liberal reform, John Stuart Mill was the foremost spokesman of this more tempered doctrine of liberalism. His conceptions of personal freedom, precisely and eloquently expressed, have had a persistent appeal to people everywhere who admire the ideal of liberty.

Mill was a follower of Jeremy Bentham, the founder of a philosophy called "utilitarianism." According to Bentham, who took an atomistic view of human society (p. 450), the most acceptable way of evaluating social institutions is to measure their total utility (usefulness) to all the affected individuals—looking to "the greatest good of the greatest number." Mill defended this view, explaining that the measurement of the "greatest good" must take into account *qualitative* differences in human satisfactions. He believed that the highest satisfactions can be reached only under conditions of personal freedom, and he set out to specify those conditions and work for their achievement. Mill's carefully reasoned essay *On Liberty* (1859) remains the classic statement of the historic liberal view of individual rights in relation to society.

The book accepts Aristotle's conviction that the purpose of human life is the harmonious development of one's abilities (pp. 83–84). This purpose, declared Mill, requires two conditions: "freedom" and "a variety of situations." He would give to each individual, therefore, the utmost freedom in relation to society and the state. Each person's freedom he regarded as sacred: "The only purpose for which power can be rightfully exercised over any member of a civilized community, against his will, is to prevent harm to others." Mill justified this position not by resorting to the outmoded doctrine of "natural rights" or the "social contract" (pp. 450–451) but on the utilitarian ground that freedom is essential to the greater happiness of the individual and the species.

He included females as well as males in his philosophical judgments. His partner in writing *On Liberty* and other major works was a woman, Harriet Taylor. A close intellectual associate for many years, she at last became his wife. Mill, unlike other writers of the nineteenth century, viewed women as equal to men in intelligence. He helped found the first woman's suffrage society in England in 1867 and published, soon after, *The Subjection of Women,* a persuasive statement of the case for female political rights.

Mill abhorred the drift toward large bureaucracies and cultural conformity. The state itself, he insisted, is worth no more than the individuals who make it up: "A State which dwarfs its men, in order that they may be more docile instruments in its hands even for beneficial purposes, will find that with small men no great thing can really be accomplished." He opposed increases in public services by government, even when done for the benefit of individuals. He preferred that citizens and groups act on their own initiative to forestall the "deadening hand" of centralized power and uniformity.

But Mill's first concern was the preservation, at any cost, of liberty of thought and discussion. This, he thought, is crucial to the health of the individual and society. He denied the right of any government, popular or despotic, to interfere with free expression: "If all mankind minus one were of one opinion, and only one person were of the contrary opinion, mankind would be no more justified in silencing that one person, than he, if he had the power, would be justified in silencing mankind." The evil of forbidding the expression of an opinion is more than the injury to an individual, Mill asserted: it hurts the human race, and it hurts those who dissent from the opinion more than those who hold it. "If the opinion is right, they are deprived of the opportunity of exchanging error for truth; if wrong, they lose, what is almost as great a benefit, the clearer and livelier impression of truth, produced by its collision with error."

THE NATIONALIST IDEAL: MAZZINI

While many people applauded Mill's sentiments, others gave priority to nationalism over individual freedom. Except in some countries of western Europe, the boundaries of *states*—that is, territories and populations under sovereign governments—were not the same as those of *nations*—that is, self-aware ethnic and cultural groups (*Map 12.3*). The Germans and the Italians lived under many more or less powerful independent rulers, and in the empires of eastern Europe—Austria, Russia, and Turkey—many subject nations lived under the rule of a single imperial power. In these nations, the desire for national unity and independence overshadowed all other aims. They did not despise individual freedom, but the history of the freest countries, Britain and the United States, seemed to show that freedom itself was rooted in the unity and independence of the nation. Unlike Mill, who took Britain's power for granted, the nationalists on the Continent did not glorify the individual, "free" of interference by the state; they regarded the building of a powerful state as the necessary means to full nationhood and individual realization.

The special form and tone of this idea, in the first half of the century, were expressed by the Italian patriot Giuseppe Mazzini. Though inspired by the humanitarian and egalitarian ideals of the Enlightenment, Mazzini was caught up in the Romantic and nationalist passion of his own generation. In him, the "religion of liberty" became the "religion of the fatherland."

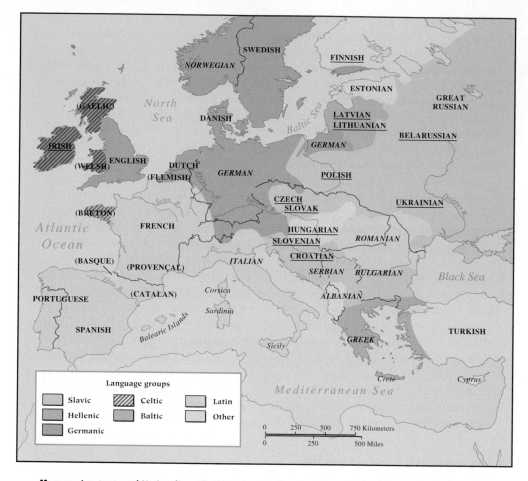

Map 12.3 Language and Nationalism. The thirty-six major European languages of today are mostly descended from those of the ancient Romans and of early medieval Germanic and Slavic invaders. In 1815, languages most of whose speakers lived in united and independent countries amounted to only about one-quarter of the total (names in Roman type). European nationalism now made language the main mark of nationhood. The italic (1815–1914) and underlined (1914–present) names mark the change to a Europe where speakers of three-quarters of languages (exceptions in parentheses) form independent nations.

The nationalist ideal, as described by Mazzini, was linked to a sentimental concern for all humanity. He set forth his feeling in a series of essays, *The Duties of Man,* written at mid-century and directed to the Italian working class. "You are men," Mazzini told his readers, "before you are citizens or fathers." The "law of life" requires that individuals embrace the whole human family in their love, confessing their faith in the unity and brotherhood of all peoples. But the lone individual, declared Mazzini, is powerless to work for the benefit of all: "The individual is too weak, and Humanity too vast." Effective action requires fraternal cooperation among individuals who can work together—those of a common language and culture—in other words, a nation. Starting with this line of reasoning, Mazzini went on to glorify the nation as divinely created for serving humanity.

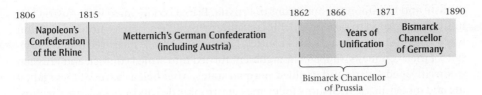

Mazzini saw the independent nation as a promoter of individual liberty and equality: "A Country is a fellowship of free and equal men. . . . The law must express the general aspiration, promote the good of all, respond to a beat of the nation's heart." But in fact, the push for national strength through unity often reduced freedom, especially when freedom involved dissent from national objectives. Nationalism could readily become *statism,* as it did north of the Alps. The historian Heinrich von Treitschke, writing later in the century, declared that the individual's first duty is obedience to the state. This influential professor at the University of Berlin gave academic and philosophical respectability to the German drive for discipline, unification, and dominance.

THE ACHIEVEMENT OF NATIONAL UNIFICATION

The unsuccessful liberal-nationalist uprisings of 1830 and 1848 had failed because of inadequate organization and power. It is significant that the eloquent Mazzini, who labored tirelessly to rid Italy of foreign occupation, spent most of his years as a revolutionary exile. Mazzini lived to see the achievement of a united Italy in 1870, but his liberal ideals were far from realized. Italian unification came about as part of a wider struggle that also brought about German unification and was mostly conducted not by peaceful change or popular uprisings but by wars among states.

Germany. The practical means to national unification were most forcefully demonstrated in Germany, and the consequences for Europe and the world were most profound. After the disappointment of 1848, German nationalists looked for more effective means of bringing their dreams to fulfillment. One of them, Count Otto von Bismarck, was sure he knew the way. Born into an aristocratic landowning family, he rose to power as a high official of the Prussian kingdom. In the tradition of Frederick the Great (p. 413), Bismarck admired autocracy and militarism. He had despised the liberal leaders of 1848 and had urged the Prussian king to use the army to restore order and civil obedience. (Many German liberals later supported Bismarck, however, because his methods proved effective in building national power.)

Bismarck was convinced that the German princelings would never join together through their own efforts, and he had only contempt for what "the people" might accomplish. The important decisions and actions had to be undertaken, he thought, by the ruler and ministers of the leading German state, Prussia. "Not by speeches and majority votes," Bismarck declared, "are the great questions of the day decided—that was the mistake of 1848 and 1849—but by iron and blood." Appointed chief minister to the Hohenzollern king of Prussia (p. 413) in 1862, Bismarck acted on this conviction and sought to remove, by diplomacy and war, whatever stood in the way of German unification.

Austria was clearly the chief obstacle, for Metternich had managed to establish and maintain Austrian dominance in central Europe, and he and his successors looked with distaste and fear upon the ambitions of Prussia. Prussia cooperated with Austria in a military campaign to take the duchies of Schleswig and Holstein (whose population was mostly German) from Danish control, but the two powers quarreled over the division of their conquests. In 1866, the argument turned into armed conflict, and Prussian troops invaded Austria and its allied German states. After half a century of reorganizing and modernizing their army following catastrophic defeats by Napoleon, the Prussians were able to defeat Austria in no more than seven weeks. The Austrians gave up all influence over northern Germany to Prussia. Metternich's German Confederation (p. 476) was abolished, and Bismarck raised in its place the North German Confederation, under the presidency of the king of Prussia. This new political grouping had a firm economic foundation, for Prussia had previously led the way in establishing a customs union (*Zollverein*) that equalized tariffs among the states that joined it. The union included most of the German states outside Austria.

It was now France's turn to be uneasy, for the French, like the Austrians, had traditionally opposed a strong and united Germany. Aggressive factions in both Prussia and France viewed a military showdown as inevitable; diplomatic maneuvering and reciprocal insults led, in 1870, to a declaration of war by France. The whirlwind Franco-Prussian War was another brilliant success for the Prussian armies, resulting in the death of one empire and the birth of another. Napoleon III, humiliated by defeat and capture, lost his throne, and in 1871, William I of Prussia was proclaimed the emperor (*Kaiser*) of a united Germany. Four south German states, which had remained aloof from the North German Confederation, took their places in the proud new empire (*Map 12.4*). Bismarck, now the imperial chancellor, had achieved the central ambitions of his career: Prussia was supreme in Germany, and Germany was supreme in Europe.

Italy. Meanwhile, the rulers of the Italian kingdom of Sardinia had been playing the same role in unifying Italy as Prussia in Germany, with the Sardinian prime minister, Camillo di Cavour, in the role of Bismarck. Since Sardinia was not a great power like Prussia, it needed outside help—above all against Austria, since 1815 the dominant power in Italy. Cavour won the support of Austria's great power rivals—first of all Napoleon III's France and then, when Napoleon cooled toward Italian unification, Bismarck's Prussia. With their help, Cavour was able to bring about Sardinian takeovers of territories in northern and central Italy, notably the States of the Church (p. 311). Meanwhile, in southern Italy, he was able to win the cooperation of the famous insurgent leader, Giuseppe Garibaldi. By 1870, a united kingdom of Italy already existed, but the pope still ruled in Rome, protected by troops of Napoleon III. Finally, when the French troops withdrew because of the war against Prussia, the kingdom of Italy sent in forces and annexed Rome, thereby completing national unification.

Italy and Germany, both of which had been divided for centuries, now became independent members of the European state system. This would be the central fact of international relations during the years to follow. The greater power, Germany, which had achieved unity and strength by the methods of authority, discipline, and militarism, was determined to win its "place in the sun" after its late arrival as a state. The successful revolutions of national unification were thus a prelude to European and global struggle, climaxed by the First and Second World Wars.

Map 12.4 A New Balance of Power. By 1871, the wars of Bismarck and Cavour had finally destroyed the European balance of power that had existed since 1648 (*Map 9.2*, p. 399). The old balance had involved powerful rival dynasties and had depended on keeping Germany and Italy weak and divided but independent of any one of their stronger neighbors. Now united Germany was the single most powerful Continental country, dynastic rivalries were turning into national ones, and the crumbling of Ottoman rule was creating a new area of weakness and division in the Balkans.

RECOMMENDED READING

The Conservative Reaction T. C. W. Blanning, ed., *The Oxford Illustrated History of Modern Europe* (1996), is an up-to-date general introduction to European political, social, and cultural history from the late eighteenth century to the present. E. J. Hobsbawm, *The Age of Revolution, 1789–1848* (1962); R. Gildea, *Barricades and Borders: Europe, 1800–1914* (1987), and M. Broers, *Europe After Napoleon: Revolution, Reaction, Romanticism* (1996), include concise accounts of the period of conservative reaction.

R. Nisbet, *Conservatism: Dream and Reality* (1986), is an excellent brief introduction to the main themes of conservative thought and action from the late eighteenth century to the present. On individual thinkers, see R. Kirk, *Edmund Burke: A Genius Reconsidered* (1997); J. V. Price, *David Hume* (1991); R. Scruton, *Kant* (1982); and P. Singer, *Hegel* (1983).

The Romantic Spirit in Literature, Art, and Music The following introductions to Romanticism in all fields of literature, the arts, and thought are recommended: M. Cranston, *The Romantic Movement* (1994) (Europe and the Americas), and S. Pritchett, *The Romantics* (1981) (England). I. Berlin, *The Roots of Romanticism* (1999), is an interpretive essay by a renowned scholar. C. M. Bowra, *The Romantic Imagination* (1949), and N. Frye, *A Study of English Romanticism* (1995), are works of a high order dealing with English literary Romanticism. On individual authors, see R. Wokler, *Rousseau* (1995); R. Noyes and J. O. Hayden, *William Wordsworth* (1991); and V. Lange, *The Classical Age of German Literature, 1740–1815* (1982) (Goethe).

D. Irwin, *Neoclassicism* (1997); W. Vaughan, *Romantic Art* (1978); and K. Clark, *The Gothic Revival: An Essay in the History of Taste* (1962), are excellent introductions to the art and architecture of the period. J. Rushton, *Classical Music: A Concise History from Gluck to Beethoven* (1986), and A. Whittall, *Romantic Music: A Concise History from Schubert to Sibelius* (1987), are readable, authoritative, and nontechnical.

The Spread of Liberal Democracy and Nationalism E. J. Hobsbawm, *The Age of Capital, 1848–1875* (1979), and B. Waller, ed., *Themes in Modern European History, 1830–1890* (1990), are excellent introductions to all aspects of European development in the mid-nineteenth century. The following introductions to liberalism are recommended: L. T. Hobhouse, *Liberalism* (1911) (a classic statement of the British liberal tradition); J. Gray, *Liberalism* (1986) (Britain and the United States); and J. Manent, *An Intellectual History of Liberalism* (1994) (France). J. Dunn, ed., *Democracy: The Unfinished Journey, 508 B.C. to A.D. 1993* (1992), includes essays on nineteenth-century democracy in Europe and America. H. Schulze, *States, Nations, and Nationalism from the Middle Ages to the Present* (1994), is a wide-ranging work on the rise of nationalism and nation-states; L. Kramer, *Nationalism: Political Cultures in Europe and America, 1775–1865* (1998), is a concise account of the era of nationalism's triumph.

P. M. Pilbeam, *The 1830 Revolution in France* (1991); P. N. Stearns, *The Revolutions of 1848* (1974); and R. J. W. Evans and H. Pogge von Strandmann, eds., *The Revolutions in Europe, 1848–1849: From Reform to Reaction* (2000), are concise and readable accounts of the revolutions of the period. On individual countries and leaders, see E. J. Evans, *Parliamentary Reform, 1770–1918* (1999) (Britain); J. Breuilly, *The Formation of the First German National State, 1800–1871* (1996); B. Waller, *Bismarck* (1997): M. Clark, *The Italian Risorgimento* (1998); and H. Hearder, *Cavour* (1994).

⃰ INFOTRAC COLLEGE EDITION

Visit the source collections at **http://academic.cengage.com/infotrac,** and use the Search function with the following key terms:

Romanticism   Goethe   John Stuart Mill

WESTERN CIVILIZATION RESOURCES

Visit the Brief History of the Western World Companion Web Site for resources specific to this textbook:

http://history.wadsworth.com/greerbrief09/

Also, the CD in the back of this book and the World History Resources Center at **http://history.wadsworth.com/west_civ/** offer a variety of tools to help you succeed in this course, including access to quizzes; images; documents; interactive simulations, maps, and timelines; movie explorations; and a wealth of other sources.

CHAPTER 13

The Impact of the Machine

OVERVIEW

The nineteenth century was the great turning point in the rise of the modern West. Not only the traditional power structure, but also much of thought, literature, and art, as well as social and economic structures that were older than civilization itself, were revolutionized in the course of a mere hundred years.

The single greatest nineteenth-century shift in civilization was what contemporaries themselves called the Industrial Revolution. The revolution began in eighteenth-century Britain with the invention of the steam engine and its use as a source of reliable power for machines to mass-produce cotton textiles. In the nineteenth century, the partnership of machines to produce and use power on an unprecedented scale spread to every branch of industry and agriculture, and from Britain to many other Western and non-Western countries. Fast-moving technical advance, leading to new products, new production processes, and the rise and fall of entire industries, became a seemingly permanent feature of Western civilization.

The result was the greatest change in human ways of life since the Agricultural Revolution (pp. 11–16). Giant capitalist corporations arose to finance and manage the new industries arising from technical advance. The elite came to be made up mainly of captains of industry, stock exchange tycoons, and government bureaucrats, rather than nobles. The sons and daughters of peasants crowded from the countryside into the cities to supply the vast forces of factory and office workers needed by the new industries. New social conflicts arose between management and labor over the distribution of the increased wealth produced by technology. New ideologies and new political and social movements, mostly of Marxist or Christian inspiration, arose in response to social and technical change.

In the nineteenth century, too, science took its place beside religion as one of the main influences on the outlook and way of life of Western civilization. The progress of scientific discovery, gradual since the seventeenth century, became a broad advance on many fronts. Human understanding of the basic features of the physical universe and of the nature of living things expanded and changed out of all recognition, and this growth of theoretical knowledge became the main engine of industrial change. Impressed by these successes, social scientists (such as economists and sociologists) and human scientists (such as anthropologists and psychologists) began to apply measurement, observation, and experiment more or less systematically to society, culture, and human nature itself.

One particular scientific advance, Charles Darwin's theory of evolution, removed God's guiding hand from yet another vast area of the natural world—the origin and development of living beings. The result was renewed and bitter ideological conflict over the relationship between science and religion. Darwin's idea of the "struggle for existence" also became a source of inspiration for many secular ideologies—capitalist, nationalist, imperialist, Marxist—which saw human society as an arena of combat, and wanted to feel that the victory of their side was both a scientific certainty and good for the human race.

The overwhelming nineteenth-century changes also had their effect on literature and the arts. The pull of the medieval, the classical, and even the Christian past began to weaken. Instead, to a greater extent than in previous eras, writers and artists found their themes in the life and objects of their own times—weary passengers in an overcrowded railroad car, for instance, or a middle-class woman awakening to the meaninglessness of her life of pleasing her husband. To depict such themes, new and contrasting styles evolved. The Realists treated their subjects in full and accurate detail, often accompanied by fierce denunciation of social evils. The Impressionists stripped detail to the bare minimum and carefully avoided social comment, so as to leave the most hauntingly evocative "impression" of the scenes they portrayed.

Because the Realists and Impressionists rejected so much that had traditionally seemed essential to the beauty and nobility of art, they were controversial. But they lived in a civilization that was in any case transforming itself amid dispute and conflict—a pattern that from now on became normal in the arts, too, as the West approached the great cultural divide that marked the beginning of the twentieth century.

The Industrial Revolution

The Industrial Revolution was unplanned. Perhaps the most remarkable thing about it was that it ever happened, for the turning of an agrarian society into an industrial one is not something that comes about easily or naturally. But many of the developments that had transformed Europe and the rest of the world from the late Middle Ages onward had also paved the way for the Industrial Revolution. The rise of capitalism had created a class of merchants and manufacturers who were willing to take risks, as well as new forms of business organization that were adaptable to the needs of large industrial enterprises (p. 331). In the technical field, waterwheels had accustomed manufacturers to using stronger sources of power than human or animal muscles, printing had set a precedent for complex mass production operations, and clocks had provided an example of accurately functioning automatic machines (pp. 240, 306–307). The Scientific Revolution had aroused the expectation that scientific discovery would result in practical benefits (p. 422). The growth of colonial empires had brought much of the world's trade to the countries of western Europe, giving them the wealth to invest in new technology and worldwide markets for their resulting products (pp. 331–332). And as it happened, by the eighteenth century, all these developments had gone far-thest in one European country: Britain. It was there that the Industrial Revolution began; the pattern of change then spread to the European continent, the Americas, and the Far East.

THE AGRARIAN TRANSFORMATION

Preceding and accompanying the Industrial Revolution were significant changes in agriculture. In the course of the eighteenth century, English landlords had substan-tially increased their holdings and revenues by speeding up the practice of land enclo-sure, which had been going on since the end of the Middle Ages. Under the old manorial regime, the lord's tenants had enjoyed access to the common lands of pasture, meadow, and wood lot (pp. 234–236). By successive parliamentary acts of enclosure, these lands were gradually removed from common use and were rented to individuals to farm. Over the same period, the "open fields" of cultivated strips were also switched into single plots and fenced in for individual use. In this process of redistribution, the land-lords usually gained additional land, while tenants often found that they could no longer make a living.

Although the redistribution brought hardship to thousands of farm families, it put large tracts of land under more efficient management. Whereas the typical small farmer clung to old-fashioned ways, the more ambitious landlords were willing to ex-periment with improved methods. They tried new farming tools and fertilizers, planted soil-renewing crops, and developed scientific breeding of livestock. The result was a substantial rise in output. This revolution in agriculture also created a pool of displaced farm workers, both men and women, who desperately sought employment. Some hired themselves out to successful farm operators; others turned to spinning or weaving. They were ready to go wherever they could earn better wages.

THE MECHANIZATION OF INDUSTRY AND TRANSPORTATION

By 1750, Britain had built up a globe-circling trading system, and rich profits awaited those who could increase their exports. Among the goods that British merchants traded across the world were cotton textiles, a product of India that was popular in many markets because it was comfortable, decorative, and cheaper than similar cloths such as fine linen or silk. But the profits would be all the greater if cotton cloth could be manufactured in Britain rather than bought in India. To begin with, cotton textiles were produced, like woolen ones, by the domestic system—but it so happened that cotton fibers were strong enough to be spun and woven even by relatively crude machines.

The first breakthrough, about 1760, was a hand-powered, multispindled spinning wheel or jenny. Soon afterward came Richard Arkwright's water-powered spinning "frame," which spun stronger threads than the jenny. Advances in spinning were soon matched by the development of powered weaving looms. At first designed for use in the cotton industry, these inventions were from the 1830s onward adapted to woolen pro-duction as well.

The logic of events led next to the building of factories. Spinning and weaving under the domestic system (pp. 300–301) were to persist for many years, but the new machines were not well suited to household use. They were a substantial capital invest-ment; therefore, they had to be operated around the clock. Moreover, they required a source of power, which at first was supplied by the traditional waterwheels (p. 240); thus factories could be built only on the banks of swift-running streams. For these reasons, as well as for reasons of maintenance and supervision, power machines were set up in special establishments. Arkwright launched the first spinning mill in the 1770s, and soon he was employing hundreds of workers, who attended thousands of spindles. Other entrepreneurs soon followed his example.

The greatest boost to the building of factories came from the development of effi-cient steam engines, which could be built to be more powerful than waterwheels and were not confined to riverbanks. The steam engine was initially developed by Thomas Newcomen about 1700 in response to a problem in coal mining: the tunnels, always liable to fill with underground water, were being dug too deep for the water to be drained from them by animal-powered pumps as in the past. Newcomen, though no scientist himself, knew about seventeenth-century discoveries concerning the behav-ior of water when heated and cooled, and used his knowledge to build a machine that would do the job. In this way, the steam engine was the first modern technical device to owe its existence to the progress of science.

Later in the eighteenth century, James Watt and other practical inventors made important improvements on Newcomen's machine, greatly increasing its power and harnessing it to turn a wheel. As a result, the steam engine eventually became the chief source of power in the factories and was adapted to both water and land transporta-tion. The "age of railways" began in 1825 when the steam locomotive pioneer George Stephenson opened a stretch of line between the coal mining town of Darlington and the harbor of Stockton, 20 miles away, from which the coal moved to homes and facto-ries by sea (*Fig. 13.1*). Five years later, Stephenson linked two much more important centers—Manchester, the headquarters of the industrialized cotton industry, and Liv-erpool, the seaport through which Manchester imported raw cotton from the United States and exported finished textiles to customers in every continent. Within twenty years, steam trains were running between all the principal cities of Britain. With its cities linked by steam transportation, its coal mines deep beneath the earth, its mecha-nized cotton industry, and other industries following cotton's example, Britain pro-vided the pattern for future industrialization around the world.

DEVELOPMENT OF A "PERMANENT" INDUSTRIAL REVOLUTION

At the middle of the nineteenth century, Britain's industrial productivity and techni-cal progress were unique, but it did not keep this position for long. In the second half of the nineteenth century, with astonishing speed, the Industrial Revolution spread to other countries of western Europe, North America, and the Far East.

Many countries in these regions possessed more or less the same features that had enabled Britain to pioneer the Industrial Revolution. They too had resources of coal and iron ore. They too had middle-class businessmen who were eager to build factories and landless country-dwellers who were eager to earn wages in them. Even landowning nobles wanted to farm their land more efficiently and profit from the coal and iron ore that might lie beneath it. National monarchs, for their part, struggling to keep what they could of their political power, were well aware that industrial wealth and ad-

©Time Life Pictures/Getty Images

Fig. 13.1 The Stockton and Darlington Railway. This engraving of the inaugural run on the first steam-powered railroad depicts a combination of engineering advances. The steam engine has become compact and powerful enough to move both itself and a whole wagon train, helped by iron rails that guide the wagons with minimal friction, and by bridges and embankments that keep the track level. The top-hatted celebrators are sitting on piles of coal from local mines, the railroad's main revenue-earning traffic. To keep fuel moving to Britain's multiplying factories and spreading cities, mass transportation has arrived.

vanced weapons could only make them stronger. In the second half of the nineteenth century, other countries besides Britain joined in the push for technical invention.

By the end of the century, Britain was but one among a global spread of industrial countries, and was no longer even the most advanced or productive. In Europe, that position had been taken by Germany, while other countries such as France, Belgium, Italy, and Austria-Hungary were also important industrial producers. In the Far East, the ancient empire of Japan, responding to the threat of U.S. and European imperialistic control, was well on the way to becoming a modern industrial country (pp. 553–554). But the most advanced and productive of all the industrial countries, thanks to its vast natural resources, its hardworking population (swelled by immigration), its scientific progress, and its technical know-how, was the United States.

Industrialization not only spread from country to country, it also progressed. More and more traditional products came to be manufactured by the new methods, and more and more new products and manufacturing processes were invented. With the rapid increase in scientific knowledge in the nineteenth century (pp. 523–532), more and more industrial firms recognized the connection between "pure" and "applied" science and sought to exploit it. Practical engineers and backyard tinkerers could still make significant breakthroughs, but more and more inventors were professionally qualified scientists. Indeed, invention itself became an organized activity, as industrial companies and national governments began to invest large sums in research and development. Purposefully conducted and linked to the seemingly limitless progress of pure science, the surge of technological progress has continued down to the present day.

The new age of a permanent Industrial Revolution linked to science began shortly after the middle of the nineteenth century. It was inaugurated by the development of new processes in the iron industry—mostly arising from better understanding of the chemistry of metallic ores—that enabled iron to be rapidly and cheaply transformed into a stronger form of the metal, steel. By the end of the century, steel had largely replaced iron for rails, bridges, shipbuilding, and other types of construction where superior strength was required. Meanwhile, advances in the physics of heat, gas, electricity, and magnetism led to revolutionary inventions in the field of power production and distribution (p. 524). A new and far more powerful form of steam engine, the turbine, was coupled with generators that turned steam power into electrical energy so as to make electric light and power.

At the end of the nineteenth century, steam and electrical power were joined by the internal combustion (gasoline or diesel) engine. Fueled by previously untapped petroleum resources—which could be located thanks to the rapidly developing science of geology (p. 527)—the new type of engine brought about yet more revolutions in transportation. Small, light, and yet powerful, it made possible the twentieth-century development of both automobiles and aircraft. With petroleum available in vast amounts to supply the needs of motorists and pilots, chemists also found ways to produce from it an endless variety of textiles and plastics. Other twentieth-century scientists, building on basic discoveries in physics from the late nineteenth century onward, created a whole range of electronic devices that have transformed the transmission and processing of information: radio, television, recording devices, and computers.

Each of these and many other inventions of the last century and a half has amounted to a revolution in itself. Whole industries—such as steel, oil, plastics, electronics, automobiles, and aircraft—have sprung from nothing to produce and sell these inventions. Usually in not more than twenty or thirty years after the initial invention, each new industry has developed its giant corporations, its massive production plants, and its labor force of hundreds of thousands.

This permanent worldwide Industrial Revolution has been far from painless. It has led to massive changes, usually accompanied by conflict and hardship, in the way businesses are organized and run and in the patterns of the work and life of ordinary people. It has given rise to radical ideologies that have promised relief from the evils of capitalism and industrialization but in practice have often brought their own forms of mass suffering. It has altered the balance of power in the world, giving dominance to the advanced and productive nations, subjecting nonindustrial ones to imperialistic control, and providing the weapons to fight wars more terrible than any in history. Much of this and the following chapters is concerned with exploring these aspects of the impact of the machine.

The Business Corporation and Capitalist Expansion

As industrial operations grew in number and size, entrepreneurs had to raise capital from sources other than their own profits. Large undertakings, calling for heavy initial investment in buildings and equipment, required the pooling of money from hundreds of thousands of individuals. The device that business leaders developed for raising and controlling such funds was called the *limited company* in England, the *corporation* in the United States.

THE STRUCTURE AND CONTROL OF THE CORPORATION

The distinctive feature of the corporation or limited company is the financial protection it gives its stockholders. Its forerunner, the *joint-stock company* (p. 331), had first appeared in the seventeenth century as a means of financing commercial and mining ventures. Joint-stock companies had sold transferable shares and had served as a means of risk sharing, but the stock owners collectively had been liable for the debts of the enterprise. The corporation, on the other hand, is a clever legal invention, a "fictitious person" created by law. It is authorized to hold property, borrow money, and sue and be sued—without direct involvement of the stockholders. Should the assets of the corporate "person" be lost, the stockholders would lose only the value of their shares of stock.

This idea of "limited liability" is of crucial importance, since it permits individuals far removed from the control of a business to invest money in its stock without the risk of losing other property that they hold. They delegate direction of the firm's operations to a small body, the board of directors, who are elected (usually routinely) by an annual vote of the stockholders. The board, in turn, chooses the executive officers of the firm. So long as the managerial group—the directors and the executives—produces profits for the stockholders, it normally remains in control. In fact, corporations grew in size (especially after 1900), and as stockholders became increasingly numerous, more and more power went to the managers—a process that has been aptly called the "managerial revolution."

The modern large corporation, whose development was a direct response to the massive use of machines, has become the main functioning unit of Western capitalism. Because these enterprises affect the lives of people everywhere, it is worth examining how they function. The typical large corporation is multinational, conducting operations around the globe. It is owned by thousands of stockholders, whose primary concern is to receive regular dividends or to gain from an increase in the value of their stock. It employs thousands or hundreds of thousands of people, provides commodities for millions, and pays taxes to national, state, and local governments. The corporation's assets may run into billions of dollars; its gross income may exceed the revenue of many states and nations. Yet this vast economic empire is controlled by a small group of corporate managers and professional experts. Their decisions, made within the limits of law, finance, and consumer acceptance, determine the flow of investment, research, and development—and thereby influence the tastes and habits of the public.

THE GLOBAL REACH OF CAPITALISM

Large corporations, from the very beginning, usually had important foreign interests. They sometimes sought to eliminate competition in world markets through private agreements (cartels), and by extending their investments abroad, they controlled the rate of economic growth in many lands. Industrial capitalism thus became a global force, with money and business seeking the best rates of return and with an international elite of owners, managers, bankers, and promoters. The push of industrialization was a major factor, along with liberalism and nationalism, in shaping Europe and the world in the nineteenth and twentieth centuries.

Risk capital was especially drawn to "backward" countries by the promise of extraordinary profits. Labor was cheap there, the demand for capital was high, and in some cases rich resources were awaiting exploitation. Overseas investments also aided the creation of an interdependent global economy geared to the interests of the industrial ("advanced") countries. Thus European capital built railways in Africa that brought out raw materials to be manufactured in Europe and sold in markets around the world.

The industrialists of Great Britain had the jump on those of other nations. By 1914, British private investments overseas amounted to more than $18 billion. French capitalists were next, with some $7 billion. These figures are a fair index of the two nations' comparative penetration and influence in the "backward" continents. (United States capitalists had only $3 billion in foreign investments in 1914; by 1970, the figure was close to $150 billion.)

As early as 1900, some thoughtful observers began to ask whether the concentration and expansion of economic power could go on without seriously disturbing political relations within and among nations. The corporate leaders knew well enough that their wealth was guiding politics both at home and abroad. They saw nothing wrong in this; in fact, they felt that their political influence was essential to the full development of the world's resources. Encouraged by the doctrines of economic liberalism, they believed that they could serve humanity best by the unrestricted pursuit of profit.

ECONOMIC LIBERALISM: THEORY AND PRACTICE

Such political and economic views were quite different from the doctrine of mercantilism, which was widely accepted up to the end of the eighteenth century. Mercantilism held that economic activities should be used to strengthen the state and that the state, in turn, should guide industry and commerce (p. 411). The Scotsman Adam Smith had been the most effective critic of mercantilism during the eighteenth century. His classic work, *The Wealth of Nations* (1776), attacked the system and called for a new order of "liberal" economics. Basing his ideas on Hobbes's atomistic view of society (pp. 417–418) and the widely held idea of natural law, he argued that there exists a "natural" economy geared to human selfishness. People, if left free to follow their own nature and interests (a doctrine known as *laissez-faire*), will be led by an "invisible hand" to promote the economic welfare of all.

Smith's writing had reflected the general optimism of the Enlightenment, but later theorists—the developers of "classical" economics—presented a darker outlook as far as the working class was concerned. One such theorist was David Ricardo, a financier who had made his fortune in England during the Napoleonic Wars. In his *Principles of Political Economy and Taxation* (1817), he set forth the main "laws" governing economic affairs, such as the "law of supply and demand." He is best remembered, perhaps, for his "iron law of wages." Ricardo declared that in a free market economy with a plentiful supply of labor, wages must remain close to the level needed for bare subsistence of the workers. More than that would allow more of the workers' children to survive; this would increase the supply, which in turn would lower the "natural" price (wages). On the other hand, should wages fall so low that some workers died off, the supply of labor would then decrease, which would raise wages back to the subsistence level.

One can see why the teachings of "free market" economists gave a feeling of hope-lessness to wage earners. But the "dismal science" of economics did not dishearten the captains of trade and industry. On the contrary, it furnished them with respectable and compelling justifications for keeping wages down, for seeking profit when and where they could, and for working toward the elimination of unwanted government interference. They proved generally successful in striking down controls that were not to their liking and in promoting government action that favored their interests. Toward the end of the nineteenth century and on into the twentieth, the latter practice became increasingly common as economic and political realities moved further away from the models of Adam Smith. His doctrines nonetheless persisted—as a kind of mythology—to be called up or ignored, according to the interests of particular industries.

The Reaction of Labor and Government

"To every force there is an equal and opposing force." Readers familiar with Newton's third law of motion should have expected that bigness in business would call into being an opposing force (or forces). And indeed, by the turn of the twentieth century, Big Business was being confronted by Big Labor and Big Government. The "autono-mous" (self-directed) individual found independent actions ever more limited by huge, "autonomous" organizations.

THE APPEARANCE OF TRADE UNIONS

There is no doubt that in the long run, industrialization raised standards of living and lightened the burden of manual labor. But the transfer of production to factories from family farms and workshops weakened the traditional family unit, for it took away one of its foremost functions. Work henceforth became associated, rather, with class. Fur-ther, working conditions in the early factories were dangerous and oppressive, hours were long, and wages were low. The factory owners beat down the workers' protests and plowed profits back into more efficient machines. The capital accumulation and investment of the nineteenth century were thus drawn from the unhappy laborers, whose only choice was to work or starve. Often, in fact, even that choice was denied them. Nineteenth-century capitalism was a dynamic, unstable system. Good times (booms) alternated with bad times (depressions). Wage earners, whose daily bread de-pended on their pay envelopes, were hardest hit when the factories laid off workers. Under the doctrines of economic liberalism, they were bound to suffer for as long as the system endured.

The conditions typical of the early factories gave rise to bitter discontent. In some respects, conditions were little worse than those under the domestic system of produc-tion (pp. 300–301). But the factory system, by bringing large numbers of workers to-gether, made workers more aware of their common plight and gave them a sense of what their united power might be. Alone, the laborer was at the mercy of a large-scale em-ployer. With a surplus of hungry workers seeking jobs, an employer could run a factory without the help of any single wage-hand. Wage-hands, however, often had no place to turn should they lose their jobs. In the early part of the nineteenth century, therefore, there was no bargaining over wages and hours; they were set by the employer, and the worker could either take them or leave them.

Collective action for the purpose of bargaining with employers or influencing legislation offered some promise of relief to the laborers. They discovered, however, that whenever they tried to organize, the odds were against them. Local "trade clubs" had existed in England before the Industrial Revolution, but only in a few skills (printing, tailoring, weaving) and only in certain communities. When artisans tried to organize on a wider basis, their combinations were broken up by the joint action of employers and the government. Generally viewed by the courts as "conspiracies," trade unions had been prohibited in both France and England by 1800. Governments feared that they might lead to riots or uprisings; employers feared that they might lead to higher costs. Later legislation in England (1825) allowed unions to exist but closely limited their activities.

Nevertheless, by the middle of the nineteenth century, steps had been taken in England to organize some skilled workers on a nationwide basis. The cotton spinners, for example, began to gain recognition for their associations and to develop modern collective bargaining procedures (supported by the power of strikes). Many legal battles still had to be fought and won by British labor unions, but by 1900, two million workers, skilled and unskilled, had been organized into effective bargaining associations. A similar pattern of struggle—legal, economic, and political—followed in the United States and in other industrial countries.

THE TREND TOWARD STATE INTERVENTION

Many workers also looked to legislation as a means of remedying certain evils of industrialism. In England, the laboring classes themselves had virtually no political power until after mid-century; even before that, however, other social groups succeeded in bringing about some needed reforms through legislation. Most disinterested observers had come to agree that protective measures by the state (contrary to the doctrines of economic liberalism) were essential to the health and safety of the nation.

Reform legislation was initiated by the Tory Party, which represented primarily the interests of the landed aristocracy. Since the landowners did not usually have large investments in industry, they could best afford to promote humane treatment of factory workers. Numerous intellectuals and humanitarians, without respect to party, also supported the Tory proposals. And it is only fair to add that some of the industrialists themselves, after accumulating their fortunes, supported reforms. Factory owners as a group, however, bitterly fought all proposed limitations on their freedom to conduct their enterprises as they saw fit.

A series of parliamentary acts, beginning in 1833, removed the worst conditions in British industry. Employers were forbidden to hire children under nine years of age, and the labor of those under eighteen was restricted to nine hours a day. Women and children were excluded from mine labor (*Fig. 13.2*), and better hours and safety devices were required in the mines. Government inspectors were hired to ensure that the regulations were observed. After wage earners themselves gained the right to vote (in 1867), additional measures were enacted for their protection and welfare.

On the continent of Europe, France and Germany began to catch up to the English in industrial growth. Napoleon III established the Second Empire in 1852 with the active support of the French bourgeois (p. 495). He took effective measures to pro-

Fig. 13.2 Child Labor. There was nothing new about children working at exhausting, tedious, or dangerous tasks—bringing in grain at the harvest, straightening threads for weavers, or fetching powder for gunners aboard warships. Only in the Industrial Revolution did this practice come to be regarded as abusive and horrifying. This picture of a boy hauling coal along a mine tunnel comes from a report to the British Parliament in 1842. The working classes had little power in Britain at the time, but such depictions influenced middle- and upper-class politicians to pass labor legislation.

mote agriculture, manufacturing, and commerce. The popular emperor also showed sympathy toward the industrial working class, legalizing labor unions in 1864 and providing many social welfare institutions.

In the latter part of the century, as Germany became Europe's largest industrial producer, it also took the lead in social legislation. Labor unions, intellectuals, and religious groups helped bring about these reforms. After Bismarck became imperial German chancellor in 1871 (p. 500), he used social legislation as a means of increasing the loyalty of citizens to the new German Empire. The crowning regulatory measure was the Industrial Code of 1891, which guaranteed uniform protection to workers (with respect to hours and conditions) throughout the nation. Equally significant were later laws providing for sickness and accident insurance and old-age pensions for workers. The Social Insurance Code of 1911 became a model for other industrialized countries.

In adopting measures of this nature, the United States was at least a generation behind western Europe—though in another field of government intervention, America was ahead. Giant industries developed rapidly after the Civil War; by 1890, mergers, trusts, and other forms of business combination were eliminating competitors and making huge profits. Many liberals, labor leaders, populists, and small entrepreneurs became alarmed by the growing concentration of economic power. They demanded legislation to check the expansion of monopolies and to keep enterprise "competitive and free."

Thus in the name of liberalism, the power of the American government was called up as a counterforce to Big Business. The Sherman Antitrust Act of 1890 declared illegal "every contract, combination, or conspiracy in restraint of interstate commerce." The passage of this law was only the starting point of a long and tough contest in which government has sought to protect the public against the excesses of private economic powers; it was looked upon by those powers, however, as an encroachment on their freedom.

Urbanization and Standardization of Society

Although the move from farm to town had begun in the high Middle Ages as a response to the revival of commerce (p. 241), for centuries the flow was insignificant. It was the Industrial Revolution, along with a sudden rise in population—and in eastern Europe the belated end of serfdom, giving the peasants freedom to move and change their occupations (p. 495)—that brought about the rapid expansion of European cities.

Population figures before 1800 are only estimates, but it is evident that the number of people in Europe had risen very slowly until that time. The nineteenth century saw a startling increase, however. From 1800 to 1914, the population of western Europe grew from about 150 million to nearly 450 million—an increase greater than that of the preceding ten centuries (p. 238). (The total figure would have been still higher except for mass emigration—the largest movement of people in history. The big wave began to roll after 1870. From that year until 1914, over 26 million Europeans left their homes for the New World, more than half of them for the United States.) The extraordinary increase was the result of many factors that led to a lowering of the death rate. Chief among them were increased food production (aided by agricultural improvements), planting of more nutritious crops (the potato and Indian corn), advances in sanitation, and control of epidemics. In addition, the Industrial Revolution provided more purchasing power in the manufacturing countries, and that power was used to import more food from overseas.

By 1910, Germany, with 58 million inhabitants, had the largest population of any western European nation. Britain was next, with 42 million; then France, with 41 million; and Italy, with 36 million. The most striking growth, everywhere, was taking place in the cities. At the start of the Industrial Revolution there were only four English cities with over fifty thousand inhabitants; by 1850, there were thirty-one of that size, and half the population of Britain was living in cities—a proportion unprecedented in European history. Manchester, in the cotton-manufacturing region, was the largest and best known of the new industrial communities. Formerly a market town of 25,000 people, it had grown to half a million by 1850.

The nineteenth-century growth of cities led to a momentous change in the way of life of the Western peoples. For thousands of years since the Agricultural Revolution (pp. 11–16), the average man or woman had lived on the land, either as a smallholding peasant or as an agricultural laborer. As late as the year 1800 in most European countries, 80 to 90 percent of the population was occupied in agriculture and only 10 to 20 percent earned a living from industry or commerce. By the late twentieth century, the proportion was exactly reversed. In western Europe and the United States, less than 10 percent of the population worked in agriculture, and much of the rest of the world was moving in the same direction.

Map 13.1 Population Growth in Europe, 1820–1900. In 1820, Europe had under 50 people per square mile, except for a narrow belt, probably dating from the Middle Ages, between northern Italy and the Netherlands. A single lifetime later, most of Europe had over 50 people per square mile, and the area of heaviest population stretched from Sicily to Scotland and right across Germany. The population grew in agrarian southern Italy and eastern Europe as well as industrial Britain and Belgium, and the increase in rural Europe fed North American as well as European cities.

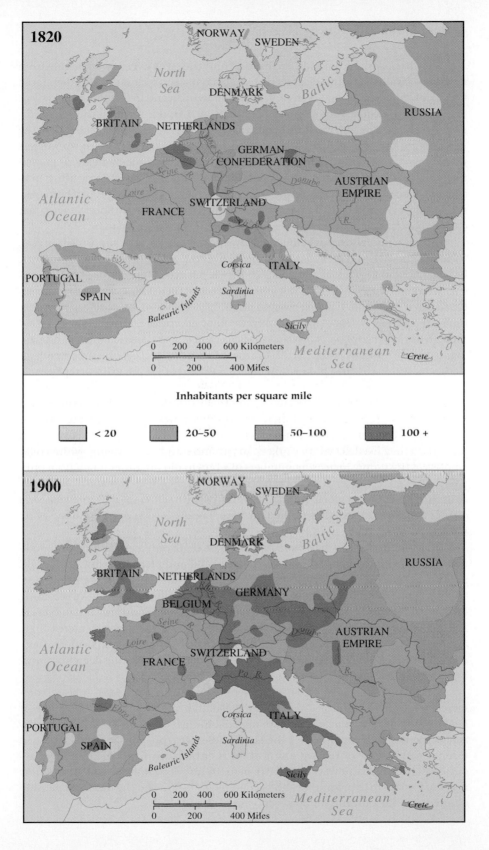

1820

NORWAY
SWEDEN

North Sea

DENMARK

Baltic Sea

RUSSIA

BRITAIN

NETHERLANDS

GERMAN CONFEDERATION

Seine

Loire R.

Danube

AUSTRIAN EMPIRE

Atlantic Ocean

SWITZERLAND

FRANCE

R.

Ebre R.

Corsica

ITALY

PORTUGAL

SPAIN

Sardinia

Balearic Islands

Sicily

0   200   400   600 Kilometers
0   200   400 Miles

Mediterranean Sea

Crete

Inhabitants per square mile

< 20   20–50   50–100   100 +

1900

NORWAY
SWEDEN

North Sea

DENMARK

Baltic Sea

RUSSIA

BRITAIN

NETHERLANDS

GERMANY

BELGIUM

Seine R.

Loire

Danube

AUSTRIAN EMPIRE

Atlantic Ocean

SWITZERLAND

FRANCE

R.

Po R.

Ebre R.

Corsica

ITALY

PORTUGAL

SPAIN

Sardinia

Balearic Islands

Sicily

0   200   400   600 Kilometers
0   200   400 Miles

Mediterranean Sea

Crete

The "backwash" from industrialization and the swift overflow of people from towns and farms overturned deep-set patterns of family and community life that traced back to the Middle Ages and even earlier. As it brought an end to the traditional way of life, the factory carried the Western peoples from a world in which they were surrounded and dominated by nature to one that was more of their own making. And the new environment was ugly. The cities lacked sewers and paving. Housing for workers was cramped, rickety, and drab. Into the crowded, soot-blackened tenements poured the refugees from rural poverty—strangers in their own land. The chronic urban maladies of alienation, disease, and crime have persisted ever since. All this had been foreseen by the classic liberal Thomas Jefferson, who had written in 1800, "I view great cities as pestilential to the morals, the health, and the liberties of man."

Cities, in time, also brought much that was positive: better education, medical care, theaters, libraries, and merchandise from all over the earth. Even these advantages, however, were shared unequally, and poor people felt even more deprived in the presence of commodities they could not afford. Moreover, they seldom found the satisfaction in their daily labor that had brought meaning to the life of the craftsman in earlier times. The factory system reduced workers to the attending of machines and subjected them to its rigid discipline. Narrowing specialization of tasks chained them to deadening, repetitive motions. Workers, like the machine and all its parts, became standardized, replaceable cogs in a production line that turned out standardized, replaceable things.

Alongside the factory, there grew up another institution that shaped the lives of millions of people from the late nineteenth century onward: the office. Big Business and Big Government needed office workers and other "white-collar" employees even more than they needed factory workers. In pay and standards of living, white-collar employees (including increasing numbers of women) did not differ much from ordinary "blue-collar" workers, but since they did not do heavy or dirty manual labor, they considered themselves more respectable. Together with self-employed small business owners and storekeepers, they formed the lower middle class as opposed to the working class.

Mass production and maximum profits required not only standardized commodities but also mass demand. In order to keep capital and plant working at their full potential, advertising was developed to force-feed natural desires. Organized "buy" appeals supported and expanded the media of mass communication—overcoming local resistance and tending to make the demand for goods uniform and universal. As the twentieth century proceeded, the individual came to be viewed increasingly as a consumer of goods, a permanent target of the commercial persuaders. Daily choices (whether conscious or not) would be governed to a mounting degree by enticing propaganda.

Mass culture thus came into being, essentially as we know it today—plastic, commercialized, and conformist. Though it included numerous and varied subcultures, it held to one constant value: concern for material things. The materialism and secularism of the West, on the rise since the late Middle Ages (pp. 303–304, 336–337), had reached new heights by the beginning of the twentieth century. The Westerners' acquisitive character had always opened them to the lure of worldly goods. The machine now enabled them to produce wealth beyond their dreams, and the new salesmanship ensured that those dreams would never cease.

The Development of Socialist Thought and Action

The impact of the machine provoked a wide range of intellectual responses. In alternating moods of gloom, bewilderment, and hope, people sought to understand where the machine was leading them and how to adapt it to human ends. Since the machine was identified in the nineteenth century with the system of industrial capitalism, that system became the focus of analysis and criticism.

We saw earlier in this chapter that many workers turned to unions and social legislation to protect themselves and their families. But some workers and intellectuals became convinced that reform within the system was insufficient. Reacting to the social reality of nineteenth-century capitalism, they believed that the only hope for a better economic life and a just society lay in a radical change of the system itself. Most of these critics, though their ideas ranged across a broad spectrum, may be classified generally as socialists.

UTOPIAN SOCIALISM

Among the socialist thinkers of the nineteenth century, the major division was between "utopians" and Marxists. The former belonged to a tradition reaching back as far as Plato (pp. 82–83). Their general approach was to turn from the evils apparent in the existing order and to seek in their imagination something closer to their ideal of life and society—as Sir Thomas More had done in the sixteenth century in his depiction of an ideal society on the imaginary island of Utopia (Greek for "no place"; p. 360).

In France, the utopians pursued two distinct lines of thought. Count Henri de Saint-Simon proposed a reorganization of society from the top, with state ownership of the means of production and control by a national board of scientists, engineers, and industrialists (technocrats). The purpose of industry would be production rather than profit, and workers and managers would be rewarded according to individual merit. In his chief work, *The New Christianity* (1825), Saint-Simon stressed philanthropic motives: "The whole of society ought to strive toward the amelioration of the moral and physical existence of the poorest class; society ought to organize itself in the way best adapted for attaining this end." Saint-Simon's disciples in France, some of whom became leaders in politics, were among the first modern advocates of a nationally planned society.

Charles Fourier, a younger contemporary of Saint-Simon, took a different approach. Resisting the idea of centralized economic control, he favored the creation of thousands of small production units, which he called "phalanxes." Limited in size to four hundred families, each phalanx would contain a residential hotel, school, market, health service, and other public facilities—in addition to its own farms and manufacturing plants. All these were to be community property, and the rule governing labor and distribution would be *"From each according to his ability; to each according to his needs."* (The Marxists were later to adopt this slogan.) Surplus production would be exchanged for other goods by barter among the phalanxes; within each plant, workers would change jobs often in order to reduce the monotony of performing repetitive tasks.

Fourier's ideas attracted numerous followers, and a few isolated phalanxes were actually established in America—notably Brook Farm, near Boston. Each phalanx had its own internal problems, and each was doomed to failure. Success for Fourier's plan would have required the development of an extensive system of phalanxes, and there was scarcely a chance that this could have come into being.

The efforts of Robert Owen, an industrialist and utopian planner, failed for the same basic reason. A successful cotton mill owner in New Lanark, Scotland, Owen was distressed by the poverty, ignorance, and immorality of his employees. He determined to change matters and succeeded in setting up a model factory and community in New Lanark. He was not satisfied, however, with his own local reforms and sought to reform the whole industrial order. Owen observed that the factory system had not freed work-ers—it had enslaved them. Under laissez-faire, their condition remained at a miserable level. Morals had fallen along with material standards of living, and the traditional ties of compassion between master and servant were missing in the new industrial order. Owen had fair success in promoting remedial factory legislation, but this served only to check the worst abuses. After failing to persuade factory owners to follow his example at New Lanark, he proposed that the poor be organized into cooperative, self-sufficient villages.

Owen's plan won commendation in the British press and in Parliament, but noth-ing more. Abandoning his appeals to the leaders of government and industry, he next turned to the working people themselves. Out of his efforts grew several producers' co-operatives, including one overseas—at New Harmony, Indiana. Founded in 1824, this venture, like the others, lasted only a few years. Owen nonetheless left his mark on public thought and on the struggle to lighten the harshness of industrialism. But it took another, more rigorous thinker to produce a tougher brand of socialism that would meet the capitalist system head on.

SCIENTIFIC SOCIALISM: THE SYNTHESIS OF MARX

Karl Marx brushed aside "utopian" ideas as sentimental and unrealistic; in this he shared the opinion of most of the capitalists of his time. Marx's study of history told him that events are shaped by underlying economic developments, rather than by ide-alistic reformers, and he believed that these developments were leading toward the collapse of capitalism. Therefore, he insisted, the proper task of workers and intellectu-als is to understand the trend of history and to participate in its forward movement. While accepting some of the observations and principles of Owen and Fourier, he felt that their appeals distracted people from the "correct" course of thought and action.

It was in this sense that Marx and his followers regarded his doctrine as "scien-tific." Marx set forth certain theories and sought to prove them by the evidence of his-tory. Materialist, rationalist, libertarian, and revolutionist, Marx was an heir of the En-lightenment—who drew upon the leading scientific, economic, and philosophical ideas of the nineteenth century. But reflecting also the Romantic spirit of his age, Marx's teachings contain strong elements of faith and feeling as well as of reason and science.

Marx and Engels. Born in the Rhineland (Germany) of a middle-class Jewish family, the youthful Karl attended the universities of Bonn and Berlin. His father (a convert to Lutheranism) was a lawyer, and the son began to prepare for the same profession. Soon, however, Karl became attracted to the study of history and philosophy and would have liked to qualify himself for a professorship. But he feared that his Jewish identity and his liberal political views would block his chances of winning a university ap-pointment, for this was the period of the conservative reaction in Germany. Caught up by the revolutionary stirrings of the 1840s, he turned instead to journalism and pamphleteering.

With his lifelong friend and partner, Friedrich Engels, Marx organized revolutionary groups and wrote *The Communist Manifesto* in 1848. After participating in the insurrections of that year in the Rhineland, he escaped to London, where he remained for the rest of his life. He was one of the first critics to stress the international character of working-class movements—thus placing himself in opposition to the mounting spirit of nationalism in Europe (pp. 495–496). From London, Marx continued his association with revolutionary movements in various countries and helped found the First (Socialist) International in 1864. He also spent long hours in the British Museum studying history and economics.

Class Struggle and Revolution. The most famous product of Marx's labors, *Das Kapital* (Capital), consisted chiefly of theory and analysis and is closely related to the writings of the classical liberal economists (pp. 510–511). Working largely from their stated "laws" and principles, Marx concluded that all economic value is produced by human labor and that the capitalist unjustly takes over a portion of this value. The system, he claimed, promises nothing but misery to the laborers and contains contradictions that ensure its own destruction.

But Marx's economic conclusions were perhaps the least original, least proven, and least important of his ideas. His enormous influence would come from the fact that he was able to join his criticism of capitalism with a revolutionary program based on a unified view of history, politics, and morals. The philosopher Hegel gave Marx the key to his general view. History is an unceasing process, said Hegel, governed at any moment by the struggle between a dominant idea and its opposing idea (pp. 479–480). Marx was excited by Hegel's dialectic principle, but he had no use for the notion that ideas are the prime forces in history. After much study and reflection, he concluded that the "mode of production" (the way in which society is organized to produce material goods) is the main determining force in a given society; its opposing force arises from technological changes that are no longer appropriate to the established economic structure. Thus did Marx "turn Hegel upside down." The flow of history and the growth of ideas and institutions, Marx thought, are all shaped by changes in the mode of production. And this evolution had passed through four principal stages: "the Asiatic, the ancient, the feudal, and the modern bourgeois methods of production."

Each mode of production, Marx said, involves "class struggle," for each serves a particular "ruling" class, which takes advantage of its opposing "exploited" class. The ancient world had its masters and slaves, and the feudal age, its nobles and peasants. As for the capitalist age, it had its increasingly wealthy and powerful class of business owners, managers, and stockholders and its increasingly numerous and poverty-stricken class of industrial wage-hands. Marx called the first of these groups by the French name for better-off townspeople, the *bourgeois,* and the second by the Latin name for propertyless citizens of ancient Rome, the *proletarians.* Marx believed that the ruling class of each age provides laws and institutions to guarantee its continued exploitation of the opposing class. The state itself thus becomes a mechanism of suppression. The government of the nineteenth-century capitalist state, he declared, was "a committee for managing the common affairs of the whole bourgeoisie" (the bourgeois class).

Social revolutions occur, according to Marx, when a new mode of production—taking shape within the framework of the old—bursts the bonds of established laws and relationships. The agents of the revolution are the "new" class, which in time becomes the ruling class. Thus, he argued, the seventeenth- and eighteenth-century revolutions in England, North America, and France, as well as those of 1830 and 1848, had been "bourgeois revolutions," promoted by the bourgeoisie. The effect of these revolutions had been to overthrow feudalism and its noble ruling class, thereby paving the way for a new capitalist economic order in which the ruling class would be the bourgeoisie. Marx regarded the bourgeoisie's exploitation of the proletariat (the proletarian class) as the most brutal in history. Nevertheless, he felt that the bourgeoisie had played a constructive and progressive role, essentially by destroying the previous feudal order and creating the liberal state, within which the proletariat could prepare for its own proletarian revolution. This was in keeping with his (and Hegel's) view of history as moving irresistibly toward higher and higher goals of human fulfillment.

Proletarian Revolution, Socialism, and Communism. But the hour had struck for the bourgeoisie, as it had earlier for the European nobility. The potential of expanding technology could not be realized within the structure of private capitalism; and the capitalist system of production, hit by increasingly severe depressions, was stumbling toward its end. In accordance with the dialectic principle, the old system had already brought into existence the class that would overthrow it and build a new order upon the ruins. This class, the proletariat, was being drawn into the industrial centers in ever-larger numbers. All it needed in order to help history along was Marxist instruction and organization.

Marx predicted that the mounting clashes between the proletariat and the bourgeoisie would lead to the triumph of the working class—either by peaceful means, within the framework of the liberal state, or more likely through violent revolution. This victory would bring an end to the historic class struggle, for all individuals would then be included in one body of workers. Dismantling the old social order and taking over the means of production would be carried out under a temporary "dictatorship of the proletariat." This would be followed, in turn, by an intermediate period of democratic "socialism," during which individuals would "work according to their ability and receive according to their output." Socialism would lead eventually to pure "communism."

Once communism had been reached, the state would "wither away," Marx believed, because without a class struggle, there would be no reason for the existence of a state. Thus would come into being, for the first time in civilized history, "true" liberty for all. In the vaguely outlined communist society, voluntary associations would plan and carry out production; individuals would work according to their abilities and receive according to their needs; private persuasion and restraint would replace police, prisons, and war.

Even if we grant a measure of truth to Marx's analysis of the past, his vision of the future was a Romantic one—as demonstrated by failures of Marxist societies in the last decade of the twentieth century. If accepted at all, it had to be accepted on faith. Indeed, the followers of Marx found in his doctrines a kind of religion; they called it the "religion of man," and Marx was its prophet. There were Marxist equivalents of apostles and saints—as well as despised heretics. The sacred books were Marx's writings, defended by "dialectical" theologians. The Party was the Church, and true believers had to have unquestioning faith in its gospel and its works. The Marxist heaven was their idealized society to come. At a time when the foundations of "old-fashioned" religion

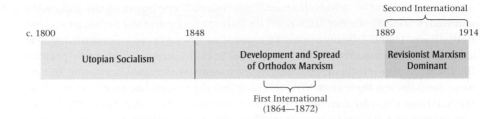

and liberalism were being challenged, Marx created a new worldview of the facts, theories, and hopes of the industrial age. Its promise appealed to the working class, but it appealed also to many intellectuals who felt alienated from industrialism and were looking for some kind of total reorientation. Partial critiques and actions based on a mix of traditional values (as in utopianism) left such people unsatisfied. Marxism offered a unified view and a psychological substitute for traditional religion.

THE INTERPRETERS OF MARX: REVOLUTIONARY AND EVOLUTIONARY

The Marxist "truth," however, has been open to differing interpretations. Had capitalism faltered and collapsed during the nineteenth century, as Marx himself expected, the division among his followers might have been less profound. But the established order proved much tougher, much more adaptable, than he had expected. Reform laws and unions strengthened capitalism (as did Marxist criticism), improved the distribution of purchasing power, and bettered the conditions of the workers. The rich were getting richer, as Marx had predicted, but the poor (at least in the West) were not getting poorer. And in the United States, the young giant of capitalism, no strong revolutionary feeling or class consciousness appeared among the wage earners.

How did the Marxists deal with this indefinite postponement of the day of revolution? Most socialist workers tended to make their peace with the existing system. True, a small group of Marxists stuck by the "hard" line, scorning "legalism" and "gradualism." But the larger group recognized that such a stand would not appeal to the bulk of workers. They stated frankly that Marxist doctrine would have to be revised if it were to continue as a major force.

The "revisionists" mapped a much longer (and different) road to the ideal society. They stressed democracy, parliamentary methods, and class cooperation as means of achieving further reforms. Eduard Bernstein, a German socialist, was the leading advocate for this view. (The "Fabian" socialists of England, though non-Marxist, held a similar position.) The broad term "social democratic" can be applied to most of the labor parties in European politics after 1890; they represented the "evolutionary" wing among the heirs of Marx. The "revolutionary" wing remained significant only in eastern Europe, where the absence of effective representative government prevented change by peaceful, legal methods. It was there, in a relatively backward country, Russia, that the revolutionary Marxists would achieve the first great victory of socialism (pp. 569–570).

A different sort of attack upon the established order of the nineteenth century took the form of anarchism. This view holds that any use of authority—economic, religious, or political—is an unjustified interference with the individual. Believing that human beings are basically good, the anarchists claim that voluntary, harmonious relationships could be achieved among individuals if the power of the state were removed. Some, like the Russian writer Leo Tolstoy (p. 533) and the American essayist Henry David Thoreau, firmly opposed the use of violence as a means of realizing their ideas. But others pursued what they considered to be the direct and necessary route to the abolition of government: assassination of government officials, terrorism, and insurrection. Though these anarchist ideas were first expressed in western Europe, it was Mikhail Bakunin, a Russian nobleman, who exerted the largest influence. Bakunin died in 1876; his followers succeeded in killing (among others) Tsar Alexander II of Russia, President Sadi Carnot of France, King Humbert I of Italy, and President William McKinley of the United States. Such acts of terror horrified the powerful everywhere but failed to produce an effective movement for social change or for the abolition of state power. Nevertheless, these acts were forerunners of terrorist killings in the twentieth century (p. 628).

THE CHRISTIAN RESPONSE

It was unthinkable that the established churches of the West could ignore the impact of industrial capitalism or the Marxist (and anarchist) attack upon it. While the one appeared destructive of certain Christian values and virtues, the other appealed openly to class hatred and violence. Both were roundly condemned, at last, by the most powerful spokesman of Western Christendom, the pope. In 1891, Leo XIII addressed his bishops through a formal letter (encyclical) entitled *Rerum Novarum* (Of New Things). In this carefully drawn, comprehensive statement, he set forth the position of his church on the relations between capital and labor.

The pope's immediate concern, as expressed in his letter, was for the "misery and wretchedness which press so heavily at this moment on the large majority of the very poor." The workers, he went on, "have been given over, isolated and defenseless, to the callousness of employers and the greed of unrestrained competition." Going still further, he declared that "a small number of very rich men have been able to lay upon the masses of the poor a yoke little better than slavery itself."

But the socialist remedy, the pontiff declared, called for the destruction of private property. Such action would be unjust to the present lawful owners of property and would deprive workers of the main object of their labors. He also rejected the socialist idea of equalizing wealth as being "against nature." The overriding mistake of the Marxists, however, was their feeling that social classes must be mutually hostile, "that rich and poor are intended by nature to live at war with one another." On the contrary, stated Pope Leo, "it is ordained by nature that these two classes should exist in harmony. . . . Capital cannot do without labor, nor labor without capital."

Quoting freely from the leading Catholic philosopher of the Middle Ages, Thomas Aquinas (pp. 270–271), who was known for his efforts to harmonize conflicting positions, the pope urged a Christian "middle course." Moderation and cooperation should guide the common affairs of employers and employees. Working people must give honest work and never injure the owners or their property; the owners must never make excessive demands on their employees' labor or pay them less than the needs of their families require. For the purpose of mutual help and wage bargaining, workers should be allowed to form unions; and if workers find themselves too weak to defend their rightful interests, the government must intervene with protective legislation.

At the same time, however, the government must preserve absolutely the sanctity of private property.

Rerum Novarum gave little comfort to aggressive entrepreneurs on the political right or to angry critics of capitalism on the left. But it offered a guide for moderates who wished to see the rewards of labor improved while avoiding industrial violence. It also prompted the founding of new Catholic trade unions and Catholic political parties in most of the countries of Europe. These organizations have exercised notable influence to the present day. Finally, *Rerum Novarum* pointed the way, morally and philosophically, to the democratic "welfare states" of the twentieth century (pp. 582–585).

Because of its organizational structure, it was possible and logical for the Roman Catholic Church to present a unified response to the disturbing economic changes of the nineteenth century. The response by Protestant churches, on the other hand, reflected their historical divisions into numerous national and denominational groups. In the wake of scientific findings and rising secularism in the Western world, Christian (and Jewish) believers were already torn between "modernists," who accepted the new science, and "fundamentalists," who rejected it and adhered to the "higher truth" of the literal Bible. Now another serious split was developing with respect to the impact of industrialization. Most Protestant preachers and congregations remained essentially conservative on economic issues, but an activist minority began to speak out for increased social consciousness, measures to assist the poor, and greater "economic justice."

In England and America, the Anglican Church played a prominent role in these efforts, often called the Social Gospel. And aside from the well-known churches, a new evangelical movement, the Salvation Army, was founded in 1865 by William Booth. He began this campaign in England, but it soon became a visible international operation. The "army" sent its "soldiers" (male and female) onto the city streets seeking to "save souls" but also to collect contributions for helping the needy with food, clothing, and shelter. This unique organization and the many other carriers of the Social Gospel would continue their humanitarian work into and through the twentieth century.

The Accelerating Progress of Science

Accompanying the technological progress, social changes, and class conflicts of the nineteenth century were great leaps in pure science. The foundations of scientific organization and method had been laid in the seventeenth century (pp. 422–425), and science had continued to progress in the eighteenth century. But now the increase in knowledge became so fast as to make science what it has remained ever since—the intellectual enterprise that more than any other decides the destiny of the human race.

It was chiefly the progress of pure science that drove forward the Industrial Revolution after the middle of the nineteenth century (pp. 507–508). In many other ways, too, the influence and prestige of science rose to new heights. Generals, industrialists, statesmen, theologians, and philosophers sought to ally themselves with scientific doctrines. Social researchers of various sorts tried to model their methods of inquiry on those of mathematics, physics, or biology—and in the process to establish new branches of "social knowledge" that might draw the kind of respect paid to natural science. Moreover, due especially to the work of Charles Darwin, science once again called into question traditional ideas on the place of humanity in the universe and its relationship to God.

ENERGY AND MATTER

Physical scientists continued to build on the foundations of Galileo, Newton, and Boyle (pp. 419–425). One of the most important subjects of their investigations was energy. Experimenters proved the equivalence of heat and energy and formulated two basic laws of thermodynamics. The First Law states that the total energy (or heat) in the universe remains constant, though it is continually changing its form. The Second Law states that energy systems tend toward degradation (heat, for example, flows from a hotter body to a colder one); hence the amount of useful energy is diminishing in the universe. These generalizations, supplementing the Newtonian laws of motion (pp. 423–424), gave fresh understanding to physicists, chemists, astronomers—and even philosophers.

In addition, major theoretical discoveries were made, with far-reaching practical applications, about electricity, magnetism, and light. Newton had observed that when sunlight passes through a prism, it spreads into a band of colors, or a *spectrum*—red at one end and indigo (dark blue) at the other. Scientists of the nineteenth century discovered that each chemical substance, when heated to incandescence (strongly enough to emit light), yields a spectrum distinct from every other. Spectrum analysis was developed as a tool for chemists—and for astronomers in studying sources of light in space (p. 641). In addition, researchers made progress in identifying the actual nature of light as a series of vibrations or waves: in the spectrum, red is longer-wavelength light, and indigo is light of shorter wavelength.

These results were in turn linked with new findings about the nature of electricity and magnetism. Ever since the Renaissance, researchers had been investigating these two forces and had gradually come to suspect that they were in some way closely related. Finally, about the middle of the nineteenth century, Michael Faraday proved that this was so, and devised many ingenious experiments in which he used magnetism to produce electric currents and vice versa. In others, he used electricity in one coil of wire to cause a flow of current in another with which it was not connected. Out of these experiments, inventors soon developed electrical generators and motors, and Alexander Graham Bell devised the first telephone; thus the modern electrical and communications industries were born.

Meanwhile, in 1861, a brilliant Scottish physicist, James Clerk Maxwell, used Faraday's results to produce an exact mathematical description of the behavior of electricity and magnetism. Remarkably, Maxwell's laws for the behavior of electricity and magnetism turned out to be exactly the same as those already discovered for the behavior of light. Evidently, all three were simply different forms of one and the same phenomenon—*electromagnetism*. True, only light was visible to the human eye, but invisible electromagnetism, too, must be able to travel in wavelike form with no obvious pathway to conduct it. As a result of Maxwell's findings, in 1887 Heinrich Hertz was able to build the first devices to transmit and receive these invisible electromagnetic waves.

The nineteenth century also witnessed many discoveries in chemistry and the theory of matter. The ancient Greek Democritus (p. 79) had theorized that matter was reducible to invisible, indivisible particles or atoms. John Dalton, a British schoolteacher, accepted this general notion but found, early in the nineteenth century, that each chemical element was composed of atoms of different weights. Scientists later assumed the existence of *molecules*—combinations of atoms of the same or different elements. Most material substances, they concluded, are made up of molecules. In the nineteenth and early twentieth centuries, much chemical research was devoted to the analysis of molecules and the synthesis (artificial creation) of new ones, with astonishing results: basic understanding of the way in which atoms combine to form molecules; the invention of new dyestuffs, explosives, drugs, and the earliest plastics; and the identification of many substances found in living tissue.

THE ATOM, SPACE, AND TIME

All these advances took place within the understanding of the workings of nature that had developed on the basis of Newton's discoveries (pp. 423–424), but further developments starting shortly before 1900 began to correct or modify this "classical physics" in various ways. Toward the end of the nineteenth century, it was discovered that certain chemical elements, such as uranium, emitted rays, so to speak, "of their own accord" (without being heated, electrified, or otherwise stimulated)—a phenomenon that the Polish scientist Marie Curie, who was mainly responsible for identifying the elements concerned, called "radioactivity."

Subsequent research showed that radioactive and other types of rays in fact consisted of streams of tiny particles, which were evidently smaller than the atoms out of which the emitting substances must be composed. Clearly, for this to happen, something must be going on within the atoms, which must themselves be built up of still smaller particles. By studying various forms of radioactivity, Ernest Rutherford and Niels Bohr introduced their model of the atom (about 1910), which they saw as a miniature solar system, containing a nucleus of one or more *protons* with encircling *electrons*—and like the solar system, consisting mainly of empty space. Later research would show the atom to be even more complex than Rutherford or Bohr at first believed (pp. 642–643), but their concept was the starting point for modern atomic physics.

In this way, one of the main assumptions of classical physics, the solidity of objects, began to dissolve. At the same time, the German physicist Albert Einstein attacked some other major classical assumptions—those that concerned mass, energy, space, and time. In his special theory of relativity, announced in 1905 and later extended to a general theory, Einstein recognized that Newtonian physics "worked" well enough for ordinary purposes, but he believed that it did not truly describe the universe of nature. Newton and his followers had conceived of space and motion as *absolute*. They assumed the existence of an "ether," a kind of immovable substance that fills the universal void (empty space). All changes in positions of objects, they thought, could be measured absolutely by reference to this ether. But experiments in the late nineteenth century proved that no such substance exists, thus destroying any fixed basis for reference.

Einstein met this puzzlement with a radically different approach. Matter and motion are not absolutes, he declared, but are *relative*. They can be measured only from a given point or system in time and space. (What is the velocity of a fly buzzing about inside a speeding aircraft?) Einstein believed, further, that objects have a *space-time* dimension that affects their length, breadth, and thickness. Bodies moving toward or away from a given point have shifting proportions of length and mass with respect to that point. The alterations are not noticeable in ordinary motions, but they become significant as bodies approach the speed of light. The speed of light is the one constant he found in the universe; it remains the same for all physical systems. In another way, too, mass is not an absolute but can be converted into energy. The tiny atomic "solar systems" that make up physical objects can be completely destroyed, releasing all the enormous energy contained within them—the basic concept behind the development of nuclear power and nuclear weapons (p. 644).

MEDICINE AND THE STRUCTURE OF LIFE

Alongside these spectacular advances in physical science, the nineteenth century was just as much the century of biological and medical progress. Drawing on seventeenth-century descriptions of cellular structure in plants, Theodor Schwann developed the cell theory to explain organic (living) matter. It was realized by about 1835 that all living things consist of tiny cells whose health and growth determine the physical fate of the total organism, and a special branch of biology (cytology) was established for the study of cells.

Bacteriology, an outgrowth of the germ theory of disease, opened for examination the world of microorganisms. These tiny forms of life had been seen through the primitive microscopes of the seventeenth century, but little attention was given to them until after 1850. It was a French chemist, Louis Pasteur, who first theorized that bacteria (germs) were the cause of many deadly illnesses. Physicians knew of the existence of bacteria but thought them the result, rather than the cause, of disease. After years of ridicule, Pasteur at last had the opportunity to demonstrate the correctness of his theory and the practice of preventive inoculation (vaccination). His first successful test was against an epidemic of anthrax disease in sheep.

Once the germ theory was accepted, it led quickly to the identification, treatment, and prevention of countless bacteriological and viral diseases, as well as to antiseptic procedures in surgery and improvements in public hygiene and sanitation. The mass killers—bubonic plague, typhus, smallpox, and cholera—were at last subject to human control. No other development in science can match the importance of the germ theory in its effect on the world's death rate—and the consequent upward curve of human population.

THE DEVELOPMENT OF LIFE: EVOLUTION

The work of Charles Darwin, the main originator of the theory of evolution, may be compared with that of Isaac Newton, who lived two centuries earlier. As Newton completed the overturn of ancient ideas about the physical universe and its governing principles, so Darwin completed a revolution of thought with respect to the earth's creatures—the human species in particular. Scientific opinion, until about 1850, had supported the idea of the fixed nature of each species, within a "Great Chain of Being." A Swedish botanist, Carolus Linnaeus, was in part responsible for the persistence of this idea. His work as a classifier (in the 1730s) helped develop the notion that all creatures had been placed in a neat and permanent overall scheme. Linnaeus assumed, and most of his readers believed, that all members of a particular species could be traced back, without change, to an original pair formed at the time of the Creation.

Before the nineteenth century, there had been insufficient evidence either to prove or to disprove this theory. But by 1850, discoveries in comparative anatomy, embryology, and geology were pointing toward one inescapable conclusion. Even before Darwin published *On the Origin of Species by Means of Natural Selection* in 1859, the theory of change in species had been accepted by a number of naturalists and philosophers. Darwin focused his life's work on that theory and established it securely on the basis of his observations, collected data, and reasoned explanations.

The Process of Evolution. Though the evolutionary theory raised many thorny problems, it won acceptance because it suited known facts better than did rival theories. According to Darwin, all forms of life are descended from a few original creatures. Each individual (and the species of which it is a part) has come into existence as the result of an unbroken competitive struggle. Continuing slight variations in physical qualities give an advantage to some creatures over others; the losers in the struggle die out, while the winners pass on their distinctive qualities through heredity. Darwin called this process the "survival of the fittest."

Without the concept of geological time, Darwin could not have convinced even himself, for the process of "natural selection" required a sweep of centuries beyond human imagination—to produce, in tiny steps, the kinds of changes that carried upward from plankton to mammals. But Charles Lyell, an English geologist, had opened the door to Darwin's theory. Prior to the appearance of Lyell's *Principles of Geology* in 1830, most educated individuals believed that the earth's history had been relatively short and that the earth's surface had undergone sudden and drastic changes ("catastrophism"). Lyell helped to reverse this view, holding that geological change had been slow and gradual and that the earth's age ran into hundreds of millions of years.

Second only to Lyell in direct influence on Darwin was Thomas Malthus, whose *Essay on the Principle of Population* (p. 478) offered a key to the process of natural selection. Malthus pointed out that reproduction in animals advances at a rate that outstrips the supply of food. Hence the fate of all nature's creatures is one of struggle for survival. This point was crucial to Darwin's doctrine, for without the elimination of some individuals and the survival of others, there would be no selection among the variant creatures.

The Process of Inheritance. The least satisfactory portion of Darwin's theory concerns the means by which survival characteristics are transmitted to succeeding generations. He believed this to be essentially a matter of superior individuals passing along their physical characteristics to their offspring. But already in Darwin's time, research by the Austrian botanist Gregor Mendel was laying the basis for a different explanation of heredity. By lengthy experiments with successive generations of plants and careful analysis of the results, Mendel was able to show, among other things, that a plant could carry what he called "hereditary factors" for particular characteristics even if it did not possess those characteristics itself: thus a short plant could carry the "factor" for tallness.

Later researchers in the new science of genetics used Mendel's results to correct Darwin's understanding of heredity in a way that actually strengthened the theory of evolution as a whole. Evolution, they said, depended not so much on the physical characteristics of individuals as on an entire species' supply of "hereditary factors," or, as they came to be called, *genes*. Only widespread *mutations* (changes) in gene supply could cause a change in the species.

Early in the twentieth century, the new theory of genes was linked up with the results of research into the cells of which all living things are composed. Nineteenth-
century cytologists (cell researchers; p. 526) had discovered that both the growth of
living things, and also their reproduction (the generation of new living things by existing ones) take place by means of cell division (the splitting of one cell into two).
They had also discovered that when a cell divides, threadlike structures called *chromosomes* form within it, and these are transferred by various processes into the new cells.
In 1911, the American geneticist Thomas H. Morgan suggested that Mendel's genes are
tiny physical entities that are somehow strung out along the chromosomes—thereby
moving from cell to cell in both growth and reproduction so as to determine and regulate the physical characteristics of new organisms. This insight not only further filled
in the picture of evolution; but out of it the twentieth-century science of molecular
biology would eventually be born (pp. 644–645).

DARWINISM IN PHILOSOPHY AND SOCIAL THOUGHT

The first and most obvious impact of Darwinism, outside the field of science itself, was
on religion. Severe attacks were mounted against the theory by religious thinkers and
devout Christians. Though some Darwinists argued that the divine hand can (and does)
work its will through evolution, critics of the theory preferred to think that humans
had been fashioned directly in God's image. The Copernican theory had dwarfed the
importance of the earth in the heavens (p. 426); the Darwinian theory now reduced
the importance of human beings by associating them with animal evolution (*Fig. 13.3*).
Moreover, it contradicted the literal reading of the Book of Genesis. It is small wonder
that many Christians were shaken by what appeared to be another blow to their faith
and pride.

All the same, by the end of the nineteenth century, the theory of evolution had
come to be generally accepted by educated people, and from the start, there were philosophers, statesmen, industrialists, and theologians who welcomed the doctrine and
sought to extend it beyond the biological field. Herbert Spencer, a brilliant and self-
educated advocate of evolution, was one of those most excited by Darwin's writings. It
was he who stressed Darwin's phrase "survival of the fittest" to describe the governing
principle in nature, and more significantly, Spencer asserted that the principle applies
not only to living creatures but to human institutions, customs, and ideas as well. All
of these, he reasoned, have their cycle of origin, growth, competition, decay, and extinction. Thus there can be no "absolutes" of religious or moral truth; there is only the
passing truth of ideas that have evolved and have (so far) survived.

These convictions, however, did not drive Spencer to atheism (p. 427). Like some
church leaders of his day, he adapted his faith in God to the new facts of science. Behind these facts, he believed, there must exist a supernatural power—one that humans
cannot fully know. He believed, however, that moral standards can be established on
the basis of what we do know. Spencer put forward a "science" of ethics based on the
principles of natural evolution: moral acts are those that contribute to human adaptation and progress. Moral perfection will be reached, he concluded, by "the completely
adapted man in the completely evolved society."

Spencer's philosophy of morals did not pass unchallenged in the nineteenth century. If morality is geared to the evolutionary processes of nature, what becomes of

MR. BERGH TO THE RESCUE.

THE DEFRAUDED GORILLA. "That *Man* wants to claim my Pedigree. He says he is one of my Descendants."
MR. BERGH. "Now, Mr. DARWIN, how could you insult him so?"

Fig. 13.3 Evolutionist and Humanitarian. Among the most disturbing of Darwin's ideas was the claim that humans had not been created by God in his own image but had evolved from lower animals. The notion inspired both indignation and—as in this cartoon by the American Thomas Nast—laughter. But here the laughter has a double target. The gorilla's friend is Henry Bergh, founder of the American Society for the Prevention of Cruelty to Animals. Nast mocks both Darwin for ruthlessly lowering humans to the animal level, and Bergh for sentimentally raising animals to the human level.

one's own moral responsibility and freedom? What has science to do with ethics? A further objection was that nature itself had been shown by Darwin to be ruthlessly amoral (lacking in moral concern). How, then, could nature serve as a foundation for morals? Some, indeed, saw magnificence in the new view of nature; Darwin himself found it thrilling: "Thus, from the war of nature, from famine and death, the most exalted object which we are capable of conceiving, namely the production of the higher animals, directly follows. There is grandeur in this view of life . . . from so simple a beginning endless forms most beautiful and wonderful have been, and are being evolved." But this creation so admired by Darwin had been achieved through monstrous waste and universal conflict. The sweet Mother Nature of the Romantic poets (pp. 482–483) had revealed another and terrible face.

It soon became clear that Darwinism could be interpreted and applied in conflicting ways. All could agree on one central point: the idea of a static world, of fixed relations and values, had been overthrown and replaced by the idea of continuous change and struggle. But how people should think and act in relation to the struggle, especially human struggle, was a question that drew profoundly different answers.

The implications of Darwinism for social action had far-reaching consequences. After reading *On the Origin of Species,* Karl Marx declared that it furnished a "basis in natural science for the class struggle in history." Marx gave Darwin a copy of *Das Kapital,* but it is doubtful whether the scientist read it. Darwin was, rather, inclined to agree with the classical economists of his time, who saw the social struggle as a "natural" expression of human competition. As his friend Herbert Spencer explained, "The poverty of the incapable, the distresses that come upon the imprudent, the starvation of the idle, and those shoulderings aside of the weak by the strong, which leave so many 'in shallows and miseries,' are the decree of a large far-seeing benevolence."

The American billionaire John D. Rockefeller once used an attractive metaphor to explain how natural selection worked to the advantage of all. The man who had built Standard Oil into a giant monopoly by beating out his competitors compared his work to the breeding of a lovely flower. The American Beauty rose, with its splendor and fragrance, could not have been produced, Rockefeller told a Sunday school audience, except by sacrificing the buds that grew up around it. In the same way, the development of a large business is "merely survival of the fittest . . . merely the working-out of a law of nature and a law of God."

Rockefeller and other titans of industry were unashamed promoters of what was later called *Social Darwinism.* Essentially, it approved a no-holds-barred struggle of "all against all," in the manner of the jungle. And the idea readily passed from one of battle among individuals to one of battle among races and nations. Darwin's theory strengthened the convictions of slave owners, racists, militarists, and extreme nationalists. Many individuals, including some respected philosophers, glorified war as a "pruning hook" for improving the health of humanity. "Making war is not only a biological law," declared a famous general, "but a moral obligation, and, as such, an indispensable factor in civilization."

DEVELOPMENT OF THE SOCIAL AND HUMAN SCIENCES

Science first began to influence ways of thinking about human society and human nature as early as the seventeenth century. Hobbes's image of human beings as driven by countervailing "motions" of desire and fear, the mercantilist notion of the "balance of trade," and the rise of the idea of the European "balance of power" were early applications of scientific concepts of motion, force, and balance to what would later be called psychology, economics, and international relations (pp. 399, 411, 417).

In the eighteenth century, rulers and their advisers began carefully observing and measuring the societies they governed. Systematic surveys and censuses provided quantitative information about matters that were highly relevant to the balances of trade and power, but which had earlier been a matter of guesswork—the value of imports compared with exports, for instance, or the number of young men of military age, or the fertility of taxpaying peasant farms. Statistical information of this kind then helped classical economics to become a well-developed field of knowledge and analysis by the early nineteenth century (pp. 510–511). Later in that century, economics acquired the scientific features of an exact vocabulary, advanced mathematical techniques, and methods of prediction.

Meanwhile, as the progress of the natural sciences became more and more impressive, more and more thinkers deliberately took them as a model for the investigation of society, culture, and human nature, and the result was the rise of a whole range of what now came to be known as "social" and "human" sciences.

Sociology and Anthropology. One of the first such thinkers was the Frenchman Auguste Comte. A disciple of Saint-Simon (p. 517), Comte was a lifelong reformer. He shared with Saint-Simon the view that society is best managed by "experts," but he believed that the experts needed a more reliable body of knowledge about people and their social relations than was at hand. Scorning "knowledge for its own sake" and narrow academic specialization, Comte believed that learning should serve human needs, and he felt that all studies should be directed to that purpose.

He believed that the most useful knowledge is the sort that rests upon empirical evidence (pp. 341–342)—"positive" knowledge, he called it—which was to be found in his day only in the natural sciences. But empirical methods can and must, he insisted, be extended to form a "science of society," which Comte was the first to call *sociology*. Human conduct is neither random nor altogether unpredictable, and it can be "quantified," analyzed, and classified. From the resulting social "laws," the proposed managers of society would be able to draw guidance for social regulation and planning.

Comte died in 1857, before he could complete his ambitious studies directed toward reconstructing knowledge and society. (Before breathing his last, he is said to have sighed, "What an irreparable loss!") But the foundations of sociology had been laid, and they were extended by the energetic Herbert Spencer (pp. 528–529). At about the same time, a companion discipline, *anthropology,* came into being. This word means, literally, the "study of human beings," but the study has focused on physical evolution, prehistoric cultures, and comparative social institutions.

Psychology and Psychoanalysis. While anthropology analyzed and classified the broad patterns of social conduct, observed over time and geographical space, a new discipline, *psychology,* concentrated on individual human actions. In 1872, Wilhelm Wundt established in Leipzig, Germany, the first laboratory for the observation and testing of human and animal subjects. Soon thereafter, a Russian, Ivan Pavlov, gained worldwide notice by his remarkable experiments with dogs. He discovered the "conditioned reflex," a principle that could (and would) be extended to humans.

By 1900, psychology was moving in several directions. Followers of Pavlov's experiments developed a view called *behaviorism.* Believing that human thoughts and actions can be understood on a purely physiological basis, they dismissed as meaningless such concepts as "mind" and "soul." They studied the various systems of the body—nervous, glandular, muscular—and the mechanisms of "stimulus" and "response," and measured them. From the accumulation of such data, the behaviorists hoped to develop "positive" knowledge of human nature. Most theologians, philosophers, and humanists found such ideas distasteful. They argued that a person's true being is spiritual rather than physical—or, if only physical, that it is far more complex than the behaviorists imagined.

Other investigators, meanwhile, were trying to penetrate the dark interior of the individual by means of *psychoanalysis.* The Austrian physician Sigmund Freud was a bold leader in this effort to investigate the subconscious and unconscious depths underlying thought and action. His methods were neither quantitative nor statistical but rather clinical. Each human subject was examined, by means of free discussion and dream recollection, for clues to the inner self. (The broader philosophical and social significance of Freud's thought will be developed in Chapter 16; pp. 649–650).

Freud's onetime associate, the Swiss psychologist Carl G. Jung, also stressed the importance of the unconscious as a major part of "psychic wholeness." Jung believed that each individual, as a result of biological evolution, possesses a "collective" unconscious in addition to a "personal" unconscious. The "collective" contains emotion-filled instincts and images connected with long-past experiences of the species. Jung called these "archetypes"—such as the "Great Mother" figure, the Hero, the Sage, the

Betrayer, the Savior-God, and other images that appear widely in popular myths and religions. In keeping with this view, he held that "great" works of art and literature are seen as great because they portray such figures—projected from the collective unconscious of their creators.

History. One of the most ancient studies concerned with human affairs, history also flourished in the nineteenth century. Much of the writing, though marked by careful research and literary merit, was essentially Romantic and nationalistic. The effort to apply scientific methodology centered in Germany, where Leopold von Ranke started the "objective" school of historical writing. He announced that he and his students would describe the past as it "actually happened." Sentiment and national bias were to be set aside, and historical documents were to be collected and interpreted in a rigorously critical fashion. Near the end of the century, the "scientific" approach was carried by historians from German to American universities.

Ranke wrote some excellent histories, and his insistence on correct method was wholesome. He did not convince all historians, however, that it is possible to reconstruct a single true picture of what "actually happened." Serious philosophical and practical objections have been raised against his assumptions, and most twentieth-century historians concluded that the account of individuals and societies can never be told with anything like the precision of natural science. There are indeed "lessons" of history, but they are interpreted in different ways by different writers. For example, a prominent group of twentieth-century French authors (the school founded by Fernand Braudel) holds that events in history can be presented properly only in their total context—including climate, geography, and cultural heritage—a method referred to as "structuralism." Still others ("deconstructionists") argue that words in any source document are but words and can never truly equate with reality (p. 707). At any rate, the fact is that the Muse of history, Clio (p. 84), has never felt altogether at ease among the social sciences. She is more at home with the humanistic disciplines, especially philosophy, literature, and the arts.

Literature and Art in the Machine Age

Writers and painters responded sharply to the changes in civilization triggered by science and the machine. They developed, by the middle of the nineteenth century, new goals and forms that would eclipse Romanticism in European literature and art (pp. 481–488).

EXPRESSIONS OF SOCIAL CHANGE: REALISM

The new trend in literature was known as *Realism.* It started in France with Honoré de Balzac, who began writing successful novels late in the 1820s. (His collected works were later published as *The Human Comedy.*) Balzac placed under close examination men and women of all stations in society. A keen observer, he set the style of insightful reporting of human strengths and weaknesses that marked French literature for the rest of the century.

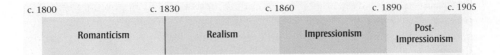

c. 1800	c. 1830	c. 1860	c. 1890	c. 1905
Romanticism	Realism	Impressionism	Post-Impressionism	

In England, Realism spotlighted the social effects of the Industrial Revolution. Charles Dickens, one of the most popular authors of the era, called the attention of his readers to the cruelties and hardships of the urban working class. In the generally light-hearted *Pickwick Papers* (1837), he nevertheless exposed the grim debtors' prisons; in *Oliver Twist* (1839), he revealed the horror of the English workhouses (places of forced labor for the poor). Though his many novels range widely over human themes and problems, they have a strong note of social protest, and Dickens's books contributed, no doubt, to the reform legislation of the nineteenth century (p. 493).

The Continental writer who addressed himself most directly to the problems of his day was a Norwegian, Henrik Ibsen. Though he is today recognized as one of the prime molders of modern dramatic form and technique, his reputation at first rested on the social content of his dramas. The son of a once-prosperous businessman, Ibsen grew up with contempt toward his own society, especially the new bourgeois. In *Pillars of Society* (1877), he revealed the corruption and hypocrisy he had observed among "established" Norwegian families. His next plays dealt with such issues as female emancipation (*A Doll's House*) and the conflict between commercial interests and personal honesty (*An Enemy of the People*). Not surprisingly, these works brought hostile reactions from the middle-class audiences. In his later plays, Ibsen gave up his challenges to the social system and created memorable portraits of individuals (*Hedda Gabler*).

George Bernard Shaw, a brilliant Irish author, was among Ibsen's admirers, and he turned his own pen to the cause of social criticism. A most prolific writer, Shaw composed nearly fifty plays during the course of his long life. Virtually every one of them contains both satire and "message"; his characters, accordingly, tend to be two-dimensional, serving mainly as bearers of intellectual argument.

The relation of literature to social questions during the latter part of the nineteenth century is underlined by the fact that Shaw was a self-taught economist and one of the founders of English socialism. "In all my plays," he once said, "my economic studies have played as important a part as a knowledge of anatomy does in the works of Michelangelo." The drama that first attracted public attention was his *Widowers' Houses* (1892), a condemnation of slum landlordism. This was followed by *Mrs. Warren's Profession,* showing the economic roots of modern prostitution, and *Arms and the Man,* satirizing the military profession. Later dramas dealt with such matters as poverty, war, religious faith, and eugenics (human genetic improvement).

The grand tradition of the Russian novel began in the Romantic era, with Nicolai Gogol. His *Taras Bulba* (1835) tells of adventures and conflicts among the high-spirited Cossacks, those warrior-horsemen who fought the Tartar enemies of Russia (p. 297). But later in the century, the finest Russian novelists, Feodor Dostoevsky and Leo Tolstoy, worked under the influence of Realism. Both were concerned primarily with the inner life and struggles of the individual while describing at the same time the color and detail of Russian life. The best known of their works are Tolstoy's epic historical novel, *War and Peace* (1868), and Dostoevsky's profound *The Brothers Karamazov* (1880).

Fig. 13.4 *The Third-Class Carriage.* Artists traditionally depicted groups of people as united by some event like Christ's death or a wedding feast (*Fig. 8.1*, p. 345; *Fig. 9.3*, p. 389). In Daumier's painting, nothing is happening, and the only thing that holds these weary people together is that they are sitting in the same railroad car. Still, the nursing mother and the woman with the basket are movingly noble, patient, and strong. Daumier both reports on a feature of working-class life in the age of mass transportation and expresses his veneration for the people who have to live it.

THE RESPONSE OF THE ARTIST: REALISM, IMPRESSIONISM, EXPRESSIONISM

In the arts, social protest was expressed in the works of only a few individuals. Most prominent among them were two French artists of the Realist school: Gustave Courbet and Honoré Daumier. Both rebelled against the Romantic tradition, sympathized with the poor, and felt that art should correspond to social facts. While Courbet stressed the simple and truthful representation of nature, Daumier pictured the poverty and despair of the working class. He is perhaps best known for his thousands of lithographs (prints) caricaturing all levels of French society; they complement the word pictures of his contemporary, Balzac, in revealing the "human comedy." One of Daumier's masterpieces in oil, *The Third-Class Carriage,* reveals his ability to paint, with sincerity and compassion, the ordinary people of his time (*Fig. 13.4*). He experienced in his own life the miseries recorded in his art—he died a pauper in 1879.

Daumier's artistic techniques, particularly the "unfinished" effect of his canvases, continued beyond his death. They influenced the style of Impressionism, the most important development in nineteenth-century painting. The Impressionists, however, had nothing to do (as artists) with social satire or protest. They tended to be strictly formal, wishing to record images with optical accuracy and without concern for any kind of message.

Fig. 13.5 *Impression: Sunrise.* Monet carefully studied Turner, but unlike the sunset in *The Fighting Téméraire* (*Fig. 12.4*, p. 488), this murky dawn over a busy seaport is not meant to inspire awe. Instead, the paint-dappled surface of Monet's canvas guides the viewer's imagination to form an "Impression" of a complex, changing scene. The waves are streaks of paint, the fishing boats are blobs, the cranes and masts and smokestacks are fuzzy scribbles. The effect, as the French writer Émile Zola said, is "living, profound, and above all truthful"—exactly because it does not try to be accurately realistic.

Claude Monet represented most fully the aims and achievements of Impressionism. He desired to record physical appearances immediately as he saw them. In order to do this faithfully, he disciplined himself to suppress his prior knowledge of the shape and detail of things—a break with traditional painting. Fascinated by the change in appearances resulting from alterations in light, Monet insisted on working in the open air, putting his visual impressions to canvas in rapid strokes, almost as though he were making a sketch. As the eye, in glancing, sees only a few objects clearly, he deliberately left major areas of his pictures blurred or "unfinished."

This absence of clear detail in Monet's work at first called forth the scorn of critics. In 1874, in an exhibit with other painters of the new style, he showed a picture of a harbor seen through morning mists. He called it *Impression: Sunrise* (*Fig. 13.5*). From this title, an unfriendly observer coined the term "Impressionists" as a label for these artists. In time, critics and public alike grew to appreciate the special aims of this kind of painting. Some of the Impressionists associated their techniques with the methods of scientific observation. Most, however, simply yielded to the delight of producing their riches of color and tone. Among such painters were, notably, Auguste Renoir in France and Mary Cassatt in the United States. Renoir was admired especially for his voluptuous nudes, Cassatt for her charming portraits of young children with their mothers.

Fig. 13.6 Solid Objects. "Still lifes"—finely detailed paintings of food and utensils—were pioneered by seventeenth-century Dutch painters who recorded everyday life. In the nineteenth century, Cézanne leaves details to photographers. Instead, he looks for the inner structure that gives objects solidity and permanence—"treating nature," as he put it, "by the cylinder, the sphere, the cone." But there is no single perspective, so that together, these luminously solid objects form a flat pattern on the surface of the canvas. In his search for underlying truth, Cézanne, like Monet, has stepped away from reproducing exact appearances.

The ultimate success and popularity of the Impressionists gave all artists a fresh sense of freedom and power. Any chosen combination of forms and colors might now be considered a legitimate work of art. Gone were the rules that had required "dignified" or "worthy" subjects, "correct drawing," "rules of perspective," and "balanced composition." This indicated perhaps an even deeper sense of alienation from society than that which inspired the Realism of Daumier. Rather than trying to speak for the downtrodden or to change society, most artists now turned their backs on society, seeking escape into a separate world of art where painters could impose whatever rules they desired upon elements of their own creation. Impressionism itself, however, was a beginning, not an end. Toward the close of the nineteenth century, there came new stirrings in art—largely reactions to Impressionism. Paul Cézanne, who came to Paris in 1861, had adopted many of the techniques of the new style. He objected, however, to what he regarded as the airy, temporary quality of Impressionist paintings; he longed to combine the brilliance of their coloring with more substantial forms.

As may be seen in his *Still Life* (*Fig. 13.6*), one of hundreds of such studies that Cézanne painted, he tried to develop solidity in his works. As a means of furthering this aim, he slightly shifted eye levels in looking at the various objects in the painting, thus creating several angles of view on a single canvas. He also distorted the natural

Vincent van Gogh Museum

Fig. 13.7 *Wheatfield with Crows.* Van Gogh moves even farther than Monet or Cézanne toward conveying a truth that is different from "what things actually look like." In this landscape painted not long before he shot himself, the wheat and crows, the sky and the rutted track, are still recognizable. But the intense colors and the jagged and twisting streaks of paint convey something else—the turbulence and menace that the artist finds in the scene, and which originate in himself. The truth here is not about the landscape but about the artist.

shapes of objects and avoided symmetrical lines, thereby rearranging nature into what he considered a more satisfying balance of light and form.

A younger artist, Vincent van Gogh, had different objectives. Like Cézanne, van Gogh learned the special brush techniques of the Impressionists. But he was not really interested in the outward appearances of things; he wanted to express his own deep feelings about nature and life. Van Gogh was thus the pioneer of the modern school of Expressionist painters.

Extraordinary spiritual and mental stress marked van Gogh's brief life. The son of a Dutch Protestant minister, he sensed a divine creative force within nature and all forms of life and sought to show this force in his paintings. His works were the products of an emotional frenzy that passed into periods of mental illness. Finally, when he feared that he would no longer be able to paint, he took his own life (1890).

But in the years before his death, beginning with a stay at Arles in southern France, he produced a series of remarkable canvases. Stimulated by the sun-drenched countryside, he painted it with fevered excitement, applying color with greater vigor and freedom than any painter had done before him. He did not try to imitate the hues of nature; the colors represented his feelings. Yellow, his favorite color, was his means of expressing the ever-present love of God. Blue, pale violet, and green expressed rest or sleep. A striking example of van Gogh's last works is *Wheatfield with Crows* (Fig. 13.7), a view of a landscape near Paris finished just before his death. It presents "vast stretches of wheat under troubled skies," expressing, as he wrote, "sadness and the extreme of loneliness." Such was the final response of a great and sensitive talent in the closing years of the nineteenth century.

Expressionism took a somewhat different turn in Germany. An exemplar there, Käthe Kollwitz, focused more on human subjects than on nature. She chose, most often, to portray the emotional life of women—their joys and sorrows—in their numerous roles, occupations, and endeavors. And instead of using the paintbrush, she usually worked in the print media (woodcuts, etchings, lithographs), as well as in sculpture.

RECOMMENDED READING

The Industrial Revolution P. M. Deane, *The First Industrial Revolution* (1979), is an excellent introduction to all aspects of the Industrial Revolution in Britain down to the mid-nineteenth century; K. Morgan, *The Birth of Industrial Britain: Economic Change, 1750–1850* (1999), concisely summarizes recent research. D. Landes, *The Unbound Prometheus: Technical Change and Industrial Development in Western Europe from 1850 to the Present* (1969), is a readable standard work; T. Kemp, *Industrialization in Nineteenth-Century Europe* (1969), is a briefer account. W. Licht, *Industrializing America: The Nineteenth Century* (1995), is a concise introduction to the rise of the world's largest industrial economy. P. N. Stearns, *The Industrial Revolution in World History* (1993), discusses nineteenth- and twentieth-century industrialization across the globe.

D. Cardwell, *The Norton History of Technology* (1994), includes readable and nontechnical treatment of all major technologies of the Industrial Revolution. E. D. Brose, *Technology and Science in the Industrializing Nations, 1500–1914* (1998), is an introduction to the relationship of science and technology.

The Business Corporation and Capitalist Expansion R. L. Heilbroner and W. Milberg, *The Making of Economic Society* (1998), is a classic introduction to the development of capitalism in modern times. M. G. Blackford, *The Rise of Modern Business in Great Britain, the United States, and Japan* (1998), is a concise discussion. G. Porter, *The Rise of Big Business, 1860–1910* (1973), deals with the United States; M. Klein, *The Flowering of the Third America: The Making of an Organizational Society, 1850–1920* (1993), explores the social and cultural impact of the rise of American corporations.

A clear exposition of economic theories since the eighteenth century is R. L. Heilbroner, *The Worldly Philosophers: The Lives, Times, and Ideas of the Great Economic Thinkers* (1992). D. D. Raphael et al., *Three Great Economic Thinkers: Smith, Malthus, Keynes* (1997), is brief and authoritative.

The Reaction of Labor and Government J. R. Gillis, *The Development of European Society, 1770–1870* (1983), all social groups. S. P. Hays, *The Response to Industrialism: 1885–1914* (1995), is a classic short account of political and social change in the industrializing United States.

D. Geary, *Labour and Socialist Movements in Europe Before 1914* (1989), and M. Dubofsky, *Industrialism and the American Worker, 1865–1920* (1985), are up-to-date short introductions to labor history. T. Katsaros, *The Development of the Welfare State in the Western World* (1995), includes discussion of nineteenth-century social legislation in Europe and America. See also such general histories as R. Gildea, *Barricades and Borders: Europe, 1800–1914* (1987); E. J. Hobsbawm, *The Age of Capital, 1848–1875* (1979); and B. Waller, ed., *Themes in Modern European History, 1830–1890* (1990).

Urbanization and Standardization of Society The general histories listed in the previous section include up-to-date treatments of social change in the nineteenth century. P. M. Hohenberg and L. H. Lees, *The Making of Urban Europe, 1000–1950* (1995), and Z. L. Miller, *The Urbanization of Modern America: A Brief History* (1977), are good introductions to the rise of cities; W. Rösener, *The Peasantry of Europe* (1994), deals with change in the countryside. M. Livi-Bacci, *A Concise History of World Population* (1992), explains increases in and movements of population.

The Development of Socialist Thought and Action A. Lindemann, *A History of European Socialism* (1983), is concise and comprehensive. R. Levitas, *The Concept of Utopia* (1990),utopian socialism . G. Lichtheim, *Marxism: A Historical and Critical Study* (1964), discusses Marxist theory from its origins to the rise of Stalinism. I. Berlin, *Karl Marx: His Life and Environment* (1978), is a balanced biography, including treatment of Marx's ideas; P. Singer, *Marx* (1980), is a brief interpretation.

The Accelerating Progress of Science S. F. Marron, *A History of the Sciences* (1962), is a good nontechnical account of the physical and life sciences in the eighteenth and nineteenth centuries; S.

G. Brush, *The Rise of Modern Science: A Guide to the Second Scientific Revolution, 1800–1950* (1988), is more detailed and includes treatment of experimental psychology and psychoanalysis.

J. W. Burrow, *The Crisis of Reason: European Thought, 1848–1914* (2000), is a concise and authoritative account of all major intellectual trends. Specifically on Darwinism, J. Bowler, *Evolution: The History of an Idea* (1984), is a standard work on evolution as a scientific concept; his *Charles Darwin: The Man and His Influence* (1990), assesses Darwin's place in the development of the concept.

R. Hofstadter, *Social Darwinism in American Thought* (1955), is clear and provocative; P. J. Bowler, *Biology and Social Thought, 1850–1914* (1993), covers Europe as well as America. P. Dickens, *Social Darwinism: Linking Evolutionary Thought to Social Theory* (2000), deals with the implications of evolutionary ideas down to the present.

R. Smith, *The Norton History of the Human Sciences* (1997), is a clear general account of the rise of sociology, anthropology, and psychology. W. M. Simpson, *European Positivism in the Nineteenth Century: An Essay in Intellectual History* (1963), is a concise and readable standard work; A. R. Standley, *Auguste Comte* (1981), is an excellent brief introduction. M. Wertheimer, *A Brief History of Psychology* (1970), includes treatment of the rise of experimental psychology. A. Storr, *Freud* (1989), is a good brief introduction. P. Rieff, *Freud: The Mind of the Moralist* (1979) discusses his general influence. D. M. Robinson, *An Intellectual History of Psychology* (1995), relates both experimental psychology and psychoanalysis to their philosophical and scientific background.

Literature and Art in the Machine Age L. R. Furst, *Realism* (1992), is a collection of statements by nineteenth-century western European Realist authors and of later critical responses, with a useful introduction; on American Realism, see D. Pizer, *Realism and Naturalism in Nineteenth-Century American Literature* (1985). G. K. Chesterton, *Criticisms and Appreciations of the Works of Charles Dickens* (1911), and G. B. Shaw, *The Quintessence of Ibsenism* (1913), are brief and enjoyable critical classics.

L. Nochlin, *Realism* (1970), is a concise and readable standard work on the visual arts. B. Thomson, *Impressionism: Origins, Practice, Reception* (2000), and B. Denvir, *Post-Impressionism* (1992), are reliable introductions. B. Denvir, *The Impressionists at First Hand* (1987), is a short and interesting documentary history. On individual artists, see R. Verdi, *Cézanne* (1992); W. Seitz, *Claude Monet* (1960); and M. McQuillan, *Van Gogh* (1989).

INFOTRAC COLLEGE EDITION

Visit the source collections at **http://academic.cengage.com/infotrac**, and use the Search function with the following key terms:

Industrial Revolution	Karl Marx	Charles Darwin
industrial development		

WESTERN CIVILIZATION RESOURCES

Visit the Brief History of the Western World Companion Web Site for resources specific to this textbook:

http://history.wadsworth.com/greerbrief09/

Also, the CD in the back of this book and the World History Resources Center at **http://history.wadsworth.com/west_civ/** offer a variety of tools to help you succeed in this course, including access to quizzes; images; documents; interactive simulations, maps, and timelines; movie explorations; and a wealth of other sources.

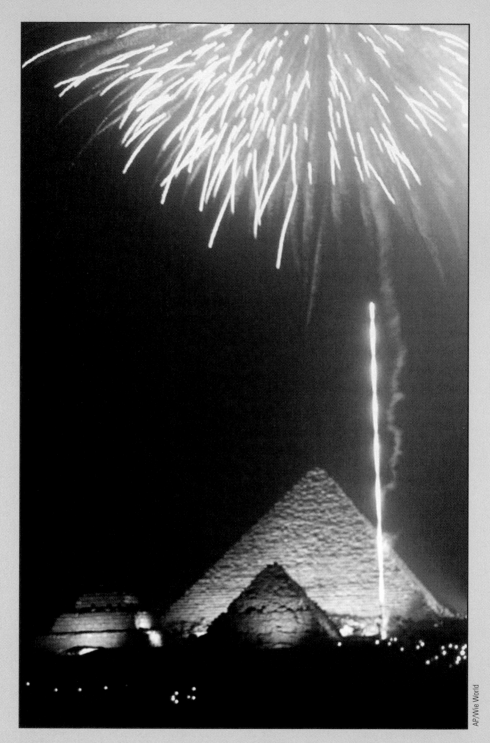

Fig. V.1. Antiquity Greets Modernity. Fireworks explode and a laser beam shoots upward at Giza, Egypt, on January 1, 2000, to mark the new millennium; behind them loom the pyramids of King Menkaure and two of his queens (*Fig. 1.8*, p. 39). Symbolic of the endurance of civilization, the 4,500-year-old monuments of the pharaohs look down upon a twenty-first-century celebration; symptomatic of the global reach of Western civilization, a date in the Western time reckoning is marked by a predominantly Muslim country.

Part Five

THE WEST
AND THE WORLD
IN THE ERA
OF GLOBAL
CIVILIZATION

PART FIVE

The West and the World in the Era of Global Civilization

A As spectacular as were the nineteenth-century shifts in Western civilization, by the end of that century they had only begun to make their full impact felt. Science and technology, capitalism and urbanization, liberalism and nationalism, and artistic and cultural experiment were forces that had almost limitless potential for change. Furthermore, these forces could not be confined to Western civilization's European and North American heartland but were bound to take effect throughout the world.

The results, from the late nineteenth to the early twenty-first century, have been continued spectacular change within Western civilization, a rapid merging of Western and non-Western civilizations, and the growth of a new pattern of modern global civilization, replacing the traditional pattern of the past.

Over the last century and a half, the Western changes have moved in different and often shifting directions, and the terms of the merger between West and non-West have been continually redefined. This is because both are the outcome of an immensely complex process of interaction among individuals, nations, social classes, cultural groups, and civilizations that still continues today. At stake in this process are both the organization of modern global civilization—its distribution of wealth and power among all those groups—and its culture and values—its prevailing patterns of thought and art, feeling and behavior.

To a great extent the shaping of modern global civilization has involved processes of conflict within both Western and non-Western civilizations as well as among them. The era has been one of continual upheavals of social, political, and international orders, among them the rise and fall of colonial empires, of fascism, and of communism. The era has also been one of erosion of old beliefs, values, and patterns of behavior by new ones: the challenge of secular ideologies to traditional religions; drastic alterations in artistic techniques of representing human experience; a historic shift in the balance of status and power between men and women. The era has also seen the deliberate infliction of suffering on the largest scale in the history of the human race—the trench warfare and indiscriminate bombing of the world wars, the genocide of the Jews, the Soviet gulag and the Chinese "Cultural Revolution," the killing fields of Kampuchea and Rwanda.

In the twenty-first century, the cultural conflicts, power struggles, and atrocities accompanying the birth of global civilization continue—disputes within Islam (and between Islam and Western countries) over the veiling of women, opposing responses within both Western and non-Western civilizations to the assertion of power by the United States, terrorist attacks on an unprecedented scale of horror.

Just as important in the coming into being of modern global civilization, however, have been processes of peaceful accommodation and interchange. In Western democratic countries, captains of industry and finance consent to government intervention in the economy and the creation of welfare states, in the interests of economic stability and social peace. National governments, Western and non-Western, pool some of their treasured sovereignty in regional and worldwide trading and financial organizations, in hopes of spreading the benefits and limiting the damage of economic globalization. Critics of global mass culture complain of the "McDonaldization" and "Coca-Colonization" of the world by the United States while, less conspicuous but just as pervasive, martial arts academies and Chinese take-outs spring up at countless U.S. street corners and shopping malls.

This worldwide accommodation and interchange is perhaps best symbolized by global civilization's "patron saints"—revered figures who express its yearning for a harmonious future. Notable examples are Mohandas Gandhi, India's leader against both foreign colonialism and its own caste system, eager student of Western literature and thought, and Hindu holy man; and Martin Luther King, disciple of Gandhi, campaigner for African American civil rights in the name of racial harmony, and Bible-quoting Protestant minister. Such people combine in their persons and their deeds ancient religious traditions, modern secular goals, Western and non-Western origins and influences, canny use of mass organization and propaganda, and the waging of bitter conflicts without the use of force.

The realities of the coming into being of global civilization are often very different from the ideals that such people embody. But a civilization that has common ideals, and leaders who express them, has at least a chance of developing into a diverse and harmonious community.

	POLITICAL, SOCIAL, AND ECONOMIC DEVELOPMENTS	RELIGION, SCIENCE, AND PHILOSOPHY	HISTORY AND LITERATURE	ARCHITECTURE, ART, AND MUSIC
1850	Growth of nationalism			
	French Second Empire:			
	Napoleon III	Kierkegaard		Courbet
	German unification and empire:	Mill	Ranke	Daumier
	Bismarck	Spencer		
		Maxwell		Impressionism:
		Pasteur	Ibsen	Monet
	Rise of corporate big business		Dostoevsky	Renoir
	Rise of labor unions		Tolstoy	Cassatt
	Urbanization of Western society			Cézanne
			Shaw	Expressionism:
	Exploration of Africa	"Social Gospel"		van Gogh
		Leo XIII		Kollwitz
		Nietzsche		Verdi
		Freud		
	The new imperialism	Jung		
	Triple Alliance	Einstein		
		Planck		
1900	British Empire at full extent	Pavlov		Schönberg
	Russo-Japanese War			Stravinsky
	Triple Entente			
	First World War	Rutherford, Bohr, Curie	Joyce	Organic style:
	League of Nations	Barth	O'Neill	Wright, "Falling
	Russian Revolution:		Wharton	Water"
	communism		Proust	International style:
	Lenin		Eliot	Gropius
	Stalin		Woolf	Bauhaus
	Rise of fascism and nazism:	Heisenberg		Mies van der Rohe
	Mussolini	Hubble		Seagram Building
	Hitler			le Corbusier
	Franco			Kandinsky
	The Great Depression (1930–1940)			Picasso
	Roosevelt and New Deal			
	Second World War and Holocaust	Existentialism		
	Atomic bomb:	Tillich	Orwell	
	"unlimited" warfare		Beckett	
	United Nations		A. Miller	
1950	The Cold War (U.S. and USSR)	World Council of Churches	Braudel	Pollock
	End of colonialism:	Crick, Watson	Sartre	Moore
	Gandhi	"Liberation Theology"	Huxley	Calder, *La Grande*
	Kenyatta	Graham	Frost	*Vitesse*
	Mao	John XXIII	Mailer	Saarinen
	Indochina War (Vietnam):	Second Vatican Council	Pasternak	Pei
	Ho Chi-Minh	Paul VI	Solzhenitsyn	Lichtenstein
	European Economic Community	New sexuality		Porter
	National liberation movements:	Revival of hedonism		Gershwin
	Castro	Gell-Mann		Armstrong
	Israeli-Arab wars:	Man on moon: Armstrong		Ellington
	Sadat			Lerner
	Begin			Loewe
	Student movement and			
	youth culture			

POLITICAL, SOCIAL, AND ECONOMIC DEVELOPMENTS	RELIGION, SCIENCE, AND PHILOSOPHY	HISTORY AND LITERATURE	ARCHITECTURE, ART, AND MUSIC	

Emergence of "Third World"
  Allende
Struggle against racism:
  King
  Jackson
  Malcolm X
Women's movement:
  Beauvoir
  Friedan
  Steinem
World population and resources
  crisis
Resurgence of Japanese power
 	
U.S.-China renewal: Nixon
East-West détente
Conservative reaction
	Postmodernism:
	  Foucault
	  Derrida
	  Lyotard
		Updike
		Heller
		Márquez
		Borges
			Presley
			Lennon
			Jackson
			
			Postmodernism:
			  Flack
			  Smithson
			  Kiefer
			  Chicago
				1970

Iranian revolution: Khomeini
International terrorism
	John Paul II	Postcolonialism:
		  Said
		  Rushdie
				1975

Cold War renewal:
  nuclear arms race
Thatcher, Reagan "revolutions"
	Islamic revival
	Christian "fundamentalism"
		Postmodernism:
		  Eco
		  De Lillo
			Postmodernism:
			  Johnson
				1980

Gorbachev revolution	Pentecostals Space probes of solar system			1985

End of Cold War
USSR dissolved
Persian Gulf War:
  Iraq versus the UN
Clinton
Apartheid ended: Mandela
General Agreement on
  Tariffs and Trade
Treaty of Maastricht:
  European Union
Yugoslavia civil war
Palestinian negotiations:
  Rabin
  Arafat
  Barak
  Sharon
	Internet
	Genetic engineering
			Gehry	1990

Palestinian-Israeli conflict Kostunica Bush September 11 attacks Iraq War NATO: expansion to Russian border			Libeskind Childs	2000

CHAPTER 14

The West Divided: Imperialism, World War, and Competing World Orders

OVERVIEW

The rise of global civilization began with three closely related developments between the late nineteenth and the mid-twentieth centuries: the spread of Western influence across the world by means of imperialism; the undermining by the First World War of the world order resulting from imperialism; and the subsequent rise of competing would-be world orders.

In the late nineteenth century, a few countries in which the Western economic, social, and political changes had gone farthest—most of them in Europe, but including also the United States and Japan—became more powerful than the rest of the world. These countries swiftly divided up the world among themselves, bringing about the first genuinely worldwide order in history—one where all peoples were interconnected by Western capitalism and imperialism, but where Western democracy and national independence were privileges of a few peoples.

This world order was unstable, however—mainly owing to conflicts among the privileged peoples, who continued their long-standing Western tradition of mutual strife. Out of the competitive imperialisms and rival nationalisms of the rulers and peoples of Europe there emerged two opposing groupings of great powers, and in 1914 they went to war. In the already close-knit world of the early twentieth century, the war eventually became a struggle between two intercontinental coalitions—Britain, France, Russia, the United States, and Japan against Germany, Austria-Hungary, and the Ottoman Empire. But most of the fighting was in Europe, where the progress of technology made the war the most devastating in history so far.

In the end, victory went to the most powerful members of the larger coalition, which were also homelands of capitalism, nationalism, and liberalism: Britain, France, and the United States. The losers were undemocratic hereditary monarchies and multinational empires: Russia (defeated in 1917), and Germany, Austria-Hungary, and the Ottoman Empire (all defeated in 1918). The winners now hoped to reform the prewar world order by widening the privileged group of nations entitled to democracy and independence, making imperial rule more benevolent, and resolving conflicts through collective international action.

Out of the turmoil of the war, however, there emerged two formidable movements against the existing order of Western and worldwide civilization: communism and fascism. Each was inspired by a different secular ideology that had arisen within Western civilization, and their rise led to an era of struggle over the future organization of the West and the world that lasted for most of the twentieth century.

Communism, derived from nineteenth-century Marxism, took power in defeated Russia. It stood for the revolutionary overthrow of the existing world order on behalf of the victims of capitalism and imperialism, leading to a world of ideal social justice and international harmony. As Russian rulers, the communists concentrated on remaking the vast country into a formidable power base, the Soviet Union, through centralized economic control and massive bloodshed and coercion. Their worldwide following grew, however, as capitalism sank into depression and colonial peoples grew restive under imperialism.

Fascism gained power in other defeated countries or ones where the spoils of victory had been unsatisfactory—notably Germany, Italy, and Japan. Its sources were injured national pride, resentment at the war's unavailing bloodshed and its aftermath of depression and unemployment, fear of rising communism, and in Europe, hatred of the Jews. Influenced by nineteenth-century social Darwinism, fascism gloried in the "struggle for existence" among nations and races. European fascists also yearned for a Leader with a capital "L"—a man of brutal authority and power who would embody the collective might of the nation and its collective anger at its enemies within and without.

In Britain, France, and the United States, victory confirmed liberal and national ideals, but their societies were damaged by wartime bloodshed and postwar unemployment. Political and labor movements arose that promised to change the workings of capitalism, and governments brought the welfare state "safety net" into being. The basic features of capitalism—private ownership and competition—remained largely untouched, however, for these changes were meant to uphold the existing social and political order by reforming it.

It was also up to these countries to uphold the existing order worldwide against its fascist and communist opponents. But the victor countries feared a renewal of bloodshed, and many of their citizens admired one or the other rival system. The communists, too, wanted peace so as to build their power base in the Soviet Union. For the fascist nations, this was the chance to exploit the hesitations and mutual distrust of all their rivals. They swept aside the treaties that had ended the First World War, began the Second World War on favorable terms, and won its early stages in both Europe and the Far East.

For a few short years, especially in Europe, fascism came into effect on an international scale, and proved itself the most sinister and destructive system that ever governed a sizable region of the world. But the fascist countries' ideology of brutality and force made them reckless. They united the United States and Britain, the undefeated guardians of the existing world order, with the Soviet Union against them, and the superior combined resources of this new coalition enabled it eventually to crush the fascist challenge. The first round of the struggle over the future organization of Western and world civilization had ended. The next round was about to begin.

Imperialism and Europe's World Dominion

Broadly defined, *imperialism* means control by one group of people over other groups of people beyond its borders, and as such, it is as old as organized human society itself. Usually, imperialistic expansion is driven by a combination of motives, among them greed for the wealth, power, and glory that imperialism brings; fear that the alternative to conquering is to be conquered; confidence in one's own military superiority, so that the opportunities seem to be there for the taking; and the self-serving belief that one can rule other peoples better than they can rule themselves. The results of imperial expansion range from vicious exploitation by conquerors and savage revolts by the conquered to welcome prosperity and cultural exchange for both sides. Most imperialist peoples lose their power in the end, but the social and cultural changes that they bring can outlast them for hundreds or even thousands of years.

All these things had happened over the centuries between Persian, Roman, Arab, Turkish, and many other conquerors and the peoples they dominated, but mostly on a regional or continental scale. Now the same was about to happen between European and non-European conquerors and the peoples they dominated throughout the world. The long-term result of this new era of imperialist expansion, outlasting the actual empires themselves, was a worldwide expansion of Western civilization.

The New Imperialism. The expansion of Western civilization had already begun in the fifteenth century and proceeded steadily into the eighteenth (pp 318–333), but about 1750 it slowed down for a time. For more than a century thereafter, Europeans were busy at home with their liberal-nationalist restructuring of the political and social order, and with the Industrial Revolution (Chapters 11–13). As a result, however, the countries in Europe and elsewhere that underwent these revolutions built up a much wider margin of political, military, and technological supremacy over the rest of the world than ever before. Thus when overseas expansion resumed after 1870, a small group of advanced countries soon came to dominate the entire world.

Nineteenth-century overseas expansion differed in important ways from earlier colonial efforts. The countries that took part were no longer exclusively European, but included two non-European nations that had undergone similar political and industrial changes—the United States and Japan. The forms of overseas expansion included not only simple conquest but also more indirect penetration and domination. Moreover, just as the imperialist countries had undergone changes, so also the motives for expansion (pp. 321–322) had changed. Alongside the desire of the clergy to spread the Christian gospel there appeared the nonreligious belief in racial superiority; more powerful than the desire of monarchs for dynastic power and glory was that of whole peoples for nationalistic self-assertion; and the desire of the merchants for gold was replaced by that of industrialists for raw materials and markets, and of bankers for investment outlets.

But this "new imperialism," as it is usually called, had one thing in common with the old: its competitive nature. The imperialist countries were not collaborators but rivals, and their rivalries played a major part in bringing about the world wars of the twentieth century.

Methods of the New Imperialism. Earlier empires had often used indirect methods of domination, taking tribute from subject peoples and enforcing obedience on them without actually ruling them. Likewise, the new imperialism did not always mean colonies;

control could be informal as well as formal. In fact, many economic and political experts preferred informal control, because it was cheaper and enabled a nation to avoid many risks and responsibilities. Prior to 1870, the British, with their shipping and financial responsibilities, had proved especially skillful at securing economic privileges abroad. But informal and formal relations were woven together into a single fabric of empire: trade with informal control if practicable, trade with rule when necessary. The United States pursued a similar strategy in the Western Hemisphere, where it was the dominant power. Though it annexed Puerto Rico and secured special constitutional privileges in Cuba (1898), the United States controlled the rest of the Caribbean republics through economic influence ("dollar diplomacy"), aided when necessary by the Marines.

When rival states began to challenge British economic privileges in particular areas, Britain responded by seeking exclusive arrangements. Thus after 1870, its Foreign Office sought treaty rights, "spheres of interest," and colonies. Germany and Italy, as well as the older European nation-states, joined in the sweepstakes. The "underdeveloped" or declining countries of Asia and Africa found themselves helpless before this combined onslaught. Even more than in the case of earlier confrontations between Europe and the non-Western world (pp. 318, 331), the Europeans held the advantages of aggressive purpose, superior organization, and advanced technology.

MOTIVES FOR NINETEENTH-CENTURY EXPANSIONISM

What was it specifically that moved the Europeans, Americans, and Japanese to strike out across the seas and force themselves upon the other peoples of the world? The economic motive, arising from the growth of industrial capitalism, was certainly powerful. We saw in Chapter 13 how surplus profits found their way to "backward" countries (pp. 509–510). The urge to secure raw materials, markets, and investments gave a mighty push to overseas penetration.

J. A. Hobson, an English socialist, wrote an influential analysis of the economic causes of expansionism. His book *Imperialism* (1902) attacked the system of overseas exploitation as "a depraved choice of national life, imposed by self-seeking interests." Hobson suggested that since wage earners lacked the purchasing power to buy all they produced, manufacturers had to go abroad to sell part of their output and invest their profits. He claimed that colonial administration and defense were costly and dangerous, and that economic problems could be better solved by providing higher wages and better social services at home. By these means, the home market would be expanded, and capitalists would have better opportunities to invest their funds there. In effect, Hobson was urging a change in policy that would bring British capitalism closer to humanistic aims.

Vladimir Lenin took a different tack. He accepted Hobson's analysis of imperialism, but as a Marxist (pp. 518–522), he viewed imperialism as the inevitable last stage of capitalism. In *Imperialism, the Highest Stage of Capitalism* (1916), Lenin declared that profits flowed overseas because they produced a higher rate of return there. And only in a colony, under formal political control, did investments yield their maximum return. Colonies had extended the life of capitalism by bringing into existence *new proletariats*. But now that the globe had been parceled out, the capitalist states were being driven by their economic systems to wage wars against one another. These, he predicted, would be followed by proletarian revolutions, the establishment of socialist states, and the death of imperialism. Though Lenin's argument is inadequate, its par-

c. 1860	1871		1914	1918
Unification of Italy and of Germany		Era of the New Imperialism	First World War	

tial confirmation by events and its acceptance by communist leaders throughout the world made it enormously influential.

The economic motive, no matter how interpreted, was only one of the forces behind imperialism. Probably more important was the drive for national power and prestige. European nationalism had come of age by 1870, as we saw in Chapter 12 (pp. 497–500). The pride and effort that went into achieving self-determination for nations (nationalism) led easily to the desire to control other nations and peoples (imperialism).

Now intellectuals began to speak and write of their nation's "civilizing mission." Along with the soldiers and merchants came hundreds of Christian missionaries, responding to the challenge of bringing the Gospel to heathen lands. In addition, many members of the upper and middle classes sought careers in the overseas services. Ordinary citizens, too, thrilled to phrases like "advance of the flag," the "white man's burden," and "manifest destiny." Men, women, and children of all classes studied the new global maps showing their nation's overseas possessions in distinctive colors. The vocal minorities that protested against imperialism on practical or moral grounds were swept aside as "small-minded" or unpatriotic.

THE SCRAMBLE FOR AFRICA

The assault on Africa began in earnest after 1870. In earlier centuries of trade and exploration, Europeans had had extensive contacts on more or less equal terms with the Muslim peoples of North Africa and with many coastal peoples elsewhere in the continent. But the interior of Africa south of the Sahara had remained virtually unknown to the Western world and was therefore thought of by Europeans as the "Dark Continent."

The conditions of Africa and the slight knowledge of it by outsiders restricted the avenues for penetration and conquest. Nineteenth-century ventures nevertheless showed the Western capacity for investigation, missionary activity, and greed for wealth. David Livingstone was the first white person to explore substantial areas of the interior. Livingstone, a Scottish physician and missionary, survived some thirty years among the Africans, doing medical and religious work; during that time he had traveled the upper courses of the great rivers. When he was reported in Europe and America as being "lost" in the jungles, a New York newspaper sent a reporter to find him—as a journalistic stunt. Henry Stanley "found" the good doctor in 1871, decided to conduct further travels of his own, and later publicized his adventures in a book called *Through the Dark Continent.* More important, Stanley saw the possibilities of extracting wealth from central Africa. He succeeded at last in interesting King Leopold II of Belgium in his promotional plans.

Belgium, a small country that had gained independence only a generation before (p. 492), had no overseas possessions. Leopold's venture was entirely private—in keeping with the buccaneering spirit of the times. He formed a company, with himself as president, and sent Stanley and other agents into the Congo region. Taking the view that the African interior was open for sale to the white race, Leopold acquired "possession" of an enormous area by making "treaties," in exchange for trifling gifts, with hundreds of tribal chieftains. He thus created a "Congo Free State" under his personal rule—recognized as legal by the major powers in 1885. The boundaries enclosed an area equal to that of the United States east of the Mississippi River.

Though Leopold claimed scientific and humanitarian purposes for his venture, his prime purpose was personal gain. His eye was fixed on the booming industrial demand for rubber: the Congo had rubber trees and a large supply of African laborers. But the Africans were infected with tropical diseases and proved unresponsive to European work incentives; they could be forced to work only by the harshest methods.

Leopold's agents used up the trees and people of the Congo without restraint, and the annual value of its rubber exports reached $10 million by 1908. But Leopold used much of the income for personal extravagance and borrowed huge sums from the Belgian government. In return, he mortgaged the Congo Free State to the government, which took it over at his death. As the Belgian Congo, the region received somewhat better treatment, but it remained a shocking example of human and resource exploitation.

Leopold's taking of the Congo attracted the attention of other European states to the prizes of Africa. A conference was called in 1885 to give some order to the carving up of the remainder of the continent. Certain ground rules were agreed upon: a nation with possessions on the coast had a prior right to the related hinterlands, but for a claim to any territory to be recognized, it must be supported by the presence of administrators and soldiers. The conference agreement was thus a signal to all competitors to move in with civilian and military forces.

The methods employed were similar to those used by Leopold's agents. White men trekked into the interior in search of tribal chiefs who would sign treaties. The chiefs seldom understood what the treaties meant or had the authority to transfer property rights, but the whites acted as if they did. These "rights" were then transferred to some European government, and a colony was thereby established. The only serious difficulties arose when rival nations secured overlapping grants in the same region. Such problems were usually referred to the European capitals for settlement.

By 1914, almost the entire continent had been partitioned. France held most of the bulge of West Africa, which was largely desert; the British held the richest lands, running from South Africa in the south to Egypt in the north. The main possessions on the southern and eastern coasts and in the central region were those of Portugal, Germany, Italy, and Belgium (*Map 14.1*, p. 552). Of the continent's many nations, only the ancient East African kingdom of Ethiopia had managed to preserve its independence.

THE PARTITION OF ASIA

In Asia, unlike Africa, there were no "dark" or "unoccupied" zones. China and Japan, for example, were historic empires, well mapped and administered, that shared a common civilization that had originated in China. Both had done their best to insulate themselves from earlier Western influences (p. 329), but now they faced intrusions that they could not resist. The vast Chinese empire, too unwieldy to cope easily with European imperialists, became their victim; Japan, smaller and more adaptable, joined the ranks of the imperialist powers.

Decline of the Chinese Empire. Chinese civilization, like that of India, traced back to 2500 B.C. Over thousand of years, China had developed into a single empire that had

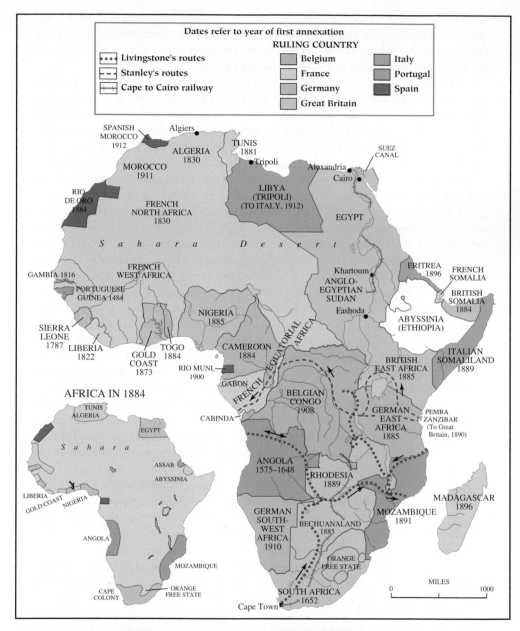

Map 14.1 The Scramble for Africa. In 1884, most of Africa was independent. Then, in about thirty years down to 1912, the entire continent except for Ethiopia and Liberia was divided among seven European powers. In North Africa, the Europeans took over existing Muslim states; elsewhere, the new borders reflected what each European country could lay its hands on before its rivals, regardless of existing tribal and ethnic groupings. The situation shown here lasted mostly unchanged for about forty years down to the 1950s. Then, in another twenty years, the short-lived European rule in Africa collapsed (*Map 15.3*, p. 606).

endured far longer than that of Rome, had absorbed many nomadic invaders, and had spread its civilization to neighboring countries, including Japan. The country's wealth and power, as well as the excellence of its practical and fine arts, scholarship, philosophy, and literature, had impressed European travelers ever since Marco Polo (p. 320). But China did not match the scientific and technological advances of the West after 1500 and in the eighteenth century had deliberately kept European contacts to a minimum (p. 329). Thus when the Europeans eventually decided to penetrate the Chinese "wall" of isolation from foreigners, they possessed superior military equipment and made effective use of it. What the Europeans wanted initially were trading privileges. They coveted the luxury goods of China (silks, precious stones, porcelain) and wanted to secure them in exchange for their factory-made products. Unfortunately, the Chinese did not want such articles. The one item they would buy in substantial quantities was the narcotic drug opium, grown in India and sold by British merchants. When the Chinese government tried to stop the importation of opium, Britain started hostilities (the so-called Opium War).

The treaty forced upon China at the end of the Opium War (1842) was the first of countless impositions on that country. According to the treaty's terms, the opium trade was to be resumed without further interference. In addition, Britain demanded and won possession of the strategic Chinese city of Hong Kong. Within the next few decades, other countries made their own demands. Under the "treaty system," a dozen Chinese port cities were opened to European traders (Map 14.2), and in each port city, the leading European powers were allowed to establish their own settlements, free from Chinese authority. European nationals, under further agreements, were allowed to travel inside China, subject only to the laws of their own homelands. The Chinese government was deprived of control over its external commerce; the European powers required that no tariff of more than 5 percent be placed on imports and that the tariffs be collected by Europeans. A good portion of this revenue was then siphoned off as "war indemnities" to the invaders. Small wonder that the Chinese felt growing resentment toward the "foreign devils"!

The results for China were massive economic and social dislocation. The entry of low-priced manufactured goods in the nineteenth century upset the structure of the Chinese economy, above all in trade and industry. By building factories in the free ports and using the cheapest labor, the Europeans undermined Chinese handicrafts and demoralized the regular workforce. Quick fortunes were made from these enterprises by foreign traders and manufacturers, but the cost to the Chinese people was beyond measure.

The Modernization of Japan. The Japanese were more fortunate. Like the Chinese, their leaders feared the influence of Western ideas on their tightly organized society. After unhappy experiences with Portuguese and Dutch traders, the Japanese had closed their ports to foreign vessels in the seventeenth century. They did not reopen them until 1854. It was then that the American commodore Matthew Perry, by threatening naval bombardment, persuaded the ruling power to negotiate a commercial treaty. The Japanese soon yielded to the idea that they must accept industrialization if they were to survive in the modern world. But they were determined to develop it themselves, without disruptive interference by foreigners. They jealously guarded control over their finances and tariffs, and in an extraordinary national effort, they modernized their economy and armed forces.

By 1890, the Japanese were able to meet the Westerners on their own terms and even to become an imperialist power in their own right. In 1894, they drew China into war over clashing rights in Korea, and their Western-style army won easily. China was

Map 14.2 Asia in 1914. In the mid-nineteenth century, the British already ruled India and the Dutch held the East Indies. Britain then continued to expand its territories and spheres of influence, and other countries joined in. By 1914, only five Asian countries—Afghanistan, China, Japan, Siam, and Persia—were legally independent. Only Japan was strong enough to become an imperialist country itself, but its share of the spoils was small. It would shortly begin an effort to expand its share that would end in the collapse of all imperial rule, including its own (*Map 15.2*, p. 605).

compelled to cede to Japan the large island of Taiwan (known in the West as Formosa), as well as its claims to Korea (*Map 14.2*).

The Struggle for the Far East. The Europeans were astonished by this demonstration of Japanese will and strength. Now that it appeared that China might be falling prey to greedy neighbors, they decided to protect their interests by seizing control of whatever territories they could. The Germans, French, Russians, and British pressured the Chinese government to give them vital coastal zones, in addition to their settlements in the "treaty ports." Only suspicions and disputes among the great powers saved the rest of China from complete partitioning at this time.

The intervention of the United States, which had become a Pacific power in 1898 when it took the Philippine Islands from Spain, had only a minor effect on the situation. The Americans feared that their commerce with China would be cut off if the foreign interests already there succeeded in spreading their territorial holdings. The secretary of state, John Hay, therefore pushed vigorously in 1899 for the acceptance of an "Open Door" policy in China, which would guarantee the "territorial integrity" of the country against further losses and extend to all nations equally the commercial privileges that had been won from the Chinese government.

Britain supported the Open Door policy, for it promised to block the threat of more annexations by China's neighbors. The other powers viewed it coolly, however, for they hoped to pounce on portions of the faltering empire. Ignoring the Open Door principle, Japan determined to tighten and extend its grasp. In both Korea and Manchuria, Japan faced a rival imperialist power, Russia. The Russians had begun, about 1850, to develop their long-neglected Siberian possessions (p. 414), founding the city of Vladivostok ("Ruler of the East") on the Pacific Ocean. Then they, too, had turned their attention to Manchuria and Korea. After failing to negotiate an agreement for two separate "spheres of influence" and fearing Russian advances, the Japanese decided to settle the issue by force.

Japan opened hostilities in 1904 with a surprise naval attack on the Russian fleet and base at Port Arthur in China, declaring war a few days afterward. This strike was a glaring violation of international law (repeated by the Japanese some forty years later in their sneak attack on American forces at Pearl Harbor; p. 589). The tsarist government never recovered from this opening blow and was roundly beaten on sea and land (in Manchuria) during the Russo-Japanese War. As a result, Russian expansion in this area was checked, and Japan strengthened its special rights in Korea and Manchuria, as well as in Port Arthur. Japan also gained enormous international prestige for having humbled the supposedly mighty Russian Empire.

Meanwhile, the rest of Asia had been gobbled up. Over the years, the French had taken control of large areas of Southeast Asia; they combined them in 1887 to form French Indochina (*Map 14.2*). The British had begun to plant settlements in India back in the seventeenth century; in the nineteenth century, the crown assumed direct control of the Indian government and extended its grip to Burma and Malaya. The Dutch widened their earlier holdings in the East Indies (p. 327), while Persia and Afghanistan were split into British and Russian spheres of influence (1907). Russia also established a "protectorate" over Mongolia in 1913.

THE NEW IMPERIALISM, THE WEST, AND THE WORLD

At last this era of fabulous conquest came to an end. In not much more than half a century, the relationship between the West and the rest of the world had been transformed. The ancient civilizations and cultures of Africa and Asia, which had so far not felt the full force of Western influence, and even the Latin American countries with their regional version of Western civilization—nearly all were by 1914 directly ruled or indirectly controlled by a small group of Western or Westernized countries. The new imperialism had added 5 million square miles to the British Empire: in 1900, Queen Victoria ruled nearly 400 million subjects, with overseas territory forty times larger than the home island. French possessions had expanded by almost as much. Substantial areas had been acquired by Germany, Russia, Belgium, Portugal, and Italy. And Japan and the United States had joined the list of imperial powers.

In some ways, imperialism brought advantages to colonial peoples. It pushed them abruptly into the mainstream of world development. Roads, railways, sanitation, hospitals, and schools were introduced, while tribal wars and the slave trade were stopped. But these benefits must be measured against the physical and psychic blows inflicted by imperialism: forced labor, heavy colonial taxes, land confiscations, inferior status compared to European immigrants, destruction of traditional institutions and ways of life. The new imperialism left its subject peoples with a lasting sense of confusion, defeat, and degradation.

But the newly arisen empires were destined to short lives. This was partly because they were the work of countries most of which more or less wholeheartedly accepted individual freedom, national independence, and material well-being as universal principles. Like all empires, those of the nineteenth century were vehicles of cultural exchange, and in this case, at least to start with, the main influences were from the imperialist countries to the subject peoples. Ironically, to the extent that the colonial peoples learned and sought to imitate the ways of their rulers, this led them not to submission but to resistance and rebellion—to demand the freedom, independence, and prosperity that the imperial nations proclaimed as the birthright of the whole human race.

In addition, the outward thrust of the new imperialism had intensified the forces that were pushing the Western nations, above all those of Europe, toward war among themselves. Europeans claimed to look after the problems of "backward" peoples, but they proved unable to solve their own. Europe was about to explode in a frightful conflagration, leading to the eventual collapse of the colonial empires.

The First World War and the Decline of Europe

The two "world wars," one starting in 1914 and the other in 1939, are closely linked. Both were products of the international political system created and legitimized by the European powers. The First World War ended not with a stable peace but with a truce; the Second World War was its nightmarish sequel. Together the two wars ended the imperial dominance of Europe and opened the world to competition between rival political, social, and economic orders.

Yet on the eve of 1914, there were few who could see what the future held. The trend of surface events had indeed been deceptive. Europe had been spared a general war for one hundred years—since the downfall of Napoleon (pp. 470–471). The advance of science, liberal institutions, and material well-being was indisputable. The years before 1914 were a time of expansiveness and optimism, with the promise of the Enlightenment (pp. 430–431) apparently nearing fulfillment. Given another half century of peace, Europe might have made the liberal order secure.

But there was another, gloomier side to the European picture. Technology had created forces that were dissolving the foundations of traditional liberalism, and imperialism had opened wounds, both in Europe and overseas, that continued to fester. There was, too, a rising romantic mood, irrational and illiberal, associated with mystical ideas of racial purity and national "soul." But Europe's fatal flaw was excessive nationalism—especially when it became connected with militarism and military alliances among the great powers.

NATIONALISM, MILITARISM, AND THE ALLIANCE SYSTEM

By the close of the nineteenth century, the nationalist ideal of Mazzini (pp. 497–498) had hardened into a self-centered and self-destroying passion. Its characteristics were the same in every Western land: the people of each nation believed in their own superiority, sovereignty, and special mission in the world. They saw the advancement of national power and glory as the supreme aim of all citizens. Nationalism, the "religion of the fatherland," was in fact the true faith of most Europeans at the turn of the century. Each nation viewed itself as the chosen instrument of God; its founders and heroes were its apostles and martyrs; its political charters were revered as holy texts.

This patriotic enthusiasm fell hard on certain ethnic minorities within states— groups suspected of having less than total loyalty to the larger community. Most Jews, for instance, were seldom accepted as full citizens of the states where they resided. Reacting to this feeling, some Jews began to think of securing a national state of their own; this fitted in with an age-old yearning following the Jewish Diaspora of ancient times (p. 52). In 1897, an Austrian journalist, Theodor Herzl, founded the World Zionist Organization. It sought to create a Jewish nation in Palestine; Zion is the name of the hill that had once been the site of King Solomon's temple and palace (p. 51). Herzl and his successors appealed to world leaders to support their cause, leading, a half century later, to the creation of the state of Israel (pp. 607–611).

The armed forces of each European nation became the principal embodiment of its sovereign spirit and honor. They served, at the same time, as the ultimate means of pursuing national aims; both pride and interest, therefore, moved public officials and citizens to respect and strengthen the army and navy. Bismarck's wars had shown that Germany had taken the lead in the art of land warfare, but the other powers worked to catch up militarily as rapidly as possible. All except Britain adopted universal male conscription and military training. Competition in weaponry accompanied the rise of huge standing armies; by the end of the century, Europe had become a bristling camp. Nationalism and militarism were fatefully joined.

Stated simply, *militarism* is the belief that preparation for war provides sound moral training and the best safeguard of peace and the national interest. Militarists aim, therefore, to build ever-stronger military power—greater, if possible, than that of any likely combination of enemies. "Peace through strength" is their slogan. But strength is relative, and each of the major nations wanted to be the strongest. When the European peoples embraced militarism in the nineteenth century, they took off on an unrestricted arms race.

Unwilling or unable to agree on principles for peaceful coexistence, the European powers were left to the deadly consequences of their own nationalisms. For in relations *between* states, there was no enforceable law comparable to that which existed *within* states. Because each sovereign power recognized no authority superior to itself, the ultimate resort was to go to war. The situation then, as now, has been correctly called *international anarchy*.

Metternich's "Concert of Europe" (pp. 476–477) had been an attempt to deal with the problem of international anarchy by harmonizing the interests of the great powers.

But this idea, basically at odds with nationalism, was doomed from the start. During the course of the nineteenth century, a few farseeing individuals tried earnestly to modify the sovereignty principle, strengthen international law, and establish international courts of justice. Peace conferences were called, notably those at The Hague (in the Netherlands) in 1899 and 1907. Representatives of twenty-six nations, assembled at The Hague, tried and failed to agree on a proposal for arms control, but they did conclude several treaties on the "law of war" and the "rules of warfare." They pledged not to use poison gas or other weapons that were considered especially inhumane or indiscriminate. They also created an international court of arbitration to which countries might submit their disputes. Moreover, numerous "peace societies" were formed in various parts of Europe and America during the prewar period.

These efforts were forerunners of more substantial moves toward replacing anarchy with international order. But the responsible leaders of the era believed that the only path to security, beyond keeping their own nation strong, was to enter into alliances with "friendly" powers. Thus nationalism and militarism led to the alliance system of the late nineteenth century. Like the arms race, the alliances were competitive, and they added strength only in relative terms. The European states did not find safety from war in either arms or alliances. The pursuit of both served only to make the war fires hotter and more widespread when they flared up.

THE ROAD TO WAR

Most of Europe's leaders, even as late as 1914, declared that war was unthinkable. Some said war would not happen because it was "too expensive" or "too frightful" or "too irrational." In addition, until 1914, there had been grounds for optimism about keeping the peace in the fact that a number of international crises had been settled without resort to arms. But the pressures for war were cumulative, and the right type of crisis at the right time was virtually certain to strike the igniting spark, regardless of the expense or frightfulness or irrationality of war.

Rival Alliances. At the center of the European power struggle stood Germany, for its triumphal unification in 1871 had made it the dominant power on the Continent. Bismarck, Germany's unifier (p. 500), wished to maintain his country's new dominance. His motives were no doubt defensive; he feared that the French, stung by their defeat in the Franco-Prussian War (1870), would seek revenge. And so he arranged an alliance with another vanquished rival, Austria-Hungary, in 1879. Italy joined this pact a few years later, making it the Triple Alliance (*Map 14.3*). At the same time, he took care to keep Germany on good terms with the other two leading great powers, Russia and Britain. He was respectful of Russia's interests in eastern Europe and of Britain's position as the leading worldwide power. He hoped in this way to preserve German dominance without fighting: his friendships and alliances were designed not to fight a war but, by their overwhelming strength, to deter it. But if Germany's allies and friends ever lost their trust in Germany as a peaceful partner, they would turn against it, and Bismarck's war-deterring structure would crumble.

This began to happen when the isolation of France, shrewdly arranged by Bismarck, was broken soon after he fell from office in 1890. His fall was due in part to the ambitions of the new German emperor (*Kaiser*), William II, who replaced Bismarck's

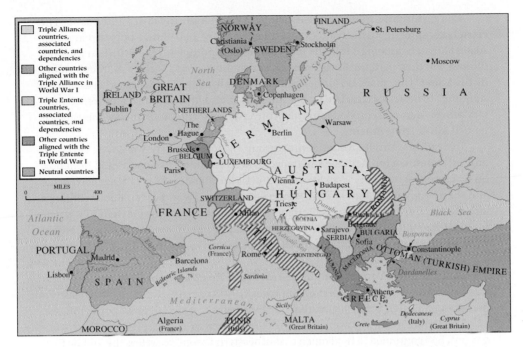

Map 14.3 Balance of Power. The map shows the rival alliances of 1914: the Triple Entente of Britain, France, and Russia and the Triple Alliance of Germany, Austria-Hungary, and Italy. It also shows wartime shifts in these alignments, most importantly Italy fighting on the Entente side and the Ottoman Empire allied with Germany and Austria-Hungary. But the basic balance of forces never changed. A stronger but scattered group of countries confronted a weaker but more compact one. The stronger group would win in the end, but it would take four years of slaughter and ruin.

cautious policy with one that would propel Germany into its "rightful" place as both a Continental and a world power. The emperor's policy was an open challenge to both Russia and Britain, and both responded by developing closer relations with France.

The French, of course, had not forgotten 1870 and had long been seeking military partners. They looked first to the power on Germany's eastern border. Russia—autocratic and conservative—was ideologically and socially in sharpest contrast to liberal and progressive France. But internal differences between states do not necessarily stand in the way of common goals in foreign policy, and the two countries entered into a Dual Alliance in 1894. This action confronted Germany with the threat that Bismarck had most feared—the possibility of a two-front war.

All the same, William II was determined that Germany should find its "place in the sun"—overseas as well as in Europe. Convinced of the importance of sea power to overseas commerce, colonies, and national prestige, he was determined to have a great navy as well as the world's finest army. Beginning in 1898, Germany began to lay out huge expenditures for a fleet of warships. Britain, alarmed, reacted with still larger sums, insisting on the principle that its navy remain the equal of any other two. And though traditionally committed to "splendid isolation" from European "entanglements," the British now began to consider European alliances to counter the rising power of Germany (*Map 14.3*).

As a result, Britain found itself swinging ever closer to France and Russia. The French accepted British advances in Africa that they had earlier opposed and persuaded Russian diplomats to settle long-standing disputes with the British in the Middle East. For their part, the British were growing more worried with each "tough" move by the Kaiser. They made no formal military commitments, but in 1907 a "close understanding" (*entente*) was reached by Britain, France, and Russia. British and French military officers began to carry on joint staff conversations. The Dual Alliance was thus extended into a Triple Entente.

Instead of a single overwhelming group of powers, there were now two rival groups. Statesmen on each side still hoped to keep the peace by what would from now on be mutual deterrence. They liked to think of the alliances as balancing each other and thereby giving stability to the Western-dominated world order. But the alliance also created a deadly danger: if deterrence failed and any two powers went to war, the other alliance members would have little alternative but to join in. Any local conflict was almost certain to turn into a general European war.

The Balkans: Local Nationalisms and Great Power Rivalries. What brought this about was a combination of local and great power conflicts in the Balkans (southeastern Europe, *Map 14.3,* p. 559), a region that had long been an object of great-power interest.

The Ottoman Turks, in spite of losses of territory from the seventeenth century onward, had continued to hold much of southeastern Europe, as well as the Middle East, until after 1815 (pp. 412–413, 416). In the first half of the nineteenth century, however, the Balkans began to respond to the spirit of nationalism that was spreading through all of Europe. The Greeks, for example, had won their independence in 1829 (p. 491), and the Romanians, Bulgarians, and others were waiting for a chance to throw off the Turkish yoke. But the Balkan nations were divided among themselves. Most of them were of Slavic ethnic origin, but some belonged to other ethnic groups that had lived in the Balkans for longer than the Slavs; most were Eastern Orthodox Christians, but some were Roman Catholic or had become Muslim under Turkish rule; and each was eager to claim the largest possible share of territory and population for itself, at the expense of fellow subject nations as well as the Turks. (For the background of religious and ethnic conflict in the Balkans, see Chapters 5 and 7.)

This was a situation that was bound to lead to interference by the great powers— each with different and competing aims. In the 1870s, the power with the greatest ambitions in the area was Russia, which had three objectives: to liberate fellow Slavs and Orthodox Christians, to win control of the Black Sea coasts, and to secure a "warm water" outlet (that would not be icebound in the winter like Russian ports on the Baltic Sea and Arctic Ocean) through the straits linking the Black Sea and the Mediterranean. But Austria, which wanted to expand trade and influence in the region and was afraid of the spread of Balkan nationalist unrest to its own territory, resented growing Russian prestige there. In addition, so long as Bismarck kept Germany's interest in the Balkans to a minimum, Britain considered Russia its main opponent there. Russia's southward push seemed a threat to Britain's own "line of empire," which ran through the Mediterranean to India, and it therefore sought to keep Russia bottled up in the Black Sea.

The tsar nearly achieved Russia's objectives in 1878 when he invaded the Turkish Empire and crushed its forces. But Austria and Britain demanded, upon threat of war, that the Russians reduce their peace demands. At the ensuing Berlin Conference, presided over by Bismarck acting as an "honest broker," Russia gained only a few harbors and border territories. But Romania, Serbia, and Montenegro were recognized as independent states, and Bulgaria secured self-rule under the Turkish sultan (ruler).

The alarmed sultan now tried to check the decay of Turkish strength by playing off the great powers against one another. But he had to pay a price: in return for continuing diplomatic aid against Russia, he permitted Britain to occupy Cyprus and the Austrians to administer the provinces of Bosnia and Herzegovina (*Map 12.4*, p. 501). Egypt, nominally part of the sultan's empire, was occupied by the British in 1882 as part of their colonial schemes in Africa. The island of Crete broke free from Turkey in 1896 and became part of Greece; in 1908, Austria-Hungary formally annexed Bosnia and Herzegovina (took them over as part of its own territory). Finally, in 1912, Serbia, Montenegro, Bulgaria, and Greece invaded and liberated most of what remained of European Turkey—and immediately went to war among themselves over the division of territory and population. Another international conference gave independence to the last of the Turkish-ruled Balkan nations, mostly Muslim Albania. (Albanians who lived in the territory of Kosovo, however, came under Serbian rule, as in medieval times it had been mainly inhabited by Serbs and was still regarded by them as sacred national territory; p. 298). By 1914, almost nothing was left of the dying Ottoman Empire's European territories.

But liberation from Ottoman rule did not bring the local and international rivalries in the Balkans to an end. Competition among the great powers for influence there grew more intense than ever, particularly when the assertive Germany of William II joined in. To open up the Middle East to German economic and political penetration, the Germans had begun work on a Berlin-to-Baghdad railway. This ambitious project required understandings with the Balkan states through which the railway passed, as well as with the Turkish sultan. Britain, Russia, and France regarded the German enterprise as a source of unwelcome aid to the Turkish Empire and an invasion into their own spheres of interest, and Britain now began to see Germany rather than Russia as the main threat to its interests in the Balkans and the Middle East.

The most serious and irrepressible conflicts, however, were between some of the Balkan nations and the empire of Austria-Hungary. The Habsburg emperor ruled an empire consisting of a dozen different nationalities, which stretched from central Europe to the Balkans. In the Balkans, the empire included several "South Slav" nationalities—Catholic Croats, Muslim Bosnians, and Orthodox Serbs—who were closely related to or actually identical with what were now independent Balkan nations living farther east in the Balkans—above all, the Serbs. The leaders of Serbia had an ambitious sense of national mission and wanted to unite all the South Slavs—including those who lived in Austria-Hungary—into a single independent state. As a first step, the leaders of the "Greater Serbia" movement began agitation and subversion in Bosnia and Herzegovina, where Serbs, Croats, and Muslim Bosnians lived side by side, in an effort to win over the allegiance of these fellow Slavs and bring about their liberation from Austria.

The statesmen in Vienna were understandably worried. A Serbian success would pull important territories away from the Austrian Empire. Still more dangerous was the force that such a success would set in motion. The Magyars (Hungarians) had already gained self-rule within the empire (in 1867), alongside the emperor's traditionally dominant subjects of German nationality. But the Czechs, Slovaks, Romanians, and other nationalities were still treated as subordinate peoples. For the moment, they were seeking only equality with the privileged Germans and Hungarians, but if the South Slavs won independence, they would probably demand it too.

The explosive situation also affected the alliance system, on which the general peace of Europe seemed to hang. If Austria-Hungary were to break apart, the Triple Alliance would be decisively weakened. Germany, the senior partner of the alliance, therefore kept in anxious touch with Vienna. On the opposing side, the Russians did all they could to encourage the Serbs to seek independence. Here was a conflict between two great powers that that was important enough to draw them into war, and with them, their friends and allies.

The Alliances Go to War. The Serbian nationalists, knowing that their country was militarily weaker than the Austrian Empire, resorted to terror to further their "holy" cause. Their efforts reached a climax in the streets of Sarajevo, Bosnia, in June 1914. A young terrorist assassinated the Archduke Francis Ferdinand (heir to the Austrian throne) and his wife. World leaders were shocked by the murders, and the Austrian government—having made sure of German support—decided to use the occasion for a showdown with Serbia. Believing that the Serbian government was involved in the assassination plot, the Austrians sent a harsh ultimatum (a demand, backed by threat of action if not agreed to). The Serbs—having in turn made sure of Russian backing—accepted most but not all of the requirements. The Austrians rejected their response as unsatisfactory, broke off diplomatic relations, mobilized their army, and declared war on Serbia.

The decisive step in widening the war was the tsar's order to mobilize the Russian army. A week or more was needed before an army could be made ready for battle, and German leaders decided that they could not stand by while Russian mobilization went ahead. They sent a telegram demanding that the Russians halt their call-up within twelve hours. Failing to receive a positive reply, the Germans declared war on Russia on August 1, 1914. The French, who had urged Russia to avoid any compromise that might be humiliating to the Triple Entente, could not now abandon their closest ally, and refused a German demand to stay out of the fighting. As a result, Berlin declared war on France as well. The catastrophe that nobody wanted but many feared had at last come about.

Though Britain had made no public pledge to aid France, its ministers had privately promised to help if the French were attacked by Germany. Parliament put aside any reluctance it might have had to make good on this promise when the Germans, according to their war plan, invaded Belgium. Britain, as one of the guarantors of Belgian neutrality and security (p. 492), now had a legal basis for action. Parliament declared war on Germany on August 4. Japan, Britain's treaty partner in the Pacific, soon entered on the side of the "Allies," while the Turks, renewing their struggle with Russia, joined the "Central Powers" (Austria and Germany). Italy, a member of the Triple Alliance, remained neutral until 1915, when secret promises of extensive territorial rewards won it over to the Allied side. Many smaller nations were gradually drawn into the war (at least formally), but they did not influence its outcome.

THE COURSE AND CONSEQUENCES OF THE WAR

The strategy of the First World War was basically simple. The Allies, with control of the seas, were sure of winning a long war of attrition. The Central Powers aimed for a quick, decisive victory based on superior military technique and forces already in place. They also enjoyed the advantage of interior lines of communication, which meant that they

Fig. 14.1 Trench Warfare. Allied soldiers on the First World War's Western Front hold a forward position, consisting of trenches to protect them against German fire. The soldier at left stands next to a machine gun; behind him are water-filled shell holes, the work of the other main killer weapon of the war, heavy artillery. Water and gunfire between them have turned the landscape to mud. Beyond the soldiers stretches "No Man's Land"; somewhere on the other side are the Germans, living in exactly the same circumstances.

could concentrate their troops swiftly on chosen fronts. The Germans, wishing to avoid dividing their army between west and east, had planned to strike an overwhelming first blow against France and then turn against the Russian forces, which would be slower in mobilizing. In executing their plan, the German generals did not hesitate to sweep through tiny Belgium, violating the treaty guaranteeing Belgium's neutrality. The treaty, explained the Germans, was but a "scrap of paper"; the invasion was a matter of "military necessity."

The Routine of Slaughter. The German attack, which aimed to roll up the French army in a grand, wheeling movement, stalled at the Marne River, near Paris. After the first few weeks, the battle on the Western Front changed from one of movement to one of fixed positions. Now the advantage shifted to those who were on the defensive. Trench warfare, with its barbed wire, machine guns, artillery barrages, and bayonet charges, became a routine of slaughter for the next four years (*Fig. 14.1*). Some new types of weapons were tried, aimed at breaking the military stalemate there: tanks by Britain, poison gas and submarines by Germany, and aircraft by both sides. These weapons failed to change the course of the conflict, but two of them—tanks and aircraft—would develop into decisive forces during the next world war (pp. 588–590).

On the Eastern Front the Germans quickly gained the upper hand. The soldiers of the tsar, brave but poorly supplied, suffered disastrous losses and were practically out of the war by 1917. This military loss to the Allies was more than balanced, however, by the entrance of the United States on their side in 1917. Americans had been generally sympathetic with the British and French from the start of the war, and in the end, the country's traditional opposition to "entangling alliances" was overcome by a combination of forces: the American government, fearing the strategic consequences of a German victory, pushed for intervention on the side of the Allies; and the public, alarmed by reports of German atrocities and the sinking of commercial vessels by German submarines, rallied to support the government. By bringing in fresh troops and equipment and by pledging the resources of their continent, the Americans ensured ultimate victory for the Allies. Bowing to the inevitable, the Germans at last responded favorably to President Woodrow Wilson's offer of a moderate settlement on Allied terms—a "peace without victory." In November 1918, they agreed to lay down their arms.

The Peace Treaties: War Guilt and National Self-Determination. At the peace conference, which met at Versailles and other suburbs of Paris, separate treaties were arranged with each of the Central Powers. None of the defeated nations was given any effective voice in the settlements; it turned out to be a victor's peace after all, in which France, Britain, and the United States laid down the conditions. Delegates from the Central Powers protested bitterly, but they were compelled to accept under threat that the war would be renewed. In a vengeful stroke, the French required the Germans to sign their treaty in the Hall of Mirrors at Versailles (*Fig. 9.9*, p. 394), where in 1871 Bismarck had proclaimed the German Empire.

Under the provisions of the treaty, Germany lost the provinces of Alsace and Lorraine (which had been taken from France in 1871), its overseas colonies, and valuable lands on its eastern frontiers. Germany also had to surrender most of its merchant shipping and to dismantle its armed forces. But the most objectionable part of the Versailles treaty, from the German point of view, was the "war guilt" clause—which stated that Germany and its partners accepted responsibility for all loss and damage caused by the war. The Germans did not feel that they alone were to blame, and the historical facts indicate that other powers shared the responsibility. The guilt clause no doubt reflected popular sentiment in the Allied countries, which had been fed strong propaganda by their wartime governments. It was put into the treaty to justify huge damage claims by the victors. Only small amounts of these claims were ever collected, but the "war guilt" clause aroused among Germans a violent and lasting hatred of the treaty (p. 579).

The treaties with the other defeated powers (1919–1920) provided for the remaking of the map of central and eastern Europe, for now three empires (the Russian, Austrian, and Turkish) were in partial or total dissolution (*Map 14.4*). The guiding principle in drawing the new frontiers was Woodrow Wilson's principle of "self-determination" for nationalities. Seven new national states came into being. In northeastern Europe, there were Finland and the Baltic states of Estonia, Latvia, and Lithuania. In central Europe, there were Poland and Czechoslovakia (where there lived two closely related Slav nations, the Czechs and Slovaks). In the Balkans, there was Yugoslavia,

Map 14.4 Twenty Years' Truce. The map shows the new European frontiers and countries following the First World War. There were more nation-states than before, but Europe was divided into "satisfied" ones that gained territory, such as France, Poland, Czechoslovakia, and Romania, and bitterly "dissatisfied" ones, such as Germany, Hungary, and the multinational Soviet Union. It was the same kind of situation that had led to war in the first place. As a French delegate to the Paris Peace Conference said, "This is not a peace; it is a twenty years' truce."

FINLAND

NORWAY

SWEDEN

Oslo

Helsinki

Leningrad
(St. Petersburg,
Petrograd)

Stockholm

ESTONIA

*North
Sea*

Baltic Sea

LATVIA

DENMARK

LITHUANIA

Memel

UNION OF SOVIET

SOCIALIST

REPUBLICS

Copenhagen

Danzig

EAST
PRUSSIA

The
Hague

NETHERLANDS

POLISH
CORRIDOR

Posen

Warsaw

Kiev

Berlin

POLAND

Rhine

Brussels

BELGIUM

GERMANY

GALICIA

UKRAINE

LUXEMBOURG

Prague

Paris

CZECHOSLOVAKIA

Versailles

ALSACE-
LORRAINE

BESSARABIA

Prut

Munich

Vienna

Budapest

Berne

AUSTRIA

HUNGARY

ROMANIA

*Black
Sea*

SWITZERLAND

S.
TYROL

ISTRIA

B
A
L
K
A
N
S

FRANCE

Milan

Fiume

YUGOSLAVIA

Bucharest

Belgrade

Danube

Sarajevo

BULGARIA

I
T
A
L
Y

Sofia

Constantinople

*Adriatic
Sea*

ALBANIA

*Bosporus
Dardanelles*

Rome

TURKEY

Naples

GREECE

*Aegean
Sea*

Athens

Mediterranean Sea

TERRITORY LOST BY:

Germany   Austria-Hungary

Bulgaria   Russia

MILES

0   300

which fulfilled the dream of the Serb nationalists who had started it all at Sarajevo—the new country's name meant "Land of the South Slavs" in the Serbian and other local languages. Within Yugoslavia's borders, there lived not only Orthodox Serbs, but also Catholic Croats and Slovenes, Muslim Bosnians and Albanians, and other groups. Austria and Hungary were separated and reduced to small landlocked states.

Turkey lost all of its Arab-inhabited Middle Eastern territories and was supposed to give up much more territory—in the west to Greece and in the east to the rival Muslim nation of the Kurds. But nationalist revolutionaries led by a Turkish army officer, Mustapha Kemal, refused to accept the peace treaty, and in a brutal war with Greece, they were able to form an independent Republic of Turkey that included all of Asia Minor and a small area in Europe surrounding Constantinople. One and a half million Greeks were compelled to leave their 2,700-year-old communities in western Asia Minor (p. 62), making way for about a million Turks expelled from Greece. The Kurds, on the other hand, remain under Turkish rule to the present day, often rebellious and often harshly repressed (p. 727).

Having brought an independent and united Turkish nation into being in defiance of the West, Kemal then ruled as a dictator, working fast and ruthlessly to Westernize his nation as Peter the Great had done with Russia two centuries before (p. 415). He repudiated (refused to pay) the debts of the former Ottoman Empire to foreign bankers, and instead used Turkey's resources to build up government-owned modern industries. He broke with Turkey's Muslim past, decreeing among other things the separation of Islam from the state, the replacement of the Arabic by the Latin alphabet, the abolition of the fez (the customary Muslim male headgear), and the prohibition of Muslim groups that he considered too intensely religious. The revered Muslim mosque in Constantinople that had formerly been the revered Christian cathedral of Hagia Sophia (pp. 202, 298) became a museum, and the city itself was now officially known by its Turkish name, Istanbul.

Kemal succeeded with these radical measures because he was a leader of nationalist triumph—the Father of the Turks (Atatürk) as he called himself, who had defied the West, expelled the Greeks, and held down the Kurds. After he died in 1938, his successors were able to turn Turkey into a more or less democratic state. Secular and Islamic political groups coexisted uneasily but were usually held together by their common Turkish nationalism. Once in a while, when Islamic or leftist groups were too successful at the polls, the army would step in to correct the course of democratic politics.

Despite the general application of national self-determination, the problem of national conflict continued to plague Europe. The diverse nationalities were so intermixed that no state boundary could be drawn that did not leave a national minority on the "wrong" side. Since the boundaries were drawn by the victors, these minorities usually came from nations that had lost the war: the new nation-states of central Europe and the Balkans were full of aggrieved minorities of Germans, Hungarians, and Turks. And in Yugoslavia and Czechoslovakia, nations that were ethnically related but divided by history and religion had endless opportunities for conflict within their "joint" nation-states.

The Threat to the Liberal Order. The deeper consequences of the war went far beyond the treaties and the breaking and making of states. The war had brought a catastrophic loss of lives and treasure. Of the more than sixty million men mobilized, some nine million were killed. Total civilian deaths, direct and indirect, amounted to more than thirty million; economic costs ran into trillions of dollars. The spirit of Europe, especially of its surviving aristocracy, was broken. The youth who had lived through the war, and wondered why, regarded themselves as a "lost generation." The old beliefs and slogans had for them become mockeries; traditional morals, manners, and standards seemed, at best, irrelevant.

Men and morals were not the only casualties of the war. The liberal order, which in 1914 had appeared firm, was badly damaged. France and England, the leading liberal states, were crippled. In addition to their irreplaceable losses in manpower, their world positions had been shaken. In prosecuting the war, both nations had found it necessary to sell off a large portion of their overseas investments. Moreover, the spectacle of Europe at war with itself stripped away the awe with which colonial peoples had viewed their conquerors. The Western powers had given them reason to hope that they might one day send the imperialists packing.

The loss of physical and psychological power by the liberal states was equaled by the injury to their professed ideas and institutions. Liberalism was rooted in the Enlightenment, with its optimistic faith in humanity, reason, nature, and progress. But this faith had been crushed in the agony and futility of the war. Could liberalism survive after its supporting faith had collapsed? Disenchanted Europeans were unsure. Some drifted into skepticism (doubting all), cynicism (scorning all), or nihilism (rejecting all). Other Europeans were drawn toward Marxist socialism or toward fascism, a new and more virulent strain of nationalism.

The war had undermined specific liberal institutions as well. This was most evident in the economic sphere, where "free enterprise" had been jealously guarded during the nineteenth century. Every nation at war was forced to clamp controls on business; just as the draft on manpower was compulsory, so was the call on economic resources. Raw materials, exports and imports, banking, wages, prices—all had been regulated in the pursuit of victory. Laissez-faire principles (pp. 510–511) had been ignored "for the duration," and this experience of government planning and direction continued into the future. The war had also disrupted the intricate mechanism of international trade, and a chain of financial dislocations after 1918 marked the end of historic laissez-faire. It would be demonstrated time and again that private enterprise, both domestic and international, was not always "self-regulating" in the public interest. To maintain employment and save business from mass failures, Western governments would be called on to take action.

The war had been fought, declared President Wilson, to make the world "safe for democracy." As he looked at Europe from Versailles in 1919, he might well have thought that the goal was now within reach. Prussian militarism had been defeated, long-standing empires had been reduced to ruins, and proud monarchies had been toppled. Democracy (as well as nationalism) appeared triumphant. Yet Wilson and others of liberal-democratic convictions were to suffer bitter disappointment. For most of the new democracies were only superficially democratic, and the older democracies were soon to lose their once-liberal character. Moreover, the shock and aftershock of the war were to open the doors of revolution in several countries. From the underground of the nineteenth century sprang the promoters of new social and international orders— who were radically opposed, in theory as well as in practice, to both liberalism and bourgeois democracy. The world was about to enter an era of struggle between rival social systems and global orders that would continue for most of the century.

Communism in Russia

All the rival social and global orders shared a general tendency toward *collectivism—* that is, more or less restriction of individual choice and freedom in the collective inter-ests of society. In other respects, however, they were profoundly different ways of orga-nizing society and the world as a whole. Communism and fascism intended to overturn and rebuild both, whereas liberal democratic reformers intended to preserve and re-form them. Here we are concerned with the first and longest-lasting of the movements to overturn the existing social and worldwide order, that of communism, in a period when it was confined to a single country, Russia.

RUSSIA BEFORE THE REVOLUTION

Strangely, the first communist state was established in a country where modern forces had scarcely started to develop. Autocratic Russia was a century or more behind the changes that had swept over western Europe. In 1917, the position of the Romanov dy-nasty was not far different from what it had been more than two centuries earlier under Catherine the Great (p. 416). It resembled, in its pretensions and ignorance, the Bour-bon monarchy of France in 1789 (pp. 456–459).

Russia had created a vast empire of many distinct nationalities, stretching east-ward from central Europe to the Pacific Ocean (pp. 414–416, 555). But most of the pop-ulation lived in European Russia (which then included Poland and the Baltic lands), and in 1900 it totaled about 100 million. More than 80 percent of these people were peasants, and most of them had only recently been freed from serfdom (1861). They held more than half the arable land of the country, either as individual owners or through their village organization (*mir*), and they had gained limited political rights. Nevertheless, they remained largely illiterate and were regarded by the landed aristoc-racy (less than 10 percent of the population) as an inferior caste. Over all was the heavy hand of the Russian Orthodox Church, which resisted Western ideas and supported the tsar's "divine" rule of Holy Russia and its empire.

Western influences had nevertheless reached into Russia. The late nineteenth cen-tury saw the rise of a new social element, the *intelligentsia,* made up of educated mem-bers of the aristocracy and the small urban middle class. Though the intelligentsia usu-ally identified themselves with Slavic traditions, they were familiar with Western books and ideas. Writers like Tolstoy and Dostoevsky were members of this group (p. 533). Their popularity in the West reflected a growing common ground of culture. Russia also produced musical composers, philosophers, and poets, as well as some outstand-ing mathematicians and scientists.

The Industrial Revolution served as the chief spearhead of Westernization. After 1880, with the help of outside funds, the capitalist pattern of economic growth began to take shape in Russia. Substantial investments went into factories, mines, and rail-roads, and Russia became active in the world trading system. Capitalist development, however, was still limited in comparison to that of England or Germany. Industrial wage earners made up only a small fraction of the total labor force in 1914, and their work-ing conditions resembled those in England fifty years earlier. The capitalist class was very small and had to share the economic field with numerous state-owned enterprises.

Though in theory an absolute monarch, Nicholas II was troubled by a wide range of domestic criticism and opposition. Around 1900, the rising business and professional class, in combination with liberal landowners, had formed a political party known as the Constitutional Democrats. Eager to follow the example of western Europe, they wanted to convert Russia's autocracy into a liberal, constitutional government. At about the same time, two radical parties were founded—the Social Revolutionaries and the Social Democrats, both drawn mainly from the intelligentsia. The former was an agrarian party; its goals were to give more land to the peasants and to strengthen the functions of the *mir*. The Social Democrats were a Marxist group. They viewed the peasants as hopelessly backward and believed that social change would have to follow Marxist theory—that is, the continuing growth of capitalism followed by the rise (and triumph) of an urban proletariat.

In 1905, a large body of protesting workers had gathered in front of the tsar's Winter Palace in Saint Petersburg and had been fired on by troops. This "Bloody Sunday" set off insurrections across the country that were supported and used in various ways by the opposition parties. As a means of restoring order, the tsar promised a constitution and civil liberties and further agreed to the creation of an elected legislative body, the Duma. But discontent still rumbled among most classes of the population. Only by means of a hated secret police was the tsar able to keep down the opposition. Even so, some revolutionaries resorted to terrorism, and no public official was safe from assassination. The grandfather of Tsar Nicholas, Alexander II, had been killed by a bomb, and Nicholas's prime minister was shot dead in 1911.

THE COLLAPSE OF THE TSARIST REGIME AND THE TRIUMPH OF LENIN

Russia's military disasters in the First World War, following defeat in the Russo-Japanese War (p. 555), opened the way to revolution: they laid bare the inadequacy of the tsarist administration and heaped disgrace upon it. Soldiers and sailors, poorly supplied and hungry, at last refused to continue the hopeless fight against the Germans. In March 1917, food riots and strikes in Petrograd (formerly Saint Petersburg) led to mutinies among the garrisons of the capital (*Fig. 14.2*). The tsar, then at the front, abdicated on the advice of his generals; thus the Romanov dynasty ended, and Russia became a republic. A provisional government, composed chiefly of the reformist leaders in the Duma, now assumed power. This government was challenged, however, by the Petrograd Soviet (Council) of Workers' and Soldiers' Deputies, a body dominated by the radical parties. Local soviets had first appeared during the insurrection of 1905. They were formed again in 1917, supposedly speaking for the peasants, city workers, and soldiers, and the Petrograd Soviet began to act as a shadow government. The country's future now hinged upon the struggle for power between the provisional government and the Soviet.

In April 1917, Vladimir Lenin arrived in Petrograd. The son of a middle-class civil official, Lenin had enjoyed a comfortable childhood. But in 1886, at the age of sixteen, after the execution of his elder brother for alleged participation in a terrorist plot, he had thrown himself into opposition to the tsarist regime. Depending on friends for his livelihood, he made revolution his life career. Lenin spent most of his years in exile— first in Siberia and later in western Europe.

An early convert to Marxism, Lenin worked to make the Russian Social Democratic party a disciplined revolutionary organization. The "revisionist" wing of the party (p. 521) appeared to outnumber Lenin's faction, but at a meeting in 1903, he temporarily secured majority backing for the radical position. His followers thenceforth called

© Sovfoto/Eastfoto

Fig. 14.2 "Comrade Workers and Soldiers, Support Our Demands!" The words on the banner show that these women know they are not alone. They are demonstrating against high bread prices as part of the first street protest that led to the fall of the tsarist government of Russia in March 1917. In fact, workers were already on strike, and soldiers refused orders to disperse the protesters. Compare *Fig. 11.3*, p. 463.

themselves Bolsheviks, from the Russian word meaning "majority"; their reformist rivals came to be known as Mensheviks (from the word for "minority"). In 1912, the Bolsheviks broke away completely from the Social Democrats and formed an independent revolutionary party. They changed the name to Communist in 1918.

During most of the First World War, Lenin promoted international Marxist activities from Switzerland. His return to Petrograd in 1917 was aided by the Germans, who hoped that his activities there would help to overthrow the new government and take Russia out of the war—which is what Lenin succeeded in doing. First, however, he had to take power from the provisional government, which was making an earnest effort to restore internal order and uphold Russia's obligation to its allies to continue fighting the Germans. But conditions grew steadily more desperate in the country. Though Russia's economy had not developed to the point at which a proletarian revolution in the Marxist pattern could be expected, Lenin became convinced that the war had opened a shortcut to socialism. He saw that the bulk of the Russian people wanted three things above all: peace, land, and food. The provisional government, headed after July by Alexander Kerensky, a Social Revolutionary, had failed to satisfy these longings.

Lenin's road to power was through the Petrograd Soviet. Though the Bolsheviks were a minority within the Soviet when Lenin arrived, he cleverly outmaneuvered his opponents (the Mensheviks and the Social Revolutionaries), and his repeated promises of peace and land won growing popular support for the Bolsheviks. In October 1917, Lenin's faction won the upper hand in the Soviet and elected Lenin's close ally, Leon Trotsky, chairman. As Kerensky's power slipped and as soldiers once more began to desert their units, Lenin decided to move against the provisional government.

The seizure of power, on November 7, was carefully planned and swiftly executed. With the support of the Petrograd military garrison, a revolutionary force occupied the telephone exchanges, power plants, and railway stations of the capital. The cruiser *Aurora,* stationed on the Neva River (fronting the Winter Palace), trained its guns on the building and fired the signal for the main attack. Kerensky found no troops to defend his government; he escaped, and the rest of his ministers fled or were captured.

On the afternoon of the coup, according to plan, Lenin arranged a meeting in Petrograd of delegates from soviets in other parts of the country. This "all-Russian" congress, controlled by the Bolsheviks, declared the provisional government at an end and claimed full authority. It approved decrees for an immediate peace with Germany and for the distribution of land to the peasants. The congress also elected a Council of People's Commissars (Deputies) to conduct the government, with Lenin at its head. These formalities could not conceal the fact that a small group, shrewdly and boldly led, had moved into the confused situation and had taken command. Could such a government, facing enormous internal and external problems, keep itself in power? Its only organs of administration were the Communist party, the soviets, and the Council of Commissars. The commissars established a secret police and authorized the recruiting of a new military force, the Red Army. The military commissar, Trotsky, was to be its builder and leader.

One of the early tests of the new government came with the arrival in Petrograd in January 1918 of delegates to a national Constituent Assembly. This body had been authorized months before by the provisional (reformist) government and was to write a liberal constitution for the country. The delegates had been chosen in a general election in which 36 million citizens voted, and a majority of them belonged to Kerensky's Social Revolutionary party. But Lenin refused to surrender power to the "malignant bourgeoisie" and sent a company of sailors to stop the meetings of the assembly.

Not long afterward, in March 1918, the new Soviet government signed a peace treaty with the Central Powers, by which it agreed to surrender control of Finland, the Ukraine, much of Poland, and the Baltic territories of Lithuania, Latvia, and Estonia— all historically parts of the former Russian Empire. It was a bitter defeat, but it freed the Soviets' hands to face the next challenge to their rule. Former tsarist generals organized and led counterrevolutionary forces (the Whites) in several regions of the country. They were joined by property owners, reactionaries, liberals, and anti-Bolshevik revolutionaries. In addition, the Western Allies sent military units to aid the Whites against the Reds; the Allies were trying to keep Russia in the war and wanted to help destroy communism. But after two years of frightful civil war, marked by the use of terror on both sides, the hardened Communists emerged victorious.

The Red triumph owed much to the extraordinary will of Lenin and to the military and organizing genius of Trotsky. And it owed something to the confusion and splits among the counterrevolutionary groups and their association with foreign powers. But in the last analysis, it owed most to the attitude of the common people. Many of the commoners, to be sure, opposed the new regime. But the majority feared that a White victory would probably lead to the withdrawal of land from the peasants and to a restoration of the old order of autocracy, caste, and privilege. Though they also feared the Communists, they preferred them to the reactionaries. And popular support, in the fluid, guerrilla-type struggle, proved decisive. After 1920, with the bloody ordeal over, Lenin and his party sought to bring order out of chaos.

BUILDING A SOCIALIST SOCIETY

The task of pulling together a battle-torn country (formerly the multinational empire of the tsars), and at the same time overhauling its social structure, was staggering. The violence of civil strife had brought more distress than had the war against the Central Powers. During the fight with the counterrevolutionaries, the government had resorted to temporary measures—later called "war communism." These included the drafting of workers into labor teams and forced deliveries of food from the peasants, in order to relieve hunger in the cities. Lenin was eager to start building socialism, but economic conditions were still so bad in 1921 that his plans had to be postponed.

Policy Changes and Power Struggles. Food was the primary problem; drought had made matters worse, and famine now stalked large areas of the country. In accord with the Soviet land distribution decree of 1917, the peasants of each community had divided the properties of the landed aristocracy among themselves, and something had to be done quickly to spur their efforts and encourage them to market their produce. The New Economic Policy (NEP), launched in 1921, aimed at doing just that. Now peasant farmers were permitted to hire laborers and to sell or lease land as they saw fit. Forced food deliveries were stopped, and the growers could market as they wished. The NEP was also extended to industry and commerce. While the state kept its grip on public utilities and other large industries (which had been nationalized in 1918), it encouraged private entrepreneurs to undertake new business ventures.

This temporary return to capitalistic methods brought about substantial recovery of production. But it fell short of the hopes and promises of the Communists. By 1928, output was at about the same level as it had been in 1913, and the momentum of the NEP seemed to slacken. Meanwhile, in 1924, the revered Lenin had died, and his former colleagues were maneuvering to take his place. Trotsky was the best known, probably the most talented, and certainly the most radical. In 1926, he openly criticized the NEP, complaining in particular about the new bourgeois and about the richer farmers or *kulaks* (from the Russian word for "fist," expressing their reputation for toughness). He called for the *collectivization* (government takeover) of agriculture, vigorous expansion of heavy industry, and a master plan for balanced and rapid economic growth, as well as for the promotion of Marxist revolution in countries beyond Russia.

But Trotsky could not gain the support of the majority of the party. Joseph Stalin, who held the post of party secretary, had quietly and skillfully built a following for himself as Lenin's heir. He appealed to those who wanted to concentrate on the revolution inside Russia, to those who looked inward rather than to the world. The party congress expelled Trotsky in 1927; he was first sent to Siberia and then deported. Branded a communist heretic ("deviationist"), Trotsky was assassinated in Mexico in 1940—probably by agents of Stalin.

Planning, Liquidations, and Purges. With Trotsky and other rivals out of the way, Stalin in 1928 commenced the building of "socialism in one country"—using the policies of rapid planned development that Trotsky had called for. He announced the party's first Five-Year Plan, which concentrated on the collectivization of farming and the accelerated development of industry. State-controlled planning was the fulfillment of an idea that had been worked out by Marx's partner, Friedrich Engels (p. 519), many decades before. Engels had noted that planning was indispensable to the efficient operation of individual factories and industries. The logical and ultimate goal, he thought, was the creation of a unified and complete national plan, embracing all parts of the economy.

Stalin's first plan ran into near-ruinous resistance. His officials scoured the countryside, joining private farms into large collectives of 1,000 or more acres each. Strictly speaking, the farmers of each collective, as a "cooperative" unit, retained possession of the land, but individual farmers no longer controlled any portion of the land as their own. The poorer peasants usually submitted to these forced measures, but the kulaks fought collectivization bitterly.

The government at last decided to coerce the resisting kulaks by "liquidating them as a class." Most of the two million kulaks and their families were shipped off to labor camps in Siberia; others were forced into obedience, and many were killed. Some of them, in a final act of defiance and sabotage, destroyed their animals and implements before yielding. The heavy losses, and government manipulation of the surviving supplies, brought renewed famines in the early 1930s. Nevertheless, the collective-farm program was driven through; Stalin pursued it as a means of effecting complete state control over the rural population and of increasing agricultural efficiency and output. He believed that the collectives could make better use of machinery and scientific methods than the single-owner farm. However, there was a loss of personal incentive in this system.

Stalin's farm policy aroused sharp protests within the ruling bodies of the Communist party. His most notable critic was Nikolai Bukharin, a veteran activist and theoretician, who was a longtime associate of both Lenin and Stalin. Bukharin condemned the use of force against the peasants; he supported a flexible economic policy, based on persuasion, compromise, and gradual development.

But Stalin outmaneuvered his opponents. In 1930, Bukharin was shunted out of party influence and was later denounced as an "enemy of the revolution." Following a rigged show trial, he was sentenced to be shot in 1938. Had Bukharin and his allies succeeded in stopping Stalin, the course of Soviet history might have been quite different. Many other communist leaders, together with almost all the Old Bolsheviks who had belonged to the party before the Revolution, together with millions of lower-ranking party members, government officials, and ordinary citizens, were also arrested in a series of massive purges, which probably originated in Stalin's determination to suppress criticism and opposition but developed a momentum of their own. The victims were coerced into confessions, usually of crimes involving treason, espionage, and sabotage, and sent to labor camps or in many cases shot.

While the painful and destructive events were taking place in the countryside, positive advances were being made in industry. The rate of growth in the 1930s surpassed that of any Western nation during that decade. Much of the new development was located east of the Urals, in central Asia, where it altered the life and culture of a vast region. It was the combination of socialist planning and state exploitation of labor that made rapid modernization possible—and without the aid of foreign capital. This example captured the attention of other underdeveloped countries around the world. The industrial successes, of course, were trumpeted to Russian workers and peasants, who developed a fierce pride in Soviet material accomplishments. They found deep satisfaction in the feeling that "backward Russia" was at last catching up, scientifically and industrially, with the West. Access to education and the arts was also extended, and most Soviet children enjoyed greater opportunities than their parents had.

Communist Totalitarianism. The price of all this, in addition to the early years of bloodshed, losses of property, and severe hardships, was the domination of life by the Communist party and government (*totalitarianism*). The Orthodox Church was stripped of its property and influence; other traditional faiths were barely tolerated. (Marxism became, in effect, the state religion.) There was no free press, free speech, free unions, or freedom of assembly. Political power remained a monopoly of the party, which was supported by the feared secret police. Dissenters, under Stalin, were put down or destroyed by systematic terror: show trials, purges, labor camps, and mass executions. Using these modern tools of control, the Soviet government succeeded in deadening virtually every nerve of resistance.

The major political institutions of the new state had been formed before Lenin's death. According to the constitution of 1923, the Union of Soviet Socialist Republics (USSR) was a federal, democratic state. The former Russian Empire had embraced some fifty nationalities, and the Communists wanted to avoid openly suppressing national feeling. Each major nationality became a republic (or a self-governing region within a republic). By 1940 there were fifteen republics; by far the largest was the Russian, which contained over half the USSR's total population of 200 million. The Ukrainian Republic (retaken by the Reds during the Civil War) had about half as many inhabitants as the Russian Republic, and the White Russian (Byelorussian), about one-tenth. Most of the other republics were relatively small, with one to six million inhabitants each.

Each republic had its own administration for its internal affairs. The highest body in the federal structure was the Supreme Soviet, which enacted national legislation. However, this body met for only a short time each year, when it elected a Presidium of some thirty members, to which its functions were delegated. The Supreme Soviet also chose the Council of People's Commissars, whose members served as the executive heads of the federal government. The Soviet capital was moved in 1924 from Petrograd—renamed Leningrad—to Moscow.

The controlling power of the USSR lay in the Communist party rather than in the agencies of the state. It was not a party in the liberal-democratic sense but a disciplined organization whose self-appointed mission was to run the country. Accordingly, the constitution of 1923 authorized it to carry out this special role. Thus while one did not have to be a party member to vote or run for office in the Soviet Union, party representatives determined whose names would be placed on the election ballot. Within the party itself, organization and authority followed the principle of "democratic centralism": officers and delegates to higher bodies were elected at several levels—from the level of the smallest party "cell," to intermediate bodies, to the All-Union Party Congress, which normally met every other year.

Though the Congress was recognized as the highest party authority, actual control resided in its Central Committee, to which the Congress delegated its power. After the time of Lenin, power tended to go more and more to the top. And once policy was decided upon there, it was the duty of every Communist to work for its fulfillment. Without the party organization and its carefully selected and trained membership, the Soviet state could not have transformed, as it did, a country that covers one-sixth of the land surface of the earth. On the other hand, this monopoly of power by a single party—with its stultifying bureaucracy and lack of accountability—would prove incapable, in the long run, of satisfying the desires of the subject peoples.

INTERNATIONAL COMMUNISM

Although the Bolsheviks succeeded in "building socialism in one country," they were less successful in spreading socialism abroad. As Marxists, they believed in and worked for world revolution (as Trotsky had urged), but they made little headway in that direction. Marx himself had given socialism its international character, regarding national states as narrow creations of the bourgeoisie. In 1864, he had organized the First (Socialist) International. During the rest of the nineteenth century, however, the international socialist movement proved weak. It was troubled by internal differences—ideological and personal—and ultimately by rival patriotisms. A Second International, associating the socialist parties of many nations, fell to pieces with the start of the First World War. A radical minority refused to support their war governments, but most "reformist" socialists supported the "patriotic fronts" of their homelands.

Lenin, who had predicted the war as a natural outcome of capitalist imperialism, scorned the reformist parties as bourgeois. In 1919, he invited left-wing socialists throughout Europe to join the Soviet Communist party in forming a Third International. This, Lenin declared, would be a "pure" successor to Marx's original organization. Free of the reformist socialists, it pledged itself to worldwide revolution and the dictatorship of the proletariat.

Left-wing socialists of other countries, impressed by Lenin's stand and by the Russian Revolution itself, readily accepted radical leadership. During the 1920s, the methods of the Soviet party were adopted by the new association. Tight organization, centralized control, and the name "Communist" were imposed on the international body and on each of its national parties. As a result, sharp hostility arose between rival groups of Marxists outside the Soviet Union. The reformist socialists viewed with horror the violence used by the Communists, especially under Stalin, and despised the intolerance of party leaders toward members with different views.

Having alienated the large majority of Marxists outside the Soviet Union, the Third International (known as the Comintern) had little chance of success. It was the reformist (democratic) socialists, strengthened by their break with revolutionary Marxism, who made impressive gains in the Western nations. After the failure of several Communist-led uprisings immediately following the war, the reformists worked to preserve the existing order by legal and democratic reforms in France, Germany, Scandinavia, and Britain. Though some European democracies, notably France and Germany, had large and legal Communist parties, they were generally excluded from governing power. Proletarian revolution was clearly not coming soon in the industrial countries of the West.

All the same, Communist parties, with Moscow's support and direction, were at work in fifty or more countries, militantly opposing capitalism and imperialism and serving as arms of propaganda and espionage for the USSR. The principal international influence of communism came not through the activities of the Comintern but through the fact that the Soviet Union existed as a world power. Collectivists of all shades could point to it as a concrete alternative to liberalism and capitalism. Though they objected to many characteristics of the Soviet Union, they could use it as a working example of state planning and cooperative social principles.

Fascism in Italy and Germany

The fear of communism helped push several European nations into revolutionary changes of another sort. In Italy and Germany, the fascist revolutions sprang from two conditions: a social crisis that arose in the wake of the First World War and the inadequacy of liberal-democratic government. (Wherever governments effectively handled their problems, they were able to resist subversion.) Moreover, the revolutions in Italy and Germany were propelled by violent nationalisms growing out of the frustrations of the war. Whereas the Communists focused on *class* and interclass struggle, the fascists stressed the *nation* and international struggle.

There is another significant difference between the two kinds of revolution. The Communist uprisings in Europe had been anticipated in the decades of Marxist organization, propaganda, and threats of action. Fascism, on the other hand, came as a surprise. As an explicit doctrine, it had no ideological founders, no authoritative books, and no forces in evidence before 1918.

Its explosive appearance can now be understood as a breaking out of strong ideas and passions, some open to view and some hidden, that were opposed to liberalism, democracy, and rationalism. Though revolutionary, fascism had a broad appeal to privileged groups as well as to ordinary people. Its militant nationalism aroused all patriots, and its support of class interests (including those of the military) satisfied individuals of property and power.

FASCISM IN ITALY: MUSSOLINI

Italy after 1918 provided a favorable setting for the rise of fascism. Its parliamentary institutions were less than fifty years old and had never won much loyalty or enthusiasm from the people—in fact, even most male citizens were not entitled to vote until 1912. Furthermore, the Italian legislature seemed incapable of dealing with postwar inflation and unemployment, and most Italians were bitterly disappointed over their country's role in the war. Though they finished on the side of the victors, their armies had experienced hardships, losses, and humiliating defeats. And at war's end, the Allies gave Italy only a portion of what they had promised as a reward for Italy's entering the conflict on the Allied side (p. 562).

The Breakdown of Parliamentary Government. Many voters turned to the Socialists in the hope that they would do something about the worsening economic situation. The elections of 1919 gave the Socialist party one-third of the seats in the national Chamber of Deputies; with the Catholic Popular party, the Socialists might have developed a constructive program for the country. Mutual distrust between Catholics and Marxists made such cooperation impossible, however, and the Socialist trade unions began to take direct action. In 1920, unionists occupied a number of factories and tried unsuccessfully to operate them. The workers soon withdrew, but their action had given the

1860	1870		March on Rome 1922	1943
Period of Unification		Constitutional Monarchy	Mussolini (Fascism)	

propertied classes a fright. In the following year, the Socialist party split over the question of whether or not to join the Communist Third International (the Comintern; p. 575), thus losing what chance it might have had of becoming a dominant political force. It was on this scene of confusion, discontent, and fear of communism that Benito Mussolini presented himself as the national savior.

Born into a Socialist family, the son of a blacksmith, Mussolini was a man of the laboring class. He went to school to become a teacher but turned to journalism and radical agitation. In 1912, he secured the position of editor of the Socialist party newspaper in Milan and soon gained a reputation as a dynamic radical leader. As a Marxist, he had initially opposed war and had escaped military conscription by going to Switzerland, but in October 1914, he reversed himself by urging Italian entry into the war against Germany. For this he was expelled from the party and from his newspaper. Thereupon he founded a journal of his own, which he used to publicize his new convictions and to advance his political career.

Mussolini served in the war as a corporal until he was injured in an accident in 1917. Resuming the editorship of his paper, he tried to stir popular support for the flagging war effort. He turned wholly against socialism after the Russian Revolution, growing more and more militant and nationalistic. He opposed the floundering parliamentary government of his own country and, like many other veterans of the war, became attracted to violence as a way of life and as a means of securing change. He started organizing his followers into paramilitary black-shirted units (*fasci di combattimento*—hence the name *fascist*). These units took it upon themselves to take part in street fighting with socialists and others they disliked, smash opposing party and newspaper offices, and assassinate some of the opposing leaders.

Mussolini next organized his forces into a fascist political party, even though he had only contempt for the parliamentary party system. In the national election of 1921, the Fascists won thirty-five seats in the Chamber of Deputies. As their leader, Mussolini made fiery nationalist appeals and attacks on socialism. He began to gain widespread support, especially from the shopkeepers and white-collar class, but from the rich as well. Young people were strongly attracted by the uniforms, parades, mass rallies, and calls for action. In 1922, his Blackshirts drove the legally elected socialist governments from control of Italy's northern industrial cities, and later that year, a huge Fascist assembly in Naples called for a march on Rome.

The constitutional king of Italy, Victor Emmanuel III, was now faced with the prospect of black-shirted bullies converging on his capital. His prime minister, unable to secure an effective legislative majority, urged him to declare martial law. But the king decided to do otherwise; he invited Mussolini to come from Milan and form a new administration. The Fascists, camped near Rome, marched on the city while Mussolini arrived by railway car to take over the government.

Fascist Dictatorship. The new prime minister, who preferred his party title of *Duce* ("Leader"), was not long in consolidating his position. The Chamber of Deputies, which had surrendered to the Blackshirt threat without a fight, quickly voted Mussolini dictatorial power for one year. In the election of 1924, the party won about 70 percent of the total national vote. Despite its unclear aims and its fondness for violence, the party received the support of many moderates who hoped that they could exercise a restraining influence on the Duce. Within a few years, he had eliminated almost all opposition and had established a fascist state.

The collapse of Italian democracy was clearly due to its own failures, but Mussolini's triumph resulted from a variety of factors. Critical among them was the backing of the army and the great industrialists of the country. Mussolini did not have to create a new army (as did Lenin), for the regular army came readily to his side. Many of its high officers had had fascist sympathies from the beginning, and the Duce's glorification of militarism and his extravagant support of the army gained their active loyalty.

The industrial leaders, for their part, had been uncertain about Mussolini at first. They approved his smashing of the Socialist party and the unions, but they were worried about his intentions toward business. In 1925, the associated industrialists signed an agreement with the Duce. In return for their support of the Fascists, the industrialists were given a recognized position in the government, with the authority to regulate the nation's industrial affairs. The major employers in agriculture and commerce were later given similar authority. Together with handpicked labor and professional bodies, these regulatory groups made up what Mussolini called the "corporate state." In theory, this state represented a harmonizing of all the economic and social interests in the country. In fact the corporate state was an instrument of the dictator, through which he permitted the leading capitalists to administer the nation's economic affairs.

Mussolini completed his structure of power by negotiating an alliance with the pope. Ever since the move for national unification had begun, in the middle of the nineteenth century, state and church in Italy had been in opposition (p. 500). After lengthy and difficult discussions, Mussolini and Pius XI signed the Lateran Treaty and Concordat of 1929. By their terms, the pope gained sovereignty over the area of Vatican City, which includes Saint Peter's Basilica and its immediate environs. The Church also secured state financial aid and a special position in the educational system. In return, Pius gave his weighty support, and that of the Italian clergy and laity, to the fascist state. Mussolini was himself an atheist, but like Napoleon before him (p. 468), he sealed his position as dictator by a bargain with the Church. Afterward, not surprisingly, he violated the terms of the Concordat as he saw fit.

The political institutions of Italy underwent a steady evolution under Mussolini. The corporate associations, which guided economic affairs, gradually became the basis for political representation in the national legislative body. But the true power in all fields was the Fascist party, headed by the Duce. The party resembled, in many ways, the Communist party of the Soviet Union (p. 574). It was the only legal party, it consisted of only a fraction of the total citizenry, and its members were carefully drawn from the ranks of select youth organizations. Corresponding to the Communist Central Committee was the Grand Council of Fascism. Its members generally held high offices in the government in addition to their party positions; this connection, too, paralleled the interlocking of party and state officials that existed in the Soviet system.

The Fascist Ideology. Though fascism stressed action and was anti-intellectual in tone and character, it nevertheless developed a distinctive ideology. In the beginning, as Mussolini himself admitted, it was largely a negative movement: against liberalism, democracy, rationalism, socialism, and pacifism. This negative feeling flowed from Mussolini's personal experience and that of countless other Europeans during and after the war. They had been cast adrift, let down by failed hopes of progress and happiness. The Fascists found an answer to this emptiness by arousing extreme nationalism. One could get an emotional lift by forgetting one's problems as a person and by giving oneself to something larger and grander—the nation. Mussolini and his associates developed this idea into the myth of the "organic state."

The Fascists asserted that the state is a living entity, above the individuals who compose it. "The state," declared Mussolini, "is a spiritual and moral fact in itself." It encompasses every sphere of life (totalitarianism); the state alone can "provide a solution to the dramatic contradictions of capitalism." And as a living organism, the state must expand in order to express its vitality. This meant a continuous and disciplined *will to power,* which requires unity within the nation, militarism, imperialism, and war.

The fascist myth rejected the liberal reliance on reason and replaced it with a mystical faith. Stridently anti-intellectual, it held that the "new order" would spring from the conviction of the "heart." Fascists therefore looked upon intellectuals as outmoded and suspicious characters, unduly concerned with their private mental fancies. Yet most Italian intellectuals willingly cooperated with the Fascists, thus confirming Mussolini's view that they were lacking in honesty and courage. The few who opposed the government were either silenced or forced into exile—the Fascist secret police struck down any active opposition.

Most ordinary Italians accepted fascism with enthusiasm. The individual, who formerly felt alone and unneeded, enjoyed a new sense of "belonging"; this feeling of personal identification and participation was deepened by the paternalistic measures of the government and by various other means. Many types of workers wore distinctive uniforms, and mass rituals were staged in the great public squares of Rome and other cities. By 1930, fascism appeared to have gained the firm support of most of the Italian people, as well as the admiration of many conservatives abroad.

Fascist ideology frankly supported rule by an elite (the "chosen" best). While Marxists taught that the state and its officeholders would gradually disappear after the abolition of capitalism (p. 520), the Fascists believed in permanent rule by their "natural" leaders. These would be individuals of rare intuitive power, capable of rising above self-interest and of sensing the character and desires of the nation. Their superiority, the Fascists declared, came chiefly from action rather than from thought: it was basic that the leaders would have fought for the fatherland, taken part in the Fascist revolution, and helped build the "new order."

THE NAZI COMPOUND OF FASCISM AND RACISM: HITLER

Just as the ideas of communism carried beyond the borders of the USSR, so the fascist philosophy spread quickly across Europe—and the world. It won a substantial following in Austria, Portugal, Spain, and Argentina; but its world-shaking triumph was in Germany. Here fascism as a doctrine fused with deeper and older forces in the German tradition; here the fierce words of elitism and imperialism turned into deeds of conquest and genocide (race murder).

Germany's humiliation at Versailles (p. 564), coupled with severe economic problems after the war, prepared the ground for Adolf Hitler and his National Socialists (Nazis—originally a slang term used by opponents, which derived from the German word for "National"). The Germans adopted a democratic constitution in 1919, but the new government was inexperienced, it suffered from the usual stresses and divisions within liberal states, and it was associated with the crushing military defeat. (In the closing days of the war, the German generals had shrewdly withdrawn and left the country's surrender to a civilian government hastily appointed by the Kaiser.) In little more than a decade, it fell under the weight of its unsolved problems.

The Nazi Rise to Power. One of its problems was Adolf Hitler, who had been born of middle-class parents in a small Austrian town. Early in life, he had become an ardent German nationalist, and though he spent some of his formative years in Vienna, he found its cosmopolitan atmosphere distasteful. A moody drifter, he did not find a place for himself until the outbreak of the First World War. When he enlisted in the German army, Hitler experienced the comradeship and discipline of military life and exulted in his service to his adopted fatherland.

In 1919, embittered by the war's outcome, he went to Munich, capital of the south German state of Bavaria. Large numbers of unemployed veterans and political dissidents had congregated there. Hitler joined a budding group that called itself the National Socialist German Workers party and soon became its Leader (*Führer*). This new role provided an outlet for Hitler's deep-seated animosities and ambitions. He attracted to the National Socialist banner others who shared his intense nationalistic feeling and hatred for Jews. Among his supporters were Hermann Goering, a swaggering pilot-hero; Dr. Josef Goebbels, a university-trained journalist; and General Erich Ludendorff, an archconservative and one of Germany's chief military commanders during the First World War.

Hitler threw himself fully into the life of politics and national "regeneration." Though he had but limited formal education, he had an intuitive grasp of the concerns that were disturbing his fellow Germans, especially the middle class: deep anxieties about the decline of "culture," the threat of social revolution, and the mixing of the races. And like Mussolini, he had a gift for rousing speech-making. The early 1920s were a time of restlessness and disorder in Germany; street clashes and rioting were commonplace. In 1923, Hitler led an attempted coup (*Putsch*) against the Bavarian state government. It was stopped in the streets of Munich by police fire, and the Nazi party seemed to have been crushed by the government reprisals. Hitler was imprisoned for nearly a year, during which time he wrote *Mein Kampf* (My Struggle), the statement of his life and beliefs. Upon his release from prison, he refounded the party.

For a while the revived party made little headway, but the international economic crisis of 1930, a product of the dislocations stemming from the war, gave the German revolutionary parties their great opportunity. Rising numbers of unemployed men were looking desperately for work. Many of them found "jobs" as brown-shirted Nazi storm troopers, similar to Mussolini's Blackshirts (p. 577). The party gained electoral strength steadily during the years of economic hardship. And when at one point it ran out of funds, some powerful industrialists came to the rescue. In January 1933, Hitler received from them a promise to pay the wages of his storm troopers and the party's debts. German business leaders generally preferred the familiar conservative politicians to Hitler. But in this time of crisis, they turned to the Nazis as a "bulwark against communism"—and to insure themselves against the possibility of a Nazi victory in the elections.

A few weeks later, backed by conservative politicians and generals, Hitler succeeded in pressuring the aged president of the republic, Paul von Hindenburg, to appoint him

1871	1918	1933	1945
Hohenzollern Empire (Reich)	Democratic Republic	Hitler Third Reich	

head of the national government (chancellor). The Nazis had the largest number of elected delegates in the legislature (Reichstag), but they still did not have a majority. However, after the Reichstag building was mysteriously burned, Hitler enforced a suspension of constitutional guarantees. He banned the Communist party and had its leaders imprisoned; the Social Democrats were the only opposition party left. The Nazis, with the support of other conservative parties, then passed the Enabling Act of March 1933, giving the government power to rule by decree for a four-year period. Hitler next replaced the flag of the republic with the Nazi swastika (the "crooked cross") and declared the beginning of the "Third" Reich (Empire)— successor to the medieval and Hohenzollern German empires (pp. 223, 500).

Soon afterward, Hitler outlawed all parties save his own; by mid-1933, his political opponents were either in jail or in exile. A year later, after Hindenburg's death, he assumed the office of president in addition to that of chancellor. This act was ratified in a vote of overwhelming approval by the German electorate. Thus the mad Austrian became the sole ruler of one of the most educated and civilized nations of the world. He proceeded, with the cooperation of the army and leading industrialists, to marshal the country's manpower and resources. Hitler's aim was to make Germany the most powerful nation in Europe and, ultimately, the world.

Nazi Ideology. Nazism had much in common with Italian fascism. Both rested on the myth of the "organic state," the importance of struggle and will, the glorification of militarism, insistence on authority and discipline, rule by an elite, and a mystical faith in the Leader. But in Germany, there were added elements of violent racism, neo-Romanticism, and nihilism. The first two were largely out of the nineteenth century; the last was mainly an outgrowth of the war and took the form, essentially, of a mindless lust for power.

For the Jews of Europe, the Nazi racial theories led toward genocide. In the course of the nineteenth century, the liberal philosophy of equal civil rights for all had liberated Jews from the ghetto in most parts of Europe. However, the decline of discrimination on *religious* grounds was counterbalanced by the rise of new theories of *racial* differences. Some writers in France, England, and Germany began to assert the supremacy of Nordic "races" over others—especially over the Semitic and Negroid.

Hitler and his associates, resentful of resurgent Jewish social and cultural influence in postwar Germany, embraced these racial ideas and made them a central part of their program. They became vicious anti-Semites, portraying the Jew as a seducing, bloodsucking fiend who longed to pollute Nordic "purity." Building on that passion, they enacted discriminatory legislation, outlawed marriage and sexual relations between Jews and citizens "of German blood," forced Jews to wear a humiliating badge, burned their synagogues, and laid plans for the systematic annihilation of the Jewish people (Hitler's "final solution"—the inhuman death camps of the Holocaust).

Like the Fascists, the Nazis had contempt for reason and intellectuals. Hitler saluted the "simple and honest" values of the German peasantry and declared that those values were the foundation of Nazi goals. Yet under Hitler, the country became increasingly industrialized and urbanized. Cleverly, the Nazis covered up the disturbing reality of technological change by encouraging popular belief in the myths of rustic purity and racial superiority. Millions became converts to the Nazi faith during the 1930s. It suited the traditional romantic yearnings of most Germans, offered a total view of life in place of fragmentation and alienation, and appealed strongly to national and racial pride. Finally, it released the urge to violence. Nazism led, by successive steps, not only to the murder of Jews and political opponents but to the wider catastrophes of the Second World War.

Although Hitler roused powerful support for his measures in Germany, some individuals and groups struggled to resist him. The Roman Catholic hierarchy criticized many of the Nazi policies, but the Church generally looked to its own survival first and was able to secure its functioning while enduring an uneasy relationship with the state. For his part, Pope Pius XII, in Rome, kept a discreet silence with respect to the systematic destruction of the Jews, in the belief that moral condemnation of the Nazis by the pope would only make the situation worse for both Jews and Catholics in Germany.

Less fortunate were the German Protestant churches, which Hitler determined to organize into a supporting force for his party. Most of them yielded to the relentless threats and pressure, but some individuals refused; they formed a separate "Confessing Church," which openly opposed Nazi power. They failed to stop Hitler and paid the high price of conscience: their chief leader, the Lutheran pastor Martin Niemöller, was arrested in 1937 and remained in a concentration camp until liberated by the Allies at the end of the war. Also arrested, imprisoned, and executed (in 1945) was the distinguished theologian Dietrich Bonhöffer, among many others.

Democratic Collectivism: Evolution of the Welfare States

While societies built on totalitarian lines were taking shape in Germany, Italy, and the USSR, the shift from liberalism went forward in a different manner in the still-democratic countries of the West. In the Scandinavian lands, France, Great Britain, and the United States, the major prewar social institutions appeared to hold firm. But none was secure from the disturbances that followed the war or from the ceaseless march of science and technology.

In response to these forces, democratic governments intervened more and more in matters formerly considered to be private. And as their functions expanded, governments left behind some of the principles and practices of historic liberalism. They created, without full-scale planning, forms of *democratic collectivism*. Some observers called this "social democracy" or "creeping socialism," but a more fitting term is the capitalist *welfare state*.

A EUROPEAN EXAMPLE: BRITAIN

Events in Britain after the war illustrate the evolution of the welfare state. This country had been identified, more than any other, with the historic liberal spirit and principles. Britain in the nineteenth century had stood as the chief stronghold of capitalism and free trade; furthermore, its people enjoyed an extraordinary tradition of stability.

Prior to 1914, one would hardly have expected this nation to move toward any form of collectivism.

Yet as we have seen, even before the war, the British had traveled a substantial distance away from liberalism (p. 512). Trade unions had become a distinct force between individual workers and their employers, and Parliament had passed numerous laws regulating industrial conditions. By 1914, the foundations had been laid also for compulsory national insurance, which protected workers against the costs of accident, sickness, unemployment, and old age. The revenues to support such programs were to be drawn in large measure from progressive income taxes. The First World War then brought new problems that demanded further action by the government. During the war itself, additional regulations were viewed as a matter of necessity; that experience made it easier for the British to accept growing state intervention in the postwar period.

England had suffered severe losses of manpower and wealth during the struggle against Germany, and its most pressing problem at war's end was to recover its financial and trading position in the world. One obstacle to the effort was Britain's aging industrial plants. Another was organized labor: the unions, accustomed to high wages during the war, would not agree to lower wages afterward. For these principal reasons, Britain failed to regain the lost markets, and after 1921, the country fell into a chronic depression that lasted until the Second World War. Unemployment and poverty became a way of life for several million Britons.

Organized labor grew into a powerful force in British politics during the 1920s. The unions, in combination with moderate socialists, had formed the Labour party in 1892. By 1924, it had the largest number of seats in Parliament and stood as a challenge to the dominant Conservative party. The working class discovered, however, that its exercise of political power did not guarantee a better standard of living for workers or a solution to the country's economic problems. The domestic policies of Labour governments did not, in fact, depart sharply from those of Conservative governments. Both parties agreed that the protection and advancement of the public well-being required continuing and widening intervention by the state.

As the British depression grew deeper during the early 1930s, laws were passed that ended the traditional policy of free trade. Tariffs were enacted to guard the home market against imports, especially from the United States. (This action was explained as a countermeasure against high tariffs in America.) The government also went off the gold standard in 1931 and devalued its money, the pound, in terms of other currencies. The latter step was taken as a means of aiding British exports, but its effect was shortly undone by corresponding devaluations of other currencies in capitals around the world. When key industries, like coal, proved unable to compete, they were voted subsidies by Parliament. Extensive plans were also laid by the government for the general development of British industry and agriculture.

THE AMERICAN EXPERIENCE: ROOSEVELT

As a consequence of the First World War, the United States became the strongest capitalist country. During the 1920s, the nation pulled away from its military adventure overseas and from the domestic controls imposed during the mobilization for war. It was the decade of "normalcy," a word coined by the amiable and easygoing President

Warren Harding. Though laissez-faire was more myth than reality, the power of big business and finance was seldom checked by the governing Republican party.

Normalcy, however, soon proved anything but normal, and the government of the United States, during the 1930s, was pushed into the kind of intervention that had become common in other Western democracies. The economic boom of the postwar years had brought temporary prosperity to the nation, but the boom was driven by artificial and unstable forces. In the spectacular stock market Crash of 1929, many of the inflated values were wiped out within a few hours. More serious, the Crash signaled the coming of the Great Depression—a long and bitter experience for millions of Americans. During that time, they discovered the underlying shortcomings of the "free-market" economy.

The Great Depression. President Herbert Hoover, the Republican leader, was in office when the Crash occurred. A competent administrator and a well-meaning humanitarian, Hoover never understood that a system and an era had ended. Although he approved limited government measures to assist certain financial institutions and railroads, he held stubbornly to the view that business in general would recover by itself. (The restrictive fiscal and monetary policies of his administration actually dampened the prospects of business.) While Hoover was telling a worried public, repeatedly, that recovery was "around the corner," production and employment skidded downward. They struck bottom during the winter of 1932–1933. By then, physical production had fallen nearly 40 percent from the 1929 level; wages were down by the same proportion; farm income was reduced by half. Construction had nearly ceased, and about fifteen million people were out of work.

Depressions were by no means a new experience in capitalist countries (p. 511). This depression, however, was the worst in history, and there was reason to believe that "normal" recovery forces were unlikely to prove effective. This was due to several factors: rigid price and wage structures, rapid technological advances in industry (which displaced workers), and the near-hopeless situation of farmers, who were producing for a depressed and uncontrollable world market. Given enough time, some kind of balance in the economy would no doubt have come about through "natural" forces. But the economy had grown so complex and interdependent that these forces would have been too slow. So many individuals and families would have been crushed in the process that the strain on the social system could have proved intolerable.

Roosevelt and the New Deal. In the presidential election of 1932, the American people turned to Franklin D. Roosevelt, who promised that he would act in this crisis—that he would lead the federal government in an attack on the depression as if it were an attack on a physical enemy. The temper of the country was such that had he not promised to act, more radical leaders might well have gained a mass following. After an overwhelming electoral victory for his Democratic party, Roosevelt began the first hundred days of his "New Deal" program. This program marked a shift from the traditional policy of limited governmental interference to one of acceptance by the government of responsibility for the "general welfare."

The New Deal was new only to a degree, since it built on the ideas and policies of earlier American "progressives" as well as the wartime experience of industrial mobilization (p. 567). But Roosevelt realized that the challenges were now far greater and that they demanded a new boldness. He proposed remedies in a frankly experimental fashion, with no developed ideology. The New Deal was not anticapitalist; on the contrary, it aimed at preserving and strengthening the capitalist system.

Roosevelt classified his measures under the headings of relief, recovery, and reform. Among the most important and enduring were legislative provisions for the Social Security system, bank deposit insurance, regulation of the securities exchanges, stabilization of agricultural production, direct relief for needy citizens ("welfare"), guarantees for labor collective bargaining, and natural resources conservation. The New Deal programs did not cure all of the nation's ills, but most of them worked, at least to a degree, and they placed the federal government in a new and generally accepted role in the social and economic life of the country. Though FDR, a well-to-do landowner, was attacked by some of his opponents as a "traitor to his class," he saw himself, simply, as a popularly elected president making necessary reforms in light of new economic realities.

The democratic welfare state, in America as in Europe, did not lose sight of the individual. In a technological, mass society, it aimed to do what was needed for the protection and well-being of the majority of individuals. In many respects, Western men and women have had less economic freedom in the twentieth century than they had in the nineteenth. On the other hand, the greater wealth and economic security resulting from advances in technology and social organization have offered them expanded areas of freedom in their personal lives. These areas include education, leisure and travel, the arts, books and magazines, entertainment, and material consumption.

The Second World War and Its Consequences

When President Woodrow Wilson led the United States into the First World War in 1917, he declared that it was a "war to end war." When that conflict ended, Wilson began a determined effort to make his promise come true. He urged the Allies to put into effect the peace proposals that had persuaded the Germans to quit the war (p. 564)—his widely publicized "Fourteen Points." These included the goals of "open" diplomacy (no more secret treaties), freedom of the seas, arms reductions, removal of trade barriers, and political "self-determination" (independence) for peoples everywhere.

The fourteenth and crowning point was Wilson's proposal for a "general association of nations," to guarantee their independence and boundaries. And with a view to ensure that this association be established, Wilson traveled to Paris after the war and took part personally in the peace conferences. At his insistence, the plan for a League of Nations was written into the Treaty of Versailles in 1919 (p. 564).

THE FAILURE OF THE LEAGUE OF NATIONS

Most of the European diplomats at Paris, still nationalists to the core, had little enthusiasm for the League. They approved it largely to please Wilson, who, in return, made concessions to them on the other provisions of the treaty. Wilson believed that the League, once established, could correct such injustices and lay the foundation for a warless world—an emerging idea that now had substantial popular support. Ironically, the Treaty of Versailles, including the League plan, was later ratified by all the Allied governments except the United States. Its defeat in the Senate was due to a combination of factors: persisting nationalism, disillusionment with the late "crusade" in Europe, Wilson's refusal to accept amendments to the treaty, and the constitutional requirement of a *two-thirds* affirmative vote for ratification. (A simple *majority* did vote for the treaty.)

Whatever chance the League may have had to fulfill its high purpose was crippled by America's failure to join it. Both Germany and the Soviet Union were excluded from membership for a number of years, so the organization was far from being universal. Nevertheless, it had some strong supporters, and it carried on in the hope that the United States would one day become a member. Disillusionment with the war and the later miseries of the Great Depression, however, turned Americans inward.

The League performed many useful international functions, including the conduct of plebiscites (popular votes) in disputed territories, returning prisoners of war to their homelands, and providing aid to refugees. Through its commissions, it also arranged for the exchange of scientific and cultural information and the collection of social and economic statistics. Its sponsorship of disarmament conferences proved completely fruitless, for the participating nations viewed proposals for arms reduction as another arena for the continuing power struggle.

The primary purpose of the League, as planned by Wilson, was to prevent war. The treaty required that member states submit their disputes to arbitration (decision by an impartial umpire) and, if that failed, to the Council of the League. The Council, which consisted of representatives of the principal countries, could, by unanimous vote only, call for economic or military actions ("sanctions") by member states against any aggressor state. The principle underlying this provision was that of "collective security," that is, the idea that if *all* "peace-loving" countries acted collectively against *any* violator of the peace, the violator would be overwhelmingly defeated. Potential aggressors, once convinced that collective action against them was a certainty, would not start acts of conquest.

Collective security might have worked if the leading powers (including the United States) had put an overriding priority on stopping aggressors. In and out of the League, however, each nation continued to pursue its own particular aims and refused to act except when its own immediate interest seemed to be threatened. Furthermore, a number of powers (notably Japan, Italy, and Germany) were conspiring to support one another's seizure of territory. The balance between countries wishing to preserve territorial boundaries and those prepared to use force to break them proved to be too nearly equal for the collective security idea to succeed.

Japan was the first country to test the will of the League's members. In 1931, Japanese soldiers occupied Manchuria, driving out the legal Chinese authorities. Responding to China's appeal, the League sent an investigating commission to Manchuria; in 1932, the commission concluded that Japan was guilty of aggression and recommended appropriate action. But the Council of the League could not agree on sanctions. Britain, with extensive interests in the Far East, was reluctant to offend the Japanese, who had a powerful Pacific fleet. Unable to secure a guarantee of assistance from the United States should sanctions lead to war with Japan, the British decided that nothing should be done. And Britain was the most influential member of the League and its Council.

The exultant militarists in Tokyo, having successfully defied the League, strengthened their grip on Japanese politics and prepared for more ambitious conquests in China and beyond, and the League's failure encouraged aggressors in Europe as well. Little more than a decade after the First World War, the Wilsonian hope for collective secu-rity lay shattered. The great powers were already on the road to the Second World War.

FASCIST CONQUESTS AND DEFEAT

Benito Mussolini viewed the League's failure with special satisfaction. In keeping with the fascist ideology of militarism and imperialism, he was seeking to expand Italian control in Africa (*Map 14.1*, p. 552). During the 1920s, he had attempted by negotiation to gain a foothold in the ancient empire of Ethiopia. But the Ethiopian emperor, Haile Selassie, had stubbornly refused. Mussolini, after observing the impotence of the League, decided to move by force of arms.

Selassie's tribesmen, armed with primitive weapons, could not hold out against the artillery and aerial bombardment of the Italians. Within a year, Ethiopia was beaten and annexed to Italy (1936). In this affair, Britain had been more deeply aroused than in the case of Manchuria; it had persuaded the Council of the League to call for eco-nomic sanctions against Italy, the declared aggressor. The measure was only partially effective, however, and Mussolini continued to receive needed supplies from Germany. Italy resigned from the League; Japan and Germany had already pulled out.

By now it was becoming clear that these three nations were linked in a plan for wide-ranging conquest. The "Rome-Berlin Axis," joining the two fascist states of Eu-rope, was formalized in 1936. In the following year, the militaristic and profascist gov-ernment of Japan joined Germany and Italy in signing an Anti-Comintern Pact. The pact was intended, supposedly, to check the spread of communism by the Comintern (Communist International) in Moscow (p. 575); actually, it was a general defensive-offensive military alliance. And the strongest member of the alliance, Germany, was preparing to strike. In 1935, Adolf Hitler had announced his decision, in defiance of the Treaty of Versailles, to rearm Germany. His army and air force were growing steadily in strength. Though he moved cautiously at first, Hitler continued to violate the 1919 peace settlement. His troops crossed into Austria in 1938, and the Führer announced the absorption of that state into the new German Empire (the Third Reich; p. 581).

A year earlier, Hitler had extended his influence southward by supporting an army rebellion, led by General Francisco Franco, against the newly established Republic of Spain. The government—which had been elected by a "Popular Front" of democratic, socialist, and communist parties—appealed to the Soviet Union for help against the rebels, and the war soon became a bloody theater for the ideological struggle between Left and Right in Europe. It also proved to be a testing ground for new weapons and tactics of war. Hitler and Mussolini sent equipment, troops, and pilots in decisive num-bers to Franco (now called *Caudillo*, "Leader"). The war ended in 1939 with total vic-tory for the fascists. With the support of the Spanish Church, Franco established a tough, repressive government that was to endure until his death in 1975.

Britain and France were by now thoroughly alarmed, but popular antiwar senti-ment and political incompetence kept them from responding effectively to the fascist threat. The Soviet Union seemed to be the only power that could check Hitler. France had concluded a defensive alliance with the Soviets in 1935, but the agreement proved short-lived.

One reason for the collapse of the Franco-Soviet alliance was the failure of France and Britain to honor their treaty obligations to defend Czechoslovakia. (The Soviets also had an agreement to aid the Czechs—but only if the French acted with them.) At Munich, in September 1938, the two Western powers, ignoring Soviet concerns, agreed to Hitler's demand for a portion of Czech territory. (Six months later, the Nazis took over the rest of Czechoslovakia.) Joseph Stalin's suspicions of the Western powers were strengthened by their act of "appeasement." The Soviet dictator feared (rightly) that some British diplomats were secretly hoping that Hitler would smash eastward into the Soviet Ukraine, thus reducing or eliminating one or both of the Nazi and Soviet threats. Stalin now chose to remove the threat of an invasion of his country by working out a deal with Hitler: the Nazi-Soviet Nonaggression Pact of 1939 came as a shock to British and French diplomats. It provided, in return for mutual pledges of non-aggression (and territorial promises to the Soviet Union), that Stalin would not interfere with Hitler's next territorial grab in Europe.

The ink was hardly dry on the pact when the Nazis, without warning, pounced on Poland on September 1, 1939. In a desperate effort to deter or contain Hitler, the British and French had given "last-minute" pledges of assistance to the Poles. This time they stood by their word and declared war on Germany. The Second World War was under way. Poland was crushed militarily within a month as the Germans displayed new tactics of mobile warfare. Swift tank formations, supported by aircraft and paratroops, paralyzed and surrounded the Polish troops. Soviet troops, meanwhile, by prior agreement with the Nazis, moved into the eastern portion of Poland. To create a further "defensive buffer," on the Baltic Sea, the USSR also occupied and annexed the newly independent states of Estonia, Latvia, and Lithuania (p. 564; *Map 14.5*, p. 590). In 1940, the Netherlands, Belgium, and France fell before the German *Blitzkrieg* ("lightning war"), and Italy formally joined the conflict on the side of the Germans (*Fig. 14.3*). Hitler, ignoring his nonaggression pact with Stalin, savagely attacked the Soviet Union in June 1941.

In Russia and elsewhere in eastern Europe, the Germans not only sought swift military victories but also launched a ruthless program of exterminating all Jews and a portion of the Slavic peoples, whom they regarded as racially inferior (*Untermenschen*). The operation grew gradually in scale and intensity between 1939 and 1942 as the German armies advanced eastward into territories that had held the majority of the world's Jews since the western European persecutions of the Middle Ages (p. 288). The Germans began by separating the Jews from the rest of the local population and placing them in ghettos or in concentration camps, where many died from brutality, hunger, and disease. Mass shootings and gassings by special "task forces" followed. Then came extermination camps, most infamously at Auschwitz, Maidanek, and Treblinka in Poland, to which Jews from all over Europe were transported and selected either for immediate gassing or for hard labor under conditions that usually resulted in death. In all, six million Jews perished, together with about three or four million non-Jews.

The extermination campaign required an enormous German diversion of men, supplies, and transport from the war effort. It benefited from the cooperation of governments and often of non-Jews in general throughout occupied Europe, as well as from the passivity of the Allied governments, the Christian churches, and Jews themselves in Allied countries. More than any other of the horrific events of the twentieth century, the Holocaust stands as a warning of the possibilities of evil released by the combined technical advances and inner conflicts of modern civilization in general and Western civilization in particular.

The fascist forces, having seized the initiative, scored astonishing gains in the early period of fighting. They secured control of most of continental Europe and much of

AF/Wide World

Fig. 14.3 Hitler Triumphant. Adolf Hitler is seen here in an unusually joyful mood. He has good reason to be happy. The date is June 1940, and his aides have just brought him the news of France's acceptance of German cease-fire terms. Germany has not only conquered France but also become the dominant power on the mainland of Europe.

North Africa, while Britain held out defiantly against Nazi bombers and threats of invasion. Meanwhile in Asia, Japanese forces had occupied large areas of China before 1941, and hoped for further gains as a result of the defeats suffered by the main European imperial powers in the Far East, Britain, France, and the Dutch. But they had run into determined opposition from the United States, and six months after the German attack on Russia, they struck the United States' Pacific fleet at Pearl Harbor, Hawaii. They then launched spectacular moves—winning mastery of the western Pacific Ocean and its islands and conquering the British colonies of Burma and Malaya, French Indochina, the Dutch East Indies, and the American-controlled Philippine Islands (p. 555). By 1942, the fascist power was at its height in both Europe and the Far East, and all the major powers were involved in the war by land, sea, and air.

The population and resources of the Allies were vastly superior, however, and in the end, they achieved unconditional victory. Soviet armies and United States air power proved to be among the decisive factors in the final outcome of the six-year war. The Nazis, after their surprise attack on Russia, had penetrated deep into the country and had nearly toppled the regime. But they were stopped at last, just short of Moscow, having suffered heavy losses. At this point, the Russians turned to the offensive, at Stalingrad (since renamed Volgograd; *Map 14.5*). In the largest single battle in history, they surrounded and destroyed twenty-two Nazi divisions, numbering some three hundred thousand soldiers.

Meanwhile, in the war in the air, the Americans had first pursued a tactic called "strategic bombing"; it aimed to destroy key transport and production facilities whose elimination would cripple the enemy's war machine. This type of bombing, which depended on "pinpoint" accuracy and spared the civilian population, was only partly successful, however. In the last year of the war (1944–1945), the Americans switched to

Map 14.5 The Second World War in Europe and North Africa. The basic strategic pattern was the same as in the First World War. The Axis powers confronted a stronger but scattered group of opponents. This time, however, the opponents were hesitant and mutually distrustful, and they faced the additional threat of Japanese expansion in the Far East. For a time, the Axis powers made spectacular conquests in western Europe, eastern Europe, and North Africa until the rival coalition mobilized enough resources, determination, and mutual cooperation to squeeze and crush the bloated Axis domain.

the British method of bombing: massed attacks on enemy cities—contrary to traditional "rules of warfare" (pp. 399–400, 558). (The Allies were not the first to bomb cities, but when they did so, they bombed on an unprecedented scale.) Fire raids on Hamburg and Dresden were among the deepest horrors of the war against Germany.

By mid-1943, the Axis powers were generally on the defensive, both in the Pacific and in Europe. On D-Day (June 6, 1944), Allied combined forces based in Britain, under the command of American General Dwight D. Eisenhower, executed a massive landing on the beaches of Normandy, in northwestern France. Once on the Continent, they moved cautiously but relentlessly toward Berlin while their Russian allies advanced from the east. The Germans surrendered in May 1945, thus ending the conflict in Europe.

Meanwhile in the Pacific theater, American forces had "island-hopped" to bases within aerial range of the Japanese home islands before the end of 1944. The enemy's population centers and their air defenses were now open to unlimited attacks from the sky. By mid-1945, virtually every Japanese city had been reduced to ashes by giant

Fig. 14.4 Ground Zero. Hiroshima after the explosion of a single atomic bomb in 1945. By the standards of nuclear weapons fifty years later, the weapon that wreaked this destruction was puny.

© Eettmann/CORBIS

bombers (B-29s). This new kind of "unlimited" warfare was most dramatically demonstrated by the dropping of the world's first atomic bombs on Hiroshima and Nagasaki (*Fig. 14.4*)—cities that the Americans had spared from earlier bombings so that they could better measure the destructive power of the new weapons. Each of the two weapons (small in power by present-day standards) incinerated tens of thousands of men, women, and children. The public justification for using atomic bombs against these defenseless cities was that this "shock" action was necessary to bring a quick end to the war—and thereby save millions of lives that would otherwise have been lost in a military invasion of Japan. These superscientific devices for mass killing assured the quick and total victory of the Allies; Japan surrendered unconditionally in August 1945. ⋗ In addition, the new weapons confirmed a radical shift in the nature of all-out warfare: from attacking opposing armed forces to destroying whole populations.

RECOMMENDED READING

Imperialism and Europe's World Dominion M. W. Doyle, *Empires* (1986), compares imperialism through the centuries from Athens and Sparta to the nineteenth-century scramble for Africa. W. J. Mommsen, *Theories of Imperialism* (1980), is a succinct guide to the main interpretations. E. J. Hobsbawm, *The Age of Empire* (1987), is an excellent treatment of European imperialism in general.

B. Davidson, *Africa in History: Themes and Outlines* (1988); C. Schirokauer, *A Brief History of Chinese and Japanese Civilizations* (1989); and P. Bakewell, *A History of Latin America: Empires and*

Sequels (1997), give general background on those regions of the world. R. Oliver and A. Atmore, *Africa Since 1800* (1994); J. K. Fairbank, *The Great Chinese Revolution, 1800–1985* (1986); and Bakewell's book describe the impact of nineteenth-century imperialism.

On individual imperialist powers, see F. Quinn, *The French Overseas Empires* (2000); W. O. Henderson, *The German Colonial Empire* (1993); T. O. Lloyd, *The British Empire, 1558–1995* (1996); T. Parsons, *The British Imperial Century, 1815–1914: A World History Perspective* (1999); E. R. May, *Imperial Democracy: The Emergence of the United States as a Great Power* (1961); and A. Stephanson, *Manifest Destiny: American Expansionism and the Empire of Right* (1995). The books by Parsons and Stephanson are brief interpretations; the others are readable detailed treatments.

The First World War and the Decline of Europe   R. Gildea, *Barricades and Borders: Europe, 1800–1914* (1987), includes treatment of the political, social, and cultural forces making for war. A. J. P. Taylor, *The Struggle for Mastery in Europe, 1848–1918* (1954), is a readable account of the long-term diplomatic background; L. Lafore, *The Long Fuse: An Interpretation of the Origins of World War I* (1971), is a fascinating story of the diplomatic step-by-step to war. On the Balkans, see S. K. Pavlowitch, *A History of the Balkans, 1804–1945* (1999); on imperialistic conflicts, see E. J. Hobsbawm, *The Age of Empire* (1987).

J. Keegan, *The First World War* (1989), is a first-rate military history; M. Ferro, *The Great War, 1914–1918* (1987), deals with the war as a social and cultural upheaval; S. Robson, *The First World War* (1998), is an up-to-date introduction. The experience of the war is unforgettably conveyed by works of fiction and personal narratives. Among the most memorable of these are E. M. Remarque, *All Quiet on the Western Front* (1929) (German); R. Graves, *Goodbye to All That* (1929), and S. Sassoon, *Memoirs of an Infantry Officer* (1930) (British); and C. A. Brannen, *Over There: A Marine in the Great War* (1996) (American). P. Fussell, *The Great War and Modern Memory* (1975), is a general account of the traces left by the war in modern consciousness; the war's wider impact on culture and values is the subject of M. Eksteins, *Rites of Spring: The Great War and the Birth of the Modern Age* (1990).

A. Sharp, *The Versailles Settlement: Peacemaking in Paris, 1919* (1991), is a concise and comprehensive account of the treaties that ended the war.

Communism in Russia   J. N. Westwood, *Endurance and Endeavour: Russian History, 1812–1986* (1987), is a detailed and readable standard work dealing with all aspects of nineteenth-century imperial Russia and the Soviet Union. R. Pipes, *Russia Under the Old Regime* (1995), and T. H. von Laue, *Why Lenin? Why Stalin? Why Gorbachev?* (1993), are excellent brief accounts of the rise and fall of imperial Russia and the Soviet Union, respectively. P. Waldron, *The End of Imperial Russia, 1855–1917* (1997), concisely describes the political, social, and economic changes that led to the downfall of imperial Russia.

On Marxist ideology in general, see the books listed for Chapter 12, "The Development of Socialist Thought and Action." P. Pomper, *The Russian Revolutionary Intelligentsia* (1970), briefly describes the social and cultural roots of the Russian revolutionary tradition, both Marxist and non-Marxist. The best short account of the 1917 Revolution and the consolidation of Bolshevik rule is S. Fitzpatrick, *The Russian Revolution, 1917–1932* (1982); on the Revolution's leader, see B. Williams, *Lenin* (2000).

A. Nove, *Stalinism* (1981); R. G. Wesson, *Lenin's Legacy: The Story of the CPSU* (1978); G. Stern, *The Rise and Decline of International Communism* (1990); and R. J. Hill, *The Soviet Union: Politics, Economics, and Society from Lenin to Gorbachev* (1989), are authoritative introductions to the workings of Stalinism, the Soviet Communist party, the worldwide Communist movement, and the Soviet government, economic, and social system.

Fascism in Italy and Germany   W. Laqueur, *Fascism* (1996), is a good introduction to fascism in the past and present and its future prospects; M. Neocleous, *Fascism* (1997), is a brief interpretation that seeks to define the basic features of fascist ideology; H. Arendt, *The Origins of Totalitarianism* (1973), deals with the ideological origins of the fascist movements. S. J. Lee, *The European Dictatorships, 1918–1945* (2000), deals with the emergence of dictatorship in Europe between the world wars; R. J. Overy, *The Inter-War Crisis, 1919–1939* (1994), is a brief guide to the political and economic failures that led to the emergence of fascism.

F. Chabod, *A History of Italian Fascism* (1963), is a classic brief account by a distinguished Italian scholar who lived through the period; A. De Grand, *Italian Fascism: Its Origins and Development* (2000), is an up-to-date introduction. J. Whittam, *Fascist Italy* (1995), concisely describes the workings of the fascist state; D. Mack Smith, *Mussolini* (1983), is a readable biography of the Italian dictator.

On Hitler's methods of gaining and exercising totalitarian power, and his personality and ideology, see E. Jäckel, *Hitler's World View: A Blueprint for Power* (1981), and I. Kershaw, *Hitler* (1991). P. Bookbinder, *Weimar Germany: The Republic of the Reasonable* (1996), and F. McDonough, *Hitler and Nazi Germany* (1999), are good brief accounts of politics and government in Germany before and after the Nazi takeover. R. Bessel, *Life in the Third Reich* (1987), vividly describes the impact of Nazi rule on many aspects of German life and culture.

J. Katz, *From Prejudice to Destruction* (1980), is a reliable general history of anti-Semitism; A. S. Lindemann, *Anti-Semitism* (2000), is a brief interpretation of anti-Semitism as a historical phenomenon; G. L. Mosse, *Toward the Final Solution: A History of European Racism* (1978), analyzes the racist element in anti-Semitism.

Democratic Collectivism: Evolution of the Welfare States   C. P. Kindleberger, *Manias, Panics, and Crashes* (1978), is an enjoyable brief interpretation of these features of capitalism by a leading economist; the same author's *The World in Depression, 1929–1939* (1986) is a somewhat more technical account of the worldwide economic crisis; and J. K. Galbraith, *The Great Crash, 1929* (1955), describes the economic collapse in America. M. Beaud, *A History of Capitalism, 1500–1980* (1983), includes brief and nontechnical discussion of the crisis of the 1930s. T. Katsaros, *The Development of the Welfare State in the Western World* (1995), concisely describes the formation of welfare states in Europe and America and their development down to the present.

P. Clarke, *Hope and Glory: Britain, 1900–1990* (1996), is a readable and up-to-date general history, including coverage of the crisis of the 1930s; specifically on the impact of the crisis and the British response, see K. Laybourn, *Britain on the Breadline: A Social and Political History of Britain Between the Wars* (1991).

A classic brief history of the New Deal era is D. Perkins, *The New Age of Franklin Roosevelt, 1932–1945* (1957); R. Edsforth, *The New Deal: America's Response to the Great Depression* (2000), is an up-to-date introduction. W. Leuchtenburg, *Franklin D. Roosevelt and the New Deal, 1932–1940* (1963), and T. H. Greer, *What Roosevelt Thought* (1958), treat the nature of the Roosevelt revolution and its central ideas. E. D. Berkowitz, *America's Welfare State from FDR to Reagan* (1991), is a useful account. For the development of the welfare state in Scandinavia, see M. Childs, *Sweden's Middle Way on Trial* (1990).

The Second World War and Its Consequences   A. P. Adamthwaite, *The Making of the Second World War* (1979), summarizes the events leading to war, as well as scholarly debates over the war's origins, with documents. G. Wright, *The Ordeal of Total War, 1939–1945* (1968), is an excellent introduction to the war in Europe; R. A. C. Parker, *The Second World War: A Short History* (1997), covers all theaters; and, for focus on the Russian front, see A. Werth, *Russia at War, 1941–1945* (1964). In C. Wilmot, *The Struggle for Europe* (1971), a critical Australian journalist views the strategy of the war.

The victims of Nazi genocide are the subject of L. Dawidowicz, *The War Against the Jews, 1933–1945* (1975); W. Benz, *The Holocaust: A German Historian Examines the Genocide* (1999), is an excellent brief interpretation; and P. Levi, *Survival in Auschwitz: The Nazi Assault on Humanity* (1961), is a vivid and horrifying personal narrative. J. Hersey, *Hiroshima* (1986), gives a moving account of the effects of the first atomic bomb on its victims.

℗ INFOTRAC COLLEGE EDITION

Visit the source collections at **http://academic.cengage.com/infotrac,** and use the Search function with the following key terms:

imperialism	Russia Revolution	Versailles Treaty
World War, 1914–1918	Bolshevik	

WESTERN CIVILIZATION RESOURCES

Visit the Brief History of the Western World Companion Web Site for resources specific to this textbook:

http://history.wadsworth.com/greerbrief09/

Also, the CD in the back of this book and the World History Resources Center at **http://history.wadsworth.com/west_civ/** offer a variety of tools to help you succeed in this course, including access to quizzes; images; documents; interactive simulations, maps, and timelines; movie explorations; and a wealth of other sources.

CHAPTER 15

The West Reunited: The Cold War, Decolonization, and the End of Communism

OVERVIEW

With the defeat of fascism in the Second World War, the second round of the struggle over the future organization of Western and world civilization began. This time, the contest was between the guardian countries of the existing world order and the communist movement that wished to overthrow it.

To safeguard the existing order, its guardian countries, now led by the United States, made more drastic reforms than ever before. Departing from the Western tradition of power struggles, they formed a single group of liberal democratic and capitalist nation-states upheld by overwhelming American power. Other war-winning countries like Britain and France, as well as the defeated fascist ones, gave up their claims to world-wide power and empire, and were content to be junior partners in this wide democratic-capitalist grouping.

Political differences, economic competition, and the linking of many countries in the European Community did not change this basic pattern of cooperation under the leadership of a superpower. Together, the democratic-capitalist countries dominated the international economy; pursued the modern Western goals of health, education, leisure, and abundance for all more vigorously than ever before; and built up massive military power. As a result, they continued to be powerful guardians of the existing world order.

The communist challenge to the world order grew far more formidable than before, however, as communism spread from the victorious Soviet Union into eastern Europe and the Far East. Up to the 1970s, communist planned economies grew faster than those of many capitalist countries, and European communist dictatorships dominated their societies in spite of occasional revolts. The vast size and state-controlled economy of the Soviet Union enabled it to build up armed forces that eventually matched those of the United States. Thus communism became a second group of countries under the leadership of a superpower.

The communist and capitalist-democratic rivalry was primarily a conflict within Western civilization, pitting the countries of its North American and western European heartland against its outlying region of Russia and eastern Europe. Meanwhile, the non-Western peoples of Asia and Africa, together with the Western outlying region of Latin America, underwent the single greatest change in the world order that resulted from the war: *decolonization.* Following the war, defeated imperial countries lost their empires and spheres of influence, victorious but weakened countries more or less willingly and completely gave them up, and intercontinental empires vanished even more swiftly than they had arisen a century earlier.

The former subject peoples of imperial rule or indirect control, however, were not sure what they wanted next or how to get it. Did they, like ex-colonial India, want to share the Western privileges of national independence, individual freedom, and widespread prosperity? If so, should they work with or against the democratic-capitalist nations, which already had these privileges? Would they seek the communist goal of overthrowing the existing world order in the name of social justice and national power? If so, would they be vassals of the Soviet Union, or its competitor like ex-colonial China? Would they turn their backs on these rival goals and values of divided Western civilization in the name of some updated version of non-Western traditions like Islamic fundamentalism? The ex-colonial peoples endlessly argued, wavered, and fought over these and other ends and means, or pursued varying combinations of them. And this worldwide ferment also interacted with the overriding rivalry of the democratic-capitalist and communist groups.

In earlier times, the two sides would certainly have gone to war like the rival European alliances in 1914, but in the age of nuclear weapons, they settled for something less—the *Cold War.* They built up world-threatening armaments against each other that they intended never to use. They competed for influence and control over the ex-colonial world, and they encouraged or were drawn into bloody postcolonial conflicts, such as those in Korea and Vietnam, which never basically changed the balance of power. But they generally respected each other's vital interests, built up enough mutual trust to avoid mutual annihilation, and sometimes practiced partnership as well as rivalry.

Even so, the democratic-capitalist countries constantly feared losing their grip on the world order, as the Soviet Union quelled occasional rebellions in its camp, but ex-colonial countries sometimes "went communist." In the 1980s, however, the dictatorships and state-run economies turned out to be too rigid to adapt to the latest round of technical advance, the information revolution. Production stagnated, living standards dropped, and the burden of the arms race became ever harder to bear. Communism lost appeal in the ex-colonial world, where the fastest-growing economies were those that limited state planning like South Korea or Taiwan—or even China, which also loosened economic controls.

Finally, leaders took over in communism's superpower who tried to restructure the system drastically. Not content with relaxing economic controls, they permitted freedom of information and discussion, and even the formation of noncommunist political organizations. The result, however, was not reform but the shriveling of communist power. First the eastern European countries broke away, and then the Soviet Union itself peacefully disintegrated. The democratic-capitalist countries had outlasted the communist challenge. For the moment, the schism within Western civilization had ended, and its heartland countries once again controlled the world order.

The Bipolar World Order

The human toll in the Second World War exceeded that of any previous conflict. Of the more than 100 million persons mobilized for military service, some 17 million were killed. Civilian deaths, direct and indirect, amounted to more than 40 million; among these were 6 million Jews, victims of the Nazi Holocaust (p. 588). The political consequences of the war were decisive. Japan was stripped of imperial sovereignty and placed under American military occupation, Italy lost its possessions in Africa, Germany was divided into occupation zones by the leading victor countries—the United States, Britain, liberated France, and the Soviet Union—and fascism was destroyed in all the defeated countries.

But Britain and France, as well as Germany, Italy, and Japan, all of them countries that a generation before had dominated global affairs, had now fallen to the rank of secondary powers. Instead, the United States, untouched at home by the ravages of battle, emerged as the strongest military and economic power in the world. The Soviet Union, however, though it had suffered enormous losses and damage from the Nazi invasion, extended its control in both Asia and Europe (*Map 15.1*, p. 598). As it recovered from the war, determined leaders built it into a military superpower, and communism continued to have worldwide appeal (pp. 574–576). The time was ripe for a lengthy conflict between the supporters of the democratic-capitalist world order and their communist challengers. The result, for the moment, was a *bipolar* world order in which the two superpowers were usually rivals and sometimes partners.

THE END OF ALLIED UNITY

President Franklin Roosevelt, who had been the principal leader of the victorious alliance until his death in April 1945, anticipated the new distribution of power. During the war, he had joined in top-level ("summit") conferences with the British prime minister, Winston Churchill, and with the Russian dictator, Joseph Stalin. The "Big Three," by working together despite grave differences, succeeded in defeating their common enemies. Roosevelt hoped that when the war was over, the major powers could continue to cooperate for peace as they had for victory. The key to this accomplishment, he thought, was American-Soviet understanding.

It was in part to develop such understanding and cooperation that Roosevelt proposed a new international organization, the United Nations. Its general outlines were approved by the Big Three at the Yalta Conference (1945), and the organization came into being some months later, after Roosevelt's death. In planning it, Roosevelt had sought to avoid what he regarded as the visionary and rigid aims of his predecessor, Woodrow Wilson.

Though the United Nations was similar in structure to the disbanded League of Nations, it was not based on the failed principle of collective security (pp. 585–587). Nor was it viewed as a world government or anything approaching it. The organization, thought Roosevelt, might be a step in that direction, but its immediate function was to serve as an instrument that would enable the two superpowers to maintain world order.

Within a few months of the president's death, a chill descended on East-West relations; as this chill deepened into the Cold War, hopes for cooperation evaporated. The reasons for the deterioration in relations have been sharply debated by diplomats and scholars. On the Soviet side, there were fear and suspicion of the Western powers,

Map 15.1 Europe Following the Second World War. The map shows the main changes that took place in Europe during and after the war—the Soviet Union's expansion at the expense of its western neighbors, the westward shift of Poland, the division of Germany and Austria among four occupying powers, the communist takeovers in eastern Europe, and the line along which NATO confronted the Warsaw Pact. This was to be the shape of Europe for more than forty years, and most postwar frontiers in eastern Europe have lasted to the present day.

tracing back to their intervention in Russia after the Bolshevik (Communist) Revolution (p. 571). On the Western side, there persisted a deep-seated fear of communist expansion. This fear also traced back to 1917, but now it was heightened by the presence of Soviet military power in central and eastern Europe.

Shortly after Roosevelt died, Churchill had proposed to the new American president, Harry Truman, that prior agreements about Allied military occupation zones in Germany be ignored by the Western powers. Truman turned down that proposal, but the Americans and British protested vainly against Stalin's failure to provide free elections (as he had promised) and the imposition of communist-dominated regimes in Poland, Romania, Bulgaria, Hungary, Yugoslavia, and Albania. In 1946, Churchill declared that Stalin had lowered an "Iron Curtain" between East and West.

When communist-led guerrilla fighters threatened the Western-supported government of Greece in 1947, President Truman responded vigorously by sending military and economic aid to Athens. More important, he declared a general American policy of communist "containment," which pledged military assistance to *any* regime threatened by "armed minorities or by outside pressure." In support of this policy, he undertook a multibillion-dollar program of aid for economic recovery and integration in western Europe (the Marshall Plan, named for his secretary of state). The Greek anti-communists prevailed in a brutal civil war, but in 1948, communists seized power in the only more or less democratically ruled country among those that the Soviets had occupied, Czechoslovakia (*Map 15.1*).

In 1949 came the final steps in the division of Europe into two rival blocs. The Americans, British, and French joined in merging their occupation zones into an independent German state (the Federal Republic of Germany). The North American and western European countries concluded a twelve-nation military alliance (the North Atlantic Treaty Organization, NATO) for unified defense against the Soviets. This treaty was later supplemented, for defense of areas outside Europe, with alliances in the Middle East (the Central Treaty Organization, CENTO) and in Southeast Asia (SEATO). Huge arms expenditures by the United States, corresponding to these expanding overseas commitments, would lead to creation of the most powerful military strike forces ever assembled.

The Soviets responded with a military buildup of their own, and in 1955, they formed a military alliance to counter NATO. Consisting of the communist states of eastern Europe (except Yugoslavia), it came to be known as the Warsaw Pact. In addition, the Soviet zone in eastern Germany became the German Democratic Republic (GDR), one of eight "satellite" states that now existed in eastern Europe (*Map 15.1*). The satellite states nearest to western Europe, the GDR, Czechoslovakia, and Hungary, gradually turned their western borders into a real Iron Curtain of barbed wire, watchtowers, and minefields so as to prevent an exodus of discontented citizens. What became the most infamous portion of this barrier was the Berlin Wall, built in 1961 by the GDR to stem the outflow of its citizens to the more prosperous Federal Republic. Its physical destruction in 1989 would signal the end of the Iron Curtain and the Cold War (*Fig. 15.2*, p. 636).

The American nuclear monopoly was the most decisive single fact in world politics immediately after the war. It caused deep worries in Moscow, where leaders feared that some American generals might gain backing for a "preventive" war against the USSR. Soviet scientists worked feverishly to build a bomb of their own as a counter to the American weapon, aided by secret information supplied by agents in the West. This they succeeded in doing in 1949, much to the surprise of scientists and military leaders in the United States.

It soon became evident that even without the help of spies, the Russians were a match for the Americans in advanced technical undertakings. When the United States exploded its first *hydrogen* (fusion) device in 1952, the government revealed that the energy released was hundreds of times greater than that of the Hiroshima (fission) bomb. Within a year, the Soviets announced the explosion of their own hydrogen bomb, and in 1957, they became first in space by rocketing *Sputnik,* the first artificial satellite, into orbit around the earth. In a real sense, these Soviet demonstrations lent a degree of stability to the international situation. With each side in the Cold War capable of destroying the other (with aircraft or intercontinental missiles), a new kind of balance was struck—a "balance of terror."

THE "FREE WORLD" CONFRONTS THE "SOCIALIST CAMP"

During the years of the Cold War, from the 1950s through the 1980s, the two blocs were the most powerful forces in both upholding and destabilizing the bipolar world order. Besides its geographical north and south poles, the world now had military and political "West" and "East" poles, in Washington and Moscow. The term "the West," previously used to mean the North Atlantic and western European heartland of Western civilization, acquired a second meaning. It also came to be used—as it still is today—to refer to the political and military grouping of the NATO countries. The West, together with other countries with both Western and non-Western traditions of civilization that were aligned with it, formed the "free world." "The East," in addition to being often used to describe non-Western civilizations in general, now also meant the communist countries, though their prevailing ideology had originated within Western civilization and they preferred to call themselves the "socialist camp."

As time passed, the rival blocs gradually grew less solid than in the earlier postwar period. The international scene was marked by growing national independence, a wide variety of sociopolitical systems, and numerous insecure governments. Even the superpowers were in no position to run the world as they wished. The United Nations remained a forum of political discussion and debate, but it appeared unable to act as a "collective" power, and there was no evidence of a trend toward a unitary world or even a world "police force." However, the two groupings remained cohesive enough for the balance of terror between them to provide worldwide stability of a sort, even while their rivalry caused or worsened endless brutal local conflicts.

The Socialist Camp. The monolithic ("rocklike") unity of the socialist camp began to dissolve soon after it appeared. Even before Stalin died in 1953, Marshal Tito of Yugoslavia, though a communist, took actions that were increasingly independent of Moscow. After Stalin's death, the new Soviet leader, Nikita Khrushchev, uncovered the massive crimes committed by Stalin and initiated a policy of internal relaxation, "peaceful coexistence" with the West, and somewhat greater freedom of action for the satellite countries.

Khrushchev's "thaw" was not supposed to undermine communist dictatorship or ultimate Soviet control of the satellite countries, however. He and his successors still expected the worldwide victory of communism. The limits of the freedom of the satellite countries were driven home to the Hungarians in 1956, when "de-Stalinization" ended in the overthrow of the communist regime until Soviet troops intervened to restore it. In 1968 there was another Soviet military intervention, this time to suppress a liberalization movement for "socialism with a human face" in Czechoslovakia.

Leonid Brezhnev, who succeeded Khrushchev, later declared that his country had the right to intervene in any country of eastern Europe where "socialism" was threatened. In the West, this declaration was called the "Brezhnev Doctrine," and it revealed the primary fear of Soviet military strategists. They were convinced that the defection of the satellite states, most of which were historically anti-Russian, would deprive the Soviet Union of its "defensive buffer" against the West and swing the world balance of power against it. Sure enough, when Polish labor unions (the "Solidarity" movement, led by Lech Walesa) challenged communist authorities in the 1980s, the Polish government, under threat of yet another Soviet intervention, repressed Solidarity temporarily by placing the country under martial law.

China. Most weighty of the changes within other communist lands was the growing power of China (which faced the southern and eastern borders of the Soviet Union; *Map 15.2*, p. 605). In 1949, Mao Zedong had led his revolutionary forces to victory over Chiang Kai-shek's Nationalists, bringing the most populous country on earth under

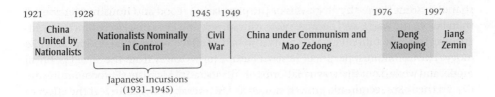

1921	1928		1945	1949		1976	1997
China United by Nationalists	Nationalists Nominally in Control		Civil War	China under Communism and Mao Zedong		Deng Xiaoping	Jiang Zemin

Japanese Incursions
(1931–1945)

the Red banner. Chiang transported his retreating army from the mainland to the nearby island province of Taiwan, which had been returned by its Japanese conquerors in 1945. There he established a rival "Republic of China," with its capital at Taipei and a claim to authority over the whole nation.

After a period of dependence on Soviet aid, the Communist Chinese (the "People's Republic") began to regard Mao as the principal ideologist of Marxism, and Beijing as the true capital of proletarian revolution. By 1962, a bitter split had opened between the two communist giants. Mao accused the Soviets of ideological "revisionism" (backsliding toward capitalism) and collaboration with the United States; Brezhnev replied with charges of Chinese defection from the socialist camp. The harsh verbal exchanges during the 1960s were accompanied by military clashes along their common frontiers in central Asia, and in 1965, China successfully tested a nuclear weapon—to deter the Soviet Union as much as the United States.

Soviet concern over the growing power of China grew stronger during the 1970s when the United States reversed its policy toward the People's Republic. John Foster Dulles, the American secretary of state under President Dwight D. Eisenhower, had previously sought to contain the communist regime through diplomatic and economic strangulation. But as other nations recognized and opened commerce with China, it became apparent that the Dulles policy had failed. President Richard M. Nixon, a long-time opponent of communism, made the practical decision to abandon the American policy and come to terms with the People's Republic. Guided by his national security adviser (and later secretary of state), Henry A. Kissinger, Nixon made a dramatic visit to Beijing in 1972. Diplomatic missions were soon afterward established in the two capitals, and "friendship" replaced hostility.

The Chinese aim was clear: to neutralize the American threat as a means of improving their position with respect to the Soviets. By pursuing at the same time a policy of relaxation toward the Soviets, Nixon and Kissinger thus initiated a *triangular* power relationship among the three rival nations. President Jimmy Carter strengthened the China ties by extending formal recognition in 1979.

The Rise of Europe. While the communist bloc was becoming less monolithic, the Atlantic alliance (NATO) was being similarly transformed, due in large measure to the swift postwar recovery of western Europe. The recovery, made possible by large American loans, was linked to the creation in 1957 of the European Economic Community (EEC)—the "Common Market." It consisted initially of six countries: France, West Germany, Belgium, the Netherlands, Luxembourg, and Italy. In 1973, Britain, Ireland, and Denmark joined the EEC, which sought to draw the separate European economies into a single trading area. Tariffs and trade restrictions were steadily reduced within the Community, and a common set of tariffs was adopted for imports from outside the EEC.

The consequences were dramatic: during the 1960s and 1970s, Europe experienced the most rapid economic advance in its history, and the rising standards of living were shared in some degree by all classes of the population. Food and housing were better than before the war; travel became more widespread, and class lines were blurred by increasing social mobility. This prosperity also had its effects on internal politics and ideology. The Communist parties of western Europe turned away from the Soviet political model and worked out their own platforms of "democratic" Marxism (Eurocommunism).

In the 1980s, economic growth slowed as EEC members began to feel the effect of such factors as oil price rises, decreases in birthrates, and increased costs of their welfare states. European countries inside and outside the Community continued to believe in it as the key to their economic and perhaps also their political future, however. New members joined (Greece in 1981, Spain and Portugal in 1986), commissions were appointed to coordinate national plans for investment and development, and the Single European Act of 1986 provided for free movement of capital and labor across the frontiers of the member countries.

While the western European nations now accepted lesser roles in global affairs, they felt a mounting urge to reassert their traditional character and independence. France in particular, under the guidance of President Charles de Gaulle, enjoyed a cultural as well as an economic resurgence. French leaders desired to reduce or eliminate the strong influence that American politicians, generals, and business representatives had exerted in Europe after the Second World War, and de Gaulle acted openly against the dominant role of the United States in NATO. By 1963, he had established, independently, a French nuclear strike force, and in 1966, he ordered U.S. military forces and bases out of France. Within the EEC, he opposed any growth in power of the Community's central institutions at the expense of national governments while trying to build up France's influence in Europe in partnership with Germany. Though somewhat softened, de Gaulle's policies have been carried on ever since by his political successors in Paris.

Détente. A contributing factor in Europe's mounting spirit of independence was a lessening of the earlier fear of the Soviet Union. The American-Soviet balance of terror cast a protective cloak over Europe, and Kremlin policy after Stalin's death gave no indication of a desire for military adventure on the Continent. Britain, whose scientists shared atomic secrets with the United States during the Second World War, developed its own nuclear force in the late 1950s. Responding to this new situation, the chancellor of the German Federal Republic, Willy Brandt, sought to turn off the Cold War on the Continent. In 1970, he undertook successful talks in Moscow, accepting for his prospering country the postwar political boundaries of central and eastern Europe.

Brandt's initiative marked a dramatic step toward an easing of tensions (*détente*) between once-hostile groups of states. It was capped in 1975 by a summit meeting at Helsinki, Finland, where heads of thirty-five countries (including the United States) signed a pact for European "security and cooperation." The Helsinki agreement, pledging the signatories to ensure "human rights" for their own citizens, gave formal support to East-West détente. European political leaders, like Helmut Schmidt of West Germany and Valéry Giscard d'Estaing of France, saw no alternative to détente in their dealings with the Soviet Union.

Even so, neither bloc showed any sign of dissolving. Within the socialist camp, the economy and armed forces of the Soviet Union dwarfed those of all its allies as well as those of its rival, China, and most of the eastern European countries remained faithful satellites of Moscow. In the West, the dominance of the United States was less oppressive. It rested on an unwritten but well-understood bargain with the European and other allies. The United States would use its military power to defend its allies and even bear more than its fair share of defense costs. In all diplomatic and military matters, it would act in their interests as well as its own and consult them whenever it expected their cooperation. The allies, for their part, would accept U.S. military command, consult the United States when making major diplomatic moves, and in times of crisis act together under U.S. leadership. (France did not usually fulfill the first two of these conditions, but even under de Gaulle, it held to the third.) In spite of détente and the loosening of ties within the blocs, therefore, so far as there was a world order during the Cold War, it remained bipolar.

The Liquidation of Imperial Rule

Besides the rivalry of the "free world" and the "socialist camp," the other great change to come out of the Second World War was *decolonization*—the end of the intercontinental empires that had grown up in the nineteenth century.

Most of the countries that had built those empires, such as Britain, France, and Japan, had been weakened or defeated in the war. In most cases, imperial rule had produced leaders in the colonial countries who opposed imperialism in the name of Western ideas of nationalism and progress. These leaders now saw the chance to steer their nations to independence.

Sometimes the imperial countries resisted the demand for independence, and the result was brutal wars of colonial liberation. For the most part, however, the empires now seemed no longer a source of strength and prosperity for their owners but an economic and military burden. As for the superpowers, though they both had their own imperialist traditions, they opposed the practice of imperialism by anyone else. For all these reasons, the colonial empires mostly disappeared over about twenty years between the late 1940s and the 1960s.

Decolonization was not just a struggle between the colonial peoples and the imperial countries, however. Often it involved bitter conflicts among the colonial peoples themselves as they disputed control of the territories that the imperial countries gave up—conflicts that in many cases are still unresolved today.

THE END OF THE BRITISH EMPIRE

The British took the most realistic and enlightened view of decolonization, in hopes of salvaging what they could from the colonial wreckage. Already in the eighteenth century, the loss of the American colonies had taught the British that overseas empires were hard to hold together by force (pp. 453–454). In the nineteenth century, at the height of their worldwide power, the British had begun granting self-government to countries like Canada and Australia, where the people were mostly European immigrants. These countries had come to be linked with Britain in friendship and cooperation.

Britain's leaders now sought to follow the same policy with countries where the people were mostly non-European, changing the "British Empire" into the "British Commonwealth of Nations." They hoped thereby to keep a measure of political influence around the globe and to benefit from established ties of commerce and culture. Perhaps the best sign of the organization's success, ironically, is the fact that the word "British" was eventually dropped from its name. The many formerly colonial nations that be-

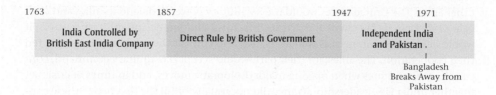

longed to the Commonwealth valued it enough to want to feel that it was their common property, not that of any one member.

India and Pakistan. The freeing of India from British rule was the largest single step in the ending of colonialism. The subcontinent, with its 400 million people at the time, had been granted limited self-rule before the Second World War. This had not satisfied Indian nationalists, however, and at the war's end, they insisted on full independence. The chief obstacle arose from the demand by Muslim leaders in India for a state separate from that of the Hindu majority. At last, in the hope of avoiding widespread violence, the last British viceroy, Lord Louis Mountbatten, agreed in 1947 to partition the colony into two independent states. The larger, mainly Hindu portion of the subcontinent took the name of India. Two smaller, mainly Muslim portions formed the state of Pakistan (*Map 15.2*). Both India and Pakistan, by their own action, became members of the British Commonwealth.

Unfortunately, the violence that Mountbatten had hoped to avoid took place. Thousands of Muslims and Hindus, dissatisfied with the terms of the division, launched reciprocal atrocities and expulsions. There was bitter fighting over the northern territory of Kashmir, where a Hindu prince, who had ruled a majority Muslim population under ultimate British control, handed over his authority to India. In 1949, the territory was divided along a cease-fire line that has remained in place ever since, but this has not prevented many disputes and armed conflicts between India and its unwilling Kashmiri citizens, as well as between India and Pakistan.

The two territories of Pakistan, one in the west and the other in the east of the subcontinent, were separated by nearly 1,000 miles. In 1971, the eastern territory rebelled against the central government, which was located in the west. After months of fighting, the rebels established an independent state, Bangladesh. This poor, war-torn land thereafter depended on aid from India and other outside powers. The remaining state of Pakistan encountered stubborn difficulties in achieving stability, arising out of the conflict with India, ethnic divisions, political corruption, and the rise of Islamic fundamentalism (pp. 621–624). After some ten years of military rule, a civilian government—headed by a woman, Benazir Bhutto—was voted into power. In 1990, under allegations of incompetence and corruption, her party suffered defeat at the polls—and a return to political influence by the military.

India, for its part, also faced mounting economic and political problems. In 1975, the Indian prime minister, Indira Gandhi, suspended constitutional guarantees and tightened her personal control over the country. Shortly afterward, the voters reacted by defeating the prime minister and her Congress party in parliamentary elections. But the opposition groups soon fell apart, and in 1980, Gandhi and her party were swept back into power.

A few years later, the country suffered a severe shock as a result of fighting between government forces and Sikh separatists in Punjab state (northern India). The Sikhs are a

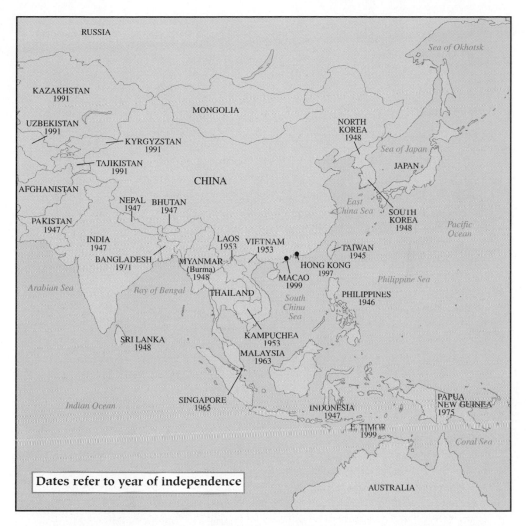

Map 15.2 Decolonization in Asia. In 1939, central Asia and the Far East were mostly divided among five imperial domains, those of Britain, France, Japan, the Netherlands, and the Soviet Union. There were only six shakily independent countries in the region: Afghanistan, China, Japan, Mongolia, the Philippines, and Thailand. Fifteen years later, British, French, Japanese, and Dutch rule had mostly ended, and Soviet rule collapsed swiftly in 1991. Today, the region consists of twenty-nine independent countries.

reform sect of Hinduism. Militants among them, members of Indira's bodyguard, shot her dead as an act of revenge for earlier government killings. Her son, Rajiv Gandhi, was elected to take her place as prime minister in 1984. He raised fresh hopes for national reconciliation. But tension and violence persisted, and Rajiv was voted out of power five years later by a coalition of opposition parties, to be assassinated in his turn in 1991.

Africa. In Africa, the British granted freedom to the Gold Coast (Ghana) in 1957 and to Nigeria in 1960. Within a brief span, most of Britain's other African territories became independent members of the Commonwealth (*Map 15.3*).

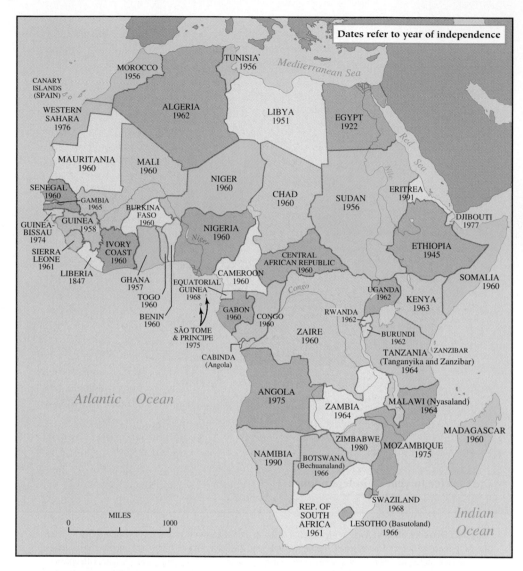

Map 15.3 Decolonization in Africa. As late as 1956, nearly all of Africa was ruled by Belgium, Britain, France, Italy, and Portugal. The main exceptions were South Africa (ruled by a minority of European settlers) and Egypt. The Europeans then swiftly abandoned their possessions, and by 1964, most of Africa gained independence, except in the south, where the opposition of Portugal and South Africa delayed independence until the 1970s and 1980s. Cuban forces, with Soviet help, supported Marxist regimes in the 1980s, and France still supports several governments. Nevertheless, the continent today counts forty-nine independent countries.

In some African territories of the British Empire, the end of imperialism was slowed by the fact that the European population did not consist only of soldiers and administrators who could easily be withdrawn. There were also communities of European settlers who were unwilling either to leave countries that had become their homes or to give up their position as privileged elites. In Kenya, in East Africa, a white minority resisted black participation in the government, and the result was a rebellion by blacks, involving

"Mau Mau" terrorists. Once the rebellion was crushed, however, in 1963 Britain granted independence to Kenya under the leadership of Jomo Kenyatta. Though the British had earlier detained Kenyatta on suspicion of being involved in the Mau Mau movement, it was he who launched the first African experiment in multiracial government.

In southern Africa, a longer and still more bitter racial fight took place. In Southern Rhodesia, where there was a large and privileged European minority, an all-white government headed by Ian Smith unilaterally declared independence in 1965. Britain, by now determined to liquidate imperial rule even over the opposition of settlers, reacted with economic sanctions against Southern Rhodesia, and some blacks formed bands of armed resistance. It was not until 1980 that the British succeeded in bringing all parties to agree on a new constitution and free elections. The black majority chose a former guerrilla chief, Robert Mugabe, as the new leader, and they changed the name of the country to Zimbabwe (an ancient capital of the region).

By 1990, only one of Britain's former colonies remained under white rule: the Republic of South Africa—not coincidentally, the territory where the white population was by far the largest. Originally, South Africa had been a Dutch colony, but in the nineteenth century, it came under British rule. Thanks to its resources of gold, diamonds, and coal, it developed into the wealthiest and most advanced country in Africa south of the Sahara, and in 1910, it became a sovereign state within the British Empire (p. 603). The business elite and professional classes were mainly of British origin, but a larger population of working-class and farm-owning Afrikaners ("Africans" of Dutch origin) ran the government through their elected representatives.

This arrangement was at the expense of the native Africans, Indian immigrants, and "Coloureds" of mixed race, who outnumbered whites by ten to one. The better jobs and advanced education were reserved for whites, and very few nonwhites were able to vote. As was inevitable in a relatively advanced industrial society, nonwhites made gains all the same, and in the late 1940s, radical Afrikaner politicians came to power who were determined to hold the nonwhites down. The new leaders institutionalized the privileges of whites in the system of *apartheid* ("separate development"), which prohibited interracial marriage, mandated residential segregation, deprived native Africans of permanent residential rights outside their tribal "homelands," and obliged them to carry "passes"—identification documents that were used to track their employment and movements.

For twenty years while empires collapsed around it, South Africa functioned more or less successfully as a democracy for whites and a police state for most nonwhites. The main African political organization, the African National Congress, was banned in 1960. Its leader, Nelson Mandela, was convicted of sabotage in 1964 and spent the next quarter of a century in prison. But the "wind of change" was blowing against South Africa. In 1961, ex-colonial nations who were now the majority in the British Commonwealth forced South Africa out. In the 1980s, as South Africa became increasingly isolated in the world and its northern neighbors Angola, Mozambique, and Zimbabwe came under African rule, apartheid began to unravel.

The Middle East and the Arab-Israeli Conflict. In the Middle East as in the Indian subcontinent, the end of the British Empire led to lengthy feuding among the peoples it formerly ruled—above all in Palestine (*Map 15.4*). In ancient times, the territory had been the homeland of the Jews, but under Roman rule, the Jews became a minority there, and after the rise of Islam, most of the population were Arabs.

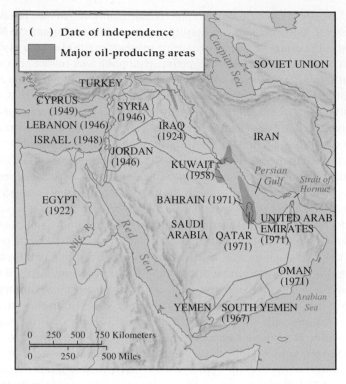

Map 15.4 Decolonization in the Middle East. In 1939, the Middle East was mostly ruled by local monarchs under Britain's more or less direct control. In Syria and Lebanon, France was dominant, and Iran and Saudi Arabia were more fully independent. After 1945, British and French control weakened, Israel established itself as an unwelcome local presence, the Persian Gulf region became the world's main supplier of petroleum, and the Soviet Union and the United States strove to inherit Britain's dominance. The United States prevailed and soon became the main target of local grievances and resentments.

The British had taken political control from the dissolving Turkish Empire at the close of the First World War (p. 566), and this opened the way for Jews to return, inspired by the Zionist ideal of reestablishing their "national home." Zionism as an organized movement had appeared in Europe at the turn of the century (p. 557). It was seen by many Jews as the only permanent solution to their age-old problem of repeated persecution and discrimination in Christian states. During the First World War, the British cabinet had responded to Zionist appeals by promising support for a national home in Palestine (the Balfour Declaration of 1917).

Following the Nazi extermination of two-thirds of Europe's Jews a generation later, the need for a place of refuge seemed even more desperate; thousands of Jews (chiefly from central and eastern Europe) made their twentieth-century exodus to the "Promised Land." The Arabs of Palestine (and elsewhere) saw this migration as a new form of Western imperialism. They believed the Jews, with their European ways, to be an expansionist colony on the Arab shore.

Violence broke out between Jewish and Arab armed factions in 1946; there were also terrorist acts, by both sides, against each other and the British. Two years later Britain withdrew, and the United Nations voted for an independent Palestine, divided into two separate states, Arab (Palestine) and Jewish (Israel). Many Arab states of the Middle

Proposed Jewish state,
UN partition, 1947

Other areas occupied,
1948–1949

Areas occupied, 1967

Israel and Its Neighbors

East and North Africa, newly liberated from British and French rule, refused to accept this division and joined with the Palestinian Arabs in unsuccessfully trying to overthrow the new state of Israel. During the war, Israeli forces expelled many Palestinians, and afterward the Israeli government refused reentry to many more who had left to avoid the fighting. Most ended in refugee camps in Palestine and surrounding territories, where their descendants still live today. Only one Arab country, Jordan, was willing to give Palestinian refugees full citizenship, though in any case the Palestinians had an interest in maintaining a separate identity so as to keep their claim on Palestine. Meanwhile, many Jews fled government harassment and mob violence in Arab countries and settled mostly in Israel.

The Jewish state gained recognition from most non-Arab nations, and defended its existence against continuing Arab pressures and threats. It soon found allies—to begin with, Britain and France, which were eager to keep what they could of their influence in the Middle East. In 1956, the three countries tried to overthrow Gamal Abdel Nasser, the nationalist leader of Egypt, who had sponsored guerrilla attacks against Israel, nationalized the British-owned Suez Canal, and helped an Algerian revolt against French rule (p. 611). In spite of spectacular military successes, the attempt came to nothing because the United States and the Soviet Union, both of which opposed any continuation of European imperial power, pressured all three nations to call off the war.

The Suez affair was an important moment not only in the Middle East, but also in the changing balance of world power in general. From Suez, the French drew the lesson that Britain and America were not to be relied on, so that France could never again exercise worldwide influence except as a member of the European Community. The British decided that they would never again act independently of the United States, but that they also needed to be part of Europe. Israel decided that in future, it must rely for its survival, apart from itself, on the United States alone. All three countries have held to these decisions ever since.

Israel's most impressive demonstration of strength was in the "Six-Day War" of June 1967. In a lightning attack against a threatening Arab mobilization, Israel smashed larger surrounding forces of Egyptians, Syrians, and Jordanians. They wrested the West Bank of the Jordan River from Jordan, the Golan Heights from Syria, and Gaza and the Sinai from Egypt. But the Arabs continued to refuse to recognize Israel and its occupation of their territories. They acquired new arms from the Soviet Union, which desired to expand its own influence in the Middle East. The UN Security Council passed a resolution calling in general terms for Israeli withdrawal in return for a settled peace. Not all Arab states accepted the resolution even in principle, however. Furthermore, many Zionists felt that Israel both needed the West Bank and Gaza for its security and had a historic right to those areas. Israel therefore held on to the occupied territories and began to settle its citizens in them.

Eventually, the Egyptians and Syrians, after six years of waiting, opened a surprise attack on the Jewish holy day Yom Kippur in October 1973. Israeli forces, hastily reinforced by weapons from the United States, recovered from heavy initial losses and turned to the offensive. With the United States and Russia poised to enter the war, each to protect its client states, the United Nations stepped in and secured acceptance of a cease-fire in the "Yom Kippur War."

Pressure against the Jewish state mounted when the Arab oil-exporting states imposed, as a war measure, an embargo on shipments to all nations supporting the cause of Israel. Since the industrialized countries were critically dependent on oil, they pressed Israel to come to an agreement with the Arabs.

Egypt, meanwhile, shifted from its reliance on the Soviet Union to a close relationship with the United States. It now realized that only the United States (exactly because it had become the only ally that Israel relied on) was in a position to influence the Israeli course of action. Henry Kissinger, the American secretary of state, became an intermediary among the contesting parties in 1974, but his "step-by-step" diplomacy did not bring a peaceful settlement to the Middle East.

The growth of American influence in the Middle East led to the first break in the feud between Israel and the Arabs. In 1977, Anwar Sadat, the Egyptian president, made a "surprise" flight (in fact the result of lengthy secret negotiations among Egypt, Israel, and the United States) from Cairo to Jerusalem. With his nation desperate for peace, he proposed a permanent settlement to Menachem Begin, the Israeli prime minister, on the basis of "land for peace"—Israel would return the Egyptian territory that it occupied in Sinai, in return for recognition by Egypt and the establishment of normal diplomatic relations. Begin responded favorably, and in 1978, the terms were painstakingly worked out at a series of summit meetings outside Washington, D.C. (at Camp David, Maryland), chaired by President Jimmy Carter.

The Arab states (in particular Libya, Syria, Jordan, Iraq, and Saudi Arabia) viewed Sadat's negotiations as a "separate peace" with a common enemy, and they furiously denounced the Camp David agreements. Nevertheless, the understandings between Israel and Egypt were largely fulfilled.

The most controversial issue, that of a homeland for the Palestinians, remained to be settled, and in 1982 Begin, a believer in the historic right of the Jews to possess the West Bank territories, made an effort to settle the issue on terms favorable to Israel. The Israeli army invaded the neighboring country of Lebanon to clear out anti-Israeli guerrilla units of the Palestine Liberation Organization (PLO) that were based there, and at the same time to destroy Palestinian hopes that the PLO would ever form an independent government under its leader, Yassir Arafat. In addition, the Israelis hoped to install a friendly government in Lebanon, dominated by Christians who would follow the Egyptian example and sign a peace treaty.

In the course of the invasion, the Israeli forces killed thousands of Lebanese civilians and caused heavy damage to towns and cities by bombings. There was revulsion in Israel against the savagery of these methods, and the Israeli forces suffered painful losses from continued Lebanese guerrilla attacks. Meanwhile, U.S. president Ronald Reagan ordered American peacekeeping forces to the capital, Beirut, which were seen by most Lebanese and other Arabs as military support for the Israeli effort to set up a client (dependent) government. During battles around Beirut between pro- and anti-

Israeli militias in 1983, a suicide bomber drove a truck full of explosives into a barracks building that was being used by U.S. marines. More than 240 marines died in their beds in one of the worst disasters in Marine Corps history. The president accepted responsibility for the losses and declared that such terrorist acts would not force the United States to run out on its commitments. Within a few months, however, American ground and naval forces were pulled out of Lebanon. Israeli troops also withdrew gradually; after 1985 they occupied only a small "security" strip north of Israel's border, which they eventually evacuated in the course of peace negotiations with the neighboring Arab state of Syria in 2000.

The Lebanon war made it clear to the Israelis that in spite of their military superiority, they were not strong enough to impose peace on any Arab country by force, and Arab militants drew the lesson that both the Israelis and the Americans would back down in the face of truck bombs. Syria, which had encouraged the guerrilla campaigns against both countries, became the dominant influence in Lebanon. Its troops occupied most of the country and brought an end to fighting among Christians, Sunni Muslims, Shiite Muslims, and Palestinians that had been going on since 1972. In the 1990s, Lebanon developed into an uneasily functioning democracy, where different religious groups each had their share of power and Syria had the last word.

THE END OF OTHER EUROPEAN EMPIRES

In contrast to the British, the French at first attempted to bring their colonies into closer political association. They offered them membership in a "French Union," which integrated overseas territories with continental France. This approach proved a failure; it appealed only to a limited number of colonial subjects who had been educated in French schools and who had come to respect and admire French culture. Moreover, Charles de Gaulle, who led the Free French movement during the Second World War, had promised the colonies that assisted him a free choice of status after peace was won. They chose independence, though most of them joined the French Community, a short-lived association that resembled the British Commonwealth. Regardless of their political choice, the former French territories in Africa have continued to rely heavily on French military aid, investment, and trade.

In two areas—Algeria, where there was a large minority of European settlers, and Indochina, where the independence leaders were communists—the French resorted to war in a vain attempt to hold political power. After brutal fighting and heavy losses, they were at last compelled to withdraw from both. Algeria became independent in 1962. Portions of Indochina—Laos and Cambodia (now known as Kampuchea)—secured their independence from France in 1954, but the remainder—Vietnam—was temporarily divided by an international conference into a communist-ruled north, with its capital in Hanoi, and a noncommunist south, ruled from Saigon. The two halves soon fell into a prolonged and bloody civil war, and now that the French had given up, the United States took up the struggle and intervened to forestall an expected communist victory in the southern half of the country (pp. 617–618).

The smaller colonial nations—the Netherlands, Belgium, and Portugal—tried to regain or hold on to their colonies after the Second World War. The Dutch, who had lost their rich holdings in the East Indies to Japanese forces in 1942, sought to reestablish their control. But they were compelled in 1949 to recognize the newly formed state of Indonesia, with a population of nearly 100 million. Belgium made little preparation for the transition of the Belgian Congo to independence, but in 1960, the rising tide of nationalism forced the Belgians to agree to freedom—without adequate preparation. The result was temporary chaos, followed by the formation of the independent state of Zaire under military rule (*Map 15.3*, p. 606).

The Portuguese were determined to keep their grip on the vast southern African territories of Angola and Mozambique, which they continued to view as part of Portugal. The native resistance forces, however, through guerrilla tactics, at last broke the will of the colonial masters. Portuguese commanders in the field, observing the futility of their own military efforts, brought about a turnover in the imperial home government in Lisbon. The new Portuguese government, veering toward the political left, granted independence to both these territories in 1975.

In Mozambique, where the resistance movement remained unified, the turn to independence went ahead on schedule. But in Angola, the Portuguese withdrawal was followed by a civil war among three competing parties; this struggle was complicated by intervention from outside powers (South Africa, Zaire, the United States, the Soviet Union, and Cuba). An "official" peace was at last negotiated in 1991, but sporadic fighting has persisted. In neighboring Namibia, formerly a German colony, South Africa continued an illegal occupation until 1990. An international agreement in that year provided for independence and free elections in Namibia.

RACIAL EQUALITY IN THE UNITED STATES

One of the justifications for nineteenth-century imperialism had been the idea of the superiority of the white race over the other races of the world. The nonwhite races, imperialists argued, were incapable of governing themselves on the Western level, or at least they would need many decades or even centuries of white rule before they were up to the task.

These ideas had always been contested even in the imperialist countries, and the Nazi atrocities had shown the horrors to which racism could lead. After the Second World War, the fact that so many white imperial countries were losing their empires made it hard to claim that peoples of European origin were in some way superior to other peoples of the world, and in any case, biology was discrediting the very idea of race as a classification of human groups (p. 10). As a result, the idea of white racial superiority ceased to be respectable even among whites themselves, and social and political orders based on this idea came to be recognized as oppressive.

Among the countries that were most affected by this result of decolonization was the United States. Its overseas empire—that is, the countries that it directly ruled, as opposed to those that it indirectly influenced—had never been large, and some of those countries, such as the Philippines, had already won independence before the Second World War. But unlike every other imperialist country, the United States had itself come into being as a result of European expansion. It had wrested its actual home territory from earlier inhabitants, and within that territory it had practiced slavery on a massive scale. Accordingly, racism and racial oppression had a long history within the borders of the United States. While other imperialist countries gave up their overseas empires, America underwent—and is still undergoing—a painful process of "internal decolonization."

Racism in the territory of the United States began with the early European settlers in New England and Virginia. It was directed first against the Native Americans, whom they called "Indians" and whom they viewed as "savages" and "pagans." From the seventeenth century onward, the tribes were pushed constantly westward; they were nearly annihilated over the years and their culture destroyed. It was not until the administration of President Franklin Roosevelt that the Indian policy was reversed (1934). The new policy aimed at respecting and protecting the cultures of the surviving Native Americans (nearly two million individuals)—though other serious problems affecting their welfare have persisted.

Racism has been directed also toward other minority peoples in the United States. These include Hispanic Americans (Latinos) and Asian Americans—both of whom are rapidly growing in numbers. But the most visible victims are African Americans, who have played a special role throughout U.S. history.

The end of legal slavery in 1865 left African Americans still in a very inferior condition; this condition included the lynching of black men accused of serious crimes against whites. It was not until the middle of the twentieth century that African Americans began to approach equality with whites in civil, political, social, and economic affairs.

Their aspirations were lifted in 1954 by a landmark decision of the U.S. Supreme Court, *Brown* v. *Board of Education of Topeka*. This decision put an end to the earlier principle of "separate but equal" education for black children and called for progressive integration of the races in public-supported schools and colleges. The decision was bitterly resisted by whites in many communities, but by 1970, it appeared to have been widely accepted in principle. In practice, however, the tradition of the "neighborhood school" and resistance to the busing of children to different schools "for racial balance" kept schools substantially segregated in spite of the ruling.

Black leaders also worked harder than ever to end "Jim Crowism" (separate seating in transportation and public service facilities) and to place more blacks on voter registration rolls. These efforts, backed by sit-ins, boycotts, mass demonstrations, and civil disobedience, proved largely successful during the 1960s. In the forefront of the drive were aggressive legal actions guided by the National Association for the Advancement of Colored People (NAACP) and the leadership of the Baptist minister Dr. Martin Luther King Jr.

King stood squarely for full integration of the races, equal opportunity, and nonviolence (p. 660). In the late 1960s, however, some of the younger members of the black community began to fall away from his leadership. Blacks still endured poor food and housing, especially in the urban ghettos, and unequal opportunity for jobs, health care, and schooling. Some concluded that more forceful methods were needed to persuade the white power structure that more must be done for blacks. Among them was the eloquent Malcolm X (Malcolm Little), whose *Autobiography* (1967) gained a wide readership. Cries arose for "black power," militancy, and violence. The police became a particular target of hatred; in the eyes of most blacks, they patrolled black neighborhoods like soldiers of an occupying army. Clashes with the police sometimes erupted into ugly riots, burnings, and lootings—such as those in the Watts neighborhood of Los Angeles (1965) and in Detroit and Washington (1967).

The assassination of Martin Luther King in 1968 was a shocking and demoralizing blow to the black movement. It had the effect of pushing the movement further toward militancy—toward more radical leaders. This was reflected in the growing numbers of black converts to Islam, motivated in part by dissatisfaction with their situation in a society dominated by white Christians. A "white backlash," meanwhile, heightened racist feelings and sharpened the "law and order" issue in the country. Police forces were enlarged and more heavily armed; they sought out militants (like the Black

Panthers), kept them under surveillance, raided their headquarters, and often brought court charges against their leaders.

In the 1970s and 1980s, violence and threats of violence diminished, but racial tension remained high. Within the African American community itself, division grew between those who favored continued efforts toward integration and a small minority who favored racial separation as a goal. In any event, blacks who were "successful" displayed a stronger spirit of pride, independence, and energy than ever before. This spirit showed itself in virtually all the arts and professions—most visibly, perhaps, in the advance of black athletes in competitive sports.

Business recessions have borne most heavily on nonwhites, especially the young, in spite of "affirmative action" programs designed to employ more minorities in industry and public service. In any case, the white majority of the country (especially males) has resented these programs as "reverse discrimination" and supported moves to repeal them. Nevertheless, the result of civil rights and affirmative action has also been the growth of a large and prosperous black middle class, as well as a growth in political and government power, especially at the local level, with African American mayors elected in many large cities—notably, Detroit, Los Angeles, Philadelphia, Atlanta, and Washington, D.C. At the national level, Jesse Jackson became the most consistent and outspoken leader in calling attention to this frustration. A more controversial figure was Louis Farrakhan, leader of the Nation of Islam. Perhaps the most notable indication of rising status, ironically, is the prominence of black Republicans—distinctly a minority among African Americans—in the upper reaches of the George W. Bush administration.

The Third World and the West: Resistance, Cooperation, and Islamic Fundamentalism

The leaders of the liberated peoples of Asia and Africa—as well as of Latin American nations that hoped for freedom from foreign dominance in the newly decolonized world—knew that there was no going back to the old times before the colonial empires. Instead, what they wanted for their peoples was the chance to reproduce some of the achievements of their former imperial rulers—in particular, national freedom, unity, and power, and the possibility of health, wealth, and leisure for all. Independence was to be the first step in political and economic *development*—the building of powerful nation-states and wealthy industrial economies—so that the nations of Asia, Africa, and Latin America could take their rightful place in the world.

The ex-colonial leaders also knew very well that in the world in which they had won independence, the former imperial nations still had the lion's share of wealth and power—even if those nations were now divided between the West (the NATO countries) and the socialist camp. In the rush of optimism that followed independence, many Asian, African, and Latin American nations hoped to change the bipolar world order into a "tripolar" one that would better reflect their interests and values. A conference at Bandung, Indonesia, in 1955 led to the formation of the so-called nonaligned movement of mostly ex-colonial nations—a united movement of the *Third World,* as it came to be called, that would stand apart from both the rival blocs of the First (capitalist) and Second (socialist) Worlds.

The ideal of a united Third World as a pillar of a reformed world order still has great appeal in the ex-colonial nations, but from the start, many realities worked against it. The Third World countries had widely different traditions of civilization—Islamic, Hindu, Chinese, and (in Latin America) Western. In many cases, their borders had originally been drawn by colonial powers regardless of these differences, as well as of well-established ethnic and tribal territories. Many Third World countries were peasant societies in which a few powerful groups—such as landowners, religious and tribal leaders, and generals—held most of the wealth and competed fiercely for power. All this often led to corruption, government instability, rule by dictatorial strongmen, and horrific international and civil wars.

In addition, it was hard for Third World countries to escape their traditional economic role as suppliers of raw materials and foodstuffs to the countries to whose empires they had earlier belonged. They continued to depend on these countries for access to markets, financial credit, and technical aid, and as often as not, for help in upholding their governments.

As a result of these internal conflicts and economic weaknesses, many Third World countries found that even after independence, they were still caught in a web of political and economic dependency on their former rulers or on the United States—that is, on the leading countries of the West.

Given these realities, there seemed to be two possible paths along which Third World countries might find their way to national power and industrial wealth. One was the path of resistance—to treat development as a continuation of the struggle for liberation, and hence to oppose the political and economic dominance of the West on the pattern of earlier opposition to imperial rule. The other was the path of cooperation—to acknowledge the West as a senior partner in an interdependent world in the hope that junior partnership would speed development and lead in the end to equality.

Few Third World countries chose either of these paths exclusively, and many altered course from time to time when the chosen path led to failure or conflict. In Muslim countries, in the course of such failures and conflicts, an international movement of Islamic fundamentalism grew up that rejected both partnership with the West, as well as resistance just for the sake of escaping political and economic dependency. Instead, the new movement proclaimed Jihad (holy struggle, p. 204) against the West in the name of the one truth about the one God. It still sought unity and power, but on a religious rather than a national basis. It was not necessarily opposed to the pursuit of wealth, health, and leisure for all—so long as these things were pursued by societies that upheld the one Islamic truth.

THE PATH OF RESISTANCE

Many Third World countries found one or another leading nation of the West still standing in the way of their hopes and ambitions even after independence. Others were on fairly good terms with the West, but their governments nevertheless wanted to declare economic and social as well as political independence. All such countries were likely to follow the path of resistance more or less wholeheartedly. Internally, they were likely to take such measures as nationalizing foreign-owned companies and introducing government planning. Externally, they sought to take advantage of the bipolar world order by playing one bloc against the other so as to get the maximum help from both without depending on either.

But there were also Third World countries where the West—most often, the United States—wielded indirect control through wealthy and corrupt elites, which were then undermined by national and social liberation movements. These movements would bring down on themselves the anger of the Western patron country and turn for support to the socialist camp. And resistance would turn into confrontation—not just between local radicals and the patron country, but also between the rival blocs. The most noteworthy of these confrontations took place in Cuba and Vietnam.

Cuba. The Caribbean island of Cuba won independence from Spain with the help of the United States in 1898, but this did not lead to real independence either before or after the Second World War. The United States kept a heavy hand in Cuban affairs. From 1933 through 1959, it exerted its influence chiefly through one man, a former army sergeant—Fulgencio Batista. With or without elections, he remained the real force in most of the Cuban governments of that period. But in 1959, Fidel Castro led a revolutionary movement that ousted the hated dictator. One of Castro's first acts in power was to nationalize the country's agriculture and industry, both of which had been owned in substantial part by Americans. Cuba thus became an authoritarian model of "national liberation" from a foreign-controlled political and economic establishment.

The underlying aim of Castro's movement, as of similar efforts to uproot the remains of colonialism elsewhere, was to put the resources of the country at the disposal of its own people. But Castro and the other leaders were well aware that continued independence and the effective use of resources depended on health care and improved education; universal literacy was essential if their purposes were to be understood and their programs successfully carried out. They stressed technical education in particular, so that the young men and women of each new nation could operate the complicated machines that promised a better future. But the new leaders discovered that the cost of education was high indeed and that resources were usually unequal to requirements. The result, often, was popular disappointment and frustration. In Cuba, for example, many thousands fled their homeland to seek a freer and more comfortable life in the United States (usually in south Florida—only ninety miles distant).

In carrying his program forward, Castro faced not only grave internal handicaps but an external enemy as well: the United States. Despite public professions of the right of all peoples to self-determination, the American government (both Democratic and Republican) took a hostile attitude toward social revolutions—on the ground that they violated "human rights" and that they were or might become "communist." In keeping with this policy, the United States has maintained a trade embargo against Cuba, and President John F. Kennedy in 1961 approved the "Bay of Pigs" invasion by anti-Castro Cubans, guided unsuccessfully by the Central Intelligence Agency. Following the invasion's failure, the CIA subsequently plotted (though it did not carry out) the assassination of Castro.

Kennedy's successor, the Democrat Lyndon B. Johnson, sent troops into the Dominican Republic in 1965 for similar reasons; he further announced the "Johnson Doctrine"—that the United States would feel free to intervene in any country of the Western Hemisphere that appeared threatened by communism. President Richard M. Nixon, a Republican, pursued the same general policy after his election in 1968, but his "Nixon Doctrine" proposed a shift in means for areas outside the hemisphere. Native troops (with American arms) would be expected to do their own ground fighting against rebel "communist" forces there. If United States combat assistance were needed, it normally would be limited to air and sea units. President Gerald Ford, Nixon's successor, confirmed this strategy in 1975. The next president, Jimmy Carter, followed a more restrained policy of intervention, but Ronald Reagan, who became chief executive in 1981, ordered stronger action and a buildup of American military forces overseas (p. 632).

Vietnam. In Vietnam (*Map 15.2,* p. 605), what had begun in 1946 as a Vietnamese revolt against French colonial rule led by a communist and nationalist revolutionary, Ho Chi-Minh, turned into a desperate civil war between North and South (p. 611) and then into a traumatic Cold War confrontation. After the French pulled out in 1954, Americans replaced them in South Vietnam—first as "advisers," then as special forces (combat soldiers). In 1965, as the South Vietnamese proved unable to suppress a guerrilla uprising inspired from the North, President Johnson decided on full-scale American involvement.

Johnson sent hundreds of thousands of troops to South Vietnam to aid the Saigon army; they were supported by hundreds of warships and thousands of aircraft, which also ranged northward to pour bombs on "enemy" installations. By the end of the war, the total tonnage dropped by the United States in Indochina amounted to more than three times the tonnage dropped by the United States in all areas during the Second World War.

It became clear by 1968, however, that the communist forces, supplied by the Soviet Union and China, would not give up—and that the American voters were becoming increasingly opposed to the continuing slaughter. American war deaths already exceeded forty thousand; Vietnamese deaths were estimated at more than a million; dollar costs had risen to hundreds of billions. (It was these huge expenditures and borrowings that opened the door to runaway price inflation and federal debt in the 1970s.) President Johnson at last stopped the military escalation and announced that he would not run for reelection.

The next president, Richard Nixon, was elected on a platform that included a "secret plan" for peace in Vietnam. The plan called for the "Vietnamization" of the struggle and the gradual withdrawal of American combat forces. The plan also called for carrying the war into neighboring Cambodia and Laos as a means of "facilitating" U.S. withdrawal from Vietnam.

By 1971, it became apparent that what the Nixon administration desired was a "Korean-type" solution (p. 620): limited United States units would remain in the South indefinitely as guarantors against a takeover by the North Vietnamese. But Nixon's critics in Congress called for total withdrawal of American forces from Vietnam and the rest of Indochina. The war had become a central issue of domestic politics in the United States. By the summer of 1971, the antiwar movement had displayed growing strength in persistent acts of protest and mass marches on Washington and other cities.

Nixon, mindful of the approaching presidential election of 1972, sent his security adviser, Henry Kissinger, to conduct peace talks with the North Vietnamese. Kissinger found that there were irreconcilable differences in political objectives between the North and the South. Just before the election, he nonetheless claimed that he had negotiated "peace" in Vietnam and the withdrawal of all American troops "with honor." Most voters chose to believe that the Nixon-Kissinger "magic" had ended the fighting for good and cast their ballots heavily for the president.

The following year, 1973, brought a time of reckoning and revelation for Nixon and the American people. The communist forces of Vietnam, convinced that South Vietnam would never permit the political compromises suggested in the Kissinger agreement, resumed hostilities. With most American forces now withdrawn, the Saigon armies began to give ground. The climax of the war came suddenly in 1975, when all of South Vietnam was swiftly taken over by "liberation" troops. Since then, the leaders in the North have tried, painfully, to consolidate the two halves of the country, repair the enormous damages left by the war, and develop a workable national economy. During the 1980s and 1990s, considerable foreign investment came in. The United States, following the lead of other nations, at last extended full diplomatic recognition to the Hanoi regime in 1995.

A disastrous sequel to the Vietnam War unfolded in Cambodia (since renamed Kampuchea). Caught in the drawn-out Indochina battle, Cambodia fell to the Khmer Rouge, an extreme Marxist group that had fought for years as guerrillas against various governments in Phnom Penh, the capital. Its leader, Pol Pot, sealed off the country in 1976 (save for contacts with China) and proceeded to transform the nation by force into a collectivized agrarian society. People were uprooted from the cities and compelled to clear new lands or work on irrigation projects and farms. As a result of these shocking dislocations and accompanying repression, malnutrition, and disease, several million Cambodians perished.

In 1978, this genocidal government was overturned by Cambodian rebels and Vietnamese troops, though the Khmer Rouge (and other groups) fought on as guerrillas. The Vietnamese, unpopular in Cambodia, subsequently withdrew, and the United Nations intervened to attempt to settle the political and military situation but could not prevent further prolonged fighting. During the periods of chaos, thousands of refugees fled Cambodia, as well as other parts of Indochina, over land and by sea (many in desperation as "boat people," loaded onto rickety vessels headed for any foreign port that would accept them).

Finally the UN succeeded, in 1993, in establishing a democratic government in Phnom Penh headed by a respected constitutional monarch, the former ruler Norodom Sihanouk. At first, the Khmer Rouge refused to participate, but in 1996, a large group came over to the government. Since then, the country has been largely free of civil war, though the democratic legitimacy of the present prime minister, Samdech Hung Sen, who staged rigged elections in 1998, is questionable.

Latin America. In the 1970s, Chile was the scene of an effort to pursue the path of resistance through peaceful and democratic methods. Salvador Allende, an avowed Marxist, was elected president in 1970 by regular constitutional procedures. He had the direct support, however, of only a *plurality* of the voters, not a *majority.* While in office, Allende sought authority for sweeping landholding reforms and for state ownership of banks and basic industries; with equal vigor, he defended democratic methods, legality, and civil liberties. The president's conservative opponents made full use of the press, their control of the Chilean Congress, and their economic power to block Allende's legislative program and his efforts to increase national production. Faced with staggering inflation, internal unrest, and secret intervention by the American CIA, Allende had reached an impasse by 1973. Then, as some observers had predicted, his generals and admirals struck against his democratic government in a bloody military coup. Allende, holding to his principles to the end, stayed at his desk in the presidential palace, where he was gunned down by the rebel soldiers.

The new military government, headed by General Augusto Pinochet, proceeded to destroy its opponents by relentless harassment, torture, and executions. It was promptly recognized by the United States government, and with the aid of American loans and financial advisers, Pinochet set out to establish a laissez-faire economy within the bounds of his anticommunist dictatorship. The Chilean economy was thus stabilized, though it later stagnated. Meanwhile, the experience of dictatorship led moderate left-wing and right-wing forces to cooperate against the regime, and in 1989, Pinochet left office. Ten years later, he managed to avoid prosecution for the crimes of his regime on grounds of age and ill health.

Elsewhere in Latin America, most countries remained under the control of the wealthy, the Catholic Church, and the military—even when democratic forms of government were adopted. Though liberalism had been the declared ideal of the first independent states of Latin America (p. 491), the twentieth century brought chiefly dictatorships and repression. However, while the higher clergy continued generally to defend the established social order, many parish priests began to preach, toward the end of the century, a new "liberation theology"; this aimed to improve the conditions of the poor. Catholic power as a whole was diminished by the rapid spread of evangelical Protestant faiths in the area. In any case, it was economic modernization that became the principal goal of the Latin nations, and with it came the impact of foreign capital. American business was the major outside influence, buttressed by the CIA.

In the 1970s, there was a determined effort to break away from "Yankee imperialism." Mexico, for example, attempted with some success to conduct a foreign policy free of American influence. In Brazil, tough military rulers, while making use of foreign investment, pursued a generally independent course of "directed" economic growth. (This program ultimately failed and led to unmanageable inflation, massive foreign debt, and overthrow of the regime.) In the Caribbean region, tiny Panama in 1978 regained control of the Canal Zone, which had been occupied by United States forces in 1903. (The handover did not take place until 1999.) The treaty of transfer, submitted to the Senate by President Jimmy Carter, was ratified over furious objections by some senators. And in 1990, United States power was once again asserted in Panama when President George H. W. Bush sent an invasion force to topple its dictatorial "strongman," Manuel Noriega.

In nearby Nicaragua, in 1979, the Sandinista National Liberation Front brought down the regime of the corrupt Somoza family, longtime American clients. The Sandinistas, headed by Daniel Ortega, quickly installed a socialist government, and this time, in spite of ideological reservations, President Carter responded with cautious friendship and assistance. However, his successor, Ronald Reagan, reversed this position in 1981 (p. 632).

THE PATH OF COOPERATION: THE EAST ASIAN MODEL

For a variety of reasons, many Third World countries sought national power and industrial wealth through cooperation with the West rather than resistance to it. Following independence, some felt more threatened by the Soviet Union or China than by the United States or their former colonial rulers, or they hoped for the West's help in disputes with other Third World countries. Others had unpopular governments that needed the help of the West in order to hold on to power or were so poor that they could not keep going without aid from their former rulers. Such countries were likely to welcome Western investment, to keep their economies on a resolutely capitalist path, and to align themselves more or less closely with the West against the socialist camp.

Cooperation was not a certain and speedy path to development any more than resistance, but some Far Eastern countries had spectacular success with it, so that their particular form of cooperation—the *East Asian model* of development—in time became the most attractive one for Third World countries to follow.

Japan. The East Asian model originated in Japan, a non-Western country that had already learned from the West so successfully that it had joined the ranks of the imperialist powers (pp. 553–554). Following their crushing defeat in the Second World War, the Japanese had powerful reasons to cooperate with and learn new lessons from the West—a benevolent U.S. occupation, fear of its communist neighbors the Soviet Union and China, and most of all, perhaps, the obvious failure of militaristic confrontation to bring Japan a dominant place in the world. Thus postwar Japan was bound by its peace treaty and its constitution to a nonmilitary foreign policy, it renounced emperor worship and adopted a fully democratic system of government, and it relied for security on a close alliance with the United States.

In addition, as befitted a loyal member of the "free world," Japan followed a capitalist pattern of economic reconstruction—but it was capitalism in the service of national prosperity and power. As well as competing, companies worked closely with each other and with the government to identify new markets and promote new technologies. Business leaders successfully limited the power and independence of labor unions, but they did so, in part, by rarely or never laying off or dismissing workers. Many formal and informal barriers prevented foreign investors from gaining control of Japanese companies, and made it difficult for competing foreign goods to enter the Japanese market.

As a result, over a quarter of a century, Japan first transformed itself from a devastated country into a competitive, low-wage supplier of basic industrial products and then became a high-wage exporter of every kind of high-quality manufactured goods. By 1970, Japan had surpassed its huge neighbor, China, in gross national product (GNP) and ranked third in the world.

South Korea. As the Japanese economy grew, it pulled along with it the economies of various Third World countries in its neighborhood. Among them was the southern half of Japan's former imperial possession of Korea—a nation adjacent to China that was given divided independence by the victors of the Second World War (*Map 15.2*, p. 605). The northern half was turned into a communist state under Soviet guidance; the southern half, under American guidance, was organized as a "democratic-capitalist" state. Each area was ruled by a dictatorial strongman dependent on one of the superpowers.

In 1950, North Korean troops, with Soviet arms, attacked the south, which was saved only by swift Western military intervention, authorized by the United Nations Security Council but carried out mainly by the United States. China, in turn, intervened to prevent the Americans from overrunning the north. After hard fighting, a cease-fire was arranged in 1951, but two more years of drawn-out negotiations passed before a final truce was signed. Korea, bloodied and devastated, remained divided at the 38th parallel.

South Korea, traditionally the agricultural half of the country, came out of the war as a devastated peasant society, kept going by United States aid and held together by military rule. Then, in the 1960s, the increasingly prosperous Japanese began to look to South Korea as an outlet for investment and a source of low-cost components for their advancing industries. The South Koreans needed Japanese money and machinery, but they were afraid of yielding control of their economy to their former imperial occupiers. The answer was to use Japanese methods as a precaution against the

Japanese—close cooperation between government and business, barriers to foreign control of South Korean companies, and guaranteed employment to keep workers loyal. Since this still left plenty of room for the Japanese to invest profitably in South Korea, the country's economy took off, and by 1980, it was well on the way to becoming an advanced industrial society—though still, for the time being, under the authoritarian government of generals or ex-generals.

Meanwhile, the communist dictatorship in North Korea had followed exactly the opposite trajectory, from speedy recovery in the 1950s to stagnation and poverty. The country's problems were made worse by the grotesque cult of its "Great Leader" Kim Il Song and by the pursuit of military superiority over the south, to include, in time, nuclear weapons (p. 702). By 1980, the contrast between the two halves of Korea was already deeply embarrassing to the socialist camp in its competition with the West.

In addition, by 1980, Japanese investment and Japanese-style economic and industrial practices were also bringing prosperity to other Far Eastern countries, above all Taiwan, Malaysia, Singapore, and Thailand. Famous companies in leading American and European industries now vied for markets with Far Eastern competitors—Volkswagen with Hyundai, Harley-Davidson with Yamaha, IBM and Philips with Hitachi and Sony. The United States, Japan's conqueror and protector, owed that country billions of dollars and could not persuade it to change its restrictive policies on imports. The path of cooperation had turned the East Asian countries into both partners and rivals of the West.

ISLAMIC FUNDAMENTALISM

Islam, like other monotheistic religions, claims for its believers a special knowledge of and a special closeness to the one almighty God (p. 49). It has traditionally been a formative and directing force in countless societies that stretch right across the Eastern Hemisphere from West Africa to Indonesia. In recent centuries, however, it has been challenged by new secular ideologies and by deep social changes, and as a result, a new division has appeared in the Islamic world. On the one hand, there are "modernizing" Muslims who are influenced by secular ideologies and are optimistic about the effect of social change. On the other hand, there are *fundamentalists* who wish to uphold traditional beliefs and practices at all costs.

The split between modernizers and fundamentalists is found in Christianity and Judaism too, but with Islam, there are two differences. First, the changes and challenges that Islam faces today originated outside the Muslim world, in the West. Hence Muslim modernizers are not just seeking to adapt to new ways and beliefs in general, but also to introduce into their societies the values and ways of a different civilization. Second, Muslim modernizers have in general failed to give Islamic societies a place in the world equal or superior to that of the West. "Enlightened" nineteenth-century Muslim monarchs introduced many reforms, but all the same their countries mostly ended as part of one or other European-ruled empire. Then came decolonization, and a new generation of modernizing leaders of Islamic countries who were committed to the Third World goal of reproducing the achievements of the West. But there were also Third World problems such as corrupt elites, ethnic and tribal rivalries, struggles over the inheritance of the colonial empires, and dependency on one or other of the power blocs.

These problems were worst in the Middle East, where both blocs were determined to wield the maximum influence as they both had vital interests there. The Western industrial societies needed Middle Eastern oil in order to survive, and the Soviet Union did not want the West to become too powerful in a region that lay directly on its southern border. In addition, the Middle East was the scene of the Islamic modernizers' single greatest failure—the inability of secular-minded Arab nationalist leaders to stop the Jewish state of Israel from coming into being, developing into the region's most successful modern country, continuing to expand its area of settlement, and conquering Jerusalem (pp. 608–610).

Mainly for these reasons, fundamentalism has been more radical in Islam than in Christianity or Judaism. Its appeal is felt exactly among those groups in Islamic societies whose lives have changed the most under Western influence, such as peasants who move to the towns or college students. In spite of its traditionalism, its belief and practice are far more rigorous than was usual in the Islamic past and are promoted by up-to-date Western-style methods of organization and propaganda. Thus fundamentalism amounts to a kind of religious dictatorship that is actually an innovation in Islam. And far more than Christian or Jewish fundamentalism, the Islamic variety sees the ultimate source of evil as an outside enemy, namely the West—above all, Israel as the Western "bridgehead" in the Muslim world and the United States, as Israel's closest ally, the West's leading country, and the main exporter of Western (non-Islamic) values.

Iran: Westernizing Monarch and Islamic Reaction. The first major collision between Islamic fundamentalism and the West came in Iran (*Map 15.4*, p. 608). Known as Persia until 1935, Iran had a history dating back before Islam to the ancient Persian Empire (pp. 45–48). After the rise of Islam, it remained a separate state with its own Muslim rulers (*shahs*), and it became the main center of the minority Shiite branch of Islam with its highly organized clergy (p. 207). Iran managed to keep its independence during the era of imperialism, though Britain and Russia competed vigorously for influence there—especially after the discovery of huge oil reserves in the early twentieth century. After the Second World War, Iran turned to the United States as a counterweight against Soviet pressure from the north. Then, in 1951, a nationalist leader, Muhammad Mossadeq, came to power and took control of the oil fields away from American and British companies. With American help, Iran's ruler, Reza Shah Pahlavi, overthrew Mossadeq and for the next quarter of a century ruled Iran as an absolute monarchy.

Shah Pahlavi made full use of American aid and his government's oil revenues. He lavished funds on his armed forces and started a program of rapid modernization and industrialization. The oil prosperity was shared by many members of the Iranian middle class, but most of the benefits were channeled to a privileged few. The shah's modernization efforts were also directed against Islamic tradition. He used repression and harassment to undermine the power of the Shiite clergy, made clear his sympathy with Western secular ways, and promoted a cult of himself as successor of the Persian kings of the times before Islam. Public resentment grew in the 1970s, involving numerous groups and parties, but religious leaders (the *mullahs* and *ayatollahs*) were the principal promoters of the swelling protest. These leaders called for a fairer economic order as well as a return to religious tradition.

In 1979, the pent-up pressures exploded against the shah. Riots and street demonstrations mounted in anger and violence. Thousands of people were imprisoned, tortured, or killed by the military during this period, but at last the shah's soldiers refused to shoot at their rebelling fellow Iranians. Though his American support continued, the monarch was compelled to flee for his life; and the Ayatollah Khomeini, who had been guiding the revolt from his exile near Paris, returned in triumph to the capital, Tehran.

Once the revolutionaries were in power, they moved to establish the theocratic (clergy-controlled) Islamic Republic of Iran. The new Revolutionary Council tracked down hundreds of the shah's military and civilian officials, put them on trial, and executed them. It enforced strict Muslim rules and punishments respecting dress and behavior, especially for women. At the same time, the regime mobilized women in political and social organizations, recognized their right to vote and stand in elections, and continued the shah's policies of expanding women's education at every level from grade school to college. What the Iranian fundamentalists wanted to do was not to oppose every aspect of modern society but to build a modern society on a foundation of Islamic religious values instead of Western secular ones.

The confrontation with America began in November 1979 when the hated shah was received in New York City for medical treatment. Iranian militants protested by seizing the American embassy in Tehran and taking the staff hostage. In return for their release, the militants demanded return of the shah (for trial), recovery of the enormous wealth he had transferred abroad, and an end to American interference in Iran's affairs.

The public reaction in the United States was one of surprise and anger. Some people called for a military response, but President Carter's concern for the lives of the hostages overruled the desire to resort to force. Carter did react with tough economic steps: he froze Iranian assets in the United States (amounting to many billions of dollars) and cut off all trade with Iran, including imports of oil. He also appealed to the United Nations and his European allies to take diplomatic and economic actions against these flagrant violators of international law. (Embassies have always been considered part of a nation's territory abroad.) But the Iranians did not yield. They remained in the grip of nationalistic excitement, hatred for the American government, and religious fanaticism. It was not until 1981, after a failed rescue mission by the Americans, that they finally released the hostages. They did so in exchange for the unfreezing of Iranian assets and a pledge of noninterference in Iranian affairs.

The "loss" of Iran was a heavy blow to American prestige and interests. The Carter administration feared that the oil fields of the entire Middle East, on which the American economy so greatly depended, were endangered. Carter recognized the danger of Iranian-style revolutions spreading to nearby oil states, and also the possibility of a Soviet march southward into a weakened Iran. He responded by increasing the number of American warships in the Persian Gulf and by starting up a "rapid deployment force" for use in the Middle East.

Afghanistan. The Soviets, for their part, though at first delighted by the humiliation of the United States, feared that the revolutionary Islamic tide might flow from Iran to a neighboring Muslim country, Afghanistan—or even to the millions of Muslims who lived in the southern republics of the U.S.S.R. It was this concern, in part, that moved the Soviets to send troops into Afghanistan late in 1979 to install a pro-Soviet regime. This move, in turn, caused a negative reaction in the United States and Europe, jeopardizing the frail détente with Russia (pp. 631–632)—and also making the Soviets as much the target of Islamic fundamentalist hatred as Israel and the United States.

Thus the fundamentalist movement in Iran not only brought upheavals within that country but also had serious effects beyond its borders. It also brought war to Iran from neighboring Iraq in 1980 (*Map 15.4*, p. 608). This conflict further split the Islamic world and continued to run its bloody course until the United Nations mediated a cease-fire in 1988. Because of Iran's suspected support of international terrorism (p. 628), the United States placed a trade embargo on that nation.

Worldwide Problems of the 1980s

Forty years after the end of the Second World War, the rivalry and partnership of the capitalist First World and the communist Second World, with the Third World uncomfortably straddling the other two, seemed a permanent fact of the world order. But in the 1980s more than before, leaders and peoples of all the three worlds came to realize that the world as a whole faced grave threats arising out of the spectacular growth of modern civilization's technical and industrial capacities and its vulnerability to disruption.

One of these threats involved the interrelated problems of population growth, resource use, and pollution. Connected with this was the issue of the economic relations between the First and Third Worlds. Another problem was posed by the development and large-scale manufacture of nuclear and thermonuclear weapons. A third was the increasing use of terrorism as a weapon in international, ethnic, and social conflicts.

There was a great deal of argument about whose fault these problems were and how they should be solved, as well as about which problems were truly serious enough to count as grave dangers to the human race as a whole. Was the earth getting warmer, and if so, was it because power stations and automobiles were pouring carbon dioxide into the atmosphere or because of long-term natural trends? Was deterrence or disarmament the most reliable means of avoiding nuclear war? Was terrorism more the fault of terrorists who committed atrocious deeds or of oppressors whom they blamed for their grievances? Disputes over these and similar questions have continued down to the present. But few disagreed that the human race faced worldwide threats that needed worldwide measures to counter them.

POPULATION, RESOURCES, AND POLLUTION

Advances in science and technology, as we have seen (pp. 507–508), were primarily responsible for sweeping changes in social conditions. After 1800, the decrease in death rates, flowing chiefly from improvements in food production and medical practices, led to a sharp rise in the number of people in the world (p. 514). The rate of increase grew even steeper in the twentieth century; the numbers being added to the world's population each year were greater than ever before. In the decade of the 1980s, the cumulative increase amounted to more than one billion people—bringing the total to more than five billion in 1990. By the year 2000 the total reached six billion.

For the time being, the food supply kept up with population growth but allowed little improvement in nutrition. The so-called Green Revolution, which introduced better grain seeds during the 1970s, lifted yields, but the increases were limited by inadequate supplies of water and fertilizer. The poor two-thirds of the globe (Asia, Latin America, Africa), where numbers rose the fastest, suffered from endemic malnutrition, and in Africa in particular, there were periodic famines. Overconsumption in the rich one-

Fig. 15.1 Nuclear Meltdown. Nuclear power stations split atoms in radioactive materials contained in reactors, and use the resulting heat to produce steam to drive electricity-generating turbines. The picture shows a reactor at Chernobyl, USSR (present-day Ukraine), the day after an explosion caused by over-heating and melting of the fuel in 1986. The wreckage shows the violence of the blast, and radioactive steam is still spewing into the atmosphere. Eight thousand people eventually died from the effects of radioactivity in Ukraine, and food products were contaminated across eastern and northern Europe.

third of the globe intensified the feeding problem. The average American or European consumed many times more calories and proteins than the average Asian or African.

Other resources also came up short. Residents of the industrialized countries were shocked into an awareness of this reality by the unexpected Arab oil embargo of 1973 (p. 610). Suddenly, the wheels of factories and automobiles slowed. For the first time in their lives, many consumers in the West became aware of the extended and intricate resource network on which their lifestyle rested. Even after the embargo was lifted, the fourfold increase in oil prices indicated the true value of a substance that previously had been bought cheaply and squandered recklessly. The dramatic price hikes by the Organization of Petroleum Exporting Countries (OPEC) upset the importing nations, the flow of international monetary payments, and the world balance of economic power.

Atomic energy, produced by nuclear reactors, was urged as a replacement for fossil fuels (oil and coal). Here was another illustration of the predicament of modern technologists: while the reactors helped fill energy needs, they created new problems such as operational safety, disposal of radioactive wastes, and the possible misuse by terrorists of the plutonium produced (p. 628). The world was sharply alerted to such dangers by a reactor disaster at Chernobyl, in the USSR, in 1986 (*Fig. 15.1*). And dozens of other nuclear plants around the globe could be similar disasters "waiting to happen."

Beyond these special problems was the general threat of environmental pollution caused by rising energy consumption, industrial wastes, and the use of chemicals. These dangers were highlighted in 1985 by the accidental release of a deadly gas from an American plant in Bhopal, India. Thousands of people were killed by this gas in a matter of hours or days. Degradation of the earth's air and water, as well as overheating of the earth's atmosphere, seemed serious possibilities as the upward trend in energy use continued. Many scientists came to believe, therefore, that the survival of the species demanded a leveling off in total population and a reduction in energy and resource consumption.

THE THIRD WORLD AND THE
ADVANCED COUNTRIES

The problems of population and resources also had a decisive influence on relationships between the poor of the Third World and their economic betters. In order to reach at least survivable standards of living, the poor ("have-not") countries asked for the creation of a "new international economic order" based on fairness and sharing rather than on power and inequality. They wanted control, for their own benefit, of whatever resources and natural advantages they possessed. And they demanded changes in the terms of trade, the relation between prices received for their exports and prices paid for their imports.

For their part, the satisfied ("have") countries accepted the fact of global interdependence, but they insisted on being the ones to decide what "adjustments" were to be made. The "North-South dialogue" of the 1970s and 1980s (between the rich and the poor nations) produced little help for development of the Third World. The poor countries, partly because of their own mistakes in economic planning and execution, were worse off in the 1980s than they were in the 1970s.

A side effect of the contrasting living standards among nations was a steep rise in the number of immigrants to the better-off states. In the nineteenth century, millions of Europeans migrated to the New World (p. 514). In the twentieth century, as Europe became more prosperous, the main flows of emigration came to be from Third World countries, either to the United States or to former imperial ruling countries in Europe. These migrants were joined by refugees from political repression, "ethnic cleansing," or social chaos (as in Rwanda, Somalia, and the former Yugoslavia). A United Nations study documented the alarming increase in the numbers of refugees: their count in 1973 was 2.5 million; within twenty years, in 1993, it was 19 million. And the number was swelled by millions more who migrated for the simple reason of crushing poverty in their homelands. Private humanitarian aid agencies were unable to meet the needs, and governments were strained to deal with them.

Most of the industrialized countries faced the inflow—Germany, France, Britain, the United States, and others. Immigration, legal and illegal, became a daunting problem, especially for housing, education, and medical care. The resulting financial cost, job competition, and social frictions with the newcomers disturbed the established residents and produced worrisome consequences. Antiforeign and racist sentiments mounted, and in some of the affected nations, such as France and Germany, extremist right-wing political parties began exploiting the situation to their advantage.

NUCLEAR WEAPONS AND TERRORISM

In the bipolar and ex-colonial world of the 1980s, the relative distribution of strength was military as well as economic. Recognition of this fact speeded the race for weaponry, both nuclear and "conventional." The superpowers, notwithstanding their existing "overkill" capabilities and their lip service to arms control, spent hundreds of billions of dollars annually in a technological struggle for superiority. This contest struck many observers as futile and wasteful, for military power is only relative; as each side matched the escalation of the other, neither gained in security or influence. On the other hand, if either side fell behind, it might lose in security and influence by no longer having the capacity of *deterrence*—to deter the other side from attacking it by the threat of retaliating in kind.

The Superpower Balance of Terror. The most dangerous and costly contest was in nuclear arms. The race had started in 1945 with the dropping of the first atomic bomb on Japan (p. 591). This action by the Americans let the world know of their ability and will to use these "ultimate" weapons when they saw fit. The Soviets responded by building nuclear bombs of their own (p. 599); during the 1950s, the race went onward for more efficient warheads (explosive charges) and for faster and more accurate means of delivery. In this race, the Americans generally kept ahead, both in technological advances and in numbers of deliverable warheads.

Though many types of weapons were designed—for such purposes as short-range ("tactical") use against armies and for use at sea against submarines—the most critical area of competition was in long-range ("strategic") weapons that could reach the homeland of the other superpower. The Soviets put most warheads of this type into land-based missiles, placed in underground "silos." The United States put most of theirs in nuclear-powered submarines, as well as in land-based missiles and bombers.

No matter what the differences in numbers and locations, it was clear by 1970 that each side had more than enough warheads to wipe out the population of the other side. Nevertheless, each side sought a breakthrough, by technological advance or sheer numbers, that would give it superiority over the other side. Essentially, this meant gaining a *first-strike* capacity: that is, the ability to destroy enough of the opponent's nuclear weapons (in a surprise attack) so that the opponent's retaliatory strike would cause only limited losses to the attacker. The nation that gained first-strike capacity would thus have superiority—and with it, supposedly, the final say in disputes with the other superpower. That is why each side wanted the advantage—and, even more important, why it could not permit the other side to gain it.

As it became obvious that neither side would be permitted to win superiority by adding more offensive weapons (because the other side would add more also), nuclear war planners turned to defensive weapons as a way to gain the advantage. If one side had a "near-perfect" defense against enemy warheads while the other did not, the first side would then have gained the desired first-strike capacity. So a race began about 1970 to build "antiballistic missile" (ABM) defenses.

It was shortly realized, however, that this simply added another threatening and expensive side to the arms race—one that, again, neither side could win nor yet afford to lose. In 1972, President Richard Nixon and the Soviet leader, Leonid Brezhnev (p. 600), signed a treaty limiting the building of ABM systems. This agreement was followed by further efforts to achieve "arms control" (limitations or reductions) of offensive weapons. A promising advance was achieved in 1979 when a Strategic Arms Limitation Treaty (SALT) was signed by Brezhnev and a new president, Jimmy Carter. However, the U.S. Senate failed to ratify the treaty, and the race in offensive weapons remained open.

Nuclear Proliferation. Britain, France, and China were also producing nuclear arms (pp. 601, 602). They did so chiefly for national prestige; a nation, to be considered a first-class power, now had to belong to the "nuclear club." But none of these nations was in the same league as the superpowers. Their relatively small supply could hardly give them a first-strike capacity, and they viewed their weapons only as a last resort—to be held as a deterrent threat against any nation that might plan to attack them. In addition, Israel possessed nuclear weapons, and India had tested a weapon so as to prove that it could build them. Iraq, North Korea, and Pakistan were trying to acquire such weapons, and many more countries had the capacity to build them if they chose. This "proliferation" (spread) raised the risk of a "small" nuclear catastrophe somewhere, which might also ignite a *total* catastrophe should the major nuclear powers become involved.

Terrorism. Most other countries, however, did not desire, nor could they afford, to "go nuclear." They contented themselves with a buildup of other types of arms, whose power and accuracy were also growing remarkably. In addition, the vulnerabilities of modern civilization made *terrorism* attractive as a type of armed force.

Deliberate and indiscriminate killing and destruction in order to inspire wide-spread fear, cause societies to cease to function, and thereby achieve political and military goals are nothing new. Conquerors throughout history have suppressed uprisings by massacring villagers and burning their crops; all sides in the Second World War in-discriminately bombed cities. But to achieve their purposes, these deeds were always on a vast scale, whereas terrorism generally involves not large-scale but relatively small-scale (though still indiscriminate) killing and destruction. Modern civilization itself then spreads the fear through the mass media, and widens the damage through its complex web of transport and communications.

This is what makes terrorism a suitable weapon for small unofficial groups claiming to represent repressed populations. It expresses rage against real or imagined injuries arising out of ethnic, social, and national conflicts, and it satisfies the need for revenge. To crush terrorist groups costs efforts out of all proportion to their size, and often leads repressors to atrocities that keep hatred against them alive. Even if a terrorist group does not achieve its stated political and military goals, therefore, it can produce a bloody stalemate that hurts the repressors as much as the terrorists.

To begin with, in fact, terrorism sometimes did achieve its goals. Following the Second World War, it was successfully used by some nationalist movements against weakening imperialist countries—for example, by Arab nationalists against the French in Algeria and by Zionist extremists against the British in Palestine. The success of these early campaigns, together with new opportunities for spectacular operations presented by the growth of airline travel, led to new campaigns in the 1960s and 1970s—by Cuban opponents of the government of Fidel Castro, by Palestinian exiles against Israeli and Jewish targets following the 1967 Six-Day War, and by Irish nationalist opponents of British rule in Northern Ireland.

These new campaigns had much less chance of success. Car bombs might encourage the British to evacuate Palestine, which was not a vital national interest for them. Against airplane hijackings intended actually to overthrow communist rule or the Jewish state, however, the governments of Cuba and Israel had no choice but to stand and fight. But from the point of view of the terrorists, however, bloody stalemate was better than no conflict at all. This view was shared by the rulers of countries under Arab nationalist or Islamic fundamentalist rule like Syria or Libya, which sponsored terrorism as a weapon against adversaries like Israel or the United States. By the 1980s, terrorism had become common enough to constitute a recognized worldwide problem, though it was not generally regarded as so serious as nuclear proliferation or the balance of terror. In the 1990s, however, the priorities would change and the problems would merge.

End of the Postwar (Cold War) Era

During the 1980s, changes got under way in the political and economic order that had existed throughout the West since the Second World War. There was a widespread sense of frustration with the functioning of the welfare state, which came to seem a brake on economic growth and rising standards of living. A new militancy appeared in relations with the socialist camp, whose worldwide power seemed to be increasing even while oppressive dictatorships continued to rule its home countries.

Neither of these changes represented a total break with the past. No Western political leader seriously tried to dismantle the welfare state, and few politicians of any stripe doubted that the socialist camp would be the West's rival and partner for the indefinite future. But meanwhile, frustrations and disappointments were growing among the political leaders of the socialist camp as well. At the end of the decade, it was the socialist countries that made a total break with the past, and of their own accord gave up the effort to build a world order alternative to that of the West.

POLITICAL AND ECONOMIC CHANGES IN THE WEST: THATCHER AND REAGAN

During the 1980s, many Western countries swung toward conservative domestic policies. This was primarily a reaction against the liberal policies that had generally prevailed in the West from 1933 until about 1980. The terms *liberal* and *liberalism,* of course, no longer meant what they had meant in the eighteenth and nineteenth centuries. In that earlier time, liberalism had been equated with individualism and with the revolt against hereditary privilege and absolute monarchy (pp. 496–497). In the twentieth century, liberalism still stood for individual rights (civil liberties) and openness to social reform but came to be most strongly identified with social democracy and the welfare state (pp. 582–585). The social and moral changes that accompanied the welfare state also came to be linked with liberalism.

"Thatcherite" Britain. Although the conservative reaction to these changes proceeded unevenly in most countries of the West, it took decisive form in Britain and the United States. Margaret Thatcher was chosen as leader by Britain's Conservative party in 1979, and she led her party to victory in Parliament during the ensuing decade. With large majorities in the elected House of Commons, she was able to enact sweeping reforms. Many government-owned enterprises were *privatized* (sold off to private corporations); the educational system was overhauled at all levels—and at reduced cost; the power of trade unions was curbed; and taxation policies shifted ever more to favor the rich. Although these changes were not altogether pleasing to many British voters, Thatcher gained and held power largely because of splits within the opposition Labour party. By 1990, her public support had fallen sharply; she was replaced as party leader and prime minister by John Major, a member of her cabinet. But many of the "Thatcherite" changes survived their originator's downfall to become permanent features of the British way of life.

The "Reagan Revolution." In the United States, the conservatives did not achieve a full grip on the federal government. This was due to the constitutional provision for "checks and balances," which distributes authority among the legislative, executive, and judicial branches. The election and reelection of Richard Nixon as president in 1968 and 1972 had signaled widespread disillusionment with liberal social reforms, but Nixon had disappointed conservatives by upholding both the welfare state and détente. He had then left office in 1974 under threat of impeachment, following the discovery of his role in covering up a political burglary at the Watergate office and apartment complex in Washington, D.C., as well as in numerous other abuses—illegal financial contributions, misuse of government agencies, campaign "dirty tricks," and obstruction of justice. It took several years for the conservatives to regroup and rally under another leader—Ronald Reagan, the governor of California.

By 1980, conservative opinion makers were also setting the national mood. Writers and television commentators like William Buckley and George Will were displacing, in the public view, well-known liberals like Arthur Schlesinger and John Kenneth Galbraith. The conservatives, like the liberals, had a considerable range of interpreters. But the central thrust of the movement was becoming quite clear. Their common wish was to conserve—actually, to restore and keep American institutions and lifestyles as they were thought to have been around 1930 (or even earlier). They therefore objected to many of the features of the welfare state (introduced in 1933 by Franklin Roosevelt's New Deal; p. 584) and to some of the social and ethical changes that had come about during the period of liberal control (pp. 654–660). Many liberals themselves, who found that these changes had gone farther than they had expected or wanted, changed their political allegiance and became *neoconservatives.* Opposition was thus a principal part of the conservative program—opposition to the expanding functions of government (business regulation, welfare services, deficit spending, high taxes), and opposition to social "permissiveness"—feminism, abortion, pornography, and busing to improve racial balance in the public schools.

The affirmative aims of American conservatives included a more nationalistic foreign policy, military "superiority" over the Soviet Union, restoring laissez-faire economic policies, strengthening "law and order," rejuvenating the traditional family and morals, and returning to religious "fundamentals." This last concern reflected a widespread demand for prayers in public schools and massive responses to television preachers. Best known among them is the Reverend Billy Graham, who for some sixty years addressed hundreds of thousands in America and around the world—urging them to "commit to Jesus as their Savior."

The issues between conservatives and liberals found clear focus in the elections of both 1980 and 1984. The Republican party, which had stood in opposition to most of the reforms of the New Deal, remained the political stronghold of conservatism. The Democratic party, beginning with the New Deal, had become identified with liberalism. The Republicans won the presidency for Ronald Reagan in 1980, as well as control over the Senate. The election results signaled that conservatives had gained the balance of power in the nation—politically, psychologically, and philosophically—and the new president began to pursue a genuinely conservative agenda, the "Reagan Revolution."

As president, Reagan sought to reverse the tendency, which dated back to Franklin Roosevelt, of looking to government as a positive agency for solving the nation's problems and aiding its citizens. Reagan, rejecting that view, declared that "government is not the solution; it is the problem." In keeping with that declaration, he cut income tax rates, which in turn put heavy pressure on Congress to make up for the loss in government revenues by cutting spending on social programs. But Reagan insisted, at the same time, on large increases in military spending. As a result, the federal budget could not be balanced, and the huge annual deficits (money shortages) had to be made up through government borrowing, much of it from foreign investors. The tax cuts left more money for businesses to invest and consumers to spend and thereby stimulated substantial economic growth, but it left the country with a mountain of government debt (in addition to an unprecedented level of private debt). Payments of interest alone on the federal debt were estimated at $250 billion for the fiscal year 1991—a sum equal to the appropriation that year for the entire Department of Defense.

Reagan and his advisers downplayed the deficit problem, declaring that a growing economy would eventually yield higher revenues even with lower tax rates. But the debt soared even higher until in 1990 his successor, President George H. W. Bush, yielding at last to the views of financial experts around the world, decided to face up to making substantial cuts in the annual deficit. In the 1990s, deficits were reduced and for a time disappeared. But the burden of existing debt on the economy—and essential public services—continued and began to increase again in the new millennium.

In addition to reducing tax rates, Reagan pushed for deregulation of the economy. This was favored by the business community but contributed to some serious negative results. Lax supervision of the savings and loan industry, for example, was a factor in permitting gross mismanagement and fraud there. And since Congress had guaranteed depositors' savings accounts, the losses to taxpayers would run into hundreds of billions of dollars. Reagan sought also to eliminate numerous federal agencies that had been established to safeguard the public (like the Environmental Protection Agency). In most cases, he was unable to gain congressional approval for abolishing them, but he often succeeded in cutting their funds—and in choosing agency heads who would limit their effectiveness. But his most lasting impact was upon the courts of the land. During his eight years in office, Reagan was able to name hundreds of federal judges, most of whom shared his conservative political and social views—and whose lifetime tenure on the bench would run many years beyond the time of their appointment.

Reagan's second term was less "revolutionary" than his first. Widespread support for his conservative policies contributed to his reelection, but much of his support came from his personal appeal: his good looks, humor, and confident public assurances. Other conservative candidates, generally, did not fare as well as he did at the polls. In subsequent congressional elections, Republicans lost control of the Senate to the Democrats. With Democrats controlling both houses of Congress after 1986, a legislative gridlock developed in the confrontation between conservatives and liberals. Reagan's vice president, George H. W. Bush, sustained the conservative position by keeping the presidency in Republican hands in the election of 1988, but proved unsuccessful in trying to bring about a majority for his party in either the Senate or the House of Representatives. In 1992, the swing of the political pendulum was completed when President Bush lost the White House to the Democratic candidate, Bill Clinton.

Relations with the "Evil Empire." Reagan became president at a time when the Soviet Union had engaged in a lengthy buildup of nuclear and conventional arms. This was partly in order to force the United States to treat it as an equal in their bipolar partnership, but it was also to gain the advantage in their bipolar rivalry. Soviet intervention in Afghanistan (p. 623), as well as their support for the spread of left-wing governments and guerrilla insurgencies in Central America and southern Africa, seemed to be changing the bipolar balance of power and thereby undermined détente. Reagan, whose intense anticommunism went back to his earliest years in politics, was eager to take up the challenge. As president, he aimed, through a military buildup, to deal with the Soviets from a "position of strength"—which meant superior strength. He believed that this policy would stop communist expansionism and, by overstraining the Soviet economy, would lead to the undermining of the "evil empire."

In confrontations with communism throughout the world, Reagan took a hard line. When the Caribbean island of Grenada fell into a political crisis under its Marxist leaders in 1982, he sent United States military forces to occupy the island and install a prodemocratic government there. He supported the government of the Central American republic of El Salvador in a brutal war against Marxist guerrillas, while also backing guerrilla uprisings against Marxist governments in neighboring Nicaragua and in the southern African republic of Angola. None of these wars was as easy to win as that against Grenada, and in all three countries they dragged on, at huge cost in human suffering, until the end of the Cold War. Once the Marxists could no longer count on Soviet support and the United States no longer saw the opponents of the Marxists as allies against communism, the conflicts ended in compromise.

Besides redressing the general balance of power with the Soviet Union, Reagan was eager to change the nuclear balance of terror in favor of the United States. By 1980, the nuclear arms race with the Soviet Union had come to a standoff (pp. 626–627). The superpowers had reached rough equality ("parity") in offensive power. But Reagan and his advisers were not satisfied with parity, and they began steps to regain nuclear superiority—which the United States had enjoyed right after the Second World War (p. 599). They believed this could be done through a massive buildup of arms: annual military spending doubled from $150 billion for the year 1981 to about $300 billion in 1985—and continued to increase thereafter. The Soviets, however, matched the buildup, and the strategic standoff persisted.

With the effort to gain superiority through offensive weapons at a dead end, in 1983 Reagan proposed to build a defensive system against intercontinental nuclear missiles. This was a return to an earlier idea in the arms race, which had been rejected by both sides in 1972 (the ABM treaty; p. 627). But advances in technology—lasers, computers, space mirrors—had led some weapon scientists to advise the president that another try should be made. Reagan therefore determined to give up the "stability" of the existing nuclear balance and seek to construct a space-based system—one that could give the United States a first-strike capacity (p. 627). Reagan called his plan the Strategic Defense Initiative, but it was quickly dubbed "Star Wars" by the news media. It soon became clear that even if the technical problems could be solved, a workable Star Wars system would cost hundreds of billions of dollars, and the Soviets indicated that if the system went into operation, they would build up their offensive missile force so that it would overcome any defense system by sheer weight of numbers. Neither side was eager for a new round of the arms race that would be more costly than any before it, and the time seemed ripe to reduce tension between the superpowers.

The Star Wars issue was one of the main subjects discussed at the Geneva summit meeting in November 1985 between Reagan and a new Soviet leader, Mikhail Gorbachev. Responding to concessions and fresh initiatives from Gorbachev, Reagan displayed a definite shift in his tone and words to the Soviets. This shift was welcomed by America's European allies and by people everywhere who feared war between the superpowers. It proved to be a critical turning point, built upon later by both leaders, toward slowing down the arms race between the superpowers, and the Star Wars project was eventually shelved. In addition, the revelation that what the Soviet leaders called the "correlation of forces" was not moving in their favor contributed both to the end of the Cold War and to the fall of communism.

THE REVOLUTIONS IN EASTERN EUROPE: GORBACHEV, YELTSIN

While conservative reforms were gradually taking shape in western Europe and America during the 1980s, the eastern (communist) bloc showed little change on its surface—until the end of the decade, when the region exploded in radical political, social, economic, and cultural changes.

For some seventy years since the Russian Revolution of 1917, the Communist party's grip on the Soviet Union had appeared to be unbreakable. So too seemed its forty-year grip on the satellite countries of East Germany, Poland, Czechoslovakia, Romania, Hungary, and Bulgaria. There had been some outspoken dissidents, like Aleksandr Solzhenitsyn (pp. 662, 711), but the socialist camp's instruments of control and repression were seemingly so systematic and so powerful that no major change could erupt from below. That made the sudden collapse of communism, when it came, the "historical surprise" of the century.

Although largely unknown to foreign observers, serious doubts about the viability of the communist system had begun to grow among some of the higher officials of the Soviet party even before 1980. As far back as the 1930s, Nikolai Bukharin had criticized the Stalinist regime and had called for greater flexibility in the economy (p. 573). And after Stalin's death in 1953, Nikita Khrushchev, as party chief, introduced some measures of relaxation (p. 600). Such views and actions, however, were not sustained by the party as a whole.

It was not until a generation after Khrushchev that disenchantment with the system became a rising force. More and more party members (as well as ordinary citizens) were concluding that the longtime promises of communism—and centralized economic control—were not being fulfilled. They viewed with envy the rising prosperity of the capitalist West, and they were discouraged by the failure of many years of weapons buildup to change the "correlation of forces" between the Soviet Union and the United States. As a result, they became convinced that changes had to be made to rescue their faltering economy—and that if only to lighten the crippling burden of military spending, these changes must include an end to the worldwide power struggle with the West.

Perestroika and Glasnost. In 1985, the central committee of the party chose Mikhail Gorbachev as their agent of change. He moved quickly in two directions: what he called *glasnost,* the "opening up" (democratization) of Soviet society. and *perestroika,* the "restructuring" of the economy. Similar efforts were also being made in other states within the Soviet orbit.

With respect to foreign affairs, Gorbachev urged "new thinking"—for his own and other countries. (He supported his words with action by pulling Soviet troops out of Afghanistan in 1988; p. 623.) The Cold War and its confrontational policies had proved enormously wasteful "dead ends." A new era of cooperation in addressing the real problems of the planet was called for. These goals, articulated and vigorously pursued by Gorbachev, were the main factors that precipitated the revolutions of eastern Europe. Worldwide recognition of his historic role was symbolized by the awarding to Gorbachev of the Nobel Prize for Peace in 1990.

The progress of change within the Soviet Union itself was uneven. Gorbachev had powerful domestic critics on both "left" and "right" (those who wanted to move faster and those who tried to hold back reforms). Nevertheless, swift action was taken to implement glasnost. Thousands of political prisoners were released, and free expression and free assembly were permitted. Perhaps the most significant constitutional reform was the abolition of the Communist party's monopoly on political power (p. 574). New elections took place throughout the USSR, with rival nonparty groups vying for office.

Gorbachev's principal frustrations lay in the area of perestroika—the restructuring of the economy. Some individuals wanted to move as quickly as possible from the existing system of centralized control to a full-fledged market economy. Others believed that such a rapid move would be too disruptive and painful to workers and consumers; they favored a "go-slow" approach. Gorbachev, walking the tightrope, proposed a plan combining features from both sides. In October 1990, his compromise was approved by the newly elected Soviet Parliament—and he was authorized, as president, to set it in motion by executive decree.

But Gorbachev's economic plan proved to be too little and too late. (Ironically, it served only to identify him, in Soviet eyes, with the collapse of the USSR.) The underlying causes of the system's failure were numerous: critical mistakes, over the years, by the central planning establishment; lack of provision for individual incentive and initiative; gross neglect of ecological considerations; and overall political and social rigidity. Beyond these intrinsic causes was perhaps the most decisive single cause—the waging of the Cold War with the United States and its NATO allies (pp. 597–603). Diversion of resources and manpower from peaceful production to pursuit of the extravagant arms race severely strained the American economy and left it with a huge burden of debt; but the arms race brought to the "enemy" Soviets what Washington had sought: the fatal crippling of their economic system (pp. 626–627, 632–633).

The Breakup of the Soviet Union. The worsening economic situation was aggravated by the dissolving of the ties that had held the Soviet Union together. Gorbachev's general policy of repudiating the use of military force to keep the country unified opened the door to long pent-up desires for independence from the multinational state. The three Baltic republics (p. 588) were the first to declare their own individual sovereignty. The Russian Republic, the largest by far of the fifteen (p. 574), quickly followed, along with Ukraine, Georgia, Azerbaijan, and most of the other republics. How could a multinational economic plan work if each of the now sovereign states took off on its own plans? This dilemma was highlighted in the case of the Russian Republic. Boris Yeltsin, a former Communist turned radical reformer, was elected president of that new republic in 1991. He declared, with the support of the republic's parliament, that Russia would press toward a market economy by a much faster route than Gorbachev had envisioned.

The momentous happenings of August 1991 gave added force to Yeltsin's plan. The political "right," backed by the secret police (KGB), ranking army officers, and Communist party conservatives, launched a coup against Gorbachev (still officially the president of the USSR) and the reformers in the Russian Parliament. But the coup lasted only seventy-two hours as thousands of Muscovites filled the streets to defend their parliament—and the deployed army units pulled back. Opinion elsewhere in the country, and in the world, strongly condemned this effort to overthrow the legal order.

The failed coup thus damaged the reactionaries—and gave decisive impetus to the supporters of democracy, market economy, and independence for the constituent re-

🐌 **Map 15.5 Europe After Communism's Collapse.** The map of the new Europe reflects the triumph of national-ism. Germany is again united. The multinational Soviet Union, Yugoslavia, and Czechoslovakia have been divided into states in most of which one nation predominates. There are still many minorities on "wrong" sides of the national borders, and Russia has lost all the territory it gained in four centuries of westward expansion (*Map 10.2*, p. 414). The challenge of the future will be for the European nations to fulfill the ideal of national unity and in-dependence leading to harmony among nations.

publics. Within days, the reformers in the Parliament initiated far-reaching measures: to deprive the Communist party of any effective role in government, alter drastically the functions of the secret police, loosen controls over the media, and ensure that the armed forces were kept under the command of loyal officers. The way was also cleared for achievement of complete independence by the individual republics—whose elected leaders would now be free to negotiate their relations with one another and with for-eign countries.

Shortly after these actions, the governing organs of the USSR ceased to exist. In early December 1991, the presidents of three of the new republics—Russia, Ukraine, and Belarus (formerly Byelorussia)—met and announced the creation of a substitute version of the union, which they called the Commonwealth of Independent States (CIS). This association was quickly joined by most of the other new republics. Modeled after the idea of the British Commonwealth of Nations (p. 603), the CIS functioned as an international organization with limited powers. Many of its members have since taken steps for economic cooperation, and in 1997, Russia and Belarus agreed on a "union" with a common currency and citizenship, though still remaining separate and independent states. In addition, the three presidents agreed on a declaration that the Russian Republic was to be accepted as the principal inheritor of the assets and obligations of the Soviet Union—including, especially, control over its nuclear missiles

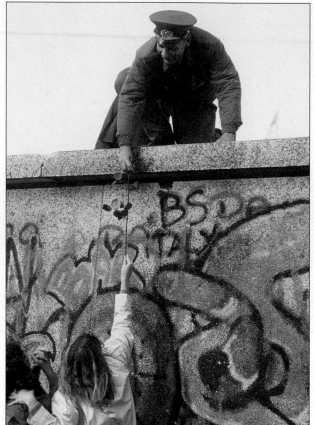

Fig. 15.2 "Tear Down This Wall!" The "Antifascist Defense Wall" was built around West Berlin in 1961 by the East German government to stop its citizens from emigrating to the West. Visiting the Berlin Wall in 1987, Ronald Reagan challenged Mikhail Gorbachev to tear it down, not really expecting that this would actually happen. Now, however, in November 1989, an East German policeman reaches down from the wall for a rose offered by a West German woman. The Cold War has ended, the wall is about to come down, Germany will soon be reunited, and communism itself will pass into history.

and its commitments to reduce their numbers. This declaration was welcomed by the United States and the European Community.

On Christmas Day 1991, Mikhail Gorbachev, responding to these events, officially resigned his empty office as president of the now-dissolved multinational state. Gorbachev had aimed to "reform" communism and to maintain the unity of its political domain. But in the country's critical "time of troubles" he was swept aside by the swelling popular demand for radical economic change and national self-determination.

The Liberation of Eastern Europe. The unraveling of the Soviet Union was paralleled by the breaking away of the satellite countries of eastern Europe (*Map 15.5*, p. 635). They had been held as allies of the USSR under the Warsaw Pact of 1955 (p. 599). At that time, the Soviet leaders viewed them as a needed buffer—to help protect their war-ravaged homeland from any future attack by a resurgent Germany and the West. The economies of these states had suffered from the same growing paralysis that the Soviets were enduring. Once Gorbachev signaled that force would no longer be used to hold them in tow, popular movements exploded against their communist regimes (all the more despised because they were imposed by a foreign power). Thus democratic revolutions (mostly nonviolent) followed in 1989 and 1990 in Poland, East Germany (*Fig. 15.2*), Hungary, Romania, Bulgaria, and Czechoslovakia. Following complex negotiations in which the West Germans persuaded both its allies and its adversaries that it would not use reunification as a springboard for reversing the results of the Second World War, West Germany and East Germany were reunited to form a single country. Czechoslovakia, on the other hand, was divided in 1993, by joint consent of its two predominant nations, into the Czech Republic and Slovakia. Though Yugoslavia had not been part of the Warsaw Pact, that country took a similar course of democratization and separation into its component republics—followed in this case by civil war.

All of these states, like the former Soviet republics, faced a complicated transition to a new kind of economy—from state-owned enterprises and central planning to privatization and production for the free market. The long struggle between the West and the socialist camp had ended in the socialist camp's voluntarily admitting defeat and seeking to join the West. Communism had collapsed suddenly, easily, and relatively peacefully. The process of replacing it, however, would be long, hard, and full of conflict.

RECOMMENDED READING

The Bipolar World Order   D. S. Painter, *The Cold War: An International History* (1999), is a good brief introduction; S. J. Ball, *The Cold War: An International History, 1947–1991* (1998), is more detailed, and covers the debates over Cold War origins.

R. Pearson, *The Rise and Fall of the Soviet Empire* (1998), deals readably with the satellite countries under Soviet domination. E. E. Moise, *Modern China: A History* (1986), concisely puts Communist China against its background of traditional Chinese civilization and Western imperialism; A. Lawrance, *China Under Communism* (1998), is an excellent introduction to the period of Communist rule; and R. E. Barrett and F. Li, *Modern China* (1999), concentrates on the country's economic and social life.

On the postwar recovery of Europe, see W. Laqueur, *Europe in Our Time: A History, 1945–1992* (1992), and G. Ambrosius and W. H. Hubbard, *A Social and Economic History of Twentieth-Century Europe* (1989).

The Liquidation of Imperial Rule   A. D. Smith, *Nations and Nationalism in a Global Era* (1996), assesses the status of nationalism in the present-day world. M. E. Chamberlain, *Decolonization: The Fall of the European Empires* (1985), is a good brief guide, concentrating on the British Empire; F. Ansprenger, *The Dissolution of the Colonial Empires* (1989), has more on other European empires; R. F. Beth, *Decolonization* (1998), is a brief interpretation of the passing of imperialism as a social and cultural development. For the experiences of the leading opponent of apartheid in South Africa, see N. Mandela, *Long Walk to Freedom* (1995); the viewpoint of an African American militant is articulated in *The Autobiography of Malcolm X* (1965).

The Third World and the West   C. Clapham, *Third World Politics: An Introduction* (1985), briefly describes the patterns of rule that have emerged in Africa, Asia, and Latin America since decolonization.

F. Fitzgerald, *Fire in the Lake: The Vietnamese and the Americans in Vietnam* (1972), is a moving account by a gifted writer. A frank explanation of the mistakes in prosecuting this war can be found in R. S. McNamara, *In Retrospect: The Tragedy and Lessons of Vietnam* (1995). E. Reischauer, *The Japanese Today* (1988), is an excellent study of a people on the rise.

On the revolution in Iran, see S. Akhavi, *Religion and Politics in Contemporary Iran* (1980); useful also is R. K. Ramazani, ed., *Iran's Revolution: The Search for Consensus* (1990). For Iraq, see S. Al-Khalil, *Republic of Fear* (1989).

Worldwide Problems of the 1980s   Sound and readable treatments are P. R. Ehrlich, *The Population Explosion* (1990), and G. Myrdal, *The Challenge of World Poverty* (1970). L. Evans, *Feeding the Ten Billion: Plants and Population Growth* (1998), is a nontechnical introduction to the interaction of population and agriculture from the Agricultural Revolution to the twenty-first century. The critical issue of birth control is discussed in G. Hardin, *Living Within Limits: Ecology, Economics, and Popular Taboos* (1993). M. Friedman and R. D. Friedman, *Free to Choose* (1980), is a popular exposition of monetarism and laissez-faire economics. D. K. Fieldhouse, *The West and the Third World* (1999), discusses the historical background and present state of relations between the two, and assesses the prospects of Third World countries in the global economy. The ferment in portions of the Third World is set forth in F. Fanon, *The Wretched of the Earth* (1966). An early work on the rising terrorist threat is W. Laqueur, *The Age of Terrorism* (1987).

End of the Postwar (Cold War) Era W. C. Berman, *America's Right Turn: From Nixon to Clinton* (1998), is a concise and readable account of U.S. politics in the 1970s and 1980s; on neoconservatism, see M. Gerson, *The Neoconservative Vision: From the Cold War to the Culture Wars* (1996). E. J. Evans, *Thatcher and Thatcherism* (1997), examines the British model of conservatism.

On the end of the Cold War and the collapse of communism in the satellite countries, see the books by Ball, Painter, and Pearson listed for "The Bipolar World Order." On the Soviet Union, see T. H. von Laue, *Why Lenin? Why Stalin? Why Gorbachev?* (1993), for a good brief account; B. Nahaylo and V. Swoboda, *Soviet Disunion* (1990), for the critical nationalities problem; and M. Galeotti, *Gorbachev and His Revolution* (1997), for the life and policies of the last Soviet leader. A. Zwass, *From Failed Communism to Underdeveloped Capitalism: Transformation of Eastern Europe, the Post–Soviet Union, and China* (1995), describes the uncertain economic future of the postcommunist world.

INFOTRAC COLLEGE EDITION

Visit the source collections at **http://academic.cengage.com/infotrac**, and use the Search function with the following key terms:

Cold War	Decolonization	Europe communism
Soviet Union relations with the United States	Khrushchev	Perestroika
	single European market	

WESTERN CIVILIZATION RESOURCES

Visit the Brief History of the Western World Companion Web Site for resources specific to this textbook:

http://history.wadsworth.com/greerbrief09/

Also, the CD in the back of this book and the World History Resources Center at **http://history.wadsworth.com/west_civ/** offer a variety of tools to help you succeed in this course, including access to quizzes; images; documents; interactive simulations, maps, and timelines; movie explorations; and a wealth of other sources.

CHAPTER 16

*The Revolution
in Western Culture*

OVERVIEW

The rise of global civilization has taken place amid an explosion of invention and discovery and of new ways of thinking, feeling, behaving, and creating. Most of these changes have originated in Western civilization, but non-Western peoples have increasingly participated in them.

These drastic changes have had strongly opposing effects on the mentality of modern global civilization. On the one hand, there is a heady sense of liberation from traditional ignorance of the workings of nature and the mind, irrational codes of behavior and morality, and conventional limits on the themes and methods of art. But there also is a disturbing awareness of loss of tradition and stability, of individual helplessness against social forces or government and commercial manipulation, of the littleness of humanity compared with the vastness of nature. In these respects, modern global civilization experiences in sharpened form humanity's age-old combination of feelings when reflecting upon itself and the universe: consciousness of freedom, knowledge, and power, and a sense of weakness, perplexity, and fear.

The sharpening of this double feeling has resulted above all from the progress of science and technology. Today, humanity is reaching toward ultimate understanding of the universe as a whole and the medium of space and time in which it exists, as well as of the almost infinitely tiny yet unimaginably complex "worlds" that make up both living and nonliving matter. Technology, firmly hitched to the scientific juggernaut, has provided safety, comfort, and abundance on a scale that earlier generations would have considered miraculous. Yet science has also made the human race seem unimportant and unexceptional as part of the universe and made whatever ultimate reality lies behind the universe seem more distant than ever, while technology has given the human race the power to enslave and destroy itself.

The effect of the rise of science has been especially strong on philosophy and religion, because it is these that have traditionally guided the human race's thinking about itself and the universe. Philosophers often restrict themselves to studying and refining the basic methods of philosophy, or they protest against a universe that seems indifferent and unknowable and societies that seem materialistic and conformist. In the monotheistic religions, "fundamentalist" believers hold to their sacred books as authoritative guides to knowledge about humanity and the universe, and oppose changes in traditional codes of behavior and morals. "Conservatives" accept both the universe of science and the one God who exists beyond it and has given humanity a unique place in it, but find no way of combining these into a single whole. And "liberals" regard traditional beliefs as no more than compelling myths, while affirming drastic changes in behavior and morality.

Of all these changes, perhaps the most far-reaching are those that Western civilization is now undergoing—and which are more or less rapidly spreading across the world—concerning sexual behavior and family life. The balance of status and power between men and women that seemingly arose with the Agricultural Revolution is breaking down, and single motherhood and homosexuality claim acceptance as part of the social order alongside heterosexuality and marriage. These changes, too, have a double nature. The emancipation of women, for instance, was partly driven by vast and impersonal social forces—by the tide of industrialization that swept millions of women out of homes and families and deposited them in factories and offices. Yet women's liberation, the most recent stage of emancipation, sprang from the protest of the mid-twentieth-century "counterculture" against mass society in the democratic-capitalist countries, with its manipulation of individuals into accepting predetermined social roles.

The arts, too, have reflected the conflicted and changing mentality of modern global civilization. The most admired artists have generally depicted the complexities and problems of the modern world. Often, they have found the traditional conventions of storytelling and depicting appearances inadequate to their purpose, preferring to view human experience through the lens of their own or others' subjective consciousness. Even when artists have used more traditional methods, they have done so mostly in order to cry out against the horrors of modern civilization. Celebrating the consensus values of society, an important function of art in traditional civilizations, is now mostly left to second-rate artists and to mass entertainment.

The Onrush of Science and Technology

The accelerating nineteenth-century progress of science (pp. 523–530) turned in the twentieth century into a headlong rush of discovery that left no aspect of nature unexplored. The distribution of galaxies across the endless reaches of space, the movement of continents across the face of the earth, the ages of prehistoric artifacts and human remains, the "language" in which bees communicate with each other in the hive—over an astonishingly wide range of matters that until recently were completely mysterious, science can now provide systematic knowledge and explanations.

From the lonely activity of a few researchers, moreover, science has become a large-scale social undertaking, employing tens of thousands of highly trained people and supported by massive state subsidies (though these are only a small fraction of total government budgets). Scientists used to boast of doing experiments "with string and sealing wax," but much scientific equipment has become spectacularly huge and complex. Fourteen European nations pooled their resources to build the Large Electron-Positron Collider, opened near Geneva, Switzerland, in 1989—a machine that hurls subatomic particles at each other over a distance of more than 50 miles so that physicists can produce collisions violent enough to break the particles down into their still more basic constituents. Likewise, in 1990 and 1993 the United States devoted two space shuttle missions to placing the Hubble Space Telescope in orbit and then repairing it, so that astronomers could get pictures of distant features of the universe unobscured by the earth's atmosphere.

Furthermore in some ways the pursuit of scientific knowledge has become the single most highly respected of human endeavors. Of all the ways in which the present-day world honors individuals as benefactors of humanity, perhaps the most prestigious are the Nobel Prizes, established by the Swedish industrialist Alfred Nobel in 1904. Of the six prizes annually awarded, one each is given for literature, economics, and peace, and the other three (physics, physiology and medicine, and chemistry) are all given for science.

The reason for this high valuation of science is not just that science has unlocked so many secrets of nature. It also has to do with the fact that the explosion of scientific knowledge has transformed every other aspect of human life on this planet: politics and warfare, industry and the economy, social life and culture. Most of the matters dealt with in the last three chapters of this book, from the atom bomb to the "pill," and from the Green Revolution in agriculture to the revolution in politics produced by television, would never have happened without the onrush of science, towing technology in its wake at vastly accelerated speed.

PENETRATING THE SECRETS OF THE PHYSICAL UNIVERSE

Among the countless twentieth-century achievements of science, perhaps the most significant—both as discoveries in themselves and in their consequences for human life and thought—are those that have taken humanity to the outermost edges of the universe, and to the innermost structure of both nonliving matter and living organisms.

The Expanding Universe. In astronomy, the twentieth century saw the "discovery of a new cosmos" comparable to that which took place in the sixteenth and seventeenth centuries (pp. 418–425). These advances in cosmology (understanding of the workings of the universe) are partly the result of other scientific and technical discoveries, which have enabled astronomers to see ever farther into space. Already in the nineteenth century, spectrum analysis (p. 524) of the light emitted by stars showed that they are made of the same basic elements known on earth; comparison with geological estimates of the earth's age also indicated that the stars must somehow have the capacity to "burn" hot and bright for billions of years. From about 1900 on, huge new telescopes revealed that stars are clustered throughout space in galaxies similar to our Milky Way, the aggregation of 200 billion stars in which the sun was already known to be located. Further, spectrum analysis of the galaxies themselves indicated that they are moving away from one another at vast speed. In the 1920s, the American astronomer Edwin Hubble made the fundamental discovery on which the new cosmology rests: that the farther apart galaxies are, the faster they seem to move away from each other. This was clinching proof that the totality of galaxies—that is, the universe itself—must be expanding.

This, in turn, led astronomers to a scientific theory about the probable origin of the universe—one as imaginative and ingenious as any earlier creation myth or philosophical speculation (pp. 21, 25, 79–80, 426–427). If the universe has been growing larger over time, it seemed to follow that there must have been a moment in the past—most likely about fifteen billion years ago—when it was infinitely small; and if the galaxies are still today hurtling away from each other, then the reason must be that "in the beginning," the original tiny universe exploded outward with unimaginable violence. In the 1960s, confirmation of this theory was provided by a new type of observing device, radio telescopes, which detect radio signals emitted by stars and other objects in space. It turned out that the entire universe is saturated with radio signals, all of the same very short wavelength, that have no source in any individual object—the remains, it is believed, of the mighty outburst of electromagnetic radiation (p. 524) given off by the original "big bang."

Relativity and Space-Time. To explain these discoveries, and for guidance in searching for such things in the first place, astronomers turned to the concepts of Albert Einstein's theory of relativity (pp. 525–526). Only the large-scale conversion of matter into energy, as proposed by Einstein, could provide a "fuel" powerful enough to keep the stars "burning" for billions of years at a time. Only the concept of space and time, matter and energy, being related to one another allowed astronomers to conceive of how all four could originally have been packed into a tiny point, and then have expanded outward into a universe that grows without having an actual boundary but where space and time simply curve back on themselves. This new view of the universe did not invalidate the view developed by Copernicus and Kepler, Galileo and Newton, as their view had invalidated that of Aristotle and Ptolemy (pp. 419–424). But it became clear that what the sixteenth- and seventeenth-century giants had discovered was only the tip of the iceberg. Their twentieth-century successors were exploring the full outlines of the whole awesome structure of mass and energy extending through time and space.

Inside the Atom: Waves, Particles, and Uncertainty. Alongside the astronomers' search for the origins of the universe there also proceeded the quest of the physicists for the inner secrets of the atom. What drove this quest forward were questions raised by the early-twentieth-century discovery of Rutherford and Bohr (p. 525) that the atom is not a basic unit of matter, but itself a tiny structure or system, with its own constituent parts. What exactly are these constituent parts, or *subatomic particles*? What forces keep them in balance with each other to form a stable system, and what kind of changes within the atom produce such things as radioactivity or light? What is the best way of describing the particles and forces at work in the atom, and how can such tiny entities be detected and measured? In the course of the twentieth century, atomic physicists came a long way toward answering many of these questions.

The theories that gave guidance in answering these questions were devised mostly between 1900 and 1930. What they said was that, just as on the ultralarge scale of the universe as a whole, so in the ultrasmall world of the atom, the "classical" (p. 525) scientific concepts that seem to do well enough for the vast range of "middle-sized" items, such as falling apples or planets in their orbits, do not apply. Thus, to make sense of the world of the atom, it turned out to be necessary to think of many subatomic particles sometimes as tiny pieces of matter orbiting within the atom, and sometimes as tiny packets of energy lapping wavelike around it. Likewise, forms of energy that might be emitted by the atom, such as light, which it had become customary to think of as traveling in waves, now came to be regarded also as streams of tiny particle-like packets of energy, or *quanta.* Major contributors to these new concepts were Einstein—the most universal of scientific theorists since Newton—together with Max Planck and Erwin Schrödinger.

It was also necessary to define most carefully what it was, within the world of the atom, that was to be observed, and how this could be done. In the 1920s, Werner Heisenberg announced a new basic concept of physics: the *principle of uncertainty,* which states that it is impossible to observe at the same time both the position and the motion of a subatomic particle. The reason is that the particle is so tiny that there is no way of observing it without significantly influencing either its position or its motion.

Many physicists, including Einstein, feared that the uncertainty principle would make the internal workings of the atom unknowable, but this turned out not to be so. True, physicists had to give up hope of ever "looking" at an individual atom, as Galileo had looked at Jupiter and its moons (p. 421). Still, physicists could theorize on the basis of large numbers of atoms so as to predict what the "average atom" would most likely do—rather as a market research company can never know for certain what brand of breakfast cereal an individual consumer will buy, but given data about many consumers, can predict with very high probability which brand the average one will purchase. And even if subatomic particles could not be directly observed inside the atom, they could be knocked out of atoms by powerful beams of rays or streams of other particles; their probable paths could be indirectly tracked and measured once they had been released in this way; and from these data it was possible, by complex calculations, to "read back" to conditions within the atom. Thus an array of increasingly powerful "atom-smashing" and later "particle-smashing" devices has made atomic physics one of the most spectacular and expensive branches of science.

With the help of concepts and devices such as these, physicists were able to perceive how the atom works to produce many features of the physical world as we know it. By the 1930s, it was known that the differences among chemical elements are due to the different numbers of various subatomic particles among the atoms that make up the elements; and that radioactivity, electricity, and light are the result of the emission of particles by atoms, the flow of particles among them, and the change of position of particles within them. This theoretical knowledge had far-reaching practical consequences. Thus, it was the understanding of the flow of electrons among atoms in certain types of solid materials—the "semiconductors"—that made possible the miniaturization of electronic components, enabling complex devices like televisions and computers to become cheap, compact, and hence widespread.

Fission and Fusion. As for the actual workings of the atom as a system in itself, from the 1930s onward, the original model devised by Rutherford and Bohr, of a proton-filled nucleus with electrons orbiting around it (p. 525), grew increasingly complex. New atom- and particle-smashing devices revealed ever more subatomic particles that theoretical physicists then had to incorporate into the model; or the theorists themselves, in order to account for discrepancies in the model, would think up new particles, or new forces acting on the particles, for which the atom- and particle-smashing devices would sooner or later provide actual evidence.

Some of the most significant discoveries made in this way concerned the structure and behavior of the atomic nucleus. This turned out to consist of two kinds of particles, protons and neutrons, clamped together by the action of a hitherto unsuspected force, the "strong interaction." Nevertheless, in 1938, Enrico Fermi succeeded in breaking apart some of the relatively large clumps of particles that formed the nuclei of uranium atoms. About ten years later, it became clear that the relatively small clumps of particles that formed the nuclei of hydrogen atoms could be forced together to create larger nuclei.

Either way, these processes of *nuclear fission* and *nuclear fusion* involved the conversion of tiny amounts of mass into vast amounts of energy (according to Einstein's principles; p. 526). Furthermore, they released neutrons that would hit the nuclei of neighboring atoms and start the same processes there, initiating *chain reactions* of enormous power. These discoveries led to the atom and hydrogen bombs (pp. 591, 599), which make use of uncontrolled fission and fusion chain reactions, respectively; and to the use of controlled fission in nuclear power stations (p. 625). Scientists still hope to learn how to control fusion reactions so as to fulfill the dream of cheap, plentiful, and nonpolluting energy.

Recently, the complex picture of particles and forces at work in the atom has been simplified in various ways. In the 1960s, physicists began to suspect that many of the newly discovered particles could be regarded as differing combinations of no more than three still tinier entities—*quarks,* as these perhaps truly basic constituents of matter were christened by one of those mainly responsible for the idea, the American Murray Gell-Mann. Another American, Steven Weinberg, together with a Pakistani, Abdus Salam, showed that two of the forces at work within the atom, electromagnetism and the "weak interaction" among particles outside the nucleus, were in fact one and the same force.

Atomic physicists hope that discoveries such as these are stepping-stones toward a "Grand Unified Theory," which in the not too distant future may show that all the various forms of matter and energy in the universe are all manifestations of a very few basic particles and perhaps only a single force. If this is in fact achieved, at least some physicists believe, it will mark the end of a stage in the Western quest for rational understanding of the physical "nature of things" that began in ancient Greece more than 2,500 years ago (pp. 79–80).

DISCOVERING THE MAKEUP OF LIVING ORGANISMS

Similar progress toward what seems like an ultimate explanation of one of the main features of the natural world has been made by scientists investigating the basic structure of living organisms and the ways in which they reproduce and grow.

Already in the nineteenth and early twentieth centuries, there had been many advances in this field (pp. 526, 527–528). Biologists had found that organisms are built up of cells, and that growth and reproduction take place by means of cell division. They had come to believe that hereditary characteristics are transmitted from one organism to another by means of *genes* and that the genes are somehow present in the central structure of the cell, the *nucleus.* Chemists had found that cells are made up of some of the same elements, formed in the same way into molecules (although far bigger and more complex) as nonliving matter. They had identified many of the resulting substances, which seemed to be basic building blocks of life, as well as two substances of unknown function within the cell: *ribonucleic* and *deoxyribonucleic acid* (RNA and DNA).

Later twentieth-century researchers assembled these scattered pieces of evidence and followed where they pointed—and more and more, the researchers found that they were led to the mysterious substances RNA and DNA. By the 1940s, it was known that the molecules of both consist of extremely lengthy strands built up of four basic units, the order of which continually varies along the strands. Experiments with bacteria (p. 526) showed that a bacterial variety with a rough-coated exterior could be altered to have a smooth exterior when "fed" with DNA from a closely related, smooth-coated variety. It seemed, then, that somehow, within its molecular structure, DNA carried the genes, and had the ability to transfer them from one cell to another. But how did it do this?

In 1953, an Englishman, Francis Crick, and an American, James D. Watson, opened the way to answering this question with their famous "double-helix" model of the DNA molecule. The molecule consists, they said, not of one but of two identical strands, interconnected along their lengths and twisted around each other. In the course of cell division, the two strands break apart and untwist, so that each can carry its genes into a new cell. Then, as each strand settles down within the newly formed nucleus, by chemical combination with surrounding substances it produces for itself a new "partner" strand. Thus these two, in turn, can separate when the time comes, thereby transferring their genes to yet further cells.

On the basis of this insight, molecular biologists have been able to build up as full a picture of the inner workings of the living cell as physicists have done with the atom. All of the following are now fairly well understood: the way in which DNA strands sometimes replicate themselves in the slightly different form of RNA; how RNA, in turn, combines with surrounding substances to produce the many complex chemicals that make up living organisms; the actual "genetic code," the different sequences of the four basic chemical units along the strands of DNA and RNA; and details of the ways in which these processes are speeded, blocked, or altered so as to foster or discourage cell growth, or to produce different kinds of cells and hence different organisms.

THE ADVENT OF HIGH TECHNOLOGY

Ever since the link between science and technology was forged in the nineteenth century, the human race has lived in a state of "permanent" industrial revolution (pp. 506–508). But in the twentieth century, this revolution accelerated as science reached the point of unlocking truly cosmic powers, and technology found ways of harnessing these powers for use (and abuse) by society. The result, from about the middle of the century onward, was an explosion of new types of machines, processes, materials, medicines, and weapons that seemed so marvelous (or so threatening) that as a group they came to be called "high technology."

Of course, the rise of high technology was not the result of scientific advance alone. To translate "pure" scientific knowledge into usable technology takes "applied" scientists and engineers obsessed with technical problems, and corporation executives hungry to stake the biggest claim in new and profitable markets; in the second half of the twentieth century, more than in earlier times, it also often took generals and admirals bent on victory in wars or arms races. The fact that the United States had plenty of all three types, as well as massive resources for investment and a massive home market for new products, helped make it, more than any other country, the homeland of high technology.

Computers and Electronics. That, for example, is why the United States led the world in the single most spectacular field of high technology, computers. It was advances in the "pure" mathematical field of information theory that made computers possible, and discoveries in the "pure" science of semiconductor physics that made them cheap and small enough to be everywhere. Generals and admirals, wanting to win the Second World War and then the Cold War, spent the money to jump-start many computer technologies at a time when they seemed too risky and unprofitable for private companies. In the 1940s, the U.S. Department of Defense sponsored the first-ever computer in hopes of speeding up the production of mathematical data needed for heavy artillery; in the 1950s, it invested in computer-controlled machine tools that would accurately make complex parts for state-of-the-art warplanes; in the 1960s and 1970s, its scientists developed ways of linking military and government research computers into "interactive networks" that would be so decentralized that not even a hydrogen bomb hit could totally knock them out. And once all these basic technologies had been proved, the engineers and corporation executives moved in. The results were mainframes and desktops, automated factories and "smart" photocopiers, the Internet and the World Wide Web.

Biotechnology. At the end of the twentieth century, another, very much older field of technology had been pulled forward by "pure" science to the point where it was producing just as spectacular results as computers—that of biotechnology.

For thousands of years, humans have manipulated living things, or products derived from living things, by such processes as selective breeding, cooking, brewing, and distilling. What turned biotechnology into high technology was the rise of new methods and processes derived from "pure" biochemical understanding of the living cell as a chemical "factory." In the 1970s, an American molecular biologist, Paul Berg, managed to "cut" DNA strands and recombine the pieces in a different order, thereby altering also the order of their basic chemical units to produce new types of genes. Many different types of *recombinant DNA* were developed, which could be implanted in the DNA of bacteria to alter their genetic makeup. In this way, new strains of bacteria could be created, with the "hereditary" capacity to produce biological substances useful to humans—for example, insulin, an essential medicine for people with diabetes.

The result, in the 1980s and 1990s, was the growth of a whole new industry of *genetic engineering.* In this new industry, "pure" and "applied" science were hard to tell apart. As a result, "pure" scientists were often directly involved in genetic engineering, and it was mainly sponsored by civilian bureaucrats eager to get a return on government funding for pure science, and by college presidents dreaming of patent royalties from discoveries made by their biochemistry departments.

In any case, genetic engineering became a massive industry as computers had before, and early in the twenty-first century, it passed an important milestone. In the 1990s, scientists came to realize that for this new industry to reach its full potential, it would be necessary to be able to identify the location of the genes in the DNA molecules of various species, ranging from bacteria to mice, that were commonly used in genetic engineering—and also, most ambitiously, of humans themselves. Without this information, genetic engineers were like readers in a library with many stacks, tens of thousands of books, and no catalogue or floor plan. The completion in 2000 of the human "genome-mapping" project meant that the catalogue and floor plan were now available to anyone who needed them, though most of the books themselves were still unopened.

THE CHALLENGE TO CONTEMPORARY CULTURE AND BELIEFS

In all these and many other ways, the onrush of discovery brought humanity to previously unsuspected realms of knowledge, while its technological applications transformed daily life. In addition, the rise of science to become the predominant intellectual enterprise of the human race could not fail to affect many other fields of thought and culture—and very often the result was unsettling.

Partly this was because science, precisely because it was so successful at explaining the material universe, left many other matters all the more mysterious. Human beings, it seemed, could be explained as complex assemblages of molecules that interacted in just the same way as those that made up plastics and dyestuffs. Where, in such an explanation, did such things as consciousness and free will fit in? The universe, physicists hoped, would soon be explained as the outcome of the interactions of a few grandly simple forces and particles. Where, in this explanation, did a creating and intervening God fit in? Earlier mythologies, theologies, and philosophical systems had generally contrived to link the material universe, human consciousness, and religious faith into a single whole; but science, by its very success in explaining the first of these things, seemed to shoulder the other two aside.

Moreover, the procedures of science, with its theories that were constantly modified or discarded in the light of new knowledge, and its principles of uncertainty and relativity that explained phenomena in terms of probabilities and the viewpoint of observers, seemed to go against traditional philosophical, religious, and artistic ideals of truth. Even if the physicists realized their dream of a Grand Unified Theory, the total insight into the material universe that it would provide gave little promise of having much to do with the age-old human quest for "ultimate" or "absolute" reality.

Likewise, the achievements of technology were in many ways double-edged. On the one hand, technology enormously increased human freedom and power; on the other, it raised the question whether creatures so used to being at the mercy of each other and the universe as humans could live with all this freedom and power. At the beginning of the twenty-first century, the World Wide Web seemed a kind of symbol of the new freedom—an enormous marketplace where everyone was equal, and where even an ancient and prestigious institution like the British monarchy was just another "vendor," offering its wares of information, entertainment, and products to the passing surfer (*Fig. 16.1*). But the surfer's path from Web site to Web site could be tracked keystroke by keystroke by anyone who had the expertise and equipment to do so, just as the genetic "destiny" of individuals could be tracked from gene to gene.

Thus technology also offered the possibility of an "anthill society" where individuals were controlled and manipulated—as well, of course, as the threat of environmental disaster or nuclear extinction. In some ways, it made the individual seem even more than before at the mercy of vast impersonal forces in society and the universe.

Fig. 16.1 The British Monarchy's Web Site. At right, the royal home page announces a religious service for deserving subjects whom the queen has honored by conferring on them knighthood and other distinguished titles. At left, there is a link to information on photos and photographers of the "royals." The monarchy still presides over the nation as it has done for a thousand years, but it is also part of the global culture of mass information and mass entertainment. Either way, it needs the Internet to reach its subjects and the world.

Of course, many other forces were at work in the cultural life of the twentieth century besides the onrush of science and technology. But there is no doubt that alongside the traumatic happenings of that century, science and technology have had a great deal to do with several differing trends in modern culture. Many writers, artists, and architects have glorified scientific and technical mastery in their work; others have abandoned the external world to science and technology, and retreated into an inner world of human consciousness, usually imagined as irrational and subjective; still others have imagined the individual as alone in an indifferent or hostile society or universe. Some philosophers have tried to imitate scientific method, with its gradual approach to limited truth through provisional theories; others have developed the idea of the lonely individual struggling against vast natural and social forces. And many religious thinkers have challenged the idea that science provides the only knowable kind of truth, and continue to proclaim an absolute spiritual truth beyond the material truth of science.

Reconstruction in Western Philosophy and Religion

One of the areas most affected by the onrush of science was philosophy. Many philosophers, impressed by Einstein's relativity theory and Heisenberg's uncertainty principle (pp. 525–526, 643), virtually gave up efforts to explain objective "reality." They generally agreed that no such explanation is possible. The two most influential schools of philosophy in the twentieth century were those of the "linguistic analysts" and the "existentialists." The former held that nothing significant could be said about "being in general"; they focused attention, therefore, on limited intellectual problems, especially the applications of symbolic (mathematical) logic. The existentialists insisted that our very humanity prevents us from seeing things in themselves.

As in all times of change and upheaval, inherited beliefs and ways died hard. The idea of progress, born of the Enlightenment, still persisted—especially in the United States. As we saw in Chapter 14, "old-fashioned" liberalism in Europe had become discredited by 1919 (p. 567); and the void was filled, in part, by Marxism, fascism, or extreme nationalism.

Some disillusioned Westerners turned, or returned, to traditional Christian doctrines. The crimes and horrors of world wars and revolutions heightened their awareness of "evil" and man's "sinful nature," and their quest for truth beyond the findings of science led them to the centuries-old intellectual system of Christian theology. In response, certain religious leaders—notably, the American Reinhold Niebuhr—rekindled Augustinian teachings (pp. 178–179) and called for a resurgence of orthodoxy and ritualism.

THE IMPLICATIONS OF DEPTH PSYCHOLOGY: FREUD

The source of the twentieth-century challenge lay as much in the new psychology as in the new physics: John Locke's simplistic view of the mind (pp. 429–430) was as completely superseded as Newton's mechanics. The major figure of modern psychology was Sigmund Freud, the pioneer of the discipline (p. 531). Freud was a practicing physician whose initial interest was in curing the mental ailments of his patients. In the course of his clinical work, however, he discovered aspects of the human mind and personality that had long lain hidden. Freud published his first significant work, *The Interpretation of Dreams,* in 1900, but his broader impact on thought was not felt until after the First World War.

Though Freudian psychology has been disputed and amended (especially his views on female sexuality), much of its substance gained acceptance. Freud held that human beings are not rational machines, consciously directing their appetites and will. On the contrary, the conscious life and its expression are but a covering of the "real" person. Beneath the surface are unconscious and subconscious drives, which are the chief engines of motivation; these include the desire for sexual gratification, love, power, and even death. In addition, behavior is influenced by physiological responses and acquired attitudes.

Society, Freud wrote in *Civilization and Its Discontents* (1930), compels individuals to *repress* many of their "natural" desires, and without some repression, civilization would be impossible. The "normal" person accepts the damage without breaking down, but the neurotic (or psychotic) person cannot do so. The Freudian view of the individual in relationship to society posed a sharp challenge to traditional morals, religion, and politics. All those had rested on a base of supposed rationality and conscious control. According to the new view, those traditions were not geared to psychological reality and might therefore be dangerously false. Freud believed that human personality would suffer even under "enlightened" social codes of behavior, because there exists an inescapable conflict between personal drives and the social order. Hence, "perfectionist" social dreams can never be fulfilled, and the goal of complete individual happiness is a tormenting mirage.

REJECTION OF TRADITIONAL SYSTEMS AND VALUES: NIETZSCHE, KIERKEGAARD, SARTRE

Friedrich Nietzsche, a German philosopher who died in 1900, lived in Freud's time and shared many of his views on human nature. And the impact of both men was most strongly felt in the twentieth century. Nietzsche's influence was perhaps wider than Freud's, for he challenged not only the traditional view of human nature but the entire institutional and ideological heritage of the West. When he said, "God is dead," he meant not only the God of the Judeo-Christian faith but the whole range of philosophical *absolutes,* from Plato down to his own day. Because all Western values had been linked to those ultimate "eternal" values, they crashed to earth with "God's death."

Nietzsche's most revealing work is his most poetic, *Thus Spake Zarathustra* (1884). In it he allowed his unconscious self to speak freely, without regard to logical organization. The book is a flowing stream of images, symbols, and visions, some of which have not yet been fully understood. In *Zarathustra* and other works, notably *Beyond Good and Evil* (1886), Nietzsche considered the various conditions of human beings and their relation to the universe. He was one of the first thinkers to stress the absurdity of human existence: the inability of our reason to comprehend our surroundings—though we are born to try.

All existing systems, whether based on reason or revelation, appeared false to Nietzsche. He focused his attack on the bourgeois civilization of the late nineteenth century: on science, industrialism, democracy, and Christianity. As an untamed individualist, he rejected theism (belief in God as Creator and Ruler), mechanism, and any other idea that would deny human freedom. What he hated most was the reduction of people to narrowly specialized creatures and their subjection to a Christian ("slave") morality. Nietzsche presented these particular ideas most fully in *The Genealogy of Morals,* published in 1887. He longed for a return to the heroic Greek idea of the "whole man"; this goal could be achieved only by the overthrow of current values and the permitting of determined individuals ("supermen") to recover their wholeness through disciplined struggle and sacrifice. Nietzsche left unanswered many questions as to how these aims could be accomplished. His importance lay primarily in his bold challenge to "sacred" beliefs and in his bitter protest against the smothering of the individual by the "herd."

A thinker of different temperament was Søren Kierkegaard, a Danish theologian-philosopher. Though he was born a generation earlier than Nietzsche, the influence of both was felt at about the same time. Writing from widely separated points of view, they were the forerunners of twentieth-century existentialism. It was in fact Kierkegaard who gave special meaning to the word "existence" (though his works were scarcely read until after the First World War). He defined existence as a unique attribute of human beings. They alone exist "outside" nature, possessing the power to think about the universe and to choose what they will believe and how they will act. This very freedom, thought Kierkegaard, gives individuals both responsibility and anxiety (*Angst*). They must suffer anxiety, for they can never be certain about the consequences of their own free choice.

Kierkegaard, like Nietzsche, attacked Hegel's view that the world is rational and that it represents the unfolding of a divine plan (pp. 479–480). How can any person, a particular part of an uncompleted scheme, know what the completed form will be? If the world is a system, only God can know it! It follows, therefore, that people cannot presume that they occupy a specific place in a known scheme of things. One must act, rather, from day to day, as best one can, always unsure of the consequences.

Kierkegaard had a profound influence on Christian theologians, but his writings appealed also to individuals of agnostic or atheistic leanings—especially, modern "existentialists." These people were impressed by Kierkegaard's assertion of the individual's nakedness and loneliness in the universe—"condemned to be free." They saw the individual increasingly depersonalized and alienated by the forces of modern society: huge economic organizations, mechanization, bureaucratization, and the high level of abstraction encountered in most phases of living. Following this observation, the existentialists sought to awaken in each person a sense of individuality and the possibility of an "authentic" life.

Jean-Paul Sartre, more than any other writer, brought the existentialist view to the educated public (through *Nausea, No Exit,* and other works). Sartre, partly through his own experience in the French Resistance against the Nazis, came to believe that personal commitment and action are essential to genuine living. He felt this especially during the war, in his daily decision making and risk taking. He proved to himself that even in extreme situations, the individual possesses the irreducible liberty of saying "no" to overpowering force. Such a force, Sartre inferred, might be an occupying army—or it might be the conformist cultures in which most of us live (p. 516). The freedom to say "no," even to "disaffiliate" oneself from the system, is the individual's ultimate defense against being swallowed up as a person.

Sartre himself in later years severely modified his wartime view of the degree of individual freedom. He conceded (as a Marxist) the powerful grip of social conditioning—yet insisted that each individual nevertheless has the ability (and the responsibility) to "make something out of what is made of him." Sartre's idea of limited freedom contrasted with the optimistic, rational liberalism of the Enlightenment (pp. 428–431). It was closer to the "tragic view" of the ancient Greek poets and dramatists, who likewise saw pain and absurdity in the human condition, yet held that one remains responsible for what one is and does within an established order (pp. 87–88).

REVISION IN CHRISTIAN THEOLOGY: BARTH, TILLICH

The blow to "systems" and "absolutes" in philosophy was paralleled by a rethinking of Christian doctrines. Here, too, Kierkegaard was the pioneer. A deeply committed Christian, Kierkegaard insisted that rational proofs for the existence of God, promoted by some liberal theologians, were irrelevant. In order to become a Christian, asserted Kierkegaard, one must make an inward choice: a leap into faith. All other human choices, he insisted, are secondary to that one. And that choice must be made without knowledge of whether it will lead to salvation or damnation. Thus a true Christian lives in a kind of despair. (Kierkegaard attacked most modern churches for enjoying and preaching a "comfortable" but counterfeit Christianity—"the opposite of what is in the New Testament.")

The leading theologians of the twentieth century advanced, in their own ways, this fundamental view of Kierkegaard's. Karl Barth, an influential Swiss Protestant theologian, stressed human dependence on God, but concluded that there is no straight line from the mind of humans to God: "What we say breaks apart constantly . . . producing paradoxes which are held together in seeming unity only by agile and arduous running to and fro on our part." Rather than preaching that there are compelling reasons for believing in God, religious thinkers like Barth would say, "This community of faith invites you to share in its venture of trust and commitment."

In addition to seeing religious faith as a matter of trust instead of something "objectively" proven, many theologians of the twentieth century sought to reconstruct the ancient symbols and myths. They believed that the traditional Christian image of God and the universe had crumbled under the bombardment of scientific findings and historical scholarship. The vision of reality expressed in the Bible no longer served as a believable frame of reference for many educated people. They were convinced that if Christianity was to endure as a meaningful teaching, it would have to create images that fitted with scientific knowledge.

To some religious thinkers, this was another way of saying, "God is dead." For the German American theologian Paul Tillich, the phrase meant simply that the ancient image of God had passed into history. This did not mean that Christianity was obsolete but rather that it had to find, as it had found in the past, new forms to carry its message to the living. The idea of a Supreme Being "out there" or "up there" is not an essential part of Christian truth. Tillich dissented from Barth's view that God lives outside humankind; he insisted that God is not a special part of creation but rather Ultimate Reality itself. Modern men and women, Tillich suggested in *Shaking of the Foundations* (1948), must look for God as the depth and center of their culture and their lives.

THE MOVEMENT TOWARD UNITY: POPE JOHN XXIII

Though the Protestant churches were more absorbed than the Roman Catholic Church in theological reappraisal, all the major branches of Christianity gave serious attention to closer relations with one another. The period following the Second World War, especially, was marked by a lessening of interfaith hostility and a growing sense of Christian oneness. This was due in part to the consciousness that all churches were being challenged, as never before, by secularism in general and Marxism in particular. Religious leaders could see that many people were turning toward agnosticism (no belief) and that a more united front would strengthen the appeal and power of Christianity.

On the Protestant side, an important step was taken in 1948 when the World Council of Churches was formally established at Geneva, Switzerland. One of its primary purposes was to bring some two hundred separate denominations into closer association. It included in its supporting membership most Protestant churches, Anglicans, and Eastern Orthodox groups (pp. 178, 278–279, 380–384). The Vatican held aloof at first but later opened formal relations with Geneva.

The election by the College of Cardinals (p. 233) of Pope John XXIII in 1958 gave a decisive boost to the movement toward unity. As leader of the largest organized body of Christians, John was in a position to aid greatly, and he did so with the full force of his warm personality. Though he did not abandon the papal claim to being the "one shepherd" of the Christian flock, John broke down centuries-old barriers to communication with Protestants. At the same time, he started a sweeping program for *aggiorna-*

mento (bringing the Roman Church up to date). This included a fresh attitude of humility and affection toward the "separated brethren" (no longer "heretics")—and toward "men of good will" beyond the fold (no longer "atheists").

The most complete expression of Pope John's thought and feeling was his encyclical *Pacem in Terris* (Peace on Earth), issued in 1963. This document, an extraordinary appeal to reason and humane sentiments, called for the harmonious coexistence of all faiths and social systems. John's work for peace, both religious and secular, was carried on after his death by Pope Paul VI and the reforming Second Vatican Council (1963–1965). Paul dramatized the new responsiveness of the papacy by breaking its historic confinement to Rome and making visits to such places as the Holy Land, India, Latin America, and the United Nations headquarters in New York. Paul secured friendlier relations with the Eastern Orthodox churches and renounced the traditional Christian hostility toward Jews. On issues of Catholic faith and morals, he remained a conservative. His immediate successor, in 1978, was the reputedly liberal John Paul I, but he died unexpectedly within months of becoming pope. In his place the College of Cardinals elected a conservative pontiff, in the mold of Paul VI.

JOHN PAUL II: RENEWAL OF CATHOLIC TRADITIONALISM

The new pope, who took the name John Paul II, was the first non-Italian elected to the office in over four hundred years. Formerly the archbishop of Cracow, in Poland, he was a learned and appealing figure—known especially for his resistance to the Communist government there. During his long reign as pope, John Paul urged the clergy to uphold traditional roles and rules, and he reinforced his advice by appointing bishops of established conservative views. A notable result of this policy occurred in Brazil, the world's largest Catholic country. The leading archbishop there, who had endorsed "liberation theology" (p. 619), was replaced in his position in 1995 by a conservative archbishop—one strongly opposed to social reform in Brazil.

John Paul disappointed many liberal Catholics who were looking for some sign of change on such pressing issues as clerical celibacy, the use of contraceptives, and admission of women to the priesthood. On this last issue, the Anglican Church in Britain and the United States broke with centuries of tradition and ordained women as priests (1993); but the pope remained firmly opposed to the change for the Roman Church.

Though insisting that the Catholic clergy must not hold any political office, the pope traveled widely around the world and spoke freely on political issues. He consistently urged national leaders to avoid war, and he approved an important "pastoral letter" of the Catholic bishops of the United States condemning nuclear weapons. Their letter, *The Challenge of Peace,* was sent out in 1983 as a "teaching" of the Church. It opposed any "first use" of nuclear arms (p. 627), and it appealed for immediate international agreements to end their testing and production.

John Paul attacked what he called the modern "culture of death," including abortion, "mercy killing," and capital punishment. With respect to relations with other Christian churches, the pope followed the path of Paul VI, pursuing closer ties with the Orthodox churches. In 1995, he hosted a historic meeting at the Vatican with Bartholomew, patriarch of Constantinople (Istanbul), generally recognized as the ranking patriarch of Eastern Orthodoxy. They sought to strengthen their own positions of Church leadership and to work together toward checking the growing influence of

Protestantism and secularism. A divisive issue, however, was an ongoing dispute over zones of Christian religious activity. Following the fall of communism, Roman Catholic bishops and missionaries entered the historically Orthodox lands of the former Soviet Union—an intrusion much resented by the patriarchs of those countries.

John Paul established a unique legacy of his reign in March 2000. During the course of the liturgy of the Sunday Mass in Saint Peter's Basilica, the seventy-nine-year-old pope offered the most sweeping apology for past sins "by children of the Church" ever publicly expressed. As the new millennium opened, he asked God's forgiveness for errors made during the preceding two thousand years. He declared that this "purification of memory" was essential as the Church moves forward with its evangelical mission. Though not specifying individual events, he placed them in seven categories: general sins; sins in the service of truth; sins against Christian unity; against the Jews; against respect for love, peace, and cultures; against the dignity of women and minorities; and against human rights.

The Shifting Ways of Society

Religious and philosophical teachings and problems, no matter what their character, did little to alter the continuing social revolution in the West. Technology was the chief engine of this revolution, but psychologists, educators, and advertisers accelerated the rate of change.

THE NEW SEXUALITY

The most visible, and perhaps the most profound, of these changes were new sexual attitudes and practices (the "sexual revolution"). Sex has been a demanding concern in all societies: how to value sex and how to deny, repress, or channel it. Sex can be regarded as any or all of the following: an instinctive impulse, a source of pleasure, the means of creating children, an expression of physical love, the bond of faithfulness in marriage, a sign of gender, and a personal property. Social and moral codes of behavior aim to contain and balance the multiple functions of both male and female sexuality.

During the nineteenth century, while scientific and technological innovations were altering the economy and society in the West, religious and civic leaders made a determined effort to prevent changes in traditional sexual mores. Thus during the Victorian Age (1840–1900), a cloak of puritan morality obscured the realities of sexual behavior. It was Sigmund Freud who, by reporting his clinical observations, showed that sexual repression could cause psychic illness . Freud, by bringing sexuality into the open, revealed it as a normal and powerful force in human behavior.

As the twentieth century progressed, other physicians, psychologists, and educators challenged all types of authoritarian controls over individuals—not only in sexual matters but in personal behavior as a whole. Traditional taboos began to fall, especially after the two world wars; the age of "permissiveness" and "self-fulfillment" was at hand. With moral, social, and legal restraints loosened, men and women gave freer rein to their instincts for self-gratification. In 1960, scientific medicine gave a liberating boost to worry-free sex: a new means of birth control, the "pill," made sex easy and "safe."

(In the 1980s, however, the appearance of the AIDS disease brought fresh worries to the sexual scene; p. 660.)

The sexual revolution was quickly exploited by profit-seeking publishers, theatrical producers, broadcasters, and filmmakers. Sex manuals flourished; no one any longer had to be ignorant. Magazines and books catered to the newly released desire for titillation, and the walls of literary censorship were leveled in nearly every Western nation (p. 663). Pornography, hard and soft, became readily available—in both verbal and pictorial forms. The ultimate in pictorial pornography seemed to have been reached in X-rated videotapes for home use—until the advent of pornographic Web sites.

Among the sexually provocative magazines, the most respectable and successful in the United States is *Playboy,* first issued in 1953. Its self-made publisher, Hugh Hefner, also built a thriving entertainment business around his magazine—geared to the theme of guilt-free sensual enjoyment. His *Playboy* "philosophy" is a modern form of historic hedonism (p. 80).

The new hedonism reaches, of course, beyond the frontiers of sexuality. Huge industries have been built around the popular hunger for every sort of pleasure. Given good health and sufficient income, people in the West today enjoy limitless opportunities for personal gratification. There is, unfortunately, another and darker side of the pleasures of freedom. This is best exemplified by the widespread consumption of illegal drugs throughout the Western world. The drug problem is now recognized as a serious threat to the health of millions of individuals—and to the functioning of every technological society. It also feeds a related problem: organized crime. Though enormous human and financial resources have been marshaled to fight against both drugs and crime, the battle seems far from won. A leading cause of this failure is the stress placed on personal freedom within most democratic countries, which tends to counter the efforts of law enforcement. Thus many activities ("evils") that "good citizens" deplore—such as drugs, crime, and pornography—are closely linked to freedom itself.

THE YOUTH CULTURE

The changing ways of Western society have had their main effect on men and women born after the Second World War. Their fathers and mothers were, as a rule, too rooted in older ways to alter their own views or behavior. But the immediate postwar generation in most Western countries grew up within a radically different culture. Especially for the middle classes, the postwar period was a time of widespread affluence and leisure. The dominant materialistic morality placed high value on competitiveness, achievement, and "success." As pointed out by the existentialists (pp. 650–651), it was an era of bureaucracy, depersonalization, manipulation, and social "adjustment." All this, moreover, was seen and heard each day in the "instant" world of radio, television, films, records, and tapes.

The 1960s: The Counterculture. Parents expected their children to accept these cultural gifts with appreciation—and many of them did—but a substantial minority experienced a disturbing sense of alienation. Not having to struggle for a livelihood, as most of their Depression-reared fathers and mothers had done, they found more time to reflect on the surrounding culture and their relation to it. These young people found much to object to. Taking for granted the ability of "the system" to satisfy their basic physical needs and pleasures, they saw in its workings a lessening of their personal identity and a great deal of hypocrisy, violence, and injustice.

These perceptions arose at a time when the philosophical and psychological barriers to doubt and idol-breaking had largely dissolved under the influence of thinkers like Freud, Sartre, and Tillich. By the 1960s, many among the postwar generation felt free to move in their own way—toward creating a "counterculture." While uncertain and groping, they appeared to share some central goals: humaneness in personal relations, self-discovery and independence, sexual freedom and equality, simple enjoyments, love of nature and peace. As a badge of these beliefs, the young revolted against adult styles of dress and began to develop styles of their own. The long hair, beards, fatigue jackets, and jeans—so repugnant to older believers in clean-shaven, starch-shirted efficiency and conformity—were symbolic challenges to the established order of values. Likewise, the young tended to be suspicious of governments, corporations, and military organizations. And they often scorned intellectualism in favor of "spontaneous experience."

The freshness of their approach and their willingness to try something new offered promise of creative ideas and remedies where old methods had failed. The parents of this generation, having recovered from their initial shock and disapproval, seemed increasingly to recognize some promise in their children. In the United States, for example, a constitutional amendment was passed in 1971 that lowered the voting age from twenty-one to eighteen years.

The 1960s: The Student Movement. The youth activity found its focus in colleges and universities; from there it spread, in considerable measure, to the rest of society. Students thus formed a leading part of the larger youth culture, but much of their concern was naturally with the campus environment. Universities had mushroomed after the Second World War. They had become, especially in the United States, vast aggregations of researchers, teachers, and students. They represented hundreds of millions of dollars in capital investment and served as the principal workshops for the production and spread of specialized knowledge. Many students saw their universities as examples of corporate bureaucracy—a huge machine that reduced the individual to a number. They conceived of the university also as a service center ("multiversity") for the larger society—preparing technicians for business and industry, conducting research for the military establishment, and turning young people into pliable servants of the state. Individual courses and curricular requirements often appeared to them as arbitrary and sterile—lacking in "relevance" to them.

In the 1960s, student discontent was translated into protest—then rebellion—at many educational centers around the world. In the United States, the movement began at the University of California at Berkeley. The "Free Speech Movement" of 1964 sought a larger exercise of student political rights on campus; it also demanded (among other things) that the highly regarded and highly paid professors spend more of their time teaching students. Demonstrations, sit-ins, and classroom "strikes" followed in support of these demands.

The protests soon spread to hundreds of other campuses, and "local" demands often were combined with demands on the nation as a whole: end the war in Vietnam (pp. 617–618), check the power of the "military-industrial complex," stop discrimination against African Americans and other minorities. The student actions were generally led by small numbers of committed radicals, who hoped to bring on a general dislocation and change of the social order. Their immediate demands, however, often had sufficient merit and attractiveness to win the support of moderate students as well. When college administrations overreacted, still larger numbers of students joined the action.

Protest fever ran high in 1969 and reached a climax in May 1970, immediately following the United States invasion of Cambodia. In response to student violence at Kent State University in Ohio, National Guardsmen were called in to restore order. During a "clearing maneuver," they shot and killed four students; a few days later, state patrolmen killed two youths in a confrontation at Jackson State College in Mississippi. A severe reaction against the student movement promptly set in. Many Americans were shocked by the killings; others blamed the students for damaging property and thus bringing on the ugly consequences.

After Kent State, "the movement" lost much of its force. Most students recoiled from the violent turn it had taken; others became convinced that it had reached a dead end; still others thought that "the system" had been opened up a bit. Actually, the American student protests of the 1960s seldom achieved great immediate successes. In many instances, however, they gave added force to university reforms that expanded student rights and benefits.

In Europe, Japan, and Latin America, during these same years, students protested against grossly inadequate facilities and outmoded curricula. They also sought wider power over national affairs. A student revolt in Paris in 1968 very nearly toppled the government of President de Gaulle; strikes and demonstrations had to be forcibly put down in Mexico City and Tokyo. Discontent and protest are by no means novel among university students. But seldom before had protest been linked so closely to the profound alienation of youth from the established culture and order.

In the 1970s, college campuses, particularly in the United States, grew peaceful once again. Students withdrew to more personal concerns: to careers, to greater "inner awareness," to religion, or even to self-centered ways that have been called narcissistic (the "me" generation). They were sobered, too, by the fewer job opportunities, and in the 1980s and 1990s, preparing for a good job became the first concern of a majority of students. But another important reason for their changed attitude and conduct was that most of them now possessed the freedoms of lifestyle that previous students had worked for in the 1960s.

THE WOMEN'S MOVEMENT

The youth culture, in its core values, was linked to the long tradition of humanism in the West (pp. 336–344). And that tradition, in its current expression, supports equality for both young and old—and for both women and men. It is a cruel yet undeniable historical fact that women have suffered severe deprivation in most civilizations; education and political rights have been withheld from them, and the professions have been generally closed to them. In the United States, after the end of the Civil War in 1865, some energetic feminists undertook a long and painful campaign to win equality of opportunity with men. Women gradually moved into jobs in industry, commerce, and education and began to insist on broader legal and political rights. Most notable among their leaders were Elizabeth Cady Stanton and Susan B. Anthony.

Their demand for the right to vote (suffrage) met with strong resistance—from some females as well as males. Opponents charged that the feminine intellect was unable to deal with problems of government and that political equality with men would diminish feminine charm and loosen family ties. But the "suffragettes" pushed on toward their goal. Finally, the politicians responded. Impressed by the contributions of women to the American effort in the First World War, Congress at war's end proposed the Nineteenth Amendment to the Constitution. Eliminating all restrictions on voting based on sex, the amendment was ratified by the states in 1920. Since then most other Western nations and Japan have extended the suffrage to women, but the female vote, by itself, appeared to make little immediate difference in the course of politics and legislation.

The 1960s Renewal of Feminism: Women's Liberation. Interest in women's rights in America was subdued for some forty years after approval of the Nineteenth Amendment. But in the 1960s, efforts started up again, and by the early 1970s, the women's liberation movement was in full swing. Social conditions had altered a great deal since 1920: more women were working outside the home, and improved contraceptive devices (as well as more easily obtained abortions) were making it practicable for women to control their traditional role of childbearing.

At first, the expanding ideas and goals of feminism were limited to a small number of "emancipated" women; but books, magazines, and the mass media soon aroused the enthusiasm of hundreds of thousands. A key work, *The Second Sex,* by the French author Simone de Beauvoir, called worldwide attention to numerous false assumptions about women. But it was chiefly *The Feminine Mystique,* written by an American, Betty Friedan, and published in 1963, that sparked the popular response. She pointed to the social and psychological pressures that kept women in the home, the false notions about female sexuality, and the persisting stereotypes of female intellect and behavior. Friedan became a political activist in order to further her cause, founding the National Organization for Women (NOW) in 1966. Another leading activist and author was Gloria Steinem, cofounder of *Ms.* magazine, a popular journal speaking to and for women, especially feminists.

The women's movement—in part organized, in part unorganized—has employed both advocacy and political action. Its leaders demand an end to discrimination in legal rights, education, and jobs. Feminists in the United States achieved initial political success in bringing about the passage in Congress of a proposed "equal rights" amendment to the Constitution (ERA); it was submitted to the fifty states for ratification in 1972. Opposition to the ERA came from men and women with traditional views, plus some women who feared that it might take away from them such existing advantages as exemption from military conscription, protective laws for women in hazardous occupations, and other established legal benefits. The proposed amendment narrowly failed to win approval by at least thirty-eight states, as required by the Constitution for adoption. President Ronald Reagan and the Republican party opposed the ERA, but Democratic leaders have supported it, and they reintroduced the amendment in Congress in 1985 and in subsequent years. The ultimate fate of the proposal remains in question.

Feminism embraces a wide spectrum of beliefs about social institutions (like marriage and the family), sexual relations, and lifestyles. But contrary to what is alleged by some critics of the movement, very few feminists desire to exchange roles with men. Most of them desire, rather, to open all social roles to both sexes. An increasing number of men, for their part, express agreement with this goal and view its achievement as an enrichment of life for themselves as well as for women. In keeping with this growing feeling for sharing, family relations and responsibilities have become more flexible than in earlier times. In fact, the traditional family unit itself is being challenged by variant forms: the one-person household, the childless household, the single-parent household, and the same-sex household are rising in numbers.

The Abortion Controversy. Probably the most controversial issue affecting American women during the 1980s and 1990s was abortion. In most parts of the world, abortion is and has been permitted, but in the United States, it had been illegal until 1973—though it was in fact widely practiced. In that year, however, the antiabortion laws of two states, Texas and Georgia, were under challenge in the federal courts on the grounds that they violated the constitutional protection of a woman's rights. The resulting decision of the U.S. Supreme Court, by a 7–2 vote, concluded that no state could prevent a woman from having an abortion during the first six months of her pregnancy. The Texas and Georgia laws were therefore declared invalid, and this principle obviously extended to similar laws in other states as well.

This landmark case (*Roe* v. *Wade*) was hailed by feminists and others as a triumph for a woman's "right to control her own body." But a fierce opposition to the ruling also erupted—from many church groups and individuals who asserted that a fetus is a person and therefore abortion is murder. They protested actively (under the "pro-life" banner) and were encouraged during the Reagan years to expect changes in the judicial makeup of the Supreme Court. Reagan's conservative appointments to the high bench (p. 631) did bring about a decided shift in its outlook on abortion and other civil rights matters. In a series of cases in 1989 and 1990, the Court reopened the issues raised earlier by *Roe* v. *Wade* and indicated that some state laws relating to abortion could be constitutional. It was even hoped by the antiabortionists that *Roe* v. *Wade* might be overturned in its entirety. The issue, still controversial, has continued to stir bitter debate throughout the nation and remains an important factor in electoral politics.

Abortion proved to be a prominent issue also at the Fourth United Nations Conference on Women, held in Beijing, China, in 1995. (This influential gathering meets once every ten years.) Attended by five thousand delegates from 189 countries, it reflected a worldwide awakening of women to their individual and collective needs. The conference's concluding "Platform for Action," approved overwhelmingly, contains a declaration that all women possess the right of sexual and reproductive control over their own bodies—part of the conference's stress upon universal human rights. Most of the delegations from Muslim and Roman Catholic countries registered their dissent from this particular declaration. However, there was total agreement by all delegations on the central thrust of the conference deliberations—demands for the economic and political empowerment of women and their protection from physical violence.

Homosexuality. The women's movement, along with growing sexual permissiveness in the West, encouraged the rise of still another social movement, "gay liberation." Homosexuals, historically subject to contempt and abuse, called for the right to live freely according to their own sexual natures. In the 1970s, gay men and lesbians sought changes in laws and institutional practices that would prohibit acts of discrimination against them. Because their aims ran counter to traditional Judeo-Christian moral teachings and ingrained social attitudes, the movement to win public acceptance for sexual diversity encountered fierce hostility.

This feeling was intensified in the 1980s by the sudden appearance of a mysterious viral disease that seemed to affect, mainly, homosexual men. Eventually named the acquired immunodeficiency syndrome (AIDS), this disease is transmitted through bodily fluids and is usually fatal. In the 1990s, however, the AIDS threat receded in advanced Western societies as drugs to manage the disease were developed and the general level of tolerance for male and female homosexuality seems to have increased. However, the rise of homosexuals to the status of an organized interest group challenging traditional values and practices has also led to fierce conflicts over such issues as "gays in the military" and hate crimes legislation.

BELIEFS IN VIOLENCE AND NONVIOLENCE

The frustrations of youth, women, and other groups outside the mainstream gave rise in the 1960s and 1970s to a widespread rejection not only of some institutions but of the accepted ways of altering institutions. The liberal-democratic tradition had generally given citizens a healthy respect for "law and order." The principles of majority rule, proper channels, and legitimate authority had been emphasized by politicians, parents, teachers, and preachers. But in the years of the Vietnam and Middle East wars, some nonconformists began to raise provocative questions: Is it consistent to assert that individual or group acts of violence are "senseless" while governments spend billions on armaments for the mass killings of "enemy" peoples? Are laws necessarily right—or are they simply the products of might?

The answers to such questions are not self-evident. Some individuals argued that it is the aim, rather than the means, that is most important in social actions. The use of violence toward a good end, then, would be permissible; its use to defend a bad institution would be condemned. This line of reasoning led to a belief in "acceptable" violence, supported by arguments drawn from the writings of Luther, Jefferson, Marx, Bakunin, and Nietzsche. The belief appealed most directly to the frustrated and despairing person, the adventurous, and the instinctive rebel; its connection with terrorism (p. 628) is apparent.

"Idealistic" violence generated its opposite: idealistic *nonviolence*. Nonviolence, whether religious or philosophical, has been for centuries a way of life for some men and women in both the Western and the non-Western worlds. In the twentieth century, this historic practice was modified to serve as the basis for a new method of social change. Its advocates were convinced that the use of violence brings on counterviolence, and that even when violence achieves an immediate goal, it creates new tensions and problems that perpetuate the chain of inhumane actions and counteractions. The leader of the Indian national independence movement, a deeply religious Hindu, Mahatma Gandhi, saw this truth most clearly and turned to *satyagraha* (militant nonviolence) in order to free his people from British imperialism.

Gandhi's ideas impressed Martin Luther King (p. 613). Both Gandhi and King saw nonviolence as the preferred method for all social change. Their idea was by no means one of cowardly passivity. They urged their followers to strive for social goals through courageous but nonviolent action; this often involved acts of civil disobedience, which might bring down violence on the "offender." They taught that one must never respond with hate; one must try, through feelings of love, to win opponents over to a just point of view. Their conviction rests on certain key assumptions: that everyone has an inner decency that can be appealed to and that people possess the capacity to live together nonviolently.

Modernism in Literature and the Arts

Literature and art were parts of the twentieth-century transformation of Western society, thought, faith, and action. We saw in Chapter 13 how writers and artists reacted to the impact of machine civilization during the nineteenth century (pp. 532–537). Some mirrored society; some wanted reform; still others turned inward upon themselves. Writers and artists continued these efforts into the twentieth century, but their striving to convey changing human experience in a changing civilization often led them to break with traditional methods of depicting reality, whether in words or in visual images. Supporters of this new artistic tendency thought of it as a natural reflection of Western civilization's growing break with its past, while opponents saw it as a symptom of regrettable cultural decadence. Either way, the tendency seemed to be something typically "modern," and hence it came to be known as the *Modern movement,* or *Modernism.*

NEW FORMS AND NEW INSIGHTS IN LITERATURE

Modernist literature flourished from shortly before the First World War. The decades that followed until about the middle of the twentieth century brought radical innovations in the forms of writing; the content brought daring new insights into the human condition.

The Search for a New Language of Expression. The key element in Modernist literature was its emphasis on *subjectivity.* As in modern psychology, philosophy, and religion, the tendency was away from seeing the individual as an object geared to an orderly and purposeful environment. The new view held that everyone is unique and can be comprehended only through his or her internal experiences. Authors now desired to penetrate the minds of their characters more deeply, to enter into the characters' private thoughts. The reader, then, also became intimate with their internal experiences. The effect was sometimes accomplished by the stream-of-consciousness technique, in which the author puts down words in the way in which ideas appear in the mind; the result is a running jumble of sense and nonsense, a mixture of past, present, and future.

Numerous literary experiments were tried in the endeavor to communicate "inner truth." In many of these, set plots and well-developed characters are missing. The traditional models of dramatic structure are abandoned as artificial. The moment-by-moment, existential reality is all.

James Joyce was a pioneer of the new literature. Born in Dublin, Ireland, he abandoned his homeland and his Catholic faith to live on the European continent. He made himself the subject of his work, and by examining his own experience, he sought to understand the general human problems of his times. In *A Portrait of the Artist as a Young Man* (1916), he drew on the first twenty years of his life.

The hero of Joyce's novel, Stephen Dedalus, struggles with major crises during his youth. In early years, he is indoctrinated with religion, and a love affair at sixteen brings on a period of tormented guilt feelings. During his years in college, Stephen at last abandons religion, turns his back on conventional society, and takes up the artistic life. His departure from Ireland is also a symbolic rejection of his cultural heritage and a seeking for goals and forms of his own making. The escape does not bring him contentment; it is only the beginning of a lonely and bitter search. In his story, Joyce deals hardly at all with action but presents an association of words that flow through consciousness.

In his later works, notably *Ulysses* (1922), Joyce continued to draw from his personal experience. In doing so, he developed further his unusual use of language. In its complexity and obscurity, his writing reflects the loneliness and alienation felt by many artists (and others) of the time. He was an inspiration to authors of his own and later generations. Many of them, using a variety of styles, have explored his method of "interior monologue." One of the most successful was the Frenchman Marcel Proust, famous for his *Remembrance of Things Past* (1913-1927). This seven-volume novel draws upon Proust's detailed recollections of figures in fashionable society that he had known in Paris around the turn of the century.

Another who experimented in similar fashion was Virginia Woolf, a distinguished English literary critic and author. In one of her best novels, *To the Lighthouse* (1927), she followed Joyce's stream-of-consciousness technique as a means of revealing the interior complexity of her characters. Woolf also used her writing skills to advance the cause of equal opportunity for women—for education and careers. Her views are eloquently set forth in a book-length essay, composed in the form of a lecture for college girls. She entitled it *A Room of One's Own* (1929), a unique and challenging blend of autobiography and advocacy.

Prophesy and History. Besides these Modernist writers, some leading authors of the times followed traditional methods of writing. The brilliant Englishman, Aldous Huxley, was one of these. He turned his talent to numerous topics; one was the society of the future. In his novel *Brave New World* (1932), Huxley reveals a "probable" world to come, based on the rapid strides in the physical and social sciences. He sees a world state—achieved, at last, as the only means of avoiding suicidal nationalistic warfare. And to eliminate conflicts within the society, he sees the planned use of genetic engineering, social conditioning, easy sex, and safe drugs. Efficiency and "happiness" are the goals of this future society—at the cost of losing individuality, dissent, and struggle. Another "anti-utopia" of the period is a gloomier novel by another Englishman, George Orwell's *1984*. Published in 1949, it is the prophecy of a future society built on totalitarian lines, one even more repressive than that of *Brave New World*. It uses psychological terror, rather than pleasure, as the primary means of social control.

In the Soviet Union, where totalitarianism was a fact, not a prophecy, some great literature appeared in the tradition of Dostoevsky and Tolstoy (p. 533). Notable is Boris Pasternak's *Dr. Zhivago* (1958), an epic historical novel about Russia before, during, and after the Communist revolution, which was also made into a memorable film. Another giant is Aleksandr Solzhenitsyn, a voice of furious dissent against totalitarianism (pp. 574-575). He first became known for his gripping novel *One Day in the Life of Ivan Denisovich* (1963). It draws on the author's experience as a prisoner in a Russian labor camp and highlights the struggle of one individual to uphold his personal spirit against determined efforts to crush it.

In the United States, some of the finest prose writing of the century was that of Edith Wharton. Among her numerous works, the best known are her romantic, ironic novel *Ethan Frome* (1911), which takes place in rural New England, and *The Age of Innocence* (1920), set in her native New York City. This novel focuses on the wealthy upper class of society and describes in rich detail its strict code of customs, dress, and manners. Underlying these, Wharton exposes the universal conflict between peer pressure to conform and the individual's own aspirations.

Experiment in Poetry and Drama. The major Modernist poet was the American-born T. S. Eliot, who, like Joyce, became an expatriate. Eliot found his spiritual home in England and deep meaning in the Christian religion. The writings of Eliot, like those of Joyce, are self-searching and rich in symbols and imagery.

Eliot moved to London in 1914 and soon began to write poems and literary criticism. His early works reflect a profound disenchantment with modern civilization, a sense of its emptiness and sterility. "The Love Song of J. Alfred Prufrock" (1917) was followed by other poems in the same mood, notably "Gerontion," "The Waste Land," and "The Hollow Men." These are scholarly works, full of echoes from the literary past. These "confessional" poems blame the failures of civilization on the loss of religious spirit; after Eliot's confirmation in the Anglican faith, he began to write more cheerfully about the human condition. If the waters of God's grace have dried up within us, he said, we must discover how to make them flow again. In a bid to reach a wider public, he turned to the theater; his most successful dramatic work, a modern morality play, is *Murder in the Cathedral* (1935). Other American poets—who chose to remain in their native land—included the gifted Robert Frost, who gave sympathetic expression to the charms and hopes of America.

Drama, like prose and poetry, came under subjectivist and experimentalist influences. Such notable playwrights as Eugene O'Neill, Tennessee Williams, and Arthur Miller dealt with ancient themes in new ways; they did not hesitate to alter methods of staging, as well as plot, form, and dialogue. The "theater of the absurd" reflected meaninglessness and the failure of human communication. The Irishman Samuel Beckett was perhaps the best known of the "absurdists." In *Waiting for Godot* (1948), his characters find themselves trapped in a nonsense world of neither logic nor decency. Theatrical producers in the late 1960s pressed experimentation still further, including the novelty of having nude characters on stage (notably in *Oh, Calcutta!* and *Hair*).

The End of Censorship. A trend common to all forms of literature in the last decades was the steady sloughing off of restraint. Legal censorship of books and plays diminished in most Western countries, while reader resistance was shattered by ever-greater shocks to traditional sensibilities. Each adult was thought to be the sole and proper judge of what he or she would see or hear. Thus the once-suppressed writings of authors who dealt frankly with sexual themes, like D. H. Lawrence and Henry Miller, became readily available—as did later works containing sex and violence, like those of Norman Mailer, Philip Roth, and Jerzy Kosinski.

Technology and Art: The Mass Media. The twentieth century brought four entirely new means of expression to world culture: the motion picture, radio, television, and the Internet. Producers of motion pictures drew on most of the established arts, including writing, drama, music, and photography; but what they created was a unique art form. As a product of technology, this form seemed perfectly suited to the new era. It was associated with rapid movement and possessed virtually limitless capabilities

Fig. 16.2 *A Violin Hanging on the Wall.*
The title of Picasso's painting proclaims
it a still life—an exploration of the outward appearance of everyday objects, which
Cézanne had turned into an analysis of
their underlying forms (*Fig. 13.6*, p. 536).
Picasso turns analysis into abstraction. He
takes the violin to pieces and rearranges it
so that it is no longer a realistic object in
three-dimensional space but a mysterious
yet coherent pattern of flat colored surfaces. In mischievous contrast, he depicts
the wood veneer patterns of the furniture
with meticulous realism.

(not always utilized). From experimental beginnings prior to the First World War, films
grew into an immensely popular medium of entertainment. They are truly international in character, with writers, directors, and actors coming from many cultures. But
the largest single source of filmmaking is the United States (chiefly, Hollywood). Motion pictures have been generally subject to censorship, but by the 1980s, restrictions
in most Western countries had become minimal.

Radio broadcasting was developed during the 1920s, offering a flexible and powerful new dimension in the field of communications. It has flourished worldwide, fea-
turing information programs and music of all types. However, radio has been overshadowed since about 1940 by still another new medium: television. In some respects,
TV is a projection of motion pictures, but it has special capabilities that give it enormous
influence on its own. Millions of viewers in Western nations faithfully watch the daily
"soaps," talk shows, and "sitcoms"; and most persons now rely mainly on television
for news and for watching sports events. This medium has also become a prime carrier
for commercial advertising and has revolutionized the conduct of political campaigns
in democratic countries.

THE PRIVATE WORLD OF PAINTERS AND SCULPTORS: PICASSO, MOORE

Modernism in the purely visual arts, like painting and sculpture, expressed many of
the same feelings and ideas that moved the serious novelists and poets of recent times.
The artistic protests of the late nineteenth century (pp. 537–538) became a storm of rebellion in the first half of the twentieth century.

Fig. 16.3 "War Is Sweet to Those Who Have Not Tried It." Before Picasso, artists aroused pity and terror at the horrors of war by showing what those horrors actually looked like (*Fig. 7.1*, p. 293; *Fig. 12.2*, p. 486). Picasso's *Guernica*, however, treats war like his violin on the wall (*Fig. 16.2*). He shows nothing of the bombing of Guernica but assembles images that could be of any war—screaming women, a dead baby, a terrified horse, a warrior's corpse still grasping a broken sword. The resulting combined pattern "abstracts" (summarizes) the terrible essence of war in general.

Pablo Picasso, a Spaniard who made his home in France, is the giant of Modernist art. His productive life spanned the major developments in art since Paul Cézanne and Vincent van Gogh (pp. 536–537). A gifted draftsman, trained at the Barcelona Academy of Fine Arts, Picasso began painting in a fairly conventional manner and quickly achieved mastery of the Expressionist style (p. 537). But he moved restlessly on through successive experiments (he called them "discoveries"). From Cézanne he took the idea of building solidity into his works, of reducing natural subjects to their basic "cubes, cones, and cylinders." Picasso thus became a leading exponent of Cubism, perhaps the most fruitful movement in painting during the first half of the twentieth century.

Though it appeared in numerous varieties, Cubist art involved essentially a breaking down and reordering of nature. For example, in Picasso's treatment of a violin (*Fig. 16.2*), he has not only taken the instrument apart; he shows the parts at whatever angle and in whatever degree of distortion he desires. More precisely, he projects onto the canvas his own thoughts and feelings about a violin, about handling and looking at it. At the same time, he arranges the pictorial elements in an aesthetically pleasing composition. The finished work, then, is Picasso's private, disciplined response to the *idea* of a violin. Like Joyce's literature, Picasso's painting is *radically subjective*, personal, unique: it is not a copy or an imitation of something, but a *special creation* of the artist.

Such inward creations have not been easily understood by the general public. If alienation influenced artists to paint private and secret visions, such paintings only lengthened the distance between them and the public. But informed and sensitive viewers were able to grasp Picasso's intent. They understood, too, that his technique could be more than a visual reduction of objects to geometrical forms; it might also reflect the breaking down of traditional culture and values. The latter possibility is starkly displayed in Picasso's *Guernica* (*Fig. 16.3*), a commemoration of the bombing of a small town during the Spanish Civil War (1937). The fascist general Francisco Franco (p. 587) had used German bombers in a terror raid against the civilian population. Picasso, who

Fig. 16.4 *Number 1, 1950 (Lavender Mist).* Works of art usually show images that can be identified in words—prehistoric rhinoceroses (*Fig. 1.1*, p. 11) or *The Birth of Venus* (*Fig. 8.8*, p. 351) or even Picasso's violin (*Fig. 16.2*). Jackson Pollock's painting is identified only as the first that he made in 1950, and its subtitle is simply the name of a standard commercial paint shade. The painting is about nothing that can be conveyed in words or recognizable images, but it expresses an inner force that acts through the artist to leave its tracks on the canvas.

was both antifascist and antimilitarist, responded by painting this large canvas (12 by 26 feet) in black, white, and gray. It is a masterful protest—using techniques of Cubism and Expressionism—against the indiscriminate and hideous character of modern war.

Generally, however, painters were absorbed in problems of their craft, especially the problem of form. After the Second World War, the principal trend in Modernist art was abstractionism—work completely divorced from any objective model. A Russian, Vassily Kandinsky, had begun to paint such works as early as 1911. His research into the psychological properties of color, line, and shape led him to conclude that a "pure" art, not connected with representation, could be developed. This would be visual art on its own terms, corresponding to the purely auditory art of music.

Though the new idea took various forms, perhaps the most exciting was Abstract Expressionism. This combined spontaneity with nonobjectivity and was most forcefully advanced by an American, Jackson Pollock. Pollock used unorthodox techniques in order to express most fully his vigorous feeling for lines, shapes, and colors. He preferred to begin painting with no pattern in mind, allowing one stroke to lead to another and responding almost subconsciously to his strong inner feelings. He spoke of his designs as creating themselves; he did not know what the final appearance would be while he was "still in the painting." In order to achieve desired effects, Pollock sometimes worked from a scaffold—pouring, spraying, and dripping his paints on a large canvas below—often achieving a hauntingly beautiful effect, as in his *Lavender Mist* series (*Fig. 16.4*).

Fig. 16.5 Penetration into Reality. Henry Moore's *Recumbent Figure* exemplifies his belief that "because a work does not aim at reproducing natural appearances, it is not, therefore, an escape from life— but may be a penetration into reality." Here Moore combines the natural appearance of the human body with that of the masses and hollows of ancient weathered stone, transforming the appearance of both to suggest a female figure of superhuman power and permanence. Unlike Michelangelo's human forms, this one is not "liberated from the stone" (p. 355). Instead, the figure and the stone are one.

As in painting, the general trend in sculpture was away from traditional forms of representation. The Englishman Henry Moore, one of the most distinguished of modern sculptors, was comparatively conservative in this respect. Many of his figures, though distorted, do suggest a subject. His primary interest, however, lies in the materials and forms. One of Moore's best-known works is his *Recumbent Figure,* done in 1938 (*Fig. 16.5*). The figure suggests the idea of woman, or femaleness; but it is at the same time a remarkably fashioned stone creation. The sculptor, by freeing himself from the requirement to reproduce naturalistic details, can concentrate on curves, texture, and the balance of masses.

The American sculptor Alexander Calder also took a novel approach to three-dimensional abstract form. He was the first sculptor to design works that moved, called *mobiles*. Typically, Calder linked components of wire and flat pieces of carved metal and suspended them (usually from a ceiling) in a carefully balanced assembly. He preferred "natural" movement to mechanical means; his mobiles are usually activated by air currents or a slight touch. Thus space and motion, rather than mass, dominate in his sculptures—transmitting a kinetic (moving) sensation to viewers as they watch the ever-changing assembly.

Calder, schooled in mechanical engineering, also found that he could construct static forms that transmit a feeling of motion. His *stabiles,* sometimes designed as large outdoor sculptures, project a sense of movement—and they change continually in appearance as the viewer walks around them. A splendid example is the Calder centerpiece

Fig. 16.6 *La Grande Vitesse.* Abstract sculpture is not obliged to use specialized materials like bronze or marble that lend themselves to reproducing natural appearances. In Alexander Calder's sculpture, industrial materials—steel beams and plates—are fabricated into a complex shape that suggests "high speed"—the meaning of *La Grande Vitesse* and a pun on the name of Grand Rapids, Michigan, where the sculpture stands. The small midwestern city is proud of the sculpture, which appears on its street signs and municipal letterheads and lends it some of the international prestige and progressive image of modern art.

for the civic plaza of Grand Rapids, Michigan: *La Grande Vitesse* (*Fig. 16.6*). Completed in 1969, it consists of giant, curved steel plates linked together in dynamic (energetic) unity of form.

TECHNOLOGY IN ARCHITECTURE: WRIGHT, GROPIUS

Architecture was affected far less than painting and sculpture by the urge to express the inner world of the creator. Architects can never simply express themselves, since the buildings that they design have to meet the needs of the people who live and work in them. But overwhelming changes in life and work, as well as in the materials and technologies of building, led in the first half of the twentieth century to Modernist innovations in styles of architecture that paralleled those in the other visual arts.

Architecture in the nineteenth century had been a mixture of revival styles, none of which came from the spirit or technology of the times (pp. 489–490). During the 1890s, a number of designers in Europe and America began to express dissatisfaction with the state of architecture. They pointed to the contradiction in putting up a structure by modern engineering methods and then covering it with a façade (facing) of "historical" ornamentation.

Frank Lloyd Wright, an American, was the pioneer of a new architecture. One should break entirely, he declared, with the forms and decorations of the past. One

Fig. 16.7 The Kaufmann House ("Fallingwater"). Modern building technology makes it possible to create a house out of geometrical forms that flow in and out of each other not unlike the elements that make up Picasso's violin (*Fig. 16.2*) yet also seem to grow from the natural landscape. The architect, Frank Lloyd Wright, called the house an "extension of the cliff beside a mountain stream, making living space over and above the stream upon which a man who loved the place sincerely, one who liked to listen to the waterfall, might well live."

should try to utilize whatever kind of beauty modern technology and materials are capable of producing and allow "form to follow function." An authentic (true) style is one that provides the kind of space suited to a particular kind of human activity (work, rest, or play); its beauty will lie in the character of the building materials themselves. Because his structures were designed around the needs and desires of the individuals who occupied them, and because they preserved the natural appearance of the materials, Wright called his style "organic."

Wright began building residences at the turn of the century. In order to maximize the free flow of space inside and to join that space with its natural surroundings, he made effective use of the cantilever method of construction. The cantilever, an outgrowth of the post-and-lintel method of the ancient Greeks (p. 89), provides for an unsupported extension of the horizontal members. Traditional construction materials, like stone, wood, or cement, can be used only in a limited way as cantilevers. But steel or ferroconcrete (concrete reinforced by steel rods or mesh) can be boldly employed in this method of building.

Wright's Kaufmann House ("Fallingwater"), built as a mountain retreat for a Pittsburgh industrialist in 1936, is a spectacular example of organic architecture using cantilevered elements (*Fig. 16.7*). This home, built over a rustic waterfall, appears to grow out of its surroundings. Inside the house, free space and a sense of contact with nature are maintained. While Wright is especially respected for his designs of private dwellings, he also created impressive structures for public and industrial uses.

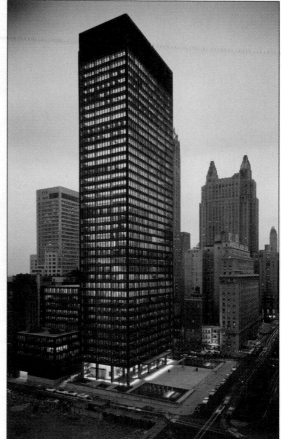

Fig. 16.8 The Seagram Building. Mies van der Rohe's building is a simple geometrical form with unadorned walls of tinted glass to retain heat and admit light. But the walls are held in place by strips of expensive bronze; by day they reflect the urban landscape, and at night they glow with internal light. The building uses the architectural language of simplicity and utility to proclaim elegance, luxury, and power on behalf of a modern capitalist corporation just as effectively as a Baroque palace did for an absolute monarch (*Fig. 9.9*, p. 394).

© Ezra Stoller/ESTO

Outside the United States, leading architects were deeply impressed by Wright's functional ideas. Perhaps the most influential among them was a German, Walter Gropius. He designed a complex of buildings for the Bauhaus ("House of Architecture," the name of a school of art and architecture that he headed) in the eastern German town of Dessau according to the new principles. Gropius, like Wright, emphasized that attention to function is the first principle of architecture; a good design in an object, no matter what it is, ensures its beauty. His Bauhaus became a model of what today is called the International Style. Especially as applied to large buildings—factories and offices—this style aptly expresses the precision and efficiency of the machine age.

The most brilliant architect in the International Style was Ludwig Mies van der Rohe, Gropius's successor as director of the Bauhaus, who emigrated to the United States after the Nazis came to power. Mies held that function alone is not enough to ensure beauty. His stunning skyscrapers please the eye because of their balanced proportions, richness of materials, and painstaking details. His shimmering glass walls hang upon frames of cantilevered steel. Mies's masterpiece, the Seagram Building in New York (*Fig. 16.8*), has been appropriately described as "dignified, sumptuous, severe, sophisticated, cool, consummately elegant architecture for the twentieth century and for the ages."

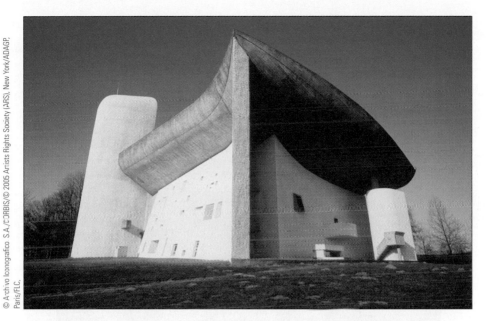

Fig. 16.9 Notre-Dame du Haut. Modern technology enables buildings not only to express engineering logic but also seemingly to defy it. In Le Corbusier's chapel of Our Lady of the Hilltop, reinforced concrete is bent into irregular curves intended to suggest features of Christianity: hands folded in prayer; the wings of a dove, standing for both peace and the Holy Spirit; and the image of the Church as a ship navigating the stormy seas of this world. Here, modern architecture speaks neither of well-being through technology nor of luxury and power, but of ancient religious faith.

Another leading exponent of functionalism was the French-Swiss architect Le Corbusier, a strong believer in the principle that if architecture used modern technology uncompromisingly in the service of utility and convenience, the result would be aesthetically satisfying buildings: "A house," he declared, "is a machine for living." Yet late in his life, he used the resources of technology to produce some striking examples of an architecture that appears to reject the machine. His chapel of Notre-Dame du Haut (Our Lady of the Hilltop) near Ronchamp in a mountainous region of eastern France, completed in 1955, is startling and mysterious in its sculptured masses (*Fig. 16.9*). Lacking in symmetry or evident plan, and lit by shifting beams of daylight through its narrow windows, its interior suggests a primitive sacred cave or the half-light of Romanesque churches (p. 259).

Numerous other architects subordinated function to interesting forms. Outstanding was the Finnish American Eero Saarinen, who is best known for his design of airports. An airport combines enormously complex movements of people, ground transport, and aircraft. Most world travelers are familiar with Saarinen's TWA Building (1961) at Kennedy International, near New York, and his Dulles International, near Washington, D.C. In the capital itself stands a superb achievement by the Chinese American architect I. M. Pei. This building (*Fig. 16.10*), built in 1978, is an intricately designed annex to the National Gallery of Art, which was built a generation before. Notable for its skylight illumination of the masterpieces it houses, the structure is prominent among Pei's many creations. Each of these named architects has one thing in common with Wright and the Internationalists: they all abandoned the backward-looking imitativeness of

Fig. 16.10 National Gallery of Art. This glass-roofed central hall in a new wing of the gallery was designed by I. M. Pei, a strong believer in what he calls the "tradition" of the pioneers of Modernist architecture. But Pei carries the tradition a step further. His simple geometrical forms and self-revealing structures combine, contrast, and interlock to make a hall that is spacious and monumental yet also varied and intimate. Instead of intimidating visitors with Modernist austerity, the hall leads them on to explore the surrounding exhibits.

the nineteenth century and committed themselves to an architecture that is modern in both spirit and materials.

NOVEL PATTERNS OF TONALITY AND RHYTHM: SCHÖNBERG, STRAVINSKY

The changes that swept through the visual arts around the turn of the century affected music as well. Romanticism continued to dominate concert and operatic performances (pp. 490–491); a leading composer carrying forward this musical style was the Russian Sergei Rachmaninoff. Other composers, however, began to embrace new aims and methods. Some turned to Impressionism, which was inspired in part by the movement in painting (pp. 535–536). Musical Impressionism, as developed by the Frenchman Claude Debussy, was anticlassical as well as anti-Romantic. It sought to record the composer's fleeting responses to nature (clouds, sea, moonlight). Departing from traditional patterns of melody, tone scales, and rhythms, Debussy's music has a dreamy, shimmering quality.

As in painting, Impressionism in music was followed by Expressionism. Expressionist composers were not interested in responding to their environment; they sought, rather, to record musically their inmost, even subconscious, feelings. (This motive corresponded to the literary subjectivism of Joyce; pp. 661–662.) Viennese composer

Arnold Schönberg was one of the earliest Expressionists. Just before the First World War, he turned from the large orchestral productions of the nineteenth century and began writing string quartets and other forms of chamber music (p. 442). Abandoning tonality, Schönberg stressed melodic distortion and the chance coincidence of notes—often producing a harsh dissonance. Later in life, he adopted a unique tone scale of his own invention. Musically, Schönberg was not unlike van Gogh or Picasso (pp. 537, 665–666) in seeking vigorous and disturbing means of expression.

Modernist composers, like painters or sculptors, freed themselves from the traditions of their craft and chose whatever musical elements they wished. The result was an unbounded diversity of individual styles. One of the best known and most successful of the musical Modernists was Russian-born Igor Stravinsky. Younger than Schönberg, he, too, worked with established forms before discarding them. He also decided to ignore public tastes (as the painters had done) and to write "abstract" music to suit his own ideas. The chief characteristics of his mature works were stress on polyphony, free use of dissonance, and quickly changing rhythms.

In popular culture, the Broadway-type "musical" proved highly successful in the United States and Europe. The leading geniuses of this entertainment medium were three Americans: Frederick Loewe, Alan Jay Lerner, and Cole Porter; their most acclaimed productions included *My Fair Lady, Camelot,* and *Kiss Me, Kate.* (These live shows were also adapted for films and sound recordings.)

The most original American contribution to world music, however, was *jazz.* Europeans, who had been creators and exporters of classical compositions for centuries, became eager importers of jazz. African rhythms are the foundation of this musical innovation, which flowered chiefly among the talented writers and musicians of black America. But the principal feature is its unending novelty and the improvisations of its interpreters; among the greatest of these were the prolific composer-conductor, "Duke" Ellington, and the trumpet-playing "Ambassador of Jazz," Louis Armstrong. A brilliant white composer, George Gershwin, created a unique blend of jazz rhythms and classical styles. He is best remembered for his piano *Rhapsody in Blue* and the folk opera *Porgy and Bess* (first performed in 1935). More than any other type of artistic expression, jazz seems to incorporate the spirit of rebellion against traditional forms and restraints. It is plainly an antidote for the tensions and frustration that are a part of contemporary living.

Rock music, which first became popular in the 1960s, has a similar appeal. It grew out of black rhythm and blues and white country and western music into its own unique form. Rock is directed mainly at young adults; its sensual beat, electronic amplification, and frank lyrics excite audiences around the world. By means of the mass media, it quickly created idols (and legends) like Elvis Presley, John Lennon, and Michael Jackson. The power of rock was further extended in the 1980s through another new art form: music video (MTV).

These and other forms of mass entertainment, the world-changing outcome of the encounter between art and technology, originated in nineteenth-century universal education and high-speed printing, but it was twentieth-century electronic technology that made them central to the lives of individuals and societies. In the global village of the twenty-first century, mass entertainment plays the same role that gossip among neighbors, religious rituals, and community celebrations play in real villages. It is a glue that holds a changing world together, as civilization breaks with its past and moves toward whatever the future holds.

RECOMMENDED READING

The Onrush of Science and Technology   T. Williams, *Science: A History of Discovery in the Twentieth Century* (1990), covers technology as well as pure science and is excellently illustrated. J. Abbate, *Inventing the Internet* (1999), and S. Aldridge, *The Thread of Life: The Story of Genes and Genetic Engineering* (1997), are clear and up-to-date accounts. H. Collins and T. Pinch, *The Golem: What You Should Know About Science* (1999) and *The Golem at Large: What You Should Know About Technology* (1998), present case studies of recent scientific and technical achievements that undermine the view that advances in these fields result from an inevitable and infallible process.

Many leading twentieth-century scientists have written accounts for the general reader of their own discoveries and those of their colleagues. Among the most notable of these are J. D. Watson, *The Double Helix* (1968), by one of the discoverers of the structure of DNA, and S. Weinberg, *Dreams of a Final Theory: The Scientist's Search for the Ultimate Laws of Nature* (1992), in which a Nobel Prize–winning physicist describes the origins and present status of Grand Unified Theories, as well as their implications for the other sciences, philosophy, and theology.

Reconstruction in Western Philosophy and Religion   R. C. Solomon, *Continental Philosophy Since 1750: The Rise and Fall of the Self* (1988), deals with the tradition of thought leading from Hegel to existentialism and beyond; A. J. Ayer, *Philosophy in the Twentieth Century* (1982), concentrates on the "linguistic analysis" school and its forerunners. P. Roubiczek, *Existentialism: For and Against* (1964), presents two opposing viewpoints; and M. Warnock, *Existentialism* (1996), is an excellent brief introduction to the intellectual background and the thought of the leading existentialist thinkers.

Recent developments in Christian thought and action are discussed in a thoughtful treatment for the general reader, D. L. Edwards, *Christianity: The First Two Thousand Years* (1997).

The Shifting Ways of Society   For the youth culture, T. Roszak, *The Making of a Counterculture: Reflections on the Technocratic Society and Its Youthful Opposition* (1969), is helpful; J. A. Califano Jr., *The Student Revolution: A Global Confrontation* (1969), is a concise worldwide review of the campus agitation of the 1960s. C. Lasch, *The Culture of Narcissism: American Life in an Age of Diminishing Expectations* (1978), is a provocative statement on contemporary attitudes and values; currents of dissent in Europe are effectively analyzed in H. S. Hughes, *Sophisticated Rebels* (1988).

S. de Beauvoir, *The Second Sex* (1952), is the classic modern study of the status of women; up-to-date treatments, including the history of the women's movement, will be found in G. Fraisse and M. Perrot, eds., *Emerging Feminism from Revolution to World War* (1992), and F. Thébaud, ed., *Toward a Cultural Identity in the Twentieth Century* (1994) (vols. 4 and 5 of G. Duby and M. Perrot, eds., *The History of Women in the West*). The concept of nonviolence is explained in depth in E. H. Erikson, *Gandhi's Truth* (1969).

Fresh Directions in Literature and the Arts   On literature, E. Wilson, *Axel's Castle* (1931), is a respected study of imaginative writing from 1870 to 1930, and P. Faulkner, *Modernism* (1977), is a good introduction to English-language literature in the early twentieth century. For the period since 1930, see L. Trilling, *The Liberal Imagination: Essays on Society and Literature* (1950), and I. Howe, *Celebrations and Attacks: Thirty Years of Literary and Cultural Commentary* (1979).

E. Lucie-Smith, *Visual Arts in the Twentieth Century* (1996), is an excellent general account of the various movements and schools in painting, sculpture, photography, and architecture. C. Crouch, *Modernism in Design, Art, and Architecture* (1999), is a brief interpretation of the twentieth century's leading artistic tendency. E. Lucie-Smith, *Movements in Art Since 1945* (1984), chronicles the decline and fall of Modernism. On architecture, W. Gropius, *New Architecture and the Bauhaus* (1935), is a classic work by a pioneer of Modernism. D. Ghirardi, *Architecture After Modernism* (1996), is a good introduction to the architecture of the last thirty years; A. L. Huxtable, *The Unreal America: Architecture and Illusion* (1997), is a personal view by a distinguished critic.

For music, S. Bechet, *Treat It Gentle* (1960), illuminates the spirit of jazz; R. J. Gleason, *Celebrating the Duke et al.* (1956), offers readable sketches of the leading jazz heroes. I. Whitcomb, *Rock Odyssey* (1983), is by a musician of the 1960s.

⍾ INFOTRAC COLLEGE EDITION

Visit the source collections at **http://academic.cengage.com/infotrac**, and use the Search function with the following key terms:

the New Belle Epoque	social problems	Equal Rights Amendment
feminism	*Roe* v. *Wade*	Kent State

WESTERN CIVILIZATION RESOURCES

Visit the Brief History of the Western World Companion Web Site for resources specific to this textbook:

http://history.wadsworth.com/greerbrief09/

   Also, the CD in the back of this book and the World History Resources Center at **http://history.wadsworth.com/west_civ/** offer a variety of tools to help you succeed in this course, including access to quizzes; images; documents; interactive simulations, maps, and timelines; movie explorations; and a wealth of other sources.

CHAPTER 17

Western Civilization
in the World of Today

OVERVIEW

The fall of communism opened a new stage in the worldwide process of conflict, accommodation, and interchange that is shaping the future organization of Western and world civilization. Having triumphed in the Cold War, the Western partnership of North American and western European capitalist and democratic countries now hoped to steer the world in a direction that would correspond to both their ideals and their long-term interests. Their goal was a harmonious worldwide community of independent nation-states, sharing the Western privileges of democratic freedom and capitalist prosperity, of which they would be the leaders and guardians.

True, changes were under way within the Western partnership. The U.S. capitalist economy grew both harsher and more productive than those of its partners as it shrank its welfare state safety net. As the western European countries pooled their resources in the European Union, however, they came to wield almost as much economic power as the United States. Even so, the Western partnership continued close enough to remain the single strongest influence in world affairs, and the United States was still its senior partner.

The rest of the world, however, had a mind—in fact, many minds—of its own about being steered by the West. There was widespread distrust of Western sincerity, particularly in the economic field. The West proclaimed the spread of capitalist prosperity through *globalization*—the unhindered worldwide movement of people, goods, and money—but Western countries made sure to shelter powerful domestic groups like bankers and farmers from globalization's hardships. The West, it seemed, was protecting its own interests at the expense of the rest of the world. How, then, could the world trust the West to steer it to prosperity?

In addition, many of the world's peoples were locked in national, ethnic, and religious conflicts that for them took priority over the pursuit of harmony, prosperity, and freedom. Some of these conflicts were newly released by the fall of communism, above all the brutal wars in Yugoslavia. Others were already of long standing, unleashed by the earlier disappearance of colonial empires—Israel and the Arabs, India and Pakistan, and a whole series of ethnic and religious wars in Africa. Either way, these conflicts came to be regarded both inside and outside the West as a test of its ability to steer the world.

Western mediation and more or less wholehearted military intervention, United Nations sanctions and war crimes tribunals, and help from Western-backed volunteer organizations often damped these conflicts down or relieved the suffering they caused. But the conflicts were mostly neither stopped before they inflicted tragic devastation, nor truly ever resolved. Furthermore, the postcolonial conflicts, resentment and distrust of Western power and influence, and growing evidence that Western power was not unlimited all strengthened three formidable challenges to the order of global civilization that the West wished to establish: militant Islamic fundamentalism, nuclear proliferation, and terrorism.

Meanwhile, a controversial new movement in thought and art developed in the late-twentieth-century West—that of *Postmodernism.* In thought, Postmodernists denied the possibility of finding ultimate truth through either reason or faith and instead held out the hope of human fulfillment through the liberation of inner human energies. In social life, Postmodernists opposed both rules of behavior that all must obey and highly organized power structures that required and enforced such behavior. Rather, they spoke up for groups that broke the rules or were held down by power structures, especially in the areas of gender, race, and sexuality. In literature and art, Postmodernists produced works that embodied their view of the irrationality of the world, reacted against the idealized abstraction of Modernism, or proclaimed the nobility and suffering of the groups they supported.

One of the main targets of Postmodernists was Western civilization itself, since most of the traditions of thought and art that they criticized were Western ones. Doubting the possibility of finding truth and undermining social conformity for the sake of fulfilling desire were themselves ancient Western traditions, however, and Postmodern thought and art were mainly influential within the lands of Western civilization.

Early in the twenty-first century, Islamic tensions and resentments that had grown since the fall of communism exploded in terrorist attacks on the United States. In response, the United States launched an ambitious effort to change the way in which the West steered the world, by using force or the threat of it more readily than before and by purposefully encouraging the spread of secular democratic government to Islamic countries. In the service of these aims, it invaded Iraq and overthrew its tyrannical regime. Rather than remolding Iraq according to its own design, the United States soon came to be involved in a complex process of negotiation and compromise among the religious and ethnic groups that it had liberated. If it ended well, the process might perhaps form a precedent for future interactions between Islam and the West.

The West and the Postcommunist World: The Ideal of an International Community

With the collapse of communism, the bipolar world order had come to a relatively peaceful end. It no longer seemed appropriate, in this world with neither blocs nor colonial empires, to speak of the free world and the socialist camp, the imperial and colonial nations, or even of the First, Second, and Third Worlds. Another term was needed—one that would express the world's renewed hopes for harmonious diversity. Much more than before, government leaders, diplomats, and journalists began to speak of the world as a single community of nation-states—an *international community.* Now that the blocs had disappeared, it seemed, the time had come for this community truly to emerge.

Like all communities, this one had its common institutions, principally the United Nations (UN) and its affiliated organizations. It had its volunteer groups which summoned dedicated activists to help solve its problems—*nongovernmental organizations* (NGOs) like Amnesty International (which devoted itself to the plight of political prisoners), Oxfam (the Oxford Committee for Famine Relief), or Médecins sans frontières (Doctors Without Borders). But the community also had its bitter internal conflicts, which often tore apart individual nation-states—*failed states,* as such victims of conflict came to be called—and which the common institutions could hardly contain. And there were also *rogue states*—outlaws who would not obey the community's rules, and whom the common institutions were not strong enough to master.

In addition, the international community had its leading citizens, members of the world's most exclusive club: the *Group of Seven* (G7) leading democratic and capitalist countries, whose leaders had met yearly since 1975 to discuss world affairs in a relaxed and informal atmosphere. Six of these countries—Britain, Canada, France, Germany, Italy, and the United States—were located in North America and western Europe, the heartland of modern Western civilization. The seventh, Japan, was the non-Western country that had most successfully striven to gain equality with the West by adopting and adapting Western ways of doing business and running countries.

All of the G7 countries had already been prominent and privileged in the world at the end of the nineteenth century, and had managed to keep this position through all the ups and downs of imperialism, two world wars, decolonization, and the Cold War. Together with the smaller western European countries, they now formed the political and economic West—with Japan, in spite of its non-Western traditions of civilization, counting as fully Western in this political and economic sense. Now, at the end of the twentieth century, these countries hoped to steer the international community according to their capitalist interests and their democratic ideals.

For this to happen, the democratic-capitalist countries would have to continue to share the ideals and interests that had held them together during the twentieth century. In addition, the peoples of the rest of the world, in spite of their enormous diversity and endless conflicts, would have to feel that they too had a stake in a capitalist-democratic world order. If the West maintained its unity, followed its ideals as well as its interests, and was able to operate by consensus with the rest of the world, then perhaps it could steer the world to the benefit of all. Ethnic, religious, and international rivalries would be contained, economies would be able to grow, and nations outside the Western heartland besides Japan would gain influence and power equal to that of the West. In that case, the international community might turn from a hope to a reality, and democratic freedom and capitalist prosperity might be genuinely shared among the nations of the world.

Alternatively, the democratic and capitalist countries might become divided, follow their interests and neglect their ideals, and seek to impose their will on the rest of the world. In that case, the result would be a far less benign world order. There would be a fierce "struggle for existence" among nations, ethnic groups, religions, and economic competitors, and the "fittest" countries, Western and non-Western, would hold down the rest by economic power, technical supremacy, and military force. And there were even worse possibilities—of gradual environmental disaster produced by an over-industrialized world, or of sudden catastrophe resulting from the use of nuclear or other weapons of mass destruction by states or terrorist groups.

If the best alternatives came about, the democratic and capitalist countries would certainly have to share the credit with the rest of the world. If the worst possibilities were realized, it would just as certainly not be the fault of these countries alone. For the moment, however, the single strongest influence on the future distribution of wealth and power within global civilization was theirs, for it was they that had won the Cold War.

The West in the 1990s:
Continuing Partnership, Evolving Partners

The end of the Cold War was a victory not just for democracy and capitalism but also for the new international power structure that had grown up within the Western heartland. In the past, Western civilization had sometimes been ruled by universal empires like Rome's and sometimes been divided among many rival states. Since the Second World War, however, the West had become a partnership in which the United States was the senior partner but usually operated in consensus with its junior partners, mostly in western Europe. This new power structure remained very much in effect in the 1990s, in spite of the disappearance of the communist adversary that had brought it into being. Shared democratic values, economic links of trade and investment, and the dangers and uncertainties of the postcommunist world were strong forces binding the partners together, even though their economic and social policies were growing apart, and the European partners were forming stronger links among themselves.

THE UNITED STATES: ECONOMIC SUCCESS AND ITS COSTS

Bill Clinton was elected president in 1992 as a centrist Democrat who would concentrate on improving the U.S. economy. The conservative Republicans remained a powerful force, however, and from 1994 onward, Clinton faced opposing majorities in both the House and the Senate, committed to a program of shrinking the U.S. welfare state. Clinton found that when he proposed extensions of the welfare state, such as a plan for universal health care, the Republicans could defeat him. On the other hand, if he himself proposed less drastic versions of Republican policies, he could siphon off their support among voters and make them look dangerously radical.

With this strategy, Clinton won reelection in 1996 and kept control of government policy out of the hands of the Republican majorities. The fury and frustration of the Republicans led them to look for scandals that could bring him down. Their efforts came to a head when the House of Representatives impeached him on charges arising out of his efforts to conceal improper relations with a White House intern. The Senate acquitted Clinton, and the affair added a great deal of poison to the political atmosphere.

Meanwhile, economic expansion that had begun in the mid-1980s continued into the Clinton years. The president and his advisers benefited from the "Cold War dividend" (a reduction in defense spending following the disappearance of the Soviet threat) and made politically astute concessions to the Republicans' desire to cut welfare spending. As a result they were able to reduce the federal deficit in gradual steps, thereby avoiding the negative impact upon the economy of sudden cuts in government spending. With shrinking deficits and a lower tax burden, consumers had money to spend to keep the economy growing, and unemployment was low. Much of the consumers' spending went on goods imported from abroad, so that the United States regularly imported more than it exported. But foreign investors, confident in the size and strength of the U.S. economy, were willing to lend money to make up the difference between what the United States sold and what it bought in foreign countries.

The economic system that came out of the uneasy cooperation between the president and the Republicans was harsher than in the era before the rise of conservatism under Reagan. It offered less security, particularly for unemployed people, and the jobs it created were mainly in low-paying service industries, since technology and global competition were reducing the need for high-paid workers in manufacturing. But at a time when many other advanced industrial economies were stagnant or beset by crises, the United States seemed a model of capitalist economic success.

At the end of the Clinton presidency this success was dimmed by the collapse of a speculative stock market boom, an economic downturn, and a rise in unemployment. The recovery that followed under the conservative Republican President George W. Bush was slow in producing jobs and was accompanied by unprecedented government deficits. The new administration was committed to one conservative principle, that of low tax rates, but not to its accompanying principle of cutting government spending. Instead, the administration was betting that as the economy recovered from recession, the government would take in more money in taxes even if tax rates were low. Meanwhile, however, the government had to borrow money from domestic and foreign lenders on a huge scale, while imports still ran far in excess of exports. If the administration lost its bet on economic growth, the confidence of lenders in the U.S. economy might waver, and the U.S. model of capitalism was likely to face a painful crisis.

WESTERN EUROPE: WELFARE STATES AND CLOSER UNION

The U.S. economy produced goods and services and created jobs on a massive and growing scale, but it did so in part by making workers work long hours for low pay and by shrinking the welfare state safety net. Most western European countries, reacting to the same trends of industrial advance and worldwide competition, preferred to uphold the welfare state safety net and regulation of pay and hours, so that their economies did not grow like that of the United States. All the same, the western European countries worked more intensively than ever on a project that, together with their partnership with the United States, represented a historic change in the power structure of Western civilization: the pooling of some of their national sovereignty (independent government) in common institutions.

"Eurosclerosis." In the 1990s, the western European economies hardly grew at all and sometimes even shrank, since government spending on welfare states left less money to invest in factories and businesses. Western Europe also lost millions of jobs, since employers were not eager to hire workers to whom they would be compelled by law to pay high wages. Economists and business leaders considered this lack of growth an

alarming economic ailment, which they called "Eurosclerosis." But western European voters—even those who were unemployed, since there was no time limit to their bene-fits—mostly accepted the trade-off between jobs and production on the one hand, and welfare state security on the other.

Western European governments often announced policies of privatization (sell-ing state-owned businesses to private corporations; p. 629), budget trimming, and con-frontation with labor unions, but in most countries these measures were less radical than in the United States. The basic features of the system were maintained, regardless of which parties ran governments, under the socialist president François Mitterrand in France (1981–1995) and his conservative successor Jacques Chirac (1995–), as well as under the conservative chancellor Helmut Kohl in Germany (1982–1998) and his so-cialist replacement Gerhard Schröder (1998–). By the early twenty-first century, how-ever, as government spending on welfare states continued to grow, worldwide compe-tition increased, and ten low-wage eastern European and Mediterranean countries prepared to join the European Union (p. 682), the western European countries faced difficult problems upholding their model of capitalism.

The policies of Margaret Thatcher, the pioneer of conservative revival in Britain, were in general far more radical than those of her fellow European leaders (p. 629). Even she did not try to tear down the welfare state safety net, however, and in 1990, after she had insisted on pushing through Parliament a local government tax system that favored the wealthy, her support among voters rapidly dropped and her own party forced her to resign. Her successor, John Major (1990–1997), followed more moderate policies until his Conservative party, divided by arguments over how far Britain should join in the strengthening of the European Union, lost to a revived and reunited Labour party under Tony Blair (1997–).

Blair upheld both the welfare state safety net and those Thatcherite reforms, such as privatization, that seemed both beneficial and popular. So far as he made changes, they were in other areas, including *devolution* (self-government within the United Kingdom) for Scotland and Wales and a historic action removing hereditary peers (no-bles) from membership in the House of Lords, a privilege they had held for some eight hundred years.

The European Community and the Treaty of Maastricht. The process of building com-mon institutions had been under way among the western European nations since shortly after the end of the Second World War (pp. 601–602). In 1957, it had passed an important milestone with the founding of the European Economic Community (EEC) or Common Market. The building of common institutions had never gone smoothly, for too many national interests and identities were at stake. But year by year, the com-munity's *acquis* ("accumulation"—the body of commonly applicable treaties, laws, and regulations) grew larger and more complex, and from time to time, the community gained new members (pp. 558–560). By the time of the fall of communism, the origi-nal six nations (Belgium, France, West Germany, Italy, Luxembourg, and the Nether-lands) had been joined by Britain, Denmark, Greece, Ireland, Portugal, and Spain, so that the community included most of western Europe.

After communism's fall, the *acquis* grew faster than ever before, above all because of the reunification of Germany. The Germans, once again the most powerful single na-tion in Europe, did not want their western neighbors to turn against them as had hap-pened before the two world wars (pp. 558–560, 587–589), and those neighbors were eager not to allow Germany too much freedom of action. For both sides, the answer seemed to be to pool still more of their sovereignty. The result was the Treaty of Maastricht, signed in 1993, which changed the community's name to the European Union (EU) and announced measures to establish a common citizenship, a common currency, common economic and social policies, and common foreign and security policies.

Building the European Union. The Treaty of Maastricht made membership of the EU much more demanding on the individual nations than before, and progress in putting it into effect was uneven. The member nations were unable to agree on specific common foreign and security policies, which would have limited their ability to pursue their individual national interests. In economic matters, member nations gained exemptions from or simply disregarded some of the Maastricht demands. Thus when the common currency, the *euro,* came into use in 2002, three countries—Britain, Denmark, and Sweden—kept their national currencies, which their citizens prized as symbols of sovereignty and identity. Larger and more powerful countries were liable to break the stricter EU rules when it suited them. For example, France and Germany have for several years run budget deficits at a higher rate than permitted by the European Central Bank, which oversees matters affecting the value of money such as interest rates and government spending. As a result, the European Commission (the EU's central administration, headquartered in Brussels) has sued the two countries in the European Court of Justice, the EU's supreme judicial body.

The pooling of sovereignty has also led to bitter conflicts over the distribution of government power. In the Council of Ministers, the body through which national governments control EU policies, small countries fear being outvoted by large ones, and large ones complain of being underrepresented as against small ones. In every EU country, the public complains of being at the mercy of remote and imperious "Eurocrats." This "democratic deficit" could be reduced if the European Parliament, which is directly elected in each country, gained greater power over the actions of the Commission and the Council of Ministers than it has so far been given. But any increase in the power of the European Parliament would have to come at the expense of the power of the national legislatures—something that public opinion in every EU country would certainly also resent.

All these disputes have arisen because the EU countries remain independent nation-states, each pursuing its own national interests. Even so, the member nations have found it in their interests to pool enough of their sovereignty to turn the EU into an economic superpower whose production of goods and services is not much smaller than that of the United States.

Furthermore, following the fall of communism, many more European nations found it in their national interests to pool some of their sovereignty in the EU. Austria, Finland, and Sweden, neutral countries that had stayed out of the EEC so long as the blocs existed, joined in 1995. (Among western European countries, only Norway, where the voters have twice disallowed efforts by their government to join the EEC and then the EU, is still outside the union.) In 2003, ten more, mostly ex-communist countries were admitted: Cyprus, the Czech Republic, Estonia, Hungary, Latvia, Lithuania, Malta, Poland, Slovakia, and Slovenia *(Map 15.5,* p. 635). This eastward expansion of the EU is likely to lead to difficult economic adjustments for both its old members and the newcomers, and to make it even more quarrelsome than before. But it is also a sure sign that the European nations see their future as one of community.

The European nations, however, did not find it in their interest to pool enough of their sovereignty to turn Europe from an economic into a military and political superpower. The Cold War bargain with the United States, whereby they accepted U.S. leadership and military command in return for being able to influence U.S. policy and save money on defense (pp. 602–603), was still very much in their interests. Without it, they would have had difficulty upholding their welfare states and would hardly have been able to pursue their project of building their community. Even so, their influence for good or ill on the world order of global civilization was second only to that of the United States, and that seemed a good reason for the United States to hold to its end of the Cold War bargain.

The Global Economy: "The West and the Rest"

The postcommunist era of rising hopes for a single international community was also an era of economic globalization. People, goods, money, and information moved across the world on an unprecedented scale, and expectations grew for the reshaping of worldwide trade, industry, and finance into a single international economy.

The globalization of the 1990s was the latest stage in an increase of worldwide travel and trade that had been going on for more than a thousand years. The main milestones of this process had been the rise of Islam, which strengthened links among the civilizations of the Eastern Hemisphere; European exploration and empire building, which linked the Old World and the New; and the first revolution in transport and communications, the nineteenth-century invention of steamships, railroads, and telegraphs (pp. 208, 318–333, 505–510). In the second half of the twentieth century, the increase of travel and trade passed another milestone, as transport and communications were once again revolutionized, this time by commercial jet aircraft, new methods of handling cargoes at seaports, and advanced technologies such as the Internet.

In addition, for most countries of the world, the end of communism meant the end of any hope of finding prosperity by following a path of resistance to the West (pp. 614–616). Only one path remained open: that of seeking prosperity within the Western-dominated worldwide capitalist system. The great question of globalization was whether it would in fact provide such a path.

THE WASHINGTON CONSENSUS AND FREE TRADE

Western governments, banks, and multinational corporations (those doing business in many countries; pp. 509–510) insisted that globalization would indeed bring worldwide prosperity, so long as all countries accepted it as quickly and completely as possible. They must abolish restrictions on movements of goods and money across their borders, privatize their economies, and cut both taxes and government spending so as to release money for businesses to invest and consumers to spend. Their economies, wide open to the increasing movement of people, goods, money, and information, would grow in step with the increase in travel and trade, and this would bring prosperity to their peoples.

This updated version of laissez-faire economics (pp. 510–511) became known as the Washington Consensus, because it was shared by four economic policymaking institutions based in the U.S. capital that together had considerable power to steer the global economy: the U.S. Treasury and the Federal Reserve Bank, which set policy for the largest national economy in the world, the World Bank, which lent money to countries in need of economic development; and the International Monetary Fund (IMF), established after the Second World War to help prevent worldwide economic crises like that of the 1930s (p. 584) by lending money to countries in financial trouble while supervising economic reforms.

The confidence of these institutions in laissez-faire economics grew from the fact that in the 1990s, the new and harsher U.S. economy grew faster not only than the EU economies, but also faster than Japan's. Since the end of the Second World War, Japan had grown into a mighty economic power partly as a result of deliberate government intervention—fostering exports, discouraging imports, helping companies identify markets and develop new products, and raising barriers to foreign ownership of companies (pp. 619–621). These policies were successfully imitated by other Far Eastern countries, so that many economists and business leaders came to speak of a Far Eastern model of capitalism, distinct from and more productive than the U.S. and European models. At the beginning of the 1990s, however, Japan's growth ended in a spectacular financial crash followed by seemingly endless economic stagnation. Japan still had the world's second largest economy and its people continued on the whole prosperous and secure, but the Far Eastern model of capitalism no longer seemed nearly so impressive as before.

Now, the Washington economic policymakers as well as U.S. business leaders and bankers believed, it was the turn of the United States to be the economic model for the world. True, in the World Bank and the IMF, the United States shared power with the EU countries and Japan. But however reluctant these other countries might be to adopt the laissez-faire model for themselves, their leaders tended to share the U.S. belief that unfettered globalization was good for the world as a whole.

President Clinton applied this belief to the United States itself, against considerable resistance from labor unions that supported his own Democratic party, with the signing in 1993 of the North American Free Trade Agreement (NAFTA). The agreement provided for gradual elimination of barriers to the movement of goods and money among the United States, Canada, and Mexico and anticipated the later addition of the other countries of the Western Hemisphere.

More sweeping still was the 1993 revision of the General Agreement on Tariffs and Trade (GATT), an arrangement for mutually agreed reductions of tariffs that was first signed in 1947 and had been periodically updated since then. The latest round of cuts, arrived at after years of hard bargaining by the major trading powers, was expected to have the effect of ending most tariffs on manufactured goods. The revised GATT also established, for the first time, an authorized agency for settling trade disputes among the signatory countries: the World Trade Organization (WTO).

THE HARDSHIPS OF GLOBALIZATION: THE POSTCOMMUNIST COUNTRIES, THE GLOBAL SOUTH, AND THE FAR EAST

In practice, globalization according to the strict requirements of the Washington Consensus often turned out to restrict the spread of capitalist prosperity. Rapid privatization enabled speculators to bribe government officials and buy up valuable industries at knockdown prices, while workers in uncompetitive industries that no one wanted to buy lost their jobs overnight. That was one of the main reasons for the economic troubles of Russia and other postcommunist countries (p. 690).

Furthermore, the Western countries and Japan refused to apply the Washington Consensus to their own farmers. They used tariffs and subsidies to foster domestic and export sales of products like sugar, soybeans, and rice, thereby locking many farmers in the rest of the world out of the benefits of globalization. Partly for this reason, in the 1990s, much of what now came to be called the *global South*—Africa and Latin America—made little or no progress along the path to economic growth and capitalist prosperity. Early in the twenty-first century, resentment in the rest of the world against Western agricultural protectionism seemed to be growing. A WTO conference in Cancún, Mexico, broke down over this divisive issue, and it seemed unlikely that a further round of worldwide tariff reductions, scheduled for 2005, would be completed on schedule.

The Crisis of Far Eastern Capitalism. In addition, the loosening of currency controls combined with high technology made it possible to send tidal waves of money rushing across the world with a few computer keystrokes, thereby damaging many economies. Among the countries that suffered most from this were ones in the Far East that had successfully followed the Japanese model of economic growth, but unlike Japan, were vulnerable to international speculators because they depended heavily on foreign investment and credit. In 1997, several Far Eastern countries faced massive unemployment and business bankruptcies when speculators who had been scrambling to take advantage of the rise in value of those countries' currencies against the U.S. dollar suddenly grew nervous and pulled their money out.

The IMF then took advantage of the crisis to try to enforce the Washington Consensus and dismantle the Far Eastern model of capitalism. In order to get IMF loans to pay off debts to foreign banks and currency speculators, Thailand, South Korea, and other countries had to cut many links between governments and private corporations and eliminate barriers to foreign ownership of those corporations. Their governments also had to balance their budgets by reducing spending on such activities as keeping down food prices to unemployed consumers or helping companies in financial difficulties. In Indonesia, where in 1998 the director of the IMF personally enforced exceptionally harsh terms on the country's corrupt and dictatorial President Suharto (*Fig. 17.1*), the result was violent street protests and the overthrow of the regime. Elsewhere there were no revolutions, but for many Far Eastern countries with basically sound economies, the 1990s ended not in prosperity but in hardship.

GLOBALIZATION AND THE SPREAD OF PROSPERITY: INDIA AND CHINA

In spite of these hardships, many countries benefited from globalization—particularly ones that were large and powerful enough to ignore outside pressures to enforce the Washington Consensus rigorously, and instead were able to adopt it selectively. Among these countries were two that between them had one-third of the world's population—India and China.

India. Ever since independence, India had done its best to follow the Western model of the capitalist welfare state (pp. 582–585), with many state-owned industries alongside private corporations, a great deal of government planning, and strict controls on the

Fig. 17.1 Controlling Gaze. Michel Camdessus, director of the International Monetary Fund, looms over President Suharto as the Indonesian leader signs an agreement in 1998 stipulating that in return for a multibillion-dollar loan, his bankrupt country will undertake economic reforms inflicting widespread hardship on its people. Camdessus later said that his schoolmasterlike pose was unintended: there was nowhere to sit, and his mother had told him always to fold his arms when standing in public. But there was fury throughout the Far East at this endlessly rebroadcast TV image of an Asian country being subjected to Western insult as well as to Western injury.

movement of money in and out of the country. These policies had not brought prosperity to India's growing population, which was expected to reach one billion early in the twenty-first century. In the late 1980s, as socialism was plainly failing throughout the world, India's government followed a different Western example and began to privatize state-owned industries and loosen currency controls. All the same, the government did not give up fostering manufacturing industries, especially those using high technology, and it made great efforts to promote education in advanced technical fields.

When Hindu nationalists came to power in 1998 (p. 700), they continued these policies. As Hindu believers, they were suspicious of Western religious and cultural influences, but as nationalists, they believed that India must build its prosperity and power within the Western capitalist world. As a result, the Indian economy boomed, a rising middle class enjoyed some of the fruits of capitalist prosperity, and the country became a more influential member of the international community than ever before.

China. China, which had once competed with the Soviet Union to lead the communist challenge to the Western-dominated world order (pp. 600–601), began its long march back to capitalism in 1976 with the death of Mao Zedong and the rise to power of Deng Xiaoping, a veteran communist whom Mao had earlier persecuted for his relative moderation.

Deng's first move was to dissolve the large collective farms of the Mao era, returning land ownership to individual farm families. (Eighty percent of the people of China live on or near farms.) In the following years, Deng decentralized the management of the vast state-owned industrial enterprises, permitting greater flexibility and individual initiative. However, the government made sure to control the pace of change. It allowed domestic and foreign capitalists to invest in new industries, but moved very slowly to privatize existing ones. It held down the value of China's currency against foreign currencies, so that Chinese products would be cheap for foreigners to buy and exports would grow. And unlike the Soviet reformers of the Gorbachev era, Deng ruthlessly upheld the dictatorial authority of the Communist party. In 1989, inspired by the Soviet and east European example, a swelling "democracy movement," centered in the universities and supported by many workers dissatisfied with their pay and conditions, challenged the party's authority. Finally, however, the army attacked thousands of demonstrators camped out in Beijing's central public space, Tiananmen Square. Perhaps as many as 2,600 people were killed, and the democracy movement collapsed.

The effect of this combination of political dictatorship and carefully managed economic liberalization, at least for the time being, was to channel the energies of the Chinese population into striving for prosperity within the global economy. Throughout the 1990s and on into the twenty-first century, China's economy grew without a pause, and in 2002, under Deng's successor, Jiang Zemin, the government showed its confidence in the country's global future by joining the WTO. In China as in India, millions began to enjoy modest fruits of capitalist prosperity.

But there were many millions in both China and India to whom capitalist prosperity did not spread, and bitter contrasts appeared between the newly rich and the still poor. In both countries, the dream of wealth, leisure, and well-being for all had been only partly realized, and disappointed hopes could still lead to social conflict.

GLOBALIZATION AND THE WEST

Economic globalization led to disputes and conflicts within Western countries just as in the rest of the world. The main wielders of economic power in governments, corporations, banks, and stock exchanges wholeheartedly supported it. Many labor unions, churches, and charitable organizations, as well as a widespread, mostly youthful, international protest movement, criticized and opposed it.

For and Against Globalization. The opponents of globalization blamed it for many evils and hardships within the West and throughout the rest of the world. The loss of high-paying industrial jobs and the decline of union membership in the West, the desperate poverty of the global South, the ruthless exploitation in Asian sweatshops, the overuse of natural resources, and the destruction of the natural environment—all were laid at the door of economic globalization. In 1999, the annual meeting of the WTO in Seattle was accompanied by massive protest demonstrations that turned violent. Such demonstrations, with or without disorders, became a regular accompaniment to the meetings of the World Bank and the IMF as well as the WTO.

Defenders of globalization insisted that the loss of industrial jobs was due to automation rather than free trade, and that cheap imports from overseas raised the standard of living of consumers. They claimed that Asian workers who found jobs in sweatshops, however badly they were exploited, were still taking a first step away from alternatives that were even worse, such as starvation and prostitution. They argued that in tropical lands, peasants in need of farms to feed their families destroyed just as much rain forest as multinational corporations eager to sell timber or soybeans on the global market.

The arguments on both sides were much the same as those that had raged in the nineteenth-century Industrial Revolution over such issues as the growth of cities, conditions in the factories, and tariffs and trade (pp. 510–513). As with nineteenth-century industrialization, many on both sides of the argument recognized that globalization was unstoppable. The real questions were how much and in what ways it could be managed and controlled, and who should manage and control it.

Globalization and Western Legitimacy. Outside the countries of the Western heartland, this last issue aroused more concern than any other. As disturbing as the destruction of the environment or conditions in sweatshops might be, the single biggest source of public indignation was the feeling that the leading countries of the West were using globalization to exploit the rest of the world.

In actual fact, the West did not escape some of the hardships of globalization, and many countries in the rest of the world gained from it. In 1996, furthermore, the G7 countries put into effect a policy of forgiving part of the many billions of dollars owed them by the most heavily indebted poor countries, and extended this measure in 1999. But although the international community's richest citizens could afford to be generous once in a while, from time to time they also did not hesitate to use their power to solve their economic problems at the expense of the rest of the world when they saw a chance to do so.

In the 1993 GATT negotiations, for example, the West held out for free trade in financial services (such as banking and stockbroking), where it had an overwhelming competitive edge—but successfully resisted free trade in farm products, which would expose Western farmers to the competition of cheap foodstuffs from the global South. Likewise, the IMF's solution to the Far Eastern financial crisis of 1997 threw millions of workers out of jobs and enabled Western investors to buy up businesses at bargain prices—but it also ensured that no Western bank went out of business, although imprudent Western loans and currency transfers to the Far East had helped cause the crisis in the first place.

In 1998, furthermore, when the Far Eastern financial crisis led to crises in North America and Europe as well, the Federal Reserve Bank helped organize a multibillion-dollar loan to Long Term Capital Management, a huge private financial company that faced bankruptcy as a result of failed international speculations in government bonds. If the Federal Reserve had not intervened, the company's failure might well have led to a severe and lengthy stock market crash that would have thrown many U.S. workers out of their jobs. But this was just the kind of action that the IMF, with Washington's backing, was forbidding to one Far Eastern government after another, regardless of the loss of Far Eastern jobs.

Nothing was more damaging to the legitimacy of the Western countries as would-be leaders of the international community—that is, to the community's willingness to accept their leadership as rightful and beneficial—than their unwillingness to abide by the rules that they tried to decree for the global economy as a whole. The image of the director of the IMF seemingly treating an Indonesian leader, however brutal and corrupt, like a misbehaving schoolboy (*Fig. 17.1*, p. 686) symbolized a new division that threatened to appear within the world—a division between what observers of the global scene began to call "The West and the Rest."

In addition, the mistakes and failures of globalization under Western leadership contributed to other problems and conflicts in both the postcommunist countries of eastern Europe and the postcolonial world of Asia and Africa.

The Former "East": Trying to Join the West

From Germany's eastern borders all the way to the Pacific Ocean, two dozen countries that had once belonged to the Soviet Union or been its satellite states coped with the aftereffects of the collapse of communism (*Map 15.2*, p. 598; *Map 15.5*, p. 635). Except for the predominantly Muslim states of central Asia, most of the ex-communist countries had been outlying territories of Western civilization, with religious and cultural identities not too different from those of the Western heartland. What their peoples now mostly wanted was quickly and easily to join the democratic-capitalist world order on equal terms with its leading countries. In practice, the process turned out to be long and hard, and success was uneven.

THE FORMER SATELLITES: MOVING WESTWARD

For the peoples of eastern Europe, democratic freedom and capitalist prosperity were unthinkable unless they first won genuine national independence. They were not certain of achieving this simply by breaking their ties of subjection to their eastern neighbor, Russia, for they also had a western neighbor that had traditionally threatened their independence—newly reunited Germany. What the eastern Europeans believed they needed was some kind of structure that would protect them against Russia, prevent their being dominated by Germany, and also suppress their own mutual rivalries and conflicts which tempted their neighbors to intervene in their affairs. Most eastern European leaders were convinced that they could find this structure as members of the North Atlantic Treaty Organization (NATO; p. 599). NATO was now far stronger than Russia; it included Germany; and within it, Germany was balanced by other powerful countries including the most powerful of all, the United States.

As for the existing NATO countries, all of them (including Germany) were willing to do whatever was necessary to prevent the collapse of communism being followed by chaos in eastern Europe. Accordingly, they decided in 1994 that NATO should expand eastward, and in 1999 the westernmost former satellites, the Czech Republic, Hungary, and Poland, joined the alliance. Five years later, NATO further expanded to include all the other former satellite countries—Albania, Bulgaria, Romania, and Slovakia; two countries that had been part of Yugoslavia (pp. 691–694)—Macedonia and Slovenia; and three Baltic countries that had belonged to the Soviet Union—Estonia, Latvia, and Lithuania.

Meanwhile, the westernmost ex-communist countries, the Czech Republic, Hungary, Poland, Slovakia, and Slovenia, seemed to be making harsh but successful political and economic transitions to Western-style democracy and capitalism. In many cases, the transitions involved cooperation and conflict among leaders of anticommunist resistance who now became national heroes, eager privatizers who wished to introduce free-market capitalism overnight, and Communist parties that changed their names, accepted democracy, and called for slower economic changes.

This call had wide appeal, for the adjustment to capitalism proved to be much harder than expected. Many noncompetitive industries had to be closed down almost overnight, causing massive unemployment. Hasty privatization led to corruption, stock market crashes, and sell-offs of assets to Western companies and local speculators. People began to miss the economic security of communism, even while they rejoiced in democratic freedoms. Late in the 1990s, government regulation and intervention made free markets less chaotic, and the large numbers of well-educated and unemployed workers began to attract global corporations to build plants and offices. In 2003, all five countries joined the European Union—a sign of their continued confidence, as well as that of the EU itself, in their democratic and capitalist future.

With this expansion, the EU reached the early medieval border between Catholic and Orthodox Europe (p. 224). Beyond that line, the problems of economic and political adjustment were much worse. Romania and Bulgaria, traditionally much poorer countries than those farther west, were nevertheless expected to join the EU by 2007. In the countries fringing Russia in Europe, the Caucasus, and central Asia, however, poverty and corruption were endemic, and former Communist party bosses had in many cases made successful transitions to become nationalist dictators.

RUSSIA: A TIME OF TROUBLES

In Russia itself, Boris Yeltsin, the victor over both the Communist conservatives and the Communist reformers in 1991 (p. 634), promised as president to turn Russia almost overnight into a modern capitalist democracy. Yeltsin was the third Russian ruler—the first two being Peter the Great and Stalin (pp. 413, 573–574)—to seek equality of wealth and power with the West through a program of breakneck Westernization. He was far less successful than either of the other two.

Yeltsin presided over almost a decade of Russian national misfortune and humiliation. True, there seemed to be general acceptance (even within the still powerful Communist party) that traditional communism was dead and would never be resurrected, and a rough-and-tumble version of democratic politics seemed to have won legitimacy. But in the ten years after the end of the Soviet Union, most Russians sank into poverty and squalor far worse than those of communism. Privatization led not to the modernization of industry and the economy but to the plundering of the country's assets by wealthy tycoons and gangsters, the spreading of the Far Eastern financial crisis to Russia in 1998, and an IMF loan to prevent bankruptcy. Instead of growing, the economy's production of goods and services declined to two-thirds that of flourishing China. In international affairs, Russia fell far from its former status as a superpower, and lost much of its influence even in countries just outside its borders: the newly independent Baltic republics made their way into NATO, and U.S. oil companies took over oil fields in central Asia. The Russian government could not collect taxes, the armed forces were in decay, and the space program, once the pride of the Soviet Union, was kept going only by U.S. subsidies.

Yeltsin's handpicked successor, Vladimir Putin—elected president in 2000—promised to strengthen the state, rein in the tycoons and gangsters, and restore Russia's standard of living and pride in itself. By 2004, he had gone some way toward accomplishing the first two of these objectives, and Russia's economy had begun to grow again.

Few Russians had become more prosperous as a result, but Putin nevertheless gained widespread trust and respect among the voters and was reelected president in a landslide, even though his methods included manipulation of the mass media and intimidation of opponents.

Both Yeltsin and Putin had to deal with an ethnic and religious conflict within Russia's borders that was unleashed by the collapse of the Communist dictatorship. Chechnya, a territory within Russia whose Muslim population had a long history of resistance to rule from Moscow, moved in 1995 to achieve complete independence. Yeltsin treated the matter as a test of the strength of the Russian state and his own effectiveness as president, and decided to use force to put down the secession. A bitter war ensued between the Russian army and Chechen militants in which the Russians suffered many setbacks and eventually withdrew, leaving Chechnya apparently set for eventual independence. But Islamic fundamentalist forces in Chechnya provoked Moscow with raids on neighboring territories and terrorist bombings, and the conflict resumed in 1999. This time, the Russians reoccupied the territory with savage bombardments and systematic destruction but were left with an apparently unwinnable guerrilla war on their hands.

The Chechen war weakened Russia at a time when turning it into a prosperous and powerful modern country was a vast and still unaccomplished task. If only because Russia still had a world-destroying arsenal of nuclear weapons left over from Soviet times, the Western countries were usually careful to treat it respectfully. In 1997, Yeltsin was invited to the annual meeting of the G7 leaders, who from then on became the G8. NATO treated Russia as a partner to be consulted rather than an adversary to be contained. The partnership was severely strained by NATO's eastward expansion, but in 2002 a NATO-Russia Joint Council was established that provided for the partners to take joint decisions and actions to deal with common threats. For the moment, however, Russia remained in a state of resentful dependence on its former capitalist rivals, and was still a long way from truly joining the West on equal terms.

CHALLENGE TO THE WEST: THE YUGOSLAV WARS

The fall of communism in eastern Europe unleashed many long-suppressed national conflicts, but usually these conflicts did not lead to war. The most destructive national passions in the region had already been released, and mostly satisfied, in an orgy of genocide and expulsions of national minorities during and after the Second World War. Most eastern European nations were therefore content with their existing borders, and even dissatisfied ones knew that nationalist wars would lay them open to German or Russian interference and prevent them from fulfilling their overriding ambition to join the West on equal terms. Furthermore, the United States and the EU countries, which were now the outside powers with the strongest influence in the region, were determined to damp down national conflicts.

The Yugoslav Background. In the Balkan country of Yugoslavia, however, national ambitions were still unsatisfied. Early medieval barbarian invasions, the schism of the Greek and Latin churches, and centuries of Turkish rule had made this territory one of half a dozen small, mostly Slavic nations, and of three religions—Catholic, Orthodox, and Muslim. Rival nationalisms, great power intervention, and two world wars had often turned these nations against each other. After the First World War, they had united for the first time in their histories to form Yugoslavia, but their rivalries and disputes had continued. (For details see Chapters 5, 7, and 14.)

Following the Second World War, the Communist party, headed by Marshal Tito, took over power (p. 600). Tito avoided ethnic persecutions and expulsions. and organized Yugoslavia as a federated state of six republics. In each republic, one or other nation predominated, but in all of them except the northernmost republic of Slovenia, there were strong minorities of other nations.

Communism and federal ties both weakened after Tito's death in 1980, and thwarted nationalist ambitions resurfaced, first of all in the Serb republic. The Serbs are an Orthodox nation with a glorious medieval past (p. 295) and a more recent history of resistance to foreign rule and conflict with neighboring nations. They dominated Yugoslavia's federal government, but many of their nation lived as minorities in the neighboring republic of Bosnia-Herzegovina (alongside Roman Catholic Croats and Muslim Bosnians), as well as in the main Croat territory, the republic of Croatia. A Serb Communist leader, Slobodan Milosevic, reinvented himself as an extreme nationalist and revived the movement for a "Greater Serbia," to include the entire nation, that had precipitated the First World War in 1914 (p. 561).

Breakup and War. Partly out of fear of Serbia and partly to fulfill their own national ambitions, most of the republics declared their independence in 1991, and at that point their hostilities exploded. Serbia was the principal inheritor of the former federal state and its army. Together with the neighboring republic of Montenegro, also mainly inhabited by Serbs, it formed a new and smaller Yugoslavia, but it also tried to use its power to gain control of the territories of Serb minorities in Croatia and Bosnia. Serbs most of all, but also Croats and Bosnian Muslims, attacked the other groups, forcing them out of the areas they lived in, occupying those areas with their own people, and giving this common twentieth-century practice a new name—"ethnic cleansing." Only ethnically homogeneous Slovenia avoided massacres and ethnic cleansing, and was able to join less troubled eastern European countries on the path to EU membership.

The United Nations decreed sanctions against Serbia and established a war crimes tribunal in the Dutch city of The Hague. The European Union negotiated cease-fires, and NATO sent in western European peacekeeping troops. In spite of all these measures, the ethnic cleansing and accompanying massacres went on for four years. The main reason was that the armed forces of the EU countries were not strong enough to intimidate the warring parties, and the United States was unwilling to risk its own forces in this European dispute.

Finally, however, an alliance of Bosnian Croats and Muslims, and an army from the Croatian republic organized and armed with unofficial U.S. help, tipped the balance against the Serbs. A U.S. initiative then succeeded in bringing the parties to a general peace agreement. Bosnia, Croatia, and Serbia recognized each other as independent states with the same borders that they had had as republics within the old Yugoslavia. In Bosnia, a joint Muslim-Croat region and a Serb region were to be created, with NATO forces and a NATO administrator to keep the peace. United States, British, French, and other NATO forces moved into Bosnia in December 1995 (*Map 17.1*).

The Serbs struck again in 1999, this time against the main ethnic minority in the Serb republic, ethnic Albanians of Muslim faith in the province of Kosovo (p. 561). The Albanians were seeking to regain the autonomy they had enjoyed under Tito as a first

Map 17.1 The Breakup of Yugoslavia. The map shows the division of Yugoslavia to the benefit of the Croats, Macedonians, Serbs, and Slovenes in 1995. All the new states except Slovenia had large and discontented national minorities—Serbs in Croatia, and Albanians in the rump Yugoslavia (later renamed "Serbia and Montenegro") and in Macedonia. Bosnia, where no nation had an absolute majority, was held together by NATO forces. In 1999, the Albanians of Kosovo won de facto independence under NATO protection. Today, the lands of former Yugoslavia remain balanced between nation building and further redrawing of borders.

step toward independence and possible union with the neighboring independent country of Albania (*Map 17.1*). The Yugoslav army, helped by some local Serbs, drove the Albanians out of their province. The world community was shocked by this ruthless example of ethnic cleansing. The United Nations failed to act for fear of a veto in its Security Council by Russia, which sympathized with the Serbs as a Slav and Orthodox nation. All the same, the members agreed that the Serbian crimes must be stopped and the refugees allowed to return.

After long hesitation, the United States used its military power to enforce this decision. Its air forces attacked the Serb army and targets inside Serbia until Milosevic gave in. Most Muslims returned to their smashed homes, and some fled to other countries.

Once again, NATO troops and administrators moved in, and normal life was gradually restored for most of the Albanian population; the Serb minority retreated to the northern part of the province, under pressure from Albanians thirsting for revenge.

The Fall of Milosevic. This renewed disaster finally led to the ouster of Milosevic as leader of Serbia. In 2000, he was defeated in a bid to win reelection as president against opposition forces led by Vojislav Kostunica, and when he tried to hold on to power in spite of the elections, he was forced out by massive street demonstrations in the capital city of Belgrade. Kostunica's victory was welcomed by the NATO countries, and it meant the end of Serb efforts to unite their entire nation within a single state.

With the fighting stopped and Milosevic out of the way, the United States and the EU encouraged the leaders of the various republics of the former Yugoslavia, now nearly all independent states, to cooperate with each other. To the extent that they did so, they received financial help and were offered the hope of eventual membership in the EU. The same inducements were offered to the leaders of the various national groups within the republics to work together.

The governments of the republics were also expected to arrest suspected war criminals and send them for trial before the tribunal at The Hague. The Serbs handed over Milosevic himself in 2002, and he behaved in the courtroom as a defiant victim of a Western conspiracy against the Serb nation. Victims of ethnic cleansing were given shelter, food, and help with returning to their homes. Often this help came from NGOs based in western Europe and the United States that mobilized dedicated and idealistic volunteers more efficiently than governments, and for this reason gained official cooperation and financing.

Repairing Failed States: Nation Building and Civil Society. In Yugoslavia, the West faced an open challenge to its hopes for a harmonious postcommunist world order. It tried to deal with the challenge partly by applying lessons derived from the experience of western Europe during and after the Second World War. Military force and what amounted to military occupations would restore order and force warring nations apart. Financial help would ease the task of reconstruction. Reconciliation and cooperation among states would bring prosperity and harmony so that national grievances would no longer matter. The punishment of war criminals by legal trials would discourage vengeance and make nations repent of the crimes committed in their names.

In addition, the approval of the United Nations would provide legitimacy and a guarantee of impartiality for these and other measures. After all, the West was acting not just for the sake of its own interests and values but in the interests of peace and order in the international community. The community should therefore give its approval after due debate and consultation, in its own interest as well as that of the former Yugoslav nations and of the West.

It seemed, however, that Yugoslavia, with its complex ethnic and religious mosaic and its peoples unfamiliar with modern democratic government, needed more than the experience of postwar western Europe to help solve its problems. Accordingly, Western leaders turned from the lessons of their own recent past to two seemingly promising theoretical concepts.

One of these was the concept of *nation building*. This idea had originally been developed by political scientists, notably the U.S. scholar Reinhard Bendix, reflecting in the

1960s on the processes whereby Western nation-states had come into existence, and on how to apply the lessons of these processes to the decolonized nations of Africa and Asia. According to Bendix, a human group acquires the status of a nation in three ways. It acquires a feeling of common identity that supersedes earlier tribal, ethnic, and religious allegiances; it develops economic links of trade, travel, and communication that overcome the isolation of the smaller communities that make it up; and it creates a powerful and effective yet democratic government. These three processes, furthermore, interact so as to push each other forward: an effective democratic government in which all members of the group participate, for example, helps to give them a sense of common national identity.

The concept of nation building had obvious relevance to the newly independent Yugoslav republics, especially Bosnia and Kosovo. NATO administrators in those lands must wield sticks and carrots, NATO peacekeeping troops must stand guard, and Western NGOs must provide disinterested help and advice, to promote reconciliation and economic development, and foster effective government institutions in which all groups would have a stake. In this way it would be possible to turn the Muslims, Croats, and Serbs of Bosnia into Bosnians, and the Albanians and Serbs of Kosovo into Kosovans, without either destroying their ethnic and religious individualities or using repression and force.

An idea allied to that of nation building was the concept of *civil society*. This idea dated back to Enlightenment beliefs about the social contract and about rulers as agents of society (pp. 450–451), and it was revived in the 1970s by dissidents (opponents of communist rule) in eastern European communist countries, notably the Polish thinker Leszek Kolakowski. Under communism, the state had tried to control all organizations and activities, no matter how remote from politics, whereas Kolakowski believes that the direction of control should be exactly the other way round. For Kolakowski and like-minded thinkers, "civil society" denotes grassroots networks of organizations and activities separate from the state but influencing and controlling it, which in their view form the foundation of democracy. Inspired by this school of thought, Western government leaders and diplomats believed that NATO administrators and NGOs must now help the peoples of Bosnia and Kosovo develop such civil societies, and thereby lay the foundations for true democracies and effective nation-states.

The Results of Western Intervention. The combination of force, aid, processes of punishment and reconciliation, and grassroots reforms, all in the name of the international community, was successful in important ways. It stopped the massacres and ethnic cleansing, and enabled many victims of cleansing to return to their homes. In addition it persuaded the former Yugoslav states to cooperate with each other on matters of common concern.

The more ambitious efforts for reconciliation and grassroots rebuilding were less successful. The trials at The Hague were essential in the interests of justice, but caused more resentment than repentance among the nations to which the defendants belonged. National minorities within each state lived in their own enclaves, guarded by peacekeepers, resenting and resented by the majority population. Perhaps the most serious difficulty was that Albanians, Croats, and Serbs were not simply ethnic or religious groups, but members of nations that had already undergone lengthy processes of building. Now they were in effect being told to abort these nation-building processes and rebuild themselves as Bosnians or as Kosovans. Many among all three groups, however, continued to see themselves as members of historic nations with the same right to fight for independence and unity as, for instance, Germans and Americans.

The Postcolonial World: The Limits of Western Leadership

Along with the conflicts and rivalries let loose by the fall of communism, those that had earlier been unleashed by the end of colonialism in Africa and Asia continued just as before. When postcolonial ethnic and religious disputes exploded or threatened to explode into war, the Western countries, as leaders of the international community, could not easily avoid responsibility for settling these disturbances of the community's peace and order. Thus every postcolonial dispute was to a greater or lesser extent a challenge to the West.

In meeting these challenges, the Western countries were at a disadvantage in many ways. With so many challenges to deal with, Western governments had limited time to spend on any one of them, and they spent much of that time arguing among themselves over what was to be done and which government was to bear the burden of doing it. In any case, Western voters were reluctant to spend money and risk lives in peacekeeping interventions, let alone in ones where their troops might actually have to fight. Often, too, Western countries were interested parties in the disputes they claimed to judge. Trade, travel, and the Internet might be shrinking the world, but it was still too large and untidy for anyone easily to steer it.

THE HOPE OF HARMONY: THE GULF WAR AND THE END OF APARTHEID

Closely following the end of communism came two events that held out the promise of what the U.S. president, George H. W. Bush, called a "New World Order"—one of harmonious diversity where the international community would combine to punish the breakers of its rules.

The Gulf War. The first great challenge to the postcommunist international community came in the Persian Gulf in August 1990, when Iraq occupied the neighboring country of Kuwait (*Map 17.2,* p. 728). Western countries had favored earlier expansionist efforts by the Iraqi leader Saddam Hussein against Islamic fundamentalist–dominated Iran (p. 624). Kuwait, however, was a pro-Western Arab state with rich oil fields, and the occupation looked like Saddam's first step to conquering Saudi Arabia, the West's single largest oil supplier.

A month later, in an unprecedented show of unity and determination, the United States led a coalition of powers within the United Nations (including many Arab countries as well as the Soviet Union) to declare and enforce a total trade embargo against Iraq as an aggressor state. In January 1991, when it was clear that this measure was insufficient to compel Saddam to withdraw his army, the UN Security Council authorized the coalition powers to resort to military action.

The coalition forces, headed by the United States, quickly and decisively routed the Iraqis in Operation Desert Storm. Kuwait's independence was restored. A U.S.-backed rebellion by the Kurds, a nation living in the north of Iraq whom Saddam had earlier repressed with poison gas attacks, achieved self-government. UN inspections forced

Saddam to dismantle all or most of his programs to develop atom bombs, poison gas, and killer germs.

This successful demonstration of collective action in turning back aggression raised hopes for developing effective means for providing global security. In some ways, however, it showed the limits of what collective action could do. The Gulf coalition's Arab members did not want a Western-led coalition to overthrow their fellow Arab, Saddam. As Sunni Muslims, they distrusted the Shiites of Iraq who had also rebelled—a feeling that the Western governments shared, since the Shiites were presumed to be pro-Iranian fundamentalists (pp. 207, 621–623). For these reasons, Saddam was able to stay in power, cruelly repress the Shiites, and in various ways violate his obligations under the cease-fire agreements. Trade sanctions stayed in place, and from time to time, U.S. and British air raids retaliated for Saddam's misdeeds. The international community had won, but the outlaw was still able to show his defiance.

The End of Apartheid. Not long after the Gulf War came the dismantling of the last outpost of colonial rule, the Republic of South Africa. Ever since the 1940s, the leaders of the Afrikaners (white South Africans of Dutch origin) had tried to build a state and society based on apartheid—separation of races, which in fact had the effect of making whites a privileged ruling group (p. 607). Even during the Cold War, this had isolated South Africa in the world, since both the rival blocs, as well as the decolonized countries, proclaimed their official belief in racial harmony.

In the 1970s, the countries on South Africa's borders gained independence and majority rule. Dissension grew among the whites, for English-speaking South Africans, though they too benefited from apartheid, saw themselves as part of a larger world that had mostly turned against them. Growing unrest in the black communities led to countless protest marches, clashes with police, and hundreds of deaths and imprisonments. The most prominent black leaders were Nelson Mandela, the chief of the banned African National Congress (ANC), the main black political organization, who was serving a life sentence for treason; and an Anglican priest, Desmond Tutu, whose church did not accept apartheid and promoted him to become archbishop of Cape Town. Both men gained a worldwide moral status like that of Gandhi or Martin Luther King—not only because they resisted racial oppression but also because they preached racial harmony. All the same, a well-trained army, an efficient secret police, and South Africa's continued trading and financial links with other advanced capitalist economies successfully upheld apartheid into the late 1980s.

Then, however, partly at Tutu's urging, South Africa's main economic partners, the leading Western countries, began to cut their commercial and financial links with the country. African American leaders in the United States, for instance, ran successful campaigns to persuade financial institutions to stop making loans to South African companies or buying shares in them. South African business leaders joined the calls for an end to apartheid, the sense that the end was near encouraged blacks and discouraged whites, and the regime was faced with possible collapse.

F. W. de Klerk, an Afrikaner and a strong supporter of apartheid who became prime minister in 1989, now came to believe that only one policy and only one leader could save South Africa from civil war. The policy was to end apartheid, and the leader was Nelson Mandela.

Over the next five years of contentious partnership between de Klerk and Mandela, apartheid was peacefully ended and South Africa became a multiracial state with majority rule under Mandela as president. To banish the ghosts of the past, Tutu headed a Truth and Reconciliation Commission that —uniquely, after such a drastic regime change—investigated and exposed the crimes of apartheid without putting anyone on trial, and criticized misdeeds of antiapartheid groups, including the ANC, as well as those of the former authorities.

The restructured state had plenty of problems. There was massive unemployment among blacks as well as continued hostility between the races and among black ethnic groups. AIDS (p. 650) was spreading disastrously, though the government for a long time ignored this problem under Mandela's successor, Thabo Mbeki, elected president in 1999. All the same, South Africa remained an advanced economy, a regional power, and an example of peaceful resolution of a historic conflict.

THE THREAT OF ANARCHY: FAILURES OF THE INTERNATIONAL COMMUNITY

Besides these spectacular victories of the international community, however, there were also spectacular defeats. In the postcolonial world of Africa and Asia, many other conflicts arose that the international community was unable to prevent from exploding into war, massacres, and ethnic cleansing. There were other postcolonial conflicts that smoldered on amid repression and terrorism without actually bursting into full-scale war, but which the international community could not resolve.

Asian and African Wars. In Asia, the international community took no action to stop a vicious ethnic war accompanied by ethnic cleansing between two former Soviet republics, Armenia and Azerbaijan, that lasted from 1992 to 1994. In that same time span, a U.S.-led peacekeeping force failed to stop a chaotic civil war in the East African country of Somalia (*Map 15.3*, p. 606), and finally withdrew after both U.S. and Pakistani troops were killed in skirmishes with local armed gangs. And in the summer of 1994, ethnic fighting in Rwanda, in central Africa, killed at least half a million people, besides another hundred thousand who died of disease in refugee camps. It was the worst single act of genocide since the atrocities in Kampuchea in the 1970s, and the international community, under the leadership of the triumphant West, did nothing to stop it.

Other African civil wars were more successfully ended by interventions authorized by the United Nations and carried out sometimes by French or British troops and sometimes by local peacekeepers led by regional powers such as Nigeria. Very often, the United Nations and Western-based NGOs supplied food relief, medical aid, and help with reconstruction. But the chaos in Africa in particular showed the limits of the international community's capacity to maintain peace and order, and of the West's ability and willingness to lead the community when its own vital interests were not involved.

Israel and the Arabs. The end of the Cold War, the end of apartheid, and the united action of Arab states under U.S. leadership in the Gulf War all seemed to point to an end to another lengthy conflict, that of Israel and the Arabs. Already it was clear that the Arabs could not destroy Israel by force, and a leading Arab country, Egypt, had recognized the Jewish state a dozen years before. The Israelis had learned in Lebanon (pp. 610–611) that they were not strong enough to force Arab states to make peace simply by invading and occupying them.

Since 1987, furthermore, Israel had faced an uprising of Palestinians (the *intifada,* or "shaking off") in the lands west of the river Jordan (the West Bank) and the huge refugee camps of Gaza, which it had conquered in 1967 (*Spot Map,* p. 609). It was clear that the Jewish state could hold on to these territories only by endless repression and force. In addition, the United States, Israel's main supporter and the backer of many Arab governments as well (p. 610), was eager for a settlement that would help consolidate a harmonious international community under U.S. leadership.

The key to settlement of the conflict, it seemed, was a settlement between Israel and the Palestinians in the West Bank and Gaza. In 1993, a crucial agreement was at last concluded. The Israeli government of Yitzhak Rabin officially recognized the Palestine Liberation Organization (PLO), headed by Yassir Arafat, as the sole representative of the Palestinian people in return for the PLO's recognition of Israel. It also granted limited Palestinian self-rule in Gaza and the city of Jericho on the West Bank, under an interim government known as the Palestinian Authority, of which Arafat was elected president. This agreement was followed by an Israeli peace pact with the neighboring kingdom of Jordan.

The Israeli-Palestinian agreement was not in fact a final peace, but the beginning of a "peace process" that would require painful sacrifices from both sides. The Israelis would have to give up most or all of the lands they had occupied in the West Bank. The Palestinians would have to give up hope of returning to the homes they had lost in what was now Israel. Furthermore, the two sides would have to reach agreement about Jerusalem, which both sides claimed as their national capital and which was holy to both Judaism and Islam as well as to Christianity.

Strong forces on both sides opposed compromise on any of these issues, and the official leaders of both sides were in some ways unwilling to challenge the opponents of compromise. No Israeli government could bring itself to stop the confiscation of land and expansion of settlements in the West Bank and end oppressive restrictions aimed at keeping Palestinians a minority in Jerusalem. Arafat made only token efforts to stop terrorism by Islamic and nationalist groups, who now began the practice of sending suicide bombers on missions to kill civilians inside Israel.

In 1995, the Palestinian Authority's area of control was extended to include most large Arab towns in the West Bank, which had always been expensive and dangerous for the Israelis to occupy. The countryside, however, with its land available for settlement, stayed under Israeli control. Finally, the Israeli prime minister, Ehud Barak, elected in 1999, made a renewed effort for peace with all Israel's neighbors. He withdrew Israeli forces from southern Lebanon and began negotiations for peace with Israel's other northern neighbor, Syria, as well as for a final settlement with the Palestinians.

But intensive negotiations between the Israelis and the Palestinians, leading to face-to-face meetings of Barak, Arafat, and Clinton in the United States, only revealed the depth of the remaining disagreement. Barak for the first time appeared willing to end the occupation of most of the West Bank, but Arafat could not bring himself to make the necessary compromises over Jerusalem and the return of Palestinian refugees. The result was an outbreak of fierce fighting between Palestinians and the Israeli army and the election as Israeli prime minister of Ariel Sharon, a believer in the historic right of the Jews to make their homeland in all of the lands west of the Jordan and the main backer of the settlements. Meanwhile, negotiations with Syria were stalled by disagreement over Israeli evacuation of Syrian territory captured in 1967, and then by the death of Syrian President Hafiz Assad after many years of power.

In all these dealings between Israel and the Arabs, the United States had been active in coaxing and pressuring both sides to compromise, and the western Europeans had supported the peace process as best they could by subsidizing the Palestinian Authority.

The halting of the peace process showed the limits of the power of the Western countries to end conflicts when one party or both parties were unwilling to make the sacrifices necessary for compromise.

India and Pakistan. The same was also true of Western power to influence another long-standing conflict, that of India and Pakistan. The two countries had compromised as well as fought each other in the past, but in the postcommunist era, rival fundamentalisms drove them onto a collision course.

In Pakistan, there was an uneasy balance of power between the army and increasingly fundamentalist Muslim political parties, which had growing success in elections. Army generals were usually able to overthrow politicians whom they considered corrupt, or who tried to bring the military under civilian control. But overthrowing politicians was one thing, and challenging the growing power of fundamentalist Islam was quite another. The generals themselves had to compromise with fundamentalism or risk revolution in the country—and mutiny among their own troops. In 1991, in a period of civilian rule, the Pakistani parliament passed legislation making *Sharia* (Islamic religious law; p. 205) valid in many legal matters, and the army did not challenge this measure. Besides, the army and Islamic fundamentalists had an important common project: that of undermining Indian rule over a Muslim majority in the part of the disputed territory of Kashmir that India controlled (p. 604).

There were parallel developments in India—a secular democracy under firm civilian control, but one where Hindu nationalism became an increasingly powerful force. Hindu nationalism, like Islamic fundamentalism, is a movement that reasserts traditional religious belief in a stricter form than was usual in the past, despises other religions, and is deeply suspicious of cultural influences emanating from the West. Unlike Islamic fundamentalism, however, it is not an international movement but a nationalist one. Indian Hindu revivalists have made little effort to spread their influence to other Hindu peoples in southern Asia, but they have been intent on building up the power and prosperity of India.

During the 1990s, Hindu nationalist parties became an increasingly formidable threat to the secular Congress party, which had steered India to independence and had nearly always been the main governing party since then. The rise of Hindu nationalism was accompanied by repeated bloody clashes with India's religious minorities—Sikhs, Christians, and above all the country's 140 million Muslims, who make up nearly one-sixth of the population. In Kashmir and elsewhere, Hindu militants burned Muslim shrines and tried to turn them into Hindu temples. Finally, in 1998, the main Hindu nationalist party, the Bharatiya Janata (Indian People's) party, took over from Congress as the largest party in the Indian parliament.

One of the new governing party's first decisions was to authorize underground tests of three atomic weapons and of two more after the United States imposed mild economic sanctions. India had already tested a nuclear device in 1974, but since then, as the Indians knew, Pakistan had been working hard on its own nuclear program. The main point of holding tests now was to show that India was a great Hindu nation that could not be trifled with—not by Pakistan, nor by the United States. The Pakistanis quickly assembled and detonated their own atom bombs two weeks later and celebrated their own Islamic triumph. Once again, the United States imposed mild sanctions.

A year later, in 1999, the two South Asian nuclear powers almost went to war after Muslim militants based in Pakistan made incursions into Kashmir, and U.S. diplomats hastened to mediate a military stand-down by both sides. But that made no difference to the fact that two important non-Western members of the international community had shown that they could ignore the community's wishes, in particular those of its leading Western member.

REBELS AND OUTLAWS: ISLAMIC FUNDAMENTALISM, TERRORISM, AND WEAPONS OF MASS DESTRUCTION

In Chechnya and Yugoslavia, in Palestine and Kashmir, and in other postcommunist or postcolonial conflicts, Muslims were involved as both victims and oppressors. The hatreds resulting from these struggles helped nourish the one international ideology that still rejected and sought to overthrow the Western-dominated world order, Islamic fundamentalism (pp. 621–624)—and fundamentalist Islam, in turn, added fuel to the flames of many conflicts. In addition, the continuing conflicts also made two of the threatening problems of the 1980s (pp. 627–628) even more menacing than before: terrorism and the proliferation of nuclear and other weapons of mass destruction.

Islamic Fundamentalism. In the 1980s, Islamic fundamentalism had developed into an international movement opposed to the existing world order like communism before it. As with communism, there were countries where Islamic fundamentalism was in power, countries where it was a strong movement without actually being in power, and countries where it was repressed. Of course, unlike communism, it had no worldwide appeal but affected only Muslim communities—and exactly for that reason, even countries that repressed it had to find a way of living with it. In addition, unlike communism, Islamic fundamentalism was an unstructured movement with no single claimant to worldwide authority—but that, if anything, helped it to spread.

The leading Islamic fundamentalist country remained Iran (pp. 622–623). If Iran was any guide, the future of Islamic fundamentalism as a Muslim alternative world order did not look promising. After the disastrous war against Iraq in the 1980s, Iran no longer sought to subvert governments in other Muslim countries, and restored normal relations with most Western countries other than the United States. Internally, there were signs of a reaction within Iranian society against extreme fundamentalism. The relatively moderate Mohammad Khatami was elected president in 1997, and a struggle began between "reforming" and "conservative" groups. The result was a stalemate in which the conservatives usually had the upper hand. But even the conservatives had lost their militancy, and so far as they were in control, the country seemed condemned to political and economic stagnation. If the reformers ever won, the result might well be a liberalized though still strongly Islamic society but no longer a militant challenge to the world order.

As Iranian militancy died down, the lead in Islamic extremism passed to Afghanistan. Soviet troops had been withdrawn from that country in 1988, and after years of civil war, the fundamentalist Taliban ("students of religion") movement came to power in 1996. The new regime imposed the strictest version of Islamic law yet seen, including prohibitions on any kind of activity by women outside the home—in contrast to the Iranian fundamentalists, who mobilized women for their own religious and political purposes. The Taliban regime was ostracized by most of the world, and had unfriendly relations even with Iran—partly because the Taliban, who were Sunni Muslims, regarded the Shiite Iranians as infidels.

The failure of Islamic fundamentalism in the main country where it was in power did not prevent the movement from spreading widely across the Muslim world. Besides its appeal to religious tradition and resentment of the West, it used many modern methods, such as political parties, TV stations, and Web sites. In chaotic and poverty-stricken Muslim regions, such as Gaza or Shiite districts in Lebanon, fundamentalists often brought food relief and medical help—performing the same tasks, in fact, as Christian missionary organizations and Western NGOs, and gaining supporters in the process.

Often, Islamic fundamentalism was an opposition movement, seeking to overthrow both secular Arab nationalist governments like those of Iraq, Syria, or Algeria, and those that were backed by the United States, like that of Egypt. In all these countries, it was cruelly repressed, but in others, like Pakistan, the territories under the Palestinian Authority, Saudi Arabia, and Nigeria, fundamentalist movements had more or less freedom to operate and a larger or smaller share of government power. Even countries that repressed fundamentalist opposition, however, had to give the movement some room. Often they allowed stricter religious preaching and practice and permitted radical propaganda against the United States, Israel, and the West in general.

Nuclear Proliferation and Terrorism. In the postcommunist era, India and Pakistan were not the only countries that wanted nuclear weapons as a symbol of national power and a deterrent against attack. Atom bombs remained expensive and difficult to produce, however, and some countries also looked to new and deadly poison gases as well as to new and lethal strains of bacteria as cheaper substitutes.

Iraq's efforts to make such weapons were ended by UN inspection after the Gulf War, and seemingly were not successfully revived even after it expelled the inspectors in 1998. But late in the 1980s, North Korea, losing the protection of the dissolving Soviet Union and alienated from an increasingly capitalist China, began to develop nuclear weapons. In the 1990s, to help solve the problems of making atom bombs, it exchanged nuclear technology with Pakistan—and also with Iran, where both conservatives and reformers were eager for nuclear prestige and power against Israel and the United States. Other countries, such as Libya and Syria, where the rulers also wanted the reassurance of possessing weapons of mass destruction (WMDs), concentrated on the more easily developed poison gas and killer germs.

Most of these WMD efforts made slow progress in the 1990s, but terrorism became increasingly formidable. It kept all its old attractions as a way for unofficial groups to carry on conflicts against organized states, and for weaker states to harass stronger ones (p. 628). State-of-the-art communications technologies, the Internet, and e-mail made it easier for terrorist groups to organize and spread their messages. And terrorist deeds became harder to stop as perpetrators appeared who were not hampered by the wish to save their own lives—suicide bombers.

Suicide bombing had first been used by Syrian-backed Muslim groups against U.S., French, and Israeli troops in Lebanon in the 1980s (pp. 610–611). In the 1990s, the use of suicide bombers against civilians became widespread. The Tamil Tigers, an organization fighting a brutal war for independence for their Hindu ethnic group in the South Asian country of Sri Lanka (formerly Ceylon; *Map 15.2,* p. 605), sent suicide bombers against politicians and ordinary people belonging to the Buddhist majority. Suicide bombing was then taken up by Hamas (the Islamic Resistance Movement), a Palestinian fundamentalist organization, as a way of disrupting the peace process by infuriating the Israelis and weakening the Palestinian Authority.

Both the Tamil Tigers and Hamas had widespread support among the peoples they claimed to represent, and mass media throughout the Arab world acclaimed the anti-Israeli suicide bombers as "martyrs." Saddam Hussein saw to it that the families of such "martyrs" received large gifts of money, and both Arab nationalist Syria and the Iranian hard-line fundamentalists sheltered and helped terrorist groups in various ways.

Al Qaeda. Alongside these long-established terrorist organizations, a new and formidable terrorist group or network of groups was arising, which seemingly received little or no support from the traditional state backers of terrorism. This was partly because its creator, Osama bin Laden, was the son of a wealthy Saudi Arabian building contractor with a vast fortune of his own. A Sunni Muslim fundamentalist who despised the secular dictatorships of Syria and Iraq as well as the no-longer-militant Shiite fundamentalism of Iran, bin Laden first "invested" his wealth in recruiting fighters against the Soviet occupation of Afghanistan (p. 623). On arrival in that country, the recruits had to register in camps or "bases" financed by bin Laden, and soon he began calling his recruitment organization "The Base"—in Arabic, Al Qaeda.

In addition, after the Soviets evacuated Afghanistan, bin Laden turned his organization into a global network of terrorist groups, headquartered first in the east African country of Sudan, and later in Afghanistan under the rule of the Sunni fundamentalist Taliban movement (p. 701). He also chose a new target that was more dangerous to attack than Israel or rival Arab countries—the United States.

For bin Laden, as for most militant fundamentalists, the United States was the single most deadly threat to Islam. It was the source of cultural contamination, the backer of the Jewish state, and the puppetmaster of many Arab governments, including that of Saudi Arabia. Above all, by stationing its unbelieving troops in Saudi Arabia during and after the Gulf War, the land of the holiest of mosques in the cities of Mecca and Medina (p. 204), it insulted God himself. In retaliation for these offenses against Islam, in 1995 and 1996 groups affiliated with Al Qaeda carried out truck bombings of U.S. installations in Saudi Arabia, and in 1998 there followed the car bombing of the U.S. embassy in Kenya.

Terrorism was of its nature a threat to the international community, both because of its inhumanity and because it was a kind of private violence on an international scale. In addition, the international community was in principle opposed to the development of WMDs. Treaties against the development of nuclear and biological weapons had been negotiated in the 1970s, and most nations had signed on to them; and in 1993, a similar treaty went into effect against chemical weapons. Terrorism and the proliferation of WMDs were certainly against the interests of the international community's leading Western members, against whom they were mostly directed.

Compared with the wars in Yugoslavia or Africa, however, the casualties of terrorist attacks were few and the dangers of proliferation seemed remote. In 1995, the bombing of a government building in Oklahoma City by a U.S. antigovernment group made domestic terrorism an issue for a time. But there were no more such atrocities, and in 1998, the bombing of the embassy in Kenya and the retaliatory U.S. air raids on Al Qaeda training camps in Afghanistan preoccupied the public for a far shorter time than the yearlong drama of the president's sex life.

Meanwhile, however, bin Laden and his collaborators were making plans. None of their attacks so far had involved suicidal "martyrs," and nearly all had been far from the United States. They wanted to strike a devastating blow against the United States itself that would unite all Islam behind Al Qaeda. Already in 1993, a Muslim extremist group that was perhaps affiliated with Al Qaeda had unsuccessfully tried to destroy the World Trade Center in New York, for them a unique symbol of the American wealth and power they detested, with a truck bomb. Perhaps another effort, combining the old terrorist technique of airplane hijacking (p. 628) and the newer method of suicide bombing, would be more effective. By the end of the 1990s, a horrific deed was already in the making that would lead to a more drastic upheaval in the international community than any single event since the fall of communism.

Between Protest and Affirmation: The Postmodern Outlook

In the era of the Cold War, the fall of communism, and the postcommunist buildup of problems and conflicts, Western thought and art continued to respond to and influence changes in the civilization of which they were part. Just as the late nineteenth century saw the rise of Realism and Impressionism and the first half of the twentieth century was the era of the rise of Modernism, so in the late twentieth century a movement arose that came to be known as *Postmodernism*. Like the earlier movements in their eras, Postmodernism was one of many competing schools of thought and art within Western civilization, and it gave rise to bitter disputes. All the same, as a general outlook and way of thinking, its influence has been widely felt in the Western and to a lesser extent the non-Western world.

The name of the movement came from the fact that it criticized some features of the Modernist thought and art of the first half of the twentieth century (pp. 661–673). In particular, Postmodernism attacked the claims of competing twentieth-century ideologies to control the lives and thoughts of individuals, the tendency to regard works of art as objects separate from and above the life of their times, and the assumption that the experience of Western civilization in thought, art, and every other field should establish the norm for the human race as a whole.

The name Postmodernism suggested that the movement it described came after Modernism, and that Modernism, in the sense of the art and thought of the first half of the twentieth century, had therefore come to an end. In fact, however, Postmodernism took many of its basic features from the secular ideologies and Modernist artistic styles that it criticized, as well as from earlier Western thinkers and artists back to the ancient Greeks. Postmodernism is best seen as a new phase of Modernism and of Western thought and art in general, which has developed as the West encounters the rest of the world in the era of the birth of global civilization.

THE BACKGROUND OF POSTMODERNISM

One of the main themes of Western thought and art has been that of the search for a single truth about the universe and the human race. However, there is also an opposing Western tradition of denying the existence or the possibility of finding such a truth and questioning the motives of those who search for it. The two traditions often react to each other, and Postmodernism, the latest version of the tradition of doubt and denial, has arisen in opposition to recent developments in the tradition of searching for a single truth.

The Search for Truth. The Western search for truth has taken many different forms over the centuries. There has been the philosophical search of thinkers from Plato onward, the religious search of Jewish prophets and Christian saints, the scientific search of Newton and Darwin. These and other searchers after truth have often and bitterly debated whether they have actually found it or not. Whatever their differences, however, most Western searchers after truth have proclaimed that a single truth exists; that it is valid for the world and the human race as a whole; that all societies throughout the world ought to reflect and uphold it; and that all individuals ought to recognize and obey it.

In ancient and medieval times, Western societies had only limited power to enforce truth within their own territories, let alone in the rest of the world. But in modern times, when exploration and empire building gave Western civilization worldwide reach, and individuals became part of highly structured mass societies, Western hopes grew high of spreading knowledge of truth and making individual human behavior conform to it throughout the world.

Efforts to bring this about took many different and often opposing forms. Christian missionaries tried hard to bring to pass the biblical prophecy that "at the name of Jesus, every knee shall bow, and every tongue shall confess that he is the Lord." Enlightenment thinkers proclaimed that mankind must liberate itself from tyranny and superstition so as to achieve universal freedom, equality, and progress. Communist activists summoned the masses with Karl Marx's call, "Proletarians of all countries, unite!" Much of the history of the coming into being of modern global civilization so far has involved conflicts among world orders inspired by these and other rival Western versions of truth.

Doubt and Denial. Meanwhile, however, thinkers and artists throughout Western history have also found many different ways of questioning and undermining the search for truth and the enforcement in its name of individual behavior. Doubting philosophers since the ancient Greek Sophists have argued that truth and moral standards vary for different individuals and communities, or that language cannot describe any truth beyond what we immediately see and feel, or that there is no way of proving that the same causes will always be followed by the same effects (pp. 80, 270, 479). Likewise, writers and artists have endlessly celebrated the theme of desire bursting through social constraints and group boundaries. They and their publics have delighted in scenes of eager young couples courting at the back door while suspicious parents guard the front door, of Christian knights carried away by passion for beautiful Muslim captives, or of the little love god amusing himself by driving gods and humans alike into helpless sexual frenzy (pp. 274–275; *Fig. 9.4,* p. 390).

In the nineteenth and twentieth centuries, with their highly structured mass societies and their secular ideologies proclaiming many competing versions of universal truth, thinkers such as Nietzsche, Kierkegaard, and Sartre turned doubt and denial into outright protest against the ideas of the search for truth and the enforcement of behavior (pp. 650–651). In addition, proclaimers of rival ideologies themselves undermined each other's searches for truth by declaring them to be motivated by one form or another of the urge to power. Marxists claimed that the Enlightenment values of universal freedom and equality were disguises for bourgeois exploitation of the proletariat, while bourgeois opponents of Marxism insisted that the idea of the dictatorship of the proletariat actually meant the tyranny of self-appointed intellectuals (pp. 320–321). Meanwhile, science set limits to its own search for truth with the principles of relativity and uncertainty, and Freudian psychoanalysts portrayed the human personality as a battleground between the conscious mind, formed by external social pressures, and formless urges welling up from within (pp. 649–650). Postmodernism has drawn on all these sources in its own protest against the search for truth and its own celebration of liberated desire.

POSTMODERNISM IN THOUGHT

Postmodernism as a body of thought originated in France in the 1960s. Like most leading Western countries at the time, France had a capitalist-democratic social order bolstered by a burgeoning consumer society. In addition, it had a powerful Communist party, but the party was losing its revolutionary zeal to consumerism, and in any case, the heavy-handed Soviet dictatorship was discrediting communism as an ideal. There was also a thriving and widespread student counterculture, and in 1968, massive student demonstrations in Paris almost overthrew the government (p. 657). When the protests threatened to spread to workers who had been left behind by consumer society, however, the Communist party joined forces with the government to suppress the movement.

The events of 1968 confirmed the belief of some Marxist thinkers that democracy and consumerism were means by which capitalism manipulated the masses, and that the Soviet-led international communist movement, so far from overthrowing capitalist conformism, was actually in league with it. It was among these disillusioned French Marxists that Postmodernism was born.

Foucault: Discourse, the Other, and Desire. One of the most influential pioneers of Postmodern thought was a historian, Michel Foucault. Impressed by the power and resilience of the capitalist and democratic world order of the West but convinced that it was fundamentally oppressive, Foucault looked into the past to discover the origins of this oppression and found it in the tradition of the search for truth and the enforcement of behavior.

Foucault's criticism of this tradition, and especially of the way it has developed in modern times, was the most radical in Western history. Essentially he turned upside down one of the basic assumptions behind the Western scientific outlook: that if we perceive the truth about something, we can control it or at least predict how it will behave. Foucault, on the contrary, made the basic assumption that how we perceive things depends on our need to control them. We develop means of *representing* (describing) them, such as written or spoken language, numbers, or pictures (all of which Foucault called *texts*) in accordance with this need for control. We then form texts into *discourses*—general systems of interpreting the world in such a way that it becomes subject to our power.

According to Foucault, one such discourse is that of truth as something outside and apart from human beings and their needs. Another is that of human beings themselves as standing outside and apart from each other and the rest of the world, and able to acquire knowledge by observing each other and the world. These discourses are what make it possible to claim that power is exercised in the name of known truth, and that claim in turn justifies power in the eyes of both those who wield it and those who are subjected to it.

In one of his most influential books, *The Order of Things* (1966), Foucault examined how these discourses operated in the medical, social, and human sciences. These sciences, he said, did not objectively describe and predict true facts as they claimed. Rather, they controlled the human body, mind, and behavior by framing general laws that enabled distinctions to be made between the "normal" *One* and the "deviant" *Other.* In other books, Foucault applied this concept to the history of insane asylums, hospitals, and prisons, where individuals defined as mad, sick, or criminal are subjected to the *gaze* (controlling observation) of doctors and guards.

Foucault's last work, *The History of Sexuality* (1976–1984), was a sustained attack on modern scientific attitudes to sexual behavior. Far from liberating people from sexual ignorance and repression, he claimed, the "sciences of sex" were discourses that controlled the most intimate aspects of human feeling and behavior, defining only one behavior (heterosexual marriage) as normal and all others as deviant. This was an example of how, in the name of reason and mind, modern Western discourses operated to hold down the underlying urges of the human personality, which Foucault called *desire.* These urges, he believed, are capable of taking many different shapes in human feeling, thought, and action. Consequently, true freedom would consist in allowing desire to fulfill all its possibilities of expression.

Derrida: Texts, Authors, and Deconstruction. Another leading Postmodern thinker, Jacques Derrida, shares many of Foucault's basic ideas but concentrates on one particular means of representation in thought and art, written language. Like Foucault, he believes that language is not an instrument with which we can perceive ourselves and the world exactly as they are; on the contrary, the structure of language determines what we perceive. Furthermore, language is an instrument with a life of its own. Individual words have a long history and are used in many different ways, so that they have many different meanings and evoke many different associations today. "Art" can mean anything from creative endeavor to common slyness (as in "artful"); the associations of "thought" range from the deepest wisdom to Tweety Bird (as in "I tawt I taw a puddy tat").

As a result, Derrida believes, authors (all who compose written texts in any field of thought, art, or everyday life) cannot be sure that their words will have the same meanings and associations for their readers as for themselves. Hence they cannot be sure that readers will grasp exactly what they intend to say. In fact, since authors formulate their own intentions in slippery words, and since their intentions are ultimately determined by shapeless desire, they themselves cannot know what they intend to say. Written texts, therefore, are ambiguous (carrying multiple meanings) and indeterminate (not the product of a single definable intention on the part of an author), and have an existence of their own, independent of authors. Derrida's name for the process of analyzing a text so as to reveal this indeterminacy, ambiguity, and independent existence is *deconstruction.* The concept of deconstruction has had wide influence on philosophical argument and literary criticism, on writers themselves, and in other fields of art.

Lyotard: Knowledge Production and Narratives. Of the leading Postmodern thinkers, Jean-François Lyotard was the one who dealt most directly with political and social matters. It was Lyotard who first used the term "postmodern" to describe late-twentieth-century culture and society in general in his book *The Postmodern Condition* (1979).

Lyotard shared the Postmodern belief that freedom consists in the release of desire to take what forms it will. People and groups *produce* knowledge to satisfy desire, he believed, rather than *acquiring* knowledge by the use of reason. The production of knowledge takes place by means of *narratives*—systems of interpretation that are much the same as Foucault's discourses. Such narratives must necessarily be *incommensurable* (mutually contradictory), but that is what freedom is all about. A free society is one in which many different individuals and small groups use *little narratives* to produce "knowledges" that they recognize as true only for themselves and do not wish to impose on others.

Often, however, the process of knowledge production takes place through *grand narratives* that claim that the knowledge they produce is true everywhere and always and for everyone. Examples of such grand narratives are Christianity, Marxism, and the *Enlightenment project*—the hope, first proclaimed by thinkers of the eighteenth-century Enlightenment (pp. 428–431), of mastering nature and reconstructing the human race on the basis of truths discovered by reason. In postmodern society, Lyotard believed, all grand narratives have been discredited, but large social structures such as governments, corporations, and the mass media can still control the production of knowledge and thereby manipulate individuals. The result is repression without violence and without grand narratives to justify it.

Individuals and small groups must therefore insist all the more on their own little narratives. They should seek to influence politics, for example, not by forming permanent mass parties but through coalitions of groups uniting for specific short-term purposes and then going their separate ways, or through larger and longer-lasting movements, each of which unites around a single issue. Many recent political movements, such as the antiglobalization campaign (p. 687) and the efforts of various underdog contenders in recent U.S. struggles for nomination as presidential candidates, have indeed taken this form, though without so far bringing about basic changes in the economic or political order. In any case, Lyotard saw postmodern society as one in which the mass power of governments, corporations, and the media can be caught off guard by what amounts to political guerrilla warfare.

Postcolonialism. Such themes as those of knowledge as power and control and the normal One versus the deviant Other are obviously relevant to the relationship between the Western heartland countries and the rest of the world, whether Western or non-Western. The most influential thinker to explore this relationship from a Postmodern viewpoint was Edward W. Said, a Palestinian American cultural historian and literary critic. His most influential book, *Orientalism* (1977), dealt with the Western study of other civilizations of the Eastern Hemisphere. Said did for orientalism, especially the Western study of Islam, what Foucault did for the study of criminality or madness. He attacked orientalism as yet another controlling discourse, which defined "West" and "East" as opposites, subjected the East to the West's controlling gaze, and described the features of both in such a way as to establish Western domination and Eastern subjection as the natural order of things.

Said focused mainly on the West, but other Postcolonialists have explored the social and cultural life of non-Western or Latin American groups, treating them as *marginalized* or *subaltern* (subordinate) Others interacting with the North American and western European One. These Postcolonialists look for colonial discourses of resistance and subversion emerging under the Western gaze, but also for signs of both Western and colonial discourses changing and even merging as a result of their mutual encounter.

Postcolonial thinkers criticize not only social and cultural attitudes of the Western heartland but also those of the ex-colonial countries themselves. The Postcolonialists reject such Western discourses as those of nationalism, progress, and traditional Christianity, all of which have considerable appeal in the non-Western world, as well as locally produced grand narratives such as Islamic fundamentalism. For this reason, Postcolonialism has actually had less influence on the non-Western world than on the Western heartland and Latin America. Edward Said, for example, was a very prominent figure, revered by some and despised by others, in literary and cultural circles in the United States and other Western countries. However, the revolutionary nationalists and Islamic fundamentalists who dominate Palestinian affairs paid little attention to him. So far, at least, the main effect of Postcolonialism has been to modify attitudes within Western civilization to the rest of the world.

Critics of Postmodernism: Conservatives, Liberals, Marxists. Postmodern thought has quickly come to pervade Western societies, and few can escape its influence. Today, people who feel neglected and ignored complain of being "marginalized," debaters tearing apart opponents' arguments see themselves engaged in "deconstruction," and those who say one thing and mean another are distrusted for having "subtexts." None of these items of everyday speech existed before the 1970s. Postmodern thought has altered the way people speak—a sure sign that it has also altered the way they think.

But this does not mean that the Western doubters and deniers have won their age-old battle with the Western searchers after truth. On the contrary, the battle rages more fiercely than ever before, and on many fronts. Conservatives accuse Postmodernists of actually suppressing individual freedom by defining knowledge and consciousness in terms of ethnic, gender, and sexual group identities—gay and straight discourses, white male and African American female narratives, and so on. Among liberals, the German philosopher Jürgen Habermas, a strong believer in the ideals of universal freedom and progress and the breaking down of barriers to communication among human beings, sees Postmodernism as itself conservative because it denies these ideals and erects barriers to communication. And Marxists see Postmodernism, with its rejection of grand narratives of "overthrow" and "revolution" in favor of little narratives of "subversion" (undermining society) and "transgression" (breaking rules), as actually working to uphold capitalist oppression. In Marxist eyes, Postmodernism functions as a safety valve in conformist modern society, relieving pressure so as to prevent an explosion.

All these criticisms of Postmodernism are variations on the traditional replies of searchers after truth to doubters and deniers. If there is no such thing as truth or if it cannot be discovered, how can the doubters know that what they themselves say is true, and why should others take them seriously? If societies cannot establish rules for all to follow that are generally accepted as good according to some truthful standard, how can societies exist at all? And if we think that a society's rules are in fact bad, how can we make that judgment and change that society unless we know the good rules and the truthful standard that we wish to adopt?

Feminism Between Grand and Little Narratives. The present-day social movement that has felt the force of the arguments for and against Postmodernism more than any other is feminism. On the one hand, Postmodern ideas have great attraction for many feminists because these ideas correspond in various ways to their hopes and experiences. On the other hand, it is only by operating as a grand narrative that feminism has brought about actual changes in the status and power of women in society.

Already before Postmodernism, Simone de Beauvoir (p. 658) described Western thought in general as a system in which man is central and woman marginal, serving as the Other against which man can define himself. More recently, a leading French thinker, Luce Irigaray, has advocated that women should construct their own "feminine symbolic order" (system of thought and culture) parallel to and separate from that of men. Many feminist thinkers have carried the Postmodern logic even farther, claiming that since women are in fact divided by such factors as class, race, and sexual orientation, there can be no grand narrative for all women but rather there must be many feminine little narratives.

Ever since it began, however, feminism has sought to replace one set of social rules, enforcing the superiority of men to women in status and power, by another set of rules, enforcing the equal status and power of men and women. It has done so in the name of equality, freedom, and justice—standards recognized as true for both men and women, by which male superiority is judged to be bad and gender equality is judged to be good. These are the assumptions that inspire the work of women's organizations like the National Organization for Women in the United States when it campaigns for laws against sex discrimination in the workplace or for the election of women to public office. Many feminists therefore reject Postmodernism, in the belief that without a standard recognized as true for men and women alike and social rules to enforce that standard, neither women nor men can ever be truly free.

This dilemma between grand narratives and little narratives is felt even by Postmodern feminists. They often claim that because female discourses express the desires of marginalized women, they are *truer* than male discourse. Underlying the thought of all thinkers claiming to represent nonwhite, nonmale, and nonheterosexual groups is the belief in a standard of equality and freedom that allows them to declare it *wrong* for their groups to be marginal Others. Derrida himself recognized that this dilemma is one of Postmodernism in general when he wrote: "I cannot conceive of a radical critique [of society and culture] that would not be motivated by some sort of affirmation, acknowledged or not."

Thus in spite of being a movement of doubt and denial, so far as Postmodernists wish to influence society, they cannot do without the ideas of truth and order that they oppose. And perhaps Western searchers after truth and enforcers of behavior, for their part, cannot do without the humility that ought to come from thinking it possible they may be mistaken.

Postmodern Literature and Art

Postmodern forms of literature and art first appeared in the 1960s, when many writers and artists came to feel that the continuing Western social and cultural changes had outstripped the potential of the prevailing modern styles to express human experience. Abstract painting and "stream of consciousness" writing (pp. 660–661, 664–668), as practiced in the middle of the twentieth century, seemed to convey little or nothing of the changes in individuals' perceptions of the world brought by mass media or consumer culture, of the horrors of totalitarianism and genocide, or of the irrationality and chaos that haunt highly structured modern societies.

Writers and artists had consciously striven to depict changing human experience within a changing society and culture ever since the middle of the nineteenth century (pp. 532–537), and the pioneers of Modernist literature and art had continued this striving. At the beginning of the twentieth century, in *Ulysses* (p. 661), James Joyce had used the writing styles of the mass media of the time, such as small-town newspapers and girls' romance stories, when these seemed suitable to the experiences he wished to convey. In the 1930s, in *Guernica* (*Fig. 16.3,* p. 665), Pablo Picasso had used the techniques of abstraction in painting to convey the essence of war's savagery in a manner that was all the more powerful because it was deeply personal.

All the same, many writers and artists of the 1960s felt that more recently, Modernist literature and art had deliberately turned away from life. Modernism had become "high art"—the status symbol of a privileged few, who looked down on the low pleasures of mass entertainment. It had become self-absorbed, concentrating on empty word play and experiments with visual form and color, instead of expressing or commenting on human experience. It was time, it seemed, for art to go back to depicting life—the endlessly fluid and changing life of the mid-twentieth century, where there seemed to be more information and less certainty than ever before, where universal freedom was preached yet everyone lived as part of huge organizations, and where dreams, realities, and nightmares seemed to merge.

To begin with, the writers and artists who shared these beliefs worked independently of Postmodern thought, but in the 1970s and 1980s, many of them took Postmodernism as their inspiration and guide, both in criticizing Modernist and earlier Western literature and art and in their own creative endeavors. All the same, Postmodern literature and art are a continuation of the modern Western striving to depict changing experience in a changing society and culture, not a break with it.

POSTMODERN LITERATURE

This continuity was strongest in prose literature, where traditional methods of storytelling in fact often proved equal to the task of conveying the trauma and confusion of the twentieth century. In the 1950s, writers like Pasternak and Solzhenitsyn successfully used realistic narrative to depict the bitter experiences of the Russian Revolution and the Soviet gulag (p. 662). The British author Evelyn Waugh, in his series of novels *Sword of Honour* (1952–1961), used a style of disciplined elegance to mock (among other things) the irrationality lurking within a huge and highly structured organization, the British Army in the Second World War. A moving novel by the Italian writer Primo Levi, *The Truce* (1963), used a narrative form dating from the Renaissance—the tale of comic adventure like Cervantes's *Don Quixote* (pp. 359–360)—to convey the chaos of eastern Europe just after the war as experienced by a Jewish prisoner newly released from Auschwitz.

Other writers, however, stretched the rules of storytelling farther than ever before. Joseph Heller's *Catch-22* (1961) did for the U.S. Air Force in the Second World War what Waugh did for the British Army, but it did so by deliberately breaking the rule that fictional events should follow the pattern of real life. The U.S. Air Force never had the "Catch 22" of the title—the rule that anyone who applies to be discharged from the air force on grounds of insanity must be sane because any sane person would want to leave the wartime air force, so the application must be denied. But the improbable invention vividly conveys the lunatic logic of large organizations at war.

Likewise, in *One Hundred Years of Solitude* (1967), a story of a fictional Latin American community by the Colombian writer Gabriel García Márquez, supernatural events occur alongside natural ones, and flashbacks from the long past take place as if in the present. By breaking the flow of time and the rules of probability, this technique of "magic realism" ties together the past and the present, realities and illusions, to encapsulate the total experience of Latin America since the Spanish conquest.

More recently, the Indian Postcolonial writer Salman Rushdie, resident in Britain, "rewrote" the life of the Prophet Muhammad in *The Satanic Verses* (1989) in a way that mixed fact with fantasy. Rushdie's work was in line with the Postmodern belief that one way to deconstruct grand narratives—in this case, fundamentalist Islam—and thereby weaken their power is to "transgress" them in spectacular ways. Ayatollah Khomeini, the supreme leader of Iran at the time (p. 623), convened a council of Muslim jurists that issued a *fatwa* (decree) condemning Rushdie to death for blasphemy, the sentence to be executed by any Muslim who had the opportunity. Rushdie went into hiding, and cultural leaders around the world protested against the *fatwa* in the name of the Western grand narratives of religious tolerance and freedom of speech. The *fatwa* was lifted in 1998, but Rushdie's transgression had deconstructed Islamic fundamentalism only in the eyes of people who already opposed it.

The Postmodern outlook is memorably expressed in *The Name of the Rose* (1984), by the Italian Umberto Eco. It is a tale of the medieval past, set in a Benedectine monastery (p. 183) with its routine of work and prayer, its mountaintop serenity disturbed by loves and hatreds among the monks and by the conflicts of the outside world, and its library, a vast and mysterious warren of texts, brooding over all. But the novel is also a detective story, in which a peerless reasoner and his naive companion investigate a seeming murderous plot within the community. In the end, the great detective's search for truth leads him to a conclusion that makes no sense: "There was no plot, and I discovered it by mistake!" Unquestionably, however, the events in the monastery are linked with a clash between rival versions of ultimate truth, those of the Catholic Church and its heretic opponents. About this, too, the investigator comes to a conclusion: "The only truth lies in learning to free oneself from the insane passion for truth."

The works of such writers as García Márquez and Eco have not only been acclaimed by critics familiar with their ideas and literary techniques, but have also been widely read and admired by readers who do not necessarily know or share the outlook and convictions that inspire these authors. The reason is that Postmodern writing at its best is simply a new way of doing justice to the richness and strangeness of human experience, which is fiction's traditional task.

POSTMODERN ART

The keynote of a great deal of work in the visual arts that is identified as Postmodern has been to turn back some or all of the way from abstraction to the depiction of things as they appear to the eye. The general intent has been to bridge the gap between art and life that appeared to have been opened by abstraction. However, the purposes of bridging that gap, the methods of bridging it, and the views of life that artists have expressed have all varied widely—often under the influence of Postmodern thought.

Pop Art and Superrealism. Artists, like writers, began to turn away from the dominant trend in Modernism even before they discovered Postmodern thought—first and most

Fig. 17.2 *Hopeless.* Roy Lichtenstein's painting was inspired by a frame (single picture) that appeared in a romance comic book, *Run For Love!* in 1962. The original frame was of course part of a strip telling a story. By showing the frame without the story, Lichtenstein focuses the viewer's attention on the general character of comic books: their bold drawing and coloring, their strong and simple emotions, and their Americanness. The girl in the original frame was a brunette, but Lichtenstein made her into a more "American" blonde.

spectacularly with the Pop Art movement. Pop Art began in Europe in the 1950s as a way of criticizing the consumer culture of the time, and spread to the United States, where artists used it for the opposite purpose—to celebrate that country's culture of mass entertainment.

A "classic" example is Roy Lichtenstein's *Hopeless* (1963; *Fig. 17.2*). The painting re-alistically shows a young woman weeping, but it is not in fact a depiction of hopeless-ness. Instead, it is an outsize (4-foot-by-4-foot) picture of a comic-book picture of a young woman weeping, accurate down to the dots of the color printing process, which are faithfully reproduced by the painter's brush. The "subject" of the painting is the way comic books depict teenage emotion. The painting, a single handmade permanent object just like the *Mona Lisa* (*Fig. 8.10*, p. 353), affectionately and even admiringly imi-tates a mass-produced throwaway comic-book picture. It is as if Lichtenstein is an-nouncing the merger of popular art (which appeals to people on a level of basic enter-tainment) and high art (which is supposed to appeal to people on a more idealistic and intellectually demanding level).

The merger of traditional painting and other media, as well as of mass entertain-ment and artistic tradition, was carried farther still by a later school of painting, Super-realism. A leading artist of this school is the American Audrey Flack. Her painting *Marilyn* (1977; *Fig. 17.3*) is a still life—a highly traditional form dating back to the seventeenth

Collection of The University of Arizona Museum of Art, Tucson, AZ. Museum Purchase with funds provided by the Edward J. Gallagher, Jr. Memorial Fund

Fig. 17.3 *Marilyn.* An ordinary girl finds a magic spell that brings her beauty, fame, and untimely death. Audrey Flack's painting tells this ancient myth in a traditional manner, with realistically depicted objects that convey symbolic meaning (compare *Fig. 8.5*, p. 348). The objects that tell the story, however, are mostly modern ones: photographs, makeup items that are the tools of enchantment, an hourglass in a plastic frame. And the myth is in fact a contemporary one: the transformation of Norma Jean Baker into the ill-starred sex goddess Marilyn Monroe.

century. Still lifes of that period depicted objects of everyday life with detailed accuracy, often including some objects that symbolized the passage of time and the brevity of life. *Marilyn* follows this tradition, with its faithfully depicted hourglass, watch, and burning candle. Among the accurate details, however, there are also photographs, and in general the painting does its best to look like a photograph—a blown-up one, since it is 8 feet by 8 feet in size. Furthermore, the painting commemorates a tragic event, involving an iconic figure of mass entertainment, that has remained a media legend ever since it happened in 1962—the suicide of Marilyn Monroe.

Neo-Expressionism. Besides the breaking of boundaries between high art and the mass media and between traditional themes and modern events, another motive for stepping back from abstraction has been the desire to express the experiences and identities of human groups. Anselm Kiefer's *Nigredo* (1984; *Fig. 17.4*) depicts another traditional subject, in this case a landscape. The depiction is not painstakingly detailed like those of Lichtenstein and Flack, but the huge 18-by-11-foot painting is realistic enough to suggest a vast, dark, and brooding scene—the painting's title is a Latin word meaning "blackness." The atmosphere is not unlike that of Van Gogh's landscapes (*Fig. 13.7,*

Fig. 17.4 Darkness Darker Than Dark. The title of Anselm Kiefer's *Nigredo* is a technical term in the mystical art of alchemy, the transformation of base metals (those thought to be of lower quality) into the noblest of metals, gold. The term describes a stage of "darkness darker than dark," before metals in process of transformation gain the brightness of the sun. The belief is a myth, but for Kiefer it symbolizes the horrific deeds and experiences of twentieth-century humanity and the hope of a more noble future.

p. 537), and Kiefer's style of painting is often called Neo-Expressionism. Are the rows of white lines graves of fallen soldiers or the stubble of fields where battle has raged? Are the dark objects in the foreground tents or huts of some kind of camp? Perhaps Kiefer himself was not sure, though for him the color black, so prominent in the foreground of the painting, symbolized both death and the transformation of substances by fire, in line with ancient scientific and mystical ideas. Through suggestion and symbolism, the painting is intended to evoke the deeds and experiences of the German nation in the recent past which still haunt the present.

Reinventing Artistic Creation. Mass entertainment and consumer culture, symbolism and different levels of meaning, and the collective experience of groups are also themes of Postmodern thought. Many recent artists have specifically sought to express or embody Postmodern ideas in their works—especially the Postmodern criticism of the idea of human beings as standing apart from and objectively observing the rest of the world. This has led them to try to revise the process of artistic creation so as to create new kinds of art objects.

The traditional process of artistic creation, such artists claim, is a controlling discourse just like the idea of humans objectively observing the world. The process begins with an artist standing apart from human experience, subjecting it to his gaze, and imposing a pattern on it. The artist then creates an object that itself stands apart from the experience and duplicates the pattern that he has imposed. Finally, the object is exposed to the gaze of viewers so as to uphold the controlling discourse that it incorporates. If by any chance a work of art incorporates the discourse of a marginalized Other, it is itself marginalized—for example, by being placed in a museum. According to the

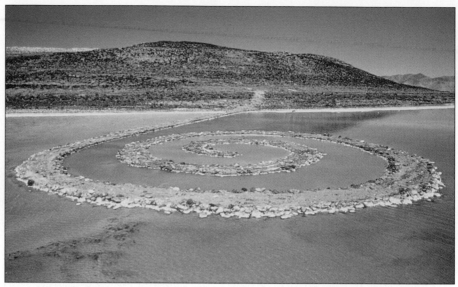

Fig. 17.5 *Spiral Jetty.* "He would raise each rock up and roll it around, then he would move this one, change that one until it looked exactly right. He wanted it to look like it was a growing, living thing, coming out of the center of the earth." That was Robert Smithson's creative procedure, according to the building contractor from whom Smithson rented two dump trucks, a tractor, and a front-loader to build this most famous of twentieth-century earthworks.

Postmodern artist Robert Smithson, "Museums, like asylums and jails, have wards and cells—in other words, neutral rooms called 'galleries.' . . . The function of the warden-curator is to separate art from the rest of society. Next comes integration. Once the work is totally neutralized, ineffective, abstracted, safe, and politically lobotomized, it is ready to be consumed by society."

One way in which Smithson hoped to solve this problem was by means of a new art form, the *earthwork.* His best-known creation of this kind is *Spiral Jetty* (1970; *Fig. 17.5*). The work is not exactly realistic; that is, it does not accurately depict something different from itself. Instead, it actually is what its title says it is—a jetty (a structure extending into a body of water) that is spiral in form. All the same, it is intended to express something other than itself, namely the play of earth forces that Smithson perceived in the scenery on the shoreline of the Great Salt Lake, Utah, where the jetty is located. But the jetty is not separate from the scenery, let alone confined in a museum. Instead, it is part of the scenery and changes with it, disappearing beneath the water when the lake is full and appearing above water only in times of exceptional drought. For Smithson, the idea of a human depiction of nature as part of the nature that it depicts was part of an environmentalist discourse of humans as one with nature, as against the discourse of humans separate from and controlling nature.

Postmodern feminism, too, sees the traditional artistic process as part of a controlling (in this case male) discourse and looks for ways to replace it. A notable example is Judith Chicago's *Dinner Party* (1979; *Fig. 17.6*). The work is an *installation*—an object that escapes the bonds of museum confinement and the viewer's gaze in the opposite way to an earthwork: instead of being part of the scene that it depicts, it creates and encloses the scene, setting up an environment that also includes the viewer.

Fig. 17.6 *The Dinner Party.* This triangular table, 48 feet on each side with place settings for thirty-nine notable women from history, was the work of two hundred craftswomen under the direction of the feminist artist Judith Chicago. Opinions among feminists about this work were divided. Some praised it for asserting female against male narratives and for subverting male phallic obsessions through the explicit female imagery of the dinner plates. Others criticized the installation for emphasizing embroidery and other traditional "women's work," and for reducing women to their sexual and reproductive functions.

In this case, both the artwork and the scene itself are a table set for dinner. The work is made not by the traditional process of an artist observing experience, but by a process of "women's work" (pp. 14–15)—exercise of the crafts traditionally assigned to women such as needlework and china painting. There is plenty of symbolism. The triangular shape of the table is an ancient female symbol, the thirteen place settings on each side are the number of witches in a coven, and the plates are painted with patterns of butterflies and female sexual organs, standing for liberation and female sexuality. As in much Postmodern art, there is written text as well as a visual presentation—both of which count as text in Postmodern thought. In this case, the names of thirty-nine principal guests, including the Egyptian pharaoh Hatshepsut, the U.S. women's rights activist Susan B. Anthony, and the British writer Virginia Woolf (pp. 30, 657, 662), appear at the place settings, and the names of 999 other distinguished women are inscribed in the floor.

In seeking to deconstruct old discourses and construct a new one, this piece continues a long-standing Western tradition of didactic art (that seeks to teach a social or moral lesson). The lesson, however, is ambiguous. Like Postmodern feminism in general, *The Dinner Party* speaks both of women's separate identity from that of men and of their underrated role in a civilization that they share with men.

As unprecedented as art forms like Smithson's earthwork and Chicago's installation may be, the themes that they treat have occurred before in both Western and non-

Western art. Readers can decide for themselves whether an earthwork conveys the sublimity (awe-inspiring quality) of nature as vividly as a Romantic seascape (*Fig. 12.4*, p. 488). They can also judge whether an installation depicts the equal dignity of women and men as convincingly as an ancient Egyptian sculpture (*Fig. 1.8*, p. 39), or portrays female sexuality as compellingly as a Renaissance nude (*Fig. 8.9*, p. 352).

POSTMODERN ARCHITECTURE

At first sight, it would seem impossible for a building, especially a large one, to be Postmodern. Postmodernism stresses fluidity, indeterminacy, and little narratives. A large building, however, has to have a massive and unchanging structure and has to be the work of a highly organized society. To build it, clients (usually wealthy and powerful organizations), real estate developers, local governments, architectural design bureaus, construction companies, trucking firms, and industrial manufacturers all have to work toward a single common end. Any large building, in fact, is a grand narrative in steel and concrete.

All the same, Postmodernism has been a leading trend in present-day architecture; in fact, it was in the architectural field that the word "Postmodernism" was first used in the sense of a turning away from Modernist styles of art. The reaction began in the United States in the 1960s with the publication of two influential books, Jane Jacobs's *Death and Life of American Cities* (1961) and Robert Venturi's *Complexity and Contradiction in Architecture* (1966). Both attacked the "glass box" style of Modernist architecture (p. 670), Jacobs for destroying the human scale and unplanned diversity of city life and Venturi for frustrating the human need for variety and complexity. Against Mies van der Rohe's Modernist slogan "less is more," Venturi proclaimed that "less is a bore." That did not mean, however, that either was opposed to bigness as such. Venturi, a practicing architect, designed individual residences, but he also praised bigness so long as it was also playful and showy—the hotel architecture of Las Vegas, for example. And many of the most striking Postmodern buildings have in fact been large ones.

The way that Postmodern architects strive to make large buildings interesting is by rejecting the idea that form should follow function—that the appearance of a building should reveal its structure, as in Modernist buildings or Gothic cathedrals (pp. 262–263, 670–671). Instead, they follow a rival architectural tradition of using the structure of a building to support an exterior that proclaims its own message. The columns on the west façade of Saint Peter's Basilica in Rome, for instance, do not support the structure, which consists of the walls and internal arches (*Fig. 9.8*, p. 393). They are an external decoration, intended to impress worshipers with the majesty and permanence of the Roman Catholic Church. The messages that Postmodern buildings send are different, but their method of sending them is the same as in Baroque structures.

Sometimes the message that Postmodern buildings are intended to send is simply one of transgressing the grand narrative of Modernism, and of freedom to choose among the decorative styles of the past. A well-known example is the AT&T Building in New York City, which recalls the massive entrance arches and vertical stone ribs of skyscrapers at the turn of the twentieth century, as well as the elaborately carved tops of colonial-style chests of drawers (*Fig. 17.7*). The designer, Philip Johnson, had a change of heart after collaborating with Mies van der Rohe on the severely modern Seagram Building (*Fig. 16.8*, p. 670). With its playful mixture of old-fashioned styles,

Fig. 17.7 Yesterday and Today. Philip Johnson's Postmodern AT&T Building, completed in 1984, makes an old-fashioned contrast with the surrounding modern office blocks. A quarter of a century before and a few streets away in New York City, the Seagram Building, which Johnson helped design, also contrasted with its neighbors—only the contrast was between a modern office block and old-fashioned apartment buildings (*Fig. 16.8,* p. 670). "Glass boxes" are now yesterday's style, and the style of the day before yesterday has become the style of today. How will today's style contrast with that of tomorrow?

the AT&T Building forms an ironic contrast with the glass boxes in its neighborhood—so far as any 660-foot corporate skyscraper can be playful and ironical.

Other recent buildings celebrate the Postmodern delight in chaos and confusion. Perhaps because it is hard for organizations to do business or people to live in structures that are designed to be disorienting, most buildings of this kind are intended to be visited rather than lived and worked in. Most of all, in spite of the Postmodern distrust of places where art objects are subjected to the public gaze, they tend to be galleries and museums.

The best-known such building is the Guggenheim Museum in Bilbao, Spain (*Fig. 17.8,* p. 720), designed by the Canadian architect Frank Gehry. Architectural theorists call the museum's style Deconstructivist, from Derrida's term for the process of revealing ambiguity and indeterminacy in texts (p. 707). Gehry himself has a simpler description of his preferred style: "Every architect who's any good, no matter what they say, is trying to make some kind of personal mud pie." But to make this particular "mud pie" and fit it onto an internal load-bearing structure took ingenious design that stretched computer technology to the limit. The building's sleek and fluid lines, so complex and indescribable that they seem almost to stretch the limits of three dimensions, make an unforgettable statement of the ancient idea that change governs all (pp. 79–80).

At the present time, architects influenced by Postmodernism face a challenge that is both daunting and inspiring—that of replacing a complex of buildings that had been a symbol of global capitalism in such a way as to revive that symbol yet also express the

Photograph by David Heald © Solomon R. Guggenheim Foundation, NY

Fig. 17.8 Architecture and Sculpture. "I don't know where you cross the line between architecture and sculpture. For me, it is the same. Buildings and sculpture are three-dimensional objects." The Guggenheim Museum in the Spanish industrial city of Bilbao expresses this belief of its designer, Frank Gehry. Its mostly windowless titanium-clad exterior is like the surface of a piece of modern sculpture, allowing the eye to follow the complex curves and irregular masses into which it is "carved."

response of a nation to a horrific deed. The twin towers of the old World Trade Center were Modernist buildings, intended to impress by reason of the simplicity of their design (*Fig. 17.9*). To replace them with replicas that would never be quite the same as the originals seemed the wrong way to commemorate them. But can Postmodern architecture, with its dislike of structure and consensus, proclaim a grand narrative of national grief and hope combined with capitalist wealth and power?

The definitive plans for the site, mainly the work of the American architects Daniel Libeskind and David Childs, show how far architecture has traveled since the 1970s (*Fig. 17.10*). The twin towers were simple, definite shapes, pointing abruptly upward from the city and clear-cut against the sky. Childs's Freedom Tower tapers and twists with its upper levels, housing wind generators, unenclosed. It shares the skyline with Libeskind's cluster of buildings surrounding the memorial "footprints" of the twin towers. The new World Trade Center, it seems, will grow out of the city and fade into the sky. It will, perhaps, be less directly assertive of wealth and power than the twin towers, but it may well be powerfully suggestive of grief and hope.

September 11, the West, and the World

Ten years after the fall of communism, the project of an international community steered toward harmony, prosperity, and freedom by the West was very much a work in progress. Globalization had spread prosperity in many poor countries but also inspired resentment between the West and "the Rest." Postcommunist and postcolonial

Fig. 17.9 The Twin Towers. The Modernist skyscrapers of the old World Trade Center were huge and self-contained objects, like Egyptian pyramids. In this view, the Statue of Liberty seems to be holding her torch high as if to illuminate them, but this does not disturb their massive immobility.

Fig. 17.10 The Freedom Tower. The Postmodern-influenced principal building of the new World Trade Center will also be a huge structure, but it will not be complete in itself. This architect's rendering shows the tower sloping away to the right but visually balanced by the trade center's lower buildings, while the broadcasting mast rising from its vertical left face seems to acknowledge the upraised arm of the Statue of Liberty.

conflicts were usually damped down or died down in the end, but remained a continually renewed source of destructive anarchy. The Islamic fundamentalist challenge to the Western-dominated world order was mostly held down by repressive governments in the Muslim world, but had increasing popular support in Muslim countries where it was not in power. Many states that the West suspected of seeking nuclear weapons had been blocked from making progress in developing them, but India and Pakistan had found ways around the obstacles, and North Korea was near to doing so. Terrorist movements within the countries of the Western heartland were mostly losing momentum, but Islamic terrorism was more active and better organized than ever before.

Such was the state of the world when Al Qaeda attacked and destroyed the World Trade Center in New York City and badly damaged the Pentagon in Washington on September 11, 2001.

THE U.S. RESPONSE: RESTRUCTURING THE INTERNATIONAL COMMUNITY

The attacks were not just against the buildings that suffered, or even against the United States, but against the whole idea of a harmonious international community with the West at the helm, and at first, the result seemed to be to reinforce the community's solidarity as Iraq's attack on Kuwait had done ten years earlier. In 2002, with the approval and cooperation of NATO and the United Nations, the United States crushed the Taliban regime that had harbored Al Qaeda in Afghanistan. Peacekeeping troops from Britain, France, Germany, and other NATO countries, UN advisers, and nongovernmental volunteers moved in to help the Afghans with the task of building a nation and a civil society, according to the recipe for rebuilding failed states that had been devised in Bosnia and Kosovo.

In the next few years, millions of Afghan refugees, displaced by twenty years of civil war and brutal repression, returned to their homes and resumed something like their normal lives. Rival ethnic and religious groups hammered out a constitution that was democratic but far from secular: it declared itself to be adopted by "We the people of Afghanistan," acting "In the name of God, the merciful, the compassionate." Contrary to the nation-building recipe, however, most of Afghanistan's ethnic and religious groups lived separate lives under the control of local warlords. Meanwhile, a Taliban guerrilla movement troubled much of the country, and for the time being, at least, Osama bin Laden lived free and unpunished in the wild lands on the border of Afghanistan and Pakistan. Afghan nation building was a difficult and uncertain undertaking, but at least the United States and its Western partners were working in harmony to accomplish it, and they had the more or (in the case of most Muslim states) less enthusiastic blessing of the rest of the world.

In the United States, however, September 11 aroused not only national sorrow, pride, and anger, but also a widespread feeling of frustration at the way the world had operated since the fall of communism. For ten years, the United States, a solitary giant in a world full of dwarfs, had tried to operate by consensus, and the result had been the first successful attack on its mainland territory since the British burned Washington during the War of 1812. President George W. Bush expressed this mood in his speeches declaring a general "War on Terror," implicitly threatening countries that did not wholeheartedly join it, and naming three specific countries that sought nuclear weapons—Iraq, Iran, and North Korea—as an international "Axis of Evil."

Bush thereby gained a stature as president that he had not enjoyed since his election, having lost the popular vote but won in the electoral college thanks to a Supreme Court verdict upholding his narrow and disputed victory in Florida. He then invested this newly acquired political capital in an ambitious effort to change the way the international community operated.

Quite soon after the September 11 attacks, the Bush administration decided that in the future, the United States would use force—including preemptively (without having been attacked first)—or the threat of force against all the outlaw and rebel states and movements that had troubled the world since the fall of communism. Terrorist movements and states that aided them, states that tried to acquire nuclear and other weapons of mass destruction, Islamic fundamentalist states and movements—all would be liable to U.S. attack.

The Bush administration's first step in applying this policy, it decided, would be to act on a decision that the Clinton administration had already taken but not put into effect: to overthrow the Iraqi dictatorship of Saddam Hussein. This deed, the administration believed, would achieve three aims. It would end Iraq's efforts—which most knowledgeable experts throughout the world believed were probably still under way—to develop WMDs. It would make a spectacular example of Saddam that would intimidate other rebels and outlaws. And it would replace Saddam's sadistic tyranny with a beneficent U.S. occupation that would remake Iraq into a secular democratic model for the Islamic world.

The plan derived partly from the traditional U.S. conservative belief that the United States should accept no limits on its freedom of action and no resistance to its will. It was also much influenced by the neoconservative (p. 630) idea that Islam had no legitimate grievances against the West, and that Muslim resentments were the work of intolerant clerics and nationalist dictators from whom Islam must be freed.

In addition, both types of conservative questioned the legitimacy of the institutions of the international community. They pointed, for example, to the fact that the UN Human Rights Commission had been taken over by countries that were tyrannies and dictatorships, and that in 2002 these countries had elected Libya, where torture and imprisonment without trial were routine, to be the commission's president. Did not the United States, the world's pioneer and model of democracy and human rights, have far greater moral authority than the feeble and hypocritical United Nations to be the lawgiver and law enforcer of the international community?

In the course of heated arguments within the U.S. administration, international-minded Republicans, notably Secretary of State Colin Powell, were able to make NATO collaboration and UN authorization part of the plan. At U.S. urging, the UN Security Council would issue an ultimatum to Iraq to readmit UN inspectors, whom it had earlier expelled, to search for WMDs; Iraq would refuse, or not cooperate properly with the inspectors; and the Security Council would then authorize the United States to go to war as its enforcer.

If the U.S. administration could not get cooperation from the institutions of the international community, however, it was determined to act without these institutions, and to replace them with a "coalition of the willing"—that is, of those countries that would be willing to join with it against Iraq. One way or another, the United States would save the world from rebels and outlaws and nightmarish threats. Either the institutions of the international community would follow its lead, or it would set those institutions aside and dominate the community through a league of states directly headed by itself.

THE IRAQ WAR AND THE ORGANIZATION OF GLOBAL CIVILIZATION

The Bush administration's project meant that the United States would take a much stronger and more purposeful hand in shaping the organization of global civilization than it had done before. The administration believed that the country was up to this task for three reasons. First, it had such overwhelming military power and economic strength that it could fight wars and reconstruct countries without devastating bloodshed to itself or even its adversaries, and without overburdening its taxpayers. Second, since the United States would be using its might to overthrow brutal dictatorships, end terror, and spread democracy and freedom, sooner or later its actions would command the assent of the world even if at first they caused consternation or resentment.

Third (and perhaps, in the U.S. administration's view, most important), the overthrow of Saddam and the building of a secular democratic Iraq would both administer a healthful shock to the Islamic world and give it an attractive example to follow. This would in turn lead to reconciliation between the Arabs and Israel, and to the victory of moderate Islam. All this would take time, and the War on Terror would certainly be a lengthy undertaking like the Cold War. Sooner or later, however, the Islamic fundamentalist challenge to the world order would collapse like the communist challenge before it.

As often happens with the most ambitious enterprises of nations, the early course of this one did not follow the most optimistic expectations of those who launched it. The undertaking was sure to have a historic effect on the organization of global civilization, but it was far less certain exactly what the effect would be.

In one respect, the U.S. venture did go exactly as its launchers expected: in Afghanistan and again in Iraq in 2003, the United States won lightning victories against conventional armies with only limited bloodshed on either side. In both countries, however, it then got involved in lengthy guerrilla wars. Neither insurgency had the kind of massive outside aid that had brought the Spanish success against Napoleon or helped the Vietnamese communists outlast an earlier U.S. campaign (pp. 470, 617). The United States would therefore probably defeat both insurgencies in the end, but the end was likely to be a long time in coming. Meanwhile the United States had nearly a third of its army tied up in two countries, and much of the rest was retraining and reequipping after its efforts.

In addition, the Iraq venture turned out to be much more expensive than President Bush and his advisers had hoped. Originally the U.S. administration seems to have believed that the reconstruction of Iraq would be paid for out of the country's oil revenues. In fact, however, Iraq's basic equipment and services, including the oil industry, had been almost destroyed by years of war and sanctions, and it soon became clear that the United States would have to finance the rebuilding. The projected cost of the war and reconstruction eventually rose to not much less than $150 billion. The U.S. administration's undertaking seemed to be straining the military and economic resources even of the United States, at the same time as it strained the relationship of the United States with much of the rest of the international community.

U.S. Worldwide Legitimacy. At least to start with, only a minority of governments and almost no peoples were prepared to accept the United States in the role it intended to fill, of reliable trustee for the interests of the world. The reason was that just as the

United States was dissatisfied with what it regarded as the feebleness and hypocrisy of the international community, so much of the community was discontented with what it perceived as the high-handedness of the United States as its single leading citizen.

Partly, this was because the United States was the main target of resentment among "the Rest" against "the West" for its self-interested globalization policies (pp. 688–689). But issues were also arising that pitted the United States even against its Western partners. Already under Clinton, the U.S. Senate, controlled by Republicans, had in 1999 refused to ratify (confirm as binding on the United States) the Comprehensive Nuclear Test Ban Treaty, which 150 nations had already signed. Since the advent of the Bush administration in 2001, such divisive issues had multiplied.

The new administration went to great lengths, including threatening to veto the financing of UN peacekeeping operations, to get its armed forces exempted from the jurisdiction of a newly established Permanent War Crimes Tribunal in The Hague, which was intended to be ready in advance to do justice against any future perpetrators of atrocities like those in Rwanda and Bosnia. Meanwhile, many nations including the United States, meeting in Kyoto, Japan, in 1997, had agreed upon a protocol (amendment to an earlier international treaty) establishing a procedure for reducing emissions of burned fuel suspected of causing global warming (pp. 624–625). The Bush administration, however, refused to submit the Kyoto Protocol to the Senate for ratification.

There were certainly arguments in favor of these U.S. decisions. It is still uncertain, for example, whether global warming is taking place at all, and if so, how fast it is taking place and whether it is caused by humans, by natural climatic processes, or by both. Most nations that accepted the Kyoto Protocol did so on what climatologists call the "precautionary" principle—namely, that with global warning, it is better to be safe than sorry. The United States had every right to refuse to subject itself to painful economic constraints on the basis of an uncertain judgment about what might happen with global warming, even though this judgment was taken seriously by most of the nations of the world.

Now, however, the United States wanted the nations of the world to risk the lives of their troops in war and peacekeeping on the basis of its own uncertain judgment about what might happen with Iraqi WMDs. Having refused to accept the judgment and obey the will of the international community, the United States now wanted the community to accept its judgment and obey its will. The United States, of course, claimed that this was justifiable since it was right about both global warming and Iraqi WMDs. Most of the community, on the other hand, believed that the United States was wrong about global warming, and was wary of a leading citizen that intended to command but refused to obey.

The Iraq War and the International Community. As a result, the United States did not lead a united international effort as it had done in the Gulf War and against Afghanistan. Instead, the United States dragged the international community along behind it, with some governments going farther and more eagerly, and others pulling back with all their might. Britain, true to its twentieth-century "special relationship" of mutual loyalty with the United States, sent a third of its army to take part in the invasion of Iraq. Other western European governments took part in postwar peacekeeping, believing this to be their duty as members of the Western partnership. Eastern European governments also sent forces, since they looked to the United States as their protector against their larger neighbors on the east and the west.

Russia, however, was embittered by its post-Soviet weakness and by what it considered to be bullying treatment by the United States, such as the expansion of NATO to countries on its borders. Together with the leading non-Western powers, India and China, it held aloof from both the war and postwar peacekeeping. Germany, whose chancellor, Gerhard Schröder, believed he would lose an election if he did the United States' bidding, broke ranks with the Western partnership and also refused to take part. And France, true to its own tradition of accepting U.S. leadership only in times of clear and present danger as in Afghanistan, pushed its opposition to the point of threatening to veto the Security Council resolution that would have authorized the invasion of Iraq.

For all of these countries and many others, Iraq's possible WMDs seemed less threatening than the prospect, as they deemed it, of an international community that was dominated and its institutions commandeered by the United States. As a result, the United States and its closest allies went to war without UN backing.

Following the war, however, the resisters of the U.S. action all voted in favor of legitimizing and authorizing UN cooperation with the U.S.-led occupation administration in Iraq. In this way, by confronting the institutions of the international community with an accomplished fact and daring them to oppose it, the United States was able to extract a measure of agreement from them. But the agreement was not enthusiastic, and to judge from opinion polls, even in countries whose governments stood by the United States, their peoples were mostly against the war. The majority in the United States supported the war, but there were wide swings of opinion afterward, influenced partly by the events of the occupation and partly by the gradual and surprising revelation that on the eve of war, Iraq had not possessed the WMDs, or active programs for developing them, that it was thought to have had.

The Iraq War and Islam. Perhaps the single most compelling inspiration for the U.S. invasion of Iraq was the idea that the Islamic world was withdrawing from and opposing the trend of global civilization, and that the Islamic world must therefore be made to change. In the short run, it might resent U.S. intervention, but in the long run, it would be integrated into a global civilization based on secular democracy.

Sure enough, in the short run this project did not make spectacular progress. The United States did succeed in intimidating both Iran and Libya into being more forthcoming about their efforts to develop nuclear weapons. However, it was unable to compel the Palestinian Authority to act against Islamic and nationalist terrorist groups (p. 702) or to force Yassir Arafat, whom it blamed for the authority's refusal to act, to give up his power. Instead, the Israelis began building a barrier against suicide bombers that took in part of the disputed West Bank territories, and they talked of evacuating their settlements in Gaza. It seemed that they were preparing for a long struggle to defend themselves against Palestinian terrorism and to hold the most valuable gains that they had made at Palestinian expense. Evidently they did not believe that even after the Iraq war, the United States had the power to impose a settlement on either the Palestinians or themselves.

Meanwhile, some undemocratic Muslim governments that the United States supported, including Kuwait and other states in the Persian Gulf, introduced or promised measures to increase popular participation in government. Generally, however, these measures were designed to make sure that Islamic religious parties, which often had the widest popular support, would be unable to win majorities in legislatures, or to control governments if they did win majorities. And other undemocratic governments

in Muslim countries, such as outright dictatorships in Tunisia and Uzbekistan, continued exactly as before, apparently confident that so long as they were pro-Western and
repressed fundamentalist Islam, the United States would not bother them.

However their governments reacted, most of the peoples of the Muslim world responded to the war with fury and dismay. They considered it a brazen U.S. effort to impose its values and its will, gain control of Middle Eastern oil fields, and bully the Arabs
into submission to Israel. The main U.S. hope of changing this mood rested on rebuilding Iraq as a prosperous, secular, and democratic state.

Rebuilding Iraq. The U.S. administration did not spell out in detail what a rebuilt Iraq
would look like, but journalists and scholars who were knowledgeable about the Middle East and sympathetic to the administration's plans often advised that Iraq follow
the secular and democratic model of a neighboring Muslim country, Turkey.

Since the fall of the Ottoman Empire at the end of the First World War, Turkey had
followed the path of Westernizing itself in order to achieve equality with the West
(p. 566). It had remade itself into a country with democratically elected political parties and governments, as well as a free-market economy. Islam, practiced by millions of
believers, was both subsidized but also supervised by the state, and was officially restricted in many ways from exercising the kind of open influence on society and politics
that would be considered normal for all religions in Western countries. The army from
time to time ousted democratically elected politicians who seemed too much influenced by Islam or by objectionably left-wing ideologies. Even so, an Islamic-influenced
party had recently come to power, but its leaders made a point of proclaiming their belief in secular government and politics. In fact, intense Turkish nationalism, shared by
all parties, was the glue that held the state together.

Presumably, then, the U.S. administration intended to rebuild Iraq on this pattern, minus the nationalism. The administration also seemingly expected that the
United States would be the one to design the future Iraq, and that the Iraqi people,
grateful for liberation from Saddam Hussein's tyranny, would eagerly set to work to rebuild their country under U.S. direction and following the U.S. blueprint.

In fact, however, not many people inside Iraq seemed to want it to become the
kind of country that the United States planned for it to be, nor did they have their own
united vision of what kind of country they wanted to live in. Iraq had come into existence in 1920, by decree of the British following the collapse of the Ottoman Empire
(p. 566). The three main Iraqi ethnic and religious groups had no strong sense of common nationhood, but each had its own historic identity and its own vision of a future
Iraq, which turned out to be different from that of the United States (*Map 17.2*).

The deepest wish of the non-Arab and Sunni Muslim Kurds, a fragment of a large and
ancient nation the rest of which lived under harsh repression in Syria and Turkey, was
not to be part of Iraq at all. For the time being, the Kurds wanted a semi-independent
territory in the north of Iraq that would be the core round which a united and independent Kurdistan would one day form.

The Shiite Muslims, Arabs living mainly in the south of Iraq who formed about
two-thirds of the population, hoped for an Iraq where they would be the dominant
force. They were eager to live in a democracy but did not want it to be a secular one. They
did not seem to want direct clerical rule as in Iran, but it soon became clear that in any
Iraqi state that responded to the will of the majority, Islamic values would be upheld
and Shiite ayatollahs (p. 622) were bound to have vast political influence.

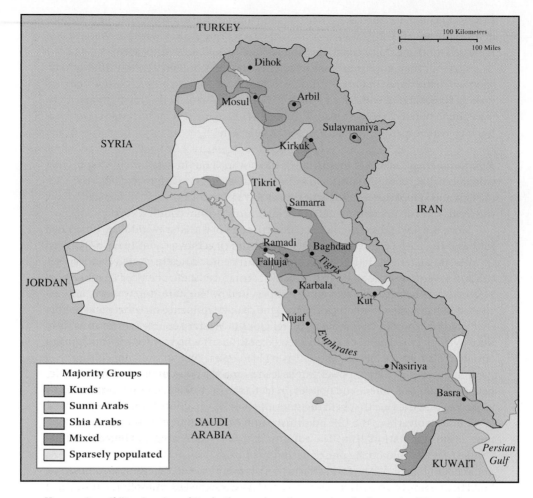

Map 17.2 Iraq: Shiites, Sunnis, and Kurds. The map shows the areas where the three main religious and national communities predominate, as well as areas of mixed population. All three communities are part of larger groups extending well beyond Iraq. Non-Arab Iran is mostly Shiite, and Shiite Islam is thickly scattered across the Arab lands of the Middle East. Sunni Islam is the predominant religion of the Arab world. The Iraqi Kurds, who are also Sunni Muslims, are a fragment of a large nation that lives mainly in Turkey, and also in Iran and Syria.

The Sunni Arabs were more secular-minded, but they had been privileged under Saddam Hussein. Their territories in central Iraq were the scene of vicious guerrilla warfare against the U.S. occupation, and of terrorist attacks against Iraqis who cooperated with it, that persisted even after the capture by U.S. forces of the former dictator.

Thus the Coalition Provisional Authority (the Iraq occupation administration, run by the United States) faced what was becoming a constant problem of would-be nation builders—how to impose its idea of a nation on groups that had definite and conflicting ideas of their own.

The United States attacked this problem in several ways. It began pouring billions of dollars into Iraq to rebuild the country's basic equipment and services. It established an Iraqi Governing Council, whose members were selected by the occupation administration from among returned exiles who were more or less respected in the Shiite, Sunni, and Kurdish communities, as its Iraqi partner. It started to train an army and a police force that would not be controlled by any one group. It involved its soldiers in many small-scale projects that were intended to win the trust of Iraqis at the grass roots. It sponsored elected city councils that took local and small-scale decisions under its watchful eye.

Even so, it soon became clear that although most Iraqis were overjoyed to be rid of Saddam Hussein and well aware that they could not do without U.S. money and troops, the expected gratitude and devotion to their liberators were not forthcoming. Even more threatening to the U.S. project than the Sunni insurgency was the fact that the Shiite majority soon began to lose patience with their status as wards of a non-Muslim and non-Arab occupation regime. In the face of this growing tension (together with growing doubts among U.S. voters), the administration changed course. Though it intended to keep troops in Iraq until the guerrilla resistance was crushed, it announced a handover of sovereign power to an Iraqi government by the middle of 2004.

The United States still hoped, however, to have the deciding voice in the shaping of the new Iraq. It intended that the new government would not be elected, and planned in particular that a new constitution would be drafted for a sovereign Iraq by an assembly chosen through caucuses (small local groups) appointed by the occupation administration. This was partly because there were genuine administrative problems in holding elections at all soon. But the United States also believed that the longer elections were delayed, the greater its chance of handing over power to an Iraqi government that would share its vision of a secular as well as democratic Iraq, and the greater the chance of Iraqis who shared this vision winning elections when they were finally held.

Early in 2004, this policy ran into trouble when the most influential Shiite cleric, Ayatollah Ali al-Sistani, called massive demonstrations against the U.S. caucus plan, on the grounds that any legitimate Iraqi government and constitution must reflect the will of the people as revealed by elections. The ayatollah also let it be known, however, that he would accept delayed elections if the United Nations confirmed that immediate elections were an administrative impossibility.

Hastily, the United States turned to the institution of the international community that it had thought of setting aside. A UN delegation arrived, and split the difference between the occupiers and the ayatollah. Caucuses, it declared, were politically unacceptable, but elections could not be held until early in 2005—which was sooner than the United States had wanted. In Iraq, it seemed, the irresistible force of the world's only superpower had met an immovable object in the form of a leader who wielded the formidable power of Islam over the life and society of its believers. Both, however, had for the moment submitted to the verdict of the main institution of the international community as a basis for their dealings with each other.

Contentious negotiations involving the Iraqi Governing Council and the Coalition Provisional Authority then produced an interim constitution under which a sovereign Iraqi government would operate until a permanent constitution could be presented to the people. The constitution proclaimed the unity of the "Iraqi homeland," but also described the country's Kurdish territories as "Kurdistan" and declared the Arabs of Iraq "an inseparable part of the Arab nation." It made many provisions for democracy and human rights, including setting as a goal that one-quarter of the members of the eventual elected National Assembly should be women, but also declared Islam the state's official religion and a source of law. It confirmed that the assembly must be elected by early in 2005 as the Shiite majority insisted, but provided for a minority veto on the future definitive constitution as the other groups wished.

Essentially, the provisional constitution met some wishes and denied other wishes of all the parties involved, including the occupying power. The United States still wielded vast power to influence events in Iraq, for without its troops and money, the country would collapse. But rather than being the designer of the new Iraq and the recruiter of the Iraqis to follow its lead, the United States had become one player, alongside the three main Iraqi communities and the United Nations, in a complex game that would determine the country's future.

This state of affairs was seemingly not at all what President Bush and his advisers had expected when they decided to attack Iraq. It did not, however, necessarily mean that their venture had failed. That could certainly still happen, but it could also happen that the game in Iraq would end well. Iraq might become a country where the interaction between the values and social structures of Islam and those of the West would be carried on according to new rules—for instance, without either fundamentalist terrorism, brutal secular dictatorship, or the attempted exclusion of religious influence from democratic public life. In that case, Iraq would indeed serve as an example, not just to Islam but also to the United States, to the West, and to the world as a whole. It would show that global civilization must come about not only through conflict, but also through negotiation and compromise among the groups that must merge to form it.

All local and national communities that have come into existence in the past have had to deal with basic issues concerning their structure and values. Who is to be the community's lawgiver and law enforcer, and how far should these functions be combined? How are the community's wealthier and more powerful members and its poorer and weaker ones to share the benefits of community life and the power to make community decisions? What beliefs and values are to prevail within the community, and how much freedom is to be given to those who dissent from or transgress these values—including those who hold to older values when the community's values change? Within Western civilization alone, such questions as these have received countless different answers—from democratic and oligarchic Greek city-states; from pagans and Christians in the Roman Empire; from the medieval Catholic Church and present-day Postmodernists; from nobles and peasants; from factory owners and labor unions. More than any event since the fall of communism, the U.S. undertaking in Iraq has raised these issues for the international community in its turn.

The outcome of the undertaking will in turn affect the answers to still broader questions concerning the destiny of global civilization as a whole. Will it fulfill its yearning for harmonious diversity, or collapse under the pressure of its internal conflicts? Will it become a single worldwide entity, or will new individual civilizations arise, or updated versions of old ones, for which global civilization will provide no more than a common basic pattern? Will Western civilization preserve its individuality and its dominance, or will it be submerged by other civilizations that learn from it and then surpass it? All these questions are suggested by humanity's experience of the past. Only the future can answer them.

RECOMMENDED READING

The West and the Postcommunist World: The Ideal of an International Community On world affairs in the 1990s, K. Robbins, *The World since 1945: A Brief History* (1998), is a concise guide. I. Clark, *The Post–Cold War Order: The Spoils of Peace* (2001), is a detailed and thoughtful treatment.

The West in the 1990s: Continuing Partnership, Evolving Partners W. C. Berman, *From the Center to the Edge: The Politics and Policies of the Clinton Presidency* (2001), is a clear and concise account of all aspects. T. C. Reeves, *Twentieth-Century America: A Brief History* (2000), readably covers the general development of the United States in the 1990s.

S. Henig, *The Uniting of Europe: From Discord to Concord* (1997), is an excellent brief guide. E. Pond, *The Rebirth of Europe* (2002), treats the 1990s in more detail.

The Global Economy: "The West and the Rest" On economic and cultural globalization in general, T. Friedman, *The Lexus and the Olive Tree: Understanding Globalization* (1999), takes a positive view; B. R. Barber, *Jihad vs. McWorld* (1995), is more skeptical. J. Stiglitz, *Globalization and Its Discontents* (2002), is a critical assessment of the free-market globalization of the 1990s by a leading economic policymaker. D. Held and A. McGrew, *Globalization/Anti-Globalization* (2002), is an excellent brief summary of current discussion of economic and cultural globalization.

P. Sunner-Smith, *India: Globalization and Changes* (2000), and P. Benewick and P. Wingrove, *China in the 1990s* (1995), give concise coverage of the era of globalization.

The Former "East": Trying to Join the West J. F. Brown, *The Grooves of Change: Eastern Europe at the Turn of the Millennium* (2001), is an insightful survey of eastern Europe including the Balkans. For Russia under Yeltsin, see D. W. Treadgold and H. J. Ellison, *Twentieth-Century Russia* (2002).

Yugoslav wars are covered in S. P. Ramet, *Balkan Babel: The Disintegration of Yugoslavia from the Death of Tito to the War for Kosovo* (1999). The Yugoslav mood on the eve of breakup is conveyed in B. Hall, *The Impossible Country: A Journey Through the Last Days of Yugoslavia* (1994).

R. Bendix, *Nation-building and Citizenship: Studies of Our Changing Social Order* (1977), and E. Gellner, *Conditions of Liberty: Civil Society and Its Rivals* (1994), explain the ideas that currently inspire Western efforts to repair failed states.

The Postcolonial World: The Limits of Western Leadership The Gulf War, the latest phases of the Arab-Israeli conflict, and all other aspects of recent Middle Eastern history are covered in W. L. Cleveland, *A History of the Modern Middle East* (2000). D. Ottaway, *Chained Together: Mandela, de Klerk, and the Struggle to Remake South Africa* (1993), tells the story of the partnership between the leaders who presided over the end of apartheid.

J. Ciment, *Palestine/Israel: The Long Conflict* (1997), is a concise and factual guide. In D. Cohn-Sherbok and D. El-Alami, *The Palestine-Israeli Conflict: A Beginner's Guide* (2002), scholars from each side briefly and forcefully present the Israeli and the Palestinian versions.

I. Talbot, *India and Pakistan* (2000), surveys the national, social, and religious struggles between and within the two countries. S. Bose, *Kashmir: Roots of Conflict, Paths to Peace* (2003), analyzes the dispute from its origins to the present. P. Robb, *A History of India* (2002), briefly and readably covers the country's development in the 1990s.

On Islam and the modern world in general, B. Lewis, *What Went Wrong? Western Impact and Middle Eastern Response* (2002), portrays Islam as having become dysfunctional in the face of the rise of the modern West. K. Armstrong, *The Battle for God* (2000), depicts Christian, Islamic, and Jewish fundamentalism as forming a single basic feature of modern civilization. L. Davidson, *Islamic Fundamentalism* (1998), is a brief factual guide.

C. C. Combs, *Terrorism in the Twenty-first Century* (1997), is a concise and thorough survey. M. Taylor and E. Quayle, *Terrorist Lives* (1994), gives insights into the lives and thoughts of terrorists. W. Laqueur, *The New Terrorism: Fanaticism and the Arms of Mass Destruction* (1999), describes the most horrific forms that terrorism may take. Y. Alexander and M. S. Swetnam, *Usama bin Laden's al-Qaida: Profile of a Terror Network* (2001), is a sober and well-informed account.

M. Schram, *Avoiding Armageddon: Our Future, Our Choice* (2003), is a well-informed nontechnical guide to the threat of nuclear, biological, and chemical WMDs. In S. D. Sagan and K. N. Watte, *The Spread of Nuclear Weapons: A Debate Renewed* (2003), leading experts present contrasting views of proliferation as leading either to nuclear disaster or to peace through deterrence.

Between Protest and Affirmation: The Postmodern Outlook T. Woods, *Beginning Postmodernism* (1999), is a readable introduction to Postmodernism in all fields of philosophy, social thought, art, and mass culture. A more detailed guide is S. Sim, ed., *The Routledge Companion to Postmodernism*

(2001). D. Harvey, *The Condition of Postmodernity: An Enquiry into the Origins of Cultural Change* (1989), treats postmodernity as a global economic and political as well as cultural development.

M. Sarup, *An Introductory Guide to Poststructuralism and Postmodernism* (1993), covers developments since Existentialism in an understandable way. R. Solomon, *Continental Philosophy since 1750: The Rise and Fall of the Self* (1988), puts Postmodern philosophy in its historical context.

Postmodern Literature and Art A. B. Kernan, *The Death of Literature* (1990), has shrewd and entertaining remarks on many aspects of the late-twentieth-century literary scene. S. Baker, *The Fiction of Postmodernity* (2000), describes the influence of Postmodern thinking on Postmodern fiction.

David Hopkins, *After Modern Art: 1945–2000* (2000), and Edward Lucie-Smith, *Movements in Art since 1945* (2001), include Postmodernism and its roots in earlier Modernist art. D. Ghirardi, *Architecture after Modernism* (1996), is a good introduction to recent architecture.

September 11, The West, and the World K. Booth and T. Dunne, *Worlds in Collision: Terror and the Future of Global Order* (2002), and M. L. Dudziak, *September 11 in History: A Watershed Moment?* (2003), assess the immediate impact of the September 11 attacks and the U.S. response on the future of the international community.

Influential books attempting to predict the long-term development of the postcommunist world are F. Fukuyama, *The End of History and the Last Man* (1992), and S. Huntington, *The Clash of Civilizations and the Remaking of World Order* (1996). Fukuyama envisages the rise of a harmonious global civilization based on benign Western models, and Huntington expects a lengthy period of conflict among the cultures and values of different types of civilization.

INFOTRAC COLLEGE EDITION

Visit the source collections at **http://academic.cengage.com/infotrac**, and use the Search function with the following key terms:

Postmodernism	Jean-François Lyotard	Freedom Tower
Michel Foucault	Salman Rushdie	
Jacques Derrida	earthworks, art	

WESTERN CIVILIZATION RESOURCES

Visit the Brief History of the Western World Companion Web Site for resources specific to this textbook:

http://history.wadsworth.com/greerbrief09/

Also, the CD in the back of this book and the World History Resources Center at **http://history.wadsworth.com/west_civ/** offer a variety of tools to help you succeed in this course, including access to quizzes; images; documents; interactive simulations, maps, and timelines; movie explorations; and a wealth of other sources.

INDEX

A page number in italics indicates an illustration. No separate number is given for related text on the same page.

Years shown in parentheses ( ) following the name of a ruler are the years of reign. For other individuals, years shown are for birth and death.

Index entries marked by an asterisk (*) are important historical terms. The meaning of each term is explained on the pages of text shown for that entry.